Sheppard Frere was born in 1916 and educated at Lancing
and Magdalene College, Cambridge. He directed the
Canterbury Excavations from 1946 to 1955 and the
Verulamium Excavations from 1958 to 1961. He has been a
lecturer at Manchester University and a Reader and Professor
of the Archaeology of the Roman Provinces at London
University and is now Professor of the Archaeology of the
Roman Empire at Oxford. He was made a Fellow of the British
Academy in 1971. He is the editor of the annual publication
Britannia for the Society for the Promotion of Roman Studies.
His publications include *Verulamium Excavations Vol I* and
Problems of the Iron Age in Southern Britain (editor).

To B. W. T. Handford who first encouraged my interest in
Ancient History and Archaeology

BRITANNIA

A History of Roman Britain

Sheppard Frere

CARDINAL edition published in 1974
by Sphere Books Ltd
30/32 Gray's Inn Road, London WC1X 8JL

First published in Great Britain by
Routledge and Kegan Paul Ltd 1967
Copyright © S. S. Frere 1967, 1974

Set in Intertype Lectura

Printed in Great Britain by
Hazell Watson & Viney Ltd
Aylesbury, Bucks

ISBN 0 351 16310 7

CONTENTS

LIST OF
ILLUSTRATIONS

ACKNOWLEDGMENTS

The author and publishers would like to thank the following for supplying photographs for use in this volume: Aerofilms Ltd, Plates 1a, 3, 16a; Major G. W. Allen, Plates 9a, 9b, 10a, 10b; Ashmolean Museum, Oxford, Plates 9a, 9b, 10a, 10b; Arnold Baker, Plate 2; David Baker, Plate 12a; M. B. Cookson, Plates 11a, 11b, 14b, 15a; Otto Fein, Plates 12b, 14a, 15b; Dr St Joseph, Plates 1b, 4, 5a, 5b, 6a, 7, 8a, 8b, 16b; Royal Commission on Historical Monuments in England, Plate 13; Warburg Institute, Plates 12b, 14a, 15b.

LIST OF TEXT-FIGURES

PREFACE

The advances made during the last twenty-five years in our knowledge of the history and archaeology of Roman Britain can be best illustrated by the extent to which R. G. Collingwood's great summary of the subject in *Roman Britain and the English Settlements* (1936) is now out of date. But the inspiration of his book when it appeared will not be forgotten by those who read it at the time, and there is no doubt of the value of a general summary of existing knowledge, if only as a spur to advance.

The present book is one of a series, by various authors, on the Provinces of the Roman Empire. Here I have tried to present the history of Roman Britain, using the available literary and epigraphic sources, and the results of archaeological research. I have not attempted to describe the archaeology of Roman Britain as such, and in those chapters which deal with the towns and countryside and the economics and religion of the province I have confined myself of set purpose to a selective historical interpretation rather than a general description of all available remains.

No one who sets out to write a book of this size on such a subject can well avoid making great use of the thoughts and works of other scholars in the field, some of which have become adopted imperceptibly into my own thoughts through constant reading, lecturing or discussion; and it may be that not all have been adequately acknowledged in footnotes or in the bibliography. This I hope will be taken by those concerned as a compliment. In particular, of course, I owe much to the earlier writings of Haverfield, Collingwood and Sagot, and much also to the published works of my friends and colleagues Mr A. L. F. Rivet, Professor E. Birley and the late Sir Ian Richmond. Professor Birley and Sir Ian Richmond have very kindly answered one or two questions which have arisen during the writing of the book, and I have also had help on particular topics from Mrs M. A. Cotton, Lady (Aileen) Fox, Mrs K. Hartley, Miss A. S. Robertson, Mrs A. Ravetz, Mr R. P. Wright, Dr J. C. Mann, Dr J. Wilkes, Mr J. S. Wacher, Dr J. P. C. Kent, Mr F. H. Thompson, Mr C. E. Stevens, Dr J. Morris, Mr H. C. Bowen, Dr G. Webster, Dr I. M. Stead and Professor W. G. Hoskins, all of whom I desire to thank. Above all, I owe much to the friendly criticism and suggestions of Mr B. R. Hartley, who has kindly read the whole book in its first typescript, to its great advantage. In most cases I have taken his advice, and always on questions of chronology, but he is not responsible for errors which may be due to my holding to my own opinion where we disagreed.

The great corpus of Romano-British inscribed stones, *The Roman Inscriptions of Britain*, Vol. I, by R. G. Collingwood and R. P. Wright, appeared too late for me to use it while writing, but I have revised all references to inscriptions mentioned in the text, to give the *RIB* numbers, in the belief that this will now be standard practice. References to Dio's Roman History are to the text in the Loeb edition, and those to *Panegyrici Latini* are to the Oxford Text of Sir Roger Mynors. Reference by footnote is normally made to works specifically mentioned in the text: a wider selection of modern sources will be found in the bibliography at the end. I have often referred to general works from which primary references may be obtained, for otherwise the bibliography would have extended to inordinate length. Because Otto Seeck's edition of the *Notitia Dignitatum* was reprinted in 1962, I have not thought it necessary to print the British lists of the Notitia.

This book was written during 1964 and 1965 while I held a post at the Institute of Archaeology at London University. I have taken account of a few publications of later date. I have to thank Mr H. M. Stewart for much help with the maps, most of which are entirely drawn by him, and Miss H. Fuller for her careful typing and retyping of the text. I am also very grateful to Dr J. K. St Joseph, Mr Arnold Baker and Mr B. W. Cunliffe for providing photographs and to Lt-Col M. A. Lloyd for his drawing of the Verulamium inscription.

S. S. FRERE

January 1966

PREFACE TO SECOND EDITION

The resetting of this book for a paper-back edition has enabled me to undertake some revision. The archaeology of Roman Britain is a rapidly expanding subject. During the seven years which have elapsed since its first appearance, there have been important new discoveries as the result of excavation, field-work and aerial photography, some of which have changed historical perspectives or have thrown new or more detailed light upon questions discussed in the first edition; and there have also been numerous works of synthesis or discussion as well as publications of basic evidence, such as Mr B. R. Hartley's 'The Roman occupation of Scotland: the evidence of samian ware' in *Britannia* iii (1972), which have compelled radical reconsideration of opinions formerly held. I have tried to include as much of the new evidence as is relevant to the main themes of the book, within the limits of what can properly be called revision, but without attempting to rewrite the whole work. There are other fields, such as the Iron Age, or the fifth to seventh centuries, where comparable advances in knowledge or revolutions in outlook – and indeed in method – are being achieved, which would have involved a considerable lengthening of treatment. This has not been attempted: I have confined myself, in the main, in these sections of the book, to the correction of mistakes. The periods which precede or follow Roman Britain deserve their own books and are receiving full-scale treatment at other hands, as in B. W. Cunliffe's *Iron Age Communities in Britain* (1974), Leslie Alcock's *Arthur's Britain* (1971), J. N. L. Myres' *Anglo-Saxon pottery, the Settlement of England* and John Morris' *The Age of Arthur* (1973).

Thanks must be expressed to Professor P. A. Brunt, Mr A. R.

Burn, Professor B. W. Cunliffe, Mr J. P. Gillam, Dr W. H. Manning and many other friends who have helped me to eradicate mistakes in the text or to include new information, and to Mrs M. Cox for re-drawing the maps.

S. S. FRERE

January 1974

ROMAN BRITAIN

Inchtuthil

CALEDONIAN
CONFEDERACY

Carpow

DAMNONII

VOTADINI

SELGOVAE

NOVANTAE

IRON

COAL

◎ Coloniae or Municipia
● Civitas capitals
○ Other towns
■ Fortresses
Civitas boundaries approximate only.

Roman Miles
0 — 50 — 100

CARVETII

Carlisle

Corbridge

COAL

LEAD

LOTOVARES

TEXTOVERDI

JET

Kirkby Thore

LEAD

Catterick

Isurium
Brigantum

YORKSHIRE
POTTERIES

LEAD

CORNAVIOVICES

York

PARISI

SETANTII

Brough
Petuaria

Templeborough

COAL

COAL

QUERNS

Caistor

Anglesey

COPPER

COPPER

DECEANGLI

LEAD

Wilderspool

Buxton

Deva

Salinae?

LEAD

Lincoln

Horncastle

CANGANI

COAL

ORDOVICES

CORNOVII

DERBYSHIRE
POTTERIES

POTTERY

Ancaster

SALT

CORITANI

Margidunum

COPPER

Viroconium
Cornoviorum

Pennocrucium

LEAD

Wall

Mancetter

Rocester

Letocetum

Corianorum

Rotae

IRON
STONE

Great Casterton

POTTERY

SALT

Caister

Venta
Icenorum

Durobrivae

POTTERY

SALT

ICENI

POTTERY

DEMETAE

SILURES

GOLD

Kenchester

Salinae?
Alcester

Towcester

Irchester

Godmanchester

Cambridge

CATUVELLAUNI

Great
Chesterford

Braughing

TRINOVANTES

POTTERY

Camulodunum

Carmarthen

Isca

IRON

Glevum

Corinium
Dobunnorum

DOBUNNI

Alchester

OXFORD
POTTERIES

Dorchester

Verulamium

POTTERY

Caesaromagus

OYSTERS

SALT

Venta Silurum

COAL

STONE

Bath

Cunetio

Sandy Lodge

BELGAE

NEW FOREST
POTTERIES

Calleva Atrebatum

ATREBATES

FARNHAM
POTTERIES

Londinium

Richborough

STONE

Durovernum
Cantiacorum

Dover

CANTIACI

IRON

REGNENSES

Lympne

Venta
Belgarum

Bitterne

Clausentum

Noviomagus
Regnensium

Isle of
Wight

Boulogne

Ilchester

Lindinis

DUROTRIGES

Dorchester
Durnovaria

PURBECK MARBLE

SHALE

DUMNONII

Isca
Dumnoniorum

TIN

TIN

I

The background:
the earliest British Iron Age

The civilisation of Roman Britain was a synthesis of things Roman and Celtic. Though it owed an incalculable debt to introductions from abroad and its preponderating element was imported from the civilisation of the Mediterranean, this civilisation took root in a Celtic land and enjoyed a native contribution: 'Romano-British' is a term not wholly synonymous with 'Roman'. Britain formed part of the Roman Empire for close on 400 years, a not inconsiderable slice of her total recorded history; and during this time there was ample opportunity for interaction and development. But a study of Roman Britain sees not only the processes of time at work; there were the powerful influences of geographical environment, as well as previous regional differences in the inheritance of the inhabitants, to modify and colour the history of the province. In this chapter and the next we must examine this environment and these differences, so that a picture can be formed of the British contribution to the synthesis.

The insularity of Britain has always been a factor, and in recent centuries an important factor, in her history. The complete security from invasion which she has enjoyed for 900 years, however, has been due to the existence of a strong central government and to the conscious development of naval and military policies impossible without centralisation. In more primitive times the existence of the Channel meant that, though settlement from overseas was possible, it rarely took the form of a full folk-migration, owing to difficulties of transport; invaders came and conquered, but their numbers were usually small enough to be gradually absorbed. Episodes such as the Roman conquest have been rare, partly for the reason stated and partly because the inhabitants of the opposite coasts for the most part lived in a disorganised barbarism almost as completely un-centralised.

Britain, lying as she does off the coast of north-west Europe, is accessible from various directions, and in different periods of history each direction in turn has achieved significance. Due west was Ireland, wealthy enough for trade but too small to be the source of more than raids, and facing a mountainous and on the whole in-hospitable shore. Due east the wide and stormy North Sea provided security until the appearance of more sea-worthy shipping in the late Roman period. The narrow waters of the English Channel give com-paratively easy access from similar lowland country on the plains of northern France; and it was from the coastlands stretching round from the Rhine delta to Brittany that most of the early settlers came. But a fourth route is available to maritime initiative from the western estuaries of France, from north-west Spain and ultimately indeed from the Mediterranean itself through the straits of Gibraltar; this leads to the south-western parts of Britain and both sides of the Irish Sea. This route was of great significance for the famous pre-historic tin trade of Cornwall, and enabled south-western Britain, and Ireland too, to maintain a tenuous contact with Mediterranean civilisation in the centuries following the fall of Rome. The travels of the Celtic Saints at that epoch match those of the neolithic settlers over the same waters 3,000 years earlier.

With access so easy to adequately equipped settlers from so many directions, it is not surprising to find that the human pattern of Iron Age Britain provides much variety. But the character of the Island itself offers very different environments in its various parts, such as would accentuate or foster differences, both in settlement pattern and in methods of livelihood. With primitive equipment and without a highly organised and centralised society, it was impossible for early settlers to do more than acquiesce in the facts of physical environ-ment. These were controlled by the influence which the geology of the country, in association with climate, exerted on vegetation. Even the highly organised Romans could do no more than modify these in-fluences. Indeed, their effect is still apparent today.

The geography of Britain shows a broad division into highland and lowland zones; the former, in the west and north, being an area of old hard rocks rising into moderate mountain chains up to 2,000 feet high or more, and for the most part barren and inhospitable owing to heavy rainfall and the leaching of the soil; the latter, in the east and south, consisting of more recent, less upstanding geological formations, softer and more readily weathered, and bearing more fertile soils. This broad distinction is of profound importance in itself, and is accentuated by the fact that much of the highland zone extends northwards into areas where inclement climate is an additional handicap to agriculture. In detail, of course, there is much variation. The highland zone is not a unity like the lowland, for Dumnonia is small and separated from Wales by the Bristol Channel, and Wales from the North by the Cheshire gap, a westward extension of the Midland Plain. In the highland zone pockets of lower, more fertile ground exist on which agricultural settlements can grow. But even where these areas were fully settled they were often cut off by inhospitable hills which prevented easy communications or mature political growth. In the lowland zone also the pattern was complex; comparatively large areas of light well-drained subsoil, such as gravel, chalk or limestone, are separated by belts of heavy clay which in primitive conditions were so heavily afforested that they formed barriers to intercommunication. Trackways developed along the ridges of well-drained hill-ranges, such as the famous Icknield Way, or the 'Pilgrims' Way' along the North Downs, or the 'Jurassic route' along the Cotswolds and through Northamptonshire up to Lincolnshire. Few rivers in Britain can compare with the rivers of Gaul for facilities offered to transport, but the role of the Thames in this respect should not be forgotten. It was one of the most outstanding contributions of Rome in Britain that she broke through the successive belts of forest with her new main roads (pl. 10a), and for the first time knit together the various habitable belts in one unified transport network, which for the most part radiated from London. Another was the construction of new towns on sites whose selection in most cases has been justified by the verdict of posterity. In the Iron Age nucleated settlement was conditioned for the most part by primitive considerations, such as the position of chieftains' strongholds or the existence of good agricultural soil. Only towards the close of the pre-Roman period did recent settlers, the Belgae, begin to develop large settlements on lower ground at river-crossings, which hint at the growth of trade. Such sites as Canterbury or Colchester illustrate this process, but the large settlements concerned were hardly to be described as towns. To Rome we owe the choice of such sites as London, York, Gloucester, Lincoln or Exeter where large modern towns still thrive, while sites like Reading or Shrewsbury or Norwich are but little removed from the position originally selected.

Evidence of Iron Age agriculture is well attested in south-east Britain, and as far north and west as the Jurassic belt; but beyond the Gloucester–Lincoln line a different economy seems to have been practised, that of pastoralism eked out by garden cultivation. Julius Caesar, though he did not penetrate within 100 miles of such people, was well informed when he wrote: 'The people of the interior for the most part do not sow corn but live on milk and meat, and dress in skins'. The wealth of such people, like that of the patriarchs of the Old Testament, was reckoned in cattle and sheep. Very large areas were required for pasturage, so that tribal lands might be very wide yet not heavily populated, and the people themselves may have been semi-nomadic, as they accompanied their flocks and herds in search of fresh pasture, and in the seasonal alternation from summer to winter grazing-grounds. It is evident that the control of such people posed a novel problem to the Roman authorities completely different from that of the settled agricultural peoples of the south. The former were more mobile, not tied to landed property or to valuable permanent homes, and probably they were physically tougher in war. Moreover, to move forward sufficient forces into such territory involved logistic complications over the supply of corn for the troops; it now had to be brought great distances from the growing-grounds. It is not surprising to find that a determined effort was made in the early years of the Roman occupation to limit the province to the lowland zone, at first with a frontier based on the Fosse Way, and, when that proved impossible, with another based on the line of the Severn; and that the intractable problem of the occupation of the rest was solved by a power able to develop transport facilities, including water transport, and willing to encourage the extension of intensive agriculture into areas which had not previously known it.

Yet advance into the highland zone was inevitable, not only because of the intransigent character of the inhabitants, whose immemorial custom it was to supplement their livelihood with booty or tribute exacted from the settled farmlands of their neighbours, but also because the mineral wealth of Britain lay very largely in the mountains. Of metals, only iron was to be found in the lowland zone, in the rich clay deposits of the Weald of Kent and Sussex and in the limestone of Northampton and Lincolnshire; lead from which silver could be won was present only in Somerset and copper in east Cheshire, though these last deposits were curiously neglected in the Roman period. Larger lead fields were to be sought in North Wales, Derbyshire or Yorkshire; copper in Wales and Anglesey; gold in Wales, tin in Cornwall and iron in the Forest of Dean. Apart from these minerals and others (like coal) of more restricted exploitation, the wealth of Britain lay in its corn lands, which produced an exportable surplus, in the leather and woollen products of its herds and flocks, and in its overflowing manpower, which Rome could put to good use in her armies on other frontiers. The value of Britain to the Empire, though not undisputed at the time,[1] is shown by the maintenance there for almost four centuries of a garrison amounting to a tenth part of the entire imperial army.

The general historical effect of Britain's geographical character is that the lowland zone, being nearer the continent and easier to over-run, has been the frequent recipient of new cultures which its agricultural wealth enabled to flourish; whereas the highland zone beyond lies farther from the source of new cultures, and by its very nature has been unable to receive them unmodified. These results are very apparent in the period of the Roman occupation of Britain, in which a flourishing Romano-British civilisation took root in the lowlands, while the highland zone was almost continuously a zone of military occupation held down by force, in which little spontaneous civilising development took place among the natives. But this is only the generalised pattern, for in detail quite large areas within the highland zone are, as we have seen, lowland in character, and some of them had always been accessible to the influence of the sea routes: in these areas, if military fluctuation allowed, civilisation of a sort could take root. Such areas are the plain of Glamorgan, parts of Yorkshire, the valley of the Eden and some of lowland Scotland. On the other hand, the conservative character of the north and west, with its ability to resist intrusion, had the effect of enabling traditions of Romano-British civilisation to survive there, if only faintly, long after the collapse of Roman Britain itself. And these traditions could be nurtured by contacts, via the western sea-ways, with surviving centres in Gaul and in the Mediterranean basin itself.

The relatively small numbers to which invading or migrating bands were confined by the difficulties of crossing the sea, and the consequent survival in Britain of older strains of culture unsubmerged, had the effect of giving the British Iron Age a strongly insular character. Though some originality can be seen in the development of its art or, on a lower plane, of special weaving appliances, it is insularity which is strikingly demonstrated in such mundane features as the ubiquitous employment of round rather than rectangular houses: for the round house is an insular feature continuously employed from the Bronze Age, while on the Continent rectangular houses were in fashion.[2] Because of this insularity, the cultures of the British Iron Age, though they derive from continental cultures, do not strictly correspond in detail. There is much overlapping. The use of continental cultural descriptions is thus apt to be misleading, nor, of course, can we yet discern or use the names of actual tribes; and an insular terminology has accordingly been evolved. In the British Iron Age three principal cultural groupings have been recognised, and classified as Iron A, Iron B and Iron C. These cultures had their histories, but the terms A, B and C are cultural not chronological; the A culture, though the first to start, could overlap or outlast in some areas the development of B or C cultures in others, and Iron B and Iron C will be found to continue in adjacent regions side by side. The chronology of the Iron Age is best dealt with by division into Periods as follows: Period I 650–350; Period II 350–150; Period III 150–the Roman Conquest. As could be anticipated, the growth of knowledge has shown the cultural pattern to be complex, but regional differences can be classified by geographical and numerical qualifications, such as Southern First A or South-Western Third B. Such a system of classification requires an intellectual effort to master it, but granted the complexity of the pattern, this effort of memory is less than that required if purely cultural labels derived from type sites, such as the 'All Cannings Cross' or 'Hunsbury' cultures, were to be used instead, since the former system contains its own clues. In recent years, it is true, some have expressed the wish to resume the use of cultural labels in accordance with the normal practice in Prehistory; but as yet no general system of that kind has been fully stated or agreed, such as could be used with any clarity as an alternative to that set out in this and the following chapters. Here it will not

19

be necessary to survey the Iron Age cultures of Britain in detail from the beginning: rather an attempt will be made to give a general outline as a background for the more detailed survey of Britain on the eve of the Roman conquest which is offered in Chapters 2 and 4.

Iron A

The expansion of European societies and the migrations of peoples had already resulted in the movement of groups into Britain during the Late Bronze Age and the forging of strong cultural links with the continent. This process was still continuing as the knowledge of iron-working became diffused: the innovations now introduced were further examples of contacts which had been intermittently maintained for 500 years, and the settlers who brought the first iron-using cultures to these islands were but following in the footsteps of their kindred. Knowledge of the new metal, however, was to prove a great advance: for iron is much more widespread than copper or tin, and thus in time metallic tools became available more cheaply and to a wider section of society.

The earliest users of iron reached Britain probably quite late in the seventh century BC. Already at that date men had been coming individually and in small groups to penetrate the eastern coasts; and in South Wales, too, finds near Cardiff and at Llyn Fawr in Glamorgan show penetration, perhaps in search of iron deposits. The type of sword (Hallstatt C) currently used by warriors on the mainland of Europe was introduced here and soon copied locally, and these British copies are themselves found on the continent: before long, however, for whatever reason, the use of swords was discontinued. By the end of the sixth century workshops had been established here which were manufacturing a specifically British kind of dagger; they were to continue producing for two centuries. Thus indigenous peoples were quick to take advantage of the new technology. The culture of these early adventurers and settlers was the continental Hallstatt culture, the first to have the use of iron in Europe. This began to be superseded in parts of western Europe by the culture known as La Tène about the middle of the fifth century; and later settlers of this early phase of our Iron Age were already being affected to greater or lesser extent by La Tène developments. These developments did not, of course, appear everywhere on the Continent at once, and people living in the extreme north-western fringes might remain unaffected, or only partially affected, for some time. Iron A, therefore, is a Hallstatt and La Tène amalgam. Exact dating of settlement sites in this phase, and indeed generally in Iron Age Britain, is a matter of some difficulty, owing to the extreme scarcity of datable metal objects – cauldrons, daggers, brooches, swan-necked pins or swords – in association with the plentiful finds of pottery. Pottery-making was a domestic industry and was subject to a natural conservatism, whereas styles in metal objects tended to change more rapidly, and the objects themselves were often either imported or made by craftsmen in touch with continental developments. It is our misfortune that objects of metal are usually found by themselves, unassociated with pottery. Nevertheless, an outline chronology is provided by the former, and there is sufficient development in the pottery sequence, aided by occasional associations, to allow some measure of equation.

In east Yorkshire a settlement at Staple Howe of Iron A produced association with Hallstatt C razors of the late sixth century, and another settlement at Scarborough was probably about as early. The earliest pottery at All Cannings Cross and other early sites in Wessex shows close similarity to pottery of even earlier type (Hallstatt B) from sites in eastern France, as does some from the Thames basin with Urnfield pottery farther north. At Fengate near Peterborough an iron pin with bronze disc-head of north German type dates from the fifth century at the latest.

These and other examples show that settlers were arriving in the late sixth and fifth centuries, bringing a late Hallstatt culture with them, and regional differences in their equipment show that they were coming from various parts of north-west Europe. From the later part of the fifth century and into the fourth, subsequent arrivals were bringing possessions that show the influence of the early La Tène culture now spreading from eastern France. Sites connected with such people are those at Long Wittenham in Berkshire and Chinnor in Buckinghamshire; while at West Harling in Norfolk the apparent difficulty caused by the association of pottery showing undoubted La Tène influence with pottery of distinctly earlier character is lessened once it is realised that they are the waste from two successive huts. In the dagger series there are parallel close contacts with developing continental practice. None of these settlers arrived in large groups; all were adventurers or refugees. They were all, however, both culturally and racially akin, and their influence spreading out over southern Britain created a culture which is essentially uniform, and which is classified as Iron A.

It was a culture based on agriculture. Though the swords and daggers skilfully produced by specialist craftsmen hint at the existence of rich patrons among the chieftains, the great bulk of the population were peasant farmers of no outstanding wealth. Settlements were mainly undefended, and consisted either of simple farmsteads working small estates of up to seventy or one hundred acres or else of larger village-groupings standing in bigger areas of fields. These fields are of the Celtic type, small square or oblong areas only a few hundred feet in dimension (pl. 10b), whose shape and size suggest the use of a light and primitive form of ox-drawn plough, and they represent an agricultural tradition which had already been implanted for a thousand years in parts of Britain. They survive today mainly on the chalk downs, demarcated by lynchets – the banks which accumulate as the soil is slowly ploughed or weathered to the lower edges of the cultivated area. Aerial photography suggests that formerly such farms extended over flatter areas of light soil, for instance the gravel spreads of the major English rivers such as those of the middle Thames, the Warwickshire Avon or of the rivers round the Fens, where subsequent cultivation has removed all surface traces.

At harvest time the seed-corn was separated from the rest and carefully preserved in small square or oblong granaries. The food-corn was first parched, to make it crisp and to prevent germination, and then stored in deep pits lined, no doubt, with basketry or leather. When required, the grains were ground on simple saddle-querns. The pottery was hand-made, without a wheel, probably mainly at home, but there is evidence also for specialist potters trading wares over long distances. The cooking vessels were very crudely made; their shapes are either rounded in the Hallstatt tradition or angular in imitation of shouldered bronze buckets; the finger-tip decoration on the angle is reminiscent of the rivets on the latter, and the red colour-coat resulting from the application of a haematite slip was also intended to recall the sheen of bronze. Finer vessels, often beautifully made and expertly polished, were used for cups and dishes, but these, also, in the details of their shape and decoration usually recall bronze prototypes. The bronzes themselves, however, were expensive, and probably rare except in chieftains' houses; in any case their value as scrap-metal when worn out has usually precluded their survival. Spinning and weaving were other industries carried on in the home with simple equipment. The houses were circular, but some were large and possessed elaborate timber-framing. Cows and sheep as well as pigs and goats supplemented the economy and so did hunting; but basically it was an agrarian landscape. The crops sown were barley, rye or beans and early forms of wheat; an important development by this period was the use of spelt, which being a hardier plant enabled winter sowing to supplement the spring-sown crops. This introduction not only lessened the labour to be undertaken in the spring but involved a further innovation in farming practice, since it became necessary to stall the herds to obtain manure; random dunging by herds cropping the stubble in the winter was only possible in spring-sown fields. That cattle-ranching on a larger scale also played a part in Iron A is suggested by areas of downland with no traces of ancient ploughing, where linear ditches suggest the boundaries of grazing areas. This picture of Iron A farming is necessarily generalised, being built up from evidence mainly from the chalklands of the south. That there were regional differences is suggested by the almost total absence of storage pits from early sites in East Anglia and in the south-west.

Little Woodbury is the classic site of a Wessex farmstead of Iron A. Here a palisaded farmyard of more than three acres contained two successive circular houses, the earlier and larger being fifty feet in diameter. Little evidence survived for the nature of the upper structure of the huts, apart from the plan of the timber framework: they were probably walled in clay or terre pisée between the framework, which is the traditional local manner. The renewal of post-holes in the house and in subsidiary structures such as drying racks and granaries pointed to long life, and it was noticed that throughout the lifetime of the farm certain areas in the yard tended to be associated with certain activities.

As well as the structures already mentioned, there were frequent storage pits, and also a large area riddled by successive bench-like hollows thought to be a working area where at successive harvests winnowing was carried out by hand. All these features seem to be characteristic of Iron A farmsteads on the chalk.

In Devon and Cornwall the sites at Kestor and Bodrifty, though of Iron A, reveal a slightly different pattern. The circular huts are mainly from twenty to thirty feet in diameter, and though they have a timber framework, revealed by a ring of post-holes, the main outer wall consists of a double wall of boulders filled in with rubble. At Kestor twenty-seven huts are loosely scattered along the sides of a ridge, in the vicinity of a larger hut set in a walled yard; they stand among the lynchets and field walls of a contemporary field system. At Bodrifty about a dozen similar huts stand mainly within a walled enclosure of three acres, and many others are scattered in the vicinity. At neither site were any storage pits discovered; thus, though corn-growing is attested at both sites, it is possible that cattle-rearing played a more important part in the economy in the south-west than it did in Wessex.

The hill-forts of Iron A are no longer to be regarded as examples of defensive methods newly introduced; they are developments of types which had been current in Britain for at least 400 years; since 1000 BC defences on this side of the Channel had developed parallel with those in adjacent areas on the continent. More or less well-dated examples of Bronze Age hill-forts are now known at Dinorben (ninth century), Ivinghoe Beacon (eight-seventh century), and elsewhere, such as at Crickley Hill. Continental ramparts of the Hallstatt period are primitive copies of Mediterranean urban walls; their essential characteristic is that the rampart core is enclosed front and back by dry stone revetment walls, producing a stout vertical rampart behind the ditch. Timber framing is usually employed, taking the form of spaced vertical timbers recessed front and back in the face of the walling, and tied to each other transversely through the body of the rampart. In Britain this type of fortification is found, but there are insular differences, possibly connected with the absence of suitable material for dry stone walling in most of the areas of primary settlement. Instead, after the ditch, perhaps eight feet deep and twice as wide, had been dug, the produce was often piled up behind a timber fence. In this way an almost vertical wall-face was created, the front consisting either of continuous vertical logs set in a foundation trench, or (more usually) of horizontal ones held back by spaced uprights. Normally this revetment is tied back to a parallel row of verticals behind, though these are not always so numerous as the front row. Occasionally, when suitable stone could be found, drystone walling was employed between the posts in the continental manner, as in the outwork or barbican which was added to the original entrance at Maiden Castle; elsewhere it is possible that rough dry walling in unsuitable materials such as chalk or flint nodules was sometimes attempted. In Cornwall the promontory fort of Maen Castle, near Lands End, had a thick wall of granite blocks packed in soil, for here suitable rock was available. At the gates tree trunks large enough to carry a rampart-walk over the gate were often set up, and the gate itself is often slightly set back within the incurving ends of the rampart. The arrangement in these early examples is not sufficiently pronounced to be styled an inturned entrance,[3] but it is definite enough. Such a timber-revetted type of fortification would be effective for about fifteen or twenty years, until the timbers rotted; then it collapsed unless repaired. Its character suggests the primitive nature of warfare in the earlier centuries of the Iron Age with no weapons but spears or daggers and a few slings, and no engines of war to effect a breach.

The primary area of Iron A in Britain lies south and east of a line from Scarborough to Gloucester. But beyond that line in the west the sea routes had led to scattered settlements on the coast of Wales, as at Dinas Powys in Glamorgan, at Caldy Island, or at Castell Odo on the northern peninsula, and possibly also farther round still, in Cheshire and Shropshire. At most sites, however, the scarcity of pottery which accompanies the pastoral way of life makes definition difficult. Along the east coast the sea routes led to eastern Scotland, but here also the pattern of settlement is still very imperfectly known. The agricultural basis of the culture was hard to establish in the adverse conditions of the north, and finds of datable objects are once again very rare. But Scotland had had its contacts with the Continent in the Late Bronze Age, and examples of timber-laced ramparts in Scotland have been shown to go back to the sixth or seventh centuries. In addition to finds of metal-work, round houses similar in design to the homesteads of Iron A in south Britain are known, and in two cases these are undefended, excavation in both producing 'flat-rimmed' pottery which is clearly akin to the Late Hallstatt types current farther south. There are also settlements surrounded by palisade-enclosures very reminiscent of sites like Staple Howe, and these are often found to precede and underlie the ramparts of hill-forts subsequently erected on the site. At Jarlshof in Shetland there is a well-explored settlement of this date which gives an interesting picture of the adaptations to environment forced on the new arrivals to the far north.

In many parts of Britain, then, evidence exists for elements of new culture introduced by fresh arrivals. The previous inhabitants, however, were not exterminated or driven out. Side by side with the settlers, whom they far outnumbered, they lived on, accepting, adapting, intermingling. In this way Iron A, and subsequently B and C as well, attained their insular specifically British character; for the native element made a considerable contribution to each.

1. Appian (*Roman History*, preface §5), writing in the second century, says that the Romans hold the most important half of Britain, but do not need the rest of it; for even the part they do occupy is not profitable to them.

2. In recent years many rectangular building-plans have been recognised in Britain, some of which may have been houses; but they are still relatively uncommon and appear in the main to be a feature of the earlier centuries of the Iron Age.

3. True inturns, with the gate set far back in a narrow passage, formed by turning the rampart-ends inwards through a right angle, were a later development.

2

Iron B and Iron C in Britain

A number of the hill-forts in Britain can now be seen to originate in
the period before 500 BC, but many were still being constructed
during the century following 400. This may be partly due to the
growing pressures induced by expanding population, but it is also
undoubtedly true that the years around 300 saw a renewal of migration from the Continent. What Celtic migration was like can be
gathered from accounts of the earlier Celtic invasion of Italy cul-
minating in the sack of Rome about 390, or the slightly later invasions of Greece and Asia Minor about 279; but in the case of
Britain there was the Channel to cross, and this as usual prevented
mass migration. Nevertheless, the arrival of chieftains and of warrior
bands can be deduced from the considerable changes which now took
place. New methods of fortification appear; the ancient Hallstatt
type of vertical wall passes out of use. And not only do new types of
pottery begin to be seen and new methods of finishing its surface,
but La Tène art-styles, applied to the decoration of metal-work and
even of pottery, are introduced and quickly take root. At the same
time the workshops which supplied the earlier British daggers go out
of production; a new style of dagger with anthropoid hilt is introduced; and long swords make their appearance for the first time for
three centuries. Though much of the new metal-work and many of
the new swords seem to have been made in Britain itself, and might
therefore be represented as native developments, this explanation
does not explain their genesis or cover the other changes: the comparatively sudden appearance of new styles of metal-work at this
date seems best explained by the arrival of new craftsmen following
in the wake of new patrons. Such new arrivals need not, and probably were not, large in numbers; they are much more likely to have
consisted for the most part of comparatively small yet powerful

war-bands under princely leaders, whose power both politically and culturally was out of all proportion to their numbers. This power may have been based on a new weapon of war – the chariot – itself an aristocratic accoutrement in the main, and one able to support the wide influence of the few. The use of chariots at this date in the south may perhaps be inferred from bridle bits now appearing for the first time, and is supported by the existence of certain linear earthworks, as in the Chilterns, which appear to be designed to prevent it. A century or so later chariots were still found in burials in East Yorkshire, although chariot burials on the Continent had long gone out of fashion. They are, it is true, not yet widely attested from Britain south of the Humber, but rich burials of any kind are so excessively rare that this is not in itself an insuperable difficulty. The Yorkshire group of settlers maintained their own traditions in conditions of relative cultural isolation.

This period of change and new introductions marks the appearance of Iron B, which is essentially a La Tène culture. From the new arrivals (First B) the influence of the new styles became widespread as they were adopted by the original inhabitants. This leavening of the older culture is known as Second B, and it took on varying characteristics in the different regions. The regionalism just mentioned may mark the growth of tribes or groups of tribes; but there was to be much more migration from across the Channel before more than a few of the historically attested tribes of the eve of the Roman conquest can be recognised. These regional groups of Iron Second B developed at various dates from the late third century and through the second. Moreover, the culture as a whole was socially stratified as well as regionally diversified. We know little at present of the dwellings of the rich, but parts of their equipment for parade, warfare or domestic furnishing are better attested, and have been much studied, most brilliantly perhaps by Sir Cyril Fox.[1] Their wide distribution gives a certain unity to the diversity seen in the peasant groupings. This unity was facilitated by intercourse along the Jurassic ridge between the Bristol Channel and the Humber, and by trade routes following the Thames Valley. At first metal was scarce, especially bronze: we find ponies' bits or parts of chariots made of iron and thinly sheathed in bronze; not until the first century BC were such things produced wholly in cast bronze. It was from the ports of the Bristol Channel that supplies of bronze were made available – so the distribution suggests – and some of the principal workshops of Iron B are thought to have been in this region. Contact was maintained with the Continent, for new swords and scabbards of La Tène II type appear, but they also soon develop distinctively insular characteristics and were made in British workshops. Some of this acquaintance with new continental features may have resulted from contact with the earliest groups of invaders of Iron C.

The La Tène culture of the Continent had developed a highly original art. Though based on classical forms such as the tendril or palmette and on eastern animal patterns, it translated these forms into abstract, non-representational figures, delighting in curving patterns, asymmetrical yet balanced, or in flowing interlocking scrolls; these could be emphasised by rounded relief or by elaborate hatching in the flat. This art was transplanted to Britain in Iron B, and there took on new life with original features. Sword-scabbards, horse-trappings, the metal parts of chariots, shields, tankards and even brooches or domestic pottery, all could be decorated with bewildering, skilfully drawn patterns in the La Tène style. Apart from the pottery, which does show regional variations reflecting the local peasant traditions of its makers, the principal examples of this art are found on expensive pieces of metal equipment which illustrate the background of patronage. Certain schools of craftsmen have been recognised, though not exactly located; but the distribution of objects transcends the tribe or individual region. Products of master-craftsmen travelled freely and probably so did the smiths themselves; debris from the workshop of a travelling bronzesmith has been found at Gussage All Saints in Dorset.[2] Perhaps the most surprising area of finds is Dumfriesshire in south-west Scotland. Here, it is clear, Second B chieftains had settled by the end of the third century, probably from Yorkshire, though possibly by the western sea-ways; and here they maintained themselves, as later finds of metal-work show, down to the first century AD. A traditional connection between this region and Yorkshire accords well with later historical situations, both in the time of Venutius (p. 119) and in the second century AD. The Stainmore Pass affords a connecting route of high antiquity and easy access.

Thus, elements which reflect aristocratic culture are widely diffused: the regional differences are largely a matter of pottery, which reflects the cultural divisions of the common people. Southern Second

B was perhaps the earliest. Pottery jars in black polished wares develop with new round-shouldered forms, and other shapes next appear which seem to copy wooden bowls. Rather restrained and simple curvilinear decoration is frequently applied to these vessels. Fresh forms of bronze brooch begin to spread. Eastern Second B is best illustrated in east Yorkshire, where the remains clearly exhibit a La Tène aristocracy ruling over a native population far less receptive of new influences than most. There are features, such as their rect-angular ditched burial-enclosures as well as imported metal-work and Mediterranean coral to decorate their brooches, which link them directly with the Continent. Further down the Jurassic belt the decorated pottery of Hunsbury is a classic example of Second B pottery at its most developed. Though highly decorated, it employs distinctively different art-forms from the pottery of Glastonbury.

In Gloucestershire and beyond there was a pottery development parallel with that in the southern region with slight differences in shape.[3] Crouched inhumation-burials appear to be typical.

The Cornish peninsula had long been in commercial contact with the Continent over the sale of tin, as the recorded visit of Pytheas of Marseilles about 320 BC reminds us.[4] Diodorus, in a famous passage which is derived probably from Pytheas, tells us of the inhabitants of *Belerium* (Lands End) who worked the tin and carried it to *Ictis* (St Michael's Mount): there it was bought by merchants who took it to Gaul, and ultimately after a journey of about thirty days they brought their wares by pack-horse to the mouth of the Rhone. It seems clear that this trade was flourishing before the beginning of the third century; there is a wide scatter of Greek coins in southern Britain (some at least of which are likely to be evidence of trade), and brooches of Iberian pattern suggest even earlier contact with Spain. In the second century intercourse continued, as is shown by the hoard of coins from Paul: these are coins of north Italian type, datable to the second half of the second century, and they illustrate at once the far end of the trade route and also the absence in Corn-wall, or indeed the whole south-west, of nearer coinages. This, as we shall see, has a chronological bearing on the date of foreign settlement.

The first contact between the south-west and the La Tène culture of Brittany was peaceful, being brought about by the intercourse of traders; and it should date to the third century. During the second century intercourse continued, and now a South-Western distinctive local culture can be recognised.[5] Breton-type pottery occurs in Cornwall, and cliff-castles – a form of hill-fort occupying a sea-girt promontory – such as are well known in southern Brittany, are found here too. These cliff-castles are usually defended by multiple ramparts to provide a defence in depth; and this feature, together with the step sometimes provided on the back of the rampart – another Breton feature – shows that the sling was the weapon in common use. Thus, there was close contact between the two regions, and we may suspect that some cliff-castles, such as Gurnard's Head and Sennen, were defended trading stations from about 200. Decorated pottery of an elaborate kind, with Breton affinities, can be dated almost as early at Castle Dore; this is a small multiple-enclosure fort of a local south-western type, where accordingly we may recognise the development of a native culture.

Somewhat later, beginning perhaps soon after 125, we find considerable signs of increasing contact with Normandy; the type-sites are the Rumps and St Mawgan in Pyder, where there are defended settlements with much pottery copying shapes current across the Channel. But the absence of local coinage in Cornwall carries the implication that these movements occurred before the Armorican coinage had developed in the homeland.[6]

It may have been from Cornwall that the idea of multiple ramparts spread to other areas in the south-west and west, for there was undoubtedly contact by coast-wise trade. But in these other regions they are constructed on quite a different scale, and may well be an independent local development born of internecine strife. Yet sling warfare was certainly employed in some, as was proved at Maiden Castle, and Armorican merchants were certainly active on the coasts of Dorset and Hampshire. The cross-channel trade reached its climax in the half century before Caesar's Gallic War, as is shown by the scatter of Armorican coins along the coast and by the settlement at Hengistbury Head.[7] This site was also in trade-contact with Italy at this time, as the many finds of amphorae of Dressel form 1 A show.[8] Breton influences can be seen in the internal rim-grooves and counter-sunk handles of its pottery; other pots seem to copy bronze bowls. The weaving equipment underwent modification, and multivallation spread among the hill forts. Here once again a date of c. 125 is suggested for the formative phase of this culture, for other-

31

wise Armorican silver coinage would have been transplanted to Dorset. During the first half of the first century, the inhabitants had begun using iron currency bars as a means of exchange and of hoarding wealth. These bars are sword-shaped; their distribution suggests a dispersion along the Jurassic way, where examples in Northamptonshire and Lincolnshire may, however, have been made locally. Another form of bar, spit-shaped, and slighter in form and weight, seems to have been made around the lower Severn valley. If these various forms of bar were used as primitive currency, they soon yielded before the spread of coinage proper from the south-east. For as it was, Dorset was overrun by Belgic chieftains with a different coinage tradition (see p. 35) perhaps about 80–70 BC; but these soon changed from a gold to a silver standard under the influence of cross-channel trade.

It may have been the stimulus of this same Breton trade, fertilising a stock made more artistic by contact with the craftsmen of the metal workshops, that at length contributed to the development (*c.* 100 BC) of another group in the Bristol Channel area.[9] The type-site is Glastonbury, a crannog village, difficult of access in the marshes of Somerset. Here a well-sheltered harbour gave access to a trackway leading to the metalliferous Mendips, and a large and long-lived settlement developed. It is chiefly remarkable for the highly decorated pottery of its later phases. Pottery of a similar type is widely distributed, though in small quantities, in Somerset, Devon and Cornwall, where, as we have seen, it had developed under Breton influence. It is probably simplest to attribute the origin of Glastonbury and Meare to traders coming up from Devon and Cornwall in the later second century.

The rich trade with the tribes of Armorica which for so long had exercised a powerful influence on south-western Britain came to an end with Caesar's conquest of Brittany in 56. The navy of the Veneti was destroyed and the tin-trade was disrupted. This had important economic consequences (p. 56).

A further group can be identified in western Britain.[10] These settlers had contacts with Northern Spain (an area which had had earlier connections with south-west Britain) via the western sea-route; they pushed up the Bristol Channel and settled in western Gloucestershire and Herefordshire. Their characteristic stamped pottery is found also, though sparsely, in Cornwall. They, too, seem to have been interested in metallurgy, for they obtained control of the iron-producing area of the Forest of Dean. In south-eastern Britain another group represented by a distinctive type of pottery is found in Surrey and Sussex (another iron-producing district), and sporadically round the Thames estuary.[11] Its origins are uncertain.

The hill-forts also must be reckoned to reflect the aristocratic element in society, and the various types current in Iron B very often transcend the boundaries of the peasant cultures. Down to about 400 they had continued to multiply, but thereafter a tendency can be seen for power to become concentrated in fewer but more powerfully defended strongholds. Second B, as we have seen, represented a transformation of Iron A, and the hill-forts show no great variation save that the ramparts when reconstructed are in simple dump construction: that is, they rely not on a vertical wall as did the Hallstatt type, but on a continuous glacis from ditch bottom to rampart top. Some hill-forts were greatly enlarged, but at Maiden Castle, where this was done at a date reckoned as *c*. 200 BC, the culture had not yet been seriously affected by Second B. In west Devon, Cornwall, west Somerset and south Wales a local variety known as multiple-enclosure forts is found, whose distribution points to the use of the sea-routes and whose form to the herding of cattle; in Cornwall they are not found in the same area as the cliff-castles. In east Devon, Dorset, western Hampshire and east Somerset the hill-forts are defended by close-set bivallate or multiple ramparts often of enormous size and strength; from this region they extend up the Jurassic belt as far as Northamptonshire and also along the Welsh Marches. This spread of multivallation in the south-west reaches a climax in Third B. In south-eastern Britain univallate hill-forts of simple dump construction were still being built by Second B folk, and at a later stage some of these were refortified with partial bivallation, probably against intruders from Belgic Gaul. In all this development there is a tendency for greater attention to be paid to entrances, where the gates are often set well back in a long narrow passage framed by inturns of the ramparts. Such a move could be introduced at the old hill-fort at the Trundle in Sussex in its latest phase, even though no other steps were then taken to elaborate the defences. In rocky areas, especially in the west, stone revetments are found on the face and sometimes even within the rampart; elsewhere dry stone walls of great strength are employed. Horizontal transverse timber lacing is also a method sometimes used to solidify the rampart.

Hill-forts are not uncommon anywhere save in eastern Britain and the Pennine area, but it is true to say that the vast majority of those in England concentrate in Wessex with its adjoining areas and in the Welsh Marches. Sometimes, as in Sussex and parts of Wessex, it is possible to see that one large hill-fort dominates a natural region and might therefore be considered as a communal defensive centre; but despite these signs of greater centralisation of power, the proliferation of hill-forts in general suggests an 'anarchy', a period of increasing baronial lawlessness, when each chieftain with his retainers was compelled to fortify because of the uncontrolled aggressiveness of the others. This might be due to growing land-shortage in Wessex or to successive waves of refugees from Western Third B, Belgic and then Roman expansion in the Marches.

Iron C

Meanwhile in Eastern Britain a new series of incursions was beginning, which after a period of turmoil were to mould her peoples into the tribes known when history first throws light on the situation. These are the invasions, attested by Caesar, of the Belgae, tribes who inhabited the area soon to become Gallia Belgica between the Seine, the Marne and the Rhine. These Belgae were culturally quite distinct from the tribes of Armorica whose activities affected the south-west; both their coins and their pottery and even their fortifications are easily distinguished. Formerly it was thought that they came in two main migrations, but Mr D. F. Allen's reappraisal of the coinage has demonstrated a much more complicated and realistic pattern. The earliest coins are continental. They do not indicate the presence of traders, for they are not found in the wealthier areas of Iron B such as east Yorkshire or Gloucestershire, but only in the regions of known Belgic settlement. Indeed, before the production of small change in silver and copper later in the period, high-value gold coins do not represent a money-economy, but rather an ostentatious method of storing wealth and of rewarding service. Like the subsequent groups of gold coins of similar continental origin which in due course gave rise to native issues, they must represent the arrival of chieftains and war-bands. A true trading pattern is seen rather in the distribution of Armorican silver coins in Britain, which is almost entirely coastal.

The coins can be arranged in a chronological series of groups on the evidence not only of design and typology but also of decreasing weight and specific gravity; these groups have been called Gallo-Belgic A-F. The distribution points to a complex series of movements into south-eastern and eastern Britain: it does not correspond with what we know of the position of later tribes or kingdoms, but represents an altogether earlier formative phase of raiding and migration by bands of adventurers. In the end successive bands succeeded in bringing over quite large parties of settlers, sufficient not merely to impose a new aristocracy but to supplant the culture of the peasant population.

The date of the earliest arrivals is difficult to fix with any precision. Owing to the earliest phases being those of movement and conquest, there is an absence of settlement material, and the relevant burials have not been found. The newcomers are represented at present only by their coins. The earliest of these [12] can be dated well before 100 BC, and possibly almost as early as 150. This would place them well back in La Tène II, whereas the developed culture of Iron C is associated with features of La Tène III. They should be accompanied by altogether earlier cultural characteristics, and it is likely that some at least of the La Tène II swords in Britain, many of which have been found in just the appropriate areas, should be assigned to them.

The third coin-series was the first imported coinage to be copied in Britain itself;[13] already on these the design, originally modelled on the gold coinage of Philip II of Macedon, had seriously deteriorated from the standard of Gallo-Belgic A. Of the copies, British A are found in Sussex, Surrey, Hampshire and southern Oxfordshire, and later were themselves copied by British B, whose distribution extends through western Hampshire into Dorset; there the two types gave rise to the tribal coinage of the Durotriges. As a worn coin of British B was found in the Le Catillon hoard, buried in Jersey at the time of Caesar's Gallic wars, and as the same hoard showed that ordinary Durotrigan silver coins were already in circulation, it is evident that British B must go back at least to *c.* 70 BC, and British A earlier still; while for Gallo-Belgic C, which gave rise to both, a date of *c.* 100 BC is entirely reasonable. The arrival of settlers or refugees from the Continent continued. A very numerous Gallo-Belgic coinage [14] appears to date from about the time of Caesar's Gallic wars; it may represent a comparatively large-scale movement of refugees from his conquest. Caesar himself [15] mentions the flight hither of leaders of the Bellovaci in 57, and later alludes to intervention from Britain in the Gallic wars.[16] Last of all the continental coin-series to reach Britain is one which must have been brought over after Caesar's wars, as is shown by the extreme scarcity of the actual imported pieces (for Caesar suppressed the issue of gold in Gaul); rare though they are, however, they gave rise to a numerous native coinage, British Q, which later shows itself to be connected with the name of Commius. This man, too, appears in the pages of Caesar, first as friend and then as bitter foe; and his subsequent flight to Britain, probably in 50, is recorded by Frontinus (p. 56).

The coins of Gallo-Belgic F and British Q have on the reverse a horse with a triple tail. The coins of Commius and the earliest coins of his son, Tincommius, kings of the Atrebates, are practically identical with these, save for the added names. The triple-tailed horse seems to be the badge of the Atrebatic kingdom, and the distribution of the coins, uninscribed as well as inscribed, gives us an approximate picture of the extent of Commius' realm. But the triple-tailed horse appears also on a second group of coins (British R) which can be associated with the historical Dobunni: the reverse of these is closely similar to, and clearly derived from, British Q, while the obverse carries a badge resembling a palm-branch. It seems obvious that the early rulers of the Dobunni were Belgic, and that they arrived from Commius' kingdom. But while the later coins of the southern dynasty, from Tincommius onwards, diverged into much more classical designs, those of the Dobunni stayed obstinately conservative: the original design remained intact until Boduocus about AD 43 placed his name BODVOC on the obverse in place of the palm.

Other derivatives of Gallo-Belgic C, termed British H and British I, were circulating in Lincolnshire and the Midlands, in the area later known to belong to the Coritani; here too we can be sure that Belgic chieftains had conquered the Iron B population, and Belgic pottery is known from a number of sites in Lincolnshire. The later inscribed coins of the Coritani bear double names such as ESUP-ASU, VOLISIOS-DUMNOCOVEROS, or VOLISIOS-DUMNOVELLAU, which, as Mr D. F. Allen has suggested, may indicate a dual magistracy: we might see here the results of the fusion of the two groups represented by British H and I into one single tribe. In Norfolk and Suffolk also the early coinage of the Iceni is in part derived from Gallo-Belgic C, and in part from British L; here, too, we should recognise a Belgic royal house ruling over earlier groups, though there is little Belgic material culture among the Icenian peasants themselves until the eve of the Roman conquest. The Trinovantes also must be considered to be at least partly Belgic, for Gallo-Belgic A coins are found in their territory; and though they appear to have resisted later attempts at conquest, they did at last succumb to the users of Gallo-Belgic E. In 54 BC they were being attacked by Cassivellaunus from their western flank; but this fact does not prove them non-Belgic, for in this early phase of settlement conflicting chieftains were warring for living room: there was no united army of conquest.

The picture of Britain that emerges from a study of the coins and other archaeological material is that in Kent, Hertfordshire and Buckinghamshire, and in eastern Hampshire, West Sussex and Berkshire successive Belgic migrations had produced a large body of settlers: beyond these regions conquering chieftains had asserted their authority over subject populations, but actual settlement by Belgic peasants was thin. In these areas the conquerors could be absorbed by the conquered. The Durotriges had been conquered thus; but their close mercantile connections with the tribes of Brittany, who used silver coins, caused them to abandon the gold standard and themselves change over to a silver coinage. As we have seen, this had already happened by Caesar's time, and after his wars these connections were disrupted. The other Belgic rulers later issued silver and copper coins, but only as small change for their continuing gold currencies. Their appearance, however, from about 20 BC meant the emergence of a true money-economy.

By the time that settlement and burial material of the Belgae become frequent enough to be recognised, they have entered the La Tène III phase. Their culture differed in several respects from that of Iron B. In the first place they cremated their dead; cremation cemeteries mark the areas of full settlement. Those at Aylesford and Swarling in Kent are recognised as type sites. The poor had their ashes placed in an urn which was sometimes accompanied by subsidiary vessels containing a viaticum. The wealthy were often buried in elaborate richly furnished tombs, sometimes surmounted by a barrow. Many of the more elaborate tombs, especially in the area of the Trinovantes, date from the decades after 50 BC, and are often accompanied by Italian wine-amphorae (in one tomb with a total capacity of over twenty gallons) and other provision for feasting, such as spits, fire-dogs and vessels of pottery or even of silver. One earlier tomb at Aylesford contained imported bronze vessels of Italian origin.

Their pottery was made on the potter's wheel. The application of rotary motion to this device, and to querns or hand-mills for domestic corn-grinding, was an invention of which knowledge was now spreading in Gaul; and it is occasionally found in the south-west also, especially on imported pottery. The use of the potter's wheel in Iron C was a step towards the professionalisation of the pottery industry. Much of the pottery was probably now made by specialists instead of domestically in the home: probably, then, by men rather than by women. The pedestal urn, which had had a long history in Gaul, was one of the types now introduced, and it was much used for burials, even after it had begun to disappear from the household range. Bead-rim vessels, often heavily combed, were another new type, based ultimately on metallic prototypes; and in the first century AD many new forms modelled on the platters and precious-metal cups of the classical world appear.

Hill-fort building was not much undertaken by the Belgae in Britain. Their own oppida are much larger than the normal hill-fort and do not seek out the hill-tops. In the early phase of settlement in the south-east, indeed, or in the areas where a Belgic ruling caste was holding a down a conquered people, pre-existing hill-forts are re-used and even refortified, as at Bigbury in Kent or Maiden Castle in Dorset. But Wheathampstead, which also dates to this phase but was a creation of the Belgae themselves, is double the size of Maiden Castle and lies not on a hill-top but beside the marshy flood-plain of the River Lea. Caesar speaks of a stronghold in Kent hidden in the woods and possessing strong natural and artificial defences, and of Cassivellaunus' oppidum he writes that it was defended by woods and marshes, and large enough to contain many men and cattle. 'The Britons call it an oppidum,' he goes on, 'when they have fortified thickly wooded spots with a rampart and ditch, as a place to retire to in order to avoid the attacks of their enemies.' Later Belgic oppida, like Camulodunum, Bagendon or Selsey, constructed in more settled times by more powerful rulers, occupied far larger areas defended partly by natural features, partly by banks and ditches. The dykes of Camulodunum enclose twelve square miles, though much of this area was no doubt devoted to pasture or market gardens.

Belgic settlement thus began the exploitation of heavier soils in valley bottoms or in the widespread loam-lands of eastern Britain. Their ability to do this was no doubt due to the greater availability of iron tools, such as axes for clearing the vegetation. It used to be thought that they introduced a heavier plough, equipped with coulter, whose use facilitated the exploitation of such soils. But the evidence for this idea does not stand up to examination. Only three of the so-called coulters are known; and they differ fundamentally in shape and weight from the undoubted coulters of Roman Britain; moreover, the latter seem themselves to be a development only of the later Roman period. The Belgic 'coulters' were probably bill-hooks, and with this recognition the case for a heavy Belgic plough collapses. Nevertheless, the Belgae were assiduous farmers, and aerial photography has supplemented the evidence of excavation for the widespread distribution of the small farms of this period. Corn storage was now for the most part carried out in large pottery vessels – another benefit of improved pottery – and the use of storage pits diminishes, though it does not entirely disappear.

The Belgae greatly stimulated the metal industries of Britain. Iron became much more plentiful in supply, and so did bronze. Exploitation of the iron field of the Weald was greatly expanded, if indeed it did not now for the first time begin; and metal was probably traded from the Forest of Dean and other iron-fields such as Northampton-shire. The skilful craftsmanship of the Belgic blacksmith can be seen in the surviving fire-dogs, the Welwyn amphora-stand, or in the slave-chains with elaborate neck-shackles which enabled captives to be controlled on the estate or for the foreign slave-market. The Belgic leaders, like the chieftains of Iron B, continued to patronise the bronze-smiths of Britain, and much of the fine late La Tène art of Britain is of Iron C. There were several innovations. The staved wooden vessels from Aylesford and Marlborough, decorated with bronze bands bearing repoussé decoration, are likely to have been imports, but they had their influence over here. On them and on other bucket mounts of a humbler sort we see a much more realistic por-trayal of animal and human figures. Further examples of staved vessels are to be found in the tankards, which were a Belgic introduction, though the type later spread westwards among other tribes. Many bronzes are decorated with studs of red enamel *en cabochon*, recalling the coral studs used in earlier times for the same effect; subsequently, areas of red enamel in champlevé technique are found decorating bronzes usually connected with pony harness. Outstanding works of art such as the Battersea shield or the Waterloo helmet illustrate the rich panoply of Belgic warrior leaders, just as the plainer scabbards of La Tène III type point to that of the ordinary warrior. The famous gold torcs from the Snettisham treasure, whatever the explanation of their find-spot, illustrate the wealth and the magnificent craftsmanship at the disposal of royal princes or Druidical high priests in this Belgic society as do those from Ipswich. On a lower plane, many of the coin-designs illustrate aspects of life and art, ranging from quintessential horses, boars, or wolves, through martial equipment like the carnyx (the war-trumpet with animal mouth) to horse- or footmen armed with a variety of weapons: some illustrate peaceful aspects of life, such as dress, smithing or music.

After about 30 BC great changes can be seen to affect the character of Iron C. In the first place political stability began to take the place of conflict, as the long settlement phase drew to a close. Following the lead of Commius, other kings began to inscribe their names and titles on coins, and in this way something of the political history of the period can for the first time be discerned: this will be described in Chapter 4. Secondly, this political stability in Britain, leading on to more settled and unified government over far wider territories than previously, coincided with the new stability introduced into the affairs of Rome by Augustus. There could not fail to develop an intercourse with the Roman Empire, which manifested itself on the political as well as on the economic plane. By the opening of the first century AD we have plentiful evidence of ever-increasing trade, while Roman imports give a new precision to archaeological dating, as well as illustrating the growing wealth of Britain.

1. *A Find of the Early Iron Age from Llyn Cerrig Bach, Anglesey* (Cardiff, 1946); *Pattern and Purpose* (Cardiff, 1958).
2. *Antiquity* xlvii (1973), 109 ff.

3. This is classified as Western Second B.

4. Much earlier contacts, in the sixth century, are recorded in Avienus, *Ora Maritima*. Fifth- and fourth-century Greek pots are known from two sites in Cornwall and from elsewhere in Britain. See A. Fox, *South West England* (London, 1964), p. 116.

5. South-Western Second B.

6. It is possible that some of the makers of cordoned pottery were refugees from Caesar's conquest of the Armorican peninsula in 56, but if these came in any number the absence of coining is striking. The site at St Mawgan itself seems to belong to a later phase, but this does not invalidate the date here suggested for the beginning of the migration.

7. In Dorset the variant culture produced by this intercourse is called Southern Third B.

8. D. P. S. Peacock, in M. Jesson and D. Hill, *The Iron Age and its Hill-forts* (1971), p. 173.

9. South-Western Third B.

10. It is classified as Western Third B.

11. South-Eastern Third B.

12. Gallo-Belgic A and B.

13. Gallo-Belgic C.

14. Gallo-Belgic E.

15. *B.G.*, ii, 14.

16. *Ibid.*, iv, 20.

3
Caesar's Expeditions

In the previous chapters we have traced the prehistory of Britain in the Iron Age down to the time when contact was established with the world of Rome. Mediterranean civilisation had developed on the foundation of the city state, and this was still the essential local unit; but above it had sprouted the grandiose visions of world empire which the west inherited from Alexander. Under the Roman Republic the Senatorial Government had tried to limit their expansion to the Mediterranean sea-board, despite the pressure of the mercantile class for wider opportunities of exploitation. But in the first century BC the government was fast losing, if it had not already lost, control, and power was falling more and more into the hands of powerful dynasts, such as Sulla, Pompey and Caesar, who commanded large armies and controlled influential political organisations. By the time that Britain passed fully under Roman rule the process was complete, and the Augustan Empire had been established. To such a state world-rule was part of its philosophical inheritance; it did not have to be justified, but might be limited by temporary considerations of empirical convenience.

In 58 BC Caesar had undertaken the governorship of the provinces of Illyricum and of Cisalpine and Transalpine Gaul. The latter was Provence, the hinterland of the Rhone mouth and the coastlands which guarded the route to Spain. In the years that followed he became involved in defending and extending Roman interests in Gaul beyond the boundaries of this province. Having dealt with the attempted migration of the Helvetii and the dangerous nuisance of Ariovistus and his Germans in 58, he was drawn on to intervene the following year in Belgic Gaul. He had become convinced that Roman control was necessary for the defence of the Rhine against renewed German penetration, and seems at first to have intended a protec-

42

torate over Gaul itself, leaving the inhabitants very largely to manage their own affairs under governments friendly to himself. But this protectorate became less and less possible as the pattern of resistance followed by intervention recurred. In 57 he defeated the Belgic confederation of tribes in north-west Gaul, and also received the surrender of the maritime tribes of Normandy and Brittany.

He could not have been operating in this region for long before becoming aware of the influence exerted by Britain on Gallic affairs. The tribes of Armorica were in close commercial contact with the south-west of Britain, which was the source of considerable mineral wealth. When Armorica revolted in 56, military assistance was received from Britain; and in Belgic Gaul also he found that there were close political and military contacts with tribes across the Channel. Within living memory Divitiacus, king of the Suessiones (round Soissons), had ruled in Britain as well.[1] Malcontents could escape the Romans by flight across the sea, as happened in 57 when chieftains of the Bellovaci had fled thither.[2] There were, therefore, sound military reasons for intervention in addition to considerations of economic gain; nor must we under-estimate the prestige which would accrue from a successful intervention in Britain. For at that time it was still regarded as a mysterious isle, only vaguely known to the classical world: it lay beyond the Ocean, which the popular outlook still regarded as bounding the habitable world.

There are good reasons for suggesting that Caesar had planned a British expedition for 56, the year before he actually came; but because his plans came to naught they received scant publicity from Caesar himself. In that year the ocean-going fleet of the Veneti was to hand, its pilots long experienced in the Channel routes leading to the south-west. In 57 Publius Crassus had been operating in Brittany with one legion, and later wintered near the mouth of the Loire: it is very probably he to whom Strabo[3] is referring when he tells us of a visit to the Cassiterides or tin islands (probably the Scillies) by a Roman of this name, which resulted in increased geographical knowledge. This sounds very like a reconnaissance of the western route. Moreover, elsewhere Strabo[4] gives as one of the motives for the Venetic rebellion of 56 the fear that an invasion of Britain would interrupt their commerce. Invasion, then, was certainly in the air at this time, though, as we have seen, not yet mentioned in Caesar's own Commentaries. In the winter of 57 large forces were stationed in

43

western as well as in Belgic Gaul, where they would be conveniently available for embarkation. But in the event, the rebellion in 56 of the Armorican tribes and the necessity of destroying the Venetic fleet nullified these plans, and the plan which succeeded them involved an invasion of the Belgic south-east of Britain in 55. In late 56, therefore, we find Caesar hastening to subdue the Morini and Menapii, who controlled the Channel coasts in the neighbourhood of the Straits of Dover. In fact, however, the invasion of 55 was delayed, partly owing to the difficulty of bringing these tribes to battle and more seriously owing to a new, large-scale invasion of Germans from across the Rhine. Much of the summer of 55 was taken up with these matters and with a short demonstration in strength beyond the Rhine; it was not until August that he was free to turn his attention to Britain.

There were not sufficient transports available for more than a small force, but neither was there time for more than a reconnaissance. This Caesar determined to attempt. He tells us that from Gallic merchants he had been unable to obtain much information of military value, but he had received offers of surrender from a number of British tribes once his plans had become known. The political situation in Britain was as fluid as had been that in Celtic Gaul and tribes under attack from their neighbours were glad to obtain Roman support. Plainly there were immediate advantages in retaining the initiative and in going to see for himself: and behind these reasons lay the deeper personal motives only discernible from a study of the Roman political scene. Mr C. E. Stevens has shown [5] that the legality of an invasion of Britain, however strategically desirable, was doubtful, or at best uncertain. The penalties for a governor illegally acting outside his province were heavy, and Caesar had powerful political enemies eager to bring him down. A small, short expedition would test public opinion in Rome; and if this were unfavourable the exploit could be represented as a mere punitive excursion similar to the one already made across the Rhine. In the event the verdict was overwhelmingly favourable, and the Senate even voted a thanksgiving of twenty days, five longer than that given in 57 for the subjection of Gaul itself. Part of the enthusiasm was undoubtedly fired by the achievement of campaigning beyond Oceanus and thus opening a new field to Roman endeavour. The way was clear for the conquest of Britain, and the necessary time was available as well. For early in 56 had occurred the conference of Luca, as a result of which he had obtained a five-year prolongation of his command. With Gaul apparently pacified, this left six campaigning seasons available for overrunning Britain, amply sufficient for the reduction of the lowland zone.

On 26 August, therefore, Caesar crossed the Channel, intending only a limited stay. He assigned two legions, the Tenth and Seventh, and about 500 cavalry to the task, but the cavalry did not arrive owing to contrary winds. The approach of the season of equinoctial gales in late September meant that he had less than a month for action before return would become imperative. Though, as we have seen, he had other motives, the immediate purpose of such a short and limited expedition must have been reconnaissance for the larger invasion planned for 54. Much of the original intelligence collected will have related to Wessex and the south-west, and his more recent enquiries had told him nothing of the size of Britain, or the character of its interior, or the fighting qualities of its inhabitants. The confused state of military information about the south-east is shown by his use of Commius as an envoy. This Atrebatic chieftain had the reputation of possessing much influence in the south-east, but in fact was arrested as soon as he landed. The Atrebatic settlers lay farther west.

Commius had been sent over with the returning ambassadors from those British tribes who had offered hostages and obedience. His orders were to visit as many tribes as possible and persuade them to make their peace. Caesar had also sent ahead a trusted tribune, C. Volusenus, with a single warship to carry out a naval survey of the coast and discover a landing place. This officer was away five days, and will certainly have explored the coast from Hythe to Sandwich. The curious fact is his failure to discover the harbour of Richborough, which was so successfully used a century later. Whatever its cause, this failure had profound effects on the campaign both this year and next, for on both occasions Caesar had to land on an open beach, and on both occasions his transports were gravely damaged by storms.

Perhaps Volusenus did not go as far north as Richborough, or perhaps he did not care to explore too closely inside coastal inlets in a single ship. We have no evidence to suggest coastal changes in the century between Caesar and Claudius, though this part of the coast

45

has, of course, changed profoundly in the period between Caesar and the present day; it is certainly curious that, even if Richborough was missed by Volusenus, it was not discovered by patrols after the landing. Another possibility is that the harbour of Richborough was not as splendid as its modern reputation; but there must have existed some sort of inlet at the mouth of the Stour, even if it was not large enough to accommodate the whole fleet, and Caesar does not appear to have known of its existence. This was undoubtedly the penalty paid for the absence of the cavalry. Short of actual archaeological identification of Caesarian earthworks, no better indentification of the landing-place is likely to be available than that offered by Rice Holmes's masterly and very full examination of the evidence. The point of departure was Portus Itius, convincingly identified with the later Gesoriacum, the harbour of Boulogne. Eighteen transports had been held up by contrary winds eight miles farther up the coast at Ambleteuse, and these were assigned to the cavalry; but they missed the tide and next day were blown back by contrary winds.

Caesar himself with the two legions – about 10,000 men – set sail at midnight, and by nine the next morning was off Dover, where he saw the formidable cliffs lined with defenders, and realised the impossibility of landing thereabouts. He lay at anchor till three o'clock, to await the slower-moving transports, and employed the time in briefing his officers. When the rest of the fleet arrived he moved northwards and ran the ships ashore in the neighbourhood of Walmer and Deal. The Britons had followed along the coast, and were there to oppose the landing. The shelving beach compelled the soldiers to jump down into deep water, and the heavily armed legionaries were at a disadvantage; but Caesar was able to use the lighter warships with their artillery and complements of slingers and archers on the left flank, and he also manned smaller boats with reinforcements under orders to support any bodies of troops seen to be in difficulties. The eagle-bearer of the Tenth legion bravely leapt into the water, and the soldiers plucked up heart to follow him. Eventually a foot-hold was gained on the beach, and a determined charge put the enemy to flight. It was now that the lack of cavalry made itself felt, for the rout could not be made final. Nevertheless, the mercurial temperament of the Britons at once compelled them to seek terms; they handed over Commius, surrendered some hostages and promised more. They also dismissed their levies, and soon a trickle of distant chieftains began to appear, to ask for peace.

Four days later the cavalry transports were sighted: but before they could make land they were scattered by a storm and with difficulty returned to the Continent. The same storm coincided with a full moon and an exceptionally high tide. The beached warships were badly damaged and the transports which had been riding at anchor were soon in grave difficulties. Some were lost, the rest found to be unusable.

This disaster turned the tables. The Britons took fresh hope and began to slink away to raise their forces once again: the Romans were without means of retreat or of supply. But Caesar was equal to the emergency. Forage parties were organised, and the rest of the army, working with great energy, repaired all but twelve ships, using the material from these to patch the rest. While this was going on the Seventh legion, whose turn it was to forage, was ambushed by a British force consisting largely of chariots and cavalry. It was saved by the sharp eyes of the cohorts on guard duty at the camp who observed an unusual cloud of dust in the direction taken by the legion. Caesar hastened to the rescue and drove off the enemy, but once again his lack of cavalry prevented effective pursuit. Nevertheless, his success produced a further offer of British hostages, and taking advantage of this success, such as it was, Caesar set sail that night with his whole force and returned to Gaul.

The first British expedition had not enjoyed the success intended. The non-arrival of the cavalry and the naval disaster had ignominiously pinned him to the coast of Kent, and more determined leadership on the part of the British might have placed him in considerable jeopardy. From a different point of view, however, his success had been spectacular. The fact that the Ocean had been crossed and surrenders made by the barbarians of Britain was what appealed to Rome and resulted in the unprecedented grant of a *supplicatio* lasting twenty days. And Caesar himself had learnt the character of British fighters; had encountered war-chariots for the first time and had seen how to deal with them; had found that an invading army could seize sufficient corn in Britain for its needs; and had discovered what seemed a suitable landing place for next year's campaign. The risks which are inseparable from success in war had been faced, and the balance in the end was satisfactory.

In 54 operations were on a much larger scale. As many as 600 transports had been constructed to a special design during the winter, as well as twenty-eight warships; including last year's ships and some privateers, over 800 vessels were to cross the Channel in one fleet. The new transports were lower in the beam than usual, for ease of loading and beaching, and rather wider than normal to carry more cargo, and they were all fitted with oars as well as sail. Caesar had assembled a large army at Boulogne: five of his eight legions and 2,000 cavalry were chosen to accompany him. There were thus many more animals as well as men to transport, and for a full-scale expedition a heavy baggage train was required. Labienus was left with the remaining three legions and 2,000 cavalry to keep the peace in Gaul, and to see to the proper supply of corn and the security of the ports.

Owing to various delays the expedition did not finally set sail till the beginning of July; on 29 August Caesar wrote to Cicero that he was shortly going to re-embark his forces, and the evacuation was probably completed by about the middle of September. Caesar thus spent just over two months in Britain, and during that time, despite a second serious naval disaster, he defeated and imposed terms on the Belgic confederacy which opposed him. No one could have done more: many ancient generals would have achieved less. In fact, his success is closely parallel, in its scale and in the time taken, with that of Aulus Plautius a century later; and the latter's task was simplified by the centralisation of Belgic power which had occurred in the meanwhile.

The expedition sailed at nightfall about 6 July, and in the morning Britain was seen on the left. The wind had dropped at midnight, and the fleet was drifting with the tide up Channel. Then the tide turned, oars were got out and a landfall made at a point chosen as best for the purpose the previous year. These facts make it certain that the landing took place in the area between Deal and Sandwich. It was unopposed. As he soon learnt from prisoners, the Britons had been alarmed by the unprecedented size of the fleet and had retired to high ground inland. Everyone was on land by midday and a camp was built. As soon as he had discovered the whereabouts of the enemy he decided on a bold stroke. A night march would bring him to the Stour crossing, which they were massing to defend twelve miles away, before he was expected. He left ten cohorts and 300 cavalry under Q. Atrius to guard the camp. The beach was open and gentle, and he took the risk of leaving the ships at anchor instead of consuming valuable time hauling them up to security.

In the early morning he reached the Stour and easily drove the Britons from the crossing. The principal ford lay at the future site of Canterbury. No settlement yet existed on this site, but a hill-fort lay on the heights above at Bigbury, 1½ miles beyond the ford. This must be the place in the woods with strong natural and artificial fortifications previously prepared for inter-tribal war, which Caesar describes, and to which the defeated Britons retired. His night march had paid its dividend.

The entrances to the earthwork were blocked with felled trees, and from the edges of the wood the Britons sallied out in small groups and impeded the advance. However, the Seventh legion formed a dense column with shields locked over their heads, and captured the hill-fort by assault across a causeway made by filling the ditch with earth and faggots. Caesar never had the same trouble over British hill-forts as he encountered in Gaul: it would have been a different story, perhaps, if his plans to invade the south-west had come to anything.

The capture of Bigbury terminated that day's fighting: pursuit was postponed, for a camp had to be constructed. This camp has still to be located. It must occupy some 150 acres, perhaps at Harbledown. The next day he had just despatched three columns of mixed cavalry and infantry in the pursuit – already he had mastered the tactics necessary to cope with British chariots – when messengers arrived from Q. Atrius with the news that disastrous damage had been suffered by the fleet in a storm the night before: almost all the ships had been driven on shore. He recalled the battle-groups which were not yet quite out of sight, ordered a retreat to the coast, and himself went on ahead to assess the damage. Forty ships proved to be a total loss, but an inspection showed that the rest might be repaired. This was a serious set-back. The damage itself was the least of his worries: precious time had to be wasted hauling up everything beyond the reach of the waves and in constructing a strong landward fortification. Messengers were sent to Labienus for crafts-men from the Continent, and with orders for the legions there to start constructing ships. By working night as well as day the task of beaching and fortification was completed in ten days: the repair of the surviving ships would, of course, take longer.

The beaching of 760 ships was an enormous task, and enormous, too, must have been the area to be included in the new ramparts. It is easy to see why on first landing he had not delayed his march until such a task had been undertaken; and it is important to remember that, even if he had done so, the thirty-six hours or so available before the onset of the storm would not have sufficed to avert more than a very small part of the disaster. The real fault lay in not having discovered a suitable harbour. If Richborough was too small, or for any reason now unknown to us unsuitable, a landing somewhere in the Thames mouth might have been wiser, though it would have meant a longer voyage and one into unknown waters. This difficulty over suitable harbourage may have been one of the factors which influenced Plautius a century later to cross in three divisions.

We may conclude that Caesar's judgement of the risks was not at fault. Speed – the famous *Caesariana celeritas* – was ever the secret of his success. The ten days' delay now enabled the Britons to do what he had hoped to prevent. Submerging their differences, they chose Cassivellaunus as supreme commander. Cassivellaunus, 'the first British historical personality', ruled beyond the Thames: though Caesar does not say so, it is probable that he was king of the Catuvellauni, who are later vouched for in the Hertfordshire–Buckinghamshire–Cambridgeshire area north of the Thames. Their area of settlement at this stage was probably neither so widespread nor so well defined, but Cassivellaunus was undoubtedly a distinguished war-lord. Under his command a much larger confederate army drawn from all sources was awaiting Caesar in the neighbourhood of the Stour crossing. This time there was no set battle. British cavalry and charioteers kept up a running fight with the Roman cavalry, but were unable to prevail, unless they could cut off groups which pursued too far. They were aided by their knowledge of the surrounding woods: later in the day, when the Roman camp was being constructed, they unexpectedly appeared in a fierce attack on the troops on guard and succeeded in eluding two cohorts sent to cut them off.

The Romans had not encountered chariot-warfare in Gaul, and at first found it hard to adapt themselves to it. Chariots had a complement of one warrior and one driver. They were drawn by two ponies, but although certain classical authors, confusing them with Persian chariots, credit them with axle-scythes, such things are neither mentioned by Caesar nor attested by archaeology. Their tactics were to drive swiftly over the battlefield, hurling javelins and creating confusion and panic with their dashing horses and the noise of the wheels. If they could get among the cavalry the warrior dismounted to fight, and the charioteer retired to be at hand to aid a speedy retreat. The chariot gave the fighter the mobility and speed of cavalry, without preventing him exhibiting the virtues of infantry as well. Daily practice gave great skill in manoeuvring at speed over rough ground. The warrior would even dash out along the pole and stand on the yoke while travelling at full gallop. The secret of the chariot was its resilient wheel made of a one-piece felloe – an invention, it seems, of the Celts. The Roman legionaries, weighed down with heavy armour, could not pursue when the enemy gave ground, nor did they dare to leave the close formation in which they had been taught to fight. The Roman cavalry could master the chariots, but when enticed too far from the supporting legions by simulated flight, they in turn failed before the dismounted warriors. Ancient cavalry was poorly mounted, and they had no stirrups. The correct tactics to employ against the chariots, as Caesar soon learned, was to keep cavalry and infantry in touch and acting in concert. After that they caused no further trouble.

The next day the opportunity came for a decisive Roman victory. The Britons attempted to repeat their success of the previous year against a detachment on foraging duty. But this time the column, commanded by C. Trebonius, consisted not only of three legions but the whole of the cavalry. The Romans were able to turn the tables, and flight became a rout as the Roman cavalry, emboldened by the support of the legions, kept up the pursuit. This failure took the heart out of the Britons: the allies melted away and no further pitched battle took place. Cassivellaunus was left as the objective, and Caesar now pressed on towards the Thames, which formed the southern borders of his kingdom. The river was fordable, Caesar says, at one point only, and there only with difficulty. This crossing had been protected with stakes on the bank and others under water, but the passage was forced – the legionaries up to their necks in water as they waded over – and the Romans were across.

The identification of this ford has been confused by the natural eagerness of antiquaries to place it at spots such as Brentford or Walton where stakes have been recorded. In fact, however, these points are all too far upstream for probability, and the remains in question would be more easily explained as fish-weirs or pile-dwellings.[6] The Claudian army in AD 43 found a ford at London,[7] and it is hard to see how Caesar could have missed it; and as shortly afterwards he found himself in Trinovantian territory (Essex), this strengthens the case for London. There is not the least need for the stakes to have survived; indeed, it is hard to see how they could have, even had they been allowed to obstruct the crossing after the war.

Cassivellaunus now pinned his faith on guerrilla tactics. The country north of the Thames was much more thickly wooded than Kent, but it was his home ground, and his people knew all the tracks. Dismissing his infantry, he retained only 4,000 chariots. With these he kept up worrying skirmishes and cleared the Roman route of inhabitants and cattle alike. Caesar was compelled to keep his cavalry near the column for fear of ambushes, and his policy of devastation was in consequence much restricted. However, he still had one card up his sleeve.

Mandubracius, a prince of the Trinovantes, had fled to Caesar in Gaul when his father, their king, had been killed by Cassivellaunus. The Trinovantes now sent envoys to Caesar offering surrender, and asking for the young prince to succeed his father as king. They sent hostages and grain, and for their part were protected from devastation by Roman troops as well as from attack by Cassivellaunus. When this became known, other tribes (otherwise unknown to us) – the Cenimagni, Segontiaci, Ancalites, Bibroci and Cassi – joined them in surrender. Cassivellaunus in this way paid for his previous aggressive policy, and Caesar learnt from his new allies the whereabouts of Cassivellaunus' oppidum. This was quite close, but its secret had been preserved through the effectiveness of Cassivellaunus' scorched-earth policy.

If this oppidum was Wheathampstead it lay on the west bank of the River Lea. Caesar remarks on the strength of its defences, but he attacked it on two sides and soon broke in, capturing large numbers of cattle – no doubt those previously swept from his path – and killing or taking prisoner many Britons. The strategic skill of Cassivellaunus and his powers of leadership are mostly clearly seen now in the closing stages of the campaign. With Caesar already at his gates, he had sent orders to the four kings who ruled in Kent to attack the naval camp: and despite the black appearance of his prospects these orders were obeyed. It was a shrewd blow aimed where it could damage Caesar most dangerously. But the attack did not succeed: the Britons were easily routed by the garrison, and when the news reached Cassivellaunus he determined to give in. This he did, using the mediation of Commius.

This last fact probably means that Caesar had taken the initiative in offering acceptable terms. He had every reason to do so for, as he himself makes clear, it would have been easy for his enemy to prolong opposition until the end of the campaigning season. Moreover, it is likely that disturbing news had come from Labienus, sufficiently unsettling to cause him to alter his original intention of wintering in Britain. It may have been in connection with this news and change of plan that he paid a visit to the coast about 5 August. He does not record this himself, but we learn of it from a letter of Cicero's. The visit must have been snatched in mid-campaign, as a short consideration of dates will show. The landing had taken place about 6 or 7 July. The wreck and ten days' reconstruction take us to about 19 July before the campaign can have been restarted. Trebonius' victory will have occurred about 21 July. The march to the Thames and beyond can hardly have been over in little more than a fortnight; and if it was, there is a long unexplained delay thereafter, for as we have seen Caesar had still not yet evacuated Britain by 29 August. The visit to the coast can hardly have been connected with the attack on the naval camp, for this cannot have occurred so early, since it is associated with the closing events of the campaign. The visit in fact seems to have taken place while the army was safely in Essex, and the motive was probably the necessity for urgent and rapid communication with the Continent. Caesar himself tells us that one of his reasons for deciding to winter in Gaul was the danger of sudden uprisings there, and it was known that the harvest that year had been poor.

Both sides were thus interested in coming to terms, and these were quickly agreed. Hostages were given, an annual tribute was fixed, and the security of the Trinovantes from aggression was arranged. The army now returned to the coast, where the fleet lay repaired. Owing to the number of prisoners and shortage of vessels, Caesar decided to evacuate in two stages; but few of the empty vessels were able in the event to return to Britain because of contrary winds, and after a long wait he crowded everyone into the ships he had and on a calm night sailed for Gaul.

1. *B.G.*, ii, 4.
2. *Ibid.*, ii, 14.
3. *Ibid.*, iii, 5, 11.
4. *Ibid.*, iv, 4, i.
5. *Antiquity*, xxi (1947), 3–9.
6. Bede, for instance (*H.E.*, i, 2), says the stakes were still visible in his day, as thick as a man's thigh and sheathed in lead. This sounds more like the piles of a Romano-British bridge. He does not give the position.
7. Changes in the relative level of land and sea in post-Roman times have resulted in the tides reaching far higher up the Thames than they did in Caesar's day. Recent work has suggested the likelihood that there was a ford near Tilbury. If so, and if it was the one used by Caesar, it would bring him more easily to the territory of the Trinovantes; and it might throw light on the location of Cassivallaunus' territory, which, we are told, adjoined the river. I am grateful to Mr W. Rodwell for knowledge of the ford.

4
Caesar to Claudius

Caesar had come and gone. The future denied him the opportunity of ever returning, but this failure to complete his work in Britain was only to be certified by the passage of time. A century and a half later the historian Tacitus summed up the situation as it then appeared to him by saying that Caesar had revealed rather than bequeathed Britain to Rome; and Claudius could go so far as to claim to be the first Roman to reduce the barbarians beyond the Ocean to obedience. Thus, subsequent generations came to overlook what had been achieved. But to contemporaries, and for more than a generation after the expedition, the picture was probably different. Mr C. E. Stevens has pointed out that in his description of the conditions of surrender Caesar employs legal and technical terms such as *dedito* and *vectigal*, which specifically indicate the first steps in forming a province out of conquered territory.[1] The final steps, as it turned out, were never taken; but for some time to come the possibility of taking them remained, and there are indications in contemporary writers that this fact was recognised down to 40 BC and even later. However, treaties had been made and tribute imposed, and hostages taken to secure obedience. It is often carelessly stated that the tribute was never paid; but there is no evidence for this, and it is most unlikely. The treaties with Cassivellaunus and the Trinovantes would have been binding so long as the rulers concerned survived: only when they died would a new situation develop. Cassivellaunus is unlikely to have broken his agreements while Caesar lived, and for Mandubracius and the Trinovantes, whose submission had altered the whole course of the campaign by leading the wavering tribes into alliance with Rome, strict compliance with Roman requirements was even more necessary in their own interests. Some reflection of the fruits of Roman friendship can be seen in the large number of Italian wine-amphorae which now begin to appear in the tombs of the Trinovantian nobility.

Thus, for Britain a new era had opened. The Roman empire now reached the Channel, and its menace or its friendship were ever-present political choices; for what had been done once could be done again. The old-established trade-routes had been disrupted; tin for the time being was no longer exported to Armorica from the South-West and meanwhile the development of Spanish tin-production captured the market; for more than a generation there is little sign, except in Essex, of cross-channel contacts between the Belgic South-East and Roman Gaul. Instead, it has been suggested that new contacts were sought across the North Sea. There is, however, little evidence of this at present, and indeed south-eastern Britain had few exports which were likely to find a market in barbarian Europe.[2]

In one other respect the situation was altered. Commius had been a friend of Caesar, as we have seen, and had been generously rewarded for his services; but after the British expeditions he took the side of Vercingetorix in the great Gallic rebellion, and played a prominent part in the resistance. Labienus had attempted to have him assassinated, but he escaped with a severe head-wound; a second attempt to kill him failed, and when he finally submitted it was on condition that he should never again have to meet a Roman. Shortly after this, probably in 50 BC, he seems to have made his escape to Britain, for Frontinus recounts the strategem whereby he eluded pursuit by spreading sail although the rising tide had not yet floated his ships: the Romans, thinking him afloat, abandoned the chase. In Britain coins bearing the name of Commius derive from the uninscribed British Q series, which is otherwise identical and presumably represents the earliest issues of the group over which he eventually attained supremacy. The distribution suggests an entry in the Chichester area and the establishment of a kingdom south of the middle Thames. He will have been joined by many refugees from Gaul; but, as we have seen, he already possessed connections among the earlier settlers in these parts. His successors, Tincommius, Eppillus and Verica, each describes himself as *Commi filius*. This introduces a certain chronological difficulty, since Commius was active in 54 BC and Verica still alive in AD 43; but it is probably better to accept this than to imagine that the Commius of the coins is not the historical Commius or that *Commi F.* on the coins means other than what it says.

The establishment of this southern kingdom of Belgae was to have far-reaching results. Though Belgic settlers in its area were probably not as numerous as north of the Thames or in Kent, and its subjects largely consisted of native peoples ruled over by a Belgic aristocracy, it did result in the spread of Belgic civilisation over much of southern Britain which had escaped the earlier migrations. Even in the early days its existence circumscribed the expansion of the Catuvellauni, who were already debarred from expansion eastwards. Later on, by an ironical development of events, it became closely associated with Rome in Augustus' policy of creating a balance of power in Britain; but this was not until after Commius' death, when his son Tincommius was king. As we shall see, this new policy of the son of the man who had vowed never to set eyes on another Roman was not to meet the unqualified approval of his followers.

The political history of the period is largely to be inferred from a study of the coins. In the northern area Cassivellaunus did not inscribe coins, and it is not even possible to be sure what coins he issued. The choice seems to lie between Gallo-Belgic E, which have too wide a distribution to be ascribed solely to him but might be the coins of a confederation, and British L, which are thought to be too late in date. The first Catuvellaunian king to issue inscribed coins was Tasciovanus, who is not otherwise attested in history. He probably began his reign *c.* 20 BC, and might perhaps have been Cassivellaunus' grandson. By now the capital was at *Verulamium* (Prae Wood), as the mint-marks show. His earliest coins derive from British L, though later in the reign more sophisticated designs appear.

Among the early issues is a very scarce type bearing the mint-mark of *Camulodunum* – Colchester. This was the capital of the Trinovantes, and these coins show that Tasciovanus had resumed expansion eastwards. This was contrary to Caesar's arrangements, but not necessarily in breach of them unless the treaty had been renewed. However, even if Cassivellaunus' successors had not felt bound to renew their agreement, the Trinovantes would surely have felt a compulsion to remain under Roman protection. This attack on them, then, may have involved an appeal to Rome, and in any case cannot have been pleasing to the government of Augustus, since it would bring a hostile power to the coast. A Roman defeat on the Rhine in 17 BC may have emboldened Tasciovanus to take this step, but the presence of Augustus himself in Gaul in 16 almost certainly caused him to withdraw. For this must be the meaning of the scarcity of the issue, and the dates fit the position of these coins in the sequence of Tasciovanus' issues.

Tincommius succeeded his father perhaps about 25–20 BC. His earlier issues closely resemble those of his father, but later in his reign completely new types suddenly appear which not only closely resemble Roman coin-types but are also so well made that they are certainly the work of Roman die-cutters. This suggests a technical mission, which, as G. C. Boon has said,[3] is hardly likely to have been confined to mint-improvement. Later kings of his line boasted the title REX on their coins, which strongly supports the idea that they had entered into treaty-relationships with Rome, and had been granted this title of recognition, which was not British. Tincommius himself did not enjoy this distinction, but it seems very probable nevertheless that he entered some sort of agreement with Augustus, for later on we find him a refugee and suppliant in Rome. The date of such an agreement is again probably *c.* 16 BC, for now, or shortly after, Roman imports and pottery begin to appear at *Calleva* his capital, and one of the coin types copied is an Augustan issue of between 15 and 12 BC. If so, we can begin to see the establishment of a new Roman policy towards Britain. Earlier in his reign Augustus seems to have kept open the possibility of a reoccupation of the island. In 34 and again in 28 and 27 BC military expeditions were planned, but were postponed owing to more pressing commitments; and for some years after this the idea of intervention was kept alive in the works of court poets. The motive may have been, as Dio once suggests, to complete the work of Caesar, but the occasions for a demonstration may also have been the need to re-establish the treaties with new rulers: and in 27, Dio tells us, the Britons would not come to terms. Later in the reign, however, we hear no more of intervention, and indeed a changed relationship with Britain is reflected in an ode of Horace published in 13 BC, though written perhaps two years earlier.

By giving support to Tincommius, Augustus probably intended to effect a balance of power between the two chief Belgic kingdoms of Britain, which would make reoccupation unnecessary. This, indeed, had already been delayed so long that it could not have been achieved without a full-scale expedition. If such was his intention, it seems to have been successful, at least for most of his reign. Tincommius, it is true, was eventually expelled and fled to Rome some time before AD 7; but the expulsion seems to have been the result of domestic intrigue rather than Catuvellaunian aggression, for he was succeeded by his brother Eppillus. Augustus therefore did not attempt to restore Tincommius; instead, with greater realism, Eppillus was granted recognition as *Rex*, and Verica after him. Eppillus had only a short reign at *Calleva*, to judge by the rarity of his coins with this mint-mark. He seems to have been soon ousted by his younger brother Verica, and thereafter gained himself a principality in Kent. Verica was certainly ruling during the reign of Tiberius, since some of his coins copy Tiberian types, and without doubt he is to be recognised as the Berikos of Dio's Greek text, who fled to Claudius on the eve of 43. Roman influence in the southern kingdom is reflected not only in the frequent copying of Roman coin-types, and the occasional presence of Roman die-cutters, but also by the symbol of the vine-leaf on certain coins of Verica, which indicated the prominence attached to Roman trade connections.

In the northern kingdom Tasciovanus continued to rule down to about AD 5–10. Under him the Catuvellauni, though prevented from overrunning the Trinovantes, continued to expand. The kingdom stretched from Northamptonshire to the Thames, and may even have included part of Kent west of the Medway. Some of his coins bear the title RIGONUS, which appears to be the Celtic counterpart of Rex, and hint thus at a war of propaganda which is more obviously reflected in the ear of barley appearing on the coins of Cunobelin, his son; for this barley not only advertises the agricultural wealth on which the kingdom's prosperity rested but also, perhaps, opposes the idea of British beer to the luxurious imports of wine suggested by Verica's vine-leaf. This was only propaganda, for in fact large quantities of wine reached the tables of Catuvellaunian nobles, as the surviving amphorae attest.

In Essex the earliest inscribed coins bear the name of Addedomaros, who was an approximate contemporary of Tasciovanus. The distribution and character of his coins show that he maintained himself against his western enemies; but in the end he was supplanted, or succeeded, by Dubnovellaunus, who had been the first king to inscribe coins in Kent. It now seems probable that it was Addedomaros who was buried in the Lexden tumulus at Colchester. It is likely that Dubnovellaunus had been driven from Kent by Eppillus, some time about AD 1, whether or not he already possessed territory north of the estuary. Dubnovellaunus then ruled at *Camulodunum*, but not for long. His name appears in Augustus' *Res Gestae* along with that of Tincommius, and this probably means that he had been driven out before AD 7; it probably also implies that, like Tincommius, he had had previous dealings with Augustus. He was supplanted at *Camulodunum* by Cunobelin, son of Tasciovanus; and from this date onwards the Trinovantes were finally submerged in the new Catuvellaunian empire.

Cunobelin was the greatest of the Belgic kings, and he had a long reign of almost forty years, during which he gained control of most of south-eastern Britain. Suetonius could call him *Britannorum rex*. It is evident that his seizure of *Camulodunum* and conquest of the Trinovantes was contrary to Roman policy as so far traced, but nevertheless it was successfully accomplished. If the conquest of the Trinovantes occurred in AD 9 or soon after, taking advantage of Roman weakness created by Varus' disastrous defeat and loss of three legions in the German forests that year, it is possible that Cunobelin was acting in pure defiance of Augustus. On the other hand, Augustus had already been ruling nearly forty years, and it is not unlikely that he had altered his ideas about Britain, where in any case the supplanting of the Trinovantian king Addedomaros by Dubnovellaunus of Kent had already confused the Caesarian position.

Now the geographer Strabo, writing soon after Augustus' death and giving reasons for non-intervention in Britain, states that certain British rulers had obtained Augustus' friendship by embassies and courtesies, and had set up offerings on the Capitol, thus making the island virtually Roman.[4] This certainly cannot refer to the fugitive princes Tincommius and Dubnovellaunus, who came in person, and could have no claim to set up offerings in the Capitol; nor could their presence in any way suggest that Roman control in Britain had been advanced, but rather the reverse. The passage records submissions or alliances from Britain itself. And as this not inconsiderable diplomatic success is unrecorded by Augustus himself in his *Res Gestae*, it is probable that it occurred after AD 7, when that document is thought to have been last revised. One of the kings is likely to have been Verica who received, as we have seen, recognition as *Rex*. Another may well have been Cunobelin himself, who certainly at one period issued bronze coins bearing the title *Rex*, and whose new capital at *Camulodunum* has been found to be so full of products imported from the Roman empire. Cunobelin has often been considered as anti-Roman in policy, but there is no real support for this view in the first half of his reign; and while he no doubt pursued an independent path, he was probably sufficiently realistic to see the advantages of a timely gesture whereby the consequences of his march to the coast might be averted. Another friendly gesture occurred in AD 16, when some ship-loads of Roman soldiers belonging to Germanicus' army were wrecked on the British coast and were returned to the Continent. On the Roman side, alliance with both British kingdoms would have obvious advantages. It would end the dangers of being involved in support of the less powerful Atrebates, and would open wide commercial possibilities north of the Thames. As Strabo put it, there was now no political reason to intervene, and Rome received much profit from import and export dues without having to finance an occupying army. The exports of Britain, he tells us, were corn, cattle, gold, silver, iron, hides, slaves and hounds; while ivory ornaments, amber and glass and other manufactured trinkets were imported in return. To the list of British products pearls should be added: Caesar had dedicated a breastplate studded with them in the temple of Venus Genetrix.

Under Tiberius relations with Britain remained static. Cunobelin overran east Kent and expanded his kingdom also beyond the upper Thames north of the Kennet. Nor was the southern kingdom to remain unmolested. Epaticcus, another son of Tasciovanus, is seen by the distribution of his coins to have been creating a kingdom for himself in the northern part of Verica's territory, and it is probable from the coins and pottery types found there that *Calleva* itself fell to him about AD 25. Cunobelin's power by this time was so paramount that these events cannot have taken place without his consent.

This encroachment on the Atrebatic kingdom could not have been achieved without protest at Rome from the victims, but the government of Tiberius was set against foreign adventure, and considered itself bound by Augustus' testament that the empire should be contained within existing bounds. Moreover, if Cunobelin himself was a Roman ally, as we have suggested, the situation may not have seemed so dangerous: it could be represented as a mere internal struggle of little interest outside Britain. The fact remains, however, that Verica's territory was gradually reduced to little more than the west Sussex coastal plain, and even this was lost by AD 42 or 43 when Verica fled to the Court of Claudius. While Cunobelin lived there seemed little cause for action, but when he died in 40 or 41, the situation seriously and quickly deteriorated, as we shall see, with the succession of his sons Caratacus and Togodumnus, two young men with no sense of restraint or of diplomatic moderation.

This, then, is the probable political history of the period. The evidence on which it is based is numismatic and archaeological. The coins of Commius whose find-spots are known are too few for their distribution to show where the focus of the kingdom lay in his day. *Calleva*, the Belgic site at Silchester, first appears by name as the mint-mark of Eppillus' coins, but it is probable from the archaeological finds that it was already the capital of Tincommius. Lying in the heaths and forests of the Berkshire–Hampshire border, it misses the opportunities that a site on the Thames would have given. A southern capital and mint probably also existed near Chichester. Coin finds are numerous in the vicinity, and the Chichester Dykes are probably best understood as its outer perimeter, perhaps dating from the last years of Verica.

Whether or no Wheathampstead had been the original nucleus of the Catuvellauni, their capital had been established at *Verulamium* by the start of Tasciovanus' reign and here also a mint was in operation. The site, lying above the valley of the Ver, enjoyed better communications north-westwards and westwards than had Wheathampstead. Not much is known of the site itself, but its defences have been traced over an extent of three-quarters of a mile along the valley crest. The bank and ditch in question were of very moderate strength, and formed probably little more than the boundary of the inner nucleus of a much wider and more sprawling settlement. Scattered traces of occupation, and the debris of the mint itself, are now known in the valley below beneath the later Roman city and outside it to the south; fragments of much stronger dykes are known to the north and beyond the river to the east, and these perhaps are all that are left of the real perimeter. Such enclosure dykes, as those of *Camulodunum* show, might delimit a very wide area within which settlement was sporadic, the remainder being devoted to pasture and tillage or market gardens. The inner defences of Prae Wood itself were strengthened at a date which is probably the eve of the Claudian conquest.

More is known of *Camulodunum*. Here on the plateau between the Roman River and the Colne twelve square miles of land are demarcated by powerful rectilinear dykes, and within this area an inner nucleus, defended by the Sheepen dyke, proved to be the capital of Cunobelin. But *Camulodunum* itself is attested before the date of his accession, and it is probable that the earlier nucleus lay at Gosbeck's Farm, south-west of Sheepen, where some curving dykes of contour type seem to pre-date the rectilinear ones. Here, then, around a sacred site – the shrine and hill, no doubt, of Camulos, the war god – lay the original *Camulodunum*, capital of Addedomaros and the Trinovantes. The site was well chosen. It has a gravel subsoil, and lies within easy reach of the estuaries and harbours of the coast, while the upper waters of the rivers give easy access across their watersheds to the chalk country beyond. It is protected by the convergence of the two valleys and by the added defences of the dykes. Enclosing the large area they do, these suggest a different tactic from that of the older hill-forts, and it has been thought that the dyke was the Belgic answer to the threat of chariotry. Against chariots these earthworks were an effective obstacle, but in undertaking their laborious construction Cunobelin was committing the common error of preparing for the last war rather than the next. The dykes of *Camulodunum* were destined to meet an army and a method of attack against which they had not been designed.

Camulodunum had fallen to the Catuvellauni, as we have seen, about AD 5–10. This drive to the east was full of significance for their later history, since in effect it converted them from an inland power, hemmed in by the isolation of marshes and forests, to a maritime one able to develop and exploit new commerce with the freshly established markets and production centres of the Roman Rhineland. It thus assured the continued ascendancy and wealth of the Catuvellaunian royal house and ensured that the advantages of continental trade should not become the prerogatives of the princes of Kent and Sussex. Of the Sheepen site itself little could be recovered by excavation owing to the thoroughness of later destruction there. The habitations were for the most part small huts of prehistoric character. Industry is attested by the working of bronze and iron, and by the manufacture of pottery. Trade is indicated by the large quantities of imported amphorae once containing wine and oil, and of imported plates and drinking vessels whose presence in such large numbers points to a revolution in manners, such specialised vessels being earlier quite unknown. The amphorae are in the main Italian, but there are some examples from Spain; the table-services are either in Arretine ware from Italy or in a variety of Gallo-Belgic wares from Northern Gaul and the Rhineland. Some of these vessels – but only imported ones – are inscribed with owners' marks, suggesting that literacy was beginning to spread among the wealthier classes who could afford the better wares. The local potters, who felt it necessary to imitate the potters' stamped signatures seen on imported plates and cups, rarely achieved more than a series of illiterate strokes.

Another large Belgic oppidum lay at Canterbury on both sides of the Stour. Nothing is known of its defences, but huts and drainage gullies have been found over a wide area, and the place was probably important enough to be the capital of some of the Kentish princes. The huts are circular or subrectangular, and sometimes recessed some two feet into the ground. Crudely baked slabs of clay were used for the hearths, the first tiles to be made in Britain, and plentiful oysters attest the growth of a trade which was to become highly organised in the subsequent period. A unique silver coin inscribed VODENOS is among the finds: this prince seems to have ruled about the beginning of the first century AD. But Kent was not a unified kingdom: another large oppidum, which possessed a mint, lay beneath Rochester. Both sites are low-lying or valley sites, and illustrate the changes of settlement-pattern introduced by the Belgae.

Beyond the metropolitan area of Belgic settlement lay other tribes, whose use of coin and further features of Iron C show that, if not wholly Belgic in ethnic character, they were at any rate ruled by Belgic princely families. This indeed was largely the case also in the southern kingdom. It was a state of affairs brought about by the confused Belgic migrations described in Chapter 2. In East Anglia north of the Trinovantes lay the Iceni. Their inscribed coins, which about AD 30 succeeded an uninscribed gold and silver series, give the following sequence of royal names. The first is CANS DVRO, which may perhaps be a dual name indicating magistrates: there follow ANTED, ECEN, AESU and SAENV, the first being the only king to issue gold coins as well as silver: the others issued silver only. Gold was, of course, less useful for ordinary commerce than silver, and the growing use of coinage for everyday commerce is shown by the numerous silver and bronze issues of Tasciovanus and Cunobelin: early coinages solely in gold were probably mainly used for princely bounties. It is also probable, however, that gold was increasingly difficult to obtain for the Iceni; if indeed they are to be recognised as the Cenimagni who surrendered to Caesar, much of their gold may have drained away over the years in tribute to Rome. The main nucleus of the tribe occupied south-west Norfolk and north-west Suffolk, and hostility towards the Catuvellauni must have developed as the frontiers of Tasciovanus approached their borders. Under Cunobelin actual encroachment took place, to judge by the aristocratic burial of Catuvellaunian type from Snailwell, and perhaps that at Elvedon too. Another concentration of population existed in the Norwich area, and as we shall see in the next chapter was perhaps not always under the same ruler as the other. The main body of the peasantry seem to have been poor and backward, but the treasure of Snettisham and other finds of rich decorated metal-work show that the aristocracy and priesthood were wealthy. Many of the surviving examples of horse- or chariot-equipment date from the last days of Icenian independence about AD 60, when the territory had already been penetrated by artistic and commercial influences of a Romano-Belgic kind from Colchester, but it is clear that the aristocracy they represent had enjoyed a long prosperity, which Iron B chieftains had helped to found.

Farther north-east in Lincolnshire, Leicestershire, Nottingham and Rutland and northern Northamptonshire lay the Coritani. Belgic pottery is known in this area, especially from Dragonby near Scunthorpe and Thorpe near Newark; from Old Sleaford, the site of a mint, where this pottery was associated with decorated wares of the Iron B tradition, as it was also at Ancaster; and from at least one brine-boiling establishment on the Lincolnshire coast. Belgic bronze brooches are known from Dragonby and South Ferriby. Similar pottery, perhaps of slightly later date, is known from Leicester itself, but it is not yet certain how far, if at all, its presence there is connected with a Roman military base at the site. The coins themselves are, as we have seen (p. 36), derived from Gallo-Belgic originals through British H and I; and since in the subsequent inscribed series we find coins bearing a double name, it can be suggested that the tribe was ruled by dual magistrates. If such existed, they must have held office for several years each, since there are not enough names to cover the period if they were annually changed. In any case, it seems likely that the arrangement commemorated the fusion of two originally separate groups. The coins in question were once thought to be Brigantian, but their distribution makes attribution to the Coritani unquestionably correct. Both gold and silver were minted. This tribe also had a common boundary in Northamptonshire with the expanding empire of Cunobelin, and is likely to have been hostile to him. They occupied a territory which was rich both in iron and in horse-pastures, and they controlled the north-eastern half of the ancient trade route known as the Jurassic way.

The south-western half of this route lay in the territory of the Dobunni. We have seen that the earliest uninscribed coins, British R, existing in this area are closely connected with those of British Q and the coins of Commius. They reflect an intrusion into south Gloucestershire by a Belgic group from Commius' realm some time between 30 and 20 BC, and this means that the Dobunni, too, were a partly Belgic tribe, though in their case the rest of the population (Western Second and Third B) were far more culturally advanced than was the case among the Coritani or Iceni. Objects such as the Birdlip mirror which are the products of the earlier group demonstrate the advanced nature of their culture.

The history of the Dobunni from this time on is one of gradual expansion south-westwards into Somerset as far as the Mendips, and north-eastwards farther into Gloucestershire, where the oppidum of Bagendon was founded; and thence as far afield as Worcestershire and western Oxfordshire. Vivid traces of this process can be seen in the massacres at Worlebury and Bredon Hill. At or shortly after this time the coins become inscribed, perhaps *c.* AD 20. The abbreviated names of kings appear in the following sequence: Anted, Eisu, Catti and Comux; last of all come Corio and Bodvoc. The last four names, to judge by the distribution of their coins, ruled over parts of the kingdom only, Catti and Comux being succeeded by Corio and Boduocus (as his full name may have been) respectively. It is a significant fact that all these kings and their unnamed predecessors continued to mint the traditional triple-tailed horse on their coins and were quite uninfluenced by the Roman types of Tincommius and his successors. Only Boduocus showed any originality, and the significance of the good Roman lettering of his coins will be discussed in Chapter 5. It seems probable that the Dobunni refused to follow the lead of Tincommius in adapting himself to Roman policy, preferring to maintain the attitude traditional among refugees from Gaul. Excavations at Bagendon, one of their chief oppida and mints, showed that the site had been established perhaps about AD 15, and that already by this date commercial relations with the Catuvellauni had begun; for not only is there at Bagendon much pottery of Catuvellaunian type – and the defences of the oppidum are also inspired from there – but also the many imported vessels can hardly be derived from any other source. It is true that a trade-route was maintained with the Durotrigan harbour at Poole, but there is no suggestion that this port saw the introduction of luxury pottery from the Continent. If during Cunobelin's reign this peaceful intercourse was allowed to develop across his western border it seems likely that Cunobelin received corresponding commercial advantages – the import of iron and copper and tin – which outweighed the desirability of conquest in this direction. Indeed, as well as raw materials, we may consider the likelihood of trade in actual manufactures from western workshops and the hiring of master-craftsmen trained therein.

South of the Dobunni lay the Durotriges, in Dorset and the southern parts of Wiltshire and Somerset. Here again we seem to have a Belgic aristocracy ruling over a tribe which was basically of Iron B. In Chapter 2 we saw the development of trade with Brittany and the introduction or local development of multivallation in the hill-forts. The coins, however, are derived from the Belgic British B coinage, and the evidence of the Le Catillon hoard shows that this intrusion of a Belgic ruling caste had occurred well before the time of Caesar's Gallic War; but under the influence of Armorican trade the original gold standard had been converted to a silver currency. The Gallic wars for a time disrupted trade connections with the Continent, and thereafter the Durotrigan coinage began a process of degeneration both in metal-standard and in execution. It was never inscribed. The new culture which accompanied the coins introduced several changes in the way of life as well as new pot-forms; the burial-rite however, remained inhumation, and this suggests that the new Belgic leaders were not very numerous. At Maiden Castle the main rampart was refortified with a timber palisade and storage-pits were no longer used. The pottery is still basically for the most part of Iron B type, but now often made on the wheel; the influence of Armorican pottery is also apparent; but there are some new types of obvious Belgic character. Some of these, as for instance the tazza or pedestalled cup, show links with the Catuvellauni and are probably to be explained by trade contacts; for the reality of trade with the Catuvellauni is demonstrated by fine lathe-turned urns of Kimmeridge shale which are not infrequently met with in chieftains' graves in Cambridgeshire and Essex.

The Durotriges possessed several very sizeable and well-defended oppida, among them Hod Hill, Hambledon, South Cadbury Castle and Maiden Castle; and on the edge of their territory an important fortified post lay at Hengistbury Head, which has some claim to be the Dunium of Ptolemy's Geography. Many other powerful hill-forts continued to be occupied down to the Roman conquest, and this suggests that after the decline of Durotrigan prosperity consequent on the Gallic Wars, the normal process of political unification was halted, and that the tribe continued in political anarchy under a large number of rival nobles, each in his stronghold. A tradition of hostility to Rome survived until AD 43: it had not been mitigated as elsewhere by the nearer threat of Catuvellaunian domination, nor had it been mollified by the undoubted trade in wine which amphora-fragments attest.

East and north-east of Durotrigan territory the area of Salisbury Plain has produced evidence of Belgic occupation. Coins of British Q stretch across north Wiltshire, and the coins of Commius and his sons reach westwards to the Swindon neighbourhood; but in the region south of this the Belgic occupants used no coins. This must mean that they were or became independent of Atrebatic rule,[5] and the fact is reflected in the creation here, later on, of the Roman *civitas* of the Belgae. This is an ethnic not a tribal title and implies that this civitas was an agglomeration of petty groups. The multivallate hill-forts, however, extend eastwards across this area as far as the Test; they suggest resistance by Iron B groups to expansion from the primary Belgic area east of this river, an expansion which is vouched for at several of them, where Belgic occupation and sometimes even refortification succeed the Iron B phases at these camps.

Beyond the outer ring of Belgic or partly Belgic kingdoms and tribes lay other groups with earlier cultural traditions. In south Somerset, Devon and Cornwall the origins of the Dumnonii can be traced to the South-Western Second B culture, though they were reinforced especially in Cornwall by Breton immigrants, some of whom may have arrived as refugees as late as Caesar's conquest of Armorica. The burial-rite is crouched inhumation in a stone cist. Trade in metals was still active both along the south coast and especially up the Bristol Channel to the ports of the Dobunni. In Devon, west of the Exe, the siting and planning of settlements point to stock-herding as one of the principal activities, but east of the river the land becomes more suitable to arable. Here the type of hill-fort is different and multivallates occur. It seems certain that this land was a zone of contention between the Durotriges and the Dumnonii, and that the former were successfully expanding into it. Quite soon the south Somerset plain had been overrun, since many of the Duro-trigan coins found there are of early type: evidence of penetration towards Exeter is provided at Hembury, where the earlier Dum-nonian hill-fort was taken over and reconstructed by people using Durotrigan pottery. The occurrence of this pottery at Exeter itself, however, is likely to be due to introduction by the Roman army and its camp-followers. The lake-villages of Glastonbury and Meare give us the most intimate glimpse of Dumnonian culture owing to the survival there of such rich finds; these included the skilled wooden products of carpenters and lathe-turners, the workshop debris of bronze-smiths and enamellers, and a wide variety of iron tools. Other finds illustrated trade in Cornish tin, local lead from the Mendips, Dorset shale from Kimmeridge and spit-shaped iron currency-bars from the Forest of Dean.

Across the Bristol Channel lies South Wales. Here the plain and hills of Glamorgan formed the homelands of the Silures, whose eastern boundary was no doubt the Wye, since beyond it Dobunnic coins circulated. Northwards they will have extended to the upper Wye valley and perhaps beyond. They thus lay westwards of the distribution both of Western Second and Third B sites, and were probably in the main aboriginal descendants of the Bronze Age and earliest Iron A settlers of the region; occasional discoveries of decorated metal-work, however, point to the presence of wealthy leaders with a taste for the culture of Iron B. Some of these finds may be the product of trade, but others were certainly made locally, perhaps by itinerant craftsmen. Occasional elements also of Iron C culture, such as pottery and brooches, appear on Silurian sites; but these were probably introduced by the followers of Caratacus after AD 43, and do not point to pre-Roman Belgic penetration, as the absence of a coinage shows.

Much of Silurian territory is high barren plateau, poorly drained and boggy. The slopes of the hill-land were densely wooded, and so were the valley floors. The strength of the tribe, to judge by the distribution of defended settlements, lay on the coastal plain and in the valleys of the Wye and upper Usk. Almost certainly they were largely pastoral by occupation, and their territory contains similar multiple-enclosure earthworks to those of the Dumnonii, which are thought to have been designed for herding. The people themselves were described by Tacitus as swarthy and curly-haired, which made him think them of Iberian stock.

The Pembroke peninsula and adjacent areas were the home of the Demetae. The elevation of the land here is lower, the hills more rounded and the earth more fertile. It is possible that the Demetae were exposed to Silurian aggression, for the scarcity of Roman military establishments in their territory suggests that they became philo-Roman. On the other hand, large hill-forts are rare in their territory; instead there are numerous small defended enclosures of very doubtful defensive value, and these do not afford a picture of a people under heavy pressure.

The core of the Ordovices lay in north-west Wales, in Caernarvonshire and Merionethshire, another mountainous and difficult district. It is possible that they were a confederacy of tribes rather than a single people, for Anglesey was certainly within their overlordship, and so presumably was much of central Wales.[6] They, too, will have been largely pastoral, deriving agricultural produce from Anglesey and the Lleyn peninsula, just as the Silures derived theirs from the coastal plain behind them.

The fourth tribe known from Wales was the Deceangli, who inhabited Flintshire and Denbighshire, an area rich in copper and lead. This tribe and its south-eastern neighbour the Cornovii lay astride the route northwards up the Welsh Marches, whose use by invaders and refugees is graphically illustrated in the numerous great hill-forts of the region, which often show many periods of refortification. The proliferation of hill-forts here and among the Silures probably points to a lack of political coherence, such as was suggested for the Duro-triges also. The Cornovii occupied the land between the estuary of the Dee and the headwaters of the Trent and Severn. Much of this area was lowland forest; the core of the tribe lay in the more open lands of southern and western Shropshire. There are indications that the Cornovii were friendly towards the Romans, and this may mean that they were under pressure from the Ordovices. Roman forts, in-deed, long occupied parts of their territory, but these may have been as much for protection as for control. On the other hand, locally independent chieftains may not all have been trustworthy.

North of the Cornovii and Coritani lay the Brigantes. These Tacitus describes as numerically the largest tribe in Britain, while Ptolemy states that they stretched from sea to sea. Their precise southern boundary is uncertain, but is usually thought to run from the Mersey to the Humber, curving southwards to include the Peak district of Derbyshire; for Coritanian coins hardly extend in this direction be-yond the vale of Trent except for three hoards in southern Yorkshire, which are clearly out of context and deposited by refugees. The north-eastern limits of the tribe lay on the Tyne as epigraphic, literary and archaeological evidence converge to show: here Hadrian's frontier of Britain virtually coincided with the tribal boundary. But north-westwards of this Brigantian land probably ex-tended beyond the Roman wall to include the fertile basins of the Lyne, Esk and Annan. East Yorkshire, however, was excluded. This was the territory of the Parisi, whose ancestors had introduced the Eastern B culture to this area long before. The Parisi maintained their independence and may even have been developing commercial relations with the middlemen of *Camulodunum* or directly with the Roman continent.

The Brigantes, however, were far less sophisticated. Despite the presence of areas of fertility, little trace of pre-Roman agriculture is known in their territory: the economy was based on flocks and herds. Julius Caesar had described their way of life when he wrote, 'the people of the interior for the most part do not grow corn but live on milk and meat and dress in skins', though the same description might apply to the peoples of Wales. Much of the vast area attributed to this tribe is barren mountain moorland or bog. The centres of popu-lation were separated by these hills, and themselves lay in favourable valleys or plains of lighter soil: some fifteen such major concentrations can be recognised.[7] The scattered nature of the grouping no doubt then as now gave rise to regionalism, but the absence of agriculture inhibited the development of powerful independent principalities. Instead a single kingdom had emerged, whether by consent or conquest, but its power was shaky. However, the primitive nature of Brigantian economy should not blind us to their military power, or to the wealth enjoyed by the nobility, which is reflected for us in the metal-work, for instance, of the Stanwick hoard. The known finds, however, are almost all of late date, and they suggest that the prosperity of the Brigantian kingdom was related to its status as a Roman client power, and even that the unification of the territory was a fairly recent one. One surprising feature of the whole region is the great scarcity of hill-forts, and some of these were probably erected after AD 43. Their shortage is very likely to be explained by the relatively primitive and semi-nomadic culture of the inhabitants, but among the few are some of the most impressively inaccessible in Britain, such as Ingleborough, Mam Tor and Carrock Fell. That at Almondbury near Huddersfield – which has been suggested for the site of Queen Cartimandua's headquarters – is multivallate and may have continued to be occupied at a relatively late date under Iron B influence coming via the Marches. The picture of the Brigantes that emerges is of a primitive and pastoral though numerous population ruled by Iron B chieftains, many of whose families may have themselves been recent arrivals; and of political centralisation only in process of achievement by AD 43.

Beyond the northern boundary of the Brigantes lowland Scotland held four tribes. The Votadini occupied the eastern lowlands and the coast north of the Tyne, with the Selgovae in the central region to their west. North of the Solway, Dumfriesshire and Galloway were in the territory of the Novantae, north of whom lay the Damnonii embracing the Clyde valley. Beyond the Forth–Clyde isthmus, in the area later to become the homeland of the Picts, Ptolemy gives us the names of eleven tribes, of whom little can be said individually except that the most northerly of them, the Cornavii, and the Damnonii, too, have names which recall those of tribes in southern Britain and may be offshoots from them; but the Cornavii may take their name simply from the headland of Caithness.

The territory of most of these tribes is characterised by numerous hill-forts, and in this respect they differ from the Brigantes. The presence of so many fortifications suggests a rather more advanced culture, with greater agricultural resources. Many of the hill-forts have timber-laced ramparts and some of them are now known to have been built at the very beginning of the Iron Age or even earlier. The character of the local rock often led to a curious but unintentional result when fire was applied to the timbers; the stones fused and the ramparts became in large part vitrified. Vitrified forts, of course, are not, as was once thought, a special category; vitrification could happen anywhere, at any period, if the geology were suitable. Some hill-forts in Scotland have a long history of occupation. Objects found, such as ring-headed pins and La Tène Ic brooches, show that the material culture had much in common with that of southern Britain, though pottery is in general more rare: possibly containers of wood or leather were used instead. Later fortifications, as in the south, no longer employed timber-framing; instead, increasing use was made of stone walls and – where the rocks allowed – of ditches. Iron B features appear in the metalwork and perhaps suggest some immigration from the south, and refugees from Roman rule may also be expected. It is noteworthy that Professor K. H. Jackson's study of the linguistic problems of the origin of the Picts has led him to a similar conclusion.[8] The differences in dialect between the Iron Age inhabitants of Scotland north of the Forth and those of the rest of Britain would be accounted for if the former spoke a Hallstatt dialect, while the language of the latter had undergone change from new arrivals in Iron B and C.

North of the Great Glen and extending thickly through the Orkneys and Shetlands, a completely different type of fortification is dominant – the brochs. These defended homesteads – the apogee of the hedgehog principle – indicate a way of life based on the family rather than on any wider unit, the families concerned being occupied with primitive farming and fishing, and perhaps with piracy. The mutually exclusive distribution of brochs and hill-forts suggests both that the brochs developed later than the hill-forts and that their occupants were opposed. Mutual plundering and slaving raids would compel both to maintain fortifications, but the social and geographical organisation of the broch-builders was such as to compel individual rather than group protection. Internecine strife between the two peoples is the context of the 'submission' of the Orkneys to Claudius in AD 43, though in fact the gesture was premature, for

73

Roman arms did not arrive to suppress the hill-fort people until another forty years had passed.

Though hill-forts with timber-laced ramparts were the earliest type of hill-fort to reach Scotland (succeeding the palisaded enclosures mentioned on p. 25), other types followed in due course, including multivallates. South of the Forth–Clyde isthmus great numbers of hill-forts exist, especially in the country of the Votadini and Selgovae, though these hill-forts are usually small in size. The Votadini, whose western border was roughly the line of Dere Street and the upper Tyne valley, had a large oppidum at Traprain Law, which became of considerable importance in the later Roman period. The Selgovae had an important oppidum on Eildon Hill North, which had attained an area of thirty-nine acres when it was destroyed in 79, but showed two previous lines of successively enlarged fortifications. This indicates the long history of Iron Age development in this part of Scotland; but the co-existence of great numbers of smaller fortresses points to general insecurity, and shows that tribal cohesion and centralised control had not proceeded very far. The Selgovae were perhaps the more powerful tribe of the two, and their hostile pressure on the Votadini may have caused that tribe to turn early to Rome for support. The former, however, for long retained an unremitting enmity towards Rome, which carefully planned military occupation could usually control but not abate.

This, then, was the state of Britain on the eve of the Roman conquest. That conquest itself was the work of Claudius in 43, but only because the attempted invasion of Gaius in 40 had ended in fiasco. Tiberius had died in 37. Gaius, his youthful successor, quickly became perverted by power, and the record of his reign is hopelessly confused by the hatred and ridicule of its historians. In 39 the emperor left hurriedly for Germany to suppress a conspiracy; but he had already planned a military expedition across the Rhine for that year. The troops, however, proved poorly disciplined and out of training, and while he was restoring the situation his attention was directed to Britain by the arrival of Adminius, a son of Cunobelin, who had been exiled by his father. This prince, it appears, too easily persuaded Gaius that Britain was ripe for plucking, but when the army was assembled at Boulogne a mutiny broke out. Three years later the legions certainly showed reluctance to embark for a land which lay outside the circle of the civilised world, and that the same reluctance was encountered by Gaius seems both likely enough and the best explanation of the garbled accounts which are all we have for guidance. The expedition was abandoned, and its sole memorial was the great lighthouse which Gaius had caused to be erected at Boulogne.

Gaius was murdered in 41, and it fell to Claudius, his uncle and successor, to revive the British project. There were sound reasons both of a personal and political kind for this, whatever we may think of Gaius' motives. In the first place, Claudius himself, though the son of Drusus and brother of Germanicus, both of them distinguished generals, had led a sheltered life owing to physical deformity. He had been despised by his family and allowed little part in public affairs. He possessed, however, his share of the pride for which the Claudii were famous, and he now felt particular need for military success in order to establish himself in the regard of the army to whose loyalty to his family he owed his throne. The personal motive behind the conquest must not be underrated: world rule was part of the psychological inheritance of the Caesars, its consummation merely attending on convenience. Moreover, if foreign conquest was to be undertaken there were good reasons to choose Britain for its object. In the first place much of the necessary staff-preparation must already have been completed for Gaius. Then in Britain the situation required action. Cunobelin had recently died, leaving his kingdom divided between Togodumnus and Caratacus. These young men were headstrong and ambitious, and they began a programme of aggression and enlargement. It is probable that they overran the Dobunni; this in itself would not affect their relations with Rome, but when they overran the remnants of the Atrebatic kingdom and expelled Verica the situation was different. Verica was a Roman ally; his arrival in Rome presented more than an excuse for intervention: failure to take action now would be damaging to Roman prestige already tarnished by the failure of Gaius. The Augustan precedent of recognising the alternative successor could not be followed, since the kingdom itself had ceased to exist. Moreover, the flight of Verica was followed by an impudent demand for his extradition; and when it was not complied with disturbances broke out. Whether Sir Ian Richmond was right in suggesting that these disturbances took the form of raids on the Gallic coast, or whether they were riots which threatened the lives of Roman merchants in Britain, there is little evidence to decide;[9] but in either event the long summer of peaceful relations with Britain was over.

Gaius had raised two new legions,[10] and this meant that the Rhine garrison, to which they had been added, was dangerously powerful, the careful balancing of the strength of army-groups being one of the secrets of successful imperial statecraft. Even if two legions were to be used to strengthen the defences of the British-facing coast, they would still be in Gaul. The safer, as well as the bolder, course would be to deal with Britain by placing the necessary forces in the island itself, where they would form a separate army-group beyond the sea, and where their supplies could be charged to the new province. Moreover, there was now available more exact knowledge than Caesar had had of the mineral wealth of Britain, the *pretium victoriae* as Tacitus put it,[11] and the vast manpower of the island would be a useful asset – a sort of invisible export balancing the costs of occupation – for conscription overseas. Thus, the new province might be expected, in the long run, to pay for itself.

One further point is relevant. Britain had the reputation of being the home of Druidism; but in Gaul Augustus, Tiberius and Claudius all took steps to stamp out the savage rites associated with this priesthood. While H. Last was no doubt correct [12] in stressing that this aspect of Roman policy was based on cultural rather than political motives, one cannot doubt that one of its results was to imbue surviving Druids with hostility, and it is a fact that in Britain this priesthood did nourish the opposition. Suppression of Druidism in Gaul can never have been completely successful with Britain unsubdued, and for its conquest therefore the existence of Druidism on the island may have formed a subsidiary motive.

1. *Antiquity*, xxi (1947), 3–9; *Aspects of Archaeology in Britain and beyond*, ed. W. F. Grimes (London, 1951), 332–44.
2. There are two British coins from Denmark and one from Belgium. The Belgic bronze bowl from Poland (*Antiq. Journ.*, xliii (1963), 27–37), should not be forgotten.
3. G. C. Boon, *Roman Silchester* (London, 1957), p. 219, note. 28.
4. Strabo, iv, 5, 3.
5. It has been suggested that the inhabitants of Salisbury Plain, like the Dobunni, rejected the Romanising policy of Tincommius.

6. The name of one component, the Gangani of the Lleyn peninsula, has been preserved by Ptolemy.

7. The names of five of these groups or *pagi* can be recovered: the Gabrantovices in north Yorkshire (perhaps really part of the Parisi), the Setantii in Lancashire (the Fylde), the Textoverdi in the upper valley of the (south) Tyne, the Lopocares round Corbridge and the Carvetii in the upper Eden valley. The last became an independent civitas in the third century (p. 214). The Corionotatae (*RIB*, 1142) were probably a sept of the Selgovae.

8. K. H. Jackson, in Chapter vi, *The Problem of the Picts* (*ed*. F. T. Wainwright, Edinburgh, 1955).

9. I. A. Richmond, *Roman Britain* (London, 1955 and 1963), 18. *Britanniam . . . tumultuantem ob non redditos transfugas* is the phrase Suetonius (*Divus Claudius* 17) uses: it supports the latter view.

10. For arguments that it was Gaius, not Claudius, who raised xv Primigenia and xxii Primigenia see Balsdon, *JRS*, xxiv (1934), 13–16.

11. *Agricola*, 12.

12. *JRS* xxix (1949), 1–5.

5

The Claudian Conquest: the rebellion of Boudicca and its aftermath

In AD 43 the conquest of Britain was begun. An army of four legions with auxiliary troops, amounting in all to about 40,000 men, had been assembled at Boulogne. The legions were the II Augusta, IX Hispana, XIV Gemina and XX Valeria, and the general was Aulus Plautius, hitherto governor of Pannonia. Legio IX had accompanied him from his province, but the other three were drafted from the Rhine garrison, Legio II from Strasbourg, Legio XIV from Mainz (both in Upper Germany), and Legio XX from Neuss.[1] The sailing was delayed by a mutiny, since the soldiers affected the superstition that the Ocean, part of which separated them from Britain, marked the boundary of the proper world of mankind: beyond it lay unknown hazards. It was not until Narcissus, one of Claudius' freedmen ministers, had been sent from Rome to address them that they returned to their senses, influenced not by any words of his but by the ludicrous humiliation of seeing an ex-slave on the general's tribunal. Their sense of humour exerted itself, and with cries of 'Io Saturnalia' – a reference to the festival when slaves assumed their masters' clothes – the angry tension was released, and embarkation followed at once. But by now time had been wasted; it may already have been past the end of April.

Dio, who is our only considerable source for these events, says that the expedition sailed in three divisions so as not to be hindered in landing, but was driven back on its course; we are left to judge whether three separate landings took place or whether after diversionary movements the army re-united at a single landfall. Excava-

78

tions at Richborough have revealed an early Claudian defensive beach-head perimeter which is clearly the scene of the main and probably the only landing. Otherwise the possibilities resolve themselves into two alternative theories. Some, struck by the pattern of the roads in east Kent, have suggested landings at Dover and Lympne, from which converging movements would unite at Canterbury. In favour of this theory is the probable inability of Richborough to house the vast invasion fleet; warned by Caesar's naval disasters, Plautius may have determined to get as many of his ships as possible into the safety of harbours. Against this, however, it can be said that hitherto no evidence has been found of early military activity at either Dover or Lympne; that the roads can hardly have been built at the time of the advance, and that after it only one supply-port, Richborough, would be required; and that excavations at Canterbury have given no indication of the large military base which would seem to be thus indicated there. The other theory recalls that one of the reasons for the expedition was the restoration of Verica, and so suggests a landing in West Sussex. Against this can be urged the folly of committing a force sufficiently large to be useful to a landing so far away that it could play no part in the decisive phases of the campaign. No sensible general would so divide his army initially; for the objective could be more easily attained by applying decisive force in the decisive place. Furthermore, the detachment which is attested as operating along the south coast a year later is *Legio* II, and this is known to have been in Kent in 43.

At Richborough, then, the army landed. The site was well chosen, for it has a sheltered harbour and occupies a slight rise in the surrounding flats: at this time it was not yet an island, despite frequent assertions. In the late Roman and early Saxon periods land-subsidence led to this result, but no general bent on a victorious invasion would be so timid as to land on an island, from which he would then have all the trouble of relanding on the mainland.

Unlike Caesar, Plautius did not have to face an opposed disembarkation. The Britons, misled by news of the mutiny, were expecting another fiasco, and at first Plautius had difficulty in finding an enemy to fight. However, in two skirmishes somewhere in east Kent both Caratacus and Togodumnus were successively routed, and they then retired to the line of the Medway, presumably to gather stronger forces. Disunity of this sort was often a factor in Celtic defeat. Soon after this, part of the Dobunni surrendered, no doubt the half of the tribe ruled by Boduocus. 'Bodunni', indeed, is the name here given us by the text of Dio, but no such tribe is known, and in any case the surrender of part only of some small local tribe in east Kent would seem too insignificant to mention. The emendation to 'Dobunni' gives us a known tribe, the surrender of part of which would be a political gain of noteworthy magnitude; but it does not involve the supposition of a Roman expeditionary force operating in Gloucestershire, as has sometimes been thought, for the surrender could have been made either by embassy or in the field itself. Moreover, such action by Boduocus at this time is plausible. He himself is known from coins whose Roman lettering distinguishes them from all their predecessors; his tribe had enjoyed friendship and trade with the Catuvellauni in Cunobelin's time, as the distribution of coins and other objects shows. But this amicable intercourse had ceased with Cunobelin's death and the more domineering policy of his sons (Dio states that the tribe was now under Catuvellaunian control). A timely surrender to the winning side was clearly to his interest.[2]

The Roman forces were still east of the Medway when this occurred, and Plautius built a fort before advancing farther: at a guess this may have been placed near Harbledown to overlook the crossing of the Stour at Canterbury, where a large Belgic settlement existed. The Britons meanwhile had massed to oppose the crossing of the Medway, and thither Plautius now arrived to fight what was to be the decisive battle of the campaign. There was no bridge, so some Celtic or German auxiliaries who were trained to swim in full equipment were first sent over; and when these had caused considerable confusion by attacking the chariot-horses more troops, including the Second legion under its legate Vespasian, followed under the overall command of Flavius Sabinus. Even so, the result hung doubtful and the battle was renewed next day, an unusual event in ancient warfare. At last victory was achieved by an attack led by Hosidius Geta.

Where did this battle take place? Though Dio does not name the river, it can hardly not be the Medway. The Roman army had to advance along existing tracks, for its own supply-roads came later. The best known ancient track westwards from Canterbury is the so-called Pilgrims' Way, and this has been suggested as the route used by Plautius, leading to a battle at the Medway crossing at Aylesford. However, more recently the existence has been demonstrated of a Belgic settlement under Rochester, important enough to have possessed a mint; and it can hardly be doubted either that trackways connected it with Canterbury or that it presented in itself an important military objective. Furthermore, in 1957 a hoard of thirty-four Roman gold coins, the latest being issues of Claudius of AD 41, was found at Bredgar near Sittingbourne. This sum is too small to represent a subsidy to some native prince, but it is too large to be the savings of an ordinary legionary soldier: moreover, the coins show progressive decrease in wear from the earliest to the latest, which suggests that they represent a cross-section of the currency such as might be obtained from the sale of property or repayment of a debt. Such a large sum (three months' pay of a centurion) was probably the property of an officer, concealed before some skirmish, and it reinforces the view that the army passed north of the Downs by the route later laid out as Watling Street. Thus, we can picture the battle taking place near Rochester, and the width of the river there is more consistent with the recorded difficulty of crossing than it is at Aylesford. When the army moved forward once more a fort must have been left to guard the Medway-crossing: it is certain that no fort exists at Aylesford, but there is a suitable site for one beneath Rochester Castle.

The Britons now fell back on the Thames near London 'near where the river flows out into the ocean and at high tide forms a pool'. The Romans found the fords hard to discover, but auxiliary troops once more swam across, and others found or built a bridge upstream,[3] perhaps near Westminster. The marshy valley of the Lea, however, and the thickly wooded country near it presented difficulties. The Romans suffered losses in skirmishes, and though Togodumnus was killed in one of these, British resistance was strengthened rather than weakened by his loss.

So far the campaign had followed that of Caesar fairly closely, except that the main battle had taken place at the Medway rather than in east Kent. But there is no need to suppose that Plautius was taken by surprise at the Medway (not finding it in his Caesar), as R. G. Collingwood suggested, or that his staff were so poorly provided with military intelligence that they were reduced to leaning heavily on Caesar's memoirs as a hand-book. South-eastern Britain had been increasingly penetrated by Roman merchants since Augustus, and there had been much political intercourse as well. We need not doubt that the Roman Staff was perfectly acquainted with the geography and other features of the area in which the army had to operate.

Claudius himself was naturally anxious to be present in person at a decisive moment in the campaign, and Plautius had instructions to send for him if a check occurred. At this point, therefore, the advance was halted and the army retired behind the Thames to await the Emperor. If, in fact, the decisive battle had already been won, at least he could enter *Camulodunum* as a conqueror. It was now about the beginning of July, and Claudius will have arrived about the middle of August – bringing with him detachments of the Praetorian Guard, probably under their prefect, Rufrius Pollio, and possibly vexillations from other legions;[4] he also brought elephants, though more from determination to conquer in style than for their practical use, frightening though they would appear.

There was still time to capture *Camulodunum* and level its inner defences, but Claudius remained no longer than sixteen days in Britain; leaving orders with Plautius to continue the campaign, he departed probably about the beginning of September to cross the Channel before the equinoctial gales began. He travelled back slowly through Gaul, and arrived in Rome after an absence of six months early in 44, when he celebrated the triumph which the Senate had voted him. While at *Camulodunum* he had received the surrender of numerous tribes, some already conquered, others anxious to join the winning side. The former were disarmed; the others received treaties which regulated their relations with the Roman governor. The Senate voted Claudius and his legates permission to negotiate binding agreements without reference back, and to this power is probably due some distinctly original arrangements.

On the inscription of his triumphal arch dedicated in 51 he claims to be the first to have reduced barbarian tribes beyond the Ocean to Roman obedience (thus tacitly forgetting Caesar's achievements) and records the surrender of eleven British kings. One of these was probably Caratacus whose capture in 51 came just in time for inclusion; another might possibly be some chieftain from the Orkneys who was curious enough or hopeful enough to send an embassy, for Eutropius records the addition of these islands by Claudius to the empire.[5] The identity of some of the others will be discussed shortly.

Claudius had left the government of the Empire in the hands of a trusted colleague, Lucius Vitellius, with whom he had shared the consulship in the first six months of 43, and was naturally accompanied to Britain by a high-ranking staff. Among consulars known to have been here in addition to Plautius the commander were M. Licinius Crassus Frugi (later to be executed), A. Didius Gallus, Servius Sulpicius Galba, D. Valerius Asiaticus, Cn. Sentius Saturninus and probably M. Vinicius. Saturninus may have played some active part in affairs, since he is singled out by Eutropius [6] as responsible, with Plautius, for the conquest, and it has been suggested that it was he who was plenipotentiary in the restoration of Verica's kingdom. Didius Gallus, later to return to Britain as governor, seems to have been in command of the cavalry in Britain for a short while before being despatched to Moesia. Among senior holders of praetorian rank were T. Flavius Sabinus, Vespasian's elder brother, and Hosidius Geta, both of whom were promoted to the consulship in c. 45, no doubt for the distinguished part they played in the Medway battle. The latter may be the general who distinguished himself in Mauretania the year before.[7] Both of these were on Plautius' own staff. There was also T. Plautius Silvanus Aelianus,[8] who being related to Aulus Plautius was also probably on his staff. Vespasian himself, of comparatively junior praetorian standing, was legate of Legio II Augusta:[9] the names of the other legionary legates are not recorded. Of lower rank were C. Stertinius Xenophon, Claudius' doctor, and Ti. Claudius Balbillus, both serving as *praefecti fabrum*, and P. Graecinius Laco, procurator of Gaul. Claudius also brought his two sons-in-law, L. Junius Silanus Torquatus and Cn. Pompeius Magnus (son of M. Licinius Crassus Frugi). All these senators were awarded triumphal ornaments; nevertheless, the care which Claudius took to leave the empire in safe hands during his absence suggests that some of them may have been brought to keep them under his own eye. Saturninus had been consul in 41 when Gaius was murdered, and had advocated a restoration of the republic. Asiaticus was suspected of aiming at the throne on the same occasion. Galba was very well connected and did in fact become Emperor in 68; Silanus and Pompey and the latter's father, too, were executed or driven to suicide later in Claudius' own reign, and so was Vinicius.

The further stages of the military campaign were assisted by the political alignments already existing in Britain as the result of previous Roman policy and the expansionist activities of Cunobelin and his sons. The southern dynasty had had a long tradition of friendship with Rome, and now the leaders of other tribes were anxious to become allies, partly from motives of self-preservation and partly because they, too, were hostile to the house of Cunobelin. The best known of these princes are Cogidubnus, who succeeded to the realm of Verica, Prasutagus of the Iceni and Cartimandua of the Brigantes. A fourth, as we have seen, was very probably Boduocus.

The origins of Cogidubnus are not clear, but that he ruled at Chichester is testified by the undated dedication of a temple to Neptune and Minerva found there in the eighteenth century; on this he calls himself Tiberius Claudius Cogidubnus, thus emphasising the Roman citizenship given him by the Emperor over any royal descent he may have enjoyed in his own right. He also proclaims the titles of *Rex* and *Legatus Augusti in Britannia*.[10] Tacitus [11] tells us that he survived loyal to within living memory, which in the context must mean into the seventies; and he also tells us that this loyalty had been rewarded by the addition of further *civitates* to his kingdom; but we are not told when he became king. Verica had lived long enough to seek refuge with Claudius and to provide a pretext for invasion, as we have seen; and it is perhaps simplest to suppose that Verica was restored in 43, to be succeeded soon afterwards by a much younger and more energetic kinsman. Julio-Claudian policy was normally against the perpetuation, without good reason, of client-kingdoms by succession, but in this case there were special circumstances – the old age of Verica, the evident philo-Romanism of Cogidubnus (who had himself perhaps been an exile in Rome) and the political obligation inherent in having supported Verica's cause.

Prasutagus presents a difficulty in that though he is known to have died in AD 60, the date of his accession is obscure. Client-kings did not usually retain the right of coinage, and no coins of Prasutagus are known. But one coin hoard found in 1960 near Lakenheath included issues of Claudius in association with three native coins bearing the legend SVBIDASTO round a head modelled on a Roman prototype: it seems likely that at least one ruler of the Iceni, not Prasutagus, issued coins after 43. Furthermore, a native coin-mould was found at Needham, Norfolk, in association with pottery of Claudian date. The easiest explanation is that Prasutagus himself did not succeed till *c.* 47 (or else previously ruled only a part of the tribe) and after that date entered into closer relations with Rome. Mr D. F. Allen has indeed suggested that Antedius continued to rule over part of the tribe until this date (and so could qualify as one of the *xi reges* who surrendered to Claudius), and that the ECEN coins were those of Prasutagus after 47, issued on behalf of the confederacy of Iceni.[12] But there is a clear contrast between the successful and ambitious romanising efforts of Cogidubnus and those of Prasutagus, who did indeed open his territory to the activities of merchants and financiers, but has left no such solid achievements as temples or inscriptions or the creation of urban life.

Cartimandua has been seen as a Belgic princess, but this was a deduction from the coinage once thought to be Brigantian but now correctly attributed to the Coritani. She is first mentioned in 51, and her actions show that she had by then entered into treaty-relationship with Rome. How much earlier this had taken place is not certain, but surely at latest in 47, when the Roman frontier marched with hers. On the whole, it is likely that she already ruled the Brigantes in 43 and had made her peace with Claudius then, and is one of the *xi reges*. We are hampered by the loss of Tacitus' account of the conquest period, but the assumption is implicit in his later statement that Venutius, Cartimandua's husband, in the governorship of Didius Gallus had long been loyal and had even been protected by Roman arms. This can only refer back to the events of 48, when Ostorius had intervened in Brigantia, which he was under no obligation to do unless there was a treaty already in existence. Cartimandua will have calculated that alliance would strengthen her position at home, as indeed was the case.

Boduocus is known to us only from his coins, which come at the end of a sequence of issues of Dobunnic rulers; and a study of their distribution and related dating evidence shows that perhaps just before AD 43 this tribe was divided. Boduocus' coins, with the good Roman lettering of his name replacing the traditional Dobunnic emblem on the obverse, circulated in Gloucestershire, while the more conservative coins of Corio . . . circulated both north and south of this principality. As already explained, it is very likely that it is to Boduocus the historian Dio is referring when he describes the surrender of a part of the 'Bodunni', which can be taken as a textual corruption of Dobunni; and if so Boduocus will be another of the *xi reges* to have been awarded a treaty; though in his case mutual interest soon demanded that his territory should be garrisoned against the raids mounted by Caratacus from South Wales.[13] As neither Corio's nor Boduocus' coins seem to appear much before 43, they must both be allowed reigns after that date: but when Corio . . . at length made his surrender his kingdom was suppressed and was made part of the composite *civitas Belgarum* (p. 68).

The names of the other five kings who made their peace are lost to us, but it is likely enough that both the Coritani, who had been under pressure from Cunobelin, and possibly also, now or later, the Cornovii, were also among those who made their submission. Thus, once the power of the Catuvellaunian kingdom and its subsidiaries had been broken – as happened in the first year – the progress of the campaign was simplified. There remained no enemy of outstanding power this side of Severn or Trent. Small expeditionary forces consisting of single legions and their auxiliaries, or even of vexillations, were sufficient to fan outwards over the lowland zone putting down such opposition as still resisted, strengthening and supporting friendly régimes, and establishing lines of communication. The immediate flanks were in safe hands, East Anglia under Prasutagus or his predecessor, and Sussex and Hampshire under Verica and Cogidubnus.

The whole army had advanced on Colchester. Now Legio IX was pushed forward round the Fens towards the Trent and Humber, and Ermine Street was garrisoned by forts a day's march apart. In the absence of careful excavation, military remains in this part of Britain cannot always be safely distributed between the conquest campaigns and those undertaken against Boudicca. But a conquest-period fort lay at Chelmsford, and another later reduced in size and then strengthened during the alarm of AD 60, is known at Great Casterton; another fort not yet explored exists at Water Newton, and others can be assumed with greater or less assurance at Ancaster, Godmanchester and Cambridge (Fig. 2, p. 88). A large marching camp have been seen from the air at Home near Newark and at Newton.

The fortress of Legio IX was eventually established at Lincoln, where tombstones, of two soldiers lacking cognomina, have been taken to show occupation before 60. Other datable material indicative of the Claudian period is at present so rare at Lincoln as to suggest that the fortress was not founded before the governorship of Didius Gallus (52–57) and maybe later.[14] The aerial photography of Dr J. K. St Joseph has discovered two fortresses of about thirty acres, the one at Longthorpe near Peterborough, the other at Newton-on-Trent, due west of Lincoln. Fortresses of this size are not sufficiently large for a whole legion, but would be adequate for part of one possibly brigaded with some auxiliary cavalry. Other comparable fortresses are now known in other parts of Britain and will be mentioned later; they reinforce the deduction that columns or battle-groups of less than full legionary size were commonly employed on a permanent footing. In the case of Legio IX, it seems very probable that it was divided into three vexillations, and that these were given independent winter-quarters in the early years, the legion being reunited at Lincoln only when the strategic situation had altered.[15] This new situation might be the preoccupation of Didius Gallus with Brigantia or the regrouping of Paullinus after Boudicca's rebellion.[16] Even then the small size of the new fortress – $41\frac{1}{2}$ acres as against 46 acres at Gloucester, 49 acres at Caerleon and $52\frac{1}{4}$ acres at Inchtuthil – may suggest that a vexillation was still expected to be permanently outposted.[17]

A reserve force probably consisting of part of Legio XX and some auxiliaries was kept at Colchester. The fortress occupied part of the site of the later *colonia* and its garrison is attested by two well-known tomb-stones, one of M. Favonius Facilis, a centurion in the Twentieth, the other of Longinus Sdapeze son of Matucus, a *duplicarius* in an auxiliary cavalry regiment, the First Ala of Thracians. These, both being serving soldiers, probably died before the garrison left in 49; and the condition of their tomb-stones suggests that these were overthrown by Boudiccan rebels in AD 60.[18] What was probably a military supply depot of this date at the mouth of the Colne was unfortunately destroyed virtually without record in gravel-workings at Fingringhoe. Here supplies of men and equipment could be landed directly from the Rhine mouth, and hence supplies collected at *Camulodunum* could be shipped coastwise, for instance to the Witham.

Little is known yet of the activities of Legio XIV, which must have advanced over the Midlands; but though the initial advances in all cases will have made use of native trackways, road-building, if only in a preliminary way, must soon have followed; and just as the Ermine Street shows the way to Lincoln, so the Watling Street can

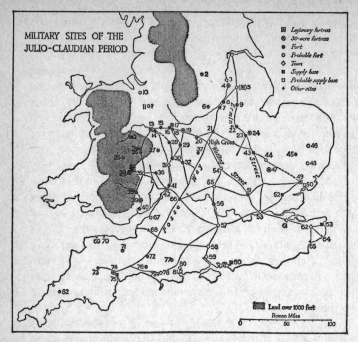

2 Military sites of the Julio-Claudian period

1 Winteringham	20 Mancetter	38 Abergavenny
2 Templeborough	21 Leicester	39 Usk
3 Littleborough	22 Great Casterton	40 Coed-y-caerau
4 Newton-on-Trent	23 Water Newton	41 Kingsholm
5 Lincoln	24 Longthorpe	42 Gloucester
6 Broxtowe	25 Nantmel	43 Godmanchester
7 Margidunum	26 Leintwardine	44 Cambridge
8 Thorpe by Newark	(Jay Lane)	45 Ixworth
9 Ancaster	27 Cleobury Mortimer	(Pakenham)
10 Chester	28 Greensforge	46 Scole
11 Whitchurch	29 Metchley	47 Great Chesterford
12 Caersws	30 Droitwich	48 Coddenham
13 Wroxeter	31 Worcester	49 Colchester
14 Leighton	32 Alcester	50 Fingringhoe
15 Red Hill	33 Clyro	51 Verulamium
16 Stretton Mill	34 Clifford	52 Chelmsford
17 Kinvaston	35 Kenchester	53 London
18 Eaton House	36 Cannon Frome	54 Towcester
19 Wall	37 The Lunt, Baginton	55 Alchester

88

be taken to indicate the track of the Fourteenth; and the first alignment of this road goes only as far as the Fosse Way at High Cross, south-west of Leicester. So far we know little of military posts along its course, except at *Verulamium*, but sites like Dunstable, Towcester or Whilton Lodge are spaced at appropriate intervals, and forts might be expected at them. Leicester itself is a likely place for a fortress for part at least of the legion.

The progress of Legio II is better known since its legate Vespasian later became Emperor, and Suetonius' Life records that in thirty battles he reduced two very powerful tribes, over twenty hill-forts and the Isle of Wight – a campaign which probably lasted three to four years. Excavations at Fishbourne near Chichester have revealed military store-buildings at the head of Chichester harbour, and this site in friendly territory would be a suitable base for mounting an attack on the Isle of Wight. Later, as the advance moved on into Dorset beyond Southampton Water, Fishbourne would be out of touch, but early samian has appropriately been found at Hamworthy on Poole Harbour, where perhaps an advance base was established, and another early military site has been found near Wimborne. Naval activity would in any case be required for the conquest of Wight, and sea-borne supplies carried to suitable harbours along the south coast would ease the problems of transport. The twenty *oppida* can be safely placed in Durotrigan and neighbouring territory, where actual traces of fighting are known at three of them. At Hod Hill a barrage of *ballista* bullets illustrates the capture of the hill-fort, and even more dramatic evidence was discovered at the excavation of the war-cemetery at Maiden Castle. Here skulls with sword-cuts, and even a spinal column deeply pierced by a Roman iron arrowhead, were found among the burials of the casualties. The great defences of Maiden Castle are among the most impressive known in Britain; but at neither hill-fort is there any trace of siege-works, of rampart-breaches or of causeways filling ditches. The gates were well defended and skilfully protected by earthwork, but they were of wood. The hill-forts themselves were not designed to face the long-range fire-power of Roman field artillery. Once the defenders had been driven from the ramparts by *ballista*-fire the gates yielded to burning as happened at South Cadbury. To capture hill-forts became a routine; the only difficulty lay in their number, not their strength. If the Durotriges were one of the two powerful tribes encountered by Vespasian the other was probably the Dumnonii. Both have many hill-forts, and both, in fact, put up so stout a resist-ance that their territory had to be extensively garrisoned for a generation. Conquest-period forts are known at Hod Hill, near Blandford (pl. 1a), and at Waddon Hill, near Bridport; another has been destroyed at Ham Hill, near Ilchester, to judge by the relics found in quarrying; and undated forts are known also at Wivelis-combe, Somerset, and at North Tawton, Devon. Beyond Exeter the occupation of Cornwall was postponed, for a fort at Nanstallon near Bodmin seems to have a Neronian origin; other supporting forts remain to be found. If Hod Hill is typical the garrisons of some of these were mixed, consisting of a vexillation of legionaries brigaded with auxiliaries; and in effect Legio II, despite heavy fighting, would have been bogged down in this area by the reduction of its man-power, withdrawn in static garrison duties. The legionary head-quarters and base at first may have been established at Wimborne or at Dorchester, Dorset, where legionary equipment, early samian ware and the behaviour of the main road all hint at such a con-clusion as a possibility; but a fortress must soon have been estab-lished farther forward at Exeter; alternatively, this legion, like the Ninth, may have been divided. Unfortunately the point is not yet certain. Ptolemy, the second-century geographer, used first-century sources for his description of Britain, but for legionary dispositions he seems to have used an independent and more recent list. He knows, for instance, that Legio VI is at York (where it did not arrive before the reign of Hadrian) and Legio XX at Chester. Legio II he places at *Isca Dumnoniorum* (Exeter), and this has usually been held to be a mistake for Silurian Isca (its fortress at Caerleon after 75). Confusion there certainly has been; but it would be easier to explain if it were founded on fact. A military origin for Exeter in this period is vouched for by early Claudian samian and by an unusual quantity of early coins, and recent excavations have revealed barracks and other military buildings as well as a very large bath-house; the latter can only be explained by the presence of the legion. Furthermore, excavation below the yard of the later town baths revealed part of a timber-framed building whose presence there at the very least implies a radical change of plan in the layout of the city, but is probably best seen as a military building earlier than the civil town: its plan can be interpreted either as part of the centurion's end of a normal barracks or as a building in the *canabae* outside the fortress. Elsewhere in Exeter early buildings were demolished in the period 65–70, which is just the time when Legio II is likely to have moved to Gloucester, leaving the area free for the foundation of the town (p. 109). Such a fortress at Exeter at this date may have been much smaller than full legionary size, and this may account for the *praefectus castrorum* being in charge of it in AD 60.

In 47 Plautius' term of office came to an end, and he returned full of honour to Rome to celebrate an ovation, the last recipient of this honour in history. His tenure of Britain had been mostly occupied with the military and political exigencies. Legionary vexillations had been established in permanent quarters near the limits of the advance. Colchester was still the main base, with at least the headquarters of a legion there, but another important centre for supplies had been established at Richborough. A network of auxiliary forts guarded the lines of communication and the zone of the frontier itself; for by 47 most of the lowland zone of Britain had been overrun and a frontier had been constructed based on the Fosse Way. This remarkable road runs from Exeter to Lincoln, whence its line is continued north to the Humber by the Ermine Street. Along and in advance of this connecting route forts are known or suspected,[19] and the road itself shows by its engineering and design – never deviating more than six miles from the direct alignment – that its conception was both unitary and military. Collingwood, who first recognised it as a military *limes*,[20] connected it with the next governor, Ostorius Scapula, and with the famous emendation of a corrupt sentence in Tacitus' Annals – *cunctaque cis Trisantonam et Sabrinam fluvios cohibere parat*.[21] But Webster has more recently shown [22] that this connection is not consistent with the military situation confronting Scapula. It is too complete to be considered merely a temporary stage of consolidation, nor would we expect such a stage in mid-campaign or between one governorship and the next. As the basis of a *limes*, it marks the intended limits of the first Claudian province, and it follows that imperial policy at first envisaged occupation only of the lowland zone. This makes sense. For though much of Britain's mineral wealth lay beyond the area thus defined, protectorates beyond the frontier could be expected to take it into account, while the position of the frontier itself at the northern limit of the native arable was convenient to the commissariat. The history of the next two centuries was to illustrate the difficulties of attempting to control the semi-nomadic economy of the sturdy pastoral tribes beyond, while ever deeper involvement would call for radical overhaul of the food-supply.

Wales and Brigantia

However, this early frontier was not to last: the tribes of Wales and even the nominally allied Brigantes would not let well alone. P. Ostorius Scapula, the succeeding governor, arrived to find the frontier in flames. Caratacus, Cunobelin's surviving heir, had fled to Wales, and his commanding personality was able to rouse both Silures and Ordovices to aggression. Late in 47, attempting to take advantage of the new governor's arrival after the close of the campaigning season and his lack of local knowledge, one or other of these tribes – we are not told which – raided 'allied' territory. This must mean either the kingdoms of Boduocus and Corio . . . or the territory of the Cornovii. Ostorius, however, drove them out, and by the next year he had assessed the situation and was ready with planned action. The frontier left by Plautius was already out of date in its middle sector, since here it made no contact with the real centre of anti-Roman activity in the north-west, the Ordovices of North Wales. Between lay the Cornovii, themselves a possible source of trouble, but more probably an allied tribe who were sharing the brunt with their southern neighbours the Dobunni. Ostorius made preparations to advance beyond the province into the gap between the headwaters of Trent and Severn. But first he must secure his rear. Plautius had established the province and had defined its boundary. Now tribes within it, whether allied or not, were to be disarmed. This measure amounted to an application of the *Lex Julia de vi publica* [23] which forbad the possession of arms except for hunting or self-defence on a journey; indeed, it may have been a somewhat arbitrary extension of its terms, since conquered territory had already been disarmed by Claudius, and allied tribes were bound by treaty rather than by Roman law. These treaties were arbitrarily altered, for Ostorius now distinguished between *civitates foederatae* within the province and the other *socii* beyond it; but the Iceni, who had never been overrun but had voluntarily entered Rome's alliance, resisted, and were joined by neighbouring tribes. They took up arms and concentrated at a spot defended by a rampart with narrow entrance so that cavalry should not break in. But Ostorius moved swiftly up with auxiliary forces only, and using his dismounted cavalry to augment his infantry, took the place by storm. In the battle the governor's son distinguished himself. The site of these operations has not been identified. The 'neighbouring tribes' would seem to indicate at least the Coritani, so the rallying point can hardly be one of the north Norfolk hill-forts; it is more likely to be found in the Cambridge or Peterborough region. A possible site is Stonea Camp, where remains of this date have been found. A study of the distribution of Icenian remains, particularly their coinage, suggests that the tribe had more than one focus; it is quite possible that it was the westerly group, ruled perhaps by 'Subidasto', who joined with its neighbours in this adventure, and that Prasutagus was ruler of one of the other groups which did not join in, and that as reward he had his territory extended. It is hard to see otherwise how he could have survived rebellion, or have been allowed to succeed a rebellious father.

With his rear thus made safe. Ostorius early in 48 advanced towards the Cheshire gap. With fine strategical insight he had quickly realised its significance: penetration here would divide the tribes of Wales and the Marches from those of the Pennines, and so would limit the objectives of subsequent operations in the west by cutting off the enemy from the possibilities of either reinforcement or retreat. More particularly, his choice of objective would seem to indicate the source of aggression the year before. We have already seen that the tribes in the hills were in any case more mobile than their lowland-zone contemporaries, but now their numbers were swelled by considerable groups of dissidents fired by desperation and with a wider vision of resistance: these would pass from tribe to tribe, inflaming aggression as they went. A successful campaign was in full swing and was already overrunning the Deceangli of Flintshire when disturbances broke out in Brigantia.

The federal character of the Brigantes made close control by Cartimandua difficult, and some of the western groups in the tribe had close connections with the Marches: for this area had long been a corridor for migration from the south, or of northward retreat before successive conquests by Western Third B peoples, princes of the Belgic Dobunni, and the Roman army itself. The reaction of these groups to Ostorius' thrust was beyond the power of Cartimandua to control, and opposition to her policy may have been fanned by the Druids of Anglesey, who saw themselves soon to be isolated from their sources of support in Brigantia [24] and doomed to extinction.

Ostorius wisely broke off his campaign when to continue would be to arouse the north as well as the west. The value of the flank-protection afforded by Cartimandua's régime was still pre-eminent: the queen received military support and the governor turned his attention to the Silures on his left front. Yet the failure to close the trap in 48 had its foreseen results in 51, when Caratacus moved into North Wales and later escaped to Brigantia. Meanwhile, however, the land between Upper Trent and Severn was held, and it seems likely that large vexillations of Legio xiv were stationed in new fortresses at Wall and Kinvaston and probably Metchley.

About twenty miles east of Wroxeter a very large fort has been found at Kinvaston near Penkridge. Originally it enclosed twenty-six acres, but in a later occupation was reduced to eighteen acres. Both forts are much larger than the size required for even the largest auxiliary unit, but too small for a complete legion. Like Longthorpe and Newton-upon-Trent, they probably represent the winter-quarters of a battle-group, a vexillation of legionaries with perhaps some auxiliaries, and the most likely time for the arrival of such a formation in this area is Ostorius' campaign of 48; but a trial trench did produce a sherd of samian pottery which falls best in Nero's reign, and which perhaps indicates the period of the second occupation. A second large fort of sixteen acres is known at Metchley, where once again a smaller fort later took its place, though this time of normal size; while at Wall the known extent of military occupation of this date implies a comparable or larger size.

The Silures in south-east Wales, guided at first by Caratacus' brilliant leadership, were to prove themselves the toughest and most successful opponents which the Roman army was to encounter in these islands, and herein they were assisted by the character of the terrain. This is for the most part broken and well wooded and very difficult to penetrate: ambuscades are easy. Before mounting a campaign Ostorius had to regroup his army. The Roman frontier was protected by a network of auxiliary forts whose garrisons, normally 500 strong, were adequate for police work but powerless against well-conceived raids in strength, and in the campaigning season many of their effectives might be away on active service. Legio xiv had been newly advanced, as we have seen is probable, to the Wall-Penkridge area; and Watling Street was now extended westwards to the Severn bank at Wroxeter, close to which an auxiliary fort is now known, and there is a tombstone of a cavalryman from a part-mounted cohort of Thracians to testify to the garrison.

Wroxeter itself is a superb site with a wide prospect up the Severn Valley into the very heart of central Wales, and was later to become a legionary fortress. Other forts to hold the line of the road were probably now established at Stretton Mill near Penkridge and at Red Hill, while at Leighton a very large fort seen from the air probably also pre-dates the arrival of legionaries at Wroxeter. Legio II was still fully stretched in the occupation of the south-west, with headquarters perhaps at Exeter and Dorchester, and Legio IX was equally stretched in the north-east behind the Trent. The remaining legion, xx, was still based at Colchester, though no doubt detachments from it had been used on campaign, This legion was the obvious choice now that the time had come to concentrate against South Wales. A fortress was built near Gloucester in 49, the site being well chosen – the lowest possible place for a bridge, and so sited as to outflank the ford in the Arlingham bend of the Severn lower down. That the troops placed there were, in fact, from the Twentieth is suggested by a tombstone of a member of that legion found at the site.[25] To maintain security after it had gone, permission was obtained to found a *colonia* at Colchester. Here, therefore, veteran legionaries, newly discharged, were settled with grants of land; and for a time at any rate, while vigour lasted, they would form an effective military substitute in case of need. The official title of the colony, Colonia Victricensis, may even suggest that the veterans were those of Legio xx Valeria Victrix; but the title more probably commemorated the British victory of Claudius, and the

95

title Victrix may not have been awarded to the legion, as it certainly was not in the case of the Fourteenth, till after the part it played against Boudicca.[26]

At Gloucester the legionary fortress whose site was later taken over by the colonia is now known to date from *c.* 67, and was built for Legio II Augusta. The fortress of Legio XX probably lay nearby at Kingsholm, where much military equipment has been found. Kingsholm is the goal of the original road-system here and, as we have seen, may previously have been occupied by an auxiliary fort, the garrison of which is attested by the tombstone of Rufus Sita, cavalryman in the sixth part-mounted cohort of Thracians. The fort will have been part of the original garrisoning of Boduocus' kingdom against the early raids of Caratacus, and perhaps a foundation of Plautius. There would be no necessity for this regiment to remain once the legion had come.

It was not sufficient to thrust forward these two legions. The fortresses had to be connected by lateral roads with each other, and more roads built for communication in the triangular salient thus advanced west of the Fosse; and suitable routes for these roads had first to be surveyed. Forts had to be provided to protect the roads.[27] Military roads run from Penkridge and Wall to Metchley, and thence to Gloucester. Another road from Wroxeter to Gloucester keeps east of the Severn with forts at Greensforge, Droitwich and probably Worcester. A third road far forward of this takes the Church Stretton gap (pl. 2) and runs past Leintwardine, where a pre-Flavian fort exists, then back to Gloucester through Hereford. Other roads between the two are partly known, and the existence of a fort at Cleobury Mortimer far from any known route illustrates the gaps in present knowledge. Probably the Leintwardine route marks the end rather than the beginning of the campaign, and is more probably the work of Didius Gallus, the next governor.

All these preparations took time, and that they were more widespread still is suggested by the discovery that the small fortlet at Old Burrow over 1,000 feet above the Bristol Channel on the edge of Exmoor was constructed at this time. It watches shipping in the estuary and seems designed as the eyes of a fleet; this hints at the widespread character of Silurian raids. Caratacus was seriously alarmed by the turn events had taken. He foresaw the slow penetration of Siluria from Gloucester and its gradual encirclement from Wroxeter up the Severn Valley. To anticipate this, and to throw the Roman offensive off balance he decided to remove its objective to a more distant sphere, and therefore transferred resistance in 51 to the territory of the Ordovices. The heart of their country was Snowdonia, an almost inpenetrable fastness, but not well suited to the presence of large forces, and easily cut off from retreat. He decided to mass his forces in an impregnable position among steep hills, a river in front and the easier approaches defended by piled stones, and there teach the Romans a lesson. Tacitus' description of this site does not make its identification obvious, but Dr St Joseph has suggested a position just west of Caersws,[28] which is plausible, and where remains of earthworks strengthen its claim. Here after some struggle the Romans broke in. The battle was lost and Caratacus' wife, children and brothers captured; but he himself, undaunted, took horse for Brigantia, where he could hope to raise his standard once more and rally anti-Roman elements. For Cartimandua, the danger was serious. If Caratacus succeeded, her rule was over. Moreover, she was bound by her alliance and by bonds of gratitude. Caratacus was arrested and handed over a prisoner: he was sent to Rome, and there made a dignified public spectacle.[29]

But in Britain the struggle continued. The Silures kept up their resistance unflagging. Roman attempts were made to penetrate the difficult territory west and north-west of Gloucester; here, once the upper Wye valley is reached near Hereford, a choice of routes is offered, either due west up the Wye or south-west via Monmouth towards Usk. Tacitus tells us of a legionary force under the senior staff officer, the *praefectus castrorum*, which was attempting to build forts in Silurian territory, but which nearly suffered disaster in a surprise attack. Help arrived just in time, but not before this officer and eight centurions had been killed. At Clyro in the upper Wye valley there is a large fort of 25½ acres, resembling in size those already discussed at Kinvaston, Longthorpe and Newton-upon-Trent. It has not yet yielded decisive evidence, but it is reasonable to suggest that Clyro was the scene of this event; its size is suitable for the accommodation of some twenty legionary centuries and perhaps two auxiliary cavalry regiments. But only 2½ miles away another very large fort of sixteen acres has recently been discovered at Clifford: it lies in a less good position and may therefore pre-date Clyro, and it offers an obvious alternative venue. At Usk itself, on the other line of penetration, military remains are of a slightly later date.

Guerrilla warfare continued inconclusively. But in 52 Ostorius Scapula died, worn out by the struggle and his lack of success. Before his successor Didius Gallus could arrive a legion itself – perhaps the Twentieth – had been defeated, and the situation further deteriorated with widespread Silurian raids.

The governorship of Ostorius was a period of progress. The original aim of Claudius, to hold the lowland zone with a buffer of friendly protectorates beyond, was seen to be impracticable, and further advances were made to the limit of the mountains. The menace of Caratacus was removed; but even this did not lead to the establishment of a peaceful frontier in the Marches, and the military problem of Wales was to tax imperial patience for a generation yet. Ostorius showed himself a skilful general with a fine grasp of strategic and tactical possibilities, and with a slow patience shown in his determination never to move rashly or without due preparation and consolidation of existing gains. He was great enough to accept a check when a more headstrong man might have stirred up a hornets' nest, as in 48, when he rated the security of his northern flank in Brigantia above the possession of the Cheshire gap. His choice of Kingsholm for a fortress stood for twenty years.

Internally also there was advance. The province was consolidated by enforcing a distinction between *civitates foederatae* within the frontier and the allied states beyond it. The former, as in Gaul, became independent only in name and for internal politics; they were no longer allowed to bear arms. By degrees their local independence was to be still further reduced, as one by one they were absorbed on the death of existing rulers. It was probably about this date that Boduocus ceased to issue coins. Britain began to take on the aspect of a normal province, and as part of this process Ostorius took the first steps to foster Romanisation of civilian life. The *colonia* at Colchester, indeed, had a dual purpose, military as well as civil: *subsidium adversus rebelles et imbuendis sociis ad officia legum*: it was both a garrison and a school of the Roman way of life. Here, too, was introduced the provincial centre of the Imperial Cult, which had a parallel purpose. Romanisation worked at first through towns, and this was a beginning. But Ostorius did more than this, for to his rule must also be ascribed the foundation of *Verulamium* as a municipium probably of 'Latin' citizens.[30] Thus both the model of a full Roman community and the hope of achieving local self-government in native communities were laid before the eyes of Britons, sufficient progress in this field for the moment. London, however, must already have been rapidly growing as a port, and it is possible that some of the native *civitates peregrinae*,[31] for instance in Kent and Hertfordshire, had also been begun; certainly Cogidubnus was making parallel progress in his allotted area. Tacitus' reference to his loyalty, and also to the presence of allied troops in the fight with the Iceni in 48, may go far to explain the augmentation of his kingdom and his unique distinction of being both client king and imperial legate. The latter term implies membership of the Senate, which in precisely this year Claudius, taking the opportunity of the census then being held, had extended to certain Gallic notables: it also probably implies praetorian status.[32] Much of the rest of the province was still under direct military rule administered through local garrison commanders; but in Somerset a beginning had been made, under legionary control, of exploiting the Mendip lead.[33]

Ostorius' successor was Aulus Didius Gallus (52–7). He had been consul in 36, and had (it seems) accompanied Claudius to Britain as general of cavalry, later campaigning in the Crimea and rising to the proconsulate of Asia; he was by now both distinguished and very senior.[34] On arrival he found, as we have seen, that the position in Britain had already gone from bad to worse since Ostorius' death: the Silures had defeated a legion, and were now raiding far and wide. Didius seems to have contained them, but he did not press on with the advance. Tacitus scornfully records that he merely acted on the defensive; but in doing this we may be sure that Didius was acting on instructions from the Emperor, whose representative he was. Provincial legates were carefully selected with an eye to what was to be required of them, and will have received careful briefing on appointment; and throughout their tenure they were in close touch with Rome. Claudius, in other words, in his last years was still convinced of the correctness of his original policy of holding lowland Britain only; he was anxious to avoid the conquest of Wales and ordered a disengagement on this front. We are not told how Didius solved the difficult problem of expelling the raiding Silures from the province and then keeping them out, without a repetition of the costly campaigning of Ostorius. The answer is one for archaeology to give, for it must lie in a really efficient frontier system of roads and forts. Indeed, the one good mark this governor receives from Tacitus is for having pushed forward certain forts. Perhaps the Church Stretton–Leintwardine road is his construction rather than that of Ostorius, and the early foundation of Usk may be due to him. The first fort there is at least fourteen acres in size, but it is unnecessarily low-lying, and in Roman times was liable to flood; this would suggest that one of its functions was as a supply port at the base of a road. A few sherds of about this date are known from Abergavenny, and if the road through it from Usk to Kenchester, there joining the Leintwardine road, could be attributed to Didius it would suit the known situation and have the effect of debarring the Silures from the more low-lying parts of their eastern border-lands. Another fort recently identified at Coed-y-caerau nearer the mouth of the River Usk may belong to the same system, for it seems too close to Caerleon to be contemporary. The fortress at Clyro may also be the work of Didius.

The fortress at Wroxeter used to be attributed to the foundation of Ostorius, but sufficient datable material from the site is now available to make it virtually certain that its foundation was not so early. It was perhaps Didius who brought together the detachments of Legio XIV once more and advanced the whole legion to Wroxeter. Such a move might well account for his greater ability to check the Silures, and would firmly anchor the northern end of the Leintwardine–Church Stretton road. But alternatively, and more probably on present evidence, the movement may have been initiated by Veranius and the fortress completed by Suetonius Paullinus.[35] That the fortress existed by AD 60 is suggested by the progress of Paullinus' campaign in North Wales, and is more certainly shown by datable pottery as well as by the tomb-stones of two soldiers of Legio XIV who lack cognomina – an early characteristic – and on which the title Martia Victrix is not given to the legion. That this fortress was ever a double legionary fortress is a mistaken inference from the presence of a tomb-stone of a soldier of Legio XX; but this man was a *beneficiarius* detached from normal duty to serve on the governor's staff.[36]

At any rate, by vigilance and good management Didius brought the Welsh front under control. The scene now shifted to Brigantia.

It was probably Cartimandua's act of surrendering Caratacus which led to a breach with her husband Venutius; on him Caratacus' mantle, as leader of resistance, now fell. Tacitus' chronology is confused. At first the discord was internal, and Cartimandua held her own by laying hands on Venutius' relatives. Then the struggle grew more intense, and Didius despatched auxiliary forces to her aid, which for a time restored the situation: the first fort at Templeborough may mark the station of one of these. Later a legion under its legate Caesius Nasica (no doubt Legio ix) had to intervene more massively. The struggle seems to have lasted most of Didius' time, that is down to 57. But Venutius – 'pre-eminent in military skill' [37] – needed no further lessons that nothing could be successfully achieved while Roman forces were free to intervene. He bided his time even in 61, but was quick to seize it in 69.

Didius Gallus was succeeded, probably in 57, by Q. Veranius. His choice as the first governor under Nero's administration is interesting, for he was in the prime of life; born c. AD 12, he had held the consulship in 49 and had a great military reputation won some ten to fifteen years earlier in Asia Minor against hill-tribes comparable to the Silures. Suetonius (§ 18) mentions in passing, though without giving any indication of date, that Nero had thought of evacuating Britain, but desisted for fear of belittling Claudius' achievements. If Nero's decision was the result of an appraisal at the outset of his reign the decision will have been made by 57, for the despatch to Britain of a man like Veranius, and Suetonius Paullinus after him, shows that by then he had determined on conquest. Another possible, and perhaps more likely, moment for doubt about holding Britain would be on first hearing the shattering news of Boudicca's rebellion. Certainly the surrender of a province which already contained a Roman colony, and on which so much blood and money had been spent, can hardly have been contemplated save for the most pressing reasons. Mere caprice or the chance reading of Veranius' will can have had nothing to do with it. A possible incentive for considering the matter early in the reign may have been affairs in the East, where Armenia had been lost and the Romans at first were almost powerless to take counter-measures owing to the total demoralisation of their troops. In these circumstances the transfer of the powerful Army of Britain to reinforce more vital interests may have been momentarily conceivable, but in the event unnecessary.

By 57, at any rate, Nero had decided that Claudius' policy in Britain was too expensive, and that the proper course was to complete the conquest of Wales. We know nothing of Veranius' activities there, except that, when he died within his first year of office, he stated in his will that if he had had a full three years he would have completed the task. That he achieved much in a brief time is indicated by subsequent events. Suetonius Paullinus, his successor (after two years' successful campaigning in which he put the finishing touches to Veranius' work), is found invading Anglesey. A campaign so far away and the employment there of part of Legio xx (if this is a justifiable inference from its presence in his column shortly afterwards) would be quite inconceivable while Silurian vigour remained untamed. Veranius must have penetrated Siluria, and Suetonius completed its defeat. Nothing more is heard of the Silures for seventeen years, but the full occupation of their territory was prevented by the outbreak of rebellion in East Anglia.

Archaeologically there is not yet much to show. Seven marching camps of legionary or larger size are known in South Wales, indicating campaigns as far west as Neath or Llandovery, but temporary camps are notoriously difficult to date, and some at least may date from the campaigns of Frontinus in 74. At Nantmel an earthwork which is likely to be a Roman fort lies far too close to Castell Collen to be part of the regular fort-system in Wales initiated by Frontinus, and may turn out to be a fort established in an earlier campaign.

For at least thirteen years (47–60) there had been almost unceasing military activity on the Welsh frontier, but by 58 a breakthrough had been achieved. Paullinus finished the resistance in South Wales and in 60 was attacking Anglesey. This island had a double importance both as a Druidical stronghold of nationalism and as a granary of the Ordovices. The end of Welsh ability to resist was clearly within sight when the outbreak of Boudicca's rebellion brought last-minute reprieve, and postponed final occupation for fifteen years. Yet long and successful though the resistance of the Welsh tribes appears, we must not forget that at first, during Claudius' life-time, his governors were not primarily bent on the conquest of Wales but on the establishment of a satisfactory frontier along its borders. Once this policy had been reversed, as it was in 57, the three-year estimate of Veranius was not wide of the mark.

At present little can be said of the civilian side of the administration of either Didius or Veranius. Didius in particular had both opportunity and inclination for administration, but the details elude us. There was much building to be undertaken at Colchester; existing roads laid out for an immediate military purpose needed more solid reconstruction, and the road system itself called for augmentation; there are hints of early growth in towns like London, Canterbury and Silchester; interesting wooden buildings of this period were taking the place of the abandoned depot at Fishbourne, and the export of Mendip lead is attested.[38] Britons, too, were clearly being conscripted for service in the army; a British unit is mentioned in a diploma, or discharge certificate, of the year 80 granting Roman citizenship after twenty-five years' service. As the army developed its widespread network of forts in the frontier regions, the problem of supply will have become more complex. The development of the great supply base at Richborough during this period with its massive warehouses illustrates the steps taken, but other similar store-centres remain to be found. Possibilities exist at Topsham near Exeter and Sea Mills near Bristol.

The Rebellion of Boudicca

C. Suetonius Paullinus, like his predecessor, had a great military reputation, for early in Claudius' reign he had learnt in Mauretania the wisdom of swift advance over the mountains to the enemy's sources of corn-supply: this was the strategy we see him operating in Britain. But after his consulship (c. 43) he had been unemployed — as far as is known — until sent to Britain on the death of Veranius, probably early in 58. After two years of successful operations, during which, as we have seen, he must have dealt finally with the Silures, we find him in 60 mounting an offensive against Anglesey.[39] Probably 58 sufficed for the Silures, since 59 would be required for over-running the Deceangli in preparation for the campaign against Anglesey. This island lies far along the coast of North Wales, and to attack it would have been impossible without security in the south. But once this had been achieved, the island became an important objective. Not only was Anglesey rich in copper ores but it was also the granary of the Ordovices and the sustainer of their resistance; in addition, it was full of political refugees, and was also an important Druidical centre (perhaps even their headquarters). This priesthood had been forbidden in Gaul by Tiberius and Claudius because of its savage rites. The Romans were tolerant of most native cults, but the human sacrifice practised by the Druids put them beyond the pale. A chance find of objects, made during the construction of an aerodrome on Anglesey in 1942 at Llyn Cerrig Bach, and brilliantly studied by Sir Cyril Fox, has been shown to represent offerings at a Druidical shrine, and illustrates the wide connections with all parts of Britain enjoyed by the cult. The offerings, accumulated from pilgrims for more than two centuries, had been either individually consigned to the spirit of the waters or more probably concealed at the time of the Roman attack.

Suetonius had prepared a fleet of flat-bottomed transports: the obvious base for this work is the estuary of the Dee, and there is reason to suppose that an auxiliary fort had occupied the site of Chester before the foundation of the legionary fortress some fifteen years later. At the Menai Straits the invading army was faced by a horrifying multitude on the farther shore. Black-clad females, long-haired and brandishing torches, mingled with the men, resembling Furies; and beyond stood the Druids with potent magic calling down curses with uplifted arms. For a moment the Roman forces hesitated, as well they might; but then they recovered and surged forward, the infantry in boats, the cavalry swimming. The rabble was cut down; the sacred groves, red with the blood of Roman prisoners, were destroyed; and a fort was constructed for a Roman garrison.

But at this moment terrible news was brought of the rebellion of Boudicca. Prasutagus, king of the Iceni, famed for his wealth, had died. With his death his treaty lapsed; and as he had no son, the kingdom was due to be incorporated in the Roman province. If he had hoped, by naming Nero as part-heir, to preserve the kingdom to his daughters – and this is not certain – such measures could have no effect on Roman policy, which favoured the gradual suppression of client-kingdoms in Britain. Slaves from the procuratorial office arrived to take over the property, and centurions from the governor's staff to reduce the kingdom to provincial status. With the governor himself campaigning far away, control was lax and outrages took place. Boudicca herself, the widow of Prasutagus, was flogged and her daughters violated. The nobility of the Iceni were given rough treatment and arrests were made. This harsh brutality sparked off the rebellion, but it was nurtured on grievances more widely spread. The

Trinovantes had suffered much from the insulting arrogance of the colonists at Colchester, who treated their lands as *agri captivi* and helped themselves at will to more than their allotted plots, evicting the rightful owners. There could be no security or peaceful growth under such conditions, but justice could not be obtained from the military arm, who turned a blind eye to abuse, in secret hope of similar licence when their turn should come. Excavation at *Camulodunum* has revealed the harsh conditions under which the natives lived as they quarried and made tiles for the new colonia. The leaders of other tribes were oppressed partly by the exactions of Roman money-lenders, to whom they had to have recourse for the capital expenditure required of them in the expensive processes of Romanisation – new towns, country houses in the Roman style, education in the new civilisation – and in particular in the costly service of the newly introduced Imperial Cult. This had been organised at *Camulodunum* with the new colony, and it was intended as a focus of loyalty. At first probably centred on an altar to Rome and Augustus on the Gallic model, the cult was now being extended by the addition of a large and expensive temple to the deified emperor Claudius. To serve the cult there must have been set up a provincial council, to which each *civitas* sent delegates, and the annual priesthood of the province was filled by election from these. In the early days there were too few candidates eligible for office, since not many *civitates* had yet been organised; and accordingly, the expense fell heavily on too few shoulders. Many felt themselves facing ruin, and would once again apply to the money-lenders. Chief among these, according to Dio, was Seneca the philosopher, Nero's tutor, who had been calling in the vast sums he had lent. Finally, Catus Decianus, the procurator of the province, himself had been trying to exact the subsidies that Claudius had paid to friendly Britons, on the ground that they were loans. Thus, when the moment came, the Iceni were not left to resort to arms alone.

Colchester was the first objective of the rebels. Here the colonists had been lulled by the false reassurances of secret sympathisers with the Icenian cause. The town was still open and undefended, and no emergency rampart was built, nor were the non-combatants evacuated. The colony was now eleven years old, and the original veterans were well past the flower of vigour; no help could come from Paullinus in Anglesey, and the procurator, apparently already operating from London, when appealed to could despatch barely 200 men. These were of little avail against the large horde of tribesmen which now appeared before the town and settled in an armed camp on the ancient site of Cunobelin's oppidum near by. The Roman town of half-timbered houses was burnt with no time to salvage the contents of shops, and a last stand in the stone temple was overwhelmed in two days.

News of the uprising had reached Petillius Cerialis, legate of Legio ix; but as he hurried south to the rescue he was ambushed, his infantry was massacred, and he himself had to gallop back with his cavalry to the security of his fortress. This was a grave set-back to the Roman cause, but the losses cannot have been as heavy as Tacitus implies. A legion consisted of some 5,000 infantry, but after the rebellion the legionary reinforcements sent over to make up the losses amounted to only 2,000 men, so it appears that Cerialis had only a vexillation of his legion to hand in the emergency. Indeed, it is very likely that the Ninth was still brigaded in two or more fortresses, and that Cerialis set out with part of the legion from Longthorpe. Meanwhile Catus Decianus the procurator withdrew to Gaul, leaving southern Britain leaderless.

Paullinus, however, was equal to the emergency. His infantry, consisting of Legio xiv and part of xx with their auxiliaries, would take at least two weeks to cover the 250 miles to London from Anglesey: with his cavalry he pushed ahead of them down Watling Street through unknown risks to the defence of London. Legio ix was now immobilised, but orders were sent to summon Legio ii (from Exeter?). The legate of this legion was absent, and the commander for the moment was Poenius Postumus, the *praefectus castrorum*. He disobeyed his orders and refused to march: the sudden responsibility was too great. The distance, the uncertainty and possibly the dispersed state of the legion were cumulatively too difficult.[40] Thus, when Suetonius Paullinus reached London he realised there were too few troops to defend it. There was no alternative but to withdraw. London would have to be sacrificed. Those who could march came with him: the rest remained to die. At *Verulamium* the scene was re-enacted, and both cities fell to Boudicca. Excavation at each has revealed the burnt debris of her destruction, and Tacitus quotes the official figure of 70,000 slain, citizens and allies, at the three sacked towns. The Britons, he says, had no thought of taking prisoners but only of slaughter, the gibbet, the fire and the cross.

When the governor rejoined his column he found that, with auxiliaries gathered from the nearest forts, he had some 10,000 men. These were all too few to meet a horde reckoned even with exaggeration at twenty-three times that number. Yet everything from instinct and policy to growing shortage of supplies bade him fight soon. He chose a site protected on its flanks and rear by woods and hills, with an open plain in front, and there he met Boudicca. Where this spot was it is now impossible to say: reasonable guesses have placed it close to Watling Street, north-west of Towcester or near Mancetter, south-east of Atherstone.

Roman discipline and superior armament prevailed after a long struggle, and the retreating British were entangled in their own wagon-lager drawn up behind their lines as a grandstand for their women. It was said that 80,000 British fell, for the loss of only 400 Roman slain. When news of the victory reached him Poenius Postumus knew what must be done: he fell on his sword.

The province had been gloriously recovered, but Paullinus was unbendingly stern towards the rebellious. Legio xiv, which had borne the brunt, received the titles Martia Victrix, and Legio xx may also have received the title Victrix.[41]

Reinforcements – 2,000 legionaries, eight auxiliary infantry and two auxiliary cavalry units – were sent from the Rhine. The whole army was concentrated against the rebel tribes, whose territory was thoroughly laid waste. Boudicca by now was dead. The new auxiliaries were brigaded together in new winter-quarters; a likely site for this has been identified at Great Chesterford. Other forts were built in East Anglia at Chelmsford, Coddenham and Pakenham near Ixworth, and perhaps at Scole. To free forces for these new duties forts farther west were abandoned, as at Waddon Hill, or else were redesigned for a new unit, as at Cirencester. At the latter traces of at least two different forts have been found partly superimposed, and we have the tomb-stones of two troopers from different cavalry-units, Dannicus of the Ala Indiana and Sextus Valerius Genialis of the Ala i Thracum. But the military grip was tightened on territory far wider than that of the Iceni. A new fort is known at Baginton near Coventry; existing forts were maintained at Great Casterton and Dorchester-on-Thames. It is clear that Paullinus' thoughts ran primarily upon repression and punishment: military forts mean military government. His ravages were to impoverish East Anglia for a generation.

Operations thus continued into 61, but now new hope dawned for the British. The new procurator sent out to succeed Catus Decianus was named C. Julius Alpinus Classicianus. This man took a statesman's view of the situation and was not afraid either to oppose the governor or to report to Rome adversely upon the fiscal effects of his policies: what was now required, he submitted, was a new man with a new policy. Nero despatched Polyclitus, one of his trusted freedmen, to hold an enquiry; and though in his report faces were saved, opportunity was taken shortly afterwards to recall Paullinus on the pretext of the loss of some ships. He was superseded by Petronius Turpilianus, who had just laid down the consulship (61), but he did not retire in disgrace. Five years later he was given the honour of a second consulship, and we find him playing the part of a senior marshal on Otho's side in the civil war of 69.

Classicianus died in office and was buried in London, and his tombstone, now reassembled in the British Museum, gives us interesting information about his background. His name and tribe both suggest that he was of provincial origin, probably from the country round Trier, and that his father or grandfather had obtained Roman citizenship at the latest from Augustus: the grant might even have been made by Caesar earlier still: one from Gaius to Classicianus himself – the only other possibility – is unlikely. His wife was Julia Pacata, daughter of Indus. Julius Indus was a well-known man in his time, from the same part of Gaul, who had taken the Roman side in the rebellion of Florus in AD 21; a cavalry regiment raised by him, the Ala Indiana, later formed part of the garrison of Britain. The new procurator was thus a member of the new provincial aristocracy of service now emerging to take increasing share in imperial administration. What Romanisation in a barbarian province should involve was within his family experience, and these ideals he was applying in Britain. His outlook was wider than that of Paullinus: though Tacitus denigrates his motives, he had the greater wisdom; and, as Collingwood affirmed, he was the real hero of the story 'who stood up to Suetonius in his hour of victory as the champion of the British people'. His tomb is a precious historical possession.

P. Petronius Turpilianus had been consul in the first part of 61; he governed Britain till 63. Under him the war·was ended, and his mild administration, though it won no praise from Tacitus, suited the requirements of the situation. His successor was M. Trebellius Maximus, consul in 56, who had just served on a commission to revise the census lists and tax assessments of Gaul. This experience was doubtless one of the factors in his choice for Britain, for what was still required was a period of peaceful rule and tactful settlement. His governorship was successful, for he remained in office until 69; and the continuity of administration thus effected, together with the liberal policies of Classicianus, did much to heal old wounds. Security indeed was so assured that in 66 the most famous legion of the British garrison, Legio xiv, was withdrawn for service in the East. This left the Wroxeter fortress empty, which with Wales unconquered was dangerous; and it must have occasioned a reorganisation of the line of battle. When Agricola was legate of Legio xx he and his legion took a major part in the campaigns of Cerialis in the north; and this suggests that Legio xx had taken over the Wroxeter fortress after the departure of Legio xiv. This would necessitate moving Legio ii Augusta to take the place of the Twentieth at Gloucester; but part of it was probably outposted immediately at Usk,[42] and in any event after only a few years the legion moved forward in 74 to take up what was to prove its permanent home at Caerleon in the heart of Siluria. Exeter then will have ceased to be held by a legion in 67, and the site soon developed as the capital of the Dumnonii.[43]

Despite Tacitus' hints that Romanisation was proceeding, archaeology has little to tell of the governorships of Turpilianus or Maximus. On the frontier the forward policy of Nero's early years was perforce abandoned for a while, but the situation did not remain entirely static. Although in the north Cartimandua's kingdom continued to provide security, in the west preparations were eventually put in hand for further action. The occupation of Cornwall may have been effected c. 61 – a task of limited difficulty.[44] The continued watch on the Silures is illustrated by the new fortlet at Martinhoe which now replaced in more permanent form the fortlet at Old Burrow, with the same function of watching for landings from across the Bristol Channel. But on the Welsh border recent discoveries have shown that active preparations for a major campaign were in hand. In addition to the new fortress at Gloucester itself, an even larger base (of fifty-one acres) now replaced the earlier fort at Usk. Part of it was a supply base, but its size suggests the concentration of a very considerable advance force. The disappointed anticipation of booty, to which abandonment of these preparations during the Civil War would give rise, gives point to Roscius Coelius' complaint that the legions were 'despoiled and impoverished',[45] and to Tacitus' comment [46] on the resulting mutiny: 'accustomed to campaigns, the troops ran riot in time of peace'.

Within the province the work of reconstruction must have been begun with the refoundation of the colony at Colchester and with the rebirth of London. By 60 London had already become an important mercantile centre, and its early development as a great port and supply base is illustrated by the main roads which radiate from London rather than from Colchester. The fact that Classicianus died and was buried at London supports the view that already in his day primacy of administration was passing to it, and what we know of his predecessor suggests that even earlier the procurator had his office there. But when Boudicca rose, London had not yet achieved self-governing status as a colony or *municipium*: it was a growing *vicus* not yet stabilised, but with a very large population. Status we can assume came soon, but we have no facts. How quickly reconstruction advanced at Colchester or London we do not know, but at both there was incentive, Roman prestige at the former, at the latter mercantile activity. The curious fact is that at *Verulamium*, the third of the sacked towns, where we do possess some facts, it is certain that reconstruction was very much delayed; the centre of that city was not rebuilt for fifteen years or more.[47] It will have been in these years that the future emperor Titus served in Britain as a military tribune and won a high reputation for energy and integrity: Suetonius (*Titus* § 4) remarks upon the number of statues and busts with inscriptions to him which were to be seen in Britain.

In 68 the Roman world came to the edge of disaster. A rising in Gaul against Nero's misrule drove him to suicide, and a struggle for power began – the Year of the Four Emperors. Conflicting Army-groups put forward rival candidates for the purple, and though the Army of Britain did not actually intervene with its own candidate, vexillations were sent from all three legions to support Vitellius; the Fourteenth was supporting Otho. This reduction in strength meant the postponement of the projected Welsh campaign, and the troops were discontented at the loss of opportunity for booty; Maximus' character was not sufficiently military to impose discipline by force of personality or by exercise. Outright mutiny broke out from which the governor escaped with his life but without prestige; the leader of the opposition was Roscius Coelius, legate of Legio xx, whose sedition became so successful as to drive Trebellius to quit his province and take refuge with Vitellius. He was not restored: Vitellius in 69 despatched Vettius Bolanus to succeed him.

The rule of the three governors who succeeded Suetonius Paullinus put Britain on her feet once more and restored her self-respect. The credit must go principally to Trebellius Maximus. There was never a repetition of Boudicca's rebellion; indeed, we find British regiments serving ten years later in Agricola's army. It was these governors who laid the essential foundations for the great advances in all fields in the Flavian period. But a policy favourable to the province could be unpopular with the army; it was Trebellius' misfortune that the outbreak of civil war made control of his troops almost impossible.

1. We have no list of the auxiliary troops concerned, but the following regiments are attested in Britain before AD 70 and so were probably part of the expeditionary force; but it must be remembered that eight infantry cohorts and two alae of cavalry were sent as reinforcements from the Rhine in 61.

Ala 1 Thracum (Colchester); Ala Indiana and Ala Thracum (Cirencester); Cohors vi Thracum (Gloucester); another Cohort of Thracians (probably ii or i) (Wroxeter). Dio, lxii, 12, 3 mentions archers. Tacitus, *Histories*, i, 59, ii, 66, mentions eight cohorts of Batavians who were attached to Legio xiv. It would be tempting to equate these with the eight cohorts sent to reinforce Paullinus in 61, but to do so would not allow them sufficient time to acquire their great reputation in Britain. More probably they were the 'Celts' whom Dio (lx, 20, 2) describes as swimming both Medway and Thames in full equipment, a habit easily acquired in their home districts, and one repeated at the Po in 69 (Tacitus, *Histories*, ii, 17). The Thracian regiments also perhaps came in 43, but 46 or 47 is a more likely date, for in 46 Thrace became a province. Though it did not become a province till that year, Tacitus (*Annals*, iv, 46) tells us that as early as 26 there was a rebellion in Thrace against Roman conscription: thus, though Longinus at Colchester had served fifteen years (*RIB*, 201), he can still have been buried before AD 49. The Ala Indiana could have formed half the thousand cavalry sent in 61; it left Britain again *c*. 69 for Lower Germany.

2. The matter is fully discussed by Professor C. F. C. Hawkes in E. M. Clifford, *Bagendon, A Belgic oppidum* (1961).

3. It is not clear whether Dio is referring to an existing bridge (*pontem* in his source) or to pontoons (*pontes*) constructed for the purpose. For an alternative site for the crossing, see p. 54, n. 7.

4. *CIL*, xiii, 5093, mentions a tribune of Legio IV, who was recalled to the colours for the British expedition. For the Praetorian Guard in Britain see *CIL*, xi, 395, and for Rufrius Pollio, Dio, lx, 23.

5. Eutropius, VII, xiii 2–3. *Brittanis intulit bellum, quam nullus Romanorum post C. Caesarem attigerat, eaque devicta per Cn. Sentium et A. Plautium, inlustres ac nobiles viros, triumphum celebrem egit. Quasdam insulas etiam ultra Brittanias in oceano positas imperio Romano addidit, quae appellantur Orchades.* . . . If Vespasian was sent by Claudius on a return mission to the north it might explain poetic references to his 'conquest' of Thule and Caledonian groves, which as Professor Momigliano has shown (*JRS*, xl (1950), 41–2), refer to this period of his career, and also Suetonius' reference to his achievements under Claudius' own command: for Claudius had left Britain before his south-coast campaign began. See p. 73 for the situation in the north.

6. See previous footnote.

7. Or he may be his brother: see *PIR sub nomine* and Syme, *American Journal of Philology*, 77 (1956), 270.

8. *CIL*, xiv, 3608. . . . *legatus et comes Claudii Caesaris in Britannia.*

9. Tacitus, *Histories*, iii, 44. *CIL*, iii, 6809, gives us the name of the senior staff-officer of this legion, P. Anicius Maximus, *praefecto castrorum Leg. II in Britannia . . . donato ab. imp. donis militaribus ob expeditionem honorato corona murali et hasta pura ob bellum Britannia.*

10. *RIB*, 91. The significance of the latter title is discussed on p. 99 and n. 32 below.

11. *Agricola*, 14.

12. *Britannia*, i (1970), 16.

13. Early forts for auxiliaries lay at Cirencester and probably at Kingsholm, near Gloucester.

14. This suggestion cannot be regarded as a certainty owing to the small amount of material from early levels; but it conforms with what evidence there is.

15. In spite of the tomb-stones, the account of Cerialis' defeat in 60 suggests very strongly that the legion was still divided at that date and not yet at Lincoln; for not only was he probably operating with less than a full legion, but Longthorpe might seem a fortress more suitable to the geographical context (see p. 106).

16. The consistent absence of Claudian finds from excavation in the fortress and its defences almost compels a date after his reign for its foundation. But the Fosse Way and Ermine Street, roads which converge on Lincoln and presuppose a military post there, were certainly built by 47. This difficulty can be overcome by assuming the presence of an original auxiliary fort at Lincoln, perhaps under the castle, where exacavation has never taken place (cf. *RIB* 266). Finds at the east gate of the fortress support this by proving that the site was occupied before the fortress gate was built (*Archaeologia* civ (1973), 144), and excavations at Longthorpe have confirmed the presence there of legionaries and cavalry, and suggest that the site was given up soon after 60 (*Britannia* v (1974)).

17. This suggestion, if accepted, itself supports a comparatively late date for Lincoln. The fortress was held by the Ninth till 71. If the fortress was built in 47 for most of the legion, there is ample time before 71, and opportunity in the various subsequent regroupings, for the remaining detachment to have returned and for the fortress to have been enlarged to a convenient size; whereas if the fortress dates from soon after 60 the detached vexillation need never have returned until the advance to York. The York fortress is of fifty acres.

18. There is also a pre-Flavian *mortarium* from Colchester inscribed before firing with the words, IVSTI SVPERI; this implies a military potting establishment.

19. The spacing of the sites at Broxtowe, Mancetter, Alcester, Gloucester and Sea Mills at a uniform distance apart and at a uniform distance beyond the Fosse is systematic and significant. A fort at Littleborough would complete the system by guarding the lowest crossing of the Trent.

20. *JRS*, xiv, 252–6.

21. 'He made preparations to occupy everything this side of Trent and Severn.'

22. *Arch. Journ.*, cxv, 49 ff, following a suggestion of T. Davies Pryce, *Antiq. Journ.*, xviii (1938), 29 ff.

23. *Digest*, xlviii, vi, 1.

24. Sir Cyril Fox, *A Find of the Early Iron Age from Llyn Cerrig Bach, Anglesey* (1946), 62, Fig. 34.

25. *RIB*, 122, found at Wotton, just outside Gloucester.

26. Alternatively, *Colonia Victricensis* may commemorate the refounding of an original *Colonia Claudia*, after its destruction by Boudicca, with new drafts from both these legions.

27. An interesting indication of troop movements at about this time is given by the reduction of the existing fort at Great Casterton; the reduced accommodation implies a change of garrison and a smaller unit.

28. *Antiquity*, xxxv (1961), 270–1.

29. It was in Rome he asked the famous question: 'Why do you, with all these great possessions, still covet our poor huts?'

30. See pp. 231 f., 450.

31. See pp. 231–3 for this term.

32. Claudius had previously (AD 41) given consular rank to Agrippa I and praetorian rank to Herod of Chalcis (Dio lx, 2–3). But an alternative suggestion which is attractive is that Cogidubnus owed his promotion as legatus to long-standing friendship with Vespasian and outstanding support to him in 69 (B. W. Cunliffe, *Excavations at Fishbourne, 1961–1969* (1971), 13 f.).

33. For the growth of the lead industry see p. 321 ff. below.

34. *American Journal of Philology*, 69 (1948), 218–22; *Hesperia*, x (1941), 239–41; *L'Année Epigraphique*, 1949, 11.

35. A similar foundation-date for Clyro is very possible.

36. *RIB*, 293.

37. Tacitus, *Annals*, xii, 40.

38. See p. 321 ff. for the development of this industry.

39. Tacitus dates the event to 61, but Sir Ronald Syme (*Tacitus*, ii, 765) has shown the difficulty of assigning all the recorded events to this single year, and suggests that the outbreak of Boudicca's rebellion, and hence the North Wales campaign, belong to the year before.

40. If the fire which destroyed part of Winchester at this time was caused by hostile unrest south of the Thames, this may have been an additional factor in his decision. That there was rebellion even nearer at hand has been suggested by recent excavations at South Cadbury.

41. The title is not certainly attested before this date, e.g. the Wroxeter tombstone, which could be earlier than 60, lacks it (*RIB*, 293).

42. The new Gloucester fortress enclosed only 43¼ acres.

43. Legio XIV was sent back to Britain by Vitellius in 69, but next year was sent to help crush the revolt of Civilis in Lower Germany; it did not return to Britain, nor do we know where it was stationed during its short stay in 69–70. The fort at Cirencester seems to have been evacuated about now, probably as part of the same reorganisation.

44. The fort at Nanstallon was occupied at this date, as the samian shows; excavations by Lady Fox have shown that its initial construction fell within the decade 55–65 (*Britannia*, iii (1972), 56–111).

45. Tacitus, *Hist.*, i, 60.

46. Tacitus, *Agricola*, 16.

47. See pp. 134, 282.

6

The Flavian Period

The crisis of the Empire in 69 ended with the victory of Vespasian. The new Flavian dynasty, two of whose emperors had seen service in Britain, was now to inaugurate a new era in the province with far-reaching advances both in the military sphere and in that of cultural development. Roman control was established over Wales, and in the North conquest was to embrace almost the whole island before the necessity of moving troops to more pressing fields of war compelled curtailment. The military advance was the work of three governors of distinguished military ability, Petillius Cerialis (71–4), Julius Frontinus (74–8) and Julius Agricola (78–84). At least two of these, the first and third, had been chosen for their previous knowledge of the province. The logic of strategy would advise the elimination of Wales, because of its dangerous position on the flank, before advancing far into Brigantia; but in fact this logical order was inverted by the force of inherited events. It was in the governorship of Vettius Bolanus (68–71) that the situation in the north had begun to crumble, and the events of 69 must be scrutinised more closely if the situation is to be understood.

The rise and fall of Galba and Otho had not directly affected Britain or the loyalties of the British garrison. Only Legio XIV, already withdrawn from the province in 67, had become involved on Otho's side; the three legions still in Britain took no part until Vitellius marched against Otho, when 8,000 legionaries were summoned thence to support him. Vitellius sent Vettius Bolanus to succeed Trebellius Maximus as governor, and after his victory over Otho at Bedriacum in April 69 he sent the Fourteenth back to Britain. Here it remained until the next year, when it left to share in the suppression of the rebellion of Civilis in the Rhineland, being thereafter posted to Mainz. Bolanus, therefore, faced a difficult situation.

His legions were of divided loyalty, and three of them were at half strength. A further demand, this time for auxiliaries, from Vitellius met with an evasive reply, for not only was Vitellius' future becoming increasingly uncertain as Vespasian's fortunes rose but the military situation in Britain itself was growing steadily more serious. Discipline had disappeared in the last year of Maximus, and Bolanus lacked the means of restoring it. He had seen service in the East under Corbulo in 62, and had held the consulship in 66: according to Tacitus he was an honourable if easy-going man, and popular, though lacking authority. In the circumstances of the moment even a martinet might doubt what steps to take. But Bolanus was not left in idleness.

Since the days of Claudius the Brigantian client kingdom under Queen Cartimandua had protected the northern flank of the province and had made unnecessary a massive deployment of force in that quarter. It stretched from sea to sea and blocked the entire north. The arrangement was worth some effort to preserve, and earlier governors had been sensitive of the need. But the kingdom lacked basic stability (pp. 71, 94), and was further weakened by dynastic strife. Cartimandua's internal troubles began when she had surrendered Caratacus in 51. Venutius, her husband, had assumed the leadership of the anti-Roman elements in Brigantia, but by 57 a series of checks from Roman troops had taught him that he must bide his time. Even in 60 he was not ready to intervene, or Cartimandua was strong enough to stop him. Since then the situation had further deteriorated. Thinking to undermine his power by winning over his supporters, the queen had divorced him, taking as new consort his squire Vellocatus, who was, of course, of noble birth and aristocratic connections. But her calculations were at fault. Venutius' strategic insight told him that now was the chance he had so long awaited. The Roman world was dissolving in civil war. The British legions were weakened and divided. In Brigantia rebellious elements were ready to strengthen his hand, and he had powerful allies in the north.[1] He made war on his wife, and drove her to appeal for Roman aid.

Bolanus had to act, but the extent of his power to do so, and of his success, is uncertain. Tacitus tells us that a force of auxiliary infantry and cavalry was despatched, which after some indecisive fights succeeded only in rescuing Cartimandua. This suggests that

Bolanus could not afford to use his legions, depleted as they were and still undisciplined; he was unable to defeat Venutius or restore the client-kingdom. 'The throne was left to Venutius: the war to us.' The poet Statius, on the other hand, paints a rather different picture in a poem in honour of Bolanus' son: he mentions the establishment of forts and the winning of a breastplate from a British king. One important step worth taking would be to garrison the Parisi, who were more Romanised than the Brigantes, and may have feared them, and whose conquest by Venutius would lose him an important position on the flank. Perhaps to Bolanus should be ascribed the early fort at Brough-on-Humber and what may be a fortress of the 30-acre type already discussed (for a legionary vexillation or group of auxiliary regiments organised as a battle-group) at Malton. Whatever his successes, Bolanus failed to quell Venutius. This failure meant that an actively hostile power now faced the northern frontier of the province; and when Petillius Cerialis arrived in 71 to take over from Bolanus this was the situation with which he was instructed to deal urgently. The breakdown of the Brigantian alliance had far-reaching consequences. If it could have achieved stability Rome would have been saved long years of war, and once Wales had been subdued and tamed, the costly garrison of Britain might have been reduced. The logical alternative was to attempt the conquest of the whole island, after which the same results might flow. But the character of the hill-men, strengthened and embittered by contingents of refugees from farther south filled with the spirit of resistance, proved in the end too unrelentingly hostile, and the military effort beyond what Rome could conveniently afford. The break with Brigantia was a turning-point of history matched only by the retreat from Scotland a generation later: from this time onward Rome was committed to keeping very large forces in Britain for an indefinite period. But this was a burden for the future: for the present the empire was still in a phase of confident expansion, and such forebodings were far from the thoughts of those who framed Flavian policy.

Q. Petillius Cerialis was a friend and relative of Vespasian, and to this he owed his advance. He was a man of dashing, even headstrong, character, and with a flair for action rather than patient consolidation. He had been legate of Legio ix during the Boudiccan rebellion, when his rashness had resulted in serious defeat. His first consulship was held in 70, and he was sent at once to the Rhine to deal with the rebellion of Civilis. The following year he was sent on to Britain, bringing with him Legio II Adiutrix to replace the Fourteenth and to restore the garrison of Britain to four legions. This legion was newly raised and not yet experienced. It was placed in the fortress of Lincoln, while Cerialis honoured his old Legion IX, formerly in garrison there, by using them as the spear-head of his advance. A new fortress was built at York for this legion: it appears to be of full size (50 acres), but was not at first constructed in any great strength, for the ramparts were rebuilt only some ten years later. Nevertheless, the choice of York showed brilliant topographical insight, and no doubt was the result of previous acquaintance with the area: York held the keys of Brigantia and has remained the military centre of northern England ever since.

The extent of Cerialis' activities is hard to make out in detail. Tacitus merely tells us that after a number of battles, some of them bloody, he conquered much of Brigantia and overran more of it. Elsewhere he mentions that Agricola, now legate of Legio XX, was given a share in the work, and this, as we have seen, implies that his legion was now at Wroxeter. The difficulty of tracing the footsteps of Cerialis in detail is due to his neglect of fort-building. At Brough and Malton military establishments were held at this date, Brough being a normal fort and Malton something much larger. These are usually taken to be foundations of Cerialis, but it has been suggested above that Bolanus may have been responsible.[2]

At any rate, whether or not the Parisi were being invaded for the first time, it was wise to approach the Vale of York from the east, for here there was good dry ground all the way, and the Humber crossing presented the only difficulty; the alternative route from the south involved skirting round many miles of very marshy ground, with the danger of Brigantian flank attacks from the hills driving the columns back against the marsh.[3] The fortress of York can more certainly be attributed to Cerialis, since the authority of Tacitus is against the moving of a legion by Bolanus; and once York was founded as a legionary fortress, a large base at Malton loses much of its point. It was, however, continuously occupied until *c*. AD 79, when a smaller but still very large fort (8½ acres) of normal pattern replaced it. But in all the rest of Brigantian territory the known forts go back no earlier than Agricola's governorship, wherever excavation has tested the matter. Only at Carlisle is there a suggestion of anything pre-Agricolan: it is possible therefore that a base was created here to make contact with the sea after an advance from York. That such an encirclement was the plan of campaign is suggested by the results of excavation at Stanwick and by the existence of pre-Agricolan marching camps in the Stainmore pass.

At Stanwick a 17-acre hill-fort of the normal type appears to have been constructed in the early fifties – just about the time of Venutius' first breach with Cartimandua – and there were two subsequent enlargements which converted the site from a hill-fort into a vast perimeter defended by massive dykes. The first enlargement enclosed 130 acres, mainly of level pasturage, and care was taken to include a water supply: the second increased the area to 730 acres. The first enlargement could be dated c. AD 50–70; the second was subsequent but did not yield closely datable evidence, save that it had not been quite completed when it was destroyed.

Stanwick occupies a strategic position near Scotch Corner, where the Roman road across Stainmore diverges from that running north to Corbridge. These roads follow routes of high antiquity, and the position is well chosen for summoning aid both from the north-east and the north-west. The site lies beyond the immediate range of Roman troops operating from the old province, and thus in every way suits the context of Venutius' struggle with Cartimandua and with Rome, which its archaeological dating suggests. The place may have been originally chosen and built by Venutius in the governorship of Didius, and the first enlargement fits in with his actions in the governorship of Bolanus, as does the third with that of Cerealis, whose rapid advance found it still under construction. The purpose was to mass and defend a large body of tribesmen and especially their herds; the dykes recall those of *Camulodunum*, the most advanced fortifications known to native Britons. But advanced though they were by British standards, they could not hope to stand up to legionary attack, while the very size of the perimeter made it impossible to defend. The excavators found that though some of the contemporary pottery was of local Brigantian home-made type, much of it was of superior wares imported from the south of Britain or beyond, which demonstrates the dependence of even anti-Roman persons outside the province on luxuries brought in from the Roman market.

At Stanwick, then, we may place Venutius' last stand. At the summit of the Stainmore pass beyond lies the marching-camp of Rey Cross (20 acres) of legionary size, and with especially massive ramparts because of the impossibility of ditch-digging in the rock. Its relationship with the Roman road (which cannot be thought later than Agricola's governorship) shows the camp to be earlier, and the details of its castrametation also point to this conclusion, being old-fashioned by Agricolan standards. Two other marching camps of the same series are known beyond it, a day's march apart, at Crackenthorpe and Plumpton Head. They point the path of a legion advancing towards Carlisle: the campaign of Cerialis seems the earliest context for this.

When Cerialis was recalled to hold a second consulship early in 74 the Brigantes were battered and leaderless; but no steps seem to have been taken as yet to police the territory adequately, or to incorporate it formally in the province. This process was not put in hand for six years. Instead, the conquest of Wales was first undertaken.

Sextus Julius Frontinus, who succeeded Cerialis, had been praetor in 70, and had played a distinguished part in the suppression of the Gallic rebellion. The date of his consulship is uncertain, but it was probably held in 73. Frontinus became an eminent elder statesman in later life: remaining unemployed during most of the tyranny of Domitian, he was put in charge of the aqueducts of Rome by Nerva, and composed a manual on the subject which tells us much about his conscientious and reforming administration. He received a second consulship in 98 and a third in 100. Another of his books was *Stratagems*, but this throws less light on Britain than might have been hoped.

His first task was to conquer the Silures. Nothing is recorded of this tribe since 57, but by now a new generation of warriors was growing up, and any lessons taught by Veranius or Paullinus were passing into oblivion. It may well be that the reason for breaking off the Brigantian settlement so abruptly was that the Silures were already on the move. Of the details of Frontinus' campaigns we know nothing, but from the apparent ease with which the Roman army this time swept over South Wales, we may suppose landings on the plain of Glamorgan rather than another attempt to breach the natural land defences of Siluria. Certainly new forts are found at harbours all along the South Welsh coast – at Cardiff, Neath and Carmarthen – and Legio II Augusta was now placed in a new fortress at Caerleon near the mouth of the Usk. From these positions valleys lead conveniently into the interior: the Towy valley in particular running north-eastwards from Carmarthen, and the Usk valley leading inland from Caerleon and curving westwards to Brecon, both offer easy routes and between them almost cut off the larger part of Silurian territory. Brecon itself is another key point from which valleys radiate. In all these valleys roads were built and forts placed a day's march apart. Thus, a net-work was constructed which cordoned off each separate block of hills: unauthorised movement on any scale became impossible. Naturally these forts could not be placed in isolated positions before a crushing victory had been won; the first stage of the conquest must have been the search for, and destruction of, the main war-bands of the tribe, and it is to this stage that we must ascribe the marching-camps. In contrast to the forts, these lie on the high plateaux: only there was rapid open movement possible to a large body of troops. A total of seven marching-camps is known at present in South Wales. Two successively at Y Pigwn (37 and 25 acres) and one at Arosfa Gareg (45 acres), both near Llandovery, and one at Ystradfellte (21 acres) mark routes skirting or penetrating the Brecon Beacons; three others near Neath (61 acres), Aberdare (16 acres) and Pontypridd (37 acres) represent troops operating in the Glamorgan uplands. None of these are dated, but some at least will belong to this campaign. The differences in size between these camps, even making allowance for irregular ground, are striking. It is impossible to trace the march of a particular force as could be done in the Stainmore pass; and clearly many others remain as yet undiscovered. The camp near Neath is particularly noteworthy for its size. A camp of 61 acres would theoretically hold three legions. This one occupies partly broken ground, but even so a very large force indeed was involved. Several others are of larger than legionary size.

The fuller account which Tacitus doubtless wrote of Frontinus' work in Britain in his *Histories* is unfortunately lost. All we possess is a summary sentence in the *Agricola*. This mentions only the Silures as objects of his conquest, but no weight can be put on this limitation. They were by far the most famous people in Wales, and in this thumb-nail sketch serve only to indicate that Frontinus was not fighting the same enemy as Cerialis. There is no doubt that the

Ordovices were also overrun by Frontinus. At first Legio xx from Wroxeter probably joined in the Silurian campaign by advancing into central Wales by the Severn valley. But before the end of his term of office Frontinus had almost certainly begun the construction of the fortress of Chester for Legio ii Adiutrix, though water-pipes were still being installed there in the early months of 79. The threat to the Ordovices of a fortress in this position is obvious. The Deceangli in between had probably been subjected since 60; lead pigs from mines in their territory are dated as early as 74. But the Ordovices were more than threatened. Garrisons were being installed in their country, for they destroyed one of these – a cavalry regiment – shortly before Agricola's arrival. Yet the conquest was not quite complete when Frontinus left, for Agricola rounded it off in his first year with the capture of Anglesey. To find garrisons for at least twenty new auxiliary forts must have meant a radical reorganisation of troop-positions in southern Britain. The forts in the Dumnonian peninsula at least will have been abandoned now. The bearing of this on the development of local self-government will be discussed shortly (p. 134); evidence, too, is beginning to accrue, for instance at *Verulamium*, of Frontinus' interest in the growth of towns.

Gnaeus Julius Agricola is the most famous of the governors of Britain, because of the biography written by his son-in-law Tacitus. Were it not for this, our knowledge would be dark indeed, for only three inscriptions of this governor have so far come to light.[4] Nevertheless, the *Agricola* is an early work of Tacitus and does not represent his mature view; this, unfortunately, is lost to us in the missing portions of his *Histories*. The biography is partisan: it tends to ignore or play down the achievements of its hero's predecessors in order to focus attention on his own. To perceive this is one thing, but to remedy it quite another, where evidence is short. Agricola served in Britain as military tribune on the staff of Suetonius Paullinus, and had probably been present on the earlier Anglesey expedition. Eight years later, after his praetorship, he was sent back to Britain by the government of Vespasian to take over from Roscius Coelius command of Legio xx, whose discipline and loyalty were both in question. Under Bolanus there were no opportunities for distinction, but under Cerialis Agricola was given field experience, at first in command of his legion, later of larger forces. He earned good reports, and on return to Rome was promoted patrician. After governing Aquitania he was elected to the consulship. The date of this is not exactly known, but was probably late in 77; and immediately after it he was appointed to Britain. Here he will have arrived half-way through the summer of 78; it is probable that Frontinus had already left, for no campaign was in progress and the army was relaxed. But the Ordovices had just destroyed an *ala* stationed in their territory, and since Agricola already knew the ground, he was able swiftly to mount a punitive expedition which cut to pieces almost the entire tribe. He thus no doubt averted the development of a much more serious situation the next year, and his action illustrates the wisdom of the Flavian choice of 'specialist' governors who already knew the province. No stranger would have dared to plunge into this difficult country so late in the season. He then went on to capture Anglesey by a *coup de main*, not bothering to wait for transports but making his auxiliaries swim beside their horses. This sounds like the Batavi again.

The conquest of Wales having been thus consolidated, he was able to turn his attention to the north. Here the Brigantes had been beaten by Cerialis five years before, but the task of occupying their territory had been left incomplete. It is possible that Vespasian now had in mind only the reduction of Brigantia, but he died in June 79 while the first campaign was still in progress; and if so Agricola had no difficulty in getting Titus' permission to go farther. A strong case could be made for overrunning the Selgovae and Novantae also, the tribes from whom Venutius had derived support.

Tracing the course of Agricola's six campaigns in the north has always been a matter of considerable difficulty, owing to the scarcity of topographical information given us by Tacitus. His account can, however, be supplemented by the evidence of archaeological discovery and especially of aerial photography, both of which have yielded a rich harvest. In 79 the advance northwards was begun. The only indications of its direction and extent given by Tacitus are the statement that Agricola himself chose the sites of camps and himself reconnoitred estuaries and forests, and the information that the following year's campaign ended at the Tay. Though personal reconnaissance of estuaries and forests is a stock attribute of good generals in Roman literature, it does suggest the western rather than the eastern side of the Pennines; and there is, in fact, no evidence that Cerialis had ever overrun this difficult area. The plan of campaign

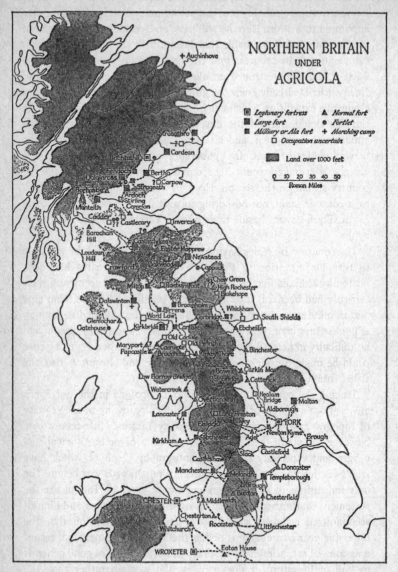

3 The forts of Agricola in the north.

may have involved two parallel columns, one marching north from York and the other from Chester, contact being made from time to time across the passes. This is a deduction from the road system which Agricola soon established (Fig. 3), no doubt on lines now explored, and it is one which suits the geography of north Britain. The roads were necessary to link the forts which, as we shall see, he established as he advanced.[5] No doubt Agricola himself led the western column, giving the place of honour to his own division, Legio xx.[6] The tactics were terrorising raids followed by offers of reasonable terms. In this way he won over many peoples who had till then maintained their independence, and he stationed garrisons in their territories. Traces of this campaign can perhaps be seen in the slighted ramparts of the native strongholds on Ingleborough and Carrock Fell, if indeed these particular hill-forts had not fallen previously to Cerialis. The Tyne–Solway isthmus was perhaps the limit of the first campaign and, as we have seen (p. 71), this line was approximately the northern boundary of the old Brigantian kingdom.

The next year, 80, however, saw the advance continued, and this time new tribes were encountered; for by the end of it devastation had been carried to the Tay estuary.[7] Despite bad weather, enemy resistance was beaten down, and once more forts were constructed so that garrisons could winter in conquered territory. As a result of this reconnaissance to the Tay, the advantages of the Forth–Clyde isthmus as the site of a fortified frontier were appreciated: next year, 81, forts were established on this line, and the troops were also employed in consolidating the gains already made. This would be the moment for more thorough road-building than had been possible so far, and for a more thorough disposition of forts at strategic points.

The exact character of the boundary established at the isthmus by Agricola is uncertain. It used to be supposed that his forts lay beneath those of the later *limes* on this line known as the Antonine Wall; but an absence of Flavian pottery from the majority of these sites compels a reconsideration of this view, nor are the sites of the independent forts of the Agricolan system necessarily the best for forts attached to a linear barrier. At Bar Hill and Croy Hill fortlets underlie the Antonine Forts; these could conceivably be Agricolan, granted that they were occupied for too short a period for broken pottery to accumulate (AD 81–3); but it has been suggested that they represent a preliminary phase of the Antonine arrangements, like the fortlet at Duntocher.[8] One Agricolan fort lies at Camelon, about two miles north of the Wall; two others may have lain near but not precisely at the Antonine Wall forts of Castlecary and Cadder; another may have existed near Mumrills.[9]

It seems probable that the emperor Titus had decided, on the basis of Agricola's reports, to limit conquest to southern Scotland. Not only did the northern isthmus provide a conveniently short line for the frontier but, as we have seen (p. 73), it was also to some extent a linguistic and cultural boundary. All to its south could be described as Britons, whereas the Caledonian tribes to its north were of different stock. Tacitus mentions that they had reddish hair and large limbs, which made him think them akin to the Germans. The northern lands could be looked on as almost a different island.[10]

Of the two main Roman roads through southern Scotland, one runs north from Carlisle up Annandale; once over the watershed, this road divides, one branch going to the Clyde valley, the other to Inveresk on the Forth. The other main road runs up from Corbridge over the Cheviots to Newstead and on to Inveresk. Both are heavily garrisoned with forts. The eastern road is approximately on the western border of the Votadini, and the effect of both roads is to cordon off the Selgovae from their neighbours. This effect is heightened by at least two other cross-roads which cut through Selgovian territory. The whole system pivots on the large fort of Newstead, which lies in the valley below the slighted oppidum of the Selgovae on Eildon Hill North (p. 74). In contrast to the treatment of the Selgovae, Traprain Law, perhaps even at this time the principal oppidum of the Votadini, has produced Roman pottery of Flavian date: evidently it was allowed to continue. And the territory of the Votadini contains remarkably few Roman forts. This tribe in later times was traditionally friendly to Rome, and it is likely that this tradition goes back to their first contact with the Roman army. Other tribes – the Brigantes or Selgovae – whose experience of it was bitter, remained unrelenting in their hostility for over a century. We may deduce that the Selgovae and the Novantae were the chief foes in the Lowlands, and that Agricola came to some arrangement with the Votadini. Such a state of affairs would be typical both of Celtic reaction to Rome and of Roman statecraft: Tacitus remarks that alliances between two or three tribes were rare in Britain. The Selgovae were a powerful and formidable enemy; but it is probable that they were bewildered by the speed of the Roman advance, and we have seen (p. 74) that the numerous small hill-forts in their territory imply a lack of political centralisation which may have proved disastrous when the moment of crisis so swiftly arrived. The moment passed and the Selgovae found themselves cut off from their neighbours and from each other, and subject to military rule.

The turn of the Novantae came next year, in 82. The great promontory of south-west Scotland lies on the flank of that part of the Lowlands already conquered. The Novantae, who occupied its southern portion, had been isolated from the Selgovae by the cordon of the Annandale road. But their hostility presented a continuing menace not only to that road with its garrisons but also to the Cumberland coast across the Solway. The reduction of this flank, then, could be postponed as a temporary expedient, but not permanently neglected, difficult though much of the country is. In 82 Agricola crossed the estuary at the head of a sea-borne invasion. This method of attack had a twofold advantage: not only will it have been unexpected by the Novantae but by it his columns will have been enabled to march with the lie of the land instead of across it, since all the river valleys on the south coast run north and south. In the course of this campaign the army encountered tribes hitherto unknown – presumably groups in Ayrshire, for the Novantae themselves must have been well known.

Until recently archaeology had little to show in this area, and there are still many sites to be discovered. A Roman road runs westwards from Castledykes down the Irvine valley past a fort at Loudoun Hill, and making, no doubt, for a harbour near the river's mouth. As a result of aerial photography in the dry summer of 1949, later confirmed by excavation, Agricolan forts are now known at Dalswinton (pl. 1b) and Glenlochar in the Nith and Dee valleys; and west of the latter a fortlet of Flavian date, possibly Agricolan, has been discovered at Gatehouse of Fleet. Clearly a road connected these sites too, penetrating the southern borders of the Novantae, and probably making for a port near Stranraer. We can assume that there was a north–south link road along the west coast. Agricola's army certainly reached the south-western extremity of Galloway which faces Ireland, and the general was of the opinion that that island could easily be conquered. He had received a fugitive Irish prince, who would be useful if it came to the point; and he had found that information on Irish harbours and approaches was to be had from merchants who traded there. It was his estimation, surely optimistic, that one legion and a few auxiliaries would suffice for the work. However, if he made recommendations to Rome on these lines, they were turned down. Titus had died in September 81, and the new emperor Domitian, impressed perhaps with the speed and success of Agricola's campaigns, seems to have decided that if further military advances were to be made, it would be more realistic to complete the conquest of Britain. He accordingly reversed the decision to stand on the Forth–Clyde line. This must be the meaning of Tacitus' obscure remark on the subject of this frontier, that here, still short of the limits of the island, a halting-place was found – 'if the valour of our armies and the glory of the Roman name had allowed it'. It was necessary to his purpose to avoid giving Domitian the credit for allowing his hero the advance which led to his great victory. At the same time Domitian himself was about to embark on an important war in Germany in 83, and called for vexillations from all four British legions.[11] If Agricola could advance without these troops he was free to do so.

In 83 accordingly the advance northwards was resumed, but this time geography imposed a different plan of action. The hitherto successful advance in two columns each side of the central spine of hills was no longer possible, as a glance at the map of the Highlands will show. This was already known to Agricola from naval reconnaissance. Plutarch tells us how at Delphi in 83–4 he met a Greek schoolmaster from Tarsus, named Demetrius, recently returned from Britain, who had taken part in the exploration of the western islands. This reconnaissance took place perhaps in 82. There are echoes of an eye-witness, too, in Tacitus' description of the wide domain of the sea in Caledonian latitudes, 'which is not limited to the coast as elsewhere, but penetrates sinuously deep inland, mingling with mountain ranges as though in its own element.' Two alternatives were left. One was to penetrate the Highland massif itself, which Agricola was too good a general to attempt before the enemy had been broken; the second was to advance with his entire force up the eastern plains, which encircle the Highlands on two sides. A successful battle after that might bring the whole land within his grasp. Northwards of Inverness lay the country of the broch-builders (p. 73). These may well have been friendly to Rome because of hostility to the Caledonian hill-fort builders and, if so, presented no serious military problem.

The drawback to such a march lay in the insecurity engendered by a single lengthening life-line. The long supply route marked by the road running north from Stirling to Stracathro was easily vulnerable to surprise attack issuing from the mouths of Highland glens beside its path. Agricola took steps to deal with this grave problem, and nothing shows his qualities as a commander more convincingly. The tactical problem was solved by placing a fort to block the exit from each glen: [12] the strategic difficulty was solved by increasing use of waterborne transport. But the fleet had a further purpose also. Its appearance in the north gravely disturbed the consciousness of security which the remoter Caledonians had hitherto enjoyed; a series of landings far behind the lines might stimulate the enemy to abandon the wise strategy of guerrilla warfare and risk the crushing defeat which alone could end the war.

News of his intentions had already reached the Caledonians, or perhaps the early naval explorations had warned them of their danger, for a confederacy had been formed which was already massing large forces. A Roman fort was attacked, and Agricola learnt that the enemy was approaching in several columns. He therefore divided his own army into three divisions, and the camp of one of these, Legio IX, was attacked. This legion was below strength, as we have seen; but Agricola himself came up in time with relief, and the enemy was put to rout, only to escape into the marshes and woods. After this the advance was maintained with renewed confidence, and may have reached the neighbourhood of Aberdeen if the reference to frequent meetings with the fleet has any meaning. Summer ended, however, indecisively. It will have been in this year that the decision was reached to place a legion – probably Legio XX – in a new fortress at Inchtuthil on the Tay. This fortress guarded the main exit from the Highlands through the Tay gorge at Dunkeld, and formed the hub of Agricola's system for the occupation of the north. A short distance north of it runs the Cleaven Dyke, an obvious Roman boundary guarded by a watch-tower. This does not extend far enough to mark an actual frontier. It probably defined the territorium of the legion, a provision area under strict military control.

In 84 it remained to force a battle, and this was at last achieved by sending the fleet ahead to raid and burn, so that the enemy's

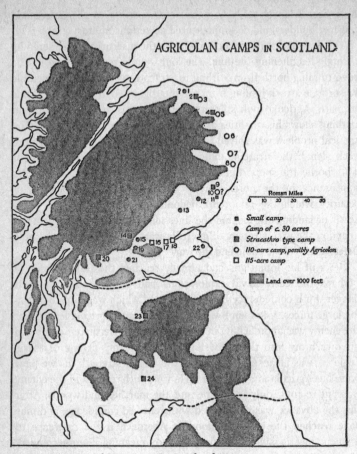

4 Agricolan marching camps in Scotland

1 Bellie
2 Auchinhove
3 Muiryfold (Pass of Grange)
4 Glenmailen (Ythan Wells)
5 Glenmailen (Ythan Wells)
6 Kintore
7 Normandykes
8 Raedykes
9 Stracathro
10 Logie (?)
11 Dun (Montrose Basin)
12 Finavon
13 Cardean
14 Dalginross
15 Dornock
16 Dunning
17 Abernethy
18 Carpow
19 Ardoch
20 Menteith
21 Dunblane
22 Bonnytown
23 Castledykes
24 Dalswinton

remaining areas of supply lost all security. The result was a full-scale mobilisation of all the remaining Caledonian states. They are said to have raised more than 30,000 men, who awaited Agricola's approach at the Mons Graupius. The exact position of this famous battle is still uncertain, but it should be sought in the approaches to Inverness at some point where the natural features enabled the Roman route to be foreseen. A line of Roman marching-camps running up the eastern side of Scotland has long been known, and in recent years aerial photography has filled in some of the gaps; but it has also added complications. It can now be said that they represent more than one campaign (Figs. 4, 8, p. 202). One series of camps is of great size, c. 130 acres. Camps of this area are sufficiently large for a force of 30,000 men, or three legions and an equal number of auxiliaries. One of these camps can be shown to be later than a permanently established signal station near Ardoch: it is probable that they represent the campaigns of Severus. A second series of camps, 63 acres in size, closely resembles the 130-acre series in shape and proportion and also appear to be of early third-century date (p. 200f.). In addition there are three, or perhaps four, other groups. One, represented by squarish camps of c. 115 acres at Dunning and Abernethy, is taken to have been built on Agricola's march to the Tay in 80. A second group has areas in the region of 30 acres, and the third, though varying considerably in acreage, has a distinctive type of *clavicula* at the gates (the 'Stracathro type'). There are good grounds for assigning both of these series also to Agricola's forces, and some at any rate of them to the year 83 when his army was marching in three divisions. A fourth group may be indicated by four camps in the far north which are of c. 110 acres; it is not yet certain whether these represent the final stages (with depleted forces) of Severus' campaign, or whether they are to be connected with Agricola's last campaign in 84. Certainly the absence of evidence for a concentration of his forces before Mons Graupius has hitherto been an embarrassment; but further camps of this size must be found to the south before the group can be attributed to Agricola with any certainty. Be this as it may, at the furthest site of all to the north-west yet discovered, a camp of Stracathro type at least 30 acres in extent has been identified from the air at Auchinhove near the pass of Grange. The site of Mons Graupius should be looked for beyond this camp.

The Caledonians had many leaders, one of the chief of whom was Calgacus, into whose mouth Tacitus puts a speech of great imagination. In the battle which followed, Agricola stationed his legions in front of the Roman camp, but behind his line of battle, which consisted entirely of auxiliary troops. He placed 8,000 infantry (some twelve or sixteen regiments which included formations enrolled in southern Britain) in the centre, and 3,000 cavalry (five or six alae) on the flanks. The legions stood in reserve, and in fact were not employed. The Roman line lacked superiority of position, for the Caledonian forces could be seen rank on rank up the slope behind their chariotry, and Agricola had to extend his line for fear of being surrounded. His problem was to get the Caledonians off the higher ground, and this he achieved by allowing his centre to fight itself to a standstill on the slope: once the enemy, attracted by this sight and contemptuous of the small number of men fighting, had moved down in hopes of sweeping round the Roman rear, he routed them with four fresh cavalry regiments held in reserve for this purpose. Ten thousand Caledonians were said to have perished for the loss of only 360 Roman troops.

The victory had been gained late in the season. There was no time for further campaigning. Agricola led his army into the lands of the Boresti and there took hostages (presumably from all the defeated tribes). The Boresti are otherwise unknown, but their name has been connected with Forres in Moray. The fleet was ordered to sail round the north of Britain, and thus established that it was an island; on this voyage, too, they explored the Orkneys and received their surrender. On land Agricola slowly returned to winter-quarters farther south. When the news of the victory reached Rome, Domitian awarded him triumphal ornaments, and arranged for his recall. Agricola had been in Britain more than six years, an unusually long term for the Governor of this province: the routine exploitation of victory could be left in accordance with precedent to his successor.

It remains to sum up Agricola's achievements. There is no doubt that on the military side he had a distinguished record in Britain.[13] In six years he had almost doubled the area under Roman control, granted that Cerialis had done the hard work in Brigantia. He had an eye for country, and his fort-sites were well chosen: many remained occupied for centuries. Moreover, he was an innovator in fort-design. Again, and unlike most Roman generals, he had a masterly appreciation of the role of sea-power in extended military operations and was notably successful in his use of the fleet both for aggression and for supply. In both these aspects of strategy he may have built on the experience of Frontinus, whose fort-system in Wales was equally well planned and who may have similarly used his fleet. Nevertheless, the military problems of Scotland were not identical with those of Wales, and Agricola's instinct never faltered there. The rapidity and sheer competence of the reconnaissance which found the way for his columns and the key positions for his forts must command respect; and when the policy of cordoning the hills foundered on the geography north of the Forth Agricola was not at a loss. In the final battle, too, he used new tactics. The conception of a decisive battle fought by auxiliaries only, with the legions looking on, had never been successfully attempted before. It is true that in 70 Cerialis at the battle of Vetera had placed his legions in the second line, but in this muddled battle they were soon engaged in heavy fighting, and there is no indication that the general had planned otherwise. The battle of Mons Graupius was a notable advance on this. Tacitus tells us that the idea was to save *Roman* manpower; but that is a propaganda point which tells only part of the truth. The auxiliaries themselves were potential Romans, who received citizenship on discharge. They were, however, more expendable; yet the real significance of these tactics, as Professor Richmond pointed out,[14] is that provincials – even Britons – were now able to play a major part in Imperial defence. Already leading provincials had risen to high rank in the administration (p. 108); but now the rank and file had shown their reliability. The provinces were on the way to partnership in Empire.

In his civilian administration Agricola was imaginative. Born in Narbonensis of provincial Roman stock, he lacked the arrogance of the true Roman aristocrat and was able to sympathise with the difficulties of provincials. In his very first winter in Britain he checked various administrative abuses, small perhaps in themselves, but cumulatively leading to hatred of Rome. The *annona*, or corn tribute, which had to be delivered by the provincials to the military authorities, was a case in point. The Britons, says Tacitus, submit to taxation cheerfully, provided there is no abuse. But the arrangements for the annona had fallen into the hands of profiteers who would compel delivery to far distant forts instead of conveniently adjacent ones if their price was not met, and there were even cases known where Britons had had to buy back from Roman granaries at greatly inflated prices in order to meet their obligations. All this was stopped.

In his second winter we are told that he embarked on a more ambitious programme of education and of romanisation. 'With private encouragement and public aid he pressed forward the construction of temples, forums and town-houses, praising those who were keen, censuring those who were not. Thus, competition for his favour was as effective as compulsion. The sons of leading men were educated in the liberal arts, and he stated his opinion that the natural ability of the Britons was superior to the studied industry of the Gauls. The result was that refusal to learn Latin was replaced by a desire to excel in it. In the same way Roman dress came into fashion and the toga was everywhere seen.'

The educational part of the policy is illustrated by the story of Demetrius of Tarsus, already quoted. The presence of a Greek teacher in Britain just at this time can hardly be either coincidental or unique. The growth of literacy is illustrated by late first-century business documents found in London, and that it went deeper is suggested by the fact that just at this time literate potters' stamps begin to appear on local pottery. As for the urbanising policy, an illustration came to light at *Verulamium* in 1955 with the discovery of the forum inscription bearing Agricola's name, and dated to the winter of this very year, 79. The policy itself must have taken several years to implement,[15] and the *Verulamium* forum had probably been begun under Frontinus; but the dedication of the new forum of a municipium doubtless involved the governor's presence, and it may have been this event which fixed the date in Agricola's, and thus in Tacitus', mind.[16] The reference to forums in the account of the new policy implies, indeed, that the reforms went further, for the forum with basilica was an integral part of the physical trappings of local self-government. But in truth the extension of self-government by the establishment of new areas of local administration, or *civitates*, was an essential preliminary to Agricola's northern campaigns. Though the number of pre-Flavian forts yet discovered in southern Britain is small (fig. 2, p. 88), it is already clear that many of them lay in places like Exeter, Cirencester, Chelmsford or Dorchester-on-Thames which subsequently became civilian towns. This must surely mean that much of southern Britain down to the Flavian period was under one form or another of military rule (p. 235). But Agricola's campaigns into Scotland involved the construction of over sixty new forts as winter-quarters of auxiliary troops. These forces had all moved forward from original bases farther south. Thus the necessities of the military situation compelled new arrangements for the control of this region. Self-governing civitates were accordingly established in areas which were ripe for the step after forty years of supervision. Once again, this process had probably been begun by Frontinus, who required troops for the occupation of Wales, and who may have established at least the Dumnonii as a civitas. Elsewhere, however, forts continued to be occupied down to Agricola's time, for instance at Great Casterton among the Coritani, and Dorchester-on-Thames among the Catuvellauni. The extent of Agricola's work in this field remains to be established as excavation produces more exact information about the date of the evacuation of forts. But meanwhile we may note the evidence already accruing of a Flavian date for the construction of the forum at Cirencester in addition to those at Exeter and London. The forums at Silchester and Winchester may be a few years later, perhaps about 100, while the establishment of a capital for the Iceni at Caistor by Norwich is usually placed about 70: the troops holding this territory may have been moved by Cerialis or Frontinus. It was probably in connection with this big programme of civic development, coupled with the governor's pre-occupation with military affairs, that we begin to find provincial law-officers – *legati iuridici* – appointed to Britain (pages 224–5).

At present Agricola's most striking mark on Roman Britain remains his system of roads and forts devised for control of the north (fig. 3, p. 124). In the lands up to the Tyne–Solway line at least forty forts were held, of which all but seven were new foundations: [17] in lowland Scotland there were at least a further twenty forts or fortlets, and north of the Forth another nine or ten in addition to the legionary fortress. The construction of over sixty forts was a major work in itself, but the organisation of supply for this large and scattered force called for administrative genius. Not least it called for the survey and construction of a minimum of 1,300 miles of road. The map of this road-system shows how the blocks of hill-land are penetrated and surrounded, so that patrols could prevent unauthorised movement and quickly reach the sources of trouble. Beyond the northern isthmus the discovery by aerial photography of the fort at Stracathro shows that the whole of Strathmore was permanently occupied right up to the point where the mountains approach the sea at Stonehaven.

Many of these forts shows signs of originality. Some, like Newstead, Castledykes, Bochastle, Oakwood or Milton, display novel experimentation in the plan of ditch systems or ramparts, designed to strengthen the gate. Some, like Malton, Newstead or Dalswinton (pl. Ib), are of large size, designed for the occupation of a composite force. Others again, like Chew Green, Cappuck, Oxton or Gatehouse of Fleet, are of very small size, designed for the reception of part of a unit only. It is noteworthy that the majority of these small forts are in Scotland, which suggests that as the area of conquered territory extended northwards, shortage of manpower began to be felt. In north-west Wales the fort at Pen Llystyn was replaced about this time by a fortlet occupying less than a quarter of the original area. In the second century, when more facts are available, we know the names of some sixty-five auxiliary regiments in Britain: the real total may have been slightly, but not much, larger. Agricola's army may have been rather more numerous than this, since auxiliaries were probably later withdrawn both by Domitian (to accompany Legio II Adiutrix to Moesia) and by Trajan; but there is no reason to think that it can have exceeded the ninety auxiliary regiments required to hold the known forts, and even this total is surprisingly large.[18] Clearly he had reached the limits of his resources despite the subdivision of certain units between fortlets. It would have been impossible for him to exploit his victory and occupy the coastal plain round to Inverness, let alone garrison the Highlands, without substantial reinforcements. These he might hope to obtain from the emperor who had authorised the advance north of the Forth in 83; but if so, his hopes were disappointed. Thus, an impasse had been reached at the time of his recall, full of possibilities for misunderstanding between the general and his Emperor.

Agricola, then, had been a great and energetic governor, but his tenure of Britain was the climax of his career. He had hopes of the command in Syria, but it was not forthcoming, nor was he given a command in the Danube wars; and later the Emperor made it clear that he was not to put in for the proconsulship of Africa or Asia, two offices regarded as the crowning honour of a senatorial career. Part of the reason for this, no doubt, was the limitations of Agricola's experience: his whole military life had been lived in Britain, and it may be the Britons were still underestimated as enemies. This, however, in itself is not sufficient to account for his eclipse. Part of the cause may lie in Agricola's own character, which had always been subservient to those above him, part perhaps in his lack of powerful connections. Nor must we discount the reason given by Tacitus – the jealous and suspicious nature of Domitian himself: very soon steps had to be taken which made it impossible any longer to hold even the land already occupied north of the Forth, and the rift between the two became complete.

These steps were necessitated by events on the Danube, where in 85 there occurred a serious invasion of Dacians; the invaders were expelled, but when in 86 a punitive expedition crossed the river it was disastrously defeated and its general killed. A second expedition had to be prepared and larger forces assembled. The year 87 was spent in preparation, and in 88 a great victory was won on Dacian soil. Legio II Adiutrix is known to have arrived in Moesia by 92,[19] and it may have been withdrawn from Britain to form part of the new army late in 86 or, more likely, in 87. Thus, more vital Roman interests compelled the reduction of the garrison of Britain, and this in turn meant that insufficient troops remained to encompass the occupation of Scotland. Legio II Adiutrix had been stationed at Chester since about 77; with its departure a vital gap opened in the legionary dispositions in Britain which could only be filled by withdrawing the legion (probably Legio XX) at Inchtuthil. Excavation has shown that the fortress at Inchtuthil had not been completely finished when dismantling began; and a coin minted perhaps in 87 shows that occupation continued at least till that date. With Legio XX at Chester, the fortress at Wroxeter, hitherto kept in working order though without garrison, was finally demolished and its site made over to the civitas of the Cornovii for the construction of their capital.[20]

The problems connected with the total evacuation of Scotland will be discussed in the next chapter. Here we need only to note that it took place in more than one stage, and that on the accession of Trajan all lowland Scotland south of the Isthmus was still held – though with fewer forts. When Tacitus, therefore, summing up the events of Roman history between AD 68 and the death of Domitian in 96, states *perdomita Britannia et statim missa* – the conquest of Britain was completed and then let slip – his epigram is not to be taken too seriously; and yet in a sense it is true. For Agricola had won the victory which should have enabled the occupation of all Caledonian territory; he left the province to his successor quiet and safely held;[21] but by removing a legion and still more by refusing auxiliary reinforcements, Domitian let slip the opportunity of following up the victory. It was inevitable in the wider interests of Rome at that moment. Nevertheless, if Domitian was the Emperor who had authorised the invasion of Scotland north of the isthmus in the first place, his action in preventing the consummation of the conquest must have appeared particularly arbitrary to Agricola and his circle. It was, too a decision of destiny. Subsequent generals might campaign as far afield, but never again was there to recur the opportunity to unify the whole island in one province.

1. When Tacitus says he summoned help from outside the words must indicate the tribes of southern Scotland, all other directions being ineligible.

2. The question is not one which can be decided without further evidence. We do not even know whether Cerialis arrived in Britain in time to utilise the campaigning season of 71; if he did so, the conquest of East Yorkshire might usefully be attributed to the first of his three campaigns. But we do not know whether the Parisi resisted Roman occupation or welcomed it as a protection from Brigantian aggression; but the fewness of the forts in their territory supports other scanty evidence that they were friendly to Rome. In this case their occupation would not require a major campaign and could therefore be within Bolanus' power. If the first fortress at York was of full size there remains the question what forces held the fortress at Malton, if founded by Cerialis; it would fit well with Bolanus, as a fortress for a mixed battle-group of normal type. As for Cerialis, even when Venutius had been crushed, there still remained the fifteen or more septs of the Brigantes (p. 71f.) to overrun against bitter opposition – task enough, surely, for three campaigns.

3. The indecisive nature of the fighting attributed by Tacitus to Bolanus might be accounted for by the hazards of this latter route.

4. Two at Chester, already mentioned, on lead water-mains, and the other from the Forum at *Verulamium* (pp. 134 and 232 (fig. 9)).

5. *civitates . . . praesidiis castellisque circumdatae* is the Tacitean summary of the operation (*Ag.* 20), giving pride of place to the forts rather than the roads; no doubt the latter were at first mere tracks,

later to be improved, but in fact the two elements were mutually indispensable, and the policing system now laid down remained in force for the rest of the Roman period.

6. Legio IX was still commanded at this time by C. Caristanius Fronto (*ILS*, 9485). In later years Agricola's own winter headquarters were at York, to judge by Demetrius' dedication there to the gods of the governor's residence (*ILS*, 8861). His other dedication to Ocean and Tethys makes his identification with Plutarch's Demetrius (p. 109) certain. See R.C.H.M.. *Roman York* (1962), p. 133; *RIB*, 662–3.

7. There is nowadays general agreement that whether Tacitus wrote *usque ad Tanaum* (*aestuario nomen est*) or *usque. ad Taum*, the estuary of the Tay is meant. See *JRS*, xxxiv (1944), 39; R. Syme, *Tacitus* (Oxford, 1958), p. 122.

8. K. A. Steer, *JRS*, l (1960), 88–90. At Bar Hill hazel roots had time to grow in the disused ditches of the fortlet before the Antonine Fort was built; unless, indeed, they were later roots which had worked their way down.

9. Sir George Macdonald's statements about the presence of Flavian pottery on certain Antonine Wall sites are inaccurate. See B. R. Hartley, *Britannia*, iii (1972), 6 ff.

10. *Summotis velut in aliam insulam hostibus* (Tacitus, *Agricola*, 23).

11. *ILS*, 1025 and 9200.

12. These forts, of course, had a strategic purpose too: that of containing the Highland tribes, whose territory could not be overrun until a victory had been won elsewhere.

13. Only the thoughts of an Irish expedition suggest doubts of his judgment; but this is not to be taken too seriously, perhaps; and certainly no detailed planning can have been completed.

14. *JRS*, xxxiv (1944), 43.

15. Suetonius' remark (already quoted, page 110) about the number of statues of and dedications to Titus which were to be seen in Britain is probably relevant here.

16. Fig. 10, p. 232.

17. On fig. 3, thirty-five forts are shown as certain; in addition, Agricolan occupation at Aldborough, Brougham, Greta Bridge, Kirkbride and Old Penrith can be assumed with reasonable sureness.

18. At least twenty Flavian forts are known in Wales in addition to those in northern Britain.

19. *ILS*, 2719.

20. This paragraph represents what may be termed the orthodox view of events. But in some ways it would be more congruous with what little evidence we have to suppose that Legio II Adiutrix remained in Britain (at Chester) until 89 or 90. In that case the withdrawal from northern Scotland, *c*. AD 87, will have been a policy decision based on the lack of auxiliary troops needed to complete the occupation of Scotland and not on lack of legionaries. Agricola's

existing arrangements there were precarious indeed unless completed, for his purpose was to contain the mountains and grip firmly the sources of enemy supply in Mar and Cawdor. The lack of sufficient auxiliaries to encompass this would be sufficient reason to write off the half-completed occupation north of the Forth. Legio II Adiutrix will have returned to Chester and Legio XX to Wroxeter. There are two tombstones of the former legion from Lincoln, covering the period 71–7, but no less than nine from Chester, covering the period from 77 to its withdrawal. This by itself means little, for the circumstances of discovery were different; but we may draw attention also to the following points. The Wroxeter fortress had been unoccupied since 83, and will have required some rebuilding. Three periods of timber military buildings have in fact been observed there: the third is difficult to account for save on the supposition that there was rebuilding here after the return from Scotland. The unfinished late-first-century bath-building at Wroxeter (p. 277), recognised by its excavator as of legionary construction, would now fall into place as the bath-house of the projected new fortress. The building opposite it may even have been begun as the principia, and the unfinished state of both will be due to the transfer of Legio XX to Chester about 90: the failure to complete them is very hard otherwise to explain. The withdrawal of Legio II Adiutrix will be seen as the result rather than the cause of the loss of Scotland. An inscription (*ILS*, 9193) records a centurion of this legion who was decorated in the Dacian war (at the latest in 89). Either, then, the legion had moved in time to take part in this campaign or, perhaps more likely, this centurion was serving in the vexillation which had left Britain in 83 and had been transferred to Moesia ahead of the main body.

21. It was probably Agricola who erected the Great Monument at Richborough, which is best interpreted as a triumphal trophy, marking the conquest of all Britain, at the gateway to the island.

1a (*above*) Hod Hill, Dorset from the west. Iron Age
hut-sites and streets can be seen in the ploughed south-eastern
corner of the hill-fort. The Roman fort lies at the
north-eastern corner

1b (*below*) Roman forts, Dalswinton and Dumfriesshire.
An Agricolan fort of 8.59 acres, with its annexe, has been replaced
by a late Domitianic fort of 10.29 acres with annexe

2 The Roman road running from Wroxeter through the Church Stretton gap and southwards towards Leintwardine

3 Hadrian's Wall near Milecastle 24 looking east. The Wall
lies under the road; the ditch to its north and vallum to the
south show clearly

4 The fort of Housesteads, Hadrian's Wall. Milecastle 37, and the Military Way looking west. The vallum is filled-in in this area

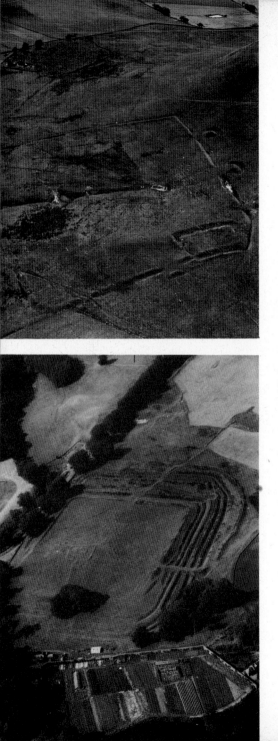

5a The south Roman
siege-camp and Roman
fortlet at Birrenswark,
Dumfriesshire, looking
west

5b The defence-systems
of successive Roman
forts at Ardoch,
Perthshire

6a (*above*) Roman *ala*-fort and civil settlement at Old Carlisle, Cumberland

6b (*below*) Roman marching camps at Pennymuir, Roxburgh, with *tutuli* at the gates

7 The Roman town and cantonal capital of the Atrebates tribe at Silchester, Hants

8a The site of *Venta Icenorum* (Caistor by Norwich) from the south-west, showing the town wall and ditch on the south side cutting through the earlier street system which appears to be bounded by two ditches further south

8b The site of *Noviomagus Regnensium* (Chicnester) from the south-west. The town wall and bastions (of mediaeval date on Roman foundations) can be seen near the bottom and following the curving road round the north-west side, returning beyond the open space, centre top

7

The retreat from Scotland: Hadrian's frontier

The period of some forty years after the recall of Agricola is darkened by the absence of any historical source; it has to be conned with the aid of archaeological discovery assisted by occasional inscriptions. The references of Juvenal to the storming of Brigantian hill-forts, and to a British king Arviragus who is evidently hostile, do not help much,[1] and may even relate to Agricola's campaigns, in which it is considered possible that Juvenal himself took part. The identity of Agricola's successor is not known for certain, nor are any steps identifiable which he may have taken to begin the consolidation of northern Scotland. The reason, as we have seen, is doubtless that there were no auxiliary troops to spare.[2] Suetonius records that Domitian put to death one governor of Britain, Sallustius Lucullus, for naming a new lance after himself. This story may disguise the possibility that he was suspected of tampering with the loyalty of the provincial army. Lucullus may or may not have been Agricola's immediate successor; but the most likely date for his execution is 89, and the most likely reason is that he was thought to be involved in the conspiracy of Saturninus, legate of Upper Germany, which was suppressed that spring. No further governors under Domitian are known except a certain Nepos, mentioned as recently governor in a diploma of 98; he has been identified as P. Metilius Nepos, consul in 91; and was probably appointed before Domitian's murder in 96. This man was succeeded by T. Avidius Quietus, who had been consul in 93. Avidius was a man of taste and cultivation; he was a member of Pliny's circle and was acquainted with Plutarch. Years earlier he had been a friend of Thrasea Paetus, put to death by Nero in 66. He was thus by now in middle age, and perhaps owed his province to the friendship of Nerva. He will have held Britain from 97 or 98 till perhaps 100 or 101. His successor was probably L. Neratius Marcellus, consul in 95, who was certainly governor in January 103, as another diploma informs us. Neratius, too, was a friend of Pliny. He was probably in Britain by 101, for a letter of Pliny, usually dated to that year, mentions a military tribunate which the writer had obtained from Neratius for Suetonius the historian. But the latter did not take up the appointment; he wrote Pliny a charming letter asking if it could be transferred to his relative Caesennius Silvanus. No other Trajanic governor of Britain is known except perhaps M. Appius Bradua, who is described on an inscription as holding this office under Hadrian, but who may have been appointed in the last years of Trajan and overlapped with the next reign. He is sometimes identified with the M. Atilius Bradua who was consul in 108, and he may have held Britain from 115 to 118.[3]

A Trajanic legate of Legio xx is known from an inscription at Chester. He was Titus Pomponius Mamilianus Rufus Antistianus Funisulanus Vettonianus, who subsequently became consul in 121.

The army of Britain was reduced before 92 by the removal of Legio ii Adiutrix to the Danube, and Professor E. Birley has shown that some auxiliary regiments, notably three Batavian units, probably accompanied it.[4] The immediate effect of this was to make it impossible to hold Agricola's conquests in the far north; when the decision was reached, perhaps as early as 87, to abandon Inchtuthil[5] and move back Legio xx to Chester or Wroxeter it became evident that the Clyde–Forth isthmus would have to be the frontier. Many forts south of this line in lowland Scotland were extensively reconstructed, though others were probably abandoned, as for instance Castledykes, Oakwood and Easter Happrew. North of it no fort except Ardoch is known to have been retained, and even at Ardoch the evidence is doubtful.[6] Beyond Ardoch there has been all too little excavation of forts; but at Fendoch and Cardean there is only one period as there is at Inchtuthil itself; and Strageath, though reoccupied in Antonine times, also shows only one Flavian period.

South of the Isthmus there were drastic changes. At Newstead, which now became a key position, the exceptionally large Agricolan fort (10·6 acres) was entirely remodelled, and a much larger fort (14·3 acres) was put in its place. Not only was the new fort of greater size; its defences were of greatly increased strength. The rampart was 45 feet thick now instead of 23 feet, and this implies a height of about 28 feet instead of the previous 15. That the date of this reconstruction was not later than about 90 was suggested by the presence of two coins of AD 86 in mint condition, which were incorporated in the filled-in ditch of the first fort. To judge by the relics, the garrison of this exceptional fort was a vexillation of legionary infantry and an *ala* of auxiliary cavalry. It was thus equipped both for striking at a distance and for heavy fighting closer at hand. This altogether unusual state of affairs emphasises the importance which its strategic position, behind the front line and at the heart of Selgovian territory, gave to Newstead in the new scheme of defence.

In South-west Scotland a comparable importance attached to Dalswinton (pl. 1b). Here also Agricola had installed a large fort (8.59 acres), of sufficient size to hold two part-mounted cohorts; and here again the late Domitianic fort was made much larger (10.29 acres), to hold perhaps two cavalry regiments. Elsewhere extensive alterations, sometimes involving changes of garrison, took place. At Milton the fort was reconstructed. At Glenlochar a new fort was built (probably for a *cohors milliaria equitata*) on a fresh site altogether, and the same thing happened at Birrens. At Broomholm the existing rampart was strengthened, as it was also at High Rochester and at the fortlet of Cappuck. Thus, the Lowlands of Scotland were the scene of tremendous activity at this time: it is clear that the Roman grip on the Selgovae and Novantae was greatly intensified, though with some economy of forces.

The occupation lasted long enough for the natives to become acquainted with Roman goods. Coins and pottery and other objects of trade began to circulate on native sites away from the forts, and the weight of their distribution appears to coincide with the area under Roman control.[7] But before the processes of Romanisation could proceed far, that control was removed. The forts were held until the turn of the century, but not long after 105 a serious setback – perhaps a disaster – occurred. Excavations at Newstead, Dalswinton, Glenlochar, Cappuck, Oakwood, High Rochester and Corbridge have shown that these forts perished by fire. Now fire alone is not proof of enemy destruction, for the Romans themselves often burnt what was not worth salvaging when they evacuated a fort.[8] But Corbridge is too far south to have been intentionally evacuated, and at Newstead were found human bones and immense quantities of equipment, including damaged armour, showing that there at least the destruction of the fort was due to hostile action. Yet it is inconceivable that the Romans should have been driven from Scotland by superior force and should have accepted the situation. It is more reasonable to suppose, though we have no certain information, that Trajan's Dacian wars, the first in 101–2, the second in 105–6, had called for reinforcements from the army of Britain. This in turn might well evoke a decision to retire from southern Scotland: such a decision was needed, for future experience was to demonstrate the truth that with only three legions in Britain it was impossible to hold permanently the lands north of the Tyne–Solway isthmus. The attacks on Newstead and Corbridge will have been the work of a new generation of Selgovians taking advantage of a moment of confusion. Not all the other burnt forts, however, were necessarily destroyed by them. Indeed, this is unlikely, since a serious outbreak would surely have called for serious counter-measures, and probably a temporary reoccupation. The retreat from southern Scotland under Trajan is, then, best regarded as a planned withdrawal decided upon after a review of manpower, and as a result of the need for more men on the Danube; and not as a retreat enforced by a victorious rising of the north.[9] There were local disturbances or attacks, as at Newstead or Corbridge, once the decision became known; but the majority of burnt forts may have been burnt by their retiring garrisons. We must remember that the timber buildings had been standing some fifteen to seventeen years, more than half the limit of their useful life: the timbers would not be worth salvaging.

The date of the withdrawal is indicated by the occurrence of a few sherds of samian pottery at Newstead and Dalswinton which are definitely later than 100, and by the discovery in the burnt debris at Corbridge of a coin-hoard in which the latest coin was minted in 98, while a coin of 103 was found in the rampart of the fort which replaced the one destroyed and another of the same date in a posttrench in the new fort. A date of about 105 would suit these events on the evidence so far available.

Where the new Trajanic frontier was now placed it is not yet completely agreed, but all the evidence suggests that it lay on the line of the Stanegate, Agricola's road across the Tyne–Solway isthmus. The alternative to this would be the Cheviot Hills, which strike farther north-east, where the present Border runs. But the fort of High Rochester, south of these hills, appears to have been burnt at this time and was not reconstructed till Antonine times; whereas on the Stanegate the Agricolan forts at Carlisle, Corbridge and possibly Whickham together with a late Domitianic one at Chesterholm were supplemented by new ones at Old Church Brampton, Nether Denton, probably Carvoran and perhaps at Castlesteads and Newbrough, while the intervals between these forts were each occupied by a fortlet. Those so far known lie at High Crosby, Castle Hill Boothby, Throp and Haltwhistle Burn. The exact dating of these additions is in dispute, some authorities holding that they date only from the beginning of Hadrian's reign; but the fortlets in particular have no place in the earliest scheme for Hadrian's Wall and mark a time when the Stanegate itself was the frontier. It was so, indeed, in the earliest years of Hadrian, before the Wall was built, but the situation then was merely a continuation of that existing in the second half of Trajan's reign: moreover, there were signs that the occupation of the Haltwhistle fortlet had not been brief. North of the Stanegate free-standing signal stations earlier than Hadrian's Wall exist at Pike Hill and Walltown Crags; it is not clear whether these are Trajanic or additions to the system made in the earliest years of Hadrian.

The main outline of events is thus dimly discernible, but the details and personalities are lost to us. That there was heavy fighting in Britain both in Domitian's reign and in Trajan's is certain. Professor Birley has shown how the Second Cohort of Asturians, which had been in Germany as late as 89, had arrived in Britain by 105 on the evidence of diplomas.[10] This movement in itself implies reinforcement of the army in Britain.[11] But, furthermore, Birley has called attention to the gravestone of C. Julius Karus, tribune of Legio III Cyrenaica at Alexandria, who died while outposted to Cyrene on a recruiting expedition. In his previous appointment Karus had been prefect of these Asturians, and had won outstanding decorations in a British war. This war, as Birley has shown, must be later than 89, when the regiment was still in Germany, and earlier than 128, when Legio III left Alexandria; he suggested that it was probably during the reign of Trajan and before 115 when the Jewish rebellion in Cyrene broke out. In fact, it may well have been earlier than 100, for two milestones erected in that year on the Cyrene–Apollonia road record construction undertaken by recruits levied in

Cyrenaica [12] – perhaps these whom Karus was sent to raise. Birley has also called attention to another regiment of the British garrison, Cohors I Cugernorum, recorded under that name in 103; by 122 it had received the titles Cohors I Ulpia Traiana Cugernorum Civium Romanorum. These were battle honours awarded by Trajan. Some of this fighting may have taken place in Wales, where the first fort at Forden Gaer was burnt about AD 90 and a new fort at Caer Llugwy was built about the same time.

There was also consolidation. All three legionary fortresses were about thirty years old, and their timbers would need renewing. In fact, we have evidence from inscriptions that all three were beginning to be reconstructed in stone, an investment which shows that no further movement was foreseen. A building at Caerleon bearing a large stone inscription was dedicated in 100; a fragment of a similar inscription, probably from a gate, at Chester dates to after 102; and a gate at York is dated 107/8.[13] The date of the Caerleon stone shows that this programme had no direct connection with the retreat from Scotland. The fort at Hardknott in the Lake District was built now, as the pottery shows, though there is also an inscription of the next reign; this fort supplements that at Ambleside, which was not founded before 90 at the earliest. A stone inscription, perhaps from the headquarters building, dedicated to Trajan, has been found at Lancaster, and the fort at Templeborough seems to have been rebuilt in stone at this time. In Wales a new fort was built at Gelligaer, and there is a fragmentary stone inscription, probably Trajanic, from Castell Collen, indicating a partial rebuilding in stone there too. The fort at Forden Gaer may also have been reconstructed in this reign. Part of the same programme, perhaps, was the erection of a fort at London just north-west of the inhabited area. It was eleven acres in size and was surrounded by a stone wall with earth rampart behind. The precise date of its foundation is uncertain, but is thought to be about 100. Its purpose was no doubt partly to accommodate the governor's guard, but the existence of numerous legionary gravestones from London suggests also that here was Army headquarters (p. 227).

Another form of consolidation which occurred about this time was the foundations of two more *coloniae*, the first at Lincoln and the second at Gloucester. The foundation date of *Lindum colonia* was probably late in Domitian's reign, about 90; the evidence – an inscription from Mainz – only defines it as Flavian, but the site was a fortress until 77, and only after Agricola's campaigns would there be suitable opportunity for discharging veterans. The date of *Glevum colonia* is defined by an inscription at Rome as occurring in Nerva's reign (96–8).[14] Both these colonies occupied the sites of previous fortresses – land, in other words, which was already imperial property, which suggests that the government was anxious not to repeat the mistakes which had marred the foundation of *Camulodunum*. Their foundation strengthened the civilising influences at work in the province, by providing further examples of Roman communities in being, both in friendly territory, but the one not far from Brigantia and the other close to the Silures.

Hadrian

The Emperor Trajan died in August 117. The event marked the termination of an era, for the period of uninhibited expansion was over. Never again was Rome able to indulge her taste for world-conquest. The emperors who succeeded Trajan were to be concerned rather with consolidating existing gains, with finding safe boundaries and with keeping the barbarians out. Defence rather than attack became the objective, and if there were from time to time advances, these were made only with the intention of finding shorter or more reliable frontier lines or for other sound defensive reasons. In Britain the new era had been born some little time prematurely; for the reign of Trajan, so glorious in the military sphere elsewhere, in Britain had witnessed retreat. But it was Hadrian, his successor, who gave up Trajan's Mesopotamian conquests on the ground that what could not be held must be liberated; and who devoted his life to the construction of efficient permanent boundary lines in many parts of the empire.

At the moment when Hadrian became emperor there was war in Britain once more. We are told no details, but the words of Hadrian's biographer, 'the Britons could no longer be held under Roman control', suggests that a rebellion, no doubt in the north, was at any rate part of the trouble. The short re-occupation of the fort at Brough on Humber about this time may have some connection with it.

The Brigantes, however, always possessed a close connection with the Selgovae and Novantae of southern Scotland: it is rarely that we find trouble with the one without the involvement of the other group; nor did ancient writers clearly distinguish between them. When in the sequel we find Hadrian constructing a wall to separate the Brigantes from their northern allies we can feel confident that the war did indeed involve them both. Whatever the details of the insurrection, it was suppressed in 118, as a reference to Hadrian's second consulship shows us on an inscription from Jarrow; this once adorned some great monument which was erected a few years later near the east end of Hadrian's Wall to commemorate the victory and the completion of the frontier. And the following year, 119, saw the issue of commemorative coins.

This victory was the work of Q. Pompeius Falco, consul probably in 108 and thereafter governor of Lower Moesia, who governed Britain from 118 to 122. In the latter year Hadrian himself, who had begun a tour of inspection of the Western provinces in 121, arrived in Britain where 'he instituted many reforms and was the first to build a wall 80 miles long to separate the barbarians from the Romans'.[15] He appointed A. Platorius Nepos as governor in 122 to carry out his policy. Nepos, who had been consul in 119, after which he governed Lower Germany, was a close friend of Hadrian at this time and possibly a kinsman, though later the friendship was broken. It is likely that he accompanied the emperor to Britain, and probably also brought over Legio VI Victrix with him; for this legion had previously been stationed at Vetera in Lower Germany, and is recorded in Britain early in his governorship (p. 160). The length of his term of office is not certain, but he probably remained till 125. The name of his successor is not directly attested; there is a governor whose name cannot be clearly read, who set up an inscription at Bewcastle not later than 128. This man was perhaps succeeded by M. Appius Bradua (p. 142), for whom the dates 128–31 may be suggested. From about 131, however, the governor was Sex. Julius Severus, consul in 127, a man with a high military reputation and a distinguished record, who like Falco had come to Britain from the governorship of Moesia, and who about 134 was transferred from Britain to suppress the rebellion of Judaea. His successor was P. Mummius Sisenna, who had been consul rather late in life in 133, and who was certainly in Britain early in 135, where his son[16] was serving as legate of Legio VI.

This is the bare skeleton of known facts concerning Britain in

Hadrian's reign, during which there is one major achievement to be described: and one still mysterious event to be placed in a suitable context. The achievement is, of course, Hadrian's Wall, one of the most remarkable constructions of any Emperor at any time. The mystery is the disappearance of Legio ix from recorded history (p. 16).

The idea of a linear frontier was a recent development in Roman planning. The early Empire had depended for its frontiers on rivers or deserts or fortified zones. The word *limes*, used for a frontier, had the primary meaning of path, and came to be used of a military road. In the time of Augustus or Tiberius such *limes* could be roads running directly into hostile territory; but by the later first century it was normally conceived of as a transverse road such as the Stanegate, carrying military installations such as forts or signal towers. Under Domitian, however, a beginning had been made in Upper Germany of strengthening the frontier with an actual fence. Hadrian in Germany developed this idea and constructed a continuous wooden palisade supported by the usual look-out and signal stations, and by forts moved up close behind its line. Such fences had little military value in themselves, but they did define the frontier, prevent small-scale crossings by unauthorised persons and channel travellers to the supervised entry-places. Moreover, the whole conception, abandoning defence in depth as it did, showed that no large-scale warfare was envisaged. The garrison could deploy forwards in case of need through gaps in the fence.

In Britain affairs were different and a much stronger barrier was constructed in stone, supported, moreover, by a system of forts and roads running back to the legionary fortresses at York and Chester. Though Hadrian's biographer, writing in the fourth century, described the wall as dividing Romans from barbarians, at the time it was constructed it served to divide the unruly Selgovae from the equally unruly Brigantes: it could rely on no peaceful hinterland. While one of its purposes was to define the frontier of the province and debar raids from the north, and in the long run to provide peaceful conditions for economic development in the region behind it, another was quite certainly to prevent that joint planning between northerners and Brigantians which had been a fruitful source of trouble in the past. Brigantian territory was still occupied, but of necessity the forts had to be considerably thinned out in order to

149

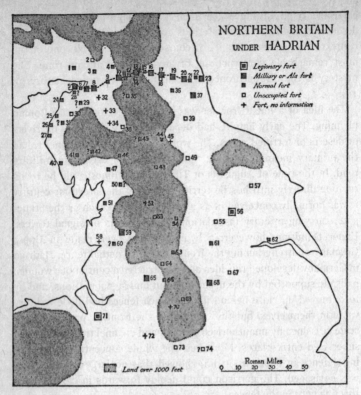

NORTHERN BRITAIN
UNDER HADRIAN

	Legionary fort
	Milliary or Ala fort
	Normal fort
	Unoccupied fort
+	Fort, no information

Land over 1000 feet

Roman Miles
0 10 20 30 40 50

5   The military occupation of the north under Hadrian (pp. 151,
182). *Note:* ? beside a fort indicates that its occupation is not entirely certain.

1 Birrens	14 Chesterholm	27 Moresby
2 Broomholm	15 Carrawburgh	28 Kirkbride
3 Netherby	16 Chesters	29 Old Carlisle
4 Bewcastle	17 Haltonchesters	30 Caermote
5 Bowness	18 Corbridge	31 Papcastle
6 Drumburgh	19 Rudchester	32 Wreay
7 Burgh by Sands	20 Benwell	33 Old Penrith
8 Stanwix	21 Newcastle	34 Brougham
9 Castlesteads	22 Wallsend	35 Whitley Castle
10 Birdoswald	23 South Shields	36 Ebchester
11 Carvoran	24 Beckfoot	37 Chester-le-Street
12 Great Chesters	25 Maryport	38 Kirkby Thore
13 Housesteads	26 Burrow Walls	39 Binchester

40 Ravenglass	52 Long Preston	64 Castleshaw
41 Hardknott	53 Ilkley	65 Manchester
42 Ambleside	54 Adel	66 Melandra Castle
43 Brough under Stainmore	55 Newton Kyme	67 Doncaster
	56 York	68 Templeborough
44 Bowes	57 Malton	69 Brough on Noe
45 Greta Bridge	58 Kirkham	(Derbyshire)
46 Low Borrow Bridge	59 Ribchester	70 Buxton
47 Watercrook	60 Walton-le-Dale	71 Chester
48 Bainbridge	61 Castleford	72 Chesterton
49 Catterick	62 Brough on Humber	73 Rocester
50 Overborough	63 Slack	74 Little Chester
51 Lancaster		

find garrisons to man the Wall (fig. 5). Thus an experiment was made: the military supervision of the Brigantes was considerably reduced, in the hopes that they might, if left to themselves, become more contented, less rebellious; and instead, the main strength of the occupying forces was used to man the Solway–Tyne isthmus.

Excavation on the line of the Wall has shown that the earliest plan for the system gravely underestimated the opposition it would arouse. A series of improvements was quickly put in hand. The Hadrianic frontier today consists of six elements. There is first the continuous wall fronted by a large ditch. Secondly, there are the milecastles, which are fortlets evenly spaced along the wall, a Roman mile apart; thirdly, the turrets, small towers, evenly spaced, two between each milecastle. The north gates of the latter carried towers corresponding with the turrets. The fourth element is the garrison forts; the fifth is the earthwork long known as the Vallum, but consisting of a wide ditch flanked some distance each side by a mound.[17] Lastly, there is the military way, the later road behind the wall. The mutual relationships, both chronological and topographical, of all these elements is complicated, and the true position has only been discovered painstakingly by excavation within the last half-century.

The earliest plan was to strengthen the Stanegate frontier with a ditch and wall provided with milecastles and turrets. The Stanegate itself with its forts lies in the valleys of the Eden, Irthing and Tyne; the barrier was placed on the north crest of the valleys, where in the central sector the basalt outcrop of the Whin Sill (pl. 4), provides an impressive ridge with craggy precipitous northern slopes.

It thus gained a good outlook northwards, where possible: only in its western part, in the region of Carlisle, does the ground fail to provide command. As originally planned the barrier ran from New-castle to Carlisle and on along the southern shore of the Solway to Bowness beyond the lowest ford of the estuary, a distance of seventy-six Roman miles. From Newcastle to the crossing of the Irthing there was to be a wall of stone ten feet thick, with a parapet walk some fifteen feet above ground: the parapet itself would give the northern face a height of some twenty feet. West of Irthing, however, it was found that there were no convenient supplies of limestone for the large quantity of mortar needed; and the wall in this sector, rather under half its length, was accordingly built of turf, twenty feet wide at the base and with an estimated height of some twelve feet to parapet walk. This turf wall could have been put up in six months, but to build the same length in stone would have added at least two years to the programme; thus the Turf Wall was in some sense a stop-gap, and its replacement in stone at leisure was in fact begun before the end of Hadrian's reign. Nevertheless turf-work was a normal method of fortification and implies no diminution of effectiveness.

At every Roman mile (1,620 yards) a fortlet was provided (c. 0·08 acre) for the patrolling garrison. These were of turf and timber in the turf-wall sector, but of stone elsewhere. They contained sometimes a pair of small barracks, but more usually only one, sufficient accommodation for eight or thirty men. Wide gateways, of massive build, pierced their north and south walls so that the troops approaching from the Stanegate might rapidly deploy from behind the screen offered by the wall itself. Here, too, civilian traffic could be scrutinised.

Though the accommodation remains constant, the milecastles fall into three types when details of their planning and of the design of their gateways are studied; these three types can be related to the three legions II, VI and XX which have left epigraphic records of their building activity. The turrets likewise fall into three types: they consist of stone towers [18] fourteen feet square internally and about 540 yards apart – a third of a Roman mile – recessed in the body of the wall. Their purpose was clearly for observation and signalling.

The building of all this, and possibly the hewing of the ditch, was the work of the British legions.[19] They were each allotted sectors, starting from Newcastle, *Pons Aelius*, where a new bridge was built over the Tyne. These sectors where identifiable were short, consisting usually of only about five miles or a little more. Within them one group of working parties laid the foundation of the wall and built the milecastles and turrets at their measured positions: the other cohorts built the wall itself on the foundation laid. Within each legionary length inscribed stones once marked each end of the lengths built by each century, cohort and, finally, by the legion itself.

Not unnaturally the parties laying the foundations and building the structures gradually drew ahead of the others, especially as they were permitted for the time being to omit the foundation here and there on the crags of the central sector. It was at the moment when the foundation builders had reached the Irthing and the ten-foot wall itself had reached the north Tyne that a change of specification was introduced for the wall, and a new plan was made under which forts were to be added to the wall itself, to house the fighting garrisons hitherto left on the Stanegate to the rear. Under the new specification the wall was to be only eight Roman feet thick; this is known today as the Narrow Wall. It was also now decided to extend the wall at its east end by another four miles (thus giving the barrier a total length of eighty miles), taking it to Wallsend, beyond which infiltration across the widening estuary of the Tyne would be more difficult: this extension consists of the Narrow Wall, and as the broad foundation is missing in this sector, the length is clearly an after-thought. The Wallsend fort is of one build with the Narrow Wall. An extension of the Narrow Wall was also made for five miles westwards from the Irthing to replace the turf wall here. The replacement took a different line from its predecessor for part of this sector, and this has enabled the Turf Wall and its structures to be studied in isolation. This extension took the stone wall to the limits of available limestone; but its construction is probably to be related to a change of garrison at Birdoswald. This fort had perhaps been planned to house a cavalry regiment, and so projected through the Wall to have three gates north of it; but it was actually garrisoned by infantry. These did not require three gates north of the wall, and the opportunity was taken to provide more space round the fort (which has a steep drop behind it) by shifting the wall to join the

153

fort's northern corners. The rebuilding in stone was then extended as far as limestone was available. Possibly plans to carry it further were interrupted by the decision to move forward into Scotland in 139.

It is not known for certain what the reason was for changing from broad to narrow wall, or whether it involved reducing the height as well as the width of the barrier. The narrow wall was normally built on the front edge of the broad foundation, and there was an offset where it joined the milecastles and turrets which had already been built to the width of the broad foundation, and which had short spurs or wing walls added on either side to take the broad wall when it should eventually arrive. The core of the broad wall has been found in some sectors to be constructed of stones set in clay or rubble instead of cement. Such a form of construction might account for its 2:3 proportions, and experience might show that such a core was liable to movement on steep hills; it has been suggested that this instability was the reason for the decision to change to the narrow-gauge wall with its concrete core. Unfortunately it is not certain whether the broad wall always originally possessed a stone and clay core. In some sectors, by contrast, a concrete core has been observed which may be original, though it might also be accounted for by rebuilding later. The narrow wall used less material and could be built more quickly. Bede, writing in the eighth century, described the narrow wall as eight feet thick and twelve feet high: it is not, indeed, absolutely certain that it was standing to its full height when he saw it, but his words seem definite and authoritative. Though the turrets and milecastles of the central sector had already been built to the height of the broad wall, it would be an easy matter to adapt them to the narrow wall, if it was of lower elevation, with three or four steps. It may well be thought likely that in addition to considerations such as these, the decision to change to the narrow gauge was part of the further decision to move the garrisons up to the wall. For once the forts had been added to the wall, the Vallum was constructed to the south of the line; and this additional barrier, together with the nearby presence of the garrison, would justify some economy in the height of the wall itself. And, after all, the reduction in height to twelve feet, if genuine, merely equalised the height of the stone wall with that of the turf wall farther west.

That the forts were a secondary addition to the wall system is shown by the fact that at Chesters, Housesteads and Great Chesters milecastles or turrets attached to the broad foundation underlie the forts; at Birdoswald the turf wall with its ditch and a turret underlie the fort, while at Halton the wall-ditch (and no doubt the broad foundation also, though this has not been found, lying as it does beneath the modern road) runs below the fort. Nevertheless, the fort at Halton, though secondary, still produced an inscription of Platorius Nepos, and another comes from Benwell. It is clear from this that the moving up of the garrison was an early alteration to the plans. The date of the change to the narrow gauge is not so directly attested; but, as we have seen, it can best be explained as part of the same new policy. In the central sector, however, where the character of the country gave greater immunity, at least one section of the narrow wall was not finished till 128 at the earliest; for at Great Chesters the narrow wall is of one build with the fort, which has produced an inscription thus dated.

There had only been seven forts on the Stanegate frontier, with perhaps another two east of Corbridge; under the new arrangements eleven forts were added to the wall,[20] the Stanegate ones being, of course, evacuated. All the new forts were for large garrisons, either alae 500 strong or milliary cohorts: the plan seems to have been [21] to place 4,000 infantry in the centre and 2,000 cavalry on either flank, leaving the bridgehead at Newcastle to be held by the 500 infantry already there. Later this scheme was slightly modified by placing smaller forts at Castlesteads, Carvoran, Great Chesters and Carrawburgh, thus reducing the gaps between the infantry forts in the centre, though leaving the same total of 4,500 infantry, and by adding a fort for 500 infantry at Wallsend at the east and Drumburgh at the west. The total garrison of the Wall forts, now sixteen in number, was thus 9,500 men.

Once the forts were in position, or at any rate once their positions had been fixed, the Vallum – or *Fossatum* – was constructed (pl. 3). This was a formidable ditch normally twenty feet wide and as much as ten feet deep, with a flat bottom eight feet in breadth, though somewhat less wide and deep where cut through rock. On each side of the ditch there is a berm of thirty feet flanked by turf-revetted mounds twenty feet wide and originally some six feet high. The effect thus created was of a boundary consisting of a ditch, impassable or very difficult to pass on foot, occupying the centre of a strip eighty feet wide defined by banks.[22] Earlier theories regarded it as the original Hadrianic frontier, but its behaviour in swerving to avoid the sites of forts shows that it was planned later than these, while the fact that it swerves to avoid a short-term turf wall milecastle in the Birdoswald sector where the narrow wall, later but still Hadrianic, takes a more northerly course with its own milecastles, proves that the difference in time is not great. The Vallum is crossed by original causeways only at forts and some of the milecastles. At the former the causeways were revetted in stone, and stone gateways have been found which were controlled from the north. At the milecastles there are gaps in the north mound but not in the south, and the berm of the ditch, lightly metalled where necessary, seems to have formed a trackway which could be patrolled, and along which supplies might reach the milecastles. Indeed, until the construction later in the century of the military way, as the Roman road is called which runs just behind the wall, this trackway was the only means of supplying the milecastles. It has therefore been suggested that the trackway is earlier than the Vallum itself, which was so constructed as to incorporate it. This would account for the regular, well-engineered course taken by the Vallum, with its straight stretches and easy gradients closely resembling those of a Roman road; though it must be admitted that the earthwork is laid out on the same principles, even in sectors where it is too distant from the Wall to have had any connection with a patrol track. This close relationship of the fort and milecastle garrisons with the Vallum disproves R. G. Collingwood's theory that the Vallum was a civil frontier manned by the procurator's staff. It clearly belongs to the military, and it is noteworthy what care was taken to make it continuous. There exist one or two places where the rock was so difficult to cut that the Wall-ditch was allowed to be left incomplete; but no rock was too hard for the Vallum. Moreover, at White Moss, where the waterlogged condition of the ground made it impossible to cut a normal ditch, the Vallum was built up like a canal and thus carried forward, as it was also at the crossing of the Poltross burn. That the Vallum should be continuous and complete was evidently felt to be important, expensive addition though it was to the system. What was its purpose? It was not a strictly military defensive system, for the ditch is not of military shape, nor are the symmetrical banks defensive; furthermore, the Vallum takes no account of commanding

156

ground. Rather it is a barrier and line of demarcation defining the rear of the Wall-zone, and preventing entry except at fixed points. Unauthorised intruders would find it hard to explain themselves; military stores would be safer; and all attempts at contact between Brigantians and their friends in the north were made very much more difficult.[23]

But the fact that the Vallum was necessary at all suggests that quite a considerable and unsettled population lived near the rear of the wall, just as the removal of the fighting garrison to the wall itself shows that hostile pressure from the north was increasing in intensity; aerial photography and field-work are beginning to show us where and how this native population lived. It was to divide these two foes that the wall was built. The eastern half of the wall does appear to coincide approximately with the boundary of Brigantia (p. 71), but in the western half the line may have cut across a salient of Brigantian territory in order to make contact with the southern shore of the Solway. It was just this sector, too, which lacked commanding views northward; and in consequence three outpost forts were maintained north of the Wall, at Birrens, Netherby and Bewcastle. These not only provided early warning of hostile movements but also maintained Roman control over the outlying parts of Brigantia. Netherby and Bewcastle, and almost certainly Birrens,[24] have produced Hadrianic inscriptions; the wording of these (except the Bewcastle example, which is too fragmentary) implies that they were in existence by 128.

The eastern flank of the wall was protected by the deep estuary of the Tyne, and by the cavalry fort at South Shields, which overlooked the mouth of the river, where no doubt a detachment of the fleet was stationed. The configuration of the coast here offered no threat. It was different at the west end, where, though the wall continues to a point below where the Solway is fordable, the coast of Cumberland continues vulnerable beyond it to crossings by boat from the opposite coast. Along this coast, therefore, the wall system was continued for another thirty-five miles. The curtain wall itself could be replaced by the shore, but a system of mile-fortlets and signal towers exactly comparable to those on the wall extends probably to St Bees Head; and there are four forts, the first at Beckfoot ($2\frac{1}{2}$ acres), the next a pre-existing one at Maryport (5·2 acres), the third at Burrow Walls ($2\frac{3}{4}$ acres) and the last at Moresby ($3\frac{1}{2}$ acres). The latter at least was constructed in or after 128.[25] These four forts are supported farther inland by others at Papcastle and Old Carlisle (pl. 6a), the latter cavalry.[26] At some later date which is not quite certain the rest of the turf wall, with its turf-built forts and milecastles, was rebuilt in stone. In this reconstruction the Wall was designed to be nine feet thick, and it is known as the Intermediate Wall. This replacement was undertaken either at the very end of Hadrian's reign or more probably about twenty years later. It will be discussed when the work of the governors Julius Verus and Calpurnius Agricola is considered (pp. 182 and 192, n. 21).

It is evident that the construction of this great system took a considerable period to complete, and was much more complicated than had at first been planned. The main features of its final form had already begun to appear before the end of Platorius Nepos' governorship, but the coastal system was being constructed in or after 128, as was the fort at Great Chesters. The fort of Carrawburgh has yielded part of an inscription of Julius Severus, governor about 130–3, which, of course, might be the date of Great Chesters too. At Carvoran the fort was being constructed even later, for the same commandant whose name appears on building records in the fort wall dedicated an altar for the health of L. Aelius Caesar, Hadrian's adopted heir, who assumed this title in 136. Carvoran is thus likely to be the work of the governor P. Mummius Sisenna. A building inscription of Julius Severus at the fort of Bowes in the Stainmore pass suggests further troop concentrations under this governor.

All this reinforces the conclusion that the building of Hadrian's Wall was much resented. Indeed, it must have interfered with traditional movement from pasturage to pasturage, quite apart from the political division which it was its purpose to enforce. For the intention of the wall itself was certainly political rather than primarily military. It was not designed as a fighting platform to be defended like a city-wall; it has few of the characteristics of such a scheme, nor were the garrisons equipped or trained for this sort of warfare. The wall was there to control movement and to give an elevated platform for observation sufficiently high to protect the sentries from molestation. The size and hostility of the adjacent populations on both sides thus made it necessary to provide a rather more powerful barrier than that constructed in Germany. Forts were then provided on the line of the wall because of increasing hostile pressure, in order that Roman reaction could be more immediate, and experience evidently soon led to further strengthening of the centre and of the west coast. But the planning of the forts and the size of the milecastle gateways, no less than the heavy provision of cavalry, demonstrates clearly that the military aspect of the wall was to act as a fortified base from which to sally out in force, and against which it would be possible to roll up enemy bands after their retreat had been cut off. The wall itself provided cover from behind which surprise sallies could be directed through whichever gates were convenient, if things came to this; but normally, of course, the army would expect to meet the enemy in the open, well beyond the Wall. Yet the absence of outpost forts in this period, except in the west, does seem to indicate that under Hadrian military planning did not envisage so extended a surveillance of the barbaricum as later experience showed to be necessary, and that therefore the Wall had a tactical function.

The forts, as we have seen, were garrisoned by auxiliary regiments of cavalry and infantry. It remains to consider how the milecastles were held. There is no direct evidence how the necessary 1,000–1,500 men were found. It is usually believed that they were a patrolling garrison of lower-grade soldiers belonging to the *numeri* recently introduced into the Roman army. These were territorial formations recruited from warlike frontier tribes, who possessed lower status and privileges than the *auxilia*. Against this view is the fact that no inscriptions attest the presence of numeri in Britain before the third century, and then only in forts. In forts also they are found on the German frontier, where they could be subjected to closer discipline. An alternative view would be that the milecastles were manned by detachments from the auxiliary regiments in garrison. Against this theory, however, there are powerful arguments: first, that the detachment of a couple of centuries from each regiment on the wall would detract from their serviceability, and since many were cavalry, the scheme would be extravagant. A more serious obstacle is the fact that the milecastles were planned and built before the forts were there to provide the suggested detachments. The probability, therefore, is that two or three cohorts of auxiliaries were spread out in vexillations along the wall to undertake this duty. In favour of this view is the probable Hadrianic altar at Milecastle 19, set up by a vexillation of the first cohort of Vardulli, and recording the erection of a shrine near by.[27] This regiment is not yet attested elsewhere in Hadrian's reign, and the nearest forts, from which otherwise the vexillation might be thought to have come for some special duty, such as repairs, are cavalry forts. This evidence is not, of course, conclusive, and the problem must remain insoluble until further evidence appears.

The western sector of the wall was the most dangerous, as we have seen, both on account of the nature of the ground and because of the hostile population beyond it. It is not surprising to find, then, that at Stanwix near Carlisle was stationed the Ala Petriana, the only milliary Ala in Britain. Such regiments are always found in the post of danger, and the prefect of this Ala was the senior officer of the whole wall garrison. Here, then, lay Command headquarters, conveniently near the centre of the line, and it has been shown that a signalling system existed along the road from Carlisle to York, which would enable the prefect at Stanwix to communicate with the legionary legate at York in a matter of minutes (p. 449).

The second topic remaining to be discussed is the disappearance of Legio IX. This legion is last attested on the York inscription of 107/8; later, its place in the York fortress was taken by Legio VI Victrix. The latter reached Britain from Lower Germany[28] in time to build the fort at Halton on the wall under Platorius Nepos, and it was probably brought over by Nepos himself in 122, for he had been governor of Lower Germany until transferred to the British command.[29] In support of an early arrival, it has been pointed out that the two large altars, both dedicated by Legio VI, the one to Ocean and the other to Neptune, and both found in the River Tyne at Newcastle, were probably consecrated at the opening of the new bridge at *Pons Aelius*, and this bridge must have been one of the earliest wall-works to be constructed. The most obvious reason for bringing in Legio VI is to replace Legio IX; and as the Ninth is not recorded, for instance, either as having taken part in Trajan's Parthian wars, or among the numerous inscriptions of the builders of Hadrian's Wall, its disappearance has usually been considered to have been due to defeat or disgrace in the warfare reported in Britain at Hadrian's accession. If it had merely suffered very heavy casualties in battle its numbers would have been made up by drafts from elsewhere or by new recruitment. Its complete disappearance would mean either total annihilation or cashiering. Annihilation is unlikely, since the names of several survivors are known; cashiering would take place after a disgraceful defeat involving, for instance, the loss of the Eagle.

Yet there are grounds for doubting whether Legio IX was lost as early as 117–18. Professor Birley has shown that the recorded careers of some of the survivors are hardly consistent with its disappearance as early as this:[30] they would be even more unduly retarded than might be expected. We have next, no knowledge of the date when Legio VI was first stationed at York: it would be difficult to prove that it was before 130. The absence of building records on Hadrian's Wall could possibly be explained if Legio IX had worked in the turf-wall sector, where the building records were in timber: the only one of these to have partially survived does not include the name of the Legion responsible.[31] The transfer of Legio VI would in this case be explained by the large scale of the work, and the requirement of large numbers of legionary craftsmen.[32]

Then, again, the destruction of a legion in battle would have called for the despatch of immediate reinforcements, We have two inscriptions [33] which record such reinforcements, which included 1,000 legionaries each from Legio VII Gemina (from Spain) and VIII Augusta and XXII Primigenia (both from Germany), under the senior centurion of Legio III Augusta (from Africa); but once again a date of about 130 would suit the careers of the men involved better than a date of about 118.[34] Finally, we have the remark of the orator Fronto writing soon after 161 to the emperor Lucius Verus, when he alludes to heavy losses in the reign of his grandfather Hadrian at the hands of Jews and Britons. Fronto is clearly referring to legionary losses: Legio XXII Deiotariana is believed to have been annihilated in the Jewish war, and the British reference can be taken as referring to the loss of the Ninth, which the order of words suggests is contemporary or later – or at least not fifteen years earlier.

The disappearance of Legio IX thus presents a difficult problem. The scattered threads of evidence all suggest serious fighting in Britain about 130, and this would suit the appointment of Julius Severus to the British command about that year, since he was one of the foremost generals of the day.[35] Sisenna, on the other hand, was undistinguished, and unlikely to be sent to a province still seriously disturbed.[36] But there remains also the probability that the legion was withdrawn from Britain at some date between 108 and 126 and that it perished unrecorded later on, either in Judaea in 132–5 or later still. Evidence which might support such a view is the discovery of a tile-stamp and a mortarium-stamp of Legio IX at Nijmegen in Holland. This site had been the fortress of Legio X Gemina until about 104, after which it seems to have been held by a mixed force of auxiliary troops. Legio IX may have replaced this force at Nijmegen about 121, or even as late as 126, and may have remained there for a few years before being sent to the east; and this seems a reasonable solution. It is difficult to see how such stamps could be explained by the mere passage of vexillations of the legion, for instance, in 83; for troops on active service do not settle down to make tiles and pottery, and in any case the troops concerned were then brigaded with soldiers from other legions. These finds certainly suggest that the Ninth may have been stationed at Nijmegen for a short time at some period after 108, the latest date known for its presence at York, and perhaps from about 126. Further evidence is needed before more can be said.

1. For Arviragus, iv, 127; for Brigantes, xiv, 196.

2. The idea, sometimes advanced, that the forts north of the Forth were built not by Agricola but by his successor has no basis in common sense, and ignores strategic necessities.

3. As Professor Birley has suggested. On the other hand, if he governed Germany first, as the inscription (*ILS*, 8824a) implies, also under Hadrian, his tenure of Britain must have come later on, perhaps in the years 128–31 (see p. 148).

4. *Roman Britain and the Roman Army* (1953), 21. A vexillation of British auxiliaries – including part of the Ala Tampiana – is known to have been sent to Pannonia at this time (*ILS*, 2515).

5. Inchtuthil, Sir Ian Richmond told me, has produced five coins in demolition contexts; four of these are of 86 and one perhaps of 87, and all were in mint condition when dropped. Moreover, construction was still unfinished when the order came to evacuate, and this must reduce our estimate of the life of these coins before loss.

6. B. R. Hartley, *Britannia*, iii (1972), 14.

7. See map prepared by Miss A. S. Robertson in Richmond, *Roman and Native in North Britain* (1958), p. 72, and her map of first-century coins in *PSAS*, xciv (1960–61), 182.

8. Not all excavators record whether nails found in the burnt

debris are bent by extraction with the claw-hammer; but this is an important criterion of intentional demolition.

9. The appearance of British numerii in Upper Germany about this time suggests that the tribes were weakened by conscription (see p. 175 and note 7).

10. *Roman Britain and the Roman Army* (1953), 22–4.

11. The auxiliary vexillation sent to Pannonia from Britain by Domitian (p. 162, note 4) can be shown to have returned here sometime between 101–2 and 122 (J. E. Bogaers, 'Die Besatzungstruppen des Legionslagers von Nijmegen im 2 Jahrhundert n. Chr.', Studien zu den Militärgrenzen Roms (1967), pp. 54 ff.: see also *Numaga*, xii (1965), pp. 10 ff.

12. For one of these see *Papers of the Brit. School at Rome*, xviii (1950), 87; for the other *L'Année Epigraphique*, 1957, 133.

13. Caerleon, *RIB*, 330; Chester, *ibid.* 464; York, *ibid.* 665

14. For Lincoln *CIL*, xiii, 6679, and discussion in *Arch. Journ.*, ciii, 29 and 64; for Gloucester CIL, vi, 3346=*ILS*, 2365, and discussion in *ibid.*, 70.

15. S.H.A., *Vita Hadriani*, 11. One of the results of his reforming zeal, no doubt, is to be seen in the Wroxeter forum inscription (p. 277).

16. This was P. Mummius Sisenna Rutilianus, whose credulous superstition was ridiculed by Lucian in *Alexander the False Prophet*.

17. *Fossatum* would be a better description, as Professor I. A. Richmond remarked, *History*, xliv (No. 150) (February 1959), 6.

18. Even in the turf wall the turrets are of stone.

19. Some small part was taken, too, by detachments from the fleet. Well over a million cubic yards of stone had to be quarried for the wall.

20. A small bridge-head fort of about 2.5 acres probably already existed at Newcastle (*Pons Aelius*) and made the twelfth.

21. There is, in fact, insufficient evidence for certainty about the nature of the Hadrianic garrisons, and the suggested scheme has been contested (*AA*⁴ xlvii (1969), pp. 15 ff.). In the absence of inscriptions naming garrisons of this period we need more details of barrack accommodation if types of garrison are to be identified.

22. The whole barrier is one *actus* wide (pl. 3).

23. A re-examination of the dating evidence at the native settlement at Milking Gap, which lies between the Wall and the Vallum, has led Mr J. P. Gillam to suggest that the Brigantian owner was expelled from the military zone when the Vallum was built. *Roman and Native in North Britain* (ed. I. A. Richmond), 62–3. In recent years plough-marks proving earlier cultivation of the soil have been found beneath the forts of Rudchester, Haltonchesters and Carrawburgh.

24 Bewcastle, *RIB*, 995; Netherby, *RIB*, 974; Birrens, Birley, *T. Dumfries and Gal. Ant. Soc.*, xxxviii (1961), 142–3.

25. *RIB*, 801.

26. The *ala Augusta* was the garrison later in the century.

27. *Archaeologia Aeliana* [4], ix, 205; *RIB*, 1421.

28. *ILS*, 1100.

29. But there is nothing to show that it did not arrive as early as 119.

30. *Roman Britain and the Roman Army* (1953), pp. 26–30; and his more recent paper in R. M. (Butler (ed.), *Soldier and Civilian in Roman Yorkshire* (1971), pp. 71–80.

31. Nevertheless, there are varieties of turret-type in the Turf Wall which make it unlikely that only one legion was responsible.

32. It would be necessary to find a fourth legionary fortress: possibly Legio ix moved to Carlisle and Legio vi took its place at York.

33. *ILS*, 2726, 2735.

34. A soldier of the Eighth, Junius Dubitatus, lost his shield in the Tyne: its metal boss is now in the British Museum (*CIL*, vii, 495; B. M. Guide: *Antiquities of Roman Britain* (1951), fig. 35). Another inscription recording the presence of this legion comes from Brougham or Kirkby Thore (*RIB*, 782). Legio xxii was once thought to be recorded at Corbridge (*Ephemeris Epigraphica*, vii, 988), but this reading is not supported by *RIB*, 1130; an inscription from Scotland (*RIB*, 2216) set up by a vexillation of this legion can hardly, in view of its find-spot, be related to the reign of Hadrian, A tile of Legio xxii is recorded from Gloucestershire (Baddeley, *A Cotteswold Shrine*, 5), but it is certainly a modern importation.

35. The civil settlement at Walton-le-Dale, Lancs., which no doubt belongs to a fort not yet found, was destroyed by fire about this time. *Trans. Historic Soc. of Lancs. and Cheshire*, 109 (1957), 1–46.

36. The fact that the Ala Tampiana was transferred to Noricum before 138 is additional evidence that the crisis was over in Britain.

8

The Antonine Wall and the frontier in the second century

On the death of Hadrian in July 138 the succession passed to Antoninus Pius (138–61). The change of emperor initiated a swift change of frontier policy in Britain. The wall of Hadrian was abandoned, and after the reconquest of the Lowlands a new barrier, built of turf, was drawn across the Scottish isthmus. The new governor, responsible for executing the new policy, was Q. Lollius Urbicus. These events are recorded only in a single sentence in Capitolinus' biography of Pius.[1] 'Through his legates he carried on many wars; for he conquered the Britons through Lollius Urbicus the governor, and, after driving back the barbarians, built another wall, of turf.' An inscription at Corbridge shows that Lollius Urbicus was putting in hand construction in preparation for the campaign as early as 139, and coins of Antoninus Pius show that the necessary victory had been gained by late in 142 or early in 143. Thus the decision was immediate.

Lollius Urbicus, a native, it seems, of Roman Africa, had shown sufficient promise as a young man to ensure rapid promotion in the emperor's service. He had enjoyed a distinguished career under Hadrian, serving on his staff in the Jewish rebellion of 132–5; later he had held the consulship, perhaps in 135, and then had governed Lower Germany. He must have been selected for the British command as one of the earliest acts of Antoninus Pius, and remained governor until perhaps 144; his successor, attested on a diploma of 146, was Cn. Papirius Aelianus.[2]

Corbridge had been the site of one of Agricola's forts; the five-acre fort which succeeded it, however, on a new site some little distance off, belonged to the Stanegate rather than to Hadrian's Wall, and the garrison had been moved away when that wall was built. Now the fort was regarrisoned and re-equipped. The earlier military phases of Corbridge's history always reflect events in Scotland rather than those on the nearer frontier. The large inscription of 139 and another of 140 show that important building was in progress during those years; and about this time also we find inscriptions recording rebuilding at the forts of Risingham and High Rochester, the latter mentioning Urbicus by name. Further inscriptions mentioning him come from the Antonine Wall itself at Balmuildy, and the wall has, of course, also produced numerous distance-slabs dedicated to Antoninus Pius and recording the lengths constructed by various legionary units. As this wall is built of turf, its identity with the work referred to by Capitolinus is certain. Though not so far illustrated by such accurately dated inscriptions, Antonine rebuilding can be shown to have taken place during this reign at the Flavian fort-sites of Newstead, Crawford, Castledykes, Glenlochar and Loudoun Hill; and new forts were built in new positions at Lanchester, Bothwell-haugh, Inveresk, Cramond and Carzield. In addition, fortlets were built at or near previously occupied sites at Cappuck, Chew Green, Lyne and Raeburnfoot, and on fresh sites at Birrenswark, Fairholm, Dalmakethar, Milton, Redshaw Burn, Wandel, Barburgh Mill and Durisdeer and perhaps Castle Greg. Thus, the military grip on the Lowlands was reasserted almost as strongly as in Flavian times, but the much greater use now made of fortlets rather than full forts is noteworthy, and will be discussed shortly (pp. 170, 185).

The Antonine Wall itself is thirty-seven miles long, running from the fort at Old Kilpatrick on the Clyde to Bridgeness on the Forth, ending a short distance west of the fort of Carriden. For much of its length, the barrier has excellent command of the ground, with wide prospects to the north. In front was a broad ditch, normally up to forty feet wide and twelve feet deep. The Wall itself, or *Vallum* as some of the inscriptions name it, rested on a foundation of stones usually fourteen feet wide, sometimes pierced by culverts. This kept the base drained, and prevented spreading. The wall itself was built of turf sods and can be calculated to have stood about nine feet high, with a rampart-walk six feet wide on its summit: a wooden breast-work would give the front of the wall an elevation of about four-teen feet. Thus, it uses not quite two-thirds the volume of turf in a given stretch that the Turf Wall of Hadrian uses; and the ditch is proportionately larger than Hadrian's, which makes possible these economies in the scale of rampart provided.[3]

The other elements of the frontier consisted of forts, fortlets, signal platforms and the Military Way. There were also outpost forts at each end. Along the line of the wall fourteen forts are known, and the spacing suggests that originally there were eighteen (or nineteen if one existed at Bridgeness). Except for Bar Hill, all these forts are attached to the rear face of the Wall. Notable peculiarities are their variation in size and their close spacing. They lie about 2 miles apart (instead of 5–7 miles as on Hadrian's Wall). The fort at Mumrills is 7·1 acres in size, amply sufficient for a cohort 1,000 strong, part-mounted; Old Kilpatrick (4·7 acres), Balmuildy (4·3 acres), Castlecary (3·99 acres), Bar Hill (3·6 acres) and Cadder (3·2 acres) were large enough for cohorts 500 strong, and the first two may have held larger garrisons. But the other forts whose areas are known are much smaller: Bearsden (2·7 acres), Westerwood (2·34 acres), Croy Hill (2·4 acres), Rough Castle (1·55 acres) and Duntocher (0·64 acres) can only have held vexillations from larger units, despite the fact that Rough Castle has produced an inscription of Cohors VI Nerviorum, a unit the whole of which it certainly could not contain. Moreover, Castlecary has produced inscriptions of two milliary cohorts; Mumrills, on the other hand, has yielded inscriptions not of a unit of the size expected but of an ala 500 strong (Ala I Tungrorum) and of a cohort of the same strength (Cohors II Thracum); nor is there much reason to suppose that these were present in garrison together.

In recent years two additional fortlets (0·23 acres) have been discovered by air-photography at Wilderness Plantation and Glasgow Bridge. These are only slightly larger than the milecastles on Hadrian's Wall, and they match a third at Watling Lodge which was destroyed in 1894.[4] It is possible that a regular series of 'interval fortlets' remains to be discovered; but those so far known occupy the middle of extra-long gaps between forts, and therefore quite probably do not form part of a regular series.

Nevertheless, as Mr J. P. Gillam has observed, there are indications that the Antonine Wall-system, like Hadrian's, suffered change during construction. The large forts with the exception of Cadder are structurally earlier than the wall (Bar Hill, being detached, offers no evidence); the reverse is true of all the small ones except

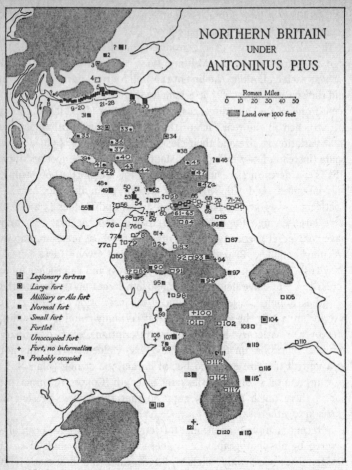

6   The military occupation of the north under Antoninus Pius (pp. 166, 175, 185).

Forts in Northern Britain under Antoninus Pius

NOTE (a) *The forts of Hadrian's Wall were under care and mainten-ance in this period.*
  (b) *The symbol 'Large Fort' means one over 7 acres.*

1	Bertha	44	Raeburnfoot	84	Whitley Castle
2	Strageath	45	Chew Green	85	Ebchester
3	Ardoch	46	Learchild	86	Lanchester
4	Stirling	47	High Rochester	87	Binchester
5	Camelon	47a	Risingham	88	Ravenglass
6	Dumbarton (?)	48	Barburgh Mill	89	Hardknott Castle
7	Outerwards	49	Carzield	90	Ambleside
8	Lurg Moor	50	Fairholm	91	Low Borrow
9	Whitemoss	51	Birrenswark		Bridge
10	Old Kilpatrick	52	Broomholm	92	Brough under
11	Duntocher	53	Birrens		Stainmore
12	Castle Hill	54	Broadlee	93	Bowes
13	Bearsden	55	Glenlochar	94	Greta Bridge
14	Balmuildy	56	Ward Law	95	Watercrook
15	Cadder	57	Netherby	96	Bainbridge
16	Kirkintilloch	58	Bewcastle	97	Brompton on
17	Auchendavy	59	Stanwix		Swale
18	Bar Hill	60	Castlesteads	98	Overborough
19	Croy Hill	61	Birdoswald	99	Lancaster
20	Westerwood	62	Carvoran	100	Long Preston
21	Castlecary	63	Great Chesters	101	Elslack
22	Seabegs	64	Chesterholm	102	Ilkley
23	Rough Castle	65	Housesteads	103	Newton Kyme
24	Falkirk	66	Carrawburgh	104	York
25	Mumrills	67	Chesters	105	Malton
26	Inveravon	68	Haltonchesters	106	Kirkham
27	Kinneil	69	Corbridge	107	Ribchester
28	Carriden	70	Rudchester	108	Walton-le-Dale
29	Cramond	71	Benwell	109	Castleford
30	Inveresk	72	Newcastle	110	Brough on
31	Bothwellhaugh	73	Wallsend		Humber
32	Castledykes	74	South Shields	111	Slack
33	Lyne	75	Kirkbride	112	Castleshaw
34	Newstead	76	Old Carlisle	113	Manchester
35	Loudoun Hill	76a	Beckfoot	114	Melandra Castle
36	Wandel	77	Maryport	115	Templeborough
37	Crawford	77a	Burrow Walls	116	Doncaster
38	Cappuck	78	Caermote	117	Brough on Noe
39	Kirkconnel	79	Papcastle		(Derbyshire)
40	Redshaw Burn	80	Moresby	118	Chester
41	Durisdeer	81	Old Penrith	119	Little Chester
42	Carronbridge	82	Brougham	120	Rocester
43	Milton	83	Kirkby Thore	121	Chesterton

Duntocher. Thus the original scheme may have been for a system resembling Hadrian's Wall in spacing of garrisons, here *c.* eight miles apart; but a closer grouping of garrisons in additional small forts may have been decided upon before many interval (milecastle-type) fortlets had been supplied.

It can be seen that the same shortage of men which is suggested by the numerous fortlets in southern Scotland may have compelled economies and simplification in the garrison of the Wall itself. The posts were filled by dividing units where necessary, but the forts were placed closer together for better supervision of the frontier and so that they could be easily reinforced. It is very unlikely that the patrolling and fighting garrisons were organised separately, as they may have been on the southern wall.

No turrets have so far come to light, but if timber signalling towers had been provided it would be almost impossible now to locate them. There are, however, a number of beacon-emplacements attached to the back of the Wall. These are not regularly disposed the length of the Wall for lateral signalling: two are known each side of Rough Castle, and two on the west slope of Croy Hill. This distribution suggests that their purpose was connected with long-distance signals linking the outposts on the north-east with the rearward fighting units.

Close behind the wall ran the Military Way, the road connecting the forts; it passed through most of these as their *via principalis*, but by-pass loops were also provided for long-distance traffic. Most of the forts possessed annexes, the purpose of which may originally have been to provide for the safety of baggage trains and stores, but undoubtedly they came to be used by civilian traders and camp-followers, and an inscription from Carriden set up by the *vikani consistentes Veluniate* prove the establishment of at least one regular *vicus*, or community with local self-government.

It has sometimes been suggested that though the Antonine Wall was less than half as long as the Wall of Hadrian, this advantage was counter-balanced by gross tactical weakness on the flanks, which rest on estuaries easily crossed by boat. This view is a misconception. A road left the western terminal at Old Kilpatrick to run beyond the wall along the north bank of the Clyde: it probably led to a harbour at Dumbarton, above which the river was not then navigable. A harbour beyond the protection of the wall implies strength not weakness, quite apart from the possibility of naval patrols. Nor was the left shore of the estuary left unprotected: a large fort recently discovered at Whitemoss (Bishopton) probably held cavalry and controlled the lowest ford, while farther west two fortlets at Lurg Moor (0·42 acres) and Outerwards (0·12 acres) kept watch over the estuary. These are remnants of a once more complete system of surveillance of this western flank.

It was the eastern end of the wall, however, which faced the larger concentration of population and the route from the north; and here the Romans boldly grasped the problem and its solution. Forts indeed guarded the southern shore of the Forth at Carriden, Cramond and Inveresk; but in addition Agricola's road north of the wall was seized and reoccupied by outpost garrisons in the forts at Camelon, Ardoch (pl. 5b), Strageath and Bertha. This garrisoning of Strath Allan and Strath Earn was not as full and intensive as that undertaken by Agricola, and it suggests a protectorate rather than an occupation. Certainly Roman objects were widely circulating on non-military sites in this area in the second century, and almost as far north as Aberdeen. Whatever the precise political arrangements, it is evident that no hostile movement could develop in this quarter unperceived.

Like Hadrian's Wall, the Antonine Vallum was constructed by legionaries; this is made quite certain by the inscriptions on the distance-slabs. What is uncertain is whether the ditch was dug by the legionaries or by native forced labour; no doubt, however, legionary labour was mainly reserved for the more skilled tasks. The forts also appear to have been built by legionaries, but probably not by the parties building the wall. In some cases the forts were clearly planned, and in many cases actually built, before the adjacent parts of the Antonine Wall; and this is especially obvious at the western end. Here the forts of Castlecary and Balmuildy have stone ramparts which pre-date the wall, and at Old Kilpatrick the fort ramparts, this time of turf, were obviously originally free-standing, since their northern corners are rounded. It can thus be deduced that the Antonine Wall was begun from its east end, but that forts at the western end were installed almost immediately, without waiting for the Wall's arrival. This conclusion was further confirmed by excavation at Duntocher in 1948–51, where it was discovered that first a fortlet and then a fort had been constructed on the site before the arrival of the Vallum. Indeed, the fortlet at Duntocher very probably belongs to a preliminary stage in the seizure of the isthmus, before the details of the wall had been planned at all, for it matches similar fortlets found below the forts at Bar Hill and Croy Hill. These were thought by Macdonald to be Agricolan, but the total absence of Flavian pottery from these sites throws doubt on his conclusion (p. 125 f.). What may be another comparable fortlet has been observed from the air at Mumrills.

Distance-slabs recorded work by all three legions. All the stones of Legio vi and all but one of Legio xx were set up by legionary vexillations rather than by the legion itself, while the stones of Legio ii do not record vexillations. This has led to the suggestion that the whole of Legio ii was working on the Wall but that the other two legions supplied detachments only, perhaps as few as 1,000 men from each. However, if that were so one would expect the distances built by Legio ii to be at least twice and probably three or four times longer than those constructed by the others. But this is not what we find; the figures in most instances agree with each other very closely. There is other evidence to suggest that in fact each legion was divided into two working parties; we may suppose that the greater part of all three legions was present, the difference in inscription-styles being left to the officers concerned. Duplicate stones were set up at each end of the lengths built by each party, but no sub-units such as cohorts and centuries left records as they did on Hadrian's Wall.

There is one peculiarity of the stones: those found between Bridgeness and Castlehill, that is to say over more than eight-ninths of the total distance starting from the east end, record the distances in *passus*, Roman paces of five feet. These distances are on average 5,357·5 yards or 3·2 Roman miles: a more realistic figure is in fact rather longer (3·66 Roman miles), since one very short length reduces the average. On the other hand, west of Castlehill the distances are recorded in feet, and average 1,233·5 yards, or only 0·74 Roman miles. It is clear, too, that great care was taken to divide up this stretch of wall equally between the various legions. When the distances allotted to the two working parties of each legion are added together the result shows that to Legio ii was assigned 7,411 feet, to Legio vi 7,381 feet and to Legio xx 7,411 feet! The reason for this change of building-length is not recorded. It is most likely to be due to an assessment of the topography, for here and here alone the Wall approaches close to unfavourable ground. The Kilpatrick Hills might have been considered as presenting a danger which could be met by closing up the working parties, so that in effect all three legions were concentrated in this four-mile sector during its construction. Concern with the security of this end of the wall had already been shown by the Roman command when they caused the forts here to be built in advance of the arrival of the Wall.[4a] It cut right through the territory of the Damnonii, and must have aroused opposition.

In recent years aerial photography by Dr J. K. St Joseph has added to knowledge of the frontier by the discovery of fourteen marching camps near the line of the Wall. Some nine at least of these, by their uniform size of just over five acres, and to some extent by their uniform spacing, suggest the housing of the construction parties.

The historian may feel some surprise in relation to the Antonine Wall, first, that it was built when it was, and secondly, that it was built at all. He requires an explanation for the sudden replacement of the Hadrianic system so recently, so expensively and so laboriously brought to perfection. He needs to know whether the prevailing use of turf and timber on this frontier carries the implication that it was regarded as a temporary expedient. The co-existence of two alternative, or parallel, frontier systems introduces a certain fluctuation into the affairs of the second century which he cannot yet chart in accurate detail.

Why was the frontier moved? There is little direct evidence. A passage in the contemporary Greek writer Pausanias has been thought to refer to these events.[5] 'Antoninus Pius never willingly made war; but when the Moors took up arms against Rome he drove them out of all their territory. . . . Also he deprived the Brigantes in Britain of most of their land because they too had begun aggression on the district of Genunia whose inhabitants are subject to Rome.' The statement is not of much value as it stands, since it is clear that Pausanias imagined the Brigantes to be outside the province, whereas they had been within it for more than sixty years; nor do we know where Genunia lay. Two explanations have been offered. The first has been argued by Birley. During this reign only in 139–40 could even a fraction of the Brigantes be thought of as outside the province, and their attack on Genunia must have taken place then, since otherwise the advance into Scotland would have been aggression, which Pausanias denies that Pius ever committed. This explanation lays emphasis on Antoninus Pius' pacific reputation. An alternative view sees in this passage a reference to the Brigantian rebellion of 154, and emphasises the deprivation of Brigantian territory. For only in the aftermath of this rebellion does a context for this appear with the re-occupation of the Pennine Forts and re-imposition of military government, and even perhaps the foundation of the colony of York (p. 213). It must be owned that neither explanation quite covers all the facts. The Gordian knot may be cut by allowing that the term Brigantes is not used by Pausanias with the same precision as it has hitherto been used in this book. If by Brigantes he can be permitted to mean 'the Brigantes and their friends in the north', or even 'the inhabitants of northern Britain', the passage acquires sense and the context becomes clear, the governorship of Urbicus.[6]

Whether or not that is what Pausanias meant, disturbances in southern Scotland were clearly the cause of the Roman advance. There the Votadini can be thought of as a philo-Roman tribe (p. 126). Their neighbours the Selgovae were not. It is possible, indeed, that fear of the Selgovae was the motive which led the former into treaty relationship with Rome. (Such a relationship is an assumption, but not one without support.) All was in their favour so long as Rome held southern Scotland, but the new frontier of Hadrian excluded them. No doubt paper arrangements were made for their security in any treaties which followed Hadrian's victory of 118; but the fact remained that the heart of their lands lay beyond effective aid from the garrisons of Hadrian's Wall. An attack on some sub-division of the Votadini by the Selgovae is the most reasonable explanation of Pausanias' statement. Hadrian's Wall, in other words, impregnable defensive barrier though it was, had been put in the wrong place for intervention farther north: it lay out of effective contact with the Lowland tribes. Rome still needed to influence events in this area, and if her influence was not accepted peaceably there was no alternative to reconquest.

The reconquest of Lowland Scotland, then, was directed primarily at the control of the Selgovae and perhaps also of the Novantae. But as Capitolinus stated in the sentence already quoted (p. 165), the Turf Wall of Pius was not built until the barbarians had been driven back. This phrase recalls that of Tacitus describing Agricola's Forth–Clyde frontier, and must mean that irreconcilable warriors from these tribes retired beyond the isthmus; this movement was to have serious repercussions in later years. Nevertheless, the military strength of the tribesmen who remained could be greatly abated by

Roman conscription. Legally they were *dediticii*: they had surrendered unconditionally. Many of their young men may have been transported to the upper German frontier and then drafted into *numeri* in the Roman army. *Numeri Brittonum*, of which at least ten are known, are first attested there by inscriptions in 145, and this fitted well with the theory that the numeri in question had been raised after the re-conquest of southern Scotland. But recently Dr Baatz[7] has shown that British numeri were in Upper Germany from considerably earlier: the first of them may have been enlisted shortly before the withdrawal from Scotland under Trajan if not earlier still. But though these discoveries upset the neatness of the old equation, there is no need to doubt that drafts were required from time to time by existing numeri, or indeed that conscripted Lowlanders would have been in demand almost everywhere on the Roman frontiers to reinforce these or other units. Those that remained soon began to trade with Roman merchants: it is not a case of wholesale depopulation.

At first, then, all went favourably for Rome. Once again Newstead occupied a key position in the scheme: the new fort, 14·7 acres in extent and now provided with a stone wall, contained as garrison two cohorts of Legio xx and a regiment of auxiliary cavalry, the Ala Augusta Vocontiorum. The auxiliary regiments which had been stationed on Hadrian's Wall were redeployed, some of them being moved up to the new wall, and Hadrian's frontier was thrown open, though garrisons still guarded the Cumberland coast. The Hadrianic Vallum was formally breached by throwing in earth from the two mounds every forty-five yards to form causeways across the ditch, and their gates were removed from the milecastles, thus allowing free access across the old military zone. The Wall-forts themselves, however, seem in most cases to have been maintained perhaps on a care-and-maintenance basis; at Benwell, Halton, Chesters, Housesteads and Great Chesters we have inscriptions which suggest the presence of legionaries at this date, no doubt skeleton detachments posted for that purpose. That at Housesteads was certainly in garrison.[8]

To maintain this greatly extended occupation more forts were evacuated in the Pennines[9] (fig. 6), and it is possible that some of the Welsh garrisons were reduced by detachments; but recent work by Miss G. Simpson has shown that the older theories of massive disengagement in Wales to find troops for northern Britain are untenable. Despite troop-shortages, however, soldiers could be spared for the Moorish campaign of 145–7; an inscription recently published from Rome records Sextus Flavius Quietus, chief centurion of Legio xx *misso cum exercitu* on this expedition. Likewise half the milliary Second Cohort of Tungrians was present in Raetia in 147, but was back in Britain ten years later.

To the second century, and probably mainly to this period in it, belongs the beginning of a change in the habitation-pattern in the eastern lowlands. Here the hill-forts are found to have gone out of use; settlements and individual farmsteads now appear on open sites, built circular-fashion of thick rubble walls faced each side with stone. Sometimes these are found overlying the abandoned ramparts of hill-forts; often there are signs of an expanding population. Their distribution is principally Votadinian, but seems to extend into the eastern boundaries of the Selgovae. This is clearly due to the impact of Rome, and the suppression of the old warlike way of life. That the Votadini were especially philo-Roman is indicated by the number of Roman objects of second-century date found at Traprain Law, their capital.

The first Antonine occupation of Scotland ended abruptly with destruction. The date of this can be fixed by indications of serious trouble in Britain between 154 and 158 given by coins and inscriptions and confirmed by troop movements. First, coins of Pius minted in 154–5 show a reverse-type of Britannia subdued. These suggest that war or rebellion had been put down by 155. That the trouble was suppressed only at the cost of heavy legionary casualties is indicated by an inscription dredged from the Tyne at Newcastle which records the arrival of reinforcements for all three British legions from the armies of both German provinces under the governor Cn. Julius Verus.

Verus was another example of the careful selection and quick promotion of *viri militares* in the imperial service. He had been legate of Legio xxx Ulpia in Lower Germany, and after holding the consulship – perhaps in 151 [10] – became Governor of Lower Germany. He may well have brought the legionary vexillations with him, and the date should not be later than 155. The troops had evidently just landed at Newcastle and had not yet been distributed. Verus was still in Britain in 158, as a building-inscription at Birrens tells us, and the scene of his activities is suggested by these two inscriptions and another at Brough in Derbyshire. This distribution – with which he associated the sentence of Pausanias already quoted – led Haverfield in 1904 to suggest that the trouble was not an invasion from the north, but a rebellion of the Brigantes in the Pennines; and this suggestion is amply borne out by the re-occupation of forts in the Pennines seen on fig. 7 (p. 183) and dated to this and the following governorships. It may even be supported by the fact that the fort at Lancaster was burnt at this time. Why else was this heavy re-occupation necessary?

It remains to consider, however, in what way a Brigantian revolt could involve the loss of the Antonine Wall. If there had been an invasion from the north which resulted in the destruction of the wall with all its forts and the loss of almost all the forts in the Scottish lowlands as well, it is strange that we hear no echo of the disaster in our written sources, scanty though these are. Even if Pausanias is referring to events at this date rather than 139–40, he mentions only the Brigantes. The explanation must be that a serious rebellion in the Pennines would necessitate the concentration of all available Roman forces on that region: and a large part of that concentration would have to be drawn from Scotland. The forts of the Antonine Wall and of the region to the south of it were, then, evacuated by the Romans and burnt to prevent them being of use to the enemy. It is very likely, indeed, that action by the Brigantian rebels was concerted with some of the tribesmen of southern Scotland. There was nothing to prevent such consultation now that Hadrian's barrier was open, and that something of the sort happened at Newstead is plain from the recovery of human bones and equipment from pits of this period there, though not in such quantity as in the previous rising. The siege-camps at Birrenswark, too, if used in real war and not just for training, would suggest the same thing, for they probably date to this period (pl. 5a). The fort of Birrens is also known to have been destroyed; its debris yielded a newly minted coin of 154.

The Roman reaction, then, was to retire from Scotland in order to crush the rebellion, for there was no strategic reserve of troops which could be called upon for such a purpose. The processes of rebellion and pacification, however, were prolonged into the next reign, for as late as 163 there was a threat of war in Britain, and Calpurnius Agricola was despatched to suppress it.[11] Inscriptions show that Calpurnius Agricola, too, was constructing forts in northern England. Moreover, in 1911 excavations at Corbridge unearthed a bronze jug containing a hoard of 160 Roman gold coins closing with an issue minted in 159–60. The hoard must have been buried in some emergency at Corbridge in 160–2 and not recovered.

It is clear that the crisis was acute and prolonged, and this view is reinforced by what is known of the calibre of the governors sent to deal with it. Verus, himself a man of outstanding ability, was succeeded in 158 or early 159 by a man whose name is incompletely recorded (. . . anus Lon(gus) or Lon(ginus)),[12] but early in 161 his place was taken by M. Statius Priscus Licinius Italicus. This man had had a remarkable career, starting with service as an equestrian officer and a decoration from Hadrian in the Jewish rebellion. After serving as a procurator in southern Gaul he was promoted to the Senate, commanded two legions in succession and governed Dacia in 157–8; he held the consulship (*consul ordinarius*) in 159, after which he governed Upper Moesia in 160–1, and came from there to Britain.[13] His rapid promotions point to ability, and it is evident that his appointment to Britain was due to the need of a first-class general. After him came Sextus Calpurnius Agricola, about whose previous career little is known; he had been consul in 158 or 159 and was appointed to Britain perhaps late in 162, or early 163; he was certainly here in 163–4 as is proved by a Corbridge inscription,[14] and perhaps remained till 166.

Excavation has shown that on Hadrian's Wall at about this period the milecastle gateways were rehung with gates, and in most cases the Vallum-crossings, inserted about 140, were removed. This implies that this Wall was being re-commissioned, and the date is probably given us by an inscription,[15] now lost, which records repairs to the face of the wall itself by Legio VI in 158. This reconstitution of Hadrian's barrier is known as that wall's period Ib, and it is further illustrated by changes of auxiliary garrison. Not all the garrisons of all the forts are yet known, of course. But Benwell, held by a cavalry regiment, as the stables show, in the reign of Hadrian, and apparently occupied by legionaries under Pius, was now – or later in the Antonine period – converted to house the milliary Cohors I Vangionum Equitata. Chesters had the same history, the Antonine garrison being the quingenary Cohors I Dalmatarum Equitata. At Carrawburgh Cohors I Aquitanorum Equitata was succeeded by

Cohors I Cugernorum; similar changes can be traced at other forts. At Carvoran the First Cohort of Hamian Archers, a Syrian regiment, returned to the fort which they had held under Hadrian, having occupied Bar Hill from 144 to 155. It is noteworthy that in this re-organisation no attempt was made to follow the Hadrianic pattern of garrisons; few of the cavalry forts regained their cavalry, and at least one of them, Chesters, though capable of housing a milliary cohort of infantry, was given a garrison little more than half this size. This suggests that the tactical problem was different.

It has usually been considered unlikely that the two walls were held simultaneously, and more probable that, if Period Ib on Hadrian's Wall started under Julius Verus or Calpurnius Agricola, the second occupation of the forts in Scotland and on the Antonine Wall was a later phenomenon. That Birrens had been rebuilt in 158 had long been known, but Birrens was an outpost of Hadrian's Wall, and its reconstruction might be no more than the beginning of Period Ib there. In 1947 Professor Richmond was able to show that the second Antonine occupation of Newstead must have followed fairly closely on the destruction of the first Antonine fort there, and more recently the same has been found at Crawford. Since Newstead and Crawford are too far north to have any connection with the phases of Hadrian's Wall, it began to seem as if southern Scotland as a whole was soon reoccupied. This view was reinforced by the knowledge that Corbridge was being reorganised by Calpurnius Agricola as a supply base. But the difficulty preventing a firm conclusion lay in the lack of dating evidence on the Antonine Wall itself. The excavations on this wall had in the main taken place in the first quarter of this century, and their records lack the scientific precision required to solve a chronological point of this sort. Sir George Macdonald had been of the opinion that the forts of the Antonine Wall had been twice destroyed and twice rebuilt, but the dates of the three occupations thus suggested could only be established on general grounds. Dr K. A. Steer has made an important advance with the convincing demonstration [16] that the second occupation of the Antonine Wall began before the death of Pius in 161. The original masonry of its fort buildings is usually so well constructed as to imply legionary work, and this inference is supported at some forts, including Castlecary, by the discovery of actual legionary building inscriptions. But the forts of Castlecary and Rough Castle have also produced auxiliary building records: these must consequently go with the rebuilding of the second period, which is notably inferior in quality. But these two auxiliary building records are dedicated to Antoninus Pius, and must have been erected before his death. At Bar Hill the case is even plainer. Here we have records of two regiments in garrison, Cohors I Hamiorum Sagittariorum, the Syrian Archers, and Cohors I Baetasiorum. It was the latter who erected the building inscription in honour of Pius, and this stone, together with a large altar also inscribed by them, was found among much broken stonework and debris filling the well of the headquarters building. Clearly this debris was the product of the final destruction of the fort at the end of the second occupation (for otherwise the well would have been cleared out); and the inscription shows that this occupation began before 161. To clinch the demonstration, some iron arrowheads, presumably left behind by the Archers, were found in the mud at the bottom of the well beneath all the later debris.

In the first edition of this book it was suggested that both walls were held in parallel from *c.* 160 to 180 and thereafter Hadrian's Wall alone until 196. The military burden imposed by this task was admittedly very great and it was shown that unless economies had been arranged by manning forts at less than full strength, or alternatively unless there were differences in the dates of occupation of individual forts within the period – differences which at the time were impossible to demonstrate – there would have been a shortfall of *c.* 9,000 men in the forces available. In 1972, however, Mr B. R. Hartley published the dating-evidence provided by samian ware for the military occupations in northern England and Scotland [17] and was able to prove conclusively that the second Antonine hold on Scotland was exceedingly brief, and that forts there were not held concurrently with those in northern England for more than a very short time. Solutions to some of the problems of the later second century are now in sight.

During the rebellion in southern Scotland and the Pennines the Roman army, as we have seen, pulled back temporarily, and Hadrian's frontier was recommissioned to bar communication with the north, though its forts may have continued to be held by small legionary vexillations. The rebuilding of Birrens in 158, as we have seen (p. 179), has uncertain relevance for the reoccupation of southern Scotland as a whole; but by the following year at the latest the Roman army was back on the Antonine Wall and in the outposts beyond it. Behind it southern Scotland, too, was reoccupied, though with some changes in garrison. The fortlet at Lyne was replaced by a full-sized fort; Carzield and Loudoun Hill were not reoccupied and several fortlets, e.g. Barburgh Mill, were also left empty. The Antonine Wall itself seems to have been held with fewer troops. Newstead was still the key position and was now held by a milliary ala instead of by the mixed force of legionaries and cavalry previously in garrison.[18]

The second Antonine occupation of Scotland was of short duration, for it did not bring peace; presumably there were not enough troops to make the system work by policing in force the whole of the huge and geographically difficult area between the Peak and the Forth. The excavators of both Lyne and Crawford have noted evidence suggesting that the occupation of these forts was brief, and at Glenlochar the small quantity of late Antonine pottery found reinforces this conclusion. Mr Hartley, too, has shown that, save at two forts soon to be mentioned, there is an entire absence of samian in the Scottish forts datable after *c.* 165.

In 163 Calpurnius Agricola was sent as governor in face of the threat of war; he rebuilt a number of forts in northern England,[19] and it was probably therefore he who decided to withdraw Roman troops once more from Scotland in order to find the men for a firmer grip on more vital territory nearer home:[20] the outbreak of trouble on the continent prevented the possibility of reinforcement from the Rhine armies. Alternatively, perhaps, it was the next governor, in 169 (see p. 186). Whatever the precise date, this time Newstead was retained; by means of its powerful cavalry garrison Roman supervision could be widely exercised. Cappuck, too, seems to have been held, which suggests that, in addition to the nearer system of outpost forts in the west, a much more extended series was maintained on the east, serviced by Dere Street. The failure of the original Hadrianic frontier had stemmed from its distance from the sources of hostility: shortage of forces compelled Calpurnius Agricola to re-establish that frontier, but his arrangements were a bold attempt to remedy its defects and at the same time to afford support to the friendly Votadini. These external arrangements explain the different order of battle now found on the Wall (p. 178f.). The re-occupation of Hadrian's Wall, however, involved replacing the Turf Wall of its western sector with a new stone wall: no doubt this turf wall had

deteriorated since 140, and its replacement was thought to be ultimately more economical than extensive repairs. The new wall was
built to an intermediate gauge of nine Roman feet; it incorporated
the stone turrets of the turf wall but was provided with new stone
mile-castles.[21]

The process of evacuating the Brigantian hill-lands had been begun
under Hadrian (fig. 5, p. 150), who retained a cordon of forts on
their south and west flanks. In his reign about 9,500 men had held
the forts on the Wall, with another 1,500–2,000 men in the milecastles; a further forty or so mile-fortlets lined the Cumberland
coast (say 1,000 men). West of a line from Ribchester to Brough-
under-Stainmore and Whitley Castle eighteen forts were certainly or
probably still held, accounting for 9,000 men; east of this line there
were only 1,500 men in Durham and north Yorkshire at three forts,
while the south edge of the Pennines was held by four or five forts
(2,500 men) with an outlying fort at Brough on Humber. The distribution shows that it was the Lancashire–Cumbrian region about
which the Romans were most apprehensive, whether from external
or internal hostility. Northern England as a whole was held by a
total of 26,000 men.

This number is well within the limits indicated by other evidence.
First, there is the information given by diplomas. These certificates,
engraved on bronze, granting Roman citizenship and legal marriage
rights, were issued to auxiliary soldiers on discharge after serving
twenty-five or more years with the colours; each individual received
his diploma, but as the discharges took place in batches, each document contains a list of all the regiments in the provincial army due
to discharge men on the same occasion. In this way they provide
valuable information concerning the identity of the auxiliary regiments in each province, and if sufficient diplomas exist, it is possible
to construct an army list which must be almost complete. For the
army of Britain there are diplomas or parts of them for the years 98,
103, 105, 122, 124, 135, 146 and 159; and in consequence the names
are known of 14 alae (1 of them milliary), 6 milliary cohorts and 38
cohorts 500 strong, which served in Britain during this period. In
addition, a further milliary cohort and 6 quingenary cohorts can be
supplied from epigraphic evidence, making a total of 65 regiments,
or 36,500 men.[22]

It is perhaps unlikely that any very large number of auxiliary

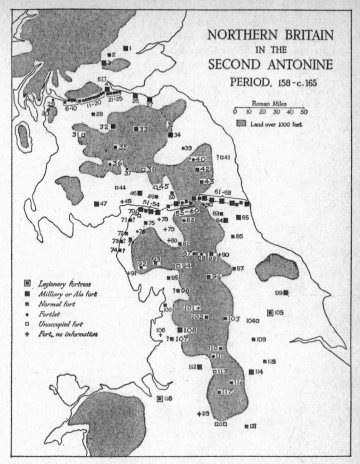

NORTHERN BRITAIN
IN THE
SECOND ANTONINE
PERIOD. 158 - c. 165

Roman Miles
0   10   20   30   40   50

■ Land over 1000 feet

■ Legionary fortress
■ Milliary or Ala fort
▪ Normal fort
● Fortlet
□ Unoccupied fort
+ Fort, no information

7 The military occupation of the north under Marcus Aurelius.
Note: ? beside a fort means that it was only probably occupied
(or unoccupied) as indicated.

1 Bertha	8 Duntocher	15 Bar Hill
2 Strageath	9 Castle Hill	16 Croy Hill
3 Ardoch	10 Bearsden	17 Westerwood
4 Camelon	11 Balmuildy	18 Castlecary
5 Stirling	12 Cadder	19 Seabegs
6 Whitemoss	13 Kirkintilloch	20 Rough Castle
7 Old Kilpatrick	14 Auchendavy	21 Falkirk

22 Mumrills
23 Inveravon
24 Kinneil
25 Carriden
26 Cramond
27 Inveresk
28 Bothwellhaugh
29 Lurg Moor
30 Outerwards
31 Loudoun Hill
32 Castledykes
33 Lyne
34 Newstead
35 Crawford
36 Durisdeer
37 Milton
38 Raeburnfoot
39 Cappuck
40 Chew Green
41 Learchild
42 High Rochester
43 Risingham
44 Carzield
45 Broomholm
46 Birrens
47 Glenlochar
48 Ward Law
49 Netherby
50 Bewcastle
51 Bowness
52 Drumburgh
53 Burgh by Sands
54 Stanwix
55 Castlesteads
56 Birdoswald

57 Carvoran
58 Great Chesters
59 Chesterholm
60 Housesteads
61 Carrawburgh
62 Chesters
63 Haltonchesters
64 Rudchester
65 Benwell
66 Newcastle
67 Wallsend
68 South Shields
69 Corbridge
70 Kirkbride
71 Beckfoot
72 Maryport
73 Burrow Walls
74 Moresby
75 Old Carlisle
76 Caermote
77 Papcastle
78 Wreay
79 Old Penrith
80 Brougham
81 Kirkby Thore
82 Whitley Castle
83 Ebchester
84 Lanchester
85 Chester-le-Street
86 Binchester
87 Brough under
   Stainmore
88 Maiden Castle
89 Bowes

90 Greta Bridge
91 Ravenglass
92 Hardknott Castle
93 Ambleside
94 Low Borrow
   Bridge
95 Watercrook
96 Bainbridge
97 Catterick
98 Overborough
99 Malton
100 Lancaster
101 Long Preston
102 Elslack
103 Ilkley
104 Newton Kyme
105 York
106 Kirkham
107 Walton-le-Dale
108 Ribchester
109 Castleford
110 Slack
111 Castleshaw
112 Manchester
113 Melandra Castle
114 Templeborough
115 Doncaster
116 Brough on Noe
   (Derbyshire)
117 Buxton
118 Chester
119 Chesterton
120 Rocester
121 Little Chester

regiments remains unknown in this period, but a further check can be obtained from the number of forts established on a permanent basis by Agricola or retained in use during his governorship. As we have seen (p. 135f.), these amounted to at least 20 in Wales, at least 57 and perhaps 73 in Northern Britain, together with 8 small forts holding perhaps half a cohort each. A conservative estimate suggests that Agricola disposed of about 90 auxiliary regiments, c. 50,000 men. In the time of Hadrian the army of Britain had been reduced by a legion, and the auxiliary troops may well have been reduced too, though perhaps not in proportion. We may guess that some 75 regiments remained, or about 42,500 men.

With 26,000 men in the north in Hadrian's reign, there thus remain some 16,500 to be accounted for. The northern garrison might be larger, seeing that 7 forts are marked as giving no information (fig. 5, p. 150), and Wales and its borders at this date had a garrison of at least 9,500 men in at least 14 forts; 8 forts in Wales yield no information, 3 were evacuated [23] and 1 reduced in size.[24]

Under Antoninus Pius the region south of Hadrian's Wall was held now by only 14 forts containing 8,000 men. North of Hadrian's Wall the lowlands were held by 17 forts (9,550 men) and 14 fortlets (700 men); the Antonine Wall had 18 forts (c. 6,500 men), and beyond it the outpost forts may have accounted for 2,500 men. Thus, the total number of auxiliaries in northern Britain was about 27,250 and of these only 33 per cent were facing an external enemy. In Wales it is likely that Gelligaer and Penydarren and probably Tomen y Mur were evacuated, leaving at least 11 forts with 7,500 men. This total of 34,750 men is still well within the limits of forces available and was achieved by skilful dispositions and the use of fortlets when possible.

In the second Antonine period, 158–63, with Scotland occupied, there is evidence of greater strain on manpower. In the Pennines about 26 forts (21,300 men) may have been held, though it is difficult to be sure in this short period; Hadrian's Wall was probably still held by small parties of legionaries, irrelevant to the present context. In lowland Scotland there were 14 forts (9,200 men) and perhaps 5 fortlets (500 men). On the Antonine Wall the garrison was now perhaps 6,250 (Bearsden was unoccupied), and beyond it were 4 outpost forts (2,500 men). Thus in northern Britain as a whole there were 30,750 auxiliaries and this total could be achieved without unduly reducing the garrison of Wales (reckoned as still 7,500 men). But this total in the north is only 2,500 more than the total in the previous period, which had proved insufficient to prevent rebellion. It is not hard to understand the pressures which led Calpurnius Agricola to abandon Scotland.

In the third Antonine period, in the reign of Marcus Aurelius, we find accordingly the garrison of northern England strengthened. In the Pennines 30 (perhaps 33) forts (with 14,300 men) and 16 on Hadrian's Wall (now with 10,000 men) contained the Brigantes with

24,300 men. North of the Wall 6 forts were held (3,750 men). In Wales, too, there were at least 14 forts (9,500 men) in occupation at this time. The total of some 37,550 auxiliaries is still, however, about 5,000 below the potential of troops available as reckoned on p. 185. The figures as a whole testify to the large native populations in lowland Scotland and in Brigantia, which are not easy otherwise to estimate.

Events after the governorship of Calpurnius Agricola are ill-recorded. There are hints of renewed trouble in Britain in 169, but we know nothing of its nature or of the steps taken unless, indeed, this was the moment when Scotland was given up.[25] Possibly, however, it was a revolt in Wales, as might be suggested by the burning of the Wroxeter forum and adjacent parts of the town about this time. At Worcester too the debris of a conflagration has been found. But it is not always certain that fires represent enemy action: Roman forts, as we have seen, were sometimes demolished and the unwanted debris burnt by the retiring garrison; and in towns which were still largely half-timbered chance fires would spread disastrously, fanned by the wind. London had been ravaged by fire in Hadrian's reign, but there is nothing to suggest that it was not an act of God, as later in 1666. A large part of *Verulamium* had been destroyed in a conflagration about 155, and though this date is more suggestive, we cannot show that it was not coincidence. Nevertheless, unrest or rebellion in Wales would seem to be suggested by certain troop-movements. The second forts at Leintwardine and at Walltown in the Marches may belong to this period, and forts were rebuilt also in Wales about this time at Forden, Coelbren and Caernarvon. The empty fort at Gelligaer seems to have been reoccupied for a short period in the second half of the century, perhaps at this time.

In 175 Britain was reinforced by 5,500 Sarmatian cavalry. At first sight this might suggest preparations to deal with rebellion or re-conquest, but in fact the circumstances were peculiar. Marcus Aurelius had been fighting on the Danube and had planned to exterminate the troublesome Iazyges, but an outbreak of rebellion in Syria compelled him to make hurried terms; under these the tribe agreed to keep well away from the Roman frontier and to furnish 8,000 cavalry. The larger half of these was sent immediately to Britain, but we cannot tell how far the reason was the military needs of the province and how far the wish to keep the Sarmatians out of harm's way and unable to escape. Nevertheless, the reinforcement must have been very welcome, though we know nothing of how it was used. The horsemen were probably formed into *numeri*, for in the next century a Numerus of Sarmatians was in garrison at Ribchester. Archaeological evidence of Sarmatians has been found also at Chesters on Hadrian's Wall, but otherwise there is no trace. This suggests that the bulk of the force did not remain in Britain long: they may not have returned after the expedition of Albinus in 196.

Q. Antistius Adventus is the next governor of Britain to be recorded: he was probably in the province from about 175 to about 178, and once again a man with a distinguished military record was chosen. He had served in the Parthian War of Verus, held the consulship probably in 166 or 167, and had governed Lower Germany. His successor was probably the (?) Caerellius whose career is recorded on an altar at Mainz.[26] These men maintained the *status quo*; but not long after the death of Marcus in 180 a serious crisis arose. Dio tells us that the greatest war in Commodus' reign occurred in Britain, when the tribes crossed the wall that separated them from the Roman garrison and slew a general (possibly the governor is meant) at the head of his forces. In great alarm Commodus sent Ulpius Marcellus against them, who inflicted terrible damage.[27] Though the exact date of this invasion is not recorded, it can be shown that Ulpius Marcellus was sent to Britain in the summer of 180.[28] By 184 a victory had been won, since in that year commemorative coins were issued and Commodus assumed the title of Britannicus; but the war was continued longer, since similar coins were issued in 185. A hoard of silver coins terminating with an issue of 186–7 found at Briglands in Kinross-shire may imply that operations continued to that date, but it may equally represent the savings of some wealthy native or trader who still had access to recent currency.

Though Dio does not specify which Wall was stormed, it is now impossible to believe that it was the Antonine Wall as stated in the first edition of this book, since the evidence, as we have seen, is against that wall having been in commission after *c.* 163–6. The Wall which was crossed, accordingly, was Hadrian's, and it is possible that the scene of the attack may be localised near Dere Street. Signs of burning and destruction have been noted at Rudchester, Haltonchesters and at Corbridge, which could conceivably be associated with this episode; they would, however, suit a context in 197–8 even better (p. 217, n. 3). On the Antonine Wall Macdonald considered that there was sufficient evidence to suggest a short third period of occupation, a rebuilding after the rebellion; but similar evidence has not appeared in recent excavations, and it is very doubtful whether the indications mean more than that preliminary preparations had been put in hand.[29]

It seems clear that Ulpius Marcellus carried out a series of punitive expeditions [30] and then withdrew once more to Hadrian's Wall. If he had planned to rebuild the Antonine Wall, he abandoned the attempt before work had proceeded far.[31] He probably also withdrew the troops occupying Newstead and other forts beyond the Wall on Dere Street. The evidence at Newstead is ceramic,[32] but we also have the evidence of a Severan inscription at Risingham,[33] which records the rebuilding about 205–8 of the fort gateway and walls 'which had collapsed through age'; it is sometimes thought that this was a euphemism for enemy destruction, but it is simpler to take it literally (p. 384) as evidence of abandonment. Moreover, two inscriptions from Benwell suggest that there was some reorganisation on the Wall itself.[34]

Such a withdrawal after a victorious campaign would have been accompanied by appropriate treaty arrangements with native states, all the more so if Roman garrisons were removed from their territories. It was surely now, as a result of these arrangements, that the confederacy of the Maeatae came into being. In the time of Severus we found Scotland divided between two great confederacies into which the individual tribes had merged themselves. The Maeatae lived 'close to the Wall which divides the island into two parts', and the Caledonii 'beyond them'.[35] It is sometimes argued that the wall referred to was the Antonine Wall; but this does not suit the context in Dio's narrative who, writing of events in 208, must mean Hadrian's Wall, recently reconditioned by Severus. The Selgovae, then – though not the Votadini, who already had their own treaty with Rome – had beccome part of the Maeatae, but the evidence of place-names shows that this confederacy included land north of the Forth which in Antonine times had been under Roman protection. We know also that in 197 the Caledonians 'had broken their undertakings'.[36] This is suggestive evidence for the work of Marcellus, who will have imposed those undertakings on the Caledonii [37] as well as forming a separate confederacy to counterbalance them in lands more easily supervised by Rome. The price paid for the friendship of this new Maeatic confederacy was withdrawal of direct control by Roman garrisons. Such a policy was fully consistent with the new policy which Commodus had already initiated on the Danube in order to bring Marcus' long wars in that region to a close. There, in return for the surrender of prisoners and deserters and the supply of 13,000 native troops, the renunciation of inter-tribal warfare and the control of assembly, the occupying armies were withdrawn and Roman subsidies were paid. It was a policy which was to be resumed in Britain with great success by Caracalla.

It had been necessary to build the Antonine Wall in order to enforce Rome's will on the refractory tribes of southern Scotland, for the Hadrianic frontier had proved too remote for active intervention. But now, forty years later, direct rule had done its work. Under Commodus a new phase opened in which Roman influence was accepted in the Lowlands in return for local autonomy, and the tribes could accordingly be used as a buffer between Hadrian's Wall and the North. The new policy was rightly conceived once its prerequisites had been achieved, and as re-established by Caracalla was to ensure almost a century of peace. But its smooth initial development was first to be interrupted in the years 196–211 by events and temptations which could hardly have been foreseen. Moreover, the third-century scheme included careful provision for Roman supervision, which the present scheme under Commodus neglected to provide.

Whether the achievement of such a result within a limited time had been the purpose of Antoninus Pius when he built his frontier in turf and timber cannot be asserted, for it by no means follows that turf-work was regarded as less permanent than stone. Roman policy was empirical, and the Antonine Wall was built in the most up-to-date techniques of Roman field-engineering, and was designed to last indefinitely.

L. Ulpius Marcellus was a stern unlikable man, of austere self-righteous character, famous for his ability to do without sleep and luxurious living, and not above play-acting to increase this reputation. Despite his victories, his governorship ended with mutiny among his forces, and he narrowly escaped execution at the hands of Commodus. The causes of unrest in the army are doubtful. Possibly the new policy in Scotland was not properly understood: possibly no donative had been given as a reward of victory; possibly the governor's heavy hand proved intolerable. At any rate the legions attempted to set up an emperor of their own, a legate named Priscus. Another cause of discontent was the fact that Perennis, Commodus' praetorian prefect, had appointed men of equestrian rank to command the legions in place of their senatorial legates, whether in reaction to the attempted elevation of Priscus or in furtherance of his own designs on the throne. His action can be illustrated by an inscription convincingly assigned to this period by Pflaum, which records the appointment of L. Artorius Castus when praefectus castrorum at York to command two British legions in an expedition sent to suppress a rebellion in Brittany.[38] The appointment of equestrian prefects to command legions became normal practice later, in the third century, but public opinion was not yet ready for the step. The displaced legates were able to win sympathy in Rome, and the British army itself sent a mutinous delegation of 1,500 to Rome to publish its grievances. These troops happened to encounter Commodus near the city, and were able to encompass the downfall of Perennis.

After this Commodus appointed P. Helvius Pertinax to Britain in 185. This man, destined on the assassination of Commodus to become emperor for three months in 193, was of lowly birth but had risen by influence and merit through the normal career of an equestrian official, during which he had served as military tribune in Britain. Later as a Senator he had shown conspicuous military ability and had held the consulship in 174 or 175. Pertinax, like Marcellus, was a disciplinarian, and his qualities were severely tested in the mutinies he had inherited from his predecessor; in one outbreak he was offered the throne, in another he almost lost his life at the hands of a legion. Despite this he had the situation in hand within a year, if coins of 186 with the legend CONCORDIA MILITUM can be taken to refer to this. Shortly afterwards, perhaps in 187, Pertinax resigned on the grounds of his unpopularity with the army. The name of his successor is unknown, but probably in 191 the governorship passed to D. Clodius Albinus, who was certainly in Britain when Commodus was assassinated on the last day of 192.

1. S. H. A., *Vita Ant. Pii*, 5, 4.

2. After him we know no governors until Julius Verus, but it should be noted (*Acta Antiqua*, ix (1961), 199) that two men, P. Cluvius Maximus and T. Flavius Longinus, had careers which suggest they may have governed Britain during this period.

3. Nevertheless, about 850 acres of turf – about 1⅓ square miles – had to be cut for the rampart, corresponding to a band 63 yards wide right across the isthmus.

4. What is possibly a fourth can be seen at Rough Castle.

4a. For another, highly ingenious, theory accounting for the change in measurement, which, however, rests on too many imponderables, see Sir George Macdonald, *The Roman Wall in Scotland* ² (Oxford 1934), pp. 393–400.

5. Pausanias viii, 43, 4.

6. Juvenal's talk of *Brigantian hill-forts* (xiv, 196) is equally loose, for Brigantia is one of the few areas where hill-forts are notably rare (p. 72).

7. D. Baatz, *Kastell Hesselbach* (Limesforschungen xii (1973), pp. 70 ff.

8. *RIB*, 1583, an altar bearing a dedication to Jupiter, Cocidius, and the Genius of the Place by *Milites Legionis II Augustae agentes in praesidio*. This lacks a date, but its context is provided by the others.

9. On present evidence these included Ebchester, Melandra, Slack, perhaps Lancaster, and probably the fortlet at Castleshaw.

10. As suggested by Birley. Degrassi proposes him for 154, but this scarcely leaves room for the Lower German command, even if he left for Britain in emergency. For his career see *ILS*, 1057, 8974.

11. Capitolinus, S.H.A., *Marcus*, 8, 7: *imminebat etiam Britannicum bellum . . . et adversus Britannos quidem Calpurnius Agricola missus est.*

12. *CIL*, xvi, 130. Better readings are probably . . . *annus Len (tulus)* or . . . *anus leg (atus)*.

13. His career is outlined in *ILS*, 1092.

14. *JRS*, xxxiv (1944), 87, No. 4; *AA*⁴, xxi (1943), 245, *RIB*, 1149.

15. *RIB*, 1389.

16. *Archaeologia Aeliana* ⁴, xlii (1964), 1–39.

17. *Britannia*, iii (1972), pp. 1–55.

18. The garrison was presumably the *Ala Petriana milliaria* which normally occupied Stanwix when Hadrian's Wall was in use. The move is not attested by inscriptions but the plan of the fort at this date seems to make it certain.

19. Calpurnius Agricola is mentioned on inscriptions at Corbridge and Carvoran, Ribchester, Chesterholm and Hardknott Castle; and there is a contemporary inscription from Ilkley (dated between 161 and 169). Of these the stones from Carvoran and Ilkley are altars

not building-records, but testify to occupation. The rest of the forts on fig. 7 (p. 183) are inserted on the map on the evidence of pottery. The heavy reoccupation of the Pennines can be appreciated by a comparison of the map with fig. 6 (p. 168), the map of forts occupied under Pius. It will be understood that the evidence on which figs. 3–7 are based is of very varying quality, and no fidelity is claimed for them in detail.

20. See p. 185.

21. The date of the Intermediate Wall, though not completely certain, is usually taken to be as stated in the text; the less likely alternative is that it was built at the very end of Hadrian's reign.

22. I have used a list of regiments compiled by Professor Birley which he kindly made available to me; the list is so nearly the same as that printed by Grace Simpson, *Britons and the Roman Army* (London, 1964), pp. 181–2, that I have not thought it necessary to print a list here.

23. Castell Collen, Trawscoed and Coelbren.

24. Tomen y Mur.

25. S.H.A., *Marcus*, xxii, 1: *imminebat et Parthicum et Britannicum bellum*.

26. *CIL*, xiii, 6806.

27. Dio, lxxiii, 8. Another governor of the same name, perhaps his grandson, is recorded in Lower Britain forty years later (p. 206).

28. *RIB*, 1329.

29. The evidence has been re-examined in detail by Steer (*AA*[4] xlii (1964), 29–39): apart from one or two repairs which might have taken place during the second occupation, the structural evidence is consistent with levelling and tidying up either in the course of evacuation or preparatory to rebuilding.

30. An inscription from Carlisle (*RIB* 946) and dated by Rostovtzeff to the reign of Commodus (*JRS* xiii (1923) 96), refers to the 'rout of a huge multitude of barbarians'.

31. There are two altars from the Antonine Wall which must be later in date than 165. The first (*RIB*, 2148), found just outside the fort of Castlecary, was set up by men of Legio vi who described themselves as *cives Italici et Norici*; Dr J. C. Mann (*Hermes* 91 (1963), 487), has shown that they are likely to be transfers from Legio ii Italica which was first raised in Italy in 165 and then served in Noricum from 171. A vexillation might have been spared to help in Britain after the conclusion of the Marcomannic Wars in 180; it cannot be as late as Severus, by whose time all the original Italians will have been discharged. The second altar was found in the fort ditch at Old Kilpatrick (*Britannia*, i (1970), 310), and was set up by *Cohors i Baetasiorum* under the supervision of a centurion of Legio i Italica (which was stationed in Lower Moesia). One possible context for the presence of this centurion in Britain is the campaigns of

Severus, for Severus relied heavily on vexillations from the Rhine and Danube legions; but there is really no indication, in archaeology or in probability, that Severus was intending to rebuild the Antonine Wall at that time (p. 201). The Baetasii were at Bar Hill in 159–63 and at Maryport later. Their presence at Old Kilpatrick, together with the centurion from Moesia, is best explained in the context of Ulpius Marcellus, whose date is close enough to 200 to cover the supposed 'early third-century character' of this altar. He too could have been reinforced with continental legionary vexillations now that the Marcomannic war was over. Both altars imply the presence of troops on at least a semi-permanent footing and thus are to be associated with the Antonine Wall third period rather than with mere passage on campaign.

There are also on record two coins, possibly of Commodus, one from Bar Hill and the other from Kirkintilloch (but they are of doubtful significance); and there is a third, better attested, of *c*. 174, from Mumrills.

32. *Britannia*, iii (1972), 53.

33. *RIB* 1234 (=*ILS* 2618): *portam cum muris vetustate dilapsis*.

34. The temple of Antenociticus (which seems to have been finally destroyed in 197) contained two late Antonine altars, one dedicated by the milliary Cohors I Vangionum, the other by Tineius Longus, prefect of cavalry (see *RIB* 1328–9). Longus was at Benwell in 180, so presumably the Vangiones arrived as the result of troop movements by Ulpius Marcellus.

35. Dio, lxxvii, 12.

36. Dio, lxxvi, 9, p. 216.

37. But it is worth noting that there are no marching camps yet known north of the Forth which can be assigned to an Antonine context.

38. H. G. Pflaum, *Les Carrières Procuratoriennes Equestres sous le Haut-empire romain* (Paris, 1960), I, 535; *CIL*, iii, 1919, 8513, 12813; *ILS*, 2770 (uncorrected). The removal of these two legions could hardly have been contemplated until a genuine settlement had been achieved in the north.

9
Severus and the third century

The assassination of Commodus, which was soon followed by that of Pertinax,[1] left open the succession to the Empire; for the provincial armies would not accept the sale of the throne to Didius Julianus by the praetorian guard which then followed. Clodius Albinus, governor of Britain, was one of the claimants, whose noble birth and constitutional reputation gained him senatorial support. There were two other provincial governors who had their armies' backing. Pescennius Niger in Syria controlled nine legions; nevertheless, he suffered the twin disadvantages of long distance from Rome and an army weaker than that which sustained his chief rival. L. Septimius Severus in Pannonia was supported by the powerful legions of the Danube and soon by those of the Rhine also – sixteen in all – and he was able to march on Rome without delay.

Clodius Albinus had the support only of three legions in Britain and one in Spain. He was given the title of Caesar by Severus, with implied right of succession, before the latter marched against Niger; and with easy-going blindness he remained content with this, whether because of the relative weakness of his forces or because of a genuine hope that the arrangement would preserve peace. But after the fall of Niger early in 194 it became evident that Severus had no intention of respecting the claim of Albinus, and a breach was soon inevitable. He was worried by the partiality shown by the senate for Albinus, and sent messengers to kill him. Escaping this danger, Albinus began his preparations;[2] he had himself proclaimed Augustus in 196, and in the autumn of that year he crossed to Gaul with as large an army as he could raise in Britain, and with the support of the garrison of Tarraconensis, Legio VII Gemina. No doubt he hoped to win over the legions of the Rhine; but though he defeated Lupus, legate of Severus, the legions did not come over. His only immediate accession of strength was the Thirteenth Urban Cohort stationed at Lyon, but control of important Gaulish recruiting grounds was now in his hands. The decisive clash took place near Lyon in February 197; Dio gives the numbers involved as 150,000 on each side: and after a hard-fought battle Albinus was defeated and killed himself. Severus exacted heavy punishment, including confiscations of estates, from all who had supported Albinus. This had serious consequences, for instance, to the wine-trade between Spain and Britain (p. 330), and its effects may conceivably be recognisable at certain villa-sites in Britain, for example, Lullingstone (p. 312). Indeed, in 197 Sextus Varius Marcellus, a relative of the emperor by marriage and a Syrian by birth, was despatched as Procurator to Britain; the reason behind this exceptional appointment of an oriental was no doubt to ensure that supporters of Albinus should be hunted out by an officer of un-impeachable devotion to the new ruler's interests.

The military balance between Albinus' legions and those of the Danube army was so adverse that it is clear he must have stripped Britain of every available auxiliary, the security of the frontier (it might be thought) being the only restraining consideration. But in reality the bulk of the forces holding Hadrian's Wall and its vicinity were removed, for the fort of Old Carlisle is the only one in all northern Britain which is known to have retained as garrison in the third century the same regiment which had served that duty in the second. At all the others of which we have record the garrison was different under Severus, and this must be due to extensive re-organisation after the movements and casualties of the expedition and to the fact that a decade passed before restoration could be undertaken.

But if Albinus hoped that existing treaties would hold the Maeatae to their duty and keep the frontier safe, he was miscal-culating the strength of temptation, and forgetting how recent were the agreements by contrast with the long tradition of hostility. Be-hind the Maeatae the Caledonians were active, and in front of them the Brigantian hill-men almost certainly broke out. In Wales also there are signs of rebellion and the destruction of forts. The result of all this was that on the recovery of Britain the government of Severus was faced throughout the military zone with the need to expel the enemy and to restore its military installations. A number of forts on Hadrian's Wall and in the Pennines had been violently destroyed.³ Others needed repairs, and almost all received a change of garrison. It is not always easy to decide whether particular examples of damage or repair were necessitated by hostile wrecking or by the processes of natural decay. The Severan reconstruction of the frontier involved the rationalisation of the turret system, in which a large number were suppressed as well as some of the milecastles. Without special evidence, it would be unreasonable to attribute the demolition of these to the enemy; in others ash from hearths may have been mistaken by early investigators for proof of arson. Nevertheless there remain many signs that Hadrian's Wall had been extensively damaged. In at least three forts destruction by fire has been noted, and at the majority of excavated forts there are indications of demolition and reconstruction, as there are also at many milecastles and turrets. The efforts of someone to lever over the north gate of Milecastle 37 near Housesteads can still be seen and dated to this time, and at other milecastles damage to, or demolition of, gate-piers has been recorded.⁴ At the forts of Housesteads and Birdoswald patches due to rebuilding can still be seen in the fort walls; elsewhere the Wall itself has been rebuilt from its foundation over many hundred yards at a time. All this work seems rather too much for natural decay alone to have caused in only forty-five years, and some of the phenomena are best explained as unhurried wanton damage by people who had no respect for government property and who were motivated by hatred of the Wall and all it stood for. But when reconstruction was put in hand it was naturally extended to other structures where repairs were required. The Wall and its forts, after all, formed a unitary system, and this is the justification for what are called Wall-periods; restorations are more likely in such a system to be widely undertaken along it rather than as unconnected individual programmes at particular forts: rebuilding necessitated by damage in one area might well trigger off a series of less urgent repairs elsewhere.

Much of this destruction must have been the work of local bands of hillmen; forts like Bainbridge and Ilkley lie too far within the hills to be the prey of invaders from beyond the wall, who if they penetrated so far South will have been in search of richer booty. In fact, however, there is little or no evidence for extensive raiding and destruction in the richer parts of northern England. Neither Catterick nor Aldborough appear to have been destroyed at this time, and it is no longer believed that the fortress of York suffered damage.[5] The destruction seems confined to the installations connected with local military control.

But the Maeatae had certainly penetrated into the province and were sustaining the resistance.[6] Virius Lupus was sent by Severus to recover Britain; and, fearing that the Caledonians were about to aid the Maeatae in breach of their agreements, and unable to obtain the forces he required from Severus, he was compelled to pay the latter a large subsidy for their withdrawal, gaining a few prisoners of war in exchange.[7] This was an application of the principle Divide and Rule: Roman policy was perforce to reconquer piecemeal. There are inscriptions recording restoration by Lupus at Brough under Stainmore (dated 197), and at Ilkley and Bowes in the same or early the following year, and an undated one also at Corbridge. The Severan inscription from Ribchester may also very probably belong to this governorship; its date is not earlier than 198. Evidently a methodical restoration of the Pennine forts was under way.[8]

The earliest records of restoration on Hadrian's Wall, on the other hand, date from 205 or later. Fairly clearly there was hard fighting to be undertaken against the Brigantian uplanders, which may have lasted almost a decade. The fort at Bainbridge has produced two inscriptions, one of 205 recording barrack-building under C. Valerius Pudens, and one of his successor L. Alfenus Senecio apparently mentioning work on the annexe wall. Bainbridge is admittedly a remote site in upper Wensleydale, and its rebuilding may have been postponed. On the other hand, the fort at Bowes in Stainmore, whose bath-building had been restored by Lupus, has also produced a building inscription of Senecio, as has that at Greta Bridge. This supports the suggestion that action against the Brigantian hill-men was prolonged;[9] renewed outbreaks may have been precipitated by the restoration of the Wall barrier.

Even so the eight years' failure to reconstitute Hadrian's Wall is curious, since the barrier would have served to cut off the rebels from help in Scotland. Though conceivably due to prolonged and fierce warfare in the Pennines, this failure is much better explained if Lupus and his successors had been instructed to punish the Maeatae by once more taking them under direct rule – in effect to reoccupy Scotland. Such a task, on top of present difficulties in the

Pennines, might well account for the long struggle, especially if the returning Roman forces were seriously depleted. And it might even provide an acceptable context for preparations to rebuild the Antonine Wall (that wall's so-called 'third period'[10]) which were noted earlier (p. 188), as well as the Severan samian noted at Newstead by Hartley. Any such attempt, however, was abandoned by 205, when we find Alfenus Senecio reconstructing the Hadrianic frontier.

Virius Lupus remained governor perhaps until 201 or 202. The date of his consulship is not known, but he was probably legate of one of the German provinces in 196, for he is certainly to be identified with the Lupus defeated by Albinus in that year. In 202 there seems to have been an interregnum, for this is the most likely date for M. Antius Crescens Calpurnianus, who was acting governor while holding office as Iuridicus Britanniae.[11] C. Valerius Pudens will have taken over from him in late 202 or 203, and was in Britain certainly until 205. After holding the command of Lower Pannonia he had been consul probably in 194 and then had governed Lower Germany before holding office in Britain. He was succeeded perhaps in 206 by L. Alfenus Senecio: the date of Senecio's consulship is not known, but he seems to have been governor of Syria [12] in 200. The date of his tenure of Britain is given by the inscription set up between 205 and the end of 207 [13] at Risingham, an outpost fort north of the Wall.

It was in Senecio's governorship that restoration of Hadrian's Wall began, to judge by the inscriptions. We find him restoring the granaries at Birdoswald and probably at Corbridge, and other buildings at Chesters and Housesteads. At Benwell, as already mentioned, his name occurs on a dedication to Victory and Dio, too, writing of 206 alludes to victories in Britain.[14] An inscription on the rock-face of a quarry just behind the Wall near Brampton records legionary work there in 207. Finally, at Risingham Senecio restored a gate and the fort-walls in 205-7. There are also a number of undated inscriptions from the Wall recording work undertaken by civitates in southern Britain – two mentioning the civitas *Dumnoniorum*, one the civitas *Catuvellaunorum*, two the Durotriges Lendinienses and one obscurely referring to a *civitas* Bricic.[15] It is certain that the civitates took no part in the original building of the wall under Hadrian, and that these inscriptions record a subsequent repair. But whether they should be ascribed to the Severan or Constantian reconstructions – or even to 369 – is not at all clear. They are usually taken to date to the time of Severus.[16]

By the end of 207, at any rate, the military re-occupation of the frontier, its hinterland and its outposts was complete. But there still remained the task of punishing the tribes of central Scotland and of restoring Roman hegemony in the Lowlands. Senecio lacked the forces necessary for such an enterprise, and according to Herodian [17] the governor wrote to Severus reporting the military situation as still serious, and asking either for reinforcements or for an imperial expedition led by Severus himself. The latter suggestion was taken up eagerly, for Severus was still ambitious for personal military renown, and was anxious to remove his sons from the temptations of court life in Rome. Despite physical infirmity, which necessitated his travelling in a litter, he made rapid preparations, and in 208 arrived with large reinforcements, including legionary vexillations from the Continent,[18] and new levies raised in Gaul and Britain, and accompanied by the empress Julia Domna, his two sons Caracalla and Geta, Papinian the praetorian prefect, Castor one of his confidential freedmen and a staff of high-ranking senators. Imperial headquarters were set up at York, and peaceful overtures from Scotland brushed aside. The campaigns were to be under the direction of Severus and his elder son; Geta, the younger, was put in charge of the province in the rear.

The accounts of the campaigns which have come down to us in the writings of Herodian and Dio are meagre in content and hostile in outlook, nor is their confusion at present greatly illuminated by archaeological evidence. According to the historians, the first objective was the Caledonians, and this campaign we may assign to the years 208–9. It resulted in a cession of territory by the Caledonians. The next year (210) saw a revolt of the Maeatae, against whom Severus could not campaign in person owing to illness, but sent Caracalla instead. Victory, however, did not end the war, for the Caledonians prepared to take a further part, and Severus was making ready for a personally conducted expedition when he died at York on 4 February 211. The whole impression given is of ineffective counter-marching and of inability to bring the Caledonian guerrilla fighters to action.

Archaeology can point to military building at Corbridge, including two granaries [19] and the great unfinished store-building known as site xi. This has been variously interpreted by Professor Birley as an unfinished headquarters building for a projected legionary fortress, and as the forum of a projected civitas; but the evidence is still in favour of its being a courtyard store-building comparable to those which exist at *Vindonissa, Novaesium, Carnuntum* and *Lambaesis*. If supplies were originally ordered to be assembled at Corbridge for an orthodox penetration up Dere Street into Maeatian territory it would seem that the plan was soon changed; for other evidence suggests that instead an amphibious expedition was substituted with objectives much farther north. An inscription from Rome, assigned on reasonable ground to this period by Pflaum, suggestively records the combination of the fleets of Germany, Moesia and Pannonia under one command with the Classis Britannica.[20] At South Shields a second supply base was built, for the fort there contains an unusually large number of granaries of this date – at least twenty instead of the normal two – sufficient, it can be calculated, to house three months' rations for 40,000 men. It has also yielded a collection of numerous lead seals, many of them bearing the heads of Severus and his sons and the inscription AVGG; these indicate the arrival of baggage and stores in bulk no later than 209. These supplies were assembled on the south side of the Tyne Estuary, which has no direct land communications northwards, but which gives ready access to the harbour. Likewise in Scotland the only forts hitherto showing Severan occupation are Cramond on the south shore of the Forth, and Carpow on the south shore of the estuary of the Tay. It is significant that with the possible exception of Newstead no forts in the Lowlands were re-occupied, though some marching camps in this area may be Severan, dating from the campaign of 210, and of course the bulk of the army proceeded by land towards the territory of the Caledonii in 208–9. Cramond was a fort of six acres; but Carpow was a much larger fortress, apparently about thirty-two acres in area, and probably intended for part of Legio VI, many of whose tile-stamps have been found there. The placing of a large legionary force at Carpow may be the context of the cession of territory by the Caledonians, though it is probable that the lands of the Votadini were enlarged at their expense also (p. 208f.). As well as these two permanent posts, there are marching camps in north-east Scotland which are likely to be Severan, though precise dating evidence is not yet available. These are the 63-acre and 130-acre camps noted earlier (p. 131), together with the four 165-acre camps leading north from Newstead which seems to have been the marshalling point of the land-forces. The 63-acre camps are earlier (but not much earlier) than the 130-acre series, and both types are closely associated in details of castrametation and often on the ground also. We may assign the smaller camps to the campaign of 208 and the 130-acre ones (large enough for three legions and an equal number of auxiliaries) to the year 209. Virtually the complete campaign of 208 can thus be traced from the crossing of the Forth near Stirling to that of the Tay at Carpow; then northwards, east of the Sidlaw hills, to the North Esk river at Keithock and back down Strathmore; it ravaged much of the fertile heartland of the Caledonii. The second campaign traverses Strathmore and penetrates beyond the North Esk at least as far as Kair House; the slightly smaller camps beyond this are perhaps unconnected (p. 131).

This distribution of forts – and camps – allows us to form certain conclusions about Severus' purpose. It is evident from his neglect to garrison the Lowlands that he was not intending a permanent occupation of Scotland. Rather we may feel confident that he wished to remain as mobile as possible and to retain the maximum intitiative for strikes deep into Caledonia from a few permanent bases on the east coast. We may also suppose that the Maeatae in the Lowlands were not at first regarded as a serious problem, for otherwise it would have been impossible to by-pass them as he did.

There is also numismatic evidence bearing on the war. Coins of 208 record the *Profectio Augustorum*, and there are also two remarkable issues of the same or the following year portraying two different bridges. The issue of Severus shows what looks like a permanent bridge with towers at either end; that of Caracalla is a bridge of boats with the legend *Traiectus*. Coins of 209 also portray Neptune and Oceanus, and other issues of this and the following two years make frequent reference to *Victoriae Brittannicae*.[21] Taken with the other evidence, these coins reinforce the idea of a sea-borne expedition, and the bridge coins may have reference to the bridging of the Forth or Tay or both. At Carpow a large enclosure has been found which is probably the bridgehead of the bridge of boats. Severus' first objective may have been Fife, for which the Agricolan road via Stirling lay too far west; and these considerable engineering works would be the context for the confused references to dyke-

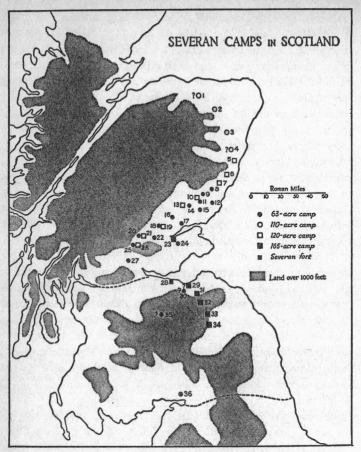

8 Severan marching camps in Scotland (pp. 131, 200–1)

building and filling up marshes (for the approach-roads) and to bridge-building, to be found in Herodian and Dio.[22] Beyond Fife the line of marching camps runs on at least to Aberdeen, reminding us of Dio's statement that Severus did not desist before approaching the extremity of the island, where he made accurate observations of the sun's height in summer and winter respectively.

Dio suggests that after the death of Severus Caracalla immediately concluded peace, withdrew the garrisons and returned to Rome. But in fact the arrival of Caracalla and Geta in Rome did not occur till late in the year, and coin issues of 212 continue to record their victory;[23] we may believe that Dio's hostility has suppressed a further campaign in 211 which brought the war to a conclusion.[24] Certainly the picture of expensive failure painted by the historians is belied by the subsequent history of the frontier. The Imperial expedition did not conquer Scotland, it is true, but the evidence proves that this was not the intention. In the event both Caledonians and Maeatae learnt their lesson and the British frontier remained at peace until 296.

Our view of Severus' Scottish intentions will affect our interpretation of another important and difficult problem. Herodian tells us that Severus divided Britain into two provinces, and the implication of his narrative is that this occurred in 197.[25] The two provinces, Britannia Superior and Britannia Inferior, soon appear on inscriptions,[26] the earliest of which, however, is later than the death of Severus. Dio implies that Chester and Caerleon were in Superior and York in Inferior,[27] while the Bordeaux inscription [28] of Lunaris tells us that in 237 Lincoln as well as York was in Inferior.[29] This distribution of legions implies that the governor of Superior was a consular and that his colleague in Inferior was of praetorian rank, and this is the situation which indeed reveals itself on the British inscriptions from Caracalla onwards. It seems clear that one of the purposes of the reform was to prevent the concentration of a large army in the hands of a single governor and thus a repetition of the affair of Albinus. Severus similarly divided the command in Syria in 194, and in 212 or 213 Caracalla reorganised Pannonia with the same end in view. But in the reign of Severus himself we have plenty of evidence for the activities of consular governors in the Pennines and beyond. Lupus, Pudens and Senecio were all men of the higher rank. Moreover, none of the inscriptions gives any hint that they were operating outside their proper province.

To explain this contradiction some scholars have suggested that in times of war the governor of Superior took command in the north by virtue of his higher rank; but if one governor were under the orders of the other it would vitiate the purpose of the reform. All we can be certain of is that the situation under Severus himself was not the same as that found later under Caracalla and his successors. There are various possibilities. Collingwood suggested that under Severus Britain was first divided between two governors of *consular* rank, and that therefore governors such as Senecio were in their own province, Inferior.[30] This might still be the correct explanation if we were sure that only vexillations of Legions II and XX, and not the entire units, were operating in the northern wars. But it is far more likely that the whole army of Britain was united for the purpose under single command, and this is implied by the inscription on an altar[31] dedicated in person by L. Julius Julianus, legate of II Augusta, in Northumberland, for the legate is unlikely to have commanded a vexillation.

Another suggestion, first put forward by Ritterling and elaborated by Birley,[32] is that Lower Britain was a procuratorial province under Severus. This suggestion is based on the curious fact that on two inscriptions of Senecio the intervention of the procurator Oclatinius Adventus is attested in the restoration of forts.[33] Certain small areas had been administered by procurators since the beginning of the Empire – the best known is Judaea – but the promotion of procurators to the control of more important provinces – *agentes vice praesidis* – is a feature which develops from the time of Severus. The suggestion, however, leads to difficulties. Not only is there no mention of the phrase *agens vice praesidis* or *proc. et praeses* in the inscriptions concerned; but Birley has been driven to admit that all three legions were probably under the governor of Upper Britain and that the procuratorial province of Inferior was centred on Carlisle with only auxiliary forces under command. This arrangement would make the defence of the frontier an impossibility, as well as once more vitiating the purpose of the reform.[34]

One solution is to reject Herodian's evidence – he is often muddled

– and to attribute the division to Caracalla, c. 213. But a reasonable and less drastic alternative may be that when Severus decreed the division of the province in 197 he did not foresee the long struggle ahead. When the recalcitrance of the Brigantes and the difficulties in the north became clear the division must have been suspended for the duration of the war. All forces must surely have been placed unequivocally under the control of the consular commander. The identity of Britannia Inferior may perhaps have been preserved by appointing a procurator to carry out its civilian administration, but there is evidence against the suggestion;[35] and we may conclude that Senecio was merely making use in the emergency of the particular talents of Oclatinius Adventus. For Herodian and Dio both record his unusual military abilities; he was sufficiently distinguished to be promoted praetorian prefect by Caracalla, and to be offered the empire itself in 217.[36] If civilian working-parties from the civitates were assisting in the work this might be an additional reason for the presence of the procurator.

Under Caracalla, once peace was restored, the two provinces resumed their normal administration. Nevertheless, the two commands even then were not entirely distinct. At Corbridge a military arsenal was occupied apparently for most of the third century by vexillations of legionaries from Upper as well as Lower Britain. In other words, troops from Superior were seconded to Inferior, and movement to and from their bases must have taken place from time to time.[37] It seems likely, too, that the governor of Superior had other rights in the Lower province, to judge by two inscriptions from Greta Bridge,[38] and one from Chesterholm mentioning *beneficiarii* from his staff on duty there. Troops might even be transferred from one province to the other, as must have happened when Cohors I Baetasiorum moved into the new fort at Reculver on the Kent coast (p. 211).

Not many governors of Britannia Superior are known. Geta Caesar had held this office in 208, at least until his elevation to the rank of Augustus in 209. It was quite probably under him that Alban was martyred at *Verulamium* (p. 371). An inscription recently found at Reculver records a consular governor Rufinus; this may have been A. Triarius Rufinus, consul ordinarius in 210, but Q. Aradius Rufinus, consul some ten or fifteen years later, is another and more likely possibility. The names of two others, C. Junius Faustinus Postumianus, who had previously served on Severus' staff in Britain, and T. Julius Pollienus Auspex, are known, but the dates of their tenures are uncertain. Auspex is thought to be identical with the man who governed Numidia *c.* 217–20, and his tenure of Upper Britain, if so, will have fallen in the period *c.* 223–6.[39]

The early governors of Britannia Inferior are better known. C. Julius Marcus is recorded on a milestone from the Military Way and on building records at Old Carlisle and Netherby: he was here in 213–4. His successor was perhaps the elder Gordian, later emperor; an inscription from Chester-le-Street[40] gives part of his name, . . . *diano.* If this is the same governor as that whose name is erased on a stone from High Rochester[41] he was in Britain in 216. It is noteworthy that the names of both these governors had been erased, suggesting that they had incurred imperial displeasure, for what reason we do not know. In 217 and 218 the province was probably held by Ulpius Marcellus the Younger. Two inscriptions from Chesters mention him in conjunction with the Second Ala of Asturians.[42] This regiment was certainly at Chesters in the third century, as two other inscriptions there,[43] dated to AD 221–2 show; and the late Antonine garrison of the fort was Cohors I Delmatarum. Chesters, like other forts in the north, seems to have experienced a change of garrison under Severus. This Ulpius Marcellus cannot therefore be identified with the governor sent by Commodus, but is likely to have been his son; from the location of his activity he must have been a governor of Lower Britain, and these years seem suitable.[44] Modius Julius was governor in 219 under Elagabalus and has left inscriptions at Birdoswald and Netherby.[45] He was succeeded by Tiberius Claudius Paulinus. This man had been commander of Legio II Augusta, after which he had been appointed to two successive governorships in Gaul before returning to take charge of Lower Britain in 220. A letter of his addressed from Tampium to a Gallic friend, Sennius Sollemnis, offering an appointment with Legio VI, survives on an inscription in Normandy, and his name recurs on a stone at High Rochester.[46] Before the end of 221 he had been succeeded by Marius Valerianus, who left inscriptions at Chesters dated 221, Netherby (222) and South Shields, and who thus overlapped the accession of Severus Alexander in March 222. His successor in 223 was Claudius Xenophon, known from inscriptions from Cawfields and Chester; he was followed by Maximus, who restored a granary at Great Chesters in 225.

The two emperors Caracalla and Geta returned to Rome in 211 after their British victory, but within thirteen months of Severus' death Caracalla encompassed his brother's murder, and thereafter was sole ruler. Geta, however, had been popular with the army, and there were protests from the troops in Italy. It seems that the Army in Britain, too, went through a period of insubordination in 212, for in 213 a number of inscriptions were set up in uniform terms throughout the north under Julius Marcus, declaring the loyalty and devotion of the troops to Caracalla and his mother. Examples have been found at Risingham, High Rochester, Carrawburgh, Chesterholm, Great Chesters, Whitley Castle, Old Carlisle, Old Penrith and perhaps Ambleside and Netherby. They have every appearance of a demonstration officially enjoined, and it was not until after this public penitence that the regiments of the British army were accorded the title *Antoniniana*, or Caracalla's Own.[47]

Caracalla's settlement of the northern frontier was based on renewed treaties with the Caledonians and Maeatae, and though the details are unknown, their general character can be assumed from similar arrangements on the Continent. Subsidies were sometimes paid in return for renunciation of inter-tribal warfare, control of assembly and the provision of troops. We are told that he withdrew garrisons; this perhaps refers to the evacuation of Cramond and Carpow.[48] We know, too, that *Brittones dediticii*, that is tribesmen who have made unconditional surrender, were transferred to the German frontier accompanied in at least one case by a staff of *Brittones gentiles*, or allied tribesmen. Control of assembly may perhaps be deduced from the record of the names of *loca* in the Lowlands, which have been interpreted as legal meeting-places, no doubt under supervision.

This experiment of a treaty relationship had been introduced by Commodus – so it has been argued (p. 188f.) – but this time a better scheme of supervision was organised. The Severan reconstruction of Hadrian's Wall, though sufficient in its reputation for Spartian writing in the fourth century to give Severus the credit for its inception,[49] differed in significant detail from the arrangements of Hadrian. The Vallum was not restored. Some turrets on the central crags were suppressed, the ruined wall being rebuilt across their recesses, and the gateways of the milecastles were narrowed – or in one case walled up altogether.⁵⁰ Clearly lateral signalling along the whole wall and the surprise appearance of large forces from concealment behind it were no longer envisaged. Instead the wall was now planned to be the base for support of forces acting well in advance of it. The Hadrianic outpost forts of Birrens, Netherby and Bewcastle were restored, and two further outpost forts were added on Dere Street at Risingham and High Rochester. At least four (the name of the garrison at Birrens is not known) were held by part-mounted milliary cohorts, and the last two by additional units as well. Risingham was the headquarters of a Numerus Exploratorum (scouts) and a vexillation of Raetian Gaesati (javelin-men) in addition to the regular Cohors I Vangionum. High Rochester had a Numerus of scouts as well as Cohors I Vardullorum. To judge by its name – Castra Exploratorum – Netherby, too, was held by scouts as well as by its attested garrison Cohors I Aelia Hispanorum. The accommodation offered by the forts is not large enough to contain all these men, the irregulars being doubtless outposted from headquarters in the forts; in this connection attention has been drawn to two inscriptions from Jedburgh relating to the first cohort of Vardulli and the Raetian Gaesati respectively. These suggest that one such outpost lay at the crossing of the Teviot. Another may have been at Tweedmouth, where a Roman military site has produced a scrap of third-century pottery.

Some forts on the Wall were similarly over-garrisoned. At Housesteads in addition to Cohors I Tungrorum, a milliary unit, inscriptions record also a Cuneus Frisiorum, a small unit of irregular cavalry, and the Numerus Hnaudifridi, a unit of Germans. At Great Chesters some Raetian Gaesati were present in addition to Cohors II Asturum, and at Burgh by Sands a Cuneus Frisiorum and later a Numerus of Moors supplemented the regular milliary cohort. Similarly Castlesteads was the headquarters of a milliary cohort, though it was a fort designed for only 500 men.

North of the Wall, which continued to limit the field of action on the south, there thus existed a heavily defended zone, beyond which the Exploratores surveyed a farther area, basing themselves upon such posts as Jedburgh or Tweedmouth; and the *loca*, which they may be expected to have supervised, extend to the Tay. It is also probable that the Votadini now received as an addition to their tribal territory some of the lands surrendered in central Scotland – they certainly possessed them in the fourth century. The unfortified farms and settlements with circular stone walls carry on in all this area in the third century, and may even extend through Fife. It is clear that the peace was guaranteed by Roman forces throughout the Lowlands, and possibly even throughout the whole area ruled by Rome in the Antonine period. In effect, a protectorate existed over the tribes of southern Scotland, and the frontier of Roman Britain more closely approximated to the true geographical border between England and Scotland. Pottery was being exported from the province, for instance to Traprain Law.

In Wales the situation is not so clear. There are, however, here and there suggestive hints of destruction at the end of the second century comparable to those found in the north. The fort at Forden Gaer seems to have been burnt once more. At Brecon the well in the headquarters was filled with rubbish, and traces of fire were found at the gates. At Caerhun the headquarters' well was similarly filled with broken building-stones. It is possible that reconstruction observed at Gelligaer belongs to this period. Extensive reconstruction was undertaken in Severan times at Caersws, Castell Collen and Caernarvon, where an inscription of 198–209 also records the reconstruction of aqueducts, and perhaps at Brecon too. This suggests that in Wales also rebellion had broken out when Albinus removed the garrisons; and the diversion of troops for its suppression may account for the difficulties of Lupus in the Pennines. But the situation was in hand by 209, since the Severan inscriptions at Caerleon and Caernarvon were erected before that year, and road repair was in progress in Caernarvonshire as indicated by a milestone of 198–209. Reconstruction, however, continued leisurely, for the amphitheatre at Caerleon and certain of the interior buildings contain tile-stamps of Caracalla or Elagabalus. This may have been partly due to the absence of detachments of Legio II Augusta in the north, which themselves reinforce the conclusion that Welsh resistance was not severe. As late as 219 vexillations of Legions II and XX from Upper Britain were assisting the reconstruction of Netherby.

Reconstruction and the provision of amenities proceeded in leisurely fashion also in the north. We have inscriptions of the reign of Caracalla recording building at Old Carlisle (213), Risingham (213 or later), Chester-le-Street (aqueduct and baths, 216(?)) and Whitley

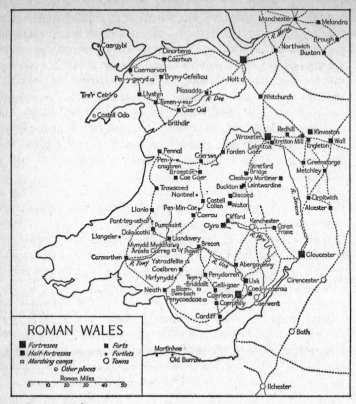

ROMAN WALES

- ■ Fortresses
- ▪ Half-fortresses
- ▫ Marching camps
- ○ Other places
- ■ Forts
- ▪ Fortlets
- ○ Towns

Roman Miles
0 10 20 30 40 50

9   Roman Wales

Castle; and at High Rochester ballistaria were under construction in
216. Under Elagabalus work is recorded at Birdoswald (east gate)
and Netherby in 219, and at High Rochester (more ballistaria) in
220. Under Severus Alexander principal buildings were being provided at Chesters in 221 and 223–5, a cavalry exercise hall at
Netherby in 222 with a temple perhaps in the same year, a gate and
towers at Chesterholm in 222–5, an aqueduct at South Shields in
222–3, granaries at Great Chesters in 225, a temple at Ribchester in
225–35 and more ballistaria at High Rochester within the same
period. At the legionary fortress of Chester reconstruction of the
principia and some barracks was being undertaken about this time.
It is noteworthy that some of these records refer to exercise halls,

temples, aqueducts or ballistaria (artillery platforms) – buildings, in other words, which are not of primary necessity – for otherwise we might have wondered whether so much reconstruction did not imply hostile activity. But the truth is probably revealed by the Netherby inscription [51] of 222 which records the completion of a cavalry exercise-hall 'whose foundations were laid long ago'. It is also remarkable that the granaries renewed at Great Chesters in 225 and the temple at Netherby were described as old and ruined (vetustate conlabsa), and this serves to remind us that not all buildings were everywhere laid flat in frontier disasters – witness the granary at Haltonchesters which survived from Hadrian till 296 with only minor repairs.

A further problem of defence, destined to become more serious half a century later, was now beginning to arise. Saxon pirates and raiders were making their appearance on the east coast, where two large inlets, the Wash and the Thames estuary, opened invitingly towards the most prosperous parts of the civil zone. Coin hoards in East Anglia, Kent and along the south coast, increasing sharply in numbers in the reigns of Marcus and Commodus, suggest insecurity here before the end of the second century: they do not occur in such numbers again in these parts until the reign of Postumus. The Classis Britannica, based partly on Boulogne and partly on British ports such as Lympne and Dover, where a second-century inscription and a fort respectively attest its presence, was not able to keep the seas clear, for ancient warships had not the range or sailing capabilities for effective permanent patrol. Early in the third century a new fort was built at Reculver on the north coast of Kent, and thither was transferred Cohors i Baetasiorum. The foundation-date is given by an inscription mentioning a consular governor Rufinus: this is probably Q. Aradius Rufinus, consul at some date soon after 225; he will have held Upper Britain a year or two later. The pottery from the primary levels of the fort would suit a date centred on 220. This fort is of a new type, transitional to the fully developed Saxon Shore Forts of the late third century, and in area is almost eight acres. This is much too large for the attested garrison, and we are left to suppose the presence of other forces, no doubt partly naval, in addition. If the Thames estuary was thus protected in the early third century it would be reasonable to expect similar precautions on the Wash, and at Brancaster there is a fort of almost identical type and size. As yet excavation has not been sufficiently extensive to produce firm dating evidence for it, and that it is contemporary with Reculver is at present a matter of inference rather than of proof. A third site which is probably connected with these early measures lies at Caister by Yarmouth at the joint mouth of the Yare and Bure.

The period after 225 becomes increasingly obscure, owing to the lack of historical sources and the growing scarcity of inscriptions. Three further governors of Britannia Inferior are known in the reign of Severus Alexander, but no dates can be assigned to them. Claudius Apellinus restored a ballistarium at High Rochester; Calvisius Rufus was responsible for a building at Old Penrith, and Valerius Crescens Fulvianus restored a temple at Ribchester. Under Gordian III (238–44) the most notable event was the refoundation of the fort at Lanchester after a period of disuse lasting from 196; but the motives behind this reinforcement of the garrison in Durham remains obscure. It was a fort of almost 5½ acres, held in the second century by a milliary part-mounted cohort; but now it was provided with a double garrison similar to the frontier forts – the Cohors I Lingonum, 500 strong, part-mounted, and a vexillatio Sueborum, irregular German cavalry. The fort was large enough to hold both groups without out-posting. Rebuilding at the site is attested under two governors, Maecilius Fuscus and Egnatius Lucilianus. The predecessor of the former had been a certain Tuccianus (the name is not quite certain), who was responsible for a building at Carrawburgh in 237 under Maximin. Lucilianus, who is mentioned also on a dedication at High Rochester, was succeeded by Nonius Philippus, whose name occurs on a dedication dated 242 at Old Carlisle. None of these men is otherwise known. The lack of information about all the governors of Britannia Inferior is no coincidence. The province was becoming a backwater of the *cursus honorum* to which prominent men were no longer sent. This gives us the measure of the success achieved by the new frontier arrangements.

It is possible that the reoccupation of Lanchester was part of a wider military reorganisation by Gordian III. Certainly by the reign of Philip (244–9) the Cuneus of Frisiones, which from the time of Caracalla had been part of the garrison of Burgh by Sands on the Wall, had been moved to Papcastle (taking the title *Aballavensium* from their former station),[52] and by the joint reign of Valerian and Gallienus (253–9) their place at Burgh by Sands is known to have been taken by the Numerus Maurorum Aurelianorum.[53] The reasons behind these troop movements are not clear.

The early third century was a period of social advance in Britain. Pausanias' reference to the deprivation of the Brigantes by Antoninus Pius of most of their territory (p. 173) has sometimes been taken as referring to grants of Brigantian lands to legionary veterans at the foundation of the colony of York at that period. But the first evidence for the colony's existence comes almost a century later, on the Bordeaux inscription of 237 (p. 219, note 28), and it is more probable that the charter was granted by Severus, not to a settlement of veterans but as a promotion of the large civil settlement which had already grown up across the river from the fortress. Grants of higher municipal status to existing towns became more common after the time of Hadrian when the practice of founding military colonies was given up; and such titular grants did not involve a redistribution of land. The Castleford milestone[54] of 251–3 records a distance of twenty-one miles from York, not because the colony possessed a territorium but because it was at that date the provincial capital. York now entered upon a period of wealth and prosperity, and as the administrative centre of the north it exerted a wide Romanising influence.

In 212, or as is now suggested, 214, Caracalla issued his famous edict conferring Roman citizenship on all free subjects of the empire.[55] The effects of this are likely to have been particularly wide in Britain, where in the nature of things Roman citizenship will have been proportionately rare hitherto. It had the effect of levelling privileges but also of increasing them for the majority; in particular, it will have enhanced the position of the towns (p. 353).

Other reforms introduced by Severus and his successors which greatly affected the military zone were the grant of the legal right of marriage to serving legionaries as well as the right to farm, and the grants of land to frontier units which could be divided among the men as allotments. The Sarmatians, originally brought to Britain in 175, were similarly provided as veterans with a block grant of land near Ribchester, and during the period there was a great development of the civil settlements which had always tended to arise round established forts. On Hadrian's Wall they were even allowed to extend into the former controlled zone north of the Vallum, spreading over its filled-in course. From such settlements, to which retired soldiers naturally gravitated, a good flow of new recruits might be expected to present themselves; for local recruitment to auxiliary regiments, whatever their titular origin, was another increasing feature of the times, though, of course, known earlier.[56] Some at least of these settlements were allowed a certain measure of self-government (p. 240), and this developed a corporate feeling.

All this naturally resulted in much greater community of sentiment between the garrisons and the local tribesmen, and in this period the long-lasting hostility of the inhabitants of the Pennines seems finally to disappear. The fact was recognised some time during the third century by the creation of a new *civitas* of the Carvetii in the Eden valley,[57] first attested in the reign of Postumus (259–68). It was perhaps centred on Carlisle, which had by now grown into a sizeable town of seventy acres; the area occupied by the *civitas* may be indicated by the location of the inscriptions mentioning it and by the milestone at Middleton giving a distance of 53 miles from Carlisle.[58] The Ribchester area, however, with its special problems, was separately administered as a regio by a *praepositus* who was also commander of the fort there. The two known holders of the office were seconded legionary centurions.[59]

With the murder of Gordian III in 244 there opened a period of grave trouble for the Roman Empire in general. In the forty years between this date and the accession of Diocletian in 284 at least fifty-five emperors or Caesars were proclaimed, and many were murdered within a short span of days or months. Not only was there a decay of political coherence and of discipline, evidenced by the elevation of so many pretenders by the various armies; there was also a series of damaging invasions across the continental frontiers of the empire in Europe and Asia; and the internal prosperity of the provinces was undermined by rapidly accelerating inflation, accompanied by debasement of the coinage. The population seriously declined, and increasing use was made of barbarian tribesmen to swell the army: an observer might readily be pardoned for supposing that the Roman Empire was nearing its end.

From all these troubles except that of inflation the provinces of Britain remained for a time relatively immune, and their successful weathering of the crisis distinguishes them from most other parts of the empire except Africa. There were two reasons for this. The English Channel placed them beyond the reach of the barbarians who swept across Gaul, and secondly, the reforms of Severus and his successors had placed the British frontier on a secure footing, and by the partition of the original province had reduced the ability of the British army to make emperors. When Postumus rebelled against Gallienus in 259 and established the Imperium Galliarum, Britain and Spain adhered to him, and the former remained part thereof until Aurelian reunited the empire in 274. Thus, for most of this period Britain remained tranquil. Road reconstruction is recorded under several emperors, notably Philip (244–9) and Decius Traianus (249–51), while at Caerleon the barracks of the seventh cohort of Legio II Augusta were completely rebuilt under Desticius Juba, consular governor of Britannia Superior within the period 253–5.[60] It is clear that the cohort had returned to base after prolonged absence probably in the north; its arrival, perhaps, was part of a rearrangement caused by the despatch of legionary vexillations and auxiliaries from Britain to aid the German campaigns of Gallienus in 255. These later accompanied the Emperor to Pannonia in 260.[61] They never returned, for by that date Britain had fallen under the sway of Postumus and remained under separate rule for fourteen years. Repairs were undertaken at the fort of Lancaster by a governor of Lower Britain named Octavius Sabinus who held office under Postumus.

It was very probably in the period 268–82 that the threat of Saxon sea-raiders first became acute. The burial of coin-hoards in unusual numbers is often a good indication of crisis, and there is a sudden steep increase in hoards belonging to these years which is most remarkable.[62] To this period, too, must belong the earth fort at Richborough, which was apparently designed to transform the great monument there into a look-out post. (pl. 16a). The exact date of this fort is uncertain, but its ditches had not been completed, nor had the entrance yet been metalled when the defences were levelled to make way for the large stone fort. The latter can be attributed to Probus (276–82), and it is evident that the earth fort must be attributed to the immediately preceding years. At Burgh Castle in Suffolk, too, a coastal fort seems to have been begun at about the same time (p. 379). Moreover, the account we possess of Carausius' rise to power (p. 376) makes it very clear how serious the danger was; and when we add to this evidence the great programme of Saxon Shore defence which he took over, and the fact that a number of town walls can be accurately dated to the period soon after 270, it cannot be doubted that although Britain was not invaded and ravaged as Gaul had been ravaged (for the sea-raiders lacked the numbers to achieve such success), nevertheless public security was deeply disturbed by what must have been a number of successful descents.[63] The navigable rivers gave daring pirates opportunity for deep penetration and complete surprise, out of all proportion to their numerical strength.

In the reign of Probus (276–82) two attempts were made to re-establish the Gallic empire. The first of these was an unimportant rising led by an Italian named Proculus, who was said to be little better than a brigand. The ringleader of the second was Bonosus, whose father was a British schoolmaster, though he himself had been born in Spain of a Gallic mother. He had been in charge of the Rhine fleet at Cologne when it was burnt by the Germans, and he rebelled to avoid the consequences of his carelessness. Probus, however, soon put him down; but his attempt may have had repercussions in Britain, where about this time an unsuccessfull rebellion was raised by a governor whose name has not survived. It was suppressed with the aid of Burgundian and Vandal barbarian forces which had been sent only a year or two previously to Britain after their surrender, which followed the great victory of Probus over the invaders of Gaul in 277. Where these German irregulars were stationed is still a problem to be solved, but their presence is a pointer to the growing barbarisation of the army which is a feature of this and the following century.

One of the causes of growing unrest in Gaul and Britain was the monetary policy of Aurelian and his successors, who attempted to reform the coinage by replacing the disgracefully debased issues of the Gallic empire with heavier, more respectable currency. The old coins, it seems, were to be exchanged for new at a very unfavourable rate, and in Britain the unpopular reform was successfully resisted: the new coins are rarely found. It is perhaps the triple facts of the unpopularity of the legitimate régime, the growing insecurity of the times and the increasing barbarisation of the army which explain the swift success of Carausius, who in 286 established a separate empire in Britain itself (p. 376).

1. At the end of March 193.

2. It is suggested below (p. 285) that the towns of Britain were put in a state of defence at this time.

3. The destruction-deposits at Rudchester, Haltonchesters (unpublished) and Corbridge, mentioned on p. 187, better suit this context because the next period at each site is Severan and a gap in the frontier, unplugged for twenty-five years, is inexplicable as well as stratigraphically undemonstrated. If, on the other hand, it was in the reign of Commodus that the Wall was both damaged and repaired, why are there no building-inscriptions of that emperor? And what would then be the significance of all the Severan inscriptions that we do have? And is it possible to conceive that the Maeatae, after wreaking so much destruction in 180, refrained from damage to the forts when they found them empty of defenders in 196–7?

The large group of pottery yielded by the 'destruction deposit' at Corbridge does contain groups of genuinely late pottery, e.g. from a burnt pottery-shop, but much else of it has been shown to be substantially earlier material. If rubbish was not reimported to level up for rebuilding, as seems unlikely since much of the burnt debris lay *in situ*, there were perhaps two fires, the main one (possibly accidental) occurring in the late sixties. A coin of Severus minted in 198 or later is recorded from the deposit. It is clear from its findspot that it came from make-up, since appropriate floor-levels had been removed within the east wing of 'Site xi', the big store-building, by terracing the foundations: the coin may therefore have been dropped after the destruction itself. The absence of 'destruction deposits' below the S-E corner of Site xi is due (a) to proximity to the fort rampart and (b) to the fact that make-up deposits had not yet been laid to level the courtyard when construction was abandoned. Attempts to redate the Corbridge destruction on the evidence of coarse pottery are thus subjective, and would in any case leave a typological gap for the period 180–200. But in the later second century the rate of typological change in coarse pottery was slowing down.

4. Milecastle 37 stands on rock, so the damage is not due to subsidence; and if the Romans themselves had desired to demolish it they would have done so methodically and with the proper tools.

5. On the occasion of rebuilding the York wall, necessitated by collapse, see Baatz, *Gnomon*, 36 (i), (1964), 88 ff.; Frere, *Arch Journ.*, cxviii (1963), 257. It should be noted, however, that recent excavations have revealed traces of a fire which severely damaged the *principia* in the late second century.

6. Dio, lxxvi 5, 4: 'Because the Caledonians did not keep their promises but had prepared to assist the Maeatae . . . Lupus was compelled to buy peace from the Maeatae for a large sum, and he received a few prisoners of war in exchange.' This must mean more

than a belated *threat* of war from the Maeatae if we are to account for the prisoners; it implies a hard-pressed governor facing great military obstacles to the recovery of his province.

7. See the important study of these events by A. R. Birley, *AA*,[4] 1 (1972), pp. 179 ff.

8. It is curious that this mention of the penetration of the Maeatae is the only hint we find in Dio of the extent of the disaster to the frontier. Perhaps we have his abbreviators to thank for this, for we only possess a summary of his account. The strong later tradition, however, which originated with the writers of the fourth century, that Severus was the builder of the Wall, bears witness to the scale of restoration which it made necessary.

9. An inscription near Halifax, dated 208, is dedicated to *Victoria Brigantia* (*RIB*, 627); and one from Benwell (*RIB*, 1337) is dedicated to the Victory of the Emperors in the time of Senecio.

10. And perhaps Virius Lupus is even more likely than Ulpius Marcellus to have been accompanied to Britain by a detachment of Legio I Italica (p. 192, note 31); the other inscription, however, is unlikely to be so late.

11. *ILS*, 1151.

12. *ILS*, 5899.

13. *ILS*, 2618; *RIB*, 1234.

14. Dio, lxxvii, 10, 6.

15. *RIB*, 1672–3, 1843–4, 1962 and 2022: see also 1629 and 2053 for work done by individuals.

16. See, however, p. 394.

17. Herodian, iii, 14, 1. But A. R. Birley (*AA*[4], 1 (1972), 186–7), notes that Herodian is here using one of his rhetorical clichés, and that his account is unreliable.

18. *ILS*, 9123. Severus in all his wars relied heavily on what was virtually a standing army largely composed of vexillations of the Rhine and Danube legions.

19. See *RIB*, 1143, for a reference to the officer in charge of these granaries *tempore expeditionis felicissi (mæ) Brittanic(æ)*.

20. *CIL*, vi, 1643: Pflaum, *Les Carrières Procuratoriennes Equestres sous le Haut-empire romain*, (Paris, 1960), No. 259.

21. For the coins see Oman, *Numismatic Chronicle*, 1931, 137–50, and *RIC*, iv (i), pp. 120, No. 225; No. 786 (=*BMC*, Pl. 52 i); 284, No. 441 (bridges); *RIC*, iv (i), p. 120, Nos. 228, 229, and *BMC*, v, p. 357, No. 5 (Sea gods); ibid., *passim* (Victory).

22. Herodian, iii, 14, 5; Dio, lxxvii, 13, 1.

23. *RIC*, iv (i), pp. 85–6.

24. Further evidence is provided by the inscription from Carpow (*JRS*, lv (1965), 223), which was not set up before 212, and proves that evacuation did not immediately follow Caracalla's return to

Rome. It shows the presence of part of Legio II Augusta at the fortress.

25. Herodian, iii, 8, 2.

26. *CIL*, viii, 2080, 2766 (=*ILS*, 2762), 5180.

27. Dio, lv, 23, 3 and 6. He states that legions II Augusta and XX Valeria Victrix lay in the upper and legio VI Victrix in the lower province.

28. *JRS*, xi, 101, *L'Année Epigraphique*, 1922, No. 116: An altar set up by Lunaris 'Sevir Augustalis of the Colonies of York and Lincoln in the province of Lower Britain'.

29. The lead seal of Lower Britain from Felixstowe (*JRS*, xlv (1955), 147), being a portable object, is not relevant to the question. Nevertheless, the province may have extended thus far to the south-east (p. 242).

30. In this case we would have to suppose that Britannia Inferior, though only possessing one legion, would be deemed worthy of a consular command because of the very large force of auxiliaries it contained: for the other explanation, that Severus intended to enlarge Inferior to include Scotland possibly with an additional legion, is ruled out, as we have seen, by the absence of any hint of an intention to occupy the Lowlands.

31. *RIB*, 1138: cf *CIL*, xi, 4182.

32. Ritterling, *RE*, xii, s.v. *Legio*, 1608–9; Birley, *Archaeologia Aeliana*[4], xi (1934), 131–7, *Trans. Cumberland and Westmorland Ant. & Arch. Soc.*[2], liii (1953), 58–62.

33. Risingham, *ILS*, 2618=*RIB*, 1234; Chesters, *RIB*, 1462.

34. Another suggestion (by J. C. Mann and M. G. Jarrett, *JRS*, lvii (1967), 61 ff.), that in the first division Lower Britain was consular and Upper Britain praetorian, lacks evidence to recommend it.

35. First Virius Lupus is described in the *Digest* (xxviii, 6, 2, 4) as *praeses Britanniae* – governor, in other words, of an undivided Britain; and Herodian himself (iii, 14, 1), refers to Senecio as 'the governor of Britain'. Next, the career of Varius Marcellus (*ILS*, 478), who, as we have seen, was appointed procurator in 197, and who must have remained in Britain several years, describes him as *procurator Britanniae*, not *Britanniarum*, as would have been the case if the division were effective: the same is true of Crescens Calpurnianus *legatus iuridicus Britanniae*, who might have been expected to specify Britannia Superior.

36. Herodian, iv, 12, 1, and 14, 1; Dio, lxxix, 14.

37. As, for instance, the Vexillations of Legions II and XX, who were building at Netherby in 219. *RIB*, 980, Birley, *Governors*, p. 88.

38. Greta Bridge, *RIB*, 745, 747; Chesterholm, *RIB*, 1696.

39. Rufinus, *Antiquaries Journal*, xli (1961), 224–8; *JRS*, li (1961), 191; Postumianus, *EE*, v, 270; Auspex, *ILS*, 8841; *JRS*, xl (1950), 63; A. Stein, *Die Legaten von Moesien* (1940), 83.

40. *RIB*, 1049. See A. R. Birley in M. G. Jarrett and B. Dobson, *Britain and Rome* (Kendal, 1966), p. 59.

41. *RIB*, 1279.

42. *RIB*, 1463–4.

43. *RIB*, 1465–6.

44. If we could assume that Ala II Asturum was moved to Chesters by Ulpius Marcellus I about 184–185 and remained there under Severus, the necessity of supposing two governors of this name would disappear. See p. 188 for similar troop movements at Benwell.

45. *RIB*, 1914; Netherby, *RIB*, 980, with A. R. Birley, *Epigraphische Studien*, iv (1967), p. 88.

46. *CIL*, xiii, 3162; *RIB*, 1280.

47. E. Birley (*Epigraphische Studien*, iv, 10 ff.), has drawn attention to a group of inscriptions attesting the presence of troops from both German provinces *c.* 217; they are thought to have provided a loyal stiffening for the British garrison.

48. Yet the gates of Carpow were rebuilt in stone at some date after 211, and pottery suggests continued occupation for some decades. It is possible that Carpow was retained as an outpost supplied by sea.

49. S.H.A., *Vita Severi*, 18: *Britanniam, quod maximum eius imperii decus est, muro per transversam insulam ducto, utrimque ad finem oceani munivit.*

50. *Archaeologia Aeliana*[4], viii, 319: Milecastle 22, perhaps because it lay close to the Dere Street gate.

51. *RIB*, 978.

52. *RIB*, 883.

53. *RIB*, 2042.

54. *RIB*, 2274.

55. For the date see *Journal of Egyptian Archaeology*, xlviii (1962), 124–31.

56. Cf. Nectovelius, *nationis Brigans*, serving in Cohors II Thracum, who died at Mumrills in the second century (*RIB*, 2142).

57. *RIB*, 933 (tombstone of a man of quaestorian rank *in C. Carvetior.*) from Old Penrith, and new inscription (1964) from Brougham mentioning the *R(es) P(ublica) C(ivitatis) Car(vetiorum)*, *JRS*, lv (1965), 224.

58. *RIB*, 2283.

59. *RIB*, 583, 587.

60. The younger Valerian, mentioned on the stone (*ILS*, 537= *RIB*, 334) died *c.* 255.

61. *CIL*, xiii, 6780 (Legio xx at Mainz in 255: legionary vexillations were always drawn from all legions in a province, so we may be sure that Legio II Augusta was represented). *ILS*, 546 (AD 260).

62. The numbers are as follows: 238–49, 19 hoards (1·7 a year); 253–68, 24 hoards (1·6 a year); 268–70, 23 hoards (11·5 a year); 270–75, 128 hoards (25·6 a year); 275–82, 41 hoards (5·9 a year).

Those closing with coins of the Tetrici (270–3), in particular, are markedly more numerous in eastern England and in the Bristol Channel region than elsewhere.

63. Several sites in Sussex, for instance, seem to have been burnt about this time (e.g. the villas at Fishbourne and Preston and the village at Park Brow).

10

The administration of Roman Britain

When Claudius left Britain he entrusted its government to Aulus Plautius, his legate, and the occupied territory became an imperial province. Under the Roman Republic all provinces had been at the disposition of the Senate; but under the imperial system, though Augustus left to the Senate the control of the more civilised and peaceful districts, where troops were not in general stationed, he himself retained under his personal command the majority of provinces in which permanent garrisons were now being maintained. In this way he was able to remain commander-in-chief of the army without obvious constitutional change. These districts formed parts of his proconsular command, but except when he happened to be present in person, their actual administration was entrusted to deputies, whose title became *Legati Augusti pro praetore*. As an administrative hierarchy evolved, senators who had served the qualifying office of praetor were sent to take charge of provinces containing either no forces at all or no more than one legion; while those with armies of two or more legions were entrusted to senators who had held the consulship. Britain was thus a consular province, but its governor, like other consulars, had the same title of emperor's deputy as his praetorian colleagues in lesser provinces. All ranked as praetors, so that the emperor's proconsular power might remain overriding.

A governor was carefully chosen from the men available for qualities consistent with the policies he was to enforce, as is clear from the careers known to us. Indeed, there is evidence for very careful original selection and subsequent training of all those who were deemed suitable for promotion in the emperor's service. That training was by experience. The Roman empire was sufficiently large to afford its administrators a wide geographical range of opportunity, and the system of promotion normally made sure that a man served in a variety of offices which tested both military and administrative capacity. The direction and level of his abilities would soon be discovered, and his appointments and promotion would be controlled accordingly. Although in theory a man might reach the governorship of Britain with military experience amounting to only a year or two as a legionary tribune at the outset of his career, and a short spell later as a legionary commander, a study of actual careers shows us that, as might be expected, the truth was not so simple or the government so naïve, and that in practice most governors had enjoyed a considerably more protracted experience, especially in the higher ranks.

Vespasian could send three men to Britain direct from their consulships; two of them had had wide previous experience of the province in war as legionary commanders (and Agricola had served his tribunate in Britain as well). This policy bore fruit at the time, but so narrow a specialisation was not usual. By the second century a fairly regular system of promotions had been evolved for those who were being groomed for the command of Britain. After the praetorship the great majority commanded a legion in Upper Pannonia, though a few were given their legion in Lower Moesia or Lower Germany. Pannonia and Moesia formed part of the Danube frontier, where the army was strong and the chances of seeing action high. Thereafter they governed a praetorian province; that selected was often Upper Dacia or else one near the scene of campaigns. After holding the consulship they were almost invariably sent to govern either Lower Moesia or Lower Germany. Then followed the British Command. For almost half of them this was the climax of their career; the others went on either to the seat of a major war or to the crowning glory either of the proconsulship of Africa or some comparable office.

In Britain a governor's duties might be largely military, as was natural to the commander of a powerful army with active frontier commitments; but besides these his responsibilities were manifold. In the first century his work was complicated by the delicate relationships which had to be maintained with client kings, those native rulers who had been left in office under treaty relationship with the

Roman power. At all times his was also the supervision of the civitates, his the responsibility for military recruitment, for road-building and for the functioning of the public courier-system. The governor, too, was the court of appeal in provincial law-suits, and he exercised primary jurisdiction not only in all cases which involved Roman citizens (a growing commitment, this) but in all cases which involved capital punishment or condemnation to the mines or salt-works, and in all civil cases which involved more than a certain sum. When not campaigning, for instance in the winter months, it was his duty to go round on circuit.

In criminal cases a Roman citizen could usually appeal to Caesar, as Paul did, though, where certain crimes and their penalties had been defined by statute, this right may have been curtailed. By the second century most cases which involved the death penalty for citizens were automatically referred to Rome for the emperor's decision, the governor's duty being merely to forward a summary of the facts. For non-citizens, *the peregrini*, the governor's was the final court, and his powers of sentence were limited only by an edict of Hadrian exempting members of the civitas councils from liability to the death penalty. In civil cases of difficulty the governor might seek elucidation from Rome, as we find Virius Lupus doing in an inheritance case quoted in *Digest*, xxviii, 6, 2, 4. By the third century, when citizenship had become universal, a system of regular appeal courts had been evolved for both civil and criminal cases.

The legal aspects of a governor's task were complicated by the variety of codes which might have to be taken into account. Roman law itself was probably binding on Roman citizens and communities, but peregrini still lived under their local Celtic codes of law save in so far as these might conflict with basic Roman principles. To assist the governor in the legal side of his work, and to relieve this heavy burden, Vespasian created a new office, that of *Legatus Iuridicus*. The iuridicus was an officer of praetorian status, responsible to the emperor, but subordinate to the governor; he acted as his deputy in legal matters. The names of five legati iuridici of Britain are known, and at least two were distinguished lawyers. The first recorded holder of the post was C. Salvius Liberalis Nonius Bassus, who was probably appointed as early as 79. He was a member of the younger Pliny's circle and had a reputation for learning. His successor was L. Iavolenus Priscus, another noted legal authority, whose term in

Britain preceded his consulship and the governorship of Upper Germany, and one of whose British cases is cited in the *Digest*.[1]

Iuridici are also found in Spain (as early as *c.* 73), Cappadocia and occasionally elsewhere: so it would be mistaken to seek to account for the creation of the office purely in terms of the needs of Britain.[2] But it is probably no coincidence that the first known holder of the British post was a colleague of Agricola, for it was that governor who doubled the area of Roman Britain, bringing under Roman control for the first time the more primitive peoples of the north, whom Roman army records perhaps distinguish from the Britanni of the lowland zone under the name Brittones. There must have been urgent need of a legal expert on the governor's staff to advise on the frequent problems which might arise over the incorporation of such people within the province, such as how best to adapt the taxation system to cover the semi-nomadic pastoralists who presented a new problem to Roman administration. In an earlier chapter, too, we have noted the achievements of Agricola in extending self-government to new civitates in the south when military government was lifted with the movement of troops to the north. In many cases towns sprang up on the sites of abandoned forts, implying a transfer of Caesar's land to native hands. All this required legal definition – a full-time task. Distinct from such problems, but no less pressing, was the need to relieve a governor so deeply involved in distant campaigns of the routine assize work of the civilian areas. Private litigation was bound to increase with the spread of civilised manners: it is no coincidence that just at this period we begin to find Roman legal terms on tablets excavated in London.

The incorporation of Cogidubnus' dominions after his death may have presented other approximately contemporary problems, but there is no evidence that this in itself had any bearing on the establishment of the post. In the first place we do not know when Cogidubnus died; in the second, such kingdoms had been incorporated before without the intervention of a special officer. The appointment was an administrative convenience which proved of permanent value. In later times we know of C. Sabucius Maior Caecilianus, who became iuridicus of Britain in the last years of Marcus, of M. Vettius Valens, who was so highly regarded that he was appointed Patron of the province, and of M. Antius Crescens

Calpurnianus, who was left as acting governor during his term of office about 202.[3]

Below the governor, and subject to his orders though appointed by the Emperor, were the legionary commanders; they, too, had the title of *Legati Augusti* (though not *pro praetore*) and were of praetorian rank. It is probable that each legion in Britain formed the core of an army district, so that auxiliary regiments would receive their orders from the commanders of the legions to which they were attached. The legates would thus naturally have some responsibility for the administration of districts under direct rule; occasionally they might administer the whole province in the absence of the governor, as happened in 69. From the time of Caracalla the command of Legio VI Victrix at York was combined with the governorship of Britannia Inferior.

Each governor, and legionary legate too, was entitled to bring with him an unofficial staff of friends, his *cohors amicorum*, who would assist him with services and advice. But there was also a regular and permanent staff attached to his *officium* or headquarters, consisting of soldiers seconded from regimental duties. This administrative staff was commanded by a centurion, the *princeps praetorii*, below whom there were three *corniculari* (adjutants), and three *commentarienses* (registrars), assisted by their *adiutores*. The governor also enjoyed the services of thirty *speculatores*, ten from each legion in the province. The duties of these were largely judicial, including the custody and execution of prisoners; but they also carried despatches, for instance, to Rome. In addition to them, there were a large number of *beneficiarii*, who seem often to have been posted in the frontier regions, or at important points on roads farther south, in a way which suggests that their responsibility included the security of supply-routes.[4] Various other grades, such as *stratores* (equerries), also existed whose precise functions are not always certain. Besides these there was a large clerical staff of slaves or freedmen, including shorthand writers, copyists and secretaries. There survives one letter which emanated from the secretariat of the governor of Lower Britain: the excellence of its drafting, in Latin remarkable for its polished terseness and lucidity[5] suggests the high standard maintained by these staffs. Finally, there was also a governor's bodyguard, the *equites* and *pedites singulares*.

The Colony at Colchester was probably intended as the capital of the province originally, replacing as it did the old capital of Cunobelin. But as early as 60 there is evidence that London was taking over its destined pre-eminence, at least for financial administration. By the beginning of the second century a large fort had been established on the outskirts of this city, probably for the governor's guard; but London has also yielded tombstones of soldiers (one of them a centurion) from Legions ii, vi and xx. The presence of men from all three legions suggests attendance at a headquarters. Even more conclusive is the tombstone of a *speculator* from Legio ii Augusta named Celsus, erected for him by one of his colleagues: for such men were detached from their legions for service in the governor's officium.

The only field in which the governor's competence was not supreme was the financial, a responsibility which was in the hands of the Procurator Augusti Britanniae. This official was a member of the Equestrian Order of Roman society which ranked next below the Senatorial. Members of this order under the Republic had enjoyed few official responsibilities, and had earned the reputation of an opposition to the Senatorial government. But under Augustus and his successors, especially Claudius, they had been given the opportunity of a larger share in the administration of the provinces; they came to form in effect a sort of Civil Service, as by degrees a regular hierarchy of office (not, however entirely excluding military posts) was evolved for them. The word *procurator* itself meant little more than steward or bailiff: the importance of the individual depended upon his position in the service. In Britain we know little about the junior procurators who must have served here under the procurator of the province; but by analogy with Gaul and elsewhere we may feel confident that there were procurators of imperial estates,[6] of mines and of the main individual taxes such as customs dues, and the death-duties to which Roman citizens were liable. At their head was the Procurator Britanniae, whose responsibility included receiving the revenue, supplying and paying the army and officials, and superintending the emperor's financial interests.

To achieve Equestrian rank it was necessary to possess capital to the value of 400,000 sesterces. Careers in the equestrian cursus were thus open to many provincials of good family as well as to retired centurions from legions or the guard. As a preliminary to administrative office they normally served what were known as the *tres militiae* in the army: these were successively the offices of prefect of an auxiliary infantry regiment 500 strong, then of military tribune, usually in a legion but sometimes as commander of an auxiliary unit 1,000 strong, and finally prefect of a cavalry regiment 500 strong. A few specially selected officers then served a fourth militia as prefect of a milliary ala, and this distinction usually pointed the way to subsequent high promotion.

Each of these commands might last two or three years, if not longer: thereafter promotion led to junior procuratorships. These men also, therefore, like their senatorial colleagues, gained a wide experience in a variety of duties in many provinces.

The provincial procurator was responsible to the emperor alone, and was not the subordinate of the governor, though his duties normally demanded close co-operation with him. But sometimes, as when Classicianus made an adverse report on Suetonius Paullinus, duty demanded otherwise; and even when it did not, there might often arise a conflict of personality. Tacitus praises Agricola for not antagonising the procurators, and in the *Digest* there is a quotation from the early third-century jurist Ulpian advising a governor not to intervene in financial matters.[7] No doubt the emperor was usually glad to receive independent reports from each official on the activities of the other, and the division of function certainly prevented the too-easy organisation of rebellion. Albinus had already been promoted Caesar before he undertook his expedition.

Procurators were graded according to their salary. The Procurator of Britain, like most other provincial procurators, was a *ducenarius*: he received 200,000 sesterces a year.[8] But though he thus ranked high, the position itself was not often held by men destined for further promotion. We know the names of ten holders of the office, and only three of them can be shown to have risen higher. Catus Decianus was presumably disgraced by Nero, and Classicianus died in office. No details are known of the careers of Ti. Claudius Augustanus (a contemporary of Agricola) or of Q. Lusius Sabinianus (a second-century procurator) or of M. Cocceius Nigrinus (who made a dedication to Caracalla), except the bare fact that they held the office. M. Maenius Agrippa had commanded the British fleet before becoming procurator early in the reign of Antoninus Pius, and this was his last post before retirement. Britain was likewise the last appointment of C. Valerius Pansa, who may have succeeded him.

Cn. Pompeius Homullus, on the other hand, who was procurator of Britain about the beginning of Trajan's reign, went on to be procurator of Lugdunensis and Aquitania in Gaul, one of the most senior ducenarial appointments, and was then promoted to the office of *a rationibus*, the emperor's secretary for finance. The remaining two were Sex. Varius Marcellus, a kinsman of Severus, who subsequently rose high in his service, and Oclatinius Adventus, whose career has already been mentioned (p. 204f.). It is interesting to note the difference in calibre required for the two offices of governor and procurator of the British province. No doubt the small size of Britain and the absence there of major financial problems accounts for the relative unimportance of its procurator.

The headquarters of the financial administration were soon established at London, perhaps even before 60. Catus Decianus certainly seems to have been operating from a centre other than *Camulodunum*, and his successor was buried in London. This city, too, has produced the wooden writing tablet stamped *Proc. Aug. Brit. Prov. dederunt* ('issued by the procurators of Britain'). On analogy with his colleagues elsewhere, the procurator will have had a staff of cornicularii and beneficiarii and other assistants seconded from the army, and will have possessed a *tabularium* or record office; but no evidence for these things survives.

Other Equestrian officials in Britain were few. The Classis Britannica was commanded by a prefect of centenarial rank. The headquarters of this fleet lay at Boulogne, but it had bases in Britain, and much of its duty was performed off the British coasts. Four of its prefects are known by name, and a fifth, whose name is lacking, is attested under Severus (p. 200). Q. Baienus Blassianus held the command under Trajan and L. Aufidius Panthera, who left a dedication at Lympne, was promoted to this post in the later years of Hadrian after serving as prefect of a milliary ala in Pannonia. His immediate successor was possibly M. Maenius Agrippa, a man who was closely connected with Britain all his official life. He had started by commanding an auxiliary regiment of Britons in Moesia, and was then appointed by Hadrian to the command of a cohort of Spaniards and sent with them *expeditione Britannica*. As we have seen (p. 161), the arrival of this and other reinforcements is best placed about 130. After further service in Moesia, Agrippa returned to Britain first as admiral of the classis Britannica and then as procurator of the province. About 150 the fleet was commanded by Sextus Flavius Quietus, who had previously been chief centurion of Legio xx and had led an expedition to aid in the suppression of a Moorish revolt in 145–7. The British fleet was his last command.

One other official of sexagenarial status is known. About 205 L. Didius Maxinus held the office of procurator in charge of the gladiators recruited and trained in Gaul, Britain, Spain, Germany and Raetia. The existence of gladiators in Britain is not without interest, and there is a little further evidence bearing on it (pp. 346–7).

Apart from the *annona*, or levy of corn devoted to feeding the army, the chief sources of revenue were the *tributum soli*, a tax based on the productivity of land, and the *tributum capitis*, or poll tax (which included other forms of property). The former was based on a very careful survey of the land in a census, when every detail of its ownership and yield was recorded. From time to time fresh censuses were carried out, and the importance attached to them can be understood from the fact that a census of Gaul occasionally called for the supervision of the Emperor in person; at other times special high-ranking senatorial *legati ad census accipiendos* were appointed. In Britain it is improbable that special legates were required, but a census may be the reason behind the appointment of Neratius Marcellus as governor about 101; for he was not the normal *vir militaris*, but moved in the upper circles of Roman society, a man more at home with administration than campaigning. From the time of Hadrian special procurators of sexagenarial status were also appointed to assist in the census. The names of two are known. T. Statilius Optatus undertook the duty under Hadrian, and followed it with a similar office in Gaul. M. Arruntius Frugi was *procurator ad census* under Antoninus Pius. Before the reign of Hadrian other sorts of *ad hoc* assistant had been employed. We know of a censitor of the Roman citizens at Colchester who held this post just about the time of Marcellus' governorship, and of a *censitor Brittonum Anavion(ensium)* who held office somewhat later in Trajan's reign,[9] perhaps about 112.

The total number of Roman officials, at least in the civil part of the province, was thus not unduly large. This was made possible by the encouragement of local self-government and responsibility among the conquered people. At first this policy was achieved very largely by the device of client kingship, whereby friendly tribes were left under the rule of their own royalty, with whom treaties were made.

Cogidubnus was the most successful of these kings, but two more are known by name, while the existence of still others may be suspected (pp. 84ff.). Cartimandua was in a class by herself, for her Brigantian kingdom lay beyond the frontiers of the province and was not really under Roman control save at the cost of special military effort. Prasutagus was also outside the province but encircled by it, and Ostorius Scapula felt justified in intervening in the affairs of the Iceni to the extent of disarming them in 47. Cogidubnus succeeded to a kingdom re-created by Roman intervention, and he amply justified the experiment. The monuments of Roman Chichester are the most distinguished of their date and kind in the province, and the early development of villas on the Sussex plain is another pointer to this king's effective Romanising influence.

By degrees, however, a more genuine system of local self-government, which had already proved successful in Gaul, was introduced. This was based on *civitates peregrinae* – self-governing communities of non-citizens. In addition, self-governing towns of Roman or Latin citizens were early established, whose buildings and institutions could serve as models for the others. A Roman colony in the first century was usually still a deliberate settlement of Roman veterans, as it was under the Republic. Colchester was founded in 49, and it had both a military and a civilising purpose, as Tacitus makes clear (p. 98). Towards the end of the first century similar coloniae were placed at Lincoln and Gloucester (p. 146f.). The veterans were Roman citizens, and they were placed in self-governing towns surrounded by a *territorium* of countryside administered from them. At Colchester native *incolae* were allowed a share in the enterprise, to judge by the size of the city. *Verulamium*, founded about the same time as Colchester, was very probably a *municipium*. This was a status given normally to pre-existing towns, and it did not involve a settlement of veterans; the inhabitants might rank as Roman or Latin citizens, depending on the type of grant. *Verulamium* itself was a new foundation but close to an important native centre; it was probably of Latin status. A municipium, like a colony, was a self-governing unit, and possessed a territorium which might embrace all or only part of the tribal lands. In the case of *Verulamium* the extent of the territorium is unknown, but it did not embrace the whole of the huge canton of the Catuvellauni, for the civitas of the

IMP·TITO·CAESARI·DIVI·VESPASIANI·F·VESPASIANO·AVG
PM·TR·P·VIIII·IMP·XV·COS·VII·DES·... G·VIII·CENSORI·PATRI·PATRIAE
ET·CAESAR·DIVI·VESPAS·... NIF·DOMITIANO·COS·VI·DESIG·VII·PRINCIPI
IVVENTVTIS·ET·O... NIVM·COLLEGIORVM·SACERDOTI
CN·IVLIO·A... RCOLA·LEGATO·AVG·PRO·PR·
MVNICIPIVM·V... RVLAMIVM·BASILICA·ORNATA

10 A possible reconstruction of
the Forum inscription at
Verulamium. (At full size the
inscription measures 13 feet
4 inches by 2 feet 4 inches.
Pp. 134, 231.) The pieces
actually surviving are stippled.
Lines 3 and 4 were
subsequently erased, after
Domitian's death and
damnatio memoriae, and they
are only faintly legible.

latter is still separately attested at a later date, though it may have been administered from Verulamium.

Below these self-governing Roman or Latin towns ranked the civitates peregrinae. The difference between them was more than a variation in the status of their respective inhabitants: it was a difference in organisation. A Roman or Latin town possessed an independent existence, being itself both the unit of administration and the legal *origo* of its inhabitants (a person's origo was not necessarily his place of birth but the registered place of family origin which each individual legally required). For the civitates peregrinae, on the other hand, the legal unit was the whole tribal area and not the town at its core. The reason for this was perhaps the absence at first of a satisfactory level of urbanisation. Many tribal areas in Gaul and Britain were of very large size, without predominating towns, and the Celtic aristocracy, which would have to take the lead in the new organisation, was by tradition based on its country estates rather than on towns.

The towns were quickly provided, of course, and were the seat of the local administration, but they did not take over the identity of their civitates until the third century in Gaul, and in Britain may never have done so. There exist sufficient inscriptions which show, on the one hand, a tribal origo [10] and, on the other, a difference of organisation between the capital town and its civitas,[11] to make it quite certain that Roman adaptability did not force an urban mould on a society not yet ready for it.

The existence of civitates in Britain is directly attested by five inscriptions which have been found at Wroxeter, Cirencester, Kenchester, Brougham and Caerwent.[12] Moreover, the capitals of the civitates can be recognised by their nomenclature, for the name of the civitas is added in the genitive to that of the town: Cirencester, capital of the Dobunni, was *Corinium Dobunnorum*. In Gaul in the third century the town name begins to be dropped, so that, for instance, *Condate Redonum* (Rennes) became known simply as Redones; but in Britain we have only one example of this.[13]

The difference between the two types of community was, however, merely one of law and organisation. From the first the Romans sought to encourage the growth of towns. City life was the basis of ancient classical civilisation: a civilised life was inconceivable to men of the Mediterranean world without a city as its stage. R. G.

Collingwood once described the philosophy of the city in a classic passage. 'Deep in the mind of every Roman, as in the mind of every Greek, was the unquestioned conviction which Aristotle put into words: that what raised man above the level of barbarism, in which he was merely an economic being, and enabled him to develop the higher faculties which in the barbarian are only latent, to live well instead of merely living, was his membership of an actual, physical city.' [14] Today our cities are too large and we have to look to smaller organisms, the school, the college, the society or small country town, to find the same nursery of community-feeling that in ancient times was embodied in the city. But city-life was something hitherto unknown to the Celts in Britain as it was to the Germans; urbanisation had to start at the beginning, and the process, although eventually successful, never produced towns of fully Mediterranean character.

Towns were needed not only as centres of local government but also to aid the spread of education and Roman civilisation. To this end models were set up at *Camulodunum* and *Verulamium* where the physical buildings as well as the methods of town life and organisation might be observed; and to this end loans were made and practical assistance in their construction given. It must not be forgotten how new all this was to the Britons of the time of Claudius. Even the oppidum of Cunobelin had been no more than an amorphous collection of round huts and unorganised squalor. By contrast, excavation at *Verulamium* has revealed some of the earliest half-timbered buildings of the new town, which bear the unmistakable stamp of imported architecture, with such close parallels both in structure and in plan to the barracks of contemporary Roman forts that we can be sure that military stockpiles of material were also made available in addition to military technicians. Though the magnitude of the task compelled a certain starkness, the essentials of a classical town were there – the straight streets intersecting at right angles and the colonnaded porticos, albeit of wood.

The organisation of new *civitates peregrinae* followed as opportunity arose and local fitness for the step became apparent. The unit was usually the existing tribal area; but sometimes, as in Kent and Hampshire, new units were created – the Cantiaci and Belgae – where there was no pre-Roman tribe of sufficient size, and in Sussex the civitas of the Regnenses was set up to replace the *regnum* of Cogidubnus. At first large areas had been kept under direct military rule, administered locally by commandants of forts under the supervision of their legionary legates, and in general the development of self-governing civitates will have taken place only when the military moved forward. This will certainly have been true of areas such as Dorset and the South-West which had resisted initial conquest; the Mendips, too, were under military government at first. We have no evidence in Britain for the military *praefecti civitatis*, who in the backward Danubian provinces were charged with the establishment of local self-government and the training of local leaders in its methods; but British tribes were equally backward, and they may have existed;[15] one is known in Holland.

The physical indication of a self-governing community was the possession of a forum with basilica, which housed the meetings of the council and the administration of local justice. The date of the foundation of such fora will give us an indication of the date of the grant of local self-government. Thus, at Chichester and Winchester the fora seem to have been built late in the Flavian period, when Cogidubnus may be expected to have died. The Silchester forum is of about the same date, and all three towns may originally have formed part of his dominion. The fora at Exeter and Cirencester are also Flavian; here this denotes the removal of military control by Frontinus or Agricola. Nowhere indeed is a pre-Flavian forum yet known, except possibly at London, but on other grounds we may expect the Cantiaci, whose capital at Canterbury was first laid out in Claudian times, to have been granted self-government as early. The main development, however, is evidently Flavian.

The erection of a forum with basilica in London in Flavian times shows us that this rapidly expanding town achieved self-government at this time;[16] and as it was never a civitas-capital, we must assume that it became either municipium or colonia. Most probably it was first the one and was later promoted to be the second. Other towns may have risen in rank as time passed, and probably did so, though the fact cannot be demonstrated with certainty in Britain. A Coritanian auxiliary soldier has his origo stated not as *Coritanus* but as *Ratis* on a military citizenship certificate of 106; and, as this class of document is meticulous in its use of terms, it has been suggested that Leicester (*Ratae*) had achieved municipal rank by this date. But the man, M. Ulpius Novantico, was already a Roman citizen as a result of a special grant in the field, and this is plainly the reason why his origo is given in this form, which is normal for Roman citizens; it has no bearing on the status of Leicester. Suggestions of a similar sort for Chester and Silchester are equally poorly authenticated.

Nevertheless, there remains the general probability, based on analogy with the history of other provinces, that some of the more advanced civitas-capitals did achieve higher status during the later second and third centuries. From the middle of the second century new grants of municipal or colonial rank became increasingly common in many parts of the empire, largely as a result of applications arising from local patriotism and rivalry.

There was also a tendency at that time to give self-government to smaller units, so that civitates became subdivided. We have evidence of this latter process in Britain, where the original civitas of the Durotriges, whose capital was doubtless *Durnovaria* (Dorchester), was later split: a new group was created, called the Durotriges Lendinienses, with capital (it has been suggested) at Ilchester. The Carvetii, too, must once have formed part of the Brigantes. But of the promotion of civitas-capitals themselves to *ius Latinum* or colonial status there is no certain evidence. We can only say that it would be surprising if towns in the south, like Cirencester, Leicester or Wroxeter, with their evidence of intense Romanisation, were not rewarded with promotion; or if towns like Carlisle, Catterick or Kirkby Thore in the north, full of retired enfranchised soldiers as they must have been, were not awarded charters. It is, perhaps, worth noting that in the Antonine Itinerary, a road-list attributable to the early third century, it is precisely *Verulamium*, Leicester, Wroxeter and Canterbury which lack their tribal suffixes (as would be the case if they had been promoted to higher status).[17] Cirencester is not mentioned; but it, together with Canterbury, Leicester and Wroxeter, are given their tribal suffixes in the Ravenna List. This, however, since it mentions the forts of the Antonine Wall, is patently based in part on sources no later than the second century, and may possibly thus give us an earlier situation for these towns.

Colonies and municipia had constitutions modelled on that of republican Rome. They were governed by a council or senate known as the Ordo, which was usually about 100 strong and membership of which was limited by a property qualification. The chief executive officers, corresponding to the Roman consuls, were a pair of *Duoviri iuridicundo*, whose title shows them to have been responsible for local justice but who also presided at meetings of the ordo or of the assembly, and bore general responsibility for public shows or religious festivals. They were assisted by two aediles, whose field was the maintenance of public buildings, drains and streets. Often there was a pair of quaestors (whose responsibility was local finance) as well. In some of the older municipia the first two pairs had the title quattuorviri, but under the Empire this had become old-fashioned, and is no longer found, for instance, in Vespasian's Spanish municipal charters. Each member of a pair could veto his colleague's decisions, but the junior magistrates were subject to the authority of the duoviri. Election to these offices was by the assembled citizen body, at least at first; but by the second century such things were left more and more to the ordo itself. Magistrates who were unavoidably absent for more than a day could appoint a prefect to act for them. There were heavy penalties for magistrates acting contrary to decrees of the ordo or failing to consult it on all important matters. Every fifth year the senior pair were chosen from persons of especial standing and enjoyed the title of quinquennales. The functions of these were akin to those of the Roman censors. They had to fill up the membership of the ordo (primarily from ex-magistrates not already enrolled), supervise the letting of public contracts and the registration of such changes of ownership as might affect taxation. The seviri Augustales, the six officials of a college of Augustales, had no administrative responsibilities, but they played an important part in the maintenance of the Imperial cult in colonies and municipia.

The constitution of the civitates peregrinae was almost exactly similar except for the normal absence of quaestors and seviri Augustales: their magistrates did not receive Roman citizenship unless Latin status had been granted to the town. Nevertheless, the prestige of office was sufficient during the first two centuries to call forth candidates despite the heavy expenditure which success involved. Not only did most communities exact a charge for election to office but successful candidates were under heavy moral pressure to pay for games or spectacles, or to donate buildings, an aqueduct, or at the very least a statue, for the public good. With the gradual rise of prices and growth of inflation office became a heavy burden, and compulsion was eventually introduced. This bore all the more heavily when responsibility for collecting taxation and forwarding it to the Procurator, which had always been part of their collective duty, was made a personal liability of decurions, who had to make good any shortage.

The possibilities of acquiring Roman citizenship through service in local government would appear to have been limited in Britain, though lack of evidence may perhaps give an unduly restricted picture. There was, however, another avenue to the citizenship. Enlistment in the auxiliary forces of the empire was regularly rewarded with a grant after twenty-five years' service, and until the reign of Antoninus Pius the grant was extended to children already born to the recipient. In the second century there existed at least nineteen auxiliary regiments recruited in Britain, amounting to 14,000 men. If as the basis of an extremely rough calculation we assume that half these soldiers survived to retirement age and that half of these again settled elsewhere than in Britain we find that 3,500 – or 14,000 a century – may have swelled the ranks of Roman citizens in Britain. The position is complicated by the fact that as time went on local recruitment became a predominant feature, so that regiments of 'Britons' on the Continent contained increasingly few natives of the island. Instead Britons will have enlisted increasingly in the regiments garrisoning Britain. Of the 42,500 auxiliaries who formed the army of Britain one-quarter – 10,625 – might on the same assumption be reckoned as eventual settlers in the province, or 42,500 a century. This, as we shall see, might amount to 2·12 per cent of the total population, a figure which would be augmented by retired legionaries and by the descendants of freedmen, of whom a number are known to have been engaged in trade and industry. How many of these new citizens settled in the civitates of the civil zone rather than in the vicinity of their old forts cannot be reckoned; but some will have done so, and those that did will have found themselves at a social advantage. An example of the process is seen on the inscription at Brough-on-Humber recording the erection of a stage-building by M. Ulpius Ianuarius, aedile of the vicus in the reign of Antoninus Pius. It is obvious from his names that his father or grandfather acquired citizenship by a grant of Trajan, no doubt after auxiliary service.

The government of the civitates was in the hands of the provincial aristocracy, to whose ranks wealth was a necessary passport. The responsibilities of the senates were entirely local, except that they did have the privilege of choosing delegates to the annual meeting of the provincial council. The *concilium provinciae* was the nearest approach we find in the Roman empire to representative government, but in the political sphere its powers were small, being practically limited to passing resolutions in praise or criticism of retiring governors. But it was the only body able to speak in the name of the provincials as a whole, and it could appoint suitably influential persons to act as patrons of the province, whose duty it was to make representations and especially to institute prosecutions on its behalf in Rome. The main purpose of the concilium, however, was to maintain the provincial centre of the Imperial Cult and its annual festival.

We know little of the provincial council of Britain: it must be assumed that the arrangements were parallel with those of Gaul. There the meeting took place annually at the altar of the imperial cult near Lyon and was attended by delegates from all the civitates, which appear to have had some system of proportional representation. A provincial high priest (or *sacerdos*) was chosen each year: he had to reside at the centre and pay for the shows and ceremonies which took place. Tacitus mentions as one of the causes of discontent in Britain, at the time of Boudicca's rebellion, that those who were chosen as sacerdotes had to pour forth all their wealth. From his account it is clear that at any rate at thi. date the British cult centre was at Colchester. But in Britain we lack the large series of inscriptions which was set up in Gaul both at the cult centre and in individual civitates in honour of provincial priests, and which throws so much light on the organisation of the council. There are two inscriptions from London, the first a dedication set up in the name of the Province of Britain to the divinity of the Emperor, the second the tombstone of a *provincialis* (perhaps a servant of the council); but these are no sure grounds for supposing that the cult and council moved with the rest of the administration to London. We possess the names of two *patroni provinciae Britanniae*, proof that the council was continuing to function down to the third century. The first was M. Vettius Valens, who had been Iuridicus of Britain perhaps about 150, and who may have been grandson of the Vettius Valens decorated by Claudius for his part in the invasion of 43. The second was C. Julius Asper, consul in 212. He was also patron of Mauretania Tingitana, but his connections with Britain are unknown.

Within the civitates were subordinate units known as pagi and vici. A vicus was the smallest unit of self-administration in the Roman provinces. The status was granted to certain sizeable villages or small towns, and it is clear from continental inscriptions that the civitas-capitals themselves ranked as either single vici or groups of vici (depending on their size) within the civitas.[18] An aedile of the vicus of Petuaria (Brough on Humber) is known, though Brough itself may have served as the *caput* of the civitas of the Parisi – if this really existed, which is not certain.[19] *Durobrivae* (Water Newton), a small town in Catuvellaunian territory, is also known to have been a vicus.[20] But certain civil settlements in the military districts, where traders and retired soldiers had combined to form sizeable villages outside forts, were also granted restricted self-government as vici. Examples are known from Hadrian's Wall and its vicinity, where at Old Carlisle a third-century inscription was set up by *vik(anorum) mag(istri)* and at Chesterholm and Housesteads inscriptions mentioning vicani have been found. The system even extended to the Antonine Wall where an altar set up by the vicani living at *Veluniate* (Carriden) has recently been found.[21]

Pagi, on the other hand, were country areas originally inhabited by sub-divisions of the Celtic tribes. We know the names of some of these (p. 77, notes 6, 7), but there are no inscriptions from Roman Britain to throw light on their local organisation. Additional hints are provided by the subdivision of the civitas of the Durotriges, which surely suggests the elevation of one of its pagi to independence, and by the nucleation of the Cantiaci, so evident on the map of Roman Britain, round the two centres of Canterbury and Rochester.

In conclusion, something must be said of the reorganisation of Britain in the fourth century. It is well known that Diocletian effected a complete reform of the administrative system of the empire, the finishing touches to which, especially on the military side, were carried through by Constantine. Their general purpose was the creation of smaller provinces to improve administrative efficiency, and the separation of the military from the civil arm (pp. 260, 382). The resulting multiplication of officials introduced the further necessity of elaborating the rather simple chain of command of the early empire.

Under the Diocletianic Tetrarchy the empire was ruled by two Augusti assisted each by a Caesar: Gaul and Britain were controlled by Constantius, Caesar to Maximian. Administrative responsibility was centralised in the hands of the Praetorian Prefects, whose numbers varied during the first half of the fourth century with the number of emperors; but by degrees a territorial prefecture of the

Gauls became permanently established whether or not an emperor was in the region, and to this the provinces of Britain naturally belonged. Within the prefecture the provinces were divided into groups or dioceses, each controlled by a deputy (*vicarius*) of the prefect. The two Severan provinces of Britain now became four, and these constituted the diocese of Britain under the control of the *vicarius Britanniarum*. If we may judge both from probability and also from the fact that the *praepositus* of the diocesan treasury [22] had his seat there, the headquarters of the Vicar lay in London.

The four provinces of Britain are named in the Verona List, a document which can be closely dated to the years 312–14, as Britannia Prima, Britannia Secunda, Maxima Caesariensis and Flavia Caesariensis. The first two are clear enough, but the curious choice of names for the second pair has given rise to speculation. Collingwood held that they were named after the two Caesars, Flavius Constantius and Galerius Maximianus. But it is hard to see why Galerius, the Caesar of the east, should have been commemorated while the two Augusti were not. An alternative view [23] would explain them as two halves of a short-lived third province entitled Caesariensis, so named after its capital, Caesariensis being the adjective of Caesarea. Though we do not know of any Caesarea in Britain, it is possible that London was given this title after its loyal welcome of Constantius in 296; and it is likely enough that one of the first actions of Constantius was to divide the two-legion command of Upper Britain, giving Chester to a new province centred on London and formed from the southern part of Inferior and the eastern part of Superior. At a later date, but before the time of the Verona list, a further reorganisation would have created two provinces out of Caesariensis, the one named Flavia after Constantius and the other Maxima in honour of the western Augustus, M. Aurelius Valerius Maximianus. If this is so, then the redivision will have taken place before the abdication of Maximian in 305. If London was given the title Caesarea in honour of Constantius it may have been changed to Augusta in that year, when Constantius was elevated to the rank of Augustus: as Augusta it was certainly known later in the century.[24]

Under Diocletian's arrangements the British provinces were all governed by *praesides* of equestrian rank;[25] but later in the century the Notitia shows that Maxima had been promoted in status, for its governor had become a senatorial *consularis*. This may have happened under Constantine, who was the first to reintroduce consulares; but there can be no certainty about the date.

It is not possible to show in any detail where the divisions between these provinces lay, but Dr J. C. Mann[26] has been able to demonstrate that Maxima and Prima were formed from the Severan province of Britannia Superior, and that the capital of Maxima was London, while Prima lay in Wales and the west of England, with its capital almost certainly at Cirencester. The remaining two, Secunda and Flavia, were carved from Britannia Inferior. York can be shown to have been the capital of one and Lincoln of the other, and if the theory of a division of Caesariensis is accepted it would follow that York lay in Britannia Secunda; again, since after Constantius' recovery of Britain the military district of the north was still controlled by a *praeses*, and the command not yet separated under the *dux*, it seems probable that the York province comprised the whole of this district. If so, the Lincoln province may have extended far enough south-east to include the civitas of the Iceni.[27]

That the northern command was at first still in the hands of the praeses is shown by an inscription from Birdoswald recording the restoration of fort buildings under his supervision;[28] subsequently, perhaps still under Diocletian, perhaps later under Constantine, a *dux* was appointed to command the garrison, and the civilian administration was separated. It is uncertain when the office of Count of the Saxon Shore was inaugurated, but it cannot have been before the reign of Constantine, who inaugurated the rank of count (*comes*). The office certainly existed in 367, for in his account of the disasters of that year Ammianus[29] refers to a *comes maritimi tractus* (p. 391), an obvious periphrasis. The problems connected with the *comes Britanniarum*, a third commander known to us in the Notitia, are discussed on pp. 261 and 268f.

In 369 a fifth British province, Valentia, was established. It was so named in honour of the reigning emperors Valentinian and Valens, and came into being as part of Count Theodosius' reconstruction of Britain. The Notitia tells us that it had a consularis as governor; its geographical position, however, is still obscure. The distribution of late Roman pottery assures us that it did not, as has sometimes been suggested, embrace the lowlands of Scotland, for nothing can be more certain than that Hadrian's Wall at this time still marked the limit of Roman Britain. Our choice seems confined either to part of northern England or to North Wales. In the latter area the fort of Caernarvon was rebuilt, but the area is hardly of sufficient importance to warrant a consularis as governor. More likely is the suggestion of Dr J. C. Mann that the York province was now subdivided; Carlisle might well have become the capital of Valentia. This idea is supported by the fact that the title of the Duke in the Notitia is *dux Britanniarum*, for this implies that his command extended over more than one province, though the forts listed as under his control all lie in northern England.

Much of the revenue of the later empire was collected in kind rather than in cash, under a method of requisition which had grown up in the inflation of the third century and was regularised by Diocletian with his system of annual indictions. When the overall requirements of the empire had been calculated tax-payers were assessed according to their individual code or *iugum*, and the duty of collecting the right total in their areas rested personally on the decurions of each city. This taxation in kind was the responsibility of the Praetorian Prefects, working through their Vicars and the governors of the provinces. The independent financial administration of the procurators of the early empire had disappeared with the merging, in the late third century, of the office of procurator with that of equestrian praeses.

There was, however, a second financial ministry controlled by an officer whose title became *comes sacrarum largitionum*. This ministry combined two departments. One was the *res summa*, which was responsible for such revenue as was still collected in gold and silver as well as for the requisition of clothing or its manufacture in state mills; it also controlled the mints and mines. The other was the *res privata*, which supervised imperial property. Both of these departments had their representatives in Britain, the *rationalis rei privatae per Britannias* and the *rationalis summarum Britanniarum*.[30] In addition, the Notitia records among the subordinates of the comes sacrarum largitionum two other British officials, the head of the treasury in London and the controller of the weaving works at Venta.[31] To judge by what is known elsewhere, the diocesan officers of these two departments disposed a numerous assortment of subordinate staff; but even so, the provincial governors were often required to assist the collection of the revenues concerned. The mint which had been established in London by Carausius continued in operation until 325–6; it was later reopened by Magnus Maximus for the production of gold and silver.

With four provincial governors and a vicarius Britain cannot have been under-administered. It was, however, upon the *curiales* – the decurions of the towns – that the imperial government relied for local implementation of central decisions, for it was the city-councils which had to appoint managers of the public post, supervisors of the state granaries and collectors of taxes in money and in kind, as well as recruiting-officers for both army and other branches of public works; and on them fell the organisation of corvées of compulsory labour and the repair of roads. Not only were such services unpaid but they might even at times be financially oppressive or even ruinous. Any shortage in the amount of taxation due could be legally extracted from the decurion responsible for its collection, and if that failed the whole council had an obligation to underwrite the deficit.

Membership of the councils had long been compulsory for suitably qualified persons and in practice became hereditary, since it was illegal to abandon the position for most other professions. Moreover, initiative was blocked by increasing supervision from above. *Curatores civitatis* had occasionally been appointed even in the early empire as special commissioners to supervise where necessary the administration of local finance; by the early fourth century these appointments had become permanent and universal.

The heavy burdens of personal expenditure, and of legal restriction and compulsory service made the position of decurion increasingly unpopular in the later empire. Those who could secured exemption, and occasionally numbers were made up by the enrolment of other persons as a penalty. Exemptions from curial duties could be obtained by promotion to the higher social status which accompanied the superior ranks of the imperial service, and such promotion could often also be secured on an honorary basis and even by bribery. By degrees the wealthier or more ambitious members of the class secured exemption, and among those that were left it was possible for the richer members to allot the heavier burdens to their poorer colleagues.

All this has some bearing on the problems presented by the prosperous villa of fourth-century Britain. Though we have little information specifically related to the curiales of Britain either in the codes or in the literature, or even from inscriptions, it is clear that decurions were compelled by legislation to live in the cities, and were forbidden to migrate to their estates.[32] These would presumably have to be run by bailiffs. In Britain some of the wealthy villas, for instance in the region of Cirencester, are close enough to the towns for it to have been possible for their owners to commute, and thus carry out their obligations. But the largest, and especially those which though more remote are yet of a luxury which proves occupation by owners, must be presumed to have belonged to families which were exempt from curial obligations, the owners having achieved equestrian or even senatorial rank.[33]

Nor must we forget that Britain was frequently used as a place of exile for distinguished and presumably still wealthy persons in the fourth century.[34] It is even possible that the wealth and comparative security of Britain in the fourth century acted as a magnet to wealth from the continental empire, land being considered a prime investment. These are problems on which little work has yet been undertaken.

1. *ILS*, 1011 (Salvius Liberalis); *ILS*, 1015 (Iavolenus Priscus); *Digest*, xxxvi, 1, 48, quoted by Birley, *Roman Britain and the Roman Army*, p. 51.

2. And cf. the situation in Spain under Augustus: Strabo, iii, 4, 20.

3. Caecilianus, *ILS*, 1123; Valens; *CIL*, xi, 383; Calpurnianus, *ILS*, 1151.

4. See also H. von Petrikovits, *Das römische Rheinland* (Köln, 1960), pp. 72–4. Beneficiarii consulares are attested at Dorchester-on-Thames and Winchester in the civil zone and at Wroxeter, Catterick, Lancaster, Binchester, Greta Bridge, Lanchester, Chesterholm, Housesteads and Risingham in the military area. A strator consularis was buried at Irchester.

5. The 'Marble of Thorigny'; *CIL*, xiii, 3162.

6. This is probably the explanation of the *principia* or headquarters restored by 'Naevius imperial freedman and assistant to the procurators' which is recorded on a third-century inscription found at Combe Down near Bath, *RIB*, 179. An imperial freedman of the time of Marcus Aurelius, named M. Aurelius Marcio, held office as procurator in Britain (*ILS*, 1477) and was thought by Mommsen (*Staatsrecht*, iii, 555, note 1) to have had charge of an imperial estate.

7. *Digest*, i, 16, 9.

8. The other grades were *sexagenarii* (60,000), *centenarii* (100,000) and *trecenarii* (300,000), the last reserved for the heads of the profession in Rome.

9. *ILS*, 1338. Pflaum, *Les Carrières Procuratoriennes Equestres sous le Haut-empire romain* (Paris, 1960), No. 95. It is not certain what or where the Britons of Anavio were. The term Brittones implies northern Britain, and they are likely to have belonged to some area under direct rule, named from a fort. *RIB*, 2243, a milestone from Buxton, reads ANAVIONE M P XI meaning eleven miles from the fort of Brough on Noe; but Richmond (*Archaeologia*, xciii, 42), has shown that this stone must read *a Navione*, 'from Navio'. The river Annan in Dumfriesshire was probably named *ANAVA* (ibid., 22), but the region of Anavio cannot have been there, as southern Scotland lay outside the province between *c.* 105 and 140, nor can Annandale be thought of as Brigantian territory. A different Anava must be sought.

10. E.g., *Nectovelius ... nationis Brigans ... RIB*, 2142.

11. In addition to those cited in *Antiquity*, xxxv (1961), 29–36, see *Germania*, 40 (1962), 83. For a contrary view see J. C. Mann in Jarrett and Dobson, *Britain and Roman* (Kendal, 1966), pp. 109 ff.

12. Wroxeter ... *civitas Cornoviorum* (*RIB*, 288); Cirencester ... *et ins(tituit) (R)espub(lica)* (*RIB*, 114); Kenchester a milestone, *r(es)p(ublica) c(ivitatis) D(obunnorum)* (*RIB*, 2250); Brougham ... *r(es)p(ublica) c(ivitatis) Car(vetiorum)* (*JRS*, lv (1965), 224; Caerwent ... *ex decreto ordinis respubl(ica) civit(atis) Silurum* (*RIB*, 311). The last is the most significant, revealing as it does the whole machinery of government. A sixth, from Brough on Humber, may have attested the *civitas Parisorum*: see *RIB*, 707, for the restoration *C(ivitas) [P(arisorum)]*. Note also the further six, from Hadrian's Wall, listed on p. 198 and p. 218, note 15.

13. The Ravenna Cosmography, compiled in the seventh century from much earlier sources, mentions ten civitas capitals in Britain: *Calleva Atrebatum* (Silchester), *Corinium Dobunnorum* (Cirencester), *Durovernum Cantiacorum* (Canterbury), *Isca Dumnoniorum* (Exeter), *Noviomagus Regnensium* (Chichester), *Ratae Coritanorum* (Leicester), *Venta Belgarum* (Winchester), *Venta Icenorum* (Caistor by Norwich), *Venta Silurum* (Caerwent), *Viroconium Cornoviorum* (Wroxeter). Some of these are confirmed by the early third-century Antonine Itinerary, which adds an eleventh, *Isurium Brigantum* (Aldborough). The Antonine Itinerary refers to Caistor by Norwich as *Icenos* (in the third-century Gallic fashion) in one list, though elsewhere it names it *Venta Icinorum*. Cf. also *Notitia Dignitatum Occ.* xi, 60: *Ventensis*, p. 337 below.

14. *Roman Britain and the English Settlements* (1936), 186.

15. For the *territorium* belonging to an auxiliary fort see *RIB*, 1049.

16. If not indeed sooner: for what appears to be an earlier and smaller forum, erected soon after the Boudiccan rebellion, has been found below the Flavian building.

17. *Durnovaria* (Dorchester) does too, but is nowhere definitely attested as a civitas-capital.

18. Constituent vici are attested in the colonia of Lincoln (*RIB*, 270–1).

19. See, however, *RIB*, 707, for the restoration C(*ivitas*)/[P(*arisorum*)].

20. A mortarium-stamp, *Cunoarus Vico Duro(brivae)* is known from examples at Castor and South Shields.

21. Old Carlisle, *RIB*, 899; Chesterholm, *RIB*, 1700; Housesteads, *RIB*, 1616; Carriden, *JRS*, xlvii (1957), 230. See also pl. 6a for Old Carlisle.

22. *Notitia Dignitatum Occ.* xi. 37: *praepositus thesaurorum Augustensium* [*in Britannis*].

23. An idea first put forward by Bury (*Cambridge Historical Journal*, i (1923), 1–9, and developed by Birley (*Acta et Dissertationes Archaeologicae*, iii (1963), 83–8.

24. Ammianus Marcellinus, xxvii, 8, 7; xxviii, 3, 1.

25. *Praeses* had long been an unofficial word for governor; now it became the official title of equestrian governors. Similarly, men of equestrian rank had been increasingly used during the third century, and especially since the reign of Gallienus, to replace senatorial governors: Diocletian merely brought the process to completion.

26. *Antiquity*, xxxv (1961), 316–20.

27. Dr Mann (op. cit.) has pointed out that the title of the Count of the Saxon Shore, *comes litoris Saxonici per Britannias*, shows that his command, which ran from the Wash to the Solent, overlapped more than one province.

28. *RIB*, 1912; see p. 382.

29. *Ammianus Marcellinus*, xxvii, 8, 1.

30. *Notitia Dignitatum Occ.*, xii, 15 and xi, 20.

31. *Praepositus thesaurorum Augustensium* (*Not. Dig. Occ.*, xi, 37) and *procurator gynaecii in Britannis Ventensis* (*ibid.*, xi, 60); see p. 337 for the identity of Venta.

32. The surviving laws on the subject (Cod. Just. viii. 10.6, Cod. Theod. xii, 18.1, Cod. Just. viii, 10.8, and Cod. Theod. xii, 18.2.), mostly apply to the eastern empire, but it cannot be doubted that the principle was general.

33. On the expansion of these orders in the fourth century see A. H. M. Jones, *The Later Roman Empire* (Oxford, 1964), pp. 525–9, 741. The family of Pelagius, one of the few fourth-century British personalities of whom anything is known, was wealthy enough to send him to study law in Rome; the law was one of the avenues of promotion open to curiales.

34. Palladius, the *magister officiorum*, Ammianus Marcellinus, xxii, 3, 3; Valentinus and others, *ibid.*, xxviii, 3, 4; Frontinus, *ibid.*, xxviii, 1, 21. A similar situation might account for the Lullingstone busts at an earlier period (pp. 312 and 319, note 9).

11

The Roman Army in Britain

The part played by the Roman army in the history of the British provinces is fully discussed in other chapters, and an estimate of its strength has been attempted on pp. 182–6. There were, however, many other ways than the application of military policy in which the substantial garrison stationed in this island affected the life of Roman Britain. For instance, in the highland zone the army formed the only contact btween the great majority of the native population and Rome. The merchants who served the garrison were not averse to trading also with the natives, and the successful intercourse of all three is seen in the great expansion of civil vici round the forts in the third and fourth centuries. For this reason, and also because the wealth of military antiquities, available for study in Britain, illustrates the archaeology of the Roman army in a way which is unique in the Roman Empire, a brief account must be given of the organisation and character of the provincial army. Finally, it is necessary to consider the bearing of the Notitia Dignitatum upon the fourth-century forces in Britain.

As is well known, the army of the early empire consisted of two distinct categories of troops. In addition to the legions of Roman citizens, the government made use of forces raised among subject peoples. Even under the Republic, Rome had called upon her allies for help in war; the still wider responsibilities of defence under the empire were far too heavy a burden for the manpower of Italy to shoulder unaided. Furthermore, certain specialist forces, such as cavalry, archers and slingers, could not be raised in Italy in the quality or quantity required. Augustus therefore balanced the legionary forces at his disposal with an approximately equal number of *auxilia*, or lighter-armed auxiliary regiments raised among the provincials.

The legions of citizen troops were recruited at first in Italy, but increasingly after the early second century from citizens in the Danube provinces and in Gaul or Spain, and ultimately from less civilised provinces, such as Britain herself. This was a process due primarily to the spread of Roman citizenship in these regions during the first century; but it was accelerated by the twin facts that the conditions of legionary service became increasingly unattractive to the inhabitants of Italy, while a growing reservoir of men eager to enlist grew up in the neighbourhood of the fortresses themselves among the children of serving soldiers.

A legion had a fighting strength of about 5,300 men, of whom 120 were mounted; in addition, a considerable number belonged to administrative grades. It was organised in ten cohorts, each of which consisted of six centuries, except the first cohort, which was formed of five centuries of double strength. The normal strength of a century was eighty men; they were heavily armed infantry whose strength lay in their weapons, their discipline and their training. Against ill-armed and ill-disciplined native levies – which for the most part was all they had to face in the first two centuries AD – they were irresistible.

The legion was commanded by a Roman senator of praetorian rank (pp. 222–4), who was assisted by six military tribunes. One of these was of senatorial family, a young man at the start of his career (the *tribunus laticlavius*); the remaining five were generally not so youthful, being men of equestrian rank (*tribuni angusti-clavii*), serving in the second of their three *militiae* (p. 227f.). Many of them would therefore tend to be in their thirties; but occasionally an older man, promoted from the centurionate, might be found among them. The duties of the tribunes were largely administrative, though the *tribunus laticlavius* ranked second in command of the legion. The real leadership was provided by the centurions who commanded the fifty-nine centuries composing the legion. These were tough experienced soldiers who had normally reached their position either by promotion from the ranks or, in rare cases, by transfer from the praetorian guard; a few were sometimes appointed directly from civilian life. The centurions were graded according to the seniority of the cohort to which they were attached. The most senior of them served in the first cohort and were known as *primi ordines*, a rank to which the leading centurions of the other cohorts also belonged;

the chief centurion (*primus pilus*) commanded the first century of the first cohort, and held a position of considerable influence and power. The second centurion (*princeps*) had charge of the administrative staff. Vegetius remarks upon the very detailed book-keeping which was maintained by the legionary staff.[1]

The auxiliary troops were not normally Roman citizens: they were raised from among the warlike tribes within the empire, whose capacities could thus be utilised for defence, and were rewarded with citizenship, occasionally after valour in battle, but normally on discharge after twenty-five or more years service. The regularisation of this system seems to be due to a reform of Claudius, and the bronze diplomas certifying individual grants throw useful light, as we have seen (p. 182), on the composition of provincial armies.

The auxiliary forces were not formed into units as large as the legions, but into cohorts (for infantry) and alae (for cavalry), both nominally either 500 or 1,000 strong. The alae were almost all of the smaller size (*alae quingenariae*); but by the late first century a few *alae milliariae* had been formed for exceptional duties at critical points, never more than one being assigned to any one province. The subdivisions of an ala were called *turmae* – sixteen of them in a quingenary ala and twenty-four in a milliary – commanded by decurions. The infantry cohorts were likewise normally of the smaller size (*cohortes quingenariae*), and either consisted solely of infantry (*cohortes peditatae*) or else included a mounted contingent of 120 men (*cohortes equitatae*). Milliary cohorts of double strength were, however, quite commonly found from Flavian times onwards, and they, too, could be either *peditatae* or *equitatae*. Their subdivisions were centuries commanded by centurions. The Dura papyri, which give a detailed picture of the internal organisation of a milliary cohort, suggest that by the early third century considerable changes had taken place in the establishment from that described by Hyginus half a century earlier.[2]

Originating as they did as territorial units, auxiliary regiments in the early empire were often commanded by the local chieftains who had raised them, and they not infrequently served in the area of their homeland. But this system broke down notably in 69 under the stress of loyalties divided by the civil war. Thereafter two steps were taken. Units now rarely served in their home areas (a precaution which it was impossible to maintain except nominally, owing to the difficulties of ensuring other than local recruitment); and, more significantly, they were regularly commanded by Roman officers centrally assigned. These commanders were men of equestrian rank serving their *militiae* (p. 227f.), all of whom held the title of prefect, except those commanding milliary cohorts, who ranked as tribunes.

Several cavalry regiments in the British garrison continued to retain in their titles the memory of the man who first raised them, for instance, the Ala Indiana, the Ala Petriana, etc.; the majority, however – and all the infantry – had territorial titles such as Cohors I Hispanorum, II Pannoniorum, etc.

Originally these regiments consisted almost entirely of men from the area named, the exceptions being a few men and N.C.O.s drafted in to stiffen or train them. A good illustration of this process is provided by Tacitus in his account of a terrible little incident which took place in 83. A cohort of Usipi had been raised in Germany and transferred to Britain: they may have been forcibly enlisted during Domitian's campaign that same year. A regular centurion and soldiers were seconded for training purposes, and these they murdered; next they stole three warships and attempted to sail home round the north of Scotland, suffering great privations from shipwreck and starvation, and being reduced to selective cannibalism, on the way. A few survivors reached the coasts of Germany, but were sold into slavery by their captors, and thus arrived eventually at the Roman frontier to make their story known.[3]

Certain regiments, such as the famous Batavi, were raised from tribes who had a treaty-obligation to provide drafts, and whose taxation was remitted in compensation; and some specialised regiments, such as the Hamian archers from Syria who served in northern Britain, probably managed to maintain their ethnic character.[4] But for the rest, the difficulty of maintaining a flow of recruits from distant sources meant that local enlistment in the area of service soon diluted their original character; they came to be manned by local romanised provincials who were attracted by the prospect of steady employment, and who saw in service an avenue to the citizenship. Indeed, it became not unknown for Roman citizens of provincial origin to serve in the auxiliaries. Thus, gradually the original character of the auxiliary forces changed, as in the calibre of their recruitment they drew closer to that of the legions: they had become part of 'the establishment'.

To remedy this state of affairs a third type of force came into existence during the late first century; these were a new type of national or tribal levy known as the *Numeri*. Like the original *auxilia*, these were regiments raised among barbarian tribes on the fringes of the empire, and transferred for service far from their native land. They were barbarian light-armed fighters, whose recruiting problem could be solved – as had been done earlier with the Batavi – by compulsory drafts levied under treaty. British numeri were serving on the Upper German frontier in the reign of Antoninus Pius, and Sarmatians raised in much the same way were sent to Britain itself in 175. Numeri are not otherwise attested in Britain until the third century (pp. 159, 208), at which period they seem to be mainly drafts sent over from Germany. Later in the century, in 277 or 278, defeated Burgundian and Vandal tribesmen were sent across to Britain in some numbers, and these, too, probably served in numeri. By this date on the Continent, it is true, lands which had become deserted after the great raids were beginning to be resettled with barbarians known as *laeti*: the term implies that they were farmers with a hereditary obligation of military service. But in Britain there is no evidence of deserted lands at this time, and little to suggest barbarian peasant settlements. Such tribesmen as were transferred were more probably drafted as regular forces.[5]

The remaining arm of the Roman forces in Britain was the Classis Britannica. Its headquarters lay at Boulogne, where a number of inscriptions testify to trierarchs and *milites* of the fleet; but during the second century it built another headquarters fort at Dover. It was from time to time used in offensive warfare, such as the Claudian invasion itself, Vespasian's campaign in the south-west, that of Frontinus in Wales or those of Agricola and Severus in the north; but its main and more enduring functions were those of transport and supply, and it is worth remembering that it contained craftsmen skilful enough to be sent to help in building the Hadrianic frontier. Down to the third century these routine functions were naturally concentrated in the English Channel, and it is between Dover and Pevensey that the tiles stamped CL BR are found; in addition to naval bases their distribution indicates involvement of naval personnel with the production of iron and timber. From the third century naval defence for the first time became important, and the system of Saxon Shore forts shows the fleet being given more extended bases to cope with a new situation; for only with the opening of the era of Saxon sea-raiding and its extension by the Irish on the western coasts did the more modern naval duty of ceaseless patrolling devolve upon this fleet – a duty well illustrated in the fourth century by Vegetius' description of the camouflaged scouting craft used for advance-warning. 'Lest the scouting craft should give themselves away by their colour, the sails and ropes are dyed blue like the waves . . . and the sailors wear blue uniforms so that they may scout more secretly by day as well as by night.'[6]

The Roman army on the march in hostile territory was accustomed to build entrenchments for the night: it was as if they carried a walled town in their packs, said Vegetius.[7] These earthworks are known as marching camps, and are quite distinct from forts and fortresses. For one thing, they usually relate to the progress of a campaign rather than to the strategic command of a district;[8] for another, they lack permanent buildings, since the army in the field camped in leather tents.[9] This meant that less space was required per man than in permanent works; a legionary fortress takes up about fifty acres, but a legionary camp[10] about twenty. Roman marching camps are an easily recognisable class of earthwork with their straight sides and rounded corners, and with their entrances defended either by *titula* – a detached length of bank and ditch covering the entrance gap to break up a rush (pl. 6b) – or else by *claviculae*, the curved horn-like extensions of the rampart which projected either inside or outside the entrance, so as to compel attackers to expose their unshielded side to the defenders. The clavicula, in every case that can be dated, is a Flavian device. Great numbers of marching camps are known in Britain, ranging in size from less than 1 acre up to 165 acres at St Leonards and other sites in southern Scotland. Often they have been discovered from the air when all surface traces have disappeared; but many notable examples still survive in Wales and the north virtually as their makers left them, and they form a unique and precious contribution to the study of military antiquities available nowhere else in such variety.

The permanent stations of the legions are termed fortresses. The best known and longest occupied are those of York, Chester and Caerleon, but others, occupied for a shorter time (though in no sense temporary in intention), are known at Lincoln, Gloucester, Wroxeter and Inchtuthil. As already mentioned (pp. 87, 94, 200), there is also a class of 20–30-acre fortresses, perhaps designed for legionary vexillations who may or may not have been accompanied by auxiliaries. Examples lie at Longthorpe, Newton on Trent, Kinvaston, Clyro, Carpow and probably Wall and Malton; apart from Carpow, they seem to belong to the early years of conquest. Only Longthorpe has yet been excavated sufficiently to throw light on the buildings, and thus on the type of garrison which they contained; it had a mixed garrison of legionaries and auxiliary cavalry.

The fortress was the legionary base and headquarters, even if for many decades detachments were absent on other duties, as clearly happened in the second and third centuries at Caerleon. Whenever possible, these fortresses were placed close to navigable rivers for ease of supply – we may recall the pilot of Legio VI, who is recorded on an altar at York [11] – and the site chosen commands the approaches to a wide region; near by lies the civil town which normally grew up to house the traders, the cult-centres and the families of the garrison. At Chester and Caerleon amphitheatres are known, the main purpose of which was to provide for arms-drill under instruction; they emphasise the continual training on which success depended. At Chester excavation has brought to light very interesting traces of a wooden amphitheatre built by Legio II Adiutrix, but replaced in stone on a much larger scale when Legio XX took over the fortress. The fullest plan of a fortress is that recovered by excavation at Inchtuthil; on it can be recognised the regular and disciplined organisation which maintained nearly 6,000 men in 50 acres: the headquarters (*principia*) in whose chapel (*aedes*) the standards and the image of the émperor were housed, the hospital covering 1·3 acres and containing wards for every century, the granaries, the workshop (covering 0·9 acre) and the centurial barracks. Only the legate's house had not been installed, though the ground had been levelled for it, when the moment of evacuation came. Here is presented a picture of a first-century timber fortress with a completeness unique in the Roman world. It has much to teach us of the character of the Roman army and the superiority of its techniques. The supply-problem alone gives sufficient food for thought, when we recollect the seven miles of timber walls required for the main frame of the men's barracks, and the eleven tons of unused iron nails which were buried at evacuation to prevent their falling into native hands;

all this and other material had to be brought up from base during active campaigns.

The forts provided for auxiliary regiments resembled legionary fortresses in miniature. Their size, of course, varied with the accommodation required. Quingenary cohorts, whether *peditatae* or *equitatae*, seem normally to have had forts of 3·5 acres, though there is variation above and below this figure; it seems probable that the former could if necessary fit into a fort only 2·8 acres in area.[12] A milliary cohort could fit a fort of only 4·52 acres, as at Fendoch, but the normal size was about 5 acres. Certainly milliary forts are as large as 6 or even 6·5 acres, but some of these may have had to accommodate extra storage space. A quingenary ala normally occupies a fort of 5·5 acres, but Carzield is almost 2 acres larger than this. Finally, the fort at Stanwix which housed the Ala Petriana Milliaria is 9·3 acres.

These figures are interesting not only because they can help to indicate the size of unit in forts where this is not otherwise attested but also because they illustrate the fact that different Roman armies had quite different rules for field-construction. If we compare these fort–garrison ratios with those of Upper Germany and Raetia we find that there the provision of space was notably more lavish: the fort-areas for the different kinds of unit are consistently larger by a factor of 1·6 or 1·7. Of course, many differences in detail also exist, such as in methods of granary-construction, but these are not nearly so striking – or so hard to explain – as this notable difference in fort-sizes.

The earliest forts in Britain go back to the Claudian period, and at both Great Casterton and Hod Hill they can be seen to lack the back gate and street (*porta and via decumana*) of later forts, and to have the *via principalis* in the middle rather than in the forward part of the fort; these characteristics have been found also in the contemporary fort at Valkenburg in Holland. The range of time covered by Romano-British forts enables us to trace the development of castrametation from these beginnings through the more familiar fort-plans of the Flavian period and second century, and on to the new Shore Forts of the third, in which gates become central once more and the bank, the rounded angles and internal towers by degrees give place to square angles and external bastions together with the omission of the earth rampart behind the wall. This corresponds to the change from an offensive to a defensive attitude of mind which characterised the later Roman army. Its forts in the first and second centuries were primarily bases for the offensive; the Saxon Shore forts and the walled towns of the later empire served as defended strongpoints against invasion (p. 291f.). Nevertheless, the conservatism of the British army is very striking. The new architectural ideas were never applied to the great mass of auxiliary forts; new ones built early in the fourth century, such as Piercebridge or Newton Kyme, and even forts rebuilt in 369 still display the castrametation of two centuries earlier. The earliest stone defensive wall in Britain is that added to the rampart surrounding Inchtuthil. More stone walls were appearing under Trajan and Hadrian, but turf forts continued to be constructed down to the Antonine period. Internal buildings were often still built of timber, even in the middle of the second century; usually, however, the principal range was of masonry, while the barracks were of wood, though even in these there is a tendency during the second century for stone footings to be provided.

Turf-work, indeed, might be called the speciality of the Roman army. We can see it under construction on Trajan's column, and we have Hadrian's own praise of its suitability for military work in his address to the army of Africa.[13] In Britain we have linear works in turf, such as the Cleaven Dyke, the mounds of the Vallum and the Turf Walls of Hadrian and Pius; we also possess a remarkable range of information concerning the ramparts and defensive systems of forts in turf and clay. Much of this knowledge is due to the work of Sir Ian Richmond, who established the angle of incline and thus the height of Hadrian's Turf Wall, and whose exacavations at Glenlochar showed that the turf of that fort's rampart had been fetched from a distance owing to the friability of the turf on the spot. The street-metalling in the fort had been obtained at heavy cost in labour by sieving the subsoil, the separated earth being used for the rampart core. Just as small details like these illuminate the hardships of military life, so the pride of a well-drilled unit can be recognised in the 4-inch spread of gravel – if we remember the raking it would require – which covered the berm between the rampart and the ditch at Glenlochar.

The turf-work of the army of Britain is another feature which distinguishes its practice from that of the army of Upper Germany.

In Britain ramparts were formed of earth or rubble held between facing cheeks of piled turf, which sloped upward at about seventy-five degrees, while in Germany fort-ramparts were often provided with a timber front of horizontal boarding held back by posts.[14]

Nowhere is the contrast between science in defence and the lack of it seen to better advantage than at Hod Hill, where the trim economy of the deadly Roman perimeter may be measured against the bulky ineffectiveness of the Celtic oppidum whose corner it occupies. Despite its enormous rampart and ditch, this oppidum appears to have fallen without difficulty to a Roman assault. The ditches of the Roman fort are only seven instead of thirty feet deep, but are planned to entice and then trap the attacker within the field of fire of javelins hurled from the rampart; the causeways leading to the gateways are (but do not appear to be) wedge-shaped, by which design an attacking rush would be cast off in confusion into the accompanying ditches; and the defence of each gate is aided by the fire of ballistae once mounted on turf platforms in the adjoining rampart. In the third-century defences of High Rochester much heavier emplacements mark the positions of stone-throwing machines (*onagri*); the balls of such machines, bigger than a man's head, have been found also at Risingham.

Skill in field-construction was valued so highly that both legionary and auxiliary troops were given special training in turf-building. This is the purpose of various small and often otherwise pointless earthworks which have come to be recognised as Practice-camps. In north Wales groups of them exist at Dolddinas about two miles from the fort of Tomen-y-Mur as well as at Tomen-y-Mur itself, and at Rhyd Sarn about two-and-a-half miles from the fort at Caer Gai; in south Wales others can be seen near Loughor and on Gelligaer Common; but by far the largest group, some eighteen in all, lies in central Wales on Llandrindod Common, a short distance south of the fort of Castell Collen. Others have been recognised in northern Britain, the best-known group being on Haltwhistle Common near Hadrian's Wall. It seems probable that these earthworks mark the sites of successive field-day operations. In building turf the chief skill is required at the carefully rounded corners, and at the claviculae or titula protecting the entrances: the majority of practice camps are of the smallest possible size consistent with these requirements.

Legionary troops underwent the same kind of training. Two camps survive from a once larger group at Bootham Stray just outside York, and at Cawthorn in the same county exist the remains of much more elaborate exercises for constructing not camps but forts, to which two successive vexillations of Legio IX were subjected. More realistic battle-practice was also staged from time to time. At Woden Law in Roxburghshire there are lines of siege-works near a hill-fort, which, since the latter was apparently unoccupied at the time, have been thought to relate to manoeuvres rather than to actual warfare. The same conclusion is possible for the famous siege-camps at Birrenswark in Dumfriesshire. Here the hill-fort was certainly under bombardment from spring-guns firing lead bullets from the great ballista-emplacements which are today so notable a feature of the site (pl. 5a).

A final class of military work has still to be mentioned, the signal stations. Britain is rich in well-preserved examples of the early Roman turf signal-post containing a timber look-out tower, from which messages could be transmitted by semaphore or fire signals;[15] both on the Gask ridge between Strageath and Bertha and in the Stainmore pass the remains of connected systems of such posts can be studied. On Hadrian's Wall the turrets represent a similar arrangement in stone, and there are also beacon emplacements on the Antonine Wall. The much larger and stronger signalling emplacements of the late fourth century on the Yorkshire coast are precious illustrations of a different type provided for a different purpose; these lie on high headlands, and were intended for liaison with the fleet (p. 395f.).

In all these aspects of the subject Britain is richly provided with illustrations. The Roman army, however, fulfilled an economic as well as a politico-military role in the province. Its mastery of building techniques in wood and stone were of the utmost importance to the growing towns, and there is no doubt also of its role in the diffusion of such arts as sculpture. To a limited extent also the army engaged in industry, and where it did so it led the field in technical ability. The legions made their own tiles and, down to about 120, much of their own pottery. At one period Legio IX seems to have worked a factory at Scalesceugh near Carlisle about which little is known, and similar establishments not yet explored existed near the fortresses of Gloucester and Caerleon. The best known of these military factories is that at Holt, Denbighshire, where a pottery and tilery of Legio xx, covering some twenty acres, lies twelve miles south of Chester beside the River Dee. Here a walled enclosure contained barrack accommodation for some two centuries, while outside it lay a bath-building, workshops, a heated drying shed and a battery of kilns of very advanced design. The whole plant seems to have been especially active in the late first and second centuries, but was not abandoned until the middle of the fourth.

It has sometimes been suggested that the metal-working depot at Wilderspool also belonged to Legio xx, but there is in fact no evidence that it was legionary or even a military establishment at all. The only site known to us where military metal-working was carried out on any scale was at Corbridge. There in the third and fourth centuries two walled compounds were established for legionary artificers seconded at various times from all three legions and engaged in large-scale armament manufacture.

Pottery and tile-making, however, are more widely attested because auxiliary forces played a part in them. A tilery is known at Pen-y-Stryd near the fort of Tomen-y-Mur, and others exist at Muncaster near the fort of Ravenglass and at Grimscar near Slack, while extensive pottery and tile works have recently come to light at Brampton near Carlisle. Pottery was made at Quernmore not far from the fort of Lancaster, and even closer associations of kilns with forts have been proved at Gelligaer and at South Shields. All these must either have been worked by soldiers or at least have been supervised by them. The evidence for military supervision of lead-mines in Derbyshire and Northumberland will be mentioned in Chapter 14 (p. 323), and to it could be added a suggestion of the same thing in Cumberland, where a building outside the fort of Caermote yielded lead-ore.

Immense quantities of leather were required by the army not only for footwear but also for items of uniform, shield-coverings and tents. Recently excavations at Catterick, immediately outside the fort, produced evidence for a depot where leather was prepared on a large scale and equipment manufactured from it during the period 80–120. The implication of this discovery is that the army itself undertook the direct supply of at any rate a large part of its own needs in this field instead of relying upon contractors, the raw material being no doubt delivered at Catterick as part of the taxation imposed upon the Brigantes. That it was delivered on the hoof is suggested by the great quantities of bones which accompanied the debris of manufacture.

Timber in bulk was another requirement, and though we have no evidence for army saw-mills, it cannot be doubted that military needs were met at least partly by establishments worked directly by soldiers. It is possible, indeed, that the sites in the Weald which have yielded stamped tiles of the *Classis Britannica* (p. 252) were concerned with timber for shipbuilding in addition to the production of iron.

Thus, the Roman army engaged in productive industry, mainly for its own purposes; it was as a consumer, however, that it made its greatest mark on the economy of Britain. Its food-requirements stimulated cereal production in the south and introduced it for the first time to some northern regions. Its consumption of pottery had to be met by imports on an enormous scale, and gave prosperity also to the numerous British firms who supplied military markets. Finally, its wealth was a standing attraction to merchants. Thus, the existence of the Roman army in northern Britain and in Wales caused a revolution in previously existing patterns of trade and civilised settlement.

In the late third and early fourth centuries the Roman army was largely reformed by Diocletian, and even greater changes in it were made by Constantine. The purpose of the reforms was partly to ensure the growth of a professional class of officers and partly to promote greater mobility by the creation of a central field army distinct from the static troops on the frontier. To achieve this not only were the civil and military branches of provincial administration almost completely separated but the numbers of legions and other formations were greatly increased; a distinction of precedence was made between the *limitanei* on frontier duties and the *comitatus* (later *comitatenses*) who formed the mobile field army. Later in the century a further distinction was recognised between the regional armies of *comitatenses* and the central core of *palatini* who served under immediate imperial control. In Britain the effect of these measures was soon apparent in the organisation, and even in the composition, of the provincial army.

Much of our information about fourth-century forces is derived from the Notitia Dignitatum. This is a collection of lists enumerating the chains of command, the civil and military officials of the empire, and the various staffs and units controlled by each. There is still disagreement between scholars about the status of this document and the exact date at which it was compiled, but there is little doubt that the lists originated in the offices of the Primicerii Notariorum, whose duty it was to keep such lists for the eastern and western parts of the empire, the lists themselves being based upon 'returns' submitted from time to time by the officials concerned. The most recent view is that the document as we have it was compiled about 395 and subsequently corrected during the next twenty-five or thirty years.[16] Yet those who hold that the Notitia was an official working copy in a government office at a date as late as 420–5 have to face two apparently insuperable difficulties. The first is that some of the lists are patently obsolete, and the second is that many others are hopelessly confused as a result of uncorrected cross-postings and promotions. An alternative and perhaps simpler view sees the Notitia as a copy of an official document of about 395, which subsequently was altered and edited to the best of his ability by some private individual, perhaps engaged on military history, who had no access to up-to-date official files. Both theories involve assumptions, but the second 'will allow us to suppose that there were rational men in the Roman Record Offices',[17] for it does not assume that they used the Notitia as it stands.

The forces in Britain are listed under three commands. In chapter xxviii of the Western Section appear the forts and troops controlled by the *comes litoris Saxonici*, while chapter xl catalogues those of the *dux Britanniarum*. The third army was that of the *comes Britanniarum*, whose headquarters staff is listed in chapter xxix, though we have to turn to chapter vii, a general distribution of palatini and comitatenses in the West, for details of the infantry and cavalry forces under his control.

This arrangement of forces certainly came into existence only by degrees. We have already noted (p. 240) that, though Diocletian first began the separation of the civil and military arms by instituting *duces* as commanders of frontier armies, the system did not become universal until the reign of Constantine, and that it was quite possibly not until the latter reign that the army of Britain was brought into line. The forces of the *dux* in Britain all ranked as limitanei, and this is the status also of the troops on the Saxon Shore; even the legions were thus graded.

Though the *dux* was probably first appointed by Diocletian or Constantine, it does not follow that the list of regiments assigned to him in the Notitia is as early. This list is in two parts. First comes a catalogue of sixteen units and their forts, all of which (in so far as they can be identified) lie in Durham or Yorkshire, except two in eastern Westmorland (Fig. 11, p. 264). Three of the units are vexillations of cavalry, a new type of formation first appearing in the third century and becoming frequent in the fourth. Two of these vexillations [18] were probably raised initially in the third century, though it seems likely that they reached Britain first under Constantine or even later; the third, the *equites Crispiani*, were clearly first raised under Constantine, since they are named after his son. The remaining units in this first part of the Duke's list are infantry, and apart from Legio vi they consist of ten numeri, only three of which show any sign of being old units.[19] The rest have local or fancy names typical of troops raised during, and perhaps late in, the fourth century, though local names are sometimes found earlier.

The second half of the Duke's list is headed *item per lineam valli* and records the garrisons of the forts of Hadrian's Wall in almost perfect geographical order from east to west, including those on the Cumberland coast, and with the insertion or addition of Chesterholm, Ribchester, *Virosidum* (accepted as Bainbridge) and *Olenacum*, which is here taken to be Lancaster.[20]

There are two curious features of this part of the list. The first is that, with two exceptions which themselves clearly go back to the third century, all the regiments are old-style alae or cohorts; these give the list an old-fashioned appearance which sharply contrasts with the other contents of the Notitia and particularly with the units appearing in the first half of the same chapter. The other is that the garrisons attributed to fourteen forts out of the twenty-three in the catalogue can be shown to have been present there during the third century, and this total might be increased by a further five where at present there is no evidence for the identity of the third-century garrisons.

Nevertheless, the catalogue cannot in fact be the third-century list itself, for in the first place the commanding officers of all infantry units, even cohorts 500 strong, are now *tribuni*; and secondly, at four forts a different garrison is listed from that known in the third century; and at one other, Olenacum, the Ala I Herculea, so named in honour of Maximian, is placed. The true explanation must be that casualties in the struggle between Constantius and Allectus were slight, and that most of the regiments returned comparatively intact to their home forts. The list must therefore represent the garrisons of these forts in the period between 296 and 367. If we are to believe that the same units remained on after 367 in the Wall-forts, we must explain how, in the great disturbances of that and the following year, when the frontier region for the first time suffered much damage despite the presence of its garrison, so great a proportion of regiments should have emerged unscathed and allowed to continue unreformed; and why, if the regiments were the same, the details of Count Theodosius' restoration of their forts should have been so radical as to suggest that a very different type of garrison was then installed (pp. 394–5).

To this view of the date two objections can be raised. One is that the list omits mention of the outpost forts beyond the Wall, which were certainly held in the fourth century, in some cases down to 367. The other is that the forts of Haltonchesters (*Onnum*) and Rudchester are listed as occupied, whereas excavations have suggested that they were not in fact occupied in the period 296–367. The first of these difficulties is not cogent, for other forts in north-west Britain which are known to have been occupied in this period are also omitted.[21] The situation at Haltonchester, and Rudchester, however, cannot yet be fully explained. Either the facts ascertained in the areas excavated are not typical of the whole or else the compiler of the list has made a slip. Why the more southerly forts of *Olenacum*, Ribchester and *Virosidum*[22] should be included in a list *per lineam valli*, it is impossible to explain. All three seem without doubt to have been occupied after 369; at Bainbridge excavations have proved this, while at Ribchester the coins go down to Valens and Gratian and at Lancaster to Arcadius and Honorius. Their significance will be considered shortly.

The list *per lineam valli* itself, then, is best taken to reflect the state of affairs in the period 296–367, even if deficiently. But the first part of the Duke's list must give an altogether later picture; and it is noteworthy that the forts in this part of the list are the only ones to figure in the Duke's insignia at the chapter's head. In the third century the forts catalogued in it had quite different garrisons (as far as they are known), which consisted of alae and cohorts. By the

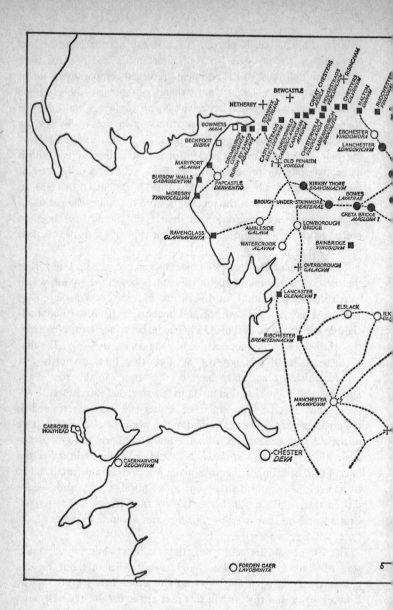

11 Map to illustrate the Duke's list in the Notitia Dignitatum
(pp. 261–8, 393–6, 405).

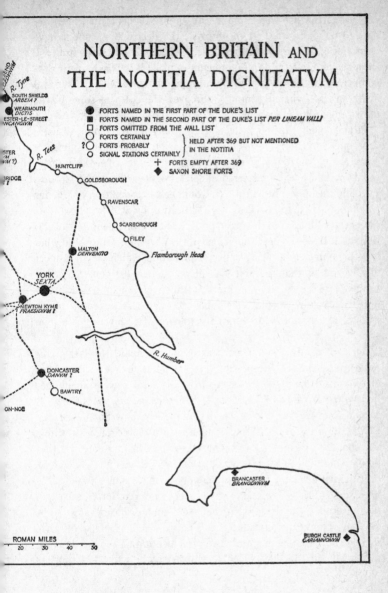

NORTHERN BRITAIN AND THE NOTITIA DIGNITATVM

● FORTS NAMED IN THE FIRST PART OF THE DUKE'S LIST
■ FORTS NAMED IN THE SECOND PART OF THE DUKE'S LIST *PER LINEAM VALLI*
□ FORTS OMITTED FROM THE WALL LIST
○ FORTS CERTAINLY ⎫
?○ FORTS PROBABLY ⎬ HELD AFTER 369 BUT NOT MENTIONED
○ SIGNAL STATIONS CERTAINLY ⎭ IN THE NOTITIA
✝ FORTS EMPTY AFTER 369
◆ SAXON SHORE FORTS

R. Tyne
—LAND
GELENDVM
SOUTH SHIELDS
ARBEIA ?
WEARMOUTH
DICTIS
ESTER-LE-STREET
NCANGIVM

R. Tees
—STER
—VM ?)
HUNTCLIFF
—BRIDGE
—E ?
GOLDSBOROUGH
RAVENSCAR
SCARBOROUGH
FILEY
MALTON
DERVENTIO
Flamborough Head
YORK
SEXTA,
NEWTON KYME
PRAESIDIVM ?
R. Humber
DONCASTER
DANVM ?
BAWTRY
ON-NOE

BRANCASTER
BRANODVNVM

ROMAN MILES
20   30   40   50

BURGH CASTLE
GARIANNONVM

date when the list was compiled all these regiments had been destroyed or transferred. If the former, the destruction cannot have been that of 296; for if we assume that Allectus used troops from the Pennines and left the Wall-regiments in place it is impossible to explain the damage to Hadrian's Wall in 296 coupled with the survival of its garrison virtually intact. Moreover, the titles of some of the units can hardly be so early.

Either, then, the list reflects the situation after some disaster subsequent to 296 (and the only one known to have been sufficiently grave is that of 367–9);[23] or it represents a time when the original garrisons had been transferred and later replaced by other troops. Virtually the only context for this would be the expedition of Magnus Maximus in 383, followed by the restoration by Stilicho about 396. But the distribution of the listed forts is not reasonable for a restoration: it does not embrace sufficient of the north nor firmly hold what it does embrace (Fig. 11). The best explanation, which seems to cover all the facts is that the first part of the Duke's list shows us what troops were left holding northern Britain after Maximus had withdrawn a large part of the available troops for his attempt on the empire. It lists not an intentional deployment of forces but a remnant.[24]

Short of a full coin-list, such as might be yielded by large-scale excavations, the evidence at our disposal is not sufficient to enable a distinction to be made between those forts which were abandoned in 383 and those which survived for another twenty years. But it is certain that the forts of Papcastle, Ambleside, Low Borrow Bridge, Watercrook, Ebchester, Elsack and Ilkley were occupied after 369, and that the first and last of these were rebuilt at that date. Yet they do not figure in the list.[25] It would be difficult to maintain, therefore, that the list gives the Duke's full command in the years 369–83; but until some of these forts can be positively proved to have been occupied after 383, the theory that they were among those evacuated by Maximus fits the available facts; this part of the Duke's list will then merely show us how much of the reorganisation of 369 survived the movements of 383, and indeed, as will shortly be suggested, those of 396.

Other forts in Wales and its borders also contributed to Maximus' expedition. The evacuation of Caernarvon must be attributed to him on the strength of its coin-evidence, and Forden Gaer, which was probably reconstructed in 369, seems to be another, as also do the forts at Brecon and Cardiff. Legio xx from Chester probably formed the nucleus of his force. It is significant that it nowhere appears in the Notitia in either the British or the continental lists, and must have been lost by Maximus, if indeed it had not been previously destroyed in the troubles of 367–9, which seems unlikely. The coin series at Chester diminishes strikingly after Valens (364–78) and Gratian (367–83).

If absence from the Duke's list is accepted as implying evacuation under Magnus Maximus, it seems to follow that the Wall forts cannot have been among those evacuated by him, for they *are* listed, even though the troops shown in them appear to belong to an earlier date. The reason for keeping this list, if it really is out-of-date, is perhaps that it preserves a record of the last regular troops to hold the wall. If Count Theodosius installed *laeti* or *gentiles* (settlements of barbarian irregulars perhaps from abroad) these would not be included in the Duke's command but would be organised in their own tribal groupings under Roman prefects. Chapter xlii of the Notitia, which catalogues the *laeti* and *gentiles* of the western empire, breaks off short before reaching Britain, and thus deprives us of confirmation.

Lancaster, Ribchester and Bainbridge remain to be considered. Though they are wrongly included in the section dealing with the wall, their appearance in the list at all should mean that they were not evacuated by Magnus Maximus. They may therefore be the only three forts held in Valentia after 383. This would account for their appearance in a different section from the rest of the Duke's forces, all of which could well lie in Britannia Secunda. However, the absence of their badges from among the Duke's insignia at the head of chapter xl should mean that their evacuation had occurred before these were compiled. Presumably, then, they were abandoned by Stilicho.

Our conclusion must be that the first part of the Duke's list reflects the position in Britain after 383, though the list as we have it is based on a later 'return'. Indeed, it is unlikely that returns were made to the western primicerius from Britain during Maximus' supremacy; and, as Mommsen first pointed out, the seconding of the chief clerk (*princeps*) of the Duke's staff from that of the Magister Militum is an arrangement which only came about after 395.[26]

From this it is clear that Stilicho's reorganisation of Britain in about 396 did not involve the movement of reinforcements for the *dux* on any scale, for otherwise strategic positions such as Ilkley and Manchester would have figured in the catalogue. Indeed, on the contrary, the evacuation may already have begun.

The list of the Count of the Saxon Shore in chapter xxviii appears to be of the same date (for his princeps, like the Duke's, is appointed from the staff of the Magister Militum), but it too probably reflects an earlier situation, that brought about in 369.[27] The office of Count itself was a development of Constantine, but the appearance of *comites rei militaris*, in charge of regional armies, is first recorded under his sons; and such counts normally commanded comitatenses. It is probable that originally this was true of the Count of the Saxon Shore, whose command, like that of Carausius, may once have covered both sides of the Channel; but by the time of the existing list the comitatenses had been withdrawn, and the continental stations had been re-organised under the *dux tractus Armoricani* and the *dux Belgicae Secundae*.[28] The Count was now in the anomalous position of controlling merely limitanei, and fewer of them than the *dux*. There are other hints, too, that the list is late. One is the presence of Legio II Augusta at Richborough. Under Diocletian the legions were still at full strength, but in later years legionary detachments on permanent posting were upgraded to legions, though they remained at about 1,000 men; the parent formations remained correspondingly reduced in numbers. It is clear that Richborough, a fort of only six acres, could not accommodate more than about 1,000 men; yet the presence there of its *praefectus* (as the commander was now called) shows that it was the headquarters of the legion. Another indication of the lateness of the list is that a former garrison of Pevensey (*Anderita*), the *milites Anderetiani*, is listed in the Notitia under the Duke of Mainz; and the *classis Anderetianorum* lies at Paris.[29] The garrison at Pevensey in chapter xxviii is the *numerus Abulcorum*.

The third commander in Britain, the *comes Britanniarum*,[30] has caused considerable confusion, owing to the belief that his office cannot have been created until after 410.[31] Collingwood was for this reason converted to the view that Britain was re-occupied later in Honorius' reign. 'The last phase of Roman government . . . began in or about 417 and ended some years before 429.' This theory has had considerable influence on subsequent writers,[32] but it has no basis in reality.

There had been at least one *comes Britanniarum* before the middle of the fourth century, when Gratian, father of the emperor Valentinian, commanded the British army in this rank.[33] This was presumably a personal appointment *ad hoc*, perhaps during a crisis which involved the despatch of comitatenses (p. 387f.); for, if there had still been a field army in Britain in 367–9, it is likely that Ammianus' fairly detailed account of the crisis would have mentioned it.

The appointment of permanent *comites* in charge of regional armies of comitatenses belongs to the late fourth or early fifth centuries, but there is no general agreement that the inception of the office dates to a period after 410, as Collingwood held.[34] In the Notitia the Count of Britain commands six cavalry and three infantry regiments, a force of some 6,000 men at the most.[35] Such an army is ludicrously inadequate to the task of recovering Britain after its loss. On the other hand, the list as it stands must date from the reign of Honorius, since one of the cavalry units has the title *equites Honoriani seniores*. Two other of its cavalry units appear to be newly promoted to the comitatenses from the armies of the Duke and the Count of the Saxon Shore;[36] and one of the legions, the Secundani iuniores, may also have been promoted from the limitanei of the latter. The force as a whole must therefore date some years after 396, and it seems reasonable to assign its creation either to Stilicho (as a counter-balance to his withdrawal of large forces of limitanei early in 402 for the defence of Italy – a withdrawal which must have virtually destroyed the commands of both the Duke and the Count of the Saxon Shore) or else to Constantine III when he removed most of the remaining troops in 407 for his invasion of Gaul. But we may bear the possibility in mind that the command was actually established earlier, perhaps by Magnus Maximus, the list as we have it merely reflecting a later situation.

One of the Count's cavalry regiments, the *equites Honoriani seniores*, appear twice in the same chapter of the Notitia, being listed also in Gaul under the *Magister equitum Galliarum*.[37] Time, therefore, has to be allowed for this transfer before the chapter reached its final form about 420. That there were still Roman troops in Britain as late as 409, is apparent from a passage in Zosimus,[38]

269

but their numbers must have been very small. The withdrawals of Stilicho followed by those of Constantine III had left the island virtually denuded of standing forces, and it is easy to understand the necessity for the cities of Britain now to undertake their own defence.

1. Vegetius, ii, 19.

2. Ann Perkins, *The Excavations at Dura-Europos*: Final Report v, part i, *The Parchments and Papyri* (Yale, 1959), p. 28; Hyginus Gromaticus, *de munitione castrorum*, 27.

3. Tacitus, *Agricola*, 28.

4. Good illustrations of Syrian archers in action can be seen on Trajan's column. Cichorius, *Die Reliefs der Traiansäule* (Berlin, 1896–1900), Scenes lxvi, lxx, cviii, cxv; See also I. A. Richmond, *Papers of the British School at Rome*, xiii (1935), 16–17.

5. A settlement of *laeti* may be the explanation of the extremely early commencement-date (perhaps as early as the end of the third century), of the Saxon cemetery outside Caistor by Norwich (J. N. L. Myres and B. Green, *Th Anglo-Saxon Cemeteries of Caistor by Norwich and Markshall, Norfolk*, Oxford, 1973, pp. 43 ff. Otherwise they must be regarded as barbarians who had obtained the *receptio* and had been allowed to settle within the empire in a depopulated region.

It has often been suggested that a century later, in 372, a similar transference of Alamannic tribesmen took place under their king Fraomar: this would amount to a settlement of *foederati* in Britain (foederati being free barbarians, under their own rulers, who were allowed to settle under treaty in return for military duties). However, a careful reading of Ammianus Marcellinus, xxix, 4, 7, shows only that after the virtual annihilation of the Bucinobantes (the division of the Alamanni of which he had been made king) Fraomar was transferred to Britain with the rank of tribune to take command of a numerus of Alamanni which was already part of the garrison.

6. Vegetius, iv, 37.

7. *Ibid.*, i, 21.

8. This is well illustrated in parts of Wales, where the camps keep to the high plateaux, where alone large bodies of troops could manoeuvre or encamp, while the permanent forts tend to be sited below, at the junctions of valleys.

9. The Latin equivalent for under canvas was *sub pellibus*; Caesar, *BG*, iii, 29, etc.

10. It is not often possible to be sure for what sized force a camp was prepared; but the problem is settled at Rey Cross, Westmorland, a camp of 20·1 acres, which can be shown by its planning to be intended for a legion (*CW*,[2] xxxiv (1934), 50).

11. *RIB*, 653.

12. The area is calculated from overall dimensions (rampart-front to rampart-front), even though this means that there will be variations due to differing widths of rampart and intervallum road. Some authorities calculate sizes on internal area, but this method has the great disadvantage that it can only be applied to excavated forts, preventing comparison with unexcavated ones.

13. *ILS*, 2487.

14. At Lincoln the fortress had a rampart of this type.

15. Compare the wooden towers seen on Trajan's Column, Cichorius, op. cit., Scene i; *Papers of t. British School at Rome*, xiii (1935), 35, fig. 14; Macdonald, *Roman Wall in Scotland* (Oxford, 1934), pl. iv.

16. A. H. M. Jones, *The Later Roman Empir.* (Oxford, 1964), iii, Appendix 2.

17. Birley, *Cumberland and Westmorland Antiquarian and Archaeological Society Transactions*,[2] xxxix (1939), 210.

18. The *equites Dalmatae* and the *equites catafractarii*.

19. The numerus barcariorum Tigrisiensium, cf. *RIB*, 601; the numerus Nerviorum, possibly an earlier cohort reformed, according to Birley; and the numerus exploratorum, cf. p. 208.

20. Castlesteads (*Uxellodunum*) and Maryport (*Alauna*, here spelt *Alione*) are out of order, and Bowness (Maia) and Beckfoot (Bibra) are omitted. Alione has been identified with Watercrook, but seems to fit Maryport better. For Lancaster, see note 22 below.

21. Such as Ambleside, Low Borrow Bridge, Watercrook, Overborough and probably Old Penrith. Nor if, in order to explain the absence of the outpost forts, we were to brush aside the difficulty over the survival of the Wall-garrisons and date the list to the period after 369, would the list even then conform to the actual position, since the forts listed on p. 266, equally absent from the list, are known to have been in occupation then.

22. There seems to be no good reason to accept the identification of *Olenacum* with Old Carlisle, th *Olerica* of the Ravenna Cosmography (*Archaeologia*, xciii, 42). In our list it is sandwiched between *Bremetenraco* (Ribchester) and *Virosido* (which is here accepted as Bainbridge on the strength of its garrison). Not only are place-names ending in *-acum* a feature of the west side of the Pennines (*Bremetennacum*, *Galacum*, *Bravoniacum*), though not north of the last (Kirkby Thore), but also the list proceeds in geographical order wherever possible. *Olenacum* is a cavalry fort (*Ala I Herculea*); this rules out Ilkley and Low Borrow Bridge, which are too small; but Lancaster would suit very well both in size and in geographical position.

23. D. Hoffmann (*Das Spätrömische Bewegungsheer* (1970), p. 350), well puts the case for a context in 369.

24. J. H. Ward (*Britannia*, iv (1973), 250 ff.), accepts this diffi-

culty but regards the distribution as evidence of a partial reoccupation in the fifth century.

25. The terminal date for Newton Kyme and Manchester within the fourth century is not so certain.

26. The Duke's title of *spectabilis* is another indication of revision no earlier than this date.

27. His command, too, includes units brought over by Count Theodosius (D. Hoffmann, *Das Spätrömische Bewegungsheer* (1970), p. 350).

28. See *Notitia Dignitatum Occ.*, xxxvii, 14, and xxxviii, 7, for two Gallic positions *in litore Saxonico*.

29. Chapters xli, 17, and xlii, 23.

30. His title is described in error as *comes Britanniae* in the heading of chapter xxix, but given correctly in line 4 as well as in chapter vii.

31. Bury in *JRS*, x (1920), 144; Collingwood, *Roman Britain and the English Settlements* (Oxford, 1936), 297–8.

32. E.g., H. M. Chadwick in Norah K. Chadwick, *Studies in Early British History* (Cambridge, 1954), p. 13.

33. Ammianus Marcellinus, xxx, 7, 3.

34. Bury himself, *History of the Later Roman Empire* (London, 1923), i, p. 118, note 3 (three years after his article in *JRS*, x) suggested that the Count of Strasbourg, an officer in every way analogous with the Count of Britain, was appointed as early as 397.

35. A. H. M. Jones, *The Later Roman Empire*, ii, 680–2; iii, 379.

36. The *equites catafractarii iuniores* and the *equites Stablesiani*.

37. Chapter vii, 202 and 172.

38. Zosimus, vi, 1, 2.

12

The towns

Something of the origin and status of the towns of Roman Britain has already been described in Chapter 10. Here their history and character will be discussed, and then an assessment will be made of the part they played in the civilisation of the province.

Urbanisation in any true sense was something new in Britain. Some towns, such as Canterbury, Rochester or Silchester, succeeded pre-Roman oppida on the same spot: others, like Colchester, *Verulamium*, Chichester or Dorchester (Dorset), succeeded their native predecessors on a freshly chosen site near by. In no case did the earlier oppidum possess the true characteristics of a town: its contribution lay in its population or prestige. The choice between building on a new site or retaining the old was decided upon grounds of accessibility and of relationship to the new road-system or to a Roman fort thereon. Dorchester at its river-crossing was a much more suitable site than Maiden Castle, high on its waterless hill-top; but the town may also owe much to an original military establishment on this spot. Colchester was an official foundation for which a new site was needed: that chosen was occupied previously by the legionary fortress, and lay half a mile from the site of Cunobelin's oppidum. Belgic Canterbury already occupied the best local site at the crossing of the Stour, as did Belgic Rochester at the crossing of the Medway: in both these cases it was necessary only to tidy the site by filling in gullies and imposing regular streets. Silchester, though not at a river-crossing, was already an important centre, with no obvious rival in the immediate neighbourhood: it, too, was adapted.

Until recently little was known of the earliest phases of the towns of highest status, the *coloniae*, save that three of them (p. 231) were veteran settlements. Archaeology had revealed only glimpses of these places in their maturity, when their remains differed little from those of other cities. But excavations in Gloucester since 1968 have thrown remarkable light on the earliest period of the *colonia* there: the veterans were accommodated in half-timbered or clay-walled hut-ments on stone cills, closely following the design and plan of the barracks of the fortress which they succeeded, but built at an even greater density. During subsequent decades these were replaced piecemeal, but only in the middle of the second century did a court-yard house of sophisticated Italianate type first make its appearance. In 1972 excavations in Colchester began to reveal a very similar pattern. There buildings belonging to the fortress, whose defences had been levelled, continued in occupation (with modifications) until destroyed in 60. These discoveries vividly illustrate the role and development of veteran coloniae (p. 98) in a way so far unparalleled in the empire, and emphasise the para-military aspect of their pur-pose. But colonies could also serve a second intention, as models of urban life: this was the first and most direct way in which the Roman army influenced the civilisation of the province.

The role of the Roman army in the development of towns was two-fold. The first, provision of technical aid, was the fruit of policy. The second, though essentially unintentional, was equally important. Roman forts tended to be placed at strategic points, especially where the new roads crossed rivers. Round them traders' settlements quickly sprang up, for 500 men with money to spend represented a market rarely available elsewhere; but if given time to take root, the settlement remained when the troops moved on. This can be seen to have happened at many sites, such as Chelmsford, Exeter, Ciren-cester or Water Newton. When the army left, the fort site was con-veyed to civilian authority, and the settlement in most cases spread over the site of the demolished military buildings. Even quite small settlements, like Great Casterton, Dorchester on Thames or Brough on Humber, were in this sense official foundations, because army lands were made available to them.

But in another sense we may distinguish between what are some-times called the large and small towns of Roman Britain, or more accurately (since sizes tend to overlap) between towns which were in-tended as administrative centres and those which were not. In colo-nies, municipia and civitas-capitals we can see the hand of the Roman surveyor at work. The streets were laid off on a rectangular grid (pl. 8a), administrative buildings were provided and a distinct effort was sometimes made to provide the colonnaded streets of a classical town. The 'small' towns were not thus treated. They resemble little more than spontaneous village growths and are called towns only because they were walled later in their history. Such small settlements might develop round the stations of the public post, where accommodation and changes of horses were provided at intervals along the principal roads, or they might grow up as local market centres; some, like Bath, owed their prosperity to a thermal establishment of note; others in the north never lost their military connection, but became thriving centres for trade, relaxation and eventual retirement in the immediate vicinity of garrison stations. Such settlements were Carlisle or Corbridge or Kirkby Thore, and the important vici at Housesteads, Chesters or Old Carlisle. Whatever the main reason for their growth, they owed little to official action, save in some cases the original transfer of military land or the occasional presence of government agencies; their prosperity was due to normal economic factors.

With the civitas-capitals it was different. Traders and manufacturers, of course, contributed to their growth, but the government intended also that the ruling classes should play their part in these. Such towns had a social and political as well as an economic role. British society, however, was not by nature town-centred; the tribal aristocrats had their country estates, and needed pressure or encouragement to take up residence in the new towns. Those who had political ambitions would soon conform; in others fashion, the need for education or the requirements of business would gradually induce a willingness to follow. Now that private warfare was no longer possible, wealth could be increased only by investing in new directions, in trade, in urban property or in manufacturing industry. An early example of such investment can be perceived in the Claudian block of shops in insula xiv at Verulamium, for the individual traders' tenements there form parts of a single larger property of unitary design. Tacitus saw evidence of the success of Agricola's educational policy in the spreading popularity of Roman language and dress, and of porticos, bathing establishments and elegant dinner parties. Nevertheless, conversion to town life was a slow process. At *Verulamium* it may have been exceptionally slow, for there no sizeably luxurious town houses with recognisable dining-rooms are known

275

before the middle of the second century; but even at Canterbury the earliest masonry house dates only from about 100, and at Silchester also those houses which can certainly be recognised as of first-century date are relatively small and simple. Even at its most developed, town life was probably for the landed aristocracy a seasonal activity, as it became again in the sixteenth and later centuries: part of the year will have been spent in the towns on official business, and after the season was over they will have repaired to their estates, where, however, the same slow development of the villa is manifest.

Something of the official nature of the assistance given to the early towns has already been seen in the new forms of building technique and design which were introduced at a very early stage (p. 234). More evidence is provided by the plans of public buildings. In Gaul the forums being built in the Flavian period were often double precincts: an oblong court had two entrances, each set in about the middle of the long sides of the building; one half of the court contained a temple and altar (the *capitolium* of the town); the other half formed the market square backed by the basilica. The forum at *Verulamium* approximates to this type, but it is exceptional in Britain, where the normal forum was not so elaborate. In this the court is much more nearly square, surrounded on three sides by porticos and shops or offices, the fourth being occupied by the basilica. The entrance lies in the centre of the short side facing the basilica, behind which lies a further range of offices. Such a plan bears an obviously close relationship to the principia of a fortress, and is certainly derived from it. This type of building had been developed for administrative convenience, and it served its new purpose well; but the adoption of this rather than the Gallic type shows that architects were not imported from abroad to plan the new cities, and is another indication of the influence of army designers in the government's urbanising programme. The absence of capitolia-precincts shows that resources were not unlimited. Nevertheless, the Romano-British type of forum could be adjusted in size to suit the needs of each city.[1]

The utilisation of building types already introduced by the army can be traced also in the plan of public baths, where the various rooms of graded heat extended in a long line behind a *palaestra* or exercise courtyard, instead of being grouped more compactly alongside it, as for instance at Pompeii. But in the middle of the second century this type of building was already being modified to suit local climate, for at Wroxeter and Caerwent and probably also at Leicester, a large hall was provided to replace the palaestra, so that exercise could be taken under cover. The idea may have been first adopted in the legionary baths at Chester.

Public buildings of this sort, which had prestige value, were, of course, early provided and on a monumental scale, and as their first appearance and later development are important keys to the history of the towns, some details must now be given. Forums and basilicas of the Flavian period have already been discussed (p. 235). Before the end of the first century *Verulamium* had been given a market building in masonry, consisting of a courtyard 136 feet long and 36 feet wide, flanked by two rows of nine shops, and a Romano-Celtic temple also in masonry had been built near by. The Triangular Temple soon followed. The implications of a thriving commerce are striking, for the city already possessed a very large forum. At Silchester the Public Baths are similarly of first-century foundation; there is a possibility that they are earlier than the forum and date from the reign of Cogidubnus (p. 326). At Canterbury a Theatre or Amphitheatre of Romano-Celtic type was provided, perhaps about 90.

The provision and maintenance of public buildings continued unabated for more than a century. At Chichester an amphitheatre was built early in the second century, and at Caistor by Norwich the forum and public baths seem both to have been provided in the reign of Antoninus Pius: the town was then already over fifty years old, and the delay must be attributable to the poverty resulting from the Boudiccan rebellion. At Wroxeter the whole development of the town began later than most, since its site was occupied by the military until about 90. The Forum was built on the site of the unfinished first-century Baths, now demolished to make room for it, perhaps under orders from Hadrian himself.[2] The building bore a dedicatory inscription to him dated 129–30. A previous military occupation of the site is probably also the reason for the Hadrianic date of the forum at Leicester. Certainly this forum and the one at Wroxeter are the only public buildings which can surely be ascribed to his reign, and possibly therefore to the emperor's personal initiative during his British visit. Fresh public baths on a larger scale than those of Silchester were provided at Wroxeter shortly after the middle of the second century on a site immediately opposite the Forum, where they were given a covered exercise hall and a very large open-air swimming bath, and were combined with a shopping precinct and the largest public latrine so far discovered in Britain. The whole insula is a notable example of town-planning. Some time about the year 165 the town-centre and many neighbouring properties were damaged by fire, but the Forum was at once restored, and a new temple of semi-classical design replaced some of the burnt shops farther south.

About ten years earlier a similar disaster had destroyed the Forum at *Verulamium* and all the central part of the town – at least 52 acres; such conflagrations were unavoidable risks when most buildings were half-timbered. But this one proved a blessing in disguise, enabling many improvements to be undertaken. A Theatre was now provided in connection with the Romano-Celtic temple near by, and new temples of classical type were added to the Forum, while the market-hall was remodelled. Somewhat later, perhaps when the town-wall was built in the early third century, two monumental arches were erected across Watling Street to mark the original limits of the town and no doubt to record its status.

At Cirencester the Flavian basilica became badly cracked by settlement of its foundations where they coincided with the buried ditches of the fort below, which had not been noticed by its builders, and was completely reconstructed about the middle of the second century; and perhaps slightly earlier a market square, much larger than the one at *Verulamium*, was added near the forum, possibly in replacement of a first-century timber predecessor.

The reign of Antoninus Pius thus saw great advances in the towns of Britain. Even at Brough on Humber (*Petuaria*), where a small town was developing on or near the site of a fort recently evacuated, a theatre was being built in this reign.[3] At Leicester public Baths, attached to what is probably a covered exercise hall similar to the one at Wroxeter, were begun about 140 and completed some ten years later; and towards the close of the century, the original Forum being found to provide insufficient market space, a big secondary market square and hall were provided north of it on a site where a derelict private house had to be demolished to make space. Thus, all through the second century public buildings were being built or improved, and notable among them are the extra market-places which came to be required. We even find a new town established during the middle of the century at Moridunum, Carmarthen, the capital of the Demetae in west Wales; it was probably based on the military vicus which had grown up there outside the Flavian fort, but now there are signs of a regular system of streets and an amphitheatre was provided. The town was laid out in time to receive the normal provision of earth and then stone defences, at the end of the century (p. 285); they enclosed about 25 acres. Whether a grant of self-government to a new *civitas peregrina* is implied is not yet certain.

As late as about 220 the original earthen theatre at Canterbury was completely remodelled, being transformed into a great masonry building of classical type. But during the third century emphasis shifted to the provision of defensive walls, and no further work is known on public buildings until its close. At that period the forums of both Caistor and Silchester seem to have been reconstructed, the latter certainly after a fire. At *Verulamium* a long porch was provided for the basilica on its Watling Street frontage, the theatre-temple was surrounded by new colonnades and the theatre itself reconstructed and enlarged; the market-hall was also rebuilt at this time, and a third monumental arch was erected, spanning Watling Street between the market and the theatre. At Cirencester the basilica was maintained throughout the fourth century, and alterations were made to the forum as also to the market-square near by; indeed, an additional market-area seems to have been provided behind the basilica by blocking off a street. Only at Wroxeter is a contrary picture given, for there the forum was again destroyed by fire towards the close of the third century and was not rebuilt, and the neighbouring temple seems to have been dismantled; the Baths, however, which may have been involved in the conflagration, continued in use and were again reconstructed.

Public baths seem to call for both aqueducts and drains, two features for which Roman civilisation was famous. In Britain we are less well informed than is appropriate about either. In the case of drains, their materials have often been subsequently robbed away, leaving little evidence of character; moreover, the streets beneath which they lie are less rewarding to the excavator than the buildings each side. Aqueducts, on the other hand, tend to escape identification because of the slight nature of their remains, which are easily destroyed by the plough. At Dorchester, Dorset, and at Wroxeter the water was tapped from streams and then brought into the upper part of the towns along open leets which follow the contours of the neighbouring valleys. For the former the River Frome was tapped more than 9 miles above the town; near Wroxeter the dam which ponded back the Bell Brook at the point of departure is still visible. The Raw Dykes at Leicester have sometimes been taken for an aqueduct, but the shape of the earthwork is that of a navigable canal, leading perhaps to docks.[4] A more remarkable system existed at Lincoln: a spring was tapped about $1\frac{1}{4}$ miles away, and the water was pumped from this on an uphill course through a pipeline sealed in concrete to withstand pressure; a large reservoir just inside the town wall, and partly supported by it, has recently been identified as the *castellum divisorium*, or distributing tank. Many other towns, such as *Verulamium* or Caerwent, must once have possessed water-supplies by aqueduct, since they show traces of distribution pipes made of hollowed timber jointed together every 4–7 feet by iron collars. At Silchester one of these pipe-lines was traced for about 700 feet across the town and then below the town-wall to a masonry foundation outside. It is possible that a water-tower here fed a gravity distribution system which had been installed before the defences were built.

Surplus water was used to flush the drains. At Wroxeter an overflow duct running along the edge of the main street provided water to flush the house-drains along its course, each of which was provided with a sluice. Analogy suggests that each householder was assigned a particular hour of the day during which he might open his sluice. The fullest evidence, however, for urban drainage comes from Lincoln. Here all the principal streets of the upper town seem to have possessed stone-built sewers big enough for a boy to walk along; into them fed smaller drains from private houses. At intervals man-holes gave access from the streets above when inspection or cleaning became necessary. Sewers of the same sort certainly served at least the larger streets at some other towns, but the system was rarely so complete: sometimes the sewer was originally built to serve some individual building, as at Colchester, or the public baths of Silchester. And at *Verulamium* a large sewer on the Lincoln scale started at the back of the forum and ran down to the river, taking subsidiary drainage from a public latrine and private houses on its way, the latrine itself being permanently flushed by two overflow ducts from elsewhere – perhaps two public fountains near the Theatre. Another sewer ran at right angles to the first along Watling Street, where it was found built into the foundations of a monumental arch; the latter was traversed also by a second channel which probably carried a clean-water supply. Other streets in *Verulamium* had wooden rain-water ducts along their sides which may also have served the houses which they passed; and the same type is known at Canterbury. Even quite small towns sometimes possessed notable drains, as for instance Kenchester.

Much money, it is clear, was spent on the provision and repair of public buildings through the centuries. But the history of a town is more than the history of its public buildings. Private houses and shops in the earliest phases of all the towns were built of cheap materials – usually clay applied to a timber framework, but some-times clay alone – partly because this was a natural architecture in the south-east and one already well proven by the Roman army, and partly because it was less costly than stone and less committing in its finality. In London the debris of a serious fire which devastated at least 65 acres about the year 130 shows that the city even then consisted largely of such buildings, and at *Verulamium* they con-tinued to be built until the fire of *c.* 155. At this city the earliest use of opus signinum for concrete floors does not appear much before 100, and almost no private buildings made use of flint and mortar for a further fifty years. Nor did mosaics make their appearance there much before 150, though at Canterbury slight traces of a destroyed mosaic of the first century have been recorded.[5] The *Verulamium* house-plans of the first and early second centuries are small rect-angular structures some 50–65 feet in length and perhaps half as wide, often set at right angles to the streets and divided into some five or six rooms, of which one or more is floored in rough yellow concrete or opus signinum, the rest in clay.

At Cirencester painted wall plaster has been found in such build-ings as early as Flavian times, and concrete or opus signinum made their appearance as early: here, too, stone began to replace timber-framing for the walls early in the second century if not earlier, doubt-less because of the ready availability of easily worked Cotswold limestone. The earliest houses which can be recognised at Silchester were slightly larger than those of *Verulamium*, being about 80 by

40 feet in dimensions; they sometimes had a corridor or veranda round three if not all four sides, and their timber-framed walls rested on flint footings. A similar style of construction is found later in the second century applied to quite large and luxurious houses at both *Verulamium* and Leicester; in the latter town a wall above its masonry footing was built of unfired clay bricks set in sand,[6] while at *Verulamium* the wall was cast in one piece by tamping the clay between shuttering.

The earliest block of shops at *Verulamium* had been destroyed in the Boudiccan sack. This event was a serious set-back for the town, and there is little indication anywhere of reconstruction for another fifteen years. Eventually, about 75, at roughly the same time as work on the Forum started, the shops in insula XIV were rebuilt on much the same lines as before, and were clearly still in single ownership. The nature of the construction, based on timber sill-beams set beneath the level of the soil, necessitated replacement of timbers every twenty-five years or so. The plans of successive rebuildings, however, show no fundamental change until about 150, by about which date it seems evident that the tenants had been able to acquire their own premises; for the buildings of the fourth reconstruction were much more individualistic, and were set for the first time at right-angles to the street, though still behind a timber colonnade. Shortly after they had been built, the whole street was destroyed by the great fire which has already been mentioned. The clearance which this effected gave opportunity for replanning much of the town, and in the second half of the second century very large private houses, built at least partly in flint and mortar, rendered fire-proof with tile roofs, and richly provided with frescoes, mosaics and tessellated pavements, make their appearance. It is clear that by the Antonine period the wealthy classes at *Verulamium* had been fully converted to town life and now invested large sums in luxurious town mansions. In plan these new houses do not much resemble contemporary villas in the countryside, but nor are they closely planned like the houses in the densely packed towns of the classical south. A Romano-British town-house type had been evolved. Each building seems to have stood in its own grounds, often at the corner of an insula, and was L-shaped, or of courtyard plan, consisting of anything from ten to thirty rooms connected by a corridor. There is little indication of an upper storey.

Verulamium seems to have been slow to grow, for at other towns

such developments probably occurred somewhat earlier. At Cirencester parts of quite sizeable masonry houses have been shown to
belong to the first half of the second century, and at Canterbury to
as early as 100. The earliest buildings in each case, however, are
always of clay or half-timber. At Cirencester a block containing
timber-framed shops of the Flavian period is known, which is
strongly reminiscent of that at *Verulamium* in plan; and here, too,
before the middle of the second century it can be suggested that
individuals had been able to buy their own premises, since about
the time of Hadrian piecemeal conversion into stone was being
undertaken in some shops but not in others. Such developments
suggest that traders were becoming increasingly prosperous. At
Wroxeter wealthy traders, who perhaps had already founded their
fortunes in the legionary *canabae*, seem to have been present from
the beginning, for detached shops some 70–90 feet long lined the
main street of the town, and no multiple blocks have yet been found
there.

Not many towns are known to have been provided with defences
in the first century. Colchester had no rampart, as Tacitus makes
clear, in 60;[7] but the early bank and ditch at *Verulamium*, enclosing
about 119 acres, are probably of Claudian date, and Silchester (pl.
7), too, was then defended in similar fashion. There were precedents for the walling of chartered cities, but earth ramparts are
difficult to parallel among the towns of the Continent;[8] and in any
case it is hard to see why Silchester alone of peregrine towns should
have defences at this date, unless this different treatment is due to
the town being part of Cogidubnus' realm at th time. and not within
the province. The late first-century colonies at Lincoln and Gloucester lay inside former legionary fortresses, whose earth ramparts they
presumably used; but at Lincoln there is evidence that the rampart,
and one of the gates, was later faced with stone some considerable
time before the town-wall proper replaced it. This reconstruction
may date from the colony's foundation; there are indications of a
similar sequence at Gloucester. No defences earlier than its town-
wall, apart from the fort, have yet been discovered in London, but a
peculiarity of its street-plan may perhaps suggest that they will one
day be found.

The other towns of Roman Britain grew up as open settlements, as
did the towns of Gaul; but unlike these, they received defences before

it was too late. In Gaul, apart from the walled colonies of the Augustan period in Provence, and a few towns dangerously exposed near the frontier which received walls in the later second or early third centuries, the great majority of the towns were still undefended when the barbarian hordes broke over the Rhine in the third quarter of the third century. The walls which were belatedly provided thereafter enclosed only fractions of the areas formerly built-up, and their foundations were largely composed of re-used masonry salvaged from the ruins. In Britain it was different. The town-wall never contain re-used masonry,[9] and the walled areas either comprise the whole town or exclude only outlying parts. It is only rarely, as at Caistor by Norwich (pl. 8a) or Silchester (pl. 7), that a definite shrinkage of the urban area can be attested, and even then the scale of the reductions is not comparable with those across the Channel.

The reason for the contrast is twofold. In the first place, of course, Britain did not suffer such serious inroads as Gaul. But in the second place it is now certain that almost all its towns received a preliminary circumvallation, consisting of an earth rampart and ditch, towards the close of the second century, at the period of their greatest prosperity.[10] When walls were added later it was naturally found easiest to cut back the front of the existing rampart and face it with the wall so that the same ditch could continue in use. In this way the new wall usually enclosed the same area as the rampart which preceded it; but sufficient examples exist where a different line was followed to show that two periods of work are involved and not merely two phases of the same programme,[11] which the dating-evidence in any case shows to be impossible.

Gaul and Britain, therefore, differ in the history of their urban fortifications, and this contrasted picture calls for explanation. Its effect is clear: the town-walls of Britain enclosed living communities, while those of Gaul formed strong-points at the heart of their former selves.

To establish the date of town defences is a task of importance to the historian, partly because once built the walls became a lasting mould, controlling expansion down to Plantagenet times and beyond (pl. 8b); partly because defences themselves are indicative of historical pressures. The *Digest* contains two passages, one of them a rescript of Marcus, which make it clear that towns could not erect defences at pleasure: imperial permission had to be obtained.[12]

Their appearance accordingly marks the application of policy, and no doubt anticipates (or follows) unrest. But imperial policy was applied on a wide front. If types of defensive structure can be identified they are more likely to be contemporary than historically haphazard. It follows that the latest date proved among members of a type should guide our dating of the rest.

Various dates in the second half of the second century have been suggested for members of the large group of Romano-British earth ramparts, depending on the evidence which each has produced.[13] The latest suggested dates are *c.* 185 at Dorchester on Thames and 'some years earlier than 200' at Chichester. At Silchester it was *c.* 160–70, and at Exeter *c.* 150. But, as we have seen, a variety of dates for the same phenomenon is very unlikely. Mass provision of earth ramparts for towns is something quite without parallel in the Roman empire, and here they must surely represent the application of a single policy in a single context which demanded the rapid simultaneous fortification of all sizeable settlements. Such a programme could only be carried out at speed in earthwork, on which large corvées could be made to labour. To build walls would be to restrict the work to the availability of skilled workmen, and thus prolong the operation.

Bearing these considerations in mind, and recalling the inherent difficulty of obtaining precisely contemporary dating evidence, we may suggest that the context for all these earthwork defences lies in the unsettled years between the death of Marcus and the recovery of Britain by Severus. Within those years the disturbances of Commodus' reign – the northern invasion and the army unrest – may be thought more remote, less likely, than the attempt of Albinus on the empire and its consequences. Britain was Albinus' base and might become his retreat; and even if a Roman invasion did not materialise, he cannot have failed to foresee the probable results of exposing the province to the barbarians by removing so large a part of the garrison. To give the towns the means of defending themselves would be the corollary, and it is certainly true that no town has yet produced signs of sack at this period. The provision of earth ramparts to protect the towns was a programme which lay within his power, whereas it is doubtful whether masonry walls could have been provided in so many places within the time at his disposal. Such a context would go far to explain the otherwise puzzling incompleteness of the second-century bank and ditch at *Verulamium*. This earthwork had to enclose an exceptionally large area, and if it had not been completed when Severus recovered the province the necessity of doing so would have passed.

At some towns the gates of these defences were probably of wood, as they certainly were at Brough on Humber; but at *Verulamium* and Cirencester monumental gateways of masonry were provided, possibly after the passing of the crisis, incorporating double carriage-ways and projecting drum-towers. These gates are of quite different plan from those later provided for the walls.[14] The only important towns which have so far failed to yield evidence of an earthwork phase in their defences are Colchester, Canterbury, Leicester, and London (p. 283). It is fairly certain that no bank pre-existed on the circuit of the walls in these towns, and if they had earlier banks these must have taken a different line.

The date assigned to the earth ramparts affects the date attributable to the masonry walls which were subsequently added. Until recently these walls themselves were thought to belong to the period of Albinus or Severus, but they must in reality be placed later in the third century. It is certain that the pottery used to date the walls of Silchester, Caerwent and Aldborough [15] has been dated too early, and at other towns, which have been more recently excavated, evidence of a considerably later period has been forthcoming.

At the end of the century a new military architecture was introduced to Britain with the construction of the main series of the Saxon Shore Forts. The walls of these were about twelve feet thick and twenty-five feet high without earth banks behind them, and without internal towers, but possessing projecting towers or bastions in front. The town-walls of Gaul, most of which can be dated within or just before the reign of Diocletian (284–305), were built in the same style. It is noteworthy that with few exceptions the town-walls of Britain belong to an earlier style than these, with internal banks even when, as at Canterbury or Verulamium, the defence was not following an earlier rampart-circuit: if towers were provided they were internal not external.[16] We can be confident that they were built before the reign of Probus (276–82) when the new series of British Shore-forts was begun, but in some cases not long before. Canterbury and Brough on Humber have both yielded coins of about 270 from their ramparts; at Dorchester on Thames pottery indicated a similar date; and the pottery contemporary with the walls of Caerwent and Witherley can hardly be earlier. The walls of Rocester, too, have been dated with fair probability to about this same time.

Some walls were thus certainly being built soon after 270, but it is possible that not all are quite so late. The walls cannot be rigidly divided into types, but it is quite probable that so large a programme of skilled work was spread over a period of thirty years or more, during which time modifications of form were introduced, best recognised in the gates.

The only towns where we have a *terminus ante quem* for the walls are *Verulamium* and London. At *Verulamium* they incorporated the two gates previously built for the earth rampart, but a third gate in contemporary style was provided elsewhere on the circuit where the road to Silchester left the town; this gate had a single carriage-way and two foot-passages, and was flanked by rectangular towers. The date is indicated by a hoard of five coins, ending with one minted in 227–9, which was concealed in the floor of one of the other wall-towers. The hoard is not likely to have been buried later than 240; so the tower – and therefore the wall of which it is a part – was in existence then.[17] The one known gate of Roman London is of very similar design to the new south-west gate of *Verulamium*, and in one of the wall-towers of the circuit were coins and forgers' coin-moulds which indicate a date of *c.* 210–20 for the building. The principal gates of Silchester were also of this design, but the minor north and south gates of the town had only single apertures eleven feet wide set behind deep incurves of the defensive wall and crowned each with a tower above: such was also the type adopted for the south gate of Caistor by Norwich. At Colchester a similar small gate set back behind an incurve has been found, but here the great Balkerne gate with its double carriage-way and two foot-passages facing the road from London belongs to an earlier tradition in which monumental style counted more than defensive capacity. The walls of all these towns have bonding courses of tile or iron-stone.

The walls of Canterbury, Brough and Caerwent have no bonding courses. The known gates at Canterbury are with one exception simple arched openings flush with the walls and only eight feet wide; retaining walls at the rear held up the bank. The gates at Brough on Humber are of almost identical simplicity, though the north gate was slightly set back between rectangular inturns of the wall and carried a tower. The north and south gates at Caerwent closely resemble those of Canterbury, being simple openings just over eight feet wide; but here the east and west gates, bridgin' the main road through the town, may have had double portals like one of the gates of Canterbury, and certainly had two towers.

Though much more evidence is needed, at present it seems possible to suggest that a programme of wall-building was begun in the first half of the third century, perhaps as early as Caracalla, matching the programme of improvement and reconstruction on the military sites of the north, and with the intention of making permanent the earth-work defences already in existence. In this programme London may have received priority of treatment. The *coloniae*, however, stood somewhat apart from it. At Colchester some stretches of the town-wall had been built free-standing at a date thought to be within the period 120–50, and had their rampart added later; but north of the Balkerne Gate the wall and bank are known to be contemporary and datable to the late second century at the earliest: this sounds like an interrupted programme completed only, perhaps, in the crisis of 193–6. Lincoln, on the other hand, and probably Gloucester too, already had narrow stone walls which had been built at or soon after the foundation of these cities as *coloniae*, in order to revet the first-century legionary ramparts which still encircled their sites. At both of them the early narrow wall was later replaced by a wider one; this is probably an early third-century development. At Lincoln there is the additional complication of the so-called 'lower *colonia*', a hitherto suburban area on the steep hillside between the *colonia* and the river Witham, which late in the second century was enclosed with an earth bank topped by a timber palisade, thus doubling the size of the defended area. At a later date, perhaps early in the third century, this bank in turn was cut back to take a stone wall. The latter may be contemporary with the new wide wall round the original *colonia*, but the upper town still retained its southward defences dividing it from the lower enclosure. It will be observed that the lower town at Lincoln exhibits the same defensive history as the general run of Romano-British cities; the existing walls of the *colonia* at the top of the hill were not considered to be sufficient protection. This fact reinforces the view that the earthwork defences of Romano-British cities were provided against a crisis. Lincoln is not alone in presenting a complicated sequence of defences: at Cirencester the late second-century rampart has been found to have been subsequently revetted by a narrow stone wall which was later replaced, though not continuously, by a wider one.

In the early third century, it was still possible to design gateways in monumental style with double carriage-ways and two square towers, or even, though rarely, still to use the plan with drum-towers; later in the century the remaining towns were walled, but now the gate-designs showed an increased concern for security and were made as small as practicable. It is noteworthy that one of the portals of the double west gateway of Silchester was subsequently blocked.

Three towns do not appear to have been walled until the beginning of the fourth century. These are Catterick, Thorpe by Newark and Great Chesterford, and at none of these were banks provided behind. This might be thought to show the influence of the new military architecture, but no external towers seem to have been supplied; the north gate at Great Chesterford was of the Canterbury type.

If the late-third-century walls suggest the growth of danger, this is confirmed by a sudden great and most striking increase in coin hoards buried during the reigns of the two Tetrici, Aurelian, Tacitus and Probus – that is between 270 and 282 – and by the construction of the main series of Saxon Shore forts which soon followed. It is worth recalling also that the forums of Silchester and Wroxeter were burnt down at some point about this period, and that the forum of Caistor by Norwich had to be rebuilt, whatever the cause.

The economic crisis of the late third century was not of sufficient duration to affect the town life of Roman Britain seriously. At *Verulamium* no building activity, apart from two arches and the town wall, can be demonstrated during the first half of the third century, but not much was required now that the half-timbered houses of the early town had been replaced in masonry; for these new buildings could be expected to last at least a century if adequately maintained. The most that can be said is that the crisis may have necessitated the postponement of major reconstruction. About 275, at the height of the crisis, a row of large semi-detached shops of masonry, linked by partial porticoes, were, however, put up along the main street on a site which had remained vacant since the second-century fire. At other towns, such as Cirencester or Caistor by Norwich, both new building and reconstruction seem to have continued perfectly normally throughout the century. The opening decades of the fourth century saw the renewal of a period of structural activity at *Verulamium*. A number of private houses were restored or enlarged at this time, as well as some of the public buildings, and more new large private mansions were built. Here as elsewhere the return of firm government and the restoration of the currency resulted in renewed confidence, while the measures taken by Diocletian and his successors to enforce attention to their duties on the curial class had immediate effects on the residential parts of the towns, whatever their later results might be. There is no doubt that in Britain, whose insularity had preserved it from the worst disasters of the third century, the curial class emerged relatively more prosperous than in many other provinces. Only at Wroxeter does the failure to re-build the forum, after its late-third-century destruction by fire, suggest a decline of initiative. No doubt the senate house and law courts were transferred to alternative premises. Little is yet known of the structural history of the large private houses which figure prominently on air-photographs of this town, but at least one was rebuilt in the early fourth century. On the site of the forum traces survived of irregular occupation during the fourth century, associated with industrial activities; these show that even if civic magnificence had waned, commercial activity continued unabated. The same phenomenon has been recorded in the lower part of Lincoln; here earlier buildings of some prominence had been dismantled by the fourth century and their place taken by more modest structures which may be shops or workshops. Here again commercial activity continued to flourish, as it did at Cirencester.

Some time after the middle of the fourth century the defences of almost all the towns in Britain were modernised by the addition of projecting towers or bastions to carry defensive artillery. Such towers were closely spaced so that covering fire could be provided along the face of the wall: well-preserved examples can still be seen at many towns in Gaul, with their arched catapult ports at or above the level of the wall-walk. The arrow-firing catapult had an effective range of about 200 yards against concentrations, and could kill individuals at 100 yards. It had long been used by the Roman army in the field and for the defence of forts, but the third century witnessed a change of tactics arising from the greater numbers and stronger organisation of the barbarian enemies who had now to be encountered. The

Roman army was compelled to adopt a defensive role, and the manning of well-defended strong-points became of greater importance than in former times, when forts had been designed as bases for the offensive. This change is well illustrated in the design of the new Saxon Shore forts in Britain (p. 255f.), where the value of artillery for defence had been appreciated from the late third century. Now this defence was applied to the towns; but the addition of bastions normally necessitated filling up the old ditch, which ran too close to the wall to allow room for towers, and a new ditch was dug farther out, often 60 or 100 feet wide, whose purpose was to disrupt and halt the enemy within convenient catapult range. The new towers vary in shape and size from town to town. They may be rectangular, pentagonal, pear-shaped or semicircular, and either solid or hollow; but all are additions to the original wall,[18] and many contain large blocks of stone taken from earlier buildings or tombs.

When did this development occur? It was certainly the result of a single decision (though several years may have elapsed before it was fully implemented), and accordingly, the latest date for any bastion should help to date the rest. A coin of 330–5 was found below a bastion at Caerwent, and at Aldborough the early ditch, obliterated to make way for the bastions, contained pottery down to the middle of the fourth century. Similar evidence has come from Chichester. But it was the excavations at Great Casterton which throw more decisive light on the problem, for here two coins minted between 354 and 358 were found associated with two different bastions. Accordingly, they can hardly have been put up before 360; and, bearing in mind the limitations of archaeological dating-evidence and the scarcity of coins of the House of Valentinian in Britain before 369, we can hardly doubt that this reorganisation of the town-defences of Britain was the work of Count Theodosius. He it was who recovered Britain in that year from the chaos and disorder of the great barbarian invasions of 367, and we have the record of Ammianus that he restored the towns.[19] His other achievements in Britain are discussed on pp. 395 ff; there is some evidence to suggest that garrisons were now provided to man the new urban defences, just as troops were certainly stationed in some of the towns of Gaul.

A noteworthy fact is that even quite small walled towns were included in the programme, and there is no doubt, therefore, of their continued value to the imperial government. Many no doubt contained official store-houses for the collection of military supplies and the posting-stations of the *cursus publicus*; but the proliferation of fortified strong-points scattered generally throughout the province also served a more general purpose. The barbarian forces of this period were formidable enemies in the field, but they lacked the ability and means to take fortified places if these were defended.[20] Moreover, invading barbarians lacked the elaborate supply-system of the Roman army and depended on forage during raids. If supplies of corn and livestock could be denied them by concentration within defended walls they could do nothing but starve or retreat. Strong, up-to-date urban defences thus had a strategic as well as a tactical role in the defence of Britain, and their provision certainly enabled the towns to hold out far into the fifth century, long after the official garrison had been withdrawn (pp. 420–22).

To modern eyes the towns of Roman Britain seem very small. London within its walls had an area of only 330 acres, Cirencester 240, and *Verulamium* and Wroxeter about 200 each. And these towns were twice the size of the remainder. Winchester with 138 acres and Canterbury with 130 were still larger than normal; and a more numerous group – Colchester, Chichester, Leicester, Silchester and Exeter – were about 100 acres (the first a little more, the last a little less). Aldborough with 60 fell considerably short. Two civitas-capitals and two coloniae were smaller still; but there were geographical and historical reasons to account for the small size of Caerwent (44 acres) and Caistor by Norwich (35), while Gloucester (46) and Lincoln (41) originated in veteran settlements tightly packed within the ramparts of former legionary fortresses. It is noteworthy that Lincoln expanded to normal size, for the extended rampart encloses 97 acres. Silchester, however, was unable to make full use of the 230 acres enclosed by the Outer Earthwork, and when the new rampart was built it reduced the town to 100 acres.

The walled areas represent what it was economical to defend in the third century. Many towns must once have been larger: Canterbury possessed a suburb across the River Stour which was excluded, as was ribbon development along the Richborough road. Extra-mural ribbon-development was excluded at Colchester too, and no doubt at many other towns. Small though they appear by modern standards, however, the majority were not excessively small among contemporary provincial towns. Roman Paris in its heyday occupied about 135 acres and Cologne 240; the walls of Avenches enclosed 375 acres, but the built-up area within occupied much less than half of this. Nor were they unduly small by medieval standards, for in most cases the Roman town walls defined the lines taken by their medieval successors. There is plenty of evidence that the towns fulfilled their purpose as centres of trade and administration as well as could be expected in a province initially quite un-accustomed to town life, and that, at least by the fourth century, developing commercial activity was providing a spontaneous impetus which more than counter-balanced any failure of the aristocracies to identify themselves completely with the town.

The ordo of a civitas normally consisted of 100 decurions, to judge by evidence from other provinces. There is indirect evidence to sup-port this figure in Britain. The central room in the range of offices behind the basilica at Silchester, which is usually identified as the *curia*, was large enough to seat 108; but if, as is more likely, this chamber was really the shrine where the Tutela goddess and im-perial images were housed, there is another hall of even larger size close by which would suit the meetings of the ordo even better. At Caerwent the central room, only 30 feet square, is hardly large enough for a full ordo, and like its counterpart at Silchester was open to the basilica; but the next room to the west could hold 110 seats comfortably. At Wroxeter a similar situation is found.

Nothing thus prevents an assumption that the normal ordo was composed of 100 decurions. But no town shows anything approach-ing 100 contemporary wealthy houses inside its walls. At Silchester and Caerwent, whose plans are most fully known, there are perhaps twenty-five such houses; and this suggests that in these places per-haps only a quarter of the curial class took up urban residence, the others remaining based upon their estates. It is not uncommon to find villas distributed in clear relationship with towns. At Wroxeter the number of wealthy houses may have been higher than at Sil-chester, and Sir Ian Richmond has suggested that here exceptional conditions obtained, causing the wealthier classes to be concentrated in the town owing to the proximity of the unsettled hill-folk of Wales: there is certainly a scarcity of villas in Cornovian territory. But at *Verulamium* also it is likely that a larger number of wealthy magnates lived in the town, and here, too, there is a dearth of large villas in the neighbourhood. It may be that at Cirencester, when the plan is better known, the same will be found true, though in this case there are some fifteen villas within 10 miles of the city.

The commercial character of the towns is illustrated partly by the shops which lined the forums and main streets, and partly by exceptional discoveries such as were made in the Wroxeter forum. Here the second-century fire overwhelmed the stalls of traders which had set up in the eastern portico, and piles of mortaria and samian vessels, and even a crate of whetstones, were discovered lying where they had fallen. These finds suggest the busy activity of a market day. Some of the chambers round the forum courtyard were evidently used for official purposes, and some perhaps as shrines or meeting-rooms for guilds; but many were undoubtedly let out as shops.

At Silchester the Rev. James Joyce, who excavated the forum in the years following 1866 with a skill greatly in advance of his time, recorded the contents of each: in one a 'singular quantity of coins' and niches in the walls which might have held strong-boxes; in a second a small bar of silver partly used; in three others the remains of numerous steelyards; in yet another the spurs of game-cocks with the skulls of four dogs buried in the floor; and in the shop next door a pottery pan, two feet in diameter, built into the corner. One of the compartments in the forum of Caerwent produced remains suggestive of an oyster-bar.

The shops which lined the main streets were often the quarters of manufacturing craftsmen who made goods to order. At *Verulamium* considerable evidence was found of bronze casting and engraving in some of the shops, where perhaps cooking utensils were turned on the lathe; in others blacksmiths had worked, and in yet another the discovery of crucibles containing a residue of gold pointed to a working jeweller.[21] In two others ovens and a long-handled shovel suggested bakers. Similar evidence comes from Cirencester, while at Caistor by Norwich and Wroxeter there is evidence for glass porduction on a small scale, and at York for the carving of jet ornaments. The craftsman Basilis, whose stamp has been found on three table-knives from London, no doubt had a similar sort of workshop.

Trade in foodstuffs, clothing and other perishables usually leaves less traces in the ground, though documentary evidence of the medieval period shows the large part played by such merchants.[22] At Cirencester part of the market-square was thought to have been occupied by butchers from the number of bones buried, and at Canterbury and London portions of large donkey-mills point to wholesale production of flour. On the Continent traders often formed themselves into Corporations (*collegia*), for example that of the butchers, who set up an inscription to Tiberius at Périgueux. In Britain we can point to only five such guilds, a *collegium peregrinorum* at Silchester, examples at Caerwent, Bath and York of type unspecified, and a *collegium fabrorum* at Chichester. The latter, a guild of artificers with many parallels on the Continent, is remarkable for the date of its appearance: it figures on the temple-inscription erected under Cogidubnus, and is important evidence of that king's early and successful efforts to introduce Roman institutions. We cannot doubt that many more such guilds existed. Their purpose was partly to further the commercial interests of their members (though their political activity was much more circumscribed than that of modern trades unions), and partly to fulfil a philanthropic or social aim. Guild feasts were held, and members' subscriptions entitled them to decent burial at the guild's expense.

At some towns other, larger, industries existed, but little is known of them in detail. Many, perhaps all, of the principal towns possessed considerable tileries and potteries in their immediate vicinity. Examples of these are known at Colchester, Lincoln and Canterbury, while near Gloucester a municipal tilery was responsible for tiles stamped *R(ei) P(ublicae) G(levensium)*, sometimes with the names of the duoviri added. Outside Canterbury a Roman chalk quarry is known, and very large stone quarries must have been in operation in the near neighbourhood of such towns as Bath, Cirencester, Wroxeter or Lincoln: an example is known at Sibson near Water Newton. Timber, too, must have been in great demand. The discovery of large deposits of bones from the heads of cattle at both Silchester and Leicester points to tanning as a local industry, and certainly leather, both for clothing and footwear, will have been in demand almost everywhere. At Silchester, too, the remains of boiling vats in an area near the west gate has been thought to suggest a cloth-dyeing quarter.

The mere existence of such industries must show that a sizeable artisan element should be included in any estimate of the population of a town. Slaves, too, undoubtedly existed in some numbers as the domestic staff of large houses and probably also in certain industries;[23] but there is little evidence for large-scale employment of freedmen in commercial enterprises by British proprietors, such as is well attested abroad. Some, however, appear to have been employed in the pottery industry, as for instance the five Sexti Valerii (with different cognomina) at Colchester, who stamped mortaria (p. 326). At *Verulamium* a large house, built in Antonine times, was clearly divided into domestic quarters at the back and commercial premises along the street-front, somewhat after the Italian manner; and we may suppose that freedmen were set up in business here, just as there is a possibility that the early shops in insula xiv, all of which show signs of single ownership, were thus let out. But such suggestive evidence is rare. The majority of shops were single buildings, most probably owned by their proprietors. The freedmen whose names we do know, for instance in the lead industry, are clearly either imperial freedmen or the representatives of Gaulish or Italian capital. Nothing is known of the status of artisans, but from the fact that many of them were literate, we may suppose them free.

The total population of the towns is hard to estimate owing to deficiency of evidence. Only at Silchester and Caerwent have we anything like a complete town-plan, but at neither is much known about the contemporaneity of buildings owing to the inadequate technique of the early excavators who first revealed them. The population of Silchester was reckoned by Sir Ian Richmond as not less than 2,500 on the showing of the plan, and possibly twice or thrice this figure on the assumption that many wooden buildings were missed by the excavators. Mr George Boon has estimated 4,000. A somewhat similar figure – between 2,000 and 3,000 – has been suggested for Caerwent. A very rough calculation shows that the amphitheatre at Silchester could accommodate something like 2,700 seats: this might approximate to the adult population of the town. The Colonies of Colchester, Lincoln and Gloucester, on the other hand, being official foundations where more purely Roman ideas of town-planning may have been applied, were probably closely built up; comparison with other coloniae of known size and settlement suggests that Colchester may have had an initial population approaching 15,000 and Lincoln and Gloucester perhaps something like 5,000 each, figures which may well have dropped towards the provincial average for towns of their sizes as time went on. Tacitus assesses the total casualties at London, *Verulamium* and Colchester during the

Boudiccan sack at 70,000, and his language suggests use of an official source. Even if exaggerated, this figure supports a population for Colchester and even *Verulamium* of about 15,000 each, and perhaps one as large as 30,000 for London.

Some check can be provided for these estimates from the population figures of those medieval towns which were still surrounded by their Roman walls. In the last quarter of the fourteenth century the estimated population of Canterbury was 3,800, Colchester 4,400, Exeter 2,300, Winchester 2,100 and Chichester 1,300; but at this period numbers had been much reduced by plague.[24] Elizabethan Leicester, it has been said, 'had no obvious means of livelihood'; it was not an industrial town, but throve by providing services to the countryside.[25] In this it invites comparison with Romano-British Ratae. In the sixteenth century its population was about 3,000, and before the Black Death had been over a thousand more. Shrewsbury, in some sense the successor of Wroxeter, had a population of 4,000 in 1545, as did Gloucester: only one provincial town in England at this time contained more than 10,000 people, and not more than fourteen others exceeded 5,000. Professor Hoskins has shown that a considerable number were at the level of 3,000–4,000 each, but that there were also a great number of active market towns with populations of about 1,500. All this by inference throws welcome light on the situation in these towns in Roman times. A few great towns like Cirencester or *Verulamium* or Colchester may have approached 20,000, but estimates of about 5,000 for the larger and 2,000–3,000 for the smaller civitas-capitals will not be wildly wrong, while the other walled centres may have had populations ranging down from 1,500 to as few as 300–500, depending on their size and function.

The larger towns were probably more cosmopolitan than our limited evidence allows us positively to assert. London in particular was the centre of a wide commerce with the continental ports and river systems, and its temples to Mithras and Isis reflect this aspect of its life. Greeks are attested at Lincoln and Carlisle as well as London, and a Caledonian set up an inscription at Colchester. Gauls are known in five towns. At Bath lived a lady from Metz, a stone-mason from Chartres and another man from the Moselle valley near Trier. M. Nonius Romanus at Caerwent also seems to have been a Rhinelander to judge by the deity he worshipped. At York one of the Seviri Augustales, despite his Greek name, was a native of Bourges

(p. 365) and was married to a lady from Sardinia; other Gauls are known at Lincoln and Cirencester. When we remember the scarcity of inscribed evidence at the majority of towns we may well believe that these are a small sample.

Many such men will have been engaged in trade, for instance the import of wine or pottery; but others will certainly have come over as teachers [26] and as purveyors of the arts, whose influence was quickly assimilated by local talent. Sculptors' workshops certainly existed in some towns (p. 358), and both mosaicists and fresco-painters were similarly based. From the towns their products, and the classical influence which they represented, reached out to the wealthy villa-owners in the surrounding districts, while the more humdrum products of trade and industry penetrated through the periodic markets to the poorest peasants of the deepest countryside.

1. The forum of Caerwent, a town of only 44 acres, measures only 251 by 182 feet; that of Silchester 313 by 275 feet; that of Wroxeter 394 by 265 feet; that at Cirencester 550 by 345 feet. The forum of London may have been even bigger.

2. This failure to complete the early baths at Wroxeter is often taken as a mark of civic bankruptcy, and it is difficult to explain it otherwise if the building was civic. But since the impetus to urbanisation in civitas-capitals was government policy, such a failure would be very remarkable, and adds support to the alternative explanation, suggested on p. 140, that the building was military. Public Baths were not normally provided in towns before the Forum: Silchester is an exception, which may be due, as suggested, to its lying in Cogidubnus' realm.

3. This theatre has not yet been found, but is attested on an inscription, *RIB*, 707, see p. 238.

4. Moreover, the level of the water is 20 feet below that of the Public Baths only 1¼ miles away; for an aqueduct this is an incredible error when water was available over 50 feet higher at a hardly greater distance from the town.

5. Other second-century mosaics are known at Silchester and Caerwent (D. J. Smith in A. L. F. Rivet (ed.) *The Roman Villa in* (1969), p. 77).

6. Unfired clay-brick construction over stone footings was found during 1965 in the earliest period at *Camulodunum*, in a building destroyed in the Boudiccan rebellion.

7. The defences of the fortress which previously occupied the site had apparently been levelled when the *colonia* was founded (*Britannia*, iv (1973), p. 302).

8. There seems to have been an earth rampart, of uncertain date, at Cologne; it may be pre-colonial. Aventicum, walled *c*. 74, had no bank.

9. The only exception seems to be the late wall (probably of the late third or fourth century) round the lower colony at Lincoln; re-used stones at Bath and Kenchester almost certainly came from bastions added in the second half of the fourth century.

10. A few had been defended earlier. At *Verulamium* the first-century defence had become obsolete by about the end of Trajan's reign and was filled in. At Silchester two successive circuits of earthwork have been attributed to the reign of Cogidubnus. At Brough on Humber earthwork defences were provided in the Hadrianic period; but it may be that Brough was still an Army supply-depot. The bank at Caerwent has been described as first-century, but it contains pottery down to the end of the second century (*Archaeologia Cambrensis*, ciii (1954), 59, where the section has clearly been misinterpreted).

11. *Verulamium* is the best example, but at Caistor by Norwich an air-photograph shows ditches on a different line, as does one at Mildenhall (Wilts); and at Brough on Humber the first bank enclosed a larger area than the second. At Caerwent the wall was built over the earlier ditch in parts of the circuit.

12. *Digest*, l, x, 6. *De operibus, quae in muris vel portis vel rebus publicis fiunt, aut si muri exstruantur, divus Marcus rescripsit praesidem aditum consulere principem debere.* Cf. *ibid.*, 1, viii, 9, 4.

13. In the absence of inscriptions, the date can only be shown to be later than the latest coin or datable sherd contained in the bank or sealed by it; but there can be no guarantee that such objects were not already old when buried.

14. The east gate at Lincoln is of similar pattern, and it, too, shows signs of being earlier than the widened town-wall. Similar gates had been provided a little earlier at the fort of Castell Collen, and a nearly contemporary example exists at Risingham.

15. The foundation-trench at Aldborough yielded a coin fairly certainly attributable to Julia Domna.

16. The style is still that of the second-century fort-defences of the Roman army in Britain.

17. It was certainly in existence before *c*. 275–85, as another coin-hoard shows; for by then this particular tower had collapsed owing to weak foundations and the second coin hoard was buried in the ruins.

18. The only apparent exceptions are those at *Verulamium* and Caistor by Norwich. Re-examination would probably show that these, too, are additions, perhaps being bonded into a wall face already decayed; for the walls at both these towns are of flint and mortar, which is quick to crumble.

19. Ammianus Marcellinus xxviii. 3.2. *in integrum restituit civitates; ibid.* 3.7: *instaurabat urbes.*

20. Fritigern leader of the Goths, *c.* 376, is reported to have said: 'For my part I am at peace with walls.' Ammianus Marcellinus, xxxi, 6, 4.

21. Gold-crucibles have also been found at Cirencester and London. We may recall the inscription from Norton: *Feliciter sit genio loci. Servule utere felix tabernam aureficinam (RIB,* 712).

22. It is worth noting that a list of the principal traders of Coventry, Northampton and Leicester in the early sixteenth century, as compiled by W. G. Hoskins (*Provincial England* (London, 1964), p. 79), includes the following: Bakers, Builders, Butchers, Drapers, Dyers, Fullers, Mercers, Millers, Shoe-makers, Tanners, Tailors and Weavers. We have no such records for Roman Britain, but the probable importance of these trades should not be forgotten, despite the difficulty of identifying undoubted archaeological traces.

23. See the inscription quoted in note 21 above.

24. See J. C. Russell, *British Medieval Population* (Albuquerque, 1948), especially chapters vi and xi. Even if inaccurate, these figures are useful as a guide.

25. W. G. Hoskins, *Provincial England* (London, 1964), p. 88.

26. *Gallia causidicos docuit facunda Britannos,* Juvenal, xv, 111.

13
The countryside

Cultivation of the soil had been the most prominent feature of the economy of southern Britain during the Iron Age, and towards its close the Belgic kingdoms had even produced an exportable surplus of corn, as we learn from Strabo.[1] Both villages and isolated farms are found in the earlier part of the Iron Age; it is possible that the Belgae made greater use of the isolated farm, to judge by the large numbers of them which Caesar saw in the south-east.[2] After the Roman conquest cultivation was intensified and certain improvements were introduced.

The new colonies at Colchester, Lincoln and Gloucester were designed to give retired veterans a stake in the land; they lived for the most part in the town, but cultivated allotments in the surrounding country. The normal method of land-division in such cases was centuriation, a carefully surveyed partition of the territorium into rectangular plots like a chess-board. No certain traces of this system have survived in the neighbourhood of the British colonies, but Tacitus describes the expropriation of Trivantian natives in the territory of Camulodunum, and we need not doubt that colonial allotments existed round these three towns. In the immediate radius of quite a number of others, too, it has been noted that villas are rare, as for instance Canterbury, Silchester, London or Caistor by Norwich; so perhaps it was normal for the inhabitants of towns to cultivate farms and market-gardens in the neighbourhood, though without centuriation.

Apart from these areas, however, the pattern of agricultural exploitation in Roman Britain as revealed by the archaeological record is on two levels. Peasant settlements, whether villages or single farmsteads, still broadly continue and develop the pre-Roman pattern in all areas, and in some they form the principal or only agricultural manifestation. In addition, and at a higher level of culture and comfort, we find Romanised buildings known as villas. These became more frequent as time went on. They can be seen as a new system growing up beside, and out of, the old. On the one hand, they clearly continue the tradition of the old isolated Celtic farmstead, but on the other, they exhibit new features in their quick adoption of Roman techniques and in their capacity to exploit new opportunities. They represent the application of capital by individual owners breaking free to some extent from the past, while the peasant settlements show the continuing rule of custom, and the cramped development imposed by traditional land-working and subdivision by inheritance. The villas belonged to men of wealth and enterprise, who could sell the timber from their estates and then cultivate the richer soils exposed; who could appreciate and exploit the superior profitability of sheep and stock-raising over arable farming, when organised on a large scale as only a big landowner could. It must not be forgotten that land was one of the safest and most sought-after investments in the ancient world. Though some of the villa-owners may have been speculators from other provinces or their agents, and others retired centurions from the garrison, the vast majority were the wealthier members of native British civitates. The very simplicity and slow development of the majority of early villas makes this clear. Such people had close political and business connections with the towns, and they needed the new roads to convey their produce thither. As a result, the villas tend to cluster in the vicinity of towns and to lie not too far from roads: they are not as ubiquitous as peasant farmsteads nor so purely rural.

The peasant settlements continued to use the 'Celtic' field system (pl. 10b), and even in some cases grain-storage pits and the ancestral round huts of wood or stone in an irregular layout; the inhabitants naturally used Roman coinage and bought their pottery in Romano-British markets, but their standard of living remained low. The only real signs of improvement are that the use of storage pits gradually disappears and that sometimes rectangular cottages are found instead of round huts, as for instance at Park Brow, Sussex, or at Studland, Dorset. Though these might achieve the comfort of quite recent dwellings of the same sort, with painted walls, glass windows and even wooden floors, they could never be confused with villas.

Before the Little Woodbury excavations of 1938–9, the pits in such settlements were interpreted as dwellings rather than as storage places, and in consequence high estimates of population gained credence and the sites themselves were regarded as villages. But the demonstration at Little Woodbury that many pits could belong to one isolated farm caused a reaction, and for some years many authorities thereafter held that the isolated farm was the sole unit of agricultural settlement in the Iron Age and even in the Roman period in Britain. But this was to go too far. Though isolated farms were certainly an important ingredient of rural settlement in both periods, excellent evidence exists for large nucleated settlements which can be called villages. Massive settlements can be seen on air-photographs of the Fens, and in other areas not only do unified tracts of fields exist which are too large for working by a single farm (as at Figheldean Down), but in parts of Wessex Romano-British settlements covering up to twenty acres, with small rectangular building platforms arranged along a street, have been identified. The agricultural basis of such villages is beyond doubt.

The Romano-British villa has been variously defined. *Sensu stricto* it should be the centre of a farm or agricultural estate, but this has not been demonstrated in every case; and undoubtedly some country houses, indistinguishable architecturally from villas, derived their *raison d'être* from other forms of exploitation, such as potteries or quarries. This is especially notable in the area of the Nene Valley potteries. There is a range of size and wealth within the category of villa, but all, whether built of stone or timber, are Romanised buildings of sufficient size or distinction to lift them out of the cottage class; they are single establishments, not parts of villages, even though many will be found to possess subsidiary outbuildings connected with their function.

This general twofold pattern of rural organisation, however, is certainly oversimplified, since archaeological investigation unaided cannot often throw light on tenure. Some villas are large and wealthy, others simple and furnished only with necessities. The former were clearly the centres of their own estates, but the latter may represent rent-paying units on the estates of others. One may have been farmed by its owner and his family; another by a bailiff and slaves. A hint that even in pre-Roman times slaves were used in agriculture is provided by the iron gang-chain found in the Belgic farmstead at Park Street; and the discovery of the skeletons of ninety-seven new-born babies in the yard of the villa at Hambleden, Buckinghamshire, suggests the exposure of the unwanted female offspring of a slave-run establishment. Different evidence for the same sort of thing has been detected at Llantwit Major, Glamorgan, where early in the fourth century the main residence was demolished but the farm buildings continued in use for another century. Here, it seems clear, an absentee landlord was acting through a bailiff. It is probable, however, that on many of the more sizeable estates the home-farm was run with the assistance of slaves and the rest let out to tenants (*coloni*). Such a relationship would explain the not infrequent areas, like that round Winchester, where villas and native settlements are intermixed. Coloni would normally hold a lease for five years, continuable annually thereafter. But by the early fourth century, their legal position had deteriorated. They had become bound to the soil like medieval serfs under a hereditary tie, paying rent in kind as often as in money, and occasionally, at any rate, having customary obligations of part-time work on what may loosely be described as manorial lands.[3]

Similarly, the peasant farmsteads may represent free owners in one district or free tenants in another; while in a third the inhabitants may have been *coloni Caesaris*, or tenants under the bureaucratic control of officials administering imperial estates. Such relationships are not documented for students of Roman Britain, and they can be established only by inference, and that infrequently.

Beyond the lowland zone where arable cultivation was normal the inhabitants of the highland zone continued to live a more primitive life. Here pastoralism remained predominant despite evidence that cereal cultivation had been introduced and become established. Villas are hardly found in these regions: either wealth did not accumulate sufficiently or the standard of Romanisation remained too low. Successful pastoralists sometimes took to mixed farming but continued to live in traditional mode, as can be seen in the large round house set up in the third century inside the old hill-fort at Dinorben in Denbighshire.

Though the Roman government did not buy corn to feed the army, but obtained the necessary supplies by means of the *annona* or corn tax, the very necessity of paying this tax in kind, as well as finding money for other provincial and local taxes, must have stimulated agricultural production from the first, while the growing demand for meat and leather as well as corn created by the new towns will have enabled farmers to enrich themselves. Increasing prosperity can be recognised at many villas. Near *Verulamium* the well-known examples at Park Street and Lockleys both began as Romanised reconstructions of previous Belgic farms after the Boudiccan rebellion, and successive enlargements in the middle second and early fourth centuries point to continuing accumulation of capital. It is noteworthy that even the earliest Roman building at Park Street occupied more than four times the area of the native structures below, and represents therefore both a material upward step in living-standards as well as a considerable capital outlay. There should be other examples of such early development in the vicinity of the new towns of the south-east. Other villas were later in starting. At Ditchley, Oxfordshire (pl. 9b), a timber house of very simple rectangular type had first been built about 70, but the first stone structure, a villa of winged corridor type, replaced it about the time of Trajan. A similar sequence, this time from a late-first-century circular hut to a later-second-century complex of two rectangular cottages set adjacent to each other in Ⅰ-fashion, is known at Catsgore near Ilchester, Somerset; at Newport, Isle of Wight, some sort of timber-framed building underlay a villa erected apparently towards the close of the second century, and at Hambleden, Buckinghamshire, a quantity of first-century samian among the published finds suggests the possibility of a similar sequence. At Bignor, Sussex, though pottery of the late first century is known from the site, the earliest structure so far identified was not erected much before 200. It was a timber-framed building apparently of corridor type, which after a fire was succeeded by a simple oblong building of masonry. Such rectangular blocks containing four to six rooms are the simplest form a villa could take, closely resembling the small early private houses found in towns; it is just this form which appears the earliest, in the late Neronian villas at Park Street and Lockleys. Simple though it was, it showed a great advance in comfort and privacy over earlier types of house which, whether round or rectangular, lacked internal subdivisions, and sheltered men and beasts without distinction. The acquisition of wealth, in other words, was introducing a social distinction between the farmer and his labourers. Simplicity of plan, however, as Bignor and the first building at Cox Green near Maidenhead show, is no indicator of absolute date: it points rather to the extent of the owner's resources. A further refinement soon added at all these villas was a corridor, so that rooms did not have to be used as passages. At or soon after this stage, projecting wings were added to each end of the building, linked by the corridor and with the ridge line of their roofs, at right-angles to that of the central block. One of the wings was sometimes used to house a bath-suite, though often these were placed in a separate building to lessen the risk of fire. Both are proofs of growing luxury.

A further indication of increasing culture is the appearance in these larger villas of a central dining-room, larger in size than the other rooms, and a sure sign of the growing Romanisation of manners. The symmetrical façade presented by such a winged corridor house with its central entrance became fashionable and no doubt indicated a certain social status, for we find such façades applied to earlier structures; sometimes, as at Bignor, in such a way as to show that it was appearance rather than purpose which was uppermost in the mind of the designer. There is thus a typological development from the simple rectangular form through to the tripartite winged corridor villa (that is, a villa having a corridor and wings at the back as well as the front), but these developments have no relationship with absolute dating; they could occur at any time according to resources. It remains true, however, that most villas show successive enlargement well down into the fourth century: in other words, agriculture was a continuously thriving industry.

The largest villas were almost all mere elaborations of the basic design already described, with the wings lengthened so as to clasp and even sometimes to enclose a courtyard. Such establishments were big indeed, and were served by a numerous household of domestic slaves and agricultural workers; they were the centres of large estates, the busy life of which is portrayed for us in contemporary fashion only in the funerary reliefs of the Moselle valley and eastern Gaul. At Bignor and at North Leigh in Oxfordshire it can be shown that the courtyard house is the climax of a long history of enlargement. The same is true of the great villa at Woodchester, Gloucestershire. In such houses the farm-buildings, which are normally inseparable even from the most luxurious establishments, are found grouped in and around an outer yard. Only at Fishbourne, Sussex, do we have in Britain an example of a classical luxury-villa apparently unconnected in its original form with estate management; and, as we have seen, this villa is anomalously early in date, and stands therefore outside the normal development of the British country house. It was the home of some exceptionally wealthy owner, either a high Roman official or more probably the royal family of the Regnenses. Nevertheless, other equally early villas are known on the coastal plain of Sussex, at Angmering in Essex, and in Kent at Eccles, and it is clear that exceptional Romanisation was active in this area. For the majority of early villa-owners, however, it was sufficiently costly to provide a Romanised permanent home of simple form; expansion and the provision of luxuries came later. Fishbourne (pl. 12a), Angmering and Eccles are the only villas so far known to have had mosaics and bath buildings in the first century:[4] at the great majority baths began to be added only in the later second century, and mosaics even later. However, many of the later villas have notably large baths, and some, like the Castle Dykes villa near Ripon in Yorkshire, even possess a separate bath building in addition to a private suite of baths. This suggests that provision was made for estate workers, for whom the baths would also form some sort of social focus. If this is so, it throws a favourable light on the relationship existing between master and man in the countryside. Mosaics, which are today often regarded as the hall-mark of the villa, are rare indeed, even in the second century. At present only seven villas – those at Fishbourne (Sussex), Boxmoor and Park Street (Hertfordshire), High Wycombe and Latimer (Hertfordshire), Well (Yorkshire) and Winterton (Lincolnshire) – are known to possess mosaics laid down in the second century. The vast majority of villa-mosaics, like the wealthy villas which they adorned, are characteristic of the fourth century in Britain.

A rather different class of building, and one of more primitive type, is the aisled house, sometimes known as the barn-dwelling or basilican villa. This is essentially a hall or barn whose roof is carried by two rows of supports dividing the building into nave and two aisles. The form is useful for many purposes. There is often a wide entrance suitable for carts at one end and a smaller doorway in the middle of one of the longer sides. At some farms the principal building recorded is one of this sort, and it can often be shown that subsequent alteration has partitioned off a set of rooms, at one end or other of the hall. In villas of this type it is not always certain that

307

the main residential building has not been missed by the excavators, since it might be some distance away; but if the type can be isolated it seems clear that part of the hall must have housed the family and the remainder served the utilitarian purposes of the farm. At other villas such a building, though displaying evident signs of human occupation, is clearly subordinate to a more conventional residence; and in these cases it has been assumed to house a resident staff of workmen, perhaps slaves. At others again it may have more closely corresponded to a normal barn. At Bignor an example lies in the outer yard, where it certainly belongs to a late stage in the history of the villa, when there was plenty of accommodation elsewhere on the premises for a resident staff; and here it is associated with other buildings for which a connection with stock can be inferred. S. Applebaum has reasonably identified it as a barn whose nave stored fodder for the fifty-five head of cattle which could be accommodated in the aisles;[5] the two small rooms divided off at one end would be for the cowherds. It has also been suggested that some at any rate of these aisled buildings served a social purpose between landlord and tenant like that of the medieval hall which they so closely resemble – perhaps for feasts or even customary courts. This is perhaps to take inference rather far, for if they served a single social purpose of wide application few large villas should lack them, and there should be more uniformity of phenomena.

The aisled house-type, though typologically simple, is not necessarily early, and does not appear to have originated in Britain, though far more plentiful here than in other provinces. Its source is not yet generally agreed, but similar buildings are known in the regions round the mouth of the Rhine. Perhaps the earliest example of the independent aisled house so far known in Britain is that at Exning, Suffolk, where the original building, all in timber, was erected in the early second century and was later partly rebuilt in stone; an earlier aisled hall, but this time incorporated with other rooms and suites in one architectural whole, occurs in the Flavian palace at Fishbourne. The architectural form was the simplest and cheapest large building which could give the appearances of Romanisation to those who were not yet ready to abandon the traditional house-byre way of life. It was thus suitable for adoption in larger establishments to house the workers, when the family itself had moved to a more commodious dwelling, but it could also be entirely devoted to livestock and their fodder.

A curious feature is the distribution of aisled houses in the narrower sense – that is buildings showing domestic sub-division at one end – for they cluster in Hampshire and in the regions round the Humber and the Fens; elsewhere if they occur at all such buildings are not certainly designed for human occupation, and are always subsidiary to the main house. It is not easy to explain this distribution, which does not appear to correspond to that of known immigrant groups or recognisable economic factors. The distribution of Romano-British barrow-burials, which originated in much the same continental region as that suggested for aisled houses, is quite different.

With the passage of time and improvement of living standards, the 'upper' end of many aisled houses was partitioned off into rooms, and a bath-suite was sometimes inserted in an aisle. It is the problem of lighting these rooms, some of which are out of contact with an exterior wall, which has given rise to the term basilican villa, since clerestory lighting would seem to be necessary. At some sites, such as West Blatchington, Sussex, where the rooms were planned from the beginning and were not added afterwards, this is likely enough; but at others, where they were afterthoughts, dormer-windows may have been inserted.

Occasionally attempts were made to give an aisled house a fashionable façade around the central doorway. At Stroud, Hampshire, two projecting wing-rooms, one at either end of the house, were part of the original design. At others, for instance Winterton, Lincolnshire, elaborate and doubtless expensive mosaics were inserted in an aisled building subsidiary to the main villa, which suggests the provision of a separate establishment for a younger generation of the family rather than accommodation for labourers. But whatever the later developments, parts of the original hall or barn at the 'lower' end always survive, and often a hearth is found at the 'upper' end of the surviving barn. This suggests that the building was still partly devoted to customary activities whatever these may have been; but the wide variety of possibilities illustrate the difficulties of too rigid a classification of such buildings.

Romano-British villas notably tend to exploit the richer soils. The lighter soils – chalk uplands, gravel terraces – though here and there supporting villas, are predominantly the areas where peasant settlements are found, on which they continued to occupy their ancestral sites. In Sussex, for instance, the South Downs were covered with settlements of this sort, some continuously occupied from Iron Age times, some new; all are, or were once, associated with traditional 'Celtic' fields. The villas, on the other hand, are found either on the coastal plain to the south or on the rich soils on the edge of the Weald north of the hills. The reason for this is not certain, because little is known of the occupation of these soils in pre-Roman times; but it is clear that their exploitation by capital would pay richer dividends than the chalk uplands, even if the complications caused by age-old traditional tenures in the latter area did not hamper development. Similar uneven distribution of villas can be seen in many parts of the country, for instance in East Anglia. In Norfolk they are concentrated along the borders of the Wash in the west of the county; much of the rest was occupied by peasant villages. In Essex the villas are in the north and west of the county; the coastal areas and adjoining lands were thickly populated by peasant settlements occupied with herding, fisheries and salt-production.

The methods of cultivation used by the villas is still obscure, but if improvements were introduced (p. 315f.) they could be applied more readily in new areas than in the old upland farms where field banks, accumulated by centuries of ploughing, resisted change of layout and indeed have yielded only in recent years to the bulldozer. Such physical difficulties would not occur, however, in the level gravel lands, and villas do make their appearance on these, for instance in the Oxford region; the tenacity of traditional farming in such areas is no doubt due to shortages of capital characteristic of large populations tied to their customary small-holdings.

The size of villa-estates must have varied considerably, and we have little evidence on which to base a calculation. The comparatively modest villa at Ditchley had a granary in the fourth century whose capacity has been calculated to reflect an estate of about 1,000 acres. At the much larger establishment at Bignor consideration of natural boundaries suggests an arable area of about 2,000 acres with additional strips of forest, downland and alluvial marsh which could be used for grazing.

In the north of England the presence of a large garrison undoubtedly had the effect of introducing arable cultivation at the expense of primitive pastoralism. Large areas of 'Celtic' fields exist in Upper Wharfedale in the neighbourhood of Grassington, and villas, which became plentiful in East Yorkshire during the third and fourth centuries, are found occasionally even in the Pennines (in Upper Airedale) and as far north as Old Durham. We have already noticed the veteran settlement of the early third century round Ribchester in Lancashire (p. 213f.), and there are hints of others in western Yorkshire.[6]

There was an obvious advantage in cereal production near the market, though much of it may have been for purely local use. But the *pax Romana* also meant a rise in native population. Parts of Cumberland and Westmorland are thickly studded with native settlements; these were probably still mainly pastoral, but such of their produce as was not taken by the tax-collector will have found a ready sale in the crowded *vici* of the region. In the limestone hills of the Peak district many peasant cultivators settled in the caves of the region; the finds from these prove that they were not temporary refuges but permanent homes. In North Wales, also, settlements with terraced fields on the hillsides seem to be a new feature of the Roman period; but here again cultivation was probably combined with cattle-keeping. Nevertheless, the discovery of an asymmetrical plough-share, almost certainly from a mould-board plough, in the hill-fort of Dinorben, where a large round house was occupied in the late third and early fourth centuries, should warn us that primitive living conditions do not necessarily imply primitive agricultural techniques.

There are two very large areas of southern Britain where the absence of villas – and even towns – is noticeable. The first of these is Salisbury Plain and Cranborne Chase. Here an area of more than 900 square miles is virtually devoid of villas, but farmsteads and villages of peasant type abound. Important road junctions at Old Sarum and Badbury Rings, which might have been expected to favour the growth of small towns, signally fail to show signs of any such tendency. Yet this area had been highly productive and fully populated in pre-Roman times: the absence of normal development is striking, more especially since villas are found on the chalk in Hampshire, and it has given rise to the suggestion that the whole area at an early date had been converted into an imperial domain, perhaps as a result of confiscation following the bitter resistance hereabouts to the original occupation: the inhabitants would accordingly have been condemned to poverty because of the heavy exactions to which they were subject. Unfortunately no inscription has yet come to light to prove the truth of this theory, but it is perhaps supported by one found at Bath set up by C. Severius Emeritus 'centurion in charge of the region'.[7] It is also supported by the fact that arrangements for local storage of the corn-harvest in pits were greatly reduced after the conquest. Professor Hawkes has brilliantly reinterpreted the results of General Pitt-Rivers' excavation of rural sites in this region, and even if his figures should have to be reduced owing to the uncertainties of exactly dating local pottery from the storage pits, it still remains true that almost a half of the harvest remains to be accounted for, no doubt by requisition; for if it were only better marketing methods, or even the introduction of barns, that were responsible for the reduced number of pits, there should be more signs of prosperity. From the later second century onwards increasing attention seems to have been paid to stock-raising, and by the fourth there may have been a very considerable changeover to ranching. This again, since it involved a transfer of population and the abandonment of farms, suggests implementation of official policy.

Imperial estates certainly existed in Britain. Nero inherited part of the royal lands of the Iceni under Prasutagus' will, and more may well have been confiscated after the rebellion. Other provinces provide better evidence of the way in which imperial possessions grew as the result of inheritance or confiscation. In Britain we may surmise that Severus enlarged the patrimonium at the cost of the supporters of Albinus (p. 195), though there is little to prove it. An inscription from Combe Down, Bath, set up in the reign of Caracalla to record the restoration of a ruined headquarters by Naevius, imperial freedman and assistant to the procurators, may have some relevance here;[8] but since restoration rather than construction *ab initio* is in question, it is perhaps more likely that the stone records an established imperial interest, possibly in the local quarries of Bath stone. Again, the villas of Lullingstone and Ditchley have been thought to have suffered a period of desertion at the beginning of the third century, and this again might imply confiscation.[9] Finally, the inscription from the villa at Clanville, Hants., erected in 282–3 to the Caesar Carinus, probably implies imperial ownership.[10] Land held by the emperor, however, was not inalienable, and could be transferred by gift or by sale; thus, the pattern of imperial ownership was ever liable to change.

The second area noticeably lacking in villas is the silts of the Fen Basin, a vast region almost three times the size of the other. Increased flooding had made virtually the whole of this uninhabitable during the Iron Age, but in the first century AD a slight change in the relative levels of land and sea allowed reoccupation. Drainage was accordingly undertaken on a large scale, and thus fairly certainly by government agency; a single authority is indicated by the single programme of surveying and levelling over the whole wide region at one time. In this the Roman scheme offers a notable contrast to the piecemeal approach which has characterised the later history of Fen-drainage. The best-known work is the Car Dyke, a canal running from the neighbourhood of Cambridge round the periphery of the Fens to Lincoln. This course enabled it to be used to divert surplus water from one river-system to the next, but it was also intended to serve the needs of transport; a further link, the Fossdyke, from Lincoln to the Trent made it possible for barges to travel by inland waterways as far as Brough on Humber or York. Military depots on the Yorkshire Ouse and even on the Tyne could receive the farm-produce of the Fens, and the returning barges sometimes brought a cargo of coal. Subsidiary canals led into the Car Dyke, and roads were also built. But though in outline the orderly appearance of the whole scheme bears an official stamp, the new land thus reclaimed was not centuriated. The settlements therein were entirely native in character and show no signs of central planning or of official land-division, which the myriad small water-courses would have made impracticable. The parallel is with the Agri Decumates of southern Germany rather than with colonial settlement. Nevertheless, it is probable that this virgin territory was public land, peasant settlers receiving farms in return for rent and no doubt being placed under the control of a *procurator saltus*.

Apart from a few exceptionally early sites dating from about 60, the settlement of the Fens seems to have started in the late first century, possibly about 80. In this first stage single scattered settlements, some apparently connected with the salt industry, were normal. But from the time of Hadrian multiple settlements became increasingly common, implying a steady rise of population and even perhaps new drafts of settlers, and it was probably now that the Car

Dyke was constructed. Indeed, it is likely that in this fuller exploitation we should recognise one of the results of Hadrian's visit to Britain, for his interest in the reclamation of waste lands is well known, and is attested on inscriptions from Roman Africa. The exact nature of the nucleated settlements cannot be defined without excavation on a large scale, but they may be loosely described as villages, provided that our picture of a village is not too closely coloured by its Anglo-Saxon form: probably they were mainly groups of farms concentrated together for kinship reasons.

Though grain-cultivation was undoubtedly an important activity in the Fens, air-photographs show large areas between settlements devoid of sub-division into fields but sometimes demarcated by dykes. This suggests that raising sheep and cattle – and perhaps horses too – played a significant part in the economy, a suggestion supported by the numbers of bones found and also by the pottery cheese-strainers which occur with notable frequency. Many sites, too, yield traces of brine-boiling apparatus, showing that salt-production was another important activity; and it was one which started on a large scale in the late first century.

Flooding was an ever-present danger, as the water-courses rose higher on their levees of silt. There seems to have been some desertion of sites already by the end of the second century, and serious flooding occurred in the early third, causing damage which was not put right for fifty years. A renewal of prosperity, however, can be traced at the end of the third century, though with less numerous settlements; it may be due to more lenient terms of tenancy if analogy elsewhere is any guide. After the opening decades of the fifth century, however, occupation of the area could no longer be maintained, for the breakdown of Roman administration in this period was soon followed by adverse changes in the relative levels of land and sea, causing renewed flooding and the end of human settlement in the region for a millennium.

The Fenland was not the only area where land-reclamation was undertaken. Both Lincoln and Gloucester had territoria which must have embraced much marshy land such as would be useless until drained; and it has been thought that this fact may have been one of the considerations determining their foundation as coloniae, since such land was of little value as it stood to its British owners, whereas Colchester had experienced the passions which might be aroused by expropriation of valuable farmlands. Another area which was reclaimed, this time under army supervision, lay in the neighbourhood of Caerleon, where an inscription from the sea-wall or embankment at Goldcliff near the mouth of the Usk shows it to have been built by legionaries.

The plough used in Iron Age Britain was a simple bow-ard whose wooden share was tipped with a short pointed iron sheath. Belgic farmers improved this plough with longer, wider iron shares, and by its means were able to exploit heavier soils than before. But it was not until the Roman period that any markedly more efficient implement was introduced. The bow-ard, especially with the addition of earth-boards or ground-wrests, is perfectly efficient in the lighter soils, and can turn the sod if the plough itself is tilted. In Romano-British times this plough was made more powerful by the addition of a coulter to cut the soil in front of the share, and of a heavy iron bar-share capable of withstanding much strain. There is also suggestive evidence in the form of asymmetrical shares that the mould-board (which automatically turns the sod) was known. But the date of these introductions is uncertain. A fragment of coulter was found at Twyford Down, apparently in an early Roman deposit, but all the other examples of bar-shares and coulters come from fourth-century contexts. It is probable that their use spread gradually through the medium of the villas, while peasants continued to use their simpler traditional equipment. Certainly the new ploughs would encourage the use of larger fields in the new villa-estates, but at present there is no secure evidence for the use of strip-fields in Roman Britain. Traces of field-systems definitely associated with villas, lying as they do on soils much cultivated in after-times, are still mainly to seek. Air photographs sometimes show small rectangular closes round the actual villa buildings, as at Ditchley, Oxfordshire (pl. 9b), or Cromwell, Nottinghamshire, but these being of small extent are almost certainly orchards or vegetable gardens or home paddocks rather than evidence for 'Celtic' fields. A firmer hint is provided at Brading (Isle of Wight), where a large area of Celtic fields exists on the Down above the villa, close enough to it to leave little doubt that they formed part of its estate. It is worth noting, too, that this villa has produced an asymmetrical plough-share, such as should belong to a mould-board plough.

Other tools now introduced, probably in the first instance by the army but of great assistance to the farmer, were the iron-tipped spade, the rake and the scythe. The last was of major importance, for it revolutionised ability to winter livestock, and the spade facilitated draining. But the wide range of lesser tools now generally available, such as chisels, draw-knives, spoke-shaves and the carpenter's plane, must have greatly increased ability to make what was necessary on the spot. A reaping-machine named the *Vallus* is mentioned by Pliny as current in Gaul, and is represented on the well-known relief from Buzenol. Though there is no evidence at present that this was used in Britain, the enormous scythe-blades, up to seven feet long (twice the length of modern examples), known from Great Chesterford and the villa at Barnsley Park near Cirencester, suggest that daring experimentation was being carried on.

Another invention whose use became widespread was the corn-drying furnace. Corn-drying, of value in times of wet harvest, and the parching of the grain both prevented germination during storage and facilitated milling. It was particularly necessary for the treatment of spelt. The practice had been followed in the Iron Age, but the exact nature of the primitive equipment in use at that time is not known. No doubt the same simple apparatus continued to be used in the first and second centuries, for spelt was a principal crop in Roman Britain. However, in the third and fourth centuries the use of carefully insulated structures with double floors and underground flues became widespread, and marked a great technological advance available alike to villa-owners and peasant farmers. Similarly, Roman technology improved the water supply of farms. A few villas, as at Abinger, Surrey, possessed an aqueduct or leet; but the great majority of farms came to depend on wells – sometimes up to 200 feet deep – the ability to dig which enabled larger flocks and herds to be maintained.

Several new crops were introduced, including rye, oats, vetch and flax, as well as the cabbage, parsnip, turnip, carrot, celery and other vegetables. Here again the winter-feeding of animals received assistance: Columella had already noted the importance of the turnip for this purpose in Gaul. A number of fruit trees are also now attested for the first time, among them being the vine, the plum, the apple, and the mulberry and walnut, and probably the sweet cherry; it is possible that specialised cultivation, following the precepts of classical agricultural treatises, was undertaken here and there. Near

316

Grimsby in north Lincolnshire an area of over twelves acres was found to be covered with a rectangular grid of closely spaced ditches, which were possibly intended for the planting of fruit trees. Much smaller plots, somewhat similar in appearance and perhaps in function, are characteristic of many of the Fenland settlements. Among flowers the rose, violet, lily, pansy and poppy are thought to be Roman importations. That animal strains were improved is not so easy to demonstrate, but there is suggestive evidence for a larger breed of horse which is likely to have been an introduction; larger cattle, too, appear more frequently than in the Iron Age, and may be due either to the import of fresh varieties or to selective breeding from existing strains. Among other introductions are normally counted the goose and the pheasant. Bee-keeping was widespread, if the large vessels used for hives have been correctly identified.

All this shows that the Romano-British farmer had many advantages over his predecessors. Corn-growing was no doubt always a principal activity owing to government pressure, but for the same reason can never have yielded outstanding wealth. It is noteworthy that the villas of East Anglia and the Midlands, which were probably then as now the main corn-producing areas, are with few exceptions of poor or medium quality. The really large and luxurious villas are clustered in the Cotswold country and in Somerset – lands which have always been best suited to sheep and cattle. But even in predominantly arable estates mixed farming was probably practised. At Bignor, for instance, certain of the outbuildings have been interpreted by Applebaum as a sheep-pen (accommodating 197 sheep), a lambing enclosure and a byre for twelve yoke of plough-oxen, in addition to the cattle-stall for fifty-five cows which has already been mentioned (p. 308); and he has recognised pig-sties at others, for instance, Pitney in Somerset and Woolaston Pill in Gloucestershire.

The climax of villa prosperity was not reached before the beginning of the fourth century. It had, however, no doubt been maturing during the third, for in 301 Diocletian's price-fixing edict could assign the maximum permitted price within their classes to two British woollen products, the Birrus Britannicus (a hooded waterproof cloak somewhat resembling a duffle coat) and the Tapete Britannicum (a woollen rug suitable for saddles or couches); clearly these products had already acquired their empire-wide reputation before this date, and they point to a flourishing woollen industry which must have been based ultimately on the villas [11] (p. 337). Nevertheless, at the beginning of the fourth century many of these establishments were rebuilt or extended, and others were constructed on new sites: to this period also, and to the succeeding century, belong the great majority of the best villa mosaics.[12]

In seeking to explain this prosperity some have suggested a flight of capital to Britain after the late-third-century troubles in Gaul and Germany. There is, however, little evidence for this save likelihood, and the prosperity can be explained in more general terms. In the first place Britain herself had survived the third century with her economy largely undamaged, and now found herself in a unique position in the western empire. Builders were sent from Britain to restore Autun by Constantius Chlorus c. 298, and in 359 Julian was able to increase the regular export of corn from Britain to the Rhineland to 600 barge-loads during an emergency. These two passing references which happen to have come down to us are pointers to the truth that, though in earlier centuries the British economy had depended on loans and the activities of continental businessmen, and had relied on imports even for its better table-wares, by the fourth century the loans had been repaid, business was in local hands and the balance of trade was favourable. This self-sufficiency is further discussed in the next chapter.

The prosperity of the countryside in the fourth century has long been recognised, but it used to be contrasted with an apparent decay of the towns: for Collingwood the success of the villas represented a flight from the towns. But, as we have seen, there is no evidence for profound urban decay before the fifth century. Villas had always had a close connection with the towns, and their prosperity in the fourth century is a sign of the continuing and increasing wealth of the British curial class as a whole. This, though characteristic of Britain, is exceptional in the Roman world; it is to be explained partly by the economic considerations already mentioned, and partly by the fact that in these provinces the aristocracy had never lost its close ties with the countryside from which it renewed its vigour and its wealth. It is not without significance that we hear little of peasant revolts in Britain, similar to the serious outbreaks which recurred in Gaul with increasing severity in the third and fourth centuries, before the opening decade of the fifth. This may mean that the peasants of Britain remained more prosperous than their Gallic counterparts, and that, as in later history, there was an absence of sharp cleavage between landlord and tenant in Britain such as gave rise to class-warfare elsewhere.

1. Strabo, iv, 199.
2. Caesar, *BG*, v, 12.
3. For *coloni* in Britain see *Codex Theodos.*, xi, 7, 2. Recent work (*Britannia* v (1974)) now suggests that the fourth-century story at Llantwit Major was different from that suggested in the text; the general point, however, remains valid.
4. First-century mosaics are also known at the incompletely excavated villa at Rivenhall, Essex (*Britannia*, iv (1973), pp. 115 ff.).
5. The width of the aisles, 14 feet 6 inches, in this and other such buildings seems to bear some relationship with the length of a beast plus the width of a feeding stall and gangway.
6. There are two dedications to *dea Brigantia* and one to *deus Bregans*: all three are dedicated by Aurelii, two of them giving their praenomen as Titus. These names suggest descendants of second-century veteran auxiliaries, one of the stones being dated to 208 (*RIB*, 623, 627, 628).
7. *RIB*, 152; *ILS*, 4920. *C(enturio) reg(ionarius)*. The scope of his office, not being further described, is likely to have been local.
8. *RIB*, 174. The villa at Combe Down also produced a lead seal inscribed *P(rovinciae) Br(itanniae) S(uperioris)*.
9. But the difficulty of distinguishing pottery of the first half of the third century from that of the late second suggests caution on this point. Nevertheless, the Lullingstone villa had belonged to a prominent Roman official in the late second century, as the portrait busts prove.
10. *RIB*, 98; but it may be a milestone reused, cf. recent finds at the Rockbourne villa.
11. As early as *c.* 220 a *tossia Britannica* – thought to be a cloak or tunic – was considered worthy of being sent by a Governor of Inferior as a presentation to a friend in Gaul. *CIL*, xiii, 3162.
12. For a contemporary view of British prosperity at the end of the third century see *Incerti Panegyricus Constantio Caesari dictus* viii (v), 11: *et sane non sicut Britanniae nomen unum, ita mediocris erat iacturae rei publicae terra tanto frugum ubere, tanto laeta numero pastionum, tot metallorum fluens rivis, tot vectigalibus quaestuosa, tot accincta portibus, tanto immensa circuitu …*

14

Trade and industry

Britain had enjoyed commercial contacts of one sort or another with the Continent from distant prehistoric times. In the first century BC the tin trade of Cornwall had begun to decline, whether the cause was Caesar's destruction of the Venetic fleet, or, more generally, the availability of richer and nearer supplies elsewhere, and it did not fully recover thereafter; for the Romans made no serious attempt to open up Cornwall before the third century. By the time of Nero, when the peninsula was occupied, sufficient tin was being obtained from Spain; and the limited exploitation of Cornwall, which is all we find in the later first century, shows that the industry could not compete with this nearer source.

Cicero, contradicting what sound like earlier anticipations, wrote to a friend in May 54 BC that it was now known that there was no trace of either gold or silver to be had in Britain.[1] But Caesar himself mentions merchants who knew the coasts, traces of whose trade we can recognise in the early Italian wine-amphorae found here and there near southern ports. The more specific account which later on Strabo gave of the imports and exports of Britain in the time of Augustus has already been quoted (p. 61). The wide market which existed for fine pottery-wares from Italy and the Rhineland, as well as for the amphora-borne products of Campania and Southern Spain, has been revealed by excavation at the principal Belgic oppida such as *Camulodunum* or Bagendon; more valuable imports, such as drinking vessels in precious metal, have come to light from time to time in chieftains' tombs.

One of the results of the Claudian Conquest was the arrival of a mass of fresh merchants, speculators and prospectors in the wake of the armies. 'Britain produces gold and silver and other metals,' writes Tacitus, better informed than Cicero, 'which are the reward of victory; ocean too produces pearls, though of poor quality.

The yield of gold, indeed, was disappointing. In earlier times Ireland had been the chief source of gold in the west, and no doubt much of the gold used in Britain during the Iron Age still came from there. Auriferous rocks certainly occur to a limited extent in Wales and Scotland and also in Cornwall, but the only known Roman workings are at Dolaucothi in Carmarthenshire, where their exploitation had to await the pacification of Wales. Even now the site is not fully explored; both open-cast workings and mining galleries are visible; and recent field work has traced at least two aqueduct systems, one of them just over seven miles long and capable of delivering about three million gallons a day to a series of large reservoirs high on the hill above the workings. The water seems to have been intended partly for breaking down the softer beds of rock, for which purpose a powerful head was necessary, and partly for washing the ore, after it had been crushed in stone mills, thus saving the necessity of carrying it to the river to wash, as had been done earlier. Fire-setting was also used to penetrate the rock. The deeper galleries, some eighty feet below ground, were drained by means of large wooden water-wheels, similar to those known from Roman mines in Spain; a portion of one of these, found in 1935 when the mines were briefly reworked, is in the National Museum of Wales. The Dolaucothi goldfield thus illustrates many of the most impressive aspects of Roman mining technology and deserves further study. It was certainly in imperial ownership and was protected by a fort. But the actual operations may nevertheless have been in the hands of contractors, to judge by the gold jewellery found at the site, which is more appropriate to lessees than to slave labour.

Silver, on the other hand, was readily available by cupellation from some of the lead ores which are easily accessible in various parts of Britain; and lead itself was a valuable by-product, some of which was exported to the Continent and the rest extensively used in bath buildings, water-pipes, lead coffins and the like. The speed with which exploitation followed the over-running of these leadfields is striking testimony to the efficiency and acumen of the prospectors. Our evidence is derived from the inscriptions cast or incised on the ingots (or pigs) – usually about 170–190 lb in weight – into which the lead was run for transport.[3]

The first area to be worked was in the Mendip Hills of Somerset.

It is clear from the distribution of ingots lost in transit that they were being exported to the Continent via Southampton Water, where a port existed at Clausentum. Two carry inscriptions dating them to AD 49, only six years after the conquest, and one found at St-Valery-sur-Somme bears the name of Nero coupled with that of Legio II Augusta. It seems likely from this that in the early years exploitation was begun by this legion, under whose control this area lay at the time. Military government, however, was not intended to be permanent, and as early as 60 we find C. Nipius Ascanius, a civilian prospector, at work: his names imply that he was a freedman; no doubt he was acting for a wealthy Roman patron. The ingot in question was found at Stockbridge, Hampshire, and is therefore probably Mendip lead, as the date and place clearly suggest, but Ascanius' name recurs on a pig from the Flintshire field.[4] The latter can hardly have been worked before Suetonius Paullinus' campaigns had over-run North Wales; the earliest dated ingot from it is one of 74 inscribed *Degeangl(icum)*. Ascanius therefore appears as an interesting example of a prospector working first in Somerset but soon extending his activities to North Wales in the wake of the army. Another slightly later illustration of this sort of 'silver-rush' is provided by three ingots of Vespasianic date found at Wells in Somerset and inscribed with the name of Tiberius Claudius Trifer(na). This man was probably an imperial freedman, and was working the Mendip field in the period 69–79; but soon after this, when Agricola's early campaigns brought the Derbyshire and Yorkshire lead-fields within the reach of prospectors, the same name occurs on a Derbyshire ingot.[5] A pig dated to 91 and bearing the inscription *Brig(anticum)* shows that the Yorkshire field, too, was put into immediate production.

After the initial period of military exploitation, therefore, which itself was due to the military government under which much of south-west Britain was placed in the conquest period, the early working of the lead was in the hands of prospectors or lessees (*conductores*); these were mainly freedmen of the emperor or of wealthy business-men, who worked either singly or in companies. Evidence for companies (*societates*) is found as early as the principate of Vespasian. A *soc(ietas) Novaec.* is mentioned on an ingot of this reign which was found at Clausentum, indicating that this company was working in the Mendips; the productions of the *societas Lutudarensis* of

Derbyshire cannot be precisely dated as yet, but are probably also of about this same period.

To judge by analogy, the mining-rights were an imperial monopoly leased out to contractors by a *procurator metallorum*; and that close supervision was exercised is attested by Pliny the elder.[6] Writing early in the reign of Vespasian he states, 'Lead is made into pipes and thin sheets. It is mined with some difficulty in Spain and Gaul, but in Britain is present in such quantity near the surface that there is a law limiting its exploitation.' Under Hadrian the Derbyshire products now carry the imperial name with the addition *Met(allum) Lut(udarense)*, and none anywhere else mentions lessees. These facts suggest that Hadrian imposed a tightening-up of monopoly and possibly also direct working by prisoners rather than by free lessees; certainly in his reign there must have been exceptional requirements for lead in the new military installations of the frontier. A generation or two later the presence of a quantity of lead ore in pebble form in the Antonine Fort at Brough, Derbyshire, points to collection of material from streams under military supervision here at this period, and in the third century the second cohort of Nervians, stationed at Whitley Castle in Northumberland, appears to have supervised the collection of lead from the Alston field; for lead seals of this cohort, bearing the word *metal(lum)*, have been found at Brough under Stainmore and point to material in transit. Thus, military control of lead-mining was continued in areas under military rule (p. 259).

How long the original system of exploitation remained in operation in the civil zone is uncertain. The latest inscribed ingots are three of Marcus and Verus (164–9) from the Mendip field. Though the lead of this region and probably of Flintshire, too, was sufficiently rich in silver to make its extraction just profitable, analysis has shown that the silver yield in Derbyshire was exceptionally low, as it was in Shropshire and Yorkshire. But the yield of silver even in the Mendips was much lower than that obtainable elsewhere in the empire, and must have disappointed Roman expectations. It seems possible that government interest in direct working of the more southerly fields was relaxed in the second half of the second century, and that the industry was allowed to fall more and more into private hands, which no longer produced large inscribed ingots. Production certainly persisted into later times, since a coin of Gordian III has been found in association with workings in Flintshire, and fourth-century finds are common in the Derbyshire mining district. In the Mendip region, too, the exceptional quantity of silver coins of the late fourth century has been taken, reasonably enough, to suggest a prosperity derived from silver production at this date. The flourishing pewter industry in the same region in the third and fourth centuries points to the same conclusion, since pewter is an alloy of lead and tin.

Imperial interest in British metals was not, of course, abandoned altogether, for private workers are thought to have been compelled to yield half their production to the state, which needed silver for its coinage. The treasury, which is attested in London in the late fourth century, may have had the collection of silver as one of its duties, and there is some evidence to suggest that silver ingots were used at this period for payments of salary instead of coin. Tin, too, was controlled, for an ingot of this metal from Carnanton in Cornwall bears a third- or fourth-century imperial stamp. About the middle of the third century the Roman government began to take a renewed interest in Cornwall, for milestones prove road-building in that period and also in the early fourth century. The purpose of this was certainly to assist the revival of the tin industry, perhaps because of the decline in Spanish production consequent on barbarian invasion, and certainly because of renewed demand for it in Britain from the manufacturers of pewter. This was a new industry which made drinking and dining vessels for the growing number of town and villa dwellers of medium wealth.

The lead–silver industry serves as a convenient illustration of the early penetration and quick exploitation of British resources by Roman enterprise, whether official or mercantile. In other industries we have hints, but no such full information. Copper, which is to be found in Shropshire, North Wales and Anglesey, appears to have been first worked in Roman times and probably by lessees who hired the mineral rights from the procurator; but very little is known of them in detail. It seems that an improved furnace was introduced which was capable of smelting up to 50 lb of copper, the metal being then run off to form a bun-shaped ingot. From stamps on these ingots the name of at least one societas is known, as well as several individual lessees. Copper was hardly ever used in its pure state in Roman Britain; stronger, harder bronze or brass alloys made with zinc, lead and tin were widely produced.[7] It has also been shown that technical knowledge was now sufficient to choose appropriate alloys for the different processes required in manufacturing cast or wrought objects.

The manufacture of bronze objects in Roman Britain was carried on at two distinct levels. On the one hand, we have craftsmen, no doubt mainly based on the towns and on the larger vici of the north, who manufactured objects in classical taste, though in provincial style. At first such people will have been immigrants in the main, but the very large quantity of material, as well as the artistic standards, show that Britons soon learnt the necessary skills. Among their products may be recognised jugs and skillets, fittings for doors and furniture, religious statuettes and personal ornaments. Most of the finer examples of the bronze-smith's art, of course, were imported ready-made from Italy or Gaul; but British craftsmen copied imported models to the best of their ability, and occasionally they achieved distinctive creations of their own, such as the enamelled cups and skillets which were sold as souvenirs of Hadrian's Wall.

Distinct from these, there still existed rural or itinerant craftsmen in the north and west trained in the old traditions of the native bronze industry of Celtic Britain, who sometimes produced minor masterpieces in which the spirit of La Tène art still breathed. Brooches of the elaborate dragonesque, fan-tailed or trumpet types seem to have come from such hands, since their distribution points to an origin in the highland zone; but even when such strongly individual production died out before the spread of more uniform fashions, we still find bronze fittings for wooden tankards or buckets, and bronze cauldrons for brewing or for seething meat. The manufacture of these never died out. They remained in demand among highland-zone households which continued in the Celtic way of life; and after the Roman period was over their continued manufacture did something to compensate for the dearth of pottery.

The timber industry was another which may have early attracted the attention of immigrant *entrepreneurs*; it must have brought great wealth to those who owned or had the control of forests. Apart from the needs of the army, which may have been met by requisition, we have only to remember the immense building programme in the first-century towns, in which almost all private buildings were of half-timber construction. Stone quarries, too, were quickly in operation where suitable rock could be found. The inscription of Cogidubnus at Chichester and that of Agricola at *Verulamium* were both carved on Purbeck Marble quarried in Dorset, and smaller pieces of this stone have been found in pits at Colchester which were filled in before AD 60; the tombstone of Classicianus in London is of Cotswold or Northampton limestone, as are the still earlier tombstones of Facilis and Longinus at Colchester; and the early baths-portico at Silchester, which is certainly of Flavian if not earlier date, is of Bath stone. The early growth of all these industries, for which technical knowledge was necessary, suggests exploitation by newcomers from abroad. The same thing might be said of the early development of the tile-making industry; a tilery in imperial ownership seems to have existed near Silchester, where a stamped tile of Nero has been found.[8] Pottery-making too, though always to some extent in local hands, was certainly stimulated and improved by foreign capital. In the Flavian–Trajanic period there were at least seven Roman citizens who stamped mortaria at Colchester, and six others who were fairly certainly working at an unidentified site in Kent. One, C. Attius Marinus, started his career at Colchester, but later worked for a brief time at Radlett near *Verulamium* before moving on to Hartshill in Warwickshire, where an enormous pottery industry subsequently developed. Most of these men were probably freedmen, notably the Sexti Valerii at Colchester (p. 296). But Q. Valerius Veranius, who came to Kent from the region of Bavai in Belgica, was the son of a citizen, and Q. Rutilius Ripanus, son of Tiberius, who made mortaria in the Radlett region, may also have been a citizen-proprietor. At this early period about a third of the potters stamping mortaria were citizens, while in the second century the proportion is distinctly lower.

The stimulus to Romano-British industries from foreign capital and immigrant speculators was matched by the exploitation of new trading opportunities by numerous continental merchants.[9] Many would come armed with contracts to supply the army with necessities and would remain to make money among the civilians of the province. Such were the importers of samian ware, the red-gloss pottery which hardly any site of the first two centuries AD fails to produce in quantity. The prototype of this class of pottery was Italian: vessels of Arretine ware from Italy reached some wealthy Belgic households before the conquest. By the beginning of the principate of Claudius, however, the Western markets were being captured by the manufacturers of similar pottery in South Gaul (at

Montans and at La Graufesenque near Millau). These continued to ship vast quantities of samian pottery to Britain until the late first century, when they began to lose ground to rival firms more advantageously placed in the Allier valley of central Gaul (at Les Martres de Veyre and Lezoux). Soon after the beginning of the second century the latter had virtually monopolised the market for fine table-ware in Britain, and their successors maintained their hold on the trade, with some rivalry from eastern Gaulish factories, throughout the second century. The well-known Pudding Pan Rock find represents the wreck of a vessel full of a cargo of samian consisting entirely of plain forms, which was lost in the late second century on its way to London. This port must have been one of the principal receiving and distributing centres in Britain for imported pottery.

During the last quarter of the second century another class of continental pottery began to be imported. This was Rhenish ware, a fine pottery with dark lustrous colour-coat, manufactured in the Cologne region, the most popular forms of which were decorated drinking vessels. Vessels of this ware continued to enjoy wide sales in the third century, but local British factories making very similar pottery had already been set up in the Nene valley, at Colchester and elsewhere in East Anglia, and probably also in Kent (p. 329).[10]

Traders in Rhenish and samian pottery were by no means the only people from the Continent who made money in the British market. Much fine glass from Alexandria or Syria was imported in the first century; when factories were established at Cologne and in Normandy during the second, their products, too, found a ready market in Britain, where the industry never seems to have established itself on a wide scale, except for window-glass. The only sites in Britain where Roman glass furnaces have been identified are Wroxeter, Caistor by Norwich, Wilderspool (Lancashire) and Mancetter (Warwickshire). However, many ordinary glass vessels are hard to assign with confidence to any particular source of origin, and the industry itself leaves such insignificant traces that it is quite possible for its place in the British economy to have been underestimated. Bronze jugs, dishes and a few lamps and candelabra from Italy, also, found a ready market among the wealthy, and smaller bronzes, sometimes decorated in enamel, were imported from Northern Gaul. In addition to these, vast quantities of wine, some olive oil (for use in Public Baths and also for lamps) [11] and possibly also fish sauce were marketed here from Spain. This trade had its beginnings before the conquest and greatly expanded thereafter, capturing the British market from Italian exporters. The earliest Spanish amphorae attested in Britain were found in pre-conquest deposits at Colchester: during the second half of the first century Spanish exporters secured a monopoly which continued until the end of the second, when the punitive measures taken by Severus against the supporters of Albinus in Spain disrupted the trade. Only two amphora-stamps from Spanish wine-producing estates after their confiscation have been found in Britain. Another widespread import was domestic hand-mills of Andernach lava from the middle Rhine which are frequently found on military as well as on civilian sites of the first and second centuries; trade in this material had begun as early as the neolithic period, and was to be resumed in the Middle Ages, but in Roman Britain the market was eventually lost to local producers of quern stones.

All these great import businesses necessarily brought over large numbers of provincials from Gaul and Spain, especially in the early days, and most of these will have returned home on retirement with the money they had made. Even more significant is the large and continuous drain of resources in the form of payments to source for the imports themselves.

This draining away of profits to the Continent was part of a process which was augmented both by the interest paid on the large loans which had been necessary to establish the early towns (which are partly attested by Dio) [12] and also by the inevitable drift back to the Continent, at least in the first century, of retired soldiers from the large British garrison whose savings were the product of British taxation. Their numbers were far larger than those of corresponding British veterans returning from abroad (p. 238). From all these causes Britain in the first century, and on a lesser scale throughout the whole of the second, was a province suffering from what nowadays would be called an adverse balance of trade, offset though this was to some extent by rising production and expansion of resources, which were made possible by new techniques and the *pax Romana*. The later prosperity of the province, especially in the fourth century, was in great part due to gradual rectification of the adverse balance, as British products gradually took the place of imports, and profits ceased to drain away overseas.[13]

How this came about may be briefly explained. We have already seen that evidence for the continued exploitation of silver–lead in its old form fails after the later second century, and that this probably means that the industry was reorganised under local enterprise, half the produce perhaps going to the state, but the other half no longer going to speculators from abroad. Such a system would explain inscriptions found on later Roman silver ingots such as that from the Tower of London; this bears the stamp *ex offe Honorini*, 'from the workshop of Honorinus', an inscription which gives no indication of connection with the government.

The import of samian pottery virtually ceased at the end of the second century, partly owing to a decline in the standards of production, but mainly owing to the disruption of the central Gaulish industry in the struggle between Severus and Albinus, from which it never recovered. A little samian from east Gaul reached Britain in the third century, and rather a larger quantity of Rhenish ware. But by this time competition by potters in Britain itself had created an industry capable of producing very tolerable table-ware which satisfied the needs of all who were content to drink from pottery. For those with more ostentatious habits the growing pewter industry in the region round Bath provided locally produced table-wares in metal, though the very rich, at any rate in the fourth century, possessed sets of imported silver, exemplified for us in the Mildenhall treasure.

Fine pottery capable of standing comparison with imported wares was probably first produced in the Nene Valley round *Durobrivae* at a date shortly before 150, and by 200 the industry had developed large-scale production – the so-called Castor ware. Manufacture continued down to the early years of the fifth century, and the sales penetrated almost all Britain. In the Colchester region similar wares were being made in the later second century, and there was even a short-lived attempt to start a samian industry, which failed owing to unsuitable clay and poor production. A similar venture, equally short-lived, attempted samian manufacture in London. The manufacture of a fine red colour-coated ware which recalled the now vanished samian, began to be developed during the later third century by the potters of the Oxford region. Their venture, which included the manufacture of mortaria, achieved a wide success in the fourth century, reaching markets as widely separated as Richborough and Caernarvon. Perhaps in emulation, the potters of the New Forest also began to produce colour-coated wares at the end of the third century, but their products never achieved a more than regional market.

Rather less sophisticated though still handsome wares, usually in grey with a white slip, were made in the Farnham district on the borders of Hampshire and Surrey; these won a regional market for themselves during the third century comparable to that of the New Forest potters farther west.

The more utilitarian domestic vessels were produced in a great number of local potteries, both large and small, all over the lowland zone and even farther north where clay and fuel were available. The wares of those who were fortunate enough to be awarded army contracts – for the army only rarely made its own pottery – achieved a wide distribution in the north; for instance, more than a third of the stamped mortaria from the Antonine Wall were made at Colchester, and many of the rest were products of kilns in the Midlands. The largest and most important of the groups of coarse ware, consisting of cooking vessels and dishes made in two categories of 'black-burnished ware', are now known to have been manufactured at a variety of centres, most of them remote from the military markets they served. Two of the principal areas for vessels of 'category 1' were in Dorset, where pre-Roman industries were expanded, and in Somerset; vessels of 'category 2' appear to have sources in East Anglia and the flanks of the Thames estuary. These factories produced pottery for the Roman army – and also for the civilian market – on a very large scale from the time of Hadrian onwards. Their products are found virtually all over the west and north of Britain; only in the south-east did sales fail to overwhelm local competitors.

Other smaller establishments achieved importance in Derbyshire and Yorkshire from the third century onwards; but in the final period, after many of them had been destroyed in the disturbed conditions of the third quarter of the fourth century, it was the factory at Crambeck which captured the military markets of the north.

If Severus destroyed the prosperity of the samian industry he also disrupted the Spanish wine-trade, and its products were now largely diverted under state control elsewhere. Thereafter the best table wines in Britain came from Bordeaux and the Moselle valley [14] but it is likely enough that local wines of a sort were developed from vines grown in the walled gardens of villas. In the monasteries of the Middle Ages wine was certainly produced as far north as Chester. For Roman Britain we have the edict of Probus of about 277 cancelling previous restrictions on viticulture in Gaul and Britain, and we have the evidence of vine plants found near the villa at Boxmoor, Hertfordshire, and of grape-pips from Silchester, Southwark and Gloucester.[15] We also have a most interesting scene illustrating the vine-harvest in barbotine on one of the Colchester vases.[16] Vines then were certainly grown in Britain, and there is no reason why wine should not have been produced from them. But alternative local intoxicating drinks were available; as well as the mead which Pytheas first recorded, a species of beer was made, the froth of which, according to Pliny, was used by women as a cosmetic.[17] This beer was priced at 4 denarii a pint in Diocletian's price-edict – twice the cost of the Egyptian variety. It is noteworthy that the fine drinking-vessels made by the British potters of the third and fourth centuries are very frequently of quart size or larger, and this reinforces the suggestion that beer largely took the place of wine in Britain after Severus; for such beakers could hardly have been used for the latter.

These changes in the pattern of industry, together with the results of agricultural improvements already described (pp. 315–17), meant that in the third century the economy of Britain became more balanced, as the wealth of the province, after the demands of taxation had been met, came to remain more and more in British hands; and much of the yield of taxation, of course, was expended in Britain on payments to soldiers and officials. Moreover, the increase in local recruitment to the army, and the measures taken by Severus and his successors to give serving soldiers a stake in the soil (p. 213), resulted in a more general settlement in Britain of retired soldiers and their capital. To this we may add the exports of the province, which, though never on a large scale, grew more numerous in the third and fourth centuries. The chief of these, woollen goods and corn, have already been mentioned (p. 317). British pearls were known to Tacitus (p. 321) and were still sold in the fourth century.[18] Another small-scale luxury-trade concerned itself with Whitby jet, which was fashioned into rings, pins, necklaces and even portrait-medallions in York. Jet was a rare substance, which with its electro-static qualities must have been highly prized and correspondingly expensive; it found a market in the Rhineland, where the absence of any trace of manufacturer's waste implies that the objects were sent ready made from York.[19] Another prized product of Britain was its hunting dogs, of which three breeds are known, one being the bulldog; bears, too, were being exported for the Roman arena as early as the time of Agricola.[20] British oysters enjoyed a certain popularity in Rome at least in the first century,[21] and British basket-work was also obtainable there.[22]

Nor was trade exclusively directed towards the continental empire. Slaves were a valuable commodity, the normal supply of which must have tended to dry up with growing frontier stability, and there is little doubt that dealers must have braved the perils of the Irish and northern seas in search of fresh sources, though such a trade leaves little archaeological trace. We may mention the discovery of Roman coins in Iceland and the Roman pot trawled up from the Porcupine Bank, 150 miles from the west coast of Ireland. There are a few finds of coins, bronze trinkets and even of pottery from Ireland itself, mainly near the north and east coasts. Evidence of trade with free Scotland is more considerable. Roman products were widely distributed up the east and west coasts, especially the former, along which commerce continued until the middle of the fourth century, when Irish raids had disrupted the western routes. This trade had its origin in Britain (perhaps in the ports of the Humber and Dee estuaries), but the goods sold were often themselves imports into Britain, such as samian and Rhenish wares or wine in amphorae, and even occasionally rare and costly painted glass vessels from Cologne, some of which reached Orkney. A dedication, apparently of the later second century, at Bowness on Solway was set up by a trader who undertook to gild its letters if sufficient profits were granted to his enterprise;[23] the Solway may have been his last port of call before the risks began.

Other traders reached southern Scotland by land. Commerce was controlled at the exits from Hadrian's Wall; at Housesteads, where the north gate of the fort is on the brink of a steep gradient, a special opening was built through the wall in the valley below at the beginning of the fourth century. Its double system of gates was clearly designed to facilitate the customs examination of travellers, and its provision at this period may point to increased commerce with the protected zone beyond. The exports of Scotland, apart from slaves, are likely to have consisted of hides, furs and wool.

Evidence for weaving, especially in the form of bone combs for packing the threads on the loom, is fairly widespread in Scotland during the Roman Iron Age, while the Roman votive model of a bale of wool from Skye points to the presence of merchants from the province in the western isles. There is evidence also from certain hoards of iron-work concealed in southern Scotland in the second century for the introduction of improved tools, and of new techniques or habits of life implicit in such articles as scythes and farriers' buttresses, cooking gridirons and lampstands, which themselves may be the products of intercourse with traders from the south or with soldiers of the garrison, though they may equally well be attributable to the influence of government policy during the period when this region was occupied.

Nothing has so far been said of the iron industry of Roman Britain, since, with the exception just mentioned, its products were not as far as we know exported; as it already had a respectable antiquity and considerable technical competence, it did not invite the same degree of development from continental newcomers as did the other industries already described. Nevertheless, it is clear that the total consumption of iron in Roman Britain soon greatly exceeded that of the preceding Iron Age; iron tools became much more common, and a greater weight of metal was employed in some of them. This enlarged production was no doubt due to the expanding economy of both town and country made possible by the *pax Romana*.

The chief iron-fields of pre-Roman Britain had been those of the Wealden area of Kent and east Sussex, the Forest of Dean, and the Northampton–Lincolnshire region. Production in each of these was greatly extended, and other less important iron deposits were exploited in Somerset, Warwickshire, west Norfolk, Yorkshire and Northumberland. Indeed, traces of small-scale smelting are even more widely distributed, since ores are entirely absent from very few parts of England. Some of these deposits were wholly or partly exploited by the military. In the Weald tiles stamped by the Classis Britannica are known from four sites, where it seems possible that naval work-shops existed (p. 252); and at Corbridge iron from the deposits near Risingham was worked by legionaries at an army arsenal. But the nature of the remains at the majority of sites suggests that the industry was in the hands of native craftsmen whose production was little interfered with by authority. Iron was not an imperial monopoly; the most that government did was to provide for roads to facilitate marketing the produce. This is especially noticeable in the Weald, though here ridgeway tracks, of pre-Roman character, were also extensively utilised.

The chief technological improvement in the Romano-British industry was the introduction of the shaft-furnace. More primitive iron-smelters had employed the bowl-furnace, which was little more than a shallow hole in the ground into which the draught had to be articially introduced by bellows, and whose capacity was very limited. The shaft-furnace was a structure sufficiently high – about five or six feet – for the required draught to be induced naturally (as in a chimney) once the furnace was alight, and one which could carry a far larger load. Known examples vary from twelve to twenty-eight inches in diameter. Bowl-furnaces, however, continued in use and show a considerable increase in size, suggesting improvements in bellow-design. After the ore had been smelted in these furnaces the resulting blooms had to be reheated in a smithing furnace so that slag still trapped within them could be hammered out. The finished lump seems usually to have weighed about 15 lbs, and could then be worked up by the smith. For large iron objects, such as the substantial six-foot iron bars sometimes used for the support of boilers above the furnaces of baths, several blooms were welded together. Most of the iron objects of the Roman period were of simple wrought iron, often showing very skilful smithing; but there was also some knowledge – though as yet little skill – in the production of harder cutting edges by the processes of carburisation and quenching, and even by pattern-welding.

Coal was much more widely used in Roman Britain than is sometimes appreciated in the south. This is because its outcrops occur only in the west and north, sufficient fuel being so readily available elsewhere as to render coal-carrying unprofitable. It was not mined, so far as is known; but wherever outcrops occurred these were quarried, yielding enough to make mining unnecessary. Its use seems to have been a discovery of the early second century, for its first dated occurrence is at Heronbridge near Chester in a deposit of 90–130; it also appears in some of the forts of the Antonine Wall and in levels of this century at Benwell and Corbridge. Large quantities have been found in forts on Hadrian's Wall and elsewhere, including about a ton in the south guard chamber of the east gate at

Housesteads (which had been converted into a store for it in the early fourth century), and an even larger quantity in the bath-building at Risingham. It is clear that coal was being officially supplied to forts. Elsewhere it was used for industrial purposes as well as for firing hypocausts. Its sulphur-content made it unsuitable for use in smelting iron, but it was used in smithing-furnaces and forges at Corbridge, Wilderspool and elsewhere, and for smelting lead in Flintshire. Many of the villas of Gloucestershire, Somerset and Wiltshire were supplied with coal, evidently from the Somerset outcrops; and this was no doubt the source of that used on the altar of Sulis Minerva at Bath, which was recorded as a curiosity by Solinus in the third century.[24] The occurrence of coal in some of the Fenland sites has already been discussed (p. 313).

The early exploitation of good stone was mentioned earlier in the chapter (p. 325f.) as one of the indications of the activities of prospectors from abroad during the first century. There was increasing production of good building-stone during the second and subsequent centuries as town buildings ceased to be half-timbered, and public and private monuments, town walls and villas all combined to increase demand. Kentish rag from the Maidstone area was used for the town-wall of London, and similar greensand rock was employed both in the town-wall of Chichester and at the villa at Bignor, whose columns, however, were of Bath stone. The limestones of the Cotswolds and of Northamptonshire and Lincolnshire were widely appreciated both for buildings and for funerary monuments and coffins, while farther north the magnesian limestone round York was much in use. In the neighbourhood of Chester the local red sandstone was employed, and it is interesting to find that in the later second century this stone was shipped to Caernarvon for the rebuilding of the earth and timber fort there, though in later reconstructions of this site local stone came to be used. There were few places in the province except part of the south-east where building-stone was not accessible, and except for special work local stone was normally employed. In the south-east flint usually took the place of cut stone, though at Colchester septaria lumps could be obtained from the London Clay. A few large public buildings in towns and some private residences of the wealthiest sort were able to use imported marbles, alabaster or even porphyry from Egypt for detailed decoration, but imports of such material can never have been on a large scale.

Some quarries specialised in the production of domestic mill-stones such as almost every household needed to buy. In the south many of these were made of greensand rock or of the conglomerate known as Hertfordshire Puddingstone, but the Millstone Grit of the Pennines was also exploited: a workshop for this exists at Wharn-cliff Rocks near Sheffield. On the whole, however, our knowledge of such undertakings is very deficient. Yet it is clear that corn was rarely converted into flour in Roman Britain before it reached the home. Two towns only have produced fragments of donkey-mills (p. 295), but the larger output which these imply may have been taken up by urban bakeries; we may recall the cake-mould from Silchester apparently figuring members of the Severan dynasty. Watermills, which are so plentiful a feature of the medieval landscape, are very rare in Roman Britain; apart from examples on Hadrian's Wall, they are attested only by the pivots surviving at Silchester and Great Chester-ford.

A quarry with a wide market for whetstones probably lay near Stony Stratford on Watling Street; its products have been found as far away as Wroxeter, Richborough, London and Caistor by Norwich, and were clearly distributed by road. Kimmeridge shale, a soft, soapy stone which had been worked for bangles and even lathe-turned drinking vessels in pre-Roman times, was now developed in an ambitious fashion for the manufacture of trays and even couches and three-legged tables of classical design; the table legs were decorated with lion or gryphon heads and claws after the model of the marble and bronze furniture of Italy. One such leg was found at *Verulamium* in a late-second-century context, but the industry maintained itself well into the fourth century.

Salt was a necessity of life, and in pre-Roman times had been obtained by boiling sea-water in vats. This industry continued and underwent considerable development, for its characteristic debris is plentiful in the Fenland and round the coasts of Lincolnshire, Essex, Kent and Sussex. In addition, the place-name *Salinae*, indicating known salt springs, was used for Droitwich and also for somewhere in Cheshire, possibly Middlewich. Ptolemy, indeed, names yet a third Salinae in Catuvellaunian territory near the Wash, but this, as Mr A. L. F. Rivet has suggested, may be a mistake for Droitwich.[25]

Leather was another necessity, at least of civilised life; but we know all too little about its production. Indications of tanneries at two towns have already been mentioned (p. 295); there must have been many more, for leather was used not only for footwear but also for workmen's aprons and even for more delicate items of attire, as the famous 'bikini' from London reminds us; and it may well have been used for jugs and buckets, as in more recent times. But in addition to the needs of the civilian population, the enormous requirements of the army had to be provided for. Leather was needed by the military authorities for a wide variety of purposes, including boots, items of uniform and equipment, and also for tents and harness. To a large extent no doubt they undertook their own tanning from hides provided by direct taxation in kind (p. 259), but there will still have remained sufficient demand to makc cattle profitable wherever suitable pasturage occurred.

The oyster industry should also be briefly mentioned. This, too, had been exploited in Belgic times, as is indicated both by the reputation of British pearls and also by the discovery of oyster shells in occupation deposits of appropriate date. In Roman Britain oysters were marketed on an immense scale, and were evidently transported alive in tanks, for there is hardly a site which does not yield shells, however distant from the sea. But of the organisation of this industry we know nothing.

Salt, leather and oysters had a continuous even history after the first expansion of production. Woollen goods, on the other hand, though at all times liable to be produced in the home, seem to be a feature primarily of the third and fourth centuries, at least as far as their export is concerned; and it was in 301 that two British items figure in Diocletian's price-edict (p. 317). In the fourth century the government took a hand in the production of cloth for the army and civil service, and weaving mills and dye-works were set up under state control. The Notitia records one such factory in Britain, the *gynaecium*, or weaving works, at Venta.[26] Unfortunately there were at least three Ventas in Britain, and the identity of this one is not certain. It is usually taken, on Haverfield's authority,[27] to be Winchester (*Venta Belgarum*); but this is by no means certain, for both Caistor by Norwich (*Venta Icenorum*) and Caerwent (*Venta Silurum*) lie near good sheep-rearing country; and in East Anglia in particular a number of pieces of large-scale weaving equipment are known. We may refer in particular to the big carding-combs from Caistor by Norwich and in the Worlington (Cambridgeshire) hoard, and to the enormous cropping-shears, 4 feet 4 inches long, from Great Chesterford, the function of which was to provide a smooth close finish to the surface of woollen cloth. Both of these must have come from wool mills, and the combs suggest some form of machinery.

Apart, then, from the state factory, it is clear that the manufacture of woollen cloth was an important part of the economy of East Anglia in the fourth century, and no doubt also in other parts of south and south-west Britain. Since the demonstration by Sir Ian Richmond that the so-called *fullonica* at the Chedworth villa is really misunderstood parts of the bath-suite, there are no clear instances where fulling can be shown to have been carried on; but the villa at Darenth in Kent, with its large tanks and enormous area of hypocausts, some of which are of unusual construction, can still be said to be probably connected either with fulling or with dyeing, though re-examination of the site is urgently required.

A striking fact about trade and industry in Roman Britain is the ease with which the problems of transport were overcome. Wherever manufactured or produced, goods were easily distributed throughout the province, and the long distances over which exceptionally heavy objects such as stone sarcophagi, large altars and other massive pieces of masonry were moved from their source is most remarkable. These facts point to the skilled development of carts and wagons equal to these demanding purposes, and to the efficient maintenance of the road-system.

The principal roads had been originally laid down for military purposes, as is clear from a detailed study of their alignments, but they also served the increasing purposes of commerce, and their effect was to unify the country as never before. Milestones were usually erected to commemorate the building or repair of roads, and though the survival of these is uneven in different parts of the country, their evidence points to a steady programme of construction and maintenance down to the middle of the fourth century. After this date detailed records cease, but the survival of many of the roads through to the Middle Ages shows that they remained in good working order, at least until the breakdown of provincial organisation.

Subsidiary to the roads in Britain, but not negligible for transport purposes, were her navigable rivers and the canals which in Cambridgeshire and Lincolnshire linked some of the most useful of them.

Finally, there was the coastal shipping, whose influence can be seen in trade with the barbarian North, or in the transport of pottery from the kilns of Colchester to the Antonine Wall, but which was also active between ports in southern Britain, as is suggested, for instance, by the distribution of pewter goods made in the south-west.

All the sea-routes which had linked Britain to the Continent in prehistoric times (p. 15) were still used. Inscriptions from Bordeaux,[28] and the trade in samian pottery, point to direct voyages from the Garonne, Loire and Seine estuaries to Britain, and military inscriptions from the Tyne [29] suggest direct links with the mouth of the Rhine. Undoubtedly for most official purposes the direct cross-channel route from Boulogne had primacy, but it seems likely that after the first century Dover took the lead from Richborough at the British end; this is suggested not only by the imposing Roman light-houses at Dover and the evident decline of Richborough in the second century but also by such details as that the street plan and gates of Roman Canterbury appear to give priority to the Dover road. The port of London, however, soon achieved supremacy in the south-east, and acted like a magnet to conveyers of continental produce. Yet in the end it was the south-western route, linking the Irish Sea and Bristol Channel with Spain and the seas beyond, which survived the downfall of the western empire; for it was by this route that tenuous mercantile connections (p. 424) were maintained between the Dark Age British kingdoms of the west and what remained of the classical Mediterranean world.

1. Cicero, *ad Fam.*, vii, 7, 1.; cf. also *Ad. Att.*, iv, 16. 7.
2. *Agricola*, 12.
3. These usually give the name of the Emperor or of the lessee of the mining rights, and often include the words *ex arg(entariis)*. Analysis has shown that the lead has not always been de-silvered by cupellation, and the term seems to mean simply 'from the lead–silver works'. The weight of the ingots seems to have been intended to render them, while still portable, difficult to steal.
4. On the Stockbridge pig the name is struck cold on the side, the cast panel bearing the name of Nero; on the Flintshire pig *C. Nipi Ascani* is cast on the top. This difference may imply stricter control of lessees in the Mendips in the Julio-Claudian period than

in Flintshire; if so, the position in the Mendips was relaxed in the next reign. It should be noted, however, that the Stockbridge pig has a similar copper-antimony content to that of Flintshire ores (Tylecote, *Metallurgy in Archaeology* (London, 1962), pp. 83–7); but it is difficult to see how the Flintshire field could have been in production as early as 60.

5. *Ti.Cl.Tr.Lut.Br. ex Arg.*, found at Pulborough, Sussex. *Lutudarum* was a lead-mining centre in Derbyshire, probably near Matlock.

6. *N.H.*, xxxiv, 17, 164.

7. At Wilderspool a furnace was found which had been designed to take at least seven crucibles at a time for the production of such alloys.

8. A single stamped tile among the many tiles at Silchester might have been suspected as a plant; but part of a second was later found at the site of a tilery at Pamber, two miles from the town (*Antiquaries Journal*, vi (1926), 75–6).

9. Even in the second century the numbers of private people making the passage to Britain caught the attention of an orator (Aristides, *Orat. Aegyptiaca*, xxxvi, 91).

10. For traders with the Rhineland see *CIL*, xiii, 8164a, a *negotiator Britannicianus* from Cologne; 8793, a *negotiator cretarius Britannicianus* (a pottery-merchant who made a dedication to Nehalennia *ob merces recte conservatas*) from Domburg in Walcheren; and 7300, another merchant, possibly of pottery *ex provincia Britannia*, from Castell by Mainz.

11. Lamps, however, are not common in Britain, even in the towns, and probably the candle remained the chief source of artificial light.

12. lxii, 2, where he records that Seneca had 10,000,000 sesterces on loan in Britain. Seneca cannot have been alone.

13. For a view of the wealth of Britain at the end of the third century see the passage quoted on p. 319, note 12.

14. Cf. M. Aurelius Lunaris, sevir Augustalis of York and Lincoln, who set up an inscription at Bordeaux in 237 (p. 219, note 28), and L. Solimarius Secundinus, *negotiator Britannicianus* also from Bordeaux, though a native of the Rhineland (*CIL*, xiii, 634). The most likely trade with Bordeaux is the wine trade, and it is to some extent confirmed by the wine barrels of silver fir found at Silchester, for this tree is not found nearer than southern France.

15. S.H.A., *Vita Probi*, 18, 8; Silchester, Southwark, *Archaeologia*, lviii (1902–3), 427; Gloucester, *Trans. Bristol and Gloucester Arch. Soc.*, lv (1933), 74. The latter find included grape-skins as well and was thought to be the debris of wine-pressing. The Boxmoor vines seem first recorded by Collingwood in Tenney Frank, *Economic Survey of Ancient Rome* (1937 and 1959), iii, 78, though the excavations were by Sir John Evans in 1851, who does not mention them in his reports; it is probable that Collingwood learnt of the vines orally from Sir Arthur Evans.

16. M. R. Hull, *Roman Potters' Kilns of Colchester* (Oxford, 1963), Fig. 53.13.

17. χοῦρμι or *cervisia*: Dioscorides, *de materia medica*, ii, 88; Pliny, *NH*, xxii, 164.

18. Ammianus Marcellinus, xxiii, 6, 88.

19. The absence of any sign of export of jet objects to free Germany is another indication that they were not made in the Rhineland.

20. Martial, *de spectaculis*, vii, 3.

21. Pliny, *NH*, ix, 169; xxxii, 62; Juvenal, iv, 141.

22. Martial, xiv, 99.

23. *RIB*, 2059.

24. *Collectanea rerum memorabilium* (ed. Mommsen, 1895), 22, 10.

25. A. L. F. Rivet, *Town and Country in Roman Britain* (London, 1958), p. 132.

26. *Notitia Dignitatum Occ.*, xi, 60: *Procurator gynaecii in Britannis Ventensis*.

27. Victoria County History, *Hampshire*, i (1900), p. 292; see now W. H. Manning, *Antiquity*, xl (1966), 60 ff.

28. See p. 340, note 4, cf. *ibid.*, note 10.

29. See pp. 160, 176.

15
The Romanisation of Britain

Romano-British culture arose from the impact of the civilisation of Rome upon the Celtic people of Britain; the result, however, was not a replacement of cultures, but rather what can broadly be described as a synthesis. A convenient illustration of this is provided at the small town of Brough on Humber (*Petuaria*), which may have been the *caput* of the civitas of the Parisi. By the middle of the second century military occupation of the area had ceased, and a civilian town was arising over the site of the fort. It possessed a theatre whose stage-building was presented by a Roman citizen, M. Ulpius Ianuarius, aedile of the vicus of Petuaria, who set up a tablet in honour of the *Domus Divina* of Antoninus Pius and the deified emperors. It would be hard to find a more Roman scene. But about the same time as this dedication was made there was buried in the cemetery just outside the town a local priest. The burial rite was inhumation accompanied by a native iron-bound wooden bucket and two sceptres. This was a native burial-rite; and as if to emphasise the non-Roman character of the ritual the two sceptres had been intentionally bent and broken to devitalise them for the journey to the other world. Nothing could illustrate better the dual character of Romano-British civilisation. Outwardly it was Roman, inwardly it remained Celtic; yet it would be wrong to suppose an inner conflict between the two aspects. The result was a synthesis, intended by Rome, and welcomed by the British people as they came to realise the advantages of peace and wealth conferred by membership of the empire.

At any one time, indeed, there was a wide range of variability within the synthesis, owing to the social stratification of Romano-British society on the one hand, and, on the other, to the widely varying conditions of life and opportunity existing in different regions of the province. At one end of the spectrum lay considerable approximation to the classical way of life and at the other a substantial survival of native characteristics. Moreover, the culture of Roman Britain should not be treated as if it were a static historical phenomenon. Through the four centuries of its existence it had its periods of development and decline, of maturity and decay, despite the comparative slowness of such processes of change in the ancient world when compared with our own. It should be studied, therefore, as far as the evidence allows, against the background not only of historical growth but also of varied social achievement.

We can measure the Romanisation of Britain only with imprecision, for we have to depend so largely upon the evidence of material things – potsherds, iron tools, bronze brooches, house-plans, towns or statues – rather than upon the much more revealing evidence of contemporary testimony. Not that the evidence of material things is of little account. Haverfield long ago made the point that when the provincial adopted the use of Roman things he could be declared civilised enough to realise their value and, further, could be seen to have abandoned any inherited hostility towards them. Nevertheless, the evidence of the written word is invaluable in such an enquiry, and Romano-British writings are denied us until the fifth century.

The Romanising agents responsible for the new culture have been mentioned in earlier chapters: they were the soldiers of the occupying army, service by Britons themselves in the Roman forces, the colonies of Roman citizens, the merchants from the Continent and, at a higher level, the policy of governors like Agricola or of client kings like Cogidubnus. The civilisation thus introduced was not really the metropolitan culture of Rome or even of Italy: it was the provincial version of this, diluted but none the less real, and sufficiently vigorous to unify an empire whose boundaries touched Scotland, the Black Sea, the Euphrates and the Sahara.

In the first century there were two distinct phases of Romanisation, the Claudian and the Flavian, divided by the setback of rebellion and its aftermath. To both of these phases the army made a considerable contribution. We have already examined the influence of its architects upon the growing towns, and it was its sculptors and stone-masons who first introduced the mind of Britain to the arts of sculpture in the round and in relief, and to monumental masonry in general. Moreover, the local garrisons and the military officers who supervised local affairs must have played their part in the spread of the Latin tongue. But even in the reign of Claudius the army alone could not provide all that was required. The temple of the Imperial Cult at Colchester clearly called for outside architectural assistance, as no doubt did the cult itself in the sphere of organisation.

With the withdrawal of the armed forces from most of the lowland zone under the early Flavian governors, further steps of this sort had to be taken to continue the training of the Britons in Roman ways. Tacitus in the *Agricola* specifically alludes to the needs of education, and the presence of Demetrius of Tarsus illustrates the sort of steps that were taken. The success of this programme is suggested by the great increase in literate potters' stamps which is a characteristic of this period, but can best be seen in the inscribed writing tablets which have survived in London. These also illustrate a thriving commerce. Much of this was undoubtedly in the hands of merchants from abroad, but not all. The Rufus son of Callisunus, who wrote to his bailiff about the sale of a slave-girl, seems to represent the first generation of Romanisation in a Celtic family, and can therefore be reasonably claimed as British.

By the end of the first century towns were rapidly developing. In them education was available, public buildings of some splendour were rising, and a Romanised life was led in which the Latin language, Roman dress and continental habits of life such as visiting the baths and giving dinner parties were becoming fashionable.[1] The great variety of plates, dishes, bowls and cooking vessels which were now available, far in excess of anything known in the Iron Age, and many of them of local British manufacture, bears witness to a complete revolution in manners. The widespread use of mortaria for preparing food similarly points to changes of diet, and the vast increase of amphorae shows that wine-drinking was now a luxury not confined to the houses of the aristocracy.

The towns were the vehicle and focus of this progress. In the country things naturally moved at a slower pace, but the owners of estates did begin here and there to Romanise their dwellings. Rectangular houses, internally subdivided into rooms and with at least the lower walls in masonry, began to appear. In this last feature they were in advance of the normal town-house, which was usually constructed of half-timber and clay at this period. But it cannot be said that in either town or country private dwellings of any great size or distinction were erected in the first century. Only in Kent, Essex, and Sussex is it possible at present to identify a few buildings of the greater pretensions suggested by mosaics or bath-blocks, as at Eccles, Rivenhall, or Angmering. Elsewhere expenditure was cautious. Nevertheless, these small villas lay at the head of a long history of development, and their occupants were undergoing the same revolution of manners as has been noted already in the towns. At a lower social level the peasantry were still largely unaffected by innovations in their way of life, though they were using coins and buying the new pottery; the benefits of peace were beginning to be reaped, but increased productivity had to cater for the demands of the tax-collector before it could yield increased prosperity.

By the close of the second century much greater advances had been made. The towns were at the zenith of their early prosperity, and in the countryside quite sizeable villas had appeared. The wealthy classes were wealthier, or at least were making greater permanent parade of their wealth. Industrially the province was, by contemporary standards, fully developed; its natural resources were known and used, and mass-production of pottery had to a great extent broken down the old regionalism of fashion. Even with objects as individual as bronze brooches it is no longer possible to discern local schools of production. In the countryside there is evidence that even the peasants were beginning to construct rectangular cottages roofed with tiles, decorated with painted plaster, provided with glass windows and even sometimes yielding evidence of wooden floors (p. 302); and at some villas baths were being provided for the estate workers, not merely for the owner. Living standards had risen in a spectacular fashion.

Mosaic floors of good workmanship and considerable technical skill were being installed in the towns, and in a few of the villas, by this time. The patterns are simple rosettes enclosed in geometric designs which sometimes give an illusion of perspective; but occasionally more ambitious representational floors, though of comparatively simple design, are found. Examples of these are the Oceanus head or the dolphins-with-cantharus pavements at *Verulamium*, and the boy on a dolphin at Fishbourne. In these scenes no attempt is made to tell a story: the figure is merely a more elaborate variation of the pattern, and where, as in the lion with stag's head floor at *Verulamium*, an attempt is made to portray action it is not particularly successful. Mosaics are rarely signed in Britain, but it is usually held that the artists responsible for them were mainly continental. This conclusion is based partly on the skill which much of this new art displays and partly on the ubiquity of mosaic patterns over the empire. In the fourth century, as we shall see (p. 360), it does become possible to identify various schools of mosaicists in the towns of Britain, but in the second century, apart from one group found at Colchester and *Verulamium*, we have not enough pavements to attempt this. Nor at present does there seem to be any continuity of mosaic production from the second to the fourth century. It is possible, then, that immigrant mosaicists set up business in one or two principal cities during the second century and constructed mosaics throughout the province where demand existed, using local materials in each case for the purpose; and that only in the fourth century did renewed demand on a sufficient scale cause a renaissance of the craft on a more regional basis.[2]

Continental also, no doubt, were the artists who specialised in fresco work for the decoration of walls, though in this craft demand may have been sufficient to support regional schools based on the larger towns. In recent years there has been considerable accumulation of evidence bearing on wall-paintings, and good second-century examples, very diverse in style, are known from *Verulamium*, Leicester and Cirencester. At *Verulamium* the peopled scroll, consisting (pl. 11b) of pheasants and panther-heads emerging from a running spiral acanthus-tendril on a bright yellow background, is the most distinguished piece, but it is entirely two-dimensional. A slightly earlier panel showing a colonnade exhibits some subtle shading to emphasise perspective. At Leicester, however, there are some more ambitious three-dimensional scenes, one showing a figure standing in a coffered niche and another a tragic mask. All these paintings are remarkable for the fully Romanised taste they display, though the general style is rather dated, recalling frescoes current in Pompeii over a century earlier. Nevertheless, it was not until the fourth century that whole scenes with three-dimensional perspective began to be attempted in mosaic.

One of the most extreme manifestations of Roman behaviour was a love of gladiatorial spectacles in the amphitheatre. Not many of the towns of Britain are known to have possessed these structures, but examples survive at Cirencester, Silchester, Dorchester (pl. 9a),

Chichester, Richborough, Caerwent and Carmarthen. As they were cheaply constructed of ramps of earth rather than in the masonry style of the Continent, they are easily destructible, and more must once have existed, for instance at the four *coloniae* and at London. A few smaller examples are known from country areas, as at Charterhouse on Mendip, but it is not certain whether these served the same purpose. Others again are known at the fortresses of Chester and Caerleon and also at least one auxiliary fort; here their main purpose was undoubtedly arms-training, though they may have served for entertainment on occasion.

Gladiatorial shows were very costly, and it is possible that acrobats and wild-beast shows were more commonly exhibited in Britain: certainly such scenes are figured on Castor ware. But we have epigraphic evidence that gladiators were recruited in the province (p. 230), and in 1965 a gladiator's bronze helmet came to light near Bury St Edmunds, Suffolk. Familiarity with the arena, too, is suggested by statuettes of gladiators from South Shields and London, and by one of the more elaborate colour-coated vases made by the Colchester potters, which bears a combat scene in barbotine. The names of the contestants and a reference to Legio xxx (part of the Rhine Army) have been incised after the vessel had been fired, and may have illustrated the owner's rather than the maker's identifications. A similar vessel comes from the Nene Valley potteries. The famous mosaic of cupids dressed and acting as gladiators at the Bignor (Sussex) villa also expects knowledge of the real thing. Probably, then, gladiatorial shows were from time to time exhibited by candidates for office at the more important towns in Britain, as they certainly were in Gaul; and this would account for the allusion at Bignor, which at the date of this late-fourth-century mosaic was one of the largest villas in Britain and clearly the property of a wealthy member of the curial class,[3] if not of someone more important still.

It has sometimes been stated that the towns of Roman Britain were in some sense failures. In part this view rests on faulty deductions about their history and in part on their lack of resemblance to Mediterranean models. It is true that in Britain we do not find the tightly packed insulae and the peristyle houses which appear even in Roman Cologne, nor do more than a few towns possess colonnaded streets such as also Cologne possessed. The Italian town-house with its peristyle is really found in Britain only among the official residences of fort-commanders and once at Gloucester. In the towns the larger houses often have a compact plan of their own, with wings ranging round three or even four sides of a courtyard. It is a different plan from that usually adopted for villas, but is distinct also from the Italian town house: it represents once again a provincial compromise.

It is evident that the Romano-British town is an adaptation rather than an adoption of the classical form of city, but in a sense this points to the vitality of the Romano-British synthesis, once granted that the internal history of the towns was more prosperous than was formerly thought. In size, as we have seen (p. 292), many of them do not fall short of their contemporaries across the Channel, and their public buildings stand comparison. The basilica of London was 500 feet long by about 120 feet wide, which was larger than any known in Gaul, and the forum areas at *Verulamium* and Cirencester are larger than those of Paris, Alesia, St-Bertrand-de-Comminges or Arles, while that at Wroxeter is only 120 square metres smaller than the last. The theatre of Canterbury has a diameter of 80 metres, four-fifths of that of Orange (103 metres), but larger than those of St-Bertrand (70 metres) or Paris (72 metres). When related, therefore, to the wealth of their respective provinces the towns of Roman Britain were not notably inferior to those of Gaul in the scale of their public buildings. In both we find that the classical city has been adapted to the climate and circumstances of northern Europe; in both we find buildings such as Romano-Celtic temples and theatres which are the product of Gallic and British provincial culture; and the same sensible compromise can be recognised in the many frescoes which represent marble veneers in paint, when cold or condensation would have made the veneers themselves an uncomfortable luxury. The latter, however, were used in public buildings.

Something has already been said of the problem of assessing the populations of the towns (p. 296). To number the population of the province as a whole is a task replete with imponderables, but an estimate must now be attempted, taking the end of the second century as the point of reference. If we calculate on the basis suggested we arrive at a figure of 117,000 for the larger towns and civitas-capitals, and some 40,000 for the other large settlements of the civil zone. To this must be added perhaps 40,000 for the inhabitants of vici near forts, though these, of course, reached their greatest

9a (*above*) The amphitheatre at *Durnovaria* (Dorchester, Dorset). This earthwork overlies a Henge-monument.

9b (*below*) Roman villa at Watts Wells, Ditchley

10a The Roman Road from *Cunetio* (Mildenhall) to *Venta Belgarum* (Winchester) looking south-east near Andover

10b 'Celtic' field system at Burderop Down

11a Bronze horse-brooch and bone dolphin from *Verulamium;* the length of the dolphin is 1.75 inches

11b 'Peopled Scroll' in painted wall plaster of Antonine date, from *Verulamium;* length 12 feet

12a First-century mosaic from Fishbourne, Sussex. At a subsequent period the room was divided by a partition across the middle

12b Fourth-century Vergilian mosaic from the villa at Low Ham, Somerset, showing Aeneas, Dido and Venus; 13 feet square

Christian Mosaic from Hinton St Mary, Dorset

14a Large stone capital decorated with Native Gods from *Corinium Dobunnorum* (Cirencester)

14b Relief of three *Matres* (mother goddesses) bearing loaves and cakes or fruits; height 2 feet 7 inches

15a Bronze statuette of
Venus from *Verulamium*;
height 8 inches

15b Relief of *Matres* in classical style from
Cirencester; height 16 inches

16a (*above*) The site of Richborough from the north, showing th
foundation of the Tetrapylon, the earth fort of the third
century, the Saxon shore fort and a short length of the Claudian
ditches

16b (*below*) The Saxon shore fort of Portchester Castle standing
at the head of Portsmouth Harbour

numbers in the third century. The army, with three legions in addition to almost 45,000 auxiliaries (p. 184f.), may be reckoned at 63,000 men, and we should add perhaps another 10,000 for dependants not included in the figure for vici. These figures amount to 270,000 people engaged in activities not primarily concerned with food-production; they must be augmented by a further estimate of those engaged in mines, the pottery industry and such activities as charcoal burning, the felling of timber and so on; perhaps 50,000 would not be excessive if we include their dependants. We have thus arrived at a total of 320,000 persons who had to be fed by the labours of the agricultural population. It is much more difficult to arrive at a reasonable estimate of the latter. Somewhat more than 600 villas are known, and the real total may be more like 800; perhaps not more than 500 of them were in occupation at the end of the second century. If purely arbitrarily we follow Collingwood in assigning an average of fifty people to each villa, this would account for 25,000. There remains the peasant class, whose numbers must have been very considerable. Not only do we have here to take account of sizeable villages in addition to isolated farms, but air photography and field-work show that large areas of the midland plain, where suitable soils occur, were thickly populated in antiquity instead of being covered by unbroken uninhabitable forest, as was once imagined. Mr Charles Thomas has recently shown that the native settlements of the Roman period in Cornwall, known as Rounds, imply a population of about 10,000, approaching that recorded in the Domesday survey of 1086. If this is true of such a comparatively undeveloped area as Cornwall it must embolden us when we approach the richer agricultural areas. The population of the Fens cannot have been less than 10,000, to judge by the recorded remains. On this sort of basis, and considering the distribution of finds it is not difficult to conclude that the rural population must have been at least a million; and when we remember the 320,000 unproductive mouths which had to be fed on the agricultural surplus we may feel that the real figure is likely to have been half as much again. Finally, in Wales and the north we have large populations of mainly pastoral folk to take into account. The Brigantes can hardly have been less than 50,000, to judge by the garrisons required to control them, and may have been twice that number; the population of Wales may have been about the same.[4] The conclusion reached, therefore, is that at the end of the second century the total population of Roman Britain may have amounted to rather over two million.[5] This figure is somewhat larger than that estimated for England and Wales at the time of the Domesday Survey in 1086, which can be used as a check on the accuracy of the guess.[6] It is clear that the population must have been considerably reduced during the immediately post-Roman centuries, and it would not be unreasonable to assume that by the time of the Norman conquest the optimum Romano-British level was once again within sight, after which the known figures for medieval England continue to rise.

We have seen that the Latin language began to spread in Britain partly as a result of intercourse with merchants or with the army, and partly as a result of the deliberate policy of governors such as Agricola who set up schools. The Celtic language, of course, survived, and in post-Roman times is found developing in the tongues spoken in Cornwall, Wales and Cumbria. Most educated Romano-Britons were no doubt bilingual, Latin being the language of law, government, business and cultured life, British that of the intimate family circle and of intercourse with the lower orders. Some such theory is necessary to account, not so much for the persistence of British place-names (for place-names are hard to kill), nor for the actual survival of Celtic (for this could have continued as the language of the peasantry), as for the presence in the latter of many loan words derived from Latin. A large proportion of these describe objects and concepts for which there was no British equivalent. Many are words connected with administration, but even more concern education or household goods, daily life, building or the calendar. They not only describe concepts new to the life of Britain but they derive in the main from experience of the middle and upper classes rather than from the agricultural peasantry. Another important factor to be taken into account is the difference between the highland and lowland zones; in the former very little Latin is likely to have been heard away from the vicinity of the forts.

It is not certain how far the art of writing was practised in pre-Roman Britain, but it is unlikely that it was altogether unknown. Caesar mentions that though the Druids did not commit their teaching to writing, the Greek alphabet was used for other purposes in Gaul. When we remember the close connections between Gaul and Britain and that schools existed in Britain at which Druids from the

Continent acquired a higher learning, we may accept the probability that the British language could be, and was, written and read. The probability is perhaps strengthened by knowledge that papyrus was imported in pre-Roman times,[7] and it is certainly supported by the occurrence of Celtic words such as *Rigonus* on Belgic coins. In Gaul, after the conquest, inscriptions in the Celtic tongue are not unknown, though now carved in Roman characters. In Britain, however, no Celtic inscription of the Roman period has been found, whether this is due to the blanketing quality of Roman education in Britain or to a proportionate infrequency of those who had had occasion to write British. What is quite clear is that even artisans could write Latin. This is proved by the many inscriptions written on tiles while they were still unfired, and therefore by the workers in the tileries.[8]

Haverfield took this to mean that 'Latin was employed freely in the towns of Britain not only on serious occasions or by the upper classes, but by servants and work-people for the most accidental purposes. It was also used, at least by the upper classes, in the country.'[9] But Professor Kenneth Jackson has suggested that though this may have been the case, the evidence quoted does not prove that Latin was their normal tongue, since 'the *only* language of writing was Latin; it would not occur to anyone to write in British, nor would they know how to do so'.[10] It is possible that he overstates the case, since as we have seen, pre-Roman British may have been written; but at least the fact remains that artisans knew and could write Latin, with all that this implies for the availability of education in and near the towns. The evidence of graffiti scored by the owners on pottery and other objects is so widespread that we can be certain that at least in the towns the use of Latin, and of Latin names, penetrated very deeply,[11] and this class of evidence extends to villas also.

But Jackson is certainly correct in denying that Latin wholly replaced British. Even in the towns, where it came nearest to doing so, the traders would need British for contact with country-dwellers on market day, and the upper classes for intercourse with the workers on their estates. Graffiti on peasant sites in the country are very rare. Education did not spread thus far, and we need not doubt that the language of the countryside continued to be British.

Thus, the British language survived, the only tongue of the peasant countryside and the bilingual partner of Latin in the towns; Latin words adopted into British were the result of intercourse between those with a cultured background and their servants or estate workers. Moreover, Jackson has been able to show that the spoken Latin of Roman Britain was of a somewhat archaic kind, different in some respects, and of a purer quality, than the so-called 'Vulgar Latin' prevalent in the western provinces as a whole. In part this may well have been the result of insularity, but he has suggested that it was also the result of schooling. Britons, in other words, maintained a purer Latin because they did not learn it in the nursery but acquired it at school. Such a theory is to some extent supported by the apology of St Patrick. He was born of good Romano-British family, but was carried off by Irish raiders in early youth; and in later life he lamented his inability to write good Latin like those who had spoken it from boyhood. Nevertheless, this sort of humility was a fashionable gambit, and should not perhaps be taken too seriously.

It is difficult to believe, with all the evidence we have of the use of Latin in Britain, that it was not spoken in the homes of the upper classes together with British; and it is perhaps better to visualise a British type of Latin, fostered indeed at first by the schools, but kept alive by the insular character of the leading families, and, for all we know, strengthened by whatever institutions Britain possessed for higher education.

The nature of these is quite unknown, but their existence is vouched for by the career of Pelagius, who is generally agreed to have received a first-class education before he left Britain, soon after 380 at the age of nearly thirty, to study law in Rome. They are also adumbrated in the early fifth-century documents usually attributed to Fastidius. Further evidence for an interest in classical Latin and Roman culture is provided by the fourth-century mosaics at the villas of Low Ham, Somerset, and Lullingstone, Kent, and the fresco from the Otford villa in Kent, which illustrate part of the *Aeneid* of Vergil or contain allusions to it. The first of these occupies a whole floor with scenes of Aeneas' arrival at Carthage and reception by Dido (pl. 12 b); the elegiac couplet which accompanies the Europa scene at Lullingstone presupposes knowledge of the epic's first book; while the wall painting from Otford carries a quotation which occurs both in book i and again in book xii. A fourth Vergilian reference is supplied by the undated graffito from Silchester (*conticuere omnes*, the opening line of book ii) which has already been mentioned.[12]

An important part in the Romanisation of Britain was played by Roman Law, which not only enforced the replacement of violence by recourse to the courts, but was also in itself an education in civilised principles. Moreover, having been evolved to meet the requirements of a more advanced civilisation, it facilitated the development of more complex transactions. Rome recognised local legal systems in so far as they did not conflict with her own law, and for the first two centuries local magistrates must have administered whatever traditional laws existed. Roman law itself was fully current only in cities with Roman constitutions or among individuals who held the citizenship. But as time went on the number of the latter increased, and in other fields the court of the governor or the iuridicus established precedents by which Roman legal concepts prevailed. With the growth of commerce and of the habits of peace, the Roman legal system must have played an influential part in the background of provincial life. With Caracalla's grant of Roman citizenship to all free members of the empire a climax in this process was reached, though it was offset to some extent by the fact that the privileges of citizenship were by now unequally applied, *honestiores* enjoying a different set of penalties upon conviction from those applied to *humiliores*. Though the decree made no difference to the constitutional status of former peregrine towns in the provinces – they do not appear to have been regraded as Roman municipia – yet imperceptibly it did affect their position. They became the legal *origo* of the citizens in their territories, and in Gaul at any rate they began to usurp the identity of their civitates. During the third century in Gaul the civitates began to take on the guise of true city-states, and it is possible that the same process went some way in Britain.

Another not insignificant factor of Romanisation was the coinage. Not only did the introduction of a large-scale, regular and consistent monetary system have an enormous influence on the growth of commerce but the propaganda effect of the legends and figure-types of the coins themselves no doubt had a considerable psychological influence. This cannot be immediately measured, but to judge by the wide use made of different contemporary types, the Imperial government had no doubt of their propaganda value. In 139, for instance, over 100 different denarius and 50 sestertius types were minted, not to mention other values. This is a very different policy from that of most other ancient states, whose coin-types were conservative to a degree. In the Roman empire, whose very size made the dissemination of news and views a peculiar problem, the coinage was perhaps the only method of reaching the eyes of every subject; the method was not neglected at least until the third century. Thereafter the types became rather more stereotyped, and no doubt their influence fell with the decay of the monetary system itself. Occasionally issues were made having special reference to Britain: it is possible that some of these were specially directed to the province, for certainly the Britannia issue of 154–5 seems remarkably common as a site find.

The depth and variety of Romanisation in Britain is accurately reflected in the art of the province, particularly its sculpture, ranging as it does from first-class imported pieces in Mediterranean marble through highly competent creations in local stone, down to very simple, and in some cases crude, attempts of no aesthetic worth. Bad though they are, however, these last are not without all value, since they show the atttractive power of classical art, even in a rural *milieu* where the Latin language itself was hardly known.

Roman art was a novelty in Britain, and its adoption was quick and thorough: it is a question whether it amounted to a revolution. In pre-Roman times a very different art had existed here. This was the insular version of the La Tène tradition of the continental Celts, with its passion for non-representational pattern based on curvilinear tendrils, and its ability, if animals or parts of the human frame were to be depicted, to transform their character into something formal, quintessential, no longer real but often horrific.

Collingwood has painted a depressing picture of the psychological difficulties of creative artists reared in this tradition, when they found themselves 'submerged beneath the tide of the dreary mediocrity of Roman provincial art'.[13] It was his view that 'throughout the Roman period British artists were working under what may perhaps be described as a permanent strain'.[14] He evolved the theory that Celtic art was somehow driven underground, to emerge once more in freedom after the collapse of Roman rule in Britain and the disappearance of its art.

Such a picture is quite unreal. In the first place it completely underestimates the achievements of Romano-British art. Secondly, we have no evidence whatever of Celtic artists practising their patterns in secret and handing them on before casting away their tools in despair. These patterns can have reappeared in the sub-Roman period only in one of two ways. Either the tradition was transmitted or it was revived by copying some chance rediscovery or survival. But the revived Celtic art of the later period does not start off where the early Celts left off. Nor was the Roman period bridged by secret strained transmission within the province: the Celtic craftsmen who still worked in the west and north during the third and fourth centuries were tinkers rather than artists and practised a peasant craft. The transmission existed, but it was open, operating in the unconquered quarters of the British Isles.

In considering, and attempting to account for, the sudden interruption of the brilliant art of pre-Roman Britain, we have to remember three of its characteristics. In the first place by the Claudian period it was already showing signs of passing its prime; the processes of degeneration had not proceeded far, but already the simple themes, which were its strength, were beginning to break up in over-elaboration and fussy detail. Secondly, it was essentially an aristocratic art, based upon the love of display which found its chief expression in objects of fine metal dedicated to personal adornment and warlike parade. It follows that there were comparatively few workshops and a lack af broad popular foundations. In another sense also it was a narrow art: it was completely divorced from nature and the observation of reality, and the field of its application was circumscribed. It is not difficult, therefore, to account for its collapse. With the Roman conquest the whole basis of society and its aspirations changed very quickly, and they became more civilised. No longer were the nobility in a position to lead their war-bands in their war-chariots, accoutred with gaily decorated panoply. At one blow the major part of the market had disappeared. A whole society had passed together with its ethos. The new society which arose in Roman Britain was able to equip itself with the new necessities of cultured life from the mass of imports which now flooded across the Channel. This process had indeed begun among the rich as early as the reign of Cunobelin, but after 43 all sections of society were able to avail themselves of the novelties of metal and pottery goods imported from the classical world, and to learn appreciation of the skill of the sculptor in stone which was hitherto unknown to them.

For the rest, the advantage of the new 'mass production' outweighed the older virtues of individual craftsmanship. We ourselves live in a comparable age. Only in Wales, Brigantia and the north did the old art linger on in areas still unsubdued, and in these regions it never totally disappeared, though reduced to small-scale activity. In Ireland, of course, and perhaps in parts of northern Scotland, Celtic artists and their patrons remained unaffected by these developments.

The rest of Britain turned eagerly to the manifestations of new techniques. In the Flavian period a great programme of public building was set on foot, with all this involved of new architectural forms and decoration. Little now survives in detail. In Britain we do not have the satisfaction of discovering masses of sculpture built into our Roman town-walls as happens in Gaul, since the British towns escaped the disasters of the third century which were responsible for so much destruction there; the sculpture of Britain has disappeared more finally into the lime-kilns and the buildings of the Middle Ages.

Whether or not the fine contemporary marble head of Germanicus from Bosham (Sussex) once adorned a shrine of the imperial cult, the nearby villa of Fishbourne contained mosaics and works of art, including an almost life-size marble head of a boy. At Bath we have a small fragment of gabled decoration [15] bearing the date 76, and a larger-than-life Bath-stone head wearing the elaborate coiffure affected by fashionable ladies of the Flavian period. And at Colchester there is the fine winged Sphinx, holding a human head between her paws, which once adorned a tomb and probably dates from the late first century.

Nor should we forget the multitude of statues and busts of Titus which, according to Suetonius, were formerly to be seen in Britain. At Richborough the great monument was covered with marble and with bronze statuary, dating from the late Flavian period; only fragments survive. At Silchester there was found in the basilica a fragment of a twice life-size bronze imperial statue wearing a cuirass of pre-Hadrianic style; this is likely to be the portrait of the emperor under whom the civitas was established, perhaps either Titus or Trajan, since Domitian's statues would not have survived his murder.

Most of these would be works of foreign craftsmen in view of their early date and the official character of most of them.[16] But these continental craftsmen had the responsibility of forming taste and setting standards. That they were not unsuccessful is indicated, for instance, by the remarkable limestone portrait head from the Bon Marché site at Gloucester;[17] this is clearly by a British artist who had succeeded in blending classical techniques with Celtic traits in a most striking, almost impressionistic, result. It is clear from this and other works (such as the second-century head of the god Antenociticus from Benwell) that British sculptors soon learnt to love and emphasise the intricate patterns which could be made from locks of hair, and also the ornamental effects to be evoked from folds of drapery (as in the statue of Juno Regina at Chesters and in numerous tombstones and religious relief throughout Britain). The most striking example of this tendency is, of course, the Bath temple-pediment with its Gorgon's locks and the flowing robes of the supporting Victories. This work is justly renowned as the masterpiece of Romano-Celtic sculpture in Britain.

Thus, the inspiration of the new art was not lost on British craftsmen who adopted sculpture as their medium; and the best of them were able to impart something of their Celtic spirit to their creations, which gave them an originality and character which is recognisably a genuine Romano-British synthesis. The same spirit inspired the best of the potters; for though the tendrils and the hunting scenes which are so characteristic of British colour-coated wares in the Nene Valley and at Colchester owe much to continental inspiration, they possess also an originality of their own in which there is a recognisable Celtic element. Indeed, their attempts at more strictly classical scenes, in which human figures take part as gladiators or charioteers, are notably less effective as works of art: they do, however, point the lesson that these potters were Roman as well as British in their outlook. The truth is that the technique of decoration favoured flowing motion rather than stylised scenes.

Thus, by the end of the second century classical art in its many forms had become a commonplace in Roman Britain, and much of it was being produced by native craftsmen. Even sculpture, perhaps the most difficult to assimilate, was being imbued with specifically local traits.

It is never easy to decide whether a particular work with provincial characteristics was made by a Gaulish or a British craftsman, and it is an easy temptation to assign anything good to an immigrant. But where, as at Bath and Cirencester, very large collections of material in local stone exist, it is surely more reasonable to recognise the emergence of a British school. Both Cirencester and Bath were wealthy cultured places with much patronage to offer, the one as the largest and richest city in the province after London, the other as a cult centre and thermal establishment with an extra-provincial reputation which attracted visitors from abroad. Both lay at the heart of good stone country. We cannot doubt that, once local schools of sculpture had been founded by Gaulish masters, the tradition took root in local talent. In fact, we have evidence of both Gaulish and British hands. At Bath there is an inscription to Sulis set up by 'Priscus son of Toutius, a stone-mason, citizen of the Carnutes' (that is, from the Chartres region); but there is also one erected to the Suleviae by 'Sulinus, son of Brucetus, the sculptor'. His name shows him to be of local origin, and another altar to the same goddesses was carved by him at Cirencester, where it was found with two mother-goddess reliefs and so much freshly cut stone-work as to suggest a workshop (or possibly a shrine).

The museum of Cirencester contains a great variety of attractive pieces, such as three well-known groups of Mother-goddesses (pls. 14b, 15b), each as different in design as in skill of execution, heads of Mercury, Minerva and a River God carved with great delicacy of feeling, and a number of fine architectural fragments; among the latter, the most outstanding is the large capital, perhaps from a Jupiter-column, which is adorned on each of its four faces with divine figures of unusual type (pl. 14 a). As far as can be judged by stylistic signs, the dates of these pieces run through the second and third centuries; the first century is represented by two military tomb-stones (which though not by local hands will have had significant visual influence), and work was still being done in the fourth century, as witnessed by the base of a column inscribed by L. Septimius, governor of Britannia Prima. Bath has an equally distinguished though more diversified collection, as might be expected of a site which drew pilgrims and patients from so wide a field. A number of military tombstones may be by regimental masons, though the men commemorated were away from their units; beside these there is a wide variety of other, principally religious, sculpture, almost all of it in local stone. The date-range here is from the late first through to the third century. Another town in the region, Gloucester, also has some distinguished pieces, though fewer in number.

It is clear that sculptors' workshops enjoyed a very long period of productive life in this region of Britain, and were highly skilled. What is more striking is the discovery that recourse to sculpture for votive purposes was had by persons in the countryside with a much less exacting taste, or at least with less commanding purses. A good illustration is provided by the pieces found in 1957 at Lower Slaughter near Bourton-on-the-Water (Gloucestershire). Here, thrown down a fourth-century well belonging to a typical peasant village in which only one rectangular cottage was found, the remaining dwellings being circular, were a number of reliefs probably of late second- or early third-century date; these had clearly once adorned a rustic shrine. The majority are crude in the extreme, but they afford good evidence of the depth to which Romanised ideals penetrated among the people of the countryside. There are many other examples of such curiously blundered reliefs from rural sites; it will be sufficient to quote that from Rushall Down, Wiltshire, now in the British Museum. Bad though they are in accomplishment, they express an awareness of the fundamentals of Romano-British civilisation.

Another centre of sculptural tradition was Lincoln, where a number of fine works of art have survived, though some are in fragmentary condition. It is likely that here, too, continental craftsmen set the early standards, being summoned to assist the adornment of the new late-first-century colony, and that stone-masons may also have been available from among the legionary veterans. But the relief of a young charioteer shows that it was not long before a distinctively Romano-British style was developed. The influence of this art once again spread far beyond the town itself. Quite competent, and in the case of the Ancaster *matres* delightful, carving is found at various sites in Lincolnshire and surrounding areas, some of them rural shrines. One of the most outstanding is the almost life-sized statue of Minerva from Sibson (Huntingdonshire), possibly in her guise as patroness of potters. No doubt other towns, such as London, exercised a similar influence in their areas; but the evidence has not survived. Most of them lie in areas where stone was not locally available and was therefore eagerly sought out for re-use in medieval times.

With her incorporation in the Roman empire Britain was once more linked to the main streams of European art; and just as society in the empire was to some extent cosmopolitan, so the art to be found in Britain was not entirely provincial (pl. 15a). Works of art in bronze and marble were imported, probably in many cases by wealthy people who themselves had come to Britain from elsewhere; craftsmen from Italy and Gaul were brought in to create works of art *in situ*; but British artists learnt their idiom from these sources, and the best of them gave a fresh interpretation to what they did which can be recognised as specifically Romano-British.

The new art was naturally based primarily on the towns and to a lesser extent on the villas; but nothing is more striking than the extent to which it reached the peasant class. No one can turn the pages of Pitt-Rivers' great reports on his excavations of the native farmsteads of Woodcutts and Rotherley without being impressed by the number of objects in bronze in everyday use (such as dish-handles, box lids or fittings, knife-handles, enamelled brooches or rings with intaglios), and others like bone pins or shale handles, which bear human and animal figures and other patterns of Roman art. The same impression is reinforced at other less fully excavated sites. It is clear that in Roman Britain art was far more pervasive than it had been in the Iron Age, and that all classes according to their means and taste could enjoy its products.

With the renewal of prosperity in Britain at the end of the third century, a new phase of mosaic production opens; artists were greatly in demand, not merely now in the towns but more particularly in the villas, especially the wealthy establishments of Dorset, Gloucestershire and Somerset, where the great majority of Romano-British mosaics have been found. Most of these seem to have been laid in the first seventy years of the fourth century, though a few can be dated later. The amount of work executed during this period and the many styles involved show clearly that British craftsmen were now at work, however close their initial training by continental masters. Here is perhaps a contrast with the situation in the second century (pp. 345–6).

It is probable that many of the towns now contained firms of mosaicists who served the surrounding districts. A comparison of patterns and styles suggests that there may have been as many as ten different 'schools', three of which have been clearly defined by Dr David Smith. The first of these was centred at Cirencester, and worked both in the town and at villas in the neighbourhood, such as Woodchester, Chedworth, North Leigh and Newton St Loe. Orpheus, surrounded by distinctively drawn birds and beasts, was one of its favourite motifs, but there are many other details of style and pattern which reveal its work. A mosaic in Trier has close stylistic connections with the Cirencester school, but it is not yet clear whether British craftsmen went to Germany (perhaps with Constantius Chlorus) or whether German craftsmen migrated to found the British firm. Another school can be identified in Dorset, perhaps working from Dorchester and serving villas such as Frampton, Hinton St Mary, Low Ham and Lufton. A third operated in the Humber region, centred perhaps at Brough or York and working at Winterton, Brantingham, Horkstow and Rudston. It is often possible to observe in the pavements that the master-craftsman executed the principal figures, leaving routine ornament – or even important detail – to his apprentices. In spite of this, very competent standards were on the whole maintained, the most notable exception being at Rudston. Many of these late mosaics contain good figure work, and the Low Ham example is notably successful as a narrative. Inspiration was no doubt obtained from pattern-books, and regional styles kept alive by the same means: but the initial training must have been supplied by immigrant masters coming from the Continent or even from North Africa.

The last subject remaining to be discussed for the light it throws on the Romanisation of Britain is its Religious Cults, in which once again a wide range of variation may be discerned between the classical and the Celtic. Broadly speaking, the religious observances of the provincials of Roman Britain, and also those of the army, may be divided between those which were officially inspired or enjoined (these being naturally Roman) and those which were more spontaneous. These last varied in their content according to the nationality and Romanisation of the individual worshipper.

The Roman empire was very tolerant of religious variety. The Romans themselves were polytheists, and the official religion of the Roman state was not exclusive. It merely demanded observance, after which the individual was free to worship what he chose. The only cults which were liable to suppression or persecution were those, such as Druidism, which involved practices (like human sacrifice) offensive to civilised thought, or those, such as Judaism or Christianity which by their exclusive claims could be thought of as endangering the safety of the empire. The reason for this attitude lay in the pragmatic character of Roman state religion, which was less a system of faith than one of contract: the gods, it was believed, would protect the state, provided that proper rituals were carried out, any human withdrawal from which – or other deficiency in their fulfilment – being accordingly perilous to the fulfilment of the divine side of the bargain.

The worship of the Capitoline Triad – Jupiter Optimus Maximus, Juno and Minerva, the chief deities of Rome – was accordingly given a high priority both in the army and in towns of official Roman foundation. A *capitolium*, the joint temple of the three, would certainly have existed in each of the four colonies and in the municipia of the province, with statues and altars to the deities concerned. No trace of any of these temples has yet been certainly identified, though it is likely that one of the buildings attached to the forum of *Verulamium* was the capitolium of that town. We have more evidence for the military version of the cult, since altars dedicated to Jupiter Optimus Maximus were renewed each year on 3 January, and the old ones were often ceremonially buried at the edge of the parade-ground.

As a focus of imperial sentiment and loyalty, the cult of the Capitoline Triad lost ground as time passed to a new state religion, the Imperial Cult. Divine honours had long been paid to rulers in the Greek Orient, and it was from Asia Minor early in the reign of Augustus that the practice spread to the west. In 12 BC the cult was formalised with the official dedication of an altar, and later a temple, at Lyon to Rome and Augustus, which were served by Gallic notables organised on a representative basis in the provincial council under an annual president (the *sacerdos Galliarum*). The living emperor was worshipped but in conjunction with the goddess Roma.

This became the pattern for the organisation of the cult in other provinces, though the precise dedication of the altar and temple may have varied according to time and circumstances. Tiberius and most of the Emperors after him refused divine honours during their lifetimes; many of them were deified by senatorial decree after death, and it became normal to offer worship to, and take oaths by, the deified emperors (*divi*) of the past and the *genius*, or more often the *numen*, of the living emperor.

In Britain the cult seems to have been introduced in or soon after

49, when a centre was provided for it at the newly founded colony at Colchester, where both an altar and a temple have been found. The precise terms of the dedication are unknown. Tacitus refers to the 'temple of the deified Claudius' and Seneca also uses expressions which suggest that it was a cult personal to Claudius;[18] from this it has usually been concluded that from the outset the British cult was anomalous in omitting Roma and offering worship to Claudius as divine (*divus*) before his death. But this conclusion is very unlikely. Tacitus is writing of the events of 60, six years after the death and official deification of Claudius; he is not describing the original dedication. Nor should the gibes and exaggerations of Seneca be taken to express historical fact. In an extant letter of AD 41 to the Alexandrians, Claudius himself wrote: 'I decline my high priest and temple establishments, for I do not wish to seem vulgar to my contemporaries, and I judge that temples and the like have been defined and set apart by all ages for the gods alone.' This makes his personal policy clear enough, and there is no reason to suppose that he altered it later; it is worth noting, however, that his words were published by the prefect of Egypt as 'the letter of our god, Caesar'.

Recently D. Fishwick had put forward an explanation which easily disperses these difficulties.[19] It is that the altar was the original feature of the cult-centre and that it was dedicated to Roma and Augustus, the living emperor, in the normal way; and that the temple is secondary, being decreed for Claudius after his death and official deification. By 60 work had advanced far enough for the temple's podium to be used in the last stand of the colonists against Boudicca.

We must not forget the reference to the *Domus divina* on the Chichester temple-inscription. This was erected within the lifetime of Cogidubnus, and is therefore hardly likely to date after the death of Vespasian, the next emperor to be deified. Cogidubnus is remarkable for his 'correct' attitude to all things Roman, and the wording accordingly can be taken to imply a wider basis for the provincial cult, now expanded, no doubt, to include the present emperor (and, by extension, the members of his family). The imperial cult achieved a genuine popularity in the province. Dedications to the *Numina Augustorum* are not uncommon, though usually attached in a secondary position to those to other gods. The Domus divina occurs again in a second-century context at Chichester itself, on a stone dedicated to Jupiter Optimus Maximus,[20] and also (among other places) on the early Antonine theatre-tablet at Brough on Humber.[21]

The reconsecration of the temple at Colchester after its destruction by Boudicca, and the maintenance thereafter of its precinct, certainly give no grounds for supposing that the provincial cult and its administration were removed to London. On the contrary, we must assume that it remained at Camulodunum. There would certainly, however, have been other temples and altars of the imperial cult in the chartered towns of the province, and perhaps also in the wealthier civitas-capitals. All, too, are likely to have possessed honorific statues of emperors, so that it is not possible to assert that the few surviving traces of such portraits must necessarily be cult objects. Thus, the bronze head of Claudius from the River Alde, though in all probability removed from *Camulodunum* itself by Boudiccan rebels, is not thought to be a temple-statue. The pre-Hadrianic fragment from Silchester has already been mentioned (p. 356); it came from the tribunal of the town's basilica, and was thus a state rather than a religious effigy. Other fragments, including a larger-than-life bronze head of Hadrian, come from London; and from within the fortress of York comes a fine head of Constantine I in local stone. None of these seems likely to have come from temples. On the other hand, a colossal marble head, perhaps of Trajan, comes from Bosham, Sussex, a parish which has also produced the head of Germanicus already mentioned (p. 356); the possibility of a cult-centre there is stronger. Moreover, three small bronze heads from various sites in the Cambridgeshire Fens, and one from Duston, Northamptonshire, seem to be provincial portraits of some of the emperors of the second century; all are made to be attached to ceremonial sceptres or staffs such as often formed part of the regalia of rural shrines, and they possibly imply that the imperial cult had a share in the observances of the temples concerned. This is, after all, no more than is implied also by such joint dedications as that at Colchester to *Numinib(us) Aug(ustorum) et Mercu(rio) deo*,[22] an example with numerous parallels elsewhere.

A part in the municipal version of the imperial cult was played by members of the corporations known as Seviri Augustales, whose membership was largely drawn from wealthy freedmen. The Bordeaux inscription already cited (p. 203) was set up in 237 by M. Aurelius Lunaris, who described himself as a sevir Augustalis of York and Lincoln. A second member of this body at York was M. Vere-cundius Diogenes, whose coffin-inscription recorded that he came from the civitas of the Bituriges Cubi (whose capital was Bourges). No seviri from other chartered towns are at present attested.

Apart from these cults, which were introduced by government policy, many other cults, both of classical and oriental deities were brought over not only by the army but also by continental merchants or officials. In the civil zone these naturally appear mainly in the towns. The Roman colony of Lincoln possessed organised guilds of worshippers, the Apollinenses and the Mercurienses, and the latter at least was connected with one of the town's constituent vici. London possessed a temple to Isis in addition to its well-known Mithraeum, the marble statuary from which provides such remarkable evidence for the wealth of its congregation. A few other towns, notably Bath and Cirencester, have produced statues or reliefs of Roman deities of completely classical type, and so have a number of the wealthier villas, where the context is more certainly Romano-British; but before these can be assessed, something must be said of Celtic religion and the effect of the *interpretatio Romana* upon it.

The early Celts worshipped the powers of nature; their deities were neither so anthropomorphic nor so departmentalised as the gods of the classical world. The Romans tended to equate Celtic gods with their own, but it is significant that the identifications were not always consistent. The Celtic gods had neither the same attributes nor the same fields of action as their classical counter-parts, and they were harder to apprehend. With the spread of Roman culture in Gaul the Celtic deities began to make their appearance in sculpture, and it is evident from the results that this process greatly assisted the Romanisation of the gods. Yet, even so, many still appear in animal form or with animal attributes such as horns; others are figured with three faces or three heads. Nevertheless, such represen-tations are often accompanied by the cock, which is an attribute of Roman Mercury, or the goose of Mars or the thunderbolt of Jupiter, and these show that an identification had been made. Conversely, a recognisable representation of Jupiter may sometimes hold a wheel, demonstrating that it is Taranis who is thus portrayed, or sometimes the hammer of Sucellus; and a figure clad in Mercury's winged hat and boots may bear the features of an aged man, and be accompanied by Rosmerta, consort of the Gaulish Mercury but without a part in classical mythology.

This clothing of Celtic deities with the attributes, appearance and personality of the Roman gods is called the *interpretatio Romana*. In many instances the synthesis is obvious, as when the physical appearance or attributes are not precisely regular, or when the identification varies, as with the 'horned god of the Brigantes' who is shown sometimes as Mars, sometimes as Mercury, and sometimes perhaps as Silvanus. But even when we are confronted with perfectly classical statues it is still rarely safe, in the absence of inscriptions, to assume that we are in touch with purely classical cults. An inscription will often give us the Celtic equation, as in dedications to Mars Lenus, or Mars Olludius or Apollo Anextiomarus; on the other hand, it may show that a classical deity is intended, as with the statuette of Mars from the Fossdyke at Torksey in Lincolnshire. Here the provincial style of work might have suggested a Celtic deity masquerading as Mars had not the inscribed base carried the legend: 'To the god Mars and the divinity of the emperor; Bruccius and Caratius, both surnamed Colasunus, gave 100 sesterces from their own money; Celatus the coppersmith made the statuette and gave a pound of bronze made at a cost of three denarii.' Here only the title *deus* labels the dedication as provincial.

In Britain we have fuller information about non-Roman deities in the north; the numerous temples in the civil zone of the province have rarely yielded evidence. Even in Gaul, where the names of 400 deities are known, only a quarter of them occur more than once. The Celtic world was full either of very local deities or more probably of many local manifestations of a few transcendent beings. Under Roman influence some of these local gods acquired distinctive character by their recognition as aspects of greater Roman deities, but few enjoyed more than local influence. The dedications mapped on fig. 12 illustrate the range of distribution, which has probably been extended by troop-movement. Many had only a single shrine with no dedications elsewhere; Coventina at Carrawburgh and Antenociticus at Benwell illustrate this. It is interesting also to note that some cults had a distribution limited in time as well as space. Antenociticus was worshipped only in the second century, and the distribution of dedications to the Matres Campestres shows that

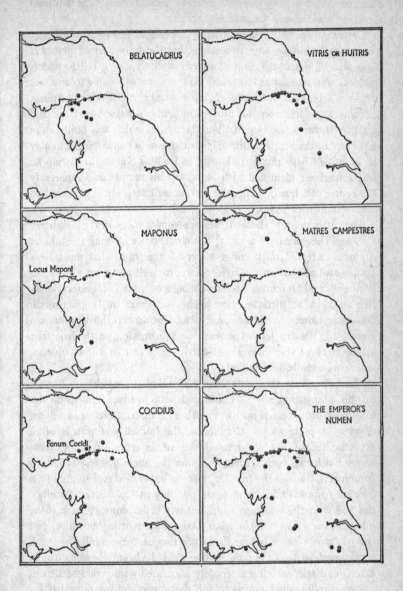

12 Distribution of dedications to some religious cults

they, too, were mainly a second-century phenomenon,[23] for southern Scotland was outside the empire thereafter.

The examples so far quoted have come from the military district of the north; but we have to assume that the same sort of picture is true also of the south. Sulis Minerva at Bath was a Celtic water-goddess who was assimilated with Minerva and who came to own one of the few temples in Britain in the classical style. She is not known elsewhere. Nodens, on the other hand, who possessed a large and wealthy shrine at Lydney in Gloucestershire, which was built in the last third of the fourth century, is also known in Lancashire, and may be identified with the deity known in Irish as Nuada. In Britain he was sometimes identified with Mars, but his temple was apparently the centre of a healing cult; the god himself seems also to have had connections with water.

The other deities whose names are known to us in the south are few, and they occur once or, at the most, twice. Among them Mars Alator is attested on a votive silver plaque from what must be a temple-site at Barkway, Hertfordshire, as well as on an altar from Wallsend, and Mercurius Andescocis once only, at Colchester. Some, like Ancasta at Bitterne, Hampshire, or Cuda at Daglingworth, Gloucestershire, or Viridius at Ancaster, Lincolnshire, have no Roman homonym. We are left to gather our information partly from the architecture of the shrines and partly from cult or votive objects, which are usually uninscribed.

These teach us the great variety of religion available in Roman Britain. Many of the great Celtic gods who are well known on the Continent are attested in Britain either on inscriptions or in reliefs, or even by place-names. Cernunnos, the horned god who is often accompanied by the ram-headed serpent, is represented at Ciren-cester (with two such serpents). Epona the horse goddess is known from inscriptions in the frontier regions, but is also represented by a figurine from Wiltshire and again possibly at Colchester. Sucellus, the god with the hammer, and Nantosvelta his consort seem to be intended on a rough relief from East Stoke, Nottinghamshire, and the god's own name is inscribed on a ring at York; while the small rural temple at Farley Heath, Surrey, yielded a bronze binding from a ceremonial staff which was crudely decorated with repoussé figures apparently intended not only for these two deities but also for Taranis. *Camulodunum*, the hill of Camulos, and (if Sir Ian Richmond is right) *Aquae Arnemetiae*, are two examples showing how place-names can reveal the presence of Celtic deities; certain river-names may possibly do the same.

The temples themselves are stereotyped in the main. A few wealthy and outstanding cults had temples of classical design, as at Bath, or of even more exotic style, as at Lydney. In the civil zone the majority had much smaller temples of the Romano-Celtic type, where the small square shrine is surrounded by a square ambulatory or portico. The building was sometimes varied by a circular or polygonal plan. Like the classical temple, it was not intended for congregational worship: people made their vows individually, and if crowds assembled on festival days they did so in the open air, or in the theatres which were occasionally provided, as at Gosbecks Farm (near Colchester) and *Verulamium*. Often the temple stands in a walled temenos, and sometimes the planning suggests the former presence of a sacred grove. At Springhead, Kent, a small temple was built over the ritual burial of four infants, interred at each corner of the building, presumably after sacrifice, in the later second century.

The Romano-Celtic temple is common in Roman Germany and in central and northern Gaul; in Britain its distribution lies south of a line connecting Norwich to Caerwent. North of this restricted area, in the civitas of the Coritani, simple round or rectangular shrines lacking the elaboration of a portico are found in the countryside, and even their more ambitious temples were probably not of Romano-Celtic form. At Thistleton Dyer, in Rutland, the temple which in the third century succeeded an earlier circular shrine resembled an aisled basilica with entrance porch, and recalls the analogous Temple B at Pesch in the Rhineland. It is possible that other equally atypical buildings existed elsewhere in Coritanian territory; at both Ancaster and Nettleham recently discovered inscriptions recorded the gift of arches to the deities concerned, but excavation has not revealed the architectural context.

There is no doubt that religious practice tends to be conservative, and in Roman Britain many primitive Celtic cults and customs continued to be observed side by side with the newer modes of worship. Thus, we find votive deposits consigned to the keeping of deities of lakes, rivers or bogs. There are many pre-Roman examples of this custom, one of the richest being the great hoard of objects from Llyn Cerrig Bach in Anglesey (p. 104). Similar deposits have been recognised in the late-first- and second-century hoards of metal-work from Carlingwark Loch and from Eckford and Blackburn Mill in southern Scotland; and even at *Verulamium* the discovery of a large number of coins together with more valuable objects in the former bed of the River Ver has been thought to represent, not casual losses, but intentional offerings to the deity of the stream, made perhaps by travellers crossing a bridge. So, too, with the large collections of fourth-century iron-work found in shafts at Great Chesterford and Silchester; these may quite possibly be due to votive rather than emergency concealment of valuable equipment. Naturally the reason for deposit is not always recoverable, but there are suggestive records of deep shafts whose contents were not the haphazard filling of an abandoned well but appeared purposive, regularly laid and often un-expected. The best known of these was at Jordon Hill near Wey-mouth, Dorset, in which a deposit of iron weapons, all (ritually?) bent, was covered by successive deposits, each containing a coin and the bones of a bird, and each being separated from the next by a layer of stone slabs. Small bronze birds, too, are not infrequent finds on sacred sites, and birds sometimes figure on religious reliefs; they can sometimes be taken to symbolise the souls of the dead, but sometimes they represent the messengers of the gods, or even, if Irish mythology is any guide, the gods themselves.

There are also traces in Roman Britain of the survival of the Celtic cult of the head. In pre-Roman times the Gauls, and the Britons too to judge by a scene on a coin of Cunobelin (Mack 260), collected and preserved the severed heads of their enemies: the head was regarded as the seat of the personality. It is not surprising therefore to find certain divinities represented by a head alone, and this is probably the significance of certain sculptured heads, often of crude workman-ship, which have been found at numerous places in Britain, mainly in Wales and the north. Occasionally, as on the well-known stone from Broadway, Worcestershire, a head or face was added to a phallic carving; this can be taken to represent the fusion of Celtic with Roman ideas. Phallic representations are numerous in Roman Britain, and they signify a Roman contribution. The phallus was re-garded in classical art as a symbol of good luck as well as of fertility: it was a talisman against the Evil Eye, and was sometimes 'demonised' by the addition of limbs, as on a remarkable unpublished stone from the temple at Wroxeter; but the addition of a face or head is probably the result of Celtic influences. Phallic representations themselves are very rare in pre-Roman Celtic art.

There was thus a great diversity of religious experience available in Britain at every level and for all tastes. The native Celtic deities of the land were recognised and propitiated even by strangers. The Roman Gods and the Imperial Cult inspired a loyalty to Rome and imparted a sense of unity within a world-wide empire. Both of these groups of cults, however, despite the round of calendered festivals about which Britain yields very little information, were on the whole impersonal. They all called for observance rather than devotion; the gods answered prayers and vows, but did not call for the soul's allegiance. This last aspect, and the insistence upon codes of conduct, was the contribution of eastern cults; and of these the most important was Christianity, since in due course this became the state religion of the empire.

There is little evidence to suggest that Christianity became widespread in Britain before the closing years of the fourth century. It was introduced, however, perhaps as early as the second, for Tertullian,[24] writing in the early years of the third, asserted that 'parts of the island inaccessible to Rome have been subjected to Christ'; and his evidence is supported a few decades later by Origen.[25] If Christianity, as is likely in Britain at this period, was a minority religion very largely confined to eastern traders, and if Tertullian may be taken literally, it is possible that merchants had made converts on voyages to Ireland or up the Scottish coasts.

That the faith had reached Britain before the time of Severus is suggested by the probability that it was in 208–9 that St Alban became the first British martyr. His death has often been attributed to the persecution of Diocletian, but there is good ancient testimony that no martyrdoms occurred in those parts of the western empire ruled by his colleague Constantius I,[26] and Britain was part of the dominion of the latter. The text of the earliest manuscript of St Alban's *Passio*, whose detailed knowledge of the topography of *Verulamium* gives it undoubted authority, describes his judge as 'Caesar', who 'without an order from the emperors commanded the persecution to cease, and reported to them that the slaughter of the Saints was stimulating rather than suppressing the spread of Christianity'.[27] This neatly fits the context when Geta Caesar was governor of the civil province during the campaigns of the two Augusti, Severus and Caracalla, in the north.[28]

Christianity, however, was likely to spread fastest in the cosmopolitan society of large ports and cities, and Britain was not at first a favourable environment. One day London may perhaps produce pre-fourth-century evidence; at the present time Cirencester is the only town to have done so, for there the famous word-square, now known to be a Christian cryptogram, is incised on wall-plaster which, to judge by its technical quality, is of second- or third-century date:[29] moreover, such a cryptogram would lose much of its significance after the Freedom of the Church. We can only say that by 314, when the Council of Arles assembled, the urban episcopate of Britain was well established. Three British bishops and a priest and a deacon attended the council;[30] and Dr J. C. Mann has shown that these represented the metropolitical churches of the four British provinces of the day.[31] Even fourth-century relics of urban Christianity, however, are curiously rare. The most substantial is the little church at Silchester, and there are the remains of what may be a cemetery-church at *Verulamium*. A third church, possibly dating to the fifth century, has left even less substantial traces at Richborough. The picture of small numbers and lack of wealth, which these small churches and the paucity of evidence elsewhere suggest, is supported by the record that poverty compelled three of the British bishops attending the Council of Ariminum in 359 to accept Constantius' offer of free transport by the imperial posting service on their journey; though it is fair to add that other British bishops refused this assistance.

Undoubtedly, however, it was through the urban aristocracy that Christianity reached the villas, where wider evidence exists for it. At Lullingstone in Kent we have the remarkable wall-paintings of the mid-fourth century, and at Hinton St Mary in Dorset a mosaic floor containing the portrait of Christ as a centre-piece (pl. 13). Both places were almost certainly chapels for worship. Other villas, such as Frampton and Chedworth, have yielded less spectacular though still authentic traces. But though the most plentiful evidence for Christianity comes from the towns and villas of the south and east, there also exists good evidence for its spread in the north, particularly in the region of Carlisle, where there was probably a bishop.

Despite the edicts of Christian emperors against pagan cults, these still continued to flourish in Britain through the middle of the fourth century, and indeed for a short time between about 360 and 380 received renewed impetus; for excavation has shown that new temples were erected at Lydney in Gloucestershire, and at Maiden Castle in Dorset during the reign of Valentinian, and repairs were carried out at others, for instance at Chew Stoke in Somerset. It is also very probable that the small column re-erected to Jupiter at Cirencester by L. Septimius governor of Britannia Prima [32] is to be dated to this same time. In London much of the fine sculpture which had adorned its Mithraeum was carefully concealed, perhaps some time in the reign of Constantine I; but if this was due, as is likely, to action by the Christian church of the city suppression was not altogether successful; for after extensive reconstruction the temple continued in use for some time thereafter. It is improbable that this pagan persistence, and even revival, had much to do with the short-lived policy of the emperor Julian; it had already long been a factor of British life, and it outlasted the apostatising movement of Julian by almost a quarter of a century. Rather it was due to the insular character of Britain itself, and to its remoteness from the sources of power which were attempting to supplant paganism by the new official cult.

By the end of the century, however, it is probable that Christianity had made considerable progress. The coin-series at many pagan temples, such as Woodeaton in Oxfordshire, seem to suffer reduction in volume soon after 380. At *Verulamium* the temple-theatre was abandoned about this time or soon after; at Chew Stoke some of the subsidiary buildings went out of use, and at Brean Down the temple itself had been converted to industrial uses as early as about 370. Concomitantly with the decay of paganism, our evidence for Christianity itself becomes richer with the emergence of historical personalities such as Pelagius, Ninian or Patrick, and with the survival of the writings of early fifth-century British Christians such as Patrick or Fastidius; while the suggestive description of the occasion in 429, when St Germanus met the *immensa multitudo* and converted it from Pelagianism to orthodox Catholicism, points to a cult now at last making headway as a popular movement. On the other hand, it is true to add that we are now entering an era when events are recorded from the Christian viewpoint. It would be wrong to regard the conversion of Britain as complete: Vortigern could still find 'magi' to consult. Nevertheless, the British church at this late date began to show a new activity with the missionary movements of Ninian and Patrick outside the old province, and was sufficiently entrenched to survive the Dark Ages. At the moment when Britain, through no wish of her own, ceased to be part of the Roman Empire she was becoming united as never before with the state religion of that empire. Yet the synthesising process was still active: the Christianity of Britain had become Pelagian Christianity, the formulation of a British heresiarch.

1. Tacitus, *Agricola*, 21.

2. Wall mosaics were also made in both periods, c.g. at Wroxeter (*Archaeologia*, lxxxviii (1938), 186) and at East Malling (*Arch. Cant.*, lxxi (1957), 238), but little survives.

3. For illustrations see J. M. C. Toynbee, *Art in Roman Britain* (London, 1962), pl. 56 (South Shields), pl. 176–7 (Colchester), pl. 193 (Nene Valley), p. 225–6 (Bignor). Eadem, *Art in Britain under the Romans* (Oxford, 1964), pl. xxxi a, b (London). For government action to reduce the cost of gladiatorial shows see *ILS*, 5163, and commentary in Pflaum, *Le Marbre de Thorigny* (Paris, 1948), p. 14 and *Hesperia* 24 (1955), p. 320.

4. The Domesday population of Wales is assessed at 100,000 by J. C. Russell, *British Mediaeval Population* (Albuquerque, 1948), p. 54.

5. This is slightly above the figure of one and a half million reached by Sir Mortimer Wheeler in 1930: *Antiquity*, iv, 95.

6. The estimate of J. C. Russell (loc. cit.) for England in 1086 is 1,105,216, to which must be added 100,000 for Wales.

7. Dr. J. P. Wild has shown that scraps of papyrus may have been used in the manufacture of British 'tin' coins (*Antiquity*, xl (1966), 139); the conclusion has been confirmed by later work: D. F. Allen in M. Jesson and D. Hill (ed.) *The Iron Age and Its Hill-Forts* (1971), pp. 127 ff.

8. The best-known examples of these are: (i) *satis*; (ii) *puellam*; (iii) *fecit tubul(um) Clementinus*; (iv) *VI k(alendas) Octo(bres)*; (v) *Pertacus perfidus Campester Lucilianus Campanus conticuere omnes* from Silchester; *Primus fecit X* from Leicester; *Austalis dibus XIII Vagatur sib(i) cotidim* from London.

9. F. Haverfield, *The Romanization of Roman Britain* (Oxford, 1915), p. 34.

10. K. Jackson, *Language and History in Early Britain* (Edinburgh, 1953), p. 99.

11. This is well illustrated by the obscene phrases scored on wall-plaster from Leicester (*JRS*, liv (1964), 182).

12. For further remarkably interesting light thrown by mosaics on classical education in Britain, and in particular on the possible ownership of illustrated manuscripts, see D. J. Smith in A. L. F. Rivet (ed.), *The Roman Villa in Britain* (1969), pp. 90 ff.

13. S. Piggott and G. E. Daniel, *A Picture Book of Ancient British Art* (Cambridge, 1951), p. 11.

14. R. G. Collingwood and J. N. L. Myres, *Roman Britain and the English Settlements* (Oxford, 1936), p. 259.

15. *RIB*, 172.

16. See *RIB*, 149, for a *lapidarius cives Carnutenus*.

17. J. M. C. Toynbee, *Art in Roman Britain* (London, 1962), pl. 8; eadem, *Art in Britain under the Romans* (Oxford, 1964), pl. viii *b*.

18. Tacitus, *Annals*, xiv, 31: *templum divo Claudio constitutum*. Seneca, *Apocolocyntosis* viii, 3: (Claudius) *deus fieri vult: parum est quod templum in Britannia habet, quod hunc barbari colunt et ut deum orant . . .*

19. *Britannia*, iii (1972), pp. 164 ff.

20. *RIB*, 89; J. M. C. Toynbee, *Art in Britain under the Romans* (Oxford, 1964), p. 164, for dating.

21. *RIB*, 707.

22. *RIB*, 193.

23. Their Benwell dedication (*RIB*, 1334), however, is of third-century date, since it was made by Ala I Asturum *Gordiana*.

24. *adversus Judaeos*, vii.

25. *Homil. iv in Ezekiel interp.*, i.

26. Augustine, Ep., 88, 2.

27. *Tunc impiissimus Caesar exanimis, tanta novitate perculsus, iniussu etiam principum iubet de persecutione cessare, referens gaudere potius religionem caede sanctorum, per quam eandem opinabantur aboleri.* Later MSS change *Caesar* to *iudex*.

28. See Dr J. R. Morris, *Hertfordshire Archaeology*, i (1968), pp. 1 ff.; W. Levison, *Antiquity*, xv (1941), 337–59.

29. *Rotas opera tenet arepo sator: Archaeologia*, lxix, 1917–18 (1920), 197; *JBAA*,[3] xvi (1953), pl. 1.

30. *Eborius Episcopus de civitate Eboracensi provincia Britannia. Restitutus episcopus de civitate Londiniensi provincia suprascripta. Adelphius episcopus de civitate colonia Londiniensium. Exinde Sacerdos presbyter, Arminius diaconus.* Part of the text is corrupt, and presumably *Lindinensi* or *Lindinensium* should be read in one or other place.

31. *Antiquity*, xxxv (1961), 316–20.

32. *ILS*, 5435 = *RIB*, 103.

16

Carausius and the fourth century

The short-lived British empire of Carausius and Allectus was the last of the separatist movements of the third century. Its rise and collapse illustrate the limitations of ancient sea-power. Britain could be held against the empire by one who commanded the Channel, but that command could not be maintained indefinitely because of the inability of oar-powered fleets to remain continuously on patrol. It required the sustaining genius of Carausius to support the experiment, and when this was removed the end came quickly.

M. Aurelius Mausaeus Carausius, like most of the military leaders of the later empire, was a man of humble origin who had risen by ability. By birth a Menapian from the Coast of Belgium, since early youth he had acquired a knowledge of the sea. He had played a distinguished part in Maximian's campaign of 286 against the Gaulish Bagaudae, those bands of deserters, displaced persons and revolted peasantry who were terrorising country and town alike, and later in the same year was given a naval command in the Channel with orders to suppress the raids of Franks and Saxons on the northern coasts of Gaul. Coming under suspicion, however, of diverting rescued treasure from its rightful owners and from the government, and even of postponing attack until the raiders were returning full of booty, he learned, so we are told, that his execution had been ordered by Maximian. Thereupon he lost no time in taking refuge in Britain, where he established himself as emperor.

This occurred probably late in 286, possibly early in the following year. But we know nothing of the reasons why Britain fell so easily into his grasp. The command of the Classis Britannica was not sufficient to outweigh the opposition of three legions: he must have enjoyed a previous popularity which perhaps can be explained by Diocletian's assumption in 285 of the title *Britannicus Maximus*, a style which he soon abandoned during the period of British independence. It was possibly therefore Carausius who had been responsible for the victory which bestowed the title, and if so he would be well known to the British legions. Nothing is recorded of the location or nature of the campaign; it may have been directed against a Saxon or Irish landing. It will be remembered that both Caistor by Norwich and Wroxeter have shown signs of destruction by fire about this time, though these may, of course, have been accidental disasters. For the rest he had sufficient funds to buy the support of the troops, and indeed the timely acquisition of treasure and the lack of opposition to his elevation by the British garrison both suggest that his ambitions were not so suddenly matured as our sources suggest. With the army in his favour, the opinion of the provincials themselves would be of secondary importance; but there is no reason to doubt that for some time they had entertained dissatisfaction with the financial policy of the central government (p. 216). It was to meet such feelings that part of Carausius' propaganda, as put out on his coins, was designed, notably the *Restitutor Britanniae* and *Genius Britanniae* legends. Nevertheless it would be an anachronism to suppose that Carausius led a nationalist movement. He was a would-be emperor of Rome, not a king of Britain.

In the early years of his reign Carausius seems to have been able to retain part of northern Gaul under his control. Maximian had his hands full with wars on the upper Rhine and against the Franks near its mouth. It was not until the autumn of 288 that he started concentrating troops and a fleet against Carausius, and though in the following spring he was able to penetrate to the coast, a naval defeat seems to have followed. The result was an uneasy peace which lasted until 293, a peace which on the Roman side was intended to gain time for further measures, but which to Carausius opened visions of recognition and legitimacy. He now brought the valuation of his coinage into line with the reformed system of the empire, and it may have been now too that he adopted the names M. Aurelius, which were those of Maximian. When it became obvious, perhaps in 292, that despite his overtures war was impending, he began to issue coin-types honouring the other emperors and stressing the triple division of supreme power, with legends such as *Pax Auggg*,[1]

Victoria Auggg, Providentia Auggg and the like; some even bore the image of Diocletian or Maximian, and one went as far as to depict the busts of all three Augusti surrounded by the legend *Carausius et Fratres sui*.

No such courtesies issued from the Roman mints, however; Diocletian was disinclined to countenance rebellion. The very existence of Carausius violated the principles of his tetrarchy, which was established early in 293 with the appointment of Constantius and Galerius as Caesars. Constantius at once opened his campaign with a swift attack upon Boulogne, Carausius' main continental base, which he cut off from naval relief with a mole across the harbour-mouth. The town fell with the surrender of its garrison, and Constantius went on to attack the Franks of the Rhine mouth, who seem to have been acting in league with Carausius. From these two blows to his prestige the latter did not recover; shortly afterwards he was murdered by Allectus.

Carausius was an able adventurer and an effective ruler. The only epigraphic evidence to survive is a milestone from the neighbourhood of Carlisle,[2] which shows that his power extended to the northern frontier. It is his coinage which provides the fullest evidence of his appearance, policy and aspirations. At first this coinage was produced with haste and little skill, partly by over-striking previous issues; two coins with the mint-mark BRI may record a temporary mint of this preliminary phase at Wroxeter.[3] Subsequently regular mints were established. In addition to one at London and another whose signature C has been taken to signify *Camulodunum, Corinium* or *Clausentum*, Carausius had at least one permanent continental mint, probably at Rouen.

That he was able to maintain his Gallic possessions so long is due no doubt partly to Maximian's preoccupation with barbarian enemies (which made the unofficial recognition of Carausius a temporary convenience provided that he kept his bargain), and partly to the military strength of Carausius himself. As well as the British legions, he controlled at least one on the Continent, for the panegyrist of Constantius mentions a 'Roman legion won over'.[4] This had probably formed part of the force originally assigned to him for the defence of northern Gaul, and it may have been Legio xxx Ulpia Victrix; this legion, normally stationed at Xanten, the nearest fortress to the

Rhine mouth, was the readiest available for transfer to Boulogne, where the walled enclosure is of fortress size.

He may well have controlled vexillations of other legions also, assigned to him for the same original purpose, for among his coins is a legionary series which names six continental legions in addition to xxx Ulpia Victrix and two of the three stationed in Britain.[5] The purpose of this issue is not certain, but it is best explained as intended for donatives to the forces concerned, for its value as propaganda is obviously minimal; and though it is inconceivable that all these legions were themselves under his control, it would be quite in accordance with the military practice of the period for detachments from them to be seconded for special service. If so, Carausius commanded powerful regular forces in Gaul, in addition to the barbarian mercenaries raised among the Franks and new forces conscripted from the ranks of Gallic merchants, which are attested by the panegyrist. But strong though he was, he lacked the power or the initiative to attempt the conquest of the Continent. Indeed, he clearly recognised the collegiate principle of empire.

His originality is clearly seen in his coinage. The legend *Expectate veni* on an early issue is a quotation from Vergil, the only one to appear on a Roman coin. For the first time for more than two generations fine silver was issued as denarii, though these coins quickly disappeared from circulation and were soon discontinued. His normal issues, however, which were minted in great quantity, were radiate *antoniniani* of a much better size and quality than those of the Gallic empire; these must have done much to restore financial confidence.

Carausius has often been credited with building the Saxon Shore forts which were provided late in the third century for the defence of the south-east coasts of Britain. In reality, however, these forts are part of a wider system of security embracing both sides of the Channel; their establishment was probably due to the initiative of the Emperor Probus (276–82). In Britain forts already existed at Brancaster and Reculver, and a small base had recently been fortified at Richborough (p. 215). The fort at Burgh Castle near Yarmouth presents some interesting problems, for it was begun in the old style with rounded corners and internal towers, but with no rampart bank; however, before the defences had been completed drastic alterations were imposed. New external towers or bastions were added to the walls and the internal ones apparently were left unfinished. Large sockets in the summits of the bastions suggest that powerful revolving onagri were mounted; but the tops of the towers are on the small side for this purpose, and perhaps the sockets served some structural purpose. Burgh, then, designed to an earlier specification, was brought into conformity during construction with the new military architecture which was being introduced for new town-walls in Gaul. Its earliest certain appearance on this side of the Channel is at the new stone fort of Richborough, which was already built when Carausius seized power.[6] At Lympne and Portchester the evidence points to the same date of construction, while the dates of Bradwell, Essex, and Walton Castle, Suffolk, are uncertain (pl. 16). Only Pevensey can be shown to belong to a later period.

There is little to recommend the view put forward by D. A. White [7] that these Saxon Shore forts were built as a precaution against Roman rather than Saxon invasion, for they would be of little tactical value against the landing of a Roman army, being too widely scattered and too thinly garrisoned, and in fact they played no part against Constantius in 296. In an earlier period the British bases of the Classis Britannica had been concentrated in Kent and perhaps east Sussex; the effect of the new measures was to create further fleet-bases along the east coast and on the south as far as Portsmouth Harbour; these were linked in each case with a land garrison with the dual function of protecting the base and of rounding up any raiders who penetrated the screen.

Similar late forts are known on the west coast at Cardiff and Lancaster, with smaller enclosures also at Caernarvon and Holyhead. These must be survivors of a once more extensive system which, like the forts on the east coast, was associated with naval activity. Caer Gybi at Holyhead closely resembles the fortified naval bases established on the Rhine and Danube by Valentinian, and the other sites are all on estuaries. But whether these forts were the work of Carausius or of Constantius, or of a later period in the fourth century, is entirely unknown.

Allectus had been the finance minister of Carausius. The words of Aurelius Victor [8] suggest that he was *rationalis summae rei*; a praetorian prefect at this date also had financial responsibilities and would have been better equipped for murder; but would hardly be described in those terms. His reign, which probably began in the autumn of 293, was uninspired and brief. In 296 Constantius was ready, and probably in September an invasion was launched. Preparations had been extensive, for the expedition was in two divisions, one fleet being massed at the Seine mouth under Asclepiodotus, Constantius' praetorian prefect, and the other under Constantius himself at Boulogne. Constantius contented himself with a demonstration in the Channel which was perhaps diversionary in intent, but Asclepiodotus took advantage of low cloud or mist to elude the fleet which was waiting for him near the Isle of Wight and landed somewhere near Southampton Water, where he burnt his boats before marching inland.

Allectus lacked the strategic genius of his predecessor, and gave way to indecision. He made the twin mistakes of leaving the naval initiative to his foes, and of being misled by Constantius' naval activity in the straits into concentrating his forces at the wrong place. These forces consisted partly, as we shall see, of regiments from the north, including the Wall, and partly of Frankish mercenaries. When the news of the landing reached him he had to hurry off to shield London, and only the weather saved him from being caught between two invading armies; for Constantius' transports were unable to make land, and the Caesar himself had to return to Boulogne. Meanwhile a decisive battle was fought somewhere in the region of Silchester, and in it Allectus lost his life. Either because of his haste, or more probably because he could not rely upon his regular troops, he was unable to deploy the whole of his strength, and the casualties were mainly among his barbarian mercenaries.[9] There are signs that Silchester itself was damaged in the resulting tumult.

Some of Constantius' own transports reached London in time to save it from the retreating Franks, and when Constantius himself arrived he was accorded a triumphant welcome. The scene is recorded for us on the great gold medallion found near Arras, which shows the *tutela* of London kneeling to welcome him at her gates, and the legend *Redditor lucis aeternae*. Relief must have been genuine, the danger only just averted. The anonymous panegyrist of Constantius uses almost the same words to describe the scene of thankfulness: *Britanni . . . tandem liberi, tandemque Romani, tandem vera imperii luce recreati.*[10] As we have seen (p. 241), this may have been the occasion for the grant of the title *Caesarea* to London, in honour of Constantius.

Once Allectus was dead, considerable reorganisation and reconstruction had to be undertaken by his conqueror. It seems probable that the two provinces of Britannia Superior and Inferior, into which Roman Britain had been divided since Caracalla, were almost at once reorganised into smaller units; and the question whether there was a preliminary separation into three provinces of Britannia Prima, B. Secunda and B. Caesariensis, before the final creation of the four which are attested in the Verona List of 312–14, has already been discussed (p. 241). These four provinces were Britannia Prima, B. Secunda, Maxima Caesariensis and Flavia Caesariensis.

Diocletian's reforms included the permanent separation of the civil government from the provincial military commands which now began to be organised under *duces*; but the new system was not everywhere applied until the reign of Constantine, and it is not certain when the division of responsibility became effective in Britain. Certainly the Birdoswald inscription shows that under Constantius the *praeses* presumably of Secunda, Aurelius Arpagius, was still in control of troops.[11]

In the north there was much to do on the frontier and in the military areas behind it. It may be that the Picts, as the Caledonians were now described, had seized the opportunity presented by the absence of the Wall-garrison to invade the protected lands north of the frontier and to attack the Wall. This act is nowhere attested by ancient sources, but it is a reasonable inference – both from the campaign, no doubt punitive in character, on which Constantius is recorded to have been engaged in the far north in 306[12] and also from the observation that some at least of the forts on the wall were damaged by fire at about this time: two have produced building inscriptions of the tetrarchy.[13] The destruction has also been recognised in some of the milecastles and turrets, though in others either the stratification has not survived or else it is not clear how far the observed repairs were necessitated by intentional damage. In addition, destruction has been recognised in some of the vici on or near the Wall.[14]

The garrisons, however, which are named in the second half of chapter xl of the *Notita Dignitatum*, in what is evidently a list of the period 296–367, are in almost every case identical with those attested in the same forts in the third century (p. 262f.). The fact that so many of them survived suggests either that any attack was small-scale or that the troops themselves were elsewhere, having been withdrawn by Allectus for his struggle with Constantius, though in the event they played little part therein. Other troops from northern Britain may have been concentrated by Allectus in addition to those from the Wall, and probably were; but since the first part of chapter xl in the *Notitia*, which contains the relevant forts, is a list of re-placements after the later disaster of 367, it throws no light on the situation now. Whatever troops were used by Allectus, they were clearly absent for so short a time that in any case the opportunity for hostile activity in the north was brief.

The wall-garrison, then, seems to have been sent back to its old stations,[15] and perhaps the only major change made by Constantius was to redeploy elsewhere the additional numeri which had sup-plemented the regular forces there during the third century; at any rate, except for the *numerus Maurorum Aurelianorum* at Burgh-by-Sands, they are no longer heard of on the Wall. The forts on the wall, however, and the milecastles and turrets too, required extensive repair. This, as the inscriptions at Birdoswald and Housesteads sug-gest, was undertaken as soon as possible, as no doubt was the re-establishment of the outpost forts. High Rochester, Risingham and Bewcastle were certainly rebuilt, and so perhaps was Netherby. Wholesale reconstruction extended also to Corbridge and to many of the Pennine forts, such as Bainbridge or Ilkley; and even York and Chester can show extensive renovation of their defences. It is not necessary, however, to imagine that all the restoration south of the Wall was necessitated by enemy action, or that it was undertaken so urgently. At Bainbridge, for instance, the headquarters building sur-vived almost unaltered from the time of Severus until 367, and this is not likely to have happened had the fort been sacked in 296. In general, excavators have not been sufficiently careful to distinguish between demolition and destruction, and the latter can be assumed with any degree of confidence only where the reports speak of wide-spread signs of fire. In the wall region these exist, but there is little certain evidence farther south. Sixty or seventy years had elapsed since the great programme of rebuilding carried out under emperors from Severus to Gordian III, and natural decay may be held responsible for much. This would certainly have caught the attention of Constantius.

At Birdoswald the inscription of the Tetrarchy furnishes support for this conclusion, since it refers to the 'praetorium which had been covered with earth and fallen into ruin'.[16] These words have sometimes been held to illustrate official euphemism intended to conceal the results of enemy action; but as with an earlier example (p. 188), it is better to take it literally. Dr J. Wilkes has shown that in the late third century the supply of equestrian commanders for auxiliary units may have been difficult to maintain in Britain,[17] and the Birdoswald inscription itself shows a centurion in command. In such circumstances the commandant's house, with its provision for the large household of a wealthy official, may well have remained unoccupied and unmaintained.

Neglect, however, extended farther than this. At Birdoswald both the headquarters building and the baths required repair. These, indeed, may have been damaged by enemy action; but elsewhere in the Pennine region forts were completely rebuilt, even though there is no certainty that their predecessors had suffered attack. No doubt the long quiescence of the frontier and the disturbed political conditions of the last thirty years had been responsible between them for much official lethargy. It is extremely unlikely that there had been a large-scale Brigantian rebellion. The Gallic empire may not have had the resources or the interest to maintain the northern frontier at full efficiency; certain regiments may have become gravely under-strength owing to slack recruitment. But there is no evidence that this state of affairs was universal.[18]

Whatever the reasons, there is no doubt that the great majority, if not all, the forts of northern Britain were extensively rebuilt about the beginning of the fourth century.[19] The date suggested for this event by the coins and pottery is necessarily ill-defined, and can sometimes be shown only to be later than about 270. However, the arrival of Constantius and the preparations for his northern campaign provide the required historical context for the initiation of the programme, which is confirmed by building-inscriptions of the Tetrarchy from Birdoswald and Housesteads, dating as they do before 305. Elsewhere in the north new forts were built at Piercebridge, Newton Kyme and perhaps at Elslack, the first, at over eleven acres, being exceptionally large; yet like the others which were now rebuilt, they show little trace of the new military architecture which had already governed the design of the forts on the Saxon Shore. Lancaster alone can be said to belong to the new type; at others the abolition of the earth rampart to make way for extra buildings, so that the fort wall is freestanding inside, is the only sign, and that perhaps coincidental, of its influence.

At Chester the north and west walls of the fortress were rebuilt very largely with material obtained from nearby cemeteries. The date of this work is certainly not earlier than the late third century, since one of the tombstones came from a burial of the time of Caracalla or Elagabalus,[20] but it cannot certainly be ascribed to Constantius. Nevertheless, when we recall the destruction of the Wroxeter forum about this time we may suspect that the damage, whatever its date, was the work of raiders from the Irish Sea. Increased insecurity in this region in the late third century can be suggested as the cause of the reoccupation of the old hill-fort at Dinorben from about 260.

At York a number of buildings previously encroaching on the rampart were demolished and sealed by a new bank, and a new defensive wall was built round the entire circuit except between the north-east and south-east gates,[21] the south-west front being equipped with eight magnificent external multangular towers. The dating-evidence for this reconstruction is meagre, but it can be shown to be later than 270, while the pottery from the accompanying ditch suggests that it began to silt up in the early fourth century. The monumental character of the south-west front, excelling in magnificence the other known fortresses of the empire and built to dominate the river and the colonia beyond it, is best understood in terms of York's position either as an imperial headquarters or more probably (since Constantius remained in Britain less than a year) as the headquarters of the *dux Britanniarum* once that command had been established.

There can be little doubt that the presence of Constantius Caesar in Britain had invigorating results in many directions; but even more important, as its influence became effective, was the return to firm government and a sounder currency. We may be sure that the restoration of the frontier and its outpost system was effected under his own supervision, but the big programme of military reconstruction elsewhere in the north, and perhaps the completion of the system of coastal defence, may have been spread out over more than one subsequent decade. This is probably true too of the revival of building activity which has been recognised at *Verulamium*. Until the middle of the reign of Constantine the influx of new coins from continental mints was very small, and existing coins remained in circulation – a fact which has tended to result in the assignment of too early a date for buildings erected in the early fourth century.

Constantius had returned to Gaul in 297, and it was not until 306 that he crossed once more to Britain.[22] By this time he had become the senior Augustus, for Diocletian and Maximian had abdicated in 305; but his health was already failing. Just as Severus a century before had campaigned far into Scotland after the defences of the province had been rebuilt, so now the time had come to carry the war into enemy territory, so that Roman terms could be imposed.

The emperor was joined at Boulogne by Constantine, his son, before the expedition sailed. The details of the campaign are unknown, but the words of the panegyrist make it plain that the far north of Scotland was reached.[23] It seems probable that Severus' amphibious tactics were employed. Pottery of appropriate date has been discovered at Cramond and Carpow, where contact could be made with the sea; but otherwise there are no known archaeological traces of the expedition. Before midsummer a brilliant victory had been won, and Constantius returned to York, where on 25 July he died. His refined features, as displayed on the Arras medallions, were reflected in the mildness of his rule, and his death was widely lamented. In 297–8 he had sent craftsmen from Britain to assist the restoration of Autun after its devastation by the Bagaudae, and Eumenius, in the speech of thanks which records this, mentions the interest he took in education. The persecution of the Christians which had been ordered by Diocletian in 303 was not strictly applied by him, and within his dominions nothing worse was enforced than the demolition of churches.

As soon as the emperor's death was known, the army at York acclaimed his son Constantine as Augustus in his place. This title, indeed, he had to surrender for a time, but succeeded in obtaining his recognition as Caesar from Galerius. A decisive part was played in his elevation by Crocus, a chieftain of the Alamanni, who had accompanied Constantius to Britain as an ally.[24] His presence illustrates the growing dependence of Roman power upon barbarian allies and the important part their leaders were coming to play in affairs of state; but there is no reason to suppose that he or his men were given land on which to settle in Britain, for there is nothing to show that he had come over for any other purpose than to take part in the campaign. But, as we have seen (p. 270, n. 5) there is evidence for a settlement of Saxons, perhaps as *laeti*, in Norfolk about this time.

Constantine had soon to leave for Gaul, and the following year received the title of Augustus. The short period of his rule as Caesar saw heavy repairs to the roads of Britain – no less than six mile-stones date from these months – and the programme was maintained for some years to come, as a further thirteen milestones indicate. Thus, his father's policy was maintained, for the care expended on the road-system can be understood as the logical accompaniment of the restoration of the forts, and as illustrating the interest of the government in the renaissance of the British economy.

During most of the first half of the fourth century Britain enjoyed peace and prosperity. At some point, perhaps in the years 315–18, Constantine assumed among other military titles that of Britannicus Maximus; but we know nothing of any campaigning which may have earned it. Both Saxon raiding and Pictish aggression appear to have died down. The edict of Milan in February 313 extended freedom of worship to the Christian Church, and in the following year three British bishops and the representatives of a fourth attended the Council of Arles; though none are known to have been present at those of Nicaea in 325 or Sardica in 343, British Christianity remained firmly in the Catholic fold.

For Haverfield the period was the golden age of Roman Britain, and we may agree that the broader basis of its prosperity surpassed that of the Antonine age. All the instruments of despotism and of soul-destroying officialdom were, it is true, to hand: yet despite them all, Britain entered an era of unexampled well-being, the causes of which have been discussed in Chapters 13 and 14.

The first sign of trouble to come occurred late in 342. The details elude us, owing to the loss of the relevant book of Ammianus' history, but a crisis became sufficiently severe to cause a hurried and apparently unexpected visit by the emperor Constans early the following year, apparently in January or early February.[25] On the death of Constantine and the division of the empire between his sons, Britain had fallen to the rule of Constantine II, the eldest brother; but from 340, after the death of the latter at the hands of his brother's troops, the western part of the empire came under the authority of Constans. It is possible that public opinion in Britain resented the killing of Constantine, and that the mid-winter visit of his brother was designed to forestall rebellion. Whether or not this was so, there were certainly good pretexts for the visit both on the northern frontier and also perhaps on the Saxon Shore; and if, as seems probable, it was on this occasion that the elder Gratian, father of Valentinian and Valens, was posted to Britain with the title of Count and a detachment of the field army, this reinforcement stresses the urgency of the situation.[26]

In the north there seems to have been an attack by the Picts, aided perhaps by the Scots (p. 390), upon the protected lands north of the Wall, for the *areani*, whose duty was to range widely beyond the frontier in search of military intelligence, were somehow involved in action taken by the emperor.[27] Moreover, the outpost forts of High Rochester, Risingham and Bewcastle were all three destroyed or badly damaged by fire at some date intermediate between their restoration by Constantius and the disaster of 367, and only the last two were rebuilt. It is not known whether Netherby, which was also restored at the beginning of the century, suffered the same fate.

Part of Constans' efforts, then, were devoted to reorganisation of arrangements beyond the frontier, where Caracalla's system of a patrolled belt was clearly still in operation: for the *areani*, whatever the significance of their name, exercised the same functions as the *exploratores* of the third century.[28] It cannot be thought that the Roman forces in Britain, especially if reinforced by *comitatenses*, were deterred from restoring High Rochester by superior power, and its evacuation can accordingly be interpreted as based upon a reassessment of policy. This fort, according to Ptolemy, lay in the territory of the Votadini, whose attitude, as far as it can be traced, had always been consistently philo-Roman (pp. 126, 274, 208f.). The act of Constans gave them greater responsibility for defence against the Picts, while still maintaining the nearer fort of Risingham as an outpost on Dere Street.

The visit of Constans can also be connected with developments on the Saxon Shore. The fort of Pevensey was an addition to the series made some time about the middle of the century, as its general coin list and the coin of 334–5 found below a bastion both testify. It could well have been built to the orders of Constans at this time, while at Richborough and Portchester also the coin lists seem to indicate increased activity. Perhaps there were troop tranfers; but it is even likely that this activity marks the establishment of the command of the Count of the Saxon Shore. Territorial counts are not recorded before the death of Constantine i, and, though the forts existed earlier, the command was probably hitherto exercised by the prefect of the Classis Britannica. The Count had certainly been established before 367: if his office originated in 343 the questions arise why it was necessary to make a change and why the new office was given the title of the Saxon Shore. Military reorganisation is usually undertaken for practical reasons, such as a breakdown of the previous system or an impending crisis.

It must be admitted that at present these questions cannot be clearly answered. Owing to the loss of Ammianus' account of these years, we have no knowledge whether Saxon raids were increasing: the distribution of coin-hoards gives little or no indication that this was so. The term *litus Saxonicum* has usually been understood as referring to the shore threatened by the Saxons, but some writers have suggested that it means the shore settled by the Saxons, these being understood as *laeti* in the Roman Service. There is little positive evidence to support this view, since the known garrisons of the Shore forts are regular troops with no Saxon connections; nor does the distribution of so-called Romano-Saxon pottery, which has been regarded (with little justification) as a hybrid fashion designed to appeal to Teutonic settlers, show any recognisable connection with the Saxon Shore. It would go beyond the evidence, then, to suggest that Constans visited Britain to arrange such a settlement; but it is worth recalling that Saxons were to be found on the north-east coast of Gaul, though the date and circumstances of their arrival there are totally unknown.[29]

During the next seven years the quality of Constans' rule degenerated and its popularity declined: early in 350 he succumbed to a conspiracy and his throne was seized by Magnentius. This man was of barbarian descent, and had started his career as a *laetus*; for his family had been settled, it seems, in Gaul, though according to one tradition his father was a Briton. Whether or not he had personal ties with Britain, his rule was welcomed there, as the aftermath made clear.[30] Magnentius' reign was brief, for he was defeated by Constantius II in a great battle at Mursa in Pannonia in 351, where the losses on both sides were very severe. That Britain was drained of troops to support the usurper must be highly probable, and it would account for the inability of the British army to control its foes which is such a feature of the next fifteen years. Magnentius maintained himself in the West for a further two years; but after his death in 353 extensive reprisals, despite the amnesty which Constantius had declared, were taken against his supporters in Britain. The agent employed for this purpose was the imperial notary Paul, whose evil repute as an investigator earned him the nickname of *Catena*, the Chain. The Vicar of Britain himself was forced to suicide after an unsuccessful attempt on his accuser. This Martinus is praised by Ammianus for his just and upright character: the charge, we are told, was brought against him because of his efforts to protect the innocent. Nevertheless, it cannot have been easy for anyone of prominence in Britain to have avoided involvement with the defeated side.[31]

Shortly after this, Constantius elevated Julian to the supervision of the west with the rank of Caesar (355). It was during 359 that, as a preliminary to his campaign along the lower Rhine, Julian caused a large fleet to be built for the transport of grain from Britain; Ammianus refers to a regular movement of corn from this side of the Channel.[32]

Some time between 354 and 358 some curious local coins, copying contemporary issues, made their appearance in Britain: they bear the name of Carausius. Who this 'Carausius II' was is quite unknown, nor is there any other record of a usurper in Britain at this period.[33]

Early in 360 the Scots (who were at this period still based on Ireland) and the Picts of central Scotland broke the terms which had been imposed upon them, presumably by Constans, and began to lay waste the regions near the frontier. Julian hesitated to cross to Britain himself because of his other commitments, especially in midwinter, but he despatched Lupicinus his *magister militum* with four regiments of comitatenses in his stead. Nothing is recorded of his achievements, but he was known for a competent general, and presumably was successful in imposing terms, for he returned to Gaul within a few months. During the interval Julian had been hailed Augustus by his troops, and some anxiety had been felt about the reactions of Lupicinus to the news, if he heard it while still in control

of the British garrison as well as of his own force; in the event, however, the precautions taken successfully kept him in ignorance until
he set foot once more in Gaul, and could be arrested.[34]

Whatever settlement was reached, it did not last long. The recur-
rent and successful raids of this decade support the suggestion that
the army of Britain was below strength due to the losses suffered by
Magnentius at Mursa. In 365 Ammianus records successful attacks by
Picts, Saxons, Scots and Attacotti, and late in 367 the position degenerated alarmingly. As the result of a *barbarica conspiratio* a concerted attack was made upon the province. The tribes responsible
were once more the Picts, Scots and Attacotti, while the Franks and
Saxons descended upon the coasts and frontiers of Gaul. Though it is
unlikely that the Saxons altogether neglected opportunities in Britain,
the main fury seems to have fallen upon the northern frontier and the
western coastlands. The Picts came down from the region north of
the Forth, the Scots took boat from Ireland; the Attacotti are of
uncertain homeland, either Irish or in the western isles, but their
savagery is vividly attested by St Jerome, who in his youth observed
their cannibal tastes in Gaul.

United planning had never been suspected of the foes of Roman
Britain before, and its success was startling. Hadrian's Wall had
always been impregnable when its garrison was there: now it was
overrun or by-passed; Nectaridus, count of the Saxon Shore,[35] was
killed and the *dux Britanniarum*, Fullofaudes, was besieged or captured. The disaster was the greater because it was unexpected: there
was treachery among the areani, who should have sent warning in
advance: they had succumbed to bribes not merely to withhold intelligence, but to betray military information to the enemy. The confusion was aggravated by a breakdown of discipline: large numbers of
Roman deserters roamed the country, and many others claimed to be
on indefinite leave. Almost certainly escaped slaves and coloni also
took advantage of the general disorder to flee their masters and
enrich themselves with plunder. The gravity of the situation was
greatly enhanced by the length of time it took to restore order:
almost two years passed before the government regained control. By
then Britain might have passed beyond recovery had conquest and
settlement been the intention of the invaders; but it was not. Their
only aim was the acquisition of slaves, cattle and portable wealth;

and when Theodosius reached London he found the country overrun by small plundering bands rather than by an invading army.

The emperor Valentinian was on the march against the Alamanni when the news reached him. He could not therefore come in person and, as sometimes happens in a crisis, a quick succession of commanders was appointed and recalled before the right man was found. The first was Severus, the emperor's *comes domesticorum*. He was soon succeeded by Jovinus, the *magister equitum*; but in the spring of 368 continuing bad reports and rumours of disaster led to the appointment of the elder Theodosius, a *comes rei militaris* whose son was later to become the emperor Theodosius I, and as a young man accompanied his father to Britain.[36]

With four regiments of the field army, the Batavi, Heruli, Jovii and Victores, he marched from Richborough to London, and from there set about rounding up the scattered bands which were plundering the countryside. Next an amnesty was issued to deserters, and his forces were strengthened with reconstituted elements of the disintegrated provincial garrison. He was now in a position to re-create the diocesan administration with the appointment of Dulcitius as *dux Britanniarum* and Civilis as *Vicarius*, and all was ready for the resumption of initiative the following year. In 369 the remaining parts of Britain were cleared of invaders and a large programme of restoration was begun, which included the establishment of a fifth province, named Valentia (p. 242f.). Indeed, Claudian hints at naval activity in the far north,[37] and victorious terms must have been dictated, for the Notitia subsequently records four regiments of Attacotti in imperial service on the Continent.

A first priority was the reconstruction of the frontier. The treacherous record of the *areani* now resulted in their removal, and this together with the decision not to re-occupy the outpost forts meant that much greater reliance came to be placed upon the federate tribes of the Lowlands; there were now no Roman forces north of the Wall. This change probably marks the inception of a new arrangement under which the Votadini were granted more complete independence with client or federate status, and the assumption of responsibility for frontier protection under their own leaders. The reality of such a change in their status at some moment in the fourth century receives confirmation from the title accorded to one of their chieftains, Paternus by name, who was the grandfather of Cunedda. In the genealogy this man figures as Padarn Pesrut, the second word signifying 'he of the scarlet cloak'; with little doubt this title indicates the award of some form of Roman military authority, and finds parallels in the gift of insignia and even of military rank to chieftains on other frontiers of the empire.[38] The date of Paternus depends upon that assigned to Cunedda, upon which there is not yet general agreement; but it will be shown later on (p. 426) that the most probable period for Cunedda's migration is about 430, which would place 369 comfortably within the *floruit* of his grandfather. A similar arrangement may possibly have been made with the dynasty of Strathclyde, whose kingdom was centred on the tribal territory of the Damnonii. The pedigree of this royal house, too, can be traced back to the fourth century, when the names of two successive rulers are given as Cluim (= Clemens) and Cinhil (= Quintilus): very approximately their *floruits* can be reckoned as *c.* 350–80 and *c.* 380–410. The adoption of Latin names at just this period is suggestive.

Undoubtedly these arrangements reflect the reduced importance of the wall itself as a frontier; its failure as a barrier had been demonstrated by recent events. Against mobile and amphibious enemies something more was required than a wall which could be so easily turned: this is the context of the increased concern for coastal and urban defences farther south which is one of the features of the Theodosian restoration.

In assessing the amount of damage done by the invaders and the localities where it took place we are hampered once again by the deficiencies of archaeological reports. The tradition of destruction at this time is so strong that any rebuilding is almost automatically assumed to be necessitated by hostile action, and it is difficult to decide how far Theodosian reconstruction was motivated by other causes, such as gradual decay or the needs of military reorganisation.

All the remaining outpost forts now ceased to be held, if indeed they had survived the troubles of 360 and 365. On the wall itself the abandonment of many civil settlements outside forts (in so far as they have been tested by excavation) is convincing evidence of disaster; and it is certainly true that extensive patching and rebuilding was undertaken in the forts themselves, and at some of them gates were walled up.[39]

The programme of restoration has also been recognised at forts farther south, such as Chester-le-Street, Papcastle, Bainbridge and

Ilkley, while the forts at Overborough and perhaps at Brough (Derbyshire) were put out of commission.

This evidence, when combined with the account of Ammianus Marcellinus, leaves little doubt that there had been a grave military disaster. Our assessment of its severity will affect the view we take of the Notitia Dignitatum and the homogeneity of its contents. In this document the garrison of the wall appears as old-style alae and cohorts with few changes from the third-century position (p. 262f.). Is it credible that all these regiments survived the disaster to appear in a list of later date or that, despite the attested activity of their general, Fullofaudes, they remained uninvolved in the struggle?

It is true that Theodosius was able to recall deserters and stragglers to the colours. Did he re-create the cohorts and alae of the wall as if nothing had happened? Two considerations suggest that he did not. The first is the changes which can now be perceived in the planning and character of the wall-forts themselves, suggesting as they do a type of garrison different from its predecessors. The second is the contrast in types of garrison shown by the two halves of chapter xl of the Notitia (p. 262). The wall-forts are garrisoned in the list by alae and cohorts, such as nowhere else in the empire appear in such numbers or uniformity; but the other forts controlled by the Duke, in Yorkshire and Durham, are shown with garrisons of a totally different type. We have seen (pp. 263–6) that this part of the Duke's list is best explained as setting forth part of Theodosius' reconstruction of the latter region. If entirely new regiments had to be formed or brought in to hold the forts of Durham and Yorkshire it is very unlikely that old regiments survived on the wall.[40]

On Hadrian's Wall the fourth period of construction, which has been recognised at a number of forts, milecastles and turrets, is firmly attributable, despite the absence of dated inscriptions, to the historical reconstructions of 369 [41] by the discovery of a coin of Valentinian well stratified beneath it at Birdoswald and by the cumulative evidence provided by a careful study of associated pottery. Some of the actual work of rebuilding may have been carried out by corvées provided by the civitates of southern Britain, and even at the expense of private individuals, if the inscriptions noted on p. 198 above may be connected with a tradition preserved by Gildas; this suggestion of Mr C. E. Stevens seems the most likely context for them,[42] and it would account for the differences observed from normal military

394

masonry. Not only is the technique of the rebuilding notably inferior to earlier work, but the regular planning which had always been a feature of Roman forts seems to have been abandoned. At Chesterholm the headquarters building was converted to provide storechambers and living-quarters, and much the same adaptations are known at South Shields and Housesteads; and at the latter fort pottery found in the granaries suggested that they, too, had been converted to domestic uses. Moreover, some evidence suggests the presence of women and children within the forts: at Housesteads trinkets were found in the barrack-rooms and at Chesters infant-burials came to light in an interval-tower.[43]

Though individually these facts have little weight, cumulatively they do suggest that arrangements for the defence of the wall were changed. The forts now seem to resemble fortified villages, as if the garrisons were no longer regular limitanei but an irregular militia. In North Africa the frontier had long been garrisoned by territorial farmer-soldiers, and in the Notitia we find control of them in the hands of *praepositi limitis* under the command of the *dux*. This cannot have been the system in northern Britain, for there the Duke's list contains no such officers. But if Theodosius transferred *laeti* or *gentiles* to the area from Germany these would be under *praefecti* independent of the Duke's command. Chapter xlii of the *Notitia*, which lists the *laeti* and *gentiles* of the western provinces, breaks off before it reaches Britain, but at Birdoswald it was noted that some of the coarse pottery of this period appeared to be of Rhineland origin, a fact which might support the suggestion of such a transfer. It is known that Alamannic soldiers were serving in Britain at this time, since in 372 Fraomar was sent over to take command of them with the rank of tribune;[44] but as both this rank and their description as a numerus both imply a regular formation, they clearly are not what we are seeking.

Farther south, forts were rebuilt in more regular manner and in a better style, as at Bainbridge and Ilkley. The contrast with the Wall-forts reinforces the deduction that the garrisons were different. A new system of signal stations seems to have been constructed along the road south of Carlisle, where two survive at Wreay Hall and Barrock Fell.

Now, too, the coast of Yorkshire and Durham was provided with a series of signal and look-out towers running from Flamborough Head probably as far as the Tyne mouth. They occupy high headlands, and contained towers which may have risen to 90 or 100 feet, and were clearly intended to co-ordinate naval action by flotillas based on the estuaries of Humber, Tees and Tyne.[45] They probably came under the Count of the Saxon Shore. It is clear that this command was re-organised by Theodosius, for at least one fort, that at Portchester, was abandoned now in favour of a new base at Bitterne near South-ampton, and troop movements at other forts best fall into place at this moment.

On the west coasts much evidence is still to seek, but in Wales the fort of Caernarvon was rebuilt and so, probably, was Forden Gaer; coin evidence suggests that other forts also were held, such as Caer-hun and Brecon, but whether they were rebuilt and how they were garrisoned are questions impossible to answer owing to the distur-bance of the upper levels by ploughing. The fleet-base at Holyhead, with its close resemblance to contemporary naval fortifications on the Rhine, also seems best attributable to Theodosius. There is evidence too for a naval yard in the Bristol Channel at this period, for a *praefectus reliquationis*, T. Flavius Senilis, dedicated a mosaic at the Lydney temple shortly after 367.

In the south of Britain the damage inflicted by the invaders is hard to detect. There seem to be no special concentrations of coin-hoards. None of the towns appears to have been affected, and signs of damage even at villas are rare. Occasionally we may suspect violent destruc-tion, as at Brislington, Somerset, where human skulls and building debris down the well and burnt roofing tiles in the villa itself suggest as much, and the coins go down to Constantius II; but in general it is only possible to say that a number of villas appears to have gone out of occupation about this time, to judge by their coin-lists, though the great majority continued to exist. Raiders frequently achieved their purpose, we may suppose, without setting fire to the house. Indeed, the disappearance of slaves and coloni amid the general confusion may well have been as disastrous to the continued life of a villa as the slaughter of its owner or the sacking of its buildings. Far too little modern work has been devoted to villas, and old accounts are too indefinite for it to be possible to map the passage of the raiders. There is a group of some seven villas in Somerset and five in Hamp-shire which may have been affected; and scattered examples, such as the Park Street villa, Hertfordshire, or Langton, Yorkshire, have been identified in other areas. On the borders of Dorset the crisis was sufficiently severe to cause the blocking of the main road from Sarum to Dorchester by an extension of the earthwork known as Bokerly Dyke; but the road was shortly afterwards re-opened. The effects of disorder in the countryside are also reflected in the history of the pottery industry. The factories which for so long had produced black-burnished ware (p. 330) seem to have gone out of production, as does the important Hartshill–Mancetter group; after 369 the military markets were supplied very largely by the kilns at Crambeck in Yorkshire. This centre had been of comparative insignificance until the disturbances of 367; but the potters then seized the opportunity presented to them of capturing the waiting market, and their production became so large and so widely distributed in the north that it has become the main means of identifying occupation during the last third of the century; indeed, its distribution has been used to demonstrate conclusively that the Wall remained the frontier of Roman Britain after 369.[46] In general, the effect of the raids appears to have been to leave much of the market in the hands of a few large production-centres, such as the Nene Valley potteries, and those of the Farnham and Oxford districts and the New Forest. Small producers for the most part disappeared, though in the south very crude wares, somewhat home-made in character, began to make their appearance. The results of this centralisation were disastrous later, when in the early fifth century these factories themselves ceased to produce.

The measures taken by Theodosius included assistance to the towns,[47] and it has been suggested on p. 290f. that it was he who ordered the external towers which were added to their walls at about this period. The purpose of these towers was to support ballistae and stone-throwing machines which could give covering fire along the face of the wall and keep attackers at a distance. Such engines would probably call for the services of a small specialist force.

There is no record of town garrisons in Britain in the Notitia, but the presence of troops in some of them seems indicated by the distribution of certain types of military belt-plates and buckles datable to the late fourth century and later. These are often popularly taken to indicate the presence of 'Germanic mercenaries'; but it is a fallacy to suppose that items of military uniform indicate nationality or pay-status. The earliest examples are of continental manufacture,

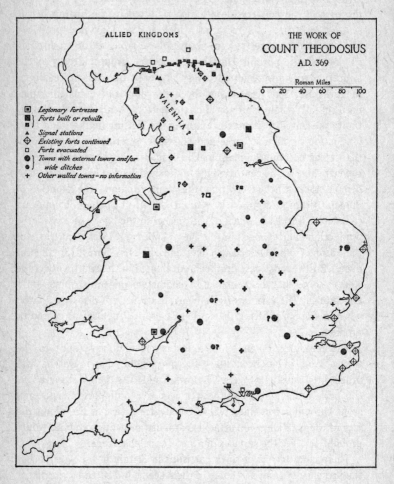

ALLIED KINGDOMS

THE WORK OF
COUNT THEODOSIUS
A.D. 369

Roman Miles

0   20   40   60   80   100

VALENTIA?

☐ } Legionary fortresses
■ } Forts built or rebuilt
▲ Signal stations
◈ Existing forts continued
□ Forts evacuated
● } Towns with external towers and/or
● } wide ditches
+ Other walled towns – no information

13   The work of Count Theodosius in Britain

398

and appear to have formed part of the uniform of regular troops transferred to Britain under Theodosius. Before long, however, British-made examples of this equipment appear as local workshops went into production. Examples of both types have been found in forts of the Saxon Shore, but they also occur in some numbers else-where in southern Britain, particularly in the towns. They must in-dicate the presence of regular troops, perhaps in small detachments; and the reason why they do not figure in the Duke's list is likely to be that they were not under his command but under that of the *vicarius*. The insignia of the Vicar of Britain at the head of chapter xxiii of the Notitia, alone among *vicarii*, consists of castellated en-closures instead of representative maidens; this must surely indicate that he controlled troops. City garrisons seem the most likely kind.

The wide range and extraordinary thoroughness of the reorganisa-tion carried out by Count Theodosius are now clear (fig. 13) and there can be no doubt of its effectiveness. It was, indeed, the last constructive large-scale intervention of the central government in Romano-British affairs, and though the action of usurpers and the deterioration of Roman military power on the Continent in due course led to the evacuation of almost all the armed forces in Britain, the work of Theodosius in the towns of the island enabled them to hold out far into the following century. Evidence is accruing that in towns as well as villas the last quarter of the fourth century was in general a period of great prosperity.

1. *Pax trium Augustorum*, etc.
2. *RIB*, 2291＝*ILS*, 8928.
3. *Viriconium＝Briconium*.
4. *Panegyrici Latini*, viii (v), 12, 1.
5. II Augusta and XX Valeria Victrix. Why Legio VI Victrix was omitted is not known. Possibly this legion had opposed his elevation.
6. See J. S. Johnson, *Britannia*, i (1970), pp. 240 ff.
7. *Litus Saxonicum* (1961), 29–30.
8. *de Caesaribus*, xxxix, 41. *Allectus . . . Qui cum eius* (sc. *Carausii*) *permissu summae rei praeesset.* Eutropius (ix, 22) calls him merely *socius eius*.
9. *Panegyrici Latini*, viii (v), 16, 2. Allectus *adeo . . . properavit ad mortem ut nec explicaret aciem nec omnes copias quas trahebat instruxerit, sed cum veteribus illius coniurationis auctoribus et mer-*

cenariis cuneis barbarorum tanti apparatus oblitus inruerit . . . nemo fere Romanus occiderit imperio vincente Romano.

10. *Panegyrici Latini*, viii (v), 19, 1–2.

11. *RIB*, 1912; see pp. 242, 384. The inscription dates to the period 296–305; probability suggests that it was erected before 300.

12. *Panegyrici Latini*, vi (vii), 7, 2: an earlier campaign in 296 or early 297 is perhaps to be deduced from the statement in the Panegyric of 297 (viii (v), 20, 3), that tribes in the far north of the island are now obedient to the emperor's will.

13. Housesteads, *RIB*, 1613, and Birdoswald, *RIB*, 1912.

14. Damage on the Wall includes the forts of Benwell (*AA*[4], xix (1941), 34), Haltonchesters (*JRS*, lii (1962), 164), Great Chesters (*AA*[2], xxiv (1903), 31, 51), Housesteads (*AA*[4], xxxix (1961), 287) and probably Birdoswald (*CW*[2], xxxi (1931), 128); perhaps milecastles 40 and 48 (*CW*[2], xiii (1913), 321) and the following turrets 49b, 50b (*ibid.*) and 44b (*AA*[2], xxiv (1903), 13). The vici at Old Carlisle and perhaps Benwell have to be included (P. Salway, *The Frontier People of Roman Britain* (1965), pp. 76, 118) and probably the villa at Old Durham. There was destruction at Corbridge (*ibid.*, p. 54), where burnt layers have been recorded (*AA*[4], xxxiii (1955), 246), and at Carrawburgh, where the Mithraeum was burnt and pillaged (*AA*[4], xxix (1951), 27). The outpost forts of Bewcastle (*CW*[2], xxxviii (1938), 208), Risingham and High Rochester (*Northumberland County History*, xv (1940), 107), were also affected. At Malton (Yorks) corn from the granaries was taken out and burnt along the rampart; the excavators took this to mark an evacuation (P. Corder, *Defences of the Roman Fort at Malton* (1930), pp. 34, 66–7).

15. At Rudchester and Haltonchesters excavations have shown that parts at any rate of these forts were unoccupied between 296 and 369. It remains to be seen whether they were wholly evacuated, or whether much smaller garrisons, needing less extensive accommodation, were present. The evidence of the *Notitia* (p. 262f.) would suggest (but does not prove) that the latter is the true explanation: if it turns out that two adjacent forts on the Wall were left empty by Constantius I close to the main eastern route southwards from Scotland, it would throw interesting light on the nature of his restoration of the frontier. At present it is difficult to see what alternative arrangements can have been made.

16. *RIB*, 1912; see pp. 242, 382.

17. In M. G. Jarrett and B. Dobson, *Britain and Rome* (1966), pp. 121 ff.

18. No coins later than *c.* 270–4 have been found in third-century deposits on Hadrian's Wall. This fact cannot in itself be taken to indicate the end of Wall-period II at about this date, for coins later than *c.* 270 but earlier than Carausius are everywhere rare in Britain. It would be more indicative of a depleted garrison in the later third century if radiates of *c.* 270 could be shown to be rare on the Wall.

The absence of published information about many excavations both old and new prevents accurate assessment; but the percentages of radiates to other coins in recent excavations at Carrawburgh (43 per cent) and Housesteads (62 per cent) – at Birdoswald in 1929 it was 17 per cent – give little support to such a theory.

19. An alternative view of events in Britain during Constantius' reign is possible. According to this, Allectus used troops from the Pennines, not from the Wall, for his operations in the south; these suffered heavy casualties and had to be replaced by new formations, much as listed in *Notitia Dignitatum Occ.*, xl, though this list as it stands incorporates later information. On his recovery of Britain, Constantius found military installations both on the Wall and in the Pennines in bad shape due to lack of maintenance, and determined on a complete restoration. There was no attack from the north in 196; indeed, the Picts sent complimentary messages (as is implied by the panegyrist of 297, p. 400, note 12 above). The signs of fire and tumbled masonry listed on p. 400, note 14, were due to the demolition of crumbling buildings, which was an essential preliminary to rebuilding. In 306 Constantius attacked the Picts in anticipation of, or retaliation for, a threat to Roman interests. This sequence of events has not been adopted in the text, since the facts on balance favour the traditional interpretation; but more evidence is needed to decide the point.

20. *RIB*, 488.

21. The *portae decumana* and *principalis sinistra*.

22. This may have been the occasion of the grant to London of the title *Augusta*, which it certainly possessed later in the century, Ammianus Marcellinus, xxvii, 8, 7; xxviii, 3, 4; see p. 241 above.

23. *Panegyrici Latini*, vi (vii), 7, 1–2.

24. Aurelius Victor, *de Caesaribus*, xxxix, 41.

25. Libanius, *Oratio*, lix (Teubner), 139–41, who mentions that Constans was accompanied by only 100 men; Firmicus Maternus, *de errore prof. relig.*, xxxviii, 6; *Codex Theodos.*, xi, 16, 5, for an edict issued at Boulogne on 25 January 343.

26. Ammianus Marcellinus, xxx, 7, 3; A. H. M. Jones, *The Later Roman Empire* (1964), p. 124.

27. As a brief reference back by Ammianus (xxviii, 3, 8), to events recorded in his lost books attests.

28. The word *areani* is usually emended to *arcani* in the text of Ammianus, to yield the meaning 'intelligence agents'. *Areani* may mean 'Men of the sheep-folds', which would have reference to the native-style farmsteads in which they now maintained themselves; alternatively, it may be taken as 'Men of the open spaces'. In either case it would be a customary, rather than official, term, derived perhaps from army slang.

29. *Archaeological Journal*, xcvii (1940), 135.

30. Cf. also the Richborough portrait-pendant, J. P. Bushe-Fox, *Richborough*, iv (1949), pl. xlii, 171.

31. Little is known of the vicarii of Britain. In 319 Pacatianus held the office (*Codex Theodosianus*, xi, 7, 2); one of Martinus' immediate successors was Alypius (Ammianus Marcellinus, xxiii, 1, 3). Two late vicars, probably both in the reign of Honorius, were Victorinus (Rutilius Namatianus, *de reditu suo*, 493–510) and Chrysanthus (Socrates, *Eccl. Hist.*, vii, 12 and 17). Still less is known of the governors. Flavius Sanctus, a connection of Ausonius, was one of them about the middle of the fourth century (Ausonius, *Parentalia* (Loeb), xviii, 7–8).

32. Ammianus Marcellinus, xviii, 2, 3; Libanius, *oratio* xviii, 82 (Teubner); Julian, *Letter to the Athenians*, 279–80, says he had 600 ships, 400 of which were built in less than ten months; Zosimus, iii, 5, mentions 800 ships.

33. For the date of Carausius II see J. P. C. Kent, *Numismatic Chronicle*,[6] xvii (1957), 78–83.

34. Ammianus Marcellinus, xx, 1; xx, 9, 9; Julian, *Letter to the Athenians*, 281.

35. Described as *comes maritimi tractus*; see p. 242.

36. *Zosimus*, iv, 35, 5.

37. Claudian, *de quarto consulatu Honorii*, 23–44.

38. A. H. M. Jones, *The Later Roman Empire* (1964), ii, p. 611.

39. There was damage at Corbridge despite its defensive walls, *AA*,[4] xxxiii (1955), 248; xxxviii (1960), 154–7; cf. the coin hoards mentioned in *AA*,[4] xv (1938), 261–2; the *mansio* seems to have been abandoned now. The vici at Benwell, Housesteads and Old Carlisle were deserted; that at Piercebridge farther south may possibly have been rebuilt in 369. The villa at Old Durham seems also to have been destroyed. On these sites see P. Salway, *Frontier People of Roman Britain* (1965). On the Wall itself signs of destruction have been noted at Chesters (*AA*,[2] vii (1876), 211) and considerable alterations after destruction or demolition at Birdoswald (*CW*,[2] xxx (1930), 169–71); at Housesteads considerable alterations took place, but there is no evidence of disaster. Attention may also be drawn here to the arm wrenched from a silver statuette of the Victory of Legio vi (*RIB*, 582), which was found in Lancashire, and to the fine gilt-bronze leg hacked off an over life-sized imperial statue which was found in Roxburghshire. Sir George Macdonald (*JRS*, xvi (1926), 7–16) showed that both represent loot, the second probably, the first certainly, from the fortress of York. They must surely be related either to the events of 196 or those of 367.

40. To avoid the logic of this conclusion it is necessary *either* to assume that, despite the evidence cited, casualties on the wall in 367 were slight, whatever happened farther south – an unreasonable solution – *or* to accept the suggestion put forward on p. 401, note 19, that the first part of chapter xl of the Notitia, listing the Duke's

troops in Yorkshire and Durham, reflects essentially the restoration of Constantius in 296. The weight of the evidence is against this theory too, and it involves rejecting a Pictish invasion in 296. Nevertheless, it would ease the dilemma of 369 by removing the necessity of believing that the list of garrisons on the wall is necessarily of different date from that of the first part of the Duke's list. Both halves of the list, the old-fashioned cohorts and alae on the wall and the new equites and numeri south of it, could now equally be regarded as surviving through the early fourth century right down to the date of the Notitia's first composition (*c.* 395). But though such a solution simplifies the problem of the Notitia, it overrides the considerable body of evidence that the military disaster of 367–8 was so serious as to make a reorganisation of forces extremely probable.

41. Ammianus Marcellinus, xxviii, 3, 7; *limitesque vigiliis tuebatur et praetenturis.*

42. *English Historical Review,* lvi (1941), 359.

43. For sprawling buildings at Birdoswald see *CW*[2], (1931), 129; for additional buildings inserted at Housesteads *AA*[2], xxv (1904), 241 ff., *AA*[4], ix (1932), 223 ff.; at Chesterholm *AA*[4], viii (1931), 195, ix (1932), 217; at Chesters, Bruce, *Handbook to the Roman Wall* (11th edition, 1957), p. 94. For principia at Chesterholm see *AA*[4], xiii (1936), 225–9; at Housesteads *AA*[2], xxv (1904), 223–5, and trinkets, *ibid.,* 235; at South Shields Richmond, *Guide to Roman Fort* (1953), p. 6; Housesteads granaries *AA*[4], ix (1932), 224; for burials Bruce, *op. cit.,* 91. At Malton twenty-nine such burials belong to the period 296–367, P. Corder, *Defences of the Roman Fort at Malton* (1930), p. 67.

44. Ammianus Marcellinus, xxix, 4, 7; see p. 270, note 5.

45. Compare the description given by Vegetius (iv, 37), of the scout-craft and warships in British waters, which are the essential complement of the scheme (p. 253).

46. J. P. Gillam, *Carnuntina: Römische Forschungen in Niederösterreich* (1956), pp. 64–77.

47. Ammianus Marcellinus, xxviii, 3, 2 and 3, 7.

17

The end of Roman Britain

In 370 Britain was once more enjoying firm government and effective defences: forty years later she ceased to be part of the Roman Empire. The civilisation and prosperity of the island during these years had never been higher; but the growing power of external barbarians constituted a danger both to Britain and to the whole western empire which by slow degrees overbore resistance. The plight of a rich people entirely dependent for defence upon a power whose interests in the final analysis were centred elsewhere is not without its interest today.

Not that consciousness of separate interest was felt in Britain. The imperial system was so old and so full of prestige that for generations to come the British continued to regard themselves as in some sense members of it still. But the repeated withdrawal of troops between 383 and 407 meant that all too soon the defence of the island devolved upon local effort. This was a responsibility which by tradition or experience the provincials here as elsewhere were all too unfitted to undertake.

A contributing cause of this situation was that very consciousness of being an integral and significant part of the empire. In 383 and again in 407 usurpers set up by the army in Britain took large forces over the Channel to support their claims to rule. Few if any of these troops returned, any more than did those who were recalled by the central government for the defence of Italy.

The rebellion of 383 was the work of Magnus Maximus. A native of Spain, he had seen service in Britain under Count Theodosius, and at the time of his revolt was probably *dux Britanniarum*. He was a capable commander, but discontented with his slow promotion; the support of his troops was easily gained, since the emperor Gratian had become unpopular with the regular army because of the favouritism he showed to his German levies. Maximus, it seems, was popular in Britain, for he was long remembered as a hero in Celtic folk-memory and tradition, and Gildas preserves a story that he was accompanied to Gaul by many British volunteers. He held the West until his death at the hands of Theodosius I in 388. Orosius judged that his vigorous and upright character would have fitted him to rule had it not been for his illegal seizure of power.[1]

His expedition involved the evacuation of many of the forts still held in Britain; the garrisons concerned were apparently those of the western Pennines and North Wales and included Legio xx from Chester (p. 266, fig. 11). These positions were never re-occupied. He is often credited with the final evacuation of Hadrian's Wall, but this view can no longer be maintained. It was based on the belief that coins later than those of Gratian (367–83) were absent from forts on the Wall, a belief now known to be mistaken. Though few in number such coins exist.[2] Their rarity can be accounted for, partly by the deficiencies of the archaeological record (and the casualness with which finds from excavations have been – and still are – treated), but mainly by the almost universal scarcity of coins of this period as site-finds throughout Roman Britain, and especially in the north. Moreover, the quantity of pottery from the levels of the latest period is normally large, and by comparison with that from earlier deposits is suggestive of a longer occupation than fourteen years.

The troops which Maximus took with him were no doubt rewarded with promotion into the field-army; and, indeed, the Notitia preserves a record of the Seguntienses – apparently the former garrison of *Segontium* (Caernarvon) – among the *auxilia palatina* in Illyricum.[3] If they were thus raised in grade it is unlikely that their return to Britain as limitanei was envisaged; and there arises the question what arrangements were made by Maximus to fill the vacuum caused by their departure. The island was beginning to be denuded of its manpower.

Now that we can believe in the continued occupation of the Wall, the problem is not so grave as it once appeared. Maximus is known to have conducted a campaign against the Picts and Scots in the year before his rebellion.[4] The success of this and the continued existence of the powerful friendly kingdoms of the Votadini and Strathclyde north of the frontier must have seemed to him sufficient security for a reduction of garrisons behind the Wall. Indeed, it is probable that he created a third friendly dynasty in south-west Scotland in the area of the Novantae: at any rate, the dark-age dynasty of Galloway, alone of those in Scotland, counted Maximus as the founder of its line.

In North Wales the situation was more serious, for with the removal of Legio xx from Chester, and the evacuation of Caernarvon, a serious gap in the defences was opened, of which the Irish soon took advantage. It used to be held that the solution to the problem which Maximus adopted was the transplantation of Cunedda and a strong force of Votadini to North Wales to replace the regular forces; but the chronology indicated by Cunedda's pedigree will not fit this supposition (p. 426). Nevertheless, the striking part played by Maximus in Welsh tradition, and the ancestry of several lines of Welsh kings attributed to him, strongly suggest that in this region too allied native kingdoms may have been established. If so, they lacked the requisite strength, for by the end of the century Scots from Ireland were settling in the Lleyn peninsula (Caernarvonshire), while in Pembrokeshire and the Gower peninsula of South Wales another Irish tribe, the Deisi, are recorded. At Wroxeter Irish attackers may have successfully looted the town. This requires confirmation by modern excavation, but Thomas Wright who dug there a century ago records two late-fourth-century coin hoards, one of them accompanying the skeleton of an old man who seems to have hidden himself in the hypocausts of the public baths: Wright considered that the baths themselves had been burnt.

After the death of Maximus the western provinces came under the rule of Valentinian ii, who was only a boy. No doubt in Britain the administration carried on, but there are indications that Picts as well as Irish continued to raid, no doubt with relative impunity. Both were sea-borne and could plunder where they willed; the Picts had no need to penetrate the philo-Roman kingdoms of the Lowlands and the unrewarding stretches of northern England, when richer plunder could be won from descents on the south. It was not until the period 396–8 that the central government turned its attention to the military problems of Britain. At that time Stilicho, the Vandal general who was the power behind the throne of the young emperor Honorius, ordered some sort of expedition, whether or not he took personal command. Our only source of information about it is found in various references to the achievements of Stilicho in the poems of

Claudian. These naturally lack precision, but they suggest naval activity against Irish, Picts and Saxons;[5] by 399 security had been achieved.[6]

But though he could mount a punitive expedition, Stilicho lacked the strength to augment the British garrison [7] (p. 267f). Indeed, even the *status quo* was impossible to maintain. Troops were pressingly required for the defence of Italy, and in 401 we find him withdrawing forces from Britain for the war against Alaric.[8] It seems clear that this movement must have deprived the command of the Duke, and probably also that of the Count of the Saxon Shore, of all effectiveness, if indeed they survived at all; and as already explained (p. 269), this is the most likely occasion for the establishment, by way of compensation, of a small field-army in Britain itself under the *comes Britanniarum*. The Notitia records a number of British regiments serving in Europe and even in Egypt and the East; some of them may have been formed from the survivors of Maximus' volunteers, but Stilicho's need was great enough to leave no possible sources of recruitment untapped. Even Attacotti were soon to be found among the auxilia palatina.[9] Thus in the interests of the empire Britain lost not only a large part of its remaining garrison, but also, it seems, many of its own young men, whose services were shortly to be needed at home.

A few years later, in 407, another and final withdrawal took place. This time it was the work of a usurper, the last of three set up, as Maximus had been, by the army in Britain. The soldiers had legitimate grievances against the central government. In the first place they were now too few to fulfil their task successfully, and the burden was considerable: Irish records, for instance, describe a harrying of the southern coasts by Niall of the Nine Hostages, a high king of Ireland, which may have occurred in 405. In the second place a clear division of interest was opening between the government's concentration on the defence of the empire's heart and the local interests of the troops, many of whom had close ties with their garrison stations. Promotion to the ranks of the comitatenses cannot have been regarded as an unqualified benefit, when it involved abandoning their homes. Nevertheless, they still possessed a sense of their ultimate responsibilities.

The chronology of the year 406 is too uncertain to tell us whether Marcus, the first of these short-lived pretenders, was made emperor in Britain as a result of these general grievances, or whether his elevation was related to the serious crisis which developed in the autumn. We know nothing of him save that he was a soldier, and was soon killed because he did not please the army. Perhaps he was the Count of Britain. Late in the year news came of a barbarian invasion of Gaul, which culminated at the end of December in a massive crossing of the frozen Rhine by hordes of Vandals, Alans and Sueves, which the Roman forces on the Rhine were too depleted to resist. The army of Britain – so Zosimus informs us [10] – became alarmed lest the enemy should cross the Channel; but the sequel suggests that he has too narrowly interpreted their feelings. Stilicho was fully engaged in Italy and in the Balkans: it was hopeless to look for timely help from him. If the West was to be saved, intervention from Britain was required. Yet in Britain itself some appear to have taken another view – that Britain held first claim on the forces it contained: it was sufficient to obey orders and defend the island.

After the short-lived Marcus, the next to become emperor was Gratian, a native Briton who was a member of the urban aristocracy.[11] His elevation took place not later than the beginning of November 406, and he reigned four months. By this time the seriousness of affairs in Gaul was becoming obvious, and the army wished to cross there; but Gratian made no move, which when his background is remembered is not surprising, and he was cut down.

Now the choice fell on Constantine III, a common soldier but one of some ability, who ably played upon the British and imperial associations of his own name, and renamed his sons Julian and Constans. There was need for speed if the Channel ports were not to fall, and at once he crossed to Gaul, sending ahead officers to take command of the surviving forces there, and by able soldiering and diplomacy he restored the situation; in the following year (408) he won control of Spain. It seems clear that Constantine represented the view that the defence of the West required an Augustus in the prefecture of the Gauls as in the time of Constans, Julian and Valentinian, and this was a view shared by the majority of the army of Britain; they realised that the defence of Britain was inseparable from that of Gaul. Marcus and Gratian, on the other hand, may have possessed a narrower vision of their responsibility which was unacceptable to the army. By the beginning of 409 Honorius himself was persuaded to see the validity of the former view, and he extended recognition to Constantine. The latter, however, again like Maximus, was led on to intervene unsuccessfully and fatally in Italy itself; his hold on Spain was broken by the rebellion there of his British *magister militum*, Gerontius; the barbarians whom he had settled in Gaul broke out once more, and he himself was compelled to surrender to the forces of Honorius and suffer execution in the summer of 411. Once again a usurper had failed to content himself with the prefecture of the Gauls, and once again he had broken himself as a result. But this time there was a difference. Britain had virtually no forces left, and Gaul itself was in a turmoil of barbarian invasion and peasant revolt. Though Honorius regained nominal control of the Gallic provinces for a short while later in 413, real power there was in the hands of the Visigoths and Burgundians; there were no troops to spare, and it was not until 417–18 that imperial forces were active once more in the north. In the meanwhile Roman control of Britain had lapsed, and in the event was never to be reimposed. How this came about must now be examined.

The separation from Rome in 410 came not as a 'withdrawal of the legions' – almost all effective forces had long ago gone to Italy or Gaul – but as a hiatus in the apparatus of central government. Our principal information about what happened comes from Zosimus, who, though not himself a contemporary, can be shown to derive much of his material from those who were. After describing the difficulties in which Constantine found himself as a result of the rebellion of Gerontius, together with an uprising of the Germans settled in Gaul which he instigated, Zosimus then proceeds:

'The barbarians across the Rhine attacked everywhere with all their power, and brought the inhabitants of Britain and some of the nations of Gaul to the point of revolting from Roman rule and living on their own, no longer obedient to Roman laws. The Britons took up arms and, braving danger for their own independence, freed their cities from the barbarians threatening them; and all Armorica and the other provinces of Gaul copied the British example and freed themselves in the same way, expelling their Roman governors and establishing their own administration as best they could.' [12]

A few paragraphs later, after dealing with other matters, Zosimus mentions a letter of Honorius to the cities of Britain in which he told them to undertake their own defence – an instruction which can best be understood as the reply to a previous message to the emperor from Britain itself, reporting the steps which had been taken and asking for help. Further information comes from a mid-fifth-century Gallic chronicle, in which a devastation of Britain by the Saxons is recorded in 410; and Procopiush summed up the situation in the following words: 'Constantine was defeated in battle. But in spite of this the Romans were never able to recover Britain, which from that time onward continued to be ruled by usurpers (tyrants)'.[13]

Much has been built upon the slender foundations of this outline. Professor E. A. Thompson, struck by the phrase 'living on their own, no longer obedient to Roman laws', has argued persuasively that what happened was not a rebellion against this or that emperor, but a total rejection of Rome and her empire which culminated in a social revolution on egalitarian lines.[14] On this theory the subsequent appeal to Honorius came from the threatened land-owning class. It is known, of course, that such a peasant pipe-dream was fleetingly successful in Brittany a few years later; but the actions reported in Britain in 410 are not consistent with a peasant revolution. They were taken by the curial class in the interests of the towns, which they freed from danger. If an outbreak of slaves and coloni did take advantage of the Saxon raid of 410 it was soon suppressed and did not play a significant part in events. The truth probably is that expulsions of Roman administrators came to be associated with such outbreaks in the fifth century, and that the motives and perpetrators of this one were not sufficiently distinguished by Zosimus.

Dr J. N. L. Myres has indicated the significance of the Pelagian heresy to the political background of this period.[15] Pelagius himself was·a Briton, but there is no evidence that he ever returned home after his departure for Rome as a young man, when about 380 he set out to embark on a legal career. In Rome he came out in opposition to Augustine's view on the part played by divine grace in the Christian life. He could not accept that man's capacity for good is most effective when his will is surrendered as a vehicle for the divine will, or believe that human beings are utterly dependent for salvation on the grace (or *favour*) of God because the frailty of their natures renders them completely unable to achieve it on their own. These ideas were repugnant to him, for he himself took what in reality was the more superficial position: that man is the captain of his soul and by the exercise of unaided human will can be the architect of his own salvation. His heresy, in fact, was a denial of original sin. Dependence upon divine grace was particularly objectionable to him because of the contemporary overtones of the word *gratia* on the human and political plane, where it stood for undue influence and favouritism.

Pelagianism had gained a strong hold on the ruling classes in Britain, as is evident from subsequent events, though there is no evidence that hitherto its ideas had penetrated the lower orders of society. Yet, since it was opposed to the corrupt practices which had long disfigured the administration of law and government, and placed great weight on man's ability to win salvation by his own efforts, it is reasonable to recognise that its influence may have strengthened the will of those who were prepared to assume responsibility for action. But the action taken was not a breach with Rome: the subsequent appeal to Honorius makes this very clear. What occurred was an ejection of Constantine's administrators in an attempt to resume relations with the legitimate emperor.

The party in Britain which four years earlier had eschewed continental adventures had now, in fact, been justified by events. Constantine had proved a total failure: he had removed the garrison of Britain, but could not even hold Gaul. The context of Honorius' letter, addressed to the civitates ($\pi\acute{o}\lambda\epsilon\iota\varsigma$) of Britain, makes it plain that there was no longer a *dux* or *comes Britanniarum* in the island, for otherwise it would have been his duty to organise the defence, and no longer a *vicarius* or governors, to whom otherwise the letter would have gone. The generals had left with their armies, and the administration had been expelled. When the Saxon raids had begun once more early in 410 many influential people had evidently come to the conclusion that resistance would be more effectively organised directly by the people whose lives were at stake than by officials who now lacked any backing. But to expel them, even if it was hoped to obtain subsequent approval or even fresh officials from the legitimate emperor, called for courage; and it exhibited the exercise of a free will which is certainly best understood in terms of Pelagian philosophy.

With the removal of the higher administration, authority must have fallen first into the hands of the provincial or diocesan council, as the only central body representing the civitates. These councils

411

were still active in other provinces, though we know nothing of the British one (p. 238f.). There were probably still small bodies of regular troops garrisoning the walled towns, but to resist the Saxons effectively a wider provincial militia had to be raised. It remained technically illegal for private citizens to take up arms, and C. E. Stevens has suggested that part of the purpose of Honorius' rescript was to authorise the breach of the *lex Julia de vi publica* which had been committed.

For some years to come it is unlikely that there was much political change: as long, indeed, as expectation remained of a resumption of Honorius' authority in Britain. Some scholars still, indeed, believe that official Roman control was re-asserted briefly between 416 and 419, and an army sent over; the theory is based on the conviction that the listing of forces in Britain in the *Notitia Dignitatum*, a document which bears traces of revision down to the 420s, must be taken seriously. This is not the view taken here, for, apart from the manifest confusion of the information contained in the Notitia, it is hard to explain why there is no trace at all in the archaeological record of the money used to pay such troops (p. 416). There were two dangers. One was the outbreak of social revolution, such as actually occurred in Brittany a few years later; the other was the seizure of power by war-leaders who might be tempted to set themselves up as 'tyrants', usurping the functions of government. The first danger was successfully evaded: we have no record of peasant republics in Britain, and much evidence that the land-owning class continued to exist. But the appearance of monarchy could not long be delayed: indeed, the right of military leaders to establish legitimate rule had for centuries been vindicated at Rome itself.

Some of these leaders may have aspired to the title of emperor: Gildas records that the parents of Ambrosius had 'worn the purple'. Such persons will have been leaders of the Romanising party. But the best authenticated British ruler of this period, Vortigern, does not seem to have made this claim. Vortigern, indeed, is a title, not a name; the word means 'high king': Gildas makes the point by referring to him as *superbus tyrannus*. It is significant that Vortigern chose a British, not a Roman, title: the somewhat garbled accounts of his contact with St Germanus show him to be a Pelagian, and we can recognise that by 425, when his rule began, there was a powerful Pelagian party in Britain, anti-Roman in sentiment, but aristocratic in background. The wealth of its members and the strength of their following is graphically described in Constantius' Life of Germanus: when they made their appearance at a large assembly they stood out 'conspicuous for riches, brilliant in dress, and surrounded by a fawning multitude'. They were the successors of what might be called the Little Britain party of 406, and their policies were directed towards maintaining the independence of the island. Vortigern was afraid of Roman intervention,[16] and his settlement of Saxon federates in Kent may have been undertaken with this in mind; indeed, he was prepared to go to dangerous lengths in his use of Saxon assistance.

Powerful though it was, however, this party did not include the majority of Britons. Myres has shown how even families could be divided on the Pelagian issue. But the appeal addressed by the British catholic bishops to the continental church, and ultimately to pope Celestine, for help against the heresy, shows the solid character of the opposition; the readiness of the church to look to Rome, and the success achieved by the mission of St Germanus, must have done much to weaken Vortigern's authority. Again, the appeal for military assistance made to Aetius in or soon after 446 – the so-called Groans of the Britons – has been recognised as originating from this same other side, which had been rightly alarmed by the scale of land-gifts made to the Saxons and was now struggling against their rebellion. Ambrosius succeeded to the leadership of this pro-Roman and catholic party, and it was under him that victory, at least for a time, was won over the German settlers.

The first visit of Germanus, who was at that time bishop of Auxerre, was made in 429, in company with Lupus, bishop of Troyes. Under papal influence they had been chosen by a council of Gallic bishops and sent to Britain to arrest the spread of Pelagianism, and to counter the influence of a certain Agricola, the son of a bishop, who was held to be its leading spirit.

Their preaching was successful, and it culminated in a great assembly at which the Pelagians were routed. Immediately afterwards the bishops visited the shrine of St Alban at *Verulamium*, and the assembly itself was probably therefore held at that town. An incident at it was the healing of the daughter of a 'man of tribunician power', a title which shows that there was still a Roman-type garrison-commander in charge of the city. Shortly after this Germanus, who had once been a general in the Roman army, won the Alleluia

Victory over a force of Picts and Saxons; it was fought in a mountainous district which was possibly in North Wales. He began the campaign by baptising the British forces, and taught them to cry 'Alleluia' at the moment of attack; the terror of this sound unnerved their adversaries, who fled. This incident vividly illustrates the plight of Britain, harassed by invaders and lacking experienced leadership, and it shows that though Christianity had made headway in the towns and among the aristocracy, the peasantry were still largely unbaptised.

Germanus retained his interest in British affairs, for some years later, perhaps in 446–7, he made a second visit, accompanied now by Severus, bishop of Trier; it was on this occasion that he encountered Elafius, *regionis illius primus*, a description which anticipates the πρῶτος τῆς πόλεως (*primus civitatis*) recorded in the southwest in the early sixth century.

These visits show the closeness of the contact which still existed between Britain and the church in Gaul. As late as 455, when the arrangements for fixing Easter were modified by Leo 1, the change was duly adopted by the Celtic church, though by the time a further alteration was introduced some forty years later, communications had been broken.

Almost the last fixed point in British fifth-century chronology is provided by the unsuccessful appeal to Aetius which was recorded by Gildas. 'To Agitius, thrice consul, the Groans of the Britons . . . the barbarians drive us to the sea, the sea drives us to the barbarians; between these two means of death we are either killed or drowned.' By Agitius he means Aetius, the *magister militum* and leading figure in the western empire from 433 to 454. His third consulship was held in 446 and his fourth in 454; the message, therefore, might date from any time between these two dates, though 446 itself is the most likely year. The appeal for help was unanswered, but the date itself has played an important part in attempts to fix the chronology of the Saxon invasions (p. 424f.).

During the first half of the fifth century the civilisation of Roman Britain was running down with increasing speed. The first slow beginnings of this process are recognisable as early as the time of Magnus Maximus. Between 378 and 388 there was a very marked decline in the amount of new currency in circulation, amounting almost to disappearance. To some extent this was offset by the sur-

vival in circulation of earlier issues; but even coins of the House of
Valentinian I are less plentiful on the majority of British sites than
those of Constantius. Though coins of the period 388–402 appeared
in somewhat larger quantity than those of 378–8, there are very few
sites where they approach the proportions of previous decades: at
these few sites, however, the percentage of Theodosian bronze is
very high. This indicates that except at a few apparently exceptional
places, where business continued as usual, or where money was
changed for the collection of taxation, the use of coinage for everyday transactions decreased very notably during the last twenty years
of the fourth century, some time before supplies were interrupted for
good. The reason may have been partly the inflation which continued
serious at this time, and partly also the intermittent difficulty of
obtaining supplies of cash: for both these conditions would favour
the revival of barter. Indeed, this tendency can be observed in
western Britain as early as the age of Valentinian I. It is worth remembering, too, that there was at least one place in Britain which
even in the third century did not use coins at all,[17] the island of
Lundy.

But another of the principal factors influencing the decreasing
availability of coinage was implicit in the government's own attitude
to currency. The foundation of the fourth-century coinage was the
gold solidus. These coins were used for the payment of government
officials and the army, and it was a main preoccupation of the state
to recover the gold thus issued. The bronze currency was used for
this purpose; the gold was recovered by taxation (much of which had
to be paid in this metal) once it had been exchanged by its recipients
for the small bronzes used for everyday transactions. In general,
then, the government was concerned to see that sufficient bronze
was in circulation to recover the gold. But in Britain from the time of
Maximus the number of troops on the pay-roll was greatly reduced,
and was shortly to be decreased even more drastically. This must
have meant a greatly decreased despatch of gold to Britain, and consequently a greatly reduced despatch of copper too: for the government was less concerned for the general utility of the currency as a
means of exchange than as a means of payment and taxation. It did
not therefore interest itself unduly in the plight of provincials, who
found themselves unable to obtain sufficient currency for everyday
purposes.

415

Sites in Britain yield very few copper coins minted after 402. Gold and silver coins are, of course, very rare as site-finds, but finds from hoards make it clear that coins in these metals continued to arrive down to about 406 and, in the case of silver, rather later. It seems probable, then, that payments in gold continued to be received down to this date, but supplies of copper were judged adequate without reinforcement from 402. Silver may have continued to arrive, though in much reduced quantity, after 406 because of the importance of Britain as a source of raw silver.

There had been a re-organisation of the western mints in 395, after which Trier and Arles produced very little bronze; but this reform did not have the catastrophic effect on British supplies of coin which was once imagined, since it has been established that the mint of Rome increased its output to counterbalance the reduction. Issues of the Rome mint in bronze down to 402 are found in some quantity in Britain, but thereafter the supply ceased. Though Constantine III did issue coins, these are very rarely found this side of the Channel, and the later issues of Honorius are virtually absent. From 407 Britain was, in effect, without new coins of any kind. Thereafter the existing coins continued to circulate, getting more and more worn; but increasingly few people found it necessary to use them. They were hoarded instead, and large numbers of these hoards were never recovered, whether because their owners perished in the disturbances of the period or because the hoards themselves became worthless. By 430, as Dr J. P. C. Kent has shown,[18] the use of coinage as a medium of exchange was a thing of the past.

For how long a period the few large potteries which had survived the troubles of 367–8 continued to produce their wares (p. 397) is a question which cannot be answered. They certainly survived down to about 400, for there is no shortage of pottery in association with coins of Honorius. Perhaps the end came about the years 410–20. The life of the factories cannot be unduly prolonged into the fifth century, for no changes of shape or ware have been recognised as succeeding those current in the last quarter of the fourth century; and at *Verulamium* a deposit which could be roughly dated within the period 420–40 contained no recognisably contemporary pottery.

The growing insecurity of transport and the escape of slaves are two factors which might easily have crippled the industry even if no raiders looted the plant. Indeed, since pottery-kilns are relatively simple to construct, it must have been the economic difficulties which were decisive. The disappearance of mass-produced pottery left a void both for the contemporary householder and for the modern archaeologist. The former was sometimes able to eke out his resources with home-made wares, some of which in the south-east bear a curious resemblance to Belgic wares of four centuries earlier. But the majority had to change their habits. Metal-workers still sold bowls and cauldrons; the rich could buy glass; and still possessed plate; for most people and for most purposes vessels of wood or leather no doubt came to suffice.

The Yorkshire signal-stations probably ceased to function soon after 400, for none has more than a single structural period, and the latest coins were not numerous. At least two, those at Huntcliff and Goldsborough came to a violent and even dramatic end at the hands of raiders, and thereafter the coastal approaches lay exposed.

It was probably about the same time that effective occupation ceased on Hadrian's Wall. The precise date is a vexed question. The type of garrison present there in the last period may not have been entitled to regular payment in cash; but despite the inadequacy of published records, it is known that coins minted later than 389 have been found at Chesterholm and Birdoswald, and in Coventina's Well at Carrawburgh, while coins at Corbridge and South Shields go down at least as late. Both Birdoswald and Chesterholm seem to have been violently destroyed,[19] and this may have happened in one of the raids at the turn of the century. Other forts, however, may conceivably have remained in occupation longer. If the second generation of occupants were of too little military value to attract the eye of Stilicho or Constantine they may well have remained in their forts until either they were overwhelmed piecemeal or they migrated to less lonely localities.

Many of the villas continued in occupation into the fifth century, and at some of them, for instance Great Casterton in Rutland or Hucclecote in Gloucestershire, new mosaic floors were laid down at the very end of the fourth century or even perhaps later. Their ultimate fate is obscure. Some, no doubt, were sacked, as the villa at North Wraxall in Wiltshire seems to have been. Here the coin-series ends with Gratian, and not only were corpses together with architectural fragments from the villa flung down the well but also two items of late Roman military uniform were unearthed, perhaps belonging to troops billeted on the owner, but more probably lost during a skirmish with the raiders. The villa may have been destroyed at any time in the early fifth century, for no great reliance can be placed on the apparent absence of the small coins of the house of Theodosius, which are in any case normally rare as site-finds. At Great Casterton, Rutland, part of the villa was burnt down in the first quarter of the fifth century, but squatter occupation continued thereafter; at Lullingstone, Kent, also, occupation of the villa ended in fire, and here also a piece of military equipment has been recorded.

The majority of villas, however, appear to have met no violent end but to have undergone gradual decay; at Bignor, Sussex, and Whittington Court, Gloucestershire, the roof-tiles were found lying where they had fallen on the collapse of the decayed rafters. The villa at Langton, Yorkshire, is one of the few at which a money-economy was active in the last decade of the fourth century or later; here again the villa seems to have been abandoned at the end, rather than destroyed.

At many villas coins become very rare from 378. This does not necessarily mean more than a growing reliance upon barter; but at King's Weston, Gloucestershire, Atworth, Wiltshire, and Ditchley, Oxfordshire, there was a perceptible decline in the standards of living. Part of the bath-wing at Atworth was converted for farm-purposes as a corn-dryer, while other rooms were crudely paved with stone. At King's Weston there was a reduction in the number of rooms in use, and the end of occupation was marked by a skeleton lying in the collapsed hypocaust; there were the marks of sword-cuts on the skull. At Ditchley fires were lit on the floor of a living-room. This sort of decline may be attributed to the growing insecurity of the times. If some of the villa-owners repaired to the security of their town-houses the estates might be left in the hands of bailiffs. The picture that St Patrick gives of his early life, however, shows that villa proprietors could continue to inhabit their villas as least down to 430, disturbed from time to time by marauding bands (who might carry off members of the staff or family into slavery), but otherwise continuing the cultivation of their estates and the practice of the Christian faith. When Patrick returned home after his captivity his father, Calpurnius, a decurion of his civitas and a deacon of the church, implored him to remain at home and undertake *munera*, or public office.

Nevertheless, there are few, if any, places where continuity can be suggested between Romano-British estates and Saxon Manors. At Wingham, Kent, very early Germanic pottery has been found in the ruins of a villa; but this does not necessarily indicate continuity, for the Saxons may have been billeted on the villa as part of a federate settlement. This may also have happened at Rivenhall, Essex. At Withington, Gloucestershire, H. P. R. Finberg has shown that the area of a seventh-century Saxon monastic estate very probably reflects that of the earlier villa; but this is evidence for the influence of geographical factors rather than for historical continuity: there is nothing to show that the villa itself survived the early fifth century, if as long.

We can feel sure that though owners might cling to their villas as long as possible, nevertheless conditions eventually became too insecure for personal safety; and that more seriously still, the slaves and coloni, upon whose labours productivity depended, were found increasingly difficult either to retain or to replace. In the majority of cases it was the economic basis rather than the physical buildings of the villas which was the first to disintegrate: when that happened the ruin of the buildings themselves would not be long postponed. It is noteworthy that Gildas, writing about 540, could describe the sack of towns; but he knew nothing whatever of villas. They had passed from the scene so long before his time that not even a tradition was left.

The state of the peasantry is less easy to analyse. As much of eastern Britain came under Saxon occupation, some of the earlier population may well have migrated westwards, and thus have swelled the numbers of those Britons who soon after the middle of the fifth century migrated to Brittany. Others, however, certainly remained; this is suggested partly by the survival of place- and river-names, partly by archaeological evidence, and also by a few historical references, such as the Life of St Guthlac, who encountered Celtic-speaking Britons in the Fens as late as 700. One of the archaeological indications is the pottery, which may genuinely be described as Romano-Saxon, from Anglo-Saxon cemeteries. This pottery, often hand-made, shows by its traditional fabric and superior techniques, often combined with Saxon decoration, that native potters were working for new masters; it must be carefully distinguished from the mass-produced wares of the fourth century which have also – and

419

too readily – been labelled Romano-Saxon from the supposed Germanic inspiration of their decoration. A few rural sites may even point to continuity of occupation, as perhaps at Elmswell, Yorkshire. But British survival is more easily demonstrated from the brooches, buckles, hanging bowls and decorative techniques, which point to the work of British bronze-smiths: some of these smiths may have been itinerant masters of high standing, but the commoner objects are more likely to be the product of local industry. Of course in the south-west, and in northern Wales and the North, beyond the immediate reach of Saxon settlers or war-bands, indications of British survival may take a less elusive form which is beginning to be better understood. For here there is growing evidence from recent excavations for reoccupation – and refortification – of the hill-forts of the Iron Age, and for the establishment of new strongholds in similar positions. The type-sites are South Cadbury and Cadbury Congresbury, both in Somerset, and Dinas Powys in South Wales; and there are others which are likely to reveal relationships with nearby sub-Roman cemeteries. The movement back to the hill-forts may have been much more widespread than at present is certainly attested: investigation of this aspect of the period is still in its infancy.

Much has been discovered in recent years to counteract the older view that the towns of Roman Britain were in complete decay from the middle of the fourth century. Excavations at the civitas capitals of *Verulamium* and Cirencester and the small towns of Catterick and Dorchester on Thames have all revealed the survival of active life well into the fifth century, and, at the two first, large houses adorned with fine mosaics were still being built in the latest decades of the fourth. These were the dwellings of aristocrats like Gratian who could accept a throne, and of the leaders who took the initiative in 410. At *Verulamium* three later phases could be recognised. In the first a large mosaic in such a mansion was sacrificed to utility, when a corn-drying oven was dug through it. This suggests a period when growing insecurity in the countryside made it wise to hurry the newly cut harvest within the safety of town-walls. The oven was in use long enough for repairs to become necessary to its furnace-room, but no contemporary pottery or coins were found in the contents of this. If precise dating was rendered impossible by the lack, at least the absence of pottery and coins suggest a period beginning no earlier than 430 for its use, when such things were no longer obtainable.

Thereafter the house itself was demolished, and its site occupied by a large buttressed hall or barn, whose wall contained a bonding-course of tiles, all of which were broken fragments recovered from earlier structures. Roman building techniques were still practised, but it was impossible to obtain new tiles. When this building in turn had perished, its site was crossed by a pipe-line of wooden tubes jointed with iron collars. Such fresh-water mains had been common in earlier centuries; the interest here is to find the technique still practised at a date which cannot be earlier than 450 and may be considerably later. Evidently the aqueduct and public fountains of the town were still in use, and Romanised life still continuing. We cannot doubt that it was the town-walls, refitted by Count Theodosius and still manned by troops in late Roman uniform, which made this sort of urban survival possible.[20]

But town life depended upon trade and ultimately upon supplies of food. With the decay of the former, decline was inevitable; yet towns would still have a function as strong-points so long as the surrounding region could be cultivated in comparative security. The date when even this ceased to be possible was naturally different in different areas; varying, too, were the destinies of each individual city. In the east Caistor by Norwich may have perished in a massacre and remained empty, while Canterbury or Dorchester on Thames could receive Germanic settlers and continue to be occupied. These lay within the regions settled by the earliest Anglo-Saxons. The Saxon laeti round Caistor, their numbers periodically replenished from their homelands, seem to have remained entirely outside the ambit of Roman civilisation; whereas the later foederati at Canterbury and Dorchester, if not less primitive, were at any rate assigned a different role, which placed them inside the towns. At York, too, there was continuous occupation of some vigour; the legionary principia continued to stand for centuries, and the defences were repaired from time to time. At what stage change from British to English town occurred excavations have not yet clearly revealed. *Verulamium* survived as a Roman city, as we have seen, well into the dark age, but today its site is empty. The date of its evacuation is quite unknown; we can only say that if life there survived until the German tide was halted late in the fifth century by the British recovery signalised for us by the battle of Mt Badon there was nothing to prevent it continuing peacefully until the Saxon victories of 571. Archaeology is

421

silent, partly because of the destruction of the upper levels by cultivation, partly because of the lack of datable material. On the whole our verdict must be against organised survival much later than 500: here and there squatters may still have inhabited the ruins, but the maintenance of buildings first put up even in the late fourth century must by then have become an insuperable difficulty.

At Silchester, too, there is suggestive evidence of continued life in the form of fifth-century metal-work and glass; and the well-known inscription carved on a stone column in the Ogham script points to the presence of an Irishman in the town at a date which can hardly be earlier than the sixth century and may be later. Round this town the late fifth-century territorium seems to be indicated by earthworks which are best understood as boundaries rather than defences as such: they mark a stage of agreement or equilibrium between the invaders and the Britons such as would suit the aftermath of Badon. The final stage of Bokerly Dyke is perhaps a similar phenomenon. It is certainly no earlier than the fifth century, as the coins show; and, now that early Saxon material is known in Hampshire and the Salisbury region, it is easier to place the dyke later in the century than was once thought likely.

Farther west again, some of the towns may have had an even longer reprieve. Unfortunately evidence bearing on the point is scarce. At Cirencester the forum was maintained to a date when coins were no longer used, and the presence of unburied bodies in the side-ditch of a street has been explained in terms of a great plague; but whether the plague of 433 or that of a century later cannot be decided. At Exeter the coin-list ends with Magnus Maximus; but this in itself means only that the supply of coinage was interrupted. The erosion of the upper Roman levels has deprived us of other sorts of archaeological evidence; William of Malmesbury, however, makes it clear that until they were expelled by Athelstan (perhaps in 928), Britons continued to live in Exeter side by side with the Saxons, in an independent community occupying their own particular quarter of the city, which was known as Britayne as late as the thirteenth century.[21] At Caerwent a fire destroyed the basilica and various shops and houses at some date in the fifth century; this town was dangerously exposed to Irish raids in the Bristol Channel, and seems to have become deserted before the revival of western trade, which began to bring in Mediterranean pottery in the later fifth century. The most profitable line of investigation of the problems of British survival in the towns is likely to be the examination of surrounding cemeteries; important evidence has been obtained at Cirencester and still more at Dorchester (Dorset), where Mediterranean pottery has also been found within the town itself.

As the material prosperity which had characterised late Roman Britain waned, so a spiritual revival took place. During the fourth century there had been a flowering of Celtic religion which is witnessed by the many sacred sites built or refurbished during that period; the process reached its climax in the last third of the century and thus may rightly be connected with the decline of civil security at that time. Christianity was not a powerful force in Britain before the last decade or two of the fourth century, but from then onwards it became the leading spiritual influence in the island, and it was Christians who took the lead in the struggle for Celtic independence and survival. Partly, perhaps because of its patriotic associations, together with the undoubted authority it had inherited from the Roman past, and partly because of its superior spiritual qualities and its links with education, Christianity now became the religion of the people, not merely of the aristocracy. It gained ascendancy through monastic foundations which were centres of learning as well as of devotion, and through the missionary activities of influential saints.

The spiritual revival of Britain, however, was not solely a matter of religion, for there was also a revival of art. This had its genesis in the West, where some of the sources of inspiration for decorated metal-work were certainly supplied by Irish settlers, but where native bronze-smiths had also kept alive the techniques of their craft throughout the Roman period, and now found their opportunity.[22] Indeed, western Britain assumed a new significance as slowly the eastern parts of the island were submerged by Germanic immigrants. Vortigern had connections with the later dynasty of Powys, and may himself have sprung from a noble Cornovian family. Much of the military strength of fifth-century Britain must have been supplied by the tribes of Wales, and this strength was sufficient to maintain the independence of the West for many centuries.

The result was a new pride, and the genesis of a new sub-Roman culture, which gave birth to the language and civilisation of early medieval Wales. The Irish Sea became the centre of a Celtic province in which western Britain and Ireland were closely linked. Long after contact with northern Gaul and the Rhineland had been interrupted by Saxon settlements, and cross-Channel trade had fallen into Germanic hands, connections with south Gaul and with the Mediterranean itself were maintained within the fifth to the seventh centuries, tenuously it is true, but sufficiently to be significant, by merchants and travellers using the western sea-ways. Pottery imported by these means has now been recognsed at a number of sites round the Irish Sea and Bristol Channel. Further evidence of contact with the Continent can sometimes be deduced from the fifth- and sixth-century inscribed stones of the Celtic West; these are suggestive of the influence of Christian missionaries from Gaul.

The three chief enemies of Roman Britain at this time were the Irish, the Picts and the Saxons. Of these, the first became a less serious menace during the second quarter of the fifth century; for with the spread of Christianity to Ireland, and the growth of friendly relations which resulted from a dynastic marriage, the raiding ceased. It was the Picts who were regarded by the British as their chief danger, and though raids by Saxons were from time to time recorded, it was to the latter that Vortigern turned when seeking help against them. The earliest permanent Saxon settlements in Britain were the result not of haphazard seizure of lands by raiders or land-hungry settlers but of planned dispositions by British authority in areas thought to stand in special need of protection or to offer outstanding strategic advantages for the defence of Britain.

One of the best-known dates of English history is 499, traditionally the year of the landing of the Saxons. It derives from Bede, and because of his great reputation as a historian the date itself has acquired more authority than perhaps Bede himself intended; for he has left evidence of his uncertainty of the chronology of the period.[23] No historian, however great, can write reliably of events almost two centuries before his own time unless he has access to reliable sources. Bede's main source for fifth-century events in Britain was Gildas, the sixth-century British ecclesiastic, whose historical sections are a subsidiary element in a work of moral exhortation. After the separation from Rome he tells of a long period of great material prosperity in which victory was achieved over Picts and Irish, who were driven home and made to abate the severity of their raiding. This period ended with renewed attacks and the outbreak of a great plague, and was followed by the invitation of the 'proud tyrant' to the Saxons to come to his assistance against the Picts. This arrangement was successful for a time, and the Saxons were kept amiable with subsidies; but at last came a rebellion of the Saxons and great slaughter and destruction of cities, ending in the enslavement of some and the escape overseas of many other Britons.

This narrative of Gildas was derived from oral tradition and not tied to dates; but the truth of its general sequence can be confirmed from other sources. Gildas did, however, quote one document which can be approximately dated, the Groans of the Britons; but there is no reason to suppose either that he himself knew the date of the third consulship of Aetius or that he placed the document in the correct position in his narrative. In fact, he placed it before the period of prosperity, and this is certainly wrong; for if the first arrival of the Saxons followed a plague, which itself followed a period of British prosperity of sufficient duration to witness victory over raiders from across the sea, the rise and fall of kings, and an increasing corruption of the people (all of which are incidents attributed to it by Gildas); and if all this long sequence has to be placed after 446, then the arrival of the Saxons becomes impossibly late, and their eventual rebellion would fall well in the second half of the fifth century. This is quite contrary both to the archaeological evidence and to what little independent historical evidence we possess. It is clear that in following Gildas over-conscientiously Bede has misdated the coming of the Saxons: his dating has no independent validity, and is twenty years too late. And since the *Anglo-Saxon Chronicle* founds its dating system on Bede, the mistake has had far-reaching consequences.

The prosperity-period of Gildas can safely be assigned to the decades following 410, during which, as Myres has pointed out,[24] we have independent evidence for the rise and fall of kings, victory over invaders and corruption (the Pelagian heresy) in church and state. The rebellion of the Saxon federates which Gildas so vividly describes is best equated with the event recorded in the contemporary anonymous *Gallic Chronicle* of 452, which under the year 442 states, 'Britain long troubled by various happenings and disasters passed under the authority of the Saxons'; for it is clear that to the composer of this chronicle what happened in Britain that year appeared as a decisive break with the past: he is not recording the

425

arrival of Saxon allies. The chronicle was published too soon after the event for the success of subsequent British resistance to be appreciated. Finally, the migrations of Britons to Brittany, which Gildas attributes to Saxon pressure after the rebellion, can be shown to have happened by about 460.[25]

If, then, the rebellion occurred in 442 the first arrival of the Saxons, in response to Vortigern's invitation, must have occurred some years before this,[26] perhaps about 430. This is a date which suits the archaeological evidence bearing on their arrival very well and is not unsupported by the documents;[27] it is also the most probable period for another but similar step taken by Vortigern. This was the transfer of Cunedda to North Wales. Cunedda's date can be worked out only very roughly. He was the great grandfather of Mailcun (Maelgwn), who died in 547, a contemporary of Gildas: allowing thirty years to a generation from a *floruit* for Mailcun about 530, the *floruit* of Cunedda would fall about 440; conversely, two generations from Paternus Pesrut (p. 392f.) in 369 would bring us to about 430. Cunedda was the first of his family for four generations to have a British rather than a Roman name, and this reinforces the view that he belonged to the immediately post-Roman period in Britain. His transfer from Manau Goddodin, the kingdom of the Votadini, to North Wales was made in order to drive out or subdue the Irish settlers there. Its result was the foundation of the royal line of Gwynedd, but the move itself was modelled on Roman statecraft, and could have been undertaken only by a strong central government controlling all Roman Britain. A context after the rebellion of the Saxons seems impossible.

The earliest Germanic cemeteries in Britain are found near the estuaries of the east coast, the Humber, the Wash and the Thames. These river-mouths are natural entries for invaders, but the cemeteries themselves, at least in their opening phase, are best interpreted as representing defenders placed in these regions to resist sea-borne Pictish invaders, and even perhaps to meet them on the seas.[28] The conclusion is reinforced by the known history of settlement in Kent, where settlement of federates is attested in history, and by the abandonment of raiding by the Picts, which suggests the successful impact of new measures. Three early cemeteries in Surrey, at Mitcham, Croydon and Beddington, seem to represent communities intentionally placed to guard the southern approaches to London.

426

Another important and very early group of burials lies in the Oxford region. The identity of their route to the centre of England was always a problem when it was assumed that the burials were those of invaders. But as a federate settlement the group makes much better sense, when we remember that the most prosperous region of late Roman Britain had lain in the Cotswolds just west of this region. Such dispositions in the east of the island were well placed to oppose and counter Pictish raiders penetrating from landfalls on the eastern coasts, and they seem to have been successful; raids from the north are no more heard of. But when the federates themselves rebelled it was all too apparent that they had been given a stranglehold on Britain. This was the context of the appeal to Aetius.

Down, then, to 442 Vortigern successfully maintained the independence of Britain. But the rebellion of his Germanic federates introduced a period of chaos fatal to the villa system, and destructive to Vortigern's own supremacy. In the later fifth century the leadership had passed to Ambrosius Aurelianus and after him to Arthur. Little is known of either. Ambrosius appears in the pages of Gildas, but Arthur does not, and his activities and personality are almost impenetrably overlaid by medieval romance. The evidence is sufficient to allow belief that he had a real existence and that he was probably the victor of Mount Badon. It is likely that he succeeded Ambrosius in the leadership; indeed, he is called *dux bellorum* in the *Historia Brittonum*, which suggests a memory of late Roman military titles, and may indicate some sort of unified command arranged between several petty kingdoms. Using mounted forces, these leaders were able to strike back at the Saxons, who had little body armour and inferior weapons. The use of cavalry enabled unexpected blows to be struck from distant bases, and it was a form of warfare in which small numbers of horsemen could rout many times their number of ill-armed barbarian foot-soldiers. It is perhaps no coincidence that eight out of twelve battles traditionally associated with Arthur were fought at fords, and so were other fifth-century battles; a well-planned charge even by a few horsemen on a force of foot soldiers crossing a stream could be expected to produce maximum confusion.

A long period of fluctuating warfare culminated at some date rather before 500 in a British victory at Mount Badon, an unidentified site perhaps in the south-west; after it there was peace for two generations. Gildas, writing soon after 540, is able to speak of 'our present security' and of a generation which had no experience of the great struggle. Soon after 550, however, the Saxon conquest was renewed. In 571 an area from Buckinghamshire to the upper Thames was overrun, and six years later came the fall of Gloucester, Cirencester and Bath. About 590 the Britons in the north suffered a serious defeat at Catterick, and by 600 most of Britain had fallen to the Saxon kingdoms with the exception of the Dumnonian peninsula, Wales and parts of the Pennines and north-west.

But though the struggle was long drawn out, two facts are clear. The official connection of Britain with the Roman empire ended in 410 and was not renewed; but the Roman framework and civilisation of the province was in some sense maintained until 442. Thereafter it was Celtic rather than Roman Britain which maintained the struggle, and the history of the dark age which followed is to be pieced together by new disciplines.

1. Orosius, vii, 34, 9.
2. *CW²*, li (1951), 4–15.
3. *Notitia Dignitatum Occ.*, vii, 49.
4. Prosper Tiro, *Chronicon, Gratiani*, iv (AD 382): *incursantes Pictos et Scotos Maximus strenue superavit.*
5. Claudian, *de consulatu Stilichonis*, ii, 250–5 (written AD 400).

> 'Me quoque vicinis pereuntem gentibus' inquit
> 'munivit Stilicho, totam cum Scotus Iernen
> movit et infesto spumavit remige Tethys.
> illius effectum curis, ne tela timerem
> Scotica, ne Pictum tremerem, ne litore toto
> prospicerem dubiis venturum Saxona ventis.'

6. Claudian, *in Eutropium*, i, 391–3.

> quantum te principe possim
> non longinqua docent, domito quod Saxone Tethys
> mitior aut fracto secura Britannia Picto.

7. The sole archaeological trace of his activities, four titles stamped HON AVG ANDRIA from the fort at Pevensey, have recently been shown to be modern forgeries: D. P. S. Peacock, *Antiquity*, xlvii (1973), 138 ff.

8. Claudian *de bello Gothico* 416–18:
> venit et extremis legio praetenta Britannis
> quae Scoto dat frena truci ferroque notatas
> perlegit exanimes Picto moriente figuras.

9. *Notitia Dignitatum Or.*, ix, 29; *Oc.*, v, 197.

10. Zosimus, vi, 3, 1.

11. Orosius, vii, 40, 4: *municeps tyrannus*.

12. Zosimus, vi, 5.

13. Procopius, *de bello Vandalico*, i, 2, 38. Procopius was writing over a century later, but C. E. Stevens has shown (*Athenaeum* (Pavia) 1957, 340–1), that he is here probably using a contemporary source. This paper is a very valuable discussion of sources and chronology from 406 to 411.

14. *Antiquity*, xxx (1956), 163–7.

15. *JRS*, l (1960), 21–36.

16. Nennius, *Historia Brittonum*, 31 (part of an early strand in this work).

17. Solinus, *Coll. rerum memorabilium* (ed. Mommsen, 1895) 22, 7: *Siluram quoque insulam ab ora quam gens Brittana Dumnonii tenent turbidum fretum distinguit. Cuius homines etiam nunc custodiunt morem vetustum; nummum refutant; dant res et accipiunt, mutationibus necessaria potius quam pretiis parant.*

18. In R. H. M. Dolley, *Anglo-Saxon Coins* (1961), pp. 1–22.

19. Birdoswald, *CW²*, xxx (1930), 170: Chesterholm, *AA⁴*, viii, 211.

20. See the study of late Roman and Dark Age military buckles etc., by S. Hawkes and G. C. Dunning in *Medieval Archaeology*, v (1961), 1–70; and *Bericht der Römisch-Germanischen Kommission*, 43–4 (1962–3), 155–231.

21. I owe this information to Professor W. G. Hoskins.

22. See the brilliant study of this industry by C. F. C. Hawkes in W. F. Grimes, *Aspects of Archaeology in Britain and Beyond* (1951), pp. 172–99.

23. In his *Chronicle* of 725 he dates the Saxon landing 449–52; in his *Church History* of 731 he three times dates it 446–7 (*H.E.*, i, 23, ii, 14, v, 23), and twice 449–56 (*H.E.*, i, 15, v, 24).

24. 'Adventus Saxonum', in W. F. Grimes, *Aspects of Archaeology in Britain and beyond* (1951), pp. 221–41.

25. J. Morris, 'Dark Age Dates', in M. G. Jarrett and B. Dobson, *Britain and Rome* (1966), 145 ff.

26. Gildas, *de excidio* 24, uses the phrase *multo tempore* of the interval.

27. Nennius, *Historia Brittonum*, 66.

28. To Gildas (*de excidio* 11) the Picts were *transmarini*: they came across the sea.

Abbreviations

AA², *AA⁴*	*Archaeologia Aeliana*, second, fourth series etc., Society of Antiquaries of Newcastle upon Tyne.
Arch. Camb.	*Archaeologia Cambrensis*, Cambrian Archaeological Association.
Arch. Cant.	*Archaeologia Cantiana*, Kent Archaeological Society.
Antiq. Journ.	*The Antiquaries Journal*, Society of Antiquaries of London.
Arch. Journ.	*The Archaeological Journal*, Royal Archaeological Institute.
BBCS	*Bulletin of the Board of Celtic Studies*, University of Wales, Cardiff.
B.M.	British Museum.
BMC	*Coins of the Roman Empire in the British Museum*, London, 1923 etc.
CIL	*Corpus Inscriptionum Latinarum.*
CW²	*Transactions of the Cumberland and Westmorland Antiquarian and Archaeological Society*, second series.
EE	*Ephemeris Epigraphica.*
ILS	H. Dessau, *Inscriptiones Latinae Selectae.*
JBAA³	*Journal of the British Archaeological Association*, third series.

JRS	*Journal of Roman Studies.*
NCH	*Northumberland County History,* Newcastle upon Tyne.
PIR	*Prosopographia Imperii Romani.*
Proc. Camb. Ant. Soc.	*Proceedings of the Cambridge Antiquarian Society.*
P. Hants. F.C.	*Papers and Proceedings of the Hampshire Field Club and Archaeological Society.*
PPS	*Proceedings of the Prehistoric Society.*
PSAS	*Proceedings of the Society of Antiquaries of Scotland.*
PUBSS	*Proceedings, University of Bristol Spelaeological Society.*
R.C.H.M.	Royal Commission on Historical Monuments.
RE	Pauly-Wissowa, *Realencyclopädie d. Class. Altertumswissenschaft.*
RIB	R. G. Collingwood and R. P. Wright, *The Roman Inscriptions of Britain,* i, Oxford, 1965.
RIC	H. Mattingly and E. A. Sydenham, *The Roman Imperial Coinage,* London, 1923 etc.
SHA	Scriptores Historiae Augustae.
Sx.A.C.	*Sussex Archaeological Collections,* Sussex Archaeological Society.
Sy.A.C.	*Surrey Archaeological Collections,* Surrey Archaeological Society.
T. Birmingham A.S.	*Transactions and Proceedings of the Birmingham Archaeological Society.*
T. Dumfries and Gal. Ant. Soc.	*Transactions of the Dumfriesshire and Galloway Antiquarian Society.*
T. Durham and N.A. Soc.	*Transactions of the Architectural and Archaeological Society of Durham and Northumberland.*
VCH	The Victoria County History.

Bibliography

GENERAL

F. Haverfield, *The Romanization of Roman Britain* (Ed. 3), Oxford, 1915.

F. Haverfield and G. Macdonald, *The Roman Occupation of Britain*, Oxford, 1924.

F. Sagot, *La Bretagne Romaine*, Paris, 1911.

I. A. Richmond, *Roman Britain*, London, 1963.

I. A. Richmond (ed.), *Roman and Native in North Britain*, London, 1958.

E. Birley, *Roman Britain and the Roman Army*, Kendal, 1953.

R. G. Collingwood and J. N. L. Myres, *Roman Britain and the English Settlements*, Oxford, 1937.

R. G. Collingwood and R. P. Wright, *The Roman Inscriptions of Britain*, I, Oxford, 1965.

M. P. Charlesworth, *The Lost Province*, Cardiff, 1949.

A. L. F. Rivet, *Town and Country in Roman Britain*, London, 1964.

A. Birley, *Life in Roman Britain*, London, 1964.

H.M. Ordnance Survey, *A Map of Southern Britain in the Iron Age*, Chessington, 1962.

H.M. Ordnance Survey, *A Map of Roman Britain* (Ed. 3), Chessington, 1956.

W. Bonser, *A Romano-British Bibliography*, Oxford, 1964.

Governors of Britain: D. Atkinson, *JRS* XII (1922), 60ff.; E. Birley in G. Askew, *The Coinage of Roman Britain*, London, 1951, 81; A. R. Birley, *Epigraphische Studien* IV (1967), 63.

C. H. V. Sutherland, *Coinage and Currency in Roman Britain*, Oxford, 1937.

K. Jackson, *Language and History in Early Britain*, Edinburgh, 1953.

J. M. C. Toynbee, *Art in Roman Britain*, London, 1962.

J. M. C. Toynbee, *Art in Britain under the Romans*, Oxford, 1964.

P. Salway, *The Frontier People of Roman Britain*, Cambridge, 1965.

C. Thomas (ed.), *Rural Settlement in Roman Britain*, London, 1966.

V. E. Nash-Williams, *The Roman Frontier in Wales* (2nd. ed., by M. G. Jarrett, Cardiff, 1969).

R. M. Butler (ed.), *Soldier and Civilian in Roman Yorkshire*, Leicester, 1971.

CHAPTER 1   The earliest British Iron Age, pp. 14–26

D. W. Harding, *The Iron Age in the Upper Thames Basin*, Oxford, 1972.

M. Jesson and D. Hill (ed.), *The Iron Age and its Hill-forts*, Southampton, 1971.

I. A. Richmond, *Hod Hill*, ii, London, 1968.

Sir Cyril Fox, *The Personality of Britain* (Ed. 4), Cardiff, 1943.

S. Piggott, in I. A. Richmond (ed), *Roman and Native in North Britain*, chapter 1.

S. S. Frere (ed.), *Problems of the Iron Age in Southern Britain*, London, 1961.

C. F. C. Hawkes, 'The A.B.C. of the British Iron Age', *Antiquity*, xxxiii (1959), 170 ff.

A. H. A. Hogg, 'Early Iron Age Wales', in I. Ll. Foster and G. Daniel, *Prehistoric and Early Wales*, London, 1965.

E. M. Jope, 'Daggers of the Early Iron Age in Britain', *PPS*, xxvii (1961), 307.

T. C. M. Brewster, *The Excavation of Staple Howe*, Scarborough, 1963.

R. E. M. Wheeler, 'Prehistoric Scarborough', in A. Rowntree, *The History of Scarborough*, London, 1931.

M. E. Cunnington, *All Cannings Cross, Devizes*, 1923.

C. F. C. Hawkes, 'The Early Iron Age Settlement at Fengate, Peterborough', *Arch. Journ.*, c (1945), 188ff.

H. N. Savory, 'An Early Iron Age site at Long Wittenham, Berks.', *Oxoniensia*, ii (1937), 1 ff.

J. N. L. Myres, 'A Prehistoric . . . Site on Mount Farm, Dorchester', *Oxoniensia*, ii (1937), 12 ff.

K. M. Richardson and A. Young, 'An Iron Age A site in the Chilterns', *Antiq. Journ.*, xxxi (1951), 132 ff.

J. G. D. Clark and C. I. Fell, '. . . Micklemoor Hill, West Harling', *PPS*, xix (1953), 1 ff.

H. C. Bowen, *Ancient Fields*, London, 1961.

G. Webster and B. Hobley, 'Aerial Reconnaisance over the Warwickshire Avon', *Arch. Journ.*, cxxi (1964), 1 ff.

G. Bersu, 'Excavations at Little Woodbury', *PPS*, vi (1940), 30 ff.

A. Fox, 'Celtic Fields and Farms on Dartmoor', *PPS*, xx (1954), 87 ff.

S. Applebaum, 'The Agriculture . . . at Figheldean Down', *PPS*, xx (1954), 103 ff.

H. Helbaek, 'Early crops in Southern Britain', *PPS*, xviii (1952), 194 ff.

C. F. C. Hawkes, 'The Excavations at Quarley Hill', *P. Hants, F.C.*, xiv (2) (1939), 136 ff.

A. Fox, 'Excavations at Kestor', *Transactions of the Devon Association for the Advancement of Science Literature and Art*, lxxxvi (1954), 21 ff.

D. Dudley, 'An Excavation at Bodrifty . . .', *Arch. Journ.*, cxiii (1956), 1 ff.

M. A. Cotton, 'British Camps with Timber-laced Ramparts', *Arch. Journ.*, cxi (1954), 26 ff.

Dinorben: H. N. Savory, *Antiquity* xlv (1971), 251 ff.

Ivinghoe Beacon: M. A. Cotton and S. S. Frere, *Records of Buckinghamshire* xviii (1968), 187 ff.

R. E. M. Wheeler, *Maiden Castle, Dorset*, Oxford, 1943.

R. E. M. Wheeler, 'Bindon Hill, Dorset', *Antiq. Journ.*, xxxiii (1953), 1 ff.

A. Fox, *South West England*, London, 1964.

E. C. Curwen, *The Archaeology of Sussex*, London, 1937.

E. Mackie, 'Radiocarbon dates and the Scottish Iron Age', *Antiquity* xliii (1969), 15 ff.

J. R. C. Hamilton, *Excavations at Jarlshof*, London, 1956.

A. L. F. Rivet, 'The Iron Age in Northern Britain', *Antiquity*, xxxvi (1962), 24 ff.

R. Feachem, *A Guide to Prehistoric Scotland*, London, 1963.

L. Alcock, 'Excavations at Castell Odo', *Arch. Camb.*, cxi (1960), 78 ff.

L. Alcock, *Dinan Powys*, Cardiff, 1963.

CHAPTER 2   Iron B and Iron C in Britain, pp. 27-41

P. Jacobsthal, *Early Celtic Art*, Oxford, 1944.

J. M. de Navarro, 'The Celts in Britain and their Art', in M. D. Knowles (ed.), *The Heritage of Early Britain*, London, 1952.

R. R. Clarke and C. F. C. Hawkes, 'An Iron Anthropoid Sword from Shouldham, Norfolk . . .', *PPS*, xxi (1955), 198 ff.

S. Piggott, 'Swords and Scabbards of the British Early Iron Age', *PPS*, xvi (1950), 1 ff.

J. B. Ward Perkins, 'Iron Age Metal Horses' Bits of the British Isles', *PPS*, v (1939), 173 ff.

E. M. Jope, 'Chariotry and Paired Draught . . .', *Ulster Journal of Archaeology*, xviii (1955), 37 ff.

J. F. Dyer, 'Drays Ditches, Bedfordshire', *Antiq. Journ.*, xli (1961), 32 ff.

Sir Cyril Fox, see p. 40, note 1.

R. J. C. Atkinson and S. Piggott, 'The Torrs Chamfrein', *Archaeologia*, xcvi (1955), 197 ff.

W. F. Grimes, 'Art on British Iron Age Pottery', *PPS*, xviii (1952), 160 ff.

I. M. Stead, 'A . . . La Tène Barrow in Eastern Yorkshire', *Antiq. Journ.*, xli (1961), 44 ff.

I. M. Stead, *The La Tène Cultures of Eastern Yorkshire*, York, 1965.

F. R. Hodson, 'Cultures of Continental type in Britain', *PPS*, xxx (1964), 100 ff.

M. A. Cotton, 'Pre-Belgic Iron Age cultures of Gloucestershire', in E. M. Clifford, *Bagendon, a Belgic Oppidum*, Cambridge, 1961.

D. F. Allen, 'The Paul (Penzance) Hoard . . .', *Numismatic Chronicle* [7], i (1961), 91 ff.

C. F. C. Hawkes, 'The Hill-forts of Northern France', *Antiquity*, xxxii (1958), 154 ff.

A. S. R. Gordon, 'The excavations of Gurnards Head', *Arch. Journ.*, xcvii (1940), 96 ff.

C. A. R. Radford, 'Report on the excavations at Castle Dore'; *Journal of the Royal Institution of Cornwall*, i (1951), 1 ff.

L. M. Threipland, 'An excavation at St. Mawgan-in-Pyder', *Arch. Journ.*, cxiii (1956), 33 ff.

D. F. Allen, 'Iron Currency Bars in Britain', *PPS*, xxxiii (1967), 307 ff.

J. P. Bushe-Fox, *Excavations at Hengistbury Head, Hampshire*, Oxford, 1915.

A. Bulleid and H. St. G. Gray, *The Glastonbury Lake Village*, Glastonbury, 1911, etc.

H. St. G. Gray and A. Bulleid, *The Meare Lake Village*, Taunton, 1948 and 1953.

K. M. Kenyon, 'Excavations at Sutton Walls', *Arch. Journ.*, cx (1953), 1 ff.

J. B. Ward Perkins, 'An Early Iron Age site at Crayford, Kent', *PPS*, iv (1938), 151 ff.

S. S. Frere, 'An Iron Age site at West Clandon . . .', *Arch. Journ.*, ci (1944), 50 ff.

M. A. Cotton, 'A Classification of Hill Forts . . .', in S. S. Frere (ed.), *Problems of the Iron Age in Southern Britain*, London, 1961, 61 ff.

A. Fox, 'South-western Hill-forts', in S. S. Frere, op. cit., pp. 35 ff.

D. F. Allen, 'The Origins of Coinage in Britain', in S. S. Frere, op. cit., pp. 97 ff.

D. F. Allen, 'The Belgic Dynasties of Britain and their Coins', *Archaeologia*, xc (1944), 1 ff.

D. F. Allen, *The Coins of the Coritani*, London, 1963.

D. F. Allen, 'The Chronology of Durotrigan coinage 'in I. A. Richmond, *Hod Hill* ii, London, 1968.

D. F. Allen, 'A study of the Dobunnic coinage' in E. M. Clifford, *Bagendon, a Belgic oppidum*, Cambridge, 1961.

D. F. Allen, 'The coins of the Iceni', *Britannia* i (1970), 1 ff.

I. M. Stead, 'A La Tène iii burial at Welwyn Garden City', *Archaeologia* ci (1967), 1 ff.

I. M. Stead, 'A La Tène burial at . . . Baldock, Hertfordshire', *Antiq. Journ.*, xlviii (1968), 306 ff.

D. P. S. Peacock, 'Roman Amphorae in pre-Roman Britain', in M. Jesson and D. Hill, *The Iron Age and its hill-forts*, Southampton, (1971), 171 ff.

A. J. Evans, 'A Late Celtic Urn-field at Aylesford, Kent', *Archaeologia*, lii (1890), 315 ff.

J. P. Bushe-Fox, *Excavation of the Late Celtic Urn-field at Swarling, Kent*, Oxford, 1925.

A. Birchall, 'The Aylesford-Swarling Culture . . .', *PPS*, xxxi (1965), 241 ff.

C. F. C. Hawkes and G. C. Dunning, 'The Belgae of Gaul and Britain',
   Arch. Journ., lxxxvii (1930), 150 ff.

W. H. Manning, 'The Plough in Roman Britain', *JRS*, liv (1964), 54 ff.

Sir Cyril Fox, *A Find of the Early Iron Age from Llyn Cerrig Bach*,
   Cardiff, 1946, for currency bars, slave-chain, etc.

J. W. Brailsford, 'A corrected restoration of the Belgic Iron Frame
   from Welwyn', *Antiq. Journ.*, xxxviii (1958), 89 ff.

R. R. Clarke, 'The Early Iron Age Treasure from Snettisham, Norfolk',
   PPS, xx (1954), 27 ff.

Ipswich Torcs: *Antiquity* xliii (1969), 208 ff.; *PPS* xxxviii (1972),
   219 ff.

D. F. Allen, 'Belgic coins as illustrations of Life . . .', *PPS*, xxiv
   (1958), 43 ff.

CHAPTER 3   Caesar's expeditions, pp. 42–54

C. E. Stevens, '55 B.C. and 54 B.C.', *Antiquity*, xxi (1947), 4 ff.

C. E. Stevens, *Latomus*, xi (1952), 3 ff. and 165 ff.

J.-J. Hatt, *Histoire de la Gaule romaine*, Paris, 1959.

C. Hignett, in *Cambridge Ancient History*, ix (1932), chapter xiii.

T. Rice Holmes, *Ancient Britain and the Invasions of Julius Caesar*,
   Oxford, 1907.

R. E. M. and T. V. Wheeler, *Verulamium, a Belgic and Two Roman
   Cities*, Oxford, 1936, for Wheathampstead.

CHAPTER 4   Caesar to Claudius, pp. 55–77

C. E. Stevens, 'Britain between the Invasions', in W. F. Grimes (ed.),
   Aspects of Archaeology in Britain and Beyond, London, 1951,
   332 ff.

D. F. Allen, papers cited on p. 436.

R. P. Mack, *The Coinage of Ancient Britain* (2nd ed.), London, 1964.

G. C. Boon, *Roman Silchester*, London, 1957.

G. C. Boon, 'Belgic and Roman Silchester', *Archaeologia* cii (1969),
   1 ff.

K. M. E. Murray, 'The Chichester Earthworks', *Sx.A.C.*, xciv (1956),
   139 ff.

R. E. M. and T. V. Wheeler, *Verulamium, a Belgic and Two Roman
   Cities*, Oxford, 1936.

S. S. Frere, 'Verulamium, Three Roman Cities', *Antiquity*, xxxviii (1964), 103 ff.

C. F. C. Hawkes and M. R. Hull, *Camulodunum*, Oxford, 1947.

D. P. S. Peacock, 'Roman amphorae in pre-Roman Britain' in M. Jesson and D. Hill (ed.), *The Iron Age and its Hill-forts*, Southampton, 1971.

S. S. Frere, *Roman Canterbury* (3rd ed.), Canterbury, 1962.

S. S. Frere, 'Canterbury Excavations', *Arch. Cant.*, lxviii (1954), 101 ff.

R. R. Clarke, 'The Iron Age in Norfolk and Suffolk', *Arch. Journ.*, xcvi (1939), 1 ff.

R. R. Clarke, *East Anglia*, London, 1960.

S. S. Frere, 'A Claudian Site at Needham, Norfolk', *Antiq. Journ.*, xxi (1941), 40 ff.

H.M. Ordnance Survey, *Map of Southern Britain in the Iron Age*, introduction.

T. C. Lethbridge, 'Burial of an Iron Age Warrior at Snailwell', *Proceedings of the Cambridge Antiquarian Society*, xlvii (1953), 25 ff.

R. R. Clarke, 'The Early Iron Age Treasure from Snettisham, Norfolk', *PPS*, xx (1954), 27 ff.

F. T. Baker, 'The Iron Age Salt Industry in Lincolnshire', *Lincolnshire Architectural and Archaeological Society, Reports and Papers*, viii (1960), 26 ff.

S. Hawkes, 'Some Belgic Brooches from South Ferriby', *Hull Museum Publications*, No. 214 (1963), 23 ff.

K. M. Kenyon, *The Jewry Wall Site, Leicester*, Oxford, 1948, 124 ff.

G. Webster, *Arch. Journ.*, cxv (1958), p. 53 on Leicester.

E. M. Clifford, *Bagendon, a Belgic Oppidum*, Cambridge, 1961.

C. W. Dymond and H. S. Tomkins, *Worlebury*, 1866.

T. C. Hencken, 'The Excavation of . . . Bredon Hill', *Arch. Journ.*, xcv (1938), 1 ff.

J. W. Brailsford, 'Early Iron Age C in Wessex', *PPS*, xxiv (1958), 101 ff.

S. S. Frere, 'Some Problems of the later Iron Age', in S. S. Frere (ed.), *Problems of the Iron Age in Southern Britain*, London, 1961.

C. F. C. Hawkes, 'Britons, Romans and Saxons . . . in Cranborne Chase', *Arch. Journ.*, civ (1947), 27 ff.

A. L. F. Rivet, *Town and Country in Roman Britain*, London, 1964 chapter vi, 'Historical Geography'.

A. Fox, *South West England*, London, 1964.

D. M. Liddell, 'Excavations at Hembury Fort, Devon', *Proceedings of the Devon Archaeological Exploration Society*, 1 (1930–32), ii (1935).

L. Alcock, 'Celtic Archaeology and Art', in E. Davies (ed.), *Celtic Studies in Wales*, Cardiff, 1963.

W. Gardner and H. N. Savory, *Dinorben*, Cardiff, 1964.

I. A. Richmond, 'The Cornovii', in I. Ll. Foster and L. Alcock (eds.), *Culture and Environment*, London, 1963

W. J. Varley and J. W. Jackson, *Prehistoric Cheshire*, Chester, 1940.

W. J. Varley, 'The Hill-forts of the Welsh Marches', *Arch. Journ.*, cv (1948), 41 ff.

R. E. M. Wheeler, *The Stanwick Fortifications*, Oxford, 1954.

A. Raistrick, *Prehistoric Yorkshire*, Clapham, 1964.

P. Corder, 'Belgic . . . pottery found at North Ferriby, Yorks.', *Antiq. Journ.*, xviii (1938), 262 ff.

I. A. Richmond, 'Queen Cartimandua', *JRS*, xliv (1954), 43 ff.

S. Piggott, in I. A. Richmond (ed.), *Roman and Native in North Britain*, Chapter i.

M. Macgregor, 'The Early Iron Age Metalwork Hoard from Stanwick, Yorks.', *PPS*, xxviii (1962), 17 ff.

G. Jobey, articles on native settlements in Northumberland and Durham, *AA* [4], xxxvii (1959), xxxviii (1960), xl (1962), xlii (1964).

R. C. H. M. (Scotland), Inventory, *The County of Roxburgh*, i, Edinburgh, 1956, 35 ff.

J. R. C. Hamilton, 'Brochs and Broch-builders', in F. T. Wainwright (ed.), *The Northern Isles*, London, 1962.

S. Piggott and K. Henderson, *Scotland before History*, London, 1958.

A. H. A. Hogg, 'The Votadini', in W. F. Grimes (ed.), *Aspects of Archaeology in Britain and Beyond*, London, 1951.

M. A. Cotton, 'British Camps with Timber-laced Ramparts', *Arch. Journ.*, cxi (1954), 26 ff.

I. A. Richmond, 'Ancient Geographical Sources', in I. A. Richmond (ed.), *Roman and Native in North Britain*, London, 1958.

R. Feachem, *A Guide to Prehistoric Scotland*, London, 1963.

S. Piggott, in F. T. Wainwright (ed.), *The Problem of the Picts*, London, 1955.

J. P. V. D. Balsdon, *The Emperor Gaius*, Oxford, 1934, pp. 88–95.

CHAPTER 5   The Claudian Conquest: rebellion of Boudicca, pp. 78–114

J. P. Bushe-Fox, *Excavations at the Roman Fort at Richborough*, iv, Oxford, 1949, 11 ff.

B. W. Cunliffe (ed.), *Excavations at the Roman Fort at Richborough*, v (forthcoming).

Aylesford crossing: A. R. Burn, *History*, 1953, 105.

Bredgar hoard: *Numismatic Chronicle*, 1959, 17 ff.

Lakenheath hoard: *Proc. Camb. Antiq. Soc.*, lvi–lvii (1963–4), 123 f.

S. S. Frere, 'A Claudian site at Needham, Norfolk', *Antiq. Journ.*, xxi (1941), 40 ff.

I. A. Richmond, 'Queen Cartimandua', *JRS*, xliv (1954), 43 ff.

E. M. Clifford, *Bagendon, a Belgic Oppidum*, Cambridge, 1961, for Boduocus.

Chelmsford: V.C.H., Essex, iii, *Roman Essex* (1963), 63 ff; *Britannia* iv (1973), 301 f.

Great Casterton: M. Todd, op. cit. on p. 449.

Longthorpe and Newton: *JRS*, lv (1965), 75 f.; lxiii (1973), 214; *Britannia* v (1974).

G. Webster, 'The Roman Military Advance under Ostorius Scapula', *Arch. Journ.*, cxv (1958), 49 ff.

M. R. Hull, *Roman Colchester*, Oxford, 1958.

B. W. Cunliffe, *Excavations at Fishbourne* i–ii, Leeds, 1971.

D. E. Eichholz, 'How long did Vespasian serve in Britain?', *Britannia* iii (1972), 149 ff.

R. E. M. Wheeler, *Maiden Castle, Dorset*, Oxford, 1943.

L. Alcock, 'Excavations at S. Cadbury Castle, 1970', *Antiq. Journ.*, li (1971), 1 ff.

I. A. Richmond, *Hod Hill* ii, London, 1968.

Waddon Hill: G. Webster, *Proceedings of the Dorset Natural History and Archaeological Society*, lxxxii (1960), 88 ff.; lxxxvi (1965), 135 ff.

A. Fox, *Roman Exeter*, Manchester, 1952; *JRS* lv (1965), 217; *Britannia* iii (1972), 344; iv (1973), 313.

Kinvaston: G. Webster, *T. Birmingham A.S.*, lxxiii (1955), 100 ff. J. K. St. Joseph, *JRS*, xlviii (1958), 94.

Metchley: J. K. St Joseph and F. W. Shotton, *T. Birmingham A.S.*, lviii (1934), 68 ff. G. Webster, ibid., lxxii (1954), 1 ff.

Wall: J. Gould, *Lichfield and South Staffordshire Archaeological and Historical Society*, v (1963–64), 1 ff.

Wroxeter, fort: J. K. St. Joseph, *T. Birmingham A.S.*, lxix (1951), 54; *JRS*, xlviii (1958), 95.

Wroxeter, fortress: *JRS*, xlv (1955), pl. xix; liv (1963), 162–5.

Gloucester: C. Green, *JRS*, xxxii (1942), 39, corrected by I. A. Richmond and H. E. O'Neil, *Transactions of the Bristol and Gloucestershire Archaeological Society*, lxxxi (1962), 14 ff.; lxxxiv (1965), 15 ff. and H. Hurst 'Excavations at Gloucester 1968–71', *Antiq. Journ.*, lii (1972), 24 ff.

Colonia Victricensis: K. S. Painter, *Antiq. Journ.*, xliii (1963), 123 ff.

A. Fox and W. Ravenhill, 'Old Burrow and Martinhoe', *Antiquity*, xxxix (1965), 253 ff.

I. A. Richmond, 'The Four Coloniae of Roman Britain', *Arch. Journ.*, ciii (1946), 57 ff.

Q. Veranius: see A. E. Gordon, *University of California Publications on Classical Archaeology*, ii (1952), 231 ff.; E. Birley, *Roman Britain and the Roman Army*, Kendal, 1963, pp. 1 ff.; C. E. Stevens, *Classical Review*, n.s., i (1961), 4 ff.

Lincoln: G. Webster, *JRS*, xxxix (1949), 57 ff. F. H. Thompson, ibid., xlvi (1956), 22 ff. D. F. Petch, *Arch. Journ.*, lxvii (1960), 40 ff.

Roman Wales: I. A. Richmond, in I. Ll. Foster and G. Daniel, *Prehistoric and Early Wales*, London, 1965, pp. 151 ff. and see Nash-Williams, cited p. 433.

Sir Cyril Fox, *A Find of the Early Iron Age from Llyn Cerrig Bach, Anglesey*, Cardiff, 1946.

D. R. Dudley and G. Webster, *The Rebellion of Boudicca*, London, 1962.

C. E. Stevens, 'Notes on Roman Chester', *Journ. Chester and N. Wales Arch. Soc.*, xxxv (1942), 49 ff.

Colchester. C. F. C. Hawkes and M. R. Hull, *Camulodunum*, Oxford, 1947; M. R. Hull, *Roman Colchester*, Oxford, 1958.

D. Fishwick, 'Templum divo Claudio constitutum', *Britannia* iii
(1972), 164 ff.

A. R. Burn, *Agricola and Roman Britain*, London, 1953.

Cirencester fort: J. S. Wacher, *Antiq. Journ.*, xlii (1962), 3 ff.; xliv
(1964), 15 ff.

Great Chesterford fort: W. Rodwell, *Britannia* iii (1972), 290 ff.

Classicianus: *RIB* 12, and references cited there.

R. Merrifield, *The Roman City of London*, London, 1965.

S. S. Frere, 'Verulamium, Then and Now', in London University Institute of Archaeology *Bulletin*, iv (1964), 61 ff.; and 'Verulamium,
Three Roman Cities', *Antiquity*, xxxviii (1964), 103 ff.

Usk: *Britannia* ii (1971), 246 f.; iii (1972), 302; iv (1973), 272.

CHAPTER 6   The Flavian Period, pp. 115–140

J. Clarke, Chapter ii in I. A. Richmond (ed.), *Roman and Native in
North Britain*, London, 1958.

R. E. M. Wheeler, *The Stanwick Fortifications*, Oxford, 1954.

Brough on Humber: J. S. Wacher, *Antiq. Journ.*, xl (1960), 58 ff.

P. Corder, *The Defences of the Roman Fort at Malton*, Leeds, 1930,
55 ff.

R.C.H.M. (England), *Eboracum, Roman York*, London, 1962.

Carlisle: J. P. Bushe-Fox, *Archaeologia*, lxiv (1913), 295 ff.

Rey Cross, etc.: I. A. Richmond, *CW* ², xxxiv (1934), 50 ff.

Roman Wales: I. A. Richmond, in I. Ll. Foster and G. Daniel (eds.),
Prehistoric and Early Wales, London, 1965; V. E. Nash-Williams
cited on p. 433.

M. G. Jarrett, 'Early Roman Campaigns in Wales', *Arch. Journ.*, cxxi
(1964), 23 ff.

Chester: *RIB* 463; R. P. Wright, *Roman inscribed . . . stones from
Chester*, Chester, 1955, 48, No. 199; F. H. Thompson, *Roman
Cheshire*, Chester, 1965.

I. A. Richmond, 'Gnaeus Julius Agricola', *JRS*, xxxiv (1944), 34 ff.

A. R. Burn, *Agricola and Roman Britain*, London, 1953.

Carrock Fell: R. G. Collingwood, *CW* ², xxxviii (1938), 32 ff.

Bar Hill, etc.: Sir G. Macdonald, *The Roman Wall in Scotland* (ed. 2),
Oxford, 1934.

Loudoun Hill: S. N. Miller (ed.), *The Roman Occupation of South Western Scotland*, Glasgow, 1952, pp. 188 ff.

Dalswinton: *JRS*, xli (1951), 52 ff.; I. A. Richmond and J. K. St. Joseph, *T. Dumfries. and Gal. Ant. Soc.*, xxxiv (1955–6), 9 ff.

Glenlochar: *JRS*, xli (1951), 52 ff. I. A. Richmond and J. K. St. Joseph, *T. Dumfries. and Gal. Ant. Soc.*, xxx (1951–2), 1 ff.

Gatehouse of Fleet: *JRS*, li (1961), 161; lii (1962), 164.

Forth *Limes*: C. E. Stevens, *Antiquity*, xxxiv (1960), 310.

I. A. Richmond, 'The Agricolan Fort at Fendoch', *PSAS*, lxxiii (1938–39), 110 ff.

Inchtuthil: *JRS*, li (1961), 158.

Cleaven Dyke: I. A. Richmond, *PSAS*, lxxiv (1939–40), 45 ff.

Roman Camps: J. K. St. Joseph, *JRS*, xlviii (1958), 86 ff.; li (1961), 123; lix (1969), 105 ff.; lxiii (1973), 216 ff.; I. A. Richmond, *Arch. Journ.*, xciii (1937), 314.

Verulamium inscription: *Antiq. Journ.*, xxxvi (1956), 8 ff.; xxxvii (1957), 216.

Dorchester on Thames: *JRS*, liv (1964), 166.

Fora: Cirencester, *Antiq. Journ.*, xlii (1962), 7; xliv (1964), 11. Winchester, *Antiq. Journ.*, xliv (1964), 204. Silchester, G. C. Boon, *Roman Silchester*, London, 1957, 67, 94. Leicester, *Britannia* iv (1973), 1 ff. Caistor by Norwich, *Britannia* ii (1971), 1 ff. Exeter, *Britannia* iv (1973), 313.

Stracathro: *JRS*, xlviii (1958), 91, 132; li (1961), 123.

Newstead: R.C.H.M. (Scotland), inventory, *The County of Roxburgh*, ii,, Edinburgh, 1956, pp. 312 ff. I. A. Richmond, *PSAS*, lxxxiv (1949–50), 1 ff.

A. S. Robertson, *The Roman Fort at Castledykes*, Edinburgh, 1964; *JRS*, xliv, 87.

Bochastle: *Transactions of the Glasgow Archaeological Society* [2], xiv (1956), 35 ff.

Oakwood: K. A. Steer and R. W. Feachem, *PSAS*, lxxxvi (1951–52), 81 ff.

Milton: *T. Dumfries, and Gal. Ant. Soc.*, xxviii (1949–50), 199 ff.

Chew Green: *AA* [4], xiv (1937), 129 ff.; *NCH*, xv (1940), 70.

Cappuck: I. A. Richmond, *PSAS*, lxxxv (1950–51), 138 ff. R.C.H.M. (Scotland), inventory, *The County of Roxburgh*, ii, Edinburgh, 1956, 354 ff.

Oxton: *JRS*, xlviii (1958), 88.

Pen Llystyn: A. H. A. Hogg, *Arch. Journ.*, cxxv (1968), 101 ff.

Wroxeter: *JRS*, liv (1964), 162.

CHAPTER 7 The Retreat from Scotland: Hadrian's frontier, pp. 141–164

J. P. Gillam, Chapter iii in I. A. Richmond (ed.), *Roman and Native in North Britain*, London, 1958.

I. A. Richmond, 'The Roman Frontier Land', *History*, xliv (1959), 1 ff.

High Rochester: I. A. Richmond, *AA* [4], xiii (1936), 171 ff.; *NCH*, xv (1940), 63 ff.

Stanegate frontier: E. Birley, *Research on Hadrian's Wall*, Kendal, 1961, chapter v.

Hardknott: *JRS*, lv (1965), 222.

Wales: I. A. Richmond, in I. Ll. Foster and G. Daniel, *Prehistoric and Early Wales*, London, 1965. G. Simpson, *Britons and the Roman Army*, London, 1964. V. E. Nash-Williams, cited on p. 433.

R. Merrifield, *The Roman City of London*, London, 1965.

I. A. Richmond, 'The Four Coloniae . . .', *Arch. Journ.*, ciii (1946), 57 ff.

Jarrow: *RIB*, 1051; I. A. Richmond and R. P. Wright, *AA* [4], xxi (1943), 93 ff.

J. Collingwood Bruce, *Handbook to the Roman Wall* (12th ed., I. A. Richmond), Newcastle, 1966.

H.M. Ordnance Survey, *Map of Hadrian's Wall*, Chessington, 1964.

I. A. Richmond, 'Hadrian's Wall 1939–49', *JRS*, xl (1950), 43 ff.

E. Birley, as above.

J. Morris, 'The Vallum again', *CW* [2], l (1950), 43 ff.

B. Swinbank and J. E. H. Spaul, 'The spacing of the forts on Hadrian's Wall', *AA* [4], xxix (1951), 221 ff.

Legion IX: J. Bogaers, 'Romeins Nijmegen', *Numaga*, 12 (1965), 10 ff. and in *Studien zu den Militärgrenzen Roms*, Köln/Graz, 1967, 54 ff.

CHAPTER 8 The Antonine Wall: the second-century frontier, pp. 165–193

J. P. Gillam, in I. A. Richmond (ed.), *Roman and Native in North Britain*, London, 1958, chapter iii.

I. A. Richmond, 'The Roman Frontier Land', *History*, xliv (1959), 1 ff.

Inveresk: *JRS*, xxxvii (1947), 165; xxxviii (1948), 81.

Lanchester: *T. Durham and N.A. Soc.*, ix (1) (1939), 112 ff.; x (4) (1953), 394.

Bothwellhaugh: S. N. Miller (ed.), *The Roman Occupation of South Western Scotland*, Glasgow, 1952, pp. 172 ff.

Carzield: I. A. Richmond, *T. Dumfries, and Gal. Ant. Soc.*, xxii (1938–40), 156 ff.

Lyne fortlet: *PSAS*, xcv (1961–62), 215 ff.

Lyne fort: *PSAS*, xxxv (1900–1), 154 ff.; xcv (1961–62), 208 ff.; *Britannia* iii (1972), 9.

Raeburnfoot: *T. Dumfries. and Gal. Ant. Soc.*, xxxix (1960–61), 24 ff.

Durisdeer, etc.: S. N. Miller (ed.), *The Roman Occupation of South Western Scotland*, Glasgow, 1952, pp. 124 ff.

Sir George Macdonald, *The Roman Wall in Scotland* (2nd ed.), Oxford, 1934.

A. S. Robertson, *The Antonine Wall*, Glasgow, 1968.

K. A. Steer, 'The Antonine Wall 1934–59', *JRS*, l (1960), 84 ff.

R. W. Feachem, 'Six Roman Camps near the Antonine Wall', *PSAS*, lxxxix (1955–56), 329 ff.

K. A. Steer, 'The Nature and Purpose of the Expansions on the Antonine Wall', *PSAS*, xc (1956–57), 161 ff.

A. S. Robertson, *An Antonine Fort, Golden Hill, Duntocher*, Edinburgh, 1957.

Wilderness Plantation: *JRS*, xli (1951), 61.

Glasgow Bridge: *JRS*, xlv (1955), 86.

Carriden inscription: *PSAS*, xc (1956–57), 1 ff.; *JRS*, xlvii (1957), 229–30.

Whitemoss: *PSAS*, lxxxiii (1948–49), 28 ff.

Lurg Moor: *JRS*, xliii (1953), 105.

Cramond: *JRS*, lii (1962), 161; *Britannia* v (1974).

Ardoch: O. G. S. Crawford, *The Topography of Roman Scotland*, Cambridge, 1949, pp. 34 ff.

Bertha: O. G. S. Crawford, op. cit., 59; *PSAS*, liii (1919), 145 ff.; *JRS*, xlix (1959), 136.

E. Birley, *Roman Britain and the Roman Army*, Kendal, 1953, pp. 31 ff.

R. G. Collingwood and J. N. L. Myres, *Roman Britain and the English Settlements*, Oxford, 1936, pp. 149, 171.

K. A. Steer, 'John Horsley and the Antonine Wall', *AA* [4], xlii (1964), 1 ff.

G. Simpson, *Britons and the Roman Army*, London, 1964; 'Caerleon and the Roman Forts in Wales . . .', *Arch. Camb.*, cxi (1962), 103 ff., cxii (1963), 13 ff.

Rome inscription: *American Journal of Archaeology*, lxiv (1960), 274.

Homesteads: G. Jobey in C. Thomas *op. cit.* on p. 433.

Julius Verus: E. Birley, 'Senators in the Emperors' Service', *Proceedings of the British Academy*, xxxix (1954), 197 ff.

F. Haverfield, *PSAS*, xxxviii (1904), 454 ff.; *AA* [2], xxv (1904), 142.

Lancaster: I. A. Richmond, *Transactions of the Historic Society of Lancashire and Cheshire*, cv (1953), 1 ff.; *JRS*, xlix (1949), 106.

Birrenswark: S. N. Miller (ed.), *The Roman Occupation of South Western Scotland*, Glasgow, 1952, p. 97.

Corbridge hoard: *AA* [3], viii (1912), 74 ff.

Newstead: I. A. Richmond, *PSAS*, lxxxiv, (1949–50), 1 ff.

CHAPTER 9   Severus and the third century, pp. 194–221

Sextus Varius Marcellus: H.-G. Pflaum, *Les Carrières Procuratoriennes Equestres sous le Haut-empire romain*, Paris, 1960, No. 237.

I. A. Richmond, 'The Roman Frontier Land', *History*, xliv (1959), 1 ff.

K. A. Steer, in I. A. Richmond (ed.), *Roman and Native in North Britain*, London, 1958, chapter iv.

E. Birley, *Research on Hadrian's Wall*, Kendal, 1961.

C. Valerius Pudens: *JRS*, li (1961), 192.

E. Birley, 'Excavations at Corstopitum, 1906–58', *AA* [4], xxxvii (1959), 12 ff.

Cramond: *JRS*, xlix (1959), 104; *Britannia* v (1974).

Carpow: R. E. Birley, *PSAS*, xcvi (1962–63), 184 ff.; see also *JRS*, xlv (1965), 223; lxiii (1973), 222.

Marching Camps: *JRS*, xlviii (1958), 93; li (1961), 123, and especially lix (1969), 113 ff.; lxiii (1973), 228 ff.

Brittones dediticii: H. T. Rowell, 'The Honesta Missio from the Numeri of the Roman Imperial Army', *Yale Classical Studies*, vi (1939), 73 ff.

Loca: Ravenna Cosmography, v, 31; *Archaeologia*, xciii, 15 and 19; *NCH*, xv (1940), 97.

Wales: I. A. Richmond, in I. Ll. Foster and G. Daniel, *Prehistoric and Early Wales*, London, 1965. G. Simpson, *Britons and the Roman Army*, London, 1964.

Haltonchesters granary: *JRS*, lii (1962), 164.

Dover: *Britannia* ii (1971), 286; iii (1972), 351.

Reculver: *JRS*, l (1960), 236; li (1961), 191. I. A. Richmond, 'A New Building-inscription from . . . Reculver', *Antiq. Journ.*, xli (1961), 224 ff. (cf. *JRS*, lv (1965), 220).

J. K. St. Joseph, 'The Roman Fort at Brancaster', *Antiq. Journ.*, xvi (1936), 444 ff.

R. Macmullen, *Soldiers and Civilians in the later Roman Empire*, Cambridge, Massachusetts, 1963, ch. i.

Ribchester: I. A. Richmond, 'The Sarmatae . . . and the regio Bremetennacensis', *JRS*, xxxv (1945), 15 ff.

P. Salway, *The Frontier People of Roman Britain*, Cambridge, 1965.

J. P. Bushe Fox, *Excavations of the Roman fort at Richborough, Kent*, iv, Oxford, 1949, 60 ff.

J. S. Johnson, 'The date of the . . . Saxon Shore fort at Richborough', *Britannia* i (1970), 240 ff.

B. W. Cunliffe (ed.), *Excavations of the Roman fort at Richborough, Kent*, v, Oxford, 1968.

CHAPTER 10 The administration of Roman Britain, pp. 222–247

E. Birley, 'Senators in the Emperor's Service', *Proceedings of the British Academy*, xxxix (1954), 197 ff.

E. Birley, 'Beförderung und Versetzungen im römischen Heere', *Carnuntum Jahrbuch*, 1957, 3 ff.

J. Fitz, 'Legati Augusti pro praetore Pannoniae Inferioris', *Acta Antiqua*, xi (1963), 245 ff.

A. H. M. Jones, *Studies in Roman Government and Law*, Oxford, 1960.

E. Birley, *Roman Britain and the Roman Army*, Kendal, 1953.

H.-G. Pflaum, *Les Procurateurs Equestres sous le Haut-empire romain*, Paris, 1950.

H.-G. Pflaum, *Les Carrières Procuratoriennes Equestres sous le Haut-empire romain*, Paris, 1960.

D. Atkinson, 'The Classical Britannica', in *Historical Essays in Honour of James Tait*, 1933, pp. 1 ff.

S. S. Frere, 'Civitas – A Myth?', *Antiquity*, xxxv (1961), 29 ff.

Verulamium: see bibliography of chapter 12 below.

London: R. Merrifield, *The Roman City of London*, London, 1965.

C. E. Stevens, 'The Roman Name of Ilchester', *Proceedings of the Somerset Archaeological Society*, xcvi (1951), 188 ff.

P. Guirand, *Les Assemblées provinciales dans l'empire romain*, Paris, 1887.

J. A. O. Larsen, *Representative Government in Greek and Roman History*, Berkeley, 1955.

D. Fishwick, 'The Imperial Cult in Roman Britain', *Phoenix* (Classical Association of Canada), xv (1961), 159, 213.

Verona List: A. H. M. Jones, *JRS*, xliv (1954), 21 ff.

A. H. M. Jones, *The Later Roman Empire*, Oxford, 1964.

CHAPTER 11   The Roman army in Britain, pp. 248–272

Classis Britannica: see D. Atkinson, op. cit., under chapter 10, and B. W. Cunliffe op. cit., under chapter 9.

I. A. Richmond, 'Roman Britain and Roman Military Antiquities', *Proceedings of the British Academy*, xli (1955), 297 ff.

Camps: *NCH*, xv (1940), and references cited under chapter 6 above. O. G. S. Crawford, 'The Topography of Roman Scotland', Cambridge, 1949. G. D. B. Jones, *BBCS*, xxi (2) (1965), 174 ff. R. E. M. Wheeler, *Prehistoric and Roman Wales*, Oxford, 1925, 220. R.C.H.M. (Scotland), inventory, *The County of Roxburgh*, ii, Edinburgh, 1956, pp. 316, 375. Rey Cross, *CW* [2], xxxiv (1934), 50 ff. *JRS*, xli (1951), pl. vi; xlv (1955), pl. xvi; li (1961), pl. ix.

Inchtuthil plan: *JRS*, li (1961), 158.

Kinvaston plan: *JRS*, xlviii (1958), 94. Longthorpe plan: *Britannia* v (1974).

Chester: F. H. Thompson, *Roman Cheshire*, Chester, 1965.

Caerleon: G. C. Boon, *Isca*, Cardiff, 1972.

V. E. Nash-Williams, *The Roman Frontier in Wales*, 2nd. ed. by M. G. Jarrett, Cardiff, 1969.

R.C.H.M. (England): *Eboracum, Roman York*, London, 1962.

Fendoch: I. A. Richmond, *PSAS*, lxxiii (1938–39), 110 ff.

Carzield: I. A. Richmond, *T. Dumfries, and Gal. Ant. Soc.*, xxii 1938–40), 156 ff.

M. Todd, *The Roman Fort at Great Casterton, Rutland*, Nottingham, 1968.

Cleaven Dyke: I. A. Richmond, *PSAS*, lxxxiv (1939–40), 45 ff.

Glenlochar: *T. Dumfries, and Gal. Ant. Soc.*, xxx (1951–52), 1 ff.

Hod Hill: O. G. S. Crawford and A. Keiller, *Wessex from the Air*, Oxford, 1928, pl. i; *JRS*, xl (1950), pl. viii *a*. I. A. Richmond, *Hod Hill* ii, London, 1968.

High Rochester, Risingham: I. A. Richmond, *AA*[4], xiii (1936), 171 ff.; *NCH*, xv (1940).

Dolddinas: G. D. B. Jones, *BBCS*, xviii (1960), 397 ff,; *JRS*, li (1961), 131.

Rhyd Sarn: G. D. B. Jones, *BBCS*, xix (1960–62), 254.

Loughor: *JRS*, xlviii (1958), 97; *Antiquity*, xxxv (1961), pl. xli.

Llandrindod Common: V. E. Nash Williams, *The Roman Frontier in Wales*, 2nd. ed. by M. G. Jarrett, Cardiff, 1969.

I. A. Richmond, 'The Four Roman Camps at Cawthorn, Yorkshire', *Arch. Journ.*, lxxxix (1932), 17 ff.

Woden Law: R.C.H.M. (Scotland) inventory, *The County of Roxburgh*, i, Edinburgh, 1956, pp. 169 ff.

I. A. Richmond, 'A Roman Arterial Signalling System in the Stainmore Pass', in W. F. Grimes (ed.), *Aspects of Archaeology in Britain and Beyond*, London, 1951, pp. 293 ff.

R. G. Collingwood, *The Archaeology of Roman Britain*, London, 1930; new edition by I. A. Richmond 1969.

Gask Ridge: *PSAS*, xxxv (1901), 15 ff.; cf. ibid., lxxiv (1940), 37 ff. O. G. S. Crawford, *The Topography of Roman Scotland*, Cambridge, 1940, 52 ff.

Scalesceugh: *CW*[2], xvi (1916), 282, 290; ibid., xxii (1922), 456 f.; T. May and L. E. Hope, *Catalogue of Roman Pottery in the Tullie House Museum*, Carlisle, 1917, 85.

W. F. Grimes, *Holt, Denbighshire*, London, 1930 (y *Cymrodor*, xli).

Wilderspool: F. H. Thompson, *Roman Cheshire*, Chester, 1965.

Muncaster: R. L. Belhouse, *CW* ², lx (1960), 1 ff.

Brampton: R. Hogg, *CW* ², lxv (1965), 133 ff.

Catterick, *JRS*, l (1960), 217 f.

A. H. M. Jones, *The Later Roman Empire*, Oxford, 1964.

J. P. Gillam, ' "Also, along the line of the Wall" ', *CW* ², xlix (1949), 38 ff.

C. E. Stevens, 'The British Sections of the Notitia Dignitatum', *Arch. Journ.*, xcvii (1940), 125 ff.

CHAPTER 12   The towns, pp. 273–300

A. L. F. Rivet, *Town and Country in Roman Britain*, London, 1964.

Dorchester and Maiden Castle: R. E. M. Wheeler, *Maiden Castle, Dorset*, Oxford, 1943, fig 1*b*, p. 15.

Chelmsford: V.C.H. Essex iii, *Roman Essex*, London, 1963; *Britannia* ii (1971), 271; iii (1972), 331 f.; iv (1973), 301.

Exeter: A. Fox, *Roman Exeter*, Manchester, 1952.

Cirencester: J. S. Wacher, *Antiq. Journ.*, xli (1961) – xlv (1965).

Great Casterton: P. Corder, *The Roman Town and Villa at Gt. Casterton, Rutland*, Third Report, Nottingham, 1961.

Dorchester-on-Thames: S. S. Frere, *Arch. Journ.*, cxix (1962), 114 ff.; *JRS*, liv (1964), 166.

Brough on Humber: J. S. Wacher, *Antiq. Journ.*, xl (1960), 58 ff.

P. Salway, *The Frontier People of Roman Britain*, Cambridge, 1965.

Verulamium: S. S. Frere, *Antiquity*, xxxviii (1964), 103 ff.; London University Institute of Archaeology *Bulletin*, iv (1964), 61 ff.; *Antiq. Journ.*, xxxvi (1956) – xlii (1962). *Verulamium Excavations* i Oxford, 1972.

Canterbury: A. Williams and S. S. Frere, *Archaeologia Cantiana*, lxi (1948), 1 ff.

Silchester: A. Fox, *Antiquity*, xxii (1948), 172 ff.; G. C. Boon, *Roman Silchester*, London, 1957.

R. G. Goodchild, 'The origins of the Romano-British Forum', *Antiquity*, xx (1946), 70 ff.

Caerwent, forum and bath: V. E. Nash Williams, *BBCS*, xv (1953), 159 ff.

Wroxeter: K. M. Kenyon, *Archaeologia*, lxxxviii (1938), 175 ff.

Verulamium market: K. M. Richardson, *Archaeologia*, xc (1944), 81 ff.

R. E. M. and T. V. Wheeler, *Verulamium, A Belgic and Two Roman Cities*, Oxford, 1936.

Canterbury: S. S. Frere, *Antiquity*, xxiii (1949), 153 ff.; *Roman Canterbury* (3rd ed.), Canterbury, 1962.

Chichester amphitheatre: G. M. White, *Antiq. Journ.*, xvi (1936), 149 ff.

Caistor by Norwich: C. F. C. Hawkes, *Arch Journ.*, cvi (1949), 62 ff.; S. S. Frere, *Britannia* ii (1971), 1 ff.

D. Atkinson, *Excavations at Wroxeter* 1923–27, Oxford, 1942.

Wroxeter Baths: K. M. Kenyon, *Archaeologia*, lxxxviii (1938), 175 ff.; G. Webster, *Antiq. Journ.*, xlvi (1966).

K. M. Kenyon, *The Jewry Wall site*, Leicester, Oxford, 1948; see also *JRS*, liv (1964), fig. on p. 161; *ibid.* xxxix (1949), 142 ff.

Leicester forum: M. Hebditch and J. Mellor, *Britannia* iv (1973), 1 ff.

Dorchester aqueduct: K. M. Richardson, *Antiq. Journ.*, xx (1940), 435 ff; R.C.H.M., *Dorset* II (iii) (1970), 585 ff.

Wroxeter aqueduct: G. Webster, *Transactions of the Shropshire Archaeological Society*, lvi (2) (1959), 133 ff.

Lincoln aqueduct: F. H. Thompson, *Arch. Journ.*, cxi (1954), 106 ff.

Silchester pipeline: *Archaeologia*, lv (1897), 422 ff.

Wroxeter ducts: J. P. Bushe Fox, *Excavations on the Site of . . . Wroxeter*, iii, (1914), Oxford, 1916.

Lincoln sewers: I. A. Richmond, *Arch. Journ.*, ciii (1946), 26 ff.

Kenchester: G. H. Jack and A. G. K. Hayter, *Excavations on the Site of . . . Magna*, ii, Hereford, 1926.

M. R. Hull, *Roman Colchester*, Oxford, 1958.

R. Merrifield, *The Roman City of London*, London, 1965.

Wroxeter: I. A. Richmond, 'The Cornovii', in I. Ll. Foster and L. Alcock, (eds.) *Culture and Environment*, London, 1963. G. Webster, 'Viroconium, A study of Problems', *Transactions of the Shropshire Archaeological Society*, lvii (2) (1962–63).

Silchester bank: G. C. Boon, *P. Hants. F.C.*, xxi (1) (1958), 9 ff. and *Archaeologia* cii (1969), 1 ff.

Silchester Wall: M. A. Cotton, *Archaeologia*, xcii (1947), 121 ff.

Lincoln defences: D. F. Petch, *Arch. Journ.*, cxvii (1960), 40 ff. F. H.

Thompson and J. B. Whitwell, *Archaeologia* civ (1973), 129 ff.

Caistor by Norwich bank: *JRS*, li (1961), pl. x; see also our pl. 8a.

J. S. Wacher, *The Civitas Capitals of Roman Britain*, Leicester, 1966.

Chichester walls: J. Holmes, *Sx. A.C.*, c (1962), 80 ff.

Caerwent walls: V. E. Nash Williams, *Archaeologia*, lxxx (1930), 229 ff. O. E. Craster, *Arch. Camb.*, ciii, 1954, 54 ff.

Aldborough walls: J. N. L. Myres, K. A. Steer and A. M. H. Chitty, *Yorkshire Archaeological Journal*, 157 (1959), 1 ff.

Gallic walls: R. M. Butler, *Arch. Journ.*, cxvi (1959), 25 ff. J. S. Johnson, *Britannia* iv (1973), 210 ff.

Witherley: A. Oswald and P. W. Gathercole, *Trans. Birmingham A.S.*, lxxiv (1956), 30 ff.

Rocester: G. Webster, *North Staffordshire Journal of Field Studies*, ii (1962), 37 ff.

Gloucester: see the papers by I. A. Richmond, H. E. O'Neil and H. Hurst, cited on p. 441.

Great Chesterford: V.C.H. Essex, iii, *Roman Essex*, London, 1963.

P. Corder, 'The Reorganisation of the Defences of Romano-British Towns in the Fourth Century', *Arch. Journ.*, cxii (1955), 20 ff.

Barbarian warfare: E. A. Thompson, *The Early Germans*, Oxford, 1965, chapter iv (from *Past and Present*, xiv (1958)).

J. Joyce, 'Account of further excavations at Silchester', *Archaeologia*, xlvi (1880), 344 ff.

Industry: I. A. Richmond, in J. S. Wacher, *The Civitas Capitals of Roman Britain*, Leicester, 1966, 76 ff.

CHAPTER 13   The countryside, pp. 301–319

A. L. F. Rivet, *Town and Country in Roman Britain*, London, 1964.

A. L. F. Rivet (ed.), *The Roman Villa in Britain*, London, 1969.

R. G. Collingwood, in Tenney Frank, *An Economic Survey of Ancient Rome*, iii (1937 and 1959).

'Report on Conference on Romano-British Villas', *Archaeological News Letter*, vi (2) (1955), 29 ff.

H. C. Bowen, *Ancient Fields*, London, 1961.

C. F. C. Hawkes, 'Britons, Romans and Saxons . . . in Cranborne Chase', *Arch. Journ.*, civ (1947), 27 ff.

G. R. Wolseley, R. A. Smith and W. Hawley, 'Prehistoric and Roman Settlements on Park Brow', *Archaeologia*, lxxvi (1926–27), 1 ff.

Studland: N. H. Field, *Proc. Dorset Nat. Hist. and Arch. Soc.*, 87 (1966), 142 ff.

S. J. Hallam, 'Villages in Roman Britain', *Antiq. Journ.*, xliv (1964), 19 ff.

Villages: R.C.H.M. (England), inventory, *Dorset*.

S. Applebaum, 'The Agriculture . . . at Figheldean Down, Wiltshire', *PPS*, xx (1954), 103 ff.

W. H. Manning, 'The Villa in Roman Britain', *Antiquity*, xxxvi (1962), 56 ff.

Park Street: H. E. O'Neil, *Arch. Journ.*, cii (1945), 21 ff.

Hambleden: A. H. Cocks, *Archaeologia*, lxxi (1920–21), 141 ff.

Llantwit Major: V. E. Nash Williams, *Arch Camb.*, cii (1953), 89 ff. A. H. A. Hogg, *Britannia* v (1974).

W. Gardner and H. N. Savory, *Dinorben*, Cardiff, 1964.

Lockleys: J. B. Ward Perkins, *Antiq. Journ.*, xviii (1938), 339 ff.; *Antiquity*, xiv (1940), 317 ff.

Ditchley: C. A. R. Radford, *Oxoniensia*, i (1936), 24 ff.

Catsgore: C. A. R. Radford, *Proceedings of the Somerset Archaeological Society*, xcvi (1951), 41 ff.

Newport: P. G. Stone, *Antiq. Journ.*, ix (1929), 141 ff.

Bignor: *JRS*, xlvii (1957), 223; xlix (1959), 131; l (1960), 234; lii (1962), 189; liii (1963), 155, and fig. 34; see also S. E. Winbolt and G. Herbert, *The Roman Villa at Bignor, Sussex* (guide book), Chichester.

Cox Green: C. M. Bennett, *Berkshire Archaeological Journal*, lx (1962), 62 ff.

North Leigh: VCH, *Oxford*, i, 1939, 316 ff.

S. Lysons, *Roman Antiquities at Woodchester*, London, 1797.

B. W. Cunliffe, *Excavations at Fishbourne* i–ii, Leeds, 1971.

Angmering: L. Scott, *Sx.A.C.*, lxxix (1938), 3 ff.; lxxx (1939), 89 ff.

Eccles: A. P. Detsicas, *Arch. Cant.*, lxxviii (1963), 125 ff.; lxxix (1964), 121 ff.; lxxx (1965), 69 ff., and following volumes.

Castle Dykes: O. G. S. Crawford, *British Association* (*Leeds* 1927) *Handbook*, xi, Leeds, 1927.

High Wycombe: B. R. Hartley, *Records of Buckinghamshire*, xvi (4) (1959), 227 ff.

Winterton: I. M. Stead, *Antiq. Journ.*, xlvi (1966), 72 ff.

J. T. Smith, 'Romano-British Aisled Houses', *Arch. Journ.*, cxx (1963), 1 ff.

S. Applebaum, unpublished D.Phil. thesis, Oxford University; see also 'Agriculture in Roman Britain', *Agricultural History Review*, vi (1958), 66 ff.

Exning: *JRS*, l (1960), 228.

Barrow Burials: R. F. Jessup, *Journal of the British Archaeological Association* [3], xxii (1959), 1 ff.

West Blatchington: N. E. S. Norris and G. P. Burstow, *Sx.A.C.*, lxxxix (1950), 1 ff.; xc (1951–52), 221 ff.

Stroud: A. M. Williams, *Arch. Journ.*, lxv (1908), 57 ff.; lxvi (1909), 33 ff.

G. A. Holleyman, 'The Celtic Field-System in South Britain', *Antiquity*, ix (1935), 443 ff.

V.C.H., Essex iii, *Roman Essex*, London, 1963.

R.C.H.M. (England), *A Matter of Time*, London, 1960.

S. Applebaum, 'Distribution of the Romano-British Population in the Basingstoke Area', *P. Hants. F.C.*, xviii (1), (1953), 119 ff.

Grassington: E. Curwen, *Antiquity*, ii (1928), 168 ff.

R.C.H.M. (England), inventory, *Westmorland*, London, 1936.

R. G. Collingwood and J. N. L. Myres, *Roman Britain and the English Settlements*, Oxford, 1936, p. 210, map 2.

J. W. Brailsford, 'Early Iron Age C in Wessex', *PPS*, xxiv (1958), pp. 101 ff.

Fens: S. J. Hallam, op. cit. (p. 453). C. W. Phillips (ed.), *The Fenland in Roman Times*, London, 1970.

J. G. D. Clark, 'Report on excavations on the Cambridgeshire Car Dyke . . .', *Antiq. Journ.*, xxix (1949), 137.

Ploughs: F. G. Payne, *Arch. Journ.*, civ (1947), 82 ff. W. Manning, *JRS*, liv (1964), 54 ff. A. Fenton, *PSAS*, xcvi (1962–63), 264 ff.

Cromwell: *JRS*, li (1961), pl. xi; see also *Britannia* v (1974), pl. 23.

Great Chesterford: *Arch. Journ.*, xiii (1856), 1 ff.

Corn-drying ovens: W. Gowland, *Archaeologia*, lxxi (1920–21), 158 ff. E. C. Curwen, *Antiq. Journ.*, xiii (1933), 109 ff. R. Goodchild, *Antiq. Journ.*, xxiii (1943), 148 ff. P. Corder, *The Roman Town and Villa at Great Casterton, Rutland*, ii, Nottingham, 1954, 19 ff.

Abinger: villa, *The Builder*, xxxvi (1878), 19 f.; *Sy.A.C.*, xxix (1916), 154 f.; leet, *Sy.A.C.*, xliv (1936), 149.

Grimsby: D. F. Petch, *Lincolnshire Architectural and Archaeological Society Reports and Papers*, ix (1961), 15; *Lincolnshire History and Archaeology* I (2), 55.

Bee hives: *Sy.A.C.*, lvii (1960), 57.

Tapete Britannicum: *JRS*, xlv (1955), 114 .

CHAPTER 14   Trade and industry, pp. 320–341

R. G. Collingwood, 'Roman Britain', in Tenney Frank, *An Economic Survey of Ancient Rome*, iii (1937 and 1959).

R. F. Tylecote, *Metallurgy in Archaeology*, London, 1962.

Dolaucothi mines: V. E. Nash Williams, *BBCS*, xiv (1950), 79 ff. G. D. B. Jones and P. R. Lewis, *Bonner Jahrb*. 171 (1971), 288 ff.; *Antiq. Journ.* xlix (1969), 244 ff. Water-wheel: G. Boon, *JRS*, lvi (1966), 122 ff.

Dolaucothi aqueduct: G. D. B. Jones, *BBCS*, xix (1960), 71 ff.

Lead pigs: G. Webster, 'The lead-mining industry in North Wales in Roman times', *Flintshire Historical Society Publications*, xiii (1952–53), 5 ff. R. F. Tylecote, op. cit.; and *JRS*, xlvii (1957), 230 f.

Brough fort: *Journal of the Derbyshire Arch. and Nat. Hist. Society*, lix (1938), 61 ff.

Lead Seals: I. A. Richmond, *CW* [2], xxxvi (1936), 104 ff.; *AA* [4], xi (1934), 101 f.

A. J. Evans, 'Coinage and Currency in Roman Britain', *Numismatic Chronicle* [4], xv (1915), 433 ff.

K. S. Painter, 'A Roman Silver Treasure from Canterbury', *JBAA* [3], xxviii (1965), 1 ff.

Pewter: W. J. Wedlake, *Excavations at Camerton, Somerset*, Bath, 1958, 82 ff.

Tin: F. Haverfield, V.C.H., *Cornwall*, London, 1924.

R. E. M. Wheeler, *Prehistoric and Roman Wales*, Oxford, 1925, 270.

R. G. Collingwood, 'Romano-Celtic Art in Northumbria', *Archaeologia*, lxxx (1930), 37 ff.

C. F. C. Hawkes, 'Bronze-workers, Cauldrons and Bucket

Animals . . .', in W. F. Grimes (ed.), *Aspects of Archaeology in Britain and Beyond*, London, 1951.

G. C. Dunning, 'The Purbeck Marble Industry in Roman Britain', *Archaeological News Letter*, i, 11 (March 1949), 15 ff.

F. Oswald and T. D. Pryce, *An Introduction to the Study of Terra Sigillata*, London, 1920.

Glass, Caistor by Norwich: D. Atkinson, 'Caistor Excavations, 1929', *Papers of the Norfolk and Norwich Archaeological Society*, xxiv (2) (1930), 93 ff. Wilderspool: F. H. Thompson, *Roman Cheshire*, Chester, 1965, Mancetter: recent work.

M. H. Callender, *Roman Amphorae*, Oxford, 1965.

R.C.H.M. (England), *Roman London*, London, 1928.

J. A. Stanfield and G. Simpson, *Central Gaulish Potters*, Oxford, 1958.

B.M., *The Mildenhall Treasure*, London, 1947.

B. R. Hartley, *Notes on the Roman Pottery Industry in the Nene Valley*, Peterborough, 1960.

M. R. Hull, *The Roman Potters' Kilns of Colchester*, Oxford, 1963.

G. Simpson, 'The Aldgate Potter . . .', *JRS*, xlii (1952), 68 ff.

H. Sumner, *Excavations in New Forest Roman Pottery Sites*, London, 1927.

M. Fulford, 'The Distribution and dating of New Forest Pottery', *Britannia* iv (1973), 160 ff.

Surrey Archaeological Society, *A Survey of the . . . Farnham District*, Guildford, 1939.

Council for British Archaeology (Research Report 6), *Romano-British Coarse Pottery: A Student's Guide*, London, 1963. Research Report 10: *Current Research in Romano-British Coarse Pottery*, London, 1973.

J. P. Gillam, 'Types of Roman Coarse Pottery Vessels in Northern Britain', *AA*[4], xxxv (1957), 1 ff.

J. P. Gillam, 'Romano-British Derbyshire ware', *Antiq. Journ.*, xix (1939), 429 ff.

J. P. Gillam, 'Dales Ware', *Antiq. Journ.*, xxxi (1951), 154 ff.

P. Corder, *The Roman Pottery at Crambeck . . .*, York, 1928; see also *Antiq. Journ.*, xvii (1937), 392 ff.

Jet: R.C.H.M. (England), *Eboracum, Roman York*, London, 1962, 141 ff.

Porcupine Bank: *JRS*, xxiv (1934), 220 f.

Roman finds in Ireland: *Proc. Royal Irish Academy* 73, Section C, No. 2 (1973), 21–97.

Skye bale: V. G. Childe, *Scotland before the Scots*, London, 1946, p. 85, fig. 20; see also *PSAS*, lxvi, 289; xlix, 66.

S. Piggott, 'Three metal-work hoards . . .', *PSAS*, lxxxvii (1952–53), 1 ff.

Classis Britannica tiles: Bardown, *JRS*, xlii (1952), 107. Cranbrook, *JRS*, xlix (1959), 137. Bodiam, *JRS*, li (1961), 196.

E. Straker, *Wealden Iron*, London, 1931.

G. Webster, 'A note on the use of Coal in Roman Britain', *Antiq. Journ.*, xxxv (1955), 199 ff.

Cake mould: G. C. Boon, *Antiq. Journ.*, xxxviii (1958), 237 ff.

Whetstones: D. Atkinson, *Excavations at Wroxeter 1923–27*, Oxford, 1942, 129; T. C. Cantrill, *Arch. Camb.*, lxxxvi (1931), 96 ff.

J. Liversidge, *Furniture in Roman Britain*, London, 1955.

Salt: R. G. Collingwood, in Tenney Frank, op. cit., 105 ff. S. J. Hallam, 'Romano-British Salt Industry in South Lincolnshire', *Lincolnshire Architectural and Archaeological Society Reports and Papers*, viii (1960), 35 ff.

Leather: R. Merrifield, *The Roman City of London*, London, 1965 ('bikini' and shoes). J. Curle, *A Roman Frontier Post . . . the fort of Newstead*, Glasgow, 1911.

Tents: I. A. Richmond, *CW* [2], xxxiv (1934), 62 ff.

Carding combs: W. H. Manning, *Antiquity*, xl (1966), 60 ff.

Great Chesterford hoard: *Arch. Journ.*, xiii (1856), 1 ff.

Worlington hoard: J. Liversidge, *Proc. Camb. Antiq. Soc.*, xlix (1955), 89.

Chedworth: I. A. Richmond, *Transactions of the Bristol and Gloucestershire Archaeological Society*, lxxviii (1959), 5 ff. R. Goodburn, *The Roman Villa, Chedworth*, London, 1972.

Darenth: G. Fox, *Archaeologia*, lix (1905), 205 ff. G. Payne, *Arch. Cant.*, xxii (1897), 49 ff.

I. D. Margary, *Roman Roads in Britain*, London, i (1955), ii (1957).

R. E. M. Wheeler, 'The Roman Light-houses at Dover', *Arch. Journ.*, lxxxvi (1930), 22 ff.

CHAPTER 15   The romanisation of Britain, pp. 342–375

J. M. C. Toynbee, *Art in Roman Britain*, London, 1962; *Art in Britain under the Romans*, Oxford, 1964.

Brough on Humber, burial: P. Corder and I. A. Richmond, *Antiq. Journ.*, xviii (1938), 68 ff.; the same, 'Petuaria', *JBAA*[3], vii (1942), 1 ff.; cf. *RIB*, 707.

Rufus, son of Callisunus: I. A. Richmond, *Antiq. Journ.*, xxxiii (1953), 206.

Verulamium mosaics: R. E. M. and T. V. Wheeler, *Verulamium, a Belgic and Two Roman Cities*, Oxford, 1936, 142 ff. S. S. Frere, *Antiq. Journ.*, xxxix (1959), 13 ff.; xl (1960), 1 ff.

Colchester mosaics: D. J. Smith, *Arch. Journ.*, cxxiii (1967), 40 ff., and in A. L. F. Rivet (ed.), *The Roman Villa in Britain*, London, 1969, 77 n. 3.

Fishbourne: B. W. Cunliffe, *Excavations at Fishbourne* i–ii, Leeds, 1971.

Mosaics: J. M. C. Toynbee, *Art in Britain under the Romans*, pp. 228 ff. D. J. Smith in A. L. F. Rivet (ed.), *The Roman Villa in Britain*, 71 ff.

Wall-paintings: J. M. C. Toynbee op. cit., pp. 213 ff.; *Art in Roman Britain*, pl. 195 ff. S. S. Frere, *Antiq. Journ.*, xxxvii (1957), 1 ff.; xxxix (1959), 1 ff. J. S. Wacher, *Antiq. Journ.*, xliii (1963), pl. xi. J. Liversidge in A. L. F. Rivet op. cit., 127 ff.

Amphitheatres: Cirencester, J. S. Wacher, *Antiq. Journ.*, xliii (1963), 23 ff.; xliv (1964), 17 ff. Chichester, G. M. White, *Antiq. Journ.*, xvi (1936), 149 ff. Caerleon, R. E. M. and T. V. Wheeler, *Archaeologia*, lxxviii (1928), 111 ff. Chester, F. H. Thompson, *Roman Cheshire*, Chester, 1965; *JRS*, li (1961), 165 ff.; lvi, 201. Carmarthen, *Britannia* ii (1971), 243 f.

Rounds: C. Thomas, *Rural Settlement in Roman Britain*, London, 1966, 87–96.

Low Ham: *JRS*, xxxvi (1946), pl. xi. J. M. C. Toynbee, *Art in Roman Britain*, pl. 235; *Art in Britain under the Romans*, pl. lviii; our plate 12b.

Lullingstone: G. W. Meates, *Lullingstone Roman Villa*, London, 1955. J. M. C. Toynbee, *Art in Roman Britain*, pl. 229; *Art in Britain under the Romans*, pl. lx.

Otford: *JRS*, xvi (1926), 238, 244; V.C.H., *Kent*, iii (1932), 122, pl. 25.

C. F. C. Hawkes, 'Bronze-workers, Cauldrons and Bucket-Animals in Iron Age and Roman Britain', in W. F. Grimes (ed.), *Aspects of Archaeology in Britain and Beyond*, London, 1951.

K. S. Painter, 'A Roman Marble Head from Sussex', *Antiq. Journ.*, xlv (1965), 178.

I. A. Richmond, 'Three fragments of Roman official statues . . .', *Antiq. Journ.*, xxiv (1944), 1 ff.

I. A. Richmond and J. M. C. Toynbee, 'The Temple of Sulis-Minerva at Bath', *JRS*, xlv (1955), 97 ff. B. Cunliffe, *Antiquity*, xl (1966), 199 ff.; *Roman Bath*, Oxford, 1969.

Lower Slaughter: J. M. C. Toynbee, *JRS*, xlviii (1958), 49 ff.

Rushall Down: B.M., *Antiquities of Roman Britain*, London, 1951, p. 53, fig. 25.5.

Lincoln: I. A. Richmond, *Arch. Journ.*, ciii (1946), 26 ff. J. M. C. Toynbee, *Art in Roman Britain*, pl. 88.

Ancaster: S. S. Frere, *Antiq. Journ.*, xli (1961), 229 ff.

Sibson: J. M. C. Toynbee, *Art in Roman Britain*, pl. 26.

Pitt Rivers, *Excavations in Cranborne Chase*, i–iv (1887, 1888, 1892, 1898).

D. J. Smith, 'Three fourth-century Schools of Mosaic in Roman Britain', *La Mosaïque Gréco-Romaine*, C.N.R.S., Paris, 1965, 95 ff., and in A. L. F. Rivet, *The Roman Villa in Britain*, London, 1969, 71 ff.

H. Last, 'Rome and the Druids: a note', *JRS*, xxxix (1949), 1 ff.

Parade ground: L. P. Wenham, *CW* [2], xxxix (1939), 19 ff.

D. Fishwick, 'The Imperial Cult in Roman Britain', *Phoenix* (Classical Association of Canada), xv (1961), 159 ff. and 213 ff., and 'Templum divo Claudio constitutum', *Britannia* iii (1972), 164 ff.

M. R. Hull, *Roman Colchester*, Oxford, 1958.

Bosham: J. M. C. Toynbee, *Art in Roman Britain*, 50; K. S. Painter, see above.

A. Ross, 'The horned god of the Brigantes', *AA* [4], xxxix (1961), 63 ff.

Foss dyke: J. M. C. Toynbee, *Art in Roman Britain*, pl. 19; B.M., *Guide to the Antiquities of Roman Britain*, London, 1951, pl. xiv.

Temple of Antenociticus: F. G. Simpson and I. A. Richmond, *AA*[4], xix (1941), 37 ff.

Shrine of Coventina: *AA*[2], viii, 1 ff.

Nodens: R. E. M. and T. V. Wheeler, *Report on the excavation of the . . . Roman . . . site in Lydney Park, Gloucestershire*, Oxford, 1932; cf. *RIB*, 616, 617.

Mars Alator: J. M. C. Toynbee, *Art in Britain under the Romans*, 328 ff. B.M., *Guide to the Antiquities of Roman Britain*, London, 1951, fig. 31.

Ancasta: *RIB*, 97.

Cuda: *RIB*, 129.

Viridius: *JRS*, lii (1962), 192.

Sucellus: J. M. C. Toynbee, *Art in Roman Britain*, pl. 78.

Farley Heath: R. G. Goodchild, *Antiq. Journ.*, xxvii (1947), 83.

Arnemetia: I. A. Richmond, *Roman Britain*, London, 1963, p. 76.

Temples: R. G. Collingwood, *The Archaeology of Roman Britain*, London, 1930; new edition by I. A. Richmond, 1969. M. J. T. Lewis, *Temples in Roman Britain*, Cambridge, 1966.

Gosbecks Farm: M. R. Hull, *Roman Colchester*, Oxford, 1958, pp. 259 ff. R. Dunnett, 'The excavation of the Roman theatre at Gosbecks', *Britannia* ii (1971), 27 ff.

Springhead: W. S. Penn, *Arch. Cant.*, lxxiv (1960), 113 ff.; cf. ibid., lxxiii (1959), 1 ff.

Thistleton Dyer: *JRS*, lii (1962), 171 f.

Ancaster and Nettleham: *JRS*, lii (1962), 192.

S. Piggott, 'Three metal-work hoards . . .', *PSAS*, lxxxvii (1952–53), 1 ff.

Verulamium, water cult: S. S. Frere, *Antiq. Journ.*, xxxvii (1957), 14 f.

Jordon Hill: C. D. Drew, *Proceedings of the Dorset Natural History and Archaeological Society*, liii (1931), 265 ff.

Broadway: C. F. C. Hawkes, *Antiq. Journ.*, xxviii (1948), 166 ff.

J. M. C. Toynbee, 'Christianity in Roman Britain', *JBAA*[3], xvi (1953), 1 ff.

W. H. C. Frend, 'Religion in Roman Britain in the fourth century', *JBAA*[3], xviii (1955), 1 ff.

M. W. Barley and R. P. C. Hanson (ed.), *Christianity in Britain, 300–700*, Leicester, 1968.

Churches: Silchester, S. S. Frere, *Archaeologia* cv forthcoming. Verulamium, I. E. Anthony, *Hertfordshire Archaeology* i (1968), 9 ff.
Richborough, P. D. C. Brown, *Britannia* ii (1971), 225 ff.

Lullingstone: G. W. Meates, *Lullingstone Roman Villa*, London,
1955, pp. 126 ff. idem, *Lullingstone Roman Villa* (Ministry of
Works Guide), London, 1962. J. M. C. Toynbee, *Art in Roman
Britain*, pl. 204–5; *Art in Britain under the Romans*, pl. liv–lv.

Chew Stoke Temple: P. Rahtz, *Proceedings of the Somerset Archaeological Society*, xcvi (1951), 112 ff.

R. Merrifield, *The Roman City of London*, 1965.

Woodeaton: R. G. Goodchild and J. R. Kirk, *Oxoniensia*, xix (1954),
15 ff.

Bream Down: *JRS*, xlix (1959), 129; *PUBSS*, x (1965), 195 ff.

CHAPTER 16 Carausius and the fourth century, pp. 376–403

D. A. White, *Litus Saxonicum*, Madison, Wisconsin, 1961.

I. A. Richmond, Chapter v in I. A. Richmond (ed.), *Roman and Native
in North Britain*, London, 1958.

I. A. Richmond, 'The Roman Frontier Land', *History*, xliv (1959),
1 ff.

R. A. G. Carson, 'The Mints and Coinage of Carausius and Allectus',
Journal of the British Archaeological Association, xxii (1959),
33 ff.

Briconium: G. F. Hill, *Numismatic Chronicle*, 1925, 336.

P. H. Webb, in Mattingly and Sydenham, *Roman Imperial Coinage*, v
(2), London, 1933, pp. 426 ff.

Burgh Castle: A. J. Morris, *Proceedings of the Suffolk Institute of
Archaeology*, xxiv (2) (1949), 100 ff. A. J. Morris and C. F. C.
Hawkes, *Arch. Journ.*, cvi (1949), 66.

Cardiff: V. E. Nash Williams, *The Roman Frontier in Wales*, 2nd
edition by M. G. Jarrett, Cardiff, 1969, 70 ff.

Lancaster: I. A. Richmond, *Transactions of the Historic Society of
Lancashire and Cheshire*, cv (1953), 1 ff.

Caernarvon and Holyhead: V. E. Nash Williams, op. cit., pp. 63,
135 ff.

D. E. Eichholz, 'Constantius Chlorus' invasion of Britain', *JRS*, xliii
(1953), 41 ff.

Arras medallion: A. J. Evans, *Numismatic Chronicle*, 1930, 221 ff.

High Rochester and Risingham: I. A. Richmond, *AA*[4], xiii (1936), 170 ff.; *NCH*, xv (1940).

Bewcastle: I. A. Richmond *et alii*, *CW*[2], xxxviii (1938), 195 ff.

Bainbridge: B. R. Hartley, *Proceedings of the Leeds Philosophical and Literary Society*, ix (3) (1960), 107 ff.

Ilkley: *JRS*, liii (1963), 129. B. R. Hartley, *loc. cit.* xii (2) (1966), 23 ff.

Piercebridge: G. S. Keeney, *T. Durham and N. A. Soc.*, ix (1939), 43 ff.

Newton Kyme: *JRS*, xlvii (1957), 209.

Elslack: T. May, *Yorkshire Archaeological Journal*, xxi (1911), 113ff.

Chester: F. H. Thompson, *Roman Cheshire*, Chester, 1965.

York: R.C.H.M. (England), *Eboracum, Roman York*, London, 1962.

Pevensey: J. P. Bushe Fox, *JRS*, xxii (1932), 60 ff.

Romano-Saxon Pottery: J. N. L. Myres, in D. B. Harden op. cit. on p. 464.

Chester le Street: *Arch. Journ.*, cxi (1954), 196; *JRS*, xlix (1959), 106; l (1960), 215.

Overborough: O. North and E. J. W. Hildyard, *CW*[2], liv (1954), 66 ff., and J. P. Gillam, ibid., 96.

Signal Stations: F. J. Haverfield, *JRS*, ii (1912), 201 ff. Barrock Fell: R. G. Collingwood, *CW*[2], xxxi (1931), 111; *Antiquity*, iv (1930), 472. Scarborough: R. G. Collingwood, in A. Rowntree, *The History of Scarborough*, London, 1931, pp. 40 ff. Huntcliff: W. Hornsby and R. Stanton, *JRS*, ii (1912), 215 ff. Goldsborough: W. Hornsby and J. D. Laverick, *Arch Journ.*, lxxxix (1932), 203 ff.

Portchester: B. W. Cunliffe, *Antiq. Journ.*, xliii (1963), 218; ibid., xlvi (1966), 39 and following volumes.

Caernarvon: R. E. M. Wheeler, *Segontium and the Roman Occupation of Wales*, London, 1924.

Lydney: R. E. M. and T. V. Wheeler, *Report on the Excavation of the . . . Roman . . . site in Lydney Park, Gloucestershire*, Oxford, 1932.

Villas: F. J. Haverfield, V.C.H., *Somerset*; London, 1906, pp. 298 ff.; V.C.H. *Hampshire*, London, 1900, 293 ff

Park Street: H. E. O'Neil, *Arch Journ.*, cii (1945), 21 ff.

Langton: P. Corder and J. L. Kirk, *A Roman Villa at Langton . . . East Yorkshire*, Leeds, 1932.

Bokerly Dyke: C. F. C. Hawkes, *Arch. Journ.*, civ (1947), 62 ff.; P. A. Rahtz, ibid., cxviii (1961), 65 ff.

J. P. Gillam, 'Roman Pottery in north Britain', *Carnuntina* (Römische Forschungen in Niederösterreich, iii), Graz-Koln, 1956, 64 ff.

S. C. Hawkes and G. C. Dunning, 'Soldiers and Settlers in Britain, fourth to fifth century . . .', *Medieval Archaeology*, v (1961), 1 ff.; *Bericht der Römisch-germanischen Kommission*, xliii–xliv (1962–63), 155 ff.

CHAPTER 17 The end of Roman Britain, pp. 404–429

C.E. Stevens, 'Gildas Sapiens', *English Historical Review*, cvi (1941), 353 ff.

Maximus: see M. P. Charlesworth, *The Lost Province*, Cardiff, 1949, pp. 26 ff.

Wroxeter: T. Wright, *Uriconium*, London, 1872.

Marcus, Gratian, Constantine: see the paper of this title by C. E. Stevens in *Athenaeum – Studi Periodici di Letteratura e Storia dell' Antichità* (Pavia), xxxv (1957), 316 ff.

Pelagianism: J. N. L. Myres, *JRS*, l (1960), 21–36. See also W. Liebeschuetz, *Historia* 12 (1963, 227 ff. and *Latomus* 26 (1967), 436 ff.

J. Morris, 'Dark Age Dates', in M. G. Jarrett and B. Dobson, *Britain and Rome*, Kendal, 1966, 145 ff.

Coinage: A. Ravetz, 'Roman Coinage of the Fourth Century in Britain', unpublished Ph.D. Thesis, University of Leeds, 1963; 'Fourth-century Inflation and R.B. coin-finds', *Numismatic Chronicle*,[7] iv (1964), 201 ff. J. P. C. Kent, 'From Roman Britain to Saxon England', in R. H. M. Dolley (ed.), *Anglo-Saxon Coins*, London (1961), pp. 2 ff.; idem, *CW*[2], li (1951), 4 ff. A. J. Evans, 'Coinage and Currency in Roman Britain', *Numismatic Chronicle*[4], xv (1915), 433 ff. K. S. Painter, 'A Roman Silver Treasure from Canterbury', *JBAA*[3], xxviii (1965), 1 ff.

Villas: Great Casterton, P. Corder, *The Roman Town and Villa at Great Casterton, Rutland*, i–iii, Nottingham, 1951, 1954, 1961. Hucclecote, E. Clifford, *Transactions of the Bristol and Gloucestershire Archaeological Society*, lv (1933), 323 ff. North Wraxall, *Wiltshire Archaeological Magazine*, vii (1862), 59 ff. Lullingstone, G. W. Meates, *The Lullingstone Roman Villa*

(Ministry of Works Guide), London, 1962. Whittington Court, H. E. O'Neil, *Transactions of the Bristol and Gloucestershire Archaeological Society*, lxxi (1952), 13 ff. King's Weston, G. C. Boon, ibid., lxix (1950), 5 ff. Atworth, A. S. Mellor and R. G. Goodchild, *Wiltshire Archaeological Magazine*, xlix (1940), 46 ff. Ditchley, C. A. R. Radford, *Oxoniensia*, i (1936), 24 ff. Wingham, excavation by F. Jenkins, 1965.

H. P. R. Finberg, *Roman and Saxon Withington*, Leicester, 1955.

J. N. L. Myres, 'Romano-Saxon Pottery', in D. B. Harden (ed.), *Dark Age Britain*, London, 1956, pp. 16 ff.

Towns: S. S. Frere, 'The End of Towns in Roman Britain', in J. S. Wacher (ed.), *The Civitas Capitals of Roman Britain*, Leicester, 1966, with references there cited; also for York, H. G. Ramm, 'The end of Roman York' in R. M. Butler (ed.), *Soldier and Civilian in Roman Yorkshire*, Leicester, 1971, 179 ff.; and for Caistor J. N. L. Myres and B. Green, *The Anglo-Saxon Cemeteries of Caistor by Norwich and Markshall, Norfolk*, Oxford, 1973, 31 ff.

Bokerly Dyke: C. F. C. Hawkes, *Arch. Journ.*, civ (1947), 62 ff.; P. A. Rahtz, ibid., cxviii (1961), 65 ff.

W. H. C. Frend, 'Religion in Roman Britain in the fourth century', *JBAA* [3], xviii (1955), 1 ff.

M. W. Barley and R. P. C. Hanson (ed.), *Christianity in Britain 300–700*, Leicester, 1968.

L. Alcock, chapter vii in I. Ll. Foster and G. Daniel, *Prehistoric and Early Wales*, London, 1965.

L. Alcock, 'Pottery and Settlements in Wales and the March, A.D. 400–700', in I. Ll. Foster and L. Alcock, *Culture and Environment*, London, 1963.

L. Alcock, 'Celtic Archaeology and Art', in E. Davies (ed.), *Celtic Studies in Wales*, Cardiff, 1963.

E. K. Chambers, *Arthur of Britain*, London, 1927.

L. Alcock, *Arthur's Britain*, London, 1971.

J. R. Morris, *The Age of Arthur*, London, 1973.

INDEX

Bertha, fort, 171, 258

Bewcastle, fort, 148, 150, 157, 208, 383, 388, 400

Bibroci, 52

Bigbury, 38, 49

Bignor, villa, 305–7, 310, 317, 335, 347, 418

Binchester, fort, 150, 245

Birdlip mirror, 66

Birdoswald, fort, 150, 153, 155, 156, 196, 198, 206, 210; damaged (AD 296 ?), 384, 400; end of, 417; inscription, 242, 382–3, 384; Theodosian reconstruction, 394, 402

Birds in cults, 370

Birley, Prof. E., 142, 145, 146, 161, 162, 176, 177, 192, 200, 204, 220, 247

Birrens, fort, 143, 150, 157, 177, 179, 180, 208

Birrenswark: fortlet, 166; siege-camps, 177, 258

birrus Britannicus, 317

Bitterne *see* Clausentum

black-burnished ware, 330

Blackburn Mill, hoard from, 370

Bochastle, fort, 136

Bodrifty, 23, 24

Bodunni, 80, 85

Boduocus, 36, 66–7, 80, 84–6, 92, 96, 98

Bogaers, Prof. J. E. A. Th., 163

Bokerley Dyke, 397, 422

Bone, 360

Bonosus, revolt of, 216

Boon, G. C., 58, 296

Bootham Stray, camps, 258

Boothby, Castle Hill, fortlet, 145

Bordeaux, inscriptions from, 203, 213, 340, 364

Boresti, 132

Bosham, sculpture from, 356, 364

Bothwellhaugh, fort, 166

Boudicca, 101–3; rebellion of, 103–7, 114, 239, 277, 282, 297, 364

Boulogne, 31, 211, 229, 252, 381; siege of, 378

Bowes, fort, 151, 158, 197

Bowness, fort, 150, 271, 332

Boxmoor, villa, 307, 331, 340

Brading, villa, 315

Bradwell, fort, 380

Brampton, 145, 198, 259

Brancaster, fort, 211, 379

Brantingham, villa, 361

Bravoniacum, 271

Brean Down, temple, 373

Brecon, fort, 121, 209, 266, 396

Bredgar hoard, 81

Bredon Hill massacre, 66

Bremetennacum, 271

Bricic, civitas, 198

Briconium, 399

Bridgeness, 167, 172

Brigantes, 71–2, 85, 87, 92, 94, 97–100, 115–20, 123–5, 132, 138, 141, 173, 205, 236, 259; control of, 177, 180–5; horned god of, 366; rebellion, under Hadrian, 147–8; under Pius, 177; under Severus, 195–7; *see also* Cartimandua

Brigantia, goddess, 319

Brigantia, population of, 71, 349, 356

Briglands, coin hoard, 187

Brislington, villa, 396

Bristol Channel, 16, 28, 32, 69, 96, 109, 339

Britain: Dark-age contact with Rome, 414; end of Roman rule in, 408–12, 428; exploitation of, 320–5; exports from, 61, 331–2; geography of, 15–16, 18; insularity of, 14; language in, 350–4; late prosperity of, 317–18, 328–32; population, 348–50; sea-routes to, 15, 18; value of, 18

Britanni, 225

Britannia Caesariensis, 382

Britannia inferior, 203, 242, 382; governors of, 205–6, 212, 215, 226

Britannia Prima, 241, 242, 358, 373, 382

Britannia Secunda, 241, 242, 267, 382

Britannia Superior, 203, 242, 382; governors of, 205–6, 215

Britannia coin-types, 177, 354

Britannicus see Commodus

Britayne, 422

British *auxilia*, 103, 111, 238

British *dediticii, gentiles*, 207

British *numeri*, 163 n. 9, 175, 250

British language, 351–3

Brittany, migration to, 15, 426; trade with, 30–1, 32, 67

Brittones, 225, 246; Anavionenses, 230

Broadway, cult object from, 370

brochs, 73, 128

bronze, 22–3, 28, 29, 324–5, 345, 346, 360, 364, 366, 415, 416, 420

brooches, la Tène Ic, 73

Brough, Derbys., fort, 177, 323, 394

Brough on Humber (*Petuaria*), burial at, 342; fort, 117–18, 147, 151, 182; inscription, 238, 246, 342, 364; mosaic centre (?), 361; theatre, 278; town, 274, 278, 342; town-defences, 286–7, 299; vicus, 240

Brough on Noe, fort, 151

Brough under Stainmore, fort, 151, 182, 197, 323

Brougham, fort, 139, 150, 164, 233, 246

Broxtowe, fort, 113

Bruccius Colasunus, 366

building materials, 281–3, 335

Burgh by Sands, fort, 150, 208, 212, 383

Burgh Castle, fort, 215, 379–80

Burgundian troops, 216, 252

burials: Iron B., 28, 52; Iron C., 37; R.B., 309, 342

Burrow Walls, fort, 150, 157

Bury St Edmund's bronze helmet, 347

butchers, 295

Buxton, 151, 246

Cadbury Congresbury, hill-fort, 420

Cadder, fort, 126, 167

Caerellius, 187

Caer Gybi, fort, 257, 380, 396

Caer Llugwy, fort, 146

Caerhun, fort, 209, 396

Caerleon, fortress, 87, 109, 121, 146, 203, 209, 215, 254, 258, 315, 347

Caermote, fort, 150, 259

Caernarvon, fort, 186, 209, 243, 266, 330, 335, 380, 396, 405–6

Caersws, 97, 209

Caerwent (*Venta Silurum*), 233; amphitheatre, 347; baths, 277; *collegium*, 294; *curia*, 293; defences, 286–7, 291, 299; fifth-century, 422; forum, 277, 293, 298; houses, 293; inscription, 246; mosaics, 298 n. 5; population, 296–7; size,

292; status, 246; water supply, 280; weaving works (?), 337

Caesar *see* Julius *and* Geta

Caesar, role of, 240, 241, 371, 390

Caesarea, 241, 382

Caesariensis province (?), 241

Caesennius Silvanus, 142

Caesius Nasica, 101

Caistor by Yarmouth, 212

Caistor by Norwich (*Venta Icenorum*), 135, 270, 301, 377, 421; baths, 277; defences, 284, 287, 299; forum, 277, 279, 289; fire, 377; glass making, 294, 327; houses, 289; (?) *laeti* at, 270 n. 5, 387, 421; size, 292; statue, 246; weaving works (?), 337; whetstone, 336

Caldy Island, 25

Caledonians, 188, 195–6, 199, 200, 201, 203, 207, 297, 382

Calgacus, 132

Caligula *see* Gaius

Calleva see Silchester

Calpurnius Agricola, Sex., 158, 177–8, 179, 181, 185, 191

Calpurnius, deacon, 418

Calvisius Rufus, 212

Cambridge, fort (?), 86

Camelon, fort, 126, 171

camps *see* Marching camps

Camulodunum see Colchester

Camulos, god, 62, 368

canals, 280, 313, 338

Canterbury (*Durovernum Cantiacorum*): Belgic, 16, 49, 64, 80, 273; defences, 286–8; drains, 281; fifth-century, 421; *foederati* at, 421; houses, 276, 283; industry and trade, 295; mosaics, 281; population, 297; Roman, 79, 103, 235, 240, 273, 301; size, 292; status, 236, 246, 273; street plan, 339; theatre, 277, 348

Cantiaci, *civitas* of, 234, 235, 240

capitals of Britain, 229, 241, 246

capitolia, 276, 362

Capitoline triad, 362

Cappadocia, 225

Cappuck, fortlet, 136, 143, 166, 181

Caracalla, 189, 199, 201, 203, 204–5, 207, 209, 226, 385; edict of, 213, 353, 388

Caratacus, 62, 70, 75, 79, 82, 86, 92, 94, 96–8, 101, 116
Caratius Colasunus, 366
Carausius, 376–80
Carausius II, 390
Cardean, fort, 142
Cardiff, forts, 121, 266, 380
Car Dyke, canal, 313–14
Carinus, inscription to, 312
Caristanius Fronto, C., 139
Carlingwark Loch hoard, 370
Carlisle: (?) bishop at, 372; fort, 119, 120, 145; Christianity, 372; inscription, 192, 378; population, 297; status, 236, 242; tile factory, 258; town, 204, 214, 275
Carmarthen: fort, 121, 279, 374; amphitheatre, 307
Carnanton ingot, 324
Carpow, 200, 201, 207, 220 n. 48, 254, 386
Carrawburgh: Coventina's shrine, 366, 417; damage (AD 296), 400; fort, 150, 155, 158, 178, 207, 212; plough-marks, 163 n. 23
Carriden: fort, 166, 170, 171, 247; *vicus*, 240
Carrock Fell, 72, 125
Cartimandua, 72, 84–5, 94, 97, 101, 109, 116, 119, 231
Carvetii, 77, 214, 236
Carvoran, fort, 145, 150, 155, 158, 179
Carzield, fort, 166, 181
Cassi, 52
Cassiterides, 43
Cassivellaunus, 37, 38, 50–7
Castell Collen, fort, 146, 191, 209, 257, 299
Castell Odo, 25
Castlecary, fort, 126, 167, 171, 179, 192
Castle Dore, 31
Castle Dykes, villa, 307
Castledykes, fort, 127, 136, 142
Castleford, 151, 213
Castle Greg, fortlet, 166
Castlehill, fort, 172
Castleshaw, fortlet, 151, 191
Castlesteads, fort, 145, 150, 155, 208, 271
Castor ware, 347; *see also* Nene valley

Catillon le, coin hoard, 35, 67
Catsgore cottages, 305
Catterick, 151, 196, 245; battle of, 428; fifth-century, 420; status, 236; tanning, 259; town defences, 289
Catus Decianus, 105, 106, 108, 228–9
Catuvellauni, 50, 57, 59, 62, 63, 65, 67, 68, 80, 86, 135; *civitas* of, 198, 231
Cavalry organisation, 250, 251, 261, 262
cave occupation, 311
Cawfields inscription, 206
Cawthorn, camps, 258
Celatus, 366
Celestine, Pope, 413
Celsus, 227
Celtic art, 354–5, 357
Celtic fields, 23, 301, 311, 315
Celtic folk tradition, 405
Celtic language, 350–1
Celtic religion, 365, 423
Celtic revival (5th century), 423
Celtic rites, 342
Celtic saints, 15
Celtic sculpture, 365
Celtic writing, 344
cemeteries, Germanic, 426–7
Cenimagni, 52, 65
censitor, 230
census, 230
centuriation, 301
centurions, 250
Cerialis *see* Petillius
Cernunnos, god, 368
chariot burials, Iron Age, 28
chariots, Iron Age, 28, 47, 50–1, 80
Charterhouse, amphitheatre, 347
Chedworth, villa, 338, 361, 372
cheese making, 314
Chelmsford, fort, 86, 107, 134, 274
Cheshire gap, 16, 93, 98
Chester: amphitheatre, 254; barracks, 259; baths, 277; Constantian (?) reconstruction, 383, 385; evacuation, 267, 405–6; fort, 90, 104; fortress, 122, 137, 142, 149, 203, 210, 253, 267; inscription, 138, 142, 146, 206; *municipium*, 236
Chesterholm, 145, 150, 205, 207, 210, 240, 245, 246, 262, 403, 417

470

Housteads – *contd*
400, 402, 403; trade route through
gate, 332; *vicus*, 240, 275, 402
Hucclecote, villa, 417
Hunsbury, 30
Huntcliff signal tower, 417
Hyginus, 250, 270
Hypocausts, 335, 338

Iavolenus Priscus, L., 224
Iceland, trade with, 332
Iceni: *civitas* of, 84, 135, 242;
coinage of, 37, 64–5, 84, 93;
rebellion (AD 47), 93, 99, 312;
rebellion (AD 60), 103–7
Icknield Way, 16
Ilchester, 236
Ilkley, fort, 151, 196, 197, 266, 268,
271; fourth-century reconstruction,
383, 395
Illyricum, 405
immigrants, 297, 320, 326, 328, 340,
346
Imperial cult, 98, 105, 239–40, 293,
344, 356, 362–4, 371
Imperial estates, 312–13, 321, 323
Imperial statues, 94, 356
Imperial tilery, 259
Imperial weaving works, 337
imperium Galliarum, 215
imports: Iron Age, 38, 40, 63; R.B.,
320, 326–8, 340, 355
Inchtuthil, fortress, 87, 129, 137, 142,
162, 253, 254, 256
incolae, 231
industry *see* bronze, leather, pottery,
etc.
infantry organisation, 250, 251, 261,
262
Ingleborough, 72, 125
interpretatio Romana, 366
Inveresk, fort, 126, 166, 167
Ipswich, torcs, 40
Irchester, 245
Ireland, 15, 127–8, 139, 332, 423–4
Irish god, 368
Irish raiders, 253, 332, 401, 406–7,
423, 424, 427
Irish settlers, 406–7, 426
Iron Age classification, 19–20; Iron
A, 20–6, 69; Iron B, 27–35, 65–7, 68,
69, 72, 73; Iron C, 34–40, 64, 70, 73

iron industry, 17, 18, 20, 39, 252,
333–4
Isis, temple of, 297, 365
Isle of Wight, 89
Itius, portus, 46
iuridicus, 135, 198, 224–5
ius Latinum see Latin right
Ivinghoe Beacon, 24
Ixworth *see* Pakenham

Jackson, Prof. K. H., 77, 351–2, 374
Jarlshof, 25
Jarrow inscriptions, 148
Javolenus Priscus, L., 224
Jedburgh inscription, 208
jet, 294, 330–1
Jordan Hill cult, 370
Jovii, comitatenses, 392
Jovinus, 392
Joyce, Rev. J., 294
Judea, rebellion in, 148, 162
Julia Domna, 199
Julia Pacata, 108
Julian, emperor, 318, 390
Julius Agricola, Cn., 109, 115, 118,
120, 122–38, 139, 140, 141, 143,
147, 184, 223, 225, 235, 252
Julius Alpinus Classicianus, C., 108–9,
110, 228, 326
Julius Asper, C., 239
Julius Caesar, C., 17, 36, 42–55, 56,
71, 228, 320
Julius Frontinus, Sex., 36, 56, 102,
115, 120–3, 133, 134, 135, 235, 252
Julius Indus, 108
Julius Julianus, L., 204
Julius Karus, C., 145, 146
Julius Marcus, C., 205, 207
Julius Pollienus, T., 205
Julius Severus, Sex., 148, 158, 161,
252
Julius Verus, C., 158, 176–7, 179, 191
Junius Dubitates, 164
Junius Faustinus, C., 205
Junius Silanus Torquatus, L., 83
Juno, 362
Jupiter, 191, 362, 364, 365, 373
Jurassic route, 16, 28, 32
Jurisdiction, 224–6, 236–7
Justus Superus, 113
Juvenal, 141, 191

Marlborough bucket, 39
Mars, 365, 366, 368
Martinhole, fortlet, 109
Martinus, *vicarius*, 390
Maryport, fort, 150, 151, 193, 271
Matlock, 340
Matres campestres, 366
Maxima Caesariensis, 241, 382
Maximian, 240, 241, 263, 376–8, 386
Maximus, governor, 207, 406–7
Mead, 331
Meare, 32, 69
Medway, river, 79–81, 83
Melandra, fort, 151, 191
Menapii, 44
Mendips, 32, 99, 103, 235, 321–4, 339, 340, 381
Mercury, 365, 366, 368
Metchley, fortress, 94, 96
Middleton milestone, 214
Middlewich, salt at, 336
Mildenhall (Suffolk), treasure, 329
Mildenhall (Wilts), 299
milecastles *see* Hadrian's Wall
milecastle 37, 196, 217
milestones, 213, 324, 338
military policy in Britain: Antoninus Pius, 165, 173, 187; Caracalla, 189, 214; Carausius, 379; Claudius, 78–84; Commodus, 189; Constans, 387; Constantius I, 381; count Theodosius, 393; Domitian, 128; Hadrian, 147–50; Magnus Maximus, 404–6; Nero, 101, 108; Severus, 201; Stilicho, 268, 406; Titus, 123, 126; Trajan, 145–7; Vespasian, 123
Military Way, 151, 170
milites Anderetiani, 268
militiae, 227–8, 249, 251
Milking Gap settlement, 163
milling, 295, 336
Milton, fort, 136, 143, 368
Minerva, 359, 362, 368
mining, 259, 321
mints: Iron Age, 57–9, 62, 65–6, 84–5; R.B., 243–4, 378; Rome, 416
Mitcham, Saxon cemetery, 426
Mithraeum, 297, 365, 375
Modius Julius, 206
Moesia, 83, 136, 137, 148; Lower, 148, 223, 229; Upper, 178
Mommsen, Th., 267

monarchy, post Roman, 412
money lenders, Roman, 105, 328, 340
monetary policy of Aurelian, 216
Mons Graupius, battle, 131–2, 133
Moresby, fort, 150, 157–8
Morini, 44
mortaria, 264, 294, 296, 326, 329, 330, 340
mosaics: town, 298 n. 5, 345–6; villa, 307, 309, 318, 319, 345–7, 352, 360–1, 372, 374, 417, 420; and education, 375 n. 12
Mummius Sisenna, P., 148, 158, 161, 163
Mumrills, 126, 167, 172, 193
Muncaster tilery, 259
municipia, 99, 231, 236, 274
Mursa, battle of, 389
Myres, Dr J. N. L., 410, 413, 425

Naevius, freedman, 245, 312
Nanstallon, fort, 90, 114
Nantmel, fort, 102
Nantosvelta, goddess, 368
Narcissus, 78
naval activity, 211, 252–3, 333, 392
Neath, camp and fort, 121
Nectaridus, count, 391
Nectovelius, soldier, 220
Needham, 84
Nene valley potteries, 329, 347, 357, 397
Nepos (?), P. Metilius, 141
Nepos Plataurius *see* Plataurius
Neratius Marcellus, L., 142, 230
Nero, 101–2, 108, 228, 312, 313, 339
Nerva, 120, 142, 147
Netherby, 157, 206, 208, 383, 388
Nether Denton, fort, 145
Nettleham inscription, 369
Newbrough, fort, 145
Newcastle: bridge at, 153, 155, 160; fort, 150, 152; inscription, 160, 176
New Forest potteries, 330, 397
Newport, Isle of Wight, villa, 305
Newstead, fort, 126, 136, 142–3, 144, 166, 175, 179, 181, 188, 198, 200
Newton Kyme, fort, 151, 256, 384
Newton St Loe, villa, 361
Newton upon Trent, fortress, 87, 97, 254
Niall of the Nine Hostages, 407

St Mawgan in Pyder, 31
salaries, payment of, 324, 417
Salinae, 336
Salisbury Plain, 68, 311
Sallustius Lucullus, 141
salt production, 310, 313–14, 336, 337
Salvius Liberalis, C., 224
Samian ware, 180, 326–7, 329, 332, 339
Sarmatians, 186, 213, 252
Saturninus, revolt of, 141
Saxon federates, 427
Saxon raiders, 211, 215–16, 387, 389,
    391, 407, 410, 411, 413, 414, 419–24
Saxon settlers, 389, 419, 421, 422–4
Saxon Shore, 252; Count of, 242, 247,
    261, 268, 269, 388, 391, 396, 407;
    forts, 211, 226, 252, 255, 256, 289,
    291, 379–80, 385, 399
Scalesceugh, 258
Scilly Isles, 41
Scole, fort (?), 107
Scotland: Celtic culture, 356, 365,
    367; Constans in, 387; Constantius
    I in, 385–6; Flavian evacuation of,
    137, 139–40, 142–4, 146; Iron Age
    in, 25–6, 29, 72–4; marching
    camps, 202–3; metal work hoards,
    370; Severus in, 199–204;
    Theodosian arrangements in,
    393–4; trade with province, 332–3;
    see also Antonine Wall *and*
    Hadrian's Wall
Scots, 388, 390–1, 405–6
sculpture and sculptors, 343, 356–60,
    364
Sea Mills, 103, 113
sea power, 120, 129, 132–3, 170, 201,
    252–3, 258, 393, 406
Secundani iuniores, 269
Segontiaci, 52
Seguntienses, *palatini*, 405
self government, local, 99, 230, 231,
    233, 234–8
Selgovae, 72, 74, 123, 126–7, 143,
    144, 147–8, 149, 174, 176, 188
Selsey, *oppidum*, 38
Seneca *see* Annaeus
Senecio *see* Alfenus
Sennen cliff castle, 31
Sennius Sollemnis, T., 206
Sentius Saturninus, Cn., 83
Septimius, L., governor, 358, 373

Septimius Severus, L., 194–6; army
    reforms, 213, 215; campaigns in
    Scotland, 199–204, 372; divisions in
    Britain, 203–5; effects on trade,
    329–31; frontier under, 195–8,
    207–9; inscription, 188; martyrdom
    of St Alban under, 205, 371; visits
    Britain, 199
Setantii, 77
Severius Emeritus, C., 313
Severn: river *limes*, 17, 92, 97, 122;
    valley, 32
Severus, bishop, 414
Severus, count, 392
Severus, emperor *see* Septimius
Severi Augustales, 297, 364–5
shale, 336, 360
Sheepen dyke, 63
shipping, trade by, 339
shops, 282–3, 293
Shrewsbury, 17, 297
Sibson, 295, 359
siege-camps, 258
signal-beacons, 170
signal towers, 131, 151, 152, 160, 258,
    396–7
Silchester (*Calleva Atrebatum*), 58,
    59, 61, 62, 103, 273; amphitheatre,
    296, 346; baths, 277, 298, 326;
    battle near, 381; church, 372;
    collegium, 295; commerce, 294;
    curia, 293; defences, 283, 285,
    287–9, 299; fifth-century, 422; fire,
    279; forum, 135, 236, 277, 279, 293,
    298; graffiti, 353; grapes, 331;
    houses, 276, 281–2; industry, 295,
    326; inscription, 422; metal hoard,
    370; mill, 336; mosaics, 298 n. 5;
    population, 296; sculpture, 356,
    364; size, 292; status, 235–6, 246;
    tilery, 326, 340; villas, 293; water
    supply, 280
Silures, 69–70, 92, 94–6, 97–103, 109,
    120–2; *civitas* of, 233
Silvanus, god, 366
silver, 18, 320, 321–4, 329, 416
Simpson, Dr G., 175, 192
Slack, fort, 151, 191, 259
slang, army, 401
slaves, 25, 295, 303–4, 332, 396, 416
Smith, Dr D. J., 360, 375
smiths: Iron Age, 20, 29, 40; R.B.,

For Max: a true animal lover—CDG

Library of Congress Control Number: 2017956186

ISBN 978-1-338-11669-4

10 9 8 7 6 5 4 3 2 1   18 19 20 21 22

Book design by Charice Silverman
First edition, February 2018

Printed in the U.S.A. 23

Scholastic US: 557 Broadway • New York, NY 10012
Scholastic Canada: 604 King Street West • Toronto, ON M5V 1E1
Scholastic New Zealand Limited: Private Bag 94407 • Greenmount, Manukau 2141
Scholastic UK Ltd.: Euston House 24 Eversholt Street • London NW1 1DB

STORMSPEAKER

1

WARRIOR'S PATH

ABEKE TOOK A DEEP BREATH AND HELD IT FOR AN EXTRA second before slowly exhaling. From the deck of the ship, in the minutes before daybreak, she could already sense a change in the air. It felt familiar. Even though they were still far away from the savannahs where she'd been raised, the breeze carried the scent, the warmth, the feel of her homeland. Nilo was on the horizon and it couldn't come soon enough.

The five Greencloaks—Abeke, Conor, Meilin, Rollan, and Anka—had been aboard the small ship for several days, and they still had a ways to travel before reaching their final destination in southern Nilo. Abeke was beginning to believe that Uraza's aversion to water was rubbing off on her. All she wanted to do was step foot on solid land . . . but they had to press on. Their priority was to hopefully find a clue about the bond tokens in the library of Takoda's former monastery.

But that hope carried an unwanted partner . . . someone Abeke and the rest of the team despised. Someone who had also returned to the monastery and who might have a few answers for them.

Kovo.

Even the thought of the Great Ape made Abeke's stomach turn. The gorilla had masterminded both the First and Second Devourer Wars, killing thousands, including Meilin's father. That was something that couldn't simply be forgotten, even if the new version of Kovo had recently helped them defeat the Wyrm.

The rising sun now streaked the sky with pink and purple rays of light, adding to the beauty of the horizon. Soon Abeke would be seeing Kovo, and she'd have to put aside all her feelings about him.

Abeke stared down into the deep blue water.

Was her anger toward Kovo similar to how people felt about the Greencloaks?

No. She shook away the comparison. It was a different situation. The Greencloaks hadn't acted willingly with the Wyrm—they'd been infected by its parasites. And the Greencloaks had been framed for the assassination of the Emperor of Zhong. Kovo, on the other hand, had done all those terrible things himself. He had taken the world to the brink of human extinction.

Twice.

The thought of Kovo and his conniving ways sent a cold shiver down Abeke's back, causing her to shudder. She had to keep her guard up around that Great Beast.

"Couldn't sleep?" Rollan asked, joining Abeke on the deck. "Or just enjoying the sunrise?"

"Neither." Abeke sighed. "Just thinking."

"Yeah, me too." Rollan leaned his back on the rail. "This rickety old ship hasn't been treating us too bad. Then again, it still has another week to go."

Abeke smiled. The Greencloaks had been lucky that Dawson, after hearing about his brother, had insisted on helping them get out of Eura. Thanks to him, they had supplies, weapons, a ship, and a two-man crew of old fishermen, Milo and Keane.

"I was actually thinking about Kovo," Abeke admitted. "Not looking forward to seeing him again."

"Can you imagine how Conor feels? Last time he was in the waters around Takoda's monastery was when he became infected with the Wyrm's parasite. This really can't be easy for him."

"You're right. I hadn't even . . ." Abeke sighed again. She'd been so wrapped up in returning to Nilo that she hadn't stopped to think about Conor. "Have you talked to him? Is he okay?"

"He'll be fine," Meilin said, walking toward them from the bow of the ship. "He's a Hero of Erdas. He's a survivor."

"I was thinking . . ." Anka suddenly appeared next to them. Her chameleon-like abilities still made Abeke uneasy. Abeke had always prided herself on her hunting skills, but this diminutive Greencloak seemed to confound her senses. "If the library doesn't have any information on the bond tokens, will Kovo tell us if he knows anything? I mean, he helped you with the Wyrm, but that was because the whole world was in peril. He's not a fan of humans . . . or Greencloaks."

"Maybe being bonded to Takoda has changed him," Rollan said. "Given him a different perspective." He glanced up at Essix circling above the ship. "Our spirit animals have changed *us*. And I'd like to think we've changed them, too."

Just as Rollan finished, Essix screeched and dove past the port side, buzzing right over the top of Rollan's head as if in protest. Essix was stubborn and head-strong, but there was no denying she had a soft spot for Rollan. They worked well together, each one fiercely independent yet always loyal.

Meilin snickered. "You've really changed her."

"Very funny, Essix!" Rollan shouted. "Way to support my point."

Essix flew around the ship one more time before coming to rest at the top of the mast.

"Maybe Essix saw something." Conor emerged from belowdecks, a concerned look on his face. He stepped closer to the railing and looked out at the horizon. "In fact, I was coming up to tell you that maybe we shouldn't go to the monastery at all."

Meilin placed a hand on Conor's shoulder. "Conor, it might be difficult for you, after what happened with the Wyrm—"

"That's not it," he interrupted. Conor took a step back and looked at the rest of the group. "I had a vision. It was brief, not a full one like I've had before with the big wave, but I think we have to go somewhere else."

"Where?" Abeke asked, quietly pleased at the thought of avoiding Kovo. "What did you see?"

"It was an enormous hole, or maybe a deep crater, and it had three land bridges . . . one on top of the other." Conor closed his eyes for a moment. "It also had a waterfall flowing from the top, past the three bridges, and into a pool at the bottom."

"And a token was there?" Anka inquired. "Like with the Wildcat's Claw, where it was hidden behind the waterfall?"

Conor shook his head. "I don't think so, but it's the first step in finding them. I'm certain of that. And it felt like we weren't too far away."

"Sounds like you're describing the sinkhole of the Taabara Chasm," Abeke said. "It's not too far from here in the northern part of Nilo."

"Northern Nilo . . . I like the sound of that!" Rollan grinned broadly. "Less time being seasick always sounds good to me."

"Well, at least you've been with your spirit animal," Meilin pointed out. "None of us have had ours during the voyage. It'll be good to bring them out."

"Maybe we should split up," Conor said, just as Essix shrieked and took flight again. "A few of us go to the sinkhole while the rest continue on to see Takoda." Conor frowned. "Just in case my vision is wrong."

"I don't know," Anka replied. "I think staying together is a better idea."

"Me too." Abeke reached over and gave Conor's forearm a squeeze. They had been through so much together, and she trusted his instincts. "I believe in your visions. . . . They haven't been wrong yet."

"Plus, sticking together might prevent a repeat of what happened with . . ." Rollan didn't finish the sentence. He had almost broken their unspoken rule.

A hush fell over the group. The experience of having lost Worthy in the cave-in was still raw for everyone. It was all they'd discussed during the first days, but then one morning, without anyone saying a word on the matter, they had stopped talking about it. It wasn't that they weren't thinking of him; they just had to place their full attention on the task at hand. Their survival depended on it.

From that point forward there was no more wondering if they had done the right thing in leaving, no more worrying whether Worthy had made it out alive, no more fearing that the Wildcat's Claw had been found by the Oathbound. The focus was on their mission. They had to find the two remaining bond tokens, Stormspeaker and the Dragon's Eye.

Anka broke the silence. "Abeke, do you know how long it'll take to get to the Taabara Chasm?"

Abeke shrugged. "Not long, but I'd have to check the map. Hold on."

Abeke sprinted belowdecks, grabbed the map of Nilo, and hurried back to her friends.

"Look." She opened it up and pointed to a spot in the ocean near the northern coast of the continent. "We're somewhere in this area. We can tell Milo and Keane to change course and go toward this river." She ran her fingers down the coastline to the mouth of a river, traced its path inland, and stopped at a place close to some mountains. "Once we dock we can make our way across the savannah, past this hilly area, and the Taabara Chasm should be right there. We might even make it there by tonight or tomorrow morning." She paused for a moment. "Maybe. I think."

"Then it's set." Rollan thrust his finger toward the sea and grinned. "Onward! To Taabara Chasm!"

"Um, yeah . . ." Meilin rolled her eyes at Rollan's over-the-top rally cry, but she couldn't help smiling. "How about I simply go tell Milo and Keane that we've had a change of plans?"

"Just remember . . ." Conor hesitated, rubbing the faint mark the Wyrm had left on his forehead. "Taabara

may only be the beginning, and not the end. I have a feeling that the bond tokens won't be easy to find."

"Well, since when have things been easy for us?" Abeke gave Conor a wink. "We like a challenge."

"Yeah, I guess." Conor turned to face the coastline, lost in his own thoughts.

The sun was directly overhead when they climbed into the small rowboat. There were no ports in the area, so Milo had anchored the ship in the middle of the river and Keane would now row with them to shore.

"So, how long should we wait for you to return?" Keane asked as they approached the riverbank lined with papyrus reeds.

Abeke bit her lip. She wanted to have access to the ship, but it didn't seem fair to leave the two old men stuck in the middle of nowhere. "The thing is . . . we aren't sure how long we'll be away."

"Well, Dawson paid us for two weeks of travel," Keane replied. "And we've got about a week's worth of food left, so it's your call."

"Could you wait here for a couple of days and then head somewhere back along the coast?" Rollan suggested as the boat drifted closer to the river's edge.

"Sure." Keane nodded. "I have a sister in Badir; it's a small port town not too far away. We could meet up there. I'll give you two more weeks, as Dawson paid us. . . . That's about all I can take of my sister anyway."

"Badir sounds good." Meilin threw a backpack filled with supplies over her shoulder as the rowboat hit the

first of the papyrus reeds. "We'll meet you there if we don't make it back here in time."

"Good luck!" Keane called out. The five Greencloaks jumped out of the boat and into water that was about two feet deep.

Abeke sloshed through the river, pushing aside reeds while her feet sank into the sand and silt with every step she took. Finally the ground became firmer and she climbed up on dry land. Once she was out of the reeds and onto the grass of the savannah, Abeke took a deep breath, relishing the hot sun that beat down on her.

She was home.

And only one thing was missing from the scene.

Abeke pushed aside her cloak and held out her arm. "Join me, Uraza."

The leopard appeared in a flash of light and raised her head to face the sun. The large cat's nostrils twitched as she took in the Niloan air and softly let out a contented purr.

"I know." Abeke stroked Uraza's arched back as they took in their surroundings. "I did the same thing. It's good to be home." The tall golden grass of the savannah rippled with the soft breeze. The rocky hills they'd have to cross loomed not too far in the distance.

Uraza stretched her legs. Abeke knew what the leopard wanted. "Go," she whispered.

Uraza immediately jumped through the tall grass, then raced across the savannah toward the hills at full speed. Abeke knew the joy Uraza felt at being free. How fun it would be to race along with her, to hunt for their next meal and savor the midday sun that was

baking her shoulders. But now was not the time. They had a mission.

"Uraza's as happy as I am not to be on that ship anymore," Rollan observed. The tall grass moved with the leopard, rustling as she sprinted back and forth. "Aren't you bringing out Briggan, Conor?"

Conor wiped the back of his neck and looked up at the cloudless blue sky. "Think I'll wait until the day isn't quite so hot."

"This is Nilo," Abeke warned. "If it's daytime, it's going to be hot."

Essix circled the group, screeched to establish her presence in the sky, then flew away once more.

"Yeah, yeah, we're moving," Rollan responded to the falcon's cry. He adjusted his green cloak, backpack, and canteen. "Everyone have their stuff?" Rollan asked.

"Since when are you the responsible one?" Meilin teased.

Rollan smiled. "Since I realized that I'd have to share my water if someone forgot theirs."

"Really?" Conor could barely hide his smile. "You mean to say you wouldn't share with Meilin?"

Abeke heard Anka giggle, even though she could no longer be seen.

They were all aware of the feelings between Rollan and Meilin, but no one usually said anything. It was only confirmed by the occasional reddening of Meilin's cheeks and Rollan's quick interest in changing the topic of conversation.

"We're wasting time. . . . Let's go." Meilin marched ahead, leaving the group behind before Abeke could check to see if her face had turned pink once again.

As the team trekked toward the Taabara Chasm, a few puffy white clouds began to gather, providing occasional relief from the heat. The terrain also changed from the grasses of the savannah to rocky hills dotted with trees. In the distance, what had at first looked like hills quietly morphed into amber-colored mountains, with scattered patches of green.

Stopping for a quick break under the shade of a wide-branched cypress tree, Conor released Briggan. The wolf burst onto the scene and, with his tail wagging, pounced on Conor, knocking him to the ground.

"Whoa," Conor laughed as Briggan placed his two front paws on Conor's chest and raised his snout to sniff the air. Conor ran his hand through the Great Wolf's gray-white fur while the wolf's cobalt-blue eyes analyzed everything. "Sense anything?"

Briggan glanced down at Conor before giving him a quick lick on his forehead. The wolf jumped off to further inspect their surroundings.

"Ha, I would take that as an all clear," Anka said, her body blending with the tree trunk she was leaning against.

Abeke opened up the map and checked their location. From the look of things, it seemed like the sinkhole that formed the Taabara Chasm should be close by.

"Are we headed in the right direction?" Meilin asked.

"Think so," Abeke answered, shielding her eyes from the glare of the sun. She scanned the land for a small stream that might feed into the waterfall of the chasm.

Briggan let out a long howl from somewhere in the distance.

Rollan stretched out his hand to help Conor up. "Sounds like your partner may have found something of interest."

Conor grinned. "Leave it to Briggan to be here five minutes and already track something down."

As they all headed toward the sound of Briggan's howl, Rollan shook his canteen. "I really hope he's found some fresh water, because I'm almost out."

Abeke shook her head. "Hm, who was talking about having enough supplies so we wouldn't have to share water later? Oh yeah, that was you."

"Hey . . ." Rollan shrugged, a mischievous smile on his face. "These muscles need the extra hydration."

At that remark, everyone laughed out loud.

"It wasn't *that* funny," Rollan mumbled.

Soon, the group came upon a small stream where Briggan and Uraza had both decided to lounge by its edge.

"Look at those two." Meilin pointed. "They're like–"

"Shhh." Abeke touched her ear. "Listen."

Besides the gurgling sound of the water bouncing off of several rocks in the stream, there was a louder, crashing sound of rushing water cascading down somewhere.

"The waterfall has to be nearby," Abeke said as Rollan filled his canteen with water. "It's got to be downstream."

Abeke and the group followed the stream until the ground dropped, disappearing into a giant sinkhole. From where they stood, at the very edge of the deep crater, they could see the stream cascade down past

three land bridges, each of which seemed to bisect the hole at different depths.

"Now what?" Rollan asked, looking down. "Do we go down into that giant rabbit hole, cross one of the bridges, or stay up here?"

"In my vision, I could see the gorge's opening high overhead. The water seemed to be falling from above." Conor patted Briggan, who had now rejoined them. The wolf nuzzled his hand. "So, I think we have to go to the bottom."

"Yeah," Rollan sighed. "I was afraid you'd say that."

Abeke looked at the western sky, where the sun was already hanging low. They had made good time, but it would be much darker in the gorge. Any remaining light would soon disappear. She could already hear a nightingale chirping in the distance. If they were going to go, they needed to be quick about it.

"What do you think, Uraza?" Abeke asked the leopard, who was peering over the edge right next to her. "Should we head down and see if there's anything there? Or wait until morning?"

Uraza responded by leaping off the rocky ledge onto the path toward the bottom.

"Guess that's your answer," Meilin said, following Uraza with a jump of her own. She looked back up at the rest of the group. "Come on!"

Once at the bottom of the crater, Meilin released Jhi. The Great Panda lumbered over to Meilin, and their foreheads touched. The genuine affection between the two was obvious to Abeke. Then Jhi waddled over to where Briggan and Uraza were lapping up water from

the edge of the small pond. The entire team spread out, hunting for a clue as to why Conor's vision had brought them here.

Abeke first searched behind the waterfall, hoping that there might be a cave like in Eura, but there was nothing there.

"Maybe it's like the Heart of the Land." Rollan touched the token that hung under his shirt. "Hidden within a rock somewhere."

"There are a million rocks here, though," Anka said.

"How about hidden along a path?" Conor pointed to a narrow chasm through the mountain walls.

Abeke walked over to him. "Are you saying we should go through there?" The opening would require them to enter single file. If it got much narrower, their spirit animals would certainly not fit. As it was, Jhi already couldn't enter.

"See how the ground is worn down in spots?" Conor pointed to the rock floor. "I think this is a path that's been used before. Used a lot."

Meilin and Rollan joined them, each peering into the long, narrow chasm.

"We should explore in there before it gets much darker," Meilin said. "Don't you think, Rollan?"

Rollan didn't answer. He only stared into it.

"Rollan?" Conor repeated his name.

Meilin placed a hand on Rollan's shoulder. "You're thinking of Tarik, aren't you?" she said. "The last battle you fought with him."

"It looked a lot like this place," he muttered. "Same type of chasm. A warrior's last path."

"But it's not that place, and we aren't battling the Devourer or the Conquerors," Meilin replied in a gentle voice.

Suddenly a sense of unease filled Abeke. This *would* be a good place for an ambush. She glanced around, her hunter instincts on full alert.

It was too quiet.

Even the nightingale had stopped singing. Something was off.

"I think we should get out of here," Abeke said in a hushed voice. "Maybe have Essix see if—"

Before Abeke could finish her sentence, a hooded figure jumped down and twirled a quarterstaff in front of them.

"Now!" came a shout from above, and suddenly warriors wearing gray cloaks rained down all around them.

First, one dropped behind Abeke. Then another in front. Then two more blocked the path forward through the chasm.

Abeke pulled an arrow from her quiver and nocked it to her bow, just as Meilin drew out her sword.

In a split second, more than two dozen cloaked figures had jumped down from the cliffs . . . all pointing their weapons at the five Greencloaks or at their spirit animals over by the pond. High above all of them, balanced on the natural bridge, another dozen attackers stood with arrows trained on Abeke and her friends.

There was no escape. . . . They were trapped!

GIANT HAIRBALL

FIGHTING A LOSING BATTLE WAS NEVER ROLLAN'S FIRST choice. He had learned on the streets of Concorba that diplomacy could work wonders. Words often yielded better results than any sword. Disarm them with a smile whenever possible.

Rollan quickly assessed the situation. Jhi, Briggan, and Uraza were surrounded, but they would be able to take care of themselves. The four Greencloaks had taken defensive stances against the hooded warriors, but Rollan wasn't sure where Anka had gone. She'd camouflaged herself so well that he couldn't see her at all. What Rollan *could* see was that these people weren't dressed in all black like the Oathbound.

Perhaps he could convince them that they weren't enemies.

"Friends, friends." Rollan lowered his dagger and took a step toward one of the figures. "We mean you no harm." He acted calm, as if the Greencloaks had the upper hand, instead of the other way around.

"Rollan . . ." Meilin's voice carried a warning that this approach might not be the best idea.

Rollan ignored her. She was a warrior at heart. Her instinct was always to fight. But he had to use his gut. He took another step. "We aren't here for a battle. We're only in search of something. Perhaps you could help."

The response came swiftly. The hooded figure in front of him spun his quarterstaff in the air, then swung it low at Rollan's knees, trying to knock his legs out from under him.

Rollan jumped over the end and quickly grabbed the pole, yanking it out of the hooded figure's hand and turning it on him.

So much for diplomacy.

"STOP!" a voice called from above. Another hooded warrior appeared from an opening near one of the land bridges. The figure ran along a path to the bottom, leaping down the last few feet to skid to a halt right in front of Rollan. "Don't harm these people. These *are* our friends."

Rollan couldn't believe it. . . . His plan had worked.

The cloaked figure pulled back his gray hood.

"TAKODA!" Meilin exclaimed.

Takoda smiled and rushed over to be embraced by Meilin, Abeke, Conor, and Rollan. "I'm so glad that you're all safe!" he exclaimed, but then lowered his voice to a whisper. "I heard what happened with the Emperor of Zhong. How could the Greencloaks do something like that? What's going on?"

"It was a setup by people impersonating us," Meilin answered. "We're trying to make things right again."

Takoda didn't hesitate. "How can I help?" he asked. "Do you want me to go with you somewhere? Maybe give you a place to hide with the monks?"

Rollan stared at Takoda. The boy had grown about four inches since he'd last seen him. He'd also become more muscular.

But along with Takoda came Kovo, who was bonded to the young monk. Rollan didn't love the idea of traveling with the once subjugator of Erdas. "Have you heard of something called Stormspeaker . . . or the Dragon's Eye?"

Takoda shook his head. "What are they?"

"Important items we need in order to clear our names and unite Erdas," Conor explained. "We believe at least one of them is found in Nilo."

Murmuring had risen from the cloaked figures. The monks still had their weapons trained on the group and their spirit animals.

"Takoda, what's going on?" someone shouted.

Takoda turned around. "Everyone, please . . . lower your weapons." He pushed down the spear of one of the nearby monks. "These are my friends, the ones I've told you about. The ones who helped defeat the Wyrm. The Heroes of Erdas. We should be welcoming them, not threatening them."

Briggan growled at one of the hooded monks and Rollan could see Uraza's muscles tense and tauten. Even Jhi was staring down the person in front of her.

"Place your spirit animals in passive state," Takoda whispered. "The monks won't relax if they're out."

Meilin, Abeke, and Conor glanced at each other. They each quietly nodded and called back their animals.

Rollan could see the hesitation among the monks, but they slowly put away their weapons and pulled back their hoods in an apparent symbol of acceptance.

Takoda had risen to become a leader in his community. This was definitely not the same boy Rollan had first encountered moping in Greenhaven. The battles underground against the Wyrm had clearly changed him . . . or was it Kovo's influence? Had the bond between him and the Great Beast caused him to grow in his command of others? Was it just a sign of growing up? Rollan wasn't sure. Perhaps Kovo had changed, too. Doubtful, but anything was possible.

"Do you know someone who might help us?" Meilin asked.

Rollan feared that the answer would be Kovo, but Takoda surprised them. "I don't know *someone* with answers, but I know *someplace* that might have them. Come with me." Takoda motioned for the group to follow him into the chasm.

"No!" The monk who had attacked Rollan leaped forward, blocking the entrance. "You can't take them into Maktaba. You'd be placing everyone and everything at risk."

"Step aside, Sodu." Takoda stared him down. "I think I've earned the right to bring four guests—four *friends*—into our community."

Sodu didn't back off. "They're wanted by the Oathbound! I've heard the rumors of what happens to those who help Greencloaks. We can't allow them

entrance. The library has never been seized, because strangers are not permitted inside."

"These four aren't strangers," Takoda argued. "They're known to everyone."

"Ahem." Anka cleared her throat. She took two steps forward, away from the mountain wall where she had been camouflaging herself, and allowed herself to be seen. "There's five of us, actually."

Takoda spun around. He hadn't noticed her, even though she'd been standing so close to him.

"Anka's with us," Meilin quickly explained. "Her spirit animal is a chameleon. We can vouch for her, though."

"You see!" Sodu mocked Takoda. "You can't even recognize danger when it's right next to you." He turned to the monks as Anka blended back into the colors of the mountain. "My brothers, we cannot let them enter. There's no telling what will happen if they do. We would be putting everything at risk."

"What I see"–Takoda spoke to Sodu through clenched teeth–"is someone who pretends to be strong, but is afraid of his own shadow."

"Look who's talking!" Sodu exclaimed. "The boy who couldn't be trusted to travel alone, but who required the guidance of a superior student to accompany him to Maktaba."

Takoda's eyes narrowed. "And when none could be found, they told me to bring you."

"Ha! Nice try, but we all know the truth," Sodu scoffed. "You are still only a boy."

"We'll see about that." Takoda sneered and took a few steps forward. He lifted his arms and addressed the

other monks in a loud, booming voice. "Brothers and sisters, you all know me and trust my judgment. These are my friends, the ones who defeated the Devourer and then helped destroy the Wyrm. They are the Heroes of Erdas, who have selflessly risked everything for Nilo . . . for the entire world. They come to us seeking answers and rest . . . something only we can offer. Isn't it our duty to share our knowledge with the righteous and stand against the Oathbound? Will you not rise up, stiffen your resolve, and aid them?"

There were whispers among the monks. A sense of purpose was filling the cavern.

"We are being called to be *part* of history," Takoda continued, "instead of just preserving the historical accounts. We cannot turn our backs on those who defended us. We have a duty, so I ask you . . ." He paused for a moment, capturing everyone's attention. "Who will join me in leading these heroes to find the answers they seek? Who stands with me and with the Heroes of Erdas?"

"I do!" shouted one monk.

"As do I!" yelled another.

"I DO!" hollered the remaining monks in unison. All except Sodu, who stayed silent with his arms crossed.

"To the Heroes of Erdas!" Takoda shouted, raising a fist in the air.

"THE HEROES OF ERDAS!" the monks roared back.

"Glad he's on our side," Rollan whispered to Conor as he followed Takoda into the chasm.

As the Greencloaks walked through the narrow passage, it continued closing in on either side. Soon it

was impossibly tight, like a fissure running up the mountain. As night fell and the light waned, Takoda lit a small lantern. Rollan glanced up the steep rock walls at the sliver of dark sky above them. He knew Essix was flying above them somewhere, giving them protection from the air.

"So what's the deal with your friend Sodu?" Rollan asked Takoda. "Not the friendliest monk I've seen . . . not that I've actually seen any before today. Except for you, of course."

"Yeah, we have some history," Takoda explained. "We were together at the other monastery before I bonded with Kovo. After everything that happened with the Wyrm, we were both sent here. He's not my biggest fan."

Rollan chuckled at the understatement. "You think?"

"Almost there!" Takoda called back to the others as the path opened up to a ledge high up on a mountain.

"Finally. I was wondering when we'd get . . . whoa!" Rollan waved his arms, trying to maintain his balance as Takoda yanked him back. In the darkness, he had misjudged where the ledge ended and almost stepped off.

"We're about two hundred feet up and it's a straight drop," Takoda warned.

"A little more notice next time," Rollan muttered over the pounding of his heart.

"Wow," Conor said as he stepped onto the ledge. "I didn't even realize the incline was taking us so high."

"The monastery is up there." Takoda pointed to a few twinkling lights in the distance. The moonlight

revealed enough of the monastery that Rollan could tell it had been built into the mountainside, about two-thirds of the way to the top.

"Guess we have to take one of these rope ladders the rest of the way up?" Rollan tugged on a pair of old ropes with wooden rungs fastened between them. None of it looked very sturdy. "It's about another two hundred feet?"

"Two fifty," Takoda corrected.

"This could explain why you don't get many visitors," Meilin added. "Though it does remind me of parts of Zhong." She grabbed the first ladder's wooden rung and hoisted herself up.

"Before we all get there, I, um . . ." Takoda suddenly seemed unsure of himself.

"Spit it out," Meilin said.

"Yeah, so, I was going to ask that you not bring out Uraza, Briggan, or Jhi when we get up there. Maktaba is, well, a sort of *particular* place, if you haven't noticed. Not that I don't want them around, but I'm not sure what the reaction would be."

"From who?" Abeke asked. "The monks or Kovo?"

Takoda sighed. "Both, I guess."

They all knew there was no love lost between their spirit animals. Kovo had killed the Four Great Beasts during the First Devourer War and had in turn been killed by them during the second. They had reluctantly worked together to defeat a common enemy, but no one truly knew what would happen if they were thrust together again. Still, Rollan didn't like the idea of having to accommodate *Kovo*.

"I think Kovo will just have to figure it out," Abeke said in a cool, unforgiving voice. "We've all had to deal with him."

"But we're guests," Conor reasoned. "Let's not stir up any trouble."

"Kovo is different now," Takoda said as they each began climbing the ladders. "You'll see."

Rollan was about to make a joke when he glanced down at the steep drop to the bottom and felt his head spin. Devastating quips would have to wait, since he needed all his concentration to not fall. As they continued up the mountain, the glow of the moon rising over the adjacent mountain peak cast a dim light over their surroundings. It was nighttime, but Rollan wasn't looking anywhere except at the rung right above him. It seemed as if everyone was focused on the climb, because no one spoke. In fact, all Rollan could hear were the occasional grunts and sighs as someone paused to catch their breath before pressing on.

Once they arrived at the monastery, Rollan turned to look back at the view. An enormous sense of peace washed over him. It was a combination of the beauty of the thousand stars above him and the moon rising silently in the sky. Wind whispered past the oil lanterns lighting the entrance to Maktaba. For the first time in weeks he felt safe, a security provided by the remote location.

"Nice, huh?" Takoda smiled, taking it all in as if for the first time. "Just be careful with the thorns that line the bushes near the entrance." He waited for the remaining Greencloaks and then motioned for them all

to follow him. "Come on, I think someone may want to see you."

"I doubt it," Abeke muttered as she walked past Rollan.

Rollan nodded in agreement. Kovo couldn't have changed that much.

The group passed several monks in the wide corridors who silently stared as they walked by. . . . It seemed that word of their arrival was spreading throughout the monastery.

"This is the Great Hall," Takoda said, entering a large room where oil lamps hung from the many rafters that crisscrossed the vaulted ceiling. There were a few monks eating at one of the long dining tables on the right side of the room, and a fire burned in the massive fireplace on the opposite end. "Figured you might want to stop and get something to eat before—"

"MEILIN! CONOR!" someone shouted while running down a darkened staircase in the corner. "ROLLAN! ABEKE!"

Takoda smiled. "Told you someone would want to see you."

A girl with white hair and almost translucent skin rushed into the light.

It was Xanthe, the Sadrean warrior Meilin and Conor had met while battling the Wyrm underground. "I can't believe you're all here!" She hurried over and pulled Meilin close to her. "Takoda and I heard about what happened to your surface elder—er, emperor. How could—"

"It wasn't us," Meilin explained. "They were imposters."

Xanthe tapped Takoda in the chest with the back of her hand. "What did I tell you? I knew it couldn't be real Greencloaks."

"And since when are you a monk, Xanthe?" Conor teased. "Or are you here for another reason?"

Takoda blushed at the insinuation, but Xanthe simply rolled her eyes. "I'm here to give a record of my people's history. Preserve the Sadrean stories for future generations."

"How are things in Sadre now?" Meilin asked.

"Still recovering. Phos Astos will never be the same, but it's being rebuilt . . . slowly."

"Sounds like several places we've seen," Anka said.

Xanthe scanned the room. "Who said that?"

"Oh." Meilin spun around. "That's Anka. I forgot to introduce the two of you. Anka, Anka, where are you?"

"Right here." Anka stepped away from a purple curtain in a dark corner of the room, her skin and clothing changing from purple to their natural coloring. "Don't mind me. Nobody does. Pleasure to meet you, Xanthe."

"Uh, yes, nice to meet you, too," Xanthe replied as Anka moved into the shadows and blended back into her surroundings.

That was when the group noticed him: a large looming figure who sat in the darkest corner of the space, draped in shadow and staring out the window. His massive back was turned to the group, but there was no mistaking him.

Kovo.

"Guess we don't merit even a glance from him," Abeke speculated.

"That's not it," Takoda explained. "Ever since we stopped the Wyrm, Kovo's gone almost completely silent. He rarely communicates with me, and he refuses to go into passive form."

Rollan cautiously drew closer to the Great Ape. "Is something wrong? Did someone take his banana away?"

Takoda shook his head. "It's part of his healing journey. Being here has given him the peace to deal with the things he's done in the past. He wants, no, he needs time for himself."

"Hmpf." Meilin didn't seem to be buying it.

"So he won't be able to give us information on Stormspeaker or the Dragon's Eye?" Conor asked.

"Afraid not," Takoda said. "He won't react to anyone." He looked to one of the corridors, where some of the monks were carrying trays of food. "I'll get you some dinner. Sit and rest for a moment."

Xanthe escorted them to one of the tables. "So those things you mentioned . . . what are they?"

"Important gifts we have to find for the Greencloaks," Abeke said, being purposefully vague.

"It's too bad Kovo can't help," Xanthe said.

"We'll see about that." Rollan got up from the table and walked over to Kovo. He stood directly in front of the gorilla, looking up at him.

"Rollan . . ." Meilin didn't sound pleased. "What are you doing?"

"I want to see if he's really as unaware as he'd have us believe." Rollan clapped his hands loudly in front of Kovo's red eyes, but the giant gorilla didn't even blink.

"Rollan!" Abeke raced over and pulled Rollan away just as he began waving his hands in front of Kovo's face.

"Are you crazy?" Abeke shook her head in disbelief. "Kovo could toss you out that window!"

"We need answers, right?" Rollan broke away from Abeke's grip and returned to stand in front of Kovo. "Listen, you giant hairball, we need to find Stormspeaker and the Dragon's Eye. If you're as smart as you pretend to be, prove it by telling us where they are."

Silence.

Rollan stood on his toes to get eye-to-eye with Kovo. "You really are one ugly, selfish—"

"Rollan!" Takoda had returned, carrying a tray with several plates of food.

Rollan continued. "Foul-smelling, mangy, good-for-nothing waste of—"

Takoda slammed the tray down on the table and began marching toward Rollan.

"An unwise move, brave Amayan warrior," an unfamiliar voice called out from the hall's entryway, stopping Takoda in his tracks. "Best not to taunt someone who can later exact revenge. Kovo can hear you; he only chooses not to react . . . yet."

Rollan's mouth twitched and he swallowed the lump that had formed in the back of his throat. He peered around Kovo's massive chest and saw an old man, his back bent down with the weight of the years, leaning on a gnarled, wooden cane for support. "Yes, well, I was only trying to provoke a reaction, so he'd snap out of it and help us."

"Reacting out of anger or fear is rarely a good decision. A lesson for Kovo . . . and perhaps for you."

Rollan was about to respond when Takoda interjected.

"Everyone, I want to introduce you to the Honorable Naveb of Maktaba." He paused as the old man gave the group a slight nod. "He's one of our esteemed elders and our greatest librarian. He knows where to find all sorts of secrets."

Meilin bowed in acknowledgment of the elder. "Sir, we're looking for information about—"

"Yes, yes." The old man raised a hand. "I may be old, but I could still hear the instigator over there while he was tormenting Kovo."

"That's not exactly what—" Rollan stopped speaking as Abeke gave him a gentle nudge. Silence was a virtue that often escaped Rollan.

"I see you're from this land." Naveb motioned to Abeke. "I hope you are brighter than your friend there."

"Sir," Abeke responded with respect, "we each have our unique strengths, which—"

"Blah, blah, blah." Naveb turned around. "Well, come on. Grab your food and let's go. I'm not getting any younger." He headed down a dimly lit hallway. "We have work to do . . . if you can pass the test."

NEFRINI'S CROWN

MEILIN EYED THE OLD MONK. HE WAS BALD, WITH A short white beard that stood out against his dark skin. His cane tapped the stone floors with a deliberate, rhythmic pattern as he led the group down the maze of corridors. At first glance, the old man appeared frail and unsteady, but to Meilin there was something in the way he had held her gaze that made her think he was much more. . . . She just didn't know what.

"Where are we going?" Meilin whispered to Xanthe.

"One of the libraries, I think," she answered. "There are several of them here."

They entered a large circular room filled with thousands of books, piled all the way to the rafters. Meilin could only marvel at the size of the place. She'd seen many libraries in her lifetime, but this one room rivaled the largest of them.

Naveb waited for them in the center of the room. He stood motionless, his eyes closed and both of his hands resting on his cane.

One minute passed, then another.

Meilin glanced at Takoda, hoping he'd reveal a clue about what was happening. He merely shrugged. The silence had become uncomfortable. They were wasting time . . . time that could be spent looking for the bond tokens. Was this part of the test he'd mentioned? Meilin considered bringing Jhi out of passive state so she could give Meilin the serenity to see things clearly, perhaps pick up on some cues they were overlooking.

"Um, Master Naveb, are we waiting for something?" Conor asked.

Naveb did not answer, but instead approached Conor. He stared at the faint mark of the Wyrm on his forehead, then narrowed his eyes in recognition of the symbol. "Ah, so you are the one. The Greencloak who took Takoda from the monastery. The one who succumbed to the Wyrm in Sadre, and eventually turned on him and all his allies."

"Yes, but what happened there . . . I didn't have a choice," Conor explained hastily.

"There's always a choice," Naveb responded sharply. "And you made yours."

"No, no. You don't understand. I had no control." Conor rubbed the mark, as if he could wipe away its stain.

Meilin's blood began to boil. She could not allow this man to insult Conor for being infected by the Wyrm, even if he was an elder. She knew how hard Conor had battled against it, what he had sacrificed, and how some of his actions while under the Wyrm's influence still tore at his heart. It wasn't fair to him and it wasn't fair to what they'd all endured.

"Regardless of what you say, you are not like the others. Not even the instigator." Naveb pointed to the door. "You will have to leave before we can continue."

"Excuse me, sir . . ." Meilin summoned up every lesson in self-control that she'd learned while growing up in the palaces of Zhong. "But you have no right to say that to Conor. I don't know what Xanthe or Takoda told you, but Conor is no less than a hero." Meilin glanced over at Conor. "He is, and always will be, one of us. If he goes, we all go."

"And do you all feel the same way?" Naveb looked toward Rollan and Abeke.

"Absolutely," Rollan said, walking to stand next to Conor. "We can always find answers somewhere else."

Abeke took Conor's hand, linking her fingers with his, and lifted their intertwined hands. "We're a team. Now and forever."

"I see." Naveb took a step back. "But you won't find answers anywhere else." He was barely able to hide a smirk beneath his beard. "You will stay and find your answers here, because you have passed my test." He walked over to a black ladder with wheels on the bottom. "It is said that those who pursue the bond tokens must be united in mind and spirit. I would never help a fractured group seeking such powerful items." He rolled the ladder along a metal railing that ran around the room. "Despite being young, you have endured much, and yet you're still united. That is why I will help."

Meilin's mouth dropped open. "So you only said those things to see if you could split us up? You didn't really mean it."

"No, I meant what I said. I always do." He stopped and climbed the first two steps. "That boy is an instigator, and the other one's choices have set him apart from his friends."

They were back to where they'd started . . . being disrespected.

"Most Honored Naveb," Takoda began, "these are the Heroes of—"

"Here it is!" Naveb pulled out a book from the shelf. He turned to look down at Takoda's concerned face. "My dear boy, I am not insulting your friends. I am merely speaking the truth." He took a cautious step down, then another. "Is the one from Amaya not an instigator? Every group needs someone to get things moving, and to lighten the mood when our burdens become too heavy."

Naveb took his cane in one hand and tucked the book beneath his other arm. "And the Euran boy, was it not his choice to stand and fight on behalf of Kovo—his once enemy—at great risk to himself? His actions have shown him to be kind and selfless. He is forgiving of others' mistakes . . . but he has yet to extend that forgiveness to himself."

The old monk hobbled over to a small desk, set down the book, and looked at Meilin. "Am I not right about your friends?"

Meilin didn't say anything, but he did have a point about Rollan and Conor.

"You know I am, warrior girl." Naveb struck a match and lit an oil lamp on the desk. He opened the book, then looked back at Meilin and chuckled.

"What's so funny?" Meilin asked.

"You," Naveb replied. Then he returned to the book, flipping through the first few pages. "A fighter who must battle herself to achieve what she truly wants."

"I don't even know what that means," Meilin scoffed, but she caught Rollan and Abeke exchanging a smirk.

Naveb shook his head and sighed. "I was once like you. Pretending to be tough in spirit. You will learn." He pointed to a page in the book. "Now, Niloan girl, come and look at this. It tells of Stormspeaker."

Abeke rushed forward and Meilin followed, peering over her shoulder at the book. In the middle of one of the pages was a drawing of a slender, dark-skinned woman with a tall, elegant bird standing by her side.

"Isn't that Nefrini, the High Chieftess of Nilo, with her spirit animal, Nazir?" Abeke asked.

The old monk nodded. "I see you know your Niloan history, but here is something you won't find in any other book or library." He turned the page to a listing of property owned by Nefrini. At the very top was the word *Stormspeaker.*

"Whoa," Abeke muttered. "Stormspeaker was hers and Nazir's."

"What does it say about the bond token?" Conor asked.

"It describes Stormspeaker as being made of gold, with a brilliant green stone in its center," Meilin said.

Abeke ran her finger down the page, looking for another clue. "But not what it is or where to find it."

"As you are a hunter, I thought you'd be more observant," Naveb chided. "Your prey is not always in front of you, but sometimes behind you."

Abeke glanced at Conor standing in the back, then realized what Naveb meant. "The earlier page. The one with the drawing."

"Perhaps there is hope for you yet," Naveb said, flipping back to the image of Nefrini.

"Stormspeaker is her crown!" Abeke exclaimed.

Anka appeared next to Abeke, squeezing past Conor, Rollan, and Meilin. "You're right. It's made of gold and the front has a bird grasping a green stone in its beak."

"Not just any bird," Naveb corrected, unfazed by Anka's sudden appearance.

"A hammerkop, also known as a lightning bird." Abeke smiled. "Like Nazir."

"But where do we find this crown?" Rollan asked.

"Ah . . . for that we will have to look in one of our other books." Naveb scanned the room. "I believe the only reference we have is in a journal left behind by a Greencloak who visited long ago." He stroked his beard. "Now, where would that book be?" He hobbled over to one of the shelves and began running his hand over the spines of several books.

"Did you meet this Greencloak?" Abeke asked.

"Oh, no." Naveb kept searching. "He visited before I was even born."

"Then it's *really* ancient history," Rollan said with a smirk.

Naveb either didn't hear him or chose to ignore the comment. "Here it is," he said, pulling out a thin, leather-covered journal with the name *Tembo* engraved in gold letters on the front, and passed it to Takoda.

"Stop!" Sodu burst in and yanked the book from Takoda's hands. "Master Naveb, you cannot trust these

killers. They should never have been allowed entry. Anything they discover might be traced to us. We could be judged as conspirators. Don't you understand? We'll be labeled traitors!"

"Sodu," Master Naveb sighed. "I understand things completely."

Takoda lunged for the book just as Sodu spun around the desk, keeping out of reach.

"Give it back," Meilin demanded, stalking Sodu around the desk, while Conor slowly approached from behind. She was waiting for the right moment to attack. "If you know what's good for you."

Sodu met Meilin's gaze, then a slight smile crept across his face. "Guess this book is pretty important, huh?"

Before Meilin could react, Sodu grabbed the oil lamp and smashed the glass on the corner of the desk.

"What are you doing?" Abeke yelled.

Sodu's eyes narrowed as he held the thin book over the open flame, the bottoms of the pages curling with the heat. "Leave now," he snarled, "or this book burns."

LETTERS

Conor and the other Greencloaks backed away from Sodu, raising their hands in surrender, knowing that the book he held over the flame might be their only lead to finding Stormspeaker. In return, Sodu's lips tipped up to form a victorious sneer. But his delight in having the upper hand lasted only for a moment.

Whack!

Sodu's eyes bulged as all the air left his lungs.

Master Naveb's cane had come flying across Sodu's back with resounding speed. Before anyone could react, Master Naveb spun his cane and slapped the book high into the air. He then twisted into a roundhouse kick, striking Sodu in the chest. As Sodu tumbled to his knees, Master Naveb slid across the room and caught the book before it could hit the floor. Slowly, he pulled himself up with his cane and dusted off the cover of the journal.

"Hold on to it a little tighter this time," he said, handing the book back to Takoda.

Conor couldn't believe what he had just witnessed.

The old monk was an incredible fighter. He was equal parts grace, strength, instinct, and speed. They could all learn so much from him.

"Master Naveb . . ." Sodu staggered up.

"Leave this library," Master Naveb ordered. "We will discuss your punishment later."

Sodu kept his gaze on the floor. "I truly meant no harm or disrespect."

"Yet you committed both," Naveb said dryly. "Your lack of trust in my decision confirms what I told Ananda when she sent you here with Takoda. I cannot teach someone who only sees with eyes of fear."

Sodu lifted his head. "No, Master." His voice had an edge to it. "I fear only *one* thing. I fear what your recklessness will bring down upon this place." He turned on his heel and stormed out of the library before anything else could be said.

No one moved. Sodu had left, but traces of the turmoil he'd brought seemed to linger.

Rollan broke the silence. "I think he may now have a fear of canes, too," he said with a grin.

Master Naveb shot Rollan a stern look and the boy's grin disappeared.

"Master Naveb, those moves . . ." Meilin said with barely restrained awe. "It was as if you were flying."

This comment seemed to please the old monk. His face softened and his shoulders relaxed. "Yes, well, once a warrior, always a warrior." He pointed to Takoda. "Go ahead and open the Greencloak's journal. If there's any information about where to find Stormspeaker, it'll be there."

Takoda gently placed the book on the desk and

opened it. He glanced sheepishly at Conor. "You should probably do this and not me," he said, stepping aside. "I'm no Greencloak."

Conor hesitated. "You might not be wearing the cloak, but you're just as much a hero as any of us. We owe you a lot, Takoda. And we wouldn't even *have* the book if you hadn't gotten us in here." He placed a hand on the boy's shoulder. "Go on, you should be the one to read it."

Takoda shook his head. "But you are—"

"Oh, for the love of—" Meilin gently pushed Conor and Takoda aside. "Why don't I just read it?"

"Well, *someone* should read the book, considering everything that just happened." Master Naveb hobbled toward the door. "Speaking of which, I should go see about that foolish Sodu. He's had enough time to contemplate his actions."

"Thank you for pointing us in the right direction, Master Naveb," Conor said as he accompanied the old monk to the door.

"Yes, thank you!" Rollan shouted in agreement.

"Meh!" Master Naveb waved them both off without turning around. "Such noise! A library is supposed to be a place of quiet contemplation," he complained, but as he turned the corner, Conor caught the slightest smile on the old monk's face.

"Come here, Conor," Abeke urged as they all gathered around the desk where Meilin was hunched over the journal, her face close to the pages.

"The lettering is faded in some parts," Meilin muttered. "And he writes in this ornate calligraphy-like style."

She scanned the first pages. "This beginning part is all about Tembo's travels . . . where he eats and sleeps." She read a little further into the journal. "Oh, and here he is talking about some earlier battles and the formation of the Greencloaks." She gasped. "He was there when Briggan and the other Four Fallen united the Greencloaks against the first Devourer! And he claims that he once rode on Uraza's back?"

"That . . . doesn't sound like Uraza," Rollan said doubtfully.

"What does it say about Stormspeaker and the Dragon's Eye?" Anka asked from an unseen location, the shadows of the library giving her even more camouflage than usual.

"Nothing yet . . ." Meilin continued reading. "But I'm beginning to think we've been walking in this Tembo's footsteps all along. According to his journal, he's the mysterious Greencloak who hid the Wildcat's Claw in Wilcoskov. And it says here that . . ." Meilin looked up, her eyes wide. "He was the one who started the tradition of Greencloak leaders passing down the Heart of the Land. *Tembo* was the first leader of the Greencloaks." She glanced down again, her finger stopping halfway on the page. "Oh, here's something even more interesting . . ."

"What?" Xanthe leaned over the desk from the opposite side.

"He's describing his approach to the monastery. Climbing a rope ladder and being greeted by several monks. They welcomed him and gave him a place to stay." Meilin turned the page. "It says that the monks

grew suspicious of him when they discovered that he was carrying two dangerous and powerful items."

"That was probably them!" Rollan interjected.

Meilin paused and raised a single eyebrow. "Are you going to let me finish?"

Rollan gave her a quick bow in mock deference. "By all means, my lady. Continue."

Meilin took a deep breath and slowly exhaled. "Yes, it says that the two objects were the crown of Nefrini, known as Stormspeaker, and an orb called the Dragon's Eye. That night a group of monks confronted Tembo. There was some type of argument. The monks tried to convince Tembo to give up the objects." Meilin flipped the page. "This can't be," she muttered, turning back to the prior page.

"What's wrong?" Rollan peered over her shoulder.

"It seems like Tembo took off and left behind this journal with a note for the monks." She turned the page again and pointed to the words written in square, blocky letters. They were different from the rest of the journal. "It says, and I quote . . ." Meilin read the words carefully. *"I depart as you wish, but in light of what is written, the orb carries on to no one, and the key to finding Stormspeaker is nowhere to be found."*

"He'd rather destroy them than have the monks guard them?" Takoda took a step back. "Why?"

"No." Conor shook his head. "A Greencloak wouldn't do that with something so important. There has to be a mistake," Conor insisted. "Read it again." His vision had led them to this place for a reason. Even though something made him wary, he *knew* they were on the right track. They were close, he was sure of it.

Rollan read over Meilin's shoulder. "That's what it says. I don't think it means that he destroyed it, but he probably hid it in such a way that he thought no one would ever find it."

The bookshelves appeared to shift under the light of the oil lamp as Anka moved away from the far corner. "Well, we have to go look for the hiding place," Anka said. "We didn't come all this way for nothing."

Xanthe sighed. "But where do you start? Do you have any other leads?"

Conor thought about the vision that had brought them here. Perhaps they weren't supposed to be searching for the bond tokens in Nilo. Maybe that was what they needed to discover. That the answers were somewhere else. "Maybe we should move on to Zhong. Try to find answers there."

"No. We can't simply move on because this didn't pan out," Anka countered. "Since when do Greencloaks give up?" She paused, allowing her words to sink in. "Stormspeaker could still be here, and Kovo might have some answers. We can ask him again," she suggested. "He probably knows about Tembo."

"You're right, but this time you can do the asking," Rollan replied. "I think I may have pushed my luck with that gorilla. Maybe he'll like that now-you-see-me, now-you-don't trick."

"No, Kovo is off-limits," Takoda stated. "I won't put him at risk. He may not look it, but he's very fragile right now."

Rollan opened his mouth to say something, but seemed to think better of it.

"Anka's right, though. . . . We have to try other

options. Why don't we look through more records?" Meilin walked around the room. "There are different libraries in this monastery, right? So there must be other books and scrolls. Maybe we can find a clue somewhere else."

"I'll go find Master Naveb," Takoda suggested, heading toward the door. "He may have an idea of where we should start. I'll be right back." Then he disappeared into the shadow of the hallway.

"So what do we do while we wait? Just start going through all these books?" Xanthe pulled a random book from the shelf and flipped to a page in the center. "Looking for what?"

"Anything. Something." Abeke opened a book on ancient Niloan homes. "Maybe someone else wrote about Tembo's visit and where he went. We can't give up."

"No one is quitting," Rollan reiterated from the other side of the room. "There's an answer here . . . somewhere."

Conor meandered around the room. "I never said anything about *quitting*," he muttered. "It was only a suggestion."

Meilin held out her hand, and with a flash of light, Jhi appeared next to her. The large panda glanced around, noticed that there was no danger in the room, and plopped down on her hind legs.

"Meilin!" Abeke exclaimed in a hushed voice. "We told Takoda we wouldn't bring out our spirit animals. Don't you think I want Uraza with me?"

"Uraza doesn't help you see all sides of a problem like Jhi does," Meilin countered, stroking the side of the panda's large neck where the white fur met the black.

"Plus, we're the only ones in here." Meilin leaned closer and whispered something to Jhi.

Jhi nodded and closed her eyes as Meilin did the same.

Conor thought of Briggan. He wanted to run his hand over the wolf's silver back and feel the energy that always seemed to fill him up when they were together. Briggan understood him like no one else. Sometimes it felt as if the two of them shared a more personal bond than any of the other Greencloaks did with their spirit animals. It was as if they were both cut from the same cloth. Twin souls.

But now wasn't the time to have him there. It was time for Conor to focus on what he could for the mission. If only he had some control over his visions. He stared at Tembo's journal, still open on the desk, willing himself into a trance. No vision came to him, but from where he stood he did notice that some of the letters in the journal seemed to be off-center.

Conor approached the desk slowly, cocked his head to the side, and squinted his eyes. He studied the words carefully. The *W* was definitely written differently than the other block letters. It was in the calligraphy-like style found in the rest of the journal.

"Um, everyone. I think you need to come over here." His eyes stayed on the page, as if shifting them away might make it all disappear.

"Do we have to?" Rollan had sat down in a corner with a stack of books on either side of him. "Can't you just tell us what you're thinking?"

"It's about Tembo and what he wrote." Conor held up the book. He may not have been the strongest reader

in the group, but he knew that the words he saw weren't the same ones Meilin had read. A smile crept over Conor's face. The poor shepherd boy had figured it out all on his own. "I think I found our next clue . . . and it was right here all along. Written in plain sight."

5

SAND SCROLL

"WHAT DO YOU MEAN IT WAS RIGHT THERE?" ROLLAN asked, slowly getting up from the floor. It was late and he didn't want to play games. "We all saw what was in the book. Tembo said he hid it somewhere that no one could find."

"Not quite." Conor set the book back down on the desk and put his fingertip on one of the last words written at the bottom of the page. "Look carefully at the letters."

Rollan and the others gathered around Conor and stared at the book. Rollan didn't understand what was supposed to be happening. The words hadn't changed.

the key to finding Stormspeaker is nowhere to be found.

"Conor, we're all tired." Rollan rubbed his right eye. "Can you just tell us what you're thinking?"

"The *w* in *nowhere*. Look. Don't you see it?" Conor pointed to the letter as Abeke stared at the book. "The

way it's written, it could be part of the word or there could be a little space after it."

"So?" Xanthe tucked a lock of her white hair behind her ear as she squeezed by Jhi to get a better look. "How does that—"

"That changes everything!" Abeke exclaimed, throwing her arms around Conor in a big bear hug. "You're a genius!"

Rollan shook his head. Maybe he was too tired after a long day of trekking through Nilo and climbing up to the monastery, but he still didn't understand what they were talking about. Usually by this point he could rely on Meilin to say something that would bring it all into focus, but she'd become quiet and pensive. Rollan knew this was Jhi's influence, allowing her to study a situation from different perspectives, but it was still unnerving to him. He liked Meilin's normal take-no-prisoners attitude.

"Look." Conor motioned for Rollan to get closer. "If you read *nowhere* as two separate words"—he placed his finger under the word—"it says that the key to finding Stormspeaker is *now here* to be found." He let out a little sigh. "But 'here' is a pretty big place, and we still don't know where to start looking."

Meilin stood still, biting her bottom lip while staring at the journal. She had one hand buried in Jhi's fur and the other just hung by her side.

"Meilin." Xanthe said her name softly. "Are you okay?"

"Mm-hm," Meilin muttered absentmindedly. Then she blinked, her mouth twitched, and the edges of her lips curled up.

Rollan could sense that the Meilin he knew was coming back. "Oh, she's got something." He felt the energy in the room shift. He loved that Meilin had that effect on people and situations.

"I knew it!" Takoda barged into the library. "I said not to bring out any of the Great Beasts and you did it anyway. Kovo is restless, and it's because Jhi's here."

Abeke's face hardened. "His being bothered by having such a kind and peaceful soul as Jhi in the monastery says more about Kovo and his lack of growth than anything else could." She rolled back her shoulders. "We needed answers, and Jhi is the only Great Beast who could, *or would*, help."

Meilin rubbed Jhi's back. "Thank you, my friend," she whispered as she held out her arm. "I'll bring you out again soon." Jhi glanced at Takoda and dipped her head. In a flash of light she disappeared, once again becoming a tattoo on Meilin's hand.

"I don't mean to be rude. . . . It's just the way things have to be." Takoda seemed embarrassed. "I couldn't find Master Naveb and then Kovo started to—"

"Doesn't matter," Rollan interrupted. "Conor figured out that the clue is here, and I think Meilin knows something more." He held back a mischievous smile. "If her highness is ready to share it with the rest of us."

Meilin rolled her eyes. "All right . . ." She walked in front of the desk, then glanced back at Rollan. "You think you can keep up?" she teased.

Rollan laughed. "Oh, I can more than keep up. Just try me!"

In the light of the broken oil lamp, Rollan could see Meilin's cheeks turning pink with their little banter.

"So what is it?" Anka asked from somewhere in the room.

Meilin pointed to the page numbers on the bottom corner of each page. "Tembo wasn't only clever about using the words *now* and *here*. . . . He also put another clue for everyone to see." She pointed to the page number written on the last page. "This page should be 147, since the one before is 146, but it's numbered 159."

"So there are pages missing," Conor reasoned. "Someone tore them out."

Meilin shook her head. "No, nothing seems to be missing, and the five in 159 isn't how Tembo wrote his other number fives. It actually looks more like an *S*."

"One-S-nine?" Rollan was puzzled. "What does that mean?"

Meilin bit her lip. "That's what I don't know."

"One-S-nine," Takoda repeated. "One *Scroll* nine. That's how we catalog all our ancient scrolls. Library One, scroll number nine!"

"Tembo could have listed the location of Stormspeaker there!" Rollan put his hands on Takoda's shoulders and turned him around to face the door. "What are we waiting for? Let's go find it."

Takoda wiggled away. "Library One is our original library, where our most ancient records are kept. No one goes in there without permission from Master Naveb. No one."

"Seriously?" Meilin put her hands on her hips. "You're not going to help us get it?"

"I don't think that's what he meant." Xanthe stepped in. "Takoda has permission to go inside. He can get

it and bring it back here for us." She glanced at Takoda and widened her eyes. "Right? Isn't *that* what you meant?"

Takoda didn't say anything, and Rollan certainly didn't like the idea. "But what if there are other clues over there? Something Takoda might overlook. Stormspeaker itself might be hidden inside."

"I wouldn't miss anything," Takoda corrected. "If it's there, I'd see it."

"Exactly." Xanthe nodded. "So Takoda will take care of it. Isn't that so, Takoda?"

"It's not the way things are supposed to work, but . . ."

Xanthe placed her hand on Takoda's arm and he grew quiet. "Then it's settled!" Xanthe said brightly.

Takoda looked down at Xanthe's hand still on his arm. He smiled and nodded.

"The window!" Xanthe abruptly shouted, pointing to the far side of the room.

Everyone turned to look as Xanthe darted toward it.

"What is it?" Anka asked, already by the window.

"A pair of eyes," Xanthe muttered, staring into the dark night. "I think it was a bird peering in, because it took off when I pointed."

Xanthe thrust open the window and looked out. The night breeze slipped into the room, causing the flame of the oil lamp to flicker.

"At this time of night, maybe it was an owl?" Takoda suggested. "Though I've never seen one up here."

A shriek in the distance echoed through the room.

Rollan knew exactly who made that noise.

Essix.

"I think I know who that was." Rollan smiled. "My faithful companion didn't want to come in. She's just letting us know she's nearby."

"But isn't Essix really big?" Xanthe leaned a little farther out the window, still scanning the sky. "I don't think this bird was that large."

"It's really dark and you were pretty far away. . . . How could you tell?" Anka asked.

"Being from Sadre, where there's no sunlight, I can usually see better at night. But maybe I was wrong." Xanthe let out a deep sigh. "My eyesight has changed since I've been aboveground . . . one of the negatives of being here, I guess."

Takoda walked over to Xanthe. "You still have the best nighttime vision of anyone I know," he said softly. "We'll visit Phos Astos soon, and then I'll be the one who can't see too well." He leaned over the windowsill and pulled the window closed. "So let's keep this closed, in case Essix changes her mind." Takoda smiled and glanced over at the Greencloaks. "At least while I go to Library One and get the scroll for all of us to read."

Rollan wasn't sure where Library One was located, but it couldn't have been too far, because Takoda returned within minutes, a little out of breath. In one hand he held a large rolled-up scroll, and in the other was an oil lantern.

"Here it is," Takoda said, hanging up the lantern. "I don't think anyone has read this in a very long time." He blew off a large layer of dust as Rollan helped unfurl the scroll over the desk.

"It's an academic study of the desert sands," Xanthe said, standing on the other side of Takoda. "Different types of minerals, how they shift with the wind, what plants grow best in each sand. Does this help you at all?"

Rollan didn't respond. He had made sure to stand next to Takoda so he wouldn't be the last one to figure out the clue this time. He wanted to prove to everyone, especially Meilin, that he had more than just street smarts.

They spent close to an hour reading through the scroll. Rollan's eyes felt as if they were beginning to cross, and the words were swimming around on the paper. He wasn't any closer to finding Stormspeaker.

"I've lived around deserts all my life–" Abeke yawned, interrupting herself. "And I never thought someone could write this much about . . . *sand*."

"Why not?" Rollan touched the Heart of the Land, the amber stone hanging on a chain under his shirt. He knew that sand, like dirt, could shape a continent. "It's a powerful part of the earth."

Abeke rolled her eyes. "You think I don't know that?" She shook her head. "Don't forget, *I'm* the one from Nilo. I've seen sand carried in a windstorm causing the sun to be blocked out and turning the day into night. It's overtaken whole villages, covering everything. You probably haven't seen anything like that in Amaya."

Conor raised both his hands to put a stop to the bickering. "Listen, we're all tired and there doesn't seem to be anything here. Maybe if we go to sleep and look at it again in the morning light, we'll figure something out."

Rollan thought back to Tembo's note. There was something written about a light. "Where's the journal?" Rollan lifted up the scroll and placed the book on top. He went to where the final note was written. He read over it again.

IN light OF what is written, the ORb CARRIES ON tO NO ONE, ANd the key tO fiNdiNG StORMSPEAkER is NOWHERE tO be fOUNd.

"Could it be?" Rollan muttered, picking up the scroll and carrying it over to where the lantern hung on the wall.

"What are you doing?" Meilin asked, following him.

"I have an idea." Rollan raised the parchment paper up to the light. "Tembo said 'in light of what is written.' Maybe he meant you needed *light* in order to see the key to finding Stormspeaker and the orb." He slowly moved the scroll across the glass of the lantern, letting the light shine through.

"There!" Anka exclaimed, showing herself to be standing next to Meilin. "There's something written on the edge!"

Rollan moved the corner of the parchment paper in front of the lantern's glass. The light from the flame revealed a previously invisible message written in the same calligraphy style as Tembo's journal. It said:

To unify all, a valiant soul must seek the face in the mountain by passing through the valley of death where skulls fill the fields in the shadow of winter, then drain the demon's blood and walk through the clouds to arrive at the edge of the land.

For when this is done the queen's glory shall be revealed.

"Valley of death? Demon's blood? Edge of the land?" Rollan grimaced. He didn't like any of it. "That doesn't sound good."

"But the face in the mountain . . ." Takoda smiled. "I think I can help you with that part." He looked at Xanthe. "Remember how Sodu kept talking about seeing a face in the mountain when he came back from the spiritual journey Naveb sent him on? He thought that it was a sign of his manhood."

"He saw a mountain spirit?" Meilin asked.

Xanthe chuckled. "No, not a spirit . . . just a rock formation in one of the mountains that's a few days east of here."

"But no one's mentioned a place called the valley of death," Takoda said. "Or a field full of skulls. Then again, this was written a long time ago. Things could have changed."

"We can go to that mountain and maybe find the valley along the way." Abeke yawned again, causing a ripple effect with everyone in the room. "We'll head out in the morning. Let our brains work on it while we sleep."

Takoda nodded as a faint tapping sound reverberated in the distance. "I'll find you some soft beds for the night."

"That's perfect." Meilin stretched her arms. "We haven't had a comfortable night's sleep in a while."

The *tap-tap-tap* noise was getting closer. Through his sluggishness, Rollan recognized what it was. "I

think Master Naveb is about to pay us another visit." He rolled up the scroll and handed it back to Takoda. "Think it's better if you're holding this when he gets here. I don't need to be scolded again."

Conor walked to the door and opened it for the old monk. The now rapid beat of the cane hitting the stone floor echoed through the hallway. "We can ask him about the—"

Conor was cut off by the old monk storming into the library. Master Naveb's brows were furrowed and his cheeks were flushed from walking so quickly.

"You must all leave at once!" Master Naveb announced. "The Oathbound are on their way!"

6

BIRD THIEF

ALL TRACE OF THE EXHAUSTION THAT HAD BEEN tugging at Conor's limbs evaporated with the announcement that the Oathbound had found them once again. It seemed that no matter what they did or where they went, the Oathbound somehow anticipated their every move. The Greencloaks were placing everyone they encountered in jeopardy.

"Are you sure they're coming here?" Rollan asked. "No one knew where we were going. *We* didn't even know that we'd end up here!"

Master Naveb nodded. "They may not have known before, but Sodu is making sure they know now."

"He betrayed us?" Conor couldn't believe it. There were traitors around every corner.

"Sodu?" Takoda repeated, his face still registering the shock of it. "It can't be." He shook his head in denial. "No, he might not have agreed with having the Greencloaks here, but I can't believe he would betray this place. He truly believes in it."

"Perhaps I was too rough with him. Backed him into

a corner." Master Naveb sighed. "Regardless of the reason, he tried to enlist a few in the monastery to go with him into town. He thinks he can strike a deal with the Oathbound. The five of you in exchange for an assurance that the monastery will be left intact."

"The Oathbound will never honor any agreement." Rollan began pacing around the room. "We need to leave right away."

"How much time do we have?" Meilin asked.

"Five, maybe six hours." Master Naveb motioned for two young monks to come into the library. They each held several bags and placed them on the floor by the window. "One of the sentries said they left about two hours ago." Master Naveb pointed to the bags. "I brought you some supplies, along with a map to help you on your journey. Don't tell any of us where you are headed. Just go . . . and be careful."

"We'll help guide them." Xanthe knelt down and opened one of the bags. "Thank you, Master Naveb . . . for everything."

Takoda grabbed Xanthe by the arm. "We can't go," he whispered. "I can't leave Kovo here in his condition, and he won't go into passive state."

"Then you stay," she answered. "I'm helping our friends. I'm a Sadrean warrior, not a librarian. I'll be more helpful outside. I know this area, and you said it yourself: No one sees better at night than me."

"Xanthe, please . . ." Takoda's eyes pleaded with her. He was caught choosing between his spirit animal and someone who was obviously special to him.

"We can go on our own," Abeke said, already slinging one of the bags over her shoulder. "We've done it before. Nilo is home for me. We don't need the extra help."

Xanthe ignored both Abeke and Takoda. "Master Naveb, did you bring my special cloak, the one I use during daylight?"

The old monk nodded. "It's over there." He pointed to a bag closest to the window. "I suspected you might want to go with them."

Xanthe hustled over to the bag, her pale skin reflecting the moonlight that streamed through the window. She slipped on a sand-colored cloak and looked at the Greencloaks. "Ready?"

"Xanthe, you don't have to do this." Conor knew how much she'd given up during the battle with the Wyrm. She was once again abandoning her home and the people she cared about. "Abeke is an amazing tracker and guide."

"No disrespect is meant by this." Xanthe's eyes met Abeke's. "But I'm your best bet to get out of here. You don't know this area like I do." She picked up one of the bags and tossed it to Meilin. "We can each contribute something to the mission."

"She has a point." Meilin flipped the bag over her shoulder. "We could definitely use her help. She's a strong fighter, too."

Xanthe looked back at Takoda. "I understand why you need to stay, but you can still help them by finding more information on the Dragon's Eye. There has to be another clue in the message." Xanthe leaned closer to Takoda and, in front of everyone, she gave him a quick kiss on the cheek. "I'll come back. Promise."

Takoda didn't say anything else. Conor wasn't sure if his silence was from the kiss or from knowing that there wasn't any point in discussing it further.

The matter had been settled. Xanthe was going with them.

The group left the monastery the same way they'd arrived: down the rope ladders and through the fissure, until they came to the Taabara Chasm. Once there, they called out Briggan and Uraza to help guard against any Oathbound attack.

For the next few hours, Xanthe led them over several rocky hills until the ground evened out and became flat. By the light of the small lanterns they carried, Conor could tell that they had entered a large savannah. According to Naveb's map, they were now just west of the mountains where Sodu had his spiritual journey and where he had described seeing the face in the mountain. If they continued at their current pace, they'd probably be there in two or three days' time.

As the group approached a small acacia tree, Anka stopped walking and leaned against its trunk. "I don't know about all of you, but I'm exhausted. I think we should make camp for a few hours. Try to get some rest."

Conor reached down and stroked Briggan, who was leaning against his leg. "I agree. It'll be daybreak in a few hours, and the sun will drain us even more. We need to be alert."

Xanthe looked around, her pink eyes searching the surroundings. "I don't see any other trees in the distance, so this is probably as good a place as any."

"Agreed." Abeke dropped her bag and sat on the savannah's grass. Uraza circled her twice before decid-

ing on a spot next to Abeke. The leopard let her long tail curl around Abeke's ankle, but the tension in her muscles showed she was not there to relax. Her ears twitched and her eyes scanned the tall grass that surrounded them. Uraza was in full hunting mode, ready to protect the group.

Conor plopped exhaustedly to the ground. His eyes were heavy and he had a hard time keeping them open. He rested his head against Briggan, knowing that the wolf would stay vigilant with Uraza.

"Maybe Xanthe should keep watch while we sleep," Anka suggested, her voice penetrating the darkness even if her form didn't. "She can see better than the rest of us."

"Of course." Xanthe nodded, sitting cross-legged in the middle of the group. "I'll make sure to wake you if I notice anything."

Meilin held out her hand and, in a brief flash, Jhi appeared. The large panda promptly curled up on the ground, squashing the tall grass around her. Meilin settled in next to her. "I won't need much time to get reenergized," she said, stifling a yawn. "Jhi helps me relax more than I could ever imagine. I'll be ready for a full day with just a couple of hours. I can switch with Xanthe at that point."

Rollan took out a piece of fruit that Naveb had packed and sat down, leaning against the tree trunk. A bird called out from somewhere in the tree.

"That sounded like a macaw," Rollan said, lifting his head to search the limbs for the bright blue feathers and yellow beak.

"Caw!" The bird repeated its call.

Rollan put the piece of fruit on top of his bag and stood up, peering into the moonlight.

A flutter of wings beat past him and snagged the piece of fruit before flying back to its perch in the tree. The thief was a fork-tailed, glossy black bird.

"Hey!" Rollan shook the tree. "That was mine!"

The bird responded by pooping right on Rollan's bag.

Everyone—except Rollan—burst into laughter.

"You just got fooled by a drongo," Abeke said, still laughing. "They're notorious for mimicking other birds in order to steal food. But it's a good thing it's here. They're also great at warning when a predator approaches."

"Yeah, well . . ." Rollan moved his bag from beneath the drongo's reach and cleaned off the top with a small rock. "Helpful or not, I'm going to have drongo stew if it drops any other presents on my stuff during the night."

"Why don't you curl up over there with Jhi?" Conor suggested. "I don't think Essix is much of a cuddler, and we all need some rest."

Rollan glanced over at Jhi's black-and-white form next to Meilin. "Think Jhi would be okay if I used her as a big pillow?" Rollan asked Meilin.

"Hrrgmmfani," Meilin muttered, already half-asleep.

"I'll take that as a yes." Rollan curled up against the panda and she gave him a big lick on the head. "Panda slobber isn't necessary, Jhi. I'm tired, not hurt."

Through half-closed eyes, Conor watched as Jhi gave Rollan another lick . . . just for good measure.

It was dawn when a shrill, metallic shriek sounded from the tree.

Briggan growled, low and guttural, and Conor immediately sat up, his sleepiness falling away like a heavy cloak.

A few feet away, Abeke was already kneeling and pulling out her bow. Uraza crouched, somewhat hidden in the tall grass, looking ready to pounce.

"Something's out there," Xanthe whispered, staring at the savannah. "But it's hidden in the grass."

Meilin was squatting, her sword in one hand, as she called Jhi back into passive state. The disappearance of the panda caused Rollan to fall back with a start.

"Hey! What's the big . . ." He glanced at everyone and quickly pulled out his dagger, taking a defensive posture. "Is it the Oathbound? Are they out there?"

"Not sure," Abeke answered. The group stayed low, putting their backs together in a tight circle formation, with an eye out in every direction. Uraza and Briggan both had their hackles raised.

Conor slowly pulled out his ax. He glanced over at Briggan, who stood stiff-legged, eyes focused on something in the distance.

Someone was definitely out there.

The drongo gave another shrill cry and flew away.

"Anka, are you up for this?" Meilin slowly moved her sword around in the air as Abeke nocked an arrow onto her bowstring.

"Seriously?" Anka said, clearly annoyed at the insinuation. "I'm a pretty decent fighter, Meilin. . . . You should know that." Anka's cloak and dark hair flickered into view as she revealed her position next to

Xanthe. She was holding her quarterstaff as Toey, her spirit animal, scampered into her boot. Then just as quickly, she blended back into her surroundings. "You've been training me, and by now I may even know all your tricks."

"Yeah, yeah, let's not get too cocky." Meilin continued staring out into the savannah, her expression focused.

Laughter rang out across the savannah. It was coming from somewhere to the east of them.

Then more laughter.

A chorus from all sides.

Whoever was out there seemed to find the entire situation very funny.

"Seriously? The Oathbound think this is a joke?" Rollan rolled back his shoulders, getting ready for the fight. "I'll show them something that's not too funny."

"No." Abeke's fingers twitched as she steadied her bow. "I recognize that sound. It's not the Oathbound."

"Who is it, then?" Conor asked, tightening his grip on his ax. "Are they dangerous?"

"Hyenas." Abeke's eyes narrowed as Uraza snarled at something in the tall grass in front of her. "And when they're in a pack, they're more than dangerous . . . they're absolutely deadly."

7

BATTLEGROUND

ABEKE COULD SENSE THE HYENAS CREEPING CLOSER through the savannah. She opened her stance, raised her right elbow, and pulled the bow's string as far back as possible to get maximum power. In that instant, Abeke became one with her surroundings. Her friends' restlessness fell away as she focused on her own breathing and heartbeat. Uraza was augmenting her hunting instincts. Abeke could smell the predators' scent in the air, feel the wind glide by her cheek, and see the slight shifts in the blades of tall grass. Her fingertips relaxed, putting enough pressure on the arrow to keep it in place until the moment demanded its release.

She waited patiently. She was no longer the hunted, but the hunter.

Thwack!

Abeke released the arrow as she caught sight of a hyena lunging toward them. "Here they come!" she yelled to her friends, knowing she'd just hit her first mark.

Uraza leaped forward, claws out and teeth bared. She grabbed one of the hyenas by the neck and flipped it over, just as two more jumped on top of her. Abeke aimed at one of the hyenas, but couldn't shoot for fear of hitting Uraza.

The leopard rolled on the ground, shaking off the doglike creatures, but not before one of them sank its teeth into her hide. Uraza roared, infuriated at being bitten, and gave chase to her attacker through the grassland.

Abeke turned her attention to Rollan and Xanthe, who had teamed up to battle against a group of smaller but persistent hyenas. They were pushing that group back toward the east. On the other side, Briggan was already in pursuit of a pack that had charged all at once. He chased them through the tall grass, losing sight of one for a moment before catching a glimpse of another and taking off in its direction.

Meanwhile, several hundred yards away, Meilin and Conor were fighting at close range against two of the larger animals. They had been forced away from the campsite, but Meilin had the upper hand, using her sword to jab and slash at the persistent hyena. Conor had taken a defensive stance behind her, wielding his ax in one hand and a knife in the other.

"Keep it up!" Meilin shouted. "We've got them on the run."

The hyenas were spreading out and seemed to be disbanding, but Abeke sensed that something was wrong. Why would these highly intelligent hunters attack a group of humans and large predators? And though the hyenas had worked together, the Greencloaks had

pushed most of them back relatively easily. Abeke spun around.

That's when she saw it . . . the real plan.

These animals were doing what they always did. A coordinated attack to get what they truly wanted . . . an easy target. Separate what they viewed as the weakest member of the herd. The large-scale attack had been a distraction to split the group into different corners, leaving the campsite with only Anka protecting their bags and food.

Anka.

Even though she was older than all of them, she would be seen as the slightest in the group. If the hyenas had spotted her at some point while the Greencloaks were sleeping, she could have become the hyenas' target.

"It's Anka!" Abeke yelled. "They're after her!" Abeke rushed back toward the tree with the other Greencloaks.

As if on cue, six snarling hyenas jumped out from the tall grass, and in the moonlight Abeke could see them surrounding Anka. Anka spun around to face each one. The colors of her clothes and skin rippled as she blended into her surroundings and disappeared from view. The hyenas paused, confused because they could still smell her. The grass shifted and Anka reappeared a few feet away. One of the hyenas was done playing cat and mouse and lunged forward.

Abeke shot an arrow straight into its neck, dropping it on the spot.

"Having a hard time believing your eyes?" Anka taunted the remaining five animals. She twirled her

quarterstaff and kicked up some dust, her cloak rippling and changing colors as she faded out of sight. The hyenas drew closer. Then one yelped as she hit it hard enough that it went flying through the air. "How'd you like that?" Anka shouted, already standing somewhere else, while another hyena whimpered in agony.

The Greencloaks watched in amazement. Anka was anything but the weakest of the group.

"Don't stand there staring!" Anka called out. "Get the rest of them!"

Meilin ran forward with her sword held high above her head while Abeke unleashed an arrow that grazed the side of a hyena. Conor, Rollan, and Xanthe charged in to help, but there was already a whooping call in the distance. The hyenas turned and retreated back into the grasslands.

"That was amazing," Conor remarked as they all regrouped at the campsite. "I didn't know you could fight like that."

"You handled them like a pro," Abeke added while pulling out her arrow from the dead hyena.

"Meilin is a good teacher," Anka said, calling Toey into passive state on her arm. Instantly her features looked crisper. Once the natural camouflage tendencies that Toey imparted were removed, Abeke could see the glimmer in Anka's eyes as she smiled. Abeke could sense that Anka was proud of herself. "Not sure how I would've done against the Oathbound, but hyenas were good for my first real one-on-one challenge."

"You've definitely come a long way." Meilin picked up her bag and slung it over her shoulder. Uraza and Briggan were nearby, each resting next to a fallen hyena

that they'd brought over. "Guess we can all eat hyena meat for our next meal."

Rollan rubbed his belly. "Yum. Well, it beats them eating some Greencloak meat for *their* next meal." He smiled. "Don't think they'd like it anyway. We're way too tough to chew."

Abeke chuckled. Rollan always had a way of lightening the mood.

Suddenly, Essix screeched and circled high above them.

"Look who finally shows up ... after the fight is over," Rollan said, lifting up his arm in case the gyrfalcon wanted to perch there.

Essix dove straight toward Rollan, twisting only at the last moment to avoid colliding with him. Abeke had to duck to escape getting pummeled.

"Hey!" Abeke glanced up at the falcon, who was swooping down once more. "He was only kidding."

Rollan frowned, his eyes trained on the majestic bird. He looked worried.

"Something's wrong." Rollan sat down on the lush grass. "Essix needs to show me something." He closed his eyes and took several deep breaths before settling into a quiet rhythm.

Xanthe pulled the map out from under her cloak. "We have to go that way ... toward those mountains." She pointed east. "But did you see who else headed that way?"

"The hyenas," Meilin and Conor answered in unison.

Abeke nodded. "They'll be tracking us. Waiting for us to drop our guard."

Rollan swayed a bit and mumbled something.

Meilin bent down next to him. "What do you see?"

Rollan didn't answer at first, but then he popped his eyes open. "Oathbound. Still pretty far, but headed this way." He stood up and pointed to the west. "Coming from that direction. I counted seven of them on camels."

"So let's go." Xanthe buttoned her hooded cloak, making sure she was fully covered from head to toe.

"And one of them has a grizzly bear as a spirit animal," Rollan added. "It was helping them track us."

"Ugh, that's really not good news." Conor grimaced. "Grizzlies have one of the best senses of smell. We have to do something to shake them off our scent."

Abeke turned to look at the remnants of their campsite. Squashed grass, dead hyenas, blood on the ground . . . anyone would know they'd been there. "Hold on," Abeke said. "Let's not go too fast."

"You sense something?" Conor asked as he gazed at Briggan. The wolf looked content to bathe in the warm sun that was rising in the east. "Briggan and Uraza seem okay."

Abeke thought about what Master Naveb had told her. A good hunter doesn't always lunge forward, but takes in what is around and behind them. They could turn this into an advantage to throw off the trackers.

"What if the hyenas had won?" Abeke mused out loud. "If they had killed us while we slept?"

"What are you saying?" Xanthe shifted her weight from one foot to another. "Are you worried that the hyenas will get us next time? Because they won't."

"No, I'm wondering if we can get the Oathbound to think that, though."

"Oh . . ." Meilin gave a slow nod. "Fake our deaths."

"Or have them think at least a couple of us died here." Conor walked around to one of the dead hyenas. "We can bloody up a couple of our cloaks and leave them here. Make it seem like the hyenas carried some of us off. Maybe they'll think we separated and there was only a small group here. Then they might go back to report what they found and start a new search."

"But won't the bear just pick up our trail when we continue across the savannah toward the mountains?" Xanthe watched as Conor ripped his bag with the corner of his ax and tossed it aside.

"Not necessarily." Abeke glanced at Rollan. "Especially if we aren't going *over* the savannah."

Rollan nodded with a smile. "That's where I come in." He pulled out the chain around his neck where the Heart of the Land hung. "We won't leave a trail over the savannah because we'll be going under it." He gave Xanthe a wink. "It'll be like going home for you."

"What? I don't understand." Xanthe watched as Rollan walked to a patch of barren, sandy dirt next to Abeke. He clutched the gila monster amulet in his fist and punched the ground.

Abeke jumped aside. She felt a small tremor, then a more powerful one, as the earth opened up right next to her, forming a sinkhole. Down at the bottom there was an opening to what looked to be a tunnel.

"How?" Xanthe had a mixed expression of fear and amazement. "What . . . what is that thing?" She pointed to the amulet in Rollan's hand.

"A bond token," Rollan said, as if that were enough of an explanation. "It has a legendary gila monster's power to move the earth."

"You're getting pretty good at using it," Meilin whispered. "Impressive."

Abeke expected Rollan to dismiss the praise with a smart-mouthed comment, but he simply smiled and stayed quiet. Meilin definitely had a positive effect on him.

"Now that we have our way out..." Conor pointed to his ripped cloak lying on the ground. "Who else wants to give up their cloak and pretend to have been eaten alive?"

Abeke knew that there was no way Rollan would relinquish Tarik's green cloak. It meant too much to him. The rest of them were wearing the nondescript cloaks they'd picked up in Eura, so it made sense for one of them to leave theirs behind.

"I'll do it." Abeke began untying the cord around her neck. "This slows me down anyway."

"No." Xanthe put a hand on Abeke's arm. "For the plan to work, it has to be me. There's no other choice."

"That's ridiculous!" Meilin exclaimed. "You're the only one who can't give up her cloak. You need to have a special covering to protect you from the sun."

Xanthe shook her head. "If the trackers came from the monastery, Sodu could have given them something from my room to track my scent. It has to be my cloak."

Essix squawked as he flew in circles above them once again.

"We don't have much time." Rollan gave Essix a signal, letting her know that he understood the message.

"What Xanthe said makes sense. Plus, we'll stay underground for most of the day. She should be fine."

"I'll give her my cloak when we move aboveground," Abeke said. "That'll help a little."

"Scatter whatever's in my bag around the campsite and let's go!" Xanthe tossed her cloak to Conor and jumped into the sinkhole, disappearing into the tunnel opening.

"I think it's a good plan," Abeke said, pulling Uraza back into passive state. "Then again, it's our only plan, so . . ."

"Um, this tunnel ends after a few feet," Xanthe shouted from down below.

Rollan peered into the sinkhole. "Yeah, I can't move that much earth at once. When we're all down there, I'll keep pushing the dirt out of the way and close it in behind us."

"Bring my lantern!" Xanthe reminded him. "You'll need it down here."

"Already got it." Rollan tapped the small lantern he'd secured to the outside of his bag. "I'll toss our bags down first."

"And I'll catch them," Anka replied from the bottom of the pit. Her skin had already shifted to mimic the coloring of the shadowy hole . . . which meant Toey was back.

"When . . . how did you . . . ?" Rollan shrugged off his own question. "Careful, this one is heavy," he said to Anka as he tossed the first of the bags.

"What do you think?" Conor held up Xanthe's blood-spattered cloak to Abeke and Meilin. It had a large rip from where Briggan had torn into it. Conor

had already staged the campsite as if there had been an epic battle, with two of the hyenas left behind as casualties, and a few items from their bags thrown around.

Meilin surveyed the area. "Looks pretty convincing," she said. She'd covered up most of their footprints in the dirt. Now it really seemed as if only two people had been at the campsite.

"Yeah, I think so too." Conor held out his arm. "Briggan, you'll probably appreciate not being in that cramped tunnel for hours." The gray wolf leaped toward Conor, disappearing in a flash and reappearing as the tattoo below his elbow.

Essix had flown back and perched herself on Rollan's shoulder. "How about it, Essix? You won't be able to track us while we're underground. Going into passive state would be—" A flash of light indicated that the gyrfalcon didn't need any more convincing.

"Guess she agreed with you," Conor said, walking to the edge of the sinkhole. "Now, let's go find that valley."

"Um, yeah, I was going to say something about that." Abeke surveyed the mountains in the distance one last time as she stood next to Rollan and Conor. "We're supposed to go to a valley of death and find a field filled with skulls . . . but have we stopped to think that those skulls might be from people entering the valley of death?"

"Oh, I've thought about it." Rollan sighed. "Just don't *like* thinking about it too much, if you know what I mean."

Conor shrugged. "It's not like we have much of a choice. We have to go wherever Tembo took Stormspeaker."

"True, but . . ." Meilin tossed her bag into the sinkhole and looked at the three other Greencloaks. "We have to be careful. Hyenas and the Oathbound may be the least of our troubles."

For a moment none of the Greencloaks said a word, breathing in the last bit of fresh air they'd have for a while. Then the four of them leaped into the shadowy pit.

8

UNDERGROUND TOUR

THE GLOW FROM THE LANTERN BOUNCED OFF THE earthen walls as Rollan continued pushing aside the ground, creating a tunnel ahead of the group and allowing it to collapse once the last person was through. They'd been crawling on their hands and knees in single file, to minimize the amount of earth Rollan had to move, but it still took considerable effort and concentration. At one point, they considered taking turns using the bond token, but though it could be used by anyone, no one knew how to use it as well as Rollan. The risk of having the tunnel collapse on top of them was too great.

It had been about six or seven hours since they'd left the campsite, or at least that's what Meilin figured, based on the growling of her stomach. Xanthe had been able to keep them headed east, using her strange ability to navigate while underground by sensing Erdas's magnetic fields.

"I think I need a break," Rollan announced, wiping his brow and rolling onto his back. "And I'm pretty

sure I've heard everyone's stomach rumble in the last few minutes."

"Should we go up and eat?" Conor asked from the rear spot in the line. "The air is becoming stagnant."

"I don't think we've gone far enough to take a chance," Abeke answered from just ahead of him. "Plus, the sun will be high in the sky, which won't help Xanthe."

"I can always stay while you go up," Xanthe offered. She'd been crawling behind Rollan while directing him where to go. "But if we're all taking a break down here, then I have an idea." She reached up and touched the hard dirt above her head. "This doesn't feel as sandy as where we were. Maybe Rollan can create an airhole. In Sadre we had them in our tunnels to help the air circulate."

Meilin peered around Xanthe to get a better look at Rollan. "What do you think? Can you do that?"

Rollan propped himself up on his elbows. "Yeah, and if we're going to be here for more than just a couple of minutes, then I think I can make this area bigger. Just give me a little space."

Meilin almost laughed at his request. Space was not something they could give. But she scooted back, bumping into Anka.

Rollan clasped the amber stone in his right hand and closed his eyes. He grimaced, as if lifting a heavy object. Tiny rocks started to rain down as the ground above them buckled and lifted. It wasn't much, maybe a few feet, but it was enough.

"You did it!" Meilin sat up, happy to be vertical once again.

Rollan took a deep breath and grunted as a crack above his head widened and burst at the surface. A ray of sunlight streamed in, highlighting the dirt floor next to Rollan.

"Whew!" He collapsed onto his back with a smile on his face. "That wasn't as easy as I thought it'd be, but you guys can call me Mr. Superstrong from now on."

"How about we not?" Abeke said, rummaging through her bag. "And instead we offer you some water, dried fruit, and jerky?"

Rollan scooted against the side of the small cavern he had created. "Fair enough. Although you have to admit, I did a pretty good job of making this place."

"Yes, you and the Heart of the Land," Conor said as Abeke passed around the food.

"But more the Heart of the Land than you," Meilin corrected. "Don't go getting a big head."

"Who, me?" Rollan acted shocked. "Never!"

They were all sitting in a circle. The cavern seemed to glow with the light from the lantern and the beam of sunlight streaming down from above. Meilin felt calm. She was with people she trusted, friends who had her back. She realized that she was relaxed because she felt safe, even as they headed toward a so-called valley of death. Everyone here would fight to the death for the others.

Xanthe stretched her arms out in front of her. "So this crown you're looking for, Stormspeaker, does it do stuff like the Heart of the Land?" she asked.

Meilin bit her lip. After everything they'd been through in Sadre, battling against the Wyrm, she trusted Xanthe. But the girl wasn't a Greencloak. She was the only one

in their group who wasn't, and it didn't seem right to discuss their mission with her. Doubt crept into Meilin's thoughts. Perhaps she shouldn't be so quick to feel safe. There had been betrayals before.

The quiet lasted too long. No one had answered Xanthe, and their silence spoke volumes.

"Guess I'm not worthy of knowing those secrets," Xanthe mumbled.

Worthy.

Meilin thought back to Worthy, and how even though he had been a Redcloak and a one-time enemy, he'd sacrificed himself for their mission. She exchanged glances with Conor, Abeke, and Rollan, but couldn't seem to find Anka in the cavern. They were all thinking the same thing. Conor nodded, as did Abeke. Rollan shrugged noncommittally.

"It does have some type of power," Meilin explained. "We just don't know what it is exactly. There are four bond tokens: the Heart of the Land, which we found in Amaya. You've seen what it does. . . ."

"The Wildcat's Claw," Abeke continued. "A sword that can cut through anything and shoots out fire. But we lost it during a cave-in while we were in Eura."

"We didn't just lose it," Conor said. "We also lost our friend Worthy, who sacrificed himself to help us escape."

"Oh, that's why . . ." Xanthe nodded with new understanding. "I get it. When I mentioned not being worthy . . . that's why you all looked at each other."

"Yes," Meilin said. "But the truth is we don't know what to expect from the remaining two bond tokens. Stormspeaker and the Dragon's Eye are still mysteries to us. We know they're probably very powerful; a bond

token in the wrong hands would be a disaster. And even creating them is dangerous, as it can rip apart a spirit animal bond. The Greencloaks hid them for a reason."

"All right, but something still puzzles me," Xanthe said. "You think finding these bond tokens will somehow clear the Greencloaks' name, but how? Won't people fear that you've become even more powerful? Isn't that what got the Greencloaks into trouble in the first place?"

"There are some things that only a Greencloak would understand, Xanthe." Anka's voice was soft but strong. "No offense, but we can't share everything with you."

The conversation ended on that point, but Meilin couldn't help wonder if what Xanthe had said was true. Olvan had sent them on this mission believing that it was the only way to save the Greencloaks, but what if he was wrong? What if this made matters worse?

After a few minutes of eating in silence, Rollan spoke up. "So how much more ground shifting do you guys think I need to do before we get to the valley?"

Abeke looked at the map. "We're probably somewhere in this area," she said, running her finger over a wide swath of what looked like empty space. "Which means we have a few more hours to go before we reach the mountain range."

"It'll probably be dark once we're there." Conor leaned over to peer up at the small ray of sunlight coming in through the airhole. "We could start hiking over the mountains with less chance of being spotted."

"I can help guide you without even using the lantern," Xanthe said. "So I like the idea. But why not simply go

under the mountains like we're doing now? Or is that something you think I shouldn't know either?"

Meilin didn't like Xanthe's tone. Sure, she had helped them before and was risking a lot now, but if it came at the price of causing division among the Greencloaks, then they would have to continue on without her. "Xanthe, if you can't accept not knowing a few things, then maybe–"

"Moving solid rock is much harder than shifting dirt and sand," Rollan said, cutting Meilin off. "Plus, in the middle of a mountain, it's not like we can go up thirty feet or so and be aboveground." He glanced at Xanthe and widened his eyes. "*And* having you guide us in the dark again will be very helpful . . . especially since we have to go to that valley of death place."

"That reminds me of something I once heard . . ." Abeke stared at the ground, where she was mindlessly making small swirls in the loose dirt with her forefinger. "What was it?"

"Something about the valley of death?" Conor rolled his head from side to side, trying to crack his neck. "Maybe you heard about it in your village?"

"Maybe," Abeke said, but she was lost in her own memories.

"Well, if Rollan's feeling rested"–Meilin put her canteen back in her bag–"then I think we should start moving again. We still have a ways to go."

"Better enter . . . valley of death . . . who can see," Abeke mumbled. She paused, then slapped her leg. "That's it!"

"Huh?" Rollan glanced over at her. "What did you say?"

"It's something the Rain Dancer in my village once said," Abeke explained. "It's an old Niloan proverb . . . *Better to enter the valley of death with someone who can see, than blindly run through life never knowing who surrounds you.*"

"You think it has something to do with where we're going?" Meilin asked.

Abeke shrugged. "No idea."

Rollan pulled out the Heart of the Land, which hung under his shirt. "Sounds like it's a warning about not being alone."

"Really?" Conor took Rollan's bag and slipped it over his shoulder. "How do you figure?"

"Well, I think it's just saying that it's better to die with someone who knows the real you than go through life never letting anyone get close." Rollan paused. Everyone was staring at him with slightly surprised looks.

"What? I can't be deep? I've read poetry before, if that surprises you." Rollan gave a sheepish smile. "Or I could be completely wrong about the whole thing."

"What you said does make sense." Meilin was already on her hands and knees, ready to start crawling again. "Goes along with our belief that united Green-cloaks are the best for Erdas."

"Xanthe, which way do we go?" Anka asked from behind Meilin.

"Open the tunnel that way." She pointed to a spot behind Rollan. "It'll keep us headed east."

The group continued crawling through Rollan's tunnel for several more hours, taking small breaks every once in a while, until they bumped into a dead end where the compacted dirt changed to solid rock. At that

point, Rollan took a deep breath and used the amulet to create a crack in the hard dirt above them, widening it to form a gaping hole.

Meilin, standing with the others, bent her head back and took in the starry sky. They were still about twenty feet down. "So, any suggestions on how to get up there?"

"Only one way," Abeke said. "Together. The lightest person climbs on top of the others and then drops a rope. Normally, that would be me, but now I think it's Anka." Abeke turned around, searching for the camouflaged Greencloak. "Don't you think, Anka? Anka? Anka, where are you?"

"I'm right here," she answered. "And yes, make a pyramid and I'll climb on top."

"Before we do anything, let me have Essix check the area," Rollan said as he released the gyrfalcon, who promptly took to the sky.

Meilin stared at Rollan. He had decided to squat down and was rubbing his temples. Under the layer of dirt that they all had covering them, his face looked flushed, and there was something about how his shoulders were drooping. "You're looking a little . . . *off*."

Rollan shook out his arms. "I'm fine. It just feels like that one time when I binged on a bag of sugar candies and my body crashed afterward. Maybe wielding all that power for hours without stopping does something similar."

From high above, Essix squawked, giving the all clear to continue.

"That's our cue." Rollan took a deep breath and slowly let it out. "Let's do this. Conor and I can form

the base." Rollan motioned for Conor to get closer. "Meilin and Xanthe can climb on top and Anka can scale all of us to get to the top."

"You sure you're okay?" Abeke asked.

"I'm a little tired . . . but when has that stopped any of us?" Rollan replied with a grin.

"All right, then, if you're sure." Conor pulled out a rope from one of the bags and handed it to Anka. "Here you go."

Anka took the rope, looping it over her head and right shoulder. As soon as the rope touched her, it began to blend into the shadows thrown by the lantern. "I'm ready."

A few minutes later each of them had made their way out of the pit and were standing under the expansive night sky and full moon. They all stretched and filled their lungs with the cool air that drifted down the mountainside.

Loosening her long braid, Meilin shook out some of the dirt and pebbles stuck in her hair. It felt good after being confined underground all day, but what she really longed for was a bath. That was a luxury she rarely got to enjoy anymore. Not that she would ever trade her life as a Greencloak for her prior life in the palace. That lifestyle was best suited for other girls . . . like Princess Song.

Meilin felt a slight pain in her chest. She hadn't thought of the princess in a while, but the two girls had much in common. Besides having grown up in Zhongese palaces, they'd both seen their fathers die violently. It was something Meilin could never forget, and she wouldn't wish it on anyone. And not only had she and

Princess Song witnessed those horrendous deaths, they'd both been forced to take charge of circumstances not of their own choosing. Meilin wondered if, after everything was over and the Greencloaks cleared their name, she and Princess Song would become friends. It felt like a distinct possibility.

"Why don't we make camp here? Give Rollan a break for a while," Anka said. "We could use the pit as a trap if any animals try to attack again."

"I just need five minutes and I'll be good to go," Rollan said, having sat down and rested his head on his knees. "We have a lot of ground to cover."

Conor and Abeke took the opportunity of finally being aboveground to release their spirit animals. Briggan and Uraza quickly took in their surroundings. Uraza first scratched the ground, then her nostrils flared. She stood motionless, having picked up the scent of something. Briggan, on the other hand, took one look around, decided that there was nothing of interest for him, and sat down to watch Uraza.

The leopard took two slow steps forward, paused, perked her ears, and then darted toward the mountain. She was on the hunt.

Conor laughed as Briggan jumped up and gave chase. "Looks like Briggan doesn't want to be left out of whatever Uraza is up to."

"Rrrr . . ." Rollan let out a quiet snore. He had passed out while sitting on the ground.

"Poor guy," Anka muttered. "He's really tired."

"He looks uncomfortable." Meilin sat across from him and began rebraiding her hair. "This should help." She called out Jhi, who, upon seeing how exhausted

Rollan was, snuggled up against him and pulled him to her chest. Rollan didn't protest and simply sank into the bear.

Rollan's five minutes turned into twenty, then thirty.

Essix had returned and was perched on a nearby acacia tree, waiting for the group to continue.

"Why don't we split up for a while?" Abeke suggested. "Conor, Xanthe, and I can head up the mountain and find a place to make camp during daylight hours. A cave or something. That way Xanthe won't have to deal with the sun. Essix can show you where we are whenever Rollan recovers."

Meilin nodded, not wanting to risk waking Rollan up. She didn't like seeing him like this. It reminded her of when he became ill with the Sunset Death when they were fighting the Devourer. So much had happened since that time . . . in the world and between her and Rollan.

"I think that's a good idea," Anka whispered. "We'll meet up with you in a few hours. Just make sure you don't go too far without us."

Conor nodded. He and the others picked up their bags to begin the hike up the mountain. Meilin watched them leave for as long as she was able to, until the darkness of the savannah swallowed her friends from sight.

She pulled the sides of her cloak tighter across her chest. There was a chill in the air. She felt fidgety not having anything to do, so she decided to take an inventory of everything in her bag. Suddenly, she felt Jhi's eyes on her.

"What?" she asked. The panda still had Rollan's head resting on top of her belly.

Jhi blinked but didn't move.

"I just don't like sitting around doing nothing," Meilin explained, repacking the medical supplies, fruit, jerky, and a small tin pot for cooking. "Don't worry, I'm not going anywhere without him. I know he needs to rest."

She sighed, leaning back on her elbows. They all needed to be at full strength if they were going to survive whatever waited for them in the valley of death.

"Anka?" Meilin listened carefully, trying to pinpoint her location. "Anka, you want to train a little more?"

"I think I'm done for the day," Anka replied, her voice coming from a few feet away. "It's too dark and I'm tired from all the crawling."

Meilin strained her eyes to see Anka, but the elder Greencloak completely blended into the night.

"You know that I have no idea where you are right now. Between the clouds covering the moon and your camouflage ability . . . it's like I'm talking into a void."

There was a brief flash of light, then Meilin could see Anka's silhouette leaning against her bag. Anka had returned Toey to his passive state as a tattoo on her wrist.

"Better?" she asked.

"Yes, it's nice to somewhat see who I'm talking to." Meilin wasn't usually one to share her feelings, but over the course of their journey, she'd grown closer to Anka. It felt good to have someone a little older around, especially someone from Zhong. It felt as if she'd gained a big sister.

"Have you thought about what you're going to do after all this is over?" Meilin asked her.

"You mean, when we complete the mission?" Anka paused, thinking about her answer. "I guess I'll return to Zhong. Help in the recovery. Unless the Greencloaks need me elsewhere. What about you?"

"I'd like to go home to Jano Rion, even if only for a little while. Rollan and I were on the way there when Olvan called for us, and then all this happened."

"You deserve the chance to go home," Anka said. "You're a legend over there."

"I don't know about the legend stuff. . . . I just want to see everyone." Meilin sighed at the thought of the people who wouldn't be there anymore. People like her father. "Speaking of seeing people," Meilin said, hoping to change the subject. "Why do you keep yourself hidden most of the time?"

"I don't know," Anka answered. "Toey likes to be out and I don't even think about it. It's like if I'm breathing, my body automatically blends into the background. In fact, I have to concentrate if I want to be seen."

"But doesn't it bother you that people forget you're around?"

Anka shrugged. "Not really. You'd be surprised at how much I get to see when people don't remember I'm there. But the truth is that *everybody* conceals themselves, at least partly. Even from our friends. I'll bet you do it, too, without really thinking about it. We skip details that are unflattering or scary, or cloak ourselves in the customs of the region we're in. There are lots of ways to hide. . . . Mine is just the most noticeable."

Meilin didn't have anything else to say. Perhaps Anka was right and she was being the most honest of them all. Meilin did keep some things hidden. Feelings and fears

that she didn't even like admitting to herself. And not just silly things like being afraid of spiders: also the real worries, like being afraid to get hurt. She'd believed that a true warrior wouldn't allow herself to be vulnerable, and that's why she always kept her emotions in check.

But was love really a weakness, or was it a strength? Meilin wasn't always sure.

VALLEY OF DEATH

CONOR STUMBLED ON THE UNEVEN GROUND AND FELL onto his right knee. He quickly popped back up as if nothing had happened, grateful that the night shrouded his clumsiness. For the last few hours, he'd been trying to keep up with Xanthe, but these mountains were more like the ones in western Amaya, where they'd first encountered Arax, than the rolling hills near his home in Eura.

"Uraza, over there!" Abeke pointed to something a few yards away.

Briggan hurdled over a rock to beat the leopard to whatever animal they'd both been chasing.

"Looks like Briggan may have won," Conor said, getting close enough to see the wolf sticking his snout into a small, rocky opening.

"Careful . . . hyraxes are tricky," Abeke warned as Briggan tried pawing his way into the hole.

"Hyrax?" Conor repeated. "I thought it was a rabbit."

"It sort of looks like a rabbit," Abeke explained.

"Except it has no tail and round ears. People call them rock rabbits because—"

"Look out, Briggan!" Xanthe called out, just as the hyrax darted between Briggan's legs and right by Uraza's snapping jaws.

The chase was on again, with Uraza and Briggan taking off after their small prey.

"Glad someone's having fun out here," Conor remarked, rubbing his knee. "Hope you're about to tell us that the path gets a whole lot smoother up ahead."

"Um, not quite," Xanthe said. "We're going to have to double back. It's narrow and steep, and it looks like the path itself has fallen away. We're going to have to find another way around."

"But going around the base of these mountains might add an extra day or two." Conor knew they'd taken the only visible path over the mountain. "We've bought some time with the hyena thing, but the Oathbound will keep looking for us. We can't waste so much time out in the open."

Abeke placed a hand on Uraza, who was now holding the dead hyrax in her mouth. "It's not like we have a choice."

"Well, we actually do. Follow me." Xanthe backtracked down the path, stopped next to a large pile of rocks, and tried pushing a large boulder out of the way. "Conor, help me with this."

Conor put his shoulder into it and the boulder shifted a few feet to reveal the opening to a dark cave. "You want to make camp in there?" He peered over some large rocks that still blocked the bottom of the entrance. He couldn't see a thing inside.

"Yes." Xanthe climbed over the rocks and went inside. "But more importantly, I'm thinking we can go through the mountain instead of going around it."

"How far back do you think this thing goes?" Abeke motioned for Uraza to stay outside while she joined Xanthe.

"Pretty far, from the vibrations I get." Xanthe's voice echoed against the walls. "But we can always have Rollan open it up whenever it dead-ends."

Conor entered and quickly lit a match. In the flickering light he could see that the cave extended into tunnels. Abeke was still close to the entrance, but he could see Xanthe's white hair as she explored the far side.

"Ow!" Conor flicked the match to the ground as the flame burned his fingertips. The cave immediately went black again, except for the fading red glow of the matchstick that now lay at Conor's feet.

"I don't think moving mountains is a good idea." Conor headed back outside where it wasn't quite as dark. "The Heart of the Land could cause a cave-in. We'd be trapped."

"But we might face a bigger risk out there with the hyenas and the Oathbound," Xanthe countered. "And this cave could stretch deep into the mountain. We can make camp in here while I go check it out."

Uraza jumped inside, followed by Briggan. They both seemed to have made their own decisions to stay inside for the remainder of the night.

"Traitor," Conor grumbled.

"Well, if there really is a field of skulls up ahead," Abeke mused, "then hopefully whatever separated the

skulls from their bodies won't expect us to come through the mountain." Abeke leaned over the group of rocks that formed a barrier to the cave entrance. She stared at the sky. "Any sort of trap would be set for those who come over or around it."

"I guess, but let's see what the others think before we decide," Conor suggested. He took a seat near the cave entrance, where he could still feel the night air.

A bird screeched somewhere outside.

Conor sat a little straighter, his hearing amplified because of Briggan. "That sounds like Essix."

Abeke pointed to something in the night sky. "It is! She knows we're here."

Briggan stretched out next to Conor. "Well, I'm guessing she'll bring the others here in the morning." Conor rubbed the wolf's belly.

Abeke took out a small blanket from her bag and laid it flat on the ground. Uraza quickly curled up at the bottom of it. "Ahem, I was going to lie there." Abeke smiled. "Guess we'll share."

As Conor drifted off to sleep, he heard the leopard purr in agreement.

Dawn was already breaking when a voice pierced through Conor's dream of running down the hillside toward his home in Eura.

"Wake up, sleepyheads!" Rollan commanded. His hands were on the rocks at the entrance of the cave as he climbed inside. Daylight streamed in from behind him. "Don't you want to see that field full of skulls and drain the demon's blood? Mwahaha!"

"Rollan, give them a minute." Meilin swung her legs over the small barrier wall and walked into the cave.

Conor opened one eye, wishing he could have five more minutes of sleep. It had been a long time since he'd seen his family, and he liked having them pop up in his dreams.

"Someone has a ton of energy," Xanthe remarked from deeper in the cave.

"You aren't kidding," Anka grumbled, clearly visible to everyone. Conor assumed she'd placed Toey in passive state. Perhaps even Anka liked to be seen once in a while.

"I think Jhi's influence made Rollan a little *too* well rested," Meilin said. "He's been chirping like this the whole walk here." Meilin pulled out her canteen and took a small sip of water. "Mental note for next time."

"Funny." Rollan stayed outside the cave and looked up at the mountain. "Did you notice that the path ends up ahead? Looks like we'll have to find a different way to get to the face in the mountain."

"Yeah, about that." Conor rubbed the back of his stiff neck. "Xanthe had an idea, but I'm not sure if–"

"Why don't we just tell them and let them decide for themselves." Xanthe drew closer, wearing Abeke's cloak to shield her from the soft morning sun.

"What's the idea?" Meilin glanced from Abeke to Conor, then back to Abeke.

"We were thinking that going around will probably take a couple of days," Abeke explained. "And if there are some sort of traps that gave the valley of death its name, they'd probably be on the typical paths around or over the mountains."

"So Xanthe found a different way?" Meilin looked over at Xanthe for more information.

"Well, last night I explored the cave a bit." She motioned behind her where one of the tunnels grew dark. "And that one extends deep into the center of the mountain."

"Uh-huh." Meilin waited for more, but Xanthe didn't say anything else. "But it ends, right? So we can't go through."

"Oh, wait. I get it." Rollan's expression changed. He snapped his fingers. "You want me to get us through the rest of it."

"I already explained that we've faced a similar situation before," Conor stated. "And we decided we couldn't use it because it was too risky. And nothing has changed."

"But it has changed. It was different with Worthy." Abeke stroked Uraza, who remained curled up on the blanket. "The cave was completely unstable back then. Any movement could've caused the whole thing to collapse. That's not the case here. And Rollan's gotten much better at using the bond token, too."

"I *am* pretty good at using it." Rollan ran his hand along the inside wall of the cave. "But I wouldn't be able to make a tunnel like I did when we were underground. There I only had to shift the dirt and sand." He knocked on the stone. "This is too solid."

"So that's that." Abeke stood up, pushed Uraza off, and shook out the blanket. "We go around and brace ourselves for whatever's out there."

Rollan pulled out a loose stone from the wall. "But maybe I can make enough cracks where we can take out the rocks and make our own tunnel."

"Rollan." Meilin pulled him aside. "Do you even know how to do that? This would probably be a lot harder than moving dirt, and if you mess up–"

"I won't mess up." He sidestepped Meilin to speak directly to Xanthe. "Do you know how far we'd have to go?"

"I tried to get a feel of the cave's vibrations like in Sadre. It's not the same because this is aboveground, but I think I could direct you to where there's another cave that comes in from the other side of the mountain. There's about ten feet or so of solid rock between them, though."

"So I'd have to make enough cracks where we can create a tunnel between the two caves." Rollan pursed his lips and nodded. "Yeah, I think I can do that . . . but I should practice first." He pulled out the Heart of the Land from under his shirt and lifted the chain over his head. He clutched the amulet in his hand and pushed against the cave wall. A rumbling and creaking noise filled the air.

"Whoa!" Meilin shouted. "Stop!"

Rollan yanked his fist away from the wall. Cracks resembling a spiderweb had already formed, boring into the stone. He dug his fingertips around one of the larger splintered pieces of rock and jostled it back and forth. Then he pulled it out, leaving behind a hole several inches deep.

"Hey, this might actually work!" Conor exclaimed.

"You doubted me?" Rollan smirked.

"Didn't doubt *you*," Conor explained. "I doubted the mountain."

"Uraza," Abeke called to the leopard. "I think it'll be easier if you make the journey in passive state."

Conor glanced over at Briggan. "You too, boy."

Both animals stepped forward and disappeared, emerging as tattoos on their respective partners.

"I'm not even going to bother asking Essix," Rollan said. "She'll either fly around and find us, or she'll follow us through the tunnel."

"So let's get started," Xanthe said, ready to lead the way. "You'll have to light the lantern. It gets very dark in there."

The group gathered their things and walked into the center of the mountain, following Xanthe through several twists and turns. Eventually, they reached the dead end Xanthe had mentioned.

"All right, then. . . . Here we go." Rollan struck the cave wall with the side of his fist while clutching the Heart of the Land.

The mountain rumbled and groaned with every hit as cracks splintered the wall. Piece by piece, bit by bit, the group took chunks out of the mountain. It was slow and tedious work that, after several hours, left many of their fingers bleeding.

"We're through!" Abeke yelled when a piece of cave wall fell back into the opening on the other side.

Conor and Meilin pushed the remaining rocks and boulders until they could all crawl through the hole. A long, winding tunnel led them to an opening where daylight streamed in. The five Greencloaks and Xanthe stood side by side, looking out at a mountain on the opposite side of the green valley down below.

"There it is." Xanthe pointed to a part of the mountain that looked like a man's profile. "The face in the mountain that Sodu described seeing and that Tembo wrote about."

It was unmistakable. The wind had chiseled out the curve of his forehead, the sunken area of his eyes, the steep angle of his nose, and a very prominent chin.

Conor gazed at the valley below, filled with bushes and a few acacia trees. There was a small stream running down the center of it. It was all very peaceful. Nothing like the barren wasteland he had imagined. "And is that supposed to be the valley of death?" he muttered.

"Doesn't quite live up to its name, huh?" Abeke replied.

"Meh, you never know." Rollan grabbed a small rock and threw it as far as he could. "It could be a trap to lull you into thinking nothing is wrong and then . . . Whack! Your head is chopped off."

"I can't see much right now." Xanthe was shielding her eyes, the hood of Abeke's cloak pulled low so it nearly covered her nose. "Do any of you see skulls?"

"No," Meilin answered. "But maybe it's been so long that they're all buried by now."

Conor looked back at Xanthe. She had stepped farther inside the cave to avoid the direct midday sun. Even with Abeke's cloak as protection, she wouldn't be able to hike in the daytime for too long. "Maybe we should wait until it gets dark. Head out then."

"No, you can't waste any time," Xanthe answered without hesitation. "I'll only be slowing you down from this point on. You have to go without me."

"But we can't leave you here." Abeke's voice was full of concern. "Nilo can be a dangerous place, especially if you're alone. You have the hyenas and other animals out here. Never mind the Oathbound."

"I'm a warrior. . . . I can take care of myself," Xanthe answered, taking another step back. "And I really should go back to see Takoda. Let him know that I'm safe." She retreated even farther into the dark cave. "I'll travel at night and I'll be fine. But you need to go finish your mission. My job was to get you to this point."

Meilin gave Xanthe a small nod of gratitude. "Thank you for helping us."

Abeke wasn't convinced. "But maybe Xanthe can wait and—"

"Good luck, my friends." Xanthe waved to them. "I hope our paths cross again soon." She turned and ran back into the cave.

"Guess she didn't want to discuss it anymore," Anka said, calling out Toey, who scampered up her cloak. Within seconds Anka's form faded from view as her skin and clothes blended against the side of the mountain.

"Xanthe understands that this is important." Meilin pointed to a way down toward the valley. "Now, let's stay alert for any traps."

Rollan and Anka followed Meilin, while Conor stayed behind with Abeke for a moment.

"I had the vision again," he whispered. "Last night."

"The one with the big tidal wave?"

Conor nodded. "I'm watching from somewhere up high, and I can see the ocean pull away just before the wave comes barreling toward me. I just wish I knew more about what it means or the circumstances around it."

"You can't force that kind of thing." Abeke touched his arm. "You have to be patient."

Conor gave her a smile. "You sound like Master Naveb."

"He definitely had some insight into each of us." Abeke paused. "Well, most of us. He didn't have much to say about Anka."

"He may not have remembered that she was there. She's pretty good at making people forget about her."

"ABEKE! CONOR!" Meilin shouted. She had reached the valley floor and was holding her sword high above her head.

Conor and Abeke sprinted down the mountain, calling out Briggan and Uraza as they ran. As both animals appeared, neither one hesitated. Each took a fraction of a second to assess the situation and race to whatever had confronted the others down below.

In his mind, Conor braced himself for what he might find. He imagined the ground covered with half-rotten skulls and something that might put his own head in jeopardy. A trap, a ferocious animal, a vicious attacker, or something completely indescribable. But he was not prepared for what he saw as he drew closer to the valley.

It was Rollan. He was sitting in the middle of the field . . . laughing hysterically.

Uraza and Briggan were pacing around all the bushes, looking as confused as Conor felt.

"What are you doing?" Abeke spun around, trying to understand what was so funny.

"The field of skulls." Rollan cupped his hand under the stem of one of the large plants. "Look!"

Conor drew closer and noticed the dried seedpods that clung to the stem. Each one looked like a small brown skull. The entire valley was full of them.

Meilin swung her sword against another plant, knocking several of the seedpods into the air. "This is what we were so worried about." She spun around, taking a swipe at another bush. "A bunch of dried-up plant parts."

"Snapdragons," Abeke confirmed. "It didn't even occur to me. When the flowers die and fall away, what's left behind are the seedpods that look like skulls."

"And here I was thinking that there would be traps trying to chop our heads off." Rollan stood and shook the dirt off his pants. "Makes me think that there may not be a demon to kill, either."

Uraza and Briggan had relaxed and were now simply inspecting the area.

Conor looked around for something that might resemble a demon. All he could see were more of the snapdragon plants and, on the other side of the valley, the small mountain with the face jutting out.

"Those trees." Abeke trekked through the snapdragon plants, mesmerized by something. Conor, Meilin, Rollan, and Anka all followed as she crossed the valley and got to the foot of the opposite mountain. "Up there. There's a cluster of them on that ridge."

"You think it has something to do with demons?" Conor tilted his head as if trying to see them from a different angle.

"They *are* the demons." Abeke smiled. "Demon trees that bleed red sap."

"So that's the blood we have to drain?" Rollan looked relieved. "Plain old tree sap? I'm really liking this part of the mission. Tembo had a good sense of humor."

"Although it looks like we might have to do some

rock climbing to get up there." Abeke stared at the sheer cliff.

"Rollan and I will do it," Meilin said. She slipped off her bag and dug around inside it.

"Um, it might be nice if you asked before volunteering me." Rollan pointed to Conor's bag. "And if you're looking for the ropes, they're over there."

"I can go with you, Meilin," Abeke offered. "It shouldn't be hard to get the sap. . . . Just nick the tree and attach one of our canteens to collect it. It might take a while, though. We'll probably have to stay up there until tomorrow, because the sap can drip pretty slowly."

"I didn't say I wouldn't go," Rollan clarified. "Just that I'd like to be asked, not told. And it does make more sense for me and Meilin to go up."

Conor and Abeke exchanged a quick glance and smiled. They both knew that Rollan liked the idea of spending some time alone with Meilin.

"What?" Rollan protested. "It's better if the two people going up are tied together, and a counterbalance works best if both people are similar in weight . . . in case either one falls, the other will be able to support them. Remember what happened when we were scaling the walls to get the Wildcat's Claw? That's why I'm saying it. Meilin and I are closer in size."

"Riiight," Conor said in mock deference. "It's just science."

Rollan had a broad smile on his face as he glanced at Meilin. "Exactly."

10

SLINGSHOT

SCALING MOUNTAINS WAS NOT ONE OF ROLLAN'S FAVOR-ite things to do, but it wasn't the worst, either. It ranked somewhere between eating seal fat and swimming in the ocean at night. But he did like spending time with Meilin. That made the climb worthwhile.

"Watch your step over here." Rollan inched his way along a long, narrow foothold where only the tips of his toes fit. "Putting another anchor in." He lodged the metal anchor into a crack in the mountain and slipped the rope that connected the two of them through it. This was much safer than when they had used vines to get to the Wildcat's Claw.

"All right!" Meilin called out. She was taking out the anchors every time she got to one so they could reuse them later on. Eventually she would collect all seven and either take over the lead or hand them back to Rollan.

They were about halfway to the ridge and making decent time. Up above them, Rollan could see plenty of handholds and a couple of narrow ledges where they'd

be able to stop, rest, and catch their breaths before continuing to climb.

"How about I go up through here?" Rollan turned to look over his shoulder at Meilin. "Meilin?"

He followed the rope and saw Meilin was already higher than he was, scaling up the mountain. "This way is better," she shouted down. "There are more crevices for the anchors over here. Shift back."

Rollan was about to argue that *he* was supposed to be leading, but it was pointless. Meilin was already putting in the second anchor. It would be more dangerous to have her come back down.

He took a careful step sideways along the tiny ledge.

No, he was definitely going to say something. They were a team. Decisions needed to be made together. Meilin had a habit of forgetting that.

"Hey, Meilin, you can't just take off and expect me to follow. We're supposed to be a unit." A rock bounced off the mountain from above, narrowly missing him as it came tumbling down.

"Yeah, but this way up was better," she insisted.

Rollan plucked off an anchor and continued along the ledge, his frustration rising with every backtracking step he took. "Doesn't matter. It's not only you up here. You aren't back in Zhong giving orders like some sort of Imperial Guard."

Meilin stopped climbing and looked back at Rollan. "That's not fair. You know I'm not like that." Another rock tumbled from above. "Plus, I've been trying—"

A flurry of rocks the size of Rollan's fist smashed against the mountainside, interrupting Meilin. But this

wasn't a rockslide from above. No, these rocks were being aimed at them from below.

Rollan looked down and saw several people jumping out from beneath the snapdragon bushes . . . slingshots in their hands. They weren't wearing the black that the Oathbound normally wore, but that didn't make them any less dangerous.

Farther back, Abeke, Conor, and their spirit animals charged across the field to do battle with the slingshot-wielding menaces. He and Meilin needed to get down there to help.

"ROLLAN!" Meilin yelled as the rocks stopped. She was pointing to a ledge high above them.

A flurry of arrows whizzed by Rollan's head, headed toward the valley.

Rollan looked up at the ridge. Several people dressed in loose-fitting, sand-colored clothing stood on the edge, with bows aimed at the valley below. Rollan followed the arrows' path and saw them land right in front of his friends. Conor and Abeke split apart, scrambling to find cover.

Essix swooped down from the sky and attacked one of the men. The archer swung wildly with his bow, using it like a bludgeon to fight her off. Rollan could hear the man scream as Essix raked her sharp talons across his face.

"SURRENDER!" a voice shouted down at them. "Do not move or we won't miss next time."

"Rollan, we have to do something!" Meilin started to climb faster, ignoring the warning. "They have the advantage up there."

"Hold on tight!" Rollan took out the Heart of the Land. He thought if he could focus all his energy on hitting the mountain, he could cause a tremor. Enough to shake the trees and maybe knock a few of the archers off the ledge. "Here it goes."

Just then another hail of stones flew at them. The slingers were back, and this time they were hitting their marks. Rollan's calf burned, and he hissed as a rock struck the back of his leg.

Another rock pegged him in the back, knocking the air from his lungs.

He glanced up at Meilin just in time to see a large rock hit the back of her head.

"MEILIN!" Rollan's voice echoed through the valley down below, but he couldn't do anything as her hands dropped to her sides, letting go of the handholds. Rollan saw her dark hair drape down her back as her body arched and peeled away from the mountain. She tumbled backward, knocking out two of the anchors as she sailed past Rollan on her way down.

Rollan braced himself. Only his counterweight would save Meilin from crashing against the rocks below. The rope's slack disappeared as it snapped tight against his chest and thrust him against the mountain, pulling him up higher as Meilin dropped several more feet. Then everything stopped. The third and fourth anchors held tight and Rollan regained his footing . . . but on the other end of the rope Meilin's limp body dangled in midair.

An arrow flew overhead, this time headed toward the ridge, striking one of the attackers. Abeke was trying to give them cover, but there was no place for them

to hide . . . nowhere to go. All Rollan knew was that he had to help Meilin. She couldn't hang like that for long.

Rollan grasped the Heart of the Land as tightly as he could and pushed against the mountain with all his might. He tried focusing all his thoughts and energy into moving the mountain. If he could create a ledge just below Meilin, he could then lower her onto it by giving the rope some slack. But he didn't even know if it was possible to force a piece of the mountain to jut out.

He had to try. Meilin's life depended on it.

Rollan concentrated, ignoring everything else in the world.

The mountain began to shake. He could hear shouting from their attackers, mixed in with the thundering rumble of rocks cascading from different areas.

He didn't care. He was going to save Meilin.

"ARGHH!" he grunted as all his energy poured out of himself and into the amulet.

Rollan didn't even realize that the fighting had stopped. He didn't know that there were no more rocks being hurled at them, no more arrows flying back and forth. His adrenaline was flowing and he was solely focused on Meilin. He could feel the weight of her body pulling on the rope.

The mountain rumbled and groaned as if in pain. Still, Rollan forced it to shift. He had never tapped into so much of the amulet's energy. Inch by inch, a narrow ledge unfolded, forming a few feet beneath Meilin.

Once it was about three feet wide, he stopped to catch his breath.

"What kind of power do you have over our mountain?" a gruff voice called out.

Rollan ignored it. He slowly climbed up, allowing the rope to slide through the remaining anchors, which in turn allowed Meilin to gently fall onto the newly formed ledge.

"Answer us!" the voice demanded, but there was no show of force to back up the words. The arrows and rocks had ceased.

"I have to check on my friend!" Rollan shouted. He untied the rope around his chest and quickly scaled down to where Meilin lay.

"Meilin," he whispered, crouching down beside her. He lifted her head and his fingers came away bloody. "Come on, Meilin. Open your eyes," he said. "We need Jhi. She can help you. You have to call her out."

Meilin's body remained limp in his arms.

"Your falcon!" a much deeper voice shouted from above. "Call it back into passive state or we will finish what we started."

For the first time since Meilin had been hit, Rollan took a good look at his surroundings.

The sun was beginning to set over the western mountains. He could hear Essix squawking. Above Rollan were warriors with arrows pointed directly at him and Meilin. Down below in the valley, Abeke and Conor were sitting among the snapdragon bushes with their hands over their heads, another group of warriors surrounding them. Uraza and Briggan were nowhere in sight. Rollan assumed that they must have been forced back into their passive states as well.

"Call off the falcon!" the voice yelled again, sounding a little more desperate.

Rollan imagined that Essix was fighting some of the warriors . . . and likely winning.

An arrow hit the ground, narrowly missing Meilin by a few inches. "Get the falcon out of here or the next one won't miss!"

"Essix! ESSIX!" Rollan wobbled as he stood up, a sudden wave of exhaustion hitting him. "Please," Rollan begged, pulling open his shirt, hoping the falcon realized that he had to do this to help Meilin. "Come!"

Essix flew away from the ridge and swooped past Rollan. Their eyes connected, and Rollan knew that the falcon understood the gravity of the situation.

A brief flash and the falcon tattoo appeared over Rollan's heart.

"She's gone," Rollan shouted. "What do you want from us?"

There was silence. Rollan gazed over at Meilin again. He had never thought of her as fragile, but that's exactly how she looked. He would do anything to protect her.

"I am Jehan, leader of the Dasat," a strong, feminine voice called down. "We saw what you did. How do you hold such power over this mountain?"

There was no way Rollan was going to tell her about the Heart of the Land. "It doesn't matter, but I can do much worse if you don't leave us alone." Rollan hoped this might be enough to frighten their attackers because, truth be told, he was far too weak to use the bond token again.

"Your friend is hurt. . . . We can help her," Jehan offered.

"You are the ones who hurt her!" Rollan countered.

Three long ropes tumbled down the mountainside toward the ledge. Rollan knew there was nowhere for them to go. And even if there were, neither he nor Meilin were in any shape to move.

"Climb up!" Jehan commanded. "That's an order."

Rollan was sitting next to Meilin once again, cradling her head. His own body was spent. Moving the mountain had drained him of all his energy. "I can't. I'm too weak." His voice shook as he spoke. "And I'm not leaving her here."

"Tie the rope around your waist and we will pull you up," Jehan offered. "Once we talk, if I'm satisfied by your answers, then I'll send a rescue team for your friend. It's the only way to save her."

Rollan didn't like the idea, but he knew there was no other way. Meilin needed to get off this mountain. She needed help. Her head had stopped bleeding, but she wasn't waking up.

He bent over and gave Meilin a kiss on the forehead. "I'm sorry," he said softly in her ear. "I hope I'm doing the right thing." He placed her head gently on the ground, tied the rope around his waist, and gave it a tug. "All right!" Rollan yelled. "Pull me up. Just get her rescue ready."

THE HUNT

ABEKE COULDN'T BELIEVE THAT AFTER EVERYTHING they'd been through, including epic wars with the Devourer and the Wyrm, the Dasat tribe had caught them completely unaware. Even Uraza hadn't spotted them until it was too late.

"Look! Here come your friends." Khai, one of the guards, pointed toward a group carrying torches down the mountain. Even though it was dark, the light from the torches revealed an exhausted Rollan using two people as support as he walked with his head hung low. Behind him, several of the Dasat carried a wooden stretcher with Meilin strapped on top. "We'll see what they have to say."

"They'll tell you the truth, just as I have." Abeke tried wiggling the ropes that held her hands behind her back. After being captured, they had all been brought to the small Dasat camp on the other side of the mountain. "We only needed to get a bit of sap from the tree, and then we would have been on our way."

Khai shook his head. "Greencloaks never want one thing. They always demand more."

"But there was no reason to attack us," Conor argued, sitting on one of the many colorful rugs strewn around the camp. He was tied together with Anka, back to back. "We could have explained what we were doing. We meant no harm."

"A Dasat hunter captures their prey first, then decides what to do with it," Khai replied, bending down to get closer to Conor. "That's why I cornered you and your wolf in the valley. But in this case, I won't be the one to decide what to do with you . . . that'll be Jehan's decision."

"Who's Jehan?" Abeke asked.

"I am." A girl not much older than the Greencloaks motioned for the others to take Meilin to one of the tents. She wore a long, golden-brown scarf over her head and had sun-kissed skin and dark hair that peeked out from the edge of the scarf. "I'm the leader of the Dasat. This is our territory. No one enters without our permission. Your friend's injuries are the unfortunate consequence of her refusal to follow instructions."

"Jehan, we meant no harm," Abeke insisted. "We were simply—"

"Searching for the edge of the land, once you'd stolen the sap of the demon blood tree, correct?" Jehan smiled as Abeke's eyebrows scrunched together. "Don't be so surprised. Your friend Rollan was most informative . . . once he was given the right incentive."

A honey badger scurried between the guards, causing them to jump aside and give it a wide berth. Abeke knew that these animals were among the most fearless

hunters in Nilo, taking on even lions many times their size. The honey badger wasn't big. In fact it looked similar to a skunk, with a white stripe down its weasel-like body. But its sharp claws and bad attitude made it a ferocious fighter. No one wanted to mess with one of these animals.

The honey badger circled Anka and Conor, pausing briefly to give a guttural hiss and bare its teeth at them.

"Livora," Jehan reprimanded the animal. The honey badger glanced back, thought better of trying to pick a fight, and trotted over to stand next to Jehan.

Abeke realized that Jehan was Marked, and that the honey badger was her spirit animal. It made sense. Abeke could see that Jehan had the respect of much older and stronger members of her group. She was probably as smart and ferocious as Livora.

"You said you would help her." Rollan glanced back at the tent where Meilin had been carried. "You'll keep your word, right?"

"Of course." Jehan unsheathed a long, sharp knife that she carried at her waist. "But you still haven't truly explained how that ledge on the mountain moved." She strolled over to Abeke and stood behind her.

"I did." Rollan gave Abeke a quick glance. "It's from my spirit animal bond. A power that comes from within me. . . . Only I can tap into it . . . no one else."

So Rollan wasn't giving away *all* their secrets. Only what was necessary to help Meilin. He hadn't told them about the Heart of the Land or the fact that anyone could use it.

"So you say." Jehan raised the knife above Abeke's head.

"NO!" Conor yelled as Jehan sliced the air with the knife, bringing it down with whiplike speed.

Abeke didn't see the blade sailing down. She only felt the parting of the air behind her back, and then her hands were free. Jehan hadn't hurt her. Instead, she'd cut the ropes around her wrists.

"No reason to have a fellow Niloan tied up." Jehan put the knife back in the leather holster. "The Dasat are an honorable people."

Abeke rubbed her wrists. "What about the others?" She pointed to Anka and Conor.

Jehan chuckled. "We're honorable . . . not stupid." She waved over one of the warriors who had shot at them with the slingshots. "Take the Niloan Greencloak to the injured girl in my tent. Once she gets better, we will escort them all back across the mountains from where they came."

"Wait." Rollan took a step forward. "I want to go with Meilin."

Jehan shook her head. "I'm sure you do, but it's not your decision."

"I know of the Dasat," Abeke said. "Your skills are legendary throughout Nilo. Growing up I would hear stories of your hunting abilities . . . but no one in my village knew if you still existed."

"We most certainly exist," Khai scoffed. "Otherwise you wouldn't be our prisoners."

"Guests," Jehan corrected him. "They don't have to be prisoners, if they agree to leave the same way they came."

"But I wonder if all the stories are true," Abeke mused. She watched as the honey badger used her large claws

to dig a burrow a few feet away. "The incredible hunts and contests that the Dasat were said to hold. Rumor had it that they never turned away from a challenge."

Conor seemed to guess what Abeke was thinking. "We've met plenty of exceptional hunters and warriors in our travels," he said. "Like the Tergesh in Zhong and the Ardu in Arctica."

"Ha!" Khai rolled his eyes. "As if they could hold a candle to any of the Dasat."

Abeke had hoped that Rollan would chime in—he was usually good at this sort of thing—but the boy kept his eyes on the tent where Meilin was being treated. He wasn't paying attention to anything that was being said.

"Perhaps we should have a contest," Abeke suggested. "Some of the stories I heard claimed the Dasat were always eager to prove their skills."

"What do you have in mind?" Khai asked, his eyes sparkling at the thought of a challenge.

"Your best against our best," Conor said.

"No." Jehan quashed the idea. "We've already proven our skills in capturing you. Soon you'll leave and be grateful that we let you live to tell the tale. We're not here for games."

Livora popped her head up from the burrow, as if something had piqued her interest. The honey badger scampered over to a barrel and, rising up on her hind legs, clawed her way to the top.

"There's nothing to eat there," Jehan said to her spirit animal.

Livora jumped down and ran between Rollan's legs. The boy blinked, as if coming to. He turned his attention away from the tent and back to the group.

"What if there's an incentive for the winner?" Rollan asked.

Abeke smiled. Rollan had been listening after all.

"Go on." Jehan's shrewd eyes watched him.

"If your challenger wins"—Rollan paused to consider his words—"I'll show you how I moved the mountain."

"I thought you said it was your spirit animal bond?" Jehan questioned, her arms folded across her chest.

"Yes, but I can show you how to work together with *your* spirit animal." Rollan pointed to the honey badger, who was busily gnawing on a rock. "That's what Greencloaks do, after all. Perhaps you could discover your own power."

Jehan seemed to entertain the idea. "And if you win . . . what is it that you want?"

"If we win . . ." Abeke spoke slowly, carefully considering what she was going to say. "You simply let us cross to get the sap."

"And you tell no one that we were ever here," Anka added.

"Ah, yes." Jehan nodded. "Rollan spoke of these Oathbound who are chasing you." The girl paced back and forth. "We're not involved in your dealings with the Oathbound. We'll take no side in your battle, as neither is a proven friend of the Dasat."

"Jehan." Khai slowly walked around Conor, evaluating him. "I know I can beat these Greencloaks. This one and his wolf tried to attack me earlier. I would enjoy battling him again."

"And you swear that you'll show me how you moved the mountain?" Jehan asked Rollan.

He nodded as several of the Dasat gathered around.

Word had already spread that a challenge had been issued.

"Then I see no harm in having a hunting contest," Jehan declared, turning to look at everyone. "Just as our old Dasat traditions dictate," she announced. "We shall give this matter over to the twin sisters of Fate and Skill, who guide every hunter's path. The first hunter to return with a significant kill will be declared the victor." She spun back around. "Our most resourceful hunter, Khai, shall be our representative."

The crowd cheered.

Jehan then looked at Rollan. "And who is your representative?"

"She is." Rollan pointed to Abeke, who stepped forward to stand next to Khai. Abeke could sense it was a stark contrast; the hunter dwarfed her in height and width.

The Dasat began laughing, and she heard murmuring rise throughout the crowd.

Khai was not pleased. "This is who you choose?" He grabbed Abeke under her arms and lifted her as if she were a small child. "This isn't a challenge . . . it is an insult. And I will not—"

Abeke swung her leg, catching him unaware. As he lost his balance, the hunter dropped her, and she landed lightly on her hands and feet. She turned and gave Khai a strong kick in the stomach that sent him flying onto his back, then quickly pressed her foot against the base of his neck.

"You're correct," Abeke hissed, bending over to get close to his face. "It doesn't seem like much of a challenge . . . does it?"

Khai glared at her and batted away her leg.

"You going to let her do that to you, Khai?" someone called out.

"Khai, how's the view from down there?" another voice laughed.

"Enough!" Jehan raised her hands and the crowd quickly grew silent. "We would all do well to remember that a hunter is not measured by his . . . *or her* . . . size." She faced Abeke. "You will not use your spirit animal during the hunt. This is a test of your skill alone. Is that clear?"

Abeke wasn't worried. She knew she could hold her own with the very best hunters. "Understood, but I will need my bow and arrows."

"Of course." Jehan motioned for one of the Dasat guards to get her things.

"What about Meilin?" Rollan asked, his voice laced with worry. "Someone needs to help her."

"Agreed." Jehan's face seemed to soften as she studied Rollan. "Since the Niloan Greencloak will be gone, I think it's best if you go to my tent and stay with your friend. The others will stay elsewhere."

"Thank you," Rollan said as the Dasat guard handed Abeke her bow and a quiver full of arrows, which she immediately inspected.

"And when does the hunt begin?" Anka asked.

Jehan lifted a single eyebrow and smiled. "It already has."

"What?" Abeke spun around and noticed that Khai had disappeared into the crowd. He not only had the advantage of knowing the terrain, but now he had a head start.

"But that's not fair," Conor protested. "There was no warning."

Jehan shrugged. "You can waste time arguing or you can begin the hunt."

Rollan's eyes met Abeke's. She gave him a slow nod. She would do this for them. And for Meilin. Failure was not an option.

Crossing the valley, Abeke kept her eyes peeled for any type of movement. She hadn't spotted any large game during the day, but there would certainly be nocturnal animals wandering the valley floor at night. She remembered seeing a watering hole as they were being brought to camp. That would be a good place to seek out game. The only problem would be if a predator turned the tables on her. This hunter had no interest in becoming the hunted.

The moonlit sky cast enough light for Abeke to see by. Every once in a while, she would hear a noise and pause, but she had yet to detect anything large enough to waste an arrow on. She contemplated shooting a very small warthog she spied hiding near a snapdragon bush, but feared that wouldn't be enough. It didn't seem like something the Dasat would consider *significant*.

She was approaching a clearing not far from the watering hole when she saw it. A lone gazelle stood placidly, foraging for its own bit of food. Abeke silently pulled out an arrow from her quiver and nocked it on her bow. She took aim and waited for the perfect shot.

The gazelle froze, sensing something was amiss.

Abeke held the arrow, watching the gazelle sniff the air.

The way the animal took in its surroundings reminded her of Uraza. Abeke's fingers trembled. It was like when she had been forced to shoot her beloved spirit animal. Abeke blinked, trying to cast out those thoughts and focus on the task at hand.

A perfectly aimed arrow flew through the night and struck the gazelle in the neck, killing it instantly.

For a moment, Abeke thought she had shot the animal, but then she noticed that her fingertips still held her own arrow.

"YES!" Khai ran past Abeke, toward the dead gazelle. "Your hesitation is my victory!" he called out.

Abeke couldn't believe it. He'd taken the kill from right under her nose. She wasn't used to being bested by anyone during a hunt. Now the Greencloaks were in serious trouble. Rollan would have to show Jehan how to use the Heart of the Land, and they would be no closer to finding Stormspeaker.

"Ha-ha!" Khai whooped it up as he tossed the gazelle over his shoulders. "And you didn't even sense me come up behind you! I'm still the king of the hunters!"

A chorus of laughter followed Khai's celebration. His eyes widened and he jolted to a stop, his body still.

Abeke knew all too well what was making that sound.

Hyenas.

Khai spun around, realizing too late that he was surrounded. Abeke thought he would toss the gazelle aside and make a run for it, but instead he pulled out his long knife. He was going to try to leave with his kill.

The hyenas pounced, attacking him from all sides. He slashed at the air, knocking a couple of them away before another one jumped on his back, snapping its jaws on the dead animal.

"Khai!" Abeke called out. "Let them have the gazelle! It's not worth it."

"Never!" he answered. A hyena bit down on Khai's leg and he cried out in pain. Khai grabbed the animal by the head and wrestled it off. "Go! This is not your fight!"

"It is now!" Abeke took aim and shot the hyena as Khai stabbed it along its flank. She called out Uraza with a burst of radiance, and the Great Leopard immediately gave chase to several hyenas. "There are too many of them for one person!" she said, firing off two more arrows.

Khai spun around. He faced one particularly determined hyena that didn't want to give up on its gazelle meal. "This is mine!" he shouted. "I will bring victory to my people or die trying!"

Abeke wasn't sure if he was speaking to her or the hyena, but it didn't matter. They were now both in the fight together.

Then, from somewhere behind her, Abeke heard a rustling sound as another hyena raced through the tall grass at full speed toward her. She nocked another arrow but didn't have enough time to aim. Just as the hyena lunged at her, Uraza leaped through the air, grasping the animal with her powerful jaws. The two fell to the ground, rolling over each other, while Uraza quickly tore at its body. It wasn't even a close match.

Abeke kept her bow and arrow ready, searching the

area for any more attacks, but the night had grown still again.

All the hyenas had disappeared . . . and so had Khai with his gazelle.

Abeke had failed her friends.

INTRUDERS

MEILIN SLOWLY OPENED HER EYES. SHE ROLLED HER head to the side and saw Rollan sleeping next to her, his hand holding on to hers. They were both lying on soft mattresses placed on colorful rugs. There was a hint of daylight coming through the fabric of the large tent they were sleeping in.

"Rollan." Her voice didn't sound like her own. It was raspy and weak. She cleared her throat and tried again. "Rollan."

Rollan sat up with a start, pulling at a shackle that chained their ankles together. "You're awake! You're awake!" He hugged her, then pulled back to double-check that she was indeed alert. "I'm sorry for arguing with you. I didn't mean any of it."

Meilin touched the bandage that was wrapped around her head. She was confused. The last thing she remembered was climbing the mountain with Rollan and arguing about whether she was too bossy. "What happened?"

"You were knocked out for a while, but you will

heal," a voice declared from the opposite side of the tent. "Based on what Rollan's told me, your spirit animal should help you far better than our herbs."

Meilin watched as a very pretty girl walked confidently over to the tent's opening. She pulled aside the fabric and called to someone outside. "Our guests are awake. Bring them some food and fresh water."

Meilin was confused. Who was this person? How did she know Rollan? And if they were her guests, then why had she shackled Meilin's leg to Rollan's? Nothing made sense. "What's going on?" Meilin asked.

"Her name is Jehan," Rollan explained. "She's the leader of the Dasat. They protect these mountains . . . as we have painfully discovered." He gave Jehan a sheepish grin and Jehan returned the smile.

Meilin pursed her lips. She wasn't sure what had happened while she was out, but she already knew that she didn't like this girl.

Jehan studied Meilin. "Rollan told me some very impressive stories about the Heroes of Erdas last night. Seems you are a formidable warrior." A honey badger scampered around the tent, climbing on top of several stacked rugs and then curling into a ball to sleep. "That's why we had to take certain precautions. We couldn't take the chance that you'd wake up during the night and try to escape."

Meilin tried to sit up, but everything seemed to spin and she fell back on her elbows. "So we're your prisoners." She didn't understand how things could have changed so much. "How long was I out?"

"About twelve hours," Jehan answered. "We tried making you as comfortable as possible . . . under the

circumstances." A guard poked his head into the tent, motioning for Jehan to come outside. "I'll be right back," she said.

"You got hit on the head pretty hard," Rollan said as soon as Jehan left. "You should have Jhi take a look at you. She'll help you feel better."

Meilin nodded, but glanced around the room. No one else was with them. "Where are the others?" she whispered, already trying to think of a means to escape.

"Conor and Anka are being guarded in another tent," Rollan answered. "You were brought here because you were in bad shape last night. I talked Jehan into letting me stay here, too."

"I'm sure it took a lot of convincing," Meilin muttered.

"Huh?" Rollan scrunched his eyebrows together. "What do you mean?"

"Nothing." Meilin wasn't sure *what* she meant, or what she was feeling exactly. "How about Abeke? Is she free?"

"Sort of," he replied. "We challenged the Dasat to a hunting contest. If Abeke wins, then . . ." Rollan stopped talking as Jehan whipped open the fabric covering the tent's entrance and stepped inside.

"You both need to stay here," she ordered, her face very stern.

"What's happened?" Rollan asked. "Something's changed."

Jehan didn't answer him. "Just do as I say and I'll be back soon. My guards will be here with your breakfast in a few minutes." She looked at the honey badger. "Livora, we need to go." She held out her hand and the

honey badger darted toward her, disappearing and then reappearing as a tattoo on her wrist.

"Something's happening," Rollan observed. "You need to have Jhi get you back to full strength. We may need to move quick."

Within the hour, Jhi had Meilin feeling better. Rollan apprised her of everything that had happened since her injury. The panda was still licking Meilin's head when a flurry of activity outside made Jhi stop. Meilin sat up, ready for action.

Outside, loud cheers erupted as the tent panels were thrust open and a guard entered carrying a basket of vines and grasses. "These are for the Great Panda," he said, placing the basket in the corner. He watched curiously as Jhi ambled over.

"What's going on outside?" Meilin asked.

The guard smiled. "We've received the signal that one of the hunters is returning. Come." He walked over to the tent panel and pulled it open. "I don't think there's any harm for you to see who won." He glanced at Jhi chewing on a vine. "But your spirit animal should stay here."

"I don't think you can tear her away from her breakfast," Rollan said, offering his arm to Meilin as she stood up.

"I got it," Meilin said, waving him off.

"I have a bad feeling about this," he whispered.

Shuffling their feet because their ankles were still chained together, Meilin and Rollan went outside. A short distance away, Meilin spotted Conor and Anka standing in front of a tent.

"Meilin!" Anka shouted and lurched forward before stumbling to a halt. Her ankle was chained to one of the tent posts. "You're fine?"

"I am!" Meilin answered.

Anka's face was awash with relief. Meilin could tell how concerned she'd been about her. It was good to have friends who cared so deeply.

"Nice to have you back!" Conor shouted.

"Look." Rollan pointed to a large man carrying a gazelle over his shoulder. The man was being congratulated by several people. "It's Khai, the hunter I told you about."

"Abeke lost?" Meilin was shocked. Abeke was the best hunter she knew.

Khai dropped the gazelle on a wooden pallet as Jehan rushed out from one of the tents. She had a serious look on her face.

"Jehan, I have brought victory once again, but I must tell you—"

"Later. I need to talk to you inside," Jehan declared, apparently uninterested in the details of Khai's hunt.

Khai's expression quickly changed. He scanned the camp, his eyes locking on Meilin. Something was wrong, but it seemed only Jehan knew what it was.

"Khai, tell us the story of your victory!" one of the guards shouted.

Khai gave him a slight smile and waved. "Not now," he said as others began to sense the unease that permeated the air. The time for hunting challenges was apparently over.

"We need to escape," Meilin whispered. "They're planning something."

Rollan nodded in agreement.

Just then the sound of a ram's horn being blown in the distance made everyone in the camp stop what they were doing. A second bellowing sound quickly followed.

"Intruders! Take your positions!" a guard yelled, and everyone rushed to grab a weapon.

"Now's our chance!" Meilin looked back at Jhi, who was chomping away at a bushel of leaves.

But Jehan was already running toward them. "We're setting you free," she announced. "You must leave the camp at once and not return." She pulled out a key and unlocked the shackle around each of their ankles.

"Why? What's happening?" Rollan asked. Across the camp, Khai was releasing Conor and Anka as well.

"The people you call the Oathbound . . . they're approaching from the mountains on the other side of the valley." She turned to one of the guards. "Bring them their bags," she instructed, then hustled to grab her own sword and a quiver full of arrows.

"This doesn't make sense," Meilin whispered as the camp emptied out and Conor and Anka rushed over. "Why wouldn't she turn us over to the Oathbound?"

Rollan shrugged; he seemed as perplexed as Meilin.

"What's going on around here?" a familiar voice shouted.

Abeke entered the nearly desolate camp, her face and clothes covered in dust. Meilin noticed that she was carrying a dead hyena over her shoulder, but they had bigger problems now.

"The Oathbound are coming," Conor replied. He pulled on his cloak and tightened the holster that once again carried his ax.

"And for some reason the Dasat have decided to let us go," Anka added.

"If you'd rather we turn you over to the Oathbound, that can still be arranged." Jehan had returned, holding a small vial in her hand. "Although Khai argued against it." She looked at Abeke. "He told me what you and your spirit animal did. You've proven yourself a worthy friend to the Dasat, and so the challenge is considered a tie. We are granting you passage through our land."

"Jehan!" Khai called out from a mountain ridge. "We await your orders."

"Here." Jehan handed Abeke the glass tube, filled with a scarlet substance. "This is the demon tree sap. Take it and go quickly. We will delay the Oathbound."

"I'm not sure what to say, except thank you." Abeke glanced up at Khai, who raised his hand in recognition.

Anka had already faded from sight and Conor had called out Briggan, who stood proudly next to him. His silver fur glistened in the morning sun.

"Hopefully the Oathbound won't be interested in the Dasat. If pressed, you can say we escaped," Conor suggested.

Jehan laughed. "That is something no one would believe." She turned to Rollan. "Last night, you mentioned that you were seeking the edge of the land. I think I know what that is. Follow me." Jehan took a few steps with Rollan while Livora scuttered behind them. Jehan pointed to a plateau in the distance. "The flat top of that mountain has an overlook. When viewed from a certain angle, it gives the impression that the world beneath you ends. It can feel like you're at the edge of the land. That might be where you need to go."

Rollan nodded. "Thank you," he said. "That's a big help."

"All right." Meilin joined them. She was feeling antsy. They were spending too much time with all this chitchat. "We need to get moving before the Oathbound arrive."

Livora opened her mouth, revealing her sharp teeth, and hissed at Meilin.

Meilin glared at the honey badger. The dislike was mutual.

Jehan placed her hand on Rollan's arm and drew closer. "I believe you're a friend of the Dasat, and I hope you choose to return one day. You'll be welcomed here."

"I'd like that," Rollan said as Meilin tugged on his sleeve.

"We have to hurry," Meilin urged. They couldn't afford to waste any more time. Jhi had already gone into passive state, and Uraza had rejoined the group. They needed to get away from the approaching Oathbound. Plus, if Meilin was honest with herself, she simply didn't like the way Jehan was speaking to Rollan.

"Of course. I, too, have to go." Jehan sprinted off to join Khai and the others, who were headed in the opposite direction. "Good luck!" she shouted back. "May Fate and Skill be with you."

Meilin scowled. This Dasat girl was annoying. But what she'd said was true enough. They would need fate, skill, and a lot of luck to complete their mission of regaining the Greencloaks' good name.

13

STORM'S WRATH

CONOR AND THE OTHER GREENCLOAKS HURRIED TO reach the plateau that Jehan had shown Rollan. Even if the Dasat slowed down the Oathbound, there was no time to spare. The Greencloaks hiked for most of the day over grueling, uneven terrain and crossed fast, slippery streams, while the blazing sun of Nilo beat down on them. By the time the group reached their final climb, the day had grown cloudy and a heavy fog rolled over everything except the tops of the mountain range. Visibility soon dropped to the point where Conor could only see Briggan if he was right next to him; otherwise the wolf simply disappeared into the mist.

"You think these are the clouds we're supposed to walk through?" Conor asked. He knew his friends were nearby, but he couldn't see anything except the gray haze.

"What?" Abeke called out from somewhere in the mist.

"The ones in Tembo's message," Conor said. "Didn't it say that after we passed the valley of death and got

the demon's blood, we'd have to go through some clouds to arrive at the edge of the land?"

"It did," Meilin answered. "And Tembo said the queen's glory would then be revealed. I can't imagine he'd make us come all the way out here if he wasn't referring to Stormspeaker as the queen's glory."

From high above them, Conor heard Essix screech.

"Keep going," Rollan called out. "We're almost out of all this fog. It gets clearer as we near the top."

Rollan was right. As Conor hiked higher up the mountain, the fog began to thin out. A few minutes later, he pulled himself over the top of a ridge and saw the flat vastness of the plateau. Stretching out in every direction was an almost barren landscape, punctuated with a few trees that seemed to rise out of the rocks. Conor tilted his head skyward to admire the streaks of purples, pinks, and oranges that the setting sun was creating.

"Look at this!" Anka called out, standing near the eastern edge of the plateau. "I think we're definitely in the right place!"

Conor and the others raced over and saw what she meant. There was a sharp drop-off that disappeared into the blanket of clouds, which covered everything up to the horizon. Without mountains to obstruct the view, it seemed as if they were floating above the world.

"It's like Tembo said," Conor whispered. "We're standing on the edge of the land, above the clouds." The beauty of the scene awed hm.

"Want to spread out while we still have a little bit of light?" Meilin asked, breaking the mood. "We can cover more area that way, and see if the 'queen's glory' is somehow revealed."

"Wait . . . look." Abeke pointed to Uraza and Briggan, who were both headed in the same direction. In the distance, Essix was flying in tight circles over one spot.

"There must be something over there," Rollan said. "Let's go."

The five Greencloaks took off running. Up ahead, Uraza and Briggan were now in a full sprint. They were in a race against time. The sun had already dipped below the horizon, and a cloud-filled night meant there would be little moonlight to help them find the crown.

Abeke had dashed ahead when she suddenly stopped, whirled around, and motioned for them all to get down. Conor crouched close to the ground, squinting into the distance at what looked like a small stone building near the far edge of the plateau.

"What do you think that is?" Anka asked.

"Some sort of lookout maybe . . ." Meilin took a few steps forward, keeping low to the ground.

High above, Essix squawked. She then swooped down, disappearing through one of the building's broken windows.

Conor held his breath until the falcon popped out of another window, going back to circling the building.

"Looks like it's empty," Rollan said. "Essix would have warned us if someone was there."

Abeke straightened up. "Then let's go quickly, before we lose the last bits of daylight."

Leaving Uraza and Briggan outside as guards, the Greencloaks entered the small stone building. Inside, Conor noticed several half-spent candles littering the floor. A wooden table had been flipped over

and chairs were tossed against a far wall. A thick layer of dust and dirt covered everything.

"Who has the matches?" Rollan asked, picking up one of the candles.

"Here." Conor had already lit a candle and carried it over.

"This place looks like it was ransacked ages ago," Meilin remarked, while she and Abeke righted the table. "I doubt anything like a crown was left behind."

"If it was hidden like the Heart of the Land and the Wildcat's Claw were, then . . ." Rollan ran his fingers along the wall, searching for a lever or notch that might reveal a secret compartment. "Maybe whoever was here before couldn't find it."

"Well, we're definitely in the right place." Abeke took one of the lit candles and walked to a corner alcove. She illuminated a statue carved into one of the stone walls, of a woman with her hands cupped in front of her. "I'm pretty sure this is supposed to be Nefrini." Abeke looked around at the sparseness of the building. "I think this might be more of a shrine than a lookout post."

Conor brought his own candle and added to the light in the alcove. He blew some of the dust off the wall beneath the statue, where something had been etched into the stone. "There's writing here."

Meilin and Rollan walked over and the alcove flick-ered with the lights of the candles. The shadows cast by the Greencloaks danced across the stones. Conor used the bottom of his shirt to wipe more of the dust off the carving.

Anka read it out loud. *"The storm's wrath has no mercy until hands drip with the blood of demons and ancestors."*

"Whoa," Rollan muttered, stepping back. "Hands dripping with the blood of demons and ancestors . . . Even knowing it means tree sap, that really does not sound good. If you ask me, I think Tembo had a little too much flair for the dramatic."

Abeke reached up and wiped the dust off the statue. "Maybe it has nothing to do with Stormspeaker."

"Right." Conor rolled his eyes. "It's just a warm and fuzzy bedtime story." Everyone turned and stared at him. "Sorry . . . guess I'm just a little tired." He walked to the window and gazed into the pitch-black night. There was no glass in the window frame and a soft breeze swept over his head, rustling his hair into his face. He brushed it away, his fingers lingering over the mark on his forehead. He couldn't help thinking about what Naveb had said . . . that the Wyrm had changed him . . . set him apart from the others, making him see things differently than they did.

Perhaps he should be thinking about their mission in a different way. Would devoting himself to fixing the things in Eura that the Greencloaks had destroyed while under the Wyrm's control be such a bad thing?

Conor glanced behind him at the others, still scanning the stone building for clues. He shook his head, dispensing with his own question. No, he loved his homeland, but the Greencloaks served everyone equally. And he couldn't imagine fighting against any of his friends.

Abeke, Meilin, and Rollan . . . each of them was so different from Conor, and from each other. They were from far-flung corners of Erdas, but the Greencloaks had brought them together to help. They *had* to regain the Greencloaks' good name, to show the world that it

was possible for every nation to unite under a common banner.

He placed his hands on the windowsill, leaned forward, and took a deep breath.

CLICK!

The frame dropped about an inch and Conor jumped back. He heard a rumbling from outside and the building began to shake. Something had been triggered.

"What did you do?" Meilin's eyes darted around the room as the candles on the table began to wobble.

"Nothing!" Conor rushed over and picked up a candle before it toppled over. "I leaned against the windowsill and something clicked."

The soft breeze blew stronger. With every passing second it picked up more dust, sand, and dirt. Suddenly, a burst of air shot through the building, blowing out all the candles.

"I think it's a sandstorm!" Abeke shouted over the high, whistling wind that was now engulfing them.

"Or a tornado!" Rollan bellowed as the chairs tumbled against the far wall. "Get away from the windows."

Conor flung the door open and stepped outside. "BRIGGAN!" he yelled, holding out his arm as a driving rain—a downpour that hadn't been there seconds before—battered his skin. The storm was fiercer than any he had ever seen. He leaned into the wind to keep his balance and yelled again. "BRIGGAN!"

Lightning flashed overhead, and in that instant he saw both Briggan and Uraza trying to make their way toward him. Uraza was crouched low to the ground, crawling toward the building, but Briggan was stumbling

and losing his footing. A storm that could stop the Great Beasts was not an ordinary storm.

"URAZA!" Abeke shouted, bracing herself in the doorway only a few feet behind Conor.

"HERE!" Conor shouted. It was a struggle just to be heard over the deafening roar that surrounded them. Another thunderbolt rocked the sky above as Briggan disappeared in a flash of his own and joined Conor as a tattoo on the back of his forearm.

A sudden gust of wind pulled the front door off its hinges, yanking Abeke from her feet and sending her tumbling to the ground. The door sailed into the night sky like a child's kite freed of its string.

"I'm fine!" Abeke called out. She braced against the storm as she stood and checked under her elbow for Uraza's tattoo.

Another lightning strike lit up the sky. Conor could see blood pouring out of a large gash over Abeke's right eye.

"You're bleeding!" Conor shouted as Abeke wiped her face.

"Get inside!" Rollan yelled, standing just inside the doorway. "None of this is normal!"

More lightning flashes followed as Conor and Abeke ran into the building, where Meilin had created a sort of barricade with the table backed into a corner.

"What do you mean by not normal?" Conor shouted over the fury of the wind and the hail that was now pelting the roof.

"All of this!" Anka yelled as they all huddled under the table. "It's like every storm's wrath put together!"

"No mercy from the storm's wrath...." Abeke crawled out from the barricade. "It's the statue!" she proclaimed. "The key to stopping the storm is there!" From her pocket she pulled out the vial of demon tree sap that Jehan had given her. "It wants this ... and my blood!"

NEFRINI

THE HOWLING WIND WHIPPED AROUND THE ROOM AS the roof began to buckle and lift. Abeke's idea had to work. They wouldn't be able to survive the storm's onslaught much longer . . . especially if they became fully exposed to the elements outside.

Abeke faced the statue of Nefrini, the wind slapping her braids against her cheeks as she opened the glass vial. She tipped it over and let a few drops of the demon tree sap fall into the statue's cupped hands.

A ripping and cracking sound echoed as the roof began to break apart, creating a gaping hole in the ceiling. Fist-sized hail rained down into the room and lightning crackled in the dark sky above.

Abeke touched the cut over her eye, smearing her fingertips until they were wet. "My blood is the blood of Nilo!" she shouted into the wind. "The blood of our ancestors!" She smeared her hands against those of the statue, letting the demon tree sap mix with her own blood.

The battering hailstorm suddenly stopped and the wind reduced its intensity, becoming little more than a strong breeze. There was one more flash of lightning, but with it the driving rain turned into a shower, then a trickle, until it stopped completely. The building rattled a few more times as the roof and walls adjusted to the sudden calm. A thick fog like the one they'd climbed through to reach the top of the plateau filtered in through the windows and torn roof.

"You did it!" Conor exclaimed. He pushed the table out of the way and picked up a battered candle from the floor.

"Do you think a spirit is going to speak to us again?" Meilin rolled her hand through the air, creating rivulets within the mist.

Rollan raised a candle he had lit and brought it over to Conor. "I think we're about to find out." He pointed to the concentration of fog swirling around Abeke.

Abeke spun around as the cloud of mist surrounding her slithered away and took the shape of a woman.

"Is that who we think it is?" Conor asked.

Abeke said nothing. If this was Nefrini, then she deserved reverence. Speaking out of turn would not be wise. Plus, if their prior experiences with the bond tokens were any indication, then only those born on the continent would be able to communicate with the spirit. That meant only she would be able to hear Nefrini's words.

"Is she saying anything?" Rollan asked.

Abeke put a finger to her lips.

"Maybe you should introduce yourself," Meilin suggested.

Abeke shook her head. Instead, she took a seat on the floor. A hunter had to be patient sometimes.

A minute passed, then two.

As the others lit more candles, creating a warm glow within the room, the fog congealed even more, revealing the woman's regal stature and kind face. There was no doubt this was Nefrini, and she was gazing down at Abeke.

Daughter of Nilo. Nefrini had a soft, gentle voice that bounced around inside Abeke's head. *You have stirred my slumber. What is it that you seek?*

Abeke glanced over at her friends, who were oblivious to what was being said. Nefrini was speaking only to her.

"High Chieftess Nefrini, we are here for Stormspeaker."

Of course you are. But why should it be entrusted to you? You are children. What have you done to deserve it?

"My friends and I, we are Greencloaks and have saved Erdas twice. But our existence as a group is being threatened. We must show that through our unity we can best serve everyone. Long ago, your bond token was given to us as a symbol of this unity, along with three others from across Erdas. The Greencloaks hid the tokens, wary of their power being misused, but present circumstances require us to retrieve all four."

I see. Nefrini floated past Abeke and paused in front of the other Greencloaks before returning to Abeke. *Bond tokens reflect the epitome of trust. Do you believe that these allies of yours are honest and true?*

"I do," Abeke answered without hesitation.

And do they feel the same about you? Nefrini asked.

Abeke turned to her friends. "She wants to know if you trust me to be honest and true."

"Yes!" they all proclaimed in unison.

Nefrini nodded in approval. Then a curl of mist flowed out from the spirit, wrapping itself around Abeke's wrist. Not of her own volition, Abeke felt herself flipping over her arm to reveal the leopard tattoo.

Your spirit animal is Uraza, Nefrini observed, letting go of Abeke's arm. *The Great Beast chose you as her human partner. . . . That is very telling.*

Abeke remained quiet.

I, too, had an incredible bond with my spirit animal, she mused. *Nazir, my hammerkop, was with me when I lost my mother and when my son was born. She gave me a perspective on life like no one else. We were inseparable.*

Abeke glanced at her tattoo. She wanted to think that way about her bond with Uraza, but Zerif had separated them for a while and pitted the two against each other. The pain of that time was still a thorn in Abeke's heart.

Nefrini bent down to get a closer look at Abeke. *I can tell that you are a hunter by nature, but I also sense the power of the Rain Dancer flowing through your bond. The Rain Dancer tradition was our gift to Nilo. I'm pleased to see it survives.*

"*You* were a Rain Dancer?" Abeke asked.

Nefrini nodded. *The first. Though truly it was Nazir's craft. And when we created our token, we gave*

a bit of that power to the land of Nilo itself. Bonds formed here are special. Some are touched by my old friend's gift. In that way, she lives forever.

Nefrini paused, studying Abeke for a moment. *In life, as with a hunt, you must always perceive what surrounds you. In front, beside, and behind.*

Abeke nodded in agreement. It was similar to what Naveb had told her.

Prepare for the future by observing the present and understanding the past. She turned without warning and pointed both fog-filled arms toward the statue. Her fingertips emanated a brilliant blue light.

"What is she—?" Abeke heard Conor begin to ask, when a single lightning bolt shot out from Nefrini's hands, hitting the statue and shattering it into dozens of pieces that went flying across the room.

"Whoa!" Meilin exclaimed as the Greencloaks all jumped against the wall.

Go to where the statue was, Nefrini instructed. *My crown is yours to use.*

Abeke quickly stepped over the broken pieces of stone strewn along the floor. Pressed against the wall was a simple gold headdress with wings on either side. A bird holding a green gem. Abeke chiseled the crown out with her fingertips.

"Stormspeaker," Abeke whispered, the crown glimmering in the candlelight. "Thank you."

"She's disappearing!" Rollan called out.

Abeke turned back to Nefrini. The chieftess had begun to fade, the fog dispersing into the atmosphere.

"Your Highness . . . please wait!" Abeke called out. "I have questions."

I'm sure you do, daughter of Nilo. Questions are good, and you should always seek answers. But I'm afraid my time here is over, Nefrini explained.

"But the crown . . . what does it do?" Abeke said, holding the golden diadem in her hand. "How do I use it?"

You have already witnessed its power. Use it wisely. But you must be careful, there is–

"Ask her where the Dragon's Eye is!" Anka said, interrupting Nefrini. "She has to tell us before she goes!"

Abeke noticed the last traces of fog shift to look at Anka. Although there wasn't much definition of Nefrini left in the mist, Abeke thought she saw the woman scowl.

Then she was gone. A gentle breeze once again reclaimed the air, and everything was silent for a few seconds.

"So?" Rollan asked. "What did she say? Did she tell you how to use it? How about where the Dragon's Eye is hidden?"

"There wasn't time," Abeke said with a sigh. "We'll have to go back to the monastery and just hope that Tembo left another clue there." Abeke inspected the gold crown in her hand, turning it slowly to see every side. "I think it controls the weather. . . . That's why it's called Stormspeaker."

"You're still bleeding," Meilin said, drawing closer to Abeke and looking at the gash over her eye. "I can ask Jhi to help you."

Abeke sat down. Her head was beginning to throb, although she wasn't sure if it was from the blow or from having Nefrini speak through her thoughts.

Jhi appeared in the room and immediately approached Abeke. The large panda pulled Abeke into a cradling embrace and gave her two quick licks over her eye.

"Panda spit works every time," Rollan said with a smile.

"We should stay the night here and get some rest." Conor unpacked his bag and laid out several items on the table. "In the morning, we can head back to the monastery."

"What if the Oathbound are still there?" Abeke asked, keeping the cut eye closed as Jhi stroked her head with her soft, furry paw.

"They've likely moved on by now," Anka said. "The Oathbound probably left and formed search parties to look for us."

Abeke glanced at Anka. Her clothes and skin had blended into the floor, but Abeke could see her shadow curled up like a cat in the corner of the room. Her thoughts went to Uraza.

She released the Great Beast. Uraza quickly evaluated her injured partner and purred with concern, rubbing her nose against Abeke's leg. "I'm fine," Abeke whispered into the leopard's ear. She then rolled away from Jhi to prove her point.

"Anka's right." Rollan stretched out his arms and cracked his knuckles before lying down on the stone floor. "The Oathbound will be on patrol, but Essix can help us scout the area. We just have to travel quick. We'll leave at first light."

"Look who's giving orders now," Meilin muttered under her breath.

"And once we get the Dragon's Eye we can head back to Eura and retrieve the Wildcat's Claw," Conor added, curling up against Briggan. "We just have to be careful."

Be careful.

The words reverberated in Abeke's head. It was what Nefrini had said before disappearing, but she hadn't had a chance to finish her warning.

"All in all, getting Stormspeaker wasn't too bad." Rollan leaned against the corner wall. "Jehan really did point us in the right direction, and we haven't seen any Oathbound the whole way."

"Hmpf . . ." Meilin scoffed at his statement and lay next to Jhi. "Only if you consider being attacked by wild hyenas, captured by the Dasat, fleeing from the Oathbound, and surviving a supernatural storm to be *not too bad*."

Rollan shrugged. "Compared to what we've gone through in the past . . . it certainly wasn't the worst. We're all still here, together."

Abeke smiled. Rollan was right. This hadn't been so bad. It seemed they'd figured out how to give the Oathbound the slip.

Perhaps the worst was truly over.

15

CAVE DWELLER

ROLLAN COULDN'T BELIEVE HOW FORTUNATE THEY were. The Greencloaks had been traveling back to the monastery for two days, only stopping for a few hours at night to rest, and they hadn't encountered any Oathbound, hyenas, or other troublemakers. They'd made good time with Essix flying overhead, scouting the mountains for potential problems and directing them along the shortest possible route.

"Essix is taking a lot longer than usual, isn't she?" Meilin scanned the sky. "It's been at least an hour since we've seen her."

Rollan grimaced. The open expanse of the savannah stretched before them. With only a couple of hours of daylight left, he didn't like the idea of being out in the open without Essix giving them the all clear. "I think we should wait to cross. She'll be back soon enough. Plus, crossing the savannah at night is probably safer."

"Actually, night is when most predators are active," Abeke reminded him, taking a seat on a nearby rock. "Hyenas and lions and all sorts of beasts. We'll still have to be careful."

"Let me see if I can connect with Essix," Rollan suggested. He closed his eyes and let his mind drift. Soon he sensed the falcon's keen vision within his mind and he could see through her eyes. However, the usual sensation of flying, of gliding through the air, was missing. Rollan quickly noticed that Essix was perched in an acacia tree, close to the base of the mountain.

The falcon turned her head, focused on a nearby cave opening, and took off toward it. Flying through the narrow entrance, Essix beat back her wings, landing gingerly on the gravel-covered ground. Taking several steps deeper into the cave, Essix stared at a figure sitting in a corner wearing a hooded cloak.

Slowly, the person lifted off the hood and smiled.

"It's Xanthe!" Rollan told the others. "Essix found her. She's not too far from here."

"Is she alone?" Anka asked.

"Or hurt?" Abeke followed up.

"No one else is there, and she seems fine." Rollan concentrated on his connection with Essix. Xanthe was saying something, but Rollan couldn't tell what it was. He felt Essix turn her head and fly out of the cave. Once again, the freedom of being in the air, the land rushing along beneath her wings, filled Rollan's spirit. He was one with Essix, but the connection couldn't last much longer. Already he felt light-headed.

He opened his eyes and regained his bearings.

"Well, what happened?" Meilin asked as Rollan took a deep breath and sat on the ground.

"I think Xanthe is waiting for night before she crosses the savannah," he said. "She was saying something to Essix, but I don't know what it was."

"So let's go find her." Abeke shook the dust off her cloak. "We can all travel together."

Essix screeched, circling overhead.

"She got here fast." Rollan pulled out a piece of jerky from his bag and lifted it in the air. Essix dove down and snatched it from his hand. "Means we don't have to go too far. Xanthe is probably hiding nearby."

Briggan led the group around the base of the mountain, following Essix's flight path high above. Uraza had disappeared once again, out scouring the area for Oathbound, hyenas, or another meal. It didn't take long before Rollan recognized the acacia tree where Essix had been perched.

"We're close," Rollan announced.

"I'm going up there." Meilin pointed to a small ridge above the cave. "I'll be a lookout in case the Oathbound decide to come our way."

"Want some company?" Rollan offered, sensing that something had been bothering Meilin ever since they'd left the Dasat camp. He just didn't know what it was.

"Sure," Meilin replied, then turned away from him. "Anka . . . why don't you come with me?"

Rollan felt a wave of disappointment. He was certain he hadn't done anything wrong, but it felt as if there were a wedge growing between the two of them.

"Already climbing," Anka said, her barely visible form blending against the rocks.

"Briggan found something." Conor pointed to the wolf standing at the mouth of the cave.

"We'll switch in a little while," Abeke offered Meilin. "So you can rest up before we cross the savannah tonight."

"Sure," Meilin called down.

Conor, Abeke, and Rollan approached the cave cautiously, but Briggan seemed at ease and lay down at the entrance. Rollan stepped around the wolf and, as his eyes adjusted to the dim light, he saw Xanthe sitting on the floor with the hood of her cloak pulled back. Her white hair shone with the bit of sunlight that reflected inside the cave.

"Hi, strangers," she greeted them all with a smile. "Had a feeling you might show up after Essix's visit. I got this far and then started to worry about you guys. Figured I'd stick around to see that you all made it back safe." She peered around the three of them. "Where's Meilin and Anka?"

"They're right above us." Rollan pointed up. "Keeping watch from the ridge."

"And Uraza's out there enjoying Nilo," Abeke added. "Hopefully, keeping an eye out for any trouble until we get back to the monastery."

Xanthe's face lit up. "Does that mean you found Stormspeaker? Is that why you're heading back?"

"Yep. We sure did." Conor dropped the bag he'd been carrying and sat next to Xanthe.

"Can I see it?" Xanthe looked over at his bag.

"It's in Meilin's bag," Abeke said quickly.

Rollan glanced at Abeke, who didn't return his gaze. He knew that Abeke had the crown, but for some reason she didn't want to show it to Xanthe. Maybe she was right, and they should keep it as hidden as possible for now.

"Um . . . yeah." Conor fidgeted a little with the strap of his own bag. "So we're going back to the monastery

in case Takoda's discovered something about the Dragon's Eye."

"But what if he hasn't?" Xanthe asked. "What's the plan then?"

Abeke's lie about the location of the crown was causing Rollan to rethink what was discussed with Xanthe. It wasn't anything against her personally, but Rollan knew it was dangerous to divulge too much information, for Xanthe and them. "We're not sure," Rollan said. "We'll have to cross that bridge once we get to it."

"But you have to start thinking of where else to look," Xanthe continued. "I mean, Tembo may have only left clues to Stormspeaker. You should try to see if there's a pattern to where the other tokens were found."

"We're looking into it." Abeke took a seat on the gravel floor. "So tell us about the last few days. Have you run into any problems? Seen any Oathbound?"

"Not really," Xanthe replied. "I've been moving at night and it's been pretty quiet." She studied the three Greencloaks. "But back to the last token . . . do you think it's still in Nilo?"

Rollan knew that they had to be honest with Xanthe. She deserved nothing less. "Xanthe, I think it's best if certain things are kept between Greencloaks. You understand, right?"

"Oh, that again. Sure." Xanthe nodded, but her mouth tightened. "Guess I keep forgetting that I'm not one of you, so I can't be trusted," she mumbled.

"It's not that," Conor replied. "We've all just been through a lot, so we're a little . . . cautious."

"Uh-huh." Xanthe eyed him carefully, lingering on the faded mark on his forehead. It was a reminder that she'd seen him at his worst and still trusted him. "Don't forget that I've been through a lot, too. In fact . . . you were there when it happened."

"We know," Abeke said softly. "And we appreciate everything you've done and are doing. But . . ." She sighed. "The less you know, the better. We don't want to put you in any more harm."

Xanthe rolled her eyes. "Riiiight. You're being secretive for my benefit. It's like what everyone warned me about."

Rollan didn't like the way that sounded. "What do you mean?"

Xanthe leaned against the wall. "People talk about how the Greencloaks think they're superior, how you think you know what's best for everyone. I've heard the stories about what happened with the Nectar and all the problems that brought. I just hope you aren't repeating the same mistakes."

The silence inside the cave was deafening, but no one had a good response. Rollan wanted to say that he too hoped they weren't making a mistake, but admitting that didn't seem like a good idea. So the four of them just sat quietly until one by one they each drifted off to sleep. A late-afternoon nap was a luxury they normally didn't enjoy.

"Fire! In the distance!" Meilin's words startled everyone.

"What?" Xanthe rushed to the cave entrance, where Briggan was sniffing the air. The sun was still out, but it was hovering over the horizon. "Where?"

"A little bit to the west," Meilin answered. "And it has to be pretty big, based on the amount of smoke."

Xanthe pulled up her hood and marched outside. Even with the sun so low in the sky, she had to squint. But Rollan could see the horror in her expression.

"It's the monastery," she said in quiet disbelief.

"No." Conor shook his head, not wanting to believe what he was seeing.

"It's got to be the Oathbound's doing." Rollan stared at the plume of dark black smoke rising in the distance. "They're burning the place down!"

Xanthe turned to the others, her pale face grave. "Takoda is there. We have to help him . . . all of them."

"Hold on." Abeke opened her bag. "I have an idea." She pulled out the gold crown and flipped it over gently in her hands.

"Is that . . . wait, I thought Meilin had it in her–" Xanthe stopped herself and crossed her arms across her chest. "Oh, right. Never mind."

"Xanthe, please understand. I think I can help Takoda and the monastery," Abeke said, placing Nefrini's crown on her head. "*This* is what the Greencloaks do . . . help others."

Meilin looked at Xanthe and then Abeke. "What's going on?"

"Nothing," they both answered in unison.

Rollan moved closer to Abeke. "You sure about this?" he asked. "We aren't totally certain what this

can do. Remember how that storm nearly pried the roof off?"

Abeke nodded. "I have to try. Now stand back." She closed her eyes, then opened one. "Better yet, go back in the cave."

Rollan and the others moved just inside the cave's entrance, watching as Abeke stood still. She closed her eyes again and tilted her head slightly back, facing the sky.

At first there was only quiet. Then, the small rustling of wind as menacing clouds formed suddenly overhead. Darkness shrouded the area, and the air grew cool, then cold. Rollan poked his head out as a strong gust of wind whipped by the cave and a dust storm swirled around Abeke. Thunder rumbled overhead. A few fat raindrops hit a nearby boulder, leaving tracks along the side of the dusty rock.

Abeke squeezed her eyes tighter.

The raindrops increased and fell to the earth in drumlike beats, yet Abeke remained dry. The rain and wind seemed to purposefully avoid her.

"You have to send the clouds across the savannah. It does no good here!" Xanthe exclaimed. "The fire is over there."

Abeke silently nodded, but the storm clouds didn't budge.

The rain slowed to a light trickle and then to an almost invisible misting of water.

The wind fluttered to a stop and the clouds parted, once again revealing the setting sun.

Abeke frowned into the sky as her shoulders drooped. "It won't move," she said.

Xanthe burst out from the cave entrance, pointing toward the smoke. "You have to try again. You have to!"

"I can't," Abeke rasped. "Nothing happens. It only stays overhead."

"Then we'll have to take the storm there ourselves." Xanthe pulled up the hood of her cloak. "Let's go!"

16

THE RETURN

MEILIN ENTERED THE TAABARA CHASM WITH HER sword drawn, ready to battle any Oathbound guards who might be lurking in the shadows. They had crossed the savannah under a cloud-filled night sky. The darkness shrouded them from any sentries keeping watch, but this place would be different. The deep crater was striped with land bridges and crevices where the Oathbound could be lying in wait for them.

"Keep alert," Xanthe whispered, leading the group to the bottom of the chasm. "Our luck may not hold much longer."

But everything was quiet.

"I don't think anyone's here." Abeke spun around, her arrow nocked and ready to fly. "Isn't that a bit strange?"

"It's very strange." Rollan looked up at Essix, who had given them the all clear. "You'd think someone would be guarding this place. At the very least guarding the fissure that leads to the monastery."

"The Oathbound may have everyone at the monastery," Anka said, approaching the entrance to the

fissure. "Perhaps they didn't expect us to come back. If we hear or see anything, get close to me. I'll camouflage us."

"I think I should go first," Xanthe suggested. "I'll be the best at spotting someone in the dark, especially if they're on the other side where the rope ladders are."

"Sounds like a good plan," Meilin concurred. "I'll bring up the rear, in case we get a surprise attack from behind."

"Then let's go." Rollan waved his arm at Essix and pointed to the crevasse. The falcon would be waiting for them on the other side.

As quickly as possible, the group made their way through the narrowing passageway. Before long, they were forced to shuffle through it sideways. Meilin reluctantly sheathed her sword. There was no room to fight at this point.

"Do you smell it?" Rollan whispered. He'd slowed down to get closer to Meilin.

"The smoke?" she answered, taking a long sniff of the air. "Yes, it's getting stronger."

"No," Rollan said. "The smell of victory. The Oathbound have no idea what we have in store for them."

Meilin rolled her eyes. She couldn't see him in the darkness, but she knew Rollan was smiling. He was always trying to lighten the mood and be the funny man. This time it bothered her.

"You don't always have to make jokes," she said. "It's okay to be serious once in a while."

"I can be serious," Rollan replied. "Not my fault if I'm just naturally likable."

"Yeah, apparently you are *very* likable." Meilin hadn't meant to sound caustic, but her feelings betrayed her.

"What are you talking about?" Rollan stopped shuffling through the crevasse. "You've been acting strange ever since we left the Dasat camp. What's going on?"

"Nothing." Meilin nudged him to keep moving, but he stayed still. They weren't going anywhere until they finished this conversation. Meilin sighed. "I just find it weird that Jehan was so friendly to you and invited you to come back after only knowing you for a day."

"Is that it?" Rollan chuckled. "You're jealous?"

"What? No." Meilin scoffed at the suggestion. "It just seems unusual."

"Well, like I said, I am a very likable guy."

Meilin could hear the snicker in his voice.

"Forget it." Meilin pushed him again, but he stood firm.

"Meilin." His voice took a softer tone. "I think Jehan was just impressed because I was able to shift the whole mountain for you. That's all."

"Wait, what?" Meilin couldn't quite believe what she was hearing. Rollan had moved an entire mountain for her?

"Yeah, well, I just knew I had to help you no matter what, so I used the Heart of the Land to create a ledge for you to land on. I guess I should've mentioned that before, but . . . I don't know . . . I just didn't."

Meilin didn't know what to say. She'd always believed that feelings and emotions weren't supposed to come into play when on a mission, but everything with Rollan was different. She was experiencing feel-

ings that she normally kept under control. Even little bits of jealousy.

After a moment of uncomfortable silence, Rollan broke the ice. "Yeah, well, you took care of me when I had the Sunset Death . . . couldn't let you continue to hold that over me. Had to do something to get us on equal footing."

Meilin tried to see Rollan's features in the darkness of the crevasse, but she could only see his silhouette. She reached over and gave him a kiss on the cheek. "Thanks," she whispered.

Rollan was about to say something when Conor interrupted with a loud "PSSSST!"

"Come on." Rollan gave Meilin a tug. "We'll talk more later."

They hurried over and caught up to the others.

"Xanthe says the ledge is up ahead," Anka whispered, relaying the message. "And there are two Oathbound on it."

"Let's do this," Rollan said.

"We're ready," Meilin confirmed.

Abeke put on the crown and sat down. It had been decide that Anka would stay with her, in case she needed to be camouflaged while the others fought the guards.

Everyone held their breaths as Abeke concentrated on bringing about a storm. The idea was to have it rain hard enough to put out the fire in the monastery. Then, with the first crack of lightning, the others would launch an attack on the guards, with the thunder masking the sounds of the fight. Timing would be critical.

The air stirred as a cool breeze filtered into the crevasse.

A few raindrops hit Meilin on the head. She pulled up her hood and unsheathed her sword. The downpour was about to begin.

A sudden storm deluged the area. The rain fell hard as the clouds rumbled above them.

Lightning flashed suddenly between the clouds overhead, illuminating the sky into shades of black, blue, and dark purple. This was it.

Xanthe, Conor, Meilin, and Rollan ran out from the crevasse, barreling into the guards as thunder boomed around them.

A swift kick to the knee. An elbow to the jaw. The pommel of Meilin's sword sideswiping a guard's head.

And silence.

It was over as quickly as it had begun.

In less than a moment, two Oathbound guards were knocked out and Conor was tying them up.

"Go, quickly," Xanthe whispered, grabbing one of the rope ladders that led up to monastery. "We don't have much time."

The group climbed up to the higher level, swiftly and silently. Once they'd scaled the overhang, they hid behind a row of thorny bushes that lined the edge of the cliff. Peering out between the leaves, they could assess what was going on in the monastery. There were Oathbound soldiers moving past the upper windows, but only one guard patrolled the raised iron gate at the front.

"Over there," Conor whispered, pointing to a smoldering part of the building. "Looks like that's what they were burning."

"It's part of the library," Xanthe explained. "Takoda would never allow that to be destroyed without putting

up a fight." Her voice faltered. "I–I should never have left. My place was with him. . . ."

Meilin put a hand on Xanthe's shoulder. She knew Xanthe had seen her people overrun by the Many during their battle with Wyrm, and had fought hard for them. "I'm sure he's all right. Takoda is smart and brave. We'll find him and beat the Oathbound."

"Is the main door the only way in?" Abeke asked, slipping on the gold headdress. "Because I can create a diversion—distract the guard with a windstorm or something."

Xanthe nodded. "Other than those upper windows, it's the—"

"Shh." Meilin pointed to the monastery's entrance. A broad-shouldered, bald man dressed all in black was talking to the guard.

"I know who that is," Anka whispered. "He was at the Citadel when the emperor was killed. They called him Sid the Generous, so I'm guessing that means he'd steal the crumbs from a street urchin's plate. No offense, Rollan."

Rollan snorted. "As if we had anything as fancy as *plates.*"

"You are all idiots!" Sid yelled to a group of warriors who had joined him by the iron gate. "Something is going on. Or am I the only one who can sense it?"

Meilin and the others froze.

"Everyone, hold hands," Anka whispered. "I'll hide us." She interlocked her fingers with Conor, causing his arms to blend into the variegated colors of the bushes.

"All of us?" Meilin asked, knowing that Anka's abilities had their limit.

"I can do it . . . trust me," she replied as everyone joined hands.

But the progression was worryingly sluggish. First Conor slowly disappeared, and then Xanthe's skin blistered into leafy green rashes. Meilin could no longer see Anka, but she heard the elder Greencloak whimper with effort.

Suddenly, Sid turned on his heel and scowled. He marched toward the edge of the cliff, right to where the Greencloaks were hiding. His eyes widened with fury.

Meilin sucked in a breath. *It's too late! He's seen us!*

But then she turned to Rollan and found that he'd already vanished. Meilin glanced down to where their fingers were interlaced and saw . . . nothing. Thorns and roots and shrubby leaves.

An animal that looked like a small bear or very large weasel trailed right behind Sid. Meilin recognized it as a wolverine—one of the most ferocious predators in the animal kingdom. Shane had once pretended his uncle's wolverine was his own spirit animal. Meilin had seen how vicious and territorial it was. It figured that would be Sid the Generous's animal partner.

Meilin's free hand reached for the pommel of her sword. She glanced back at the sheer cliff behind them. They were in the worst possible spot for a fight, but it didn't make a difference.

Any moment the battlefield could be declared, and they'd have to be ready to attack. She gripped the sword's handle.

It was now or never.

SID THE GENEROUS

THE WOLVERINE REARED UP ON ITS HIND LEGS, ITS NOS-trils flaring as it moved its head from side to side. Even though they were hidden from view, it wasn't going to be enough. Conor could see that the animal was picking up their scent.

"Change the direction of the wind," Conor whispered to Abeke. "If we're downwind, it'll only be able to smell the ashes from the fire." A few seconds later the air stirred above them. Although Conor couldn't see Abeke, he assumed she was using the crown. A strong smell of smoke floated over them and down the mountain.

The wolverine fell back on its four legs and turned to face the building, where a few fires were still smoldering. The smoke was confusing it.

"Nothing?" Sid asked his spirit animal, who had apparently lost the scent.

Conor and the others stayed still, barely breathing.

Sid the Generous was not convinced. He took a few more steps toward the bushes and stared out into the night. Waiting for a sound or a movement.

Conor considered jumping him, but they'd be giving up their most valuable weapon . . . the element of surprise. His prudence proved to be right; just a moment later, another small group of Oathbound emerged from the monastery.

"Sir . . ." A young-looking Oathbound warrior, probably not much older than fifteen, cautiously approached Sid from behind. "Um . . . one of the guards sent me to tell you that we haven't found any gold. Do you want us to keep–?"

Sid spun around and struck the boy squarely across the face with an open hand. The force from the slap knocked the young warrior to his knees. "KEEP LOOKING!" Sid bellowed. "I want results, not excuses! Now, stand up!"

The boy got up, clutching the side of his face.

Sid grabbed the young Oathbound's shirt, twisting it in one hand and hoisting him up so they were face-to-face. "Tell the guards to scour the libraries . . . every single crevice. I want some gold in my bag before the captain arrives, is that understood?"

"Y-y-yes, sir," the boy stammered.

"Good!" Sid dropped the boy, who quickly turned and ran back inside the monastery. He scanned the area one more time, then motioned for the wolverine to follow him in.

Once Sid disappeared into the building, Xanthe snuck around the bush, pulling Anka along. "Stay close," she whispered.

There was no discussion. They were all going in together. But as long as they held hands and moved slowly along the stone walls, they were virtually invisible.

As they passed several rooms and corridors, Conor noticed that there were virtually no guards inside. It seemed that they were all searching for Sid's gold, and few were searching for the Greencloaks. If only they could find Takoda and the other monks, then maybe they could outnumber these Oathbound and regain control of the monastery.

"I'm done being patient!" Sid's voice roared from the Great Hall.

Staying flush against the wall and using any shadows available, the group moved as one unit until they entered the hall. In the center of the chamber, beneath the wooden trusses that crisscrossed the ceiling, stood Sid the Generous. In front of him were the monks, lined up in a row with their hands and feet tied. Sid was staring down at Master Naveb.

Conor and the others slowly inched into the room, making sure they weren't seen as they moved along the gray stone wall.

"Foolish old man," Sid sneered. "Tell me what you know."

"Untie me and see how old and foolish I am," Master Naveb said defiantly.

"Ha! Don't make me laugh!" Sid leaned closer to Master Naveb, placing both hands on the old monk's shoulders. "Don't you care that your precious Niloan history is being lost?" he asked. "Tell me where the gold is and we'll stop destroying your libraries."

"Even if I had some, I wouldn't tell a degenerate like you," Naveb said, his voice flat. He face betrayed not a hint of emotion.

Sid's eyes blazed with fury as he lashed out at Naveb,

kneeing him in the stomach and knocking the old man to the floor. "This is what happens when you don't respect me." He pulled back his leg and kicked the old man with all his might.

"STOP!" several of the monks shouted.

"Leave him alone!" Takoda fought against the ropes that bound him.

"This wasn't part of the deal!" Sodu shouted from the end of the line. The young monk was also tied up, his face screwed into a scowl. "You gave me your word!"

"Deal? The deal was for the Greencloaks," Sid sneered. "No Greencloaks, no deal." Sid looked around the room. "And a place this vast must have its share of gold and valuable secrets."

"Secrets? I know about a secret. What if we strike a new deal?" Sodu asked, his eyes darting over to Takoda. "How about something that's valuable to the Green-cloaks? Something called the Dragon's Eye."

Anka's grip tightened around Conor's hand. He felt his stomach turn, and a lump formed in his throat. *How does Sodu know about the final bond token? Did he stumble on the clue himself in the monastery?*

"Sodu . . ." Master Naveb moaned while still on the floor. "Don't."

"Go on," Sid replied.

"Takoda knows where it is," Sodu continued, staring at the young monk. "I overheard him tell Master Naveb that he had to find a way to get word to the Greencloaks."

"I see." Sid raised a single eyebrow and strolled to stand in front of Takoda. "This is an interesting turn of events." He stared in silence for several seconds, apparently weighing his options. "Seems like we might be

able to help each other. I'd make it worth your while . . . possibly share some of the gold with you. They don't call me Sid the Generous for nothing. "

Takoda spat in his face.

Sid's eyes burned. He responded with an uppercut punch to the chin that caught Takoda by surprise, dropping him to his knees.

Conor felt Xanthe flinch, but she stayed put. Any movement away from Anka would reveal her. They had to stay together and wait for the right moment.

Kovo, on the other hand, had awoken from his trance and was making his presence known. The Great Ape roared, fighting against the heavy chains that pinned him to the wall, baring his teeth at the Oathbound who had been guarding him.

"Idiot!" Sid wiped his face with his sleeve. "I'll simply continue destroying the treasures of Nilo until you tell us where to find the Dragon's Eye and your gold." He walked around Takoda, standing behind the line of monks. "I don't understand this silence. I've shown you proof that the Sadrean girl and one of the Greencloaks have already met their deaths. Why insist on protecting their secrets?"

"Takoda, just tell him!" Sodu urged. "This will be over if you say what you know!"

Kovo suddenly stopped struggling against his chains and sniffed the air. The large gorilla's red eyes darted around the room. He quickly signed something to Takoda, who sat up and glanced curiously around.

Kovo's actions weren't lost on Sid. The Oathbound grabbed Takoda by the arm and dragged him to the center of the room. "Guards!" Sid yelled, calling out his

spirit animal at the same time. "The Greencloaks are here!"

Before the Greencloaks or Xanthe could react, Sid pulled out a knife and held it to Takoda's neck. "We've been waiting for your return, Greencloaks. Reveal yourselves . . . or he dies!" His eyes nervously searched the room. Standing beside Sid, the wolverine looked at the wall where Conor and the others were hidden and growled. "I give you to the count of three. One . . . two . . ."

Kovo roared and resumed his struggle against his chains. It was a momentary distraction, but it was all Xanthe needed. She broke away from the group, leaping out of the shadows toward Sid.

In the same instant Sid pulled another knife out from his belt and hurled it at Xanthe. The Sadrean warrior ducked but was tackled by another guard several feet before reaching Sid or Takoda.

But the knife Sid threw didn't fall to the floor.

It hung in midair for a long moment, and then the whole team's camouflage vanished, revealing their position near the back wall.

Conor turned and saw Anka, her short dark hair and cloak coming through in vibrant colors. She was completely visible, and she was clutching the knife's handle in front of her chest. A few drops of bright red blood were speckled across her shirt. Toey ran around her in a panic.

No one moved.

Not a Greencloak nor an Oathbound.

Even Sid seemed to be shocked by the apparition of the young Zhongese woman he'd just impaled.

Anka slowly pulled the knife away, revealing a growing red stain on her shirt. Her eyes dropped down to look at what the others were seeing. Stumbling, she tried to reach a table in the corner, but then her eyes locked with Meilin's.

"I'm sorry," she muttered before collapsing to the floor.

"ANKA!" Meilin cried out, but before she could run to her, Oathbound soldiers blocked her path.

"NO!" Sid yelled, pushing away the tied-up Takoda and grabbing Xanthe from the Oathbound guard. "No one move!" he yelled. "Or she also dies!"

Conor gripped the handle of his ax. One quick throw and he could lodge it into an Oathbound guard . . . but then what? Sid held the ultimate card. He was holding Xanthe in a headlock, positioning her in front of him like a shield. He had the tip of his knife pressed against the pale skin of her neck, where a tiny bit of blood was already trickling out.

"Let her go!" Takoda pleaded, struggling against his ropes. "PLEASE! I'll tell you everything! Just let her go."

Kovo's chains clanged against the floor as he continued trying to get loose.

Sid took a step back, dragging Xanthe with him. "So you wouldn't do it for yourself or your fellow monks, but you'll do it for her?" He glared at Takoda as he pressed down on the knife. "Speak quickly, because I have already lost my patience."

"Don't . . ." Xanthe's voice came out a hoarse whisper. She couldn't flinch or else her throat would be cut.

"The Dragon's Eye is in the catacombs underneath Xin Kao Dai." Takoda's words tumbled out. "Beneath

the Summer Palace. That's all Tembo wrote. I don't know anything else."

"See?" Sid smiled and pulled the knife away from Xanthe's throat, but tightened his grip on her. "Wasn't that easy?"

Takoda's shoulders slumped in defeat.

"Now, where's the gold?" Sid asked.

"There isn't any," Takoda muttered. "I told you before. The monks never had use for it."

"I don't believe you. . . ." Sid's eyes narrowed, trying to gauge Takoda's reaction. "But if that's true . . ." He paused for a moment, smiling. "Then sadly, we have no use for her either."

With that Sid the Generous plunged the knife into Xanthe's stomach and pushed her to the ground.

"NOOOOOO!" Takoda's painful scream echoed throughout the Great Hall.

Xanthe gasped, trying to catch her breath. Her eyes were fixed on Takoda as she struggled to breathe.

Takoda wiggled his way across the floor to get closer to her, but there was nothing he could do as her eyes lost focus, closed. She stopped moving.

Takoda moaned, the noise echoing hopelessly in the expansive chamber. Hearing Takoda's raw grief, Conor felt his throat close.

"Xanthe!" Abeke cried out.

A chill ran down Conor's back.

They all feared the same thing.

Was Xanthe gone, too?

CAPTAIN

R OLLAN WAS IN SHOCK. HE COULDN'T BELIEVE HIS EYES. Takoda, his feet bound and his hands still tied behind his back, was kneeling next to Xanthe, whispering something to her as she lay motionless. Sid had killed Anka and possibly Xanthe with barely a second thought. In fact, he seemed to enjoy it.

This was not the way things were supposed to go.

"Surrender or face the consequences," Sid snarled. "Because there's no way out."

"We'll see about that," Rollan replied. He'd learned on the streets of Concorba that there was usually at least one means of escape. He noticed Kovo still jerking against his chains, the ape's red eyes shining with anger. If Rollan could make it over to him, he could release the lock and unleash five hundred pounds of gorilla fury upon the Oathbound.

Sid threw back his head and laughed. "The monastery is surrounded," he said. "The four of you are completely outnumbered. And you still think there's a way out?" He laughed again.

"Greencloaks, get ready!" Meilin called out, taking a defensive stance. Her sword gleamed in her hand.

"Uraza!" Abeke yelled, calling out to the Great Leopard.

"Briggan!" Conor held out his arm as the silver-gray wolf joined him.

The Greencloaks stood together in a semicircle, facing a dozen Oathbound, many with spirit animals of their own. Sid's wolverine was already snarling, ready to face off against Briggan. A white tiger growled at Uraza.

"Jhi!" Meilin said, but her eyes were fixed on Xanthe lying on the floor. The girl was still breathing, but she was unconscious and bleeding out fast.

The large panda flashed onto the scene. Rollan knew Jhi would be a fierce fighter and improve Meilin's own battle skills, but perhaps that wasn't what the girl had in mind.

Still . . . she'd need a distraction.

Rollan scanned the room, taking in the placement of every Oathbound, every monk, and every object in the room. Behind the anguished Takoda there were spears, shields, and swords hanging on the wall. If Rollan could free the monks and get them those weapons, their numbers would increase dramatically. Between them and Kovo, the Greencloaks might have a real chance.

Xanthe might have a chance.

Across the chamber, Master Naveb coughed. Rollan locked eyes with the old man just as Naveb quickly lifted the edge of his robe and revealed a key tied to his ankle. He gave Rollan a quick nod and motioned to Kovo. Naveb had the key to unlock Kovo's chains!

"Fine." Sid grinned cruelly. "You want to fight? We'll fight."

Rollan readied himself to sprint.

A screech from somewhere in the room caught everyone's attention . . . especially Rollan's. It sounded like Essix. Rollan's eyes flicked over to the closed window. How had the falcon gotten in, and where was she now?

Another screech, but something was off. Rollan glanced upward, where he saw a tiny black bird perched in the rafters. It was the same bird that had stolen his food out on the savannah! The drongo flew onto the shoulder of a girl with curly red hair. The Oathbound fished a snack from her pocket and gave it to her spirit animal, sneering at Rollan the whole time.

That little sneak. It had imitated Essix's call.

Sid rolled his shoulders confidently and continued talking. "If you choose to fight us, all you'll accomplish is more bloodshed . . . your own. Surrender is your only option."

Meilin scoffed. "Never."

"You'll just kill us anyway," Conor added.

Abeke narrowed her eyes. "Once we're of no *use* to you."

"Now, now, friends," Rollan said, taking a small sideways step. If he could just get to Kovo, then Master Naveb would toss him the key. "Sid here seems like a smart guy. I mean, he obviously knew we were coming. I'm guessing a little bird told you."

Sid looked over at the drongo and chuckled. "Yes, Kasmira can be very useful."

This time the bird chirped like a nightingale in response.

Rollan took another step. "So you must also know that the Greencloaks have vast resources. We can make a person very wealthy."

"If it's more gold you want," Abeke said, catching on that Rollan had a plan of sorts, "we can always come to some type of arrangement." She began slowly moving away from the group in the opposite direction.

The Oathbound soldiers shifted, cautiously spreading out in order to remain in front of each Greencloak.

"Such as?" Sid asked as Conor took a couple steps forward.

"Gold, of course," Conor said. "*And* we know many influential people."

Rollan could see that Sid was interested. They just needed a little more time.

"I can't believe that you would offer him anything!" Takoda cried out from beside Xanthe. "Look what he did!"

"Hush, boy," Master Naveb scolded.

Rollan ignored Takoda's anguish and took another step closer to the window. "It would seem that you hold all the cards, so why don't you set the terms?"

Meilin lowered her sword, as if willing to entertain the idea as well. "Just tell us what you want."

Sid's expression changed as he stared at Meilin. The eager gleam was replaced by a rigid grimace. "There is nothing I want," he stated, his back straightening. It almost looked as if he were about to salute her. "My captain . . . we await your orders."

Rollan was confused, but when he turned to look at Meilin, it was the person who was standing behind her who surprised him.

Anka.

Meilin spun around and came face-to-face with the Greencloak. Anka now had a knife pointed directly at Meilin. The same knife that had stabbed her. Her shirt was no longer stained with blood.

The truth dawned slowly on Rollan. The whole thing had been an illusion. Anka had actually caught the knife and used her chameleon ability to make it seem as if she'd been mortally wounded.

"Anka?" Meilin took a half step back. "What's going on?"

"Captain, I . . . I'm glad you're not hurt." Sid's voice quavered. "I truly did not realize that—"

"Enough!" Anka stopped Sid's prattling with a wave of her hand. "Yes, Sid, your blindness has become painfully obvious. You didn't even realize that the old man has Kovo's key *in his hand*."

"I knew I didn't like you from the moment I couldn't see you," Master Naveb said.

"Oathbound," Anka called, "arrest them all!"

Each Greencloak took a defensive stance. They wouldn't go down without a fight. Rollan knew that the battle for their lives was about to begin.

Anka stared at Meilin. "Except for her. This one . . . this one is mine."

19

HONEST FIGHT

MEILIN'S HEAD WAS SPINNING. SHE COULDN'T BELIEVE Anka had betrayed them . . . that she'd apparently been working with the Oathbound all along. None of them had suspected her of being a spy.

"You seem so surprised," Anka said as she and Meilin circled each other. All around them, fighting had broken out between Greencloaks and Oathbound. Distantly, Meilin heard Abeke scream, but she didn't dare look away from the enemy facing her. "Did you think you were the only Zhongese girl to want more?"

"More what? More treachery?" Meilin turned the sword in her hand. "How could you, Anka? We were *friends.*"

"It's nothing personal," the young woman said with a shrug. "Fate put us on different sides of this conflict. You win your battles through combat. I win in my own way. Plus, you're the one who told me: 'In a real battle for life and death, you shouldn't worry about what is and isn't fair.'"

Jhi barked urgently, a low, plaintive sound that cut through the noise of the hall. Meilin spared her spirit animal a quick glance and saw that Jhi was watching Xanthe with anxious eyes.

"She's lost a lot of blood," Anka said. "Probably just on the verge of death. So what will you do? Will you sacrifice your spirit animal's help? The last time we sparred without her, I nearly beat you."

Meilin glared. "Go, Jhi. I can handle the likes of *Anka*, myself."

The panda exploded into action, loping across the chamber toward Xanthe and Takoda.

Anka smirked. "Wrong call," she crooned.

Meilin lunged at her with her sword, but Anka spun away, landing a kick against Meilin's hip at the same time. "And since you bring it up . . . my name isn't really Anka. It's Kana. Kana the Honest."

Kana disappeared, her cloak dissolving into the background like mist burning away in the sun.

Meilin jabbed at the empty air around her, unsure of where Anka . . . or Kana . . . had gone.

Then she felt her legs being swept out from under her. Meilin fell back and slammed her skull against the hard floor.

Now her head *truly* spun. Meilin forced herself up, bracing her unsteady feet. She glanced nervously around her. In a fight where she couldn't see her enemy, she had to trust her other senses.

A slight rustling sound told her what she needed to know. Meilin did a backward handspring and sliced through the air with her leg, making hard contact with the unseen Kana.

"Ugh!" Kana grunted.

Meilin struck again, landing a second kick. As she went for a third, she felt a sharp pain in her upper leg. She screamed, stumbling back and leaving a trail of blood in her wake.

Retreating to a corner of the room, Meilin held her sword in front of her. Her wound wasn't serious, but it was too difficult to fight an invisible opponent. Kana could have cut an artery if she'd struck her in a different place.

"That was a warning," Kana said, as if reading Meilin's mind.

Meilin couldn't believe Kana's skill. She was a much better fighter than she'd pretended to be. Meilin could *not* underestimate her.

"You've learned a lot," Meilin said, trying to find Kana's location through her voice.

"Ha!" Kana's laugh came from Meilin's left. "You thought I was learning how to fight. . . . I was only learning how *you* fight."

Meilin spun her sword in front of her like a protective barrier. Out of the corner of her eye she saw Conor fighting off three Oathbound warriors with his ax and a sword he'd picked up from somewhere.

"Things don't have to be this way, Meilin." Kana's voice had switched sides, now coming from the right side of the room. "You could join us. Work for me. I know how much you love Zhong. So did your father."

"Leave my father out of this!" Meilin shouted, her eyes straining to see where the voice was coming from. But the only thing she saw were her friends, battling the Oathbound. Rollan defended against two attackers,

giving Abeke cover as she shot arrows at some archers who were perched on the rafters. Uraza and Briggan were each tangled up under weighted nets that had been thrown over them.

Things weren't looking good. Meilin needed to level the playing field. She *had* to defeat Kana.

"Think about it, Meilin," Kana said. "Zhong needs more women like you. Strong and brave and unafraid to fight for what they believe in. It's why I started the Oathbound. The military wouldn't have me, so I formed my own company. The time of the Greencloaks is over, but you can still serve your nation."

"You're nothing but mercenaries," Meilin snarled. "Without the Greencloaks, the nations will be at each other's throats, and then who will you *serve*? The highest bidder? Being a Greencloak means recognizing that we're all in this together. We all bleed the same. Helping others, wherever they are, is the right thing to do."

Meilin caught sight of the large fireplace. An idea began to form. The ash could reveal Kana's location. Make it easier to fight her.

"You still don't understand," Kana answered with a sigh. She was standing somewhere to Meilin's right side.

Meilin didn't waste any more time responding. She sprinted toward the fireplace, jumping over knocked-down chairs and beating down any Oathbound who dared to get in her way.

She grabbed a handful of ash and flung it in the air.

Kana coughed as the clouds of soot hit her. Meilin could see portions of the Oathbound spy outlined in the ash. Before Kana had a chance to camouflage herself

again, Meilin tackled her, the two rolling onto the floor. Kana swiped at Meilin with her fists, but Meilin swiftly countered every one of Kana's moves, then she hopped lightly to her feet.

Spinning in the air, Meilin swung her leg, leading with a strong roundhouse kick. But Kana was ready. She grabbed Meilin's ankle, turned her leg, and slammed her down with a resounding thud. Before Meilin could roll away, Kana had the knife at her throat.

"So predictable," Kana lamented. "I thought you'd be more creative." She paused to glance over at the other Greencloaks, who were each being taken down. "But this is over. It all ends now."

20

EXPENDABLE

ABEKE WAS DEVASTATED. THE GREENCLOAKS HAD PUT up a good fight, but they were outnumbered by a group that had been waiting for them for days. The Oathbound had exploited their every weakness, and now their fate was in Kana's hands.

All the monks had been taken away, including the heartbroken Takoda, who had to be carried out kicking and screaming when the Oathbound dragged Xanthe out of the hall. The Sadrean was alive, thanks to Jhi, but she hadn't woken up since being stabbed. When Abeke last glimpsed the girl, her already pale skin was nearly blue.

The only ones left in the Great Hall were Sid, Kana, and the four Greencloaks, who were sitting on the ground with their hands and legs tied.

"We're ready, Captain," Sid announced. He held a small blue bottle in his hand. "Do I knock them out?"

"I'm reconsidering sending them to Greenhaven to be tried with the other Greencloaks." Kana paced back

and forth across the Great Hall. She was clearly visible to everyone.

Abeke noticed that now that Kana had shown her true colors, she no longer camouflaged herself as much.

"What? Why?" Sid glanced at Meilin before looking at Kana again. "Were you able to convince her to join us?"

"I'd never join you." Meilin spat out the words.

"None of us would," Rollan added.

Kana chuckled. "As if I'd accept any of you at this point." She walked over to Rollan and bent down in front of him. "Before we forget." She reached under his shirt and pulled out the Heart of the Land. She smiled as she slipped the chain over his head and put it around her own neck, tucking it under her collar.

Abeke could see the anger in Rollan's eyes. She'd felt the same way when her bag with Stormspeaker was taken away. They'd risked so much, lost so much, to get those two bond tokens, and now the Oathbound had them.

"So what are we doing with them?" Sid asked as Kana gazed out the window. "Cordelia will be waiting for them."

"Cordelia will just have to wait, then," Kana replied, watching the sunrise.

"Cordelia the Kind?" Abeke didn't want to get her hopes up too much, but if Cordelia had survived the cave-in, then maybe Worthy had, too. The Redcloaks might be able to help them somehow.

"Yes, but what's it to you?" Sid asked.

"They're worried about that heinous half-breed you captured," Kana explained, turning to face the group again. "The former Trunswick kid."

"So he's alive?" Conor asked.

"Yeah, yeah . . . he's fine," Sid said. "Well, as fine as a mash-up of animal and human can ever be." Sid shuddered for dramatic effect.

"Go ahead and knock them out with the potion," Kana ordered. "That way we don't have to worry about any feeble attempts at escaping."

"I won't swallow that," Meilin declared, struggling with her ropes.

Kana cocked her head to the side. "Please, as if you have a say in the matter. Plus, this doesn't even involve you drinking it. We're much more sophisticated."

Sid opened up the bottle and poured a little on a handkerchief. "So they *are* going to Greenhaven?" He flashed a sinister smile as he stalked toward Conor. "This should be fun."

"No, they're not," Kana said. "You'll put them on our boat."

"To Xin Kao Dai?" Sid looked confused as he covered Conor's nose and mouth with the wet cloth.

"The catacombs there are riddled with deadly traps," Kana said. She watched impassively while Conor struggled against Sid's hands. "Better to have expendables like these four go in first, don't you think?"

Sid grinned as Conor stopped moving. The boy slumped to the side, unconscious.

"Who's next?" he asked, eyeing Meilin.

"Leave her for last," Kana said. "I want her to watch each one of her friends go down."

Sid let out a big, strong laugh. He was enjoying this. He approached Abeke and poured a little more of the liquid from the blue bottle onto the cloth before covering her face with it.

Abeke held her breath, not wanting to breathe in whatever was on the handkerchief.

"Kana, stop this," Meilin pleaded, trying with all her might to free herself. "The Greencloaks are innocent. You *know* we didn't kill the emperor."

"Oh, Meilin," Kana said as Abeke tried in vain to move her face away from Sid's powerful hands. "You really don't know anything at all."

And with those words, Abeke gasped for air and her entire world went dark.

Christina Diaz Gonzalez

is the award-winning author of *Moving Target*, *Return Fire*, *The Red Umbrella*, and *A Thunderous Whisper*. Her books have received numerous honors and recognitions, including the Florida Book Award and the Nebraska Book Award, and have been named the American Library Association's Best Fiction for Young Adults, a Notable Social Studies Trade Book for Young People, and the International Reading Association's Teachers' Choice. More information can be found at www.christinagonzalez.com.

BOOK EIGHT

THE DRAGON'S EYE

Conor, Abeke, Meilin, and Rollan are four young heroes who have dedicated their lives to fighting evil. They are Greencloaks, called from every corner of the world to defend Erdas. But now the Greencloaks lie broken. The order is imprisoned, and their legendary relics have been stolen.

Something huge and terrible is coming, and it plans to swallow the Greencloaks whole. If the four friends and their spirit animals are going to stop it, then they'll have to trust in their bonds.

They'll need to become more than just heroes:
They must become legends.

scholastic.com/spiritanimals

Discover the Hidden Tales of Erdas!

There's more to explore in the Spirit Animals
world! These Special Editions reveal the secrets
of Erdas in ways you never saw coming...

SCHOLASTIC

scholastic.com/spiritanimals

All Sphere Books are available at your bookshop or
newsagent, or can be ordered from the following address:

Sphere Books, Cash Sales Department,
P.O. Box 11, Falmouth, Cornwall.

Please send cheque or postal order (no currency), and allow
7p per copy to cover the cost of postage and packing
in U.K. or overseas.

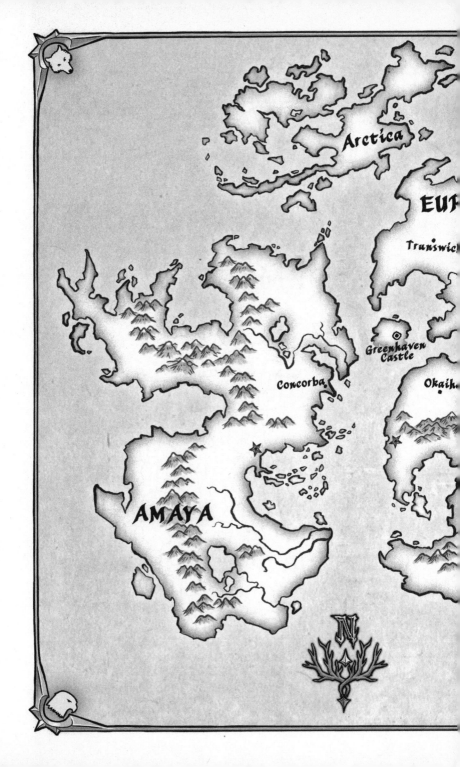

FALL of the BEASTS
SPIRIT ANIMALS

STORMSPEAKER

Christina Diaz Gonzalez

SCHOLASTIC INC.

"Your prey is not
always in front of you,
but sometimes behind."

The world is in peril.

An ancient evil is rising from beneath Erdas, and we need YOU to help stop it.

Claim your spirit animal and join the adventure now:

1. Go to scholastic.com/spiritanimals.

2. Log in to create your character and choose your own spirit animal.

3. Have your book ready and enter the code below to unlock the adventure.

Your code: NHRDH3HF2T

By the Four Fallen,
The Greencloaks

primary amendment (as explained under *Strike Out Words*, above).

- But if the primary amendment is to strike out a *paragraph*, then words struck out of that paragraph in the process of secondary amendment are *out of* the resolution regardless of the final vote on the primary amendment.

12:52 After a paragraph has been struck out, it cannot be inserted again unless the wording (or, possibly, the place) is changed in a way that presents an essentially new question. After a motion to strike out a particular paragraph has been voted down, any amendment presenting a materially new question involving the same paragraph, or any part of it, is still in order.

12:53 **Form and Example: 2(a), 2(b). To Strike Out (Words or a Paragraph).** The motion to strike out may be made in such forms as "I move to strike out the word 'concrete' before 'pavement' in Line 5"; or "I move to strike out the third paragraph of the platform statement." Variations similar to those given for inserting or adding (12:32) are applicable.

12:54 Assume that the following main motion is pending: "That the Bowling League establish a division open to the juniors and seniors of Southwood High School."

> **MEMBER A (obtaining the floor):** I move to amend by striking out the words "juniors and." (Second.)
>
> **CHAIR:** It is moved and seconded to amend by striking out the words "juniors and." If the amendment is adopted, the main motion will be to "establish a division open to the seniors of Southwood High School." The question is on striking out the words "juniors and."

12:55 From this point, the procedure is similar to that already illustrated for inserting or adding.

12:56 **3(a). To Strike Out and Insert (applying to words).** The motion to strike out and insert is especially applicable in situations where it may be impossible to secure the desired result without making the act of "striking out" inseparable from that of "inserting"—as may happen if some members are unwilling to vote for the one unless assured of the other. The two parts of this motion cannot be separated, either by secondary amendment or by a *Division of a Question.*

12:57   To avoid confusion with the form of amendment known as *Substitute* (12:69–90), which applies to paragraphs or longer elements, the word *substitute* should not be used in connection with the motion to *strike out and insert*, which applies to words.

12:58   Motions to strike out and insert fall into two types:

- those by which a different wording is inserted in the same place; and
- those by which the same wording struck out of one place is inserted in a different place.

12:59   The two parts of the motion to strike out and insert must not represent two independent questions, unless the mover receives unanimous consent to make such a combined motion; rather, the two parts must be germane to each other. Thus, in motions of the first type mentioned in the previous paragraph—to strike words out of and insert words into the same place—the words to be inserted must in some way be related to, or address the same issue as, the words to be struck out; and in motions of the second type—to strike words out of one place and insert words into a different place—the words to be inserted must not be materially different from the words to be struck out.

12:60   The first type of the motion to strike out and insert—the kind that proposes to insert a different wording in the same place—is perhaps more common.

12:61   When such a primary amendment is offered, the chair states the question on it and lets debate of its merits begin in the usual way. For purposes of secondary amendment, however, this type of motion is treated as if resolved into its two elements, with secondary amendment of each element following the rules that would apply to two separate motions for primary amendment—

one to strike out (amendable only by striking out) and another to insert (amendable in any of three forms relating to words). A single secondary amendment involving both elements of a primary amendment to strike out and insert is not in order. If a motion to strike out and insert involves enough words that several secondary amendments—particularly to the words to be struck out—might be possible, it is often best to take any amendments to the words to be struck out first, because members who wish to perfect the words to be inserted by secondary amendment may need to know exactly what language those words will replace, to be able to perfect them effectively. Amendments to the words to be inserted are then taken up after amendments to the words to be struck out have been disposed of. But the chair should make a judgment depending on the conditions as to whether the assembly wishes to follow this procedure or will find it helpful. In any event, the primary amendment remains open to debate at all times while it is pending with no secondary amendment pending, and this debate goes into the merits of both parts of the motion viewed as a single whole.

12:62 While a primary amendment to strike out and insert certain words is pending, if an admissible secondary amendment to the words to be struck out is introduced and no amendments to the words to be inserted have been proposed, the chair simply proceeds to entertain the secondary amendment, letting debate on the primary amendment resume after the secondary amendment has been dealt with. But the first time that a secondary amendment to the words to be inserted is offered—assuming a number of amendments to the words to be struck out might be possible—the chair has the option, as described in the preceding paragraph, of saying: "The chair believes it would be better to follow the procedure of taking any amendments to the words to be struck out first, as permitted under the rules. Accordingly, before entertaining the amendment just offered, the chair will ask: Are there any amendments [or "any further amendments"] to the words to be struck out?" When it appears that no one else wishes to propose an amendment to the words to be struck out, the chair then says: "The primary amendment as amended is open to debate, and secondary amendments to the words to be inserted are now in order." After reasonable opportunity to offer any amendments of the latter type has been given, secondary amendments to either element are in order. When these and any further debate have concluded, the vote is taken on the motion to strike out and insert as it stands after secondary amendment.

12:63   After a motion to strike out and insert has been adopted, what has been struck out and what has been inserted are subject to the same rules regarding further amendment during the same session, as if the striking out and the inserting had been done by separate motions: The inserted matter cannot be struck out, and the matter that has been struck out cannot be inserted again, except through a reconsideration of the vote on the amendment, or through changes in the wording or the place in a way that presents a new question (under the rules already given for *Insert, or Add*, and for *Strike Out*).

12:64   If a motion to strike out and insert is voted down, it is still in order:

- to make either of the separate motions to *strike out*, or to *insert*, the same words that would have been struck out or inserted by the combined motion that was lost; or
- to make another motion to *strike out and insert*—provided that the change in either the wording to be struck out or the wording to be inserted presents a question materially different from the one that was voted down.

12:65   When a primary amendment to strike out a passage of any length or complexity and insert a new version is pending and some members would prefer to insert something different or keep something closer to the original, it may be difficult or impossible to reach the desired end by secondary amendment. Situations of this kind can occur especially when the amendment relates to one or more complete sentences that do not constitute an entire paragraph. In such a case, a member should speak against the pending primary amendment and say that if it is rejected he will offer a new motion to strike out the same passage and insert the version he desires—which he should then state. He should present his case as strongly as possible, because if the first proposed version is inserted, it cannot be changed afterward during the same session except in connection with a different question.

12:66   As already explained in connection with the rules for the motion to *strike out*, the motion to *strike out and insert* can be used to obtain the effect of striking out or modifying separated words. To do this, a member can move to strike out of the resolution a passage long enough to include all of the words to be removed or changed, and insert the revised passage. If several changes in a paragraph are desired, it is usually better to rewrite the paragraph and offer the new version as a *substitute*, as explained below.

12:67   *Form and Example: 3(a). To Strike Out and Insert (applying to words).* As an example of a motion to strike out and insert, assume that the following resolution is pending: "*Resolved*, That the Citizens' Association endorse the Rockville site for the new Community College."

> MEMBER A (obtaining the floor): I move to amend by striking out "Rockville" and inserting "Chatham." (Second.)
>
> CHAIR: It is moved and seconded to strike out "Rockville" and insert "Chatham." If the amendment is adopted, the resolution will be to "endorse the Chatham site for the new Community College." The question is on striking out "Rockville" and inserting "Chatham."

12:68   Debate on the amendment is limited to the relative advantages of the two sites. After the amendment is debated, the chair puts it to vote, as in the case already illustrated for *Insert or Add*. Debate on the resolution can go into the question of whether the association should express approval of any site.

12:69   **3(b). To Substitute.** A motion to *Amend* by striking out an entire paragraph, section, or article—or a complete main motion or resolution—and inserting a different paragraph or other unit in its place is called a motion to *substitute*, and the paragraph or resolution to be inserted is said to be offered (or proposed) as "a substitute." A substitute can be offered for a paragraph or a main motion of only one sentence, and in such a case the paragraph proposed as a substitute can contain several sentences. (For the replacement of sentences *within* a paragraph, see below.) A substitute offered for a main motion or resolution, or for a paragraph within a resolution, is a primary amendment and can therefore be moved only when no other amendment is pending. If a motion proposes to replace one or more paragraphs that are involved in a pending primary amendment, it is a secondary amendment to which the term *substitute* is also applicable.[6]

12:70   A primary amendment to *substitute* is treated similarly to a motion to *strike out and insert* as described in 12:56–68. It is open to debate at all times while it is pending with no secondary amendment pending; and such debate may go fully into the merits of both the original text and the substitute, since this is necessary to determine the desirability of the primary amendment. But for purposes of secondary amendment, the motion to substitute is looked upon as resolved into its two elements, the paragraph to be struck out and the paragraph to be inserted. In contrast to the rules for striking out and inserting *words*, however, when a motion to *substitute* is under consideration the paragraph to be struck out as well as the paragraph to be inserted can be perfected by secondary amendment in any of the three basic forms (inserting or adding; striking out; or striking out and inserting), since this is the procedure when either of the separate motions to *insert* or to *strike out* is applied to the paragraph.

6. It is thus possible to introduce a proposed "substitute for a substitute," which cannot be amended, since it is a secondary amendment.

12:71   As in the case of a motion to strike out and insert words, the chair has the option of accepting only amendments to the paragraph to be struck out first, and then only amendments to the proposed substitute, thereafter accepting either type of secondary amendment. Following this procedure is likely to be more often indicated in the case of a motion to substitute, particularly if a substantive issue hangs on such a motion, as in the example given below. After all secondary amendments have been disposed of and after any further debate on the motion to substitute, the vote is taken on whether to make this substitution.

12:72   For replacing an unbroken *part* of a paragraph when the part to be replaced consists of (or contains) one or more complete sentences, there is an option between offering the amendment as a motion to strike out the part and insert the new matter (that is, as a motion to *strike out and insert*), or moving it in the form of a substitute for the entire paragraph with only the desired part changed. Either of these motions, as applied to the same case, will present substantially the same question when it is made, but the effect of each of them is different as to permissible secondary amendment. If much of the paragraph is involved in such a case, it is generally better to offer the desired amendment in the form of a substitute. If this method is used, however, secondary amendment can also involve the portion of the paragraph in which no change was proposed initially.

12:73   In taking the vote on whether to make the substitution, the chair should first read both the paragraph of the original text and the proposed substitute—*as they stand at the time* as amended. Even if the entire resolution or main motion is replaced, adopting the motion to *substitute* only *amends* the resolution, which remains pending as amended.

12:74   After a paragraph, section, or version of a resolution has been substituted for another, the substituted paragraph or resolution cannot be amended during the same session except by *adding* something that does not modify the paragraph's existing content—as is true of any paragraph that has been inserted.

The paragraph that has been replaced cannot be inserted again during the same session unless a material change in the wording (or possibly, the place) makes a new question—as is true of any paragraph that has been struck out.

12:75   If a motion to substitute is lost, the assembly has decided only that the paragraph proposed as a substitute shall not replace the one specified. The same proposed new paragraph can still replace a different one, or can simply be inserted. On the other hand, the paragraph that was retained in the resolution can be further amended, or struck out (if it is not the entire resolution); or it still can be replaced by a different substitute.

12:76   When a question is being considered *by paragraph or seriatim* (**28**), it is in order to move a substitute for any paragraph or section at the time that the paragraph or section is opened to amendment. But it is not in order to move a substitute for the entire document until all of the paragraphs or sections have been individually considered and the point is reached when the chair announces that the entire paper is open to amendment.

12:77   If a resolution is referred to a committee while a primary amendment—or a primary and a secondary amendment—are pending, the committee can report by recommending a substitute for the resolution, even though the substitute cannot become pending until the other amendments have been voted on in their normal order. Thus, when a committee has so reported, the chair first states the question on the secondary amendment that was pending when the resolution was committed, puts the secondary amendment to vote, and then continues with the primary amendment to which it applied. As soon as this primary amendment is disposed of, the chair states the question on the substitute recommended by the committee, and proceeds as he would with any other motion to substitute.

12:78   In a similar way, if a resolution is referred to a committee while a substitute and a secondary amendment (either to the original or to the substitute) are pending, the committee can report in favor of either version, with any desired recommendation as to secondary amendment; or the committee can recommend rejection of the pending substitute and propose a new substitute in its place. In all such cases, the chair starts with the parliamentary situation as it was when the resolution was committed; he then proceeds as with any motion to substitute, and states the question on any new amendment (recommended by the committee) as soon as it is in order for that amendment to be pending under the usual rules.

12:79 The motion to *substitute* often provides a convenient and timesaving method for handling a poorly framed resolution, or for introducing a different and better approach to the real question raised by a main motion. While changes by separate amendments are in progress, a member who feels that he has a better solution by substitution can indicate its features briefly and announce his intention of offering the substitute as soon as no other amendment is pending. If the member wishing to propose the substitute thinks it appropriate, he can try to bring the pending amendments to an immediate vote by moving the *Previous Question* (**16**) on them.

12:80 An amendment in the form of a substitute can also be used to defeat or work against the purpose of the measure originally introduced. Such a stratagem can be utilized with a view either to converting the measure into a weakened form before its final adoption, or to substituting a version that is likely to be rejected in the final vote. It should be noted that a vote in favor of a substitute for an entire resolution or main motion is ordinarily a vote to kill any provisions of the original version that are not included in the substitute.

12:81 Properly applied, the rules for the treatment of motions to *substitute* automatically operate in fairness to both sides when there is disagreement as to the preferability of the original or the substitute. Under the procedure of initially accepting amendments to each element of the primary amendment exclusively—which is generally indicated whenever such disagreement exists—the proponents of the original version are first given the opportunity to amend their proposition into a more acceptable form in the light of conditions revealed by the introduction of the substitute. When this process is correctly handled as described 12:61–62 and 12:70–71, it tends to ensure that the provisions of the version first offered receive appropriate consideration, without impeding free debate of the proposal to substitute. Furthermore, by the requirement that internal amendment of the substitute be done before the vote on the motion to make the substitution, the members are protected from having to decide whether to reject the original version without knowing what may finally replace it.

12:82   **Form and Example: 3(b). To Substitute.** As an example of a motion to substitute, assume that the following resolution is pending: "*Resolved*, That the Parish Federation undertake the construction and equipping of a new service wing for the Parish House, to be financed as far as possible by a mortgage on the present building."

12:83   Debate points strongly to a need for further investigation, but many members are determined to secure immediate authorization. The meeting seems evenly divided, and the outcome is unpredictable.

> **MEMBER A (obtaining the floor):** I move to substitute for the pending resolution the following: "*Resolved*, That the Parish Board be directed to engage appropriate professional consultants to make a survey of, and prepare a complete report on, the need, probable cost, feasible methods of financing, and maintenance of a new service wing for the Parish House." (Second.)
>
> **CHAIR:** It is moved and seconded to amend by substituting for the pending resolution the following: [reading the substitute submitted by Member A]. The motion to substitute proposes that the resolution just read shall come before the assembly in place of the pending resolution. [Debate.]
>
> **MEMBER L (who favors the *pending* resolution and is, therefore, opposed to the motion to substitute—obtaining the floor):** I move to amend the proposed substitute by adding the words "within twenty days." (Second.)

CHAIR: The chair believes it will be preferable to take any amendments to the pending resolution first, as permitted under the rules. Such amendments, if adopted, will affect the wording in which the pending resolution will come to a final vote if the motion to substitute fails.[7] Accordingly, before entertaining the amendment just offered, the chair will call for any amendments to the pending resolution, which he will first reread. The pending resolution is as follows: "*Resolved,* That the Parish Federation undertake the construction and equipping of a new service wing for the Parish House, to be financed as far as possible by a mortgage on the present building." Are there any amendments to the pending resolution?

MEMBER X (obtaining the floor): I move to amend the pending resolution by striking out everything after the word "undertake" and inserting the words "a campaign to raise funds for the construction and equipping of a new service wing for the Parish House." (Second.)

12:84   The chair states the question on this amendment, making its effect clear, and, after debate, puts it to vote. For purposes of the example, assume that the proponents of the original resolution differ on the amendment, some voting for it, others opposing it. Also, since the adoption of this amendment presumably would make the pending resolution *less* objectionable to those who feel that the proposed project is presently ill advised and who therefore hope that the substitution will be made, most of those members probably vote for the amendment. Assume that it is adopted. The chair announces the result as follows:

CHAIR: The ayes have it and the amendment is adopted. The pending resolution now reads, "*Resolved,* That the Parish Federation undertake a campaign to raise funds for the construction and equipping of a new service wing for the Parish House." The question is on the motion to substitute. [Further debate on the relative merits of the pending resolution and the proposed substitute.]

---

7. If the members are familiar with the procedure for handling motions to substitute, the chair may omit this sentence.

MEMBER L (who favors the *pending* resolution—obtaining the floor): I move to amend the substitute by adding "within twenty days." (Second.)

CHAIR: Before entertaining the amendment just offered, the chair will again ask: Are there any further amendments to the pending resolution? [Pause.] There being none, it is moved and seconded to amend the proposed substitute by adding the words "within twenty days." If the amendment is adopted, the substitute will read, "*Resolved*, That the Parish Board be directed to engage appropriate professional consultants to make a survey of, and prepare a complete report on, the need, probable cost, feasible methods of financing, and maintenance of a new service wing for the Parish House within twenty days." The question is on amending the proposed substitute by adding the words "within twenty days."

12:85   Brief debate shows that the proposed survey could not be properly carried out in twenty days. Assume that this amendment is voted down.

MEMBER B (who is in favor of the motion to substitute, but fears it will fail unless some time limit is specified—obtaining the floor): I move to amend the substitute by adding "within sixty days." (Second.)

12:86   The chair states the question on this amendment and (after brief debate) puts it to vote. Assume that the amendment is adopted. In announcing the result, the chair continues:

CHAIR: The ayes have it and the amendment is adopted. The proposed substitute now reads, "*Resolved*, That the Parish Board be directed to engage ... for the Parish House within sixty days." Are you ready for the question on the motion to substitute?

12:87   After further amendment of the proposed substitute, the chair says:

CHAIR: Are there any further amendments to the proposed substitute? [Pause.] There being none, it is now in order to offer amendments *either* to the pending resolution *or* to the proposed substitute.

12:88 When all debate and secondary amendment has concluded, the chair puts to vote the motion to substitute. Both resolutions are read, usually by the chair—the pending resolution first, then the resolution proposed as a substitute.

> CHAIR: The question is on the motion to substitute. The chair will read the pending resolution first, then the resolution proposed as a substitute. The pending resolution is: "*Resolved,* That the Parish Federation undertake a campaign to raise funds for the construction and equipping of a new service wing for the Parish House." The resolution proposed as a substitute is: "*Resolved,* That the Parish Board be directed to engage appropriate professional consultants to make a survey of, and prepare a complete report on, the need, probable cost, … within sixty days." The question is: Shall the resolution last read be substituted for the pending resolution? Those in favor of the motion to substitute, say *aye.* … Those opposed, say *no.* …

12:89 The chair announces the result of the vote and states the question on whichever resolution is left pending, as follows:

> CHAIR: The ayes have it and the motion to substitute is adopted. The question is now on the resolution: [reading the resolution directing the employment of professional consultants].

Or:

> CHAIR: The noes have it and the motion to substitute is lost. The question is now on the resolution: [reading the resolution for a fundraising campaign].

12:90 Regardless of which resolution is now pending, there may be further debate. If the motion to substitute has been adopted, the resolution now pending is in the position of a paragraph that has been inserted, and it can no longer be amended during the same session except by *adding* nonmodifying matter. On the other hand, if the motion to substitute has been lost, the resolution for the fund drive can be further amended; but in determining whether an amendment now offered presents a new question and can therefore be admitted during the same session, account must be taken of any motions to amend that were voted on before the motion to substitute was introduced, or while it was pending.

12:91   **Friendly Amendments.** The term "friendly amendment" is often used to describe an amendment offered by someone who is in sympathy with the purposes of the main motion, in the belief that the amendment will either improve the statement or effect of the main motion, presumably to the satisfaction of its maker, or will increase the chances of the main motion's adoption. Regardless of whether or not the maker of the main motion "accepts" the amendment, it must be opened to debate and voted on formally (unless adopted by unanimous consent) and is handled under the same rules as amendments generally (see 33:11–19).

Filling Blanks

12:92   Filling blanks, although not a form of amendment in itself, is a closely related device by which an unlimited number of alternative choices for a particular specification in a main motion or primary amendment can be pending at the same time. In effect, it permits an exception to the rule (12:13) that only one primary and one secondary amendment can be pending at a time, and in certain cases it has distinct advantages.

12:93   In amending by the ordinary method, a maximum of three alternatives can be pending at once, and the last one moved must be voted on first. In filling blanks, the number of alternatives is not limited; members have an opportunity to weigh all choices before voting and to vote on them in a fair and logical order. Among cases adapted to such treatment are main motions or primary amendments containing names of persons or places, dates, numbers, or amounts.

12:94 The basic procedure for filling blanks is as follows: After a blank in a pending motion has been created by any of the methods described below, members suggest alternatives to fill the blank, and these are stated by the chair. When debate on the suggestions has ended (or, if the pending motion is undebatable, when no more suggestions are offered), the assembly decides, by majority vote, which suggestion(s) shall fill the blank. The vote that fills a blank does *not* decide the question that contained the blank. As soon as the blank has been filled, the chair states the question on the adoption of the completed motion, which remains pending.

12:95 **Creating a Blank.** A blank to be filled can be created in one of three ways:

a) A member can offer a motion or an amendment containing a blank: for example, "*Resolved*, That Lodge No. 432 renovate the headquarters at a cost not to exceed $_____"; or an amendment to a main motion can propose "to add 'provided that estimates be received on or before _____.'"

b) A member can move that a blank be created. For example, assume that the pending resolution is: "*Resolved*, That Lodge No. 432 renovate the headquarters at a cost not to exceed $300,000." Any member can move "to create a blank by striking out of the pending resolution the sum '$300,000.'" If such a motion is adopted, the specification struck out to create the blank automatically becomes one of the proposals for filling it—as "$300,000" in the example. Although the motion to create a blank may appear to resemble a motion to amend by striking out and inserting, it is in fact an incidental motion (see 6:15). It is not in order to create a blank in a motion on which the *Previous Question* has been ordered. The motion to create a blank requires a second, but it is neither debatable nor amendable; it can also be made and voted on while a primary or a secondary amendment relating to the subject specification is pending. For example, assuming the same pending resolution as above, the identical motion to create a blank by striking out "$300,000" can be made while a primary amendment "to strike out '$300,000' and insert '$350,000'" is also pending. Adoption of the motion to create a blank in such a case (before the amendment is voted on) disposes of the amendment (which is thereafter ignored) and causes both specifications—the one in the pending resolution and the corresponding one in the amendment—to become proposals for filling the blank; as "$300,000" and "$350,000" in the example.

c) The chair can suggest the creation of a blank, as follows: "The chair suggests creating a blank by striking out '$300,000.' If there is no objection, a blank will be created. [Pause.] There is no objection; the blank is created." If a member objects, the chair puts the question to a vote, treating the question just as he would treat a motion to create a blank made as described above.

12:96   **Making Suggestions to Fill a Blank.** When a blank exists or has been created, the chair calls for suggestions, by asking for them in a manner appropriate to the particular question, such as by asking, "How many members shall the committee consist of?"; or, "In the pending resolution relating to the renovation of the headquarters, the amounts $350,000 and $300,000 have been proposed to fill the blank specifying the maximum cost. Are there any further suggestions?" Any number of members can then suggest different names, places, numbers, dates, or amounts for filling the blank. A member need not be recognized by the chair to make a suggestion unless he or she wishes to speak in debate on it at the same time (see below). No second is required. As soon as a member has made a suggestion (or, if the member had obtained the floor, as soon as the member has yielded the floor), the chair repeats the member's suggestion and calls for further suggestions.

12:97   No member can suggest more than one proposal for filling a blank—or, when the blank can be filled with multiple suggestions, such as in a motion to appoint members of a committee, more than the number allowed for in the blank. In the latter case, a member cannot make more than one suggestion at a time, if any objection is made, but must wait until after all other members have had the same opportunity to make their suggestions.

12:98 **Debate on the Suggestions.** Proposals to fill a blank in a debatable motion are debatable. When there is no response to the chair's call for further suggestions, the chair asks, "Are you ready for the question?" or "Is there any debate?" To speak in debate, a member must first be recognized by the chair. The member may then speak in favor of or against a suggestion made previously or make a new suggestion and speak in favor of it.

12:99 As a consequence of the rules stated in the preceding paragraphs, debate on the comparative merits of the different suggestions may take place both concurrently with the making of suggestions and after all suggestions have been made. In any event, in this debate the underlying question is that of choosing the suggestion(s) that shall fill the blank, and each member is therefore permitted to speak no more than twice per day on that question, regardless of the number of suggestions made. When no further suggestions are offered, and there is no further debate, a vote is taken on the suggestions, as described below.

12:100 Proposals to fill a blank are not amendable.

12:101 Motions to *Limit or Extend Limits of Debate* or for the *Previous Question* can be applied to the consideration of suggestions, and when voting on the suggestions has been ordered by adoption of either of these motions, no further suggestions for filling the blank may be made at the time the order goes into effect. However, if a member obtains the floor and moves the *Previous Question* before a reasonable opportunity to make suggestions has been given, the chair must call for suggestions before stating the motion for the *Previous Question*.

12:102 **Voting on the Suggestions.** The suggestions for filling a blank can be voted on by any of the regular methods (4:35ff.,

45:11ff.), in which case each of the proposals is voted on, in turn, as a separate question. (The order in which suggestions are voted on in particular cases is discussed below.) As soon as one of the suggestions (or the proper number of suggestions that will fill the blank) receives a majority vote, the chair declares the blank thereby filled, and no vote is taken on any remaining suggestions.

12:103 Alternatively, the assembly may direct that voting be by ballot or roll call (see **30**; 45:18ff.), in which case each member marks or announces his or her preference for the choice (or choices) that shall fill the blank—which need not be confined to the suggestions previously made—and the blank is filled by the choice receiving a majority of the votes cast (or the proper number of choices receiving a majority that receive the largest number of votes; cf. 46:33). Voting by ballot or roll call is seldom used except in the case of names, however, unless there is keen competition—for example, among several cities seeking a convention. When names are being voted on, the ballot has an advantage in more truly revealing the will of the voting body; frequently when the vote is by voice, those whose names are voted on first are more likely to be elected.

12:104 It should be noted that the vote that fills a blank does not decide the main question or other pending question that contained the blank. When the blank is filled, the chair must immediately state the question on the adoption of the completed motion.

12:105 Normally, blanks in a pending motion should be filled before the motion itself is voted on. However, if the pending motion is included in an adopted order for the *Previous Question*, that order must be carried out even if the blank has not yet been filled—and even if no suggestions have been offered (note, however, that a reasonable opportunity to make suggestions must always be given; see 12:101). This may happen, for example, when two thirds of those voting are confident that the motion will be rejected in any case. But if the motion is actually adopted with an unfilled blank, the assembly immediately proceeds to fill it, and no new subject (except a privileged one) may be introduced before the motion is thereby completed.

12:106 **Filling Blanks by Unanimous Consent.** If no more suggestions are offered than the number required to fill the blank, then unless the voting is to be by ballot or roll call, those suggestions are deemed inserted by unanimous consent, and no vote is taken on inserting them. This procedure is especially common when filling a blank with names (see below).

12:107 **Filling a Blank with Names.** The following principles apply to the process of filling a blank with one or more names:

a) The procedure for filling a blank with one name is practically the same as for making nominations. The chair repeats each name as it is proposed, and finally takes a vote on each in that same order, until one receives a majority.

b) If the blank is to be filled with more than one name and no more are suggested than are required, the names are deemed inserted by unanimous consent (cf. 46:40 and 50:13(b)).

c) If more names are suggested than are required, the chair takes a vote on each in the order of its proposal until enough to fill the blank have received a majority vote. The names remaining in the list as proposed are ignored, since the assembly has decided which names shall fill the blank.

d) If the number of names is not specified, the chair takes a vote on each name suggested; and all names approved by a majority vote are inserted.

12:108 **Filling a Blank with Amounts of Money.** Sometimes the particular nature of the blank determines the order in which proposals for filling it should be put to vote. Typical instances of this kind are blanks to be filled with amounts of money. In such cases it is advisable, whenever a logical order is apparent, to arrange the proposed entries so that *the one least likely to be acceptable will be voted on first*, and so on. New supporters may then be gained with each succeeding vote until a majority in favor of one entry is reached.

12:109   As an example of the procedure for filling a blank with an amount of money, assume that a resolution to renovate the headquarters "at a cost not to exceed $_____" is pending, and that it is proposed to fill the blank with the following amounts: $350,000, $250,000, $400,000, and $300,000. The character of this measure—to *spend* money—indicates that the amounts should be arranged and voted on in order from the highest to lowest. If $400,000 is rejected, the vote is taken next on $350,000; and if that is not adopted, the chair puts the question on $300,000. If that amount is adopted, no vote is taken on $250,000, and the chair immediately says, "The amount of $300,000 fills the blank. The question is now on the resolution: '*Resolved*, That … at a cost not to exceed $300,000.'" Note that if the smallest sum had been voted on first, it might have been adopted, with the result that those who preferred the added advantages possible through a larger expenditure would have been cut off from considering larger sums.

12:110   On the other hand, suppose that the motion or resolution is "to sell the headquarters for an amount not less than $_____." In the case of such a motion—to *accept* a sum of money in *settlement*—the amounts being considered should be arranged and voted on in order from the smallest to the largest. Thus, those who are willing to sell for the smallest amount, and some additional members, will be willing to sell for the next larger sum, and so on, until the smallest sum for which the majority is willing to sell is reached.

12:111   **Filling a Blank with Places, Dates, or Numbers.** When a blank is to be filled with a place, date, or number, a choice of methods for arranging and voting on the proposals can be made as follows:

a) Voting on the suggestions in the order in which they are offered, as when filling a blank with names.

b) Voting on the proposals in the order of their probable acceptability, beginning with the least popular choice, as when filling a blank with an amount.

c) (If there is no clear-cut reason why either increasing or decreasing order would be preferable), voting first on the largest number, longest time, or most distant date, and so on.

The particular circumstances must determine the order to be used.

12:112   If an amount has been struck out in order to create a blank, that amount is voted on in its proper place in the logical sequence among the other amounts. If a name has been struck out to create a blank, however, it comes first in the order of names to be voted on.

12:113   (For further examples of both creating and filling a blank, see 13:7(6), 13:8, 13:12, 13:26, 27:4, 31:3.)

§13. COMMIT OR REFER

13:1   The subsidiary motion to *Commit* or *Refer* is generally used to send a pending question to a relatively small group of selected persons—a committee—so that the question may be carefully investigated and put into better condition for the assembly to consider.

13:2   The motion to *Commit* also has three *variations* whose object is not to turn the main question over to a smaller group, but to permit the assembly's full meeting body to consider it with the greater freedom of debate that is allowed in committees—that is, with no limit on the number of times a member can speak. These forms of the motion are:

a) to "go into a committee of the whole";
b) to "go into quasi committee of the whole" (or, to "consider as if in committee of the whole"); and
c) to "consider informally."

13:3   "Informal consideration" is the simplest of the three methods and is usually the best in ordinary societies whose meetings are not large (see 52:24–27).

13:4   The term *recommit* is applied to a motion that proposes to refer a question a second time, either to the same committee that previously considered it or to a different one.

13:5   All of the rules in this section, except when stated to the contrary, apply equally to variations (a), (b), and (c) above, and to a motion to recommit.

13:6   When a motion proposes to assign a task or refer a matter to a committee when no question is pending, such a motion is not the subsidiary motion to *Commit*, but is a main motion. It is an incidental main motion if the assignment or referral is pursuant to a subject on which the assembly has already taken some action; but it is an original main motion if the matter to be assigned or referred relates to a new subject.

Standard Descriptive Characteristics

13:7   The subsidiary motion to *Commit* or *Refer*:

1. Takes precedence over the main motion, over the subsidiary motions to *Postpone Indefinitely* and to *Amend*, and over the incidental motions for *Division of a Question* and for *Consideration by Paragraph or Seriatim*. It takes precedence over a debatable appeal that adheres to the main question (or a point of order that adheres to the main question and has been referred by the chair to the judgment of the assembly and that is debatable when so referred, 23:2(2)), if no motions other than those named in the preceding sentence are pending or involved in the appeal or point of order; and it also takes precedence over a debatable nonadhering appeal or point of order to which it is applied. It yields to the subsidiary motions to *Postpone Definitely*, to *Limit or Extend Limits of Debate*, for the *Previous Question*, and to *Lay on the Table*; to a motion to *Amend* that is applied to it; to all privileged motions; and to all applicable incidental motions.

2. Can be applied to main motions, with any amendments or motions for *Division of a Question* or *Consideration by*

Paragraph or Seriatim that may be pending; can be thus applied to *orders of the day* (**18, 41**) or *questions of privilege* (**19**) while they are actually pending as main motions, and such an application is independent of, and does not affect, any other matter that they may have interrupted; can be applied to debatable appeals (or points of order referred by the chair to the judgment of the assembly that are debatable when so referred, 23:2(2)), but if such an appeal or point of order adheres (10:35) to the main question (that is, if it must be decided before the main question is decided), the motion to *Commit* can be applied to the appeal or point of order only in connection with the main question, which also goes to the committee (see also 13:19); and can be applied to nonadhering debatable appeals (or points of order submitted to the judgment of the assembly) separately, without affecting the status of any pending questions not involved in the appeal or point of order. It cannot be applied to an undebatable appeal. It cannot be applied to the motion to *Reconsider* alone—that is, it cannot be applied to a motion to reconsider a main question; and if a main question is committed while a motion to reconsider an amendment is pending or has been made but not yet taken up, such a motion to *Reconsider* is thereafter ignored. It cannot be applied to any subsidiary motion, except that its application to a main question also affects any motions to *Amend* that may be pending, as noted above. It cannot be moved after the adoption of a motion to close debate on the main question at a definite hour or to limit the total time allowed for debate; but it remains in order if only a limitation on the length of speeches is in force (see **15**). Motions to *Amend*, to *Limit or Extend Limits of Debate*, and for the *Previous Question* can be applied to it without affecting the main question. The motion to *Commit* cannot be definitely postponed or laid on the table alone, but when it is pending the main question can be definitely postponed or laid on the table, and in such a case, the motion to *Commit* is also postponed or carried to the table. It cannot be postponed indefinitely.

3. Is out of order when another has the floor.

4. Must be seconded.

5. Is debatable. The debate can extend only to the desirability of committing the main question and to the appropriate details of the motion to *Commit*, as explained below, however, and not to the merits of the main question.

6. Is amendable as follows: in the case of a standing committee, as to the committee to which the main question is to be referred; in the case of a special committee, as to the committee's composition and manner of selection; and in the case of any form of committee, as to any instructions the committee is to follow. It can be amended so as to change from any one of the five forms of the motion (listed in 13:12) to another, or a blank can be created (12:92–113) and the suggested forms voted on in the order given in 13:12.

7. Requires a majority vote.

8. An affirmative vote on the motion to *Commit* can be reconsidered if the committee has not begun consideration of the question. Thereafter, if the assembly wishes to take the question out of the hands of the committee, the motion to *Discharge a Committee* (**36**) must be used. A negative vote on the motion to *Commit* can be reconsidered only until such time as progress in business or debate has been sufficient to make it essentially a new question. Thereafter, the motion can be renewed (see 38:7).

Further Rules and Explanation

13:8   **Necessary Details of the Motion.** The motion to *Commit* usually should include all necessary details:

a) If the main question is to be considered in a committee of the whole, or in quasi committee of the whole ("as if in committee of the whole"), or if it is to be considered informally, the motion should specify which of these methods is to be used.

b) If the main question is to be sent to a standing committee (see **50**), the motion should specify the name of the committee.

c) If the main question is to go to a special (select, or ad hoc) committee (see **50**), the motion should specify the number of committee members, and the method of their selection unless the method is prescribed by the bylaws or rules of the assembly; or, if preferred, the motion can name the members of the special committee. (The word *special*, or *select*, or *ad hoc*, is not generally used in a motion to refer to a special committee; the motion is worded, for example, "to refer the question to a committee of five to be appointed by ..." See also forms of the motion in 13:25–26.)

d) Instructions to the committee can also be included in the motion to *Commit*, whether the committee is to be a standing or a special one, or a committee of the whole. These instructions, which are binding on the committee, may involve such matters as when the committee is to meet, how it is to consider the question, whether it is to employ an expert consultant, and when it is to report. The committee can be given "full power" to act for the society in a specific case and can be authorized to spend money or even to add to its own membership. The motion to *Commit* requires a majority vote for its adoption even when it contains instructions that suspend, modify, or conflict with rules of order that would otherwise apply to meetings of the committee. (See 9:35 regarding the adoption of instructions authorizing a committee to hold electronic meetings.)

Although these details can be changed by ordinary amendments, they can often be handled more efficiently by treating them as in filling blanks (12:92–113, 13:26).

13:9 **Dilatory Motion to Commit.** The chair has a duty to rule out of order, as dilatory, any motion to *Commit* that is obviously absurd or unreasonable—such as one that (because of the time involved or any other reason) would have the effect of defeating the purpose of the main question.

13:10   **Alternative Procedures When the Motion Is Incomplete.** When a motion to *Commit* merely lacks essential details—for example, when the motion is made simply "to refer the main question to a committee"—the chair should not rule it out of order. Instead, these two courses are open:

a) Members can offer suggestions or formal amendments to complete the required details, or the chair can call for them.
b) The chair can put the motion to *Commit* to vote at once in its simple form.

The second alternative is appropriate if no one is seeking recognition and the chair believes that the motion to *Commit* is not likely to be adopted, in which case time spent in completing the details would be wasted. Opponents of the motion to *Commit* may try to bring about the same result (that is, obtaining an immediate vote on the referral) by moving the *Previous Question* on it (see **16**). If the necessary two thirds (of those voting) vote to order the *Previous Question* on an incomplete motion to *Commit*, the motion is almost certain to be rejected, whatever details might be added.

13:11   In the event that any of the above procedures results in the adoption of an incomplete motion "to refer the question to a committee," the details must be completed as described in the following paragraphs. In such a case, no new subject (except a privileged one) can be introduced until the assembly has decided all of these related questions. In completing the details, the member who made the motion to commit has no preference in recognition, since he or she could have included any desired specifications in that motion.

13:12   **Completing an Incomplete Motion to Commit.** In completing a motion that simply refers "the main question to a committee"—either while the motion to *Commit* is pending or after it is adopted—the chair first asks, "To what committee shall the question be referred?" If only one suggestion is made, he assumes that this is the will of the assembly, and he states that it is inserted into the motion to *Commit*. But if different proposals are made, either in the form of primary and secondary amendments or simply as suggestions, the chair treats them as proposals to fill a blank (12:92–113) and puts them to vote in the following order until one receives a majority: (1) committee of the whole; (2) quasi committee of the whole (or "as if in committee of the whole"); (3) consider informally; (4) standing committees, in the order in which they are proposed; and (5) special (select, or ad hoc) committees, the one containing the largest number of members being voted on first. A proposal to recommit to the same standing or special committee that previously considered the question is voted on before other proposals for standing or special committees are voted on.

13:13   If it is decided that the committee is to be a special one, the chair then asks—unless the rules provide the method—"How shall the committee be appointed?" Again, if only one suggestion is made, it is inserted by unanimous consent, but if different methods are suggested or moved, they are voted on in the following order: (1) election by ballot; (2) nominations from the floor ("open nominations") with viva-voce election; (3) nominations by the chair; and (4) appointment by the chair (see also 50:11ff.). The first of these methods of selection that receives a majority vote is then inserted into the motion to *Commit* and the remainder are ignored.

13:14   If the motion to *Commit* lacks any other detail, the chair proceeds in a similar fashion to obtain completion of the motion. As soon as it is completed, if it is a *pending* motion to *Commit*, the chair states the question on it, thus opening it to additional debate during which any member can move—or the chair himself can suggest—that it be amended by adding instructions. By a majority vote, instructions can also be added to a motion to *Commit* that is being completed after its adoption.

13:15 **Naming Members to a Special Committee.** A standing or special committee may include, or even have as its chairman, one or more persons who are not members of the assembly or the society; but if the chair appoints the committee, the names of all such nonmembers being appointed must be submitted to the assembly for approval, unless the bylaws, the rules of the assembly, or the motion to appoint the committee specifically authorizes the presiding officer to appoint nonmembers (see also 50:12, 50:13(d)). When a motion to refer to a special committee has been adopted, no business except privileged matters can intervene until selection of the committee members is completed—except that if the chair is to appoint the committee, he can, if he wishes and time permits, state that he will announce the names of its members later. In such a case, however, the committee must be left with reasonable time to accomplish its purpose after the names of its members have been announced for the record and any non–society members have been approved in a meeting of the assembly as necessary under the rule stated at the beginning of this paragraph. The committee cannot act before such an announcement of its membership is made, unless otherwise authorized by the assembly, which may be done in the motion establishing the special committee or by a later incidental main motion (which can be adopted by a majority vote).

13:16 Although it is not necessary to place on a special committee the member who made the motion to *Commit*, it is usual to do so when such a person is interested and qualified. For a discussion of the appropriate size and personnel of committees under various circumstances, see 50:18.

13:17 **Designating the Committee Chairman.** If the chair appoints or nominates the committee, he has the duty to select its chairman—which he does by naming that person to the committee first—and the committee cannot elect another. The chair should not state the name of any committee member until he has decided his preference for chairman. The chair should specifically mention as chairman the first committee member he names, but if he neglects to state this fact, the designation nevertheless is automatic unless the first-named member immediately declines the chairmanship (which the member can do, and remain on the committee). If the first-named member declines to serve as chairman, the chair then names his next choice for this position. If the committee's task is heavy and will require some time to complete, it often is advisable to appoint a vice-chairman. The anomalous title "co-chairman" should be avoided, as it causes impossible dilemmas in attempts to share the functions of a single position.

13:18   If the committee is named by a power other than the chair (such as the assembly or the executive board), the body that elects the committee members has the power, at the time the appointments are made, to designate any one of them as chairman. If a chairman is not designated when the committee is appointed, the committee has the right to elect its own chairman. In the latter case, the first-named member has the duty of calling the committee together and of acting as temporary chairman until the committee elects a chairman. Since such a committee may confirm its first-named member in the chairmanship, it is important that this person be qualified and dependable.

13:19   **Effect on Motions Adhering to a Referred Question.** If a motion to *Postpone Indefinitely* is pending when the main motion is referred to a committee, the motion for indefinite postponement is dropped from further consideration. On the other hand, any pending amendments, motions for *Division of a Question* or *Consideration by Paragraph or Seriatim*, and adhering debatable appeals (or points of order submitted to the judgment of the assembly) go to the committee with the main motion, and are reported with it. (No question can be referred to a committee while an *undebatable* appeal or point of order is pending.) If, at the time a main motion is committed, a motion to reconsider an adhering subsidiary or incidental motion is pending or has been made but not yet taken up, the motion to *Reconsider* is thereafter ignored.

13:20   **Freedom of Action After Referral.** Since the purpose of referring a motion to a committee is generally to allow for a more thorough consideration of the matter, greater freedom of action is obtained once the committee commences its deliberations,[8] as follows: The usual prohibition against introducing a motion to *Amend* that raises the same question of content and effect as one already decided by the assembly at the same session (cf. 12:25) no longer applies. Therefore, a committee to which a resolution or other motion has been referred is free to consider, and recommend for adoption, its own amendments to the referred motion, or a recommendation for definite or indefinite postponement (**11**, **14**), without regard to whether or not the assembly, by either adopting or rejecting the same or related amendments or motions prior to the referral, had effectively voted against making such changes or taking such action. Likewise, when a committee reports on a motion referred to it—even if to the same meeting that made the referral—the assembly itself is free to consider any such amendments, or motions for definite or indefinite postponement, whether considered by the committee or not. (In all cases, however, any amendments actually pending at the time of referral are sent to the committee with the main motion, and, when the committee reports, they must be disposed of by the assembly before any additional amendments of the same degree may be considered; see 51:36–52.)

13:21   **Effect on Subsequent Debate and Methods of Voting.** If consideration of a referred question is resumed in the assembly on the same day on which it was referred, any members who have exhausted their right to debate (that is, those who have already spoken twice on the question that day, unless the assembly has a special rule providing otherwise) cannot speak on it again that

---

8. Such freedom of action as provided in this paragraph is not obtained, however, by informal consideration (13:3, 52:24–27).

day without permission of the assembly (by a two-thirds vote or unanimous consent; see **15**, **43**). Speeches made in committee of the whole, in quasi committee of the whole, or during informal consideration, however, do not count against a member's right to debate the same question when it is further considered by the assembly under the regular rules. When a question is referred to a committee, any orders limiting or extending the limits of debate (**15**) or for the *Previous Question* (**16**) are thereby exhausted, so that when the question is brought back from the committee, debate in the assembly takes place according to the regular rules, even if at the same session in which the motion to *Commit* was adopted. For the rules relating to the exhaustion of an order prescribing the method of voting on a question, see 30:7.

13:22 **Subsequent Instructions.** After a question has been referred to a committee and at any time before the committee submits its report, even at another session, the assembly by a majority vote can give the committee additional instructions in reference to the referred question (see also 13:8(d)).

13:23 **Vacancies in a Committee.** The power to appoint a committee includes the power to fill any vacancy that may arise in it. The resignation of a member of a committee should be addressed to the appointing power, and it is the responsibility of that power to fill the resulting vacancy (see also 47:57–58). Unless the bylaws or other governing rules provide otherwise (see 50:14, 62:16), the appointing authority has the power to remove or replace members of the committee: If a single person, such as the president, has the power of appointment, he has the power to remove or replace a member so appointed; but if the assembly has the power of selection, removal or replacement can take place only under rules applicable to the motions to *Rescind* or *Amend Something Previously Adopted* (see 50:14). Committee members are presumed to serve until their successors are appointed.

13:24   **Procedure When a Committee Reports.** For the procedure when a committee submits its report on a referred question, see **51**; see also 12:77–78.

Form and Example

13:25   The motion to *Commit* or *Refer* may be made in many forms. The following are typical: "I move to refer the motion to a committee"; "I move to recommit the resolution"; "I move that the motion be referred to the Social Committee"; "I move that the resolution be referred to a committee of three to be appointed by the chair" [or "nominated by the chair," or "elected from open nominations"]; "I move that the question be referred to the Executive Board with full power"; "I move to refer the resolution to a committee of seven, the chairman to be Mr. Brownley, six members to be elected by ballot from open nominations, and the committee to be instructed to report at the April meeting"; "I move that the Club now resolve itself into [or "go into"] a committee of the whole to consider the resolution"; "I move that the resolution be considered in quasi committee of the whole" [or "considered as if in committee of the whole"]; and "I move that the motion be considered informally."

13:26   Assume that a resolution is pending which, after debate, apparently requires careful amendment before the assembly will be willing to act on it. However, the assembly is pressed for time.

> **MEMBER A (obtaining the floor):** I move that the resolution be referred to a committee to be appointed by the chair. (Second.)
> **CHAIR:** It is moved and seconded that the resolution be referred to a committee to be appointed by the chair. [Pause.] Are you ready for the question? [No response.] How many members shall the committee consist of?
> **MEMBER B (obtaining the floor):** I move to amend the motion to commit by inserting after the word "committee" the words "of three." (Second.)

CHAIR: It is moved and seconded to amend the motion by inserting after the word "committee" the words "of three."

MEMBER C (obtaining the floor): I move to amend the amendment by striking out "three" and inserting "seven." (Second.)

CHAIR: If there is no objection, the chair suggests that the number of committee members be decided upon by the method of filling blanks. [Pause.] There is no objection and it is so ordered. It has been suggested that the committee be composed of seven and also three members. Are there additional suggestions?

MEMBER D (calling from his seat): I suggest five.

CHAIR: Five is also suggested. Are there other suggestions? [No response.] If not, the different numbers of members suggested for the proposed committee are seven, five, and three. These will be voted on in descending order. Those in favor of seven members, say *aye*. ... Those opposed, say *no*. ... The noes have it and the number seven is not adopted. Those in favor of five members, say *aye*. ... Those opposed, say *no*. ... The ayes have it and the number five is chosen for the committee membership. The question is now on the motion "to refer the resolution to a committee of five to be appointed by the chair." [Pause. No response.] Those in favor of referring the resolution to such a committee, say *aye*. ... Those opposed, say *no*. ... The ayes have it and the motion is adopted. The chair appoints Mr. Johnson as chairman, Dr. Donaldson, Mrs. Applegarth, Mr. Frank, Miss Dillon.

§14. POSTPONE TO A CERTAIN TIME (OR DEFINITELY)

14:1   The subsidiary motion to *Postpone to a Certain Time* (or *Postpone Definitely*, or *Postpone*) is the motion by which action on a pending question can be put off, within limits, to a definite session, day, meeting, or hour, or until after a certain event. (The expression "to defer" should be avoided, since it is often subject to vague usage.) This motion can be moved regardless of how much debate there has been on the motion it proposes to postpone. A question may be postponed either so that it may be considered at a more convenient time, or because debate has shown reasons for holding off a decision until later. This motion should not be confused with *Postpone Indefinitely*, which, as explained earlier (**11**), does not actually postpone the pending question, but kills it.

14:2   At the time when a postponed question is due to come up, there may be another question pending, or other business of a higher priority than the postponed question, that would delay its consideration, as fully explained in **41**. In its simple and usual form, the motion to postpone a question makes it a *general order*, which cannot interrupt pending business. To give the question being postponed a special type of priority that will enable it to interrupt the consideration of other business at the specified time, the motion to *Postpone* may, by a two-thirds vote, be adopted in a form that makes the question a *special order*. (See *Time at Which a Postponed Question Is Taken Up Again*, 14:13–17, and the illustrations under *Form and Example*, 14:20–22.)

14:3   When a motion proposes to postpone a matter that is not pending—for example, the hearing of a committee's report—such a motion is not the subsidiary motion to *Postpone*, but is an incidental main motion (**10**). If the effect would be to change action already taken by the assembly, as, for example, "to postpone for three weeks the dinner scheduled for October 15," such a motion is a particular case of the motion to *Amend Something Previously Adopted* (**35**).

Standard Descriptive Characteristics

14:4   The subsidiary motion to *Postpone to a Certain Time*:

1. Takes precedence over the main motion; over the subsidiary motions to *Postpone Indefinitely*, to *Amend*, and to *Commit*; and over the incidental motions for *Division of a Question* and for *Consideration by Paragraph or Seriatim*. It takes precedence over a debatable appeal that adheres to the

main question (or a point of order that adheres to the main question and has been referred by the chair to the judgment of the assembly and which is debatable when so referred, 23:2(5)), if no motions other than those named in the preceding sentence are pending or involved in the appeal or point of order; and it also takes precedence over a debatable nonadhering appeal or point of order to which it is applied. It takes precedence over a debatable motion to *Reconsider* when it is in order to apply it to that motion under the conditions stated in Standard Characteristic 2 below. It yields to the subsidiary motions to *Limit or Extend Limits of Debate*, for the *Previous Question*, or to *Lay on the Table*; to a motion to *Amend* that is applied to it; to all privileged motions; and to all applicable incidental motions.

2. Can be applied to main motions, with any motions to *Postpone Indefinitely*, *Amend*, or *Commit* or for *Division of a Question* or *Consideration by Paragraph or Seriatim* that may be pending; can be thus applied to *orders of the day* (14:13–17; **41**) or *questions of privilege* (**19**) while they are actually pending as main motions, and such an application is independent of, and does not affect, any other matter that they may have interrupted; can be applied to debatable appeals (or points of order referred by the chair to the judgment of the assembly that are debatable when so referred, 23:2(5)), but if such an appeal or point of order adheres (10:35) to the main question (that is, if it must be decided before the main question is decided), the motion to *Postpone* can be applied to the appeal or point of order only in connection with the main question, which is thus also postponed (see also 14:18); can be applied to nonadhering debatable appeals (or points of order submitted to the judgment of the assembly) separately, without affecting the status of any pending questions not involved in the appeal or point of order; and can be applied to an immediately pending, debatable motion to *Reconsider* (**37**) when it is in order to postpone the question or series of adhering

questions containing the motion(s) to be reconsidered, in which case all such questions and adhering motions are postponed with the motion to *Reconsider*. It cannot be applied to an undebatable appeal or to an undebatable motion to *Reconsider*; and it cannot be applied to any subsidiary motion, except that its application to a main question also affects any motions to *Postpone Indefinitely*, *Amend*, or *Commit* that may be pending, as noted above. It cannot be moved after the adoption of a motion to close debate on the main question at a definite hour or of a motion to limit the total time allowed for debate; but it remains in order if only a limitation on the length of speeches is in force (see **15**). Motions to *Amend*, to *Limit or Extend Limits of Debate*, and for the *Previous Question* can be applied to it without affecting the main question. The motion to *Postpone* cannot be laid on the table alone, but when it is pending the main question can be laid on the table, carrying to the table also the motion to *Postpone*. It cannot be postponed indefinitely or committed.

3. Is out of order when another has the floor.

4. Must be seconded.

5. Is debatable; but debate is limited in that it must not go into the merits of the main question any more than is necessary to enable the assembly to decide whether the main question should be postponed and to what time.

6. Is amendable as to the time to which the main question is to be postponed, and as to making the postponed question a *special order* (see 14:13–17; **41**).

7. Requires a majority vote in its simple and usual form. If (as originally moved or as a result of amendment) it makes a question a *special order*, however, the motion to *Postpone* then requires a two-thirds vote, because it suspends any rules that will interfere with the question's consideration at the time specified. An amendment to the motion to *Postpone* requires only a majority vote, even if it would add a provision to make the postponed question a special order

and would consequently change to two thirds the vote necessary for adoption of the motion to *Postpone*.

8. An affirmative vote on the motion to *Postpone* can be reconsidered. A negative vote on the motion to *Postpone* can be reconsidered only until such time as progress in business or debate has been sufficient to make it essentially a new question. Thereafter, the motion can be renewed (see 38:7).

Further Rules and Explanation

14:5 **Limits on Postponement and Their Relation to Meeting and Session.** Rules limiting the time to which a question can be postponed are related to the terms *meeting* and *session* (**8**), as follows:

14:6 In a case where more than a quarterly time interval (see 9:7) will elapse between meetings (for example, in an annual convention of delegates or in a local society that holds only an annual meeting), a question cannot be postponed beyond the end of the present session. In cases where no more than a quarterly time interval will elapse between sessions, a question can be postponed until, but not beyond, the next regular business session. For example, in a society that holds regular business meetings on the same day of each week, a question cannot, at one meeting, be postponed for longer than a week.

14:7 If it is desired to postpone a question to a time between regular meetings, it is necessary first to provide for an *adjourned meeting*, which is a continuation of the session scheduling it; then the question can be postponed to that meeting. If a motion to postpone a question to a regular meeting is already pending, the privileged motion to *Fix the Time to Which to Adjourn* (**22**) can be used to set an adjourned meeting, and the motion to *Postpone* can then be amended so that the proposed postponement will be to the adjourned meeting. Some societies have frequent sessions for social or cultural purposes at which business may be transacted, and also hold a session every month or quarter especially for business. In such societies these rules apply particularly to the regular business sessions, to which questions can be postponed from the previous regular business session or from any intervening meeting.

14:8   When the time to which a question has been postponed arrives and the question is taken up, it can be postponed again if the additional delay will not interfere with the proper handling of the postponed motion.

14:9   Neither the motion to *Postpone to a Certain Time* nor any amendment to it is in order if the effect would be the same as that of the motion to *Postpone Indefinitely*—that is, if it would kill the measure. For example, a motion to postpone until tomorrow a pending question of accepting an invitation to a banquet tonight cannot be recognized as a motion to *Postpone to a Certain Time*. The chair must either rule that this motion is not in order or, if the motion to *Postpone Indefinitely* is in order at the time, state the motion as such. The same would apply to a motion to postpone a question from one regular business session to the next in cases where the next business session will not be held within a quarterly time interval (see 9:7).

14:10   **Rule Against Postponement of a Class of Subjects.** As already noted, the subsidiary motion to *Postpone* can be applied only to a question that is actually pending; but an individual item of business that is not pending can, when appropriate, be postponed by means of a main motion.

14:11   It is not in order, either through a subsidiary motion or a main motion, to postpone a class of business composed of several items or subjects, such as reports of officers or reports of committees (see *Order of Business*, **41**); but each report can be postponed separately as it is announced or called for.[9] If it is desired to reach an item immediately but it falls at a later point in the regular order of business, the assembly, by a two-thirds vote or by unanimous consent (4:58–63), can adopt a motion to "suspend the rules and take up" the desired question or, equivalently, "to pass" one or more items or classes of

---

9. It should be noted that a similar rule applies to the subsidiary motion to *Lay on the Table* (see 17:3(2), 17:14, 41:38).

subjects in the order of business. After a question taken up out of its proper order by such a suspension of the rules has been disposed of, the regular order of business is resumed at the point where it was left off (see **25**).

14:12   **Postponement of a Subject That the Bylaws Set for a Particular Session.** A matter that the bylaws require to be attended to at a specified session, such as the election of officers, cannot, in advance and through a main motion, be postponed to another session. It can be taken up at any time when it is in order during the specified session (that is, either as originally convened or at any adjournment of it); and it can be postponed to an adjourned meeting in the manner explained above, after first adopting, if necessary, a motion to *Fix the Time to Which to Adjourn*. The adjourned meeting, as already stated, is a continuation of the same session. The procedure of postponing such a matter to an adjourned meeting is sometimes advisable, as in an annual meeting for the election of officers on a stormy night when, although a quorum is present, the attendance is abnormally small. If the matter has actually been taken up during the specified session as required, it also may be postponed beyond that session in accordance with the regular rules for the motion to *Postpone*. It is usually unwise to do so, however, unless completing it during the session proves impossible or impractical.

14:13   **Time at Which a Postponed Question Is Taken Up Again.** A postponed question becomes an *order of the day* for the session, day, meeting, or hour to which it is postponed. It cannot be taken up *before* the time for which it is set, except by reconsidering (**37**) the vote on the motion to *Postpone*, or by suspending the rules by a two-thirds vote. The postponed question is taken up either at the specified time or later, as follows:

14:14   Orders of the day consist of *general orders* and *special orders*. If the motion to *Postpone* does not make the postponed question a special order, it becomes a general order, which cannot interrupt pending business even if the time for which it is set has arrived or passed. By a two-thirds vote, however, a question can be postponed and made a special order, giving it priority over general orders as well as the ability to interrupt pending business. If it is desired to reserve an entire meeting—or as much of it as necessary—for the consideration of a single subject, a matter can be made *the* special order for a meeting (see 41:57).

14:15   When set for a session, day, or meeting but not for a particular hour, special orders and general orders usually have their established places in the order of business (see 41:18–26 and 41:46).

14:16   The full rules regarding the priority of orders of the day, and their relation to each other and to the order of business, are given in **41**.

14:17   When the appointed time has been reached for a postponed question to be taken up, and as soon as no other business of a higher priority interferes, the chair states the question as pending. (For examples, see 14:22, 41:19, and 41:24.) Therefore, no further motion is normally needed to bring the question before the assembly; however, if the chair fails to state the question at the correct time, any member may then demand that the postponed question be taken up as ordered, by making a *Call for the Orders of the Day* (**18**).

14:18   **Effect on Motions Adhering to a Postponed Question.** When a main motion is postponed, one or more of the subsidiary motions to *Postpone Indefinitely, Amend,* and *Commit* or incidental motions for *Division of a Question* and *Consideration by Paragraph or Seriatim* may be pending. All such adhering motions are postponed with the main question, and when consideration of that question is resumed at the specified time, the business is in the same condition, so far as possible, as it was immediately before the postponement, with the exceptions noted in the next paragraph. Similarly, when a main motion is postponed, it also carries with it any adhering debatable appeals (**24**) or adhering points of order (**23**) that the chair has submitted to the judgment of the assembly and that are then debatable. (No question can be postponed while an *undebatable* appeal or point of order is pending.)

14:19   **Effect on Subsequent Debate and Methods of Voting.** When consideration of a postponed question is resumed at a later session, any orders limiting or extending the limits of debate or for the *Previous Question* that were adopted at the original session are exhausted (see 15:18, 16:11–12), and debate takes place according to the regular rules. But when consideration is resumed at the *same* session—even on another day, as may happen in a convention—all such applicable orders remain in effect. Except for the effect of an unexhausted order limiting or closing debate as just stated, when a question is taken up *on a different day* from the one on which it was postponed, the right of members to debate it begins over again, as if the question had not previously been debated; that is, each member can again speak twice to each debatable question, regardless of whether the member had already done so before the postponement (see **43**). For the rules relating to the exhaustion of an order prescribing the method of voting on a question, see 30:7.

Form and Example

14:20   The form used in making this motion depends on the desired object:

a) Simply to postpone the question to the next meeting, when it will have priority over new business: "I move to postpone the motion [or "that the question be postponed"] to the next meeting."

b) To specify an hour before which the question will not be taken up (unless by a two-thirds vote or through reconsideration), and when it will come up automatically as soon as no business is pending and any remaining matters that have priority over it have been disposed of: "I move that the resolution be postponed until 3 P.M." [or "… until 9 P.M. at the meeting scheduled for February 15"].

c) To postpone consideration of a motion until after a certain event in a meeting, when it will immediately be taken up (unless a special order intervenes): "I move to postpone the question until after the address by our guest speaker."

d) To ensure that the question will come up at the next meeting and will not be crowded out by other matters: "I move that the question be postponed to the next meeting and be made a special order." (Two-thirds vote required for adoption.)

e) To ensure that the matter will come up at precisely a certain hour, even if it interrupts pending business: "I move that the resolution be postponed and be made a special order for 3 P.M. tomorrow." (Two-thirds vote required for adoption.)

f) To postpone a subject—such as a revision of the bylaws—to an adjourned meeting at which the entire time can be devoted to it if necessary, a motion to *Fix the Time to Which to Adjourn* must first be made and adopted, and then the motion to *Postpone* may be made in this form: "I move that the question be postponed and made *the* special order for the adjourned meeting set for next Tuesday evening." (Two-thirds vote required for adoption.)

14:21   Assume that a controversial resolution is pending at a convention and that many of the delegates who are most interested and best informed on the subject will not be able to be present until tomorrow.

MEMBER A (obtaining the floor): I move to postpone the resolution until eleven o'clock tomorrow morning. (Second.)

CHAIR: It is moved and seconded to postpone the resolution until eleven o'clock tomorrow morning. [Pause.]

MEMBER B (after obtaining the floor and stating that in his opinion further consideration of the resolution should under no circumstances be delayed *beyond* 11 A.M. the next day): I move to amend the motion to postpone, by adding "and make it a special order." (Second.)

CHAIR: It is moved and seconded to amend the motion to postpone the resolution until eleven o'clock tomorrow morning by adding "and make it a special order." [Debate, if any.] The question is on amending the motion to postpone by adding "and make it a special order." Those in favor of the amendment, say *aye*. … Those opposed, say *no*. … The ayes have it and the amendment is adopted. The question now is on the motion, as amended, to postpone the resolution until eleven o'clock tomorrow morning and make it a special order. This motion now requires a two-thirds vote. [Pause.] Are you ready for the question? [Pause. No further debate.] Those in favor of the motion to postpone the resolution until eleven o'clock tomorrow morning and make it a special order will rise. … Be seated. Those opposed, rise. … Be seated. There are two thirds in the affirmative and the motion is adopted. The resolution is a special order for 11 A.M. tomorrow. The next item of business is …

14:22   If the amendment to make a special order is rejected, the chair proceeds in the usual manner to take a voice vote on the *unamended* motion to postpone. If the motion to postpone is not adopted, he again states the question on the resolution. But if the resolution *has* been made a special order for the following day at 11 A.M., as in the above example, then at the appointed time the chair says:

> CHAIR: It is now eleven o'clock. The following resolution was made a special order for this time: "*Resolved*, That …" The question is on the adoption of the resolution. …

§15. LIMIT OR EXTEND LIMITS OF DEBATE

15:1   The subsidiary motion to *Limit or Extend Limits of Debate* is one of the two motions by means of which an assembly can exercise special control over debate on a pending question or on a series of pending questions. (The other motion serving such a purpose is the *Previous Question*, **16**. Neither of these motions is allowed in committees; see **50**.)

15:2   The motion to *Limit or Extend Limits of Debate* can *limit* debate by: (1) reducing the number or length of speeches permitted, without including specific provision for closing debate; or (2) requiring that, at a certain later hour or after debate for a specified length of time, debate shall be closed. It can *extend the limits* of debate by allowing more and longer speeches than under the regular rules (see 43:8–13). It cannot impose an immediate closing of debate, which requires a different motion—the *Previous Question.*

15:3   When an assembly adopts a motion to *Limit or Extend Limits of Debate*, it is said to adopt an "order" taking such action. (The word *order* as applied in this sense should not be confused with the technical terms *order of the day*, *general order*, and *special order* as used in **3**, **14**, and **41**.) When an order limiting or extending the limits of debate finally ceases to be in force as relates to all the motions it affected, the order is said to be "exhausted" (see 15:18).

15:4   If a motion proposing to change the regular limits of debate (for any length of time or during the consideration of one or more particular subjects) is made while no question is pending, such a motion is not the subsidiary motion to *Limit or Extend Limits of Debate*, but is an incidental main motion (although it requires a two-thirds vote for its adoption, just as the subsidiary motion does).

Standard Descriptive Characteristics

15:5   The subsidiary motion to *Limit or Extend Limits of Debate*:

1. Takes precedence over all debatable motions. It yields to the subsidiary motions for the *Previous Question* and to *Lay on the Table*; to a motion to *Amend* that is applied to it; to all privileged motions; and to all applicable incidental motions.

2. Can be applied to any immediately pending debatable motion, to an entire series of pending debatable motions, or to any consecutive part of such a series beginning with the immediately pending question. (It therefore can be made only while a debatable motion is immediately pending. If a

series of debatable questions is pending and an undebatable incidental motion is immediately pending, the latter must be disposed of before any motion to *Limit or Extend Limits of Debate* can be made.) Motions to *Amend* and (for the purpose of stopping amendment) the motion for the *Previous Question* can be applied to it without affecting the main question. The motion to *Limit or Extend Limits of Debate* cannot be laid on the table alone, but when it is pending the main question can be laid on the table, carrying to the table also the motion to *Limit or Extend Limits of Debate*.

3. Is out of order when another has the floor.

4. Must be seconded.

5. Is not debatable.

6. Is amendable, but any amendment, like the motion itself, is undebatable.

7. Requires a two-thirds vote—because it suspends the rules, and because limiting debate takes away the basic rights of all members to full discussion and may restrict a minority's right to present its case.

8. An affirmative vote on the motion to *Limit or Extend Limits of Debate* can be reconsidered, without debate, at any time before the order limiting or extending limits of debate is exhausted (see 15:18). If the order has been partially carried out, only the unexecuted part can be subject to reconsideration. A negative vote on the motion to *Limit or Extend Limits of Debate* can be reconsidered only until such time as progress in business or debate has been sufficient to make it essentially a new question. Thereafter, the motion can be renewed (see 38:7).

Further Rules and Explanation

15:6   **Effect on Pending and Subsequent Motions.** This motion's effect upon other pending and subsequent motions is closely related to its position in the order of precedence of motions (**5**) and further depends on the nature of its specific provisions, as explained below. Any relevant provisions can be included in the motion to

Limit or Extend Limits of Debate by its maker or, while the motion is pending, can be added or modified by amendment (**12**).

15:7   **Pending Motions to Which It Applies.** If, at the time the motion to *Limit or Extend Limits of Debate* is made, the immediately pending question is one among a consecutive series of pending debatable questions, the motion to *Limit or Extend Limits of Debate* can be applied, as noted in Standard Characteristic 2 above, to the immediately pending question, to any consecutive part of the series beginning with the immediately pending question, or to the entire series. If the motion does not specify to which of these questions it is to apply, then only the immediately pending question is affected.

15:8   **Subsequent Motions to Which It Applies.** Unless otherwise specified in the motion to *Limit or Extend Limits of Debate*, its effect on the debate of motions that may subsequently become pending is as follows: An order *limiting* debate applies not only to the motion(s) on which the limitation is ordered, but also to any debatable subsidiary motions, motions to *Reconsider*, or debatable appeals that may become pending *subsequently* while the order is in force. On the other hand, an order *extending limits* of debate—or one that both limits *and* extends the limits of debate, such as by limiting the length of each speech to two minutes while allowing each member to speak three times the same day on the question—applies only to the debate of the pending motion(s) on which it is ordered.

15:9   **Effect on the Making of Subsidiary Motions.** While a motion to *Limit or Extend Limits of Debate* is *pending*, its precedence prevents the making of subsidiary motions of lower rank (*Postpone Indefinitely, Amend, Commit, Postpone to a Certain Time*). After a limitation or extension on debate has been ordered, however, its effect on which subsidiary motions can be made depends on the particular form in which the order was made.

15:10   *Limitations (or extensions) that do not close debate.* If the limitation or extension that has been ordered does not provide for *closing* debate—for example, if the order was "that debate be limited to one speech of five minutes for each member," as in *Form and Example* (a) below—it has no effect on what subsidiary motions can be made.

15:11   **Limitations that close debate on the main motion.** After the adoption of an order that does provide a time for closing debate on the main question—either at a specified hour or after debate for a specified length of time, as in *Form and Example* (b) or (f) below—motions to *Commit* or to *Postpone to a Certain Time* are not in order, since providing a time for closing debate implies that at that time the question will be voted on.[10] If the assembly decides, while the order is in effect, that it wishes to commit or postpone the main motion, then it may reconsider (**37**) and reverse the vote establishing the order or, by a two-thirds vote, it may adopt a new limitation or extension of debate that has no such restriction. If motions to *Commit* or to *Postpone* were already part of a series that was pending when such an order was adopted, however, the remaining questions may be postponed or committed at the time those motions come to a vote.

15:12   When the allotted time under such an order has expired, no further debate on any pending question is allowed, no further amendments or subsidiary motions other than *Lay on the Table* (or a superseding motion to *Limit or Extend Limits of Debate;* see below) can be offered, and all pending questions are voted on immediately. In making an order that provides a time for closing debate on the main motion, sometimes it is specified that the question shall be put at that time, although the effect is the same whether or not this is explicitly provided.

15:13   **Limitations that close debate on the main motion without limiting the making of subsidiary motions.** If the assembly wishes only to limit the time devoted to the question without preventing motions to *Commit* or *Postpone* from being made during that

---

10. Under an order that provides a time for closing debate on a secondary motion or a consecutive series of secondary motions without affecting the main motion, this restriction does not apply.

time, the order can specify, for example, "that debate on the pending resolution be limited to twenty minutes, during which time all applicable secondary motions shall remain in order."

15:14   *Other limitations or extensions.* If it is desired to order a limitation or extension of debate whose effect is other than as described above, this can be specified in the order, such as in *Form and Example* (e) below.

15:15   **Interruptions While It Is in Effect.** Regardless of the form of an order to limit or extend the limits of debate, the main question and any adhering motions can be laid on the table while the order is in effect.

15:16   It should be noted that there can be a significant difference in effect between (a) an order that closes debate at a particular hour and (b) one that limits debate to a specified length of time. In the first case, if consideration of the question to which the order applies is interrupted, such as by the question's being laid on the table, and is resumed after the specified hour has passed (but during the same session, so that the order has not been exhausted; see below), no further debate is allowed. In the second case, however, any time consumed while the question is lying on the table, or during other interruptions unrelated to the question to which the order applies (such as consideration of orders of the day (**18**, **41**) or unrelated questions of privilege (**19**)), does not diminish the amount of time allowed for debate on the question.

15:17   **Adoption of a Superseding Limitation or Extension.** Unlike the case of main motions and lower-ranking subsidiary motions (*Postpone Indefinitely, Amend, Commit, Postpone*), the adoption of one motion limiting or extending debate in a certain way does not prevent another such conflicting motion from being in order. A motion to set different limitation(s) or extension(s), or to change from one to the other, or to order the *Previous Question* (**16**), can be made at any time that it is in order under the order of precedence of motions, until the pending questions affected have been finally disposed of. The reason is that the two-thirds vote necessary for the adoption of any motion to modify the limits of debate also fulfills the requirement for suspending the rules (**25**).

15:18 **Conditions for Exhaustion of Its Effect.** An order limiting or extending limits of debate is *exhausted* (that is, no longer applies): (1) when all of the questions on which it was imposed have been voted on; (2) when those questions affected by the order and not yet voted on have been either referred to a committee or postponed indefinitely; or (3) at the conclusion of the session in which the order was adopted—whichever occurs first. If any of the questions to which the order applies are postponed definitely or laid on the table, and are taken up again later during the same session, the unexecuted part of the order remains in effect. Any questions affected by an order modifying limits of debate that in any way go over to the next session—or that are referred to a committee and reported back, even in the same session in which committed—become open to debate under the regular rules. An order limiting or extending limits of debate applies to reconsiderations of the affected questions before, but not after, exhaustion of the order.

Form and Example

15:19 The forms in which this motion may be made depend on the desired object, as follows:

a) To reduce or increase the number or length of speeches: "I move that debate be limited to one speech of five minutes for each member"; or "… that Mr. Lee's time be extended three minutes"; or "I ask unanimous consent that Mr. Lee's time …" (see 4:58–63).

b) To provide a time for closing debate on the main question and taking the vote on all pending questions: "I move that at 9 P.M. [or "after twenty minutes"] debate on the resolution be closed." (Under such a limitation, motions to

Commit or *Postpone to a Certain Time* will no longer be in order.)

c) To limit time spent in debate on a secondary motion, such as an amendment: "I move that debate on the pending amendment be limited to twenty minutes."

d) To limit the time devoted to the question without preventing motions to *Commit* or *Postpone* from being made during that time: "I move that debate on the pending resolution be limited to twenty minutes, during which time all applicable secondary motions shall remain in order."

e) To fix the hour for closing debate without cutting off further amendments: "I move that debate on the pending resolution be closed at 5 P.M., after which time members may continue to offer amendments, which shall then be undebatable."

f) To combine several of the above objects: "I move that _____ and _____ [the leaders on the two sides] each be allowed twenty minutes, which may be divided between two speeches, and that other members be limited to one speech of two minutes each, provided that all pending questions shall be put to a vote at 4 P.M." (see also example in 59:82).

15:20   The form of *stating* the question on this amendable but undebatable motion is:

> **CHAIR:** It is moved and seconded that no later than 9 P.M. debate be closed and the question on the resolution be put. The motion to limit or extend limits of debate is not debatable, but it can be amended. [Pause.] Are you ready for the question on [or, "Are there any amendments to"] the motion to limit debate?

The words at the end of the last sentence, "the motion to limit debate," can be modified to suit the particular form in which the motion was made.

15:21   Unless the motion to *Limit or Extend Limits of Debate* is adopted by unanimous consent (4:58–63), the chair puts it to a vote taken by rising, as in the example shown for a motion to postpone a question and make it a special order, in 14:21. In announcing the result, the chair states the parliamentary situation as it then exists:

> CHAIR (after taking a rising vote): There are two thirds in the affirmative and the motion is adopted. The resolution will therefore be put to a vote no later than 9 P.M. and debate cannot continue beyond that hour. The question is on [stating the immediately pending question].

§16. PREVIOUS QUESTION

(Immediately to close debate and the making of subsidiary motions except the motion to Lay on the Table)

16:1   The *Previous Question* is the motion used to bring the assembly to an immediate vote on one or more pending questions; its adoption does this with certain exceptions.

16:2   Adopting or "ordering" the *Previous Question*:

1) immediately closes debate on, and stops amendment of, the immediately pending question and such other pending questions as the motion may specify (in consecutive series; see Standard Characteristic 2); and

2) prevents the making of any other subsidiary motions except the higher-ranking (**5**) *Lay on the Table*.[11]

The adoption of an order for the *Previous Question* does not prevent the making of privileged or incidental motions (**6**) as applicable, and, strictly speaking, it does not prevent a special order set for a particular hour (**14, 41**) from interrupting the pending business (see also **16:10**).

---

11. In practice it is seldom appropriate to move to lay a pending question or series of questions on the table after the *Previous Question* has been ordered on them; but a legitimate need to do so may sometimes arise, particularly in a large assembly if the vote(s) are to be taken by a method such as by ballot, standing for a count, or roll call (see also **45**, and *Misuses of the Motion to Lay on the Table*, 17:13–16).

16:3　　The motion for the *Previous Question* has nothing to do with the last question previously considered by the assembly and has a long history of gradually changing purpose.

16:4　　The *Previous Question* is not allowed in committees (**50**).

Standard Descriptive Characteristics

16:5　　The subsidiary motion for the *Previous Question*:

1. Takes precedence over all debatable or amendable motions to which it is applied, and over the subsidiary motion to *Limit or Extend Limits of Debate*; and, if adopted, it supersedes the effect of an unexhausted order limiting or extending debate, with respect to the motions to which it is applied. It yields to the subsidiary motion to *Lay on the Table*, to all privileged motions, and to all applicable incidental motions.

2. Can be applied to any immediately pending debatable or amendable motion; to an entire series of pending debatable or amendable motions; and to any consecutive part of such a series, beginning with the immediately pending question. (Under this rule it can be applied to motions that are amendable but not debatable,[12] for the purpose of stopping amendment; see page t47.) It supersedes any earlier order for the closing of debate at a future time and can be applied while such an order is in effect. In practice, this motion usually is made in an unqualified form, such as "I move the previous question," and then it applies only to the immediately pending question. In its qualified form, however, it can be applied to include consecutively any series beginning with the immediately pending question. For example, the following motions might be pending: (a) a resolution; (b) an amendment to the resolution; (c) a motion to refer the resolution and its pending amendment to a committee; and (d) an immediately pending motion to postpone all of these questions to a definite time. In this case, an unqualified motion for the *Previous Question* will apply only to (d). Such a

---

12. An example of such a motion is the motion to *Limit or Extend Limits of Debate* (**15**).

motion can be qualified to apply to (d) and (c); to (d), (c), and (b); or to (d), (c), (b), and (a). It cannot include only (d) and (b); only (d), (b), and (a); only (d), (c), and (a); or only (d) and (a); and no motion for the *Previous Question* excluding the immediately pending question (d) can be made until (d) has been voted on. No subsidiary motion can be applied to the *Previous Question*, except that when it is pending the main question can be laid on the table, carrying to the table also all adhering motions, including the motion for the *Previous Question*.

3. Is out of order when another has the floor.
4. Must be seconded.
5. Is not debatable.
6. Is not amendable. However, it has a special characteristic that permits an effect similar to amendment when the motion is applied while a series of questions is pending. When a motion for the *Previous Question* is immediately pending in such a case, it can be made again with more or fewer pending questions included (subject to the restrictions shown in Standard Characteristic 2, above), *before* the first motion for the *Previous Question* is voted on. The procedure resembles filling blanks (see 12:92–113) except that each of the motions must be made by a member who has obtained the floor, and each must be seconded.[13] For example, if one member has made this motion in the unqualified form when a series of questions is pending (so that it would apply only to the question immediately pending at that time), another member can move it on part of the series and still another can move it on *all* pending questions. The vote is taken first on the motion that would order the *Previous Question* on the largest number of motions; if this fails, then on the next smaller number, and so on, until one is adopted (by a two-thirds vote), or until all of the motions for the *Previous Question* are rejected.

---

13. For the form to be followed by the chair in granting limited recognition to a member who seeks the floor at such a time, see 16:27.

7. Requires a two-thirds vote. (If a motion for the *Previous Question* fails to gain the necessary two-thirds vote, debate continues as if this motion had not been made.) In ordinary bodies, the requirement of a two-thirds vote for ordering the *Previous Question* is important in protecting the democratic process. If this rule were not observed, a temporary majority of only one vote could deny the remaining members all opportunity to discuss any measure that such a majority wished to adopt or kill.[14]

8. An affirmative vote on the motion for the *Previous Question* can be reconsidered before any vote has been taken under the order for the *Previous Question*, but (in contrast to the motion to *Limit or Extend Limits of Debate*) it cannot be reconsidered after the order has been partly executed;[15] see also 16:13–16. A negative vote on the motion for the *Previous Question* can be reconsidered only until such time as progress in business or debate has been sufficient to make it essentially a new question—that is, only until such time as it is reasonable to assume that debate or action on any of the motions involved may have made more members desire to vote immediately on some or all of the questions still pending. Thereafter, it can be renewed (see 38:7).

---

14. Although the rules of the United States House of Representatives permit the *Previous Question* to be ordered by a majority vote, there are differences between the conditions in that body and in the ordinary organization that should be understood. Because of another House rule, an order for the *Previous Question* does not actually bring a measure to an immediate vote in Congress unless it has already been debated. If no discussion of the measure has taken place on the floor of the House, forty minutes' debate is allowed after adoption of the *Previous Question*—twenty minutes for each of the opposing sides. These rules derive from the great volume of business and the fact that under the two-party system of government by elected representatives, opposing sides often become nearly equal. At the same time, this system creates special conditions that make it unlikely that there will be unfair use of the power to curtail debate. The United States Senate does not admit the *Previous Question*, although it permits debate to be limited by means of a motion for cloture.

15. When the *Previous Question* has been ordered on a number of motions, the order is said to be partly executed (or partly carried out) if one or more, but not all, of these motions have been voted on. When all of the motions specified in the order have been voted on, it is fully executed.

Further Rules and Explanation

16:6 **Equal Application of Rules to Nonstandard Forms Such as "Call for the Question."** A motion such as "I call for [or "call"] the question," "I demand the previous question," "I move to close [or "end"] debate," or "I move we vote now" is simply a motion for the *Previous Question* made in nonstandard form, and it is subject to all of the rules in this section. Care should be taken that failure to understand this fact does not lead to violation of members' rights of debate.

16:7 Sometimes the mere making of a motion for the *Previous Question* or "call for the question" may motivate unanimous consent to ending debate. Before or after such a motion has been seconded, the chair may ask if there is any objection to closing debate. If member(s) object or try to get the floor, he must ask if there is a second to the motion or call; or, if it has already been seconded, he must immediately take a vote on *whether to order* the *Previous Question*. But *regardless of the wording of a motion or "call" seeking to close debate, it always requires a second and a two-thirds vote, taken separately from and before the vote(s) on the motion(s) to which it is applied, to shut off debate against the will of even one member who wishes to speak and has not exhausted his right to debate* (see 4:32, 43:8–13).

16:8 **Exemption of Undebated Preamble from the Previous Question Unless Separately Ordered.** When a resolution having a preamble (one or more explanatory clauses beginning "Whereas, …") is pending, if the *Previous Question* is ordered on the resolution before consideration of the preamble has been reached (10:16ff., 12:23, 28:7), the order does not apply to debate and amendment of the preamble, to which the assembly proceeds before voting on the resolution. After the chair has declared the preamble open to debate and amendment in such a case, the entire resolution can be brought to an immediate vote, if desired, by then ordering the *Previous Question* on the preamble.

16:9   **Voting on a Series of Motions Under the Previous Question; Interruption of Execution.** When the *Previous Question* is ordered on a series of pending motions as explained above under Standard Characteristic 2, they are voted on in order of rank beginning with the immediately pending question—that is, in reverse of the order in which they were made. If the series includes motions to *Postpone Definitely*, to *Commit*, or to *Postpone Indefinitely* and one of these motions is adopted, further voting stops—regardless of how many of the remaining questions were, or were not, included under the order for the *Previous Question*. But if voting is not stopped in such a manner, then, when all of the motions on which the *Previous Question* was ordered have been voted on, consideration of any questions still pending resumes under the regular rules.

16:10   If a question or series of questions (including motions on which the *Previous Question* has been ordered) *ceases to be the pending business* before all of the motions affected by the order have been voted on, *execution* of the order is said to be *interrupted*. Interruption of the execution of an order for the *Previous Question* may occur as follows:

- If a motion to *Postpone*, to *Commit*, or to *Postpone Indefinitely* on which the *Previous Question* has been ordered is adopted (as in the preceding paragraph) in a case where one or more of the remaining questions *were also included* under the order, execution of the order is thus *interrupted after it has been partly carried out.*

- *Before or after* an order for the *Previous Question* has been *partly carried out*, as already noted, it is also possible for its execution to be interrupted as a result of the question(s)'s being laid on the table, or by the intervention of a special order set for a particular hour (**14, 41**), a question of privilege (**19**), a recess (**8, 20**), or an adjournment (**8, 21**). (If the hour set for a special order, a recess, or an adjournment has arrived and the *Previous Question* has been ordered on one or more pending motions, however, there usually will be no objection to the chair's putting them all to a vote in succession before he announces the matter that intervenes.)

16:11 **Exhaustion of the Previous Question.** The *Previous Question* is said to be *exhausted* (in reference to a particular order for it) when all of the motions on which it was ordered have been finally disposed of, or when any motions not yet finally disposed of are no longer affected by the order. The conditions for exhaustion of the *Previous Question* are the same as for an order limiting or extending limits of debate—that is: (1) when all motions on which the *Previous Question* was ordered have been voted on; (2) when those not yet voted on have either been committed or postponed indefinitely; or (3) at the end of the session in which the *Previous Question* was ordered—whichever occurs first. After the *Previous Question* is exhausted, any remaining questions that come up again are open to debate and amendment just as if there had been no order for the *Previous Question*.

16:12 If the execution of an order for the *Previous Question* is interrupted and if the motion or motions that were pending come up again later, the rules in the foregoing paragraph apply as follows:

- If the questions were *referred to a committee* and are later reported, the *Previous Question* is *exhausted* and the motions are open to debate and amendment, even if it is during the same session.
- But if the interruption of execution occurred by any *other means than referral* and the questions come up again during the *same session*, the order *remains in effect*; all motions on which the *Previous Question* was ordered must be voted on immediately (unless a reconsideration of the order is possible and a motion to reconsider it has been made, or is then made; see below).
- If the questions do not come up again until a *later session*, the *Previous Question* is *always exhausted*, regardless of how the interruption of execution occurred.

16:13   **Reconsideration of a Vote That Has Ordered the Previous Question.** As noted in Standard Characteristic 8, a vote that has ordered the *Previous Question* can be reconsidered before, but not after, any of the motions affected by the order have been voted on. Consequently, it will frequently happen that a motion to reconsider an affirmative vote on the *Previous Question* itself can be made only in the brief moment after the vote ordering the *Previous Question* is completed and before the first vote is taken under the order.

16:14   If the execution of an order for the *Previous Question* was interrupted before any vote was taken under the order, and if the questions come up again during the same session, a motion to reconsider the order (if not made earlier) can be made only in the moment after the chair has announced these questions as the pending business and before any of them are voted on. In addition, the regular time limits for making a motion to *Reconsider* apply (see **37**).

16:15   It should be noted that if a motion or series of motions that is under an order for the *Previous Question* comes up after having been *postponed*, there can never be a reconsideration of the order. The reason is that the motion to *Postpone* can only have been made before the *Previous Question* was ordered, so that the order for the *Previous Question* will always have been partly executed by the vote that caused the postponement.

16:16   In practice, if a motion to reconsider an affirmative vote on the *Previous Question* prevails, the vote that adopted the motion to *Reconsider* is also presumed to have carried out the reconsideration and to have reversed the vote that is reconsidered. That is, the *Previous Question* is now presumed to be rejected and is not voted on again, for this reason: in such a case, only members opposed to the *Previous Question* would vote to reconsider it after it had been adopted; consequently, if a majority have voted for reconsideration, it will be impossible to obtain a two-thirds vote in favor of the *Previous Question*.

16:17   **Reconsideration of a Vote While the Previous Question Is in Effect.** An order for the *Previous Question* does not prevent the making of a motion to *Reconsider*, nor does it prevent the assembly from taking up a motion to *Reconsider* that was made either before or after the *Previous Question* was ordered. Whether or not debate is in order during reconsideration depends on when the reconsideration takes place. If a motion to *Reconsider* becomes pending while the *Previous Question* is in effect, the motion to *Reconsider* is undebatable and the motion to be reconsidered cannot be debated or amended. But if the reconsideration occurs after the *Previous Question* is exhausted, the motion to *Reconsider* and the question to be reconsidered are no longer affected by the *Previous Question*.

16:18   **Effect on Appeals.** An appeal is undebatable if it is made after the *Previous Question* has been moved or ordered and before the order is exhausted.

16:19   **Effect on Subsequent Motions Generally.** The general rules as to the effect of an unexhausted order for the *Previous Question* on subsequent motions that would normally be debatable or amendable are as follows:

- While one or more *motions on which the Previous Question has been ordered remain pending*, the order also applies to any other motions that may take precedence over these pending questions. (The rules stated in the two preceding paragraphs—relating to reconsiderations and appeals—are applications of this principle.)
- But if a *question of privilege* is raised and is admitted for immediate consideration (see **19**), or if a special order set for a particular hour intervenes, these questions are independent of an unexhausted order for the *Previous Question* applying to business that they interrupt.

Form and Example

16:20   The forms used in making this motion include: "I move the previous question" (to apply only to the immediately pending question); "I move [or "call for"] the previous question on the motion to commit and its amendment"; "I move the previous question on all pending questions"; and so on. Calls of "Question!" by members from their seats are not motions for the *Previous Question* and are disorderly if another member is speaking or seeking recognition.

16:21   In stating the question on this undebatable, unamendable motion, the chair does not pause or ask, "Are you ready for the question?" but *puts* the question for a rising vote on the motion for the *Previous Question* immediately, as shown below. Similarly, in announcing an affirmative result, he at once states the question on the motion that is then immediately pending.

16:22   As a first example, assume that a series of several debatable and amendable motions is pending.

> **MEMBER A (obtaining the floor):** I move the previous question [or, if it is desired that the order affect more than just the immediately pending question, "I move the previous question on … ," specifying the motions]. (Second.)
> **CHAIR:** The previous question is moved and seconded on [naming the motions].

16:23   If the assembly is not familiar with the use of the *Previous Question*, the chair should at this point explain it. In any case, the chair then proceeds to take the vote:

> **CHAIR:** Those in favor of ordering the previous question on [repeating the motion or motions], rise. … Be seated. Those opposed, rise. … Be seated.

16:24   Assume two thirds vote in favor of the *Previous Question*. The result is announced as follows:

> **CHAIR:** There are two thirds in the affirmative and the previous question is ordered on [naming again the motions to which

the order applies]. The question is now on the adoption of the motion to … [stating in full the immediately pending question]. Those in favor … [and so on, putting to vote in proper sequence all motions on which the *Previous Question* has been ordered].

16:25   If less than two thirds vote in the affirmative, the chair announces the result of the vote on the motion for the *Previous Question* as follows:

> CHAIR: There are less than two thirds in the affirmative and the motion for the previous question is lost. The question is now on … [stating the question on the immediately pending motion]. Debate may now resume. [The chair does not say, "Are you ready for the question?" here, since the assembly has just shown that it is not ready.]

16:26   The following example shows the forms used in handling alternative motions for the *Previous Question* that specify different numbers of pending questions in a series, as described under Standard Characteristic 6.

16:27   Assume that a resolution, an amendment to the resolution, and a motion to *Commit* are pending (in which case the motion to *Commit* is the immediately pending question).

> MEMBER X (obtaining the floor): I move the previous question. (Second.) [In this case only the motion to *Commit* is affected.]
> CHAIR: The previous question is moved and seconded on the motion to commit. Those in favor of ordering …
> MEMBER Y (quickly rising and interrupting the chair): Mr. President.
> CHAIR: For what purpose does the member rise?
> MEMBER Y: I move the previous question on all pending questions. (Second.)
> CHAIR: The previous question is also moved on all pending questions. The question is now on the motion for the previous question on all pending questions. Those …
> MEMBER Z (quickly rising): Mr. President.
> CHAIR: For what purpose does the member rise?

> **MEMBER Z:** I move the previous question on the motion to commit and on the amendment to the resolution. (Second.)
>
> **CHAIR:** The previous question is also moved and seconded on the motion to commit and on the amendment to the resolution. The question is first, however, on the motion to order the previous question on all pending questions. Those in favor of ordering … [and so on. Alternative motions for the *Previous Question* are voted on in order beginning with the one that would apply to the largest number of pending questions. Therefore, after admitting Member Y's motion, the chair starts to put the question on it first; but after admitting Member Z's, he returns to taking a vote on Member Y's. If one of these motions for the *Previous Question* is adopted, any remaining ones are ignored.]

16:28   If a member wishes to make a higher-ranking motion or to move a reconsideration while a motion for the *Previous Question* is pending or after the *Previous Question* has been ordered, he seeks limited recognition by rising and interrupting the chair just as in the example above.

§17. LAY ON THE TABLE

(To interrupt the pending business so as to permit doing something else immediately)

17:1   The motion to *Lay on the Table* enables the assembly to lay the pending question aside temporarily when something else of immediate urgency has arisen or when something else needs to be addressed before consideration of the pending question is resumed, in such a way that:

- there is *no set time* for taking the matter up again;
- but (until the expiration of time limits explained in 17:8) its consideration *can be resumed at the will of a majority* and in preference to any new questions that may then be competing with it for consideration.

This motion is commonly misused in ordinary assemblies—in place of a motion to *Postpone Indefinitely* (**11**), a motion to

Postpone to a Certain Time (**14**), or other motions. Particularly in such misuses, it also is known as a motion "to table."

17:2   By adopting the motion to *Lay on the Table*, a majority has the power to halt consideration of a question immediately without debate. Such action violates the rights of the minority and individual members if it is for any other purpose than the one stated in the first sentence of this section. In ordinary assemblies, the motion to *Lay on the Table* is not in order if the evident intent is to kill or avoid dealing with a measure. If a time for resuming consideration is specified in making the motion, it can be admitted only as a motion to *Postpone* (**14**), in which case it is debatable (see also 17:13–19).

Standard Descriptive Characteristics

17:3   The subsidiary motion to *Lay on the Table*:

1. Takes precedence over the main motion, over all other subsidiary motions, and over any incidental motions that are pending when it is made. It yields to all privileged motions, and to motions that are incidental to itself.

2. Can be applied to main motions, with any other subsidiary motions that may be pending; can be thus applied to *orders of the day* (**14**, **41**) or *questions of privilege* (**19**) while they are actually pending as main motions, and such an application is independent of, and does not carry to the table, any other matter that they may have interrupted; can be separately applied to debatable appeals that do not adhere (10:35) to the main question (or to nonadhering points of order referred by the chair to the judgment of the assembly that are debatable when so referred), and this application has no effect on the status of any other questions that may be pending; can be applied to adhering appeals—whether debatable or undebatable—only by laying the main question on the table, in which case the appeal and all other adhering motions go to the table also; and can be applied to an immediately pending motion to *Reconsider* (**37**), whenever *Lay on the Table* would

be applicable if the motion to be reconsidered were immediately pending, and in such a case, it carries to the table also the motion to be reconsidered, or the series of questions adhering to the latter motion. It cannot be applied to an undebatable appeal that does not adhere to the main question; and it cannot be applied to any subsidiary motion except in connection with application to the main question. No motion or motions can be laid on the table apart from motions which adhere to them, or to which they adhere; and if any one of them is laid on the table, all such motions go to the table together. The motion to *Lay on the Table* can be made while an order limiting debate or an order for the *Previous Question* is in force (see also below). No subsidiary motion can be applied to the motion to *Lay on the Table*.

Since the motion to *Lay on the Table* can be applied *only* to a question that is actually *pending*, a class or group of main questions such as orders of the day, unfinished business, or committee reports *cannot be laid on the table as a unit*. (An item of business can be reached in such a case, however, by methods that are explained in 17:14 and 41:38.)

3. Is out of order when another has the floor.
4. Must be seconded.
5. Is not debatable. It is proper for, and the chair can ask, the maker of this motion to state his reason first, however, as: "Our speaker must catch an early flight," or "Laying this question aside temporarily will ensure adequate time to consider the next item of business, which must be decided at this meeting." (The urgency and the legitimate intent of the motion can thus be established; but mentioning its purpose imposes no requirement as to when or whether the assembly will take the question from the table. An essential feature of this motion is that it cannot be qualified in any way and that, so long as the question remains on the table, the decision as to when—or if—it will be taken up is left open. For the limitations on the length of time that a question can lie on the table, see 17:8.)

6. Is not amendable.

7. Requires a majority vote.

8. An affirmative vote on the motion to *Lay on the Table* cannot be reconsidered, because it is easier and more direct to move to take the question from the table (see below). A negative vote on the motion to *Lay on the Table* can be reconsidered only until such time as the motion can be renewed. As explained in 17:11, renewal of the motion to *Lay on the Table* is permitted only when either (a) progress in business or debate has been sufficient to make it essentially a new question, or (b) something urgent has arisen that was not known when the assembly rejected this motion; see 38:7.

Further Rules and Explanation

17:4 **Laying a Question on the Table and Taking It from the Table.** Rules affecting the motion to *Lay on the Table* are closely related to the motion to *Take from the Table* (**34**), as follows:

17:5 Adopting a motion to *Lay on the Table* places on the table—that is, in the care of the secretary—the pending question and everything adhering to it. Thus, if a resolution with a proposed amendment and a motion to *Commit* are pending and the resolution is laid on the table, all of these questions go to the table at the same time and, if taken from the table, all will return together. (But a proposed amendment to anything previously adopted—existing bylaws, for example—is a main motion and when laid on the table does not carry with it what it proposes to amend.)

17:6 After a question has been laid on the table, it can be taken from the table by a majority vote as soon as the interrupting business is disposed of—or at some later time before the limits for taking it from the table have expired (see below)—whenever no question is pending, provided that business of the same class as the question on the table, or unfinished business, general orders, or new business, is in order.

17:7 When a question is taken from the table, everything is in the same condition, so far as possible, as it was when laid on the table, except as the rules relating to amendment, debate, and voting may be affected when the question is taken up on another day or at a later session, as noted in **34** (see *Status of a Question Taken from the Table*, 34:6–7).

17:8   A question that has been laid on the table remains there and can be taken from the table during the same session (**8**), or, if the next regular business session will be held before a quarterly time interval has elapsed (see 9:7), also until the end of the next regular session. If not taken from the table within these time limits, the question dies, although it can be reintroduced later as a new question. (For additional rules regarding the meetings at which a question can be taken from the table, see *Time Limits on Taking a Question from the Table*, 34:3.)

17:9   **Status of a Question Lying on the Table.** Since a motion that has been laid on the table is still *within the control of the assembly* (38:8), no other motion on the same subject is in order that would either conflict with, or present substantially the same question as, the motion that is lying on the table. To consider another motion on the same subject, it is necessary first to take the question from the table and then to move the new proposal as a substitute, or to make whatever other motion is appropriate to the case.

17:10   **Additional Steps That May Be Required When Laying a Question on the Table.** Laying a question on the table with the idea of attending to something else does not suspend any rules or set aside an order of business that may interfere with doing the thing desired at the time. Taking up the desired business may require an additional motion after the question has been laid on the table (see *Suspend the Rules*, **25**; *Taking Up Business out of Its Proper Order*, 41:37–39).

17:11   **Renewal of the Motion to Lay on the Table; Laying a Question on the Table Again.** A motion to *Lay on the Table* that has been voted down can be renewed, or a question that has been taken from the table can be laid on the table again, subject to the following condition in either case: A motion made the same day to lay the same question on the table is in order only after material progress in business or debate has been made, or when an unforeseen urgent matter requires immediate attention. (This rule is a consequence of the fact that the rejection of a motion to *Lay on the Table* or the taking of a question from the table means that the assembly wishes to consider the matter at that time.) Motions to *Recess* (**20**) or to *Adjourn* (**21**) that have been made and lost do not justify a new motion to lay the same question on the table, but the renewal might be justified after a vote on an important amendment or on a motion to *Commit*.

17:12 **Laying the Pending Questions on the Table After Debate Has Been Closed.** If debate has been closed by ordering the *Previous Question* or by the expiration of the time to which debate was limited, then up until the moment of taking the last vote under the order, the questions still before the assembly can be laid on the table. Thus, while a resolution and an amendment are pending, if the *Previous Question* is ordered on both motions, it is in order to lay the resolution on the table, carrying with it the adhering amendment. If the amendment had already been voted on, it would likewise have been in order to lay the resolution on the table.

17:13 **Misuses of the Motion.** As stated at the beginning of this section, the motion to *Lay on the Table* is subject to a number of incorrect uses that must be avoided.[16]

---

16. Some misuses of the motion to *Lay on the Table* probably arise from a misunderstanding of the practice of the United States House of Representatives, where this motion has gradually become converted to a special purpose that is not applicable in ordinary assemblies. The press of legislation in the House is so great that only a fraction of the bills introduced each year can be considered. With this volume of work under the two-party system in such a large body, the majority must be given power to suppress a measure without debate, and the agenda must be tightly regulated. The House rules therefore do not allow a question to be taken from the table without first suspending the rules by a two-thirds vote. Consequently, when a matter is laid on the table in the House it is virtually killed.

17:14   It is not in order to move to lay a pending question on the table if there is evidently no other matter requiring immediate attention. However, if members who command a majority wish to bring up a measure out of its order but lack the two thirds required to suspend the rules to do so, they may lay each intervening matter on the table in succession, until the desired matter is reached. This is proper because their evident object is not to suppress without debate the items laid on the table, but instead to advance consideration of something they consider more urgent. (See also 41:38.) At a special meeting, it is dilatory (**39**) and not in order to move to lay on the table the matter for which the meeting has been called.

17:15   The motion to *Lay on the Table* is often incorrectly used and wrongly admitted as in order with the intention of either killing an embarrassing question without a direct vote, or of suppressing a question without debate. The first of these two uses is unsafe if there is any contest on the issue; the second is in violation of the fundamental principle of parliamentary law that only a two-thirds vote can rightfully suppress a main question without allowing free debate.

17:16   If the majority were to lay a question on the table, erroneously supposing that it thereby becomes dead, some of those who voted with the majority might leave before the time of final adjournment and the minority might all stay. The real minority might thus become a temporary majority, take the question from the table, and act upon it in the absence of many interested parties. They also might take the question from the table at the next session in cases where that session is held at least within the next quarterly time interval (see 9:7).

17:17   **Correct Procedures in lieu of Misuses.** In the situations that give rise to improper use of the motion to *Lay on the Table*, the correct procedures are as follows:

17:18   If it is desired to dispose of a question without a direct vote, the suitable method is to use the motion to *Postpone Indefi-*

nitely. If it is desired to do this without further debate, the motion to *Postpone Indefinitely* can be followed immediately by a motion for the *Previous Question*. A motion that has been indefinitely postponed is killed for the remainder of the session, but is no more difficult to renew at a later session than any other motion that is subject to such renewal (38:3(2)).

17:19 If it is believed that any discussion of a particular original main motion might do harm, the proper course is to raise *Objection to the Consideration of the Question* (**26**) before its consideration has begun. For cases where *Postpone* (**14**) is the proper motion in lieu of an incorrectly used motion to *Lay on the Table*, see "Form and Example," below.

Form and Example

17:20 Forms used in making this motion are: "I move to lay the question on the table"; or "I move that the resolution be laid on the table." (It is preferable to avoid moving "to table" a motion, or "that the motion be tabled.")[17]

17:21 This motion, as explained earlier, is undebatable and cannot be qualified in any way. In moving it, a member can mention its intended purpose or name a time at which he plans to move that the question be taken from the table, but he cannot move to lay a question "on the table until after the completion of ... ," or, "on the table until 2 P.M." Rather than always ruling that such a motion is not in order, however, the chair should properly treat it as a motion "to postpone the question until ..."; that is, he should state the motion as admitted in that form unless the motion to *Postpone* is not in order at the time.

---

17. In the United States, the word "table" used as a verb often suggests the improper application of the motion to *Lay on the Table*, as explained in 17:13–16. In British usage, on the other hand, the same expression has an entirely different meaning and refers not to a subsidiary motion but to the introduction of a proposed resolution or document to be placed among items of business waiting to be considered.

17:22   Since the motion to *Lay on the Table* can be neither debated nor amended, the chair puts it to a vote immediately after stating the question on it, as follows:

> **CHAIR:** It is moved and seconded to lay the pending question(s) on the table. As many as are in favor of laying the pending question(s) on the table, say *aye*. … Those opposed, say *no*. … [and so on, as in the examples already given for motions requiring a majority vote for adoption].

17:23   For certain limited purposes not involving debate or amendment—such as to make a privileged motion or a motion to *Reconsider* (**37**)—a member can claim the floor while the motion to *Lay on the Table* is pending. To do so, the member rises and interrupts the chair by calling out "Mr. President!"— immediately *after* the chair has said, "It is moved and seconded to lay the pending question(s) on the table," and *before* the vote is taken. The chair grants the member limited recognition by answering, "For what purpose does the member rise?"

17:24   After a question has been laid on the table, if further action by the assembly is needed to reach the desired business, the chair immediately says, for example, "Is there a motion to suspend the rules that interfere with hearing the speaker at this time?" (Or, "The chair will entertain a motion to …")

CHAPTER VII

PRIVILEGED MOTIONS

*See 6:11ff. for a list of these motions and a
description of their characteristics as a class.*

§18. CALL FOR THE ORDERS OF THE DAY
(To demand to take up the proper business in order)

18:1   A *Call for the Orders of the Day* is a privileged motion by which a member can require the assembly to conform to its agenda, program, or order of business, or to take up a general or special order that is due to come up at the time (**14**, **41**), unless two thirds of those voting wish to do otherwise.

18:2   Taking up business in the prescribed order is of substantial importance, especially in conventions—which must follow a closely regulated schedule with much of the underlying work taking place off the convention floor in conferences and committees. For business to receive proper consideration, officers, committee members, and the delegates who are principally involved in major questions must be able to know the approximate times at which subjects will come up.

18:3   If the presiding officer consistently performs his duty of announcing the business to come before the assembly in its proper order, there will be no occasion for calling for the orders of the day. But the chair may fail to notice that the time assigned for a general or special order has arrived, or he may skip an item in the order of business by mistake, or delay announcing a special order set for that time because he thinks the assembly is so interested in the pending question that it does not yet wish to take up the special order. In these cases, any member has the right to call for the orders of the day.[1] The call must be simply "for the orders of the day" and not for a specified one, as this motion is only a demand that the proper schedule of business— whatever it is—be followed. In other words, while the member may remind the chair of what is scheduled, he cannot by this call obtain consideration of an order of the day that does not have first priority for consideration at that time.

Standard Descriptive Characteristics

18:4   The privileged *Call for the Orders of the Day*:

1. Takes precedence over all motions except (a) other privileged motions and (b) a motion to *Suspend the Rules* (**25**) that relates to the priority of business—although it can interrupt a *pending* question only if the neglect of a special order is involved (see below). It yields to all other privileged motions, and to any applicable incidental motions that may arise and that must be disposed of before it is disposed of. Except when a special order must be taken up, this call also yields to a motion to *Reconsider* or to the calling up (**37**) of a motion to *Reconsider* that has been made previously.

2. Is not applied *to* any motion, but is applicable as follows: (a) when the agenda, program, or order of business is being varied from; (b) when a general order that is in order at the time is not being taken up; or (c) when the time for considering a special order has arrived or passed and it is not being taken up. (For a statement of the precise times at which a *Call for the Orders of the Day* is in order, see below.) No subsidiary motion can be applied to this call.

3. If in order at the time, is in order when another has the floor, even if it interrupts a person speaking.

4. Does not require a second.

---

1. When a convention adopts a program that includes an agenda for the business session together with the times for events outside of business meetings, the events outside the business meetings are not subject to a *Call for the Orders of the Day*.

5. Is not debatable. (But the member making the call can remind the chair of the matter that is required to be taken up at the time.)

6. Is not amendable.

7. Upon a call by a single member the orders of the day must be enforced, except that a two-thirds vote can set them aside. (That is, the orders of the day can be set aside: either by a vote of two thirds in the negative on a question put by the chair as to the assembly's desire to proceed to the orders of the day; or by a vote of two thirds in the affirmative on a motion by a member to extend the time for considering the pending question, or to suspend the rules and take up the desired question; see below.)

8. Cannot be reconsidered.

Further Rules and Explanation

18:5   **Times When a Call for the Orders of the Day Is in Order.** The particular conditions under which a *Call for the Orders of the Day* is in order are as follows:

- Referring to cases (a) and (b) under Standard Characteristic 2, which do not involve the neglect of a special order: As soon as it is evident that the agenda, program, or order of business is being varied from, or that the time for the consideration of a postponed motion has arrived or passed, a *Call for the Orders of the Day* is in order whenever no question is pending. In such a case where no special order is involved, if a member starts to make a motion departing from the correct order of business, or if the chair announces a wrong item, the call must be made before any motion is stated by the chair; otherwise, it cannot be made until after the motion has been disposed of.

- Referring, on the other hand, to case (c) under Standard Characteristic 2: If the chair does not immediately announce a special order when the time set for its consideration has arrived, a *Call for the Orders of the Day* can be made at once—even while another question is pending, unless the pending question is itself a special order that was made before the one set for the present time was made (see **14, 41**). From the time when a particular special order becomes the proper order of business and until it is announced, a *Call for the Orders of the Day* is in order.

18:6   A *Call for the Orders of the Day* cannot be made in a committee of the whole (see **52**).

18:7   **Status of an Order of the Day as a Main Motion.** In contrast to the privileged *Call for the Orders of the Day*, an order of the day which such a call may bring before the assembly is itself invariably a main motion, and when it is announced and pending, it is debatable and amendable, and all of the other rules governing main motions apply to it. The orders of the day as a whole cannot be laid on the table or postponed, but an individual order of the day when actually pending can be so disposed of. As soon as the orders of the day that have interrupted business that was pending are completed, the interrupted business is taken up again at the point at which it was discontinued.

18:8   **Setting Aside the Orders of the Day.** When the orders of the day are called for, the chair can, and ordinarily should, immediately either interrupt or conclude consideration of the pending question (in accordance with the rules in **41**) and proceed to take up the business prescribed for the present time. But sometimes the chair or a member may sense that the assembly would prefer to continue consideration of the presently pending question or take up another matter first. In such cases, the assembly by a two-thirds vote can set aside the orders of the day, as follows:

     a) *At the initiative of the chair:* Instead of announcing the orders of the day when they are called for, the chair can put the question on proceeding to them: "The orders of the day are called for. The orders of the day are [identifying the business that is in order]. The question is: Will the assembly proceed to the orders of the day? As many as are in favor of proceeding to the orders of the day … [and so on, taking a rising vote].” Since to refuse to proceed to the orders of the day is an interference with the order of business similar to suspending the rules, two thirds in the *negative* are required to vote down this question and refuse to take up the orders of the day. Once the assembly has refused to proceed to the orders of the day, they cannot be called for again until the pending business is disposed of.

b) *At the initiative of a member:* When the orders of the day are called for or announced, a member can move (depending on the case) “that the time for considering the pending question be extended” a certain number of minutes, or “that the rules be suspended and” the desired question be taken up (see **25**). These motions require a two-thirds vote in the *affirmative* for their adoption, since they change the order of business, agenda, or program.

Form and Example

18:9   The form of the motion is as follows: To call for the orders of the day, a member rises and, addressing the chair without waiting for recognition, says, “Mr. President, I call for the orders of the day,” or “Madam President, I demand the regular order.” The member can, if necessary, remind the chair of the matter set for that time.

18:10   Assume that at yesterday’s meeting of a convention, a resolution was postponed and made a special order for 11:30 A.M. today. That time has now arrived, but a member is speaking on a pending question.

> MEMBER A (rising and addressing the chair): Madam President, I call for the orders of the day.
>
> CHAIR: The orders of the day are called for. Yesterday the convention postponed the resolution relating to tax reform to 11:30 A.M. today, and made it a special order. It is now 11:30. The question is on the resolution, *“Resolved,* That …”

18:11　　After consideration of the resolution is completed, the former business is resumed where it was left off:

> **CHAIR:** When the orders of the day were called for, the convention was considering the resolution "*Resolved*, That ..." Mr. Henley had the floor at that time. The chair recognizes Mr. Henley.

§19. RAISE A QUESTION OF PRIVILEGE

19:1　　To *Raise a Question of Privilege* is a device that permits *a request or main motion relating to the rights and privileges of the assembly or any of its members* to be brought up for possible immediate consideration because of its urgency, while business is pending and the request or motion would otherwise not be in order. (For types and examples of questions of privilege,[2] see 19:7–17.)

19:2　　This device operates as follows: A member rises and addresses the chair saying that he "rises to a question of privilege ..." (as explained in 19:8), and the chair immediately directs the member to state his question of privilege; the chair must then rule (subject to appeal, **24**) whether the request or motion is in fact a question of privilege and, if so, whether it is urgent enough to interrupt the pending business.

19:3　　It is important to understand the distinction between the device *Raise a Question of Privilege* and the question of privilege itself. The point to be decided in connection with the former is whether a certain question shall be admitted for consideration with the status and priority of the latter. The "raising" of a question of privilege is governed by rules appropriate to the device's high rank in the order of precedence of motions. When a question of privilege is taken up after it has been raised and has been admitted by the chair, however, depending on the form in which it was introduced, it is handled as a *request*

---

2. The term *question of privilege* is applied to any request or motion relating to the rights and privileges of the assembly or its members, whether or not it is introduced by means of the device *Raise a Question of Privilege*.

(**32**, **33**), or it is treated as a main motion and is debatable and amendable and can have any subsidiary motion applied to it—regardless of whether it interrupted, or awaited the disposal of, the pending business. Questions of privilege can also be introduced while no motion is pending, either as requests or by being moved and seconded just as any other main motion; in that case, the device of "raising" a question of privilege does not enter in.

19:4 Questions of privilege or motions growing out of them should not be confused with "privileged motions" (or "privileged questions"). The latter comprise the five highest-ranking motions in the order of precedence, among which *Raise a Question of Privilege* is assigned a position.

19:5 The eight characteristics below apply only to the device of *raising* a question of privilege; that is, to a member's obtaining recognition to state his urgent motion or request while business is pending, and to the chair's ruling on the question's admissibility as noted above (and described in 19:8–10).

Standard Descriptive Characteristics

19:6 The privileged device *Raise a Question of Privilege*:

1. Takes precedence over all other motions except the three higher-ranking privileged motions to *Recess*, to *Adjourn*, and to *Fix the Time to Which to Adjourn*. It yields to these three privileged motions, and to any applicable incidental motions that may arise and that *must* be disposed of before it is disposed of.

2. Cannot be applied to any other motion, and no subsidiary motion can be applied to it.

3. Is in order when another has the floor if warranted by the urgency of the situation. (In such cases, the raising of a question of privilege is in order after another has been assigned the floor and before he has begun to speak; it cannot interrupt a member who is actually speaking unless the object of the question of privilege would otherwise be defeated—as it

would be, however, in each of the two examples at the end of this section, 19:11–17. The raising of a question of privilege cannot interrupt voting or verifying a vote.)

4. Does not require a second, as relates to *raising* the question of privilege; that is, no second is required at any step in the process unless (after the chair has directed the member to state his question of privilege) the member states it in the form of a motion; such a motion must be seconded.

5. Is not debatable; that is, there can be no debate as to admitting the request or motion that has been raised as a question of privilege. (See, however, 19:9, allowing a brief description of the situation.) In contrast, a main motion that is pending after having been admitted as a question of privilege is debatable.

6. Is not amendable; that is, the motion to *Amend* is not applicable to the process of raising a question of privilege. (But a main motion that is pending after having been admitted as a question of privilege can be amended.)

7. Is ruled upon by the chair. No vote on the question's admissibility is taken unless the chair's ruling is appealed (**24**).

8. The chair's ruling on whether to admit the request or motion that has been raised as a question of privilege cannot be reconsidered.

Further Rules and Explanation

19:7   **Types of Questions of Privilege.** Questions of privilege are of two types: (1) those relating to the privileges of the assembly as a whole; and (2) questions of personal privilege. If the two come into competition, the former take precedence over the latter. Questions of the privileges of the assembly may relate to its organization or existence; to the comfort of its members with respect to heating, ventilation, lighting, and noise or other disturbance; to the conduct of its officers and employees, or of visitors; to the punishment of its members; or to the accuracy of published reports of its proceedings; etc. A motion to go into executive session (**9**) is a question of the privileges of the assembly. Questions of personal privilege—which seldom arise in ordinary societies and even more rarely justify interruption of pending business—may relate, for example, to an incorrect record of a member's participation in a meeting contained in minutes approved in his absence, or to charges circulated against a member's character.

19:8 **Steps in Raising and Disposing of a Question of Privilege.** In raising a question of privilege, a member rises, addresses the chair without waiting for recognition, and says, "I rise to a question of privilege affecting the assembly," or "… to a question of personal privilege."

19:9 The chair, even if he has assigned the floor to another person, directs the member to state his question of privilege. Depending on the case, the member then either (a) describes the situation briefly and asks that it be remedied, or (b) if he believes that the matter will require formal action by the assembly, makes a motion covering his question of privilege, and another member seconds it. The chair at his discretion can ask a member to put into the form of a motion a question of privilege that the member has stated as a request. Unless the point is simple enough to be promptly adjusted (as in the first example, below) or unless it is in the form of a motion and is not seconded, the chair rules whether the question is a question of privilege, and, if so, whether it is of sufficient urgency to warrant interruption of the existing parliamentary situation. From this ruling an undebatable appeal can be taken.

19:10 If the motion made as a question of privilege is seconded, and if the chair admits it as such and decides that it should be entertained immediately, he states the question on it and proceeds as with any other main motion. When the question of privilege has been disposed of, business is resumed at exactly the point at which it was interrupted. If a member had the floor when the question of privilege was raised, the chair assigns him the floor again.

Form and Example

19:11   The forms used in raising a question of privilege include: "I rise to a question of privilege affecting [or "relating to"] the assembly" (or "to a question of the privileges of the assembly"), and "I rise to a question of personal privilege." The preceding forms should always be adhered to in cases where it is necessary to interrupt a person speaking. When a question of the privileges of the assembly is raised in a small meeting without interrupting a speaker, a variation such as "A question of privilege, Mr. President!" is permissible.

19:12   The following is an example of a question relating to the privileges of the assembly that can be stated as an informal request and that can be routinely adjusted by the chair:

19:13   Assume that, while an important speech is in progress at a meeting in a large hall with upper windows, workmen begin to operate jackhammers in an alley beside the building. Member A rises and interrupts, addressing the chair:

> **MEMBER A:** Mr. President, I rise to a question of privilege affecting the assembly.
>
> **CHAIR:** The gentleman will state his question.
>
> **MEMBER A:** Mr. President, I don't think we're going to be able to hear unless some of the windows are closed.
>
> **CHAIR:** Will one of the ushers ask the building engineer to have the windows closed on the left side. May we have the sound turned up a little until the windows are closed.

19:14   The next example illustrates a question of the privileges of the assembly requiring a formal motion which interrupts pending business. In an ordinary society these occasions are rare, but in a convention or large assembly a situation of unforeseen complications may cause such a motion to become appropriate.

19:15   Assume that, to hear a prominent speaker, an association has opened one of its meetings to the public. Because of the speaker's commitments at a later hour, his address was given first, preceding the business meeting—which was expected to be brief and routine. But Member X has surprised this meeting by introducing a resolution dealing with a delicate matter of obvious importance that may call for prompt action by the association.

19:16 Member Y, sensing that consideration of this question should be kept within the organization, interrupts Member X's speech on the pending resolution by rising "to a question of privilege relating to the assembly." As directed by the president, he states the question of privilege:

> MEMBER Y: Mr. President, I believe this is a question we should consider privately. With apologies to our guests, I move to go into executive session. (Second.)
>
> CHAIR: The chair rules that the question is one of privilege to be entertained immediately. It is moved and seconded to go into executive session.

19:17 Debate or amendment follows, if needed; then the question is put to a vote. If the motion is adopted, the president expresses appreciation to guests. As soon as they have left, he states the resolution that was interrupted by the question of privilege, and recognizes Member X, who had the floor.

§20. RECESS

20:1 A *recess* is a short intermission in the assembly's proceedings, commonly of only a few minutes, which does not close the meeting and after which business will immediately be resumed at exactly the point where it was interrupted.[3] A recess may be taken, for example, to count ballots, to secure information, or to allow for informal consultation.

20:2 The privileged motion to *Recess* (or to *Take a Recess*) is a motion that a recess begin *immediately*, made *while another question is pending.*

20:3 A motion to recess that is made *when no question is pending* (whether the recess is to begin immediately or at a future time)

---

3. For an explanation of the distinction between *recess* and *adjournment*, see **8**, especially 8:7.

is a *main motion*, and the eight characteristics given below do not apply to it. Consequently, a motion to recess is privileged only when another question is pending; and a motion to take a recess at a future time is in order only when no question is pending.

20:4   The eight characteristics below apply only to the *privileged* motion to *Recess*.

Standard Descriptive Characteristics

20:5   The privileged motion to *Recess*:

1. Takes precedence over the main motion, over all subsidiary and incidental motions, and over all privileged motions except those to *Adjourn* and to *Fix the Time to Which to Adjourn*. It yields to motions to *Amend* or for the *Previous Question* that are applied to it, and it yields to the *privileged* motions to *Adjourn* and to *Fix the Time to Which to Adjourn* (but in the cases where motions to adjourn or to set a time for meeting again are "not privileged"—that is, are main motions—it takes precedence over these motions; see **21** and **22**). It also yields to any applicable incidental motions that may arise and that *must* be disposed of before the motion to *Recess* is voted on.

2. Is not applied *to* any motion. Motions to *Amend* can be applied to it. The *Previous Question* can also be applied to it to prevent amendments being moved, although this situation rarely arises in ordinary societies. No other subsidiary motion can be applied to it.

3. Is out of order when another has the floor.

4. Must be seconded.

5. Is not debatable. (But see 43:31–32 regarding allowable explanation of an undebatable motion.)

6. Is amendable as to the length of the recess; any such amendment is undebatable.

7. Requires a majority vote.

8. Cannot be reconsidered.

Further Rules and Explanation

20:6 **Declaring a Recess When It Has Been Provided For in the Agenda or Program.** If a recess is provided for in the adopted agenda or program of a convention or other meeting, the chair, without further action by the assembly, announces the fact and simply declares the assembly in recess when the specified time arrives. If the chair does not announce the recess at the scheduled time, a member can call for the orders of the day (**18**), thereby demanding that the recess be declared.

20:7 **Postponing the Time for Taking a Scheduled Recess.** The time for taking a scheduled recess can be postponed by a two-thirds vote if, when that time arrives, the assembly does not wish to recess. In the latter event, the taking of the recess is treated just as any other order of the day that is due to be taken up, and it can be set aside by any of the procedures described in 18:8.

Form and Example

20:8 Forms in which this motion may be made are: "I move that the meeting recess [or "take a recess"] until 2 P.M."; "I move to recess for ten minutes"; or "I move to recess until called to order by the chair."

20:9 If such a motion is adopted, the chair announces the result as follows:

> CHAIR: The ayes have it and the meeting stands recessed [or, "in recess"] for fifteen minutes [rapping once with the gavel, if desired].

20:10 At the end of the specified time, the chair gains the attention of the assembly and begins:

> CHAIR: The convention [or "meeting"] will come to order. The time of recess has expired. The question is on the resolution … [Or, if the recess was taken following the vote on a question or an election but before the result had been announced, the first business would be the announcement of the vote.]

§21. ADJOURN

21:1   To *adjourn* means to close the meeting (**8**). A motion to adjourn may be a privileged or a main motion depending on a number of conditions. The motion to adjourn that commonly occurs in meetings of ordinary societies is the privileged motion. The adoption of any motion to adjourn closes the meeting immediately unless the motion specifies a later time for adjourning (but if it does specify such a time it is not a privileged motion).

21:2   The *privileged* motion to *Adjourn* (which is always moved in an unqualified form with no mention of a time either for adjourning or for meeting again) is a motion to close the meeting immediately, made under conditions where some other provision for another meeting exists (so that the adjournment will not have the effect of dissolving the assembly), and where no time for adjourning the present meeting has already been set. In such a case, regardless of whether business is pending, a majority should not be forced to continue in session substantially longer than it desires, and even if no business is pending, a decision as to whether to close the meeting should not be allowed to consume time. For this reason, when there is provision for another meeting and no time for adjourning is already set, an unqualified motion "to adjourn" is afforded sufficiently high privilege to interrupt the pending question and, on adoption, to close the meeting before the pending business is disposed of. And for the same reason, such a motion has the unique characteristic that, *even if it is made while no question is pending*, it is not debatable or amendable and it remains subject to all of the rules governing the privileged motion to *Adjourn* (except those that relate to making the motion while business is pending; see *Standard Descriptive Characteristics*). Under the conditions just described, a motion to *Adjourn* is therefore said to be "privileged" or to be "a privileged motion" even when no question is pending.

21:3   A motion to adjourn is always a privileged motion *except* in the following cases:

1) When the motion is qualified in any way, as in the case of a motion to adjourn at, or to, a future time.
2) When a time for adjourning is already established, either because the assembly has adopted a motion or a program setting such a time, or because the order of business, the bylaws, or other governing rules prescribe it.
3) When the effect of the motion to adjourn, if adopted, would be to dissolve the assembly with no provision for another meeting, as is usually the case in a mass meeting or the last meeting of a convention.[4]

Under any of conditions (1) through (3) above, a motion to adjourn is not privileged and is treated just as any other incidental main motion. Consequently, a motion to adjourn at or to a future time is always out of order while business is pending in any assembly; and any motion to adjourn at all is out of order while business is pending under either of conditions (2) or (3)—which, however, do not commonly apply to meetings of ordinary societies.

21:4   In ordinary societies having bylaws that provide for several regular meetings during the year and having no fixed hour for adjournment, a motion "to adjourn," when unqualified, is always a privileged motion. In meetings of these organizations, such a motion to *Adjourn* is in order regardless of whether business is pending; and even when business is not pending, this motion is undebatable and is subject to the rules given below.

21:5   The following eight characteristics apply only to the *privileged* motion to *Adjourn*.

---

4. In state or national organizations where subordinate units choose delegates each time an annual or biennial convention is held, each convention is a separate assembly, since it is made up of a different body of delegates.

Standard Descriptive Characteristics

21:6   The privileged motion to *Adjourn*:

1. Takes precedence over all motions except the *privileged* motion to *Fix the Time to Which to Adjourn*; but it is not in order while the assembly is engaged in voting or verifying a vote, or before the result of a vote has been announced by the chair, except that, in the case of a vote taken by ballot, a motion to *Adjourn* is in order after the ballots have been collected by the tellers and before the result has been announced.[5] It yields to the *privileged* motion to *Fix the Time to Which to Adjourn* (but it takes precedence over a motion to set a time for meeting again in the cases where such a motion is "not privileged"—that is, is a main motion; see **22**). It also yields to any applicable incidental motions that may arise and that *must* be disposed of before the motion to *Adjourn* is voted on; but an incidental motion that can wait may not be entertained after a motion to *Adjourn* has been made.

2. Is not applied *to* any motion, and no subsidiary motion can be applied to it.

3. Is out of order when another has the floor.

4. Must be seconded.

5. Is not debatable (see 21:10–12, however).

6. Is not amendable.

7. Requires a majority vote.

8. Cannot be reconsidered (but see 21:13 regarding its renewal).

Further Rules and Explanation

21:7   **Effect of Adjournment on Pending Business or on an Uncompleted Order of Business.** Except as the assembly may have

---

5. When much time may be consumed in counting ballots, it is generally better to take a recess, but the assembly can adjourn if it has previously appointed a time for the next meeting. In any case, the result of the ballot vote should be announced as soon as business is resumed.

adopted rules providing otherwise, the effect of an adjournment on a pending motion or an uncompleted order of business is as follows:

a) *When the adjournment does not close the session* (as when an adjourned meeting (**9**) has been set, or in any meeting of a convention except the last one): Business is immediately resumed at the next meeting at the point where it left off, except that there may first be brief opening ceremonies or reading of the minutes (see **41**).

b) *When the adjournment closes the session in an assembly having its next regular business session within a quarterly time interval (see 9:7), and having no members whose terms of membership expire before the next regular session* (for example, in ordinary clubs and societies that hold frequent "regular meetings"): The complete order of business is followed at the next regular session. If a question was pending at the time of adjournment, it is taken up as the first item under unfinished business (or under special orders, if it was a special order)—resuming the question at exactly where it was previously interrupted. Any general or special order that was not reached is also taken up under unfinished business or under special orders, respectively (see **41**).

c) *When the adjournment closes a session in a body that will not have another regular session within a quarterly time interval (see 9:7), or closes a session that ends the term of all or some of the members* (as may happen in an elected legislative assembly or in a board): Matters temporarily but not finally disposed of, except those that remain in the hands of a committee to which they have been referred (see 9:8–11), fall to the ground.[6] They can, however, be introduced at the next session, the same as if they had never before been brought up.

---

6. In the case of an adopted motion which is the subject of a motion to *Reconsider* that was not finally disposed of, it is only the motion to *Reconsider* that falls to the ground, and the adopted motion then goes into effect.

21:8   Adjournment of Bodies Without Regularly Scheduled Meetings. The adjournment of a mass meeting or the last meeting of a convention dissolves the assembly unless provision has been made whereby it will, or may, be later reconvened. When adjournment would dissolve an assembly, the motion to adjourn is a main motion. A motion to close the session in an assembly that will thereby be dissolved, or will not meet again for a long time unless called into authorized special session under the bylaws or other governing rule, is often referred to as a motion to "adjourn *sine die*," which means to "adjourn without day" (see also 8:2(6)). If the bylaws of an organization provide for the calling of a special convention after the regular convention session has been held, this assembly should meet as a distinct session with a body of delegates and alternates that must be chosen anew under provisions established in the bylaws. However, program items normally associated with conventions of the organization need not be provided for.

21:9   If a board or committee meeting is adjourned without any provision having been made for future meetings, the next meeting is held at the call of the chairman (see also 50:21–22). Consequently, since there usually is no fixed hour for adjournment, the unqualified motion to adjourn is usually privileged in boards or committees. When a special committee has completed the business referred to it, however, it "rises" and reports, which is equivalent to the main motion to adjourn *sine die* (or without day).

21:10   Parliamentary Steps That Are in Order While the Privileged Motion to Adjourn Is Pending, or After the Assembly Has Voted to Adjourn. Although the privileged motion to *Adjourn* is undebatable, the following parliamentary steps are in order while it is pending:

- to inform the assembly of business requiring attention before adjournment;
- to make important announcements;

- to *make* (but not to take up[7]) a motion to reconsider a previous vote;
- to make a motion to *Reconsider and Enter on the Minutes* (37:46–52);
- to give notice of a motion to be made at the next meeting (or on the next day, in a session consisting of daily meetings) where the motion requires *previous notice* (see 10:44–51); and
- to move to set a time for an adjourned meeting (**9, 22**) if there is no meeting scheduled for later within the same session.

21:11 Any of the above steps that are desired should be taken care of earlier, if possible; but there may sometimes be no such opportunity, particularly in a convention or a session of several meetings that is following an adopted agenda or program (**41**), or in cases where a meeting of an ordinary society adjourns before completing its regular order of business. If any matters of the types listed above arise after it has been moved to adjourn, the chair should state the facts briefly, or a member who rises and addresses the chair for the purpose may do so—or make the necessary motion or give the desired notice—before the vote is taken on the motion to *Adjourn*. If something requires action before adjournment, the member who moved to adjourn can be requested to withdraw his motion.

21:12 Regardless of the type of motion by which it is voted to adjourn, the meeting is not closed until the chair has declared that the meeting "is adjourned" (or "stands adjourned"), and members should not leave their seats until this declaration has

---

7. Because of time limits on moving a reconsideration, a motion to *Reconsider* is allowed to be *made* and recorded (but *not* to be *considered*) while a motion to *Adjourn* is pending, or even after it has been voted to adjourn and before the chair has declared the assembly adjourned. A motion to *Reconsider* that is made at such a time normally must wait to be *called up* at a later meeting, unless it is made before the motion to *Adjourn* is voted on and that motion is withdrawn or voted down. If the reconsideration is moved after it has been voted to adjourn and it appears to require immediate attention, however, the chair must then retake the vote on the motion to *Adjourn* (see *unique characteristics* of the motion to *Reconsider*, 37:8).

been made. After it has been voted to adjourn but before the chair has declared the meeting adjourned, it is still in order to take any of the steps listed above (in 21:10), if necessary. In announcing an affirmative vote on a motion to adjourn, the chair should usually pause before declaring the meeting adjourned, saying: "The ayes seem to have it. [Pausing and resuming slowly:] The ayes have it, and the meeting is adjourned." The pause affords time for members to demand a division (**29**) on the vote to adjourn, or to take any of the other steps just described. If the chair learns, immediately after declaring the assembly adjourned, that a member seeking the floor for one of these purposes had risen and addressed the chair before the adjournment was declared, then, since the adjournment was improper and this breach was promptly noted, the chair must call the meeting back to order—but only long enough for the purpose for which the member legitimately sought the floor.

21:13   **Legitimate Renewal of the Privileged Motion and Its Abuses.** Since a motion to *Adjourn* may be voted down because a majority wish to hear one speech or take one vote, this motion must be renewable as soon as there has been any progress in business or even material progress in debate. But this privilege of renewal and the high rank of the motion are sometimes abused to the annoyance of the assembly. The chair should therefore refuse to entertain a motion to *Adjourn* that is obviously made for obstructive purposes—for example, when a motion to *Adjourn* has just been voted down and nothing has taken place since to indicate that the assembly may now wish to close the meeting. If a member who has not properly obtained the floor calls out, "I move to adjourn," such a call cannot be entertained as a motion except by unanimous consent (see *Dilatory Motions*, **39**).

21:14   **Cases Where the Assembly Can Adjourn Without a Motion.** If an hour for adjourning a meeting within a convention or other session of more than one meeting has been scheduled—either in an agenda or program or by the adoption of a motion setting a time—no motion to adjourn is necessary when that hour arrives. The chair simply announces the fact and declares the meeting adjourned, as described for a recess in 20:6. If the assembly does not then wish to adjourn, the matter is handled as a case of setting aside the orders of the day, as explained in 18:8 (see also 41:56). If such a meeting wishes to adjourn earlier, it is done by a main motion, which, however, can be adopted by a majority vote (see 21:3). The rules stated above regarding parliamentary steps that are in order after it has been voted to adjourn are applicable in this case also.

21:15   When it appears that there is no further business in a meeting of an ordinary local society that normally goes through a complete order of business (**41**) at each regular meeting (**9**), the chair, instead of waiting or calling for a motion to adjourn, can ask, "Is there any further business?" If there is no response, the chair can then say, "Since there is no further business, the meeting is adjourned."

Form and Example

21:16   The following forms may be used for either a privileged or a main motion: "I move to adjourn," or "I move that the meeting ["now"] adjourn." Additional forms in order as a *main* motion are: "I move that the club now adjourn to meet at 8 P.M. on April 10," or "I move that the convention adjourn *sine die* [or "adjourn without day"]."

21:17   Assume that while a resolution is pending in a regular monthly meeting of a local society, a member obtains the floor and moves to adjourn, and the motion is seconded. Since this motion is privileged and therefore undebatable, the chair immediately puts the question.

> CHAIR: It is moved and seconded to adjourn. Those in favor, say *aye* [continuing to take the vote as described in 4:37].

21:18   If the motion is adopted, the chair announces the result and declares the meeting adjourned (first making sure that no member is seeking the floor, as described in 21:12). If the motion is lost, the chair, after announcing the result, immediately restates the resolution that was pending when the motion to *Adjourn* was made.

21:19   After the pending resolution has been disposed of, or if there has been sufficient debate to show that the assembly now wishes to adjourn, a new motion to adjourn is in order. If such a motion is made and seconded and there is no other business, the chair, if he senses a general desire to adjourn, can suggest unanimous consent (4:58–63), as follows:

> **CHAIR:** If there is no objection, the meeting will now adjourn. [Pause.] Since there is no objection, the meeting is adjourned.

21:20   The adjournment may be signaled by a single rap of the gavel, if desired.

§22. FIX THE TIME TO WHICH TO ADJOURN

22:1   The object of the motion to *Fix the Time to Which to Adjourn* (also referred to as the motion to "fix the time for an adjourned meeting") is to set the time, and sometimes the place, for another meeting to continue business of the session, with no effect on when the present meeting will adjourn.

22:2   A motion to *Fix the Time to Which to Adjourn* is in order only if at the time it is offered there is no meeting scheduled for later within the same session. If there is such a meeting, additional meetings within the same session may be set by a motion either to *Suspend the Rules* (**25**) or to *Amend Something Previously Adopted* (**35**), namely, the previously adopted agenda or program for the session.

22:3   A motion to fix the time to which to adjourn is privileged only when it is made while a question is pending.

22:4   If a motion to fix the time to which to adjourn is made in any assembly when no question is pending, it is in order and is debatable and subject to all of the other rules applicable to main motions. If feasible, any desired motion to fix the time to which to adjourn should be made while no other question is pending. But situations may arise in which immediate establishment of the time for an adjourned meeting is important, yet there is no opportunity to make a main motion. The privileged motion to *Fix the Time to Which to Adjourn* can then be used.

22:5   The following eight characteristics apply only to the *privileged* motion to *Fix the Time to Which to Adjourn*.

Standard Descriptive Characteristics

22:6   The privileged motion to *Fix the Time to Which to Adjourn*:

1. Takes precedence over all other motions. It yields to motions to *Amend* or for the *Previous Question* that are applied to it and yields to any applicable incidental motions that may arise and that must be disposed of before the motion to *Fix the Time to Which to Adjourn* is voted on. The privileged motion to *Fix the Time to Which to Adjourn* can be moved even after the assembly has voted to adjourn, provided that the chair has not yet declared the assembly adjourned.

2. Is not applied *to* any motion. Motions to *Amend* can be applied to it. The *Previous Question* can also be moved on it to prevent amendments, although this seldom serves a useful purpose.

3. Is out of order when another has the floor.

4. Must be seconded.

5. Is not debatable. (But see 43:31–32 regarding allowable explanation of an undebatable motion, as in the example beginning 22:14.)

6. Is amendable as to the date, hour, or place; such amendments are undebatable.

7. Requires a majority vote.

8. Can be reconsidered.

Further Rules and Explanation

22:7   **Provisions as to Time and Place.** In an organized society, the adjourned meeting scheduled by adoption of this motion (privileged or main) must be set for a time before that of the next regular meeting. When the assembly has no fixed place for its meetings, the motion should include the place as well as the time of the adjourned meeting.

22:8   If an assembly holding regularly scheduled business meetings adjourns to meet "at the call of the chair," an adjourned meeting called accordingly is a continuation of the same session; but, if no such meeting is held before the next regular session, the adjournment of the previous session becomes final retrospectively as of the date the last meeting adjourned, and the chair's authority to call an adjourned meeting expires.

22:9   **Effect of the Motion.** Whether introduced as a privileged or a main motion, the effect of this motion is to establish an *adjourned meeting*—that is, another meeting that will be a continuation of the session at which the motion is adopted. Unlike a special meeting, an adjourned meeting does not require notice, although it is desirable to give such notice if feasible. An adjourned meeting should not be confused with a *special meeting*, which is a separate session called, in ordinary societies, as prescribed by the bylaws.

22:10   Because of the nature of the situations that give rise to use of the privileged motion to *Fix the Time to Which to Adjourn*, adoption of this motion is often followed by immediate introduction of a motion to *Postpone*, or of the privileged motion to *Adjourn*, depending on the purpose, as shown in the examples below. At the adjourned meeting, except for the reading of the minutes, business will be taken up from the point at which the previous meeting adjourned or at which questions were postponed.

22:11   It should be noted that the adoption of this motion does not adjourn the present meeting or set a time for its adjournment; thus, it has no direct effect on when the present meeting shall adjourn, and is very different from a motion to fix the time *at* which to adjourn (which is always a main motion).

Form and Example

22:12   Forms in which this motion may be made are: "I move that when this meeting adjourns, it adjourn to meet at 2:00 P.M. tomorrow"; "I move that when this meeting adjourns, it stand adjourned to meet at 8:00 P.M. on Wednesday, April 2, at the Riggs Hotel"; or "I move that on adjournment, the meeting adjourn to meet at the call of the chair."

22:13   In announcing an affirmative result, the chair says, for instance, "The ayes have it. When the meeting adjourns this evening, it will adjourn to meet at 2 P.M. tomorrow."

22:14   As a first example, assume that a number of members wish to set up an adjourned meeting to deal with an involved pending question, so that the remaining order of business can be completed now.

> MEMBER A (obtaining the floor): Madam President, I believe the pending resolution will require longer discussion than we have time for this evening. I move that when the meeting adjourns, it adjourn to meet here next Tuesday at 8:15 P.M. (Second.)

22:15   The chair states the question on this motion. Amendment as to time and place is possible, but no debate is in order. The chair then puts to vote the motion to *Fix the Time to Which to Adjourn*. After announcing the result—whether adoption or rejection—she says that the question is on the resolution, which she rereads or indicates by descriptive title. If the motion to *Fix the Time to Which to Adjourn* has been adopted, Member A rises once more.

> MEMBER A (obtaining the floor): I move to postpone the pending resolution to the adjourned meeting set for next Tuesday evening. (Second.)

22:16　　The motion to postpone is considered in the usual manner. If it is adopted, the chair continues:

> **CHAIR:** The ayes have it and the resolution is postponed to the adjourned meeting. The next item of business is …

22:17　　As a second example, assume that the motion to *Fix the Time to Which to Adjourn* is to be made with a view to immediate adjournment to a specified time, when this purpose cannot be reached by a main motion:

22:18　　At the annual meeting of a society, the hour is growing late. A controversial bylaw amendment is pending, on which a strong minority is determined to continue debate.

> **MEMBER X (obtaining the floor):** I move that when this meeting adjourns, it adjourn to meet at the same time tomorrow evening. (Second.)

22:19　　The motion is treated as in the first example. If it is adopted, Member X, after the question has been restated on the pending bylaw amendment, again rises and addresses the chair.

> **MEMBER X (obtaining the floor):** I move that the club now adjourn. (Second.)

22:20　　The chair states the question on the motion to *Adjourn* and immediately puts it to vote. If it is adopted, the chair announces the result, as follows:

> **CHAIR:** The ayes have it and the club stands adjourned until eight o'clock tomorrow evening.

CHAPTER VIII

INCIDENTAL MOTIONS

*See 6:15ff. for a list of these motions and a
description of their characteristics as a class.*

§23. POINT OF ORDER

23:1   When a member thinks that the rules of the assembly are
being violated, he can make a *Point of Order* (or "raise a question of order," as it is sometimes expressed), thereby calling upon
the chair for a ruling and an enforcement of the regular rules.

Standard Descriptive Characteristics

23:2   A *Point of Order*:

1. Takes precedence over any pending question out of which it
   may arise. It yields to all privileged motions and (if it adheres
   to pending question(s), 10:35) it yields to a motion to lay
   the main question on the table, in cases where these motions
   are in order at the time according to the order of precedence
   of motions. Except for yielding to the motion to *Lay on the
   Table* when it adheres to pending question(s) as just stated,
   it does not yield to any subsidiary motion so long as it is
   handled in the normal manner—that is, by being ruled upon
   by the chair without debate. Consequently, under this normal procedure:
   - If a point of order which adheres to pending question(s)
     is raised while any one of the six lower-ranking subsidi-
     ary motions is immediately pending, no other subsidiary

motion except *Lay on the Table* can be made until the point of order is disposed of; but in such a case, *Lay on the Table* or any privileged motion can be moved and must be considered before the point of order is ruled upon.

- If a point of order which does not adhere to pending question(s) is raised while *any* subsidiary motion is immediately pending, *no* subsidiary motion can be made until the point of order is disposed of, but any privileged motion can be moved and must be considered first.

- With reference to either of the above cases, on the other hand, if a motion to *Lay on the Table* or a privileged motion is *pending* and a point of order arises out of the parliamentary situation existing then, the point of order is disposed of first, although it can be interrupted by a still higher-ranking privileged motion.

In cases where the chair, being in doubt, refers the point of order to the judgment of the assembly and where the point thereby becomes debatable (see Standard Characteristic 5, below), it—like a debatable appeal (**24**)—also: yields to the subsidiary motions to *Limit or Extend Limits of Debate* and for the *Previous Question*; yields to the motions to *Commit* and to *Postpone Definitely* provided that they are in order at the time according to the order of precedence of motions; and yields to incidental motions arising out of itself.

2. Can be applied to any breach of the assembly's rules. So long as it is handled in the normal manner by being ruled upon by the chair, no subsidiary motion can be applied to it—except that, if it adheres to pending question(s), then (unless the motion to *Lay on the Table* was already pending when the point of order arose) the main question can be laid on the table while the point of order is pending, and the point of order also goes to the table with all adhering motions. If the chair, being in doubt, refers the point of order to the judgment of the assembly and it thereby becomes debatable (see Standard Characteristic 5, below), the application of subsidiary motions to it is governed by

the same rules as stated for debatable appeals under Standard Characteristic 2, 24:3(2).

3. Is in order when another has the floor, even interrupting a person speaking or reading a report if the point genuinely requires attention at such a time (see *Timeliness Requirement for a Point of Order*, 23:5).

4. Does not require a second.

5. Is not debatable—but, with the chair's consent, a member may be permitted to explain his point and knowledgeable or interested members can be heard by way of explanation. If the chair submits the point to a vote of the assembly, the rules governing its debatability are the same as for an *Appeal* (see 23:19; see also 24:3(5)).

6. Is not amendable.

7. Is normally ruled upon by the chair. No vote is taken unless the chair is in doubt or his ruling is appealed.

8. Cannot be reconsidered; that is, the chair's ruling on a point of order cannot be reconsidered. If the chair submits the point to a vote of the assembly, however, the vote of the assembly can be reconsidered.

Further Rules and Explanation

23:3 **Grounds for a Point of Order.** It is the right of every member who notices a breach of the rules to insist on their enforcement. If the chair notices a breach, he corrects the matter immediately; but if he fails to do so—through oversight or otherwise—any member can make the appropriate *Point of Order*. The presiding officer may wish to engage in brief research or consult with the parliamentarian before ruling, and may allow the assembly to stand at ease (see 8:2(4)) while he does so. In any event, when the presiding officer has made a ruling, any two members can appeal (one making the appeal and the other seconding it), as described in **24**.[1]

---

1. There can be no appeal from a ruling on a point of order that is raised while an appeal is pending.

23:4   If a member is uncertain as to whether there is a breach on which a point of order can be made, he can make a parliamentary inquiry of the chair (see 33:3–5). In ordinary meetings it is undesirable to raise points of order on minor irregularities of a purely technical character, if it is clear that no one's rights are being infringed upon and no real harm is being done to the proper transaction of business.

23:5   **Timeliness Requirement for a Point of Order.** The general rule is that if a question of order is to be raised, it must be raised promptly at the time the breach occurs. For example, if the chair is stating the question on a motion that has not been seconded, or on a motion that is not in order in the existing parliamentary situation, the time to raise these points of order is when the chair states the motion. After debate on such a motion has begun—no matter how clear it is that the chair should not have stated the question on the motion—a point of order is too late. If a member is unsure of his point or wishes to hear what the maker has to say on behalf of the motion before pressing a point of order, he may, with the chair's sufferance, "reserve a point of order" against the motion; but after the maker has spoken, he must insist upon his point of order or withdraw it. Points of order regarding the conduct of a vote must be raised immediately following the announcement of the voting result (see 45:9).

23:6   The only exceptions to the requirement that a point of order must be made promptly at the time of the breach arise in connection with breaches that are of a continuing nature, whereby the action taken in violation of the rules is null and void. In such cases, a point of order can be made at any time during the continuance of the breach—that is, at any time that the action has continuing force and effect—regardless of how much time has elapsed. Instances of this kind occur when:

a) a main motion has been adopted that conflicts with the bylaws (or constitution) of the organization or assembly,[2]

---

2. However, see 10:26(1) and the footnote there for exceptions.

b) a main motion has been adopted that conflicts with a main motion previously adopted and still in force, unless the subsequently adopted motion was adopted by the vote required to rescind or amend the previously adopted motion,

c) any action has been taken in violation of applicable procedural rules prescribed by federal, state, or local law,

d) any action has been taken in violation of a fundamental principle of parliamentary law (25:9), or

e) any action has been taken in violation of a rule protecting absentees, a rule in the bylaws protecting the secrecy of the members' votes (as on a ballot vote), or a rule protecting a basic right of an individual member (25:7, 25:10–11).

(For particular rules applicable to boards, see 23:9.)

23:7   **Remedy for Violation of the Right to Vote.** If one or more members have been denied the right to vote, or the right to attend all or part of a regular or properly called meeting during which a vote was taken while a quorum was present, a point of order concerning the action taken in denying the basic rights of the individual members can be raised so long as the decision arrived at as a result of the vote has continuing force and effect. If there is any possibility that the members' vote(s) would have affected the outcome, then the results of the vote must be declared invalid if the point of order is sustained. If there is no such possibility, the results of the vote itself can be made invalid only if the point of order is raised immediately following the chair's announcement of the vote. If the vote was such that the number of members excluded from participating would not have affected the outcome, a member may wish, in the appropriate circumstances, to move to *Rescind* or *Amend Something Previously Adopted* (**35**), to move to *Reconsider* (**37**), or to renew a motion (**38**), arguing that comments in debate by the excluded members could have led to a different result; but the action resulting from the vote is not invalidated by a ruling in response to a point of order raised at a later time.

23:8 **Remedy for Inclusion of Improper Votes.** If the announced result of a vote included votes cast in violation of a fundamental principle of parliamentary law, such as votes cast by nonmembers or by absent members, or multiple votes improperly cast by a single member, a point of order can be raised so long as the decision arrived at as a result of the vote has continuing force and effect. If there is any possibility that the vote(s) would have affected the outcome, the results of the vote must be declared invalid if the point of order is sustained.

23:9 **Remedy When Action Taken by an Executive Board Is Null and Void.** If the executive board of a society takes action that exceeds the board's instructions or authority, that conflicts with a decision made by the assembly of the society, or that falls under any of the categories listed in 23:6, a point of order can be raised at a board meeting at any time during the continuance of the breach. If the point of order is sustained, the action must be declared null and void. Alternatively, the society's assembly can adopt an incidental main motion by majority vote declaring that the board's action is null and void; or, if it is affecting business at a meeting of the assembly, the board's action can be declared null and void by a ruling of the chair relating to the affected business or on a relevant point of order raised by a member. It is also possible for the assembly to bring disciplinary measures against the board members who voted for the improper action. If the assembly finds itself in sympathy with the board's action and the action is one that that assembly could have authorized in advance, the assembly can instead ratify the action as explained in 10:54–57.

23:10 **Precedent.** The minutes include the reasons given by the chair for his or her ruling (see 48:4(10)). The ruling and its rationale serve as a precedent for future reference by the chair and the assembly, unless overturned on appeal, the result of which is also recorded in the minutes and may create a contrary precedent. When similar issues arise in the future, such precedents are *persuasive* in resolving them—that is, they carry weight in the absence of overriding reasons for following a different course—but they are not binding on the chair or the assembly. The weight given to precedent increases with the number of times the same or similar rulings have been repeated and with the length of time during which the assembly has consistently adhered to them.

23:11   If an assembly is or becomes dissatisfied with a precedent, it may be overruled, in whole or in part, by a later ruling of the chair or a decision of the assembly in an appeal in a similar situation, which will then create a new precedent. Alternatively, adoption, rescission, or amendment (**35**) of a bylaw provision, special rule of order, standing rule, or other motion may alter the rule or policy on which the unsatisfactory precedent was based.

Form and Example

23:12   When a member notices a breach of order that may do harm if allowed to pass, he rises and, without waiting for recognition, immediately addresses the chair as follows:

> MEMBER A: I rise to a point of order. [Or, "Point of order!"]

23:13   Anyone who is speaking takes his seat. If the point relates to a transgression of the rules of debate, the form used may be:

> MEMBER A: Mr. President, I call the gentleman to order.

23:14   The chair then asks the member to state his point of order, or what words in the debate he objects to.

> MEMBER A: I make the point of order that …

23:15   On completing his statement, the member resumes his seat. The chair then rules whether "the point of order is well taken" or "is not well taken," stating briefly his reasons, which are recorded in the minutes. If the chair desires, he can review the parliamentary situation without leaving the chair, but standing, before giving his ruling.

23:16   If the chair's decision requires any action and no appeal is made, he sees that the necessary action is taken before proceeding with the pending business. Thus, if the point of order relates to a breach of decorum in debate that is not serious, the chair can allow the member to continue his speech. But if the member's remarks are decided to be improper and anyone objects, the member cannot continue speaking without a vote of the assembly to that effect (see 61:11).

23:17   Before rendering his decision, the chair can consult the parliamentarian, if there is one. The chair can also request the advice of experienced members, but no one has the right to express such opinions in the meeting unless requested to do so by the chair.

23:18   When the chair is in doubt as to how to rule on an important point, he can submit it to the assembly for decision in some such manner as:

> CHAIR: Mr. Downey raises a point of order that the amendment is not germane to the resolution. The chair is in doubt and submits the question to the assembly. The resolution is [reading it]. The proposed amendment is [reading it]. The question is, "Is the amendment germane to the resolution?"

23:19   Since no appeal can be made from a decision of the assembly itself, this question is open to debate whenever an appeal would be—that is, the question submitted by the chair to the assembly for decision is debatable except when it relates to indecorum or transgression of the rules of speaking, or to the priority of business, or when an undebatable question is immediately pending or involved in the point of order. As in the case of debate on an appeal (**24**), when a point of order that is submitted to a vote is debatable, no member can speak more than once in the debate except the chair, who can speak in preference to other members the first time, and who is also entitled to speak a second time at the close of debate.

23:20 In the example given above, the question may be put as follows:

> CHAIR: Those of the opinion that the amendment is germane, say *aye*. … Those of the opinion that it is not germane, say *no*. … The ayes have it and the amendment is in order. The question is on the adoption of the amendment.

Or:

> CHAIR: … The noes have it and the amendment is not in order. The question is on the adoption of the resolution.

23:21 When a point of order is submitted to a vote of the assembly and the point relates to stopping something from being done, it is usually best to put the question so that an affirmative vote will be in favor of allowing the proceedings to continue as if the point had not been raised. Thus, if a point is made that the chair is admitting a motion which is not in order, the question should be put so that an affirmative result of the vote will mean that the motion is in order—as in the example above, or as follows: "… Those of the opinion that the motion is in order, say *aye*. … ; etc." When a member has been called to order because of indecorum in debate, the corresponding form is: "… Those of the opinion that the member should be allowed to resume speaking, say *aye*. …" If the foregoing principle has no clear application to the case, the question can be put so that an affirmative result will uphold the point of order: "… Those of the opinion that the point is well taken, say *aye*. …"[3]

---

3. It should be noted that the latter method of putting the question may often be the opposite of the first method in cases where the first method is applicable. Thus, in the example of a point of order that an amendment is not germane, as shown above, the question is put so that a vote of *aye* is a vote that the amendment *is* germane; but in that case, a vote of *aye* is a vote that the point is *not* well taken.

§24. APPEAL

24:1   By electing a presiding officer, the assembly delegates to him the authority and duty to make necessary rulings on questions of parliamentary law. But any two members have the right to *Appeal* from his decision on such a question. By one member making (or "taking") the appeal and another seconding it, the question is taken from the chair and vested in the assembly for final decision.

24:2   Members have no right to criticize a ruling of the chair unless they appeal from his decision.

Standard Descriptive Characteristics

24:3   An *Appeal*:

1. Takes precedence over any question pending at the time the chair makes a ruling from which the appeal is made. It yields to all privileged motions (provided that they are in order at the time according to the order of precedence of motions), and it yields to incidental motions arising out of itself. If it is debatable (see Standard Characteristic 5, below), it also yields to the subsidiary motions to *Limit or Extend Limits of Debate* and for the *Previous Question*, and yields to the motions to *Commit*, to *Postpone Definitely*, and to *Lay on the Table*, provided that they are in order at the time according to the order of precedence of motions. If it is undebatable and adheres to pending question(s), it does not yield to any subsidiary motion except to *Lay on the Table*; and if it is undebatable and does *not* adhere to pending question(s), it yields to no subsidiary motion.

2. Can be applied to any ruling by the presiding officer except that:

   a) if a point of order is raised while an appeal is pending, there is no appeal from the chair's decision on this point of order, although the correctness of the ruling can be brought up later by a motion covering the case; and

b) when the chair rules on a question about which there cannot possibly be two reasonable opinions, an appeal would be dilatory and is not allowed.

Rules governing the applicability of subsidiary motions to *debatable appeals* are as follows: A motion limiting or extending debate or a motion for the *Previous Question* can be applied to a debatable appeal without affecting any other pending question. Also:

- When a *debatable* appeal *does not adhere* to pending question(s)—that is, when the decision on it would in no way affect pending question(s)—such a debatable appeal can have any of the subsidiary motions applied to it except *Postpone Indefinitely* and *Amend.*
- But when a *debatable* appeal *adheres* to pending question(s)—as in the case of an appeal from a ruling that an amendment is not germane—the subsidiary motions, except the motions affecting debate, cannot be applied to the appeal alone. However, they can be applied to the main question, and if the latter is committed, postponed, or laid on the table, the appeal goes with this main question.

In the case of *undebatable* appeals:

- When an *undebatable* appeal *does not adhere* to pending question(s), no subsidiary motion can be applied to it; however,
- When an *undebatable* appeal *adheres* to pending question(s), no subsidiary motion can be applied to it alone; but the main question can be laid on the table, and the appeal then goes to the table with the main question and all adhering motions.

3. Is in order when another has the floor.
4. Must be seconded.
5. Is debatable, unless it (a) relates to indecorum or a transgression of the rules of speaking; (b) relates to the priority of business; or (c) is made when an undebatable question is immediately pending or involved in the appeal. When an

appeal is debatable, no member is allowed to speak more than once except the presiding officer—who need not leave the chair while so speaking, but should stand. The first time the chair speaks in debate on the appeal, he is entitled to preference over other members seeking recognition. He can answer arguments against the decision or give additional reasons by speaking a second time at the close of the debate. He may announce his intention to speak in rebuttal and ask if there are others who wish to speak first. Even when the appeal is not debatable, the chair can, when stating the question on it, give the reasons for his decision without leaving the chair.

6. Is not amendable.

7. A majority or a tie vote sustains the decision of the chair on the principle that the chair's decision stands until reversed by a majority. If the presiding officer is a member of the assembly, he can vote to create a tie and thus sustain his decision.

8. Can be reconsidered.

Further Rules and Explanation

24:4 **Appropriateness of Appeal.** If a member disagrees with a ruling of the chair affecting any substantial question, he should not hesitate to appeal. The situation is no more delicate than disagreeing with another member in debate. In the case of serious questions when proponents and opponents appear nearly equal, a presiding officer may welcome an appeal from his decision. By relieving the chair of responsibility in a strongly contested situation and placing it on the assembly itself, better relationships are often preserved.

24:5 **Applicability Limited to Rulings.** As explained in Standard Characteristic 2, an appeal is applicable only to a *ruling* by the chair.

24:6 No appeal can be made from the chair's response to a parliamentary inquiry or other query, since such a reply is an *opinion* rendered by the chair, not a ruling on a question that has actually arisen. For example, if, in answer to a parliamentary inquiry, the chair states that a certain motion would not be in order at the time, this reply is not subject to appeal. But the point can be put at issue before the assembly by making the motion despite the chair's opinion and, when he *rules* that the motion is not in order, appealing from the chair's decision.

24:7   The chair's judgment as to the more numerous side in a vote, or whether there are two thirds in the affirmative, also is not a ruling and is not subject to appeal.[4] If a member doubts the correctness of such an announced result, however, he should call for a *Division* (see **29**) or move that the vote be counted.

24:8   **Timeliness Requirement for an Appeal.** If an appeal is to be made, it must be made at the time of the chair's ruling. If any debate or business has intervened, it is too late to appeal.

Form and Example

24:9   A member desiring to appeal rises and, without waiting to be recognized, addresses the chair as follows:

> **MEMBER A:** I appeal from the decision of the chair. (Second.)
> **CHAIR:** The decision of the chair is appealed from.

24:10   The chair, after stating clearly the exact question at issue, and the reasons for his decision if he thinks an explanation necessary, states the question on the appeal as follows:

> **CHAIR:** The question is: "Shall the decision of the chair stand as the judgment of the assembly [or "club," "society," "board," etc.]?"

Or:

> **CHAIR:** The question is, "Shall the decision of the chair be sustained?"

---

4. If the chair made a procedural error in declaring a motion adopted or lost, for example, in declaring that a motion which received a majority vote but not a two-thirds vote was adopted when a two-thirds vote was required under the rules, a point of order may be raised to that effect.

24:11   The question is not on "sustaining the chair," because the *decision*, not the presiding officer, is in question.

24:12   The vote is taken so that the affirmative will be in favor of sustaining the chair's decision, as follows:

> **CHAIR:** Those in favor of sustaining the chair's decision, say *aye*. ... Those opposed to sustaining this decision, say *no*. ...

24:13   After the result of the vote is announced, business is resumed in accordance with the situation existing after the action on the appeal.

§25. SUSPEND THE RULES

25:1   When an assembly wishes to do something during a meeting that it cannot do without violating one or more of its regular rules, it can adopt a motion to *Suspend the Rules* interfering with the proposed action—provided that the proposal is not in conflict with the organization's bylaws (or constitution), with local, state, or national law prescribing procedural rules applicable to the organization or assembly, or with a fundamental principle of parliamentary law.

Standard Descriptive Characteristics

25:2   The incidental motion to *Suspend the Rules*:

1. Can be made at any time that no question is pending. When business is pending, *Suspend the Rules* takes precedence over any motion if it is for a purpose connected with that motion. It yields to the motion to *Lay on the Table* and to all privileged motions when these motions are in order at the time according to the order of precedence of motions—except that if it relates to the priority of business it does not yield to a *Call for the Orders of the Day*. It also yields to incidental motions arising out of itself.

2. Can be applied to any rule of the assembly except bylaws (or rules contained in a constitution or corporate charter).[5] No subsidiary motion can be applied to *Suspend the Rules.*

3. Is out of order when another has the floor.

4. Must be seconded.

5. Is not debatable. (But see 43:31–32 regarding allowable explanation of an undebatable motion.)

6. Is not amendable.

7. Usually requires a two-thirds vote (see below, however). In any case, no rule protecting a minority of a particular size can be suspended in the face of a negative vote as large as the minority protected by the rule.

8. Cannot be reconsidered (see below regarding its renewal).

Further Rules and Explanation

25:3 **Object and Effect of the Motion.** The object of this motion is to suspend one or more rules applicable to the assembly—such as rules contained in the parliamentary authority, special rules of order, or standing rules[6]—that interfere with proposed action during a meeting. A motion to "take up a question out of its proper order," or to consider one before a time to which it has been postponed, is an application of the motion to *Suspend the Rules* (see **14, 41**).

25:4 In making the incidental motion to *Suspend the Rules,* the particular rule or rules to be suspended are not mentioned; but the motion must state its specific purpose, and its adoption permits nothing else to be done under the suspension. Such a motion, for instance, may be "to suspend the rules and take up the report of the Building Committee," or "to suspend the rules and agree to [that is, to adopt without debate or amendment] the resolution ..." When the purpose of a motion to *Suspend*

---

5. Regarding the suspendibility of rules in the nature of rules of order when placed within the bylaws (or constitution), see 2:21. Nothing in a corporate charter can be suspended unless the charter or applicable law so provides.

6. For the classes of rules that an organization or an assembly may adopt, see **2**.

the Rules is to permit the making of another motion, and the adoption of the first motion would obviously be followed by adoption of the second, the two motions can be combined, as in "to suspend the rules and take from the table (**34**) the question relating to ..." The foregoing is an exception to the general rule that no member can make two motions at the same time except with the consent of the assembly—unanimous consent being required if the two motions are unrelated (see also 10:25, 27:10–11).

25:5   If a motion to *Suspend the Rules* is adopted and its object is to allow consideration of business that could not otherwise have been considered at the time, the chair immediately recognizes the member who moved the suspension of the rules, to make the appropriate motion that will bring up the desired business. Or, if no further motion is necessary (for example, if the two motions were combined as indicated above, or if the question is one that was postponed), the chair announces the business as pending.

25:6   **Renewal of the Motion.** If a motion to suspend the rules is voted down, it cannot be renewed by moving to suspend the rules for the same purpose at the same meeting, unless unanimous consent is given. It can, however, be renewed for the same purpose after an adjournment, even if the next meeting is held the same day. Any number of motions to suspend the rules for different purposes can be entertained at the same meeting.

25:7   **Rules That Cannot Be Suspended.** Rules contained in the *bylaws* (or constitution) cannot be suspended—no matter how large the vote in favor of doing so or how inconvenient the rule in question may be—unless the particular rule specifically provides for its own suspension, or unless the rule properly is in the nature of a rule of order as described in 2:14. However, a rule in the bylaws requiring that a vote—such as, for example, on the election of officers—be taken by (secret) *ballot* cannot be suspended so as to violate the secrecy of the members' votes unless the bylaws so provide (see also *Voting by Ballot*, 45:18–24).

Nothing in a corporate charter can be suspended unless the charter or applicable law so provides.

25:8 No applicable *procedural rule prescribed by federal, state, or local law* can be suspended unless the rule specifically provides for its own suspension.

25:9 Rules which embody *fundamental principles of parliamentary law*, such as the rule that allows only one question to be considered at a time (5:4), cannot be suspended, even by a unanimous vote. Thus, since it is a fundamental principle of parliamentary law that the right to vote is limited to the members of an organization who are actually present at the time the vote is taken in a regular or properly called meeting (45:56), the rules cannot be suspended so as to give the right to vote to a nonmember,[7] or to authorize absentee voting (45:56ff.). Likewise, since it is a fundamental principle that each member of a deliberative assembly is entitled to one—and only one—vote on a question, the rules may not be suspended so as to authorize cumulative voting (46:43).

25:10 Rules *protecting absentees* cannot be suspended, even by unanimous consent or an actual unanimous vote, because the absentees do not consent to such suspension. For example, the rules requiring the presence of a quorum, restricting business transacted at a special meeting to that mentioned in the call of the meeting, and requiring previous notice of a proposed amendment to the bylaws protect absentees, if there are any, and cannot be suspended when any member is absent.[8]

25:11 Rules protecting a *basic right of the individual member* cannot be suspended. Thus, while generally applicable limits on debate and the making of motions may be imposed by motions such as the *Previous Question*, the rules may not be suspended so as to deny any particular member the right to attend meetings, make motions or nominations, speak in debate, give previous notice,

---

7. In contrast, the rules may be suspended to allow a nonmember to speak in debate.

8. An elected or appointed body that lacks the authority to determine its own quorum may not suspend the quorum requirement, even if all members are present.

or vote. These basic rights may be curtailed only through disciplinary proceedings.

25:12   At a regular meeting of an organization that has an established order of business, the assembly cannot, even unanimously, vote to *dispense with* that order of business (in the sense of voting, in advance of the time when it adjourns, that the order of business shall not be gone through at all at that meeting). If the assembly, by a two-thirds vote, adopts a motion "to dispense with the regular order of business and proceed to"[9] a certain subject, it has in effect voted to suspend the rules and *pass* all classes in the order of business which normally would precede that subject (see 41:37–39). In such a case, when the matter taken up out of its proper order has been disposed of, even if it has consumed as much time as the usual meeting, the chair must return to the regular order of business and call for the items in sequence, unless the assembly then votes to adjourn (see **21**).

25:13   Rules that have their application outside of the session which is in progress cannot be suspended. For example, a policy prohibiting total contributions to any one charitable organization in excess of $500.00 in any one calendar year is a rule which has its application outside of a meeting context, and thus cannot be suspended so as to permit the adoption of a motion to make a contribution in excess of the specified amount. (Such a rule can, however, be rescinded or amended; see **35**.) Likewise, the rules cannot be suspended in order to permit postponement of a motion to a future session that will be held after the next regular business session or that will be held after more than a quarterly time interval has elapsed.

25:14   **Rules Whose Suspension Requires a Two-Thirds Vote.** The *rules of order* of a society, as contained in the manual established by the bylaws as the parliamentary authority, or as included in any special rules of order adopted by the organization (see **2**), are rules of parliamentary procedure, the suspension of which

---

9. This usage should be avoided.

requires a two-thirds vote. Some societies call all their rules "standing rules." But by whatever name a rule is called, if it relates to parliamentary procedure, it requires a two-thirds vote for its suspension.

25:15 **Rules That Can Be Suspended by a Majority Vote.** An ordinary[10] *standing rule*, as the term is used in this book, is a rule that does not relate to parliamentary procedure as such and refers, for example, to such matters as the use of recording devices at meetings (see 2:23). Standing rules can be suspended by a majority vote. Through an incidental main motion adopted by a majority vote, a standing rule can be suspended for the duration of the current session.

25:16 **Suspension of Rules by Unanimous Consent.** Frequently, when the matter is clearly not controversial, time may be saved by asking unanimous consent rather than by making a formal motion to suspend the rules. A member who has obtained the floor can say, for example, "Madam President, I ask unanimous consent to offer the courtesy resolutions before we receive the report of the special committee." The chair then asks if anyone objects and, if so, proceeds to take a vote on suspending the rules, just as if a formal motion had been made.

Form and Example

25:17 The usual form of this motion is:

> MEMBER A (obtaining the floor): I move that the rules be suspended [or "to suspend the rules"] which interfere with … [stating the object of the suspension]. (Second.)

Or:

> MEMBER A (obtaining the floor): I move to suspend the rules and take up … (Second.)

---

10. In conventions, the term *standing rule* is used in a special sense that may include parliamentary rules adopted by the convention (see 59:27ff.).

25:18   When the object is to adopt a motion without debate or amendment, the form is:

> **MEMBER A (obtaining the floor):** I move to suspend the rules and adopt [or "agree to"] the following resolution: *"Resolved, That ..."* (Second.)

25:19   A member moving to suspend the rules can briefly give sufficient information to enable the members to vote intelligently on his undebatable motion. (For the manner of taking a two-thirds vote, see 4:38–39 and provisions (d), (e), and (g) in 4:49.) In announcing an affirmative result, the chair says, for example,

> **CHAIR:** There are two thirds in the affirmative and the rules are suspended for the purpose of ... The chair recognizes Mrs. Watkins.

25:20   If such a motion does not receive the required two-thirds vote, the main motion can be taken up only in the normal way.

§26. OBJECTION TO THE CONSIDERATION OF A QUESTION

26:1   The purpose of an *Objection to the Consideration of a Question* is to enable the assembly to avoid a particular original main motion altogether when it believes it would be strongly undesirable for the motion even to come before the assembly.

Standard Descriptive Characteristics

26:2   An *Objection to the Consideration of a Question*:

1. Takes precedence over original main motions and over an *unstated* subsidiary motion except *Lay on the Table*. The objection can be raised only before there has been any debate or any subsidiary motion except *Lay on the Table* has been stated by the chair; thereafter, consideration of

the main question has begun and it is too late to object. It does not take precedence over any *pending* subsidiary motion. It yields to the motion to *Lay on the Table*, to all privileged motions, and to incidental motions arising out of itself.

2. Can be applied to original main motions (10:3) and to petitions and communications that are not from a superior body. It cannot be applied to incidental main motions. No subsidiary motion can be applied to it alone, but while it is pending the main question can be laid on the table, and the objection then goes to the table with the main question.

3. Is in order when another has the floor, until consideration of the question has begun, as indicated in Standard Characteristic 1, above.

4. Does not require a second.

5. Is not debatable. (But see 43:31–32 regarding allowable explanation of an undebatable motion.)

6. Is not amendable.

7. A two-thirds vote *against consideration* is required to sustain the objection.

8. A negative vote—that is, a vote sustaining the objection—can be reconsidered, but not an affirmative vote.

Further Rules and Explanation

26:3 **Resemblance to Point of Order.** An *Objection to the Consideration of a Question* is similar in some ways to a *Point of Order*. The presiding officer, on his own initiative, can submit his objection of this kind to a vote, just as he can raise a question of order on his own accord. An *Objection to the Consideration of a Question* is not used if a main motion is outside the society's objects as defined in the bylaws or constitution, or outside the announced purpose for which a mass meeting has been called; such a motion is not in order unless the assembly by a two-thirds vote *in the affirmative* authorizes its introduction (10:26(2)).

26:4   **Difference from Objection in Other Context.** *Objection to the Consideration of a Question* should not be confused with an objection to a request for unanimous consent (see 4:58–63).

26:5   **Effect of the Objection.** If an objection to consideration is sustained, the main motion is dismissed for that session and cannot be renewed during the same session except by unanimous consent or by reconsideration of the vote on the objection. If the objection is not sustained, consideration of the main motion proceeds as if no objection had been made. Even if the objection is sustained, the same main motion can be introduced at any succeeding session.

26:6   **Reconsideration of a Vote That Has Sustained the Objection.** As noted in Standard Characteristic 8, a vote *sustaining* an objection to consideration can be reconsidered. The motion to reconsider such a vote is undebatable and requires a majority vote for its adoption, and it can be taken up or called up only when no other motion is pending. If the motion to *Reconsider* is adopted, it is also presumed to have overturned the objection, and the chair immediately states the question on the main motion whose consideration had been objected to, without again putting the objection to a vote. (The reason for this abbreviated procedure is that only the members who wish to consider the main question would vote to reconsider the objection to its consideration; consequently, if a majority have voted for reconsideration of the objection, this implies that there are less than two thirds who wish to prevent consideration of the main question.)

26:7   **Manner of Putting the Question.** When the objection is put to a vote in its correct form (see *Form and Example*, below), members are asked to vote for or against *consideration* of the question objected to (not for or against sustaining the objection). Therefore, those who wish to *prevent consideration* of the question *vote in the negative*. The objection is sustained if there are at least twice as many negative as affirmative votes.

Form and Example

26:8   A member rises, even if another has been assigned the floor, and without waiting to be recognized, addresses the chair as follows:

> **MEMBER A:** Mr. President, I object to the consideration of the question [or "resolution," "motion," etc.].

The chair responds:

> **CHAIR:** The consideration of the question is objected to. Shall the question be considered? Those in favor of considering it, rise. ... Be seated. Those opposed to considering the question, rise. ... Be seated. There are two thirds opposed and the question will not be considered.

Or, if the objection is not sustained, the announcement of the vote may be worded as follows:

> **CHAIR:** There are less than two thirds opposed and the objection is not sustained. The question is on the resolution, *"Resolved,* That ..."

26:9   In putting the objection to vote, the chair must be careful *not* to say, "Shall the objection be sustained?" This would reverse the effect of affirmative and negative votes and might cause confusion.

§27. DIVISION OF A QUESTION

27:1   When a motion relating to a single subject contains several parts, each of which is capable of standing as a complete proposition if the others are removed, the parts can be separated to be considered and voted on as if they were distinct questions—by adoption of the motion for *Division of a Question* (or "to divide the question").

27:2   There are also certain motions which must be divided on the demand of a single member, in which case a formal motion to divide is not used (see 27:10–11). The eight characteristics below apply only to the incidental *motion* for *Division of a Question*.

Standard Descriptive Characteristics

27:3   The incidental motion for *Division of a Question*:

1. Takes precedence over the main motion and over the subsidiary motion to *Postpone Indefinitely*. If applied to an amendment, it also takes precedence over that amendment; but a motion to divide the main question cannot be made while an amendment to the main question is pending. It yields to all subsidiary motions except *Postpone Indefinitely*, *Amend*, and *Limit or Extend Limits of Debate*; to all privileged motions; and to all applicable incidental motions. Although it is preferable to divide a question when it is first introduced, a motion to divide can be made at any time that the main motion, an amendment which it is proposed to divide, or the motion to *Postpone Indefinitely* is immediately pending—even after the *Previous Question* has been ordered.

2. Can be applied to main motions and their amendments, if they are susceptible to division (see below). No subsidiary motion can be applied to it alone except *Amend* and (for the purpose of stopping its amendment) the *Previous Question*; but while it is pending the main question can be committed, postponed, or laid on the table, and it then undergoes the same process with the main question.

3. Is out of order when another has the floor.

4. Must be seconded.

5. Is not debatable. (But see 43:31–32 regarding allowable explanation of an undebatable motion.)

6. Is amendable.

7. Requires a majority vote.

8. Cannot be reconsidered.

Further Rules and Explanation

27:4 **Specification of the Manner in Which the Question Is to Be Divided.** The motion to divide must clearly state the manner in which the question is to be divided. While the motion to divide is pending, another member can propose a different division by moving an amendment. If several different proposals are made, they are treated as filling blanks; that is, they are voted on in the order in which they were proposed unless they suggest different numbers of questions, in which case the largest number is voted on first (12:92–113). Usually, however, little formality is involved in dividing a question, and it is arranged by unanimous consent.

27:5 **Motions That Cannot Be Divided.** A motion cannot be divided unless each part presents a proper question for the assembly to act upon if none of the other parts is adopted, and unless the effect of adopting all of the parts will be exactly the same— no more, no less—as adoption of the compound main question. Thus, if it is moved to establish a committee and give it instructions, this motion is indivisible because, should the part establishing the committee fail, the part giving the committee instructions would be absurd. Similarly, if a single motion proposes a series of amendments to something previously adopted (**35**)—existing bylaws, for example—and all of the individual amendments must be made, if any one of them is made, in order for the document being amended to be coherent, then the motion cannot be divided. For the same reason, multiple conforming amendments to a pending motion, as described in 12:15, cannot be divided.

27:6 Another type of motion that cannot be divided is one whose parts are not easily separated. The division cannot require a rewriting of the resolution beyond an essentially mechanical separation of it into the required parts. If possible, the division should be carried out by no more than a renumbering of phrases or clauses, prefacing each part with the formal word(s),

"That," "*Resolved*, That," or "*Ordered*, That," dropping conjunctions where necessary, or replacing pronouns with the nouns for which they stand, with or without the definite article "the," as required. Depending on how the compound main motion or resolution is worded, however, it may sometimes be necessary to repeat words in more than one part which, in the main motion, appear only once and apply to more than one element of the proposed division. Also needed in this connection may be slight corrections in syntax or phrase structure in order to render each part as a complete grammatical sentence free of awkward wording. These adjustments are permissible provided care is taken to preserve exact logical equivalence of statement and no new language is introduced.

27:7 For example, suppose that the following resolution is pending: "*Resolved*, That the Society congratulate its member Ernest Dunn on his novel *Crestwood*, and that three copies be purchased for the Society's library." Suppose also that a member wishes to divide the question so as to consider the purchase of the books separately. The first divided part obviously would be, "*Resolved*, That the Society congratulate its member Ernest Dunn on his novel *Crestwood*." The second part, with the wording adjusted no more than necessary to avoid awkwardness, would have to read, "*Resolved*, That three copies of the novel *Crestwood* by the Society's member Ernest Dunn be purchased for the Society's library." The phrasing of the second part involves both types of modification described in the last three sentences of the preceding paragraph.

27:8 As indicated in this subsection, if separating the elements of action in a proposed resolution would require recasting the parts more than described above, the resolution cannot be divided.

27:9 **Striking Out Part of an Indivisible Motion or Series of Motions.** When a question is indivisible and a member is opposed to a portion of it, he can seek the desired result by moving to *strike out* (**12**) the part to which he is opposed. In like manner, when a series of resolutions is proposed as a substitute for another series, the substitute series is indivisible if the several resolutions are not completely parallel, but a motion can be made to strike out of the series any of the component resolutions before the vote is taken on whether to make the substitution.

27:10 **Motions That Must Be Divided on Demand.** Sometimes a series of independent resolutions or main motions dealing with different subjects is offered in one motion. In such a case, one or more of the several resolutions must receive separate consideration and vote at the request of a single member, and the motion for *Division of a Question* is not used. Such a demand (which should not be confused with a demand for a division of the assembly—that is, for a rising vote) can be made even when another has the floor, as in, "Mr. President, I call for a separate vote on Resolution No. 3." This demand must be asserted before the question on adopting the series has actually been put to vote.

27:11 Similarly, a series of amendments to a pending main motion (or to a lengthy primary amendment, such as a substitute) may be offered in one motion. Unless these amendments meet the standard for conforming amendments given in 12:15, any member may demand a separate vote on one or more of them. After the others have been voted on together, the amendment(s) on which separate votes were requested are disposed of.

Form and Example

27:12 Referring to the example relating to Ernest Dunn's novel *Crestwood* in 27:7, a motion to divide the question may be made either by stating the proposed parts in their entirety or by using a shorter description of how the division is to be made, if it is perfectly clear.

27:13 In the first instance, the motion would be made thus:

> **MEMBER A (obtaining the floor):** Madam President, I move to divide the resolution into two parts as follows: [repeating them as shown in the example in 27:7]. (Second.)

The question as to whether to divide the resolution is voted on first. In this case, the chair would doubtless use unanimous consent.

27:14   Under the shorter form of the motion, it may be made instead as follows:

> **MEMBER A (obtaining the floor):** Madam President, I move to divide the resolution so as to consider separately the question of purchasing the books. [Or, "… so that the question of purchasing the books be considered separately."] (Second.)

The procedure is then the same as in the first case.

27:15   If the motion for the division prevails, the chair states each of the separated resolutions in full as it is considered.

§28. CONSIDERATION BY PARAGRAPH OR SERIATIM

28:1   A report or long motion consisting of a series of resolutions, paragraphs, articles, or sections that are not totally separate questions can be considered by opening the different parts to debate and amendment separately, without a division of the question. If the chair does not follow such a course of his own accord and the assembly wishes to do so, the procedure can be ordered by adopting a motion to *Consider by Paragraph* (or to *Consider Seriatim*). Several distinct main motions *on different subjects* cannot be considered seriatim if a single member objects.

Standard Descriptive Characteristics

28:2   The incidental motion for *Consideration by Paragraph or Seriatim:*

1. Takes precedence over the main motion and over the subsidiary motion to *Postpone Indefinitely.* If applied to an amendment, it also takes precedence over that amendment; but it cannot be applied to the main question while an

amendment to the main question is pending. It yields to all subsidiary motions except *Postpone Indefinitely, Amend,* and *Limit or Extend Limits of Debate*; to all privileged motions; and to all applicable incidental motions.

2. Can be applied to main motions and amendments of such length and structure that the method is appropriate. No subsidiary motion can be applied to it alone except *Amend* and (for the purpose of stopping its amendment) the *Previous Question*; but while it is pending the main question can be committed, postponed, or laid on the table, and it then undergoes the same process with the main question.

3. Is out of order when another has the floor.

4. Must be seconded.

5. Is not debatable. (But see 43:31–32 regarding allowable explanation of an undebatable motion.)

6. Is amendable.

7. Requires a majority vote.

8. Cannot be reconsidered.

Further Rules and Explanation

28:3 **Effect of Consideration by Paragraph.** The effect of considering a document by paragraph or seriatim is as follows: If a member exhausts his right to debate under the usual rules on one part, his right to debate begins over again as each succeeding part is opened to debate and amendment; yet no vote on adoption is taken until there has been opportunity to perfect all the parts by amendment. Keeping all subdivisions of the series open until one final vote avoids the possibility of complications which would result—especially in the case of bylaws—if amendments to later paragraphs necessitated changes in others that had already been adopted.

28:4 **Cases in Which the Chair Normally Applies the Method.** In adopting a set of bylaws or the articles of a platform, consideration by paragraph is the normal and advisable procedure, followed as a matter of course unless the assembly votes to do otherwise.

The chair, on his own initiative, can apply this method to any elaborate proposition susceptible to such treatment, unless he thinks the assembly wishes to act on the question as a whole; or the manner of consideration can be settled by unanimous consent. Should the chair neglect this, a member can move "that the resolution be considered by paragraph" (or "seriatim").

28:5   **Motion to Consider as a Whole.** If the chair suggests consideration by paragraph and a member feels that time could be saved by acting on it as a whole, the member can move "that it be considered as a whole." This motion is governed by standard descriptive characteristics identical to those for *Consideration by Paragraph or Seriatim.*

28:6   **Procedure for Consideration by Paragraph.** The procedure in considering by paragraph or seriatim is as follows: The member who moved the adoption of the document, the secretary, or the presiding officer (as the chair may decide) reads the first subdivision, and it is explained by its proponent. The chair then asks, "Is there any debate or amendment to this paragraph [or "section," etc.]?" When there is no further debate or amendment to the first paragraph, each succeeding one is taken up. Amendments are voted on as they arise, but no paragraph as amended is acted upon (as to final adoption or rejection) at that time. After all parts have been considered, the chair opens the entire document to amendment. At this time additional parts can be inserted, or parts can be struck out, or any one of them can be further amended. It is not necessary to amend the numbers of articles, sections, or other subdivisions. It is the duty of the secretary to make all such corrections where they become necessary (see 57:18–19).

28:7   If there is a preamble, it is treated in the same way before the final vote. Then the entire document is acted upon in a single vote. If the *Previous Question* is ordered before the preamble has been considered, it does not apply to the preamble unless expressly so stated.

28:8 **Application of Subsidiary and Incidental Motions During Consideration by Paragraph.** During the consideration of the separate paragraphs, any motion to *Postpone Indefinitely, Commit, Postpone,* or *Lay on the Table* can apply only to the entire series or proposition. If a motion to *Postpone Indefinitely* is made under these circumstances, it is stated by the chair, but is not debated or voted on until the paragraph-by-paragraph phase of consideration is completed and the entire document has been declared open to amendment. This rule is a consequence of two characteristics of the motion to *Postpone Indefinitely*—that amendments take precedence over it, and that while it is pending the entire main question is open to debate. Motions to *Commit, Postpone* (definitely), or *Lay on the Table*, on the other hand, are taken up as they arise; and, if adopted, they affect the entire main question immediately. If or when the main question comes before the assembly again later, the consideration by paragraph or seriatim is resumed at the point where it was interrupted. The *Previous Question* and *Limit or Extend Limits of Debate* can be applied to amendments or to the entire document but not to the individual paragraphs.

28:9 If it has been decided to consider divisible material seriatim, even if the material was divisible on the demand of a single member, it is too late to move or demand a division of the question.

Form and Example

28:10 When the chair does not initiate seriatim consideration, this form can be used:

> MEMBER A (obtaining the floor): Mr. President, I move that the resolution [or "the platform," etc.] be considered by paragraph [or "seriatim"]. (Second.)

28:11 If the chair suggests consideration by paragraph and a member feels that the proposition could be acted upon as a whole, this form may be used:

MEMBER X (obtaining the floor): Madam President, I move that … be considered as a whole. (Second.)

§29. DIVISION OF THE ASSEMBLY

29:1   Whenever a member doubts the result of a voice (viva-voce) vote or a vote by show of hands—either because the result appears close or because he doubts that a representative number of the members present have voted—he can call for a *Division of the Assembly*, thereby requiring the vote to be taken again by rising.[11]

29:2   A voice vote retaken by a show of hands is not a *Division of the Assembly*, since in large assemblies it may be less accurate than a rising vote, and since—even in a small meeting—the rising vote may be more effective in causing a maximum number of members to vote.

29:3   On an inconclusive voice vote in a very small meeting where all present can clearly see one another, if, instead of calling for a *Division*, a member asks for a show of hands, this is in the nature of a request, and the chair can retake the vote by this method unless a call for a *Division* is also made. Before or after the vote is thus retaken, however, any member still has the right to demand a *Division* if he believes it will obtain a more conclusive result.

Standard Descriptive Characteristics

29:4   A *Division of the Assembly*:

1. Takes precedence over any motion on which a vote is being taken or has just been taken. It may be called for from the moment the negative votes have been cast until the

---

11. In the earliest forms of this procedure, members in favor of a measure and those opposed were asked to rise from their seats and proceed to the opposite sides of the meeting hall—hence the name, "division."

announcement of the result is complete, or immediately thereafter (see 45:9). It does not yield to any motion.

2. Can be applied to any motion on which the assembly is called upon to vote by voice or by a show of hands. No subsidiary motion can be applied to it.

3. Is in order when another has the floor and is called for without obtaining the floor.

4. Does not require a second.

5. Is not debatable.

6. Is not amendable.

7. Does not require a vote, since a single member can demand a division.

8. Cannot be reconsidered.

Further Rules and Explanation

29:5 **Procedure for Retaking a Vote.** When a *Division* is demanded, the chair immediately takes the vote again, first by having the affirmative rise, then by having the negative rise. If it appears to the chair, when those in the affirmative rise, that the vote will be close, he can count the vote or order it to be counted. If a member desires the vote on the division to be counted, he must make a motion to that effect, which requires a majority vote (see 4:53; **30**; 45:14).

29:6 **Vote Retaken at Chair's Initiative.** The chair has the responsibility of obtaining a correct expression of the will of the assembly. If he is uncertain of the result of a vote or if he feels that the vote is unrepresentative, the chair can of his own accord take the vote again by a rising vote.

29:7 **Dilatory Use.** When it is clear that there has been a full vote and there can be no reasonable doubt as to which side is in the majority, a call for a *Division* is dilatory, and the chair should not allow the individual member's right of demanding a *Division* to be abused to the annoyance of the assembly.

Form and Example

29:8   While, or immediately after, the chair announces the result of a vote, "The ayes [or "noes"] have it and … ," a member can call for a division from his seat, without obtaining the floor:

> **MEMBER:** Division!

Or:

> **MEMBER:** I call for [or "demand"] a division.

Or:

> **MEMBER:** I doubt the result of the vote.

To such a call in any of these forms, the chair responds:

> **CHAIR:** A division is called for [or "demanded"].

The chair then proceeds to take the rising vote, as shown in 4:38.

§30. MOTIONS RELATING TO METHODS OF VOTING AND THE POLLS

30:1   The object of motions relating to methods of voting and the polls is to obtain a vote on a question in some form other than by voice, by show of hands, or by *Division* (rising); or to otherwise direct how and when voting is to be conducted. This category includes motions that the vote be taken by ballot, that it be taken by roll call (the yeas and nays), that a standing vote be counted (tellers), or that the vote be taken by an unusual method such as the use of black and white balls or a signed ballot (see 45:46). This category also includes motions relating to the conduct of a vote, such as those closing or reopening the polls, or ordering a recapitulation of a roll-call vote (see 45:51) or a recount (see 45:41).

30:2   A motion in this category is an incidental motion—and subject to the rules given here—only when a motion or election is pending or the vote on it has just been taken or announced; otherwise, it is an incidental main motion.

Standard Descriptive Characteristics

30:3   Incidental motions relating to methods of voting and the polls:

1. Take precedence over the motion being voted on or to be voted on. When applied to a vote which has just been taken, they can be moved from the moment the chair has reported the vote (see 4:43(1)) until the announcement of the result is complete, or immediately thereafter (see 45:9). They can be moved while an order for the *Previous Question* is in effect on the votes to which they apply. They yield to the privileged motions, and to a motion to *Lay on the Table* moved while the question to which they are applied is pending.

2. Can be applied to any motion on which the assembly is called upon to vote other than another motion relating to the method of voting, or a motion to close or reopen the polls.[12] No subsidiary motion can be applied to them except *Amend*.[13]

3. Are out of order when another has the floor; but, within the time limits specified in Standard Characteristic 1 above, a member can claim preference in being recognized for the purpose of making one of these motions when applied to a vote that has just been taken.

4. Must be seconded.

5. Are not debatable. (But see 43:31–32 regarding allowable explanation of an undebatable motion.)

6. Are amendable.

---

12. However, a motion to take a counted vote can be applied to any motion except to another motion to take a counted vote.

13. In principle, the *Previous Question* can also be applied to them to stop their amendment, though such a case will rarely arise in practice.

7. Require a majority vote, except a motion to close the polls, which requires a two-thirds vote.

8. The vote on a motion ordering that the polls be closed or reopened at a specified time can be reconsidered at any time before the order has been carried out. Otherwise, neither a vote to close the polls nor an affirmative vote to reopen the polls can be reconsidered; the same effect can be obtained by renewal or by the opposite motion. A negative vote on a motion to reopen the polls can be reconsidered within the period during which a motion to reopen the polls could be made originally. Other motions relating to methods of voting can be reconsidered.

Further Rules and Explanation

30:4 **Methods of Voting.** In practice, the method of taking a vote usually can be agreed upon informally. But when different methods are suggested, they are usually treated not as amendments but as filling blanks, the vote normally being taken first on the one taking the most time. (For ways of voting, see 4:34–56; **45**.)

30:5 A member who believes that a secret vote will give a truer expression of the assembly's will on a pending motion can move that the vote on the motion be taken by ballot. An order that the vote on a main motion be taken by ballot also applies to a vote on whether to postpone the main motion indefinitely. (See also *Roll-Call Vote*, 45:45ff.)

30:6 **Retaking a Vote.** As explained in **4** (see 4:34–56) and **45** (see 45:11), the regular methods of initially taking a vote are by voice (*viva voce*), by rising (division), or by show of hands—the latter two of which may also be called for by any member as a means of verifying an inconclusive vote that has just been taken (see **29**)—and the chair may order that a vote be counted or that an uncounted vote be retaken as a counted vote. After a question has been voted on in any of these ways, and within the time specified in Standard Characteristic 1 above, the assembly can still order that the vote be taken again by some method other than any of the regular ones (see *Other Methods of Voting*, 45:17ff.) or that an uncounted vote be retaken as a counted vote. But after a vote has been taken by one of those other methods, or after the assembly has ordered that a counted vote be taken, it is not in order to move that the vote be taken again. It is never in order to move that the vote on a question be taken a second time by the same method.

30:7 **Exhaustion of an Order Prescribing the Method of Voting.** If the method of voting on a motion is ordered by the assembly (and not prescribed by the assembly's rules), such an order is exhausted (1) when the question on which it was imposed has been finally disposed of, or (2) at the conclusion of the session in which the order has been adopted—whichever occurs first. If, after such an order is exhausted, the motion to which it previously applied comes to a vote (for example, during reconsideration or at a subsequent session), the order is no longer in effect. Notwithstanding the exhaustion of this order, however, a motion which has been voted on by ballot must also be voted on by ballot during any reconsideration of it, since no action is in order that would force the disclosure of a member's vote or views on the matter (see 45:21). Likewise, if the assembly adjourns after balloting for an office has begun but before the election to that office is complete (46:44–45), any additional votes needed to complete the election must also be taken by ballot, even if they are taken at a subsequent session.

30:8 **Closing or Reopening the Polls.** Motions relating to opening and closing the polls are applicable only with respect to ballot votes. It is usually better to leave it to the chair to close the polls. When the vote is taken by ballot, as soon as the chair thinks that all have voted who wish to, he inquires if all have voted. If there is no response, he declares the polls closed, and the tellers proceed to count the vote.

30:9 If a motion is made to close the polls when the voting has closed naturally, the chair can treat the motion as a unanimous-consent request and declare the polls closed. In any case, a formal motion to close the polls may not be recognized until all have presumably voted. Like motions relating to the close of debate or nominations, the motion to close the polls requires a two-thirds vote.

30:10   If members enter afterward and it is desired to reopen the polls, this can be done by a majority vote.

30:11   The time at which the polls shall be closed or reopened can be specified in the motion, or added by amendment.

§31. MOTIONS RELATING TO NOMINATIONS

31:1   While an election is pending, a member may wish to offer a motion to determine the method of making nominations[14] (when it is not prescribed in the bylaws or rules of order). Members also may wish to offer motions to close or reopen nominations.

Standard Descriptive Characteristics

31:2   Incidental motions relating to nominations:

1. Take precedence over the pending election for which nominations are to be made. They yield to the privileged motions, and to the motion to *Lay on the Table.*
2. Apply to any pending election. No subsidiary motion except *Amend*[15] can be applied to them.
3. Are out of order when another has the floor or any member is attempting to make a nomination.
4. Must be seconded.
5. Are not debatable. (But see 43:31–32 regarding allowable explanation of an undebatable motion.)
6. Are amendable.
7. Require a majority vote, except a motion to close nominations, which requires a two-thirds vote because (a) its adop-

---

14. A motion prescribing the method of nominating is an incidental motion—and subject to the rules given here—only when the election is pending; otherwise, it is an incidental main motion (see **10**).

15. See 30:3(2)n14, which also applies to these motions.

tion deprives members of a basic right—to nominate; and (b) the assembly must be protected against attempted abuse of the power to close nominations by a temporary majority.

8. Can be reconsidered, except the motion to close nominations, or an affirmative vote on a motion to reopen nominations. (In the latter cases, the same effect can be obtained by renewal or by the opposite motion.)

Further Rules and Explanation

31:3   **Motions to Prescribe Methods of Nominating.** If no method of making nominations is designated by the bylaws or rules and the assembly has adopted no order on the subject, anyone can make a motion prescribing the method of nomination for an office to be filled. When different methods are proposed, they can be moved as amendments, but are frequently treated as filling blanks (12:92–113). In that event, the vote is taken on the various suggested methods of nominating, in this order: (a) by the chair; (b) from the floor (sometimes called "open nominations"); (c) by a committee; (d) by ballot; (e) by mail; and (f) by petition (see **46**). It should be noted that not all of these methods are appropriate or desirable in average societies.

31:4   **Motions to Close or Reopen Nominations.** In the average society, a motion to close nominations is not a necessary part of the election procedure and it should not generally be moved. When nominations have been made by a committee or from the floor, the chair inquires whether there are any further nominations; and when there is no response, he declares that nominations are closed. In very large bodies, the formality of a motion to close nominations is sometimes allowed, but this motion is not in order until a reasonable opportunity to make nominations has been given; as noted above, it is out of order if a member is rising, addressing the chair, or otherwise attempting to make a nomination, and it always requires a two-thirds vote. When no one wishes to make a further nomination, the motion serves no useful purpose.

31:5   A legitimate use of the motion to close nominations would be, for example, to end delay of an election by numbers of nominations obviously intended only to honor persons who have no chance of being elected.

31:6   When for any reason it is desired to reopen nominations, this can be done by a majority vote. The closing of nominations—whether or not a formal motion to close them has been adopted—does not limit the making of further nominations at a later session at which the election is held (see also 46:6).

31:7   The time at which nominations shall be closed or reopened can be specified in the motion, or added by amendment.

§32. REQUEST TO BE EXCUSED FROM A DUTY

32:1   Occasionally the bylaws of a society may impose specific duties on members beyond the mere payment of dues. Members may be obligated to attend a certain number of meetings, to prepare talks or papers, to serve on committees, or even to accept office if elected. In these cases, a member cannot, as a matter of right, decline such a duty or *demand* that he or she be excused from it, but the assembly—except as the bylaws may provide otherwise—can grant the member's *request* to be so excused. The request can be granted by unanimous consent, or a motion to grant it, which is debatable and amendable, can be offered.

Standard Descriptive Characteristics

32:2   A *Request to Be Excused from a Duty*:

1. Takes precedence over any motion with whose purpose it is connected and can also be made at any time when no question is pending. A motion on a request that is pending yields to all subsidiary motions except *Postpone Indefinitely*, to all privileged motions, and to other incidental motions.

2. Can be applied in reference to any motion or parliamentary situation out of which it arises. All subsidiary motions except *Postpone Indefinitely* can be applied to it.

3. Is in order when another has the floor if it requires immediate attention.

4. Does not require a second except when moved formally *by the maker of the request.* A motion to *grant* the request of another member does not require a second since the maker of the request and the maker of the motion—two members—wish the question to be considered.

5. Is debatable.

6. Is amendable.

7. Requires a majority vote, but is frequently settled by unanimous consent.

8. Where the member requesting to be excused from a duty has learned of the action taken on his or her request, only a negative vote can be reconsidered.

Further Rules and Explanation

32:3   If a duty is not compulsory, a member can decline when he is first named to it or, if absent at that time, when he first learns of his election or appointment. At times other than during a meeting, such a notice of declination can be addressed to the secretary or to the appointing power. Since in these cases the duty is not compulsory, no motion to excuse the member is necessary.

32:4   A member who remains silent when presumably aware that he has been named to a duty is regarded as accepting, and he thereby places himself under the same obligations as if he had expressly accepted.

32:5   If a member who has accepted an office, committee assignment, or other duty finds that he is unable to perform it, he should submit his resignation. A resignation is submitted in writing, addressed to the secretary or appointing power; alternatively, it may be submitted during a meeting either orally or in writing.[16] By submitting a resignation, the member is, in effect, requesting to be excused from a duty. The chair, on reading or

---

16. See 13:23, 47:57–58.

announcing the resignation, can assume a motion "that the resignation be accepted."

32:6   The duties of a position must not be abandoned until a resignation has been accepted and becomes effective, or at least until there has been a reasonable opportunity for it to be accepted.

32:7   A request to be excused from a duty *essential to the functioning of a society or assembly* is a question of privilege affecting the organization of the assembly; and so also is the filling of a vacancy created by the acceptance of a resignation. In such cases, the assembly can proceed immediately to fill the vacancy, unless notice is required or other provision for filling vacancies is made in the bylaws. In the case of a resignation *from office*, unless the bylaws provide otherwise, the assembly cannot proceed to fill the vacancy immediately since notice is a requirement. But if a member is elected and declines, no notice is required to complete the election immediately or at the next meeting (see 46:46).

32:8   **Resignation from Membership.**   A member in good standing with his dues paid cannot be compelled to continue his membership so that additional obligations are incurred. His resignation should be accepted immediately, and if it is not, he incurs no obligation after his resignation has been sent in, provided he does not avail himself of the privileges of membership. It is different with members who have not paid their dues up to the date of sending in their resignations. Until they have settled their dues, the society is under no obligation to accept their resignations, and thus additional amounts may become due. If their dues are not paid within a reasonable time, instead of accepting their resignations, the society may expel them. A resignation sent in to escape charges need not be accepted. The charges may be preferred, and the trial should proceed the same as if the resignation had not been sent in.

§33. REQUESTS AND INQUIRIES

33:1   In connection with business in a meeting, members may wish to obtain information or to do or have something done that requires permission of the assembly. Any member can make the following types of inquiry or request: (a) *Parliamentary Inquiry*; (b) *For Information*; (c) *For Permission (or Leave) to Withdraw or Modify a Motion*; (d) *To Read Papers*; and (e) *For Any Other Privilege*.

Standard Descriptive Characteristics

33:2   With respect to the requests and inquiries growing out of the business of the assembly that are listed above, the following rules apply:

1. All take precedence over any motion with whose purpose they are connected, and can also be made at any time when no question is pending. A motion on a request that is pending yields to all privileged motions and to other incidental motions.
2. All can be applied in reference to any motion or parliamentary situation out of which they arise. No subsidiary motion can be applied to any of them.
3. All are in order when another has the floor if they require immediate attention.
4. A *Parliamentary Inquiry* and a *Request for Information* do not require a second. The other requests do not require a second, except when moved formally *by the maker of the request*. A motion to *grant* the request of another member does not require a second, since two members already wish the question to come up—the maker of the request and the maker of the motion.
5. All are not debatable, although they may be accompanied by brief explanations as necessary (cf. 43:31–32).
6. All are not amendable.
7. No vote is taken on a *Parliamentary Inquiry* and a *Request for Information*. The other requests require a majority vote

in order to be granted, and are frequently settled by unanimous consent. When it is too late for renewal, unanimous consent is *required* to grant permission to withdraw a motion to *Reconsider* (37:10(b)), or to withdraw previous notice of a proposed motion requiring such notice (10:44–51).

8. A *Parliamentary Inquiry* and a *Request for Information* are not subject to reconsideration. The vote on a request *For Permission to Modify a Motion*, *To Read Papers*, and *For Any Other Privilege* can be reconsidered. On a request *For Permission to Withdraw a Motion*, only a negative vote can be reconsidered.

Further Rules and Explanation (with Forms)

33:3   **A. Parliamentary Inquiry.** A *Parliamentary Inquiry* is a question directed to the presiding officer to obtain information on a matter of parliamentary law or the rules of the organization bearing on the business at hand. It is the chair's duty to answer such questions when it may assist a member to make an appropriate motion, raise a proper point of order, or understand the parliamentary situation or the effect of a motion. The chair is not obliged to answer hypothetical questions.

33:4   In making an inquiry, the inquirer arises, and without obtaining the floor, addresses the chair as follows:

> **MEMBER A:** Madam President, I rise to a parliamentary inquiry. [Or, "A parliamentary inquiry, please."]
> **CHAIR:** The member will state the inquiry.
> **MEMBER A:** Is it in order at this time to move the previous question?

33:5   The chair's reply to a parliamentary inquiry is not subject to an appeal, since it is an opinion, not a ruling. A member may act contrary to this opinion, however, and may appeal from a resulting adverse ruling by the chair. If an inquiry is made when another member has the floor and an immediate answer is not necessary, the chair can defer a reply until the floor has been yielded.

33:6 **B. Request for Information.** A *Request for Information* (also called a *Point of Information*) is a request directed to the chair, or through the chair to another officer or member, for information relevant to the business at hand but not related to parliamentary procedure.

33:7 It is treated like a parliamentary inquiry, as follows:

> MEMBER A: Mr. President, I have a request for information. [Or, "A point of information, please."]
> CHAIR: The member will state his question.
> MEMBER A: Will the convention delegates report at this meeting?

Or:

> MEMBER A: This motion calls for a large expenditure. Will the Treasurer state the present balance?

33:8 If information is desired of a member who is speaking, the inquirer, upon rising, may use the following form instead:

> MEMBER A: Madam President, will the member yield for a question?

Or:

> MEMBER A: Mr. President, I would like to ask the gentleman [or "the member"] a question.

33:9 If the speaker consents to the interruption, the time consumed will be taken out of his allowed time. The chair therefore asks if the speaker is willing to be interrupted, and if he consents, directs the inquirer to proceed. Although the presiding officer generally remains silent during the ensuing exchange, the inquiry, the reply, and any resulting colloquy are made in the third person through the chair. To protect decorum, members are not allowed to carry on discussion directly with one another.

33:10 An inquiry of this kind may also be for the purpose of reminding a speaker of a point to be made in argument, or it may be intended to rebut his position; but it must always be put in the form of a question.

33:11 **C. Request for Permission (or Leave) to Withdraw or Modify a Motion.** Conditions for withdrawing or modifying a motion depend upon how soon the mover states his wish to withdraw or modify it. *Permission* for him to do so is required only after the motion to which it pertains has been stated by the chair as pending.

33:12 *Before a motion has been stated by the chair*, it is the property of its mover, who can withdraw it or modify it without asking the consent of anyone. Thus, *in the brief interval between the making of a motion and the time when the chair places it before the assembly by stating it*, the maker can withdraw it as follows:

> **MEMBER A (who made the motion):** Madam President, I withdraw the motion.

Or:

> **MEMBER A (who made the motion):** Mr. President, I wish to modify the motion by striking out "demand" and inserting "urge."

In the same interval also, another member can ask if the maker of the motion is willing to withdraw it or accept a change in it, which suggestion the maker can either accept or reject. In such a case the chair either announces, "The motion has been withdrawn," or states the question on the modified motion. If a motion is modified, the seconder can withdraw his second. When the seconder withdraws his second to the modified motion, the member who suggested the modification has, in effect, supplied a second.

33:13 *After a motion has been stated by the chair*, it belongs to the meeting as a whole, and the maker must request the assembly's permission to withdraw or modify his own motion, according to the rules stated in Standard Characteristics 1–8, above. In such cases the procedure is as follows.

33:14   To *withdraw* a motion that is before the assembly, the member who made it may use this form:

> **MEMBER A (who made the motion):** Madam President, I ask permission [or "leave"] to withdraw the motion.

33:15   The chair treats this first as a unanimous-consent request. That is, if no one objects, the announcement is:

> **CHAIR:** Unless there is objection [pause] the motion is withdrawn.

If there is an objection, the chair of his own accord can put the question on granting the request, or any member can move "that permission to withdraw the motion be granted." If a member other than the one making the request made the motion, it does not require a second, since the maker of the motion to grant permission and the maker of the request surely both favor it.

33:16   A request for permission to withdraw a motion, or a motion to grant such permission, can be made at any time before voting on the question has begun, even though the motion has been amended, and even though subsidiary or incidental motions may be pending. Any such motions that adhere to the main motion cease to be before the assembly and require no further disposition if the main motion is withdrawn. Any member can suggest that the maker of a motion ask permission to withdraw it, which the maker can do or decline to do, as he chooses.

33:17   After a question has been divided, one or more of the parts can be withdrawn without affecting the other parts. A motion to *Reconsider* (**37**), or a previous notice of a proposed motion requiring such notice (10:44–51), cannot be withdrawn after it is too late for renewal, unless unanimous consent is given.

33:18   After a motion has been withdrawn, the situation is as though it had never been made; therefore, the same motion can be made again at the same meeting.

33:19   To *modify* a motion after it has been stated by the chair, the maker asks permission to do so, as in the case of withdrawal of a motion. If there is no objection, the chair states the question on the modified motion. If anyone objects, the chair must then determine whether an amendment equivalent to the requested modification would be in order. If not, the modification may not be made unless a motion to suspend the rules is made and adopted. If a motion for such an amendment is in order, the chair can assume it or any member can move it formally. The amendment requires a second if moved by the member who originally made the request. The rules governing consideration of amendments are followed (see **12**). A pending motion can be amended only by vote or unanimous consent of the assembly, even if the maker of the motion states that he "accepts" the amendment. (See also treatment of "friendly amendments," 12:91.)

33:20   **D. Request to Read Papers.** If any member objects, a member has no right to read from—or to have the secretary read from—any paper or book as a part of his speech without permission of the assembly. This rule is a protection against the use of reading as a means of prolonging debate and delaying business. It is customary, however, to permit members to read short, pertinent, printed extracts in debate so long as they do not abuse the privilege. If a member wishes to do so, he can, while speaking in debate, say, "If there is no objection, I would like to read … [indicating the nature and length of the paper]." The member can then begin to read unless another member objects.[17] In such a case, at any time until the speaker has finished reading, another member can interrupt him by an objection, which must be addressed to the chair. Or, if the speaker desiring to read prefers, he can formally request permission: "Mr. President, I ask permission to read a state-

---

17. The procedure of presuming permission to read until objection is raised is applicable *only in debate on a pending question.*

ment ... [briefly describing it, as above]"; and the chair then asks if there is objection. In either case, if there is an objection, the chair can, of his own accord, put the question on granting permission, or any member can move "that permission to read a paper in debate be granted." This motion requires no second unless moved by the member who made the request. Action of the assembly granting a request to read a paper can be reconsidered at any time until the reading has been concluded.

33:21   The foregoing paragraph applies only to papers or documents that are not before the assembly for action. When any paper is laid before the assembly for action, it is a right of every member that it be read once; and, if there is any debate or amendment, that it be read again before members are asked to vote on it. Except as just stated, no member has the right to have anything read without permission of the assembly. But whenever any member requests that a document that is before the assembly be read—obviously for information and not for delay—and no one objects, the chair normally should direct that it be read. If there is an objection, a majority vote is required to order that it be read. If a member was absent from the hall when the paper under consideration was read—even though absent on duty—he cannot insist on its being read again; in this case, the convenience of the assembly is more important than that of a single member.

33:22   **E. Request for Any Other Privilege.** When a member desires to make a request not covered by one of the four types explained above—as, for example, a request to address remarks or make a presentation while no motion is pending—he rises, addresses the chair, and, as soon as he catches the presiding officer's attention, states his request. Although he does not have to wait for recognition and can make his request even though another member has been assigned the floor, he should never interrupt a member speaking unless sure that urgency justifies it. Generally, such matters are settled by unanimous consent or informally, but if there is an objection, a motion can be made to grant the request. If explanation is required, it can be requested or given, but this must not extend into debate. These requests should be treated so as to interrupt the proceedings as little as is consistent with the demands of justice.

chapter IX

MOTIONS THAT BRING A QUESTION AGAIN BEFORE THE ASSEMBLY

*See 6:25ff. for a list of these motions and
a description of their characteristics as a group.*

§34. TAKE FROM THE TABLE

34:1   The object of the motion to *Take from the Table* is to make
pending again before the assembly a motion or a series of
adhering motions that previously has been laid on the table
(see **17**).

Standard Descriptive Characteristics

34:2   The motion to *Take from the Table*:

1. Takes precedence over no pending motion, and therefore
cannot be moved while any other question is pending; but,
subject to the conditions indicated in the next sentence, it
takes precedence over a main motion that has been made
but has not yet been stated by the chair. Unless it is moved
under a suspension of the rules (**25**) it must be moved at
a time when no program or rule interferes, and while business of the class to which the subject question belongs, or
unfinished business, general orders, or new business, is in
order; and it cannot interrupt a series of motions connected
with taking up a single item of business (see below). It yields

to privileged and incidental motions but not to subsidiary ones.

2. Can be applied to any question or series of *adhering* motions that lies on the table as explained in the first paragraph under *Further Rules and Explanation*, below. This motion is not in order, however, until some business or interrupting matter has been transacted or dealt with since the question was laid on the table; and if it is moved and voted down, the motion to *Take from the Table* cannot be renewed until some further business has been transacted. No subsidiary motion can be applied to the motion to *Take from the Table*.

3. Is out of order when another has the floor; but a member can claim preference in being recognized for the purpose of making this motion ahead of a new main motion, or he can claim the floor for such a purpose after a new main motion has been made but before the new motion has been stated by the chair (see below).

4. Must be seconded.

5. Is not debatable. (But see 43:31–32 regarding allowable explanation of an undebatable motion.)

6. Is not amendable.

7. Requires a majority vote.

8. Cannot be reconsidered. If the motion to *Take from the Table* is adopted, the question can be laid on the table again should any legitimate need arise to do so, according to the rules stated in 17:11. If the motion to *Take from the Table* is rejected, it can be renewed each time that any business has been transacted (see 38:7(2)).

Further Rules and Explanation

34:3 **Time Limits on Taking a Question from the Table.** A question that has been laid on the table remains there and can be taken from the table during the same session (**8**), or, if the next regular business session will be held before a quarterly time interval has elapsed (see 9:7), also until the end of the next regular session.[1] If not taken from the table within these time limits, the question dies, although it can be reintroduced later as a new question. As long as a question remains on the table, any member can move to take it from the table at a regular meeting, including a meeting that is an adjournment (**9**) of a regular meeting. At a special meeting, however, a question can be taken from the table only if: (a) it has been laid on the table earlier at the same session, or (b) the call of the special meeting specifies either the particular question that lies on the table or its subject matter.

34:4 **Right of Way in Preference to a New Main Motion.** In ordinary assemblies a question is supposed to be laid on the table only temporarily, with the expectation that its consideration will be resumed after disposal of the interrupting matter or at a more convenient time. Consequently, as soon as the business or interrupting matter has been disposed of, any member can seek recognition for the purpose of moving to take the question from the table; or, so long as it remains on the table, he can do so at any time under the classes of business listed in Standard Characteristic 1 above—except while another motion is pending or while a series of motions connected with one question is being introduced, as explained in the next paragraph. If the chair recognizes someone else as having risen and addressed the chair first, a member who rose at about the same time to move to take the question from the table should remain standing and say that he rises for this purpose, and the chair then assigns him the floor. Or, even after a new motion has been made but before it has been stated by the chair, a member who quickly rises and says that he does so to move to

---

1. If the term of all or a specified portion of the assembly's membership will expire before the start of the next regular session, as may happen in a board or an elected legislative assembly, the rule is the same as though more than a quarterly time interval will have elapsed—that is, a question can be taken from the table only until the end of the same session at which it was laid on the table.

take the question from the table is entitled to be assigned the floor. The principle is that, if the assembly so desires, a motion already within its control by being only temporarily disposed of (9:7–11, 38:8) has the right of way over a new main motion.

34:5   Even if no question is pending, a motion to *Take from the Table* cannot interrupt a series of motions connected with bringing up a single item of business, but must wait until the complete series is disposed of. For example, such a series of motions is in process of being dealt with:

- when the assembly has just voted to suspend the rules and permit a certain main motion to be introduced;
- when a question has just been laid on the table for the announced purpose of admitting another motion;
- when a previous action has just been rescinded (**35**) to enable a conflicting main motion to be made; or
- when a main motion has just been voted down after a member stated in debate that in that event he would offer a different motion covering the case.

In each of the above instances, until the main motion that was specified has been made and disposed of, it is not in order to move to take still another question from the table.

34:6   **Status of a Question Taken from the Table.** When a question is taken from the table, it is before the assembly, with everything adhering to it, so far as possible (and with the exceptions noted below), exactly as it was when laid on the table.[2] For example, if amendments and a motion to *Commit* were pending when a resolution was laid on the table, then when it is taken from the table the question is first on the motion to *Commit*. The same would be true if a motion to *Postpone to a Certain Time* were adhering to a resolution—that is, the

---

2. However, if an amendable motion is taken from the table at a later session, motions to amend it may be made without regard to whether or not the same or similar motions to amend it were either adopted or rejected during any previous session.

motion to *Postpone* would become immediately pending—except that if the resolution is not taken from the table until after the time of proposed postponement, the motion to *Postpone* is ignored. If the question is taken up on the same day that it was laid on the table, members who had exhausted their right of debate cannot speak on the question again; but if on another day, all members have their right to debate renewed with reference to each question being debated under the regular limitations (see 43:12–13). An order for the *Previous Question* or a limitation or extension of debate is not exhausted, however, if the question to which such an order was applied is taken from the table at the same session, even on another day—as in a convention.

34:7   At the next session any such order is exhausted and the regular rules of debate prevail. For the rules relating to the exhaustion of an order prescribing the method of voting on a question, see 30:7.

Form and Example

34:8   The form used in making this motion is, for example, "I move to take from the table the resolution relating to … and its amendment."

34:9   If Member A, who has risen to seek the floor for the purpose of making this motion, observes that the chair has recognized another member who rose at about the same time and who apparently intends to make a new main motion, the procedure would be as follows:

> **MEMBER A (remaining standing and interrupting):** Mr. President, I rise for the purpose of moving to take a question from the table.

Upon recognition, Member A then would move "… to take from the table the motion relating to …"

34:10   If Member A did not rise to claim the floor before the chair recognized another who already has made a new motion, then before this question has been stated by the chair, Member A can quickly rise and address the chair, thus:

MEMBER A: Madam President.
CHAIR: For what purpose does the member rise?
MEMBER A: I rise for the purpose of moving … [and so on, as in the case above].

§35. RESCIND; AMEND SOMETHING PREVIOUSLY ADOPTED

35:1　　By means of the motions to *Rescind* and to *Amend Something Previously Adopted*—which are two forms of one incidental main motion governed by identical rules—the assembly can change an action previously taken or ordered. *Rescind*—also known as *Repeal* or *Annul*—is the motion by which a previous action or order can be canceled or countermanded. The effect of *Rescind* is to strike out an entire main motion, resolution, order, or rule that has been adopted at some previous time. *Amend Something Previously Adopted* is the motion that can be used if it is desired to change only a part of the text, or to substitute a different version.

Standard Descriptive Characteristics

35:2　　The motions to *Rescind* and to *Amend Something Previously Adopted*:

1. Take precedence over nothing, and can therefore be moved only when no other motion is pending. *Previous notice* (10:44–51) of intent to offer one of these motions at the next meeting can be given while another question is pending, however—provided that it does not interrupt a speaker (see Standard Characteristic 7). These motions yield to subsidiary, privileged, and incidental motions.
2. Can be applied to anything (e.g., bylaw, rule, policy, decision, or choice) which has continuing force and effect and which was made or created at any time or times as the result

of the *adoption* of one or more main motions. (However, see below for actions that cannot be rescinded or amended.) All of the subsidiary motions can be applied to the motions to *Rescind* and to *Amend Something Previously Adopted.*

3. Are out of order when another has the floor; but previous notice of intent to offer one of these motions at the next meeting can be given after another member has been assigned the floor, provided that he has not begun to speak.

4. Must be seconded.

5. Are debatable; debate can go into the merits of the question which it is proposed to rescind or amend.

6. Are amendable, by the processes of primary and secondary amendment in any of the forms discussed in **12**, as applicable to the particular case. Thus, a motion to *Rescind* can be amended, for example, by substituting for it a motion to amend what is proposed to be rescinded. But if a motion to *Rescind* or to *Amend Something Previously Adopted* is amended so that the change proposed by the amended motion then exceeds the scope of a previous notice that was given, the effect of the previous notice is destroyed and the motion can no longer be adopted by a majority vote (see Standard Characteristic 7). When these motions *require* previous notice (as may be the case with respect to a motion to rescind or amend a provision of the bylaws or a special rule of order), such a motion cannot be amended so as to make the proposed change greater than that for which notice has been given.

7. In an assembly, except when applied to a constitution, bylaws, or special rules of order, require (a) a two-thirds vote, (b) a majority vote when notice of intent to make the motion, stating the complete substance of the proposed change, has been given at the previous meeting within a quarterly time interval or in the call of the present meeting, or (c) a vote of a majority of the entire membership—any one of which will suffice. The same vote is required for the assembly to rescind or amend an action taken by subordinate bodies,

such as some executive boards, empowered to act on behalf of the assembly. In a committee, these motions require a two-thirds vote unless all committee members who voted for the motion to be rescinded or amended are present or have received reasonable notice, in which case they require a majority vote. A motion to rescind or amend provisions of a constitution or bylaws is subject to the requirements for amendment as contained in the constitution or bylaws (see **56, 57**). If the bylaws or governing instrument contains no provision relating to amendment, a motion to rescind or amend applied to a constitution or to bylaws is subject to the same voting requirement as to rescind or amend special rules of order—that is, it requires (a) previous notice as described above *and* a two-thirds vote or (b) a vote of a majority of the entire membership.

8. A negative vote on these motions can be reconsidered, but not an affirmative vote.

Further Rules and Explanation

35:3   **Right of Any Member to Make the Motions, Without Time Limit.** In contrast to the case of the motion to *Reconsider*, there is no time limit on making these motions after the adoption of the measure to which they are applied, and they can be moved by any member, regardless of how he voted on the original question. When previous notice has been given, it is usual to wait for the member who gave notice of these motions to move them; but if he does not, any member can do so.

35:4   **Proposed Amendments Beyond the Scope of the Notice.** As noted in Standard Descriptive Characteristic 6 above, when previous notice is a *requirement* for the adoption of a motion to *Rescind* or *Amend Something Previously Adopted*, no subsidiary motion to *Amend* is in order that proposes a change greater than that for which notice was given. This is always the case, for example, when the bylaws of an organization require previous notice for their amendment, which they should do (56:50–53). It will also be the case, as a practical matter, whenever a majority of the entire membership is not in attendance at the time the vote is taken on a motion to rescind or amend a provision of the constitution or bylaws, or a special rule of order. In either of the situations described above, no subsidiary motion to *Amend* is in order that proposes a change going beyond the scope of the notice which was given, for the reason that adoption of such a motion will destroy the effect of the notice, and the motion is thus tantamount to a motion to *Postpone Indefinitely.*

35:5   **Series of Amendments to Previously Adopted Text.** It is possible to offer and adopt several amendments to previously adopted text by means of a single incidental main motion to *Amend Something Previously Adopted* governed by the rules in this section and in **10**. See 10:25 and 27:5 for the rules governing whether and how such a motion may be divided. (For an example, see 57:3.)

35:6   **Actions That Cannot Be Rescinded or Amended.** The motions to *Rescind* and to *Amend Something Previously Adopted* are not in order under the following circumstances:

a) When it has previously been moved to reconsider the vote on the main motion, and the question can be reached by calling up the motion to *Reconsider* (**37**).

b) When something has been done, as a result of the vote on the main motion, that is impossible to undo. (The unexecuted part of an order, however, can be rescinded or amended.)

c) When a resignation has been acted upon, or a person has been elected to or expelled from membership or office, and the person was present or has been officially notified of the action. (The only way to reverse an expulsion is to follow whatever procedure is prescribed by the bylaws for admission or reinstatement. For the case of an election, see 62:16 regarding removal of a person from office.)

Form and Example

35:7   When previous notice has been given, the motions to *Rescind* or to *Amend Something Previously Adopted* may be made as follows:

> **MEMBER A (obtaining the floor):** In accordance with notice given at the last meeting, I move to rescind the resolution that authorized additional landscaping of the grounds. [Or "… to amend the resolution … by adding …"] (Second.)

In such a case, a majority vote is sufficient.

35:8   When no notice of the motion to *Rescind* or to *Amend Something Previously Adopted* has been given, the motions may be made as follows:

> **MEMBER A (obtaining the floor):** I move to rescind the motion relating to … adopted at the May meeting. [Or "… to amend the motion … by inserting …"] (Second.)

Without previous notice, the motion requires a two-thirds vote or a majority of the entire membership for its adoption.

35:9   In a great many instances, the motion or resolution originally adopted is not referred to, and only the bylaw, rule, or policy to be rescinded or amended is mentioned. For example:

> **MEMBER A (obtaining the floor):** In accordance with the notice given in the call of this meeting, I move to amend Article V, Section 3 of the bylaws by striking out subparagraph (c) thereof. (Second.)

35:10   To offer an amendment to change one form of the motion into the other:

35:11   If the motion was made "To amend the motion relating to … adopted at the May meeting … by inserting …":

> **MEMBER A (obtaining the floor):** I move to substitute for the pending motion the following: "To rescind the motion relating to … adopted at the May meeting."

35:12　If the motion was made "To rescind the resolution that authorized additional landscaping of the grounds":

> MEMBER A (obtaining the floor): I move to substitute for the pending motion the following: "To amend the resolution that authorized additional landscaping of the grounds by adding 'at a cost not to exceed $100,000.'"

Rescind and Expunge from the Minutes

35:13　On extremely rare occasions when it is desired not only to rescind action but also to express the strongest disapproval, a member may move to *Rescind and Expunge from the Minutes* (or *the Record*). Adoption of this motion requires an affirmative vote of a majority of the entire membership, and may be inadvisable unless the support is even greater. Even a unanimous vote at a meeting is insufficient if that vote is not a majority of the entire membership. If such a motion is adopted, the secretary, in the presence of the assembly, draws a single line through or around the offending words in the minutes, and writes across them the words, "Rescinded and Ordered Expunged," with the date and his signature. In the recorded minutes the words that are expunged must not be blotted or cut out so that they cannot be read, since this would make it impossible to verify whether more was expunged than ordered. In any published record of the proceedings, the expunged material is omitted. Rather than expunging, it is usually better to rescind the previous action and then, if advisable, to adopt a resolution condemning the action which has been rescinded.

§36. DISCHARGE A COMMITTEE

36:1　By means of the motion to *Discharge a Committee* from further consideration of a question or subject, the assembly can take the matter out of a committee's hands[3] after referring it

---

3.　Or a committee can take it out of a subcommittee's hands.

to the committee and before the committee has made a final report on it, and the assembly itself can consider it.

36:2   So long as a question is in the hands of a committee, the assembly cannot consider another motion involving practically the same question.

36:3   The rules governing this motion are similar to those applying to the motion to *Rescind* or to *Amend Something Previously Adopted*—of which it is a particular case in certain applications, as explained in 36:10–11.

Standard Descriptive Characteristics

36:4   The motion to *Discharge a Committee*:

1. Takes precedence over nothing, and therefore can be moved only when no other question is pending. *Previous notice* of intent to offer the motion at the next meeting can be given while another question is pending, however—provided that it does not interrupt a speaker. This motion yields to all subsidiary, privileged, and incidental motions.

2. Can be applied to any main motion, or any other matter, that has been referred to a committee and that the committee has not yet finally reported to the assembly. All of the subsidiary motions can be applied to it.

3. Is out of order when another has the floor; but previous notice of intent to offer this motion at the next meeting can be given after another member has been assigned the floor, provided that he has not begun to speak.

4. Must be seconded.

5. Is debatable; debate can go into the merits of the question in the hands of the committee.

6. Is amendable. For example, the motion can be amended as to the time at which the assembly is to consider the question; or an amendment to the effect that the committee be instructed to report instead of being discharged can be moved as a substitute.

7. Since the motion would change action already taken by the assembly, requires (a) a two-thirds vote, (b) a majority vote when notice of intent to make the motion has been given at the previous meeting within a quarterly time interval or in the call of the present meeting, or (c) a vote of a majority of the entire membership—any one of which will suffice. To prevent business from being delayed by a committee, however, there are two special circumstances under which the motion requires only a majority vote (even without notice): (a) if the committee fails to report within a prescribed time as instructed, and (b) while the assembly is considering any partial report of the committee.

8. A negative vote can be reconsidered, but not an affirmative vote.

Further Rules and Explanation

36:5 **Circumstances Justifying the Motion; Alternative Procedures.** Action to discharge a committee from further consideration of a question or subject is generally advisable only when the committee has failed to report with appropriate promptness or when, for some urgent reason, the assembly desires to proceed on the matter without further aid from the committee, or wishes to drop the matter.

36:6 If the committee to which the matter was referred has not yet taken it up and if it is not too late to move to *Reconsider* (the day of its committal or the next business-meeting day), the appropriate motion is to reconsider the vote on the motion of referral, which requires only a majority vote. The motion of referral may have been a subsidiary motion to *Commit* (**13**) or a main motion, depending on the case, as explained below.

36:7 Instead of discharging the committee, the assembly can instruct it to report at a reasonable specified time. A motion to do this can be moved as a substitute (see **12**) for a pending motion to *Discharge a Committee*, or it can be introduced as an incidental main motion when no question is pending. If no instruction as to time of reporting has been given previously, this motion requires only a majority vote for adoption. If it changes a previously specified reporting time before that time has arrived, however, the vote required is the same as for the motion to *Discharge a Committee*.

36:8   No motion to *Discharge a Committee* is needed when a committee's final report on a referred question or subject has been received by the assembly, since the committee is then automatically discharged from further consideration of the matter.

36:9   **Effect of Discharging a Committee.** When a committee is discharged from considering a matter, either by the adoption of a motion to discharge it or by the submission of its final report, the committee continues in existence if it is a standing committee, but ceases to exist if it is a special committee that was appointed to take up the matter. In any case, when a committee is thus discharged, its chairman returns to the secretary of the society all papers relating to the referred matter that were previously entrusted to him.

36:10   When a committee is discharged from further consideration of a question which was pending at the time of its referral and which was referred by means of the subsidiary motion to *Commit*, the question comes before the assembly automatically at that time (unless the committee is discharged by means of a motion that includes the specification of a later time for considering it). If no later time was specified in the motion, the question can then be postponed, if desired; or if the assembly wishes to drop the matter, the question can be postponed indefinitely. If a motion to *Discharge a Committee* specifies a later time for considering the question and does not make it a special order, the question comes up under the same conditions as if postponed to that time without making it a special order—that is, it is a general order for the time named. If the motion to *Discharge a Committee* includes a provision making the question a special order, it requires a two-thirds vote, just as any other motion to make a special order. (See 14:12–17 regarding the priority to which a question is subject when it is due to come up after postponement.)

36:11   On the other hand, a motion to discharge a committee from further consideration of a subject that was referred to the committee by means of a *main* motion is a particular case of the motion to *Rescind* or to *Amend Something Previously Adopted* (**35**). When such a motion to *Discharge a Committee* has been adopted, another main motion is needed to bring before the assembly the matter that was referred; otherwise it dies.

Form and Example

36:12   The form used in making this motion, as applied to a question being considered by a *standing committee*, may be:

> MEMBER A (obtaining the floor): I move that the Finance Committee be discharged from further consideration of the resolution relating to … (Second.)

36:13   In the case of a *special committee*, the following form may be used:

> MEMBER A (obtaining the floor): I move that the committee to which was referred the resolution relating to … be discharged. (Second.)

36:14   If it is desired to take up the question at a later time, there may be added to either of the above forms, for example, the words, "and that the resolution be considered at 4 P.M." (in which case it is a general order for that time), or, "and that it be made a special order for …"

36:15   If the motion to discharge the committee is adopted and includes no provision for consideration at a later time, and if the question was referred while pending (by means of the subsidiary motion to *Commit*), the chair announces the result and immediately states the question brought out of committee. For example:

> **CHAIR:** There are two thirds in the affirmative and the committee is discharged. The question is now on the resolution, "*Resolved, …*"

§37. RECONSIDER

37:1   *Reconsider*—a motion of American origin—enables a majority in an assembly, within a limited time and without notice, to bring back for further consideration a motion that has already been voted on. The purpose of reconsidering a vote is to permit correction of hasty, ill-advised, or erroneous action, or to take into account added information or a changed situation that has developed since the taking of the vote.

37:2   Whenever it is stated in this book that a motion or a vote "can be reconsidered" or "cannot be reconsidered," specific reference is being made to the use of the motion to *Reconsider*, and not to any of the other motions or procedures that bring a question again before the assembly (see 6:25–28; **34–36**; **38**; also 10:26(3–5) to 10:27).

37:3   The motion to *Reconsider* can, in general, be applied to a vote that either adopted or rejected a motion, and it proposes no specific change in a decision but simply that the original question be reopened. It is neither a main motion nor a secondary motion, but in certain respects it assumes the character of the motion to which it is applied (that is, the motion to be reconsidered), as will be seen below.

37:4   The full procedure for reconsidering a vote involves essentially three stages, which may be summarized as follows:

37:5   First, the mere making of a motion to *Reconsider*, when seconded by another member and acknowledged by the chair, has the effect of suspending, at least temporarily, any action growing out of the vote proposed to be reconsidered (see 37:11). The general rule therefore is that *Reconsider* cannot be applied to an affirmative vote whose provisions have been partly carried out or to any vote that has caused something to be done that it is impossible to undo (see Standard Characteristic 2, below).

37:6   Second, the motion to *Reconsider* is considered by the assembly—either immediately after it is made or at some later time, depending on the parliamentary situation (see 37:14–17). Although at this stage the motion to be reconsidered is not yet pending, debate on the motion to *Reconsider* (if it is debatable; see 37:18) can go fully into the merits of that question.

37:7   Third, if the motion to *Reconsider* is adopted, the effect is— to the extent practicable, and with certain exceptions—to place before the assembly again the question on which the vote has been reconsidered, in the exact position it occupied the moment before it was voted on originally. The original vote is thus canceled, and, before any new vote on it is taken, the question is again open to debate, amendment, or any other action appropriate in the case. If, however, the motion to *Reconsider* is rejected, the vote which it proposed to reconsider, as well as any action held up because of the proposed reconsideration, goes back into effect, just as though the motion to *Reconsider* had never been made. The same result occurs if the motion to *Reconsider* is dropped without having been voted on at all. (See 37:11.)

37:8   To provide both usefulness and protection against abuse, the motion to *Reconsider* has the following *unique characteristics*, as more fully explained in 37:10:

a) Except in committees, it can be made only by a member who voted on the prevailing side.

b) Except in committees, it must be moved either on the same day the original vote was taken or on the next succeeding day within the same session on which a business meeting is held.

c) It can be *made* even when its *consideration* would not be in order, in which case it may be "called up" for consideration at a later time whose limits are longer than those for its making. Under those circumstances, action growing out of the vote proposed to be considered is temporarily suspended.

Standard Descriptive Characteristics

37:9   The motion to *Reconsider*:

1. a) With respect to *making* the motion, takes precedence over any other motion whatever and yields to nothing.[4] The making of this motion is in order when any other question is pending, and also after the assembly has voted to adjourn, if the member rose and addressed the chair before the chair declared the meeting adjourned. If a reconsideration appears to require immediate action in the latter case, the vote on adjourning must be retaken. Even while an order for the *Previous Question* is in effect on a motion which is immediately pending, until the chair actually begins to take the vote, the making of a motion to *Reconsider* an earlier vote on another question is in order.

   b) With respect to its *consideration*, has only the same rank as that of the motion to be reconsidered, but it takes precedence over, and supersedes, any new motion of equal rank that has been made but has not yet been stated by the chair. (The procedure for calling up a motion to *Reconsider* in preference to a main motion just made by someone else, and relating to another matter, is similar to that described for moving to *Take from the Table*; see **34**.) Provided that no question is pending, the reconsideration of a vote disposing of a main motion, either temporarily or permanently, can be taken up even while the assembly is in the midst of taking up the general orders.

2. Can be applied to the vote on any motion except:

   a) a motion which can be renewed (see 38:6–7);

   b) a negative vote on a motion which, at the time the motion to *Reconsider* is made, would be out of order because:

      i) it conflicts with a motion previously adopted and still in force,

---

4. The motion to *Reconsider* has a special form known as *Reconsider and Enter on the Minutes*, however, which outranks the regular form of the motion (see 37:46–52).

　　　ii) it conflicts with a motion which has been tempo-
　　　rarily but not finally disposed of and which remains
　　　within the control of the assembly, or

　　　iii) it would conflict with a pending motion if that mo-
　　　tion were adopted;

c) an affirmative vote whose provisions have been partly
carried out;[5]

d) an affirmative vote in the nature of a contract when the
party to the contract has been notified of the outcome;

e) any vote which has caused something to be done that it
is impossible to undo;

f) a vote on a motion to *Reconsider*;

g) an election that has become final as provided in 46:46; or

h) when practically the same result as desired can be obtained by some other parliamentary motion that can be
adopted by a majority vote without previous notice.

In the case of subsidiary or incidental motions that adhered
to a main motion, however, *Reconsider* can be applied only
in such a way that the reconsideration takes place while the
main motion to which they adhered is pending—either
before the main motion is voted on or when it is being
reconsidered at the same time. The same is true where one
subsidiary or incidental motion adheres to another; for example, *Reconsider* can be applied to the vote on a secondary amendment only in such a way that the reconsideration
takes place before the primary amendment involved is voted
on or while the primary amendment is being reconsidered.
(See 37:24–34.)

　　By application of these principles, it follows that certain
motions cannot be reconsidered, while in the case of others
only the vote on an affirmative result can be reconsidered,
and with still others, only the vote on a negative result.
(See pages t50–t51 for a list of the motions in each of these

---

5. Exception (c) does not apply to a motion to *Limit or Extend Limits of Debate*, on
which the vote can be reconsidered even if such an order has been partly carried out.

categories; see also Standard Characteristic 8 in the sections on each individual motion.)

The motion to *Lay on the Table* can be applied to the motion to *Reconsider*. Motions to *Postpone to a Certain Time*, to *Limit or Extend Limits of Debate*, and for the *Previous Question* can also be applied to it when it is debatable (see Standard Characteristic 5). When a motion to *Reconsider* is postponed or laid on the table, all adhering questions are also postponed or go to the table. Motions to *Postpone Indefinitely*, *Amend*, or *Commit* cannot be applied to a motion to *Reconsider*.

3. Is in order (with respect to *making* the motion) even after another person has been assigned the floor, so long as he has not actually begun to speak. The *calling up* of a motion to *Reconsider* is out of order when another has the floor. A member can, however, claim preference in being recognized for the purpose of either making or calling up a motion to *Reconsider* ahead of another who rose first for the purpose of making a new motion; see also Standard Characteristic 1(b), above.

4. Must be seconded at the time it is made. Unlike the making of the motion, which must be done by a person who voted with the prevailing side, the seconding can be done by any member regardless of how he voted on the motion to be reconsidered. The *calling up* of the motion to *Reconsider* does not require a second.

5. Is debatable whenever the motion proposed to be reconsidered would be debatable, and when debatable, opens to debate the merits of the question whose reconsideration is proposed. (See 37:29–32, however, regarding a series of motions proposed to be reconsidered, and the question that is opened to debate in such a case.) When the motion proposed to be reconsidered is not debatable—either because of its nature or because it is subject to an unexhausted order for the *Previous Question* (**16**)—the motion to *Reconsider* is undebatable (but see 43:31–32 regarding allowable expla-

nation of an undebatable motion). Similarly, if the *Previous Question* is in effect on a pending question or series of questions, and if a motion which is proposed to be reconsidered adheres to these pending question(s) in such a way that the reconsideration must be taken up before the *Previous Question* is exhausted, both the motion to *Reconsider* and the motion to be reconsidered are undebatable—even if the latter motion was open to debate at its earlier consideration and the *Previous Question* was ordered later.

6. Is not amendable.

7. Requires only a majority vote, *regardless of the vote necessary to adopt the motion to be reconsidered.* (But see 37:35 for a different rule in the case of standing and special committees.)

8. Cannot be reconsidered. If it is voted on and lost, the motion to *Reconsider* cannot be renewed except by unanimous consent. By the same principle, no question can be reconsidered twice unless it was materially amended during its first reconsideration.

Further Rules and Explanation

37:10 **By Whom and When a Motion to Reconsider Can Be Made.** As briefly mentioned above (37:8), to provide both usefulness and protection against abuse, the motion to *Reconsider* has the following unique characteristics:

a) The motion to *Reconsider* can be made only by a member who voted with the prevailing side. In other words, a reconsideration can be moved only by one who voted *aye* if the motion involved was adopted, or *no* if the motion was lost. (In standing and special committees, however, the motion to *Reconsider* can be made by any member who did not vote on the losing side—including one who did not vote at all.) It should be noted that it is possible for a minority to be the prevailing side if a motion requiring a two-thirds vote for adoption is lost.

A member who voted by ballot may make the motion if he is willing to waive the secrecy of his ballot. If the motion to be reconsidered was adopted by unanimous consent, all the members present at the time of the adoption are in the same position as if they had voted on the prevailing side and qualify to move to reconsider. Similarly, if a motion was lost but the negative vote was not taken because it was intrinsically irrelevant (see 44:9(a)), the members present at the time who did not vote in favor qualify to move to reconsider.

This requirement for making the motion to *Reconsider* is a protection against its dilatory use by a defeated minority—especially when the motion is debatable (see Standard Characteristic 5, above) and the minority is large enough to prevent adoption of the *Previous Question* (**16**). When a member who cannot move a reconsideration believes there are valid reasons for one, he should try, if there is time or opportunity, to persuade someone who voted with the prevailing side to make such a motion. Otherwise, he can obtain the floor while no business is pending and briefly state his reasons for hoping that a reconsideration will be moved, provided that this does not run into debate; or, if necessary while business is pending, he can request permission to state such reasons (see *Request for Any Other Privilege*, 33:22).

b) The making of this motion is subject to time limits, as follows: In a session of one day—such as an ordinary meeting of a club or a one-day convention—the motion to *Reconsider* can be made only on the same day the vote to be reconsidered was taken. In a convention or session of more than one day, a reconsideration can be moved only on the same day the original vote was taken or on the next succeeding day within the session on which a business meeting is held. These time limitations do not apply to standing or special committees (see 37:35). Except by unanimous consent, a motion to *Reconsider* that has not been finally disposed of cannot be withdrawn after it is too late to renew it;

that is, it can be withdrawn only within the same time limits as for making the motion in the first place.

c) The *making* of this motion has a higher rank than its *consideration*; that is, the motion can be made and seconded at a time when it is not in order for it to come before the assembly for debate or vote. In such a case it can be taken up later, even after it would be too late to move it in the first place. If the motion to *Reconsider* is introduced at a time when it cannot be taken up, the chair does not state the question on it as pending, but instructs the secretary to record the motion as made and seconded. While a motion to reconsider the vote on a main motion has this status, a member can bring the motion before the assembly at any time when its consideration is in order. When he does this, he is said to *call up* the motion to *Reconsider* (see 37:15).

37:11 **Suspending Effect of Making a Motion to Reconsider.** The effect of *making* a motion to *Reconsider* is the suspension of all action that depends on the result of the vote proposed to be reconsidered. This suspending effect lasts until:

a) the motion to *Reconsider* is adopted or rejected;

b) it is withdrawn (see 37:10(b), 33:11–18);

c) it falls to the ground without having been voted on, because it was pending, or remained temporarily disposed of, upon the final adjournment of a session under conditions stated in 21:7(c); or

d) if it has not yet been taken up, when the limits of time for calling it up have expired (see 37:15).

37:12 If the motion to *Reconsider* is adopted, the original vote on the motion being reconsidered is thereby canceled altogether; but if the suspending effect is terminated by a vote rejecting the motion to *Reconsider* or in any other way, the situation becomes the same as if there had been no such motion, and the vote which it was proposed to reconsider—and any other action held up because of the proposed reconsideration—comes into full force, as if in effect, so far as applicable, from the time the vote was originally taken.

37:13   **Reconsideration of a Motion That Is No Longer in Order Because of Intervening Action.** It should be noted that, as a consequence of the rule set forth in (b) of Standard Characteristic 2 above, action taken by an assembly may preclude the making of a motion to reconsider the vote on a previously rejected motion. For an example, assume that a motion to spend all of an available sum of money for library books is voted down, and thereafter a motion to spend the same money for athletic equipment is made and adopted. No motion to reconsider the vote on the motion to purchase library books will thereafter be in order because, if adopted, it would place before the assembly a motion which conflicts with a motion previously adopted and still in force (see 39:5). In such a case, if it is desired to reconsider the vote on the rejected motion, the subsequently adopted motion must first be rescinded (or amended in some fashion so that it no longer conflicts), or the vote on it must be reconsidered and reversed.

37:14   **Taking Up the Motion to Reconsider at the Time It Is Made.** If a motion to *Reconsider* is made at a time when it can be taken up—that is, when the motion proposed to be reconsidered would be in order initially—the chair immediately states the question on the motion to *Reconsider* as pending before the assembly. In proposing a reconsideration of the vote on a main motion, it is usually better to make the motion to *Reconsider* when no other business is pending and the motion can be taken up immediately—unless it appears that there may be no such opportunity or there is an important reason for doing otherwise.

37:15   **Calling Up the Motion to Reconsider at a Later Time.** If a motion to *Reconsider* that involves a main motion cannot be taken up when it is made, then it can be called up and acted upon whenever no question is pending and no other member has the floor, within the following limits: The motion to *Reconsider* may be called up at any meeting of the same session in which it was made. If the next regular business session will be held within a quarterly time interval (9:7), it may also be called up at any meeting of that next session, or at any intervening special meeting called for that purpose. To call it up, a member obtains the floor and says, "Mr. President, I call up the motion to reconsider the vote on the motion ... [identifying it]." (The member is entitled to preference in recognition for this purpose; see 42:13(4)(c)). No second is necessary, since the motion to *Reconsider* was seconded at the time it was made. When this motion is called up, the chair immediately states the question on it as pending (see *Form and Example*).

37:16   ***Privilege accorded the mover in regard to the time at which reconsideration takes place.*** Although any member can call up the motion to *Reconsider* as just described, usually no one but the mover of the reconsideration calls it up on the day the motion is made—at least in cases where the session is to last beyond that day and there is no need for immediate action. The reason is that the mover may wish time to assemble new information, or—if the reconsideration is moved on the same day the original vote was taken—he may want the unrestricted debate that will be allowable if the motion is taken up on another day (see below). So long as business is not unreasonably delayed and the mover of the reconsideration acts in good faith, he is entitled to have it take place at a time he feels will make for the fullest and fairest reexamination of the question.

37:17   ***Duty of the chair when failure to call up the motion may do harm.*** In cases where a failure to call up a motion to *Reconsider* may do harm, the chair has the duty to point out the situation to the assembly. Suppose, for example, that in a meeting of an ordinary society that will meet within a quarterly time interval (9:7), there has been a motion to *Reconsider* a vote to do something that can only be done before the next meeting. Should the present meeting adjourn without taking up the motion to

Reconsider, the measure proposed to be reconsidered would be killed unless an adjourned meeting or special meeting were held to consider it. Therefore, if this meeting seems on the point of adjourning before the motion to *Reconsider* has been taken up, the chair should explain the facts and suggest that someone call up the motion. If it has been moved to adjourn under these circumstances, the motion to *Adjourn* can be withdrawn or voted down—or the time can be fixed for an adjourned meeting, which can be done either before or after the vote on adjournment has been taken (see *Fix the Time to Which to Adjourn*, **22**).

37:18   **Debate on the Motion to Reconsider.** Whenever the motion to *Reconsider* is taken up, it is debatable if the motion proposed to be reconsidered is debatable, and debate can go into the merits of the question proposed to be reconsidered, as noted in Standard Characteristic 5. The right of each member to debate the motion to *Reconsider* is separate from the original consideration of the motion proposed to be reconsidered. Therefore, even if a member exhausted his right to debate in the original consideration and the motion to *Reconsider* is taken up on the same day, he still has the right to speak the regular number of times (twice unless the assembly has a special rule providing otherwise) in debate on the motion to *Reconsider*. (For rules affecting a member's right to debate in the reconsideration if the motion to *Reconsider* is adopted, see below.)

37:19   **Effect of Adoption of the Motion to Reconsider; Rules Governing Debate on the Reconsideration.** The effect of the adoption of the motion to *Reconsider* is immediately to place before the assembly again the question on which the vote is to be reconsidered—in the exact position it occupied the moment before it was voted on originally.[6]

---

6. However, passage of a motion to reconsider adoption of the *Previous Question* (16:16) or of *Objection to the Consideration of a Question* (26:6) is deemed to have resulted in the reversal of the original vote on those motions (that is, the *Previous Question* is deemed defeated or the objection is deemed overturned) without taking

37:20   Rules governing debate on the reconsideration of the vote are as follows:

37:21   *Reconsideration of a vote on the same day.* A member's right to debate the reconsideration of a vote is independent of the extent to which he took part in debate on the motion to *Reconsider*. If the reconsideration takes place on the same day as the first consideration, however, anyone who exhausted his right to debate in the first consideration will not be able to speak on it again during the reconsideration, without permission of the assembly. (But such a member can pursue an equivalent purpose while the motion to *Reconsider* is pending, since the motion proposed to be reconsidered is also open to discussion in debate on the motion to *Reconsider*.)

37:22   *Reconsideration of a vote on a later day.* Every member's right to debate in the reconsideration of a question begins over again, regardless of speeches made previously, if reconsideration takes place on a day other than that on which the vote to be reconsidered was taken.

37:23   *Reconsideration under an order limiting or extending limits of debate.* If a vote on one of a series of motions is taken under an order *limiting* debate or for the *Previous Question*, and then is reconsidered before such an order is exhausted (as explained in the sections on those motions, **15** and **16**), the same restrictions continue to apply to debate both on the motion to *Reconsider* and on the reconsideration. In the case of reconsidering a motion similarly covered by an unexhausted order *extending* limits of debate, the extension applies only to the reconsideration itself, not to debate on the motion to *Reconsider*. When reconsideration takes place after exhaustion of the *Previous Question*

---

another vote. It should also be noted that, if reconsideration of a vote taken on an amendable motion takes place during a later session, motions to amend the motion being reconsidered may be made during its reconsideration without regard to whether or not the same or similar motions to amend it were either adopted or rejected during any previous session.

or a limitation or extension of debate, these orders do not come back into force, and debate or amendment is subject to the ordinary rules.

37:24   **Reconsideration of Subsidiary, Privileged, and Incidental Motions.** Conditions under which subsidiary, privileged, or incidental motions can be reconsidered depend on what other motions are pending at the time the reconsideration is moved, as follows:

37:25   *To reconsider a subsidiary, privileged, or incidental motion: Reconsideration moved while the main question is pending.* When a main motion is pending (with or without a series of adhering motions) and it is moved to reconsider the vote on a related subsidiary, privileged, or incidental motion, the motion to *Reconsider* becomes (a) immediately pending or (b) pending at a lower position in the series, depending on whether the motion proposed to be reconsidered would then be in order if moved for the first time.

37:26   Referring to case (a) above, the motion to *Reconsider* takes precedence over all pending questions if the motion proposed to be reconsidered would take such precedence (see **5** and **6**; see also the chart on pages t3–t5), in which case the motion to *Reconsider* becomes the immediately pending question at once. For example, assume that it is moved and seconded to reconsider a negative vote on a motion to refer the pending main question to a committee. If the main question is now pending alone, or if no other questions are pending except motions to *Postpone Indefinitely* or to *Amend* (which rank below the motion to *Commit*), the chair at once states the question on the motion to *Reconsider* as immediately pending.

37:27   On the other hand, referring to case (b) above, if a series of motions is pending with the main question, and the related motion whose reconsideration is proposed would *not* take precedence over all of them, the motion to *Reconsider* does not become the immediately pending question when it is moved, but it becomes pending as one of the series, at a position corresponding to the rank of the motion proposed to be reconsidered. In such a case, the motion to *Reconsider* is taken up immediately after voting has been completed on all motions that would not yield to the motion to be reconsidered. For example, suppose that while a main motion, an amendment, and a motion to lay the pending questions on the table are pending, it is moved to reconsider a previous negative vote on referring the same main question and amendment to a committee. The order of rank, from highest to lowest, of the four motions is: (1) *Lay on the Table*, (2) *Commit*, (3) *Amend*, and (4) the main motion. This is the order in which these motions would be voted on, and the reverse of the order in which they would be made. The procedure in this instance is as follows: The chair takes note of the fact that the motion to *Reconsider* has been made and seconded, instructing the secretary to record it. He then proceeds to take the vote on the motion to *Lay on the Table*. If that motion is lost, he automatically states the question on the motion to reconsider the vote on the referral to the committee, since the motion to *Commit* is next lower in rank. If the motion to *Reconsider* is adopted, the motion to *Commit* is then reconsidered and voted on again; and if this is lost, the question is then stated on the amendment. (If the motion to *Lay on the Table* is adopted, then whenever the questions are taken from the table, the immediately pending question is the motion to *Reconsider*, and from this point the procedure is the same as above.)

37:28   If the reconsideration of a primary amendment is moved while another amendment of the same degree is pending, the pending amendment is disposed of first. Then the chair states the question on the motion to reconsider the amendment previously acted upon.

37:29   When it is moved to reconsider a debatable subsidiary or incidental motion which relates to a pending main question or a series of pending questions (in which case the motion to *Reconsider* is debatable, as noted in Standard Characteristic 5), debate on the motion to *Reconsider* can go into the merits of the motion *proposed to be reconsidered*, but not into the merits of any other pending question. For example, in the debate on a motion to reconsider an amendment to the pending main question, the merits of the amendment are open to discussion, but not those of the main question apart from the amendment.

37:30 **To reconsider an adhering subsidiary or incidental motion: Reconsideration moved after the main question has been acted upon.** If it is desired to reconsider the vote on a subsidiary or incidental motion (an amendment, for example) after the main question to which it adhered has been finally disposed of (by adoption, rejection, or indefinite postponement), the vote on the main question, or on its indefinite postponement, must also be reconsidered (see also Standard Characteristic 2). In such a case, one motion to *Reconsider* should be made to cover both the vote on the subsidiary or incidental motion whose reconsideration is desired, and the vote on the main question (or its indefinite postponement). The member who makes this motion to *Reconsider* must have voted with the prevailing side in the original vote on the subsidiary or incidental motion—that is, on the motion which will be reconsidered first if the reconsideration takes place.

37:31 The same principle applies to the reconsideration of a secondary amendment after the related primary amendment has been voted on. If such a reconsideration is desired while the main question is still pending, the primary amendment must also be reconsidered. If it is desired to reconsider the secondary amendment after the main question has been finally disposed of, the secondary amendment, the primary amendment, and the main question must all be reconsidered, and one motion to *Reconsider* should be made covering the votes of these three motions.

37:32 When a motion to *Reconsider* covers the votes on two or more connected motions, not all of these questions can be discussed in debate on the motion to *Reconsider*, but only the one that will be voted on first if the motion to *Reconsider* is adopted. Thus, if the motion is to reconsider the votes on a resolution, a primary amendment, and a secondary amendment, only the secondary amendment is open to debate in connection with debate on the motion to *Reconsider*. If this motion to *Reconsider* is adopted, the chair states the question on the secondary amendment and recognizes the mover of the reconsideration as entitled to the floor. The question is now in exactly the same condition as it was just before the original vote was taken on the secondary amendment.

37:33   If a main motion is included in a series covered by a single motion to *Reconsider*, as just described, the reconsideration is in order at the same times as if it had been moved to reconsider the main motion alone. If the motion to *Reconsider* is made at a time when it cannot be taken up, it suspends action in the way described in 37:11 and stands until called up, subject to the same conditions as if it applied only to the main motion.

37:34   If a motion to reconsider the vote on an adhering subsidiary or incidental motion (an amendment, for example) is made after the main question to which it adheres has been either postponed to a certain time or laid on the table, the motion to *Reconsider* is properly noted and is taken up in due course (37:27) if and when the main motion is again brought before the assembly. The same is true if the motion to reconsider the adhering subsidiary or incidental motion was made before, but was not called up before, the main question was postponed or laid on the table. On the other hand, if a main question is referred to a committee, no motion to reconsider the vote on an adhering subsidiary or incidental motion is in order while the question is in the hands of the committee, and any such motion to *Reconsider* that was made but not taken up prior to referral is thereafter ignored.

37:35   **Reconsideration in Standing and Special Committees.** Reconsideration in a standing or a special committee (**50**) differs from reconsideration in a meeting of the assembly in the following respects:

1) A motion to reconsider a vote in the committee can be made and taken up *regardless of the time that has elapsed* since the vote was taken, and there is no limit to the number of times a question can be reconsidered. Likewise, the rule requiring unanimous consent to renew a defeated motion to *Reconsider* does not apply in committees.

2) The motion can be made by any member of the committee who *did not vote with the losing side*; or, in other words, the maker of the motion to *Reconsider* can be one who voted with the prevailing side, or one who did not vote at all, or even was absent.

3) Unless all the members of the committee who voted with the prevailing side are present or have been given reasonable notice that the reconsideration will be moved, it requires a *two-thirds vote* to adopt the motion to *Reconsider*.

In other respects, reconsideration in a committee is the same as in a meeting of the society or its board. A vote cannot be reconsidered in a committee of the whole.

Form and Example

37:36   This motion may be made in forms such as the following:

a) For the reconsideration of a main question: "I move to reconsider the vote on the resolution relating to the annual banquet. I voted for [or "against"] the resolution."

b) To move the reconsideration of a subsidiary, privileged, or incidental motion related to the main question, while the main question is pending: "I move to reconsider the vote on the amendment to strike out 'Friday' and insert 'Saturday.' I voted for [or "against"] the amendment."

c) When the reconsideration of a subsidiary or incidental motion is desired after the main question to which it adhered has been acted upon: "I move to reconsider the votes on the resolution relating to the annual banquet and on the amendment to strike out 'Friday' and insert 'Saturday.' I voted for [or "against"] the amendment."

37:37 If the maker of the motion to *Reconsider* fails to state which side he voted on, the chair, before making any other response, directs the member to do so:

> CHAIR: The member moving the reconsideration must state how he voted on the resolution ["motion," "amendment," etc.].

37:38 If the resolution was adopted by unanimous consent, the chair asks whether the member was present at the time. If the member did not vote with the prevailing side, another member who did so can make the motion to *Reconsider*, if he desires. The motion must be seconded.

37:39 If it is in order to take up the motion to *Reconsider* when it is made, the chair immediately states the question as follows:

> CHAIR: It is moved and seconded to reconsider the vote on the following resolution [reading it].

37:40 If it is not in order to take up the motion to *Reconsider* when it is moved, the chair says instead:

> CHAIR: It is moved and seconded to reconsider the vote on the resolution relating to … The Secretary will make a note of it.

He then continues with the pending business.

37:41 When it is in order to call up the motion to *Reconsider* and a member wishes to do so, the member rises and addresses the chair:

> MEMBER A (obtaining the floor): I call up the motion to reconsider the vote [or "votes"] on …

37:42 The chair proceeds:

> CHAIR: The motion to reconsider the vote [or "votes"] on … is called up. The question is on the motion to reconsider … [etc.].

37:43   If a reconsideration that could not be taken up when it was moved is one that later comes before the assembly automatically, then when that point is reached, the chair says, for example:

> **CHAIR:** The question is now on the motion to reconsider the vote on the amendment to …

37:44   After debate on a motion to *Reconsider*, assuming that this motion is adopted, the chair puts the question and states the result as follows:

> **CHAIR:** As many as are in favor of reconsidering the vote on the resolution relating to the annual banquet, say *aye*. … Those opposed, say *no*. … The ayes have it and the vote on the resolution is reconsidered. The question is now on the resolution, which is … [etc.].

Or:

> **CHAIR:** The ayes have it and the votes on the resolution and the amendment are reconsidered. The question is now on the amendment, which is … [etc.].

37:45   Note that if the result of the vote on the motion to *Reconsider* is negative, it is the only vote taken. But if the motion to *Reconsider* is adopted, this is followed—after any debate—by the taking of the vote or votes that are consequently reconsidered.

Reconsider and Enter on the Minutes

37:46   *Reconsider and Enter on the Minutes* is a special form of the motion to *Reconsider* that has a different object from the regular motion. Its purpose is to prevent a temporary majority from taking advantage of an unrepresentative attendance at a meeting to vote an action that is opposed by a majority of a society's or a convention's membership. The effect of this form of the motion arises from the fact that when it is moved—on the same day that the vote to be reconsidered was taken—it cannot be called up until another day, even if another meeting is held on the same day.[7] Thus, with a view to obtaining a more representative attendance, it ensures reconsideration of a question on a different day from the one on which the question was put to vote. The name of this form does not imply that the regular motion to *Reconsider* is not also recorded in the minutes.

37:47 **Differences from the Regular Form of the Motion.** *Reconsider and Enter on the Minutes* differs from the regular form of *Reconsider* in the following respects:

1) It can be moved only on the same day that the vote proposed to be reconsidered was taken. The regular form of the motion to *Reconsider* can be used on the next succeeding day within the session on which a business meeting is held.

2) It takes precedence over the regular motion to *Reconsider*. Also, this motion can be made even after the vote has been taken on the motion to *Reconsider*, provided that the chair has not announced the result of the vote. In this case the regular motion to *Reconsider* is then ignored. If it were not for the rule that the motion to *Reconsider and Enter on the Minutes* takes precedence over the regular motion to *Reconsider*, the motion to *Reconsider and Enter on the Minutes* would generally be forestalled by the regular motion, which would be voted down, and then *Reconsider and Enter on the Minutes* could not be moved.

3) It can be applied only to votes that finally dispose of main motions; that is, to: (a) an affirmative or negative vote on a main motion; (b) an affirmative vote on postponing indefinitely; or (c) a negative vote on an objection to the consideration of a question, if the session extends beyond that day.

4) It cannot be applied to votes on motions whose object would be defeated by a delay of one day. For example, a motion asking a visitor to address a convention the following day cannot have this motion applied to it.

7. For an exception, see item (6) below.

5) If more than a quarterly time interval (9:7) will intervene before the next regular business session, it cannot be moved at the last business meeting of the current session.

6) It cannot be called up on the day it is made, except that when it is moved on the last day—but not the last meeting—of a session of an organization that is not scheduled to meet again within a quarterly time interval (9:7), it can be called up at the last business meeting of the session.

37:48   After a motion to *Reconsider and Enter on the Minutes* has been called up, its treatment is the same as that of the regular motion to *Reconsider*.

37:49 **Procedure for Use of the Motion.** To illustrate the use of this form of the motion, suppose that at a long meeting of a county historical society, many members have left, unknowingly leaving a quorum composed mainly of a small group determined to commit the society to certain action that a few of those present believe would be opposed by most of the membership. A member in opposition can prevent the vote on such action from becoming final by moving "to reconsider and enter on the minutes the vote on ..." To be in a position to do this, such a member—detecting the hopelessness of preventing an affirmative result on the vote—should vote in the affirmative himself. If the motion to *Reconsider and Enter on the Minutes* is seconded, all action required by the vote proposed to be reconsidered is suspended, and there is time to notify absent members of the proposed action.

37:50   If no member of the temporary minority voted on the prevailing side and it is too late for anyone to change his vote (see 45:9), notice can be given that a motion to rescind the assembly's action will be made at the next meeting. At this next meeting, provided that such notice has been given, the motion to *Rescind* can then be adopted by a majority vote.

37:51 **Protecting Against Abuses of the Motion.** The motion to *Reconsider and Enter on the Minutes* may occasionally be subject to attempted abuse, particularly in ordinary societies with single-meeting sessions, since it gives any two members power to hold up action taken by a meeting. In the average organization this motion should generally be reserved for extreme cases, and is in order only when final decision on the question could, if necessary, wait until the next regular meeting, or when an adjourned or special meeting to take it up is a practical possibility.

37:52   If an actual minority in a representative meeting makes improper use of this motion by moving to reconsider and enter on the minutes a vote which requires action before the next regular meeting, the remedy is to fix the time for an adjourned meeting (**9, 22**) on another suitable day when the reconsideration can be called up and disposed of. In such a case, the mere making of a motion to set an adjourned meeting would likely cause withdrawal of the motion to *Reconsider and Enter on the Minutes*, since its object would be defeated.

CHAPTER X

RENEWAL OF MOTIONS; DILATORY AND IMPROPER MOTIONS

§38. RENEWAL OF MOTIONS

38:1   If a motion is made and disposed of without being adopted, and is later allowed to come before the assembly after being made again by any member in essentially the same connection, the motion is said to be *renewed*. Renewal of motions is limited by the basic principle that an assembly cannot be asked to decide the same, or substantially the same, question twice during one session—except through a motion to reconsider a vote (**37**) or a motion to rescind an action (**35**), or in connection with amending something already adopted (see also 6:25). A previously considered motion may become a substantially different question through a significant change in the wording or because of a difference in the time or circumstances in which it is proposed, and such a motion may thus be in order when it could not otherwise be renewed.

38:2   The rules restricting renewal of motions do not apply to any motion that was last disposed of by being withdrawn. A motion that is withdrawn becomes as if it had never been made and can be renewed whenever it would be originally in order. The rules restricting renewal of motions also do not apply to any motion that dies for lack of a second. Although such a motion is not treated as if it had never been made, it too is a motion which the assembly was not called upon to decide,

and thus it too may be renewed whenever it would originally
be in order to make it.

38:3   Two general principles govern the renewal of motions:

1) *No motion can be renewed during the same session in which it
has already been before the assembly, except where its renewal
is permitted by a specific rule; and such a rule always implies
circumstances under which the motion has in some respect
become a different question.* (For a discussion of the rules
growing out of this principle, see *Nonrenewability During
the Same Session, and Exceptions,* below.) Whenever it is
stated without qualification that a particular parliamentary
motion "cannot be renewed," such a statement means that
the motion cannot be renewed during the same session, or,
in the case of a subsidiary or incidental motion, not during
that session in connection with the same motion to which it
directly adhered.

2) *Any motion that is still applicable can be renewed at any later
session, except where a specific rule prevents its renewal; and
such an impediment to renewal at a later session normally
can exist only when the first motion goes over to that session as
not finally disposed of, in which case the question can then be
reached through the first motion* (see 9:7–11, 38:8–9).

Nonrenewability During the Same Session, and Exceptions

38:4   The following rules are derived from the first principle stated
above, by which a motion is not renewable at the same session
unless the question has become somehow different.

38:5   **Particular Cases of the General Rule Against Renewal.** Applications of the general rule against renewal during the same session include the following:

1) A main motion, or a motion for the same amendment to
a given motion, cannot be renewed at the same session
unless there is a change in wording or circumstances sufficient to present substantially a new question, in which

case this becomes technically a different motion. If a series of resolutions voted on together is lost, however, one or more of them can be offered again at the same session, but enough resolutions must be left out to present a genuinely different question from the viewpoint of probable voting result; otherwise this procedure becomes dilatory.

2) A motion to *Postpone Indefinitely* cannot be renewed in connection with the same main question during the same session, even if the main motion has been materially amended since the previous vote against indefinite postponement. There will be another opportunity to accomplish the same object—that is, to defeat the main motion—when it comes up for a final vote.

3) A motion to *Reconsider* that has been rejected cannot be renewed in connection with the same vote. To be able to be reconsidered a second time, the original question must have been materially amended during the first reconsideration—in which case the proposal to reconsider a second time is a new question.

4) A motion to *Rescind* that has been voted down cannot be renewed at the same session unless the motion proposed to be rescinded has meanwhile been amended sufficiently to present a new question.

5) A motion to divide the same question in substantially the same way cannot be renewed at the same session.

6) When a *Question of Privilege* or a *Point of Order* has been ruled on adversely by the chair, it cannot be raised again at the same session unless an appeal is made and the chair's decision is reversed. After a decision of the chair has been sustained on an appeal, no point of order or appeal contrary to it can be made during that session.

38:6 **Motions That Can Be Renewed at a Later Meeting of the Same Session.** Following are two cases of motions which cannot be renewed at the same *meeting*, but which may have become different questions—and consequently are renewable—at another meeting of the same session (see **8**):

1) Although the motion to *Suspend the Rules* for the same purpose cannot be renewed at the same meeting, such a motion can be renewed at the next meeting or any later meeting, even if the next meeting is held on the same day or is part of the same session. This renewal is allowable because by the time of the next meeting the attendance or situation may already have changed sufficiently to justify the renewal. The mere passage of time may make it a new question.

2) The same motion to *Fix the Time to Which to Adjourn*—that is, a motion to set the same date, hour, and place for an adjourned meeting—cannot be renewed at the same meeting at which it is voted down; but if, after the first motion is rejected, the assembly decides to set an adjourned meeting for an earlier time than proposed in the first motion, then at that adjourned meeting it is in order to move to set a second adjourned meeting for the same time as originally considered for the first.

38:7 **Motions That Can Be Renewed After Material Progress in Business or Debate.** The following motions are renewable if they become new questions as described, even within the same meeting:

1) The subsidiary motions to *Commit*, to *Postpone to a Certain Time*, to *Limit or Extend Limits of Debate*, for the *Previous Question*, and to *Lay on the Table* can be renewed whenever progress in business or debate has been such that they are no longer practically the same questions. In addition, a motion to *Lay on the Table* can be renewed if something urgent has arisen that was not known when the assembly rejected this motion.

2) A motion to *Take from the Table* that has failed can be renewed after disposal of the business that was taken up following rejection of the motion.

3) A *Call for the Orders of the Day* can be renewed after disposal of the business that was taken up when the assembly refused to proceed to the orders of the day.

4) A motion to *Adjourn* or to *Recess* can be renewed after material progress in business or in debate—such as an important decision or speech. A vote on a motion to *Recess* or to *Lay on the Table* is not business of a character to justify renewal of a motion to *Adjourn*; and a vote on any of these three motions is not sufficient business to allow renewal of either of the others.

5) Motions to close nominations or the polls can be renewed after progress in nominations or voting has been such as to make them essentially new questions.

Conditions That May Impede Renewal at a Later Session

38:8 **Main Motions That Go Over to Another Session; Motions Within the Control of the Assembly, Because Not Finally Disposed Of.** Referring to the second general principle stated in 38:3, a main motion that was introduced but not adopted during one session can, except as noted in this paragraph, be renewed at any later session unless it has become absurd. Such exceptions occur only through one of the processes by which, from one session to another, a main motion can remain *within the control of the assembly* (that is, *temporarily, but not finally, disposed of*), so that *the same* motion can be considered at the later session. Four of these processes (numbered 1 through 4 below) can arise only in cases of organizations where no more than a quarterly time interval (see 9:7) will elapse until the next regular session. In such societies, a main motion cannot be renewed during the next session after a session at which it was:

1) postponed to, or otherwise set as a general or special order for, the next session (**14, 41**);

2) allowed to go over to the next session as unfinished business or as an unfinished special order (see 21:7(b), 41:18(a), 41:21–24);

3) laid on the table and not taken from the table (**17**, **34**); or

4) the subject of a motion to *Reconsider* (**37**) that was made but not finally disposed of.

Also, in any assembly:

5) a main motion that has been referred to a committee cannot be renewed until after the session at which the assembly finally disposes of the main motion—after the committee has reported it back or has been discharged from its consideration (**36**).

38:9   **Nonrenewability of Unsustained Objection to the Consideration of a Question.** An unsustained *Objection to the Consideration of a Question* (**26**) cannot be renewed in connection with the same main motion—even at a later session if the main motion goes over to that session through one of the processes stated immediately above. By deciding to consider the question, the assembly has already begun its involvement, and it is too late to make an objection. But if an original main motion is finally disposed of at one session without being adopted and is renewed at a later session, it is then a new motion and its consideration can be objected to, subject to the usual rules.

§39. DILATORY AND IMPROPER MOTIONS

Dilatory Motions

39:1   A motion is *dilatory* if it seeks to obstruct or thwart the will of the assembly as clearly indicated by the existing parliamentary situation.

39:2   Parliamentary forms are designed to assist in the transaction of business. Even without adopting a rule on the subject, every deliberative assembly has the right to protect itself from the dilatory use of these forms.

39:3   Any main or other motion that is frivolous or absurd or that contains no rational proposition is dilatory and cannot be introduced. As further examples, it is dilatory to obstruct business by appealing from a ruling of the chair on a question about which there cannot possibly be two reasonable opinions, by demanding a division (**29**) on a vote even when there has been a full vote and the result is clear, by moving to lay on the table the matter for which a special meeting has been called, by constantly raising points of order and appealing from the chair's decision on them, or by moving to adjourn again and again when nothing has happened to justify renewal of such a motion. By use of such tactics, a minority of two or three members could bring business to a standstill.

39:4   It is the duty of the presiding officer to prevent members from misusing the legitimate forms of motions, or abusing the privilege of renewing certain motions, merely to obstruct business. Whenever the chair becomes convinced that one or more members are repeatedly using parliamentary forms for dilatory purposes, he should either not recognize these members or he should rule that such motions are not in order—but he should never adopt such a course merely to *speed up* business, and he should never permit his personal feelings to affect his judgment in such cases. If the chair only *suspects* that a motion is not made in good faith, he should give the maker of the motion the benefit of the doubt. The chair should always be courteous and fair, but at the same time he should be firm in protecting the assembly from imposition.

Improper Motions

39:5   Motions that conflict with the corporate charter, constitution, or bylaws of a society, or with procedural rules prescribed by national, state, or local laws, are not in order,[1] and if any motion of this kind is adopted, it is null and void. Likewise, apart from motions to *Rescind* or to *Amend Something Previously Adopted* (**35**), motions are not in order if they conflict with one or more motions previously adopted at any time and still in force. Such conflicting motions, if adopted, are null and void

---

1. However, see 10:26(1) and the footnote there for exceptions.

unless adopted by the vote required to rescind or amend the motion previously adopted.

39:6   Motions are also improper when they present practically the same question as a motion previously decided at the same session. In addition, motions are improper that conflict with, or present practically the same question as, one still within the control of the society because not finally disposed of (see 9:7–11, 38:8). If a conflicting motion were allowed in such cases, it would interfere with the freedom of the assembly in acting on the earlier motion when its consideration is resumed.

39:7   No motion can be introduced that is outside the object of the society as defined in the corporate charter, constitution, or by-laws (see 56:18), unless by a two-thirds vote the assembly agrees to its consideration (see 10:26(2)). Except as may be necessary in the case of a motion of censure or a motion related to disciplinary procedures (**61**, **63**), a motion must not use language that reflects on a member's conduct or character, or is discourteous, unnecessarily harsh, or not allowed in debate (see **43**).

CHAPTER
XI

QUORUM; ORDER OF BUSINESS AND RELATED CONCEPTS

§40. QUORUM

40:1   As indicated in 3:3, a quorum in an assembly is the number of members (see definition, 1:4) who must be present in order that business can be validly transacted. The quorum refers to the number of members present, not to the number actually voting on a particular question.

Rules Pertaining to the Quorum

40:2   **Number of Members Constituting a Quorum.** Depending on the organization and the provision it adopts in this regard, the number of members constituting a quorum may vary. As discussed below, most voluntary societies should provide for a quorum in their bylaws, but where there is no such provision, the quorum, in accordance with the common parliamentary law, is as follows:

1) In a mass meeting, the quorum is simply the number of persons present at the time, since they constitute the entire membership at that time.
2) In organizations such as many churches or some societies in which there are no required or effective annual dues and the register of members is not generally reliable as a list of the bona-fide members, the quorum at any regular or properly called meeting consists of those who attend.

3) In a body of delegates, such as a convention, the quorum is a majority of the number who have been registered as attending, irrespective of whether some may have departed. This may differ greatly from the number elected or appointed.

4) In any other deliberative assembly with enrolled membership whose bylaws do not specify a quorum, the quorum is a majority of all the members.

40:3   To accomplish their work, voluntary societies that have an enrolled membership generally need a provision in their bylaws establishing a relatively small quorum—considerably less than a majority of all the members. In most such organizations, it is rarely possible to obtain the attendance of a majority of the membership at a meeting. Sometimes the specification of a quorum is based on a percentage of the membership; but such a method has the disadvantage of requiring recomputation and may lead to confusion—for example, when the secretary, or other officer who is in a position to certify as to the current number of members for purposes of the percentage calculation, is absent. There is no single number or percentage of members that will be equally suitable as a quorum in all societies. The quorum should be as large a number of members as can reasonably be depended on to be present at any meeting, except in very bad weather or other exceptionally unfavorable conditions.

40:4   **Note on Procedure in Changing the Quorum Provision in Bylaws.** If it becomes necessary to change the quorum provision in a society's bylaws, care should be taken, because if the rule is struck out first, the quorum will instantly become a majority of the membership, so that in many cases a quorum could not be obtained to adopt a new rule. The proper procedure is to strike out the old provision and insert the new provision, which is moved and voted on as one question.

40:5   **Quorum in Boards and Committees.** In a committee of the whole or its variations (**52**), the quorum is the same as in the assembly unless the rules of the assembly or the organization (that is, either its bylaws or its rules of order) specify otherwise. In all other committees and in boards, the quorum is a majority of the members of the board or committee unless a different quorum is provided for: (a) by the bylaws, in the case of a board or standing committee that the bylaws specifically establish; or (b) by a rule of the parent body or organization or by the motion establishing the particular committee, in the case of a committee that is not expressly established by the bylaws.

40:6 **Proceedings in the Absence of a Quorum.** In the absence of a quorum, any business transacted (except for the procedural actions noted in the next paragraph) is null and void. But if a quorum fails to appear at a regular or properly called meeting, the inability to transact business does not detract from the fact that the society's rules requiring the meeting to be held were complied with and the meeting was convened—even though it had to adjourn immediately.

40:7 Even in the absence of a quorum, the assembly may fix the time to which to adjourn (**22**), adjourn (**21**), recess (**20**), or take measures to obtain a quorum. Subsidiary and incidental motions, questions of privilege, motions to *Raise a Question of Privilege* or *Call for the Orders of the Day*, and other motions may also be considered if they are related to these motions or to the conduct of the meeting while it remains without a quorum.

40:8 A motion that absent members be contacted during a recess would represent a measure to obtain a quorum. A motion to obtain a quorum may be moved as a main motion when no business is pending, or as a privileged motion that takes precedence over a motion to *Recess* (**20**). Such motions are out of order when another has the floor; must be seconded; are debatable except when privileged; are amendable; require a majority vote; and can be reconsidered. Motions to obtain a quorum are similar to a *Call of the House,* which can be ordered in assemblies having the power to compel attendance (see below).

40:9   The prohibition against transacting business in the absence of a quorum cannot be waived even by unanimous consent, and a notice (10:44–51) cannot be validly given. If there is important business that should not be delayed until the next regular meeting, the assembly should fix the time for an adjourned meeting and then adjourn. If, instead, the members present take action informally in the absence of a quorum, they do so at their own risk. Although the assembly can later ratify their action (10:54–57), it is under no obligation to do so.

40:10   If a committee of the whole finds itself without a quorum, it can do nothing but rise and report to the assembly, which can then proceed as described above. A quasi committee of the whole or a meeting in informal consideration of a question can itself take any of the actions permitted an assembly in the absence of a quorum, but a quasi committee of the whole is thereby ended (see **52**).

Manner of Enforcing the Quorum Requirement

40:11   Before the presiding officer calls a meeting to order, it is his duty to determine, although he need not announce, that a quorum is present. If a quorum is not present, the chair waits until there is one, or until, after a reasonable time, there appears to be no prospect that a quorum will assemble. If a quorum cannot be obtained, the chair calls the meeting to order, announces the absence of a quorum, and entertains a motion to adjourn or one of the other motions allowed, as described above.

40:12   When the chair has called a meeting to order after finding that a quorum is present, the continued presence of a quorum is presumed unless the chair or a member notices that a quorum is no longer present. If the chair notices the absence of a quorum, it is his duty to declare the fact, at least before taking any vote or stating the question on any new motion—which he can no longer do except in connection with the permissible proceedings related to the absence of a quorum, as explained above. Any member noticing the apparent absence of a quorum can make a point of order to that effect at any time so long as he does not interrupt a person who is speaking. *Debate* on a question already pending can be allowed to continue at length after a quorum is no longer present, however, until a member raises the point. Because of the difficulty likely to be encountered in determining exactly how long the meeting has been without a quorum in such cases, a point of order relating to the absence of a quorum is generally not permitted to affect prior action; but upon clear and convincing proof, such a point of order can be given effect retrospectively by a ruling of the presiding officer, subject to appeal (**24**).[1]

Call of the House

40:13   In legislative bodies or other assemblies that have legal power to compel the attendance of their members, a procedure that can be used to obtain a quorum, if necessary, is the motion for a *Call of the House*. This is a motion that unexcused absent members be brought to the meeting under arrest. A *Call of the House* is not applicable in voluntary societies.

40:14   Assemblies in which there may be occasion to order a *Call of the House* should adopt a rule governing this motion and providing that if one third, one fifth, or some other number less than a majority of the members or members-elect are present, they can order a *Call of the House* by a majority vote. When a quorum is not present, this motion should take precedence over everything except a motion to *Adjourn* (**21**). If the rule allows the call to be moved while a quorum is actually present (for the purpose of obtaining a *greater* attendance), the motion at such times should rank only with questions of privilege, should require a majority vote for adoption, and, if

---

1. What happens to a question that is pending when a meeting adjourns (because of the loss of a quorum or for any other reason) is determined by the rules given in 21:7. If such a question, however, was introduced as new business and it is proven that there was already no quorum when it was introduced, its introduction was invalid and, to be considered at a later meeting, it must again be brought up as new business.

rejected, should not be allowed to be renewed while a quorum is present.

40:15 When a *Call of the House* is ordered, the clerk calls the roll of the members, then calls again the names of the absentees— in whose behalf explanations of absence can be made and excuses can be requested. After this, no member is permitted to leave, the doors are locked, and the sergeant-at-arms, chief of police, or other arresting officer is ordered to take into custody absentees who have not been excused from attendance and bring them before the house. He does this on a warrant signed by the presiding officer and attested by the clerk. When arrested members are brought in, they are arraigned separately, their explanations are heard, and, on motion, they can be excused with or without penalty in the form of payment of a fee. Until a member has paid such a fee assessed against him, he cannot vote or be recognized by the chair for any purpose.

40:16 After a *Call of the House* has been ordered, no motion is in order, even by unanimous consent, except motions relating to the call. Motions to adjourn or dispense with further proceedings under the call, however, can be entertained after a quorum is present, or after the arresting officer reports that in his opinion a quorum cannot be obtained. An adjournment terminates all proceedings under the *Call of the House*.

§41. ORDER OF BUSINESS; ORDERS OF THE DAY; AGENDA OR PROGRAM

41:1 The terms *order of business, orders of the day, agenda,* and *program* refer to closely related concepts having to do with the order in which business is taken up in a session (**8**) and the scheduling of particular business. The meaning of these terms often coincides, although each has its own applications in common usage.

41:2 An *order of business* is any established sequence in which it may be prescribed that business shall be taken up at a session of a given assembly. In the case of ordinary societies that hold frequent regular meetings, an order of business that specifies such a sequence only in terms of certain general types or classes of business and gives only the *order* in which they are to be taken up is normally prescribed for all regular meetings by the rules of the organization. The typical order of business of this kind is described in 41:5–27. In other cases, such as in a convention, an order of business expressly adopted for a particular session frequently assigns positions, and even times, to specific subjects or items of business; and to this type of order of business the terms *agenda* and *program*[2] are applicable, as explained in 41:58–70. Although the terms *order of business, agenda,* and *program* relate primarily to the business of an entire session, the same terms are also applied to a part of the whole, in speaking of "the order of business," "the agenda," or "the program" of a meeting within a session.

41:3   An *order of the day* is an item of business that is scheduled to be taken up during a given session, day, or meeting, or at a given hour (unless there is business having precedence over it that interferes). The methods by which orders of the day can be made, their division into the classes of *general orders* and *special orders,* and their treatment in cases where they come into conflict are explained in 41:40–57. General orders and special orders are also discussed with particular reference to making them by means of the motion to *Postpone* in 14:13–17 (see also *Call for the Orders of the Day,* **18**). Unless designated for particular hours or assigned positions item by item in an agenda or program formally adopted for a given session, general orders and special orders are taken up under assigned headings or in customary positions allotted to each of these categories in the

---

2. The term *program* has two senses in parliamentary usage. In the first sense, as used here, it refers to a type of order of business that may be identical with an agenda, or (in a convention) may include an agenda together with the times for events outside of the business meetings; such events are not themselves orders of the day (see also **59**). In the second sense, as used in 41:36, the term refers to a heading, often included *within* the order of business for meetings of ordinary societies, that covers talks, lectures, films, or other features of informational or entertainment value.

order of business. (Note such headings in the "standard" order of business described below.)

41:4 Within a meeting in which the only items of business that are in order have been specified and set in sequence in advance—as might occur, for example, in a particular meeting of a convention—the orders of the day are identical with the order of business (which, in such a case, is in the form of an agenda or program).

Usual Order of Business in Ordinary Societies

41:5 **Basic Headings Covering Business Proper.** The customary or "standard" order of business comprises the following subdivisions:

1) Reading and Approval of Minutes
2) Reports of Officers, Boards, and Standing Committees
3) Reports of Special (Select or Ad Hoc) Committees
4) Special Orders
5) Unfinished Business and General Orders
6) New Business

41:6 In organizations that have adopted this book as parliamentary authority and that have not adopted a special order of business, this series of headings is the prescribed order of business for regular meetings, unless the periods intervening between consecutive regular meetings are usually more than a quarterly time interval (see 9:7). This standard order of business prescribes only the sequence of the headings, not the time to be allotted to each—which may vary with every meeting. Certain optional headings are also described following the detailed discussion of the regular headings below.

41:7 The presiding officer may find it helpful to have at hand a memorandum of the complete order of business, listing, under headings (2) and (3) as explained below, all known reports which are expected to be presented, and under headings (4) and (5), all matters which the minutes show are due to come up, arranged in proper sequence or, where applicable, listed with the times for which they have been set. The secretary can prepare, or assist the presiding officer to prepare, such a memorandum. In this connection, regarding the practice in some societies or assemblies of providing each member with a copy of the expected agenda in advance of a meeting, see 41:62.

41:8   After the presiding officer has called the meeting to order as described in 3:15, and after any customary opening ceremonies (see *Optional Headings*, 41:28–31 and 41:36), the meeting proceeds through the different headings in the order of business:

41:9   **1. Reading and Approval of Minutes.** The chair says, "The Secretary will read the minutes." However, in organizations where copies of the minutes of each previous meeting as prepared by the secretary are sent to all members in advance, the chair announces that this has been done, and the actual reading of them aloud is omitted unless any member then requests that they be read. (For "dispensing" with the reading of the minutes—that is, not reading them for approval *at the regular time*—see 48:11.) If for any reason there are minutes of other meetings in addition to the last meeting that have not been read previously, they are each read and approved first, in order of date from earliest to latest. In all but the smallest meetings, the secretary stands while reading the minutes.

41:10   A formal motion to approve the minutes is not necessary, although such a motion is not out of order. After the minutes have been read (or after their reading has been omitted by unanimous consent as described in the previous paragraph), and whether or not a motion for approval has been offered, the chair asks, "Are there any corrections to the minutes?" and pauses. Corrections, when proposed, are usually handled by unanimous consent (4:58–63), but if any member objects to a proposed correction—which is, in effect, a subsidiary motion to *Amend*—the usual rules governing consideration of amendments to a main motion are applicable (see **12**).

41:11   After any proposed corrections have been disposed of, and when there is no response to the chair's inquiry, "Are there any corrections [or "further corrections"] to the minutes?" the chair says, "There being no corrections [or "no further corrections"] to the minutes, the minutes stand [or "are"] approved [or "approved as read," or "approved as corrected"]." The minutes are thus approved without any formal vote, even if a motion for their approval has been made. The only proper way to object to the approval of the secretary's draft of the minutes is to offer a correction to it.[3] It should be noted that a member's absence from the meeting for which minutes are being approved does not prevent the member from participating in their correction or approval.

41:12   The secretary's draft of the minutes is often sent to all members in advance of the meeting at which those minutes are to be approved, usually with the meeting notice. When this has been done, it is presumed that the members have had an opportunity to review these draft minutes, and they are not read at the meeting unless a member requests it. Correction and approval, however, is handled in the usual way. A draft of the minutes circulated to members must be clearly marked as such. The secretary's draft of the minutes, whether or not circulated before their approval, does not become *the* minutes—that is, the official record of the proceedings of the society—unless it is approved, and the minutes may be materially modified in the correction process. Only the secretary's corrected version of the minutes is official in such a case.

41:13   **2. Reports of Officers, Boards, and Standing Committees.** In most societies it is customary to hear reports from all officers (**47**, **48**), boards (**49**), and standing committees (**50**) only at annual meetings. At other meetings the chair calls only on those who

---

3. However, a member who believes that further investigation or redrafting is necessary in order to produce a correct version of the minutes may offer a motion to refer the minutes to a committee or to postpone their approval to a certain time.

have reports to make, as by saying (in calling upon the secretary), "Is there any correspondence?" Or, "May we have the Treasurer's report." Or, "The chair recognizes Mr. Downey, Chairman of the Membership Committee, for a report." If the chair is uncertain, he may ask, for example, "Does the Program Committee have a report?" *Standing committees* listed in the bylaws are called upon in the order in which they are listed.

41:14   If an officer, in reporting, makes a recommendation, he should not himself move its implementation, but such a motion can be made by another member as soon as the officer has concluded his report. In the case of a committee report, on the other hand, the chairman or other reporting member should make any motion(s) necessary to bring the committee's recommendations before the assembly for consideration. A motion arising out of an officer's, a board's, or a committee's report is taken up immediately, since the object of the order of business is to give priority to the classes of business in the order listed.

41:15   If an item of business in this class is on the table (that is, if it was laid on the table at the present session, or at the preceding session if no more than a quarterly time interval has intervened (see 9:7), and if the item has not been taken from the table), it is in order to move to take such business from the table under this heading (see **17**, **34**).

41:16   (For procedures to be followed in making reports and in handling recommendations arising from reports, see **51**.)

41:17   *3. Reports of Special Committees.* The special committees (**50**) that are to report are called on in the order in which they were appointed. Only those special committees that are prepared, or were instructed, to report on matters referred to them should be called on. Business incident to reports of special committees that is on the table can be taken from the table under this heading (**17**, **34**).

41:18   *4. Special Orders.* Under this heading (referring to the explanation of *Orders of the Day* in 41:40ff.) are taken up the following in the order listed:

a) Any unfinished special orders (that is, special orders that were not disposed of at the preceding meeting)—taken in sequence beginning with the special order that was pending when that meeting adjourned if it adjourned while one was pending, and continuing with the remaining unfinished special orders in the order in which they were made (that is, were set by action of the assembly).

b) Items of business that have been made special orders for the present meeting[4] without being set for specific hours— taken in the order in which they were made.

Regarding the interruption of business under this heading by special orders that have been set for particular hours, see 41:53–56.

41:19   Normally—unless an order of the day was made as a part of an agenda for a session—no motion is necessary at the time the order comes up, since the introduction of the question has been accomplished previously, as will be seen from the description of the methods by which orders of the day are made, in 41:42. When a special order that was so introduced comes up, the chair announces it as pending, thus: "At the last meeting, the resolution relating to funds for a new playground was made a special order for this meeting [or, if the special order was made by postponement, "... was postponed to this meeting and made a special order."]. The resolution is as follows: '*Resolved,* That ... [reading it].' The question is on the adoption of the resolution."

41:20   Matters that the bylaws require to be considered at a particular meeting, such as the nomination and election of officers, may be regarded as special orders for the meeting and be considered under the heading of *Special Orders* in the order of business. If a special order is on the table, it is in order to move

4. But not *the* special order (see 41:57).

to take it from the table under this heading when no question is pending (**17**, **34**).

41:21   **5. Unfinished Business and General Orders.** The term *unfinished business*,[5] in cases where the regular business meetings of an organization are not separated by more than a quarterly time interval (9:7), refers to questions that have come over from the previous meeting (other than special orders) as a result of that meeting's having adjourned without completing its order of business (21:7(b)) and without scheduling an adjourned meeting (**9**, **22**) to complete it.

41:22   A *general order* (as explained under *Orders of the Day,* below) is any question which, usually by postponement, has been made an order of the day without being made a special order.

41:23   The heading of *Unfinished Business and General Orders* includes items of business in the four categories that are listed below in the order in which they are taken up. Of these, the first three constitute "Unfinished Business," while the fourth consists of "General Orders":

a) The question that was pending when the previous meeting adjourned, if that meeting adjourned while a question other than a special order was pending.

b) Any questions that were unfinished business at the previous meeting but were not reached before it adjourned—taken in the order in which they were due to come up at that meeting as indicated under (a) and (c).

c) Any questions which, by postponement or otherwise, were set as general orders for the previous meeting, or for a particular hour during that meeting, but were not reached before it adjourned—taken in the order in which the general orders were made.

d) Matters that were postponed to, or otherwise made general orders for, the present meeting—taken in the order in which they were made.

---

5. The expression "old business" should be avoided, since it may incorrectly suggest the further consideration of matters that have been finally disposed of.

Regarding the relationship between this heading in the order of business and general orders for particular hours, see 41:49–52.

41:24　　The chair should not announce the heading of *Unfinished Business and General Orders* unless the minutes show that there is some business to come up under it. In the latter case, he should have all such subjects listed in correct sequence in a memorandum prepared in advance of the meeting. He should *not* ask, "Is there any unfinished business?" but should state the question on the first item of business that is due to come up under this heading; and when it has been disposed of, he should proceed through the remaining subjects in their proper order. If a question was pending when the previous meeting adjourned, for example, the chair might begin this heading by saying, "Under Unfinished Business and General Orders, the first item of business is the motion relating to use of the parking facilities, which was pending when the last meeting adjourned. The question is on the adoption of the motion 'That … [stating the motion].'" Later under the same heading, in announcing a general order that was made by postponing a question, the chair might say, "The next item of business is the resolution relating to proposed improvement of our newly purchased picnic grounds, which was postponed to this meeting. The resolution is as follows: '*Resolved,* That … [reading the resolution].' The question is on the adoption of the resolution."

41:25　　Any item of business (in whatever class) that is on the table can be taken from the table under this heading at any time when no question is pending (**17, 34**). To obtain the floor for the purpose of moving to take a question from the table at such a time, a member can rise and address the chair, interrupting him as he starts to announce the next item of business after the previous one is disposed of.

41:26　　It should be noted that, with the exception indicated in the preceding paragraph, a subject may not be taken up under Unfinished Business and General Orders unless it has acquired such status by one of the formal processes (a), (c), or (d) listed in 41:23. If brief consultation during a meeting leads to an informal understanding that a certain subject should be "brought up at the next meeting," that does not make it unfinished business. Instead, the matter would have to be introduced at the next meeting as new business, as explained below.

41:27   **6. New Business.**   After unfinished business and general orders have been disposed of, the chair asks, "Is there any new business?" Members can then introduce new items of business, or can move to take from the table any matter that is on the table (**17**, **34**), in the order in which they are able to obtain the floor when no question is pending, as explained in **3** and **4**. So long as members are reasonably prompt in claiming the floor, the chair cannot prevent the making of legitimate motions or deprive members of the right to introduce legitimate business, by hurrying through the proceedings.

41:28   **Optional Headings.**   In addition to the standard order of business as just described, regular meetings of organizations sometimes include proceedings in the categories listed below, which may be regarded as optional in the order of business prescribed by this book.

41:29   After the call to order and *before the reading of the minutes,* the next two headings may be included:

41:30   *Opening Ceremonies or Exercises.*   Opening ceremonies immediately after the meeting is called to order may include the invocation (which, if offered, should always be placed first), the singing of the national anthem, the reciting of the Pledge of Allegiance to the flag, a ritual briefly recalling the objects or ideals of the organization, or the like.

41:31   *Roll Call.*   In some organizations it is customary at meetings to call the roll of officers in order to verify their attendance—or, sometimes in very small societies, even to call the roll of members. If there is a roll call of this nature, it should take place at the end of the opening ceremonies unless a special rule of the organization assigns it a different position in the order of business. The chair announces it by saying, "The Secretary will call the roll of officers [or "will call the roll"]."

41:32 *Consent Calendar.* Legislatures, city, town, or county councils, or other assemblies which have a heavy work load including a large number of routine or noncontroversial matters may find a *consent calendar* a useful tool for disposing of such items of business. Commonly, when such a matter has been introduced or reported by a committee for consideration in the assembly, its sponsor, or, sometimes, an administrator, may seek to have it placed on the consent calendar. This calendar is called over periodically *at a point established in the agenda by special rule of order, at least preceding standing committee reports.* The matters listed on it are taken up in order, unless objected to, in which case they are restored to the ordinary process by which they are placed in line for consideration on the regular agenda. The special rule of order establishing a consent calendar may provide that, when the matters on the calendar are called up, they may be considered in gross or without debate or amendment. Otherwise, they are considered under the rules just as any other business, in which case the "consent" relates only to permitting the matter to be on the calendar for consideration without conforming to the usual, more onerous, rules for reaching measures in the body.

41:33   *After the completion of new business*—that is, when no one claims the floor to make a motion in response to the chair's query, "Is there any further new business?"—the chair may proceed to one or more of the following headings, in an order that may be subject to variation determined by the practice of the organization.

41:34 *Good of the Order, General Good and Welfare, or Open Forum.* This heading, included by some types of societies in their order of business, refers to the general welfare of the organization, and may vary in character. Under this heading (in contrast to the general parliamentary rule that allows discussion only with reference to a pending motion), members who obtain the floor commonly are permitted to offer informal observations regarding the work of the organization, the public reputation of the society or its membership, or the like. Certain types of announcements may tend to fall here. Although the Good of the Order often involves no business or motions, the practice of some organizations would place motions or resolutions relating to formal disciplinary procedures for offenses outside a meeting (**63**) at this point. In some organizations, the program (see below) is looked upon as a part of the Good of the Order.

41:35   *Announcements.* The chair may make, or call upon other officers or members to make, any necessary announcements; or, if the practice of the organization permits it, members can briefly obtain the floor for such a purpose. The placing of general announcements at this point in the order of business does not prevent the chair from making an urgent announcement at any time.

41:36   *Program.* If there is to be a talk, film, or other program of a cultural, educational, or civic nature, it is usually presented before the meeting is adjourned, since it may prompt a desire on the part of the assembly to take action. Although the program is commonly placed at the end of the order of business in such cases, it can, by special rule or practice, be received before the minutes are read; or, by suspending the rules (**25**), it can be proceeded to at any time during the meeting. If, in courtesy to a guest speaker who is present, the chair wishes the talk to be located at an unscheduled point within the business portion of the meeting, he can usually obtain unanimous consent for a suspension of the rules by simply announcing, "If there is no objection, we will hear our speaker's address at this time."

Taking Up Business out of Its Proper Order

41:37   Any particular item of business can be taken up out of its proper order by adopting a motion to *Suspend the Rules* (**25**) by a two-thirds vote, although this is usually arranged by unanimous consent (4:58–63). Hence, an important committee report or an urgent item of new business can be advanced in order to assure its full and unhurried consideration. If desired, before the completion of the advanced question the regular order of business can be returned to by a majority vote—by adopting a motion to lay the pending question on the table (**17**).

41:38   To take up a motion out of its proper order—for example, to introduce an item of new business before that heading is reached—a member who has obtained the floor can say, "I ask unanimous consent to introduce at this time a resolution on financing better schools." If there is any objection, or the member anticipates that there may be, he can say, "I move to suspend the rules that interfere with the introduction at this time of …" If unanimous consent is given or if this motion is adopted by a two-thirds vote, the member is immediately recognized to introduce the resolution. If only one or two items stand ahead of the item it is desired to reach, it may be just as simple to lay the intervening items on the table individually (**17**), or to postpone them as they arise (**14**). It is not in order to lay on the table or postpone a *class* of questions, like committee reports, or anything but the question that is actually before the assembly. (See 14:10–11, 17:3(2), 17:14.)

41:39   The chair himself cannot depart from the prescribed order of business, which only the assembly can do by at least a two-thirds vote. This is an important protection in cases where some of the members principally involved in a particular question may be unable to be present through an entire meeting. When such a departure from the order of business is justified, however, it is usually easy for the chair to obtain the necessary authorization from the assembly. He can say, for example, "The chair will entertain a motion to suspend the rules, and take up …"; or (for obtaining unanimous consent), "If there is no objection, the chair proposes at this time to proceed to take up …" (see also illustration under the heading *Program* above).

Orders of the Day

41:40   An *order of the day,* as stated above, is a particular subject, question, or item of business that is set in advance to be taken up during a given session, day, or meeting, or at a given hour, provided that no business having precedence over it interferes. In cases where more than a quarterly time interval (9:7) will elapse before the next regular business session of the organization, an order of the day cannot be made for a time beyond the end of the present session. If the next regular business session will be held within a quarterly time interval, an order of the day cannot be made beyond the end of that next session. An order of the day cannot be taken up before the time for which it is set, except by reconsidering (37) the vote that established the order (so long as a reconsideration is possible), or by suspending the rules (25) by a two-thirds vote.

41:41   Orders of the day are divided into the classes of *general orders* and *special orders.* A special order is an order of the day that is made with the stipulation that any rules interfering with its consideration at the specified time shall be suspended except those relating: (a) to adjournment or recess (**8, 20, 21**); (b) to questions of privilege (**19**); (c) to special orders that were made before this special order was made; or (d) to a question that has been assigned priority over all other business at a meeting by being made *the* special order for the meeting as described in 41:57. An important consequence of this suspending effect is that, with the four exceptions just mentioned, a special order for a particular hour interrupts any business that is pending when that hour arrives. Since the making of a special order has the effect of suspending any interfering rules, it requires a two-thirds vote (except where such action is included in the adoption of an agenda or program for a session having no prescribed order of business). Any matter that is made an order of the day without being made a special order is a general order for the time named.

41:42   An item of business can be made an order of the day in the following ways:

1) While the question is pending, it can be postponed (**14**) to the specified time by a majority vote (in which case it is a general order); or, by a two-thirds vote, it can be postponed to that time and made a special order.

2) A question that has not yet been brought before the assembly can be made a special order for a future time by means of a main motion adopted by a two-thirds vote. Similarly, it is possible, although less common, to make a question that is not pending a general order for a future time by a majority vote.

3) An agenda or program assigning a specific position or hour to the item of business can be adopted. The subject is then a general order or a special order, depending on the form of the agenda or program (see 41:58). For the vote required to adopt an agenda, see *Procedure for Adoption*, 41:61.

41:43   **Forms for Motions to Make General or Special Orders.** The forms in proposing to make a *pending* question an order of the day for a future time by means of the motion to *Postpone* are given in 14:20.

41:44   When a question that is *not pending* is made an order of the day, it is usually made a special order. A main motion to make a particular subject a special order can be introduced whenever business of its class or new business is in order and nothing is pending. It can be offered in this form: "I move that the following resolution be made a special order for the next meeting: '*Resolved*, That …'"; or, "I offer the following resolution and move that it be made a special order for 3 P.M.: '…'" In the case of a committee report, a resolution such as this may be adopted: "*Resolved*, That the report of the committee on the revision of the bylaws be made the special order for Wednesday morning and thereafter until it has been disposed of."

41:45   Motions in similar forms can also be used to make a question that is not pending a general order. In this connection, however, it should be noted that a majority can thus prevent a matter from coming before the assembly until a future time, but after a majority has taken such action, nothing less than a two-thirds vote can change it unless it is reconsidered (**37**). If a main motion to make a question that is not pending an order of the day for a future time is introduced, any member who would prefer to consider the matter immediately should speak in debate against the motion that would make it an order of the day. If that motion is voted down, he can then introduce the subject of the proposed order as a main question.

41:46　**Relation of Orders of the Day to the Established Order of Business.** In assemblies that follow the "standard" order of business explained above, orders of the day for a given session, day, or meeting that are not set for particular hours are taken up under the headings of *Special Orders* and *Unfinished Business and General Orders* (see 41:18–26). In cases where an ordinary society has adopted its own order of business for regular meetings, it usually includes similar headings covering such orders of the day. Where an organization's order of business does not provide such headings, special orders not set for particular hours are taken up before unfinished business and general orders, or (if there are neither of these), at all events before new business. Under the same conditions, general orders are taken up after any unfinished business (that is, business pending at the adjournment of the previous meeting, if any, and orders of the day not disposed of at the time of its adjournment), and before new business unless a later hour is specified (see below).

41:47　The most common instances of orders of the day set for particular hours occur in conventions.

41:48　In any type of assembly, in cases where orders of the day have been set for particular hours, their consideration at the proper time may cause interruption or modification of the order of business as it exists apart from these orders of the day; and different orders of the day may come into conflict. Rules governing such cases are as follows:

41:49 ***Rules of precedence affecting general orders for particular hours.*** As stated above, a general order that has been set for a particular hour cannot be considered before that hour unless the rules are suspended by a two-thirds vote, or unless the vote that made the general order can still be reconsidered. This is the principal effect of making a subject a general order for a particular hour. Since the making of a general order does not suspend any rules, even if it is designated for a particular hour, delay in its consideration when that hour arrives may arise from a number of causes. Even though the hour fixed for a general order has arrived, the order can be taken up only when all of the following additional conditions are fulfilled:

a) no other business is pending;
b) no special order interferes;
c) no motion to *Reconsider* (**37**) that may then be moved or called up interferes;
d) the category of General Orders in the prescribed order of business has been reached or passed; and
e) all general orders that were made before this order was made, except any that were set for a time that has not yet arrived, have been disposed of.

As soon after the designated hour as conditions (a), (b), (d), and (e) are met, the chair announces the general order as the pending business; but as he starts to do so, any member can rise and address the chair for the purpose of moving or calling up a reconsideration.

41:50   The rule that a general order for a particular hour does not interrupt a pending question when that hour arrives holds even when the pending question is a general order that was made later.[6] But if a general order for an earlier time is not reached by the time set for another general order that was made before

---

6. If it is desired to take up a general order at its specified hour and a pending question interferes, that pending question can, however, be laid on the table (**17**) or postponed (**14**).

it was, the general order that was made first is taken up in preference to the one for the earlier time.

41:51	*Example.* A motion is postponed to 4:30 P.M. Later, another motion is postponed to 4:15 P.M. If the 4:15 motion is taken up at that time (or at least before 4:30) and is not disposed of by 4:30, it continues under consideration and is not interrupted. But if the 4:15 motion is not reached by 4:30, the 4:30 motion, having been postponed first, has preference and will be taken up first. Unless something else affects the situation, the 4:15 motion in such a case will be considered after the disposal of the 4:30 motion.

41:52	If several general orders were made for the same time, they are taken up in the order in which they were made. If several general orders were made for the same time in the same motion, they are taken up in the order in which they are listed in the motion. If all of this business is not disposed of before adjournment, it is treated as described in 21:7 and 41:23.

41:53	**Rules of precedence affecting special orders for particular hours.** A special order for a particular hour cannot be considered before that hour except by a two-thirds vote. But when the designated hour arrives, the special order automatically interrupts any business that may be pending except: (a) a motion relating to adjournment or recess; (b) a question of privilege; (c) a special order that was made before the special order set for the present hour was made; or (d) *the* special order for a meeting, as described below. The chair simply announces the special order at the proper time, as shown in 14:22.

41:54	With the exception of *the* special order for a meeting, when special orders that have been made at different times come into conflict, the one that was made first takes precedence over all special orders made afterward, which rank in the order in which they were made. This rule holds even when special orders made later have been set for consideration at earlier hours. No special order can interfere with one that was made earlier than itself. If several special orders have been made at the same time for the same hour, they rank in the order in which they are listed in the motion by which they were made. If they were made at the same time for different hours, it is implied that the vote on each one will be taken when the hour for the next one arrives, and the same rules apply as those for taking up topics in an agenda (see 41:65).

41:55 **Example.** Assume that a special order has been made for 3 P.M. Thereafter, one is made for 2 P.M. Still later, one is made for 4 P.M. At two o'clock, the special order for that time is taken up, even if it interrupts a general order that is pending. However, if the 2 P.M. special order is still pending at 3 P.M., the 3 P.M. special order is immediately taken up—interrupting the one that is pending—because it was made first. Also, because the 3 P.M. order was made first, if it is still under consideration at four o'clock, it continues regardless of the order for that time. Even after the 3 P.M. order is disposed of, the 4 P.M. order must await completion of the prior-made 2 P.M. order, which is resumed first. Not until all of these special orders are disposed of, together with any others whose times are reached in the meantime, can the assembly return to its regular order of business, first resuming consideration of any subject that may have been interrupted at 2 P.M. It is possible, of course, to rearrange these special orders by reconsidering the votes that made them, or, if reconsideration is no longer possible (**37**), by suspending the rules and taking up each one of them in succession, only to postpone it and make it a special order for the desired new time.

41:56 It should be noted that a special order does not interfere with a recess or adjournment that is scheduled for a particular hour. When such an hour arrives, the chair announces it and declares the assembly in recess or adjourned, even if a special order is pending that was made before the hour of recess or adjournment was fixed. When the chair announces the hour, anyone can move to postpone the time for adjournment, or to extend the time of considering the pending question for a specified period. These motions are undebatable and require a two-thirds vote (see also 20:6–7, 21:14).

41:57   *The special order for a meeting.* When it is desired to devote an entire meeting to a subject, or as much of the meeting as may be necessary, the matter can be made *the* special order for the meeting (as distinguished from *a* special order for the meeting; see 41:18–20). *The* special order for the meeting will then be taken up as soon as the minutes have been approved, and the remainder of the order of business will not be taken up until this special order has been disposed of. Although *the* special order for a meeting takes precedence over all other forms of special orders, even if they were made before it was, the times of any such orders for particular hours that may come into conflict should be adjusted, as indicated in the last sentence of 41:55.

Agenda or Program

41:58   By a single vote, a series of special orders or general orders—or a mixture of both—can be made; such a series is called an *agenda*. When an hour is assigned to a particular subject in an agenda, that subject is thereby made a special order unless, by footnote or other means, it is stated that the time is intended merely for guidance, in which case the subject is only a general order. Subjects for which no hour is specified in an agenda are general orders.

41:59   In an agenda, often an hour is assigned only to such subjects as the calls to order, recesses, adjournments, and particularly important items of business where it is desired to give the members greater assurance that the matter will not be considered before that time. These, then, are special orders for the time stated, and a strict adherence to these times provides a protection to the members and invited speakers, who often come from great distances. Occasionally, a time is assigned for every item on the agenda. While this practice may be necessary in some cases, the resulting loss of flexibility often outweighs any benefits that may be gained.

41:60 **Organizations and Meetings in Which Adoption of an Agenda Is Customary.** It is customary to adopt an agenda or program for each session in organizations that do not hold frequent regular meetings, and at conventions and other sessions that may last for several days (see **59**). This is also frequently done when, for any reason, neither the standard order of business nor a special order of business established by rule of the organization is practical or applicable.

41:61 **Procedure for Adoption.** In cases in which an agenda is adopted, usually this is done at the outset of a session and the agenda is intended to cover the entire session. At a session having no prescribed or adopted order of business, such an agenda is followed as a guide by the chair pending its formal adoption and can be adopted by majority vote, even if it contains special orders; it is then the order of business for that session. At a session that already has an order of business, an agenda can be adopted by a majority vote only if it does not create any special orders and does not conflict with the existing order of business; otherwise, a two-thirds vote is required (see also 25:12).

41:62 **Agenda Provided in Advance.** In some organizations, it is customary to send each member, in advance of a meeting, an order of business or agenda, with some indication of the matters to be considered under each heading. Such an agenda is often provided for information only, with no intention or practice of submitting it for adoption. Unless a precirculated agenda is formally adopted at the session to which it applies, it is not binding as to detail or order of consideration, other than as it lists preexisting orders of the day (41:40ff.) or conforms to the standard order of business (3:16, 41:5ff.) or an order of business prescribed by the rules of the organization (2:16, 3:16).

41:63 **Changing an Agenda.** When the adoption of a proposed agenda is pending, it is subject to amendment by majority vote. After an agenda has been adopted by the assembly, no change can be made in it except by a two-thirds vote, a vote of a majority of the entire membership, or unanimous consent. (See also *Taking Up Business out of Its Proper Order*, 41:37–39; cf. 59:59.) An affirmative vote to adopt an agenda may not be reconsidered.

41:64 **Agenda in the Form of a Program.** In reference to an order of business specially adopted for a given session, the term *program* is often used instead of *agenda*; but while the latter technically includes only items of business, the former may include also the times for speakers, meals, and other nonbusiness matters.

41:65 **Taking Up Topics in an Agenda.** When the assigned time for taking up a topic in an agenda arrives, the chair announces that fact. Then he puts to a vote any pending questions without allowing further debate, unless someone immediately moves to lay the question on the table, postpone it, or refer it to a committee. If any of these subsidiary motions are moved, they are likewise put to a vote, together with any amendment to them, without debate. Besides these subsidiary motions, a motion to extend the time for considering the pending question is in order. While an extension under these conditions is seldom desirable and is often unfair to the next topic, it is sometimes necessary, and a motion for the extension can be adopted without debate by a two-thirds vote (see also **18**). As soon as the business that was pending has been disposed of as described, the chair recognizes the member who is to offer the motion or resolution embodying the scheduled topic (unless the question has previously been introduced and has come over from an earlier time, in which case the chair announces it as the pending business).

41:66 **Declaring a Scheduled Recess or Adjournment.** When a recess or adjournment has been scheduled for a particular hour (either by provision in the adopted agenda or program or by adoption of a motion setting the time) and that hour arrives, the chair announces it and, unless a member promptly seeks the floor for one of the purposes described below, declares the assembly in recess or adjourned. (However, if the *Previous Question* has already been ordered on one or more pending motions when the hour for a recess or adjournment arrives, there usually will be no objection to the chair's putting them all to a vote in succession before declaring the assembly to be in recess or adjourned.)

41:67 When the chair announces the hour, any member can move to reschedule the time for recess or adjournment, or to extend the time of considering the pending question for a specified period. These motions are undebatable and require a two-thirds vote; see also 18:8, 20:6–7, and 21:14. Before declaring the meeting adjourned, the chair must allow, in addition to the motions just described, any of the parliamentary steps that would be in order when a privileged motion to *Adjourn* is pending or has just been voted for (see 21:10–12).

41:68 In the case of a recess, any pending business is interrupted for the recess, and taken up again after the recess. In the case of an adjournment, see *Carrying Over Unfinished Business* below.

41:69 **Advisability of Providing for Unfinished Business.** At intervals or near the end of the session, an agenda should include provision for unfinished business. In agendas in which most or all of the items are special orders for particular times, it may be necessary to provide for unfinished business near the end of each day's sitting. Such provisions give the assembly a recourse whenever it needs a little more time before voting on a question. It can postpone a question to a time provided for unfinished business or, at all events, can conclude consideration of a question during such a period. Otherwise, a pending question that is merely postponed until the disposal of the next item—since it becomes only a general order—may be severely buffeted by the remaining special orders. Its further consideration would depend upon the next or some successive items taking less time than allotted, and it might soon be interrupted again by the next subject for which a time was assigned.

41:70 **Carrying Over Unfinished Business.** In sessions consisting of several meetings, if the time set for adjournment of a meeting arrives before all of the matters scheduled for that meeting have been considered, the remaining items of business are carried over to the next meeting.[7] The unfinished items of business are taken first in their order before the matters scheduled for the later meeting, provided that the agenda makes no special provision for unfinished business that day and no conflict arises with a special order. Therefore, when most items in the agenda are general orders, it is wise to schedule the more important items of business at a reasonably early meeting of a convention or to set them as special orders. (See also 59:55(10).)

---

7. For the treatment of business unfinished at the end of a session, see 21:7(b–c).

CHAPTER
XII

ASSIGNMENT OF THE FLOOR; DEBATE

§42. RULES GOVERNING ASSIGNMENT OF THE FLOOR

42:1   The manner in which a member obtains the floor is described in 3:30–35, with an initial treatment of the principal rules governing the assignment of the floor under ordinary conditions in most business meetings. More complete rules affecting the assignment of the floor are contained in this section.

Recognition of a Member

42:2   Before a member in an assembly can make a motion or speak in debate, he must claim the floor by rising[1] and addressing the chair as described in 3:31, and must be recognized by the chair. The chair must recognize any member who seeks the floor while entitled to it. The chair normally recognizes a member (thereby assigning the floor to him) by announcing, as applicable, the member's name or title, or the place or unit that he represents. If necessary, the member—either on his own initiative or at the request of the chair—should state his name, with any appropriate additional identification, as soon as the

---

1. In small boards and in committees, members generally need not rise to obtain the floor. See 49:21(1).

presiding officer turns toward him after he has risen and addressed the chair. Variations in the granting of recognition are as follows:

- If only one person is seeking the floor in a small meeting where all present can clearly see one another, the chair may recognize the member by merely nodding to him.
- If a speech is prearranged, or if several members are attempting to claim the floor at once in a large meeting, a wording frequently used by the chair in granting recognition is, "The chair recognizes Mr. Smith."

42:3 Whenever a member rises and addresses the chair at a time when the floor can be granted only for limited purposes and the chair is not certain that the member understands this fact— for example, when an undebatable question is immediately pending as explained in 42:12—the chair, before recognizing the member, asks, "For what purpose does the member [or "the gentleman," or "the lady," or, as in Congress, "the gentlewoman"] rise?" If members remain seated around a conference table and do not rise, the chair may ask, "For what purpose does the member address the chair?"

42:4 Except by unanimous consent (4:58–63), a motion can be made only by one who has been recognized by the chair as having the floor. If a motion is called out by anyone who has not obtained the floor, the chair must not treat it as having been properly moved if another member, by rising promptly and claiming the floor, shows that unanimous consent has not been given.

42:5 When assigned the floor, a member may use it for any proper purpose, or a combination of purposes; for example, although a member may have begun by debating a pending motion, he may conclude by moving any secondary motion, including the *Previous Question* (**16**), that is in order at the time.

Assignment of the Floor When More Than One Person Claims It

42:6 If two or more rise at about the same time to claim the floor, the general rule is that, all other things being equal, the member who rose and addressed the chair first *after the floor was yielded* is entitled to be recognized. A member who rises before the floor has been yielded is not entitled to the floor if any other member rises afterward and addresses the chair.[2]

42:7 Under a variety of particular conditions, however, when more than one member claims the floor at about the same time, the best interests of the assembly require the floor to be assigned to a claimant who was not the first to rise and address the chair. Such a claimant to the floor in these cases is said to be entitled to "preference in being recognized" or "preference in recognition." A member cannot rise to claim preference in recognition after the chair has actually recognized another member. However, there are a number of purposes for which a member who has been assigned the floor may be interrupted (see 42:18–19). A member who sought the floor for such a purpose before the floor has been assigned is likewise entitled to preference in recognition. Thus, if there may be no other opportunity, a member is entitled to preference in recognition to give notice of intent to introduce a motion requiring such notice (10:47–50), or to make a motion to *Reconsider* (**37**) or to *Reconsider and Enter on the Minutes* (37:46–52), even when another motion is pending or a series of motions connected with taking up a single item of business is being disposed of (cf. 42:13(2–3)).

42:8 When the chair has just reported a vote, a member is entitled to preference in recognition to make an appropriate motion that the vote be taken again by another method (**30**). Other rules governing preference in recognition may be grouped as relating to cases when a debatable question is immediately pending, when an undebatable question is immediately pending, and when no question is pending.

---

2. For modification of these rules in large assemblies, see 42:16.

42:9 **Preference in Recognition When a Debatable Question Is Immediately Pending.** While a motion is open to debate:

1) If the member who made the motion that is immediately pending claims the floor and has not already spoken on the question, he is entitled to be recognized in preference to other members. Under some particular cases or variations of this rule, the members entitled to preference in recognition are:

   a) in the case of a motion to implement a recommendation in a committee's report, the reporting member (who presented the committee's report to the assembly);

   b) in the case of a question that has been taken from the table (**34**), the member who moved to take it from the table; and

   c) in the case of a motion to *Reconsider* (**37**), the member who *made* the motion to *Reconsider,* not necessarily the one who may have called it up (see 37:10(c), 37:15–16).

2) No member who has already had the floor in debate on the immediately pending question is entitled to it again on the same day for debate on the same question so long as any member who has not spoken on that question claims the floor.

3) In cases where the chair knows that persons seeking the floor have opposite opinions on the question—and the member to be recognized is not determined by (1) or (2) above—the chair lets the floor alternate, as far as possible, between those favoring and those opposing the measure. In large assemblies, various devices are sometimes used to assist the chair in following this rule, such as having members seeking recognition hold up cards of different colors, go to different microphones "for" and "against," or the like.

42:10   In the case of an *Appeal* (or a *Point of Order* that the chair has submitted to a vote) that is debatable, the chair is entitled to speak once in preference to any member seeking the floor and a second time at the close of the debate (see 23:19, 24:3(5)).

42:11   When a member has moved to reconsider the vote on a motion for the announced purpose of amending the motion, if the vote is reconsidered he must be recognized in preference to others in order to move his amendment. This rule also applies to reconsiderations of amendable motions that are not debatable (see list on page t47), as noted below.

42:12   **Preference in Recognition When an Undebatable Question Is Immediately Pending.** When the immediately pending question is undebatable (pages t46–t47), the member who moved it has no preference to the floor. When an undebatable motion that can be amended is reconsidered for that announced purpose, however, the maker of the motion to *Reconsider* (**37**) is entitled to preference in recognition, as explained in the preceding paragraph.

42:13   **Preference in Recognition When No Question Is Pending.** Cases where a member is entitled to preference in recognition when no question is pending occur as follows:

1) When a member has been assigned to offer a motion which a special meeting was called to consider, or an important prearranged main motion at any meeting, that member is entitled to prior recognition and no other members are permitted to intervene in an effort to offer another motion in competition.

2) When a desired object requires a series of motions, each of which is moved while no question is pending, and when the assembly has disposed of one motion in such a series, the next motion in the series has the right of way; and, for the purpose of making that motion, the chair recognizes the member who is presenting the series, even if another member has risen and addressed the chair first. For example:

a) When a question has been laid on the table (**17**) for a legitimate purpose—to enable the assembly to take up a more urgent matter—the member who moved to lay on the table is entitled to preference in recognition to introduce the urgent business.

b) When the rules have been suspended (**25**) to enable a certain motion to be made, the member who moved to suspend the rules is entitled to the floor to make the motion involved.

3) Similarly, when a motion has been voted down at the urging of a member who stated in debate that in such event he would offer a different motion on the same subject (see 10:30(5)), that member is entitled to preference in recognition so that he may introduce his alternative motion.

4) When no question is pending and no series of motions has been started, and a member has risen seeking the floor to make a main motion, another member is entitled to preference in recognition if he addresses the chair and states that he rises for one of the following purposes:

a) to make a motion to *Reconsider and Enter on the Minutes* (37:46–52);

b) to move to reconsider a vote (**37**);

c) to call up a motion to *Reconsider* (in its regular or special form (**37**)) that has been made earlier;

d) to give previous notice (10:44–50);

e) to move to take a question from the table (**34**) when it is in order to do so; or

f) to make a motion for which previous notice has been given.

If members come into competition in rising for these purposes, they have preference in the order in which the six actions are listed above. Time limits on making the motion to *Reconsider*—and shorter limits on its special form, to *Reconsider and Enter on the Minutes*—account for first preference of these two motions in such cases.

42:14 **Assignment of the Floor by Vote; Appeals.** If the chair is in doubt as to who is entitled to the floor, he can allow the assembly to decide the question by a vote, in which case the member receiving the largest vote is entitled to the floor.

42:15   If at any time the chair makes a mistake and assigns the floor to the wrong person when more than one member rose and addressed the chair promptly, a *Point of Order* can be raised. Except in a mass meeting, the decision of the chair in assigning the floor can be appealed from by any two members—one making the appeal and the other seconding it (**24**).[3]

42:16   **Variations in Large Assemblies.** In large conventions or similar bodies, some of the rules applicable to the assignment of the floor may require adaptation, which, pending the adoption of appropriate convention standing rules or special rules of order, the chair may direct. For example, in a large hall where microphones are in use and members must walk some distance to reach one, members may be asked to line up at numbered microphones. They may be recognized in numerical order, or someone may list them for the chair in the order in which assistant sergeants-at-arms turned on lights affixed to the microphones. It may be provided that a member who has a priority matter, such as a point of order, may ask the assistant at the microphone to flash the light to so indicate. Should a member, called in whatever order is established, move an amendment or other debatable motion, others awaiting a turn should stand aside unless their debate is germane to the new motion. If the *Previous Question* or a motion to limit debate is moved, members who have been waiting in line cannot validly protest; as in all other cases, the chair cannot choose the occasions when such motions will be in order. He may advise the assembly that, if it wishes to continue debate and hear from those waiting in line, a minority greater than one third has this within its power.

3. In a mass meeting, the chair's decision in assigning the floor is not subject to appeal. In a very large body other than a mass meeting, if the best interests of the assembly require that the chair be given greater power in assigning the floor, a special rule that there shall be no appeal from his decision in granting recognition can be adopted (see 2:14ff.; see also, in regard to standing rules in a convention, 59:27ff.).

42:17   If ushers are equipped with hand microphones and a micro-phone is carried to each member who is recognized, the stan-dard rules in 42:6 can be followed.

Interruption of a Member Assigned the Floor

42:18   When a member has been assigned the floor and has begun to speak—unless he begins to discuss a subject when no mo-tion is pending or speaks longer in debate than the rules of the assembly allow—he cannot be interrupted by another member or by the chair except for one of the following purposes, and then only when the urgency of the situation justifies it:

a) a *Call for the Orders of the Day* (**18**) when they are not being conformed to,
b) the raising of a question of privilege (**19**),
c) a *Point of Order* or the calling of the member who has the floor to order (**23**, **61**)—or the chair's calling this mem-ber's attention to the fact that he is failing to observe the rules of speaking (61:10–11),
d) a call for a separate vote on one or more of a set of inde-pendent resolutions on different subjects, or a divisible set of amendments, that have been offered by a single motion (10:25, 12:14, 27:10–11),
e) a request or inquiry (**32**, **33**) that requires an immediate response;

or, in certain special circumstances, these additional purposes:

f) an *Appeal* (**24**),
g) an *Objection to the Consideration of a Question* (**26**), or
h) a *Division of the Assembly* (**29**).

42:19   After a member has been assigned the floor but before he has begun to speak, it is in order to take any of the steps listed above, and also, if there may be no other opportunity, to rise for the purpose of:

a) giving notice of intent to introduce a motion requiring such notice (10:44–50); or

b) making a motion to *Reconsider* (**37**) or to *Reconsider and Enter on the Minutes* (37:46–52).

42:20   If an interruption occurs for any of the reasons listed above, the member who had the floor does not lose it, although he takes his seat while the interrupting matter is being attended to. As soon as the interruption has been disposed of, the chair directs him to rise and proceed by saying, for example, "Mr. Lewis has the floor."

42:21   If a member presenting a committee report or other document to the assembly hands it to the secretary or a reading clerk to be read, the member does not thereby yield the floor, but has it again when the reading is finished.

42:22   When a member has risen to claim the floor or has been assigned the floor, it is out of order for another to call out a motion to adjourn, or a motion to lay the pending question on the table. If someone does so, or if calls of "Question!" are made, it is the duty of the chair to obtain order and protect the rights of the member who is entitled to the floor.

§43. RULES GOVERNING DEBATE

43:1   *Debate,* rightly understood, is an essential element in the making of rational decisions of consequence by intelligent people. In a deliberative assembly, this term applies to discussion on the merits of a pending question—that is, whether the proposal under consideration should, or should not, be agreed to. That the right of debate is inherent in such an assembly is implied by the word *deliberative.*

43:2   Debatability is a characteristic of all main motions and of certain other motions, depending on the parliamentary function they serve, according to principles summarized at the end of this section; and from such principles are derived the specific rules stated under Standard Characteristic 5 in **11–37**.

43:3   While the amount of debate on a motion in actual practice will depend on such factors as its importance, how strongly it is contested, etc., every member of the assembly has the right to speak to every debatable motion before it is finally acted upon; and subject only to general limitations on debate established by parliamentary law or the rules of the body as explained below, this right cannot be interfered with except by a two-thirds vote.

Summary of Procedures Incident to Debate

43:4   Until a matter has been brought before the assembly in the form of a motion proposing a specific action, it cannot be debated. As explained in **3** and **4**, the motion must be made by a member who has obtained the floor while no question is pending (or while the motion is in order, if it is not a main motion), after which it must be seconded by another member (unless it is made by direction of a board or committee), and must be stated by the chair. The chair may conclude his statement of the question on the debatable motion by asking, "Are you ready for the question?" or, less formally, "Is there any debate?" Alternatively, he may simply pause and turn toward the maker of the motion to see if he desires the floor first in debate. After the maker of the motion has had the opportunity to speak first if he wishes, other members can rise and address the chair to claim the floor for the purpose of debate, as explained in 3:30ff. and **42**.

43:5   While debate is in progress, amendments or other secondary (subsidiary, privileged, or incidental) motions can be introduced and disposed of—and can be debated in the process, if they are debatable—as explained in 10:31–35. A member may both speak in debate and conclude by offering a secondary motion, which is a particular application of the principle that a member having been recognized for *any* legitimate purpose has the floor for *all* legitimate purposes.

43:6   When debate appears to have concluded, the chair may again ask, "Are you ready for the question?" (or "Is there any further debate?") or if, after a reasonable pause, no one rises to claim the floor, the chair may assume that no member wishes to speak and, standing, may proceed to put the question.

43:7   It should be noted that, under legitimate parliamentary procedure, there is no such thing as "gaveling through" a measure. The right of members to debate or introduce secondary motions cannot be cut off by the chair's attempting to put a question to vote so quickly that no member can get the floor—either when the chair first states the question or when he believes debate is ended. Debate is not closed by the presiding officer's rising to put the question. If a vote has been taken or begun quickly and it is found that a member rose and addressed the chair with reasonable promptness after the chair asked, "Are you ready for the question?" or, by a pause or otherwise, indicated that the floor was open to assignment, then—even if the chair has announced the result of such a vote—the vote must be disregarded, the member is entitled to the floor, and debate begins or resumes. But if the chair gives ample opportunity for members to claim the floor before he puts the question, and no one rises, the right to debate cannot be claimed after the voting has commenced. If, because a member sought the floor in timely fashion, debate is resumed after voting has begun, the question must be put fully again—that is, both the affirmative and the negative votes must be called for—regardless of how far the earlier vote had proceeded. When a vote is taken a second time for purposes of verification—as when a *Division* (**29**) is demanded—debate cannot be resumed except by unanimous consent (4:58–63).

Length and Number of Speeches

43:8   **Maximum Time for Each Speech.** In a nonlegislative body or organization that has no special rule relating to the length of speeches (**2**), a member, having obtained the floor while a debatable motion is immediately pending, can speak no longer than ten minutes unless he obtains the consent of the assembly. Such permission can be given by unanimous consent (4:58–63), or by means of a motion to *Extend Limits of Debate* (**15**), which requires a two-thirds vote without debate.

43:9 When a member's time is exhausted, the chair rises and—if the member does not immediately conclude his remarks—calls his attention to the fact by an appropriate signal, or by interrupting him if necessary. The chair may appoint timekeepers to provide assistance in fulfilling this responsibility. If it appears that a minute more will afford sufficient time for the member to conclude more gracefully, the chair can ask unanimous consent to extend the member's time for a short period, or any member can do so.

43:10 Rights in regard to debate are not transferable. Unless the organization has a special rule on the subject, a member cannot yield any unexpired portion of his time to another member, or reserve any portion of his time for a later time—that is, if a member yields the floor before speaking his full ten minutes, he is presumed to have waived his right to the remaining time.[4] If a speaker yields to another member for a question (*Request for Information,* 33:6–10), the time consumed by the question is charged to the speaker.

43:11 A committee chairman or reporting member is not considered to be debating when presenting or reading the committee's report, but he is bound to obey the assembly's rules relating to debate in any speech made by him in support of the motion offered on behalf of the committee.

43:12 **Number of Speeches on the Same Question per Member per Day.** Unless the assembly has a special rule providing otherwise, no member can speak more than twice to the same question on the same day—except that in the case of an *Appeal* (**24**), only the presiding officer can speak twice (the second time at the close of the debate), all other members being limited to one speech. Merely asking a question or making a brief suggestion is not counted as speaking in debate; nor is the making

---

4. This rule reflects the traditional parliamentary principles. The House of Representatives has a different rule which permits control of all time by a single member or the leaders of the opposing sides of the question. The House rule also prevents members to whom time has been yielded for debate from making motions. See form (f) in 15:19 and, especially, the form discussed in 59:82–83.

of a secondary motion counted as speaking in debate,[5] so long as in making the motion the member makes no comment on the then-pending question. It will be seen from this rule that if debate on a pending motion is continued at the next meeting, and if that meeting is held on the same day, members who have already made two speeches on a question are not allowed to speak on it again without the assembly's permission. But if the next meeting is held on another day, all members have their right to debate entirely renewed with reference to that question.

43:13   Under this rule, each debatable motion is a separate question with respect to members' rights to debate it. Thus, if a series of debatable questions is pending and a member has, for example, spoken twice that day while the main motion is immediately pending, he has exhausted his right to debate the main motion; but, even on the same day, he can still speak twice on a motion to postpone the main question indefinitely, and twice on each amendment that may be moved, and so on. As noted under the rules for assigning the floor (**42**), however, a member cannot make a second speech on the same question the same day until every member who desires to speak on it has had an opportunity to do so once. If debate is closed before the member has an opportunity to make a second speech, none may be made.

Modification of General Limits of Debate

43:14   The general rules limiting the length and number of speeches in debate that are stated above can be modified to serve the assembly's needs as follows:

43:15   **Adopting a Special Rule.** The rule allowing each member two speeches of ten minutes' length per day on each debatable

---

5. Thus a member who has exhausted the number of speeches permitted him on a main motion may still seek recognition to move its referral or amendment, for example. In such a case the chair grants limited recognition by saying, "The member has exhausted his right to debate. For what purpose does he rise?"

question can be made either more restrictive or more liberal for all meetings of a society by adopting a special rule of order by a two-thirds vote after notice, or by a vote of a majority of the entire membership (2:14ff.; see also 10:44–51). An example of a more restrictive rule might be one setting a limit of not more than one speech of five minutes' length on the same question on the same day for each member.

43:16 **Changing the Limits for a Session.** An assembly at any session can change the limits of debate, for that session only, by means of a main motion adopted by a two-thirds vote without notice. In a convention—where the limits of debate generally need to be stricter than in a local society—such a modification is usually adopted in the form of a *standing rule of the convention* (**59**), requiring a two-thirds vote in such a case.

43:17 **Changing the Limits for the Pending Question(s) Only.** While a debatable question is immediately pending, the allowed length or number of speeches can be reduced or increased, for that question only, by means of the subsidiary motion to *Limit or Extend Limits of Debate* (**15**), adopted by a two-thirds vote. This motion can also be used to close debate at a specified future time. If two thirds of those voting wish to close debate immediately, they can do so by adopting the motion for the *Previous Question* (**16**). If a series of adhering debatable questions (10:35) is pending, either of these motions can also be applied to the entire series or any consecutive part of the series beginning with the immediately pending question. (For forms, see 15:19, 16:20, 59:82.) If it is desired to prevent any discussion of a subject—even by the introducer of the motion, who has the right to the floor first—the only way this can be done is to raise an *Objection to the Consideration of the Question* (**26**) before debate begins or any subsidiary motion (other than a motion to *Lay on the Table*) is stated. If the objection is sustained by a two-thirds vote, the question cannot be considered in any way at that time or during that session.

43:18   On the other hand, if, in considering a particular question, it is desired to retain the usual limit on the length of speeches but remove restrictions on the total number of times members can speak, the assembly by a majority vote can resolve itself into a committee of the whole or into quasi committee of the whole, or it can consider the question informally (see 52:1). Speeches made under these procedures do not count against a member's right to debate the same question if it is further considered by the assembly on the same day under the regular rules. If the question under consideration is composed of a number of sections or paragraphs—as in the case of bylaws, for example—the total number of speeches allowed each member can be greatly increased, but not made unlimited, by considering the document seriatim (**28**), in which case each member can speak twice on each paragraph, section, or unit that is taken up as a separate part.

Decorum in Debate

43:19   The following practices and customs observed by speakers and other members in an assembly assist the carrying on of debate in a smooth and orderly manner. Paragraphs 3:9–13 under the head *Pattern of Formality* should be read in connection with this subject.

43:20   **Confining Remarks to the Merits of the Pending Question.** In debate a member's remarks must be germane to the question before the assembly—that is, his statements must have bearing on whether the immediately pending motion should be adopted (see also *Principles Governing the Debatability of Motions,* 43:35–40).

43:21   **Refraining from Attacking a Member's Motives.** When a question is pending, a member can condemn the nature or likely consequences of the proposed measure in strong terms, but he must avoid personalities, and under no circumstances can he attack or question the motives of another member. The measure, not the member, is the subject of debate. If a member disagrees with a statement by another in regard to an event that both witnessed, he cannot state in debate that the other's statement "is false." But he might say, "I believe there is strong evidence that the member is mistaken." The moment the chair hears such words as "fraud," "liar," or "lie" used about a member in debate, he must act immediately and decisively to correct the matter and prevent its repetition (see **61**).

43:22   **Addressing All Remarks Through the Chair.** Members of an assembly cannot address one another directly, but must address all remarks through the chair. If, while a member is speaking in debate, another member wishes to address a question to him—which the person speaking can permit or not as he chooses, but which is taken out of his time if he does—the member desiring to ask the question rises and addresses the chair, proceeding as explained under *Request for Information* (33:6–10).

43:23   **Avoiding the Use of Members' Names.** As much as possible, the use of names of members should be avoided in debate. It is better to describe a member in some other way, as by saying, "the member who spoke last," or, "the delegate from Mason County." The officers of the society should always be referred to by their official titles. There is no need, however, to refer to oneself in debate in the third person as by the use of such expressions as "this member." A member's debate is expected and intended to be partial, and the first person is quite acceptable.

43:24   **Refraining from Speaking Adversely on a Prior Action Not Pending.** In debate, a member cannot reflect adversely on any prior act of the society that is not then pending, unless a motion to reconsider, rescind, or amend it is pending, or unless he intends to conclude his remarks by making or giving notice of one of these motions.

43:25   **Refraining from Speaking Against One's Own Motion.** In debate, the maker of a motion, while he can vote against it, is not allowed to speak against his own motion. He need not speak at all, but if he does he is obliged to take a favorable position. If he changes his mind while the motion he made is pending, he can, in effect, advise the assembly of this by asking permission to withdraw the motion (33:11–18).

43:26 **Reading from Reports, Quotations, etc., Only Without Objection or With Permission.** If any member objects, a member has no right to read from—or to have the secretary read from—any paper or book as part of his speech, without permission of the assembly. Members are usually permitted to read short, pertinent, printed extracts in debate, however, so long as they do not abuse the privilege (see also 33:20–21).

43:27 **Being Seated During an Interruption by the Chair.** If at any time the presiding officer rises to make a ruling, give information, or otherwise speak within his privilege, any member who is speaking should be seated (or should step back slightly if he is standing at a microphone some distance from a seat) until the presiding officer has finished. At that time the member can resume his speech, unless he is denied the right as a disciplinary measure. (Questions of discipline arising from disorderly debate by members are treated in **61**.)

43:28 **Refraining from Disturbing the Assembly.** During debate, during remarks by the presiding officer to the assembly, and during voting, no member should be permitted to disturb the assembly by whispering, walking across the floor, or in any other way. The key words here are *disturb the assembly.* This rule does not mean, therefore, that members can never whisper, or walk from one place to another in the hall during the deliberations of the assembly. At large meetings it would be impossible to enforce such a rule. However, the presiding officer should watch that such activity does not disturb the meeting or hamper the transaction of business.

Rule Against the Chair's Participation in Debate

43:29   If the presiding officer is a member of the society, he has—as an individual—the same *rights* in debate as any other member; but the impartiality required of the chair in an assembly precludes his exercising these rights while he is presiding. Normally, especially in a large body, he should have nothing to say on the merits of pending questions. On certain occasions—which should be extremely rare—the presiding officer may believe that a crucial factor relating to such a question has been overlooked and that his obligation as a member to call attention to the point outweighs his duty to preside at that time. To participate in debate, he must relinquish the chair; and in such a case he turns the chair over:

a) to the highest-ranking vice-president present who has not spoken on the question and does not decline on the grounds of wishing to speak on it; or

b) if no such vice-president is in the room, to some other member qualified as in (a), whom the chair designates (and who is assumed to receive the assembly's approval by unanimous consent unless member(s) then nominate other person(s), in which case the presiding officer's choice is also treated as a nominee and the matter is decided by vote).

The presiding officer who relinquished the chair then may not return to it until the pending main question has been disposed of, since he has shown himself to be a partisan as far as that particular matter is concerned. Indeed, unless a presiding officer is extremely sparing in leaving the chair to take part in debate, he may destroy members' confidence in the impartiality of his approach to the task of presiding.

43:30   In debate on an appeal (**24**) or a point of order that the chair has submitted to the judgment of the assembly (23:18–21), the foregoing rule does not apply, and the presiding officer does not leave the chair, since his participation in the debate relates to the function of presiding.

Occasions Justifying Brief Discussion Outside Debate

43:31 **Allowable Explanations and Requests When No Motion Is Pending or When an Undebatable Motion Is Pending.** As already stated, debate in a deliberative assembly is permitted only when it is germane to a debatable motion that has been stated by the chair as the immediately pending question. However, as explained in **4**, the making of a motion of any kind— whether debatable or undebatable—may be prefaced, when necessary, by a few words of explanation, which must not become a speech; or a member can first request information, or briefly indicate the substance of a desired proposal and ask for the chair's assistance in wording an appropriate motion. Similarly, business may sometimes be expedited by allowing a few words of factual explanation while an undebatable motion is pending.

43:32 The distinction between debate and asking questions or making brief suggestions should be kept in mind in this connection. Especially in large assemblies, the chair must be careful not to allow this type of consultation to develop into an extended colloquy between members or to take on the semblance of debate, and should generally remain standing while the consultation takes place, to show that the floor has not been assigned.

43:33 **Informal Consultation to Assist the Framing of a Motion.** Occasionally, brief informal consultation or discussion of a subject may assist a member in framing a proper motion. If the chair permits such discussion, he must not allow it to continue more than a few moments or longer than is reasonably necessary to arrive at a motion embodying the member's ideas.

43:34 In general, for a member to speak when no question is pending, without promptly leading to a motion, implies an unusual circumstance and requires permission *of the assembly*. But occasionally, in very small bodies, a member who has obtained the floor at such a time may state that, if there is no objection, he would like to give some explanations dealing with a specified subject and to conclude by offering a motion on that subject. If no one objects, the member can then proceed; and the chair, knowing the subject, can hold him to it as he would in debate on a motion (see also 4:7–8).

Principles Governing the Debatability of Motions

43:35   Rules as to each motion's debatability or undebatability are given under Standard Characteristic 5 in **10–37** and in the Table of Rules Relating to Motions on pages t6–t33. The following is a brief summary of these rules in relation to the principles on which they are based.

43:36   Every main motion is debatable, from the nature of the deliberative assembly itself.

43:37   With the exception of the two subsidiary motions that have to do with debate, the degree to which each of the subsidiary motions can be debated depends on the extent to which its adoption would restrict the assembly in dealing with the main question.

1) Since the motion to *Postpone Indefinitely* (**11**) will kill the main motion if it is adopted, it is fully debatable and leaves the main question open to debate.

2) A motion to *Amend* (**12**) is debatable when it is applied to the main question or to any other debatable motion, since it would alter the question it proposes to amend; but the debate is limited to the merits of the amendment, and other pending questions can be brought into the discussion only as necessary in this connection. A motion to amend an undebatable motion is undebatable, because to allow debate on it would be contrary to the purposes of the other motion's undebatability.

3) In the case of the motions to *Commit* (**13**) and to *Postpone to a Certain Time* (**14**), debate is quite limited, because the main question will be open to further debate when the committee reports or when the time arrives to which the question was postponed. Hence, debate is confined in the first in-

stance to the wisdom of referring or to the choice of personnel of the committee and to the nature of its instructions, and in the latter instance to the wisdom of postponement and the choice of a time to which the question will be postponed.

4) Motions to *Limit or Extend Limits of Debate* (**15**) and for the *Previous Question* (**16**) are undebatable inasmuch as their very object is to alter the debatability of pending question(s), and their purpose would be defeated if they were debatable; they are also in the nature of specialized motions to suspend the rules, and any such motion made while business is pending is undebatable.

5) The motion to *Lay on the Table* (**17**) is undebatable because its legitimate purpose would be defeated if it were debatable, and because its adoption in no way interferes with the right of the majority to take the question from the table (**34**) and resume debate.

43:38   The privileged motions are all undebatable because, if they were debatable, their high privilege would allow them to interfere with business. The right of debate is thus incompatible with high privilege. With reference to the two lowest-ranking privileged motions, it is, of course, the "calling" for the orders of the day (**18**) or the "raising" of a question of privilege (**19**) that is undebatable. When the order of the day or the question of privilege involved in such a case becomes the pending main motion, it is debatable.

43:39   Except as noted in this paragraph, the incidental motions are undebatable, because they have high privilege to interrupt any motions or situations to which they are incidental. In the case of an *Appeal* that relates to indecorum, the rules of debate, or the priority of business, it is assumed that debate would be a hindrance to business, as it would be if the appeal were made when an undebatable question is immediately pending or involved in the appeal. At all other times, an appeal is fully debatable so long as the debate is germane to the subject matter of the appeal. The incidental motion to create a proviso, like the corresponding subsidiary motion to create a proviso by amending a motion's enacting words (see 57:15), is debatable when the motion to which it applies is debatable. A *Request to Be Excused from a Duty,* such as a resignation, may require some discussion for its proper decision, and for this reason it is debatable.

43:40   Rules as to the debatability of motions that bring a question again before the assembly may be summarized as follows:

1) The motion to *Take from the Table* (**34**) is undebatable because debate would serve no useful purpose and would delay business, and because, if it is voted down, it can be renewed each time any business has been transacted.

2) The motion to *Rescind* or to *Amend Something Previously Adopted* (**35**) is fully debatable, and it opens to debate the entire motion that it proposes to rescind or to amend. The same is true of the motion to *Discharge a Committee* (**36**).

3) The motion to *Reconsider* (**37**) is debatable only to the extent that the motion proposed to be reconsidered is debatable, and it opens the merits of that question to debate. A motion to reconsider an undebatable motion is thus undebatable.

CHAPTER XIII

VOTING

§44. BASES FOR DETERMINING A VOTING RESULT

Majority Vote—the Basic Requirement

44:1   As stated in 1:6, the basic requirement for approval of an action or choice by a deliberative assembly, except where a rule provides otherwise, is a *majority vote*. The word *majority* means "more than half"; and when the term *majority vote* is used without qualification—as in the case of the basic requirement—it means more than half of the votes cast by persons entitled to vote, excluding blanks or abstentions, at a regular or properly called meeting. For example (assuming that there are no voters having fractions of a vote, as may occur in some conventions):

- If 19 votes are cast, a majority (more than 9½) is 10.
- If 20 votes are cast, a majority (more than 10) is 11.
- If 21 votes are cast, a majority (more than 10½) is 11.

44:2   Other bases for determining a voting result, as described below, are required under parliamentary law for certain procedures, or may be prescribed by the rules of the particular body—for decisions in general or for questions of a specified nature (see also 10:8(7)). Regardless of the basis required, a decision can be validly made only when a quorum is present (unless otherwise specified in the rules, as in the case of certain procedural actions); see **40**.

Two-Thirds Vote

44:3   A *two-thirds vote*—when the term is unqualified—means at least two thirds of the votes cast by persons entitled to vote, excluding blanks or abstentions, at a regular or properly called meeting. For example (assuming that there are no fractions of votes):

- If 30 votes are cast, a two-thirds vote is 20.
- If 31 votes are cast, a two-thirds vote is 21.
- If 32 votes are cast, a two-thirds vote is 22.
- If 33 votes are cast, a two-thirds vote is 22.

44:4   As a compromise between the rights of the individual and the rights of the assembly, the principle has been established that a two-thirds vote is required to adopt any motion that: (a) suspends or modifies a rule of order previously adopted; (b) prevents the introduction of a question for consideration; (c) closes, limits, or extends the limits of debate; (d) closes nominations or the polls, or otherwise limits the freedom of nominating or voting; or (e) takes away membership. (For a list of motions that require a two-thirds vote, see pages t48–t49.)

44:5   In determining whether a question has obtained two thirds of the votes cast, the chair takes a rising vote (or, in a very small assembly, if the chair prefers and no one objects, a vote by show of hands), and it is the chair's duty to obtain a count of the vote whenever he is in doubt concerning the result.

44:6   The chair can obtain a count of the vote initially if it appears—when those in the affirmative rise—that the result will be close; or he can retake it as a counted rising vote if he is afterward in doubt. In an assembly that has no special rule permitting a small fraction (that is, a specified fraction somewhat less than one third) of the voters to require a two-thirds vote to be counted, the chair, in judging whether to obtain a count of the vote at his own instance, must be particularly careful to leave no room for anyone to doubt the result in cases where he finds that there *are* two thirds on the side that thereby prevails. Without a count at the chair's instance under these conditions, if he announces that a two-thirds vote has been obtained and those on the losing side doubt the result, they are powerless to have it verified should those declared the winners choose to prevent a count. The reason is that—whatever may be the true result in view of the closeness of the vote in such a case—those declared the losers are no more than approximately one third of those voting, and therefore cannot command the majority necessary to order the vote counted.

Modifications of Usual Bases for Decision

44:7   By modifying the concepts of a majority vote and a two-thirds vote, other bases for determining a voting result can be defined and are sometimes prescribed by rule. Two elements enter into the definition of such bases for decision: (1) the proportion that must concur—as a majority, two thirds, three fourths, etc.; and (2) the set of members to which the proportion applies—which (a) when not stated, is always the number of members *present and voting*, but (b) can be specified by rule as the number of members present, the total membership, or some other grouping.

44:8   Assume, for example, that at a meeting of a society with a total membership of 150 and a quorum of 10, there are 30 members present, of whom 25 participate in a given counted vote (taken by rising, by show of hands, by roll call, or by ballot). Then, with respect to that vote:

A majority is	13
A majority of the members present is	16
A majority of the entire membership is	76
A two-thirds vote is	17
A vote of two thirds of the members present is	20
A vote of two thirds of the entire membership is	100

44:9   Regarding these bases for determining a voting result, the following points should be noted:

a) Voting requirements based on the number of members present—a majority of those present, two thirds of those present, etc.—while possible, are generally undesirable. Since an abstention in such cases has the same effect as a negative vote, these bases deny members the right to maintain a neutral position by abstaining. For the same reason, members present who fail to vote through indifference rather than through deliberate neutrality may affect the result negatively. When such a vote is required, however, the chair must count those present immediately after the affirmative vote is taken, before any change can take place in attendance. The negative vote is not taken, since it is intrinsically irrelevant to determining whether the motion is adopted. (See 4:35.)

b) A *majority of the entire membership*[1] is a majority of the total number of those who are members of the voting body at the time of the vote. (Thus, in a society that has both a general membership and an executive board, a "majority of the entire membership" at a board meeting refers to a majority of the membership of the board, not of the society.) In a convention of delegates a majority of the entire membership means a majority of the total number of convention members entitled to vote as set forth in the official roll of voting members of the convention (1:16, 59:25–26). The vote of a majority of the entire membership is frequently an alternative to a requirement of previous notice, and is required in order to rescind and expunge from the minutes (see 35:13).

---

1. In the case of a body having a fixed membership—for example, a permanent board—it is also possible to define a voting requirement as a majority of the fixed membership, which is greater than a majority of the entire membership if there are vacancies on the board. Thus, in a board whose membership is fixed at 12, if 2 members have died and their successors have not been named, a majority of the entire membership is 6, and a majority of the fixed membership is 7. Where a majority of the fixed membership is required for a decision, the body cannot act if half or more of the membership positions are vacant.

Otherwise, prescribing such a requirement is generally unsatisfactory in an assembly of an ordinary society, since it is likely to be impossible to get a majority of the entire membership even to attend a given meeting, although in certain instances it may be appropriate in conventions or in permanent boards where the members are obligated to attend the meetings.

44:10   Whenever it is desired that the basis for decision be other than a majority vote or (where the normal rules of parliamentary law require it) a two-thirds vote or a vote of a majority of the entire membership, the desired basis should be precisely defined in the bylaws or in a special rule of order. Whatever voting basis is used, it is also possible to include a requirement of *previous notice* for specified types of action. Previous notice means that notice of intent to introduce the proposal must be given at the preceding meeting (in which case the notice can be oral), or in the call of the meeting at which it is brought up (for a discussion of *previous notice,* see 10:44–51).

Plurality Vote

44:11   A *plurality vote* is the largest number of votes to be given any candidate or proposition when three or more choices are possible; the candidate or proposition receiving the largest number of votes has a plurality. A plurality that is not a majority never chooses a proposition or elects anyone to office except by virtue of a special rule previously adopted. If such a rule is to apply to the election of officers, it must be prescribed in the bylaws. A rule that a plurality shall elect is unlikely to be in the best interests of the average organization. In an international or national society where the election is conducted by mail ballot, a plurality is sometimes allowed to elect officers, with a view to avoiding the delay and extra expense that would result from additional balloting under these conditions. A better method in such cases is for the bylaws to prescribe some form of preferential voting (see 45:62–69).

Tie Votes and Cases in Which the Chair's Vote Affects the Result

44:12   If the presiding officer is a member of the assembly, he can vote as any other member when the vote is by ballot (see also 45:28). In all other cases the presiding officer, if a member of the assembly, can (but is not obliged to) vote whenever his vote will affect the result—that is, he can vote either to break or to cause a tie; or, in a case where a two-thirds vote is required, he can vote either to cause or to block the attainment of the necessary two thirds. In particular:

- On a tie vote, a motion requiring a majority vote for adoption is lost, since a tie is not a majority. Thus, if there is a tie without the chair's vote, the presiding officer can, if he is a member, vote in the affirmative, thereby causing the motion to be adopted; or, if there is one more in the affirmative than in the negative without the chair's vote (for example, if there are 72 votes in favor and 71 opposed), he can vote in the negative to create a tie, thus causing the motion to be rejected.

- Similarly, in the case of a motion requiring a two-thirds vote, if, without the chair's vote, the number in the affirmative is one less than twice the number in the negative (for example, if there are 59 in the affirmative and 30 in the negative), the chair, if a member, can vote in the affirmative and thus cause the motion to be adopted; or, if there are exactly two thirds in the affirmative without his vote (for example, if there are 60 in the affirmative and 30 in the negative), the chair can vote in the negative, with the result that the motion is rejected.[2] Similarly, the chair's vote might affect the result in cases where a *majority of the members* can decide a question.

2. It should be noted that if, without the chair's vote, the number of negative votes is one more than half the number of affirmative votes, the chair's vote cannot affect the result. Thus, if there are 60 in the affirmative and 31 in the negative without the chair's vote, and he were to vote in the affirmative, the resulting 61 in the affirmative would still fall short of two thirds of the total vote of 92.

The chair cannot vote twice, once as a member, then again in his capacity as presiding officer.

44:13 In an appeal from the decision of the chair, a tie vote sustains the chair's decision, even though his vote created the tie, on the principle that the decision of the chair can be reversed only by a majority.

§45. VOTING PROCEDURE

Rights and Obligations in Voting

45:1 **Voting Rights of a Member in Arrears.** A member of a society who is in arrears in payment of his dues, but who has not been formally dropped from the membership rolls and is not under a disciplinary suspension, retains the full rights of a voting member and is entitled to vote except as the bylaws may otherwise provide. (See also 1:13n3, 56:19.)

45:2 **One Person, One Vote.** It is a fundamental principle of parliamentary law that each person who is a member of a deliberative assembly is entitled to one—and only one—vote on a question. This is true even if a person is elected or appointed to more than one position, each of which would entitle the holder to a vote. For example, in a convention, a person selected as delegate by more than one constituent body may cast only one vote. An individual member's right to vote may not be transferred to another person (for example, by the use of proxies).

45:3 **Right of Abstention.** Although it is the duty of every member who has an opinion on a question to express it by his vote, he can abstain, since he cannot be compelled to vote. By the same token, when an office or position is to be filled by a number of members, as in the case of a committee, or positions on a board, a member may partially abstain by voting for less than all of those for whom he is entitled to vote.

45:4 **Abstaining from Voting on a Question of Direct Personal Interest.** No member should vote on a question in which he has a direct personal or pecuniary interest not common to other members of the organization. For example, if a motion proposes that the organization enter into a contract with a commercial firm of which a member of the organization is an officer and from which contract he would derive personal pecuniary profit, the member should abstain from voting on the motion. However, no member can be compelled to refrain from voting in such circumstances.

45:5   **Voting on Questions Affecting Oneself.** The rule on abstaining from voting on a question of direct personal interest does not mean that a member should not vote for himself for an office or other position to which members generally are eligible, or should not vote when other members are included with him in a motion. If a member never voted on a question affecting himself, it would be impossible for a society to vote to hold a banquet, or for the majority to prevent a small minority from preferring charges against them and suspending or expelling them (**61**, **63**).

45:6   **Interruption of Votes.** When a vote is being taken, no interruption is permitted from the time that any member has actually voted until all have presumably voted, unless as sometimes occurs in ballot voting, other business is being transacted during voting. For points of order regarding the conduct of a vote, see below (**45:9**).

45:7   **Rule Against Explanation by Members During Voting.** A member has no right to "explain his vote" during voting, which would be the same as debate at such a time.

45:8   **Changing One's Vote.** Except when the vote has been taken by ballot (or some other method that provides secrecy), a member has a right to change his vote up to the time the result is announced but afterward can make the change only by the unanimous consent of the assembly requested and granted, without debate, immediately following the chair's announcement of the result of the vote (see below).

45:9 **Time Limits on Efforts to Challenge, Retake, or Change a Vote.**
After the result of a vote has been announced, members can still propose or demand certain actions that may change the result. A member may raise a point of order regarding the conduct of the vote, demand a division of the assembly, move to retake the vote under another method, move for a recapitulation of a roll-call vote, or request unanimous consent to change his vote. With the exception of a point of order raised against a breach of a continuing nature (23:6–9), if any of these actions is to apply to a vote after the result has been announced, it must be taken immediately after the chair's announcement, before any debate or business has intervened. For example, it is too late to take these actions after any member has been recognized and begun to speak in debate or to give a report or presentation, or after the chair has stated the question on a subsequently made motion, or after the chair has begun to take the vote and any member has voted on another motion that was pending. For the time limits on ordering that a counted rising vote, a ballot, or a roll-call vote be recounted, see the last sentence of 45:15; 45:41; and 45:54. See also *Contesting the Announced Result of an Election*, 46:48–50.

45:10 **Assembly's Prerogative in Judging Voting Procedures.** The assembly itself is the judge of all questions arising that are incidental to the voting or the counting of the votes. In an election by ballot, for example, the tellers should refer to the assembly for decision all questions on which there is any uncertainty (see 45:33).

Regular Methods of Voting on Motions

45:11   In Chapter II are described the following methods of voting:

1) by *voice (viva voce)*—the normal method of voting on a motion;

2) by *rising*—used in verifying an inconclusive voice vote, and in voting on motions requiring a two-thirds vote for adoption; and

3) by *show of hands*—an alternative method that can be used in place of a rising vote in very small assemblies if no member objects. In some small groups, a vote by show of hands is also used in place of a voice vote as a normal method of voting.

Paragraphs 4:34–57 should be read in connection with these three methods of voting.

45:12   Also described in Chapter II is the procedure of action by *unanimous consent.* Paragraphs 4:58–63 should be read in reference to this method of transacting business.

45:13   A characteristic that the three methods of voting listed above have in common is that in each case the chair calls first for those voting in the affirmative to indicate the fact in a specified manner ("say *aye*," "rise," or "raise the right hand"), after which he calls for the negative vote, then judges and declares which side prevails.

45:14   **Verifying a Vote.** In connection with the methods of voting by voice, by rising, or by show of hands, as explained in Chapter II, if the chair is in doubt on a voice vote or a vote by show of hands, he should retake it as a rising vote and, if necessary to satisfy himself of the result, he should obtain a count of it. Any member, by demanding a *Division* (**29**), can require a voice vote or a vote by show of hands to be retaken as a rising vote—but no individual member can compel it to be counted. If the chair does not obtain a count at his own instance and a member thinks one is desirable, that member should move that the vote be counted. If this motion is seconded, the question as to whether a count shall be ordered is voted on by voice vote, or by an *uncounted* rising vote or show of hands. Where no special rule has been adopted, a majority vote is required to order a count. In organizations where it is desired to allow less than a majority to order a count, a special rule of order establishing the required vote should be adopted. Such a rule is particularly desirable with reference to motions that require a two-thirds vote for adoption (see also 44:5–6). It should be noted that a vote is never retaken by the same form of voting, although, in a counted rising vote, a ballot, or a roll call, a recount of the votes or of the tellers' tabulations can be ordered to ensure that the count is precisely correct as reported.

45:15 **Method of Counting a Rising Vote.** In small meetings, the chair can take such a count himself—with or without directing the secretary to make an independent count for verification. In a large assembly, the chair should appoint tellers to take the count. The count is taken by having those in the affirmative rise and stand until counted, then having those in the negative rise and stand until counted. The votes can also be counted by having the members pass between tellers, or having them count off by rows and be seated one at a time, although the latter process is particularly subject to confusion if great care is not exercised by the tellers. Those in the affirmative are always counted first. In all but small assemblies, the doors should be closed and no one should enter or leave the hall while a count is being taken. The form used in taking a count is as shown in 4:39. In a meeting small enough that each member present can make his own verification of a count on a show of hands, the chair can take the count by this method, if he prefers and no one objects. If written records are prepared in counting the vote, such as tellers' tally sheets, they are subject to the same retention and recount rules as ballots (45:41).

45:16 **Voting Cards.** Some organizations like to use a brightly colored cardboard card, approximately three inches wide and a foot long, in voting on most or all occasions by raising it when asked to do so by the chair. The authorization of the use of these devices in voting, however, depends on expected conditions in the meeting. If the "voters' cards" have been distributed to the voters in advance, and the chair or a member thinks a simple division vote (as described in 4:38) is called for, the chair may say: "As many as are in favor of the motion, raise your voters' cards. ... Down. Those opposed, raise your voters' cards. Down. ..." If a count is desired, however, the chair or the assembly must authorize the count as in the case of a counted division (as described in 4:39; see also **30,** *Motions Relating to Methods of Voting and the Polls*). If this method of voting is to be used, it must be authorized by a special rule of order or, in a convention, by a convention standing rule.

Other Methods of Voting

45:17   In contrast to the methods of voting mentioned in the preceding subsection, the voting methods described below are used only when expressly ordered by the assembly or prescribed by its rules.

45:18   **Voting by Ballot.** Voting by *ballot* (also known as *secret ballot*) is used when secrecy of the members' votes is desired. A ballot vote is a vote taken by instruments, such as slips of paper or electronic devices,[3] by which members can indicate their choices without revealing how individual members have voted. On a ballot vote in an election or other vote involving multiple possible choices, members are able to write in or fill in a vote for any eligible person or choice and are not confined to voting for or against candidates that appear on the ballot.

45:19   The bylaws of the organization may prescribe that the vote be by ballot in certain cases, as in the election of officers and in admission to membership. Any vote related to charges or proposed charges before or after a trial of a member or any officer should always be by ballot. In cases in which there is no requirement that a vote be by ballot, a ballot vote can be ordered by a majority vote—which may be desirable whenever

---

3. In some organizations—particularly secret societies—the use of black and white balls, deposited in a box out of sight of all but the voter, with a white ball signifying a *yes* vote and a black one a *no* vote, may be directed as a method of balloting. This method is used principally on voting on the admission of candidates to membership where one or very few negative votes are to be sufficient to cause a candidate's rejection. This custom, however, is apparently declining.

it is believed that members may thereby be more likely to vote their true sentiments.

45:20 When the bylaws require a vote to be taken by ballot, this requirement cannot be suspended—even by a unanimous vote—so as to take the vote by a nonsecret method. A vote ordering a ballot vote on a particular question (see **30**) can, however, be reconsidered as long as the balloting has not yet begun.

45:21 When a vote is to be taken, or has been taken, by ballot, whether or not the bylaws require that form of voting, no action is in order that would force the disclosure of a member's vote or views on the matter. Applications of this rule arise with regard to voting on motions to *Postpone Indefinitely* (30:5) and the reconsideration of motions that have been previously voted on by ballot (30:7). Likewise, a motion to make unanimous a ballot vote that was not unanimous must itself be voted on by ballot; even a single negative vote in such a case defeats the motion.

45:22 Whenever a vote is to be taken by ballot, it is not in order to move that one person—the secretary, for example—cast the ballot of the assembly.

45:23 Unless another method is specified by an appropriate rule or motion (see 45:42–43 regarding electronic or machine voting), a ballot vote is taken on slips of paper on which the voters mark their votes and is subject to the rules below.

45:24 *Form of the ballot.* A ballot can consist of simply a small slip of paper on which the voter writes his choice in a manner directed by the chair; but if it is known ahead of time that a vote is to be by ballot and what the exact questions are, the ballots should be prepared in advance for distribution at the proper time. In such a case, each question to be voted on appears on the ballot with a list of the possible answers beside blank spaces or boxes, so that the voter can check the answer he desires. Two or more questions can be listed on the same sheet, provided that each is marked in such a way that there can be no confusion, as illustrated below.

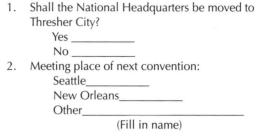

Indicate vote with X.

1. Shall the National Headquarters be moved to Thresher City?

      Yes _____

      No _____

2. Meeting place of next convention:

      Seattle_____

      New Orleans_____

      Other_____

          (Fill in name)

45:25   In elections, "for" and "against" spaces or boxes may not be used. They are applicable only with respect to votes on motions. In an election, a voter can vote against one candidate only by voting for another who has been nominated or by writing in the name of another candidate.

45:26   **Balloting procedure.** In balloting in a meeting where the voting is in the same room as the meeting, the chair appoints tellers to distribute, collect, and count the ballots, and to report the vote. The number of tellers is dependent on the number of voters, and the number of offices to be filled or questions to be answered, or the number of candidates. For a small group, two or three tellers are usually sufficient. The tellers should be chosen for accuracy and dependability, should have the confidence of the membership, and should not have a direct personal involvement in the question or in the result of the vote to an extent that they should refrain from voting under the principle stated in 45:4. Often their position with regard to the issue involved is well known, however, and they are frequently chosen to protect the interests of each opposing side. They normally vote themselves.

45:27   To ensure accuracy and to enable the tellers when unfolding the ballots to detect any error, each ballot should be folded in a manner announced in advance or stated on the ballot itself.

45:28   The presiding officer, if a member of the assembly, can always vote in the case of a ballot at the time other members do. Should he fail to vote before the polls are closed, he cannot then do so without the permission of the assembly.

45:29 When the balloting is completed, the chair directs the tellers to collect the ballots. In collecting the ballots, it is the tellers' responsibility to see that no member votes more than once—for the assurance of which the assembly should adopt some reasonable and orderly method. For example: (a) In meetings where only voters are present, members can remain in their seats and drop their ballots into a receptacle passed by a teller, accompanied by another teller as watcher and checker; (b) they can go to a central ballot box monitored by at least two tellers and deposit their ballots; or (c) they can hand their ballots to a teller—who judges by the thickness and feel of the paper that only one ballot is being cast, and who deposits them in a central ballot box. Whatever method of collecting the ballots is followed, it—like other details relating to voting—should be fixed by rule or custom in the organization and should not be subject to haphazard variation from occasion to occasion.

45:30 After all have voted who wish to, the polls can be closed on the motion of a member by a two-thirds vote (**30**); but it is usually best to rely on the chair to close the polls. When everyone appears to have voted, the chair inquires, "Have all voted who wish to do so?" If there is no response, he says, "If no one else wishes to vote … [pause], the polls are closed," thus in effect declaring the polls closed by unanimous consent. Thereafter, if other members arrive who wish to vote, a majority vote is required to reopen the polls (**30**). The tellers proceed to count the ballots—in a secluded location or in another room if the meeting proceeds to other business during the counting. Some small organizations have a custom that ballots are counted in full presence of the meeting.

45:31 *Recording the votes.* In recording the votes cast, the principle followed is that a choice has no mandate from the voting body unless approval is expressed by more than half of those entitled to vote and registering any evidence of having some preference.

Accordingly, the tellers ignore blank ballots and other ballots that indicate no preference, treating them as abstentions. (Blank ballots are sometimes cast by members to conceal the fact that they do not wish to vote.)

45:32   All ballots that indicate a preference—provided they have been cast by persons entitled to vote—are taken into account in determining the number of votes cast for purposes of computing the majority. Each such ballot is credited to the voter's preferred candidate or choice if the meaning of the ballot is clear and the choice is valid. Unintelligible ballots or ballots cast for an unidentifiable or ineligible candidate are treated instead as *illegal votes*—that is, they are counted as votes cast but are not credited to any candidate or choice. Similarly, a ballot that contains votes for too many candidates for a given office is counted as one illegal vote cast for that office, because it is not possible for the tellers to determine which candidate(s) the voter prefers.

45:33   Technical errors, like the misspelling of a word or name, do not make a vote illegal if the meaning of the ballot is clear. If the meaning of one or more ballots is doubtful, they can be treated as illegal if it is impossible for them to affect the result; but if they may affect the result, the tellers report them to the chair, who immediately submits to the assembly the question of how these ballots should be recorded. When reporting doubtful ballots, the tellers must be careful whenever possible not to show how the decision would affect any of the candidates.

45:34   If, in unfolding the ballots, it is found that two or more filled-out ballots are folded together, they are recorded as illegal votes—that is, each set of ballots folded together is reported as one illegal vote, and is not credited. On the other hand, a blank ballot folded in with one that is properly filled out is ignored and does not cause the rejection of the ballot with which it was folded.

45:35   If one or more ballots are identifiable as cast by persons not entitled to vote, these ballots are excluded in determining the number of votes cast for purposes of computing the majority. If there is evidence that any unidentifiable ballots were cast by persons not entitled to vote, and if there is any possibility that such ballots might affect the result, the entire ballot vote is null and void, and a new ballot vote must be taken.

45:36 On a ballot containing several questions or several independent offices or positions to be filled, each section of the ballot—that is, each portion that contains one question or position to be filled, or one group of identical positions (such as on a board or committee) to be filled—is treated for all purposes as if it were a separate ballot, which is counted in accordance with the rules given above. Therefore, the number of votes cast for purposes of computing the majority must be tallied independently for each section. So, too, if a member leaves one or more of the sections blank, the blank sections in no way affect the validity of the sections that are filled; nor do illegal votes on one section affect the validity of the remaining sections. Likewise, the folding together of two or more ballots that contain multiple sections creates an illegal vote only for each section that is filled out on more than one of the folded-together ballots. (Regarding the election of members of a board or committee in which votes are cast for several identical positions on one section of the ballot, see also 46:33–34.)

45:37 *Tellers' report and the chair's declaration of the result.* The chairman of tellers, standing, addresses the chair, reads the tellers' report, and hands it to the chair without declaring the result. In the case of an election, the report follows this form:

TELLERS' REPORT

Number of votes cast	97
Necessary for election (majority)	49
Mr. Miller received	51
Mr. Wilson received	24
Mr. Strong received	14
Illegal Votes	
Mr. Friend (ineligible)	7
Two ballots for	
Mr. Wilson folded together, rejected	1

45:38   In the case of balloting on a motion, the tellers' report is as follows:

TELLERS' REPORT

Number of votes cast 102
Necessary for adoption (majority) 52
Votes for motion 69
Votes against 32
Illegal votes
Two ballots against,
    folded together, rejected 1

45:39   The tellers' report does not include the number of members eligible to vote nor the number abstaining. In a local society or other body in which membership continues on a long-term basis, only the officer responsible for maintaining the membership roll, and in a convention only an immediate updated report of the credentials committee, can validly determine the number of members eligible to vote if this figure becomes needed. The reporting teller never declares the result of a ballot vote. The result is always declared by the chair, who also reads the tellers' report before he does so. In an election, the chair separately declares the election of each officer (see also **46**). In balloting on a motion, the chair announces the result.

45:40   The tellers' report is entered in full in the minutes, becoming a part of the official records of the organization. Under no circumstances may this be omitted in an election or in a vote on a critical motion out of a mistaken deference to the feelings of unsuccessful candidates or members of the losing side.

45:41   After completion of an election or balloting on a motion, unless the voting body adopts an incidental main motion directing otherwise, the tellers place the ballots and tally sheets in the custody of the secretary, who keeps them under seal until the time within which a recount may be ordered expires, and then destroys them. A recount may be ordered by the voting body, by a majority vote, at the same session at which the voting result was announced, or at the next regular session if that session is held within a quarterly time interval (see 9:7). A recount may also be ordered at a special session properly called for that purpose, if held within a quarterly time interval of the session at which the voting result was announced and before the next regular session. A motion to order a recount after the vote has just been taken or announced is an incidental motion (see **30**); if the motion is made at a later time, it is an incidental main motion.

45:42 **Electronic or Machine Voting.** In many organizations—especially in those comprising hundreds of voters—the process of verifying and counting votes is greatly simplified by the use of electronic or mechanical voting devices, such as handheld keypads or standalone voting machines. The use of such devices to conduct voting may be directed by a special rule of order or convention standing rule or, for a particular vote, by a motion relating to methods of voting and the polls (**30**). Their use to fulfill a ballot requirement in the bylaws may be directed in the same manner, provided that the devices meet the criteria for a ballot vote as stated in 45:18. Members must be able to indicate their choices without revealing how they have voted. If the devices are to be used for an election, provision must be made to allow voters to cast write-in votes. If the devices are to be used to conduct voting on several questions or several independent offices simultaneously, then they must be programmed to allow the number of votes cast for purposes of computing the majority to be tallied independently for each question or office (see 45:36).

45:43 Where such devices are to be used, the following considerations are important:

- Preparations for the meeting should be made in consultation with the person in charge of installing the devices and overseeing their use, so that all adjustments required by the particular conditions of the meeting can be provided for.
- Persons who are to tend the devices during voting must be carefully instructed in their duties, and must be able to explain the use of the devices to voters.

- If there are likely to be many voters who have never used the devices, it may be advisable to have a device available for the voters' inspection on a day previous to the meeting or to conduct a practice vote at the start of the meeting.

45:44   For the use of electronic devices in place of a roll-call vote, see 45:55.

45:45   **Roll-Call Vote.** Taking a vote by *roll call* (or by *yeas and nays,* as it is also called) has the effect of placing on the record how each member, or sometimes each delegation, votes; therefore, it has exactly the opposite effect of a ballot vote. It is usually confined to representative bodies, where the proceedings are published, since it enables constituents to know how their representatives voted on certain measures. It should not be used in a mass meeting or in any assembly whose members are not responsible to a constituency.

45:46   *Ordering a roll-call vote.* In a representative body, if there is no legal or constitutional provision specifying the size of the minority that can order a roll-call vote, the body should adopt a rule fixing the size of such a minority—for example, *one fifth of those present,* as in Congress, or some other portion of those present that is less than a majority. In the absence of such a special rule, a majority vote is required to order the taking of a vote by roll call—in which case a motion to do so is likely to be useless, since its purpose is to force the majority to go on record. In local societies having a large membership but relatively small attendance at meetings, a motion to take a vote by roll call is generally dilatory. It is in order, as one of the *Motions Relating to Methods of Voting,* however, to move "that a signed ballot be taken by tellers"; and if such a vote is ordered, the voter writes "yes" or "no" on the ballot and signs it. The votes can be recorded in the minutes just as a roll call would be, but the names of all members need not be called. A roll-call vote cannot be ordered in committee of the whole.

45:47 ***Procedure for roll-call vote.*** When a vote is to be taken by roll call (see **30** for the motion), the chair puts the question in a form like the following:

> CHAIR: As many as are in favor of the adoption of the resolution will, as their names are called, answer aye [or "yes," or "yea"]; those opposed will answer no [or "nay"]. The Secretary [or "the Clerk"] will call the roll.

45:48 The roll is called in alphabetical order except that the presiding officer's name is called last, and only when his vote will affect the result. It is too late, after one person has answered to the roll call, to renew the debate. Each member, as his name is called, responds in the affirmative or negative as shown above. If he does not wish to vote, he answers *present* (or *abstain*). If he is not ready to vote, but wishes to be called on again after the roll has been completely called, he answers *pass*.

45:49 The secretary repeats each member's name and answer aloud as it is given and notes the answers to the roll call in separate columns. A convenient method of noting the answers is to write the number *1* to the left of the name of the first member answering in the affirmative, the number *2* to the left of the second name in the affirmative, and so on. The negative answers are treated similarly in a column to the right of the names; and those answering *present* are tallied in a third column, to the far right or left. In this way, the last number in each column shows how the vote stands at any given point in the list.

45:50 At the conclusion of the roll call, the names of those who failed to answer can be called again, or the chair can ask if anyone entered the room after his or her name was called. Each of these members who then responds can be assigned the final number for his or her vote or abstention in the proper column, continuing from the last number previously in the column, although the member's number will appear in a position out of sequence. Changes of vote are also permitted at this time, before the result is announced. When this happens, the number beside the member's name is struck through, the total for that column is adjusted accordingly, and the next, final number in the proper column is entered. Changes of vote may be limited when some electronic equipment is used.

45:51   The secretary gives the final number of those voting on each side, and the number answering *present,* to the chair, who announces these figures and declares the result. The chair, at his or her discretion, may direct, or the assembly may order (see **30**), a "recapitulation"—a procedure in which the secretary calls out the names, first, of the members who voted in the affirmative, second, of the members who voted in the negative, and third, of the members who answered *present*, with the chair calling for any necessary corrections to each category after the names in that category have been called.

45:52   In roll-call voting, a record of how each member voted, as well as the result of the vote, is entered in full in the journal or minutes. If those responding to the roll call do not total a sufficient number to constitute a quorum, the chair must direct the secretary to enter the names of enough members who are present but not voting to reflect the attendance of a quorum during the vote.

45:53   In large conventions, the roll is sometimes called of entire delegations rather than of the individual members. The secretary, in calling for the votes of a delegation, states the vote entitlement, as: "Local No. 145: 8 votes." In such cases, the chairman or spokesman of each delegation, as it is called in alphabetical or numerical order, responds by giving its vote, as: "Local No. 145 votes 5 'for' and 3 'against.'" The secretary repeats this for confirmation and calls the next delegation. If any member of the assembly doubts the chairman's announcement of the delegation's vote, he may demand a poll of the delegation, in which case each delegate's name is called by the secretary, and the delegation votes individually. When all delegates have voted, the secretary announces the totals for the delegation, which are recorded.

45:54   The same rules concerning the custody and preservation of tally sheets and the authority of the voting body to order a recount that govern ballot votes (see 45:41) apply to a roll-call vote.

45:55   *Electronic roll-call vote installation.* Various forms of electronic devices have become available to take the place of a roll-call vote. Any deliberative body can use such a system with appropriate adjustments to conform as closely as possible with the rules given above for roll-call voting procedure. When used, there is usually a presumption of technical, mechanical accuracy of the electronic system if properly used by the members. Changes of votes after the result has been announced by the chair on the allegation of machine error are not entertained. On the same grounds, a recapitulation (see 45:51) is not permitted. Where electronic voting is used, it should be noted that, if it is impossible to erect a display board in the hall, members of the same delegation will not be able to ascertain how other members of the delegation vote. Also, steps must be taken to prevent members from being able to vote more than once by using a neighbor's keypad, or a member lending his keypad to a friend so that the friend can vote for him in his absence by "proxy."

45:56   **Absentee Voting.** It is a fundamental principle of parliamentary law that the right to vote is limited to the members of an organization who are actually present at the time the vote is taken in a regular or properly called meeting, although it should be noted that a member need not be present when the question is put. Exceptions to this rule must be expressly stated in the bylaws. Such possible exceptions include: (a) voting by postal mail, e-mail, or fax, and (b) proxy voting. An organization should never adopt a bylaw permitting a question to be decided by a voting procedure in which the votes of persons who attend a meeting are counted together with ballots mailed in by absentees. The votes of those present could be affected by debate, by amendments, and perhaps by the need for repeated balloting, while those absent would be unable to adjust their votes to reflect these factors. Consequently, the absentee ballots would in most cases be on a somewhat different question than that on which those present were voting, leading to confusion, unfairness, and inaccuracy in determining the result. If there is a possibility of any uncertainty about who will be entitled to vote, this should be spelled out unambiguously and strictly enforced to avoid unfairness in close votes.

45:57   **A Vote by Mail.** A vote by mail, when authorized in the bylaws, is generally reserved for important issues, such as an amendment to the bylaws or an election of officers—on which a full vote of the membership is desirable even though only a small fraction of the members normally attend meetings. Situations of this kind frequently occur in scientific societies or in alumni associations whose members may be in many countries.

45:58   For a vote by mail—so that there may be no question of the result in the event that the vote is close—it is important that the mailing list used exactly correspond to the current official roll of voting members. For this purpose, the secretary furnishes to the chairman of tellers or other official in charge of issuing the ballots a list of the names and mailing addresses of record of all persons entitled to vote, which the secretary certifies as corrected to the date as of which the ballots are issued. Each nominee may be allowed to furnish for enclosure with the ballots a brief factual statement of his service and qualifications, provided that all nominees are accorded equal opportunity and space.

45:59   If the vote is not to be secret, the following items should be sent to each qualified voter: (1) a printed ballot containing a space for the voter's signature, to ensure against votes being cast by persons not entitled to vote, together with full instructions for marking and returning by the required date; and (2) a specially recognizable, self-addressed return envelope with the name and address of the secretary, the chairman of tellers, or other person designated to receive the marked ballot. E-mail and other means of electronic communication can be tailored to comply with these requirements.

45:60   If the vote is to be secret, an inner return envelope—with a space for the voter's signature placed on its face instead of on the ballot—should be sent to the voter with the ballot, in addition to the self-addressed outer return envelope described above. The ballot sent to the voter should be prefolded a sufficient number of times so that—when returned marked and refolded in the same manner and sealed in the inner envelope—there will be no chance of accidental observance of the member's vote by the teller who removes the ballot from the inner envelope. The person designated as addressee for the returned ballots holds them in the outer envelopes for delivery, unopened, at the meeting of the tellers where the votes are to be counted. At that meeting all inner envelopes are first removed from the outer envelopes. In the procedure by which the tellers remove the ballots from the inner envelopes, each envelope and ballot is handled in the following manner: (1) the signature on the envelope is checked against the list of qualified voters; (2) the voter is checked off on the list as having voted; and (3) the envelope is opened and the ballot is removed and placed, still folded, into a receptacle. When all inner envelopes have thus been processed, the ballots are taken from the receptacle and the votes are counted.

45:61   In order to ensure the accuracy and the secrecy of such a vote by mail, special care should be taken in all phases of handling the ballots. The chairman of tellers or other person responsible must be able to certify the results from both of these standpoints. Should the recipient of the ballots receive two evidently sent in by the same voter, the above procedure permits the voter to be contacted for a determination of which is the voter's true vote and, if both are, which (the most recent) is to be counted. As with respect to nonsecret ballots, e-mail and other means of electronic communication may be able to be tailored to comply with the above requirements for secret mail balloting.

45:62   **Preferential voting.** The term *preferential voting* refers to any of a number of voting methods by which, on a single ballot when there are more than two possible choices, the second or less-preferred choices of voters can be taken into account if no candidate or proposition attains a majority. While it is more complicated than other methods of voting in common use and is not a substitute for the normal procedure of repeated balloting until a majority is obtained, preferential voting is especially useful and fair in an election by mail if it is impractical to take more than one ballot. In such cases it makes possible a more representative result than under a rule that a plurality shall elect. It can be used with respect to the election of officers only if expressly authorized in the bylaws.

45:63   Preferential voting has many variations. One method is described here by way of illustration. On the preferential ballot— for each office to be filled or multiple-choice question to be decided—the voter is asked to indicate the order in which he prefers all the candidates or propositions, placing the numeral *1* beside his first preference, the numeral *2* beside his second preference, and so on for every possible choice. In counting the votes for a given office or question, the ballots are arranged in piles according to the indicated first preferences—one pile for each candidate or proposition. The number of ballots in each pile is then recorded for the tellers' report. These piles remain identified with the names of the same candidates or propositions throughout the counting procedure until all but one are eliminated as described below. If more than half of the ballots show one candidate or proposition indicated as first choice, that choice has a majority in the ordinary sense and the candidate is elected or the proposition is decided upon. But if there is no such majority, candidates or propositions are eliminated one by one, beginning with the least popular, until one prevails, as follows:

45:64   The ballots in the thinnest pile—that is, those containing the name designated as first choice by the fewest number of voters—are redistributed into the other piles according to the names marked as second choice on these ballots. The number of ballots in each remaining pile after this distribution is again recorded. If more than half of the ballots are now in one pile, that candidate or proposition is elected or decided upon. If not, the next least popular candidate or proposition is similarly eliminated, by taking the thinnest remaining pile and redistributing its ballots according to their second choices into the other piles, except that, if the name eliminated in the last distribution is indicated as second choice on a ballot, that ballot is placed according to its third choice. Again the number of ballots in each existing pile is recorded, and, if necessary, the process is repeated—by redistributing each time the ballots in the thinnest remaining pile, according to the marked second choice or most-preferred choice among those not yet eliminated—until one pile contains more than half of the ballots, the result being thereby determined.

45:65   The tellers' report consists of a table listing all candidates or propositions, with the number of ballots that were in each pile after each successive distribution.

45:66   If a ballot having one or more names not marked with any numeral comes up for placement at any stage of the counting and all of its marked names have been eliminated, it is not placed in any pile, but instead is set aside. If at any point two or more candidates or propositions are tied for the least popular position, the ballots in their piles are redistributed in a single step, all of the tied names being treated as eliminated. In the event of a tie in the winning position—which would imply that the elimination process is continued until the ballots are reduced to two or more equal piles—the election is resolved in favor of the candidate or proposition that was strongest in terms of first choices (by referring to the record of the first distribution).

45:67   If more than one person is to be elected to the same type of office—for example, if three members of a board are to be chosen—the voters can indicate their order of preference among the names in a single list of candidates, just as if only one was to be elected. The counting procedure is the same as described above, except that it is continued until all but the necessary number of candidates have been eliminated (that is, in the example, all but three).

45:68   When this or any other system of preferential voting is to be used, the voting and counting procedure must be precisely established in advance and should be prescribed in detail. The members must be thoroughly instructed as to how to mark the ballot, and should have sufficient understanding of the counting process to enable them to have confidence in the method. Sometimes, for instance, voters decline to indicate a second or other choice, mistakenly believing that such a course increases the chances of their first choice. In fact, it may prevent any candidate from receiving a majority and require the voting to be repeated. The persons selected as tellers must perform their work with particular care.

45:69   The system of preferential voting just described should not be used in cases where it is possible to follow the normal procedure of repeated balloting until one candidate or proposition attains a majority. Although this type of preferential ballot is preferable to an election by plurality, it affords less freedom of choice than repeated balloting, because it denies voters the opportunity of basing their second or lesser choices on the results of earlier ballots, and because the candidate or proposition in last place is automatically eliminated and may thus be prevented from becoming a compromise choice.

45:70   **Proxy Voting.** A *proxy* is a power of attorney given by one person to another to vote in his stead; the term also designates the person who holds the power of attorney. Proxy voting is not permitted in ordinary deliberative assemblies unless the laws of the state in which the society is incorporated require it, or the charter or bylaws of the organization provide for it. Ordinarily it should neither be allowed nor required, because proxy voting is incompatible with the essential characteristics of a deliberative assembly in which membership is individual, personal, and nontransferable. In a stock corporation, on the other hand, where the ownership is transferable, the voice and vote of the member also is transferable, by use of a proxy. But in a nonstock corporation, where membership is usually on the same basis as in an unincorporated, voluntary association, voting by proxy should not be permitted unless the state's corporation law—as applying to nonstock corporations—absolutely requires it.

45:71   If the law under which an organization is incorporated allows proxy voting to be prohibited by a provision of the bylaws, the adoption of this book as parliamentary authority by prescription in the bylaws should be treated as sufficient provision to accomplish that result (cf. 56:49n1).

45:72   **Straw Polls Not in Order.** A motion to take an informal straw poll to "test the water" is not in order because it neither adopts nor rejects a measure and hence is meaningless and dilatory. If the assembly wishes to discuss and take a vote on a matter without the vote constituting final action by the assembly, it may instead vote to go into a committee of the whole or a quasi committee of the whole (**52**). Under these procedures, the assembly considers the matter as would a committee, and its vote while in committee of the whole (or quasi committee of the whole) serves only as a recommendation to the assembly, which the assembly is free to reject just as would be the case with regard to the report of any ordinary committee.

CHAPTER
XIV

NOMINATIONS AND ELECTIONS

§46. NOMINATIONS AND ELECTIONS

Nominations

46:1   A nomination is, in effect, a proposal to fill the blank in an assumed motion "that _____ be elected" to the specified position. In choosing someone to fill an office or other elective position in a society or assembly, a more effective freedom of choice is maintained through the practice of nominating persons for the office, rather than moving that a given person be elected as in the older British procedure. Hence, a form of ballot on which provision is made for voting "for" or "against" a candidate or candidates, as distinguished from a motion, is not proper. Since such a ballot is improper, in order to defeat a candidate for an office it is necessary to vote for an opposing candidate, thus avoiding the anomaly of an assembly refusing to elect anyone to an office.

46:2   Strictly speaking, nominations are not necessary when an election is by ballot or roll call, since each member is free to vote for any eligible person, whether he has been nominated or not. In most societies, however, it is impractical to proceed to an election without first making nominations. While members are always free to "write in," on a ballot, the name of an eligible person who has not been nominated, or to vote for an eligible non-nominee during a roll-call vote, under normal conditions it is likely that most members will confine their choice to the nominees. Without nominations, voting might have to be repeated many times before a candidate achieved the required majority.

46:3   Methods of nomination are: (a) by the chair; (b) from the floor (sometimes called "open nominations"); (c) by a committee; (d) by ballot; (e) by mail; and (f) by petition. If no method of nominating has been specified in the bylaws and if the assembly has adopted no rule on the subject, any member can make a motion prescribing the method (**31**).

46:4   As the following descriptions of the six methods of nomination indicate, not all of them are appropriate or desirable in average societies. The order in which they are listed corresponds to that in which they would be voted on if all six were proposed in motions prescribing the method of nomination.

46:5   **Nominations by the Chair.** At a mass meeting it is a common practice to have the chairman nominated by the person who was designated to call the meeting to order, but an organized society should adopt other methods of nominating for office. The chair, however, can make nominations for committee membership and similar positions (an exception being made in the case of the nominating committee), as may be provided in the bylaws or by the adoption of a motion.

46:6   **Nominations from the Floor.** Under the procedure of nominations from the floor, the chair calls for nominations at the time established by rule or custom of the organization or assembly—which may be while the election is pending or earlier, but in any case is subsequent to the report of the nominating committee if there is such a committee. Unless the bylaws or a special rule of order provides otherwise, the chair must call for further nominations at the session at which the election is held even if nominations were called for at a previous session. A member need not be recognized by the chair to make a nomination unless he or she wishes to speak in debate on it at the same time (see 46:27–29). In a large meeting or convention a member should rise when making a nomination from the floor, but in small assemblies nominations frequently are made by members from their seats. No second is required, but sometimes one or more members will second a nomination to indicate endorsement. Where more than one person is to be elected to an office, such as to a board of directors or trustees, or to a position, such as to a committee, no one may nominate more than one person for the office or position, if an objection is made, until every member wishing to nominate has had an opportunity to do so. In no event may a member nominate more persons than there are places to fill.

46:7   The same person can be nominated for more than one office, even if voting for all offices is to take place at the same time on a single ballot. If one person is elected to more than one office under these conditions, the case is resolved as described in the second paragraph of 46:31(1).

46:8   If there is no nominating committee and nominations are to be from the floor, the chair calls for them by saying, for example, "Nominations are now in order for the office of President." If there is a nominating committee, the chair calls for nominations as shown in 46:19. When the presiding officer has called for nominations from the floor, a member rises and makes a nomination as follows:

> **MEMBER:** I nominate Mr. A. [Or, in a large assembly, "Mr. President, I nominate Mr. A."]
>
> **CHAIR:** Mr. A is nominated. Are there any further nominations [or "any further nominations for the office of President"]?

The chair repeats each nomination in this way until all nominations for the office have been made. (For the procedure for closing nominations, see 46:20.) Nominations for the different offices are thus called for in the order in which the offices are listed in the bylaws.

46:9   **Nominations by a Committee.** In the election of officers of an ordinary society, nominations often are made by a nominating committee. Usually in such cases a nominating committee is chosen in advance to submit nominations for the various offices for which elections are to be held at the annual meeting.

46:10 *Designation of the nominating committee.* The nominating committee should be elected by the organization wherever possible, or else by its executive board. Although in organizing a new society it may be feasible for the chair to appoint the nominating committee, in an organized society the president should not appoint this committee or be a member of it—ex officio or otherwise. The bylaws may provide that "the President shall appoint all committees except the Nominating Committee ..." and that "the President shall be ex officio a member of all committees except the Nominating Committee ..."; the exception should not be omitted in either case.

46:11 *Nominees.* Although it is not common for the nominating committee to nominate more than one candidate for any office, the committee can do so unless the bylaws prohibit it. It is usually not sound to *require* the committee to nominate more than one candidate for each office, since the committee can easily circumvent such a provision by nominating only one person who has any chance of being elected (see also 56:25).

46:12 Members of the nominating committee are not barred from becoming nominees for office themselves. To make such a requirement would mean, first, that service on the nominating committee carried a penalty by depriving its members of one of their privileges; and second, that appointment or election to the nominating committee could be used to prevent a member from becoming a nominee.

46:13 It is desirable policy for the nominating committee, before making its report, to contact each person whom it wishes to nominate, in order to obtain his acceptance of nomination— that is, his assurance that he will serve in the specified office if elected. The bylaws can make such a practice mandatory.

46:14 *Report of the nominating committee.* The time at which the nominating committee's report is made is a matter to be determined by rule or established custom of the particular organization—depending on its own conditions. In some societies this report is not formally presented to the voting body until the election is pending; but in any organization where advance interest in the election may develop, the nominations submitted by the committee should be made known to the membership earlier. These nominations can be sent to all members, for example, several days before the regular meeting—usually the election meeting itself—at which the chair calls for additional nominations from the floor (see below). The report should always be formally presented at a regular meeting, even if the names of the committee's nominees have been transmitted to the members of the society beforehand. Sometimes—in societies that hold frequent regular meetings—the nominating committee's report is presented at the regular meeting preceding the annual meeting (**9**) at which the election is to take place.

46:15   When the nominating committee is called upon for its report at a meeting, its chairman rises and presents the report as follows:

> **NOMINATING COMMITTEE CHAIRMAN:** Mr. President, the Nominating Committee submits the following nominations: For President, Mr. A [or "John A"]; for Vice-President, Mr. B; for Secretary, Mr. C; … [and so on for each office to be filled, naming the nominees in the order in which the offices are listed in the bylaws].

46:16   A minority within a nominating committee, as a group, may propose other nominees for some or all of the offices in any case where nominations from the floor are permitted.

46:17   A nominating committee is automatically discharged when its report is formally presented to the assembly, although if one of the nominees withdraws before the election, the committee is revived and should meet immediately to agree upon another nomination if there is time.

46:18   *Call by the chair for further nominations from the floor.* After the nominating committee has presented its report and before voting for the different offices takes place, the chair must call for further nominations from the floor. This is another stage of nomination and election procedure for which a number of details should be established by rule or custom of the particular organization. In many organizations, nominations from the floor are called for immediately after the presentation of the nominating committee's report—while the election is pending or earlier. Note that the chair must call for further nominations at the session at which the election is held even if nominations from the floor were called for at a previous session. When the calling for nominations from the floor is about to begin, if some time has elapsed since the presentation of the nominating committee's report, the complete list of the committee's nominations should be read again before further nominations are called for. In any case, if the nominating committee has for any reason failed to make its report at the appropriate time, this does not prevent the assembly from proceeding to nominations from the floor.

46:19   In some organizations all nominations from the floor are completed and nominations are closed for each office before voting for any office takes place. In other organizations, when nominations for one office have been completed, votes are cast for that office and the result is announced before the chair calls for nominations for the next office (see also 46:31). If the organization has no rule on the subject, a custom based on its own conditions may determine which of the two procedures is used (see 2:25) or this may be decided by a motion (**31**). In either case, the different offices are taken in the order in which they are listed in the bylaws. The chair, as he calls for nominations, first repeats the name that was submitted by the nominating committee, thus:

> CHAIR: For President, Mr. A is nominated by the Nominating Committee. Are there any further nominations for President? [If a member nominates another person, the chair repeats the name of that nominee.] Mr. N is nominated. Are there any further nominations?

46:20   When it appears that no one else wishes to make a nomination, the chair again asks if there are any further nominations; and if there is no response, he normally declares that nominations (for that office) are closed, without waiting for a motion to that effect, as follows:

> **CHAIR:** Are there any further nominations for President? ... [Pause.] If not ... [pause], nominations are closed. [Or, "Without objection, ... nominations are closed."]

(For use of the motion to close nominations, which requires a two-thirds vote, see **31**.) After nominations have been closed, they can be reopened by a majority vote.

46:21   After nominations have been closed, voting for that office takes place, or nominations for the next office are called for by the chair, depending on the procedure being followed by the particular organization.

46:22   **Nominations by Ballot.** The object of a nominating ballot is to provide the members with an indication of the sentiments of the voting body, which they may take into account in voting in the election. The value of the nominating ballot is that it shows the preferences without electing anyone. The nominating ballot is conducted in the same way as an ordinary electing ballot except that everyone receiving a vote is nominated; the tellers' report, therefore, does not state the number of votes necessary for nomination. Since each member has the opportunity to nominate on his ballot a candidate for every office, he does not have the right then to make nominations from the floor, unless the assembly by a majority vote authorizes such nominations.

46:23   *Impropriety of making the nominating ballot the electing ballot.* Sometimes a motion is made to declare the nominating ballot the electing ballot. Such action negates all the advantages of a nominating ballot and is, in effect, the same as having an electing ballot without any nominations. If there is to be only one ballot, it should be the electing ballot, with nominations from the floor, or by a nominating committee and from the floor. A nominating ballot cannot take the place of an electing ballot in an organization whose bylaws require elections to be held by ballot.

46:24   *Impropriety of limiting voting in the election to the two leading candidates.* In some organizations using the nominating ballot, an attempt is made to limit the voting on the electing ballot to the two nominees for each office receiving the highest number of votes on the nominating ballot. This—or any attempt to limit the number of candidates for an office to two, by whatever method they are nominated—is an unfortunate practice and should be discouraged. Often the two leading candidates for a position will represent two different factions, and division within the organization may be deepened by limiting the election to them. On the other hand, it may be possible to unite the members if the assembly has the choice of a compromise candidate.

46:25   **Nominations by Mail.** In organizations whose membership is widely scattered, the method of nominating by mail is often adopted. In such a case a nominating ballot can be prepared, deposited, and counted in the same way as an electing ballot—with the secretary of the organization mailing to every member a nominating ballot, plus instructions for completing and returning it as described in 45:57–61. Or, in some organizations, a blank on which each member can submit the names of desired nominees, in a signed ballot, is used instead of a secret nominating ballot.

46:26   **Nominations by Petition.** The bylaws may provide that a member shall be a nominee upon the petition of a specified number of members. Sometimes, a nominating petition blank is sent to the members with a copy of the list of nominees submitted by a nominating committee. In large state or national societies composed of local units, the blanks are sometimes sent to these units with instructions for their distribution or processing.

46:27 **Debate on Nominations.** In large conventions, nominations are sometimes accompanied by a speech advocating the nominee's election. The nomination may then be seconded by one or more members also making speeches. In ordinary societies, however, such speeches are less common.

46:28 To give a nominating or seconding speech, a member must first be recognized by the chair while the floor is open for nominations. The member may then nominate a candidate and, without waiting for the chair to state the nomination, speak in favor of the candidate, or he or she may speak in favor of a candidate who was nominated previously. If candidates are members of the organization, speakers must exercise caution to avoid making any personal criticisms of them in debate. Rather than attacking a nominee, a speaker may advocate the election of a rival candidate. By a two-thirds vote, the assembly may adopt a motion limiting debate to any extent desired (**15**).

46:29 Some organizations adopt rules specifying that debate on nominations be conducted at a different time or in a different manner. Such a rule might, for example, allot each candidate (or his or her designee) equal time to state the candidate's credentials and to argue for the candidate's election.

Elections

46:30 In an assembly or organization that does not have a rule or established custom prescribing the method of voting in elections, the voting can be by any of the accepted methods. While some form of election by ballot is generally appropriate in organized societies, each assembly should adopt—and each society should prescribe in its bylaws—the procedure best suited to its purposes and needs. Where there is no determining rule, a motion to fix the method of voting (or any other detail of nomination or election procedure) is an incidental main motion if made before the election is pending, or an incidental motion if made while the election is pending (**30**, **31**). Such a motion can be offered containing a blank so that different methods are voted on in succession; or the chair can take votes on the methods in this way, assuming the motion, if no member objects. In the absence of a rule establishing the method of voting, the rule that is established by custom, if any, is followed, unless the assembly, by adoption of an incidental motion or incidental main motion, agrees to do otherwise.

46:31 **Ballot Election.** Two alternative procedures for the sequence of nominating and voting in elections by ballot can be prescribed or adopted, as mentioned above. The first method requires the least time, while the second affords greater flexibility in choosing officers. These procedures are as follows:

1) All nominations can be completed before any balloting takes place—in which case voting for all offices is commonly done by a single ballot. This method is suitable for use in conventions where voting takes place at a "polling place" apart from the convention meetings. It may also be a preferred method in any large meeting where the time required for balloting is an important consideration. The elections should take place early in such a meeting, to allow time for any necessary additional balloting for any office for which no candidate receives a vote sufficient for election. Votes can be cast for any person who is eligible for election, even if he has not been nominated. The procedure followed in balloting, in counting the votes, and in reporting the results is described in 45:18–43. The tellers prepare a tellers' report for each office involved, in the form shown in 45:37. When these reports are completed for all offices, the chairman of tellers, after reading them to the assembly, submits them to the chair, who, as he reads each one of them again, declares the result for that office. In each case where a candidate has a majority, the chair declares that candidate elected. For offices for which no candidate has a majority, the chair announces, "no election." When the tellers' reports for all offices have thus been read, the chair directs that new ballots be distributed for those offices for which no candidate attained a majority (see also below).

When voting for multiple offices by a single ballot, the members are not able to take the result for one office into account when voting for another office. For this reason, a candidate is never deemed elected to more than one office by a single ballot unless the motion or rules governing the election specifically provide for such simultaneous election. When there is no such provision, a candidate who receives a majority for more than one office on a single ballot must, if present, choose which one of the offices he will accept; if he is absent, the assembly decides by a ballot vote the office to be assigned to him. This question, which is debatable, requires a majority vote for adoption. The assembly then ballots again to fill the other office(s). (The assembly is free, however, to elect the same person to another office on a subsequent ballot, unless the bylaws prohibit a person from holding both offices simultaneously.)

2) Under the usual form of the second election procedure, balloting for each office immediately follows nominations from the floor for that office. The ballots are counted for one office and the result of that election is announced—after repeated balloting, if necessary—before the next office to be voted on is opened to nominations from the floor. The members are thus able to take into account the results for the offices voted on first, in deciding upon both nominations and votes for the later offices. Under this method the ballots normally consist of small slips of blank paper handed out by the tellers as each ballot is taken—on which voters write the name of the candidate of their choice (who need not have been nominated). This method is generally practical only in assemblies small enough that the votes from each balloting can be counted while the meeting briefly pauses—usually without recessing or proceeding to other business, although it can do either of these things if it wishes.

46:32 Whichever one of the preceding methods of election is used, if any office remains unfilled after the first ballot, the balloting is repeated for that office as many times as necessary to obtain a majority vote for a single candidate. When repeated balloting for an office is necessary, individuals are never removed from candidacy on the next ballot unless they voluntarily withdraw—which they are not obligated to do.[1] The candidate in lowest place may turn out to be a "dark horse" on whom all factions may prefer to agree.

46:33   In an election of members of a board or committee in which votes are cast in one section of the ballot for multiple positions on the board or committee, every ballot with a vote in that section for one or more candidates is counted as one vote cast, and a candidate must receive a majority of the total of such votes to be elected. If more candidates receive such a majority vote than there are positions to fill, then the chair declares the candidates elected in order of their vote totals, starting with the candidate who received the largest number of votes and continuing until every position is filled. If, during this process, a tie arises involving more candidates than there are positions remaining to be filled, then the candidates who are tied, as well as all other nominees not yet elected, remain as candidates for the repeated balloting necessary to fill the remaining position(s). Similarly, if the number of candidates receiving the necessary majority vote is less than the number of positions to be filled, those who have a majority are declared elected, and all other nominees remain as candidates on the next ballot.

46:34   If the multiple positions have varying terms (as may happen when terms are staggered or there is an election to fill the remainder of an unexpired term) and the differing term lengths have not been assigned different sections of the ballot, the longer terms are allocated among those receiving a majority

---

1. An organization could suspend the rules, or adopt a special rule of order, so that the nominee with the fewest votes is dropped from the list of nominees for succeeding ballots in the expectation that voters will then confine their choice to the remaining nominees. Only a bylaws provision, however, could make the dropped nominee ineligible for election so as to render illegal any subsequent votes cast for that nominee. (See 46:2.)

vote in the order in which they obtain greater numbers of votes. If there is a tie, the tied candidates may agree which of them will take a longer term; if they do not agree, the question is put to a vote on the next ballot.

46:35　　If the bylaws require the election of officers to be by ballot and there is only one nominee for an office, the ballot must nevertheless be taken for that office unless the bylaws provide for an exception in such a case. In the absence of the latter provision, members still have the right, on the ballot, to cast "write-in votes" for other eligible persons.

46:36　　An election by ballot can be conducted by mail if the bylaws so provide, as explained in 45:57–69. For such an election, however—unless repeated balloting by mail is feasible in cases where no candidate attains a majority—the bylaws should authorize the use of some form of preferential voting or should provide that a plurality shall elect, and should provide for a method of selection if there is a tie.

46:37 **Viva-Voce Election.** The viva-voce method of election finds application principally in mass meetings—or when an election is not strongly contested and the bylaws do not require election by ballot.

46:38　　When there is more than one nominee for a given office in a viva-voce election—or in an election by rising vote or by show of hands—the candidates are voted on in the order in which they were nominated. When the nominations have ended, the chair repeats the nominations and continues:

> **CHAIR:** As many as are in favor of Mr. A for President say *aye*. … Those opposed say *no*. … The ayes have it and Mr. A is elected President.

If the noes are in the majority the wording is:

> **CHAIR:** The noes have it and Mr. A is not elected. Those in favor of Mr. B [the next nominee] say *aye*. … Those opposed say *no*. …

As soon as one of the nominees receives a majority vote, the chair declares him elected and no votes are taken on the remaining nominees for that office. The other officers are elected in the same way. When a number of members are to be elected to identical offices in the nature of a single office held by more than one person—as, for example, in electing four directors—the same procedure is followed; when four have received a majority, the voting ceases.

46:39   It will be seen that, under the procedure just described, it is necessary for members wishing to vote for a later nominee to vote against an earlier one. This fact gives an undue advantage to earlier nominees and, accordingly, a voice vote is not a generally suitable method for electing the officers of organized societies.

46:40   If only one person is nominated and the bylaws do not require that a ballot vote be taken, the chair, after ensuring that, in fact, no members present wish to make further nominations, simply declares that the nominee is elected, thus effecting the election by unanimous consent or "acclamation." The motion to close nominations cannot be used as a means of moving the election of the candidate in such a case.

46:41   The assembly cannot make valid a viva-voce election if the bylaws require the election to be by ballot.

46:42   **Roll-Call Election.** Although unusual, an election can be held by roll call. Either the first or second procedure described in 46:31 for election by ballot can be generally followed, and the member (or the chairman of a delegation, as the case may be), when called upon, declares his vote or the votes of the members of his delegation for each office to be filled. The secretary records the vote(s) and then repeats them to be sure of their accurate recordation.

46:43   **Cumulative Voting.** For ballot or roll-call elections of boards, committees, delegates, or other positions held by more than one individual, the bylaws may provide for *cumulative voting*. In this form of voting, each member is entitled to cast one vote for each position, so that if, for example, three directors are to be elected, each member may cast three votes. These votes may all be cast for one, two, or three candidates, as the voter chooses. A minority group, by coordinating its effort in voting for only one candidate who is a member of the group, may be able to secure the election of that candidate as a minority member of the board. However, this method of voting, which permits a member to cast multiple votes for a single candidate, must be viewed with reservation since it violates the fundamental principle of parliamentary law that each member is entitled to one and only one vote on a question.

46:44   **Providing for Completion of an Election.** An election should be completed at the session at which it is taken up, unless it is impossible or impractical to do so. If an assembly wishes to adjourn when an election is incomplete, an adjourned meeting (**9**) should therefore be provided for. If such an adjourned meeting is not provided for and the organization will hold another regular business session before a quarterly time interval has elapsed (see 9:7), the election is taken up automatically at the next regular meeting. (Cf. 14:12.)

46:45   If, for any reason, the assembly does not complete an election at the time for which it was scheduled, it should do so as soon as possible and may do so at any time until the expiration of the term the election is to fill. In the meantime, if the term of office extends until a successor is elected (see 56:28–30) failure to complete an election leaves the incumbent, if any, in office. Otherwise, a vacancy in office arises (see 47:57–58 for procedures for filling vacancies). Once the election is completed, however, the person elected replaces anyone who filled the vacancy. Failure to hold or to complete an election at the scheduled time does not deprive the membership of its right to elect an officer of its choice.

46:46   **Time at Which an Election Takes Effect.** An election to an office becomes final immediately if the candidate is present and does not decline, or if he is absent but has consented to his candidacy. If he is absent and has not consented to his candidacy, the election becomes final when he is notified of his election, provided that he does not immediately decline. If he does decline, the election is incomplete, and another vote can be taken immediately or at the next meeting without further notice. After an election has become final as stated in this paragraph, it is too late to reconsider (**37**) the vote on the election.

46:47   An officer-elect takes possession of his office immediately upon his election's becoming final, unless the bylaws or other rules specify a later time (see 56:27). If a formal installation ceremony is prescribed, failure to hold it does not affect the time at which the new officers assume office.

46:48   **Contesting the Announced Result of an Election.** Depending on the circumstances, the voting body may be able to order a recount if an election was conducted by ballot (see 45:41), roll-call vote (see 45:54), or counted vote (see the last sentence of 45:15). In the case of a roll-call vote, a recapitulation may be possible (see 45:51). It may be possible, under some circumstances, to order that the election be voted on again by another method (see *Retaking a Vote*, 30:6).

46:49   Otherwise, an election may be contested only by raising a point of order. The general rule is that such a point of order must be timely, as described in 23:5. If an election is disputed on the ground that a quorum was not present, the provisions in the last sentence of 40:12 apply. Other exceptions to the general timeliness requirement are those that come within the five categories listed in 23:6, in which cases a point of order can be made at any time during the continuance in office of the individual declared elected. For example:

a) If an individual does not meet the qualifications for the post established in the bylaws, his or her election is tantamount to adoption of a main motion that conflicts with the bylaws.

b) If there was a previously valid election for the same term, the subsequent election of another is the adoption of a main motion conflicting with one still in force.

c) If the votes of nonmembers or absentees in the election affect the result, action has been taken in violation of the fundamental principle of parliamentary law that the right to vote is limited to the members of an organization who are actually present at the time the vote is taken.

d) If an election to fill a vacancy is held without required previous notice, action has been taken in violation of a rule protecting the rights of absentees.

e) If a number of members sufficient to affect the result are improperly prevented from voting in an election, action has been taken in violation of a rule protecting a basic right of the individual member.

46:50   Because the voting body itself is the ultimate judge of election disputes, only that body has the authority to resolve them in the absence of a bylaw or special rule of order that specifically grants another body that authority. Thus, for example, when an election has been conducted at a membership meeting or in a convention of delegates, an executive board, even one that is given full power and authority over the society's affairs between meetings of the body that conducted the election, may not entertain a point of order challenging, or direct a recount concerning, the announced election result. While an election dispute is immediately pending before the voting body, however, it may vote to refer the dispute to a committee or board to which it delegates power to resolve the dispute.

CHAPTER

XV

OFFICERS; MINUTES AND OFFICERS' REPORTS

§47. OFFICERS

47:1   As stated in 3:6, the minimum essential officers for the conduct of business in any deliberative assembly are a presiding officer and a secretary or clerk. The usual duties of these and other officers generally required in an organized society are summarized and discussed in this section. Every society should specify in its bylaws what officers it requires, how they shall be elected or appointed, their term of office, and any qualifications for holding office or any duties different from or in addition to those stated in the parliamentary authority.

Principles Applying to Holding of Office

47:2   In most societies it is usual to elect the officers from among the members; but in all except secret societies, unless the bylaws provide otherwise, it is possible for an organization to choose its officers from outside its membership. In many legislative bodies the presiding officer is not a member of the body. A large society with complex financial affairs may wish to employ a professional as treasurer.

47:3   An office carries with it only the rights necessary for executing the duties of the office, and it does not deprive a member of the society of his rights as a member. If a person holds an office in a society of which he is not a member and the bylaws make that officer an ex-officio member of the board, the nonmember is thereby a full-fledged board member with all the accompanying rights; but this does not make him a member of the society.

47:4   The bylaws may contain a provision that "No person shall be eligible to serve _____ consecutive terms in the same office." In filling vacancies for unexpired terms, an officer who has served more than half a term in an office is considered to have served a full term. As stated in 46:46–47, the term of office begins as soon as the officer is elected, unless the bylaws establish a different time (see also 56:27).

Elected Officers

47:5   **Chairman or President.** The presiding officer of an assembly ordinarily is called the *chairman*[1] when no special title has been assigned, or in a body not permanently organized, such as a mass meeting (**53**). In organized societies the presiding officer's title is usually prescribed by the bylaws, that of *president* being most common. The term *the chair* refers to the person in a meeting who is actually presiding at the time, whether that person is the regular presiding officer or not. The same term also applies to the presiding officer's station in the hall from which he or she presides, which should not be permitted to be used by other members as a place from which to make reports or speak in debate during a meeting (see also 47:12). In assemblies where committee chairmen or others will require a lectern for their papers, another lectern on the side of the platform or on the floor at the front should be provided so that the chair can maintain his presiding location. For the manner in which the chair should be addressed in a meeting, see 3:10–11.

47:6   The presiding officer of an assembly—especially of a large one—should be chosen principally for the ability to preside. This person should be well versed in parliamentary law and should be thoroughly familiar with the bylaws and other rules of the organization—even if he or she is to have the

---

1. See 3:10 regarding variations of this term which have come into use.

assistance of a parliamentarian. At the same time, any presiding officer will do well to bear in mind that no rules can take the place of tact and common sense on the part of the chairman.

47:7   *Duties of the presiding officer of an assembly.* The principal duties of the presiding officer of an assembly under parliamentary law are listed below—with references, where appropriate, to fuller descriptions elsewhere in this book. Additional information relating to the duties of the chair in particular cases will be found in the treatment of the subjects involved. It is the duty of the presiding officer of an assembly:

1) To open the meeting at the appointed time by taking the chair and calling the meeting to order (3:15), having ascertained that a quorum is present (3:3–4; **40**).

2) To announce in proper sequence the business that comes before the assembly or becomes in order in accordance with the prescribed order of business, agenda, or program, and with existing orders of the day (**41**).

3) To recognize members who are entitled to the floor (3:30–35; **42**).

4) To state and to put to vote all questions that legitimately come before the assembly as motions or that otherwise arise in the course of proceedings (except questions that relate to the presiding officer himself in the manner noted below), and to announce the result of each vote (**4**); or, if a motion that is not in order is made, to rule that it is not in order (although this may be avoided if the chair can suggest an alternative that is in order which the maker agrees to offer instead; see 4:16–18). (For a discussion of the circumstances under which the chair votes, see 44:12–13. See also the discussion of unanimous consent, 4:58–63.)

5) To protect the assembly from obviously dilatory motions by refusing to recognize them (**39**).

6) To enforce the rules relating to debate and those relating to order and decorum within the assembly (3:9–13; 4:27–32; **43**).

7) To expedite business in every way compatible with the rights of members.

8) To decide all questions of order (**23**), subject to appeal (**24**)—unless, when in doubt, the presiding officer prefers initially to submit such a question to the assembly for decision.

9) To respond to inquiries of members relating to parliamentary procedure (*Parliamentary Inquiry*, 33:3–5) or factual information (*Request for Information*, 33:6–10) bearing on the business of the assembly.

10) To authenticate by his or her signature, when necessary, all acts, orders, and proceedings of the assembly.

11) To declare the meeting adjourned when the assembly so votes or—where applicable—at the time prescribed in the program, or at any time in the event of a sudden emergency affecting the safety of those present (**8**, **21**).

47:8   At each meeting, in addition to the necessary papers proper to that meeting's business, the presiding officer should have at hand:

- a copy of the bylaws and other rules of the organization;
- a copy of its parliamentary authority (that is, this book, if it is prescribed in the bylaws);
- a list of all standing and special committees and their members; and
- a memorandum of the complete order of business listing all known matters that are to come up, shown in proper sequence under the correct headings—or with their scheduled times—as applicable.

47:9   Except in a small board or a committee, the presiding officer should stand while calling a meeting to order or declaring it adjourned, and while putting a question to vote. He should also stand—without leaving the chair—while explaining his reasons for a ruling on a point of order (if the explanation entails more than a few words) or when speaking during debate on an appeal or a point of order that he has submitted to the judgment of the assembly (**23, 24**). When speaking for the first time during debate in either of the latter two cases, he can do so in preference to other members (see 23:2(5), 23:19, and 24:3(5)). While a member is speaking in debate on any question, the presiding officer should remain seated—unless the view between him and the members would be obstructed, in which case he should step back slightly during the member's speech. At times other than those just mentioned, the presiding officer can stand or sit as he finds convenient for commanding the assembly's attention, preserving order, etc.—provided that his station is arranged so that even when seated he can see the entire hall and all present can see him (see also 3:7, 47:5).

47:10   Whenever a motion is made that refers only to the presiding officer in a capacity not shared in common with other members, or that commends or censures him with others, he should turn the chair over to the vice-president or appropriate temporary occupant (see below) during the assembly's consideration of that motion, just as he would in a case where he wishes to take part in debate (see also 43:29–30). The chair, however, should not hesitate to put the question on a motion to elect officers or appoint delegates or a committee even if he is included.

47:11   *Temporary occupants of the chair.* If it is necessary for the president to vacate the chair during a meeting, or if the president is absent, the chair is occupied temporarily by another—who also must not be precluded from presiding by any of the impediments mentioned in the preceding paragraph—as follows:

1) *A vice-president.* If the president for any reason vacates the chair or is absent, the vice-president or first vice-president takes the chair unless he also, because of involvement in the debate or for any other reason, is disqualified from presiding in the particular case; and if the first vice-president is absent or must disqualify himself, the duty of presiding devolves on the other vice-presidents in order. For this reason, the bylaws should number the vice-presidencies if there are

more than one, and persons should be elected to specific positions. It should be noted, however, that if the bylaws provide for a president-elect, they usually provide also that the president-elect shall precede the first vice-president in the right to preside.

2) *An appointed chairman pro tem.* If the president vacates the chair during a meeting and no vice-president is available, he can, subject to the approval of the assembly, as explained in 43:29(b), appoint a temporary chairman who is called the *chairman pro tempore,* or *chairman pro tem.* The return of the president, the arrival of a vice-president, or the first adjournment puts an end to this appointment, and the assembly can terminate it even earlier by the adoption of a motion to "declare the chair vacant and proceed to elect a new chairman" (see 62:11). The regular presiding officer, knowing that he will be absent from a future meeting, cannot in advance authorize another member to preside in his place.

3) *An elected chairman pro tem.* If neither the president nor any vice-president is present, the secretary—or in the secretary's absence some other member—calls the meeting to order, and the assembly immediately elects a chairman pro tem to preside during that session. Such office is terminated by the entrance of the president or a vice-president, or by the adoption of a motion to "declare the chair vacant and proceed to elect a new chairman" (see 62:11). If the assembly is to elect a chairman pro tem to hold office beyond the current session (in the event that the president and the vice-presidents are unable to perform their duties for that length of time), notice must be given at the preceding meeting or in the call of the meeting at which such election is held.

47:12   The practice in some organizations of permitting the chairman of a committee to preside over the assembly or put questions to vote during the presentation and consideration of the committee's report violates numerous principles of parliamentary law relating to the chair's appearance of impartiality and the inappropriateness of his entering into debate, not to speak of the regular presiding officer's duty to preside (see 47:5–7).

47:13 *Invited temporary presiding officer.* In certain instances in an ordinary society—for example, if an adjourned meeting or a special meeting (**9**) must deal with a problem that has intensely divided the organization—it may be that such a meeting can accomplish more under the chairmanship of an invited nonmember who is skilled in presiding. (Sometimes this may be a professional presiding officer.) If the president and vicepresident(s) do not object, the assembly, by majority vote, can adopt an incidental main motion to effect such an arrangement for all or part of a session. This motion is a question of privilege affecting the assembly (**19**). Alternatively, the rules may be suspended to authorize this type of temporary appointment, even over the objection of the president or a vicepresident. Cf. 62:13–14.

47:14 *Suggestions for inexperienced presiding officers.* The larger the assembly, the more readily it will detect the slightest weakness in a presiding officer. Efforts to capitalize on any such failing may follow with sometimes disastrous results. It is often said that knowledge is strength, and certainly that is true in this case. The presiding officer should be thoroughly familiar with the duties of the presiding officer of an assembly, as stated in 47:7–10, and should have with him the documents listed in 47:8. There is no acceptable alternative to parliamentary procedure for the conduct of business in a deliberative assembly; yet many presiding officers try to get along with a minimum of knowledge. This approach inevitably results in signs of unsureness.

47:15 A presiding officer should make every effort to know more parliamentary procedure than other members. A good first step is to read through *Robert's Rules of Order Newly Revised In Brief*—a concise introductory guide prepared by the authors of this book and fully compatible with it—paying particular attention to Chapter 15 ("President or Vice-President").

A presiding officer should also at least become familiar with 1 through 9 of this book and memorize the list of motions on page t4, in their order of precedence. The chair should be able to refer to the table of rules relating to motions on pages t6–t33 quickly enough that there will be no delay in deciding all points contained there. These steps are simple and will enable a president to master parliamentary procedure more quickly. As more difficult points arise, a careful reading of the detailed treatment of such points in the body of this book will make them readily understood and mastered.

47:16   The presiding officer must not permit members to press on so rapidly that the parliamentary steps are abridged or go unobserved. When a motion is made, he must not recognize any member or allow anyone to speak until the motion is seconded (where that is required) and he has stated the question.

47:17   The chair should take special care to make sure that the members always understand what is the immediately pending business—the *exact* question to be voted on the next time a vote is taken. Failure of presiding officers to do so is one of the greatest causes of confusion in meetings. The chair should carefully follow the directions for stating a question on a motion or resolution given in 4:15. Particularly in stating the question on an unwritten motion, the chair should always say, "It is moved and seconded that" and then give the precise words of the motion fully, no matter how clearly the motion may have been framed when moved by its maker. The chair should never try to avoid this critically important duty by saying, "You have heard the motion" or by saying, "The motion is moved and seconded" without repeating its words. The chair must be careful to be exact in stating any proposed amendment so as to make clear the effect its adoption would have on the motion to be amended. After the vote on an amendment, he should fully restate that motion as it stands as a result of the amendment's adoption or failure (see 12:33–40). Above all, just before the vote, the chair must make clear the precise question the assembly is to decide. It is far better to risk taxing the patience of an assembly by repeating the wording of a motion on which all may be clear, than to risk taking a vote whose effect may be unclear to even a few members.

47:18   When a vote is taken, the result should be announced and also what question, if any, is then pending, before any member who addresses the chair is recognized. In a large assembly where a microphone is required, the chair should insist that a member go to it and identify himself. This brief delay is often very salutary in quieting heated feelings. Efforts to abbreviate the requirements of parliamentary procedure often signal an effort to substitute the member's will for the parliamentary leadership of the presiding officer. A not uncommon instance of this kind is described in 42:13(1), where a member attempts quickly to obtain the floor to offer a motion in competition with one arranged by the officers to be offered by another member. Firmness and, at the same time, calm insistence on the regular order is a technique essential to the development of a skilled presiding officer.

47:19   While a commanding presence and knowledge are essential in procedural matters, the president of an ordinary deliberative assembly, especially a large one, should, of all the members, have the least to say upon the substance of pending questions. While providing strong leadership, he should be fair. He should never get excited; he should never be unjust to even the most troublesome member, or take advantage of such member's lack of knowledge of parliamentary law, even though a temporary good might be accomplished thereby. The president should never be technical or more strict than is necessary for the good of the meeting. Good judgment is essential; the assembly may be of such a nature, through its unfamiliarity with parliamentary usage and its peaceable disposition, that strict enforcement of the rules, instead of assisting, would greatly hinder business. But in large assemblies where there is much work to be done, and especially where there is likelihood of trouble, the only safe course is to require a strict observance of the rules.

47:20   *Administrative duties of the president of a society.* All of the duties of the presiding officer described above relate to the function of presiding over the assembly at its meetings. In addition, in many organized societies, the president has duties as an administrative or executive officer; but these are outside the scope of parliamentary law, and the president has such authority only insofar as the bylaws provide it. In some organizations, the president is responsible for appointing, and is ex officio a member of, all committees (with the exception of the nominating committee, which should be expressly excluded from such a provision, and with the further possible exception of all disciplinary committees; see 56:47). But only when he is so authorized by the bylaws—or, in the case of a particular committee, by vote of the assembly—does he have this authority and status. As an ex-officio member of a committee, the president has the same rights as the other committee members, but is not obligated to attend meetings of the committee and is not counted in determining the number required for a quorum or whether a quorum is present.

47:21   **President-Elect.** Some organizations desire to elect their president one entire term in advance, and in such cases, during the term following the election, the person chosen is called the *president-elect.* This office exists only if expressly provided for in the bylaws, in which case the members never vote on any candidate for the office of president, but elect a president-elect and the other officers of the organization. Accordingly, when a member has served his full term as president-elect, he automatically becomes president for a full term. Once a person has been elected president-elect, the assembly cannot alter its decision regarding the succession of that person to the presidency, unless he vacates office during his term as president-elect or unless ground arises for removing him from that office (see 62:16).

47:22   When the bylaws of an organization provide for a president-elect, it is usual to provide also that if the president should be absent, or if the office of the president should become vacant between elections, the president-elect shall preside, if present, or shall fill the vacancy. Unless such provision is made, the first vice-president would preside or complete the president's term. It is also customary to provide in the bylaws for some method to fill a vacancy in the office of president-elect, should one occur between elections. It is important to consider these provisions with great care. The bylaws can assign the president-elect specific responsibilities.

47:23 **Vice-President.** In the absence of the president, or when for any reason the president vacates the chair (see 43:29, 47:11, 62:12–14), the vice-president serves in his stead (see the previous paragraph, however, regarding the usual duties of the president-elect in organizations that have one). Thus, it is important to elect a vice-president who is competent to perform the duties of president. When an assembly resolves itself into a committee of the whole, frequently it is the vice-president who is appointed to preside as committee chairman (see 52:2(a), 52:7).

47:24 When a vice-president is presiding over the assembly, he or she is addressed as "Mr. President" or "Madam President" (unless confusion might result—for example, when the president is also on the platform—in which case the form "Mr. Vice-President" or "Madam Vice-President" may be used).

47:25 Where the bylaws of a state, regional, or national society make the president of each constituent unit automatically a delegate to the society's convention, the vice-president of a unit serves as the president's alternate (see 58:12) and usually acts as vice-chairman of the unit's delegation (see 58:19).

47:26 If the bylaws provide that the president shall appoint all committees, this power does not transfer to a vice-president occupying the chair, even when the president is absent (see the second paragraph of 50:13(d)).

47:27 The president and vice-president may have occasion to make reports in connection with administrative duties prescribed in the society's bylaws or other rules (see 48:19). If the president has prepared a report but cannot attend the meeting at which it is to be presented, the vice-president should present it for him. But the vice-president cannot modify the president's report, or substitute a different one for it, simply because the president is absent.

47:28　　In case of the president's resignation, death, or removal, the vice-president automatically becomes president for the remainder of the term, unless the bylaws *expressly* provide otherwise for filling a vacancy *in the office of president* (see also 56:32).

47:29　　Some societies elect several vice-presidents in an order of precedence—first, second, third, and so on—in which case the highest-ranking one present has the duty of serving in place of the president when needed. In case of the president's resignation, death, or removal, the first vice-president then automatically becomes president (unless, as indicated above, the bylaws expressly provide otherwise for the office of president). Likewise, in case of any vice-president's resignation, death, or removal, or upon his or her automatic promotion to a higher office, the next-highest-ranking vice-president, if there is one, is automatically promoted (unless the bylaws expressly provide otherwise). Thus, for example, if the first vice-president resigns, the second vice-president becomes first vice-president, the third vice-president becomes second-vice-president, and so on, with the vacancy to be filled occurring in the lowest-ranking vice-presidency. A vice-president cannot decline to take the higher office to which he has been automatically promoted; if unable or unwilling to carry out the duties of the new office, his only recourse is then to submit his resignation, upon the acceptance of which he will no longer hold either office.

47:30　　Sometimes the bylaws provide that the different vice-presidents shall have administrative charge of different departments. In many such cases, it is inadvisable for the vice-presidents to have to change their duties whenever a vacancy occurs among them, and the bylaws should therefore also provide a method for filling vacancies that expressly applies to the offices of president and all vice-presidents.

47:31   Although in many instances the outgoing vice-president (or first vice-president) will be the logical nominee for president in the next term, the society has the freedom to make its own choice and to elect the most promising candidate at that particular time, unless stated otherwise in the bylaws (cf. *President-Elect*, above).

47:32 **Secretary.** The secretary is the recording officer of the assembly and the custodian of its records, except those specifically assigned to others, such as the treasurer's books. The recording officer is sometimes called the *clerk*, the *recording secretary* (when there is also, for example, a corresponding secretary or financial secretary), the *recorder*, or the *scribe*.

47:33 *Duties of the secretary.* The duties of the secretary are:

1) To keep a record of all the proceedings of the organization—usually called the *minutes*.
2) To keep on file all committee reports.
3) To keep the organization's official membership roll (unless another officer or staff member has this duty); and to call the roll where it is required.
4) To make the minutes and records available to members upon request (see 47:36).
5) To notify officers, committee members, and delegates of their election or appointment, to furnish committees with whatever documents are required for the performance of their duties, and to have on hand at each meeting a list of all existing committees and their members.
6) To furnish delegates with credentials.
7) To sign all certified copies of acts of the society.
8) To maintain record book(s) in which the bylaws, special rules of order, standing rules, and minutes are entered, with any amendments to these documents properly recorded, and to have the current record book(s) on hand at every meeting.
9) To send out to the membership any required notice of each meeting, known as the *call* of the meeting, and to

conduct the general correspondence of the organization—that is, correspondence that is not a function proper to other offices or to committees (see also *Corresponding Secretary* and *Executive Secretary,* below).

10) To prepare, prior to each meeting, an order of business (**41**) for the use of the presiding officer, showing in their exact order, under the correct headings, all matters known in advance that are due to come up and—if applicable—the times for which they are set.

11) In the absence of the president and vice-president, to call the meeting to order and preside until the immediate election of a chairman pro tem.

47:34   In the absence of the secretary, a secretary pro tem must be elected; the corresponding, financial, or executive secretary in organizations having such officers is not an automatic replacement. If, under "Reports of Officers" in the order of business, correspondence of an official character is to be read, it is normally read by the recording secretary and not by the corresponding secretary.

47:35   ***Records of the secretary.*** When written reports are received from boards or committees, the secretary records on them the date they were received and what further action was taken on them, and preserves them among his records. It is not necessary for an assembly to vote that a board or committee report be "placed on file," as that is done without a vote.

47:36   Any member has a right to examine these reports and the record book(s) referred to in 47:33(8), including the minutes of an executive session, at a reasonable time and place, but this privilege must not be abused to the annoyance of the secretary. Members are free to share their contents with others, except for any content protected by the secrecy of an executive session that has not been lifted (see 9:26). The same principles apply to records kept by boards and committees, these being accessible to members of the boards or committees (see also 49:17–19). When a committee requires certain records for the proper performance of its duties, the secretary turns them over to the committee chairman—after consulting with the president in any cases where he or she is in doubt. The corporation law of each state frequently provides for the availability of records of any group incorporated in that state.

47:37 **Corresponding Secretary.** In larger societies, the duties of issuing notices of meetings and conducting the general correspondence of the organization as described in 47:33(9) are frequently assigned to a separate elected officer, usually called the *corresponding secretary*. When there is a corresponding secretary, the unqualified word *secretary* used alone refers to the recording officer.

47:38 **Treasurer, and Financial Secretary.** The treasurer of an organization is the officer entrusted with the custody of its funds. The treasurer, and any other officers who handle funds of the society, should be bonded for a sum sufficient to protect the society from loss. The specific duties of the treasurer will vary depending on the size and complexity of the society; but this officer cannot disburse funds except by authority of the society or as the bylaws prescribe. The treasurer is required to make a full financial report annually or as the bylaws may prescribe, and to make such interim reports as the assembly or the executive board may direct. (For the suggested form of this annual report in simple cases, see 48:22ff.)

47:39 In ordinary societies, tasks incident to the collection of dues from members are a part of the treasurer's duties unless the bylaws provide otherwise. Much clerical work may be attached to this function, however, in large organizations, in societies where dues are payable in frequent installments, or in societies that suspend the voting-membership rights of members who fall in arrears in dues payments (see 1:13n3, 45:1, 56:19). In such cases some organizations have, in addition to the treasurer, a *financial secretary*—an officer whose usual duties are to bill members for their dues and to receive payment of them, to maintain a ledger of each member's account, and to turn over to the treasurer and obtain his receipt for moneys received.

47:40 **Other Officers.** In addition to the officers described above, an organization can provide in its bylaws for any other officers it may wish—including assistant officers. Officers sometimes included, and their usual duties, are:

- *Directors* (or *trustees*, or *managers*), who sit as members of the executive board (**49**)—usually in addition to the other officers—and perform such duties as the bylaws may require. In some organizations the term *trustees* refers to officers who perform the duties of elected auditors (see 48:25).

- A *historian*, who prepares a narrative account of the society's activities during his or her term of office, which, when approved by the assembly, will become a permanent part of the society's official history.

- A *librarian*, who, if the society possesses a collection of books or other written or printed matter, has custody of these items, and—subject to the society's direction—control over members' access to them.

- A *curator*, who serves as custodian of any objects of value that may belong to the society (other than library holdings).

- A *chaplain*, who recites or leads invocations and benedictions where such prayers are offered at the opening and closing of meetings or other events, and who—if a clergyman—serves the organization in that capacity in such manner as it may require.

- A *sergeant-at-arms* (or *warden*, or *warrant officer*, as sometimes called), who, on the floor of the meeting hall, assists in preserving order as the chair may direct. In a convention or large meeting this officer may have charge of the ushers. He may handle certain physical arrangements in the hall as well, such as being responsible in some cases for seeing that the furnishings are in proper order for each meeting. In a legislative or public body that has the power to penalize or compel the attendance of its members, the sergeant-at-arms may have the duty of serving warrants or notices of fines, or of arresting absent members in the event of a *Call of the House* (40:13–16).

- A *doorkeeper* or *guard*, who, in meetings where only members or some other limited category of persons are permitted to enter, checks the credentials or eligibility of those arriving, and denies entrance to unauthorized persons.

47:41 Directors should always be elected. The other officers mentioned above are usually elected also, but the bylaws can provide for their appointment.

47:42 **Honorary Officers (and Members).** An honorary office is in fact not an office but—like honorary membership—a complimentary title that may be bestowed on members or nonmembers. When it is desired to honor a nonmember, it is more usual to elect such a person to honorary membership. An honorary officer— for example, an honorary president or an honorary treasurer— is often elected at the time of retirement from the corresponding actual office, particularly when the person has filled it creditably for a long time. If there are to be honorary officers or honorary members, they must be authorized by the bylaws. Like an honorary degree conferred by a college or university, an honorary office or membership is perpetual—unless rescinded or unless its duration is limited by the bylaws. Rights carried with the honor include the right to attend meetings and to speak, but not to make motions or vote unless the person is also a regular member, or unless the bylaws provide full membership rights.[2] Honorary presidents and vice-presidents should sit on the platform, but they do not preside. An honorary office entails no duties and in no way conflicts with a member's holding a regular office or being assigned any duty whatever. It is not improper

---

2. Some societies provide in the bylaws for electing to "honorary life membership"—or even its automatic conferment upon—a person who has been an active member for a specified long period of years, sometimes with the added requirement that he shall have attained a certain age. The bylaws may prescribe that such an honorary member shall pay no dues but shall retain full voting privileges.

to include in the published list of honorary officers the names of those who are deceased, if that fact is clearly indicated.

Appointed Officers or Consultants

47:43   **Executive Secretary.**   The term *executive secretary,* or *executive director,* is usually applied to a salaried officer who devotes full time to the position of administrative officer and general manager of an organization, especially at the national, regional, or state level; and unless otherwise indicated the term is used in that sense in this book. In most organizations, the executive secretary is employed by the board of directors under contract, but in some this officer is elected by the convention.

47:44   *Duties of the executive secretary.*   The executive secretary is in charge of the central office of the society and acts under the immediate direction of the board and the executive committee, if there is one (see 49:13). He is sometimes ex officio the secretary of the executive committee (and sometimes of the board) and is responsible for seeing that the committee's instructions are carried out. He is expected to recommend plans of work and to conduct the day-to-day business of the organization. He is often responsible for the work that would otherwise be carried out by an elected corresponding secretary. He usually hires, fires, and determines the salaries of other staff members with the approval of the board or executive committee, which may regulate this function by adopting personnel policies. The bylaws should specify the duties of the executive secretary and should describe the manner in which he is to be selected, and for how long a term.

47:45   *Relationship to the president.*   The relationship between the office of executive secretary and that of president depends on the duties and authority of these officers as defined in the bylaws. In some organizations, the executive and managerial function that would otherwise be exercised by the president is entirely split off and vested in the executive secretary. This arrangement leaves the president his duties as presiding officer and spokesman for the organization. In any case, the president may not give orders to the executive secretary independently unless the bylaws so authorize; in the absence of such a provision, the executive secretary receives his direction from the board or executive committee.

47:46 **Parliamentarian.** The parliamentarian is a consultant, commonly a professional, who advises the president and other officers, committees, and members on matters of parliamentary procedure. The parliamentarian's role during a meeting is purely an advisory and consultative one—since parliamentary law gives to the chair alone the power to rule on questions of order or to answer parliamentary inquiries.

47:47 A small local organization should rarely require the services of a parliamentarian, unless it undertakes a general revision of its bylaws; but for large assemblies and conventions or organizations where the transaction of business is apt to be complex, it is advisable to engage one. Some state or national organizations find it advisable to employ a parliamentarian throughout the year to assist with any questions that may arise in interpreting bylaws and rules, or in connection with the work of the board and of officers or committees. In such a case, the parliamentarian's duties extend beyond giving opinions to the presiding officer during meetings, and may include assisting in the planning and steering of business to be introduced.

47:48 *Appointment of the parliamentarian.* If a parliamentarian is needed by an organization, the president should be free to appoint one in whom he has confidence. The board or society must approve any fee that will be required, however. If needed for only one meeting, a parliamentarian should be appointed as far as possible in advance of the meeting at which he is to serve, since his main work should be done outside the meeting.

47:49 *Duties of the parliamentarian.* The president, knowing in advance the business to come before the assembly, should confer with the parliamentarian before the meetings open, and during recesses, in order to anticipate any problems that may arise and to avoid, as much as possible, frequent consultation during the meetings. There is no set rule for the number of additional functions a parliamentarian may be asked to perform as a permanent appointee, such as teaching classes, holding office hours during conventions, and the like.

47:50 During a meeting the work of the parliamentarian should be limited to giving advice to the chair and, when requested, to any other member. It is also the duty of the parliamentarian—as inconspicuously as possible—to call the attention of the chair to any error in the proceedings that may affect the substantive rights of any member or may otherwise do harm.

47:51 There should be an understanding between the parliamentarian and the presiding officer that there will probably be occasions when it may be essential for the chair to listen to suggestions being made by the parliamentarian, even if it means momentarily not giving full attention to others or asking the assembly to *stand at ease* during the consultation (see 8:2(4), 23:3). This practice will enable the chair to be in a position to act promptly at the correct time and be fully informed. In advising the chair, the parliamentarian should not wait until asked for advice—that may be too late. An experienced parliamentarian will often see a problem developing and be able to head it off with a few words to the chair.

47:52 Only on the most involved matters should the parliamentarian actually be called upon to speak to the assembly; and the practice should be avoided if at all possible.

47:53 The parliamentarian should be assigned a seat next to the chair, so as to be convenient for consultation in a low voice, but the chair should try to avoid checking with the parliamentarian too frequently or too obviously.

47:54 After the parliamentarian has expressed an opinion on a point, the chair has the duty to make the final ruling and, in doing so, has the right to follow the advice of the parliamentarian or to disregard it. But if the parliamentarian's advice on important procedural issues is habitually disregarded, he may find it necessary, at the end of the present engagement or session, to resign.

47:55   A member of an assembly who acts as its parliamentarian has the same duty as the presiding officer to maintain a position of impartiality, and therefore does not make motions, participate in debate, or vote on any question except in the case of a ballot vote. He does not cast a deciding vote, even if his vote would affect the result, since that would interfere with the chair's prerogative of doing so. If a member feels that he cannot properly forgo these rights in order to serve as parliamentarian, he should not accept that position. Unlike the presiding officer, the parliamentarian cannot temporarily relinquish his position in order to exercise such rights on a particular motion.

47:56   Regarding the duties of the parliamentarian in connection with a convention, see also 59:9.

Vacancies

47:57   The power to appoint or elect persons to any office or board carries with it the power to accept their resignations, and also the power to fill any vacancy occurring in it, unless the bylaws expressly provide otherwise. In the case of a society whose bylaws confer upon its executive board full power and authority over the society's affairs between meetings of the society's assembly (as in the example in 56:43) without reserving to the society itself the exclusive right to fill vacancies, the executive board is empowered to accept resignations and fill vacancies between meetings of the society's assembly. For particular vacancies, see 47:22 (president-elect), and 47:28–30 and 56:32 (president and vice-presidents). See also 13:23 (vacancies in a committee).

47:58   Notice of filling a vacancy in an office (including a vacancy in an executive board or executive committee) must always be given to the members of the body that will elect the person to fill it, unless the bylaws or special rules of order clearly provide otherwise.

§48. MINUTES AND REPORTS OF OFFICERS

Minutes

48:1   The official record of the proceedings of a deliberative assembly is usually called the *minutes,* or sometimes—particularly in legislative bodies—the *journal.* The minutes should be kept in a substantial book or binder.

48:2   **Content of the Minutes.** In an ordinary society, the minutes should contain mainly a record of what was *done* at the meeting, not what was *said* by the members. The minutes must never reflect the secretary's opinion, favorable or otherwise, on anything said or done.

48:3   To modify the rules governing what is regularly to be included in the minutes requires adoption of a special rule of order, although a majority vote may direct the inclusion of specific additional information in the minutes of a particular meeting.

48:4   The *first paragraph* of the minutes should contain the following information (which need not, however, be divided into numbered or separated items directly corresponding to those below):

    1) the kind of meeting: regular, special, adjourned regular, or adjourned special;

    2) the name of the society or assembly;

    3) the date and time of the meeting, and the place, if it is not always the same;

    4) the fact that the regular chairman and secretary were present or, in their absence, the names of the persons who substituted for them; and

    5) whether the minutes of the previous meeting were read and approved—as read, or as corrected—and the date of that meeting if it was other than a regular business meeting. Any correction approved by the assembly is made in the text of the minutes being approved; the minutes of the meeting making the correction merely state that the

minutes were approved "as corrected," without specifying what the correction was (see first paragraph of form, 48:8).

The body of the minutes should contain a *separate paragraph for each subject matter*, and should show:

6) all main motions (**10**) or motions to bring a main question again before the assembly (6:25–27; **34–37**) that were made or taken up—except, normally, any that were withdrawn[3]—stating:

a) the wording in which each motion was adopted or otherwise disposed of (with the facts as to whether the motion may have been debated or amended before disposition being mentioned only parenthetically); and

b) the disposition of the motion, including—if it was *temporarily* disposed of (9:7–11, 38:8)—any primary and secondary amendments and all adhering secondary motions that were then pending;

7) secondary motions that were not lost or withdrawn, in cases where it is necessary to record them for completeness or clarity—for example, motions to *Recess* or to *Fix the Time to Which to Adjourn* (among the privileged motions), or motions to *Suspend the Rules* or grant a *Request to Be Excused from a Duty* (among the incidental motions), generally only alluding to the adoption of such motions, however, as "… the matter having been advanced in the agenda on motion of …" or "… a ballot vote having been ordered, the tellers …";

---

3. There may be certain instances in which a main motion is withdrawn under circumstances that require some mention in the minutes. In such a case, only as much information should be included in the minutes as is needed to reflect the necessary details clearly. For example, if, at one meeting, a main motion was made *the* special order for the next meeting (41:57), or a main motion was postponed after lengthy consideration to a meeting at which it was withdrawn by consent, action at the first meeting should always be recorded, and the withdrawal at the second meeting should be stated for completeness of the minutes.

8) the complete substance of oral committee reports that are permitted to be given in small assemblies in particular cases as provided in 51:60–62;

9) all notices of motions (10:44–51);

10) all points of order and appeals, whether sustained or lost, together with the reasons given by the chair for his or her ruling; and

11) the declaration by the chair in "naming" an offending member as a part of disciplinary procedures, as well as any disorderly words that led to such naming and that the chair directed the secretary to take down (see 61:12–14).

The *last paragraph* should state:

12) the hour of adjournment.

48:5   Additional rules and practices relating to the content of the minutes are the following:

1) The name of the maker of a main motion should be entered in the minutes, but the name of the seconder should not be entered unless ordered by the assembly.

2) a) When a count has been ordered, the number of votes on each side is entered, unless the vote was on a motion that would not otherwise be entered in the minutes.

     b) When the voting is by ballot, the full tellers' report (45:37–40) is entered.

     c) When the voting is by roll call, the names of those voting on each side and those answering "present," as well as the total number in each category, are entered. If members who are present fail to respond on a roll-call vote, enough of their names must be recorded as present to reflect that a quorum was present at the time of the vote. If the chair voted, no special mention of this fact is made in the minutes.

3) The proceedings of a committee of the whole, or a quasi committee of the whole, are not entered in the minutes, but the fact that the assembly went into committee of the

whole (or into quasi committee) and the committee report is recorded (see **52**).

4) When a question is considered informally, the same information is recorded as under the regular rules, since the only informality in the proceedings is in the debate.

5) When a committee report is of great importance or should be recorded to show the legislative history of a measure, the assembly can order it "to be entered in the minutes," in which case the secretary copies it in full in, or attaches a copy of it to, the minutes.

6) The name and subject of a guest speaker can be given, but no effort should be made to summarize his remarks.

48:6   The use by the secretary of a recording device can be of great benefit in preparing the minutes, but a transcription from it should never be used as the minutes themselves.

48:7   **The Signature.** Minutes should be signed by the secretary and can also be signed, if the assembly wishes, by the president. The words *Respectfully submitted*—although occasionally used—represent an older practice that is not essential in signing the minutes.

48:8   **Form of the Minutes.** The principles stated above are illustrated in the following model form for minutes:

> The regular monthly meeting of the L.M. Society was held on Thursday, January 4, 20___, at 8:30 P.M., at the Society's building, the President being in the chair and the Secretary being present. The minutes of the last meeting were read and approved as corrected.
>
> The Treasurer reported the receipt of a bill from the Downs Construction Company in the amount of $5,000 for the improvements recently made in the Society's building. The question put by the chair "that the bill be paid" was adopted.
>
> Mr. Johnson, reporting on behalf of the Membership Committee, moved "that John R. Brown be admitted to membership in the Society." The motion was adopted after debate.

The report of the Program Committee was received and placed on file.

The special committee that was appointed to investigate and report on suitable parking facilities near the Society's building reported, through its chairman, Mrs. Smith, a resolution, which, after debate and amendment, was adopted as follows: "*Resolved,* That … [its exact words immediately before being acted upon, incorporating all amendments]."

The resolution relating to the use of the Society's library by nonmembers, which was postponed from the last meeting, was then taken up. This motion and a pending amendment were laid on the table after the chair announced that the guest speaker had received a phone message which would require his early departure.

The President introduced the guest speaker, Mr. James F. Mitchell, whose subject was _____.

At the conclusion of Mr. Mitchell's talk, the resolution relating to the use of the Society's library by nonmembers was taken from the table. After amendment and further debate, the resolution was adopted as follows: "*Resolved,* That … [its exact wording immediately before being finally voted on]."

Mr. Gordon moved "that the Society undertake the establishment of a summer camp for boys on its lakefront property." Mrs. Thomas moved to amend this motion by inserting the word "underprivileged" before "boys." On motion of Mr. Dorsey, the motion to establish the camp, with the pending amendment, was referred to a committee of three to be appointed by the chair with instructions to report at the next meeting. The chair appointed Messrs. Flynn, Dorsey, and Fine to the committee.

The meeting adjourned at 10:05 P.M.

Margaret Duffy, Secretary

48:9 **Approval of the Minutes.** In an organization that holds regular meetings at frequent intervals, such as weekly, monthly, or quarterly, the minutes of each regular or special meeting are normally read and approved at the beginning of the next regular meeting, immediately after the call to order and any opening ceremonies. A special meeting does not approve minutes of a previous session unless the meeting was called for that purpose, which is not ordinarily the case. In a session lasting longer than one day, the minutes of meetings held the preceding day are read and approved at the beginning of each day's business after the first. In particular, an adjourned meeting of an ordinary society approves the minutes of the meeting that established the adjourned meeting; its own minutes are approved at the next adjourned or regular meeting, whichever occurs first.

48:10 Procedures for the reading, correction, and approval of minutes at a meeting are shown in 41:9–12.

48:11 If the assembly does not wish to carry out the reading and approval of the minutes at the regular time, it may, by majority vote without debate, "dispense with the reading of the minutes." The minutes can then be taken up by majority vote without debate at any later time during the meeting while no business is pending, under the same rules as those governing *Take from the Table* (**34**). If the minutes are not thus taken up before adjournment, they are read and approved at the following meeting, before the later minutes are taken up. A motion to "dispense with the reading of the minutes" is not a request to omit their reading altogether; it can be made at any time while the minutes are actually pending for approval regardless of whether the minutes have already been read or corrected in some respect.

48:12 Exceptions to the rule that minutes are approved at the next regular meeting (or at the next meeting within the session) arise when the next meeting will not be held within a quarterly time interval, when the term of a specified portion of the membership will expire before the start of the next meeting, or when, as at the final meeting of a convention, the assembly will be dissolved at the close of the present meeting. In any of these cases, minutes that have not been approved previously should be approved before final adjournment, or the assembly should authorize the executive board or a special committee to approve the minutes. The fact that the minutes are not read for approval at the next meeting does not prevent a member from having a relevant excerpt read for information; nor does it prevent the assembly in such a case from making additional corrections, treating the minutes as having been previously approved (see 48:15).

48:13 Minutes of an executive session may be read and approved only in executive session, as described in 9:26–27. Common practices when approving minutes at a convention are discussed in 59:55(9).

48:14 When the minutes are approved, the word *Approved*, with the secretary's initials (or the signature of the chairman of the approving committee) and the date, should be written below them. If the minutes are approved with corrections, the secretary should prepare a fully corrected version and distribute copies to the members as well as placing it in the minute book. (As noted in 48:4(5) all such corrections should be incorporated in the minutes to which they pertain, and not in the minutes of the meeting making the corrections.)

48:15 If the existence of an error or material omission in the minutes becomes reasonably established after their approval—even many years later—the minutes can then be corrected by means of the motion to *Amend Something Previously Adopted* (**35**), which requires a two-thirds vote, or a majority vote with notice, or the vote of a majority of the entire membership, or unanimous consent. In such a case the content of the original minutes must not be altered, although it may be advisable for the secretary to make a marginal notation indicating the corrected text or referring to the minutes of the meeting at which the correction was adopted. The minutes of the latter meeting must include the full text of the motion to *Amend Something Previously Adopted*, which necessarily includes all information required to construct an accurate record of the actions taken at the earlier meeting.

48:16 **Publication of an Assembly's Proceedings.** Sometimes a society wishes to have a full record of its proceedings made available to the public, and when such a record of the proceedings is to be published (in which case it is often called "proceedings," "transactions," or the like), it frequently contains, in addition to the information described above for inclusion in the minutes, a list of the speakers on each side of every question, with an abstract or the text of each address. In such cases the secretary should have an assistant. When it is desired, as in some conventions, to publish the proceedings in full, the secretary's assistant should be a stenographic reporter or recording technician. The presiding officer should then take particular care that everyone to whom he assigns the floor is fully identified. Under these conditions it is usually necessary to require members to use a public-address system. Reports of committees should be printed exactly as submitted, the record showing what action was taken by the assembly in regard to them; or they can be printed with all additions in italics and parts struck out enclosed in brackets, in which case a note to that effect should precede the report or resolution. Any such record or transcript of the proceedings prepared for publication, however, does not take the place of the minutes, and it is the minutes which comprise the official record of the assembly's proceedings.

Reports of Officers

48:17 In principle, all reports of officers in a society are incident to administrative duties that these officers have by virtue of provisions in the bylaws or other rules. Strictly speaking, in a purely deliberative assembly, the officers make no reports.

48:18 In an organized society, the bylaws may require each of the principal officers to make a report of the year's work at the annual meeting (**9**). At any meeting at which officers' reports are made, they immediately follow the reading and approval of the minutes.

48:19 **Reports of Executive Officers.** In addition to their annual reports, the president and vice-president from time to time may wish or need to report on their activities in connection with administrative duties. Such reports are usually for purposes of information only, but may sometimes contain recommendations calling for action by the assembly. In either case, the reports should generally conform to the rules as to form, substance, and disposition that govern committee reports (**51**). Motions to adopt or implement any recommendations should be made from the floor by a member *other than the reporting officer.*

48:20 **Reports by the Treasurer.** At each meeting of a society, the chair may ask for a "Treasurer's report," which may consist simply of a verbal statement of the cash balance on hand—or of this balance less outstanding obligations. Such a report requires no action by the assembly.

48:21 In addition, the treasurer is required to make a full financial report annually, and in some societies more often. Such an annual report should always be audited. It is compiled and dated as of the last day of the fiscal year, if there is one, or December 31 if no different financial year is stated in the bylaws.

48:22 *Form and content of the financial report.* The best form for the financial report depends on particular conditions, such as the kind and size of the society, the nature of its activities, the frequency of reporting, and so on. The form used should be patterned after reports in similar organizations. In any case, since the financial report is made for the information of the members, it should not contain details of dates and separate payments, which are a hindrance to the report's being understood.

48:23 The brief model report below is in a form suitable for most small societies whose financial affairs are simple and primarily involve cash. In organizations whose finances are more involved, a double-entry set of books may be advisable or required. Such a system should be set up with the assistance of an accountant, and the report would normally consist of a balance sheet showing the society's assets, liabilities, and fund balance (or members' equity) as well as an income statement similar to the report below without the opening and closing cash balances. Other statements may be included as needed, such as a statement of changes in members' equity, a statement of sources and application of funds, and a cash forecast. This system may be on a cash or an accrual basis and will usually require review or audit by an accountant.

REPORT OF THE TREASURER OF THE L.M. SOCIETY
FOR THE YEAR ENDING DECEMBER 31, 20____

Balance on hand January 1, 20___ $1,253.25

Receipts
  Members' Dues $630.00
  Proceeds from Spring Barbecue   296.75
  Fines   12.00

  Total Receipts   938.75

  Total $2,192.00

Disbursements
  Rent of Hall $500.00
  Custodial Service Fees   175.00
  Stationery and Printing   122.40
  Postage   84.00

  Total Disbursements $ 881.40

Balance on hand December 31, 20___   1,310.60

  Total $2,192.00

                                             Richard Larson, Treasurer

Audited and found correct.
  Colleen Burke
  Randolph Schuler
    Auditing Committee

48:24   *Action on the financial report.* No action of acceptance by the assembly is required—or proper—on a financial report of the treasurer unless it is of sufficient importance, as an annual report, to be referred to auditors. In the latter case it is the auditors' report which the assembly accepts. The treasurer's financial report should therefore be prepared long enough in advance for the audit to be completed before the report is made at a meeting of the society.

48:25   When the amounts involved are very large and the reports complicated, or the organization's contributors or others require it, it is desirable to have the audits made by independent certified accountants. But in ordinary societies and those in which the expense of a professional cannot be justified, it is practical to have the financial reports audited by an auditing committee of two or more members of the society—appointed in advance if there is not a standing auditing committee. In some organizations the financial reports are audited by elected officers known as "trustees." Where professional examination is desired but the organization does not require a full audit, a "review" (as distinct from a mere "compilation") by an accountant may supply sufficient testing and verification to satisfy the organization. If the auditors' report consists only of an endorsement on the financial report—to the effect that it has been found correct, as shown in the model above—the treasurer can simply read out this certification as he concludes the presentation of his own report. After the treasurer has made his report to the assembly (and after any detailed report presented by the chairman of the auditing committee, if it is needed), the chair states the question on adopting the *auditors'* report. The adoption of the auditors' report has the effect of relieving the treasurer of responsibility for the period covered by his report, except in case of fraud.

48:26   If the treasurer presents an unaudited annual report or other financial report that the bylaws require to be audited, and if there is a standing auditing committee or if auditors have already been chosen in some other manner, the chair, without waiting for a motion when the treasurer has finished reading his report, immediately says, "The report is referred to the Auditing Committee [or "to the auditors," or "to the Trustees for audit"]." If no auditors have been chosen, the proper procedure is to adopt a motion to refer the report to an auditing committee to be appointed by one of the methods described in **50**.

48:27   **Reports of Other Officers.** Other officers as may be prescribed in the bylaws, such as a historian or a librarian, may also have occasion to report to the assembly. These reports are usually made annually and, like those of the executive officers, are generally for purposes of information only. They can, however, contain recommendations upon which it is hoped the assembly will act. If the report is to become a permanent official document of the organization, it must be formally adopted by the assembly. Thus, for example, historical accounts prepared by the historian do not become part of the official history of the society until the assembly formally adopts them, with any desired changes, after their presentation by the historian.

XVI

BOARDS AND COMMITTEES

§49. BOARDS

49:1   The essential characteristics of a *board* are stated in 1:22–23. All of the material under the heading *Types of Deliberative Assembly* in 1:9–23 should be read in connection with this section.

49:2   The authority by which a board is constituted commonly prescribes the times at which it shall hold regular meetings, and the procedure by which special meetings of the board can be called; or the board can establish such provisions to the extent that it has the authority to adopt its own rules (see 49:15).

The Executive Board of an Organized Society

49:3   Except in the simplest and smallest local societies, or those holding very frequent regular meetings, it is generally found advisable to provide in the bylaws for a board to be empowered to act for the society when necessary between its regular meetings, and in some cases to have complete control over certain phases of the society's business. Such a board is usually known as the *executive board,* or—in organizations where there is an executive committee within and subordinate to the board as described below—the *board of directors, board of managers,* or *board of trustees.* Any such body is referred to in this book as an executive board, however—regardless of whether there is an executive committee—in cases where the distinction is immaterial.

49:4   If a society is to have an executive board, the bylaws should specify the number of board members and how they are to be determined, should define the board's duties and powers, and should make provision for meetings of the board as stated above. An executive board commonly consists of those of the society's officers (**47**) who also have duties apart from the board, together with a number of directors, managers, or trustees who may or may not have other duties such as the chairmanship of important standing committees (**50**). (See Sample Bylaws, Article IV, Section 1 (56:62) and Article VI, Section 1 (56:64).) The directors usually should be elected in the same way and at the same time as the other officers of the society. Frequently it is provided that a specified percentage of the directors shall be chosen periodically in such a way that their terms of office overlap those of the others—as when, for example, there are six directors and it is provided that two shall be elected at each annual meeting for three-year terms.

49:5   A society has no executive board, nor can its officers act as a board, except as the bylaws may provide; and when so established, the board has only such power as is delegated to it by the bylaws or by vote of the society's assembly referring individual matters to it.

49:6   The amount of regular power delegated to an executive board under the bylaws varies considerably from one organization to another. If the society as a whole usually meets less often than within quarterly time intervals (9:7), or if its main purpose is other than to transact business, the entire administrative authority of the society is best left to the board between the society's meetings. Usually in organizations meeting monthly or oftener, and sometimes in those meeting quarterly, the board is not given so much power, since the society can attend to much of its business at its regular meetings. (For appropriate wordings for the governing provision in the bylaws in each of these two cases, see 56:43, 56:64(2).)

49:7   In any event, no action of the board can alter or conflict with any decision made by the assembly of the society, and any such action of the board is null and void (see 56:41 and 23:9). Except in matters placed by the bylaws exclusively under the control of the board, the society's assembly can give the board instructions which it must carry out, and can rescind or amend any action of the board if it is not too late (see **35**). It should be noted, however, that exactly the opposite condition prevails in connection with boards of business corporations, in which the board has exclusive power and authority to operate the business.

Ex-Officio Board Members

49:8   Frequently boards include ex-officio members—that is, persons who are members of the board by virtue of an office or committee chairmanship held in the society, or in the parent state or national society or federation or some allied group; or—sometimes in boards outside of organized societies—by virtue of a public office. In the executive board of a society, if the ex-officio member of the board is under the authority of the society (that is, if he is a member, an employee, or an elected or appointed officer of the society), there is no distinction between him and the other board members. If the ex-officio member is not under the authority of the society, he has all the privileges of board membership, including the right to make motions and to vote, but none of the obligations—just as in a case, for example, where the governor of a state is ex officio a trustee of a private academy. The latter class of ex-officio board member, who has no obligation to participate, is not counted in determining the number required for a quorum or whether a quorum is present at a meeting. Whenever an ex-officio board member is also ex officio an officer of the board, he of course has the obligation to serve as a regular working member and is therefore counted in the quorum.

49:9   When an ex-officio member of a board ceases to hold the office that entitles him to such membership, his membership on the board terminates automatically.

49:10   Concerning ex-officio members of committees, including the president, see 50:16.

Officers of Boards

49:11   A board that is not an instrumentality of a parent assembly or membership body is organized as any deliberative assembly, with a chairman[1] or president, a secretary, and other officers as may be needed. In general, such a board elects its own officers if the authority under which the board is constituted makes no other provision as to how the officers are to be determined. A board that is to elect its officers should meet for this purpose as soon as possible after the selection of its members (see also 49:22). In ordinary societies having executive boards, on the other hand, the president and the secretary of the society serve in the same capacities within the board (and the executive committee, if there is one), unless the bylaws provide otherwise.

Bodies Subordinate to a Board

49:12   As a general principle, a board cannot delegate its authority—that is, it cannot empower a subordinate group to act independently in its name—except as may be authorized by the bylaws (of the *society*) or other instrument under which the board is constituted; but any board can appoint committees to work under its supervision or according to its specific instructions. Such committees *of the board* always report *to the board*.

49:13   **Executive Committee.** In a society where the board is large or its members must travel from a distance to meet, it is usual for the bylaws to establish an *executive committee* composed of a specified number of board members, which shall have all or much of the power of the board between meetings (just as the board has all or much of the power of the society between the society's meetings), but which cannot alter any decision made by the board (just as the board cannot alter any decision made by the society). The executive committee is thus in reality a "board within a board" and operates under the rules in this

---

1. See 3:10 regarding variations of this term that have come into use.

book applicable to boards rather than those applicable to committees. Usually the membership of the executive committee is specified in the bylaws, rather than being left to the choice of the full board. It is advisable that the executive committee be small and, unless it has been authorized to conduct electronic meetings (see 9:30–36), that its members live near enough to each other to be able to hold frequent regular meetings and also special meetings when necessary. The executive secretary, if there is one, should work closely with the executive committee, but should be appointed by the parent body or at least by the board. A board cannot appoint an executive committee unless the bylaws so authorize.

49:14 **Committees of a Board.** Where an organization is local—for example, a society for sustaining a foster home for children—the executive board usually divides itself into committees having charge of different branches of the work during the interval between the monthly or quarterly meetings of the board. At the board meetings these committees report on the fulfillment of their assigned responsibilities. In such cases the committees are genuinely subordinate to the board and must ordinarily report back to it for authority to act (in contrast to an executive committee, which usually has power to act as the board, and in contrast to standing committees of the *society*, which are not subordinate to the board unless made so by a provision in the bylaws). Any board can appoint committees of the kind just described without authorization in the bylaws.

Conduct of Business in Boards

49:15 **General Procedure.** The executive board of an organized society operates under the society's bylaws, the society's parliamentary authority, and any special rules of order or standing rules of the society which may be applicable to it. Such a board may adopt its own special rules of order or standing rules only to the extent that such rules do not conflict with any of the rules of the society listed above. It may protect itself against breaches of order by its members during board meetings, and against annoyance by nonmembers, by employing the procedures outlined in 61:10–21, but the maximum penalty which may be imposed upon a disorderly member of the board is that he be required to leave the meeting room during the remainder of the meeting. A board that is not a part of a society can adopt its own rules, provided that they do not conflict with anything in the legal instrument under which the board is constituted.

49:16 Under the general parliamentary law, business is transacted in large boards according to the same rules of procedure as in other deliberative assemblies. In smaller boards, these rules apply as far as practicable, with the exceptions noted below. In any case, a board can transact business only in a regular or properly called meeting of which every board member has been sent any required notice (see 9:2–5, 9:13–16)—or at an adjournment of one of these meetings[2]—and at which a quorum (see 40:5) is present. The personal approval of a proposed action obtained separately by telephone, by individual interviews, or in writing, even from every member of the board, is not the approval of the board, since the members lacked the opportunity to mutually debate and decide the matter as a deliberative body. (See also *Electronic Meetings*, 9:30–36.)

49:17 A record of the board's proceedings is kept by the secretary, just as in any other assembly. Only members of the board have the right to examine the minute book kept by the secretary (cf. 47:36), unless the board orders otherwise (see next paragraph). Board members are, however, free to share the content of the minutes with others, except for any content protected by the secrecy of an executive session that has not been lifted (see 9:26–27).

49:18 The board can order that any specified person(s)—including, for example, all members of the society—be permitted to

---

2. For an adjourned meeting (9:17–19), no additional notice is required—except, of course, when it is to meet at the call of the chair rather than at a specified time—although it is desirable to give such notice if feasible.

view, or be furnished with copies of, board minutes. A motion to do so is an incidental main motion, which can be adopted by a majority vote if the minutes are not protected by executive-session secrecy. If they are protected by such secrecy, the motion requires a two-thirds vote, the vote of a majority of the entire membership of the board, or a majority vote if previous notice has been given.

49:19   Whether or not board minutes are protected by the secrecy of an executive session, the assembly of the society can adopt a motion granting such permission, or can order that the board's minutes be produced and read at a meeting of the assembly, by a two-thirds vote, the vote of a majority of the entire member-ship of the assembly, or a majority vote if previous notice has been given.

49:20   At regular board meetings the executive committee, if there is one, should be required to make a report of its activities since the last board meeting. No action need be taken on this report, which is generally intended as information only.

49:21   **Procedure in Small Boards.** In a board meeting where there are not more than about a dozen members present, some of the formality that is necessary in a large assembly would hin-der business. The rules governing such meetings are different from the rules that hold in other assemblies, in the following respects:

1) Members may raise a hand instead of standing when seeking to obtain the floor, and may remain seated while making motions or speaking.

2) Motions need not be seconded.

3) There is no limit to the number of times a member can speak to a debatable question.[3] Appeals, however, are debat-able under the regular rules—that is, each member (except

---

3. However, motions to close or limit debate (**15, 16**), including motions to limit the number of times a member can speak to a question, are in order even in meetings of a small board (but not in meetings of a committee; see 50:25), although occasions where they are necessary or appropriate may be rarer than in larger assemblies.

the chair) can speak only once in debate on them, while the chair may speak twice.

4) Informal discussion of a subject is permitted while no motion is pending.

5) When a proposal is perfectly clear to all present, a vote can be taken without a motion's having been introduced. Unless agreed to by unanimous consent, however, all proposed actions must be approved by vote under the same rules as in larger meetings, except that a vote can be taken initially by a show of hands, which is often a better method in small meetings.

6) The chairman need not rise while putting questions to a vote.

7) If the chairman is a member, he may, without leaving the chair, speak in informal discussions and in debate, and vote on all questions.[4]

49:22 **Effect of Periodic Partial Change in Board Membership.** In cases where a board is constituted so that a specified portion of its membership is chosen periodically (as, for example, where one third of the board is elected annually for three-year terms), it becomes, in effect, a new board each time such a group assumes board membership. Consequently, when the outgoing portion of the board vacates membership, all matters temporarily but not finally disposed of (see 9:8–11, 38:8), except those that remain in the hands of a committee to which they have been referred, fall to the ground under provision (c) in 21:7. (See also 50:30, regarding the continuity of matters that have been referred to a special committee appointed by the board.) If the board is one that elects its own officers or appoints standing committees, it chooses new officers and committees as soon as the new board members have taken up their duties, just as if the entire board membership had changed.

---

4. Informal discussion may be initiated by the chairman himself, which, in effect, enables the chairman to submit his own proposals without formally making a motion as described in 4:4–8 (although he has the right to make a motion if he wishes).

The individual replacement of persons who may occasionally vacate board membership at other times, however, does not have these effects.

§50. COMMITTEES

50:1   A committee, as understood in parliamentary law, is a body of one or more persons, elected or appointed by (or by direction of) an assembly or society, to consider, investigate, or take action on certain matters or subjects, or to do all of these things. Unlike a board, a committee is not itself considered to be a form of assembly.

50:2   Although the term *committee* commonly implies a relatively small number of persons appointed to give a task more detailed attention than is possible in a body the size of the assembly, this characteristic more accurately describes what are known as *ordinary committees.* An assembly can also designate all of its members present to act as a committee, which is called a *committee of the whole* and is distinguished from an ordinary committee. In large assemblies, the use of a committee of the whole is a convenient method of considering a question when it is desired to allow each member to speak an unlimited number of times in debate. Committees of the whole are treated separately in **52**. The statements in this section apply principally to ordinary committees.

50:3   Ordinary committees are of two types—*standing committees* (which have a continuing existence) and *special committees* (which go out of existence as soon as they have completed a specified task).

50:4   Generally the term *committee* implies that, within the area of its assigned responsibilities, the committee has less authority to act independently for the society (or other constituting power) than a board is usually understood to have. Thus, if the committee is to do more than report its findings or recommendations to the assembly, it may be empowered to act for the society only on specific instructions; or, if it is given standing powers, its actions may be more closely subject to review than a board's, or it may be required to report more fully. Also, unlike most boards, a committee in general does not have regular meeting times established by rule; but meetings of the committee are called as stated in 50:21–22. Some standing committees, however—particularly in large state or national organizations—function virtually in the manner of boards, although not designated as such.

50:5 When a committee is appointed "with power," this means with power to take all the steps necessary to carry out its instructions.

50:6 In large assemblies or those doing a great volume of business, much of the preliminary work in the preparation of subjects for consideration is usually done by committees. In many such bodies, in fact, it is advisable to have every main question go to a committee before final action on it is taken by the assembly.

50:7 *Standing committees* are constituted to perform a continuing function, and remain in existence permanently or for the life of the assembly that establishes them. In an ordinary society, the members of such a committee serve for a term corresponding to that of the officers, or until their successors have been chosen, unless the bylaws or other rules otherwise expressly provide. Thus, a new body of committee members is normally appointed at the beginning of each administration.

50:8 A standing committee must be constituted by name (a) by a specific provision of the bylaws or (b) by a resolution which is in effect a special rule of order and therefore requires for its adoption either previous notice and a two-thirds vote or a vote of a majority of the entire membership, if any of the following conditions are to apply:

- if the committee is to have standing authority to act for the society on matters of a certain class without specific instructions from the assembly;
- if all business of a certain class is to be automatically referred to the committee; or

- if some other rule of parliamentary procedure is affected by the committee's assigned function.

50:9   If a standing committee's assigned function does not affect a rule of parliamentary procedure in any of these three ways, it can be established by a standing rule adopted by a majority vote without notice, although, even in such a case, the committee is frequently constituted by name in the bylaws as indicated above. If certain standing committees are enumerated in the by-laws, no standing committee aside from those enumerated can be established without amending the bylaws, unless the bylaws also include a provision authorizing the creation of additional standing committees (see also 56:44–48). A standing commit-tee of a society reports to the assembly of the society, and not to the executive board or board of directors, unless the bylaws provide otherwise. In some societies, standing committees in ef-fect have charge of certain branches of the organization's work, in which case these committees are really in the nature of boards.

50:10   A *special* (*select,* or *ad hoc*) *committee* is a committee ap-pointed, as the need arises, to carry out a specified task, at the completion of which—that is, on presentation of its final report to the assembly—it automatically ceases to exist. A special com-mittee may not be appointed to perform a task that falls within the assigned function of an existing standing committee.

Appointment of Committees

50:11   **Methods of Appointment.** In an assembly or organization that has not prescribed in its bylaws or rules how the members of its committees shall be selected, the method can be decided by unanimous consent or by majority vote at the time the com-mittee is appointed, as described in 13:13; or (in the case of a special committee) the method can be specified in the motion to establish the committee. The power to appoint a committee carries with it the power to appoint the chairman and to fill any vacancy that may arise in the committee. The two paragraphs headed *Designating the Committee Chairman,* 13:17–18, should be read in connection with the five methods of appointing a committee described below.

50:12   It is possible for persons who are not members of the assembly or the society to be appointed to committees—even to the position of committee chairman—but control over each such appointment is reserved to the assembly in the individual case. From this principle, it follows that, referring to these five methods of appointment, non–assembly members may be appointed to committees by methods (a), (b), (c), and (e), as listed below. When method (d) is used and the chair appoints either a standing or a special committee, however, the governing rule regarding the appointment of non–assembly members is as stated under *Naming Members to a Special Committee*, in 13:15–16.

50:13   Methods by which committees can be appointed are as follows:

a) *Election by ballot.* This method is principally applicable to important standing committees having extensive powers. Under this procedure, nominations for committee membership can be made by any of the methods described in **46**; then the nominees are voted on by ballot just as in an election of a board, a majority vote being necessary to elect. In the event that more, or less, than the required number receive a majority, places on the committee are filled as explained in 46:33. If it is the assembly's practice—or its wish in the particular case—to select the committee chairman (rather than leave it to the committee to do so; cf. 13:18), the chairmanship can be treated as a separate position to be voted for on the same ballot with the other committee members; or, in a smaller assembly, if preferred, the chairman can be elected from among the committee's members on a second ballot, after their names have been announced.

b) *Nominations from the floor (open nominations) with viva-voce election* (usually called simply "nominations from the floor"). This is a common method of appointing members to a committee when the assembly wishes to reserve the selection to itself without requiring secrecy in the voting. When this method has been decided upon, the chair says, "Members will please nominate," or, "Nominations for the committee are now in order." The chair announces each nomination as he hears it, as shown in 46:8. No one has a right to nominate more than one person to membership on the committee until every other member has had an opportunity to nominate a candidate; and thus the nomination of more than one person at a time by a single member can be entertained only by unanimous consent.

If no more than the prescribed number of committee members are nominated, a vote is unnecessary since the fact that no more than the required number are nominated shows that there is unanimous consent that the committee should consist of these persons, which the chair declares as follows: "Messrs. A, B, and C, Mrs. D, and Mrs. E are nominated. Are there any further nominations? … Since there are no further nominations, the committee is composed of the persons just named [or he repeats the names if he feels it advisable]."

If there are more nominees than the required number of committee members, then, when there are no further nominations, the chair repeats all of the names in the order in which they were nominated, and in the same order puts the question on the election of each nominee—one at a time until the proper number have been elected—as described for viva-voce elections (46). For reasons explained in 46:37–39, those nominated last in such a case have less chance of being elected.

After the selection of committee members has been completed, the assembly can elect a committee chairman from among them, if desired; or a chairman can be elected separately, first.

c) *Nominations by the chair* (with confirmation by voice vote). This method is used when the assembly wishes to take advantage of the chair's knowledge and judgment as to suitable appointees, yet wishes to have veto power. In this case, the chair names the same number of persons as there are to be members of the committee, always naming his choice of committee chairman first, thus: "The chair nominates Mr. X as chairman, Mrs. Y, and Mr. Z.[5] The question is: Shall these persons constitute the committee?" Any member can then move to strike out one or more names—but not to insert new ones, which the chair must do if such a motion to strike out is adopted. After any changes in the original names have thus been made, the chair repeats the proposed names as they stand and puts the question on the entire list: "Mr. X, Mrs. Y, and Mr. W are nominated. Those in favor of these persons constituting the committee, say *aye*. … Those opposed, say *no*. … , etc."

d) *Appointment by the chair.* In the absence of special conditions, appointment of committees by the chair, or by the regular presiding officer, is usually the best method in large assemblies, and it is the ordinary procedure in many smaller societies as well. The president cannot assume such power, however, unless it is given to him by the bylaws or by action of the assembly in the individual case (13:8(c), 13:13, 13:15, 56:46).

When the bylaws provide that the *president* shall appoint all committees, this power does not transfer to the *chair* if someone else presides. A clause in the bylaws assigning to the president the duty of appointing all committees should therefore contain appropriate provision for its own suspension if necessary (for example, if there is occasion to appoint a special committee during a meeting from which the president is absent). In addition, a clause conferring on the president such power of appointment should exclude the nominating

---

5. The first person that the chair names is automatically chairman of the committee unless the assembly rejects that person as a committee member or unless he or she declines the chairmanship; but it is good practice for the chair to mention him or her as chairman (see 13:17).

committee, and it may be advisable for such a clause also to exclude all disciplinary committees.

Whenever it is stated in the bylaws (with or without the proper exceptions just noted) that the president "shall appoint all committees," this means that the president shall select the persons to serve on such committees as the bylaws prescribe to be established or the assembly may direct to be appointed; it does not mean that the president can himself decide to appoint and assign a task to a group and thereby give it the status of a committee of the society.

When the chair appoints a committee, no vote is taken on the appointees, except any who are not members of the assembly in cases where there is no prior authorization for the chair to appoint non–assembly members to the committee— either in the bylaws or in a motion directing the appointment of the particular committee (see also 13:15, 56:46). But the chair must announce the names of the committee members to the assembly, naming the chairman of the committee first, as in (c) above; and until such announcement is made the committee cannot act. If the assembly orders the appointment of a special committee and it is desired to let the chair select the committee members after adjournment, this delay must be authorized by the assembly; the names of the committee members must then be announced at the next meeting and recorded in the minutes.

e) *Appointment by adoption of a motion naming members of a committee.* This method finds use in the case of special committees when the rules or particular conditions do not dictate the use of another procedure. The names of the proposed committee members can be included in the motion proposing to appoint the committee, either as it is originally offered or by way of an amendment. Or, if the motion to appoint the committee is adopted without prescribing the manner of appointment, a second motion can be made "That the committee be composed of Mr. X, Mr. Y, …" In either case, the motion naming the committee members can specify the committee chairman or not as the assembly wishes. If other names (intended to replace one or more of those in the motion) are proposed while the motion is pending, all such names and those in the motion are treated as nominations and are voted on as in the case of an election (see also 13:8(c), 13:10–18).

50:14 Unless the bylaws or other governing rules expressly provide that committee members shall serve "... *and* until their successors are chosen" or for a fixed period, as "... for a term of two years" (in which case the procedure for their removal or replacement is the same as that for officers described in the second bulleted item in 62:16), committee members (including the chairman) may be removed or replaced as follows: If appointment was as provided in paragraphs (a), (b), (c), or (e) above, the removal or replacement of a committee member requires the same vote as for any other motion to *Rescind* or *Amend Something Previously Adopted*. If appointment was by the president acting alone under paragraph (d), he may remove or replace committee members by his own act (see 13:23).

50:15 A committee (except a committee of the whole, **52**) can appoint subcommittees, which are responsible to and report to the committee and not to the assembly. Subcommittees must consist of members of the committee, except when otherwise authorized by the society in cases where the committee is appointed to take action that requires the assistance of others.

50:16 The rules affecting ex-officio members of committees are the same as those applying to ex-officio members of boards (49:8–9). When the bylaws provide that the president shall be ex officio a member of all committees (or of all committees with the stated exception of those from which the president is best excluded; see 56:47), the president is an ex-officio member who has the right, but not the obligation, to participate in the proceedings of the committees, and he is not counted in determining the number required for a quorum or whether a quorum is present at a meeting.

50:17　　　The resignation of a member of a committee should be addressed to the appointing power, and it is the responsibility of that power to fill the resulting vacancy (cf. 47:57–58).

50:18　**Proper Composition of Committees.** The members of a standing committee should be chosen so as to provide the strongest possible group for the handling of any task that may arise within the province of the committee. In the case of a special committee, the purpose for which it is appointed affects the desirable size and composition, as follows:

- When a special committee is appointed to implement an order of the assembly, it should be small and should consist only of those in favor of the action to be carried out. If anyone not in sympathy with the action is appointed, he should ask to be excused.

- When a special committee is appointed for deliberation or investigation, however, it should often be larger, and it should represent, as far as possible, all points of view in the organization, so that its opinion will carry maximum weight. When such a committee is properly selected, its recommendations will most often reflect the will of the assembly. By care in selecting committees, debates on delicate and troublesome questions in ordinary societies can be mostly confined to the committees. The usefulness of the committee will be greatly impaired, on the other hand, if any important faction of the assembly is not represented.

50:19　**Information, Instructions, and Referred Papers.** Upon the appointment of a committee, it is the duty of the secretary of the society to see that all persons appointed are notified, and to furnish a list of the members of the committee to its chairman or, in the chairman's absence, to some other authorized committee member. When a subject or item of business is referred to the committee (normally at the time of its appointment if it is a special committee, or at any time if it is a standing committee), the secretary provides the committee chairman or his representative with copies of the papers, motion, or other matter formally referred to it, and whatever instructions the assembly has given. Upon the committee's request, any other papers or books necessary for the proper performance of its duties must be made available to it by the appropriate officers of the society, who can first consult with the president if in doubt whether the requested papers or books are indeed needed by the committee.

50:20   A committee should take care to preserve the papers referred to it from the society, since, after its assignment is completed, they must be returned in the same condition as when received. If the committee wishes to write on copies of the documents, therefore, it must obtain its own photocopies, unless it has been provided with extra copies specified in its instructions as for that purpose. In any case, amendments prepared for recommendation to the assembly when the committee reports should be drawn up on a separate sheet.

Conduct of Business in Committees

50:21   **Committee Meetings.** When a committee has been appointed, its chairman (or first-named member temporarily acting—see 13:18) should call it together.[6] If some members of the committee believe that the chairman has failed to call this initial meeting or any subsequent meeting when necessary, a meeting of the committee may be called by any two of its members, unless (such as for very large committees) the assembly's rules or instructions prescribe, or empower the committee itself to require, a larger number. It is the responsibility of the person or persons calling a committee meeting to ensure that reasonable notice of its time and place is sent to every committee member.

---

6. For cases in which it is impractical to bring the members of a committee together for a meeting, the report of the committee can contain what has been agreed to by every one of its members (see 51:2). Also, committees are sometimes authorized to hold "electronic meetings"; see 9:30–36, especially *Electronic Meetings in Committees* (9:35).

The quorum in a committee is a majority of its membership unless the assembly has prescribed a different quorum (**40**).

50:22 **Adjournment; Provision for Future Meetings.** When a committee intends to reconvene, it can simply adjourn, or adjourn to meet at a later time. In the first case—when it adjourns without appointing a time for another meeting—the next meeting is called as provided in the previous paragraph. In the second case—when it sets an adjourned meeting—notice of the adjourned meeting is not required (although it is desirable to give such notice if feasible), but reasonable efforts must be made to inform absent members of its time and place.

50:23 All of the meetings of a special committee constitute one session (**8**). When a special committee has finished with the business assigned to it, a motion is made for the committee to "rise"—which is equivalent to the motion to adjourn *sine die* (or without day)—and for the chairman or some other member to make its report to the assembly. The motion to rise is never used in standing committees, or in special committees until they are ready to go out of existence.

50:24 **Committee Procedure.** In small committees, the chairman usually acts as secretary, but in large ones and many standing committees, a secretary may be chosen to keep a brief memorandum in the nature of minutes for the use of the committee.

50:25 The informalities and modifications of the regular rules of parliamentary procedure listed in 49:21 for use in small boards are applicable during the meetings of all standing and special committees, unless the committee is otherwise instructed by the society (see next paragraph below); also, the rules governing the motions to *Rescind*, to *Amend Something Previously Adopted*, and to *Reconsider* are modified as stated in 35:2(7) and 37:35. In committees, the chairman is usually the most active participant in the discussions and work of the committee. In order that there may be no interference with the assembly's having the benefit of its committees' matured judgment, motions to close or limit debate (**15**, **16**) are not allowed in committees.[7]

50:26   Committees of organized societies operate under the bylaws, the parliamentary authority, and any special rules of order or standing rules of the society which may be applicable to them. A committee may not adopt its own rules except as authorized in the rules of the society or in instructions given to the committee by its parent assembly in a particular case. If a standing or special committee is so large that it can function best in the manner of a full-scale assembly, it should be instructed that the informalities and modifications of the regular rules of parliamentary procedure listed for small boards in 49:21 are not to apply to its proceedings. The parent assembly may adopt such instructions to the committee by majority vote.

50:27   When a committee is to make substantive recommendations or decisions on an important matter, it should give members of the society an opportunity to appear before it and present their views on the subject at a time scheduled by the committee. Such a meeting is usually called a *hearing*. During actual deliberations of the committee, only committee members have the right to be present.

50:28   A standing or special committee may protect itself against breaches of order by its members during committee meetings, and against annoyance by nonmembers, by employing the procedures outlined in 61:10–21, but the committee, instead of itself imposing any penalty on a disorderly member, can only report such behavior to the committee's parent body, which may then take such action as it deems advisable. However, *if there will be no*

---

7. If a member abuses his privilege of speaking an unlimited number of times in debate in order to obstruct the business of the committee, such dilatory behavior should be reported to the committee's parent, which may then remove that member from the committee, adopt an order limiting or closing debate in the committee, or take such other action as it deems advisable. However, *if there will be no opportunity for this to occur* within the time needed to effectively resolve the problem, it is the duty of the committee chairman to deny such a member any further recognition to speak in debate on the pending question.

opportunity for this to occur within the time needed to effectively resolve the problem and enable the committee to complete its assigned tasks, the committee may protect itself against such disruptive behavior by requiring the disorderly member to leave the meeting room during the remainder of the meeting.

50:29   **Continuity and Conclusion of Committee Assignment.** Since members of standing committees in ordinary societies are appointed for a term corresponding to that of the officers, such a committee is generally required to report at least once a year, usually at the annual meeting, on its activities and everything referred to it during the year. When a standing committee submits such a report at the conclusion of its members' term, the *committee* is not discharged from further consideration of referred matters on which it reports partially at that time, unless the assembly so votes (**36**); thus such matters normally go over to the new committee. The members of the old committee continue their duties until their successors are chosen.

50:30   A special committee—since it is appointed for a specific purpose—continues to exist until the duty assigned to it is accomplished, unless discharged sooner (see **36**); and it ceases to exist as soon as the assembly receives its final report. The fact that an annual meeting intervenes does not discharge a special committee. But in a body which ceases to exist or in which the terms of some or all of its members expire at a definite time, like a convention of delegates, a city council, or a board of directors, a special committee expires with the body that appointed it, unless it is appointed expressly to report at a later time. If it does not report, its life expires with that of the body to which it was to report.

§51. REPORTS OF BOARDS AND COMMITTEES

51:1   A report of a subordinate board or a committee is an official statement formally adopted by, and submitted in the name of, the reporting body, informing the parent assembly of action taken or recommended, or information obtained.

General Considerations Affecting Board and Committee Reports

51:2 **Limitation of Report Content to What Has Been Properly Agreed To.** Except as noted in this paragraph, a report of a board or committee can contain only what has been agreed to by a majority vote at a regular or properly called meeting of which every member has been notified (or at an adjournment of one of these meetings, 9:17–19)—where a quorum of the board or committee was present. A presentation of facts or recommendations made merely upon separate consultation with every member of a board must be described thus to the parent assembly, and not as an official report of the board (see also 49:16). In the case of a committee, however, if it is impractical to bring its members together for a meeting, the report of the committee can contain what has been agreed to by every one of its members. (See also *Electronic Meetings,* 9:30–36.)

51:3 **Types of Reports.** For convenience in the discussions in this section, reports may be divided into two general categories as follows:

a) *Annual or periodic reports of boards or standing committees* are usually submitted in accordance with requirements in the bylaws, are primarily for information, and should summarize important work done by the board or committee during the year or other period covered by the report. They may also contain recommendations—which may relate to general policy to be followed by the organization, or may propose specific action by its assembly (see next paragraph).

b) *Reports relating to single items of business arising during the year* fall into a number of particular forms—which are described for the case of committees in 51:30ff. As will be seen from examples there, these reports can often be quite brief unless special circumstances or instructions to the reporting body call for a detailed presentation of facts.

51:4 **Recommendations in a Report.** In any report of a subordinate board or a committee (of type (a) or (b) above), specific recommendations for immediate action by the parent assembly should be grouped at the end—repeating them if they have already been noted at separate places in the report—and should generally be cast in the form of one or more proposed resolutions. Although it is possible for a report, in the circumstances just described, to present recommendations which are not in the form of resolutions or motions, the "adoption" of such recommendations by the parent assembly may, depending on their wording or that of the motion to adopt, lead to confusion as to whether their adoption *authorizes action,* or only has the force of a declaration of intent (requiring the adoption of subsequent resolutions for implementation). A board or committee is usually best fitted to prepare resolutions to carry out its recommendations, and it should never leave this responsibility to others.

51:5 When a report is made for the purpose of presenting recommendations on a single subject—especially if it is the report of a committee to which the subject was referred—it is often best for the formal report to be confined as much as possible to the recommendations, whether they are in the form of resolutions or otherwise (see examples in 51:30–51). If this approach is followed and it is desired to bring supporting reasons to the attention of the assembly, the reporting member (that is, the person who presents the report) can include brief oral explanations with his presentation. Or, supporting reasons can be explained at greater length during debate on the report—by the reporting member, who has the right to the floor first in debate, and also by other members of the board or committee, if appropriate, as the debate progresses.

51:6 In the foregoing connection, it should be noted that under parliamentary conditions the inclusion of supporting facts or reasoning in a report proposing certain action may tend to work against the taking of that action, since some members who might otherwise have been willing to accept the proposals may be led to vote against them if they disagree with the factual background as reported or the reasoning of the reporting body.

51:7 **Form of Detailed Report.** If special conditions dictate that a report devoted to a single subject and presenting recommendations should include a full account of the details involved in the case, the body of the report is best organized according to the following topics, as applicable:

1) a description of the way in which the reporting body (usually a committee in such cases) undertook its charge;
2) the facts uncovered or information obtained;
3) the findings or conclusions derived from the facts or information; and
4) resolutions or recommendations.

If for any reason one or more resolutions or recommendations are placed within this type of detailed report before its conclusion, they should be repeated at the end, as stated above. In this way they can be more easily dealt with apart from any implied endorsement of reported facts and reasoning which some members may not accept.

51:8 **Presentation and Reception of Reports.** A report of a board or committee to an assembly is presented at the proper time by a "reporting member" of the board or committee. For the report of a board whose chairman is also the presiding officer of the assembly, the secretary or another one of its members acts as reporting member. In the case of a committee, the committee chairman is the reporting member unless—because he does not agree with the report or for any other reason—he does not wish to give it, in which event the committee chooses another one of its members.

51:9 A reporting member *makes* or *presents* a report on behalf of a board or a committee when, having been assigned the floor for such a purpose in a meeting, he does one of the following things (depending on the nature of the report and other conditions): (a) renders the report orally, if it is not in writing; (b) reads the report to the assembly and passes it to the chair or the secretary; or (c) announces that he is submitting it and passes it to one of these officers to be read by a reading clerk. When the assembly hears the report thus read or orally rendered, it *receives* the report. The terms *presentation* and *reception* accordingly describe one and the same event from the respective viewpoints of the reporting member and the assembly.

51:10 **Motions for Action on Reports.** Immediately after receiving a board's or a committee's report—unless it is a report containing only information on which no action is taken (51:53)—an assembly normally considers whatever action may be recommended in or arise out of the report. In the remainder of this section, it is explained how such action under various conditions may involve the introduction of motions—to implement recommendations or, occasionally, to adopt the entire report.

51:11 *Motions to implement recommendations.* When a report contains recommendations—except in cases where the recommendations relate only to the adoption or rejection of question(s) that were referred while pending (**13**) and consequently become pending again automatically when reported (51:37–43)—the reporting board or committee member usually makes the necessary motion to implement the recommendations at the conclusion of his presentation, provided he is a member of the assembly (see examples in 51:31–35 and 51:44–51, in which it is generally assumed that the "reporting member" is a member of the assembly). If the report is read by the secretary or a reading clerk in such a case, the reporting member resumes the floor for the purpose of making the motion immediately after the reading is completed. No second is required in these cases, since the motion is made on behalf of the board or committee (see 4:11).

51:12   If the person presenting the report is not a member of the assembly or for any other reason does not make the required motion to implement the recommendations as just described, any member of the assembly can do so; but the motion must then be seconded. Or, when the proper motion is a matter of clear-cut procedure and must necessarily be introduced to resolve the case, the chair may sometimes expedite matters by *assuming* the motion—that is, stating the question on it without waiting for it to be made.

51:13   *Motion to adopt an entire report.* In rare instances after an assembly has received a report, it may have occasion to adopt the (entire) report; an affirmative vote on such a motion has the effect of the assembly's endorsing every word of the report—including the indicated facts and the reasoning—as its own statement (see also 10:52–53). Unlike motions to take the action recommended in a report as described above, a motion "to adopt the report" should be made by someone other than the reporting member and requires a second. Adoption of an entire report is seldom wise except when it is to be issued or published in the name of the whole organization.

51:14   **Equivalence of Terms; Incorrect Motions.** As applied to an assembly's action with respect to board or committee reports or any of their contents, the expressions *adopt, accept,* and *agree to* are all equivalent—that is, the text adopted becomes in effect the act or statement of the assembly. It is usually best to use the word *adopt,* however, since it is the least likely to be misunderstood.

51:15   A common error is to move that a report "be received" after it has been read—apparently on the supposition that such a motion is necessary in order for the report to be taken under consideration or to be recorded as having been made. In fact, this motion is meaningless and is therefore not in order, since the report has already been received. Even before a report has been read, a motion to receive it is unnecessary if the time for its reception is established by the order of business, or if no member objects (see also below).

51:16   Another error—less common, but dangerous—is to move, after the report has been read (or even before the reading), that it "be accepted," when the actual intent is that of the mistaken motion to receive, as just explained, or of a legitimate motion to receive made *before* the report is read. If a motion "to accept" made under any of these circumstances is adopted and is given its proper interpretation, it implies that the assembly has endorsed the complete report.

51:17   **Applicability of Regular Rules to Questions Arising out of Reports.** When a board or committee report has been received and the chair has stated the question on the adoption of the motion, resolution(s), recommendation(s), or report—whether the question became pending automatically, or the proper motion was made or was assumed by the chair as explained above—the matter is treated as any other main question, is open to debate and amendment, and can have any of the subsidiary motions applied to it. Similarly, if a committee to which the main question was referred has recommended that it be amended or definitely or indefinitely postponed, the motion to take such action is debatable and (for primary amendment or definite postponement) amendable, under the regular rules for these motions.

51:18   In the foregoing connection it should be noted that the consideration of a matter *that was referred* to a board or committee cannot be objected to (**26**) when it is reported on—regardless of whether the matter was referred as a pending question (**13**) or as a subject on which no question was pending. The reason is that an *Objection to the Consideration of a Question* can be raised only against an original main motion at the time of its introduction; and the reported matter in no case has this status since (a) if it was referred as a pending question, it was introduced at an earlier time, or (b) if it was referred as a subject on which no question was pending, the main question introduced following the report is an incidental main motion (see 10:4–6).

51:19   **Conditions for Amendment of a Report by the Assembly Before Its Adoption.** An assembly that is to adopt an entire report which it has received can amend the report, but the text as published or recorded must not make the reporting board or committee appear to say anything different from the wording that was actually reported. For this reason, the published or recorded text must show clearly the reported version and the changes that the assembly has made—for example, by enclosing in brackets all that was struck out and underlining or putting in italics all that was inserted, and including a note explaining this notation at the beginning of the report (see also 51:13, 51:22).

Board Reports

51:20   **Occasion and Manner of Preparation.** The executive board (or board of directors) of a society reports to the assembly annually on the work done during the year, and at such other times and upon such subjects as the bylaws may prescribe or the society's business may require.

51:21   A board report is usually drafted by the president or secretary, and this draft often passes through the executive committee first, if there is one, before it comes up for consideration and adoption by the board at one of its meetings (see also 51:1–3). A board report should be signed by the president or chairman of the board and its secretary only.

51:22   **Reception and Disposition of Board Reports.** In meetings at which the executive board is to make a report, the chair calls for it at the time provided in the order of business, or, if there is no such provision, before committee reports are received or unfinished business is taken up. After the reading of the report, the reporting member moves the adoption of any resolutions included in it, which, as indicated above, should be grouped or repeated at the end. If the annual report of the board is to be formally adopted by the society before being published, an appropriate wording for the minutes in such a case is the following: "The Executive Board [or "Board of Directors," etc.] submitted its report, which, after debate and amendment [if any], was adopted as follows, the words in brackets having been struck out and those underlined [or, "in italics"] having been inserted before the report was adopted." A society need not endorse the report of its board, and can even decline to allow the report to be printed, or it can adopt only a part; but whatever it prints or records from the report must show any changes clearly marked.

Form and Reception of Committee Reports in General

51:23 **General Form of Committee Reports.** All committee reports should be submitted in writing, except as noted (for particular types of brief reports in a small assembly) in 51:60–62. In the case of such exceptions, a report can be given orally only if it is brief enough that the secretary can record its complete substance in the minutes on hearing it given—which he must do if no written copy is submitted for file.

51:24 Usually a written committee report is not addressed or dated. It is understood to be addressed to the assembly, and its date is that on which it is presented in a meeting of the assembly as recorded in the minutes.

51:25 A committee report should always be worded in the third person—that is, as shown in the next paragraph (not "I report …" or "We recommend …"). Similarly, in an assembly a committee report is always spoken of by the chair and others as, for example, "the report of the Finance Committee" or "the report of the committee to which was referred … [stating the subject]." It should never be spoken of as "the report of the chairman of the Finance Committee" and never as "Mr. Smith's report," even though it is usually presented by the committee chairman and even if he may have personally drafted it or done most of the work reported.

51:26 A committee report should begin with an identification of the committee submitting it—the name of the committee in the case of a standing committee, or the subject that was referred in the case of a special committee; thus:

[For a standing committee:]

The Committee on ... wishes to report [or, "reports"] that ... [or, "submits the following report: ..."].

Or:

Report of the Committee on ... :

[For a special committee:]

The committee to which was referred [stating the subject] reports [or "recommends"] that ...

Or:

The committee appointed to [stating the purpose] reports that ... [or, "submits the following report: ..."].

51:27   If a written committee report is of considerable importance, it should be signed by all the members concurring.[8] Otherwise, the committee can authorize its chairman to sign the report alone, in which case he adds the word *Chairman* after his signature. By so signing, the committee chairman certifies that the report has been adopted by the committee as explained in 51:2. When all concurring members sign the report, it is customary for the chairman to sign first, but this is not obligatory. In any case, he should not place the word *Chairman* after his name except when he signs alone on behalf of the entire committee. The use of the words *Respectfully submitted* preceding the signature(s) on a committee report is unnecessary and no longer customary.

51:28   **Reception of Committee Reports.** Reports of committees are called for or can be presented in a meeting as follows:

- If, as is usually the case, a place has been provided in the order of business for the reports of committees, the chair calls for the reports of standing committees first, in the order in which they are listed in the bylaws or other rules; after that

---

8. Regarding signature with an expression of disagreement in a certain particular, see 51:71.

he calls for the reports of the special committees, in the order of their appointment. (The chair omits calling for the report of any committee that he knows has no report to make; see also 41:13.) As each report is called for, the committee chairman or other reporting member rises, addresses the chair, and presents the report.

- Or, if the order of business makes no provision for committee reports, the committee chairman or other reporting member seeks to obtain the floor when no business is pending and, addressing the chair, informs the assembly that the committee has agreed upon a report which he is prepared to submit. If the chair thinks that the assembly wishes to hear the report, the chair directs the member to proceed. If anyone objects to the report's reception or if the chair is in doubt as to whether the report should be received at that time, the chair asks if there is a motion to receive the report, or the chair assumes such a motion and puts the question to the assembly:

> CHAIR: The question is, "Shall the report be received now?" Those in favor of receiving the report now, say *aye*. … Those opposed say *no*. … , etc.

This question requires a majority vote and is neither debatable nor amendable. If the vote is in the negative, a later time for the reception of the report should be set, either by unanimous consent or by a vote on an incidental main motion setting such a time. The manner of presenting the report is the same as described above.

51:29　　　(For the reception of "minority reports," see 51:69–70.)

Disposition of Particular Types of Committee Reports

51:30　　　The proper method of presenting and disposing of different types of committee reports is explained below, with sample reports being given in certain cases. Whenever a motion by the reporting member is a normal part of the procedure in the examples, it is assumed that this member actually makes the motion rather than leaving it to the chair to state the question without a formal motion (see 51:10–13).

51:31 **A Report at the Initiative of a Standing Committee Recommending Action.** If a standing committee wishes on its own initiative to recommend action by the assembly on a matter within the committee's concern, it is generally desirable, as stated above, for the report to consist of or conclude with one or more proposed resolutions embodying the committee's recommendations. Such resolutions should always be in writing. Although the reporting member in a small assembly may sometimes give accompanying explanations orally, it is usually better to submit a formal written report if it is to contain anything other than the resolutions themselves. In any event, after giving or reading the report, the reporting member moves the adoption of the resolution(s). He may make such a presentation, for example, as follows:

> **REPORTING MEMBER (reading written report):**
> The Buildings and Grounds Committee wishes to report that the clubhouse roof was extensively damaged by the hurricane last week. The committee therefore recommends the adoption of the following resolution: "*Resolved*, That the Buildings and Grounds Committee be authorized to request bids for repair of the clubhouse roof and to award a contract for the same, provided that, without further authorization, the cost shall not exceed $5,000."
>
> George Wilson, Chairman
>
> Mr. President, by direction of [or "on behalf of"] the committee, I move the adoption of the resolution just read.

51:32 The chair then states the question on the resolution, and it is considered just as any other main motion. If the report contains more than one resolution, the reporting member makes a single motion for the adoption of them all, and the rules given in 10:25 apply.

51:33 Although it is not generally the best procedure, a report may sometimes contain recommendations not in the form of motions or resolutions. In any case, as stated above, the recommendations should be placed at the end of the report even if they have been given separately before. Sometimes also, in this connection, it is moved "to adopt the committee's recommendation(s)," although, as noted in 51:4, this can lead to confusion as to the precise effect of the motion. A better method of treating a committee recommendation that is not in the form of a resolution—in a case, for example, where the recommendation is to authorize a $2,000 expenditure for a personnel consultant's fee—is to offer a motion like this: "In accordance with the recommendation in the committee's report, I move that the expenditure of $2,000 for a personnel consultant's fee be authorized." The reporting member can make such a motion after reading the report, or another member can obtain the floor to do so. In cases where the committee has offered no resolutions embodying its recommendations and the drafting of satisfactory resolution(s) covering them is likely to require the further attention of a committee, another member can move to refer the matter to the same or another committee for this purpose.[9]

51:34 **A Report on a Referred Subject on Which No Resolution or Motion Was Pending.** If a subject on which no resolution or motion was pending has been referred to a committee for recommendations, the report usually should conclude with one or more resolutions, unless the committee recommends that no action be taken. The committee's report on the subject referred to it may be presented, for example, thus:

> **REPORTING MEMBER (reading written report):**
> The committee that was appointed to recommend a suitable recreational facility for the Club to donate to the new Runny-

---

9. The motion to refer in such a case is a main motion, since the matter being referred is not a pending question (see 13:6).

mede Park project finds that no provision has been made for tennis courts. The committee therefore recommends the adoption of the following resolution: "*Resolved*, That the Club underwrite the cost of two tennis courts to be constructed in Runnymede Park."

Howard Ford, Chairman

Mr. President, on behalf of the committee, I move the adoption of the resolution just read.

51:35   The resolution is treated as any other main question, just as in the preceding case dealing with the recommendation of a standing committee. Recommendations not in the form of resolutions are also handled as described in the preceding case.

51:36   **A Report on a Resolution Previously Referred to a Committee.** When a committee reports on a resolution or other main question which was referred to it (**13**) or which the rules require to be considered by it before coming before the assembly with the committee's recommendation, the form of the report and the type of action depends on the nature of the case, as follows:

51:37   *Recommending adoption, or rejection, or (when a majority of the committee fail to agree) making no recommendation.* Such a report in a small assembly can be given orally (provided that the secretary records it in the minutes); for example, thus:

> REPORTING MEMBER: The committee to which was referred the resolution "*Resolved*, That the Federation endorse the so-called Farnsworth Plan for financing the proposed new school construction program" recommends that the resolution be adopted [or "not be adopted"].

Or:

> The committee to which was referred ... has been unable to arrive at a recommendation.

51:38   If the resolution is too long to fit into the form given above, a form such as the following may be used:

> **REPORTING MEMBER:** The committee to which was referred the resolution relating to governmental reorganization reports it with the recommendation that it be adopted as referred.

51:39   The reporting member then hands to the chair or the secretary the copy of the resolution that was turned over to the committee.

51:40   When the presentation of the report is concluded in each of the above cases, the resolution or main question becomes pending automatically and the chair states the question accordingly, no motion being necessary. If the committee recommends adoption or makes no recommendation, the chair, as soon as the reporting member has resumed his seat, proceeds:

> **CHAIR:** The committee to which was referred the resolution on ... recommends its adoption [or, "is unable to arrive at a recommendation"]. The resolution is ... [reading it]. The question is on the adoption of the resolution.

51:41   The question is always stated and put on the *adoption* of the resolution (that is, so that a vote of *aye* is a vote in favor of it). Thus, when the committee's recommendation is in the negative, the chair states the question as follows:

> **CHAIR:** The committee to which was referred ... recommends that it not be adopted. The resolution is ... [reading it]. The question is on the adoption of the resolution, the recommendation of the committee to the contrary notwithstanding. [Or, simply, "The question is on the adoption of the resolution," in which case the chair may add, "The committee recommends that the resolution be rejected."]

51:42   *Recommending action on a resolution and an amendment that were pending when referred.* If an amendment was pending when the resolution was referred, the report can be given orally in a small assembly provided that it is recorded in the minutes; and it should first state the committee's recommendation as to the disposition of the amendment, then as to the disposition of the resolution. For example:

> **REPORTING MEMBER:** The committee to which was referred the resolution "*Resolved*, That the proposed expansion of the yacht basin be authorized," together with the pending amendment "to add the words, 'at a cost not to exceed $150,000,'" recommends that the amendment be adopted and that the resolution as thus amended be adopted.

51:43   As in the preceding case, no motions are necessary, and the chair states the question first on the amendment, and after it is voted on, then on the resolution. The same principles apply if a primary amendment and a secondary amendment were pending when the resolution was referred. The report states the committee's recommendations first on the secondary amendment, then on the primary amendment, and finally on the resolution; and the chair states the questions in that order.

51:44   *Recommending definite or indefinite postponement.* If a resolution or other main question is referred to a committee while a motion to postpone it indefinitely is pending, that motion to *Postpone Indefinitely* (**11**) is ignored by the committee and by the assembly when the committee reports. But whether or not such a motion was pending at the time of referral, the committee can report the main question with a recommendation that it be postponed indefinitely or that it be postponed to a certain time (**14**). Thus, if (a) no amendment was pending at the time of referral, or if (b) an amendment was pending and the committee recommends postponement to a certain time, the reporting member makes a motion for the postponement at the conclusion of his presentation. But if (c) an amendment was pending and the recommendation is for indefinite postponement, the motion to *Postpone Indefinitely* cannot be made until after the amendment has been voted on (see *Order of Precedence of Motions,* **5**). In each of the three cases, the report can be given orally in a small assembly, provided that it is recorded in the minutes, as follows:

a) If no amendment was pending at the time of referral:

> **REPORTING MEMBER:** The committee to which was referred the resolution "*Resolved*, That ..." recommends, and on behalf of [or "by direction of"] the committee I move, that the resolution be postponed until ... [or "be postponed indefinitely"].

The chair then states the question first on the postponement, and if that is voted down, next on the resolution.

b) If an amendment was pending and the recommendation is for postponement to a certain time:

> **REPORTING MEMBER:** The committee to which was referred the resolution "*Resolved*, That ... ," together with the pending amendment [stating the amendment], recommends, and by direction of the committee I move, that the resolution be postponed until ...

The chair states the question first on the postponement as in (a); but if that is voted down, the question in this case is next on the amendment, and then on the resolution.

c) If an amendment was pending and the recommendation is for indefinite postponement (in which case the motion to *Postpone Indefinitely* is not in order when the report is made):

> **REPORTING MEMBER:** The committee to which was referred the resolution "*Resolved*, That ... ," together with the pending amendment [stating the amendment], recommends that the resolution be postponed indefinitely.

The reporting member resumes his seat without making a motion, and the chair immediately states the question on the amendment. After it has been voted on, he can state the question on the indefinite postponement (thus assuming this motion), or he can recognize the reporting member to move it by direction of the committee, and the procedure is then as in (a) above.

51:45   *Recommending amendments.* When a committee reports back a resolution or paper with amendments that it proposes, the amendments, at least, should be in writing unless they are very simple. In a small assembly, depending on the complexity of the case, the amendments can be written out on a separate sheet that is handed to the chair or the secretary at the conclusion of an oral presentation, or a more formal written report can be submitted; the latter procedure should be followed in a large body. In the report, the resolution can be included in full and be followed by a statement of the proposed amendments as in the example below; or, if the resolution or document is long and copies are available to the members, the report can contain only the amendments with enough of the context of the resolution to make them understood.

51:46   If no amendment was pending at the time of referral, the reporting member at the conclusion of his presentation moves the adoption of the amendments proposed by the committee, making a single motion covering them all. But if an amendment was pending at the time of referral, the chair (unless the committee recommends a secondary amendment, whose adoption the reporting member would first move) states the question on the referred amendment first—the reporting member making no motion until after that amendment has been voted on.

51:47   The following example (although equally suitable for treatment by the method of reporting a substitute as in 51:49–51) illustrates the presentation of a written report proposing amendments to a resolution short enough to be read in full, in a case where no amendment was pending at the time of referral.

REPORTING MEMBER (reading written report):
The committee to which was referred the resolution relating to a proposed scholarship in journalism hereby submits its report. The resolution is the following: *"Resolved,* That the Guild establish a four-year scholarship in journalism at

the State University, to be open to sons and daughters of Guild members, the recipient to be chosen annually by the Board of Directors of the Guild."

The committee recommends that the resolution be amended as follows:

1) by striking out the words "four-year scholarship" and inserting the words "scholarship covering the last three undergraduate years";

2) by striking out the words "to be open to sons and daughters of Guild members"; and

3) by adding the words "upon the recommendation of the Dean of the School of Journalism";

and the committee further recommends that, as thus amended, the resolution be adopted.

Milton Roth, Chairman
[Or (see 51:27):]
Milton Roth
John Harley
Elizabeth Norton
Elwood Quinn

Mr. President, by direction of the committee, I move the adoption of the amendments contained in the report.

51:48   After the chair states the question on the adoption of the amendments proposed by the committee, the procedure is by one of the following methods:

a) Normally the chair immediately rereads or calls for a re-reading of the first of these amendments, after which it is open to debate and secondary amendment. A vote is then taken on the adoption of the first committee amendment, after which the next one is read, and so on. Until all of the committee's amendments have been voted on, no other primary amendments are in order, but only secondary amendments as each committee amendment comes up. After all of the committee's amendments have been acted upon, other amendments which are not precluded by action taken on the committee amendments can be proposed from the floor. When these have been voted on, the chair puts the question on adopting the resolution or paper as amended.[10]

b) Alternatively, the chair puts a single question on all of the committee's amendments together, except those for which a member asks for a separate vote,[11] thus: "Those in favor of adopting the amendments recommended by the committee, except those for which a separate vote has been asked, say *aye.* ... Those opposed, say *no.* ..." This is called putting the question on the amendments *in gross.* He then takes up the remaining amendments separately in their order. This alternative, although it is in order whenever a committee reports multiple amendments to a referred resolution, may be most advisable when the amendments may be expected not to occasion debate or secondary amendment—for example, if they are reported from a committee of the whole (**52**) where they have already been open to debate and amendment.

c) By unanimous consent (4:58–63), the assembly can allow the introduction of a motion to adopt all recommendations in the report, without considering the amendments separately.

51:49 *Recommending a substitute.* If a committee reports back a resolution with a substitute that it recommends for adoption, at least the substitute should be in writing, just as in the case of any other report proposing amendments.

51:50 If no amendment was pending when the resolution was referred, the reporting member concludes his presentation by making the motion to substitute; for example, thus:

> **REPORTING MEMBER:** The committee to which was referred the resolution "*Resolved,* That the proceeds from the recent bequest to the Association from the Asquith estate be invested

---

10. The step of taking a vote on the adoption of the entire paper applies only to cases where that paper is *pending.* This step does not apply in the case of a report on a series of amendments to something previously adopted (**35**), such as bylaws that are in effect (see also **57**).

11. Separate votes may not be demanded on conforming amendments. See 12:14–15.

in stock of the Consolidated Development Corporation" recommends that, for the resolution, the following substitute be adopted: "*Resolved,* That the Executive Board be authorized to retain reputable investment counsel with a view to determining appropriate investment of the proceeds from the Asquith bequest." On behalf of the committee I move that the resolution last read be substituted for the referred resolution.

51:51 The chair then states the question on the motion to substitute. But if amendment(s) were pending when the resolution was referred, then, before the motion to substitute can be made, the question is first on the secondary amendment if one was pending, then on the primary amendment that was pending. When these amendments have been voted on, the reporting member makes the motion to substitute and the chair states the question on it (or the chair can state the question assuming the motion). In any event, the substitute proposed by the committee is treated as in the case of any other motion to substitute (see 12:69–90). If the motion to substitute is lost, the "original" resolution is open to further amendment; but if the motion to substitute is adopted, the resolution thus substituted can be amended only by *adding.* (Regarding substitutes proposed by committees, see also 12:77–78.)

51:52 In regard to referred questions reported back, see also *Resolutions Committee,* 59:67–75, 59:80–83.

51:53 **A Report Containing Only Information.** Even if a report contains only an account of work done or a statement of fact or opinion for the assembly's information, it should be in writing. Apart from filing such a report, however, no action on it is necessary and usually none should be taken. (See also *Motion to Adopt an Entire Report,* 51:13, and *Conditions for Amendment of a Report by the Assembly Before Its Adoption,* 51:19.)

51:54 **Membership and Nominating Committee Reports; Reports of Other Kinds of Committees.** When a membership committee reports on names of persons referred to the committee as applicants for society membership, the report can be rendered orally, but a list of the names of the persons recommended for membership should be submitted in writing. When such a report is made, the chair at once states the question on the admission to membership of the candidates recommended by the committee.

51:55   The report of the nominating committee consists of a written list of candidates for office, just as in the case of the membership committee's report. No vote on the nominating committee's report is taken, however; the procedure is as described in **46**.

51:56   For the handling of the report of an auditing committee, see 48:24–25.

51:57   For the report of a committee on bylaws, see **54** and **56**.

51:58   For the reports of the three principal committees that perform parliamentary functions in the organization of a convention—the Credentials Committee, the Committee on Standing Rules, and the Program Committee—see **59**.

51:59   For the report of an investigating committee appointed under disciplinary procedures, see **63**.

Oral Reports; Partial and Minority Reports

51:60   **Summary of Types of Reports That Can Be Rendered Orally in a Small Assembly.** As stated in 51:23, committee reports should be submitted in writing, with the permissible exceptions noted in the following two paragraphs (51:61–62), which apply to very brief reports in a small assembly, provided that the secretary records the complete substance of the report in the minutes as it is given orally.

51:61   With respect to a resolution or main question that was referred while pending:

1) If the committee report consists only of a recommendation as to the disposition of the referred resolution or motion, the report can be given orally if implementation of the recommendation involves:

   a) no further motion, as when the committee recommends that the referred resolution or motion be adopted, or rejected; or

   b) the introduction of a subsidiary motion that can be made orally, as when the committee recommends that the referred resolution be postponed definitely or indefinitely, or be amended by the change of only a few words.

2) If an amendment or a primary and a secondary amendment were pending with a resolution or main question that was referred and the committee has no new amendments to propose, the report can also usually be oral, in which case the reporting member simply states the committee's recommendation as to the adoption or rejection, first, of the secondary amendment, and then of the primary amendment, and finally its recommendation as to the disposition of the resolution or main motion—all before any of the referred questions are voted on.

3) When the committee wishes to propose amendments, the amendments themselves should always be in writing if they involve more than a few words; but the complete report—that is, the declaration on behalf of the committee that it recommends the amendments—can be oral or written depending on the complexity of statement required by the resulting parliamentary situation.

51:62   If a subject that was not in the form of a pending resolution or motion was referred to a committee for recommendations, and if the committee in its report presents the recommendations in one or more resolutions offered with no comment, only the resolutions need be in writing and the statement that the committee recommends their adoption can be given orally.

51:63   **Action Required by a Partial Report.** A partial report of a committee is handled in the same way as the final report. If it is a progress report only, with no recommendations or conclusions, it is treated as any other report for information only, and no action need be taken. But if the partial report recommends action, the question is put on adopting its proposed resolutions, or its recommendations, or the report itself, just as if it were the final report. A committee can be discharged (**36**) by a majority vote at the time at which it makes a partial report.

51:64   **Formal Expression of Minority View ("Minority Report").** The formal presentation of a so-called "minority report"—that is, the presentation of an expression of views in the name of a group of committee members not concurring with the committee report—is usually allowed by the assembly when such permission is requested, as explained below. Regardless of whether a minority report is submitted, however, the report adopted by vote of a majority in the committee should always be referred to as "the committee report," never "the majority report."

51:65   *Nature of committee minority's rights with respect to reports.* As indicated above, the formal presentation of a "minority report" is a privilege that the assembly may accord, not a matter of right—since the appointment of the committee implies that the assembly is primarily interested in the findings of the majority of the committee's members. But in debate on any written or oral report in the assembly, any member of the reporting committee who does not concur has the same right as any other member of the assembly to speak individually in opposition. No one can make allusion in the assembly to what has occurred during the deliberations of the committee, however, unless it is by report of the committee or by unanimous consent.

51:66   *Form of minority report; minority recommendations.* A "minority report" in writing may begin:

> The undersigned, a minority of the committee appointed to … , not agreeing with the majority, desire to express their views in the case. …

51:67   If the committee report concludes with a proposed resolution, the minority can (a) recommend rejection of the resolution; (b) recommend amendment of it; or (c) recommend adoption of some other suitable motion designed to dispose of the resolution appropriately.

51:68   If the committee report is for information only, the views of the minority may be similarly constructed or may conclude with a motion.

51:69   ***Reception of minority report.*** When the minority of a committee wishes to make a formal presentation of its views, it is customary, unless the assembly refuses permission, to receive its report immediately after the report of the committee. In such a case, the member presenting the committee report can properly notify the assembly that the minority wishes to submit its views in a separate report. As soon as the chair has stated the appropriate question on the committee report, he calls for the minority presentation unless someone objects, in which case he puts the question on the report's being received. A majority vote is required to receive a minority report; the question is undebatable.

51:70   When the minority report is presented, it is for information, and it cannot be acted upon except by a motion to substitute it for the report of the committee. Whether the views of the minority are formally presented or not, however, any member can move that resolutions proposed by the committee be amended, or that they be postponed indefinitely, or that some other appropriate action be taken.

51:71   **Indicating Agreement with a Report Except in a Specified Particular.** If a written report of a committee is signed by all who concur and a committee member is in agreement with the report except in one particular, he can, after all who agree to the report have signed, add a statement that he concurs with the report except the part that he specifies, and then sign the statement—regardless of whether a minority report is to be submitted. Similarly, a committee member who agrees with most of a minority report can sign it with an added note indicating what he does not agree with, just as in the case of a committee report. If the committee members in the minority do not agree, the assembly can allow more than one minority report to be submitted.

§52. COMMITTEE OF THE WHOLE AND ITS ALTERNATE FORMS

52:1   The *committee of the whole* and its two alternate forms, the *quasi committee of the whole* (or *consideration as if in committee of the whole*) and *informal consideration,* are devices that enable the full assembly to give detailed consideration to a matter under conditions of freedom somewhat like those of a committee. Under each of these procedures, any member can speak in debate on the main question or any amendment—for the same length of time as allowed by the assembly's rules—as often as he is able to get the floor. As under the regular rules of debate, however, he cannot speak another time on the same question so long as a member who has not spoken on it is seeking the floor.

52:2   Each of these three devices is best suited to assemblies of a particular range in size and provides a different degree of protection against disorderliness and its possible consequences—which are risked when each member is allowed to speak an unlimited number of times in debate, such risk increasing in proportion to the size of the assembly. With respect to this type of protection, the essential distinctions between the three procedures may be summarized as follows:

a) In a *committee of the whole,* which is suited to *large assemblies,* the results of votes taken are not final decisions of the assembly, but have the status of recommendations which the assembly is given the opportunity to consider further and which it votes on finally under its regular rules. Also, a chairman of the committee of the whole is appointed and the regular presiding officer leaves the chair, so that, by being disengaged from any difficulties that may arise in the committee, he may be in a better position to preside effectively during the final consideration by the assembly.

b) In the *quasi committee of the whole,* which may be convenient in *meetings of medium size* (about 50 to 100 members), the results of votes taken are reported to the assembly for final consideration under the regular rules, just as with a committee of the whole. But in this case the presiding officer of the assembly remains in the chair and presides.

c) *Informal consideration,* which is suited to *small meetings of ordinary societies,* simply removes the normal limitations on the number of times members can speak in debate, as stated in the first paragraph of this section. The regular presiding officer remains in the chair; and the results of votes taken during informal consideration are decisions of the assembly, which are not voted on again.

52:3   The complete rules governing committees of the whole, proceedings in quasi committee of the whole, and informal consideration are given below.

Committee of the Whole

52:4   Although the committee of the whole is not used extensively except in legislative bodies, it is the oldest of the three devices described above and is the prototype from which the other two are derived. Unlike the processes of quasi committee of the whole and informal consideration, a committee of the whole is a real committee in the parliamentary sense. Therefore, during the time that a meeting is "in committee of the whole," even though the committee consists of the entire body of members in attendance at the assembly's meeting, it is technically not "the assembly."

52:5   The parliamentary steps in making use of a committee of the whole are essentially the same as those involved in referring a subject to an ordinary committee. The assembly votes to go into a committee of the whole (which is equivalent to voting to refer the matter to the committee), and a chairman of the committee is appointed. The committee considers the referred matter, adopts a report to be made to the assembly, then votes to "rise and report." Finally, the committee chairman presents the report and the assembly considers the committee's recommendations—all as in the case of an ordinary committee.

52:6   **Going into Committee of the Whole.** As implied above, the motion to go into a committee of the whole is a form of the motion to commit (**13**). The motion is made as follows:

> MEMBER (obtaining the floor): I move to go into a committee of the whole [or, "I move that the assembly now resolve itself into a committee of the whole"] to consider the pending question [or "to take under consideration … (stating the subject)"]. (Second.)

Instructions to the committee of the whole can be included in this motion of referral.

52:7   If the motion of referral to the committee of the whole is adopted, the presiding officer immediately calls another member to the chair—frequently, but not necessarily, the vice-president—and takes his place as a member of the committee. In large assemblies, the secretary may also leave his seat, the committee chairman may preside from that position, and an assistant secretary may act as secretary of the committee. For the committee's use until it reports, its secretary keeps a temporary memorandum of the business it transacts, but the committee's proceedings are not entered in the minutes of the assembly. Those minutes carry only the same kind of record of the referral to a committee of the whole, the committee's report, and the assembly's action on the report, as if the committee had been an ordinary one.

52:8   **Conduct of Business.** Like ordinary committees, a committee of the whole cannot alter the text of any resolution referred to it; but it can propose amendments, which it must report in the form of recommendations to the assembly. Amendments to a resolution *originating in the committee* are in order, however; and if such amendments are adopted within the committee, they are incorporated in the resolution before it is reported to the assembly for action.

52:9   A committee of the whole is under the rules of the assembly, except as follows:

1) The only motions that are in order in a committee of the whole are to adopt (within the committee, for inclusion in its report), to amend (what it is proposed to report), and to "rise" or "rise and report"[12]—except that, among the incidental motions, a point of order (**23**) can be raised, an appeal from the decision of the chair (**24**) can be made, a division of the assembly (**29**) can be called for, and applicable requests and inquiries (**32, 33**) can be made.

2) In debate on motions to adopt or amend, unless a limit is prescribed by the assembly before it goes into committee of the whole as explained below, each member can speak an unlimited number of times under the rules given in the first paragraph of this section.[13]

If the committee of the whole wishes action to be taken which requires the adoption of any motion other than those that are in order in the committee as listed in (1) above, it must vote to rise and report a recommendation that the assembly take the desired action (see below). The motion to rise must be seconded, is undebatable, cannot be amended, and requires a majority vote. It is

---

12. As applied to committees in general, the word *rise* simply describes the parliamentary step of ceasing to function as a committee, preparatory to making a report. As stated in 50:23, the motion to rise is not used in ordinary standing committees, and in ordinary special committees it is used only when the committee is ready to make its final report and go out of existence. In a committee of the whole, on the other hand, the word *rise* applies to any case of the committee's returning to the status of the assembly—whether it is expected to be temporarily or permanently.

13. Appeals in committee of the whole are debatable under the same rules as in the assembly—that is, each member (except the chair) can speak only once in debate on them.

always in order in committee of the whole, except during voting or verifying a vote and when another member has the floor.

52:10   Among the consequences of the rules stated in the preceding paragraph are the following:

1) A committee of the whole cannot appoint subcommittees or refer a matter to another (ordinary) committee.

2) An appeal from the decision of the chair must be voted on directly, since it cannot be postponed or laid on the table in the committee.

3) The only way for debate to be closed or limited in the committee is for the assembly to specify such conditions before going into committee of the whole. If the committee develops a desire to have debate limited, it can only do so by rising and requesting the assembly to impose the desired limits, as explained below. If debate has been closed at a particular time by order of the assembly, the committee does not have the power, even by unanimous consent, to extend the time.

4) A roll-call vote or a vote by ballot cannot be ordered in a committee of the whole, nor can a counted rising vote be ordered except by the chair.

5) A committee of the whole has no power to impose disciplinary measures on its members, but can only report the facts to the assembly. If the committee becomes disorderly and its chairman loses control of it, the presiding officer of the assembly should take the chair and declare the committee dissolved.

6) A committee of the whole cannot adjourn or recess, but must rise in order that the assembly may do so.

52:11   **Rising and Reporting.** When a committee of the whole has completed its consideration of the matter referred to it, or when it wishes to bring the meeting to an end, or wishes the assembly to take any other action requiring the adoption of a motion which is not in order in the committee, the committee rises and reports.

52:12   If the committee originates a resolution, it concludes by voting to report the resolution, as perfected. If a resolution was referred to the committee, however, it votes only on any amendments that it will recommend, not on the resolution, which it reports back to the assembly with the recommended amendments. On a motion, or by unanimous consent, the committee rises and the presiding officer of the assembly resumes the chair. The committee chairman returns to a place in the assembly in front of the presiding officer, at which, standing, he addresses the chair:

> **COMMITTEE CHAIRMAN:** Mr. President, the committee of the whole has had under consideration … [describing the resolution or other matter] and has directed me to report the same as follows: …

52:13   The sample reports in the subsection *Disposition of Particular Types of Committee Reports* (see 51:31–51) may be used as guides for reporting similar cases from a committee of the whole, and the procedures for disposing of such reports as described in the same subsection are likewise applicable. If no amendments are reported, the chair states the question on the resolution that was referred to the committee or that it recommends for adoption; and this question is then open to debate and amendment in the assembly. If amendments proposed by the committee are reported, the committee chairman reads them and hands the paper to the chair, who reads them again or has the secretary do so. The chair then states and puts the question on all of the committee's amendments in gross (that is, taken together), unless a member asks for a separate vote on one or more of them. If so, a single vote is taken on all of the other amendments, and then the question is stated separately on each of the amendments for which a separate vote was asked. These amendments can be further debated and amended in the assembly, as can the main question after action on all the committee's amendments—under the same rules as when any other committee reports.

52:14   If the committee, to facilitate completion of its work, wishes the assembly to take an action outside the committee's powers that requires the adoption of an undebatable motion—for example, to limit debate in the committee—a motion to rise should be made in a form like the following:

> **MEMBER (obtaining the floor):** I move that the committee rise and request that debate be limited ... [specifying the desired limitation]. (Second.)

If this motion is adopted, the committee chairman reports to the assembly as follows:

> **COMMITTEE CHAIRMAN:** Mr. President, the committee of the whole has had under consideration ... [describing the referred matter] and has come to no conclusion thereon, but asks permission [or "leave"] to continue sitting with debate limited ... [specifying the limitation].

The presiding officer then puts the question on granting the request, and if the result is affirmative, the committee chairman resumes the chair.

52:15   A committee of the whole can also rise, before completing its work, to request instructions, in which case the nature or wording of the request needs to be agreed to before the motion to rise is made.

52:16   If the committee wishes to bring its proceedings to an end because it believes the matter can be better handled under the assembly's rules, or because it wishes the meeting to be adjourned, the motion to rise can be made in this form:

> **MEMBER (obtaining the floor):** I move that the committee rise. (Second.)

If this motion is adopted, the committee chairman then reports:

> **COMMITTEE CHAIRMAN:** The committee of the whole has had under consideration ... [describing the matter] and has come to no conclusion thereon.

With such a report, the committee passes out of existence unless the assembly directs it to sit again. In this connection, however, the committee in reporting can "ask permission to sit again," with or without specifying a time; and in granting such a request, the assembly can make the sitting a general order or a special order (**41**) for a particular time. If the assembly grants the committee permission to sit again without specifying a time, the sitting is unfinished business. A committee of the whole cannot itself arrange a future meeting.

52:17   If an hour for adjournment has been preset in the assembly and it arrives while the meeting is in committee of the whole, the committee chairman announces, "The hour for adjournment of the assembly has arrived and the committee will rise." The committee chairman then reports that the committee has come to no conclusion on the referred matter, as described in the preceding paragraph.

52:18   **Quorum in Committee of the Whole.** The quorum of a committee of the whole is the same as that of the assembly unless the bylaws provide, or the assembly establishes, a different quorum for the committee. If the bylaws do not provide a different quorum for the committee, the assembly can establish one in the particular case before going into committee of the whole, regardless of the quorum that the bylaws require for the assembly. If at any time the committee finds itself without a quorum, it must rise and report the fact to the assembly. If the assembly itself is thereupon without a quorum, it must then adjourn or take one of the other courses that are open in the absence of a quorum (**40:6–10**).

Quasi Committee of the Whole
(Consideration as if in Committee of the Whole)

52:19   A somewhat simpler version of the committee of the whole, in effect, is the procedure of consideration in quasi committee of the whole (or consideration as if in committee of the whole), which is convenient in assemblies of medium size. In contrast to a committee of the whole, the quasi committee of the whole is not a real committee, but is "the assembly acting as if in committee of the whole."

52:20 **Going into Quasi Committee of the Whole.** The motion for consideration in quasi committee is made in a form like this:

> MEMBER (obtaining the floor): I move that the resolution be considered in quasi committee of the whole [or "be considered as if in committee of the whole"]. (Second.)

This motion is debatable as to the desirability of going into quasi committee, just as any other motion to *Commit*. If it is adopted, the chair concludes his announcement of the result of the vote as follows:

> CHAIR (after declaring the voting result): The resolution is before the assembly as if in committee of the whole.

52:21 The presiding officer of the assembly does not appoint a chairman of the quasi committee, but remains in the chair himself throughout its proceedings. The assembly's secretary keeps a temporary memorandum of the business transacted in quasi committee; but, just as in the case of a real committee of the whole, the minutes of the assembly carry only a record of the report from quasi committee and the action thereon, as shown below.

52:22 **Conduct of Business.** In the quasi committee of the whole, the main question and any amendments that may be proposed are open to debate under the same rules as in a real committee of the whole—each member being allowed to speak an unlimited number of times as explained in 52:1. In contrast to the case of a real committee of the whole, however, any motion that would be in order in the assembly is also in order in the quasi committee, where it is debatable only to the extent permitted under the assembly's rules. But if any such motion except an amendment or other motion that would be in order in a real committee of the whole is adopted, it automatically puts an end to the proceedings in quasi committee. Thus, for example, if a motion to refer the main question to an ordinary committee is made in quasi committee of the whole, such a motion to *Commit* would be equivalent to the following series of motions if the matter were being considered in a real committee of the whole: (1) that the committee of the whole rise; (2) that the committee of the whole be discharged from further consideration of the subject; and (3) that the question be referred to an ordinary committee.

52:23   **Reporting.** The motion to rise is not used in quasi committee of the whole. If the quasi committee is not brought to an end as described in the preceding paragraph, then, when no further amendments are offered in response to the chair's call for them, the presiding officer immediately proceeds to report to the assembly and to state the question on the amendments as follows:

> CHAIR: The assembly, acting as if in committee of the whole, has had under consideration ... [describing the resolution] and has made the following amendments ... [reading them]. The question is on the adoption of the amendments.

The proceedings in a quasi committee of the whole are thus concluded, and from this point the procedure is the same as in disposing of the report of a real committee of the whole (52:13)—the chair putting the question on the reported amendments in gross, except those for which a separate vote may be asked, and so on.

Informal Consideration

52:24   As explained above, if a question is considered in either a real committee of the whole or in quasi committee of the whole, the recommendations of the committee or quasi committee must be reported to the assembly and then the assembly must take action on these recommendations. In ordinary societies whose meetings are not large, a much simpler method is to consider the question informally, which in effect only suspends the rule limiting the number of times a member can speak in debate on the main question and any amendments to it.

52:25   When it is desired to consider a question informally, a member makes the motion that this be done:

> **MEMBER (obtaining the floor):** I move that the question be considered informally. (Second.)

This is a variation of the motion to *Commit,* and can be debated only as to the desirability of considering the question informally. If the motion is adopted, the chair announces the result thus:

> **CHAIR (after declaring the voting result):** The question is now open to informal consideration. There is no limit to the number of times a member can speak on the question or any amendment.

52:26   The "informal" aspect of the consideration applies only to the number of speeches allowed in debate on the main question and its amendments; all votes are formal, and any other motion that is made is under the regular rules of debate. In contrast to the case of a committee of the whole or quasi committee of the whole, the proceedings under informal consideration are recorded in the assembly's minutes, just as they would be if the consideration were formal. While considering a question informally the assembly can, by a two-thirds vote, limit the number or length of speeches, or in any other way limit or close debate. As soon as the main question is disposed of, temporarily or permanently, the informal consideration automatically ceases without any motion or vote.

52:27   Before the main question is disposed of, the informal consideration can be brought to an end, if desired, by adopting by majority vote a motion "that the regular rules of debate be in force," or "that the question be considered formally."

Aids to the Crystallization of Opinion

52:28   The more traditional aids to the crystallization of opinion in societies have been, simply, to take a *Recess* or to refer the matter to a committee—often a large committee composed of members representing differing views in the society, such as a committee of the whole or one of its alternate forms. In more recent years, a practice has developed of establishing breakout groups with every member in attendance being urged to participate in a group. Each breakout group, of which there may be many, is usually kept small—frequently ten or twelve persons—and a moderator is appointed for each group. Often, the groups meet during a recess or adjournment of the assembly. Sometimes, the conclusions reached by the various breakout groups are conveyed to a committee that assembles them and attempts to report a consolidated response to the assembly. At other times, the breakout groups report through their moderators directly to the assembly after it has been reconvened and the matter under consideration is again pending. These reports are in the nature of debate. Whatever method is used, in the end, the pending measure must be returned to the full assembly for final consideration under normal parliamentary procedure—just as in the case of a referred question reported back by a committee—and the assembly must make the final decision, if whatever is to purport to be a product of the assembly is to be valid as the assembly's act.

XVII

MASS MEETINGS; ORGANIZATION OF A PERMANENT SOCIETY

§53. MASS MEETINGS

Distinguishing Characteristics of a Mass Meeting

53:1   A *mass meeting,* as understood in parliamentary law, is a meeting of an unorganized group, which—in a publicized or selectively distributed notice known as the *call* of the meeting—has been announced:

- as called to take appropriate action on a particular problem or toward a particular purpose stated by the meeting's sponsors, and
- as open to everyone interested in the stated problem or purpose (or to everyone within a specified sector of the population thus interested).

53:2   To the extent that persons in the invited category are clearly identifiable—as, for example, registered voters of a particular political party, or residents of a certain area—only such persons have the right to make motions, to speak, and to vote at the meeting, and none others need be admitted if the sponsors so choose. In any event, a mass meeting is convened—and those who attend are admitted—upon the implied understanding that the sponsors (who have engaged the hall and assumed the expenses of promoting the meeting) have the right to have the proceedings confined to the overall object they have announced; but that the entire assembly (which is made up of persons whose help the sponsors are seeking) has the right to determine the action to be taken in pursuit of the stated object. With respect to this limitation of the right of attendance— or, at least, of participation—to persons in general sympathy with the announced object of the meeting, a mass meeting differs from a "town meeting," a public forum, a "lecture-and-discussion-period" type of meeting, or an open hearing held by an instrumentality of government.

Organization of a Mass Meeting

53:3   **Call of the Meeting.** The call or announcement of a mass meeting should specify the date, hour, and place of the meeting, its purpose, and—where applicable—who is invited to attend. It may also carry an identification of the sponsorship. Depending on the funds available and the people to be reached, the call can be given the desired publicity or distribution by whatever means are expected to be most effective—announcements in the newspapers or by radio or television, a website, mailings, posters, handbills or flyers, or the like.

53:4   **Preparation.** While a mass meeting should be conducted so as to accord the assembly its proper role in determining the outcome as described above, at the same time, a certain amount of planning by the sponsors is advisable to avoid the risk of the meeting's foundering.

53:5   Before the meeting, the sponsors should agree on the following:

- whom they prefer for its chairman;
- who shall call the meeting to order and nominate their choice of chairman;
- who shall be nominated for secretary and by whom;
- what rules—if any—shall be proposed for adoption; and
- who shall make the initial talk explaining the purpose of the meeting.

(See also the detailed discussion of these steps below.)

53:6   The person chosen as chairman should be competent as a presiding officer and in sympathy with the object of the meeting, and it is an advantage if he personally knows many of the people who may attend. Depending on conditions, it is sometimes good policy to have a set of resolutions drafted in advance to submit to the meeting. Provision should also be made for occupying the time of the gathering in the event that resolutions are referred to a committee—or a committee is assigned to draft them (see below).

53:7   **The "Membership" of a Mass Meeting.** At a mass meeting, the "membership" consists of all persons in the invited category who attend. If no qualification was placed in the call, anyone who attends is regarded as a member and has the same rights as members in other assemblies—to make motions, to speak in debate, and to vote. If the call specified only a particular category of persons as invited and if no attempt is made to screen the attendance at the door, anyone attending is presumed to be entitled to participate as a member, subject only to his subsequent identification to the contrary. If only those invited are admitted, anyone legitimately admitted has the rights of a member, and a person who is discovered to have entered fraudulently can be asked to leave.

53:8   **Rules in a Mass Meeting.** Mass meetings frequently operate with no formally adopted rules, upon the assumption that the meeting will proceed according to the common parliamentary law— or that any differences of opinion on procedural questions can be resolved by citing a recognized parliamentary manual as persuasive (see 1:5, 2:18–19). Depending on the probable character of the assembly, however, it may be wise to adopt a standard parliamentary authority, which can be done by a majority vote on the motion of a member—made, as prearranged by the sponsors, immediately after the election of the secretary (see below). Other rules are seldom necessary at a mass meeting unless it is desired to modify the general rules (43:8–13) as to the allowable length and number of speeches. If such a modification is desired, the assembly can adopt a standing rule covering the desired provisions at the same time as it adopts the parliamentary authority, or at a later time. In regard to the vote required for their adoption, amendment, rescission, or suspension, standing rules of a mass meeting (or a series of mass meetings) are similar to standing rules of a convention as described in 59:32–37.

53:9   In any event, without adoption at a mass meeting and regardless of what rules the meeting may adopt, the provisions of the call, specifying the meeting's purpose and those invited to attend it, have a force equivalent to bylaws of an organized society; that is, they define the subject matter within which motions or resolutions are in order, and determine who have the right to participate as members (see also 53:7, 53:14–17). This effect is a consequence of the sponsors' rights as explained in the first paragraph of this section.

53:10   Any person at a mass meeting who, after being advised, persists in an obvious attempt to divert the meeting to a different purpose from that for which it was called, or who otherwise tries to disrupt the proceedings, becomes subject to the disciplinary procedures described in **61**.

53:11 **Opening of the Meeting; Election of Officers.** A chairman and a secretary are in general the only officers required by a mass meeting. Their election takes place immediately after the meeting is called to order, a convenient method of electing them being by voice vote. As explained in **46**, the first person nominated is voted on first under this method. In the interest of electing competent persons, it is therefore advisable that a name chosen by the sponsors be placed in nomination first for each office. Additional nominations can be made from the floor and the assembly can elect anyone it wishes, but except under unusual circumstances it is likely to elect the apparent choices of the sponsors.

53:12   Although the person who calls the meeting to order can call for nominations for chairman, and another can nominate the sponsors' choice, it is proper—and simpler—for one person to perform both functions (see *Nominations by the Chair,* 46:5). In the latter case, at the scheduled hour or shortly thereafter, this person steps to the chair and, after waiting or signaling for quiet, says, "The meeting will come to order. I nominate Mr. A for chairman of this meeting." After any additional nominations from the floor, the chair puts the question on each name in succession, beginning with the one he placed in nomination himself, as described under *Viva-Voce Election,* 46:37–41.

53:13 When the chairman of the meeting has been elected, he takes the chair and may say a few words of acknowledgment if he wishes, after which he says, "Nominations are now in order for secretary of this meeting." The person agreed upon to nominate the sponsors' choice for secretary should promptly place that name in nomination; members can also make additional nominations. The secretary is elected viva voce in the same manner as the chairman. When the secretary has been elected, he takes his seat near the chairman and keeps a record of the proceedings. If additional officers are desired, they can be elected in the same way.

Transaction of Business Specified in the Call

53:14 **Explanation of the Meeting's Purpose.** When the elections are completed, the chair says, "The Secretary will now read the call of this meeting." This reading of the call should include the names of the sponsors. The chair then recognizes the person who is to explain the purpose of the meeting more fully, or the chairman gives this presentation himself if he has been selected to do so.

53:15 **Resolutions to Accomplish the Purpose.** After the purpose of the meeting has been explained, it is in order for a member to offer a resolution, or a series of resolutions, to accomplish this purpose; or, if believed more suitable to the conditions, it can be moved that a committee be appointed to draft such resolution(s).

53:16   If the plan is for the resolution(s) to be offered immediately after the initial explanation, they can have been prepared in advance—with double-spaced reproduced copies for distribution to those in attendance—and a preselected member can now move their adoption. (For considerations to be observed in the drafting of resolutions, see *The Framing of Main Motions,* 10:9–25.) After another member has seconded the resolution(s), the chair states the question on them, they are open to debate and amendment, and the assembly proceeds to consider them, the entire procedure being as described in **4** and (for a series of resolutions) in 10:25.

53:17   In stating the question, the chair should make sure that those present understand the means by which the assembly can modify the proposals contained in the resolutions (see 10:29–30), and should provide such explanations as he believes necessary. With reference to the proposal of substitutes or other amendments—or alternative resolutions if those first introduced are rejected—any motion within the scope of the meeting's purpose as announced in the call is in order; but any motion outside of or contrary to that purpose is not in order. For example, if the announced purpose of a mass meeting is to oppose the construction of a proposed airport in a particular location, any motion or resolution directed toward preventing the airport's construction can be brought up at the meeting; but a motion whose effect would be to endorse the airport construction project is not in order.

53:18   The rules governing the assignment of the floor and debate, as given in **42** and **43**, are generally applicable. In a mass meeting, however, there is no appeal from the chair's decision in assigning the floor. The rule requiring the assembly's permission to speak for longer than ten minutes at a time in debate on pending questions applies if the meeting has adopted no other rule.

53:19   **Resolutions Drafted by a Committee Appointed at the Meeting.** If resolutions have not been prepared in advance, a committee should be appointed at the meeting to draft them. Such a procedure is appropriate when it is believed advisable to obtain expressions of opinion from persons who attend the meeting, before attempting to frame resolutions. In a small mass meeting, the chair at his discretion can permit those present to make brief statements of this nature after the initial explanation of the meeting's purpose and before the motion to appoint the committee is made. In that case, the chair should specify the time to be allowed each member—which is a matter entirely under the chair's control unless the meeting has adopted a special rule, since the procedure is in effect a relaxation of the general parliamentary rule prohibiting speeches when no question is pending (see 4:7–8). In any event, the same kind of discussion can also take place in regular debate on the motion to appoint the committee, since it is relevant to the committee's instructions to draft resolution(s) "expressing the sense of the meeting" on the specified subject, as explained below.

53:20   The person who is to make the motion to appoint the committee should be agreed upon by the sponsors in advance, as well as the matter of whether preliminary discussion is to be permitted before the motion is made. The motion may be made in a form such as the following:

> MEMBER (obtaining the floor): I move that a committee of five be appointed by the chair to draft resolutions expressing the sense of this meeting on … [the subject for which the meeting was called]. (Second.)

This is a main motion, since it is made when no question is pending. It is debatable and amendable and can have any subsidiary motion applied to it.

53:21   In a mass meeting it is usually advisable to have all committees appointed by the chair—assuming that the chairman has been well chosen. If the assembly prefers a different method of appointment, however, the procedures that can be followed are as described in **50**. When the committee has been appointed, it should immediately retire and prepare the resolution(s).

53:22   During the committee's absence from the hall, the assembly can attend to any other business related to the object of the meeting; or it can occupy the time in listening to talks, in engaging in forums or seminar-type discussions, or in watching a relevant film; or it can recess (**20**).

53:23   If the assembly does not recess and the chair sees the committee return to the room, he asks, as soon as the pending business is disposed of (or as soon as the person giving a talk closes, etc.), "Is the committee that was appointed to draft resolutions prepared to report?"

53:24   When the committee chairman has answered affirmatively, the chair says, "If there is no objection, the meeting will now hear the committee's report. [Pause.] The chair recognizes the chairman of the committee appointed to draft resolutions." (See treatment of *unanimous consent*, 4:58–63.)

53:25   If the chair does not notice the committee's return, the committee chairman, at the first opportunity, obtains the floor and says, "The committee appointed to draft resolutions is prepared to report." Unless objection is then made, the chair directs the committee chairman to proceed. If anyone objects, the chair puts the question on the report's being received (see second bulleted item in 51:28).

53:26   The committee chairman, addressing the presiding officer of the assembly, presents the report as follows:

> **COMMITTEE CHAIRMAN:** Madam President, the committee appointed to draft resolutions recommends, and on behalf of the committee I move, the adoption of the following resolution(s) … [reading them].

53:27   On the presentation of this report, the committee is discharged automatically. The chair then states the question on the resolutions, and they are considered in the same way as summarized above for the case in which resolutions are offered by a member from the floor (see also **51**).

Adjournment

53:28   In a mass meeting, unless a time for another meeting has already been set (by adopting a motion to *Fix the Time to Which to Adjourn,* **22**, or by adopting temporary rules as described below), a motion to adjourn is not in order while business is pending (see 21:2, 21:3(3)).

53:29   When the business for which the mass meeting was called has apparently been completed and no question is pending, someone should move "to adjourn," or the chair can call for such a motion. Unless a time has been set for another meeting, the adoption of this motion dissolves the assembly—so that, as explained in **21**, it is a main motion and can be debated and amended just as any other main motion. An example of an amendment to a main motion "to adjourn" might be "to add the words 'until eight o'clock Wednesday evening,'" which would thereby include in the motion a provision to set a time for another meeting.

53:30   In cases where it is desired to close the meeting before its business has been completed, the rules are as follows:

a) If the time for another meeting has already been set, the motion to adjourn is privileged, just as in a meeting of an ordinary permanent society, and is subject to the rules given in **21**.

b) If no time has been set for another meeting and a question is pending, a motion to *Fix the Time to Which to Adjourn* (**22**) should first be moved and adopted, after which the privileged motion to *Adjourn* (**21**) is in order; the procedure is as shown in 22:17–20.

c) If no time has been set for another meeting and no question is pending, any member can move, for example, "to adjourn until eight o'clock Wednesday evening," which is a main motion.

53:31   When a motion to adjourn a mass meeting has been adopted and no time is set for another meeting, the chair says, "The ayes have it and the meeting is adjourned." This announcement in effect declares the assembly dissolved. If a time for an adjourned meeting has been set, on the other hand—either previously or by means of a provision included in the motion to adjourn—the chair announces the result by saying, "The ayes have it and this meeting is [or "stands"] adjourned until eight o'clock Wednesday evening." Before declaring the adjournment, or even taking a vote on adjourning, the chair should make sure that all necessary announcements have been made.

Series of Mass Meetings; Temporary Society

53:32   If more than one mass meeting is necessary to achieve a certain objective, or if the group is working toward the formation of an organized society, a temporary organization to continue beyond a single mass meeting may become necessary. If so, the officers elected at the first meeting are designated *chairman pro tem* and *secretary pro tem*—although the words *pro tem* are not used in addressing these officers. If a permanent society is the aim of the group, the temporary officers serve until the election of permanent officers. If special rules were not adopted at the first meeting, a committee on rules can be appointed to recommend a few rules, providing for the hour and place for holding the meetings, the number and length of speeches allowed (if the general rules given in 43:8–13 are not satisfactory), and a work on parliamentary law to be used as parliamentary authority. If such rules specify periodic dates on which meetings are to be held, each meeting is a separate session (**8**) as in an ordinary society; but if the time of each succeeding meeting is set at the previous meeting or is "at the call of the chair," the entire series of meetings constitutes a single session.

§54. ORGANIZATION OF A PERMANENT SOCIETY

54:1   When it is desired to form a permanent society, the organizers proceed in much the same way as for a mass meeting, except that the meetings while the organization is being formed should usually be carefully limited to persons whose interest in the project is known. For this reason, it may be desirable to solicit attendance for these meetings by personal contact or by letter, rather than by public announcement.

First Organizational Meeting

54:2   The first meeting, at which the business portion should be kept brief, sometimes follows a luncheon or dinner. At these meetings for purposes of organization, the call to order can be delayed a few minutes beyond the scheduled time, if desired.

54:3   **Election of Temporary Officers, and Introductory Talks.** When the person designated for the purpose has called the meeting to order, he announces, "The first business is the election of a chairman." As in a mass meeting, the one who calls the meeting to order can either nominate a chairman pro tem or immediately call for nominations from the floor, and the nominees are voted on by voice. After the chairman pro tem has taken the chair, a secretary is elected, also as in the case of a mass meeting (see 53:11–13).

54:4   The chair then calls on the member most interested in the formation of the society to provide background information, or he himself can make the talk. Others can also be asked to give their opinions on the subject, but the chair should not permit any one person to monopolize the meeting.

54:5   **Adoption of a Resolution to Form a Society.** After a reasonable time for such informal discussion, someone should offer a resolution proposing definite action. Those who planned the meeting should have prepared in advance a suitable resolution, which may be in a form essentially as follows:

54:6   *Resolved,* That it is the sense of this meeting that a society for … [the object of the proposed society] now be formed [or "shall now be formed"].

54:7   This resolution, when seconded, is stated by the chair, and is then open to debate and amendment. Such a resolution, it should be noted, is only a declaration of intention; its adoption does not bring the organization into being, which is accomplished by the adoption of bylaws and the signing of the membership roll by those who initially join the society, as described below. If the meeting is a large one, it is usually better that, except for a brief statement of purpose, the resolution be offered before the introductory talks mentioned above.

54:8 **Further Business Relating to Organization.** After the resolution to organize the society is adopted, the succeeding steps generally are:

1) Introduction and adoption of a motion that a committee of a specified number be appointed by the chair to draft bylaws[1] for the society—and, where incorporation may be necessary, to consult an attorney as described below.

2) Introduction and adoption of a motion to fix the date, hour, and place of the next meeting (**22**), at which the report of the bylaws committee will be presented. If it is impractical to set a time and place for the next meeting, the motion can be that "when the meeting adjourns, it adjourn to meet at the call of the chair."

3) Introduction and adoption of a motion authorizing the committee on bylaws to provide reproduced copies of the completed draft for distribution to all who attend the next meeting. In this connection, persons seeking to form a society should take into account the fact that expenses may be involved, whether or not an organization materializes. Initiation fees or dues cannot be collected or received in the name of the society until its organization, as described in this section, is completed. Expenses advanced can be reimbursed.

54:9 Other business before adjournment may include informal discussion of aims and structure of the proposed society—which may serve to guide the bylaws committee (see also below).

---

1. Called the *constitution* or *constitution and bylaws* in some organizations (see 2:8–13). For factors affecting the appropriate size of this committee, see 56:4.

54:10   When the business of the first meeting is concluded and a motion to adjourn is adopted (see 53:28–31), the chair says either: (1) "The meeting stands [or "is"] adjourned to meet again at … [the date, hour, and place of next meeting]"; or (2) "The meeting is adjourned to meet again at the call of the chair."

Work of the Bylaws Committee

54:11   General principles for guidance in the drafting of bylaws are given in **56**. The drafting committee may find it helpful to procure and study copies of the bylaws of other organizations similar to the one being formed, although the possible applicability of their provisions must be carefully evaluated in the light of expected conditions within the new society. The committee may also find it advisable to consult a professional parliamentarian.

54:12   If it is expected that the society will own real estate, become a beneficiary under wills, engage employees, or the like, it may need to be incorporated according to the laws of the state in which it is situated (see 2:5–7). In such a case, the bylaws committee should be authorized to have one or more of its members consult an attorney to secure information and advice regarding the legal requirements that must be taken into account in drawing up the society's bylaws. If the society is to be incorporated, the same attorney should draft the charter or other instrument of incorporation, which the committee submits for approval at the second organizational meeting, before the bylaws are considered, unless there is some reason for delay (see below).

54:13   As indicated above, it is advisable to prepare double-spaced reproduced copies of the proposed bylaws—as drawn up by the committee—for distribution to each person entering the hall for the second organizational meeting. If desired, such copies can be sent in advance to everyone who attended the first meeting.

Second Organizational Meeting

54:14 **Reading and Approval of the Minutes.** With the temporary officers elected at the first organizational meeting serving until the
regular officers are elected, the first item of business at the second meeting is the reading and approval of the minutes of the
first meeting, with corrections if necessary.

54:15 **Consideration and Adoption of Proposed Bylaws.** After the minutes are approved, the report of the bylaws committee normally
is received. If there is a proposed corporate charter, that document is presented first. The assembly can amend the draft of the
charter, but any resulting modification should be checked by
the attorney, to whom the charter is returned after its adoption,
for processing under the legal procedure for incorporation in
the particular state.

54:16   If there is no proposed corporate charter, the bylaws committee chairman, when recognized for the purpose of presenting the report, begins somewhat as follows:

> COMMITTEE CHAIRMAN: Mr. Chairman, the committee ap-
> pointed to draw up proposed bylaws has agreed upon the
> following draft and has directed me to move its adoption.
> [Reads proposals in full—members following on their own
> copies—unless the first reading is dispensed with; then
> moves the adoption of the document, as follows:] Mr. Chair-
> man, by direction of the committee, I move the adoption of
> the bylaws.

54:17   No second is necessary, since the motion is offered by a
committee of more than one person. Since a complete set of
bylaws is commonly considered *by article or section* (see **28**),
the chair states the question as follows:

> CHAIR: The question is on the adoption of the bylaws as pro-
> posed by the committee. The committee chairman [or "the
> Secretary"] will now read the proposed bylaws, one article or
> section at a time. After each article or section is read, it will
> be open to debate and amendment. When amendment of

one article or section is completed, the next one will be read and considered. No section or article will be adopted until all have been opened to amendment.

54:18   Each article or section is read separately, each provision being carefully explained by the chairman of the bylaws committee, as described above; and after the last one has been completed, the chair gives opportunity to insert additional paragraphs or sections and to correct any inconsistency or oversight that may have arisen during the process of amendment, as follows:

> CHAIR: The entire set of bylaws is now open to amendment. Are there any further amendments?

54:19   If, at any point during the consideration of the bylaws, it develops that important additions or amendments are desirable but will require time or investigation to prepare, it is in order to move to recommit (**13**) the proposed bylaws, with instructions that the committee report at another meeting for which the time can be fixed. Or, further consideration of the bylaws can simply be postponed (**14**) to such a meeting. This third meeting in forming an organization, although in many cases unnecessary, in others often pays dividends in increased understanding and a larger membership. In any event, at the second or third meeting, when there are no further amendments, the question is put on adopting the bylaws:

> CHAIR: The question is on the adoption of the bylaws as amended. Those in favor of adopting the bylaws, say *aye*. … Those opposed, say *no*. … [and so on, taking a voice vote in the regular manner].

54:20   In case of doubt, the chair calls for a rising vote and, if necessary, directs that a count be made; or a member can call for a division (**29**), and can move that the vote be counted, as described in 4:50–53. Unlike the case of amending or revising the bylaws of an organization already established (**57**), the adoption of the bylaws through which a society is brought into being requires only a majority vote. The bylaws take effect immediately upon their adoption. A negative vote on their adoption can be reconsidered, but not an affirmative one.

54:21 **Recess to Enroll Members.** After the adoption of the bylaws, only those who join the society are entitled to vote in further proceedings. At this point, therefore, the meeting recesses to enroll initial members. Immediate admission to membership is contingent upon signing a permanent record sheet provided in advance by the secretary pro tem—to be filed with the original papers of the organization. This signature constitutes agreement to abide by the bylaws, and is a commitment to prompt payment of the initiation fee (if there is one) and dues for the first year or other period prescribed by the bylaws. Persons thus signing become "charter members."[2] The secretary pro tem records and gives receipt for payments received from members until the treasurer is elected and takes office.

54:22 **Reading of the Roll and Election of Permanent Officers.** After the recess the chairman pro tem calls for the reading of the roll of members, and the secretary pro tem does so. The chair then says, "The next business in order is the nomination and election of the permanent officers as prescribed in the bylaws."

54:23 The nomination and election processes are as described in **46**, the election being by ballot if the bylaws so prescribe, which they usually should. The members for whom one can vote are not limited to nominees, since each member is free to vote for any member who is not made ineligible by the bylaws. After the election is completed, the chair declares the results. Unless a proviso attached to the bylaws (57:15–17) prescribes otherwise, the newly elected officers immediately replace the temporary ones.

54:24 **Any Other Essential Business.** When the offices have been filled and the new president has taken the chair, he should call for

2. Sometimes, in forming a society, all who join before a specified date after the actual establishment of the organization are included in the roll of charter members.

any business requiring immediate attention. In a new society it is generally important that the president have time to give careful thought to committee appointments after examining the list of members. It is therefore often advisable to provide for an adjourned meeting to complete the organization before the first regular meeting. The president may find it essential, however, to name the chairmen of certain committees, such as the membership or program committees, immediately.

54:25   When the business of the meeting has been completed, or when an adjourned meeting has been provided for, a motion to adjourn is in order. If it is adopted, the chair announces the result and declares the meeting adjourned.

54:26   Subsequent meetings of the society are conducted as described in **3** and **4**. For additional information regarding the organization of a federation by a convention of delegates from prospective member societies, see **60**.

§55. MERGER, CONSOLIDATION, AND DISSOLUTION OF SOCIETIES

Combining of Societies

55:1   **Distinction Between Merger and Consolidation.** In cases where two existing societies wish to combine, there are two possible procedures, which are legally distinct:

- In the case of a *merger,* one of the two organizations continues, while the other loses its independent identity and ceases to exist, since it is merged—that is, absorbed—into the former.

- In the case of a *consolidation,* two or more organizations each discontinue their independent existence, and a new entity is formed that includes the memberships of the consolidating organizations, continues their work, and assumes their assets and liabilities.

In either a merger or a consolidation, the resulting organization may be given a new name, which may include, for example, elements of the names of each of the combining organizations.

55:2   **Cases Involving Incorporated Societies.** If one or more of the organizations involved in a merger or a consolidation are incorporated, an attorney should be consulted to draw up the proper papers and advise as to all steps necessary to fulfill the legal requirements.

55:3   **Cases Involving Unincorporated Societies.** If none of the organizations involved in a merger or a consolidation is incorporated, the respective procedures are as follows:

- In the case of a merger, the organization that is giving up its independent identity should adopt a resolution substantially as follows: "*Resolved,* That the A Society be, and hereby is, merged into the B Society as of [date] or when such merger shall be accepted by the B Society." For its adoption, such a resolution requires the same notice and vote as for amending the bylaws (see 56:50–56). This resolution should be joined with, or its adoption should be followed by the adoption of, resolutions transferring all of the assets and liabilities to the organization into which it is merging, and providing for whatever other administrative details will be required in the mechanics of transition. The society into which the first organization is being merged should adopt a resolution accepting the merger, and this motion similarly requires the same notice and vote as to amend the accepting organization's bylaws, because it so greatly alters the per-capita interest of each member. Often, resolutions authorizing and approving mergers contain stipulations and qualifications, sometimes even to the extent of naming the officers who will serve during the first year after the merger. Usually these resolutions are the work of a joint committee of the two organizations and form a part of its recommendations.

- In the case of a consolidation, the two or more consolidating organizations adopt resolutions authorizing the consolidation, similar to the resolutions described in the preceding item relating to merger. Often—but not necessarily—these meetings are held simultaneously in the same building. As in the case of a merger, the resolutions containing details relating to the mechanics of transition are usually drafted by a joint committee. After the consolidating organizations have each adopted resolutions which are substantially identical and which provide for consolidation as of a stated date, a joint meeting of the members of the consolidating groups is held for the purpose of organizing the new society that is to emerge. In contrast to the case of a merger, a new set of bylaws must be drawn up and adopted. The procedure is similar to that for the original establishment of a society as described in **54**, except that the necessary resolutions and motions normally are worded so that the date on which the new organization is established, its bylaws take effect, and its officers assume office coincides with the date on which the consolidating groups discontinue separate existence.

Dissolution of a Society

55:4   It may sometimes happen over a period of time that the needs which led to the formation of a society have largely disappeared, and the organization may wish formally to disband or dissolve.

55:5   **Dissolution of an Incorporated Society.** If a society is incorporated, the laws of the state in which it is incorporated provide in some detail the legal requirements for the dissolution of the corporation. An attorney should be consulted to draw up the necessary papers and advise the society as to the procedure to be followed.

55:6   **Dissolution of an Unincorporated Society.** In the case of an unincorporated society, a resolution should be prepared, such as: "*Resolved,* That the X Society be dissolved as of March 31,

20__." This resolution may be preceded by a preamble setting forth the reasons for the dissolution. It is in effect a motion to rescind the bylaws, and therefore requires for its adoption the same notice and vote as to amend them (see 56:50–56). The required notice must be sent to all members of record.

55:7   Such a resolution can be coupled with other resolutions stating the manner in which the society's assets shall be disposed of and attending to other administrative details—or these can be adopted separately. In certain tax-exempt organizations of a charitable or educational character, federal and state tax laws must be adhered to in the disposal of the organization's assets. Often such assets are distributed to societies with similar objectives, or to a superior body.

CHAPTER
XVIII

BYLAWS

§56. CONTENT AND COMPOSITION OF BYLAWS

Nature and Importance of Bylaws

56:1   The constitution and/or bylaws of a society, as explained in **2**, contains its own basic rules that relate to itself as an organization, except for what must be included in the corporate charter of an incorporated society. Under the preferred practice for ordinary societies today, the constitution and the bylaws— once usually separate—are now combined in a single instrument, referred to in this book as the *bylaws* (although in some organizations called the *constitution,* or—even though only one document—the *constitution and bylaws*). A precise statement of the essential characteristics of bylaws, in the sense of the combination-type instrument, and their relation to the other kinds of rules that an organization may have is given in **2**, which should be read in connection with this chapter. Because bylaws in this sense are the most important rules which an organization must compose for itself, and because certain considerations must be taken into account that affect their construction as a unified document rather than a series of separate rules, bylaws are given more detailed treatment below.

56:2   The content of a society's bylaws has important bearing on the rights and duties of members within the organization— whether present or absent from the assembly—and on the degree to which the general membership is to retain control of, or be relieved of detailed concern with, the society's business. Except as the rules of a society may provide otherwise, its assembly (that is, the members attending one of its regular or properly called meetings) has full and sole power to act for the entire organization, and does so by majority vote. Any limitation or standing delegation of the assembly's power with respect to the society as a whole can only be by provision in the bylaws—or in the corporate charter or separate constitution, if either of these exists.

Committee to Draw Up Bylaws

56:3 **Appointment of Committee.** A committee to draw up proposed bylaws is usually appointed at the first organizational meeting when a new society is being formed, as described in **54**; or, if an existing society wishes to undertake a general revision of its bylaws, a committee to draw up the proposed revision can be appointed at any regular meeting, just as any other special committee.

56:4 A committee to draw up proposed bylaws should generally be large, and should include the most judicious persons available, those who have a special interest in the rules of the society, and those who would otherwise be likely to consume much time in discussing the bylaws when they come before the assembly for adoption. Persons having writing ability of the kind required should also be included, unless a professional parliamentarian is to do the actual drafting of the bylaws. Even if the drafting is to be done by members of the committee, a parliamentarian can often be of great assistance as a consultant.

56:5 The committee should consult an attorney with reference to the considerations indicated in 54:12 if there is any possibility that the society should be incorporated. If it is to be incorporated, the committee works with the attorney to provide him with the necessary information for drafting an appropriate corporate charter, to which the bylaws must conform. The committee should review the draft of the charter before submitting it to the assembly.

56:6   **Initial Discussions; Factors Influencing Content of Bylaws.** The committee normally begins its work—with the entire committee present—in general discussion of the desired content of the bylaws. Besides reviewing the existing bylaws (in the case of a revision), it is well for the committee to study the bylaws of a number of similar organizations, or—if applicable—of other subordinate units within the same state or national society. Before any provisions from other documents are used as a pattern, however, possible differences between the conditions in the other organizations and the one for which the bylaws are being prepared should be carefully analyzed.

56:7   If the unit for which the bylaws are to be drawn up is subject to a parent organization or superior body, such as a state or a national society (or both), or a federation, the bylaws governing at these higher levels should be studied for provisions which are binding upon subordinate units in a way that must be taken into account. The bylaws of a subordinate unit need to conform to those of a superior body only on clearly requisite points. For example, if the superior body limits the size of its subordinate units to 200 members, the bylaws may not contain a higher limit. But the subordinate unit should not adopt provisions from the other document that have no local application, and the bylaws of the superior body should not require it to do so.

56:8   In order to give the organization the greatest freedom to act within its object, bylaws should be made no more restrictive nor more detailed in specification than necessary.

56:9   The description of the basic bylaw articles in 56:16–57 provides a brief indication of the framework within which the particular needs of the society should be considered in determining the content of its bylaws. A sample set of bylaws of the type that might be adopted by a small and independent local society is shown in 56:58–67. Such a model can only illustrate how a typical document of this kind is put together, however;

and the provisions must be varied, additional ones inserted, or inapplicable ones omitted, as appropriate to the individual organization.

56:10   **Drafting of Bylaws; Appointment of Subcommittee(s).** After conferences on the topics described above, the committee should appoint a drafting subcommittee, or several of them for various articles if the bylaws are expected to be long and complex. Another subcommittee may be needed in the latter case to eliminate inconsistencies, make the style uniform, and make sure that, as far as possible, everything relating to a single subject is placed in the same or adjacent articles.

56:11   The composition of bylaws is somewhat different from ordinary expository writing, in that it places greater demand on a "tight" clarity and precision in word choice, sentence structure, and punctuation. In bylaws, every punctuation mark may have an important effect; and what is omitted may carry as much significance as what is included. Indisputability of meaning and application is a more important consideration than "readability," and the latter must be sacrificed when both cannot be achieved. Each sentence should be written so as to be impossible to quote out of context; that is, either its complete meaning should be clear without reference to sentences preceding or following, or it should be worded so as to compel the reader to refer to adjoining sentences—as by beginning, "Any member so elected …" Exceptions or qualifications to statements should be included, as far as possible, within the sentence to which they apply—which can often be accomplished by ending sentences with clauses beginning "except that …" or "provided, however, that …" Where such a technique is impractical, a sentence should contain at least an allusion or reference to any exceptions to its own applicability—as in "Except as provided in Article VI, Section 2 of these bylaws, officers shall …"

56:12   Provisions of a temporary nature or relating to the mechanics of transition from old to revised bylaws should not be included within bylaws (see 57:15–17).

56:13   Regarding the inclusion of provisions in the nature of rules of order within bylaws, see 2:20–21.

56:14   **Critical Review by Full Committee.** After the first draft of the bylaws has been completed, it should be given thorough critical examination in discussions by the full committee. The probable long-range effect of each provision should be weighed, and particular care taken to detect and eliminate any remaining inconsistencies or ambiguities. It is much better to take a good deal of time in consideration of bylaws before their adoption than to find an early need for extensive amendment.

56:15   **Presentation of Report.** After the proposed bylaws are approved by the committee, the report of the committee is presented to the assembly and is considered seriatim—article by article and, whenever an article consists of more than one section, section by section. The procedure is as described in 54:15–20 and in **28**—except that:

a) especially in the case of a revision of bylaws, the motion to adopt them may include provisos relating to transition, as explained in 57:15–17; and

b) a revision of bylaws is adopted by the vote required to amend the existing ones (56:50–56), rather than by a majority vote as in the case of bylaws that bring a society into being.

In presenting the report of the bylaws committee to the assembly, the committee chairman should explain each section and—in the case of a proposed revision of bylaws—make clear what is new about each provision or how it differs from the corresponding provision of the existing bylaws.

Content of Bylaw Articles

56:16   **Basic Bylaw Articles.** While the number of bylaw articles will be determined by the size and activities of the organization adopting them, and more than those listed below will be needed in some cases, the average society will find it sufficient to include articles on the following numbered headings. The description of appropriate provisions in these articles, while in no sense exhaustive, should prove of help in framing bylaws. Articles are commonly designated with Roman numerals, and sections with Arabic numerals (see also Sample Bylaws, 56:58–67). For ready reference, it may be helpful to precede lengthy bylaws with a table of contents when they are printed or copied for distribution.

56:17 **Article I: Name.** In unincorporated societies, the full, exact, and properly punctuated name of the society should be given. In incorporated societies or those with separate constitutions, however, the bylaws can omit this article, since the official name of the organization is then stated in the corporate charter or constitution. If the name is in both locations, conflicts may creep in, and it is the name as stated in the superior document that is official.

56:18 **Article II: Object.** In unincorporated societies, the object of the society should be concisely expressed in a single sentence, the various aspects or phases being written in sequence, set off by semicolons, or in lettered subparagraphs, also set off by semicolons. The statement should be general in its application, since it sets boundaries within which business can be introduced at the society's meetings—a two-thirds vote being required to allow the introduction of a motion that falls outside the society's object. For the same reason stated above in reference to the society's name, this article also can be omitted from the bylaws in incorporated societies or in those having a separate constitution. Some societies prefer to set forth the object in a preamble to the bylaws rather than in an article, in which case the preamble precedes Article I, and the numbering of the remaining articles described below is modified as necessary. This device is especially useful in societies incorporated many years before, whose charter no longer states its object in modern terms or with the specificity now desired.

56:19   *Article III: Members.* Usually the article on members consists of several sections, covering, for example: (1) classes of members—as "active," "associate," and the like—with any distinctions between them being set forth, and, as applicable, the rights of each, and any limitation on their number; and (2) qualifications or eligibility for membership, with application and acceptance procedures, including the method of reviewing and voting on applications. Unless the financial obligations of members are especially complicated, a section of this article should also state: (3) the required fees and dues, the date(s) when payable (whether annually, semiannually, quarterly, etc.), the time and prescribed procedure for notifying members if they become delinquent in payment, and the date thereafter on which a member will be dropped for nonpayment of dues. Before a member in arrears has been finally dropped under such a provision, his voting rights cannot be suspended unless the bylaws so provide. (See also 1:13n3, 32:8, 45:1, 47:39, 56:61(3).) Members cannot be assessed any additional payment aside from their dues unless it is provided for in the bylaws. If the necessary provisions relating to the financial obligations of members to the society are too complex to be included in this article, such provisions can be set out in a separate article immediately following.

56:20   Some organizations require attendance at a certain proportion of the meetings or a specified minimum participation in the society's activities as a requirement for continued membership; this also can be done only by provision in the bylaws.

56:21   Sometimes this article also contains provisions for: (4) resignations; and (5) honorary members (see 47:42).

56:22   In a state or national body or a federation, local units or constituent clubs, rather than individuals, may be the "members" referred to in this article.

56:23   *Article IV: Officers.* As stated in **47**, every society should specify in this article of its bylaws the officers it requires, including honorary ones, and how they shall be elected or appointed. The officers rank in the order listed, so that the president should be named first, the vice-president or first vice-president next (unless there is to be a president-elect; see 47:21–22), and so on. Directors should be classed as officers.

56:24   Normally all that need be said about the duties of officers (apart from occasional references in other articles, under the topics to which specific duties relate) can be included in the section designating the officers, to the effect that "These officers shall perform the duties prescribed by these bylaws and by the parliamentary authority adopted by the Society." In cases where the extraordinary duties of officers are numerous, however, a separate article titled "Duties of Officers" may sometimes follow this article, and treat the duties for each office in a separate section. Such a procedure is advantageous in collecting related information in one place, but it results in repetition and may occasion problems of interpretation. Great care must be taken in the writing of the article not to omit any duty, since an implication that the duty is not required could be read into the omission. For this reason, if such an article is to be included, it is well to conclude the section on each office with a clause such as "… and such other duties applicable to the office as prescribed by the parliamentary authority adopted by the Society."

56:25   A method of nominating officers (see **46**) may be prescribed in a section of this article; in the absence of such a provision or any rule adopted by the society, nominations are made in accordance with established custom (if any) or as otherwise directed by vote of the society at the time of each election (see also **31**). If the bylaws provide for a nominating committee and prescribe that the committee shall nominate "candidates for each office," the committee is not limited to one candidate for each office. If it is desired to impose such a limitation, the provision should state that the committee shall nominate "a candidate for each office."

56:26   Election by ballot should usually be prescribed in the section pertaining to elections and terms of office—often with additional details of election procedure as discussed in **46**. A provision can be included to dispense with the ballot when there is only one candidate for an office, although this deprives members of the privilege of voting for "write-in" candidates in such a case. If it is desired to elect by mail, by plurality vote, by preferential voting, or by cumulative voting, this must be expressly stated, and necessary details of the procedure should be prescribed (see **45**).

56:27 The length of the terms of office should be prescribed; and unless the terms are to begin at the instant the chair declares each officer elected, the time when they are to begin must be specified. When the bylaws specify the number of years in a term of office, it is understood that the actual term may be more or less than a whole number of calendar years, owing to permissible variation in the dates on which successive elections are scheduled. For example, suppose that the bylaws provide that the annual meeting for the election of officers shall take place "in October or November," that their terms of office shall begin "at the close of the annual meeting," and that they shall serve for a term of "one year and until their successors are elected" (or simply for a term of "one year," which is not recommended; see below). If the annual meeting is held on October 20 of one year and on November 1 of the next (or vice versa), the officers elected at the second meeting take office immediately upon the adjournment of that meeting—and the previous officers remain in office until that time—even though this represents a term of office longer than (or shorter than) one calendar year. (For procedures when an election is not completed at the scheduled time, see 46:44–45.)

56:28 To ensure the continued services of officers in the event, for example, of public emergency or of difficulty in obtaining a nominee for an office, the unqualified wording "for a term of … year(s)" should be avoided, because at the end of that time there would be no officers if new ones had not been elected. The exact wording that instead ought to be used depends on a further consideration, namely, the manner in which the organization wants to make it possible to remove officers before the expiration of their normal term.

56:29   Careful thought should be given to whether, given the circumstances of the particular organization, it is preferable (1) to permit removal of officers only for cause, through disciplinary proceedings that may involve a formal trial, or (2) instead to permit their removal at the pleasure of the membership by a two-thirds vote, a majority vote when previous notice has been given, or a vote of a majority of the entire membership—any one of which will suffice (see 62:16).

56:30   To accomplish the first alternative, the bylaws may provide that officers "shall hold office for a term of _____ year(s) *and* until their successors are elected." To accomplish the second alternative, the bylaws may provide that officers "shall hold office for a term of _____ year(s) *or* until their successors are elected." (Emphases added.) Because the significant difference in effect between the use of "and" and "or" is unlikely to be clear to most members, it may be desirable (although it is not essential) to add an explanatory sentence, such as:

- For the first alternative: "Officers may be removed from office for cause by disciplinary proceedings as provided in the parliamentary authority."
- For the second alternative: "Officers may be removed from office at the pleasure of the membership as provided in the parliamentary authority."

56:31   Since a reasonable rotation in office is desirable in almost all organizations, a section of this article may well provide that "No person shall be eligible to serve ... consecutive terms [specifying the number] in the same office." For purposes of determining eligibility to continue in office under such a provision, an officer who has served more than half a term is considered to have served a full term in that office.

56:32   The method of filling vacancies may also be provided (cf. 47:57–58). Unless the bylaws clearly provide otherwise, notice of filling a vacancy in office must always be given to the members of the body that will elect the person to fill it. If the bylaws are silent as to the method of filling a vacancy in the specific case of the presidency, the vice-president or first vice-president automatically becomes president for the remainder of the term, and the vacancy to be filled arises in the vice-presidency or lowest-ranking vice-presidency; if another method of filling a vacancy in the presidency is desired, it must be prescribed and specified as applying to the office of president in particular.

56:33   *Article V: Meetings.* The first section of the article on meetings should fix the day on which regular meetings of the society are to be held—as by specifying, for example, "the first Friday of each month." If the words "unless otherwise ordered by the Society [or "Executive Board"]" are added, the date can be changed in an unusual circumstance, but only for that single meeting on that particular occasion, and not for a period of time including several meetings. To change the general rule fixing the time for meetings would require amendment of the bylaws. The hour and place at which meetings are to be held should not be specified in the bylaws, but should be established by a standing rule (**2**) adopted by the society or, if it is empowered to do so, by the executive board.

56:34   Some organizations prefer to schedule meetings by resolution. If so, the bylaws should provide for the number of days' notice required before regular meetings, since under such a practice members cannot determine the meeting dates by consulting the bylaws. Unless otherwise provided in the bylaws, the number of days is computed by counting all calendar days (including holidays and weekends), excluding the day of the meeting but including the day the notice is sent.

56:35   In a separate section it should be provided that "The regular meeting ... [specifying which one, as "on the last Tuesday in May"] shall be known as the annual meeting." As explained in **9**, this meeting is conducted in the same way as any regular meeting, except that officers are elected and annual reports are received from officers and standing committees.

56:36　　A section authorizing the calling of special meetings should state by whom such meetings can be called—such as the president, the board, or a specified number of members nearly equal to a quorum—and the number of days' notice required. It may be well to provide that no business shall be transacted except that mentioned in the call (that is, the notice) of the special meeting, although this rule would apply even if not expressly stated (see 9:15). If the bylaws do not authorize the calling of special meetings, such meetings are not permitted—except when authorized by the assembly itself, as part of formal disciplinary procedures, for purposes of conducting a trial and determining a punishment (see 63:21n9).

56:37　　The quorum for all meetings should be established in a section of this article (see **40**).

56:38　　In state or national bodies where one session—usually called a *convention*—is held annually, biennially, or at less frequent intervals, the article on meetings is titled "Conventions." While much that is stated above would be generally applicable to such an article, considerable adaptation is needed, as described in 58:6–10.

56:39　　***Article VI: Executive Board (or Board of Directors).*** As explained in 49:3–7, all but the smallest societies usually find it advisable to establish a board whose members are the officers of the society, such a body being entrusted with administrative authority and responsibility to a degree that varies with the organization. If there is to be such a board, sections of this article should:

- specify the board's composition;
- delineate the powers of the board; and
- set forth any special rules by which the board is to conduct its business, such as when and how often it is to meet, its quorum, and the like.

56:40　　In most societies this body is called the *Executive Board* unless there is to be a smaller body within it to act for the board between its meetings, in which case the full board is usually designated the *Board of Directors* and the smaller body is called the *Executive Committee* (see 49:13). The Executive Committee is then established in a separate article following the one on the complete board, with similar provisions. The bylaws may provide for how the presiding officer and the secretary of the board, and those of the Executive Committee, are to be determined. In the absence of such provisions in the bylaws, however, the president and the secretary of the society also serve in the same capacities within these bodies. Organizations may sometimes give varied names to their full boards, such as *Board of Managers, Board of Trustees, Board of Governors, Administrative Council,* etc. In such cases, the nature of the particular body as one of the types described above can be determined from the bylaw article that establishes it.

56:41 A board may never alter a decision of the society's assembly (and an executive committee may never alter a decision of either the assembly or the board), even by a motion to *Rescind* or *Amend Something Previously Adopted* or by adoption of a proposal which has been rejected, unless expressly authorized by the superior body or by the bylaws (see 49:7). Thus, for example, if it is desired that the assembly adopt an annual budget but that the board be empowered to alter it to deal with contingencies that may develop, the bylaws (or the budget resolution) must specifically confer this power on the board.

56:42 Article VI, Section 2 of the Sample Bylaws (56:64) shows an appropriate wording for defining the board's powers so that the board's authority will be limited to the power to supervise, and to determine the details of, implementation of the decisions of the society's assembly and, in a manner not inconsistent with such decisions, to attend to any business of the society that cannot wait until the next meeting.

56:43 If the organization desires to leave the entire administrative authority of the society to the board between the society's meetings—as may occur, for example, in organizations that meet infrequently or whose main purpose is other than to transact business—the same section might read:

> The Executive Board [or "Board of Directors," etc.] shall have full power and authority over the affairs of the Society except … [specifying classes of business over which the assembly of the society is to retain sole authority].

56:44 **Article VII: Committees.** The article on committees should provide for the establishment of each of the standing committees (**50**) that it is known will be required. A separate section devoted to each of these committees should give its name, composition, manner of selection, and duties. If this article names certain standing committees, no other standing committees can be appointed without amending the bylaws, unless a provision is included—usually in a separate section of the article as described below—permitting the establishment of such other standing committees as are deemed necessary to carry on the work of the society. In any event, if a standing committee is to have standing authority to act for the society without specific instructions, if business of a certain class is to be automatically referred to it, or if some other rule of parliamentary procedure is affected by the committee's assigned function, such procedure must be prescribed in a provision of the bylaws or in a special rule of order, establishing the committee by name.

56:45 The number and nature of the standing committees that may be named in individual sections of this article will depend on the size and object of the organization. The standing committees most frequently established by local societies are few in number; they may include a committee on membership, a program committee, and sometimes a finance committee. (A section relating to the nominating committee, when included, is usually located not in this article but in the article on officers, where nomination and election procedures are usually prescribed.) In national or state bodies more committees may be needed, but local units should not try to establish a committee to correspond to each one in the superior body, and the superior body generally should not require them to do so.

56:46   Appointment of special committees is usually provided for in a separate section that may also, as indicated above, provide for the appointment of additional standing committees. When this section empowers the president to appoint such special committees or additional standing committees as the society or the board shall direct, he is not thereby authorized to appoint other committees on his own initiative. If the president is to appoint committees and it is desired that he have standing authority to appoint non–assembly members to positions on the committees without submitting these persons' names to the assembly for approval, this section should contain a provision to that effect (see 13:15, 50:12, 50:13(d)).

56:47   This section may also provide that certain officers—for example, the president—"shall be ex officio a member of all committees except the Nominating Committee." In that case, the president has the right, but not the duty, of participating in the work of the committees (see also 49:8, 50:16). Without such a provision, he has no vote within the committees, nor can he attend their meetings except as invited by a particular committee. The nominating committee should always be expressly excluded in a provision making the president an ex-officio member of committees. It may also be advisable to exclude all disciplinary committees—such as trial and investigating committees—both from a provision making the president an ex-officio member of committees and from a provision authorizing the president to appoint committees.

56:48   If no article on committees is included in the bylaws, standing and special committees are established as directed by the society (see **13**, **50**).

56:49   *Article VIII: Parliamentary Authority.*   The parliamentary authority—through the adoption of which a society establishes its rules of order—should be prescribed in a one-sentence article reading: "The rules contained in the current edition of … [specifying a standard manual of parliamentary practice, such as this book] shall govern the Society in all cases to which they are applicable and in which they are not inconsistent with these bylaws and any special rules of order the Society may adopt."[1] Societies can adopt special rules of order as they are needed to supplement their parliamentary authority, as explained in **2**. It should be noted that the bylaw language recommended above does not authorize the adoption of a special rule of order that would supersede a rule that the parliamentary authority states can be altered only by a provision in the bylaws. When a particular work is adopted as the parliamentary authority, what any other book may say on any point is of no authority if in conflict with the adopted work. In other cases, it may be persuasive but is not binding upon the society.

56:50 *Article IX: Amendment of Bylaws.* The bylaws should always prescribe the procedure for their amendment, and such provision should always require at least that advance notice be given in a specified manner, and that the amendment be approved by a two-thirds vote. If the bylaws contain no provision for their amendment, they can be amended by a two-thirds vote if previous notice (in the sense defined in 10:44) has been given, or they can be amended by the vote of a majority of the entire membership. In making a requirement that notice be given by submitting the amendment at a meeting in advance of the one at which it is to be considered, the provision should always specify submission at "*the* previous meeting," and not "a" previous meeting, since the latter would permit indefinite delay and would defeat the object of giving notice—namely, to alert

---

1. Where a particular type of organization is subject to local, state, or national law containing provisions relating to its procedure—as for certain procedures in a labor organization, in condominium associations, or in an incorporated association— it may be desirable to add at this point a phrase such as, "and any statutes applicable to this organization that do not authorize the provisions of these bylaws to take precedence." However, such statutes (those that do *not* authorize bylaws to take precedence) supersede all rules of the organization which conflict with them, even if no mention is made of it in the bylaws.

the members to the proposed amendment so that all those interested can arrange to be present at its consideration. The requirement of notice restricts amendment of the proposed bylaw amendment to changes within the scope of the notice, as explained in 57:10–13 (see also 35:2(6)).

56:51   The manner prescribed for giving notice should suit the needs of the particular assembly. For some, oral notice is sufficient; others may require written notice. Some may require only a general statement of the purport of the amendment; others may require that the exact wording of the amendment be given. If the bylaws require only previous notice of an amendment without limitation of the period within which it must be acted upon, and a committee is appointed to revise the bylaws and report at a specified meeting, the appointing action is all the notice required, and the amendments can be immediately acted upon at the time the committee reports. But if it is required that the amendment itself, or "notice of such amendment," be submitted at the previous regular meeting, the revision cannot be taken up until the meeting following the meeting at which the committee submitted its report.

56:52   In societies having very frequent regular meetings primarily for presentation of a program, and also monthly or quarterly business meetings (9:1), it is well to permit action on amendments to the bylaws only at a quarterly or annual meeting or their adjournments.

56:53   Where assemblies meet regularly only once a year, instead of requiring amendments to be submitted at the previous annual meeting, the bylaws should provide for both notice and copies of the proposed amendment to be sent to the member delegates or constituent societies a specified minimum number of days in advance.

56:54   If there is a constitution separate from the bylaws, the requirement for amendment of the constitution should be made more difficult than that for amendment of the bylaws; otherwise there would be no purpose in having separate documents. In either case, however, the necessary vote should be at least two thirds.

56:55   In prescribing the vote necessary for the adoption of an amendment, the expression "a vote of two thirds of the members" should never be used in ordinary societies, especially in large organizations. In such societies two thirds of the entire membership would rarely, if ever, be present at a meeting. It is more reasonable to require "a two-thirds vote" (see 44:3–6).

56:56   The wording of this article should avoid redundant phraseology such as "amend, alter, add to, or repeal," or "alter or amend," or "amend or in any way change." The word *amend* covers any change, whether a word or a paragraph is to be added, struck out, or replaced, or whether a new set of articles is to be substituted for the old one. Efforts to define the meaning of such expressions as "two-thirds vote" should also be avoided in the wording of this article, since these definitions are found in the parliamentary authority.

56:57 **Additional Bylaw Articles.** Some societies may have cause to include additional bylaw articles, such as those mentioned above, bearing on the subjects of finance, duties of officers, and an executive committee of the board of directors. In a national organization, an article providing for constituent societies or units at regional, state, or local levels and establishing their relationships within the organizational structure may be required. In associations divided into departments, the article establishing them—titled "Departments"—follows the article establishing committees. In professional and some other societies there may be an article on disciplinary procedure; and such an article can be simple or very elaborate. Most such provisions, however, are generally unnecessary in ordinary societies, at least at the local level (see **61–63**).

Sample Bylaws

56:58   Regarding the applicability of the following model, see 56:9. Titles of sections are optional, but they may be felt to be desirable, particularly if the bylaws become elaborate, as may be the case, for example, in a complex national organization.

BYLAWS
OF THE _____ SOCIETY
OF _____

ARTICLE I: NAME

The name of this Society shall be _____.

ARTICLE II: OBJECT

The object of this Society shall be to _____; to _____; and to _____.

ARTICLE III: MEMBERS

Section 1. Maximum Membership. The membership of this Society shall be limited to two hundred members.

Section 2. Membership Eligibility and Admission Procedure. Any adult resident of _____ shall be eligible for membership, provided that such resident shall be proposed by one member and seconded by another member of the Society. A proposal for membership, signed by the two endorsers, shall be sent to the Recording Secretary, who shall report it, together with the names of the sponsors, at the next regular meeting of the Society. Voting upon the admission shall take place at the next regular meeting thereafter. A two-thirds vote shall elect to membership. A person so elected shall be declared a member of the Society upon payment of the initiation fee and the annual dues for the first year.

Section 3. Initiation Fee and Dues. The initiation fee shall be _____ dollars. The annual dues shall be _____ dollars, payable in advance on or before _____ of each year. The Treasurer shall notify members _____ months in arrears, and those whose dues are not paid within _____ thereafter shall be automatically dropped from membership in the Society.

Section 4. Resignation from Membership. Any member desiring to resign from the Society shall submit his resignation in writing to the Recording Secretary, who shall present it to the Executive Board for action. No member's resignation shall be accepted until his dues are paid.

Section 5. Honorary Life Membership. Upon the signed recommendation of one member, seconded by another member, and by a three-fourths vote by ballot at the annual meeting, honorary life membership may be conferred upon an adult resident of _____ who shall have rendered notable service to the Society. An honorary member shall have none of the obligations of membership in the Society, but shall be entitled to all of the privileges except those of making motions, of voting, and of holding office.

56:62   **ARTICLE IV: OFFICERS**

Section 1. Officers and Duties. The officers of the Society shall be a President, a First Vice-President, a Second Vice-President, a Recording Secretary, a Corresponding Secretary, a Treasurer, and four Directors. These officers shall perform the duties prescribed by these bylaws and by the parliamentary authority adopted by the Society.

Section 2. Nomination Procedure, Time of Elections. At the regular meeting held on the second Tuesday in February, a Nominating Committee of five members shall be elected by the Society. It shall be the duty of this committee to nominate candidates for the offices to be filled at the annual meeting in April. The Nominating Committee shall report at the regular meeting in March. Before the election at the annual meeting in April, additional nominations from the floor shall be permitted.

Section 3. Ballot Election, Term of Office, Removal from Office. The officers shall be elected by ballot to serve for one year or until their successors are elected, and their term of office shall begin at the close of the annual meeting at which they are elected. Officers may be removed from office at the pleasure of the membership as provided in the parliamentary authority.

Section 4. Office-Holding Limitations. No member shall hold more than one office at a time, and no member shall be eligible to serve three consecutive terms in the same office.

ARTICLE V: MEETINGS

Section 1. Regular Meetings. The regular meetings of the Society shall be held on the second Tuesday of each month from September to May inclusive unless otherwise ordered by the Society.

Section 2. Annual Meetings. The regular meeting on the second Tuesday in April shall be known as the annual meeting and shall be for the purpose of electing officers, receiving reports of officers and committees, and for any other business that may arise.

Section 3. Special Meetings. Special meetings may be called by the President or by the Executive Board and shall be called upon the written request of ten members of the Society. The purpose of the meeting shall be stated in the call, which shall be sent to all members at least three days before the meeting.

Section 4. Quorum. Fifteen members of the Society shall constitute a quorum.

ARTICLE VI: THE EXECUTIVE BOARD

Section 1. Board Composition. The officers of the Society, including the Directors, shall constitute the Executive Board.

Section 2. Board's Duties and Powers. The Executive Board shall have general supervision of the affairs of the Society between its business meetings, fix the hour and place of meetings, make recommendations to the Society, and perform such other duties as are specified in these bylaws.

Section 3. Board Meetings. Unless otherwise ordered by the Board, regular meetings of the Executive Board shall be held on the first Tuesday of each month from September to June, inclusive. Special meetings of the Board may be called by the President and shall be called upon the written request of three members of the Board.

ARTICLE VII: COMMITTEES

Section 1. Finance Committee. A Finance Committee composed of the Treasurer and four other members shall be appointed by the President promptly after each annual meeting. It shall be the duty of this committee to prepare a budget for the fiscal year beginning the first day of April, and to submit it to the Society at its regular meeting in March. The Finance Committee may from time to time submit amendments to the budget for the current fiscal year, which may be adopted by a majority vote.

Section 2. Program Committee. A Program Committee of five members shall be appointed by the President promptly after the annual meeting, whose duty it shall be to plan the annual program of the Society. This committee's report shall be submitted to the Society for its approval at its regular meeting in September.

Section 3. Auditing Committee. An Auditing Committee of three members shall be appointed by the President at the Society's March meeting, whose duty it shall be to audit the Treasurer's accounts at the close of fiscal year and to report at the annual meeting.

Section 4. Other Committees; President's Ex-Officio Committee Membership. Such other committees, standing or special, may be established by the Society as it shall from time to time deem necessary to carry on its work. Their members shall be appointed by the President unless this rule is suspended by a two-thirds vote before their appointment. The President shall be ex officio a member of all committees except the Nominating Committee and any disciplinary committees.

ARTICLE VIII: PARLIAMENTARY AUTHORITY

The rules contained in the current edition of *Robert's Rules of Order Newly Revised* shall govern the Society in all cases to which they are applicable and in which they are not inconsistent with these bylaws and any special rules of order the Society may adopt.

ARTICLE IX: AMENDMENT OF BYLAWS

These bylaws may be amended at any regular meeting of the Society by a two-thirds vote, provided that the amendment has been submitted in writing at the previous regular meeting.

Some Principles of Interpretation

56:68   In preparing bylaws and interpreting them, the following principles of interpretation—which have equal application to other rules and documents adopted by an organization—may be of assistance.

1) *Each society decides for itself the meaning of its bylaws.* When the meaning is clear, however, the society, even by a unanimous vote, cannot change that meaning except by amending its bylaws. An ambiguity must exist before there is any occasion for interpretation. If a bylaw is ambiguous, it must be interpreted, if possible, in harmony with the other bylaws. The interpretation should be in accordance with the intention of the society at the time the bylaw was adopted, as far as this can be determined. Again, intent plays no role unless the meaning is unclear or uncertain, but where an ambiguity exists, a majority vote is all that is required to decide the question. The ambiguous or doubtful expression should be amended as soon as practicable.

2) *When a provision of the bylaws is susceptible to two meanings, one of which conflicts with or renders absurd another bylaw provision, and the other meaning does not, the latter must be taken as the true meaning.* For example, assume the bylaws define the officers as "a president, a vice-president, a secretary, a treasurer, and five other members, all of whom shall serve as members of the Board ..." Assume also that elsewhere the bylaws speak of "Directors" being board members. A suggestion that the "Directors" are not officers and are additional members of the board would create a conflict within the bylaws and cannot be taken as the true meaning. The "other members" are the same as the "Directors."

3) *A general statement or rule is always of less authority than a specific statement or rule and yields to it.* It is not practical to state a rule in its full detail every time it is referred to. General statements of rules are seldom strictly correct in every possible application. The specific statement of the rule that gives the details applying to the particular case must always be examined. For instance: in the Sample Bylaws, Article III, Section 2 (56:61), it is provided that any "adult resident" shall, by a two-thirds vote, be elected to membership. This is a general statement which yields to the proviso stated in Section 1 of the same article that restricts membership to two hundred. Thus, the Society is not empowered to elect a two-hundred-and-first member by a two-thirds vote. No one has a right to quote a general statement as of authority against a specific statement.

4) *If the bylaws authorize certain things specifically, other things of the same class are thereby prohibited.* There is a presumption that nothing has been placed in the bylaws without some reason for it. There can be no valid reason for authorizing certain things to be done that can clearly be done without the authorization of the bylaws, unless the intent is to specify the things of the same class that may be done, all others being prohibited. Thus, where Article IV, Section 1 of the Sample Bylaws (56:62) lists certain officers, the election of other officers not named, such as a sergeant-at-arms, is prohibited.

5) *A provision granting certain privileges carries with it a right to a part of the privileges, but prohibits a greater privilege.* The Sample Bylaws, in Article VI, Section 2 (56:64) provide that the executive board may "fix the hour and place of meetings" of the society. The board may, therefore, change the time or the place, or both, of a society's meeting. But it may not change the day for which the meeting is scheduled.

6) *A prohibition or limitation prohibits everything greater than what is prohibited, or that goes beyond the limitation; but it permits what is less than the limitation, and also permits*

things of the same class that are not mentioned in the prohibition or limitation and that are not evidently improper. The Sample Bylaws, Article IV, Section 4 (56:62) limits a member to holding one office at a time. This limitation carries with it, of course, the prohibition of holding more than two or three offices as well. The next clause in Article IV, Section 4 prohibits officers from serving three consecutive terms in the same office. Hence, an officer cannot serve four consecutive terms, but may serve two consecutive terms. Article IX of the Sample Bylaws (56:67) limits amendments to the bylaws to those of which notice has been given and which are adopted by a two-thirds vote. Thus, the change of a single word is prohibited unless these conditions are met, and a revision of the entire bylaws requires that the same steps be taken.

7) *The imposition of a definite penalty for a particular action prohibits the increase or diminution of the penalty.* If the bylaws state that a member shall be dropped from membership on a board if he misses three consecutive regular meetings of the board, he cannot be retained by vote of the board, nor can more severe penalties be imposed, such as a fine in addition. If, for example, it is desired to allow the board to diminish or waive the penalty, or increase it, the bylaw must not make it definite or must specifically provide for diminution, waiver, or enlargement.

8) *In cases where the bylaws use a general term and also two or more specific terms that are wholly included under the general one, a rule in which only the general term is used applies to all the specific terms.* Where the bylaws provide in the basic enumeration of the classes of membership that "members may be active, associate, or honorary," the general term "member" is used to apply to all three classes of members. But if, in the article on Members, it is stated that members may be either active or associate members, or if that article simply describes "members" without classification, as in the Sample Bylaws, Article III (56:61), the term "member" applies only to those

classes or that class of members, even if honorary members are provided for elsewhere—in which case honorary membership is not real membership. Similarly, if the bylaws provide for "elected officers" and "appointed officers," the word "officers" or the expression "all officers," used elsewhere in establishing the term during which office shall be held, applies to both the elected and the appointed officers.

§57. AMENDMENT OF BYLAWS

57:1   A motion to amend the bylaws is a particular case of the motion to *Amend Something Previously Adopted* (**35**); it is therefore a main motion, and it is subject to the same rules as other main motions with the following exceptions:

1) Special requirements for this motion's adoption should be specified in the bylaws, and they should always include at least notice *and* a two-thirds vote, which (with a vote of a majority of the entire membership as an allowable alternative) are the requirements for its adoption if such specification in the bylaws is neglected (see 56:50–56).
2) Permissible primary and secondary amendment of the motion to amend the bylaws is usually limited by the extent of change for which notice was given, as explained below.
3) An affirmative vote on the motion to amend the bylaws cannot be reconsidered (**37**).
4) The rule that, when a main motion is adopted, no other conflicting main motion is thereafter in order is not applicable to the motion to amend the bylaws, since several notices of proposals representing different approaches to the same problem may have been given, and all such bylaw amendments are entitled to be considered (see 57:6–8).

Method of Handling Bylaw Amendments

57:2   The extensiveness of amendments to the bylaws will determine the method of handling them, as follows:

57:3 **Isolated Changes.** If only an isolated change is to be made in the bylaws, it can be treated as any motion to *Amend Something Previously Adopted* (**35**), subject to the particular rules indicated immediately above. When a series of isolated changes to the bylaws are needed to achieve one end—such as abolishing the office of "Historian" and eliminating all references to it—the changes should be offered in a single motion. If the changes are related in such a way that all of the individual amendments must be made, if any one of them is made, in order for the bylaws to be coherent, then the motion cannot be divided (see 27:5).

57:4 Sometimes a more extensive change is proposed involving the substitution of an entire section, group of sections, or article. In such a case, often only a few separated passages are actually involved in the changes, and they are offered in the form of a single proposed substitute in order to avoid time-consuming separate action on each change. The text of the substitute should then be given with the notice of proposed amendment, or the notice should delineate each of the actual changes, and only changes within the scope of those contained in the substitute can be considered. Portions of the substitute which remain as in the existing version cannot be amended, since they involve areas for which no notice of proposed change was given.

57:5 **General Revisions.** Changes of the bylaws that are so extensive and general that they are scattered throughout the bylaws should be effected through the substitution of an entirely new set of bylaws, called a *revision*. Notice of such a revision is notice that a new document will be submitted that will be open to amendment as fully as if the society were adopting bylaws for the first time. In other words, in the case of a revision, the assembly is not confined to consideration of only the points of change included in the proposed revision as submitted by the committee that has drafted it. The revision can be perfected by first-degree and second-degree amendments, but as in the case of any other bylaw amendment, the old document is not pending; and therefore, while the revision can be rejected altogether, leaving the old bylaws intact, the old document cannot be altered with a view to retaining it in a changed form. Consideration of a revision of the bylaws is in order only when prepared by a committee that has been properly authorized to draft it either by the membership or by an executive board that has the power to refer such matters to a committee.[2]

57:6   **Procedure of Consideration.** A revision of bylaws or a lengthy amendment involving more than one section should be considered seriatim as described in **28**. If notice is given of several amendments which conflict so that all cannot be given effect, the chair should arrange them in a logical order, much as in the case of filling blanks (**12**), generally taking the least inclusive amendment first and the most inclusive last so that the last one adopted is given effect. That arrangement of the amendments can be altered by the assembly; a motion to rearrange the amendments requires a second, is not debatable, is amendable, and requires a majority vote. An affirmative vote adopting such an arrangement is not subject to a motion to *Reconsider,* nor may a later, separate amendment be offered as a substitute for a pending one.

57:7   However, as already stated in 57:1(4), all bylaw amendments of which notice was given are entitled to be considered, as a matter of the rights of their proposers, and a bylaw amendment is not dropped simply because it would conflict with one previously adopted. This procedure does not violate the normal parliamentary rule as might appear, because when any bylaw amendment is adopted, that amendment becomes a part of the bylaws immediately; and it is the bylaw language *as thus amended,* rather than the previous language, which any bylaw

---

2. A proposal to substitute a new set of bylaws that is submitted by anyone other than such an authorized committee is not improper, but it is not treated as a general revision. In such a case, only changes within the scope of those contained in the substitute can be considered, as described in the previous paragraph (57:4).

amendments subsequently considered would now propose to modify.

57:8 If an amendment that has not been considered no longer presents a rational proposition because it was applicable only to language which has disappeared from the bylaws in this process, such a bylaw amendment must, of course, be dropped; but this situation should generally not arise if the amendments are taken up in proper order as indicated above.

57:9 The final vote on a bylaw amendment should be counted and recorded in the minutes unless it is nearly unanimous.

Amending a Proposed Amendment to the Bylaws

57:10 While amendments to a proposed bylaw amendment can be made in both the first and the second degrees (as applicable) and can be adopted by a majority vote without notice, they are subject to restrictions on the extent of the changes they propose.

57:11 If the bylaws require previous notice for their amendment (as they should), or if they do not but notice *has* been given and a majority of the entire membership is not present, no amendment to a bylaw amendment is in order that increases the modification of the article or provision to be amended (see 35:2(6)). This restriction prevents members from proposing a slight change and then taking advantage of absent members by moving a greater one as an amendment to the amendment. Thus, if the bylaws place the annual dues of members at $10 and an amendment is pending to strike out 10 and insert 25, an amendment to change the 25 to any number between 10 and 25 would be in order, but an amendment to change the number to less than 10 or greater than 25 would not be in order, even with unanimous consent. Had notice been given that it was proposed to increase the dues to more than $25 or to reduce them below $10, members who opposed such a change might have attended the meeting to vote against the amendment.

57:12   The same principle applies to an amendment in the nature of a substitute for sections or articles (short of a revision), as already indicated above; the proposed substitute is open to amendments that diminish the amount of change, but not to amendments that increase it or that introduce new changes. Thus, if an amendment is pending to substitute a new rule for one that prescribes the initiation fee and the annual dues, and the substitute proposes to alter the initiation fee but does not propose any change in the annual dues, then an amendment which recommends changing the annual dues would not be in order.

57:13   Amendments to strike out a sentence, paragraph, or section deserve special care. In such cases, the existing bylaw is not itself open to consideration, but only the amendment. If notice is given to strike out a provision of the bylaws and some members feel it should be retained with certain changes whose substance would be outside the scope of that notice, those members should immediately give notice of the amendments to the existing provisions which they think are advisable. Otherwise, friends of the existing provision will be cut off from opportunity to work out compromises for its partial retention by perfecting the existing language.

Giving Notice of Amendments

57:14   Notice of a bylaw amendment should be formally worded in a form such as "To amend Article IV, Section 2, by striking out 'March' and inserting 'April' after the words 'second Tuesday in.'" When the bylaws do not place a limitation on those who can give notice of a bylaw amendment, any member is entitled to do so. If notice is to be given at a meeting, this is usually done under new business, although it can be done at any time, even after it has been voted to adjourn if the chair has not actually declared the meeting adjourned. A bylaws committee can give notice in that part of the order of business set aside for committee reports. If notice is to be sent with the call of the meeting at which the amendment will be introduced, the society is responsible for paying the cost of sending such notice, not the member proposing the amendment. The notice should fairly inform the members of the changes contemplated. Showing the existing bylaw and the bylaw with the proposed changes in parallel columns is a good device so long as the exact amendment, stated in a formal manner, is set out at the top across both columns. When notice of a bylaw amendment is given in open meeting, it cannot be considered at that time, except to be discussed informally and briefly at the discretion of the presiding officer (see also 43:31–34).

Time at Which a Bylaw Amendment Takes Effect

57:15   An amendment to the bylaws goes into effect immediately upon its adoption unless the motion to adopt specifies another time for its becoming effective, or the assembly has set such a time by a previously adopted motion. While the amendment is pending, a motion can be made to amend the enacting words of the motion to amend by adding a clause such as this: "… with the proviso that [or, "… provided, however, that"] this amendment shall not go into effect until after the close of this annual meeting." Or, while the amendment is pending, an incidental motion can be adopted that, in the event of the amendment's adoption, it shall not take effect until a specified time. Either method requires only a majority vote. It is a mistake to encumber the bylaws themselves with provisions which have effect for only a limited time. If the mechanics of transition to operation under a revised set of bylaws will be complicated in ways for which the act of adoption must provide temporarily, such provisions can be numbered and attached to the revision draft on a separate sheet headed "Provisos Relating to Transition." The motion to adopt the revision can then be made in this form: "I move the adoption of the revised bylaws with the provisos attached thereto."

57:16   Amendments to the article on officers may raise difficulties in relation to the time at which adopted changes take effect, unless special care is taken. A society can, for example, amend its bylaws so as to affect the emoluments and duties of the officers already elected, or even to abolish an office; and if it is desired that the amendment should not affect officers already elected, a motion so specifying should be adopted before voting on the amendment, or the motion to amend can have added to it the proviso that it shall not affect officers already elected. There is virtually a contract between a society and its officers, and while to some extent action can be taken by either party to modify or even terminate the contract, such action must be taken with reasonable consideration for the other party.

57:17   It is important to note that, although the time when a by-law amendment *takes effect* can be delayed by the assembly, the amendment becomes part of the bylaws immediately upon adoption. If the amended bylaws are printed, a footnote or similar device should indicate that the amended language is not yet in effect and, if language was removed by the amendment, the text of that provision should be given if it is still applicable in the organization.

Captions, Headings, and Article and Section Numbers

57:18   It was formerly customary to permit the secretary to fill in captions, headings, and article, section, or paragraph numbers or letters, and the like, after the assembly had adopted bylaws or other long documents. Such designations were treated as mere marginal notations which could be clerically modified. It is now the usual practice to include these subtitles or identifying numbers or letters as an integral part of what is adopted by action of the assembly.

57:19   In the process of amending previously adopted documents of this kind, indisputably necessary changes in designation by number or letter may be presumed to have been included in the assembly's action even if they were not mentioned. For example, if an assembly adopts a motion "to insert after Article III a new Article IV reading as follows: … ," the secretary or a committee would, of course, raise the numerical designation of each of the later articles by one, even if the enacting motion made no reference to doing so. Only the assembly can amend captions or headings under the rules applicable to bylaws or other papers if such change could have any effect on meaning, and this authority may not be delegated. Corrections of article or section numbers or cross-references that cannot result in a change of meaning can be delegated, however, to the secretary or, in more involved cases, to a committee. An assembly may delegate its authority in this connection in a particular case, by adopting, for example, a resolution such as the following:

> *Resolved*, That the secretary [or, "the ... committee"] be authorized to correct article and section designations, punctuation, and cross-references and to make such other technical and conforming changes as may be necessary to reflect the intent of the Society in connection with ...

XIX

CONVENTIONS

§58. CONVENTIONS OF DELEGATES

58:1   As commonly understood in parliamentary law and as used in this book, the word *convention* refers to an assembly of *delegates* (other than a permanently constituted public lawmaking body), who are usually chosen specially for each session as representatives of the constituent units or subdivisions within a larger group of people, to sit as a single deliberative body acting in the name of the entire group. The most common type of convention is that of an established state or national society—in which the delegates are selected by, and from among, the members of each local unit. Other terms by which such a convention may be described in some organizations include *congress, conference, convocation, general assembly, house of delegates,* and *house of representatives.*

58:2   The term *house of delegates,* or *house of representatives,* is often applied particularly in the case of learned or professional associations, to distinguish the voting body of delegates from large numbers of other members of the constituent units, who come to the convention to attend seminars, workshops, educational or social activities, or the like. In some societies, also, *house of delegates* or *house of representatives* may describe a body of delegates who, instead of being elected only for a convention session, are elected for a fixed term during which they hold sessions from time to time as the bylaws may prescribe.

58:3   Conventions vary in size, duration, and complexity of operation. A relatively small state society may hold a one-day convention consisting of two or three meetings at which all delegates are present. A week's convention of a national scientific or educational association, on the other hand, may be divided into a number of specialized sections meeting separately at the same time, with only a few meetings when the entire body of delegates gathers in one hall.

58:4   In addition, a convention is sometimes called for the purpose of forming an association or federation; or (like a mass meeting, **53**) it may be convened to draw interested parties or representatives of interested organizations together in acting upon a particular problem.

58:5   This chapter is limited to the features common to most conventions and relates principally to the convention of an established society. (For variations of procedure applying to other types of conventions, see **60**.)

Basic Provisions in Bylaws

58:6   In the case of an established state, regional, or national society composed of constituent units, the bylaws (see 2:8–13; 56:33ff., especially 56:38) or other governing instrument of the association or parent body should:

- authorize a periodic convention;
- define its powers and duties;
- fix its quorum;
- specify its voting members;
- prescribe the qualifications of its delegates and alternates, the basis of determining their number, and the method of electing them;
- specify when, how, and to whom the call (notice) of the convention is to be sent; and
- make such provision as the particular convention may require for its organization and operation.

58:7　　Basic provision for the voting body of members may be worded in the bylaws as appropriate to the particular organization—for example, as follows:

> The voting members of the State Convention shall be the state officers (including members of the Executive Board of the State Association), the president (or, in his absence, the vice-president) of each club within the Association, and the elected delegates of each club.

58:8　　In addition, the bylaws at the level on which the convention is held should prescribe: (1) the conditions for a constituent unit to be in good standing for purposes of the right to representation—commonly including a minimum membership requirement; and (2) the number of delegates to which a unit shall be entitled depending on its size—usually by specifying, for example, that each unit shall be represented by its president, plus one additional delegate if the unit has more than a certain number of members, or two additional delegates if the unit has more than twice that number of members, and so on.

58:9　　The bylaws at the level at which the convention is held should also provide for the election of alternates as described in 58:13–15.

58:10　　To avoid a change of officers during the convention, the bylaws should provide that newly elected officers shall take up their duties at the close of the convention (see 56:27).

Convention Members and Alternates

58:11　**Ways in Which Voting Membership Comes About.** Voting membership in a convention of an established society generally comes about in one of the following ways:

1) through being an accredited delegate elected by a constituent body especially to act as its authorized representative (or one of several representatives) in a particular convention;

2) through provision in the bylaws, as in many organizations,

that the president or chief officer (or, in his absence, the vice-president) of each constituent local unit shall be the delegate or one of the delegates;

3) through being an incumbent elective officer of the organization on the level at which the convention is held—for example, an officer of a state society in a state convention, where the officers of the state society as listed in the bylaws are ex officio the officers of the convention as well as members of it, irrespective of the number of delegates that the local unit to which an officer belongs is entitled to elect; or

4) through being an accredited elected alternate and replacing, at the time of the convention, a delegate who is unable to attend or who withdraws from registered status.

58:12 **Filling of Vacancies Arising in a Delegation.** If the president of a constituent unit is unable to be present at the convention of an established society, his place there is taken by the vice-president (or by the second, third, or ranking available vice-president if necessary and if there are such officers), just as for any other duty in which the vice-president acts in the president's place. If the vice-president is himself an elected delegate but takes the president's place, the vice-president's original position as an elected delegate is filled by an elected alternate in the manner explained below—just as when any other elected delegate does not serve.

58:13 *Provision for alternates.* To ensure as complete representation at the convention as possible, the bylaws at the convention level should provide that each unit shall elect a certain number of alternates—frequently equal to the number of delegates. To maintain a uniform standard of representation, the qualifications for election as an alternate—which may include membership in good standing for a prescribed number of years—are made the same as for a delegate.

58:14 Alternates normally are elected with a designated order, in which they will be called to serve, if available, as vacancies arise in the delegation of their constituent unit. When a unit has more than one delegate, an elected alternate (other than the vice-president) is not associated with any particular delegate. The vacancy that occurs first in point of time (except one involving the president when the vice-president is able to serve in his stead) is filled by the first elected alternate or the ranking one available, and so on.

58:15   In cases where the individual delegates within a unit's delegation represent particular areas or groups, it may sometimes be desirable to make exception to the foregoing rule by providing, in the bylaws at the convention level, for the pairing of each alternate with a specific delegate. The disadvantage of such a system arises when both a particular delegate and his only alternate are unable to attend the convention—thus depriving a constituent unit of part of the representation to which it is entitled.

58:16   *Status and seating of alternates; replacement procedure.* Alternates registered as such are usually provided with badges of a different color or shape from those of delegates and are seated in sections apart from them. (In large conventions, assigned seats in the assembly hall ordinarily can be guaranteed only to the voting body.) When an alternate is officially registered by the Credentials Committee (59:14(5), 59:25) as taking the place of an elected delegate, however, he is supplied with a delegate's badge and becomes a voting delegate with the same duties and privileges as if originally so elected.

58:17   If an alternate is to replace a delegate who has registered, proper evidence of that delegate's withdrawal from such status must be presented to the Credentials Committee, and the alternate must be reregistered as the new delegate before he can sit or vote as a member of the convention. It is the duty of any registered delegate who ends his presence at the convention to see that his departure is promptly reported to the Credentials Committee, and to whatever authority is concerned with locating the proper accredited alternate if one is available. Unless the rules of the body provide otherwise, no alternate or other person can "substitute" for a delegate who remains registered. In other words, a delegate's temporary absence from the convention hall does not entitle an alternate to make motions, speak in debate, or cast the delegate's vote—even with the delegate's authorization—unless a rule of the body permits this procedure.

58:18   **Duties of Delegates.** When a member of a constituent unit has accepted election as a delegate, he has the obligation to attend the convention, with such expense allowance as the unit may provide; he should not leave it to an alternate to serve in his place except for serious reason. At the convention, the delegate has the duty to be present at the business meetings, and to be prepared on returning from the convention to present to his unit an information report of what transpired. A delegate is free to vote as he sees fit on questions at the convention, except as his constituent unit may have instructed him in regard to particular matters scheduled for consideration.

Caucuses

58:19   Prior to or during a convention, members of a delegation may need or wish to meet as a group to decide how they will act with reference to certain matters to come before the convention; a meeting of this kind is usually called a *caucus*. Unless instructed otherwise by its parent society or unit, such a caucus is governed by the rules of procedure applicable to committees (**50**), since the delegation is in effect a committee to represent and act at the convention for the constituent society or unit that chose it. If the president of a constituent society (or in his absence the vice-president) is automatically a delegate to a convention, he usually acts as chairman of his delegation; otherwise the delegation chairman is selected as outlined for the case of any other committee (13:17–18).

58:20   Sometimes caucuses are held of different groupings of delegates, as, for example, all delegates from a certain district, territory, or other geographic area as defined by the organization;

and they are similarly governed by the rules generally applicable to committees.

58:21   As in the case of any committee, in the absence of a superior rule to the contrary a constituent society or unit can instruct its delegation, although this is not always a good practice in ordinary societies. Such instructions are binding upon the delegation to the extent that the convention's presiding officer and other officials have a duty to enforce instructions of which they have been properly and officially notified. Such instructions, for example, frequently require a delegation to take a position for or against a measure expected to come before the convention, or to vote for certain candidates. As stated above, the delegates are free to vote as they see fit except where an instruction has been given; but a society can, by instructing its delegation, bind it to vote as a unit (that is, to cast all of its votes in accord with the decision of the majority of the delegation) on all issues, on a particular class of business, or on certain matters to be acted on by the convention.

58:22   The term *caucus* is also sometimes applied to a similar meeting of all the known or admitted partisans of a particular position on an important issue—in a convention or any other deliberative assembly—who meet to plan strategy toward a desired result within the assembly. Such a meeting may be held on the presumed informal understanding that those who attend will follow the decisions of the caucus.

§59. ORGANIZATION OF A CONVENTION OF AN ESTABLISHED SOCIETY

59:1   Most conventions must operate on a closely controlled schedule and transact a large amount of business quickly—often with rented facilities available only for a prearranged length of time and with each added day of meetings entailing considerable expense both to the association and to the delegates personally. Maximum effort toward a well-organized convention is therefore essential.

Advance Preparation

59:2   The work of organizing and preparing for a convention normally begins weeks or months in advance and involves many committees, under the general direction of the officers and the board of the association.

59:3   The principal parliamentary functions most directly connected with the formal organization of the convention itself are performed by three committees, each of which has been appointed by the president or the board as prescribed in the bylaws. These three committees are: (1) the Credentials Committee, which prepares and certifies to the convention the list of officers, delegates, and alternates that it has registered after finding them entitled to accreditation; (2) the Committee on Standing Rules, which drafts rules of operating procedure specially required for the particular convention; and (3) the Program Committee, which works out a convention program combining a suitable *order of business* (**41**) with special features designed to promote and develop the association or society as a whole. Because the duties of these committees are exacting, a member should never be appointed to one of them for any other reason than his ability in the field involved.

59:4   In addition, depending on the size of the convention, one or more committees concerned with the necessary physical arrangements, such as securing the hall, hotel accommodations, and related services, should be appointed. If a single committee is responsible for all of these matters, it may be known as the Convention Arrangements Committee.

59:5   Another important committee that usually works before as well as during the convention is the Resolutions Committee. This committee screens and recommends appropriate action on resolutions and original (as distinct from incidental) main motions to come before the convention.

59:6   The duties of the convention committees are more fully explained in the succeeding portions of this chapter.

59:7   Each of the regular standing committees of the association—in consultation with the presiding officer, the executive body or board, and the Program Committee—should also carefully plan the presentation and management of the convention business that is the particular committee's concern.

59:8   A preconvention meeting of the board of the association is often held in the convention city a day or more in advance of the convention opening. A number of decisions bearing on business to come before the convention may be made at this meeting.

Services of a Parliamentarian

59:9   A key consultant in the preparation for a convention should be the parliamentarian, *who should be engaged well in advance.* It is desirable that this person be a professional—the more seasoned in actual operating experience within organizations, the better. Although he has the duty of giving parliamentary advice and opinions at convention meetings (where he should be seated next to the presiding officer), the parliamentarian's most important work may well be performed before the convention opens (see 47:46–54). During the period of preparation and while the convention is in progress, he should serve as the principal adviser to the president, the officers, and the committee chairmen regarding management of the convention as it relates to the actual transaction of business. The chairmen of the Credentials Committee, the Committee on Standing Rules, the Program Committee, the Resolutions Committee, the Elections Committee if there is one, and the standing committees who are to present business to the convention should all consult with the parliamentarian during this time; and it may be advisable that he should attend certain meetings of these committees. The parliamentarian should always be present at the preconvention board meetings mentioned above.

Formal Organization Procedure at the Convention

59:10   Before a convention can transact any other business, it must officially form itself into a single voting body—which is done at the first *business* meeting. Preliminary ceremonies—whether at the commencement of the convention or at the beginning of each day—are not regarded as business. A separate formal opening of inspirational nature can be held, if desired, before the convention is officially organized. When the assembly of delegates of an established society has been so organized in accordance with the bylaws or other governing rules as described below, it then acts as and in the name of the whole society and may be referred to as "The Tenth Annual Convention of the National Society of _____" or, as common formerly, "The National Society of _____ in convention assembled."

59:11   The official organization of the convention is brought about by the separate consideration and adoption of the reports of three committees mentioned above—the Credentials Committee, the Committee on Standing Rules, and the Program Committee, in that order.

59:12   As each report comes up for consideration, it is presented to the convention by a reporting member, normally the respective committee chairman. This person concludes his report with a statement that "by direction of the committee" he moves its adoption—unless he is not a voting member of the convention, in which case anyone who is such a voting member can make this motion; a convenient practice is for the recording secretary of the convention or a qualified member of the committee to do so. No second is required if the motion is made by a member of the committee. If no one offers the motion promptly, the chair can call for it, or can assume it by stating, for example, "The question is on the adoption of the report of the Program Committee."

59:13   Each of these committee reports is debatable and amendable. In an ordinary convention of a society, however, debate or proposals for amendment of any of them seldom occur, and the reports are likely to be adopted without dissenting vote—if the committees have done their work well. (The vote *required* for their adoption is a majority for the reports of the Credentials Committee and the Program Committee, and normally a two-thirds vote for that of the Committee on Standing

Rules, as explained in 59:34–35.) With the adoption of these three separate reports, the convention is officially organized for conducting business.

Credentials Committee

59:14   **Responsibilities.** The specific duties of the Credentials Committee are listed below. Items (1) through (4) must of necessity be spread over a considerable period of time in advance of the convention. Items (5) and (6) must be performed at the convention location during the period leading up to the convention opening. Items (7) and (8) relate to the committee's duties during the convention.

1) Distribution well in advance, to each constituent body entitled to representation, of (a) information, in accordance with the bylaws, as to the authorized number of representatives and alternates, eligibility requirements, and the time and manner of their election;[1] and (b) credentials forms with instructions that they are to be returned by a specified date after having been filled in with the names of the representatives and alternates designated by the constituent unit, and having been signed by the unit's secretary and sometimes also by its president. A single form can be used for all representatives and alternates, or a separate form in the form of a card can be used for each delegate and each alternate, with different colors to distinguish delegates from alternates. If alternates are paired with specific delegates as described in 58:15, double cards can be used.

2) (a) Examination of all forms returned, to verify the eligibility of each member listed; and (b) notification to the proper constituent unit whenever an elected delegate or alternate is found ineligible (through nonpayment of dues, insufficient duration of membership, etc.), advising the unit of its right to

---

1. Some organizations include this information in a printed, general "Call to Convention."

designate one of the elected alternates named on its credentials form to take the place of any ineligible delegate (unless replacement is automatic because of pairing of alternates with individual delegates).

3) Compilation of the list of members entitled to register and the basis of this right (officer who is a convention member ex officio, unit president, elected delegate, alternate, etc.) arranged for quick reference—as alphabetically by districts, clubs, sections, or as may be suitable.

4) Arrangements for registration to take place at the convention—beginning one or two days before the convention opens (see 59:16).

5) Registration—which normally includes these steps:
   a) Submission, by the member intending to register, of evidence that he is entitled to do so;
   b) Verification by the committee, or a subcommittee of it, that the member's credentials are correct;
   c) Recording of the member as officially registered, upon his paying the registration fee (which is sometimes sent in in advance) and signing the list of registrations; and
   d) Issuing of the particular badge to which the member is entitled, the official program, and additional necessary information, such as time and place of individual section or committee meetings or workshops.

6) Preparation of the committee's first report to the convention, which can include registrations only to such an hour as will enable the chairman of the Credentials Committee to present this initial report as the first item of official business of the convention.

7) Continuation of the committee until the convention ends—to record changes in the registration rolls occasioned by: (a) additional registrations (which the bylaws or the convention's standing rules (59:27ff.) may require to be closed at a specified time slightly earlier than the final adjournment); or (b) the departure of delegates and the reregistration of alternates who replace them.

8) Submission of a supplementary credentials report—at the beginning of the first business meeting each day and at other times when required—as resulting from changes in the registration rolls.

59:15   In societies that maintain a permanent administrative headquarters, most of the clerical duties required of the Credentials Committee in advance of the convention usually develop into a routine technique preserved from year to year and performed largely by the regular paid staff; but the authority and responsibility for general direction of this work remain with the Credentials Committee.

59:16 **Times and Place of Registration.** The times and the place of registration should be announced in the printed convention program. In a convention of any size lasting for a number of days, registration may begin one or two days before the convention opens, and provision should be made to handle a heavy volume of registrations during the afternoon and evening before the opening business meeting, as well as on the morning of that meeting. This registration normally takes place in a separate room or hall whose size and equipment depend on the probable total number of registrants. Throughout the convention, a registration desk of the Credentials Committee in a convenient location should be manned a reasonable time before each business meeting begins, and should always remain open during meetings. Near the end of the convention, usually only one or two committee members stay on duty.

59:17 **Method of Registration.** The method used by the Credentials Committee to register the delegates and alternates will vary according to the size of the convention. A procedure in common use is outlined as follows:

59:18   The entire association holding the convention is divided into parts, such as states, districts, or counties, and a separate section of the register—often prepared in triplicate, as noted below—is set up for each subdivision. Each section of the register contains—arranged in an appropriate logical order—the typed names of the constituent societies or units located within the corresponding geographical area; and under each unit's name are typed alphabetically the names of the delegates and alternates that have been sent in on the unit's credentials blanks, provided that these persons have been found eligible by the committee.

59:19   During the initial period when the bulk of registrations take place, usually two committee members are assigned to a separate and conspicuously marked table or station for each section of the register. In a large convention, ushers may be helpful in guiding delegates and alternates to the proper section, where they present their credentials and sign the register to the right of their typewritten names.

59:20   At least one, and frequently two, duplicate registers (or photocopy-reproduced sets of the register pages) are desirable in addition to the Credentials Committee's master copy—one duplicate list to be submitted as an attachment to the committee's report, the other for later use by election tellers in verifying the eligibility of voters. By use of the latter copy, counting procedure in an election can be expedited by dividing the tellers into subcommittee groups for each section of the register, according to the same pattern as in the case of the Credentials Committee members during registration. The delegates' badges can also be correspondingly labeled or numbered to facilitate identification with the correct section.

59:21   Cases of contested seats in a delegation will seldom arise except in political conventions. In the rare event of a contest between two delegates or groups of delegates and serious doubt as to which is entitled to be seated, the committee should omit both from the list and report the fact of the contest to the convention as explained below. If, on the other hand, after hearing the facts, the committee thinks the contest is not justified, it should enter on the list only the names of the delegates whose claim it finds to be legitimate. The same rules apply to the more common case of delegates chosen by a local unit that is not entitled to representation or has chosen delegates in excess of its entitlement.

59:22   **Adoption of Report.** Before the Credentials Committee report is adopted, since the membership has not been established, the only motions that are in order are those related to its consideration or to the conduct of the meeting before its adoption, as well as those that are in order in the absence of a quorum (40:6–8).[2] Even, for example, a motion relating to the validity of the holding of the convention is not in order at such a time. It is, therefore, essential that the committee establish and hold itself to a deadline for registrations to be included in its first report, which will leave it time to prepare that report. The opening ceremonies will afford some opportunity for this work, and, while it is in process, delegates can continue to register—but not to be included in the committee's initial report. If the report is not ready in time, the convention may continue with other nonbusiness matters, such as speakers, or may stand at ease or take a recess.

59:23   The Credentials Committee report, which is read by the committee's chairman, states in substance that, "Attached is the list of the names of the voting members of the convention and their alternates who have been registered up until ... [indicating the hour to which the list is corrected]." This statement should be followed by whatever statistical summary is customary in the particular organization (frequently including a breakdown according to basis of voting membership as indicated in 59:14(3)), and always gives the total number of convention members *entitled to vote* and the number of registered alternates. Normally the list of delegates and alternates is not read unless a portion of it is read upon request, for information. If there is an unresolved contest between delegates, the particulars are stated, as well as the fact that the names of the contesting or contested delegates do not appear on the

---

2. But see **60** for necessary variations in the case of conventions not of a permanent organization.

roll. The committee chairman concludes the report by saying, "On behalf of the committee, I move that the roll of delegates hereby submitted be the official roll of the voting members of the convention." The report with the attached list of names is then handed to the chair or to the secretary.

59:24   Unless there is debate or proposed amendment, the chair, before taking the vote on the adoption of the report, asks, "Are there any questions on the report?" If seat(s) are contested, an amendment can be offered substantially in this form: "To amend by adding 'provided that the name of George J. Morse be added to the roll of delegates as submitted, as a delegate from the state of Missouri.'" The name of the rival delegate can then be offered in a secondary amendment, for example, "to strike out 'George J. Morse' and insert 'Frank Norton.'" Whether or not a contest is reported, it is in order to move such amendments or even to move to substitute an entirely different set of delegates for any delegation in the reported list, but no such amendment is permitted to include more names than those of a single challenged delegate or delegation all of whom are challenged on the same grounds, together with any claimants involved. On an amendment proposing changes in the list of delegates, none of the delegates involved in the case can vote. Those seated by the committee, though contested in a case not yet reached, can vote on all cases except their own. On the question of adopting the Credentials Committee's report or on motions connected with its consideration, only those persons whose names are on the list of voting members reported by the committee (as this list stands after any amendment already approved by the convention) are entitled to vote.

59:25   **Roll of Voting Members; Supplementary Reports.** When the report of the Credentials Committee is adopted, it is thereby ratified as the official roll of voting members of the convention—subject to changes through later reports. A voting member who registers after the submission of the first report assumes his full status as soon as he has done so, if his status is not questioned; if it is, it must await a decision by the committee or the convention itself. Although the Credentials Committee normally makes a supplementary report only at the beginning of each day, it may be called upon to do so at other times, such as immediately before an important vote. If there has been no change in the roll of registered delegates since the last report, no motion or vote is required; but if there are changes, the committee chairman concludes his report by saying, "On behalf of the committee, I move that the revised roll of delegates hereby submitted be the official roll of voting members of the convention." Although this motion might appear to be one to amend something previously adopted (**35**), it requires only a majority vote for its adoption, since it is always understood that the roll will be altered as delegates arrive late or leave early, and alternates may thereby be shifted in status.

59:26   The Credentials Committee's master roll of currently registered voting members of the convention must be maintained at all times in such a way that their exact number can be promptly determined. Accuracy of the list of registrants is essential, since it may affect the outcome of elections or closely contested issues. If the bylaws or the convention's standing rules do not prescribe a quorum (**40**)—which they should do—the quorum is a majority of the number of voting members who have actually registered at the convention as in attendance, irrespective of whether some may have departed.

Committee on Standing Rules

59:27   **Responsibilities.**   The Committee on Standing Rules drafts and submits for consideration a group of rules known as "The Standing Rules of the Convention," which, as adopted, will apply to that one convention only. These rules must in no way conflict with the bylaws of the society, but (in contrast to ordinary standing rules in a local society) they can involve modifications of rules contained in the parliamentary authority prescribed by the bylaws. The standing rules of a convention usually contain both "parliamentary" rules relating to the conduct of business, and nonparliamentary rules, so that in some ways they resemble a combination of special rules of order and ordinary standing rules (**2**). Since their effect expires at the close of the session that adopts them, however, they differ from either of the latter types of rules in certain respects.

59:28   The standing rules of successive conventions held by a society often become developed to a point where little change in the rules adopted by the preceding convention is necessary. On the other hand, the work of this committee may sometimes require extensive research into past proceedings of the organization. In any case, the parliamentarian should always be consulted regarding the convention's standing rules, and he often prepares a first draft for submission to this committee.

59:29   A copy of the "Proposed Standing Rules of the Convention" that the committee is to recommend—usually printed in the official program—should be handed to each person when he registers. Until the proposed standing rules are adopted, the convention is governed by the rules in the organization's parliamentary authority, such as those concerning the seating of delegates and alternates (see 58:16–17 and 59:2) and assignment of the floor (see especially 42:16).

59:30   **Presentation and Adoption of Convention Standing Rules.** The report of the Committee on Standing Rules is presented to the convention immediately after the adoption of that of the Credentials Committee. As part of this report, the proposed rules are read in their entirety—unless the rules are not substantially changed from those adopted in the last few conventions and every delegate has been provided with a copy when registering at the convention or previously, in which case the committee chairman or other reporting member may omit their reading. The report concludes by offering a motion such as the following: "By direction of the Committee on Standing Rules, I move the adoption of the Standing Rules of the Convention as printed [or, "as just read"]." (For the procedure when the person presenting the report is not a voting member of the convention, see 59:12.)

59:31   The chair states the question by saying, "It is moved to adopt the Standing Rules of the Convention as printed [or, "as just read"]," but any voting member of the convention then has the right to have the proposed rules read by the chair or secretary if they were not read by the committee chairman or other reporting member.

59:32   After debate or amendment (if any), a single vote normally is taken on the complete body of rules. It should be understood, however, that although the rules may be organized to have the appearance of being a single document, they are in fact a group of separate main motions being offered by the committee under one enacting motion. Therefore, by the demand of a voting member of the convention, a separate vote can be required on any individual rule (see 10:25, 27:10), and the procedure of seriatim consideration can be applied only if there is no objection (see **28**). If a demand is made for a separate vote—which is advisable only if a serious matter appears to be at stake—the remainder of the rules are acted on first, and then those separated out are acted on individually. If an additional rule is proposed during the consideration of the committee's proposed rules (or later during the convention), it is similarly acted on separately after the committee's proposals have been voted on.

59:33   In putting the question to a vote, the chair may initially omit reading the proposed rules. However, if they have not been read even once, any delegate then has the right to demand that they be read before the vote. Even if previously read, any delegate has the right at that time to demand the reading of any rule that has been amended since being read.

59:34   A group of proposed standing rules requires a two-thirds vote for its adoption whenever it includes any rule that would require a two-thirds vote for its adoption if voted on individually (see next paragraph below). Therefore, under the usual procedure of voting on the standing rules as a "package," a two-thirds vote will normally be required for their adoption—

because, if they are to fill the needs of the convention, they nearly always include provisions that can be imposed only by a two-thirds vote.

59:35   **Vote Required for Adoption of an Individual Rule.** If a standing rule of a convention is voted on individually, the vote necessary for its adoption is in some cases two thirds and in others a majority, depending on the nature of the rule:

1) Convention standing rules requiring a two-thirds vote for adoption (even individually) are, in principle, distinguished by the same characteristics as provisions which, in an ordinary local society or assembly, would need a two-thirds vote to be placed in effect for the duration of a meeting or session, or would require adoption as a *special rule of order* to continue in force from session to session (see **2**). An example would be a rule limiting the time allowed for debate. Rules in this class are described by the term *parliamentary standing rules in a convention* as used in this book.

2) A standing rule is individually adoptable by a majority vote in a convention if it does not fall in class (1) above, and consequently could be adopted in a local assembly as an *ordinary standing rule* (see **2**). Examples of such convention rules would be those relating to the wearing of badges or to the format in which written reports or resolutions shall be submitted.

59:36   **Vote Required to Amend or Rescind a Convention Standing Rule.** To amend or rescind a standing rule of a convention requires a two-thirds vote or the vote of a majority of all the delegates or other "voting members" of the convention who have been registered, except that a rule individually adoptable by a majority vote can be amended or rescinded by a majority vote after notice on at least the preceding day.

59:37   **Suspension of a Convention Standing Rule.** Any standing rule of a convention (except one prescribing the parliamentary authority) can be suspended for a particular specified purpose by a majority vote, even if the rule required a two-thirds vote for its adoption. Under such a suspension, however, the applicable rules in the parliamentary authority prescribed by the bylaws (or by a rule of the convention) come into force—as if the standing rule had not been adopted. To suspend a convention standing rule and also the general parliamentary rule normally applying to the same situation requires a two-thirds vote, just as to suspend the general rule when no standing rule is involved (**25**).[3] No standing rule of a convention can be suspended for the remainder of the session, and no standing rule which has only a single application can be suspended, since this would be equivalent to rescinding the rule, and the case would have to be treated accordingly.

59:38 **Sample Set of Convention Standing Rules.** The standing rules of a convention must vary with its size, type, and responsibilities. While it is not possible to frame model rules which are universally applicable, the following sample set illustrates the nature of the standing rules adopted by many conventions.

STANDING RULES OF THE _____
CONVENTION OF _____

59:39   Rule 1. (a) The Credentials Committee, directly after the opening ceremonies of the first business meeting,[4] shall report the number of delegates and alternates registered as present

---

3. The reason why a parliamentary standing rule of a convention can be suspended by a majority vote even though it requires a two-thirds vote for its adoption is as follows: In a convention, parliamentary standing rules—which are in the nature of suspensions of the regular rules of order for the duration of the convention session—generally arise from a need to give the majority more power to transact business with minimum delay, even when the majority is not large enough to command a two-thirds vote. Since it is thus likely to reduce the protection of a minority greater than one third, a parliamentary standing rule of a convention requires a two-thirds vote for its adoption; but since the same rule tends to protect a majority of less than two thirds, such a majority should have the right to suspend the rules for a particular purpose and allow the regular rules of order to come into force.

4. See 59:10–11.

with proper credentials, and shall make a supplementary report after the opening exercises at the beginning of each day that business continues.

(b) A member registered as an alternate may, upon proper clearance by the Credentials Committee, be transferred from alternate to delegate at any time during the continuance of business meetings.

59:40   Rule 2. For admission to the assembly hall, to facilitate identification and seating, members, alternates, and others shall be required to wear the badge issued by the Credentials Committee upon registration.

59:41   Rule 3. A resolution offered by an individual member shall be in writing, signed by the maker and the seconder—each of whom shall be a voting member of the convention—and shall be sent directly to the desk of the Recording Secretary.

59:42   Rule 4.[5] (a) All resolutions except those proposed by the Executive Board [or "Board of Directors," "Board of Managers," etc.] or by committees, and all recommendations made in reports of officers or committees of the convention that are not in the form of resolutions, shall be referred without debate to the Resolutions Committee; resolutions proposed by the Executive Board or by committees shall be presented by the Board or proposing committee directly to the convention.

(b) Each member who offers a resolution shall be given an opportunity to explain it to the Resolutions Committee if he so requests.

(c) The Resolutions Committee shall prepare suitable resolutions to carry into effect recommendations referred to it, and shall submit to the convention, with the Committee's own recommendation as to appropriate action, these and all other resolutions referred to the Committee, except questions which the Committee by a vote of two thirds of its members may decide not to report.[6]

---

5. Regarding variations in the rules and practices of societies relating to the handling of resolutions at a convention, see 59:68–75.

6. See 59:74–75.

(d) The convention by a majority vote may suspend this Rule 4 and may immediately consider a question, or may order the Resolutions Committee to report a question at a certain time, even if the Committee has voted not to report it.

59:43   Rule 5. No member shall speak in debate more than once on the same question on the same day, or longer than two minutes, without permission of the convention granted by a two-thirds vote without debate.

59:44   Rule 6. All reports and other material for the permanent record or printed proceedings shall be in typing and, immediately on presentation, shall be sent to the Recording Secretary.

59:45   Rule 7. Nominations for each office to be filled by the convention shall be limited to one nominating speech of three minutes and one seconding speech of one minute for each nominee.

59:46   Rule 8. Notices for announcement to the convention shall be in writing, signed by the person (or a proper representative of the persons) under whose authority the announcement is issued, and shall be sent to the desk of the Recording Secretary.

59:47   Rule 9.[7] The rules contained in the current edition of *Robert's Rules of Order Newly Revised* shall govern the convention in all cases to which they are applicable and in which they are not inconsistent with the bylaws of the Society [or "Federation," "Association," etc.] and these standing rules.

Program Committee

59:48   The Program Committee plans and submits the proposed schedule of meetings, proceedings, and special events of the convention. When the program is adopted by the voting body, with or without amendment, it becomes the *order of business* of the entire convention session (**41**). The program also commonly includes—interwoven throughout the convention timetable—

---

7. A rule on "Parliamentary Authority" is included in the standing rules of a convention only if the bylaws of the organization do not prescribe the authority. If this rule is included, it cannot be suspended as such, although a particular rule stated in the parliamentary authority can be suspended by a two-thirds vote.

a series of addresses, forums, workshops, exhibits, tours, and other activities designed for membership-training, motivational, or entertainment value.

59:49 **Responsibilities.** The nature of a convention Program Committee's responsibilities is considerably more complex than for a committee of the same name in a local society that includes a "program" as a part of each meeting. The overall program must cover all aspects of the society's work and commitments on the level at which the convention is held (district, state, national, etc.)—reviewing the period since the preceding convention and anticipating the course of the society until the next convention. In addition to enabling the convention to handle all business that it should consider within the time available, the program should be of such nature as to stimulate each delegate to an evaluation of the society's policies, accomplishments, and opportunities, inasmuch as benefit from the convention to the general membership may depend largely on the impression that each local president or delegate transmits to the unit he represents.

59:50 The Program Committee usually begins work soon after the preceding convention closes, and its duties continue throughout the convention that it plans—so that it functions as virtually a standing committee of the organization. The Program Committee should work in close contact with the president and the parliamentarian.

59:51 **Planning the Program.** Although the program must come before the convention for adoption and can be amended by it, many details must be decided far ahead. Prior to the convention, the Program Committee must have the authority (sometimes with designated members of the executive committee or board as advisers, and often acting in cooperation with a Convention Arrangements Committee) to engage outside speakers or entertainers, to work out an order of business allotting appropriate amounts of time to each subject, and to make all necessary advance arrangements.

59:52   Some societies send a tentative skeleton program to the constituent units several weeks beforehand as part of a printed "Call to Convention." The complete program that the committee expects to recommend should be printed at the latest practical time for handing to each person as he registers at the convention.

59:53   The order of business for the complete series of a convention's business meetings normally includes, in expanded form, the elements of the one followed in ordinary meetings of the society's constituent units (**41**). In the case of the convention, however, greater detail and precision are necessary for two principal reasons: (1) Adherence to a prearranged schedule is imperative if the convention is to complete its work—timing being an especially important factor if there are to be features carried by radio and television at particular hours, addresses by government officials, or appearances by professional artists. (2) Each member has the right to know at which meeting and at what approximate time a particular matter can be expected to come before the convention, so that he may avoid absence from the hall during important debates or votes.

59:54   Some organizations divide the printed convention program into two parts, the first of which gives the times and places of special events and—for each business meeting—only the hours of the call to order, adjournment, and any scheduled recesses. The second part, listing the items or classes of business set for each meeting, is then known as the *agenda* (**41**).

59:55   While it is not possible to set out a model program that would be suitable for all conventions, the following principles are commonly applicable:

1) Notice of the times of registration should be given early general distribution by mail or other means, and should also be printed in the convention program. Handing out—with the program—a schedule of preconvention meetings of the board and of committees is often advisable, although the persons directly concerned with these meetings may need to be separately informed at an earlier time.

2) When the invocation is offered, the national anthem is played or sung, and the Pledge of Allegiance is recited in opening ceremonies, they should always be in that order—that is, the invocation first and the pledge last.

3) If there is an address of welcome—often given by a local public official at the opening of the convention—it should, as a matter of courtesy, be followed by remarks of acknowledgment and appreciation by the presiding officer or his designee on behalf of the organization.

4) For each meeting, the program should specify the hour of opening and closing, and the program or the agenda should specify the order in which the subjects or classes of subjects assigned to that meeting are to come up. The extent to which such classes are subdivided should be guided by the particular conditions and probable timing problems of the individual convention. Sufficient time should be allotted for thorough consideration of each important policy question that is expected to come before the convention. For such an item of business, it is frequently advisable to set a particular hour—which *automatically* makes the matter a *special order* unless otherwise specified (see 41:58–59). Listed subjects for which no hour is specified are general orders for the meeting to which they are assigned.

5) Reports of officers are commonly presented in the order in which the officers are listed in the bylaws, the president reporting first, unless it is the desire or practice of the organization to vary from such an order. Action on the report of the auditors should immediately follow the treasurer's report. Often reports of officers that are for information only and do not require action by the convention are printed and distributed in advance. In such a case it may not be necessary to have the report read; the chair can simply pause for any questions by delegates to the reporting officer, and the reporting officer can make additional comments on his report at that time. The report of the board, if any, usually should follow the reports of officers.

6) Reports of committees that are for information only and that do not require action by the convention should, as far as possible, be brought up in succession at the same point in the order of business. Time can frequently be saved by reproducing and distributing these reports in advance, in which case it may be unnecessary to read them aloud to the convention. The chair can then simply call the name of each committee in sequence, pausing for any questions. The chairman of any committee can be permitted to make additional comments upon his committee's report at that time.

7) The report of a committee having a resolution or other motion to offer can be received at any appropriate time, but it should usually be before the report of the Resolutions Committee.

8) A time for announcements should immediately precede the adjournment of each meeting of the convention.

9) Beginning with the second day of the convention (unless a rule or resolution is adopted providing for the approval of the minutes of the entire convention by the board or a committee), the minutes of the preceding day's meetings are read immediately after any opening ceremonies at the first meeting of each day. Authority to approve such minutes is then usually delegated to the board or to a special committee, by means of a standing rule of the convention or an adopted resolution introduced by the Resolutions Committee.

10) Business unfinished at the end of a day normally is taken up after the reading of the minutes (or after the opening of the meeting, if the minutes are not read) at the resumption of business the next day—provided that the program makes no special provision for unfinished business on that day and there is no conflict with a special order. If unfinished business is not listed as such in the program each day, the planned timing should nevertheless allow for it; a listed heading of "Unfinished Business" should then be provided near the end of the last business meeting, and at

any point where it is advisable because special orders have been scheduled early in the day (see also **41**).

11) Nominations and the election of officers should take place relatively early in the convention, if possible, so that there will be time to complete balloting if more than one ballot must be taken.

12) If there is to be a formal installation of officers, this ceremony is often made a part of a closing banquet meeting, at which any presentations of gavels, pins, awards, or the like are also made.

59:56   It is often advisable to schedule a meeting of the executive body or board of the association a day after the close of the convention, asking the board members and other necessary personnel to remain in the convention city for this purpose. If such a meeting is to be held, its time and place may be announced in the printed convention program.

59:57   **Adoption of the Convention Program.** The program is the president's guide as to the order of business during the initial proceedings, even before it has been formally adopted by the convention. Directly after the adoption of the standing rules, the report of the Program Committee is presented—normally by the committee chairman—somewhat as follows: "Mr. President, a printed copy of the program as proposed by the Program Committee is in the hands of each registrant for the convention. By direction of the committee I move the adoption of the program as printed." (If the chairman or other person presenting the report is not a voting member of the convention, he omits the motion for adoption. For procedure in such a case, see 59:12.)

59:58   If last-minute changes in the program have become necessary, the chairman can make his report by saying: "Mr. President, because of ... [briefly indicating reasons], the Program Committee recommends the following modifications in its proposed program which has been printed and placed in the hands of each registrant for the convention: ... [clearly stating each change, with reference to page and line in the printed program]. By direction of the Program Committee, I move that, with these changes, the printed program be adopted." This motion is debatable and amendable. A majority vote adopts the program—even if it contains special orders. While the making of a special order requires a two-thirds vote under ordinary circumstances, the situation is different in the case of a convention program, where the special order is part of a complete order of business being adopted for the current session.

59:59   To change the program after its adoption requires a two-thirds vote or the vote of a majority of all the delegates or other "voting members" of the convention who have been registered—or unanimous consent, which can usually be obtained with no difficulty in cases where a departure from the program is justified. Thus, an affirmative vote to adopt the program cannot be reconsidered. (See 4:58–63; see also *Program* (41:36) and *Taking Up Business out of Its Proper Order* (41:37–39).) Changing the program to add additional meetings within the same session requires such a vote except that during the last meeting scheduled by the program an additional meeting may be set by majority vote through the use of the motion to *Fix the Time to Which to Adjourn* (**22**). Any proposed changes except those to which there is obviously no reasonable alternative are best referred to the Program Committee. The committee can recommend changes if and when needed while the convention is in progress, but neither the presiding officer nor the Program Committee is free to alter the program as adopted—which only the convention can do.

59:60   (For parliamentary rules applying at the expiration of the time allotted to a subject, and procedure at scheduled times of adjournment, see 18:8, 21:10–12, 21:14, and 41:65–70.)

Convention Arrangements Committee

59:61   The complex arrangements necessary to a convention generally require the coordination of many additional details that are outside the province of any of the other committees mentioned in this chapter. In the simplest case a Convention Arrangements Committee is appointed—usually by the board at the convention level. Most often the committee's membership is largely made up of members of the constituent society or societies acting as convention hosts; it should, however, include persons who have had experience in similar work at prior conventions. In cases where there has been competition between cities for the convention site, it is often well to place on this committee local members who were instrumental in obtaining the selection of their city.

59:62   The Convention Arrangements Committee may be empowered to consult experts, who may include professional convention managers. Assistance frequently is obtainable also from staff members of hotels where conventions are held, and from convention bureaus in many cities.

59:63   Depending on the size and duration of the convention, duties ordinarily assigned to the Convention Arrangements Committee are sometimes delegated to subcommittees or even distributed among separate committees. At the outset, the convention headquarters must be selected and advance arrangements made concerning room accommodations in as many hotels or motor inns as may be necessary. The committee may work with the Credentials Committee in coordinating room reservations for delegates with their registration for the convention. While the Program Committee may arrange for all speakers and entertainment, details relating to the overnight and other accommodations for these guests are usually a responsibility of the Convention Arrangements Committee. Ensuring that dignitaries and honored guests are met at the airport or other point of arrival may also be one of the latter committee's functions.

59:64   Printed or reproduced material assembled in cooperation with the Program Committee for distribution to the delegates in advance of the convention should include directions for getting to the convention by the various means of transportation available, and information about the locality, points of interest, restaurants, entertainment, tours arranged by the Program Committee, and parking facilities for those driving to the convention.

59:65   Careful attention should be given to seating arrangements within the hall, voting members always being located in a separate section if other persons are assigned seating space on the convention floor. Pages, messengers, ushers, and doorkeepers—who are essential to the good order of all but the smallest conventions—should be trained to perform their duties in a calm and courteous manner. During the convention, liaison should be maintained with the Program Committee to ensure, for example, proper seating on the platform, as the needs may change from meeting to meeting.

59:66   The staffing of an information desk throughout the convention may lie within the province of the Convention Arrangements Committee, together with additional functions in the areas of communications and public relations. If the meetings are to be covered by the press, the representatives of the various media must be kept informed of developments and provided with an area on the floor near the platform, or in some other point of vantage in the hall. It is often helpful to have facilities for typing and copying close at hand, as well as for the distribution of literature. In very large conventions it is wise to investigate existing telephone and other communication facilities and to provide for their augmentation if necessary.

Resolutions Committee

59:67   The Resolutions Committee—also sometimes called the *Reference Committee* or, in certain cases described below, the *Platform Committee*—has as its basic purpose the screening of all original main motions (**10**) that have not been screened by another committee and that come—or are to come—before the convention. It is usually not intended to require purely formal or incidental main motions to be submitted to the Resolutions Committee, or to refer to it resolutions reported to the convention by other committees (see also **51**).

59:68   **Variations in Rules Relating to the Resolutions Committee.** The establishment of a Resolutions Committee in a convention represents a limitation on the ordinary right of members to propose any number of motions from the floor without notice—such limitation arising from the need for keeping within a schedule and disposing of a large amount of business within a short time. The degree of limitation imposed and the manner in which the committee functions vary considerably, depending on the organization, in particulars such as the following:

59:69   *Variations in the time when a resolution can be introduced.* In the simplest situation a resolution is offered from the floor of the convention in the way it would be in an ordinary meeting. Such an arrangement is outlined in Standing Rules 3 and 4(a) in 59:41–42. A place in the program or agenda should then be provided at each meeting, under a heading such as "New Business," for the introduction of resolutions. Under this system, the proposer of the resolution says, "Mr. President, I move the adoption of [or "I offer"] the resolution which I have sent to the Secretary's desk." The secretary reads the resolution, announcing the names of the mover and the seconder, and the chair says, "Under the rules the resolution is referred to the Resolutions Committee."

59:70   To save even this time in a convention, an arrangement can be made whereby resolutions are submitted to the recording secretary without being formally moved and read in open meeting, and the secretary then must promptly deliver them to the chairman of the Resolutions Committee. The convention can suspend such a rule at any time, however—by a majority vote if it is a standing rule of the convention, or by a two-thirds vote if it is a higher-ranking rule (2:21)—and can thus take up a resolution without sending it to the Resolutions Committee.

59:71   If many resolutions are customarily proposed by members, a permanent rule or provision in the bylaws can be adopted by the organization requiring all resolutions to be submitted to the committee, or to the executive secretary for delivery to the committee, a number of days, weeks, or even months in advance of the convention. This system can be arranged to allow time for sending copies of all resolutions considered by the Resolutions Committee to the constituent societies and their delegates in advance of the convention, thereby giving time for consultation and, possibly, instruction of delegates. In such cases it is advisable to provide that resolutions can also be introduced at the convention if permitted by a two-thirds vote in the individual case.

59:72 *Variations in permitted origin of resolutions.* In the ordinary case only the members of the convention—that is, the delegates—are allowed to introduce resolutions for consideration by the assembly, and other members of constituent societies (who are not convention members) are allowed to speak for the purpose of suggesting motions only with the consent of the convention. Such consent can be granted in an individual case, or a rule can be adopted specifying persons who, in addition to the delegates, can submit resolutions; the latter practice has particular value when resolutions are required to be submitted in advance of the convention meetings.

59:73 In some cases any member of a constituent society, whether he is a delegate or not, is permitted to offer a resolution. In other organizations a resolution is required to have the sponsorship of a constituent society itself. A number of organizations require even the resolutions offered by standing and special committees of the organization to be screened and reported by the Resolutions Committee. In some types of organizations the Resolutions Committee originates and drafts its own resolutions for submission to the assembly. In any society, when an officer or committee simply makes one or more recommendations, the Resolutions Committee is customarily assigned the task of putting the recommendation(s) in the form of resolution(s).

59:74 *Variations in the power of the resolutions committee.* In the simplest arrangement, the Resolutions Committee has only the power to put resolutions in proper form, eliminate duplication where similar resolutions are offered, and ensure that all resolutions relating to a specific subject will be offered in a logical sequence. In other cases the committee is given the authority to make substantive alterations in a resolution, but only with the sponsor's consent; while in still others, by vote of the committee—sometimes a two-thirds vote—the substance of the resolution can be altered and the resolution can be reported to the assembly in the altered form as though the committee had originated it.

59:75   Except as the rules may provide otherwise, the Resolutions Committee is required to report all resolutions referred to it; but the committee can, if it wishes, report a resolution with "no recommendation." If the committee is given the power "not to report" a resolution—thus withholding it from consideration by the convention—a requirement of an unusually high vote within the committee (such as a three-fourths vote or a vote of two-thirds of the committee's members) should always be imposed; and the convention should always be given power to override such a decision of the Resolutions Committee and order the committee to report the resolution, by a majority vote (see Rule 4(d) in the sample standing rules of a convention, 59:42). In this connection, it should be noted that voting "not to report" a resolution, reporting it with "no recommendation," and reporting it with the recommendation that it be rejected by the convention are each quite different.

59:76   **Platforms or Policy Statements.** In political and certain other types of organizations, the Resolutions Committee is required to prepare and report a platform for adoption by the organization, setting forth its views, aims, and aspirations. Other associations occasionally require the committee to draft statements of policy or similar documents that take the form of a platform rather than of a resolution. In such a platform or statement, many of the principles applicable to drafting resolutions are followed.

59:77   If there is a preamble, instead of beginning each paragraph with the word "Whereas," a participle is used; thus, "Believing in the ... , [etc.]." Each paragraph is terminated by a semicolon and, in the case of the next-to-the-last paragraph, the word "and." The last paragraph of the preamble may be followed by the word "therefore." Each new paragraph of the preamble begins with another participle. In the body of the paper, each paragraph, instead of opening with the enacting words "*Resolved,* That," begins with a verb denoting an attitude or position—for example, "Affirms ... ," "Assures ... ," "Condemns ... ," "Calls upon ... ," and the like. As in a resolution, no paragraph should contain a period within its structure. The paragraphs of the body of the document can be linked by a semicolon and the word "and," as in the preamble, or a semicolon only can be used. The first paragraph of the body of the statement is often somewhat general. The preamble and the body of the statement may be connected by words such as "Issues this statement of ... ; and ... ." The full name of the organization can precede these words, or it can be placed before the preamble; for example, thus:

> Believing ... ;
> Recalling ... ; and
> Noting ... ;
>
> The Phoenix Improvement Association issues this statement of its basic governing principles; and
>
> Affirms ... ;
> Assures ... ; and
> Condemns ...

Or:

> The Phoenix Improvement Association,
> Believing ... ; and
> Holding ... ; therefore
>
> Issues this statement of its basic governing principles; and
>
> Affirms ... ;
> Assures ... ; [and so on].

59:78 **Courtesy Resolutions.** In addition to its duties in regard to the resolutions which are referred to it and which usually relate to policy matters, the Resolutions Committee is often charged with the duty of drafting and presenting to the assembly any courtesy resolutions that may seem appropriate. Ordinarily, courtesy resolutions express the appreciation of the convention to those who arranged accommodations for its physical needs or rendered it service.

59:79 **Meetings of the Committee.** Ordinarily the Resolutions Committee should make known, through the program or announcements, the times and places it will meet. It is best to allow any sponsor of a resolution to appear before the committee to explain it and answer any questions about it; and interested delegates also may be allowed to attend and even participate in discussion. Many times such free discussion reduces friction that may have developed concerning a resolution, and the convention as a result goes more smoothly. After any open "hearings" of this type, the committee meets in executive session (**9**) to review each resolution and prepare its report. The parliamentarian may be asked to attend the committee's meetings.

59:80 **Report of the Resolutions Committee.** In reporting, the Resolutions Committee follows the procedure of any committee reporting back a resolution referred to it, as described in **51**. Even when resolutions are submitted to the committee before the opening of the convention, the report on each resolution is treated as if it had been moved and seconded in the assembly before being referred to the committee. It is never necessary for the Resolutions Committee chairman or reporting member to move the adoption of a resolution being reported—unless the committee itself originated it, as in the case of courtesy resolutions.

59:81 When the committee recommends amendments to a resolution, in cases where it is not empowered to incorporate them itself, its chairman reports as follows:

RESOLUTIONS COMMITTEE CHAIRMAN: Mr. President, the Resolutions Committee recommends that the resolution relating to … [or "Resolution No. 6," etc.] be amended by striking out the words "…" and inserting the words "… ," and that, as thus amended, the resolution be adopted. By direction of the Resolutions Committee, I move the adoption of the recommended amendment.

If the convention members do not have reproduced copies of the resolution, the chair reads it before stating the question on the amendment. He then proceeds:

CHAIR: The Resolutions Committee recommends the adoption of the resolution with the following amendment … [rereading the amendment]. The question is on the amendment.

59:82   In instances where it is advisable for a resolution of overriding importance to be considered as a special order rather than as a part of the main body of resolutions reported by the Resolutions Committee, this is arranged through liaison with the Program Committee. The chairman of the Resolutions Committee then reports the resolution at the time prescribed for it in the agenda. If desired, the committee's report can include a preliminary motion establishing special rules for the consideration of the resolution, similar to the practice of the U.S. House of Representatives. The following is an example of such a rule:

Resolved, That at the time prescribed in the agenda the resolution relating to _____ be considered as a special order, the general debate to be limited to two hours and equally divided between, and controlled by, Mr. A, the leader for the affirmative, and Mr. B, the leader for the negative; that at the expiration of general debate the resolution shall be open to amendment, debate on said amendment(s) to be limited to two minutes for each member.

59:83   Under such a rule, the leaders for the two sides are recognized alternately by the presiding officer and can speak themselves or yield the floor to other member(s) for a portion of the time at their disposal. The leaders are usually the more ardent or persuasive advocates of the two positions, and frequently they speak first and save themselves enough time so that at the end they can close debate for their side. An alternative procedure is to assign a longer period of debate to Mr. A and Mr. B, and require other members to adhere to a shorter limit. Often it is helpful to require general debate to be conducted first before amendments are allowed, but this provision can be dispensed with.

§60. CONVENTIONS NOT OF A PERMANENT SOCIETY

60:1   A convention called only for a specific purpose not involving a permanent organization, or one called to form a state or a national society or a federation, is similar to a mass meeting as described in **53** in that when called to order it has no bylaws or officers. Because it has no bylaws, added difficulty may be encountered in determining who are the properly appointed delegates.

60:2   The group sponsoring the convention should appoint a Convention Arrangements Committee, as described above, to secure the hall and accommodations for the delegates, make the preliminary arrangements for the convention, and perform the other coordinating and arranging duties assigned to it.

60:3   Someone designated by the sponsoring group—sometimes the chairman of the Convention Arrangements Committee—calls the meeting to order and presides during any opening exercises and the election of a temporary chairman. The sponsoring group's choice for temporary chairman and the person who is to nominate him should be agreed upon in advance. After the elected temporary chairman has taken the chair, a temporary secretary is elected. Next comes the appointment of the Credentials, Rules, and Program Committees, or the ratification of the prior selection of these committees. In a convention of this type, if these committees have not been appointed in advance, all committees should be appointed by the chair. Until the report of the Credentials Committee is adopted, no business other than its adoption or the other preliminary actions described in this paragraph may be considered, except that any motions related to the consideration of such business or to the conduct of the meeting before the report is adopted, as well as those that are in order in the absence of a quorum (40:6–8), are in order.

60:4   If the Credentials Committee and other organizing committees were not appointed in advance and are not, therefore, ready to report, the time they need to prepare their reports is usually spent in listening to talks, perhaps on various phases of the convention's object. Otherwise the reports of the organizing committees are received in the same manner as that described for organizing a convention of an established association. If a permanent organization is not contemplated, a permanent chairman and secretary can, but need not, be elected at this time, after which the convention proceeds with the business for which it was called together. The principal purpose in electing a temporary chairman first and a permanent chairman later in a convention of this kind is to enable the temporary chairman to preside over the convention while it acts upon any matters relating to contested seats (see 59:21, 59:24), so that the permanent chairman can be elected by the delegates on the permanent roll of the convention as it is finally determined after all such contests have been resolved.

60:5   If the convention is called to form a permanent organization, permanent officers are not elected until later (after the adoption of the bylaws), but a resolution should be adopted at this point in the proceedings expressing an intention to form such a permanent association, as in the case of forming a permanent local society (see 54). A set of bylaws should have been carefully drawn up before the meeting of the convention, either by a Bylaws Committee appointed by the organizing group, with the appointments being ratified by the convention, or by members of the sponsoring group who thereafter hand them to a Bylaws Committee appointed at the convention. In the latter case some of those who drafted the bylaws should be appointed to the committee to avoid delay in reporting them.

60:6   After adoption of the bylaws, a Nominating Committee, selected in a manner as close as possible to that prescribed in the bylaws, nominates candidates for office, and those elected to these permanent offices take up their duties immediately, unless other provision is made.

CHAPTER

XX

DISCIPLINARY PROCEDURES

§61. DISCIPLINE OF MEMBERS AND GUESTS

61:1   In most societies it is understood that members are required to be of honorable character and reputation, and certain types of associations may have particular codes of ethics to enforce. Although ordinary societies seldom have occasion to discipline members, an organization or assembly has the ultimate right to make and enforce its own rules, and to require that its members refrain from conduct injurious to the organization or its purposes. No one should be allowed to remain a member if his retention will do this kind of harm.

61:2   Punishments that a society can impose generally fall under the headings of censure,[1] fine (if authorized in the bylaws), suspension, or expulsion. The extreme penalty that an organization or society can impose on a member is expulsion.

61:3   If there is an article on discipline in the bylaws (56:57), it may specify a number of offenses outside meetings for which these penalties can be imposed on a member of the organization. Frequently, such an article provides for their imposition on any member found guilty of conduct described, for example, as "tending to injure the good name of the organization, disturb its well-being, or hamper it in its work." In any society, behavior of this nature is a serious offense properly subject to disciplinary action, whether the bylaws make mention of it or not.

---

1. It is also possible to adopt a motion of censure without formal disciplinary procedures.

61:4   Formal disciplinary procedures should generally be regarded as a drastic step reserved for serious situations or those potentially so. When it appears that such measures may become necessary, proper and tactful handling of the case is of prime importance. It is usually in the best interests of the organization first to make every effort to obtain a satisfactory solution of the matter quietly and informally.

61:5   Cases of conduct subject to disciplinary action divide themselves into: offenses occurring in a meeting; and offenses by members outside a meeting.

Dealing with Offenses in a Meeting

61:6   **Principles Governing Discipline at Meetings.** A society has the right to determine who may be present at its meetings and to control its hall while meetings are in progress; but all members have the right to attend except in cases where the bylaws provide for the automatic suspension of members who fall in arrears in payment of their dues, or where the society has, by vote and as a penalty imposed for a specific offense, forbidden attendance.

61:7   Nonmembers, on the other hand—or a particular nonmember or group of nonmembers—can be excluded at any time from part or all of a meeting of a society, or from all of its meetings. Such exclusion can be effected by a ruling of the chair in cases of disorder, or by the adoption of a rule on the subject, or by an appropriate motion as the need arises—a motion of the latter nature being a question of privilege (see 9:25; 9:28–29; and **19**).

61:8   All persons present at a meeting have an obligation to obey the legitimate orders of the presiding officer.[2] Members, however, can appeal from the decision of the chair (**24**), move to suspend the rules (**25**), or move a reconsideration (**37**)—depending on the circumstances of the chair's ruling. A member can make such an appeal or motion whether the order involved applies to him or not.

---

2. See, however, *Remedies for Abuse of Authority by the Chair in a Meeting*, 62:2ff.

61:9   In dealing with any case of disorder in a meeting, the presiding officer should always maintain a calm, deliberate tone—although he may become increasingly firm if a situation demands it. Under no circumstances should the chair attempt to drown out a disorderly member—either by his own voice or the gavel—or permit himself to be drawn into a verbal duel. If unavoidable, however, proper disciplinary proceedings to cope with immediate necessity can be conducted while a disorderly member continues to speak.

61:10   **Breaches of Order by Members in a Meeting.** If a member commits only a slight breach of order—such as addressing another member instead of the chair in debate, or, in a single instance, failing to confine his remarks to the merits of the pending question—the chair simply raps lightly, points out the fault, and advises the member to avoid it. The member can then continue speaking if he commits no further breaches. More formal procedures can be used in the case of serious offenses, as follows:

61:11   *Calling a member to order.* If the offense is more serious than in the case above—as when a member repeatedly questions the motives of other members whom he mentions by name, or persists in speaking on completely irrelevant matters in debate—the chair normally should first warn the member; but with or without such a warning, the chair or any other member can "call the member to order." If the chair does this, he says, "The member is out of order and will be seated." Another member making the call rises and, without waiting to be recognized, says, "Mr. President, I call the member to order," then resumes his seat. If the chair finds this point of order (**23**) well taken, he declares the offender out of order and directs him to be seated, just as above. If the offender had the floor, then (irrespective of who originated the proceeding) the chair clearly states the breach involved and puts the question to the assembly: "Shall the member be allowed to continue speaking?" This question is undebatable.

61:12 *"Naming" an offender.* In cases of obstinate or grave breach of order by a member, the chair can, after repeated warnings, "name" the offender, which amounts to preferring charges and should be resorted to only in extreme circumstances. Before taking such action, when it begins to appear that it may become necessary, the chair directs the secretary to take down objectionable or disorderly words used by the member. This direction by the chair, and the words taken down pursuant to it, are entered in the minutes only if the chair finds it necessary to name the offender.

61:13 Although the chair has no authority to impose a penalty or to order the offending member removed from the hall, the assembly has that power. It should be noted in this connection that in any case of an offense against the assembly occurring in a meeting, there is no need for a formal trial provided that any penalty is imposed promptly after the breach (cf. 23:5), since the witnesses are all present and make up the body that is to determine the penalty.

61:14 The declaration made by the chair in naming a member is addressed to the offender by name and in the second person, and is entered in the minutes. An example of such a declaration is as follows:

> CHAIR: Mr. J! The chair has repeatedly directed you to refrain from offensive personal references when speaking in this meeting. Three times the chair has ordered you to be seated, and you have nevertheless attempted to continue speaking.

61:15 If the member obeys at this point, the matter can be dropped or not, as the assembly chooses. The case may be sufficiently resolved by an apology or a withdrawal of objectionable statements or remarks by the offender; but if not, any member can move to order a penalty, or the chair can first ask, "What penalty shall be imposed on the member?" A motion offered in a case of this kind can propose, for example, that the offender be required to make an apology, that he be censured, that he be required to leave the hall during the remainder of the meeting or until he is prepared to apologize, that his rights of membership be suspended for a time, or that he be expelled from the organization.

61:16   The offending member can be required to leave the hall during the consideration of his penalty, but he must be allowed to present his defense briefly first. A motion to require the member's departure during consideration of the penalty—which may be assumed by the chair if he thinks it appropriate—is undebatable, is unamendable, and requires a majority vote.

61:17   If the member denies having said anything improper, the words recorded by the secretary can be read to him and, if necessary, the assembly can decide by vote whether he was heard to say them. On the demand of a single member—other than the named offender, who is not considered to be a voting member while his case is pending—the vote on imposing a penalty must be taken by ballot, unless the penalty proposed is only that the offender be required to leave the hall for all or part of the remainder of the meeting. Expulsion from membership requires a two-thirds vote.

61:18   If the assembly orders an offending member to leave the hall during a meeting as described above and he refuses to do so, the considerations stated below regarding the removal of offenders apply; but such a member exposes himself to the possibility of more severe disciplinary action by the society.

61:19   **Protection from Annoyance by Nonmembers in a Meeting; Removal of an Offender from the Hall.** Any nonmembers allowed in the hall during a meeting, as guests of the organization, have no rights with reference to the proceedings (61:6–8). An assembly has the right to protect itself from annoyance by nonmembers, and its full authority in this regard—as distinguished from cases involving disorderly members—can be exercised by the chair acting alone. The chair has the power to require nonmembers to leave the hall, or to order their removal, at any time during the meeting; and the nonmembers have no right of appeal from such an order of the presiding officer. However, such an order may be appealed by a member.

That appeal is undebatable (see 24:3(5)(a)). At a mass meeting (**53**), any person who attempts to disrupt the proceedings in a manner obviously hostile to the announced purpose of the meeting can be treated as a nonmember under the provisions of this paragraph.

61:20   If a person—whether a member of the assembly or not—refuses to obey the order of proper authority to leave the hall during a meeting, the chair should take necessary measures to see that the order is enforced, but should be guided by a judicious appraisal of the situation. The chair can appoint a committee to escort the offender to the door, or the sergeant-at-arms—if there is one—can be asked to do this. If those who are assigned that task are unable to persuade the offender to leave, it is usually preferable that he be removed by police—who may, however, be reluctant to intervene unless representatives of the organization are prepared to press charges.

61:21   The sergeant-at-arms or the members of the appointed committee themselves may attempt to remove the offender from the hall, using the minimum force necessary. Such a step should generally be taken only as a last resort, since there may be adverse legal consequences; and a person who would refuse to leave upon legitimate request may be the type most likely to bring suit, even if with little justification. In cases where possibly serious annoyance by hostile persons is anticipated—in some mass meetings, for example—it may be advisable to arrange in advance for the presence of police or guards from a security service agency.

Offenses Elsewhere Than in a Meeting; Trials

61:22   If improper conduct by a member of a society occurs elsewhere than at a meeting, the members generally have no first-hand knowledge of the case. Therefore, if disciplinary action is to be taken, charges must be preferred and a formal trial held before the assembly of the society, or before a committee—standing or special—which is then required to report its findings and recommendations to the assembly for action. In addition, even when improper conduct occurs at a meeting, in order for disciplinary action to be taken *other than promptly after the breach occurs*, charges must be preferred and a formal trial held. However, the only way in which a member may be disciplined for words spoken in debate is through the procedure described in 61:10–18, which may be employed only promptly after the breach occurs. In some societies (depending on particular provisions of the bylaws, as explained in **62**), the same steps must also be employed if an officer of the society is to be removed from office. The procedures governing all such cases are described in detail in **63**.

§62. REMOVAL FROM OFFICE AND OTHER REMEDIES FOR DERELICTION OF DUTY IN OFFICE OR MISCONDUCT

62:1   The presiding officer and other officers have the duties set forth in this manual (see **47**) and in the organization's bylaws. This section covers procedures available if they neglect those duties, abuse their authority, or engage in other misconduct that calls into question their fitness for office. This section also covers removal from office at the pleasure of the assembly when the bylaws permit such removal.

Remedies for Abuse of Authority by the Chair in a Meeting

62:2   **Making and Enforcing Points of Order and Appeals.** In attempting to remedy any incorrect or abusive act by the chair at a meeting, the first step is for a member to raise a *Point of Order* as soon as the breach of the rules occurs.

62:3   For example, some important rules of parliamentary procedure are (a) that the chair must recognize any member who seeks the floor while entitled to it (see **42**); (b) that after a member has properly made a motion that is not dilatory (see **39**), the chair must either state the question on it, or else rule it out of order for a specified valid reason, require that the wording be clarified or be submitted in writing, or declare that it is not before the assembly for lack of a required second (see **4**); and (c) that the chair cannot hurry through the proceedings so quickly as to deprive the members of their rights to debate and to introduce secondary motions (see **43:7**).

62:4   So, if the chair ignores a member seeking the floor while entitled to it, ignores a properly made nondilatory motion, "gavels through" a motion in an improper attempt to cut off debate, or violates any other rule, any member may immediately raise a *Point of Order*.

62:5   To raise a *Point of Order*, a member rises and, without waiting to be recognized, immediately addresses the chair, saying, "I rise to a point of order," or simply, "Point of order!" The chair must then ask the member to state the point; and after the member does so, the chair is obligated either to rule whether the point is "well taken"—briefly stating the reasons for that ruling—or to submit the question to the assembly (see **23**).

62:6   Immediately after the chair makes a ruling, any member who disagrees with it may then move an *Appeal* (unless another *Appeal* is already pending or an appeal would be dilatory because there cannot possibly be two reasonable opinions on the question). The member does this by rising and, without waiting to be recognized, addressing the chair, saying, "I appeal from the decision of the chair." If the *Appeal* is seconded, the chair must state the question on it, clearly explain the exact parliamentary question at issue, allow any permissible debate, and put the question to a vote, as shown in **24**.

62:7   These procedures enable the majority to ensure enforcement of the rules unless the chair fails to respond to and resolve the *Point of Order*, fails to respond appropriately to any *Appeal*, or fails to act in accordance with the assembly's decision on the *Appeal* (or on a *Point of Order* submitted by the chair to the assembly).

62:8   If the chair ignores a point of order that is not dilatory, the member can repeat the point of order a second and third time and if the chair still ignores it, the member, standing in his place, can immediately put the point of order to a vote without debate. The question may be put as, "Is the point of order that … well taken?" If the point of order was that the chair improperly ignored another motion, the member may, instead of repeating the point of order, repeat the original motion, and if it is seconded and the chair still ignores it, may, standing in his place, put the ignored motion to a vote without debate.

62:9   Likewise, if the chair ignores an appeal appropriately made and seconded,[3] a member can repeat the appeal and if, despite its being seconded, the chair ignores it again, the member can repeat it a third time and if it is again seconded but still ignored by the chair, the member can immediately, standing in his place, put the appeal to a vote without debate. The question may be put as: "Shall the decision of the chair be sustained?"

62:10 **Removal of Presiding Officer from Chair for All or Part of a Session.** If the chair fails to act in accordance with the assembly's decision on an appeal (or on a point of order submitted to a vote of the assembly) or otherwise culpably fails to perform the duties of the chair properly in a meeting, the assembly may employ measures temporarily to replace the chair with another presiding officer expected to act in accordance with the will of the assembly.

62:11   If the offending occupant of the chair is an appointed or elected chairman pro tem (see 47:11(2–3)), a motion can be made to "declare the chair vacant and proceed to elect a new

---

3. An appeal is not allowed from the chair's ruling on a question about which there cannot possibly be two reasonable opinions (24:3(2)(b)) and is not in order in certain other circumstances (24:3(2)(a), 24:5–8), but in such cases the chair must announce that the appeal is not in order for the relevant reason, not simply ignore the appeal (unless the appeal is dilatory as explained in 39:1–4).

chairman." Such a motion is a question of privilege affecting the assembly (**19**) and is an incidental main motion requiring a majority vote for its adoption.[4]

62:12   If the chair is not an appointed or elected chairman pro tem, a motion to declare the chair vacant is not in order. However, a motion can be made to *Suspend the Rules* so as to take away from him the authority to preside during all or part of a given session.[5] When such a motion is made and seconded, after stating the motion he must turn the chair over to another following the procedure described in 43:29, and the remedy for refusal or failure to do so is that the motion may be put to a vote by its maker.

62:13   Any one motion to *Suspend the Rules* that might limit the authority or duties of the presiding officer during a meeting can remain in effect, at most, for one session. (See 8:12, 8:16.) Therefore, in order to prevent the regular presiding officer from presiding during subsequent sessions, the motion to *Suspend the Rules* would have to be renewed and separately adopted at each of the sessions. Moreover, since *Suspend the Rules* applies only when "an assembly wishes to do something *during a meeting* that it cannot do without violating one or more of its regular rules" (25:1, emphasis added), the motion cannot be used to remove from the presiding officer (even

---

4. Once such a motion is made and seconded, the chair must state it, and then, since it refers to the presiding officer in a capacity not shared in common with other members, the chair must be turned over to the secretary or secretary pro tem. The new occupant of the chair then presides during consideration of the motion to declare the chair vacant and proceed to elect a new chairman. The new occupant continues to preside until the result of the vote on that motion is announced and, if it is adopted, until the election of the new chairman is completed.

     If the presiding officer refuses or fails to turn the chair over as required, and ignores a point of order on the issue (or ignores, or does not abide by the decision on, an appeal of a ruling on the point of order) the motion to declare the chair vacant may be put to a vote by its maker as explained in 62:8–9. In such a case, the motion is undebatable.

5. This is true even if the bylaws contain a provision to the effect that the president shall preside at all meetings, since such a provision is clearly in the nature of a rule of order, which may be suspended even if in the bylaws. See 2:21.

temporarily) any administrative duties—those related to the role of an executive officer that are distinct from the function of presiding over the assembly at its meetings. (Cf. 47:20.)

62:14   If the motion to suspend the rules is adopted by a two-thirds vote, then, unless the motion names a new occupant of the chair, the ranking vice-president (or, in the absence of the vice-president, an elected temporary presiding officer; 47:11(3), 47:13) has the duty of presiding through the end of the session (or any shorter period specified by the motion to suspend the rules).

62:15   A permanent removal of the presiding officer, and removal of authority to exercise administrative duties conferred by the bylaws, requires the procedure described below.

Removal from Office

62:16   Except as the bylaws may provide otherwise, any regularly elected officer of a permanent society can be removed from office by the society's assembly as follows:

- If the bylaws provide that officers shall serve "for __ years *or* until their successors are elected," the officer in question can be removed from office by adoption of a motion to do so. The vote required for adoption of this incidental main motion is (a) a two-thirds vote, (b) a majority vote when previous notice (as defined in 10:44) has been given, or (c) a vote of a majority of the entire membership—any one of which will suffice. A motion to remove an officer from office is a question of privilege (**19**) affecting the organization of the assembly, and so also is the filling of any vacancy created by the adoption of such a motion.[6]

---

6. The assembly normally cannot proceed to fill the vacancy created by removal of an officer immediately, since notice is a requirement (see 32:7). If the president is removed from office, the vice-president thereby succeeds to the presidency, creating a vacancy in the vice-presidency which requires notice to fill. If it is desired to fill a vacancy that may be created by removal, previous notice may be given in advance of the meeting at which removal is contemplated that, should removal of the officer occur, the resulting vacancy may be filled at that meeting.

- If, however, the bylaws provide that officers shall serve *only* a fixed term, such as "for two years" (which is not a recommended wording; see 56:28), or if they provide that officers shall serve "for __ years *and* until their successors are elected," an officer can be removed from office only for cause—that is, neglect of duty in office or misconduct—in accordance with the procedures described in **63**; that is, an investigating committee must be appointed, charges must be preferred, and a formal trial must be held.

§63. INVESTIGATION AND TRIAL

63:1   As explained in **61** and **62**, the removal of an officer for cause, or the discipline of a member for improper conduct, may require that charges be preferred and that a formal trial be held. The full procedure for such cases is described in this section.[7]

Rights of the Society and the Accused

63:2   A society has the right to investigate the character of its members and officers as may be necessary to the enforcement of its own standards. But neither the society nor any member has the right to make public any information obtained through such investigation; if it becomes common knowledge within the society, it may not be revealed to any persons outside the society. Consequently, a trial must always be held in executive session, as must the introduction and consideration of all resolutions leading up to the trial.

63:3   If (after trial) a member is expelled or an officer is removed from office, the society has the right to disclose that fact—

---

7. It is possible for a disciplinary proceeding to affect an individual's status both as an officer and as a member, and a resolution preferring charges (see 63:13–63:20) may combine notice to show cause both why the accused should not be removed from office and why he should not be expelled from membership. If the bylaws make membership a required qualification for office (see 47:2), then expulsion from membership necessarily results in removal from office.

circulating it only to the extent required for the protection of the society or, possibly, of other organizations. Neither the society nor any of its members has the right to make public the charge of which an officer or member has been found guilty, or to reveal any other details connected with the case. To make any of the facts public may constitute libel. A trial by the society cannot legally establish the guilt of the accused, as understood in a court of law; it can only establish his guilt as affecting the society's judgment of his fitness for membership or office.

63:4   Ordinarily it is impossible for the society to obtain *legal* proof of facts in disciplinary cases. To get at the truth under the conditions of such a trial, hearsay evidence has to be admissible, and judgment as to the best interests of the society may have to be based on it. Witnesses are not sworn. The persons with first-hand knowledge may be nonmembers, who probably will decline to testify, and may be willing only to reveal the facts privately to a single member on condition that their names in no way be connected with the case. Even members may be reluctant to give formal testimony against the accused. A member can be required to testify at a trial on pain of expulsion, but it is very seldom advisable to force such an issue.

63:5   A member or officer has the right that allegations against his good name shall not be made except by charges brought on reasonable ground. If thus accused, he has the right to due process—that is, to be informed of the charge and given time to prepare his defense, to appear and defend himself, and to be fairly treated.

63:6   If a member or officer is guilty of a serious offense and knows that other members are in possession of the facts, he may wish to submit his resignation. When the good of the society appears to demand the departure of an offender, it is usually best for all concerned to offer him the opportunity to resign quietly before charges are preferred. The society has no obligation to suggest or accept such a resignation at any stage of the case, however, even if it is submitted on the offender's own initiative.

Steps in a Fair Disciplinary Process

63:7 Most ordinary societies should never have to hold a formal trial, and their bylaws need not be encumbered with clauses on discipline. For the protection both of the society and of its members and officers, however, the basic steps which, in any organization, make up the elements of fair disciplinary process should be understood. Any special procedures established should be built essentially around them, and the steps must be followed in the absence of such provisions. As set forth below, these are: (1) confidential investigation by a committee; (2) report of the committee, and preferral of charges if warranted; (3) formal notification of the accused; (4) trial; and (5) the assembly's review of a trial committee's findings (if the trial has been held in a committee instead of the assembly of the society).

63:8 **Confidential Investigation by Committee.** A committee whose members are selected for known integrity and good judgment conducts a confidential investigation (including a reasonable attempt to interview the accused) to determine whether to recommend that further action, including the preferring of charges if necessary, is warranted.

63:9 Accordingly, if the rules of the organization do not otherwise provide for the method of charge and trial, a member may, at a time when nonmembers are not present, offer a resolution to appoint an investigating committee. This resolution is to be in a form similar to the following:

> *Resolved,* That a committee of … [perhaps "five"] be elected by ballot to investigate allegations of neglect of duty in office by our treasurer, J.M., which, if true, cast doubt on her fitness to continue in office, and that the committee be instructed, if it concludes that the allegations are well-founded, to report resolutions covering its recommendations.

63:10   To initiate disciplinary proceedings involving a member, a suitable resolution would be:

> *Resolved,* That a committee of … [perhaps "five"] be appointed by the chair [or "be elected by ballot"] to investigate rumors regarding the conduct of our member Mr. N, which, if true, would tend to injure the good name of this organization, and that the committee be instructed, if it concludes the allegations are well-founded, to report resolutions covering its recommendations.

63:11   For the protection of parties who may be innocent, the first resolution should avoid details as much as possible. An individual member may not prefer charges, even if that member has proof of an officer's or member's wrongdoing. If a member introduces a resolution preferring charges unsupported by an investigating committee's recommendation, the chair must rule the resolution out of order, informing the member that it would instead be in order to move the appointment of such a committee (by a resolution, as in the example above). A resolution is improper if it implies the truth of specific rumors or contains insinuations unfavorable to an officer or member, even one who is to be accused. It is out of order, for example, for a resolution to begin, "Whereas, It seems probable that the treasurer has engaged in graft, …" At the first mention of the word "graft" in such a case, the chair must instantly call to order the member attempting to move the resolution.

63:12   An investigating committee appointed as described above has no power to require the accused, or any other person, to appear before it, but it should quietly conduct a complete investigation, making an effort to learn all relevant facts. Information obtained in strict confidence may help the committee to form an opinion, but it may not be reported to the society or used in a trial—except as may be possible without bringing out the confidential particulars. Before any action is taken, fairness demands that the committee or some of its members make a reasonable attempt to meet with the accused for frank discussion and to hear his side of the story. It may be possible at this stage to point out to the accused that if he does not rectify the situation or resign, he probably will be brought to trial.

63:13 **Report of the Investigating Committee; Preferral of Charges.** If after investigation the committee's opinion is favorable to the accused, or if it finds that the matter can be resolved satisfactorily without a trial, it reports that fact.[8] But if the committee from its investigations finds substance to the allegations and cannot resolve the matter satisfactorily in any other way, it makes a report in writing—which is signed by every committee member who agrees—outlining the course of its investigation and recommending in the report the adoption of resolutions preferring charges, arranging for a trial, and, if desired, suspending the rights of the accused, as in the following example:

63:14   *Resolved,* That when this meeting adjourns, it adjourn to meet at 8 P.M. on Wednesday, November 15, 20__. [For variations depending on conditions, see the first paragraph following these resolutions, below.]

63:15   *Resolved,* That J.M. is hereby cited to appear at said adjourned meeting for trial, to show cause why she should not be removed from the office of treasurer on the following charge and specifications:

     Charge. Neglect of duty in office.

     Specification 1. In that J.M. has failed to account for at least $10,000 of the Society's funds known to have been given into her custody.

---

8. If the investigating committee submits a report that does not recommend preferral of charges, it is within the power of the assembly nevertheless to adopt a resolution that does prefer charges. It is also possible for the assembly to adopt instructions to the committee specifying when it is to report, or even to adopt a motion to *Discharge a Committee* (**36**) and thereafter to consider a resolution preferring charges; but in order to provide due process to the accused, any such instructions must allow the investigating committee a reasonable and adequate time to investigate and prepare a report, and the committee may be discharged only if it has had such time yet has failed to complete its report.

Specification 2. In that J.M. has repeatedly failed to provide the financial records of her treasurership for review by the auditing committee.

63:16   *Resolved,* That from the time official notification of this resolution is delivered to J.M.'s address until disposition of the case, all of J.M.'s authority, rights, and duties pertaining to the office of treasurer are suspended.

63:17   *Resolved,* That members S and T act as managers for the Society at the trial. [See below.]

63:18   In a disciplinary proceeding against a member, an example of the second and third resolutions is:

63:19   *Resolved,* That Mr. N is hereby cited to appear at said adjourned meeting for trial, to show cause why he should not be expelled from the Society on the following charge and specifications:

Charge. Conduct tending to injure the good name of this organization.

Specification 1. In that Mr. N has so conducted himself as to establish among a number of his acquaintances a reputation for willfully originating false reports against innocent persons.

Specification 2. In that on or about the evening of August 12, 20__, in the Matterhorn Restaurant, Mr. N was seen by patrons to be the apparent provoker of a needless and violent disturbance, causing damage to the furnishings.

63:20   *Resolved,* That from the time official notification of this resolution is delivered to Mr. N's address until disposition of the case, all of Mr. N's rights as a member (except as relate to the trial) are suspended pending disposition of the case.

63:21   With reference to an appropriate date for which to set the trial, thirty days is a reasonable time to allow the accused to prepare his defense. When a trial is to be before the assembly of the society, it is generally a good policy to hold it at a meeting devoted exclusively to the matter, such as an adjourned meeting as in the example above. To devote a meeting to the trial when there is to be another regular meeting between the date of adoption of these resolutions and the date desired for the trial, the first resolution would establish a special meeting instead of an adjourned meeting (see **9**).[9] If believed advisable—and particularly when the trial is likely to be delicate, involve potential scandal, or be long and troublesome, or when the assembly of the organization is large—the resolutions reported by the investigating committee, instead of providing for trial before the entire assembly, can be worded so as to establish a committee to hear the trial and report its findings and recommendations to the assembly for action. In such a case, the first two of the resolutions above would be worded as follows:

63:22   *Resolved,* That a trial committee consisting of Mr. H as chairman and members A, B, C, D, E, and F be appointed to try the case of J.M. and report its findings and recommendations. [A special committee appointed to hear a trial must be composed of persons different from those on the preliminary investigating committee. This resolution can either be offered with the names of the members of the proposed trial committee specified as in the example, or it can contain a blank so as to leave the manner of their selection to the assembly.]

63:23   *Resolved,* That J.M. is hereby cited to appear before the said trial committee at the Society hall at 8 P.M. on Wednesday, November 15, 20__, to show cause why she should not be removed from the office of treasurer on the following charge and specifications: ... [setting them forth, as above].

The remaining resolutions would be the same whether the trial is to be before the assembly or before a special committee (see above).

63:24   A *charge* sets forth an *offense*—that is, a particular kind of act or conduct that entails liability to penalty under the

---

9. The assembly of a society may call a special meeting for purposes of conducting a trial and determining a punishment, even if the bylaws fail to provide for special meetings or the designation in the bylaws of those who can call special meetings does not include the assembly.

governing rules—of which the accused is alleged to be guilty. A *specification* states *what the accused is alleged to have done* which, if true, constitutes an instance of the offense indicated in the charge. An accused officer or member must be found guilty of a *charge* before a penalty can be imposed. If the bylaws of the society provide for the imposition of penalties for offenses defined in the bylaws or an adopted code of conduct or similar set of rules, a charge may consist of such a defined offense. If such particular offenses are not defined or are not applicable, a member may be charged with "conduct tending to injure the good name of the organization, disturb its well-being, or hamper it in its work," or the like, and an officer may be charged with misconduct of the type just mentioned or with "misconduct in office," "neglect of duty in office," or "conduct that renders him [or "her"] unfit for office."

63:25   Each separate charge contained in the resolutions must be accompanied by at least one specification, unless the investigating committee and the accused agree in preferring that this information not be disclosed outside the trial. It is best if each specification is carefully worded so as to make no broader allegation than is believed sufficient to establish the validity of the charge if the specification is found to be true.

63:26   A resolution preferring charges may (although it need not) be accompanied by one suspending all or some specified portion of the accused's authority, rights, and duties as an officer or rights as a member (except those rights that relate to the trial) pending disposition of the case, effective from the time official notification of the resolution is delivered to the accused's address.

63:27   The "managers" at the trial—referred to in the fourth resolution of the complete set shown above—have the task of presenting the evidence against the accused, and must be members of the society. Their duty, however, is not to act as prosecutors—in the sense of making every effort to secure conviction—but rather to strive that the trial will get at the truth and that, in the light of all facts brought out, the outcome will be just.

63:28 **Formal Notification of the Officer or Member.** If the society adopts resolutions ordering trial before the assembly or a committee, the secretary immediately sends to the accused, by a method providing confirmation of delivery to his address (such as registered mail with delivery confirmation), a letter notifying him of the date, hour, and place of the trial, containing an exact copy of the charge(s) and specifications with the date of their adoption, and directing him to appear as cited—even if the accused officer or member was present when the resolutions were adopted. The secretary's letter of notification can reproduce the resolutions in full and can be worded as follows:

> Dear Mr. N:
> Your attention is called to the fact that the ... Society, at its meeting on October 14, 20__, adopted the following resolutions:
> ... [Text of resolutions].
> Kindly be present at the Society hall at the time indicated above.
>
> Sincerely,
> John Clark, Secretary

63:29 It is the duty of the secretary to have at hand at the trial a photocopy, printout, or other direct reproduction of the letter of notification with the delivery confirmation attached, as proof that it was delivered to the accused's address.

63:30 **Trial Procedure.** The trial is a formal hearing on the validity of the charges. At the trial, the evidence against the accused officer or member is presented by the managers for the society, and the officer or member has the right to be represented by counsel and to speak and produce witnesses in his own defense. If the charges are found to be true, a penalty may be imposed or recommended; but if the charges are not substantiated, the officer or member is exonerated and any authority, rights, duties, and privileges of office or membership that had been suspended are automatically restored. The managers, as previously stated, must be members of the society. Defense counsel can be attorney(s) or not, but must be member(s) of the society unless the trial body (that is, the assembly or the trial committee as the case may be) by vote agrees to permit attorney(s) who are not member(s) to act in this capacity. Nonmembers who consent to testify can be brought in as witnesses at the trial, but such a witness is allowed in the room only while testifying.

63:31   If the accused fails to appear for trial at the appointed time as directed, the trial proceeds without him.

63:32   At any time before the commencement of the trial with the first of the "preliminary steps" described below, the assembly may, by majority vote, adopt a resolution to govern the trial specifying details not inconsistent with the procedures described here.[10] The resolution may include an agenda that establishes times for portions of the trial, such as time limits for opening and closing statements. If time limits are imposed, they must allow the defense at least equal time for each element of the trial as that allowed the managers, and this rule may not be suspended without the consent of the defense.

63:33   At the trial, in calling the meeting to order, the chair should call attention to the fact that the meeting is in executive session (9), and to the attendant obligation of secrecy. Preliminary steps then include the secretary's reading from the minutes the resolutions adopted by the society relating to the trial, the chair's verification—by inquiring of the secretary—that the accused was furnished with a copy of the charges, the chair's announcement of the names of the managers for the society, and the chair's inquiry of the accused as to whether he has counsel. The trial then proceeds as follows:

a) The chair directs the secretary to read the charge and specifications.

b) The chair asks the accused how he pleads—*guilty* or *not guilty*—first to each of the specifications in order, and then to the charge.

---

10. The assembly may vary the procedures described here through adoption of special rules of order for disciplinary proceedings either by previous notice and a two-thirds vote or by a vote of a majority of the entire membership.

c) If a plea of *guilty* is entered to the charge, there need be no trial, and the meeting can proceed directly to the determination of the penalty after hearing a brief statement of the facts.

d) If the plea to the charge is *not guilty*, the trial proceeds in the following order, the chair first explaining all the steps, then calling for each of them in sequence: (1) opening statements by both sides—the managers first; (2) testimony of witnesses produced by the managers for the society; (3) testimony of defense witnesses; (4) rebuttal witnesses on behalf of the society, and then on behalf of the defense, if any; and (5) closing arguments by both sides. Up until the completion of the closing arguments, no one is entitled to the floor except the managers and the defense; and they must address the chair except when questioning witnesses. Cross-examination, re-direct-examination, and re-cross-examination of witnesses is permitted, and witnesses can be recalled for further testimony as the occasion may dictate.

From the first of the "preliminary steps" described above up until the completion of the closing arguments:

i) Subject to the relevant rules and the provisions in any resolution governing the trial, the presiding officer, similarly to a judge at a trial, directs the proceedings and rules on all questions of evidence and any objections or requests by the managers or the defense, the merits of which may first be argued by the managers and the defense. From any such direction or ruling, a member of the assembly may take an undebatable appeal, or the presiding officer may in the first instance submit any such question to a vote, without debate, by the assembly. Any motion to alter a resolution previously adopted to govern the trial, which may be proposed only by the managers or defense, or a proposal by the chair to do the same, is submitted without debate to a vote by the assembly; its adoption requires the vote necessary to *Amend Something Previously Adopted*.

ii) If a member of the assembly who is not a manager or with the defense wishes a question to be put to a witness, a manager, or the defense, the question must be delivered in writing to the presiding officer, who at an appropriate point puts it, unless he rules it not in order of his own accord or upon an objection by the managers or the defense, which ruling, like any other in the trial, is subject to an undebatable appeal.

iii) The only motions in order are the five privileged motions and those motions that relate to the conduct of the meeting or to the trial itself. Any member who is not a manager or with the defense may offer such a motion, subject to the limitation in (i) above, only in writing delivered to the presiding officer,[11] who at an appropriate point reads the motion aloud, inquires whether there is a second (if required), and either rules upon it or puts the motion to a vote without debate.

e) When the closing arguments have been completed, the accused must leave the room. If the trial is before the assembly rather than a trial committee, the managers, defense counsel (if members of the society), and member witnesses for both sides remain, take part in discussion, and vote as any other members. The chair then states the question on the finding as to the guilt of the accused, as follows: "The question before the assembly [or "the committee"] is: Is Mr. N guilty of the charge and specifications preferred against him?" Each of the specifications, and then the charge, is read, opened to debate, and voted on separately—although the several votes can be delayed to be taken on a single ballot.

The specifications or the charge can be amended to conform to facts brought out in the trial—but not in such a way as to find the accused guilty of a charge not wholly included within charge(s) for which he has been tried.

If the accused is found guilty of none of the specifications relating to a charge, he is automatically found not

---

11. However, any member may address the chair to appeal a ruling.

guilty of the charge, and no vote is taken on it (or, if the vote on the charge was already taken on the same ballot as the vote on the specifications, the vote on the charge is ignored). If the accused is found guilty of one or more of the specifications but not of the charge, and if a lower degree or level of the offense charged is defined in the organization's bylaws, adopted code of conduct, or similar set of rules, then such a lesser charge may be moved and voted on.

If the accused is found guilty, the chair announces that the next item of business is the determination of the penalty. One of the managers for the society usually makes a motion for a penalty the managers feel appropriate, although any member may move that a specific penalty be imposed; this motion is debatable and amendable. On the demand of a single member both the question of guilt and the question of the penalty must be voted on by ballot.

The usual possible penalties for an officer are censure or removal from office, although in special circumstances others may be appropriate (for example, to repay into the society's treasury funds that the officer has been found guilty of misappropriating, perhaps with an added fine). For all of these, including removal from office, a majority vote is required. Penalties appropriate in disciplinary proceedings against members are discussed in 61:2. For expulsion, a two-thirds vote is required.

f) After voting is completed, the accused is called back into the hall and advised of the result.

63:34 A member who votes for a finding of guilt at a trial should be morally convinced, on the basis of the evidence he has heard, that the accused is guilty.

63:35 **Assembly's Review of a Trial Committee's Findings.** If the trial has been held before a trial committee instead of the assembly of the society, this committee reports to the assembly in executive session (9) the results of its trial of the case, with resolutions—in cases where its finding is one of *guilty*—covering the penalty it recommends that the society impose. The report is prepared in writing and includes, to the extent possible without disclosing confidential information which should be kept within the committee, a summary of the basis for the committee's finding.

63:36   Unless the report exonerates the accused, he is then permitted—personally, through counsel, or both, as he prefers—to make a statement of the case, after which the committee is given the opportunity to present a statement in rebuttal. The accused—and defense counsel if not member(s)—then leave the room, and the assembly acts upon the resolutions submitted by the committee. The members of the committee remain and vote on the case the same as other members of the society.

63:37   Under this procedure, the assembly can decline to impose any penalty, notwithstanding the trial committee's recommendation; or it can reduce the recommended penalty; but it cannot increase the penalty. The assembly cannot impose a penalty if the trial committee has found the accused not guilty.

Committee on Discipline

63:38   In some professional societies and other organizations where particular aspects of discipline are of special importance, the handling of such matters is simplified by providing in the bylaws for a standing Committee on Discipline (see **50, 56**). Its prescribed duties are normally to be alert to disciplinary problems, to investigate them, to introduce all necessary resolutions, and—in event of a trial—to manage the case for the society.

63:39   This committee may also have the duty of hearing the actual trial, in which case it should be large enough that a subcommittee can perform the confidential investigation as described in 63:8–12. Under the latter practice, the full Committee on Discipline adopts the charge and specifications, and the chairman of the committee sends the citation to the accused and presides at the trial, which is conducted just as it would be if held before the assembly. It is generally best not to empower the committee to *impose* a penalty, however, but to require it to report its recommended disciplinary measures to the society for action, just as in the case of a special committee to hear a trial.

63:40   In organizations where disciplinary matters may arise with some frequency, the system of having a Committee on Discipline has the advantages of not unduly inconveniencing the society, and of promoting the avoidance of scandal and the settlement of disciplinary problems without an actual trial.

CHARTS, TABLES, AND LISTS

I. CHART FOR DETERMINING WHEN EACH SUBSIDIARY OR PRIVILEGED MOTION IS IN ORDER

In the chart on the two following pages, the privileged, subsidiary, and main motions are listed in order of rank, the motion at the top taking precedence over all the others, and each of the remaining ones taking precedence over all those below it. A main motion is in order only when no other motion is pending.

When a given one of the motions listed is immediately pending, then: (a) any other motion appearing *above* it in the list is *in order*, unless a condition stated opposite the other motion causes that motion to be out of order; and (b) motions listed *below* the given motion which are not already pending are *out of order* (except for the application of *Amend* or the *Previous Question* to certain motions ranking above them as noted in the next paragraph; see also Standard Characteristic 2, 12:7(2) and 16:5(2)).

With respect to arrowed lines in the chart, (————) indicates applicability of all of the subsidiary motions to the main motion; (════), applicability of *Amend* to certain other motions in the order of precedence; (▬ ▬ ▬), applicability of *Limit or Extend Limits of Debate* to debatable motions in the order of precedence; and (═ ═ ═), applicability of the *Previous Question* to the motions that are debatable or amendable.

I. CHART FOR DETERMINING WHEN EACH SUBSIDIARY OR PRIVILEGED MOTION IS IN ORDER (cont.)

Order of Precedence of Motions

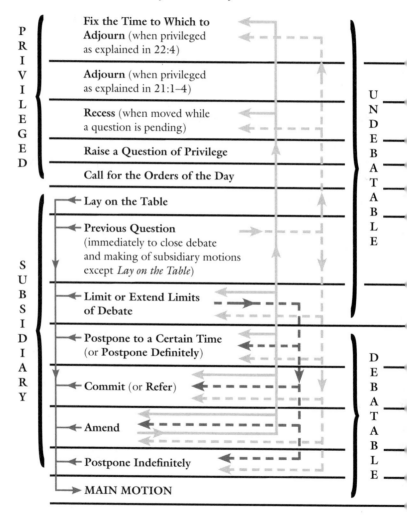

PRIVILEGED

Fix the Time to Which to Adjourn (when privileged as explained in 22:4)

Adjourn (when privileged as explained in 21:1–4)

Recess (when moved while a question is pending)

Raise a Question of Privilege

Call for the Orders of the Day

SUBSIDIARY

← **Lay on the Table**

← **Previous Question** (immediately to close debate and making of subsidiary motions except *Lay on the Table*)

← **Limit or Extend Limits of Debate**

← **Postpone to a Certain Time** (or **Postpone Definitely**)

← **Commit** (or **Refer**)

← **Amend**

← **Postpone Indefinitely**

→ **MAIN MOTION**

UNDEBATABLE

DEBATABLE

Other Conditions Affecting Admissibility
MOTION DIRECTLY TO LEFT ON FACING PAGE IS OUT OF ORDER WHEN:

- a motion to *Suspend the Rules* relating to priority of business is pending

- a *Point of Order*, undebatable *Appeal*, or one of the five *Requests and Inquiries*—not adhering to main question—is pending

- a motion which cannot be debated or amended is immediately pending

- any undebatable question is immediately pending; also when motion(s) under an order for the *Previous Question* remain to be voted on

- any undebatable question except *Division of a Question* or *Consider by Paragraph or Seriatim* is immediately pending; also when motion(s) under an order for the *Previous Question* remain to be voted on

- a motion to *Reconsider* is pending, or any undebatable question except *Division of a Question* or *Consider by Paragraph or Seriatim* is immediately pending; also when motion(s) under an order for the *Previous Question* remain to be voted on

- the application would be to the main question, and any motion except *Postpone Indefinitely* is pending; also, in any application, when motion(s) under an order for the *Previous Question* remain to be voted on

- any motion except the main question is pending; also when the *Previous Question* has been ordered

- any motion is pending

II. TABLE OF RULES RELATING TO MOTIONS

MOTION	CLASS[1]	IN ORDER WHEN ANOTHER HAS THE FLOOR	MUST BE SECONDED[2]
1. Main motion or question (**10**)	M	No	Yes
2. Adjourn, ordinary case in societies (**21**)	P	No	Yes
3. Adjourn at or to a future time, or in advance of a time already set, or when the assembly will thereby be dissolved (**8, 10, 21**)	M	No	Yes
4. Adopt, accept, or agree to a report (**10, 51**)	M	No	Yes
5. Adopt bylaws or constitution, initially in forming a society (**10, 54, 56**)	M	No	Yes[3]
6. Adopt revised bylaws or constitution (**35, 56, 57**)	M/B	No	Yes[3]
7. Adopt special rules of order (2:14ff.; **10**)	M	No	Yes
8. Adopt ordinary standing rules (2:23; **10**)	M	No	Yes
9. Adopt parliamentary standing rules in a convention (**10**; 59:27ff.)	M	No	Yes[3]

1. Key to classification symbols: M—main motions; S—subsidiary motions; P—privileged motions; I—incidental motions; B—motions that bring a question again before the assembly; M/B—incidental main motions classed with motions that bring a question again before the assembly (see 6:25ff.).

(For forms used in making motions, see Table III.)

DEBATABLE	AMENDABLE	VOTE REQUIRED FOR ADOPTION	CAN BE RECONSIDERED
Yes	Yes	Majority, except as explained in 10:8(7)	Yes
No	No	Majority	No
Yes	Yes	Majority	No
Yes	Yes	Majority	Yes
Yes	Yes	Majority	Negative vote only
Yes	Yes	As provided in existing bylaws. (In absence of such provision, same as in next line)	Negative vote only
Yes	Yes	(a) Previous notice *and* two-thirds; or (b) majority of entire membership	Negative vote only
Yes	Yes	Majority	Yes
Yes	Yes	Two-thirds	Negative vote only

2. Motions listed as requiring a second do not need to be seconded when made by direction of a board or committee.
3. In practice, motion is usually made by the reporting member of a committee, in which case it does not require a second.

II. TABLE OF RULES RELATING TO MOTIONS (cont.)

MOTION	CLASS[1]	IN ORDER WHEN ANOTHER HAS THE FLOOR	MUST BE SECONDED[2]
10. Adopt agenda or program (10; 41; 59:48ff.)	M	No	Yes[3]
11. Amend a pending motion (12)	S	No	Yes
12. Amend an amendment of a pending motion (12)	S	No	Yes
13. Amend Something Previously Adopted, general case, including ordinary standing rules (35)	M/B	No	Yes
14. Amend parliamentary standing rules in a convention, when they are not pending (35; 59:27ff.)	M/B	No	Yes
15. Amend adopted agenda or program with reference to items not yet reached (35; 41; 59:59)	M/B	No	Yes[3]
16. Amend bylaws or constitution, when not pending (35, 57)	M/B	No	Yes

1. Key to classification symbols: M—main motions; S—subsidiary motions; P—privileged motions; I—incidental motions; B—motions that bring a question again before the assembly; M/B—incidental main motions classed with motions that bring a question again before the assembly (see 6:25ff.).
2. Motions listed as requiring a second do not need to be seconded when made by direction of a board or committee.

(For forms used in making motions, see Table III.)

DEBATABLE	AMENDABLE	VOTE REQUIRED FOR ADOPTION	CAN BE RECONSIDERED
Yes	Yes	Majority; but in session with existing order of business, two-thirds if in conflict with it or sets special order	Negative vote only
If motion to be amended is debatable[4]	Yes	Majority	Yes
If motion to be amended is debatable[4]	No	Majority	Yes
Yes	Yes	(a) Majority with notice; or (b) two-thirds; or (c) majority of entire membership	Negative vote only
Yes	Yes	Two-thirds; or majority of all having convention voting rights who have been registered	Negative vote only
Yes	Yes	As immediately above, though often by unanimous consent after Program Committee's recommendation	Negative vote only
Yes	Yes	As provided in bylaws or constitution. (In absence of such provision, same as in No. 17, following)	Negative vote only

3. In practice, motion is usually made by the reporting member of a committee, in which case it does not require a second.
4. Debate on motion must be confined to *its* merits only, and cannot go into the main question except as necessary for debate of the immediately pending question.

II. TABLE OF RULES RELATING TO MOTIONS (cont.)

MOTION	CLASS[1]	IN ORDER WHEN ANOTHER HAS THE FLOOR	MUST BE SECONDED[2]
17. Amend special rules of order, when not pending (2:22; **35**)	M/B	No	Yes
18. Appeal, general case (**24**)	I	Yes, at time of appealed ruling	Yes
19. Appeal, relating to indecorum or transgression of rules of speaking, or to the priority of business, or if made when an undebatable question is immediately pending or involved in the appeal (**24**)	I	Yes, at time of appealed ruling	Yes
20. Ballot, to order the vote on pending question to be taken by (**30, 45**)	I	No	Yes
21. Blank, to create by striking out (12:95)	I	No	Yes
22. Blanks, proposals for filling (12:92ff.)	—	Can be called out when chair asks for them	No
23. Bylaw amendments, to rearrange order of consideration (57:6)	I	No	Yes

1. Key to classification symbols: M—main motions; S—subsidiary motions; P—privileged motions; I—incidental motions; B—motions that bring a question again before the assembly; M/B—incidental main motions classed with motions that bring a question again before the assembly (see 6:25ff.).

(For forms used in making motions, see Table III.)

DEBATABLE	AMENDABLE	VOTE REQUIRED FOR ADOPTION	CAN BE RECONSIDERED
Yes	Yes	(a) Previous notice *and* two-thirds; or (b) majority of entire membership	Negative vote only
Yes,[4] under rules stated in 24:3(5)	No	Majority in negative required to reverse chair's decision	Yes
No	No	Majority in negative required to reverse chair's decision	Yes
No	Yes	Majority	Yes
No	No	Majority	No
If filling a blank in a debatable motion[4]	No	Majority	Yes
No	Yes	Majority	Negative vote only

2. Motions listed as requiring a second do not need to be seconded when made by direction of a board or committee.
4. Debate on motion or proposal must be confined to *its* merits only, and cannot go into the main question except as necessary for debate of the immediately pending question.

II. TABLE OF RULES RELATING TO MOTIONS (cont.)

MOTION	CLASS[1]	IN ORDER WHEN ANOTHER HAS THE FLOOR	MUST BE SECONDED[2]
24. Chair, to declare vacant (**10**; 62:10–12)	M	No	Yes
25. Change or depart from adopted convention agenda or program, immediately to take up a matter out of its proper order (**25, 35**)	I	No	Yes
26. Commit, Refer, or Recommit a pending question (**13**)	S	No	Yes
27. Committee, to refer a matter that is not pending to (**10, 13**)	M	No	Yes
28. Consider informally (**13, 52**)	S	No	Yes
29. Consider by Paragraph or Seriatim (**28**)	I	No	Yes
30. Continue speaking after indecorum, to grant permission to (**23**; 61:10ff.)	I	No	Yes, if in form of a motion
31. Debate and amendment, to obtain immediate closing of	(See *Previous Question*, No. 70)		

---

1. Key to classification symbols: M—main motions; S—subsidiary motions; P—privileged motions; I—incidental motions; B—motions that bring a question again before the assembly; M/B—incidental main motions classed with motions that bring a question again before the assembly (see 6:25ff.).
2. Motions listed as requiring a second do not need to be seconded when made by direction of a board or committee.

(For forms used in making motions, see Table III.)

DEBATABLE	AMENDABLE	VOTE REQUIRED FOR ADOPTION	CAN BE RECONSIDERED
Yes, unless put to a vote by its maker (see 62:11n4)	Yes	Majority	Negative vote only
No	No	Two-thirds; or majority of all having convention voting rights who have been registered	No
Yes[4]	Yes	Majority	If committee has not begun consideration of the question[5]
Yes	Yes	Majority	If committee has not begun work on the matter
Yes[4]	Yes	Majority	Negative vote only
No	Yes	Majority	No
No	No	Majority	Yes

4. Debate on motion must be confined to *its* merits only, and cannot go into the main question except as necessary for debate of the immediately pending question.
5. A negative vote on this motion can be reconsidered only until such time as progress in business or debate has made it essentially a new question.

II. TABLE OF RULES RELATING TO MOTIONS (cont.)

MOTION	CLASS[1]	IN ORDER WHEN ANOTHER HAS THE FLOOR	MUST BE SECONDED[2]
32. Debate, to Limit or Extend Limits of, on a pending question (**15**)	S	No	Yes
33. Debate, to Limit or Extend Limits of, for the duration of a meeting (**10, 15**)	M	No	Yes
34. Discharge a Committee (**36**)	B or M/B[6]	No	Yes
35. Discharge a Committee, when it has failed to report at prescribed time, or while assembly is considering partial report of committee (**36**)	B or M/B[6]	No	Yes
36. Division of the Assembly (call for verification of a voting result by an uncounted rising vote) (**29**)	I	Yes	No
37. Count of vote on Division, to order, if chair does not do so (**4, 29, 30, 45**)	I	Yes	Yes
38. Division of a Question (**27**)	I	No	Yes

1. Key to classification symbols: M—main motions; S—subsidiary motions; P—privileged motions; I—incidental motions; B—motions that bring a question again before the assembly; M/B—incidental main motions classed with motions that bring a question again before the assembly (see 6:25ff.).
2. Motions listed as requiring a second do not need to be seconded when made by direction of a board or committee.

(For forms used in making motions, see Table III.)

DEBATABLE	AMENDABLE	VOTE REQUIRED FOR ADOPTION	CAN BE RECONSIDERED
No	Yes	Two-thirds	Yes; but if vote was affirmative, only unexecuted part of order[5]
Yes	Yes	Two-thirds	Yes
Yes; debate can go into question in hands of the committee	Yes	(a) Majority with notice; or (b) two-thirds; or (c) majority of entire membership	Negative vote only
Yes; debate can go into question in hands of the committee	Yes	Majority	Negative vote only
No	No	Demand of single member compels Division	No
No	Yes	Majority	No
No	Yes	Majority	No

5. A negative vote on this motion can be reconsidered only until such time as progress in business or debate has made it essentially a new question.
6. B if committee is discharged from consideration of question that was pending at time of referral and was referred by subsidiary motion to *Commit*; M/B if subject was referred by a main motion (see 36:10–11).

II. TABLE OF RULES RELATING TO MOTIONS (cont.)

MOTION	CLASS[1]	IN ORDER WHEN ANOTHER HAS THE FLOOR	MUST BE SECONDED[2]
39. Call for a separate vote on a resolution which is one of a series *on different subjects* offered by a single motion (10:25, 27:10)	I	Yes	No
40. Duty, to be excused from (**32**)	I	Yes	Yes, if motion is made by member to be excused; no, if made by another member
41. Effect, fix time for taking (**10**; **12**; 57:15ff.)	M, S, or I[7]	No	Yes
42. Extend time for consideration of pending question, or time until announced or scheduled adjournment or recess (**18**)	I	Yes, when orders of the day are announced or called for	Yes
43. Fix the Time to Which to Adjourn, if moved while a question is pending (**22**)	P	No	Yes
44. Fix the Time to Which to Adjourn, if moved while no question is pending (**10, 22**)	M	No	Yes

1. Key to classification symbols: M—main motions; S—subsidiary motions; P—privileged motions; I—incidental motions; B—motions that bring a question again before the assembly; M/B—incidental main motions classed with motions that bring a question again before the assembly (see 6:25ff.).

(For forms used in making motions, see Table III.)

DEBATABLE	AMENDABLE	VOTE REQUIRED FOR ADOPTION	CAN BE RECONSIDERED
No	No	Demand of single member compels specified separate vote	No
Yes	Yes	Majority	Negative vote only
Yes	Yes	Majority	Yes[8]
No	No	Two-thirds	No
No	Yes	Majority	Yes
Yes	Yes	Majority	Yes

2. Motions listed as requiring a second do not need to be seconded when made by direction of a board or committee.

7. See 57:15. This motion can be made as a main motion, as an amendment to enacting words, or as an incidental motion, and the same rules apply.

8. See, however, 37:9(2) and 37:30ff.

II. TABLE OF RULES RELATING TO MOTIONS (cont.)

MOTION	CLASS[1]	IN ORDER WHEN ANOTHER HAS THE FLOOR	MUST BE SECONDED[2]
45. Information, Request for (**33**)	I	Yes	No
46. Lay on the Table (**17**)	S	No	Yes
47. Minutes, to approve (when proposed by a motion) (**10, 41, 48**)	M	No	Yes
48. Minutes, to correct before adoption (when done by a motion) (**12, 41, 48**)	S	No	Yes
49. Minutes, to correct after approval (48:15)	(See *Amend Something Previously Adopted*, No. 13.)		
50. Minutes, to dispense with reading of (48:11)	I	No	Yes
51. Minutes, to take up after their reading has been dispensed with (48:11)	B	No	Yes
52. Minutes, to order the reading of a subordinate board's (49:17–19)	M	No	Yes
53. Nominations, to make (**46**)	—	No	No

1. Key to classification symbols: M—main motions; S—subsidiary motions; P—privileged motions; I—incidental motions; B—motions that bring a question again before the assembly; M/B—incidental main motions classed with motions that bring a question again before the assembly (see 6:25ff.).

(For forms used in making motions, see Table III.)

DEBATABLE	AMENDABLE	VOTE REQUIRED FOR ADOPTION	CAN BE RECONSIDERED
No	No	Is not voted on	No
No	No	Majority	Negative vote only[9]
Yes	Yes	Is not voted on (see 41:10–11)	Yes
Yes	Yes	Majority	Yes
No	No	Majority	Negative vote only[9]
No	No	Majority	No
Yes	Yes	(a) Majority with notice; or (b) two-thirds; or (c) majority of entire membership	Yes
Yes	No	Majority for election unless bylaws provide otherwise	Election cannot be reconsidered after person elected learns of it, and has not declined

2. Motions listed as requiring a second do not need to be seconded when made by direction of a board or committee.
9. A negative vote on this motion can be reconsidered only until such time as either (a) progress in business or debate has made it essentially a new question, or (b) something urgent has arisen that was not known when the assembly rejected the motion.

II. TABLE OF RULES RELATING TO MOTIONS (cont.)

MOTION	CLASS[1]	IN ORDER WHEN ANOTHER HAS THE FLOOR	MUST BE SECONDED[2]
54. Nominations, to close (**31**)	I	No	Yes
55. Nominations, to reopen (**31**)	I	No	Yes
56. Nominations, motions relating to (except to close or reopen nominations) made while election is pending (**31**)	I	No	Yes
57. Nominations, motions relating to, made while election is not pending (**10, 46**)	M	No	Yes
58. Object, to authorize motion outside society's (**10:26(2)**)	I	No	Yes
59. Objection to Consideration of a Question (**26**)	I	Yes, until debate has begun or a subsidiary motion other than *Lay on the Table* has been stated by the chair	No
60. Order, to make a special, when question is not pending (cf. No. 68) (**10, 41**)	M	No	Yes

1. Key to classification symbols: M—main motions; S—subsidiary motions; P—privileged motions; I—incidental motions; B—motions that bring a question again before the assembly; M/B—incidental main motions classed with motions that bring a question again before the assembly (see 6:25ff.).

(For forms used in making motions, see Table III.)

DEBATABLE	AMENDABLE	VOTE REQUIRED FOR ADOPTION	CAN BE RECONSIDERED
No	Yes	Two-thirds	No
No	Yes	Majority	Negative vote only
No	Yes	Majority	Yes
Yes	Yes	Majority	Yes
No	No	Two-thirds	Negative vote only
No	No	Two-thirds against consideration sustains objection	Negative vote (sustaining objection) only
Yes[4]	Yes	Two-thirds	Yes

2. Motions listed as requiring a second do not need to be seconded when made by direction of a board or committee.
4. Debate on motion must be confined to *its* merits only, and cannot go into the main question except as necessary for debate of the immediately pending question.

II. TABLE OF RULES RELATING TO MOTIONS (cont.)

MOTION	CLASS[1]	IN ORDER WHEN ANOTHER HAS THE FLOOR	MUST BE SECONDED[2]
61. Orders of the Day, to Call for (**18**)	P	Yes	No
62. Orders of the day, to proceed to (**18**)	—	Chair at his discretion puts this question when orders of the day are due to be taken up or are called for	—
63. Orders of the day, when pending (**10, 18, 41**)	M	—	—
64. Order, Point of, Question of, or Calling a Member to (**23**)	I	Yes	No
65. Parliamentary Inquiry (**33**)	I	Yes	No
66. Postpone Indefinitely (**11**)	S	No	Yes
67. Postpone to a Certain Time, or Definitely, applied to a pending question (**14**)	S	No	Yes

1. Key to classification symbols: M—main motions; S—subsidiary motions; P—privileged motions; I—incidental motions; B—motions that bring a question again before the assembly; M/B—incidental main motions classed with motions that bring a question again before the assembly (see 6:25ff.).
2. Motions listed as requiring a second do not need to be seconded when made by direction of a board or committee.

(For forms used in making motions, see Table III.)

DEBATABLE	AMENDABLE	VOTE REQUIRED FOR ADOPTION	CAN BE RECONSIDERED
No	No	Must be enforced on demand of one member unless set aside by a two-thirds vote (see 18:8)	No
No	No	Two-thirds in negative required to refuse to proceed to orders of the day	No
Yes	Yes	Majority, except as explained in 10:8(7)	Yes
No (but chair can permit full explanation and can submit question to assembly, in which case rule is as for *Appeal*; see No. 18)	No	Is ruled upon by chair (unless he submits question to judgment of majority in assembly)	No
No	No	Is not voted on, but is responded to by chair	—
Yes; debate can go into main question	No	Majority	Affirmative vote only
Yes[4]	Yes	Majority, unless it makes question a special order	Yes[5]

4. Debate on motion must be confined to *its* merits only, and cannot go into the main question except as necessary for debate of the immediately pending question.
5. A negative vote on this motion can be reconsidered only until such time as progress in business or debate has made it essentially a new question.

II. TABLE OF RULES RELATING TO MOTIONS (cont.)

MOTION	CLASS[1]	IN ORDER WHEN ANOTHER HAS THE FLOOR	MUST BE SECONDED[2]
68. Postpone a pending question to a certain time and make it a special order (cf. No. 60) (**14**)	S	No	Yes
69. Postpone an event or action previously scheduled (**35**)	M/B	No	Yes
70. Previous Question (immediately to close debate and the making of subsidiary motions except the motion to Lay on the Table) (**16**)	S	No	Yes
71. Proviso (**10**; **12**; **57**:15ff.)	M, S, or I[7]	No	Yes
72. Question of Privilege, to Raise while regular introduction as main motion is not in order (**19**)	P	Yes, but should not interrupt a person who has begun to speak, unless unavoidable	No; but if the question of privilege thereby raised is in the form of a motion, the motion must be seconded
73. Question of privilege in the form of a main motion, whether introduced when an ordinary main motion is in order or admitted by raising a question of privilege (**10, 19**)	M	Floor should be obtained in usual manner if question is brought up while main motion is in order	Yes

1. Key to classification symbols: M—main motions; S—subsidiary motions; P—privileged motions; I—incidental motions; B—motions that bring a question again before the assembly; M/B—incidental main motions classed with motions that bring a question again before the assembly (see 6:25ff.).
2. Motions listed as requiring a second do not need to be seconded when made by direction of a board or committee.

(For forms used in making motions, see Table III.)

DEBATABLE	AMENDABLE	VOTE REQUIRED FOR ADOPTION	CAN BE RECONSIDERED
Yes[4]	Yes	Two-thirds	Yes[5]
Yes	Yes	(a) Majority with notice; or (b) two-thirds; or (c) majority of entire membership	Negative vote only
No	No	Two-thirds	Yes; but if vote was affirmative, only before any vote has been taken under it[5]
Yes	Yes	Majority	Yes
No	No	Admissibility of question is ruled upon by chair	No
Yes	Yes	Majority, except as explained in 10:8(7)	Yes

4. Debate on motion must be confined to *its* merits only, and cannot go into the main question except as necessary for debate of the immediately pending question.
5. A negative vote on this motion can be reconsidered only until such time as progress in business or debate has made it essentially a new question.
7. See 57:15. This motion can be made as a main motion, as an amendment to enacting words, or as an incidental motion, and the same rules apply.

II. TABLE OF RULES RELATING TO MOTIONS (cont.)

MOTION	CLASS[1]	IN ORDER WHEN ANOTHER HAS THE FLOOR	MUST BE SECONDED[2]
74. Quorum, to take measures to obtain, if moved while a question is pending (**40**)	P	No	Yes
75. Quorum, to take measures to obtain, if moved while no question is pending (**40**)	M	No	Yes
76. Ratify, or Confirm (**10**)	M	No	Yes
77. Read Papers, to grant permission to (**33**)	I	If not granted by unanimous consent, can be moved by person requesting permission or by another while the former has the floor	Yes, if motion is made by person requesting permission; no, if made by another member
78. Recapitulation of roll call, to order (**30**; 45:51)	I	No	Yes
79. Recess, to take a, if moved while business is pending (**20**)	P	No	Yes
80. Recess, to take a, if moved while no question is pending (**10, 20**)	M	No	Yes

1. Key to classification symbols: M—main motions; S—subsidiary motions; P—privileged motions; I—incidental motions; B—motions that bring a question again before the assembly; M/B—incidental main motions classed with motions that bring a question again before the assembly (see 6:25ff.).

(For forms used in making motions, see Table III.)

DEBATABLE	AMENDABLE	VOTE REQUIRED FOR ADOPTION	CAN BE RECONSIDERED
No	Yes	Majority	Yes
Yes	Yes	Majority	Yes
Yes	Yes	Majority, except as explained in 10:8(7)	Yes
No	No	Majority	Yes
No	Yes	Majority	Yes
No	Yes	Majority	No
Yes	Yes	Majority	No

2. Motions listed as requiring a second do not need to be seconded when made by direction of a board or committee.

II. TABLE OF RULES RELATING TO MOTIONS (cont.)

MOTION	CLASS[1]	IN ORDER WHEN ANOTHER HAS THE FLOOR	MUST BE SECONDED[2]
81. Reconsider (**37**)	B	When another *has been assigned* the floor, but not after he has begun to speak	Yes
82. Reconsider, in a committee (**37:35**)	B	Cannot interrupt a person speaking	No
83. Reconsider, call up motion to (**37**)	—	No	No
84. Recount, to order (**30**; **45:41**)	I	No	Yes
85. Report, to receive when no time has been established for its reception (**51:28**)	I	No	Yes
86. Rescind and expunge from minutes (**35:13**)	M/B	No	Yes
87. Rescind, Repeal, or Annul (**35**)	M/B	No	Yes
88. Refer	(See *Commit, Committee*, Nos. 26 and 27.)		
89. Rise, or Rise and Report (in a special committee) (**50:23**)	M	No	No

1. Key to classification symbols: M—main motions; S—subsidiary motions; P—privileged motions; I—incidental motions; B—motions that bring a question again before the assembly; M/B—incidental main motions classed with motions that bring a question again before the assembly (see 6:25ff.).

(For forms used in making motions, see Table III.)

DEBATABLE	AMENDABLE	VOTE REQUIRED FOR ADOPTION	CAN BE RECONSIDERED
If motion to be reconsidered is debatable, in which case debate can go into that question	No	Majority	No
As in No. 81, preceding	No	Two-thirds; but majority if every committee member who voted with prevailing side is present or was notified	No
—	—	—	—
No	Yes	Majority	If recount has not begun
No	No	Majority	If report has not begun[5]
Yes	Yes	Majority of entire membership	Negative vote only
Yes	Yes	(a) Majority with notice; or (b) two-thirds; or (c) majority of entire membership	Negative vote only
Yes	Yes	Majority	No

2. Motions listed as requiring a second do not need to be seconded when made by direction of a board or committee.
5. A negative vote on this motion can be reconsidered only until such time as progress in business or debate has made it essentially a new question.

II. TABLE OF RULES RELATING TO MOTIONS (cont.)

MOTION	CLASS[1]	IN ORDER WHEN ANOTHER HAS THE FLOOR	MUST BE SECONDED[2]
90. Rise, or Rise and Report (in a committee of the whole) (52:4ff.)	P	No	Yes
91. Substitute	(See *Amend a pending motion*, No. 11.)		
92. Suspend the Rules (as applied to rules of order) (**25**)	I	No	Yes
93. Suspend ordinary standing rules, or standing rules in a convention (**25**; 59:37)	I	No	Yes
94. Take from the Table (**34**)	B	No	Yes
95. Take up a question out of its proper order	(See *Suspend the Rules (as applied to rules of order)*, No. 92; cf. also No. 25)		
96. Voting, motions relating to, if made while subject is pending (**30, 45, 46**)	I	No	Yes
97. Voting, motions relating to, if made while no question is pending (**10, 30, 45, 46**)	M	No	Yes

1. Key to classification symbols: M—main motions; S—subsidiary motions; P—privileged motions; I—incidental motions; B—motions that bring a question again before the assembly; M/B—incidental main motions classed with motions that bring a question again before the assembly (see 6:25ff.).

(For forms used in making motions, see Table III.)

DEBATABLE	AMENDABLE	VOTE REQUIRED FOR ADOPTION	CAN BE RECONSIDERED
No	No	Majority	No
No	No	Two-thirds—except where rule protects a minority of less than one third (see 25:2(7))	No
No	No	Majority	No
No	No	Majority	No
No	Yes	Majority, except two-thirds for motion to close polls	To close polls, no; to reopen polls, negative vote only;[10] all others, yes
Yes	Yes	Majority	Yes

2. Motions listed as requiring a second do not need to be seconded when made by direction of a board or committee.
10. The vote on a motion ordering that the polls be closed or reopened at a specified time can be reconsidered at any time before the order has been carried out.

II. TABLE OF RULES RELATING TO MOTIONS (cont.)

MOTION	CLASS[1]	IN ORDER WHEN ANOTHER HAS THE FLOOR	MUST BE SECONDED[2]
98. Withdraw or Modify a Motion, to grant maker permission to, after motion has been stated by the chair (**33**)	I	If not granted by unanimous consent, can be moved by person requesting permission, or by another while the former has the floor	Yes, if motion is made by person requesting permission; no, if made by another member

1. Key to classification symbols: M—main motions; S—subsidiary motions; P—privileged motions; I—incidental motions; B—motions that bring a question again before the assembly; M/B—incidental main motions classed with motions that bring a question again before the assembly (see 6:25ff.).

(For forms used in making motions, see Table III.)

DEBATABLE	AMENDABLE	VOTE REQUIRED FOR ADOPTION	CAN BE RECONSIDERED
No	No	Majority	As to withdrawal, negative vote only; as to modification, yes

2. Motions listed as requiring a second do not need to be seconded when made by direction of a board or committee.

III. SAMPLE FORMS USED IN MAKING MOTIONS

1. Main motion or question (original)
   [For forms see 4:4–5, 10:9–25.]

2. Adjourn, ordinary case in societies
   • I move to adjourn.

3. Adjourn at or to a future time, or in advance of a time already set, or when the assembly will thereby be dissolved
   • I move to adjourn at 4 P.M.
   • I move that the meeting adjourn to meet at 8 P.M. Tuesday.
   • I move to adjourn.
   • I move to adjourn *sine die*.

4. Adopt, accept, or agree to a report
   • I move that the report be adopted.

5. Adopt bylaws or constitution, initially in forming a society
   • On behalf of the committee appointed to draw up bylaws, I move the adoption of the bylaws submitted by the committee.

6. Adopt revised bylaws or constitution
   • On behalf of the committee on revision of the bylaws, I move that, as a substitute for the present bylaws, the bylaws submitted by the committee be adopted with the following provisos: …

7. Adopt special rules of order
   • In accordance with notice given at the last meeting, I move that the following resolution be adopted as a special rule of order: "*Resolved*, That …"

8. Adopt ordinary standing rules
   • I move that the following resolution be adopted as a standing rule: "*Resolved*, That …"

9. Adopt parliamentary standing rules in a convention
   • By direction of the Committee on Standing Rules, I move the adoption of the Standing Rules of the Convention as just read.

10. Adopt convention agenda or program
    • By direction of the Program Committee, I move the adoption of the Convention Program as printed.

11. Amend a pending motion
- I move to amend by adding …
- I move to amend by inserting the word … before the word …
- I move to amend by striking out the second paragraph.
- I move to amend by striking out "concrete" and inserting "blacktop."
- I move to substitute for the pending resolution the following resolution: "*Resolved*, That …"

[For manner in which above forms are varied in the particular case, see 12:32, 12:53, 12:67, 12:82–83.]

12. Amend an amendment of a pending motion
- I move to insert in the pending amendment the word … before the word …
- I move to amend the pending amendment by … [varying form to fit particular case, as under *Amend a pending motion*, No. 11].

13. Amend Something Previously Adopted, general case, including ordinary standing rules
- I move to amend the resolution relating to … , adopted at the September meeting, by …

14. Amend parliamentary standing rules in a convention, when they are not pending
- I move to amend Standing Rule No. 6 by …

15. Amend adopted convention agenda or program with reference to items not yet reached
- I move to amend the agenda [or "program"] by …

16. Amend bylaws or constitution, when not pending
- In accordance with notice given, I move the adoption of the following amendment to the bylaws …

17. Amend special rules of order, when not pending
- In accordance with notice given, I move to amend Special Rule of Order No. 3 by …

18. Appeal, general case
- I appeal from the decision of the chair.

III. SAMPLE FORMS USED IN MAKING MOTIONS
   (cont.)

19. Appeal, relating to indecorum or transgression of rules of speaking,
or to the priority of business, or if made when an undebatable question
is immediately pending or involved in the appeal

   [Same form as No. 18]

20. Ballot, to order the vote on a pending question to be taken by
   • I move that the vote on the pending question be taken by ballot.

21. Blank, to create by striking out
   • I move to create a blank by striking out "$10,000."

22. Blanks, proposals for filling
   • I suggest $20,000.

23. Bylaw amendments, to rearrange order of consideration
   • I move that the amendments be considered in the following order ...

24. Chair, to declare vacant
   • I move to declare the chair vacant and proceed to elect a new
     chairman.

25. Change or depart from adopted convention agenda or program,
immediately to take up a matter out of its proper order
   • I move to suspend the rules and take up ...

26. Commit, Refer, or Recommit a pending question
   • I move to refer the motion to the Program Committee.
   • I move that the motion be referred to a committee of three to be
     appointed by the chair.

   [For additional variations see 13:25.]

27. Committee, to refer a matter that is not pending to
   • I move that a committee [stating number and manner of selection]
     be appointed to conduct a survey relating to ...

28. Consider informally
   • I move that the question be considered informally.

29. Consider by Paragraph or Seriatim
   • I move that the resolution be considered by paragraph.

30. Continue speaking after indecorum, to grant permission to
- [Chair usually puts question without a motion. When done by a motion:] I move that the member be permitted [or "allowed"] to continue speaking.

31. Debate and amendment, to obtain immediate closing of
[See *Previous Question*, No. 70.]

32. Debate, to Limit or Extend Limits of, on a pending question
- I move that debate be limited to one speech of three minutes for each member.

[For variations in particular cases see 15:19.]

33. Debate, to Limit or Extend Limits of, for the duration of a meeting
- I move that during this meeting debate be limited to five minutes for each member.

34. Discharge a Committee
- [For a standing committee:] I move that the Finance Committee be discharged from further consideration of the resolution relating to ...
- [For a special committee:] I move that the committee to which was referred ... be discharged.

35. Discharge a Committee, when it has failed to report at prescribed time, or while assembly is considering partial report of committee
[Same forms as No. 34]

36. Division of the Assembly (call for verification of a voting result by an uncounted rising vote)
- Division!
- I call for a division.

37. Count of vote on Division, to order, if chair does not do so
- I move that the vote be counted.
- I move for [or "demand"] tellers.
- I move that the vote on this motion be by counted division.

38. Division of a Question
- I move to divide the resolution so as to consider separately ...

III. SAMPLE FORMS USED IN MAKING MOTIONS (cont.)

39. Call for a separate vote on a resolution which is one of a series *on different subjects* offered by a single motion
- I call for a separate vote on the third resolution.

40. Duty, to be excused from
- I move [or "ask"] that I be excused from …
- I move that the resignation be accepted.

41. Effect, fix time for taking
- I move that the amendment to the … take effect as of …

42. Extend time for consideration of pending question, or time until scheduled adjournment or recess
- I move that the time for consideration of the pending resolution be extended for twenty minutes.
- I move to suspend the rules which interfere with continuing the consideration of the motion.
- I move that the time until the recess be extended ten minutes.

43. Fix the Time to Which to Adjourn, if moved while a question is pending
- I move that when this [or, "the"] meeting adjourns, it adjourn to meet next Tuesday at 8 P.M.

44. Fix the Time to Which to Adjourn, if moved while no question is pending [Same form as No. 43]

45. Information, Request for
- I have a request for information.
- A point of information, please.
- Will the member yield for a question?

46. Lay on the Table
- I move that the motion be laid on the table.

47. Minutes, to approve
- [Normally done by unanimous consent. When proposed by a motion:] I move that the minutes be approved as read [or "as corrected"].

48. Minutes, to correct before adoption
- [Usually suggested informally and done by unanimous consent except in cases of disagreement. When done by a motion:] I move to amend the minutes by ...

49. Minutes, to correct after approval
[See *Amend Something Previously Adopted*, No. 13.]

50. Minutes, to dispense with reading of
- I move that the reading of the minutes be dispensed with.

51. Minutes, to take up after their reading has been dispensed with
- I move to take up the reading of the minutes.

52. Minutes, to order the reading of a subordinate board's
- I move that the minutes of the Executive Board's last meeting be produced and read.

53. Nominations, to make
- I nominate George Beall.

54. Nominations, to close
- I move that nominations be closed.

55. Nominations, to reopen
- I move that nominations for ... be reopened.

56. Nominations, motions relating to (except to close or reopen nominations) made while election is pending
- I move that candidates for service on the committee be nominated from the floor.

57. Nominations, motions relating to, made while election is not pending
[Same form as No. 56]

58. Object, to authorize motion outside society's
- I move to authorize the introduction of the following motion: ...
- I move that the motion just made by Member A be considered by the assembly.

III. SAMPLE FORMS USED IN MAKING MOTIONS (cont.)

59. Objection to Consideration of a Question
- I object to the consideration of the question.

60. Order, to make a special, when question is not pending
- I move that the following resolution be made a special order for 3 P.M.: "*Resolved*, That ..."

61. Orders of the Day, to Call for
- I call for the orders of the day.

62. Orders of the day, to proceed to
[Chair at his discretion puts this question when orders of the day are due to be taken up or are called for.]

63. Order of the day, when pending
[Will have been introduced earlier as a main motion.]

64. Order, Point of, Question of, or Calling a Member to
- Point of order!
- I rise to a point of order.
- I call the member to order. [Applying to indecorum]

65. Parliamentary Inquiry
- I rise to a parliamentary inquiry.
- Parliamentary inquiry, Mr. President!

66. Postpone Indefinitely
- I move that the resolution be postponed indefinitely.

67. Postpone to a Certain Time, or Definitely, applied to a pending question
- I move to postpone the question to the next meeting.

68. Postpone a pending question to a certain time and make it a special order
- I move that the resolution be postponed until 3 P.M. and made a special order.

69. Postpone an event or action previously scheduled
- I move that the dinner previously scheduled for September 15 be postponed until October 17.

70. Previous Question (immediately to close debate and the making of subsidiary motions except the motion to Lay on the Table)
- I move the previous question.
- I move the previous question on the motion to commit and the amendment.

71. Proviso
- I move to add the following to the motion: provided that this shall not take effect until ... .

72. Question of Privilege, to Raise while regular introduction as main motion is not in order
- I rise to a question of privilege.

73. Question of privilege, to offer as a main motion when an ordinary main motion is in order or after being raised as in No. 72 above
  [Is moved as a main motion.]

74. Quorum, to take measures to obtain, if moved while a question is pending
- I move that a committee of three be appointed by the chair and directed to contact absent members during the recess.

75. Quorum, to take measures to obtain, if moved while no question is pending
  [Same form as No. 74]

76. Ratify, or Confirm
- I move that the action of the Executive Board on ... be ratified.

77. Read Papers, to grant permission to
- [Usually done by unanimous consent. When done by a motion:] I move that the member [or "I"] be permitted [or "allowed"] to read ...

78. Recapitulation of roll call, to order
- I move for a recapitulation of the vote.

79. Recess, to take a, if moved while business is pending
- I move to recess for five minutes.

80. Recess, to take a, if moved while no question is pending
  [Same form as No. 79]

III. SAMPLE FORMS USED IN MAKING MOTIONS (cont.)

81. Reconsider
  - I move to reconsider the vote on the motion relating to …
  - I move to reconsider the vote on the amendment striking out … and inserting …

82. Reconsider, in a committee
  [Form similar to No. 81]

83. Reconsider, call up motion to
  - I call up the motion to reconsider the vote …

84. Recount, to order
  - I move that the ballots be recounted.

85. Report, to receive when no time has been established for its reception
  - I move that the assembly receive the report of the Finance Committee.

86. Rescind and expunge from the minutes
  - I move that the entry relating to … be rescinded and expunged from the minutes.

87. Rescind, Repeal, or Annul
  - I move that the resolution relating to … adopted on [date] be rescinded.

88. Refer
  [See *Commit, Committee*, Nos. 26 and 27.]

89. Rise, or Rise and Report (in a special committee)
  - I move that the committee rise.

90. Rise, or Rise and Report (in a committee of the whole)
  - I move that the committee rise and report.

91. Substitute
  - I move to substitute for the pending resolution the following resolution: "*Resolved*, That …"

92. Suspend the Rules (as applied to rules of order)
  - I move to suspend the rules which interfere with …

93. Suspend ordinary standing rules, or standing rules in a convention
[Form similar to No. 92]

94. Take from the Table
- I move to take from the table the motion relating to …

95. Take up a question out of its proper order
- I move to suspend the rules and take up …

96. Voting, motions relating to, if made while subject is pending
- I move that the vote on this question be taken by rising and be counted.

97. Voting, motions relating to, if made while no question is pending
[Form similar to No. 96]

98. Withdraw or Modify a Motion, to grant maker permission to, after motion has been stated by the chair
- [Usually done by unanimous consent. When done by a motion, for the case of withdrawal:] I move that the member [or "I"] be permitted [or "allowed"] to withdraw the motion.
[For the case of modification by a motion, see *Amend a pending motion*, No. 11.]

IV. MOTIONS AND PARLIAMENTARY STEPS

- **Which Are in Order When Another Has the Floor
  and Do Not Require a Second**

Can interrupt a person speaking in debate if urgency requires it.	Call for a Division of the Assembly (**29**)
	Call for separate vote(s) on one or more of a series of unrelated resolutions that have been offered by a single motion (10:25, 27:10), or on one or more of a series of amendments on which the chair has stated the question in gross (12:14, 27:11, 51:48(b), 52:13, 52:23)
	Call for the Orders of the Day (**18**)
	Calling a member to order (61:11)
	Parliamentary Inquiry (33:3–5)
	Point of Order (**23**)
	Raise a Question of Privilege (**19**)
	Request for Information (33:6–10)
	Request to Be Excused from a Duty (**32**)
	Requests, or motions to grant the request of another member, as follows:
	  For Permission to Withdraw or Modify a Motion (33:11–19)
	  For Permission to Read Papers (33:20–21)
	  For Any Other Privilege (33:22)

In order when another has been assigned the floor but has not begun to speak. (See particular rules under references given.)	Notice of intent to introduce a motion requiring such notice (10:44–51) Objection to the Consideration of a Question (**26**)

- **Which Are in Order When Another Has the Floor
but Must Be Seconded**

Can interrupt a person speaking in debate if urgency requires it.	Appeal (**24**) Formal motion to grant maker's own request, if it is not granted by unanimous consent (**32**; 33:11–22)
In order when another has been assigned the floor but has not begun to speak. (See particular rules under references given.)	Reconsider (to *make* the motion, but not to have it considered at that time; **37**) Reconsider and Enter on the Minutes (to *make* the motion; 37:46–52)

- **Which Are out of Order When Another Has the Floor
but Do Not Require a Second**

	Call up a motion to Reconsider or a motion to Reconsider and Enter on the Minutes (**37**) Nominations* (**46**) Proposals for filling blanks* (12:92–113)
	* When chair calls for them, can be offered without obtaining the floor.

V. MOTIONS AND PARLIAMENTARY STEPS

- ### Which Are Not Debatable and Not Amendable

  Adjourn (when privileged; **21**)

  Amend an amendment to an undebatable motion (**12**)

  Appeal, if it: (a) relates to indecorum or a transgression of the rules of speaking; (b) relates to the priority of business; or (c) is made when an undebatable question is immediately pending or involved in the appeal (**24**)

  Authorize a motion outside society's object (10:26(2))

  Blank in an undebatable motion, proposals for filling (12:92–113)

  Call for a Division of the Assembly (**29**)

  Call for separate vote(s) on one or more of a series of unrelated resolutions which have been offered by a single motion (10:25, 27:10), or on one or more of a series of amendments on which the chair has stated the question in gross (12:14, 27:11, 51:48(b), 52:13, 52:23)

  Call for the Orders of the Day (**18**)

  Call up a motion to Reconsider, or a motion to Reconsider and Enter on the Minutes (**37**)

  Calling a member to order (61:11)

  Dispense with reading of the minutes (48:11)

  Grant permission to continue speaking after indecorum (61:11)

  Lay on the Table (**17**)

  Objection to the Consideration of a Question (**26**)

  Parliamentary Inquiry (33:3–5)

  Point of Order (except one referred to assembly by chair on which appeal would be debatable, or one where debate is permitted at chair's discretion by way of explanation; **23**)

  Previous Question (**16**)

  Raise a Question of Privilege (**19**)

  Receive a report (51:28)

  Reconsider an undebatable motion (**37**)

  Request for Information (33:6–10)

  Request for Permission to Modify a Motion (33:11–13, 33:19)

  Requests or motions to grant requests, in these cases:

      For Permission to Withdraw a Motion (33:11–18)

      For Permission to Read Papers (33:20–21)

      For Any Other Privilege (33:22)

  Rise, or Rise and Report, in a committee of the whole (52:4ff.)

  Suspend the Rules (**25**)

Take from the Table (**34**)
Take up a question out of its proper order (14:11; **25**; 41:37–39)
Take up minutes after their reading has been dispensed with (48:11)

- **Which Are Not Debatable but Are Amendable**

Amend an undebatable motion (**12**)
Arrange order of consideration of bylaw amendments (57:6)
Consider by Paragraph or Seriatim (**28**)
Division of a Question (**27**)
Fix the Time to Which to Adjourn (when privileged; **22**)
Limit or Extend Limits of Debate (**15**)
Motions relating to methods of voting and the polls (**30**)
Motions relating to nominations (**31**)
Recess (when privileged; **20**)
Take measures to obtain a quorum (when privileged; **40**)

- **Which Are Not Amendable but Are Debatable**

Amend an amendment to a debatable motion (**12**)
Appeal, in all cases except those listed at the top of the facing page as undebatable (**24**)
Blank in a debatable motion, proposals for filling (12:92–113)
Nominations, to make (**46**)
Postpone Indefinitely (**11**)
Question of Order, when it has been referred to the assembly by the chair and an appeal on the same point would be debatable (see above, and **23**)
Reconsider a debatable motion (**37**)

- **On Which Debate Can Go into Merits of the Main Question or the Question Which Is the Subject of the Proposed Action**

Amend Something Previously Adopted (**35**)
Discharge a Committee (**36**)
Fix the time at which a motion shall take effect (**10**; **12**; 57:15–17)
Postpone Indefinitely (**11**)
Ratify (10:54–57)
Reconsider a debatable motion (**37**)
Rescind (**35**)

VI. MOTIONS WHICH REQUIRE A TWO-THIRDS VOTE

Motions marked † may also be adopted by a vote of a majority of the entire membership, even if previous notice has not been given.

Adopt agenda or program at a session already having an order of business, if it contains special orders or conflicts with the existing order of business (**10, 41**)

† Adopt parliamentary authority in an organized society if the bylaws do not designate one, previous notice also being required (2:14–22; **10**)

Adopt parliamentary standing rules in a convention (**10**; 59:27ff.)

† Adopt special rules of order, previous notice also being required (2:14–22; **10**)

† Amend an adopted agenda or program (**35**; **41**; 59:59)

† Amend or Rescind adopted constitution or bylaws containing no provision for own amendment, previous notice also being required (**35, 57**)

† Amend or Rescind adopted nonparliamentary standing rule in a convention, if notice has not been given on at least the preceding day (**35**; 59:27ff.)

† Amend or Rescind adopted parliamentary standing rule in a convention (**35**; 59:27ff.)

† Amend or Rescind adopted special rules of order (2:22; **35**), previous notice also being required

† Amend or Rescind Something Previously Adopted (general case, including ordinary standing rules), when previous notice has not been given (**35**)

Amend or Rescind Something Previously Adopted, in a committee when someone who voted for the motion to be rescinded or amended is absent and has not been notified of the motion to Amend or Rescind (**35**)

Authorize a motion outside society's object (10:26(2))

Close nominations (**31**)

Close the polls (**30**)

† Discharge a Committee, if previous notice, or a partial report, has not been given (**36**)

Expel from membership, notice and a trial being also required unless the offense is committed in a meeting of the assembly (**61**)

Extend time for consideration of pending question (**18**), or time until scheduled adjournment or recess (**20, 21**)

Limit or Extend Limits of Debate (**15**)

Make a special order (**14, 41**)

Objection to the Consideration of a Question (**26**) (two-thirds against consideration sustains the objection)

† Order the reading of a subordinate board's minutes, when previous notice has not been given (49:17–19)

Previous Question (**16**)

Reconsider in committee, when someone who voted with the prevailing side is absent and has not been notified that the reconsideration will be moved (37:35)

Refuse to proceed to the orders of the day (**18**)

† Remove from office where trial is not required (see 62:16), and previous notice has not been given

Suspend the Rules (**25**)

Take up a question out of its proper order, or take up an order of the day before the time for which it has been set (14:11; **25**; **41**)

VII. MOTIONS WHOSE RECONSIDERATION IS PROHIBITED OR LIMITED

- **Cannot be reconsidered at all:**

    Adjourn (**21**)
    Close nominations (**31**)
    Close the polls immediately (**30**)
    Consider by Paragraph or Seriatim (**28**)
    Create a blank (12:95)
    Dispense with the reading of the minutes (48:11)
    Division of a Question (**27**)
    Division of the Assembly, or ordering a rising vote counted (**29**)
    Extend time for consideration of pending question (**18**), or time until scheduled adjournment or recess (**20**, **21**)
    Parliamentary Inquiry (33:3–5)
    Point of Order (**23**)
    Proceed to the orders of the day (**18**)
    Raise a Question of Privilege (**19**)
    Recess (**20**)
    Reconsider (**37**)
    Request for Information (33:6–10)
    Rise, or Rise and Report (50:23, 52:4ff.)
    Suspend the Rules (**25**)
    Take from the Table (**34**)
    Take up a question out of its proper order (**14**; **25**; 41:37–39)
    Take up minutes after their reading has been dispensed with (48:11)

- **A negative vote cannot be reconsidered (although an affirmative vote can be):**

    Postpone Indefinitely (**11**)

- **An affirmative vote cannot be reconsidered (although a negative vote can be):**

    Accept resignation or grant Request to Be Excused from a Duty, if person was present or has been notified (**32**)
    Adopt or amend agenda or program (**41**; 59:48ff.)
    Adopt or amend bylaws or constitution, rules of order, or any other rules that require previous notice for their amendment (**2**, **54**, **57**, **59**)
    Amend Something Previously Adopted (**35**, **57**)
    Arrange order of consideration of bylaw amendments (57:6)

Authorize a motion outside society's object (10:26(2))

Commit, if committee has begun work on referred matter (**13**)

Consider informally (**13, 52**)

Declare the chair vacant (62:10–12)

Discharge a Committee (**36**)

Election, if person elected was present and did not decline, or was absent but had consented to candidacy, or had not consented to candidacy but has been notified and has not declined (**46**)

Expulsion from membership or office, if person was present or has been officially notified (35:6(c))

Grant Permission to Withdraw or Modify a Motion (33:11–19)

Lay on the Table (**17**)

Objection to the Consideration of a Question (**26**)

Order a recount, after recount has begun (**30**; 45:41)

Previous Question, after any vote has been taken under it (**16**)

Receive a report, after report has begun (51:28)

Reopen nominations (**31**)

Reopen the polls immediately (**30**)

Rescind (**35**)

VIII. TABLE OF RULES FOR COUNTING ELECTION BALLOTS

(See 45:31–36 and 46:33–34)

TYPE OF BALLOT	CREDITED TO CANDIDATE(S)	COUNTED TOWARD NUMBER OF VOTES CAST
Ballots That Indicate Preference, Cast by Member		
— if meaning of ballot is clear, and ballot indicates eligible candidate	Yes	Yes
— if ballot indicates ineligible candidate	No	Yes
— if meaning of ballot is unclear, but can't affect result	No	Yes
— if meaning of ballot is unclear, and may affect result	Submit to assembly for decision	Yes
— two or more filled-out ballots, folded together	No	Yes, but counted as one vote
— one filled-out ballot, folded together with one or more blank ballots	Yes	Yes
Blank Ballots, Ballots That Indicate No Preference	No	No
Ballots Cast by Nonmember	No	No[1]
Ballots for Multiple Positions on a Board or Committee		
— with votes for full number of positions to fill	Yes	Yes (one vote)[2]
— with votes for less than full number	Yes	Yes (one vote)[2]
— with votes for too many candidates	No	Yes (one vote)[2]

1. If there is evidence that any ballots were cast by persons not entitled to vote but those ballots cannot be identified, and if there is any possibility that such ballots might affect the result, the entire ballot vote is null and void and a new ballot vote must be taken.
2. When votes are cast in one section of the ballot for multiple positions on a board or committee, every ballot with a vote in that section for one or more candidates is counted as one vote cast.

SAMPLE RULES FOR ELECTRONIC MEETINGS

INTRODUCTION

As noted in the main text of this book, there is an increasing preference among some organizations to transact business at "electronic meetings," in which some or all of the members communicate through electronic means such as the Internet or by telephone. Regarding the proper authorization of such meetings, and their limitations, see *Electronic Meetings*, 9:30–36, wherein it is stated that when electronic meetings are authorized—which, in the case of a board or other assembly, always requires a bylaw provision—additional rules should be adopted to govern their conduct. Depending on the nature of the rules and the specific provisions of the bylaws, such additional rules may be placed in the bylaws, adopted as special rules of order or standing rules, or contained in instructions from a superior body.

The additional rules appropriate to a particular organization's electronic meetings may depend on many factors, such as the number of members in the organization, the nature and complexity of the business to be transacted, the organization's need for confidentiality in its proceedings, and the funds available. Four sets of sample rules for electronic meetings designed to meet various needs are provided here, along with bylaw provisions sufficient to authorize such meetings. These rules should, of course, be adapted as necessary for the particular circumstances of each group and the technology the organization finds most useful. It is therefore advisable to review all four sets of rules, as some particular rules from one set may prove appropriate for adaptation together with some or all of the rules from another. It is also worth noting that although the rules below are written on the assumption they would be used by a board, electronic meetings could be authorized for another type of assembly or for a committee, and the sample rules could be adapted accordingly.

Consider an organization governed by bylaws whose relevant provisions are patterned directly on the Sample Bylaws in this book (56:58–67). Each of the four sets of sample rules below shows how the organization might amend Article VI of the bylaws to authorize the executive board to conduct business by a particular type of electronic meeting. In each case, the sample bylaw provisions are followed by a number of additional rules that may be helpful in governing the conduct of that type of meeting.

The sample rules in Scenarios A, B, C, and D below are designed for allowing the board to make use of the following types of electronic communication to conduct meetings, respectively:

A. Full-featured Internet, or combination Internet/telephone, meeting services that integrate audio (and optionally video), text, and voting capabilities.
B. Telephone meetings, with Internet services for conducting secret votes and sharing documents.
C. A speakerphone in the meeting room to allow members who are not physically present to participate by telephone.
D. Telephone meetings without Internet support (and without any central meeting room).

For Scenarios A and B, it is assumed that electronic meetings will be the usual method for conducting business, with in-person meetings held only when ordered by the board or all of its members. In Scenario C, it is assumed that a physical meeting space is designated for every meeting, but individual board members may participate by telephone. In Scenario D, in-person meetings are assumed as the norm, but telephone meetings may be ordered as needed.

SCENARIO A: USE OF FULL-FEATURED INTERNET MEETING SERVICES

In this scenario, the board makes use of Internet meeting services with integrated audio (and optionally video), text, and voting capabilities as the usual meeting method, with in-person meetings when ordered by the board or all of its members.

Internet meeting services adapted to the needs of deliberative assemblies vary somewhat in the names given to their features and in how they are set up and arranged. Typically, a full-featured Internet meeting is set up as follows:

Each participant, using his or her own computer or other device, can view the current list of all participants—with an indication of which member has the floor or which members are seeking recognition by the chair—and can seek recognition, submit motions in writing, view the text of pending motions, vote, and view the results of a vote. The sample rules given below require that anonymous voting be supported (in other words, that a member who is properly logged in to a meeting can cast an "electronic ballot" that does not identify that member's vote as belonging to him or her), and they also assume that non-anonymous votes can be taken, as well.

Audio transmissions can be integrated directly via the Internet, so that participants listen and speak through microphones and speakers or headsets at their computers or other devices. Alternatively, there might be a conference call, with access codes for the participants, that is dialed into by ordinary telephone but is also linked to the Internet meeting interface, so that participants speak and listen by telephone, but use the Internet service (which remains aware of the identity of each caller) for all other features. If the participants have webcams for transmitting live video, a portion of the screen might show their faces, or else (perhaps depending on the total number of participants) just those of the chair and/or the person speaking in debate or presenting a report.

The organizers of the meeting also have access to a control panel for use by the chair, the Recording Secretary, and their assistants, which enables them to perform their duties during the meeting, such as ensuring that the text of the pending question is properly displayed, assigning the floor to a member, opening and closing the polls for taking a vote, controlling the camera view, etc.

Assuming an organization's bylaws are patterned directly on the Sample Bylaws in this book, the organization can authorize the board to meet by use of an Internet meeting service with features like those described above by adding the following sections to Article VI (56:64):

Sample Bylaw Provisions for Scenario A

Section 4. Meetings Held Electronically. Except as otherwise provided in these bylaws, meetings of the Board shall be conducted through use of Internet meeting services designated by the President that support anonymous voting and support visible displays identifying those participating, identifying those seeking recognition to speak, showing (or permitting the retrieval of) the text of pending motions, and showing the results of votes. These electronic meetings of the Board shall be subject to all rules adopted by the Board, or by the Society, to govern them, which may include any reasonable limitations on, and requirements for, Board members' participation. Any such rules adopted by the Board shall supersede any conflicting rules in the parliamentary authority, but may not otherwise conflict with or alter any rule or decision of the Society. An anonymous vote conducted through the designated Internet meeting service shall be deemed a ballot vote, fulfilling any requirement in the bylaws or rules that a vote be conducted by ballot.

Section 5. Meetings Held in Person. Some particular meeting or meetings of the Board shall be held in person either (a) when the President or First Vice-President has obtained written consent for this from every Board member, or (b) when ordered by the Board, by a two-thirds vote with previous notice of a motion to do so having been given.[1]

The board may then find it helpful to adopt rules such as the following:

Sample Rules for Electronic Meetings for Scenario A

1. **Login information.** The Corresponding Secretary shall send by e-mail to every member of the Board, at least [time] before each meeting, the time of the meeting, the URL and codes necessary to connect to the Internet meeting service, and, as an alternative and backup to the audio connection included within the Internet service, the phone number and access code(s) the member needs to participate aurally by telephone. The Corresponding Secretary shall also include a copy of, or a link to, these rules.

2. **Login time.** The Recording Secretary shall schedule Internet meeting service availability to begin at least 15 minutes before the start of each meeting.

3. **Signing in and out.** Members shall identify themselves as required to sign in to the Internet meeting service, and shall maintain Internet and audio access throughout the meeting whenever present, but shall sign out upon any departure before adjournment.

4. **Quorum calls.** The presence of a quorum shall be established by audible roll call at the beginning of the meeting. Thereafter, the continued presence of a quorum shall be determined by the online list of participating members, unless any member demands a quorum count by audible

---

1. Compare this with Sample Bylaw Provisions for Scenario D, which assume in-person meetings as the norm, but authorize electronic meetings when directed by the board or with the written consent of a majority of board members (or, in the case of a special meeting, when directed by those calling the meeting).

roll call. Such a demand may be made following any vote for which the announced totals add to less than a quorum.

5. **Technical requirements and malfunctions.** Each member is responsible for his or her audio and Internet connections; no action shall be invalidated on the grounds that the loss of, or poor quality of, a member's individual connection prevented participation in the meeting.

6. **Forced disconnections.** The chair may cause or direct the disconnection or muting of a member's connection if it is causing undue interference with the meeting. The chair's decision to do so, which is subject to an undebatable appeal that can be made by any member, shall be announced during the meeting and recorded in the minutes.

7. **Assignment of the floor.** To seek recognition by the chair, a member shall … [specifying the exact method appropriate to the Internet meeting service being used]. Upon assigning the floor to a member, the chair shall clear the online queue of members who had been seeking recognition. To claim preference in recognition, another member who had been seeking recognition may promptly seek recognition again, and the chair shall recognize the member for the limited purpose of determining whether that member is entitled to preference in recognition.

8. **Interrupting a member.** A member who intends to make a motion or request that under the rules may interrupt a speaker shall use [the designated feature] for so indicating, and shall thereafter wait a reasonable time for the chair's instructions before attempting to interrupt the speaker by voice.

9. **Motions submitted in writing.** A member intending to make a main motion, to offer an amendment, or to propose instructions to a committee, shall, before or after being recognized, post the motion in writing to the online area designated

by the Recording Secretary for this purpose, preceded by the member's name and a number corresponding to how many written motions the member has so far posted during the meeting (e.g., "SMITH 3:"; "FRANCES JONES 2:"). Use of the online area designated by the Recording Secretary for this purpose shall be restricted to posting the text of intended motions.

10. **Display of motions.** The Recording Secretary shall designate an online area exclusively for the display of the immediately pending question and other relevant pending questions (such as the main motion, or the pertinent part of the main motion, when an amendment to it is immediately pending); and, to the extent feasible, the Recording Secretary, or any assistants appointed by him or her for this purpose, shall cause such questions, or any other documents that are currently before the meeting for action or information, to be displayed therein until disposed of.

11. **Voting.** Votes shall be taken by the anonymous voting feature of the Internet meeting service, unless a different method is ordered by the Board or required by the rules. When required or ordered, other permissible methods of voting are by electronic roll call or by audible roll call. The chair's announcement of the voting result shall include the number of members voting on each side of the question and the number, if any, who explicitly respond to acknowledge their presence without casting a vote. Business may also be conducted by unanimous consent.

12. **Video display.** [For groups using video, but in which the number of participants is too large for all to be displayed simultaneously:] The chair, the Recording Secretary, or their assistants shall cause a video of the chair to be displayed throughout the meeting, and shall also cause display of the video of the member currently recognized to speak or report.

SCENARIO B: TELECONFERENCE WITH INTERNET VOTING AND DOCUMENT SHARING

Assuming an organization's bylaws are patterned directly on the Sample Bylaws in this book, the organization can authorize the board to meet by teleconference, using Internet services for conducting secret votes and sharing documents, by adding the following section to Article VI (56:64):

Sample Bylaw Provisions for Scenario B

Section 4. Meetings Held Electronically. Meetings of the Board shall be conducted by telephone, except that some particular meeting or meetings shall be held in person either (a) when the President or First Vice-President has obtained written consent for this from every Board member, or (b) when ordered by the Board, by a two-thirds vote with previous notice of a motion to do so having been given.[2] Telephone meetings of the Board shall be subject to all rules adopted by the Board, or by the Society, to govern such meetings, which may include any reasonable limitations on, and requirements for, Board members' participation, and which shall specify how motions may be submitted in writing via the Internet. Any such rules adopted by the Board shall supersede any conflicting rules in the parliamentary authority, but may not otherwise conflict with or alter any rule or decision of the Society. At telephone meetings, any ballot votes required under the rules or ordered by the Board shall be conducted electronically, using an Internet service that supports anonymous voting.

The board may then find it helpful to adopt rules such as the following to govern the conduct of telephone meetings. Note that the requirement in Rules 1 and 2 of a unique access code for each member provides greater assurance that only members

---

2. Compare this with Sample Bylaw Provisions for Scenario D, which assume in-person meetings as the norm, but authorize electronic meetings when directed by the board or with the written consent of a majority of board members (or, in the case of a special meeting, when directed by those calling the meeting).

and others specifically invited can participate than do the sample rules given for Scenarios C and D. (Cf. 9:36.)

Sample Rules for Electronic Meetings for Scenario B

1. **Login information.** The Corresponding Secretary shall send by e-mail to every member of the Board, at least [time] before each meeting, the time of the meeting, the phone number and unique access code that that member needs to connect to the telephone conference call, and the URLs and login information for the online survey tool and file-hosting service. The Corresponding Secretary shall also include a copy of, or a link to, these rules.

2. **Call-in time.** The Recording Secretary shall schedule a telephone conference call, using a free service that provides each user a unique access code, to begin 15 minutes before the start of each meeting. The Recording Secretary shall also establish accounts with a free online survey tool that supports anonymous surveys, and with a free file-hosting service.

3. **Technical requirements.** For the purposes of electronic ballot voting and file sharing, members shall maintain Internet access during the meeting.

4. **Arrival announcements.** Members shall announce themselves at the first opportunity after joining the telephone conference call, but may not interrupt a speaker to do so.

5. **Departure announcements.** Members who leave the telephone conference call before adjournment shall announce their departure, but may not interrupt a speaker to do so.

6. **Quorum calls.** The presence of a quorum shall be established by roll call at the beginning of the meeting and on the demand of any member. Such a demand may be made following the departure of any member, or following the taking of any vote for which the announced totals add to less than a quorum.

7. **Obtaining the floor.** To seek recognition by the chair, a member shall address the chair and state his or her own name.

8. **Motions submitted in writing.** Members may submit motions to the chair in writing by uploading them to the file-hosting service and notifying the chair of the URL or download link needed to access the file.

9. **Voting.** All votes shall be taken by roll call, unless required under the rules or ordered by the Board to be taken by ballot. When a vote is taken by roll call, only the number of votes on each side and the number of members present but not voting shall be entered in the minutes, unless the Board orders a fully recorded roll-call vote. Ballot votes shall be taken electronically, as follows: The Recording Secretary shall post the question using the online survey tool, and the chair shall then alert the members that the polls are open, providing any additional information that members need to cast their votes online. The polls shall be closed not less than two minutes after they have been opened by the chair. Business may also be conducted by unanimous consent.

10. **Technical malfunctions.** Each member is responsible for his or her connection to the telephone conference call and to the Internet; no action shall be invalidated on the grounds that the loss of, or poor quality of, a member's individual connection prevented participation in the meeting.

11. **Forced disconnections.** The chair may order the Recording Secretary to disconnect or mute a member's connection if it is causing undue interference with the telephone conference call. The chair's decision to do so, which is subject to an undebatable appeal that can be made by any member, shall be announced during the meeting and recorded in the minutes.

SCENARIO C: SOME MEMBERS PARTICIPATE BY SPEAKERPHONE IN OTHERWISE FACE-TO-FACE MEETING

An organization may wish to permit its board to hold meetings in which some members are physically present while others participate by telephone.

Assume an organization's bylaws are patterned directly on the Sample Bylaws in this book, and assume that no rule of the organization requires votes of the executive board to be taken by ballot. By adding the following provision to Section 3 of Article VI of the bylaws (56:64), the organization can grant board members the right to participate in meetings by telephone, subject to rules adopted by the board:

Sample Bylaw Provisions for Scenario C

Board meetings shall be held at a central location, but Board members who are not present in person shall have the right to participate by telephone, subject to any limitations established in rules adopted by the Board to govern such participation.

The board may then find it helpful to adopt rules such as the following:

Sample Rules for Electronic Meetings for Scenario C

1. **Login information.** The Corresponding Secretary shall send by e-mail to every member of the Board, at least [time] before each meeting, the time and location of the meeting and the phone number and any access code needed to connect to the telephone conference call. The Corresponding Secretary shall also include a copy of, or a link to, these rules.

2. **Call-in time.** The Recording Secretary shall schedule a telephone conference call, using equipment provided by the Society or a free service, to begin 15 minutes before the start of each meeting.

3. **Meeting-room equipment.** The society shall provide a speakerphone at each meeting, which the Recording Secretary shall connect to the telephone conference call at least 5 minutes before the start of the meeting.

4. **Location of chairman.** The chair of the meeting must be present in the meeting room.

5. **Arrival announcements.** Members who participate in the meeting by phone shall announce themselves at the first opportunity after joining the telephone conference call, but may not interrupt a speaker to do so.

6. **Departure announcements.** Members who leave the telephone conference call or the meeting room before adjournment shall announce their departure, but may not interrupt a speaker to do so.

7. **Quorum calls.** The presence of a quorum shall be established by roll call at the beginning of the meeting and on the demand of any member. Such a demand may be made following the departure of any member or following the taking of any vote for which the announced totals add to less than a quorum.

8. **Obtaining the floor.** To seek recognition by the chair, a member shall address the chair and state his or her own name.

9. **Motions submitted in writing.** Members who participate in the meeting by phone may not submit motions in writing during the meeting, but are entitled to make motions orally. Members may, however, submit motions in writing by sending them at least [time] before the meeting to the Corresponding Secretary, who shall send any such pre-submitted motions by e-mail to all members in advance of the meeting and shall provide copies to the members present in person at the meeting.

10. **Voting methods.** All votes shall be taken by roll call. Unless the Board orders a fully recorded roll-call vote, only the number of votes on each side and the number of members

present but not voting (including members participating by phone) shall be entered in the minutes. Business may also be conducted by unanimous consent.

11. **Loss of meeting-room connection.** Any business transacted while the meeting-room speakerphone is disconnected from the telephone conference call is null and void, except that the members present in the meeting room at such a time may take those actions that are in order in the absence of a quorum.

12. **Other technical malfunctions and requirements.** Each member is responsible for his or her connection to the telephone conference call; no action shall be invalidated on the grounds that the loss of, or poor quality of, a member's individual connection prevented participation in the meeting.

13. **Forced disconnections.** The chair may order the Recording Secretary to disconnect or mute a member's connection if it is causing undue interference with the telephone conference call. The chair's decision to do so, which is subject to an undebatable appeal that can be made by any member, shall be announced during the meeting and recorded in the minutes.

SCENARIO D: TELEPHONE MEETING WITHOUT INTERNET SUPPORT

Assume an organization's bylaws are patterned directly on the Sample Bylaws in this book, and assume that no rule of the organization requires votes of the board to be taken by ballot. By adding the following section to Article VI of the bylaws (56:64), the organization can authorize the board to meet by telephone conference call when desired, without using Internet services.

Sample Bylaw Provisions for Scenario D

Section 4. Meetings Held Electronically. Meetings of the Board may be conducted by telephone (a) when the President or First Vice-President has obtained written consent for this from a majority of the Board members; (b) when so directed by the Board; or (c) in the case of special meetings, when so directed by those calling the special meeting.[3] Telephone meetings of the Board shall be subject to all rules adopted by the Board, or by the Society, to govern such meetings, which may include any reasonable limitations on, and requirements for, Board members' participation. Any such rules adopted by the Board shall supersede any conflicting rules in the parliamentary authority, but may not otherwise conflict with or alter any rule or decision of the Society.

The board may then find it helpful to adopt rules such as the following to govern the conduct of telephone meetings:

Sample Rules for Electronic Meetings for Scenario D

1. **Connection information.** The Corresponding Secretary shall send by e-mail to every member of the Board, at least [time] before each meeting, the time of the meeting and the phone number and access code needed to connect to the telephone conference call.

2. **Call-in time.** The Recording Secretary shall schedule a telephone conference call, using a free service, to begin 15 minutes before the start of each telephone meeting.

3. **Arrival announcements.** Members shall announce themselves at the first opportunity after joining the telephone conference call, but may not interrupt a speaker to do so.

4. **Departure announcements.** Members who leave the telephone conference call before adjournment shall announce their departure, but may not interrupt a speaker to do so.

5. **Quorum calls.** The presence of a quorum shall be established by roll call at the beginning of the meeting and on

---

3. Compare this with Sample Bylaw Provisions for Scenarios A and B, which assume electronic meetings and require a supermajority to order an in-person meeting.

the demand of any member. Such a demand may be made following the departure of any member, or following the taking of any vote for which the announced totals add to less than a quorum.

6. **Obtaining the floor.** To seek recognition by the chair, a member shall address the chair and state his or her own name.

7. **Motions submitted in writing.** Members may not submit motions in writing during the meeting, but are entitled to make motions orally. Members may, however, submit motions in writing by sending them at least [time] before the meeting to the Corresponding Secretary, who shall send any such pre-submitted motions by e-mail to all members in advance of the meeting.

8. **Voting methods.** All votes shall be taken by roll call. Unless the Board orders a fully recorded roll-call vote, only the number of votes on each side and the number of members present but not voting shall be entered in the minutes. Business may also be conducted by unanimous consent.

9. **Technical malfunctions and requirements.** Each member is responsible for his or her connection to the telephone conference call; no action shall be invalidated on the grounds that the loss of, or poor quality of, a member's individual connection prevented participation in the meeting.

10. **Forced disconnections.** The chair may order the Recording Secretary to disconnect or mute a member's connection if it is causing undue interference with the telephone conference call. The chair's decision to do so, which is subject to an undebatable appeal that can be made by any member, shall be announced during the meeting and recorded in the minutes.

INDEX

Specific content within the Standard Descriptive Characteristics (SDCs) of motions—referenced in the index by italic paragraph numbers at each motion name—is generally not indexed. Key facts with regard to SDCs of motions are summarized in Chart I (pages t3–t5) and Table II (pages t6–t33).

The content of Tables II–VII (pages t6–t51), in which motions can be located alphabetically by category, is not indexed.

Key to locations: 1:1 to 63:40 = paragraphs (**bold number** = definition; *italic number* = SDCs);
§1–§63 = sections; t1–t52 = page numbers in the Charts, Tables, and Lists

---

Key to locations: 1:1 to 63:40 = paragraphs (**bold number** = definition; *italic number* = SDCs); §1–§63 = sections; t1–t52 = page numbers in the Charts, Tables, and Lists

---